Webster's
Home & Office
Desk Reference

Webster's
Home & Office
Desk Reference

Created in Cooperation with the Editors of

MERRIAM-WEBSTER

SMITHMARK
REFERENCE

Materials in this book were drawn from:
Merriam-Webster's Pocket Dictionary, Merriam-Webster's Desk Dictionary, Merriam-Webster's Secretarial Handbook, Merriam-Webster's Guide to Business Correspondence, and Merriam-Webster's Guide to International Business Communications. © 1993–1996.

This edition published in 1996 by
SMITHMARK Publishers
a division of U.S. Media Holdings, Inc.
16 East 32nd Street
New York, NY 10016.

SMITHMARK books are available for bulk purchases for sales promotion and premium use. For details, write or call the manager of special sales, SMITHMARK Publishers, 16 East 32nd Street, New York, NY 10016; (212) 532-6600.

Library of Congress Cataloging-in-Publication Data

Webster's home & office desk reference / created in cooperation with the editors of Merriam-Webster.
    p.   cm.
  "Smithmark reference."
  Includes index.
  ISBN 0-7651-9718-9
    1. Handbooks, vade-mecums, etc.   I. Merriam-Webster, Inc.
  AG106.W43 1997
  031.02 —dc21   96-50140
                                     CIP

Printed in the United States of America.

10 9 8 7 6 5 4 3 2 1

15.79

Contents

CHAPTER 6
Composing Letters

CHAPTER 7
Computers, Word Processing, and Office Equipment

CHAPTER 8
Desktop Publishing

CHAPTER 9
Records Management

CHAPTER 10
Basic Accounting and Bookkeeping Systems

CHAPTER 11

Telephones and Telecommunications

CHAPTER 12

Postal Services and Classes of Mail

CHAPTER 13

Travel Arrangements and International Business

CHAPTER 14

Useful Products and Services

CHAPTER 15

Math and Science Basics

Introduction

WEBSTER'S HOME AND OFFICE DESK REFERENCE has been designed as a desktop companion for both office professionals and homeowners. It brings together a unique collection of reference resources that are invaluable to have on hand when conducting personal or professional business transactions.

The book provides practical guidelines on all aspects of writing, from punctuating sentences and capitalizing names to forming the plurals and possessives of words and deciding when to use abbreviations and numerals. This book also offers clear advice on composition and grammar, notes and bibliographies, and the use of appropriate tone in business writing.

Comprehensive guidance on a variety of topics related to business correspondence is intended to help writers achieve concise, accurate, and effective communication. A section on composing form letters and memorandums demonstrates how to meet the needs of common business situations, and an overview of computer hardware and software provides a wealth of information about the best ways to create and format business documents.

Other communication and management resources are also given thorough coverage. Proven strategies for managing records and maintaining accurate accounting and bookkeeping systems encompass the needs of both large and small companies. Procedures for using domestic and international telephone, telecommunication, and mail services are also addressed, as are techniques for arranging productive overseas business trips.

Finally, this book incorporates a number of valuable references, including helpful math and science tables, a glossary of geographical names, a guide to common signs and symbols, and a quick-reference dictionary of English.

WEBSTER'S HOME AND OFFICE DESK REFERENCE was created in cooperation with the editors of Merriam-Webster Inc., a company that has been publishing dictionaries and reference books for 150 years.

CHAPTER 1

Composition and Grammar

No guide to effective communication can ignore the basic components of discourse: the word, the phrase, the clause, the sentence, and the paragraph. Each of these increasingly complex units contributes to the expression of a writer's ideas.

The simplest component of discourse is the word. The treatment of words in this chapter focuses on their grammatical function in a sentence. For a discussion of the ways in which words convey tone in writing, see Chapter 3, "Tone in Writing." General questions concerning the more complex language components of phrases, clauses, sentences, and paragraphs are also discussed in this chapter. For a discussion of the compositional topics that relate specifically to letter-writing, see Chapter 6, "Composing Letters."

Parts of Speech

Words have traditionally been classified into eight parts of speech: the adjective, adverb, conjunction, interjection, noun, preposition, pronoun, and verb. This classification system is based mainly on a word's inflectional features, its general grammatical functions, and its positioning within a sentence. On the following pages, these parts of speech are listed alphabetically and discussed briefly.

Adjective
An adjective is a word that typically describes or modifies the meaning of a noun. Adjectives serve to point out a quality of a thing named, to indicate its quantity or extent, or to specify a thing as distinct from something else.

Adjectives are often classified by the ways in which they modify or limit the meaning of a noun. The classifications commonly referred to are the following: descriptive adjectives, demonstrative adjectives, indefinite adjectives, interrogative adjectives, possessive adjectives, predicate adjectives, proper adjectives, relative adjectives, and articles.

A *descriptive adjective* describes something or indicates a quality, kind, or condition ("a *sick* person," "a *brave* soldier," "a *new* dress"). The *demonstrative adjectives,* such as *this* and *that,* point to what they modify in order to distinguish it from others. These two are the only adjectives with plural forms ("*this* child," "*these* children"; "*that* house," "*those* houses"). An *indefinite adjective* designates an unidentified or not immediately identifiable person or thing ("*some* books," "*other* hotels"). An *interrogative adjective* conveys the force of a question ("*Whose* office is this?" "*Which* book do you want?"). A *possessive adjective* is the possessive form of a personal pronoun ("*her* idea," "*his* job," "*my* car," "*our* savings plan," "*their* office," "*your* opinion"). A *proper adjective* is derived from a proper noun and takes its meaning from what characterizes the noun. It is usually capitalized ("*Victorian* furniture," "a *Puerto Rican* product," "*Keynesian* economics"). A *relative adjective* introduces an adjectival clause ("at the April conference, by *which* time the report should be finished") or a clause that functions as a noun ("the uncomfortable position of not knowing *which* course she should follow"). An *article* is one of a small group of words (as *a, an,* and *the*) that are used with nouns to limit or give definiteness to the application of a noun ("*a* condominium," "*an* honor," "*the* jetliner").

The following paragraphs describe some other types of adjectives. They also outline situations involving adjectives that are sometimes troublesome for writers.

1. **Absolute adjectives** Some adjectives (such as *prior, maximum, optimum, minimum,* and *first*) admit no comparison under ordinary circumstances (see paragraphs 3 and 4 below), because they represent ultimate conditions. These adjectives are called *absolute adjectives.* Some writers are careful to modify these adjectives with adverbs such as *almost, near,* or *nearly,* rather than *least, less, more, most,* or *very.*

> an almost fatal dose
> at near maximum capacity
> a more nearly perfect likeness

NOTE: Many writers do compare and qualify this type of adjective in order to show connotations and shades of meaning they consider less than absolute.

> a more perfect union
> a less complete account

When in doubt about the comparability of an absolute adjective, one should check the definitions and examples of usage given for the adjective in a dictionary.

2. **Adjective/noun agreement** The number (singular or plural) of a demonstrative adjective *(this, that, these, those)* should agree with that of the noun it modifies.

> these kinds of typewriters *not* these kind of typewriters
> those sorts of jobs *not* those sort of jobs
> this type of person *not* these type of people

3. **Compared with adverbs** Both adjectives and adverbs describe or modify other words; however, adjectives can only modify nouns, while adverbs can modify verbs, adverbs, and adjectives. For more on the differences between adjectives and adverbs, see paragraph 14 below and paragraphs 4–6 under Adverb in this section.

4. **Comparison of adjectives** The main structural feature of an adjective is its ability to indicate degrees of comparison (positive, comparative, superlative) by addition of suffixal endings *-er/-est* to the base word, by addition of *more/most* or *less/least* before the base word, or by use of irregular forms.

positive	*comparative*	*superlative*
clean	cleaner	cleanest
meaningful	more meaningful	most meaningful
meaningful	less meaningful	least meaningful
bad	worse	worst

5. The comparative degree is used to show that the thing being modified has more (or less) of a particular quality than the one or ones to which it is being compared. The superlative degree is used to show that the thing being modified has the most (or least) of a quality out of all of the ones to which it is being compared. The superlative degree is most commonly used when there are more than two things being compared.

> *comparative*
> prices that were higher than those at other stores
> a better report than our last one
> the more expensive of the two methods
>
> *superlative*
> the highest prices in the area
> the best report so far
> the most expensive of the three methods

6. In general, the comparatives and superlatives of one-syllable adjectives are formed by adding *-er/-est* to the base word. The comparatives and superlatives of adjectives with more than two syllables are formed by adding *more* and *most* or *less* and *least* before the base word. The comparatives and superlatives of two-syllable adjectives are variously formed by adding *-er/-est* to the base word or using *more* and *most* or *less* and *least* before the base word. When in doubt about the inflection of a particular adjective, one should consult a dictionary.

positive	*comparative*	*superlative*
big	bigger	biggest
loose	looser	loosest
empty	emptier	emptiest
narrow	narrower	narrowest
complex	more complex	most complex
concise	less concise	least concise
important	more important	most important
troublesome	less troublesome	least troublesome

7. Some adjectives are ordinarily not compared, because they are felt to represent ultimate conditions. For more on these adjectives, see paragraph 1, above.

8. **Coordinate and noncoordinate adjectives** Adjectives that share equal relationships to the nouns they modify are called *coordinate adjectives* and are separated from each other by commas.

   a concise, coherent essay
   a hard, flickering light

9. When the first of two adjectives modifies the noun plus a second adjective, the result is a pair of *noncoordinate adjectives*. Noncoordinate adjectives are not separated by commas.

   a low monthly fee
   the first warm day

10. **Double comparisons** Double comparisons are considered nonstandard and should be avoided.

    an easier method   *not*   a more easier method
    the easiest solution   *not*   the most easiest solution

11. **Incomplete or understood comparisons** Some comparisons are left incomplete because the context clearly implies the comparison. These are commonly used especially in advertising. It should be understood, however, that the use of incomplete comparisons is often considered careless or illogical in formal writing.

    Get better buys here!
    We have lower prices.

12. **Nouns used as adjectives** Nouns are frequently used to describe other nouns, and in this way they act like adjectives. For more on the use of nouns as modifiers, see paragraph 6 under Noun in this section and the discussion under Compounds That Function as Adjectives, pages 119–122.

13. **Placement within a sentence** Adjectives may occur in the following positions within sentences: (1) preceding the nouns they modify, (2) fol-

lowing the nouns they modify, (3) following the verb *to be* and other linking verbs in the predicate-adjective position, and (4) following some transitive verbs used in the passive voice.

(1) the black hat   a dark, shabby coat
(2) an executive par excellence   painted the room blue
(3) a hat that is black   food that tastes stale
     while I felt sick
(4) a room that was painted blue
     passengers found dead at the crash site

14. Predicate adjectives A predicate adjective modifies the subject of a linking verb (as *be, become, feel, taste, smell, seem*) which it follows.

She is happy.
The milk tastes sour.
The student seems puzzled.

NOTE: Because some linking verbs (as *feel, look, smell, taste*) can also function as active verbs, which can in turn be modified by adverbs, writers are sometimes confused over whether they should use the adverbial or adjectival form of a modifier after the verb. The answer is that an adjective is used if the subject of the sentence is being modified. If the verb is being modified, an adverb is used. (For more examples, see paragraph 5 under Adverb in this section.)

Your report looks good. [adjective]
The colors feel right. [adjective]
The engine smells hot. [adjective]
They looked quickly at each item. [adverb]
He felt immediately for his wallet. [adverb]
She felt the corners carefully for dampness. [adverb]

Adverb

An adverb is a word or combination of words typically serving as a modifier of a verb, an adjective, another adverb, a preposition, a phrase, a clause, or a sentence and expressing some relation of manner or quality, place, time, degree, number, cause, opposition, affirmation, or denial.

Most commonly, adverbs take the form of an adjective with an *-ly* ending added to it (*actually, congenially, madly, really*). There are many exceptions to this pattern, however. For instance, adverbs based on adjectives ending in *-ly* (*costly, friendly, likely*) do not include an additional *-ly* ending but take the same form as the adjective. In addition, some adverbs do not end in *-ly* (*now, quite, too*).

Adverbs answer such questions as the following: "when?" ("Please reply *at once*"); "how long?" ("This job is taking *forever*"); "where?" ("She works *there*"); "in what direction?" ("Move the lever *upward*"); "how?" ("The staff moved *expeditiously* on the project"); and "to what degree?" ("The book was *very* popular").

1. **Basic uses** Adverbs modify verbs, adjectives, and other adverbs.

> She *carefully* studied the balance sheet.
> She gave the balance sheet *very* careful study.
> She studied the balance sheet *very* carefully.

2. Conjunctive adverbs join clauses or link sentences. (For more on this use of adverbs, see paragraphs 13–15 under Conjunction in this section.)

> You are welcome to join our car pool; *however,* please be ready by 7:00 a.m.
> He thoroughly enjoyed the symposium. *Indeed,* he was fascinated by the presentations.

3. In addition, adverbs may be essential elements of two-word verbs commonly having separate entries in dictionaries.

> Our staff will work *up* the specifications.
> We can work them *up* later.

4. **Compared with adjectives** Adverbs but not adjectives modify action verbs.

> *not*
> He answered very *harsh.*
> *instead*
> He answered very *harshly.*

5. Complements referring to the subject of a sentence and occurring after linking verbs conventionally take adjectives but not adverbs. (For more examples, see paragraph 14 under Adjective in this section.)

> *not*
> He looks *badly* these days.
> The letter sounded *strongly.*
> *instead*
> He looks *bad* these days.
> The letter sounded *strong.*
> *and also*
> He looks *good* these days.
> He looks *well* these days.

NOTE: In the last two examples, either *good* or *well* is acceptable, because both words are here functioning as adjectives in the sense of "healthy."

6. Adverbs but not adjectives modify adjectives and other adverbs.

> *not*
> She looked *dreadful* tired.
> *instead*
> She looked *dreadfully* tired.

7. **Comparison of adverbs** Most adverbs have three different forms to indicate degrees of comparison (positive, comparative, superlative). The positive form is the same as the base word *(quickly, loudly, near)*. The comparative form is usually shown by the addition of *more* or *less* before the base word *(more quickly, less quickly)*; the superlative form is usually shown by the addition of *most* or *least (most quickly, least quickly)*. However, a few adverbs (such as *fast, slow, loud, soft, early, late,* and *quick*) may be compared in two ways: by the method described above or by the addition of the suffixal endings *-er/-est* to the base word *(quick, quicker, quickest)*. For an explanation of the uses of the comparative and superlative forms, see paragraph 5 under Adjective in this section.

8. As a general rule, one-syllable adverbs use the *-er/-est* endings to show comparison. Adverbs of three or more syllables use *more/most* and *less/least*. Two-syllable adverbs take either form.

fast	faster	fastest
late	later	latest
easy	easier	easiest
madly	more madly	most madly
happily	more happily	most happily

9. Some adverbs (such as *quite* and *very*) cannot be compared.

10. **Double negatives** A combination of two negative adverbs (such as *not, hardly, never,* and *scarcely*) used to express a single negative idea is considered substandard.

> *not*
> We *cannot* see *hardly* any reason why we should buy this product.
>
> *instead*
> We *cannot* see any reason why we should buy this product.
> We can see *hardly* any reason why we should buy this product.

11. **Emphasis** Adverbs (such as *just* and *only*) are often used to emphasize other words. A writer should be aware of the various emphases that can result from the positioning of an adverb in a sentence.

> *emphasis on the action itself*
> He *just* nodded to me as he passed.
>
> *emphasis on timing of the action*
> He nodded to me *just* as he passed.

12. In some positions and contexts, these adverbs can be ambiguous.

> They will only tell it to you.

It is not clear whether this writer means that they will only tell it, not put it in writing, or that they will tell no one else. If the latter interpretation is intended, a slight shift of position would remove the uncertainty.

> They will tell it only to you.

13. Placement within a sentence Adverbs are generally positioned as close as possible to the words they modify if such a position will not result in misinterpretation.

> *unclear*
> A project that the board would support *completely* occupied her thinking.

It is unclear whether the writer means "would support completely" or "completely occupied her thinking." The adverb may be moved to another position, or the sentence may be recast, depending on intended meaning.

> *clear*
> A project that the board would *completely* support occupied her thinking.
> *or*
> Her thinking was *completely* occupied with a project that the board would support.

14. When an adverb separates *to* from the verbal element of an infinitive ("hope to really start"), the result is called a split infinitive. For a discussion of split infinitives, see paragraph 32 under Verb in this section.

15. In some cases, adverbs modify an entire sentence rather than a specific word or phrase within the sentence. Such adverbs are referred to as *sentence adverbs,* and their position can vary according to the emphasis one wishes to use.

> *Fortunately* they had already placed their order.
> They *fortunately* had already placed their order.
> They had already placed their order *fortunately*.

16. Relative adverbs Relative adverbs (such as *when, where, why*) introduce subordinate clauses. (For more on subordinate clauses, see the section on Clauses, beginning on page 36.)

> They met at a time *when* prospects were good.
> I went into the room *where* they were sitting.
> Everyone knows the reason *why* she did it.

Conjunction

A conjunction is a word or phrase that joins together words, phrases, clauses, or sentences. Conjunctions may occur in many different positions in a sentence, although they ordinarily do not appear at the end of a sentence unless the sentence is elliptical. There are three main types of conjunctions: *coordinating, correlative,* and *subordinating.* In addition to these three types of conjunctions, the English language has transitional adverbs and adverbial phrases called *conjunctive adverbs*. These function as conjunctions even though they are customarily classified as adverbs. A definition and discussion of the three types of conjunctions and of conjunctive adverbs follows. (For information about punctuating sentences with conjunctions, see paragraphs 1–4, 23, and 26–28 under Comma, pages 55–56 and 60–61, and paragraphs 1–5 under Semicolon, pages 82–83.)

Coordinating conjunctions Coordinating conjunctions (such as *and, but, for, or, nor, so,* and *yet*) join together grammatical elements of equal weight. The elements may be words, phrases, subordinate clauses, main clauses, or complete sentences.

1. Coordinating conjunctions are used to join elements, to exclude or contrast, to offer alternatives, or to propose reasons, grounds, or a result.

    joining elements
    She ordered pencils, pens, *and* erasers.
    Sales were slow, *and* they showed no sign of improvement.

    excluding or contrasting
    He is a brilliant *but* arrogant man.
    They offered a promising plan, *but* it had not yet been tested.

    alternative
    She can wait here *or* go on ahead.

    reason or grounds
    The report is useless, *for* its information is no longer current.

    result
    His diction is excellent, *so* every word is clear.

2. A comma is used before a coordinating conjunction linking coordinate clauses, especially when these clauses are lengthy. For more on the use of Commas between clauses, see paragraphs 1–4 under Comma, pages 55–56.

    We encourage applications from all interested persons, *but* we do have high professional standards that the successful applicant must meet.

3. Coordinating conjunctions should link equal grammatical elements—for example, adjectives with other adjectives, nouns with other nouns, participles with other participles, clauses with other equal-ranking clauses, and so on. Combining unequal grammatical elements may result in unbalanced sentences.

    unbalanced (and links a participial phrase with an adverbial clause)
    Having become disgusted *and* because he was tired, he left the meeting.

    balanced (and links two adjectives)
    Because he was tired *and* disgusted, he left the meeting.
    Having become tired *and* disgusted, he left the meeting.

4. Coordinating conjunctions should not be used to string together excessively long series of elements, regardless of their grammatical equality.

> *strung-out*
> We have sustained enormous losses in this division, *and* we have realized practically no profits even though the sales figures indicate last-quarter gains, *and* we are therefore reorganizing the entire management structure as well as cutting back on personnel.

> *tightened*
> Because this division has sustained enormous losses and has realized only insignificant profits even with its last-quarter sales gains, we are totally reorganizing its management. We are also cutting back on personnel.

5. The choice of just the right coordinating conjunction for a particular verbal situation is important: the right word will pinpoint the writer's true meaning and intent and will emphasize the most relevant idea or point of the sentence. The following three sentences show increasingly stronger degrees of contrast through the use of different conjunctions:

> *neutral*
> He works hard *and* doesn't progress.

> *more contrast*
> He works hard *but* doesn't progress.

> *stronger contrast*
> He works hard, *yet* he doesn't progress.

6. The coordinating conjunction *and/or* linking two elements of a compound subject often poses a problem: should the verb that follows be singular or plural? A subject comprising singular nouns connected by *and/or* may be considered singular or plural, depending on the meaning of the sentence.

> *singular*
> All loss *and/or* damage *is* to be the responsibility of the sender. [one or the other and possibly both]

> *plural*
> John R. Westlake *and/or* Maria A. Artandi *are* hereby appointed as the executors of my estate. [both executors are to act, or either of them is to act if the other dies or is incapacitated]

Correlative conjunctions Correlative conjunctions are coordinating conjunctions that are regularly used in pairs, although they are not placed adjacent to one another.

7. Correlative conjunctions are used to link alternatives and equal elements.

> *alternatives*
> *Either* you go *or* you stay.
> He had *neither* looks *nor* wits.

equal elements
Both typist *and* writer should understand the rules of punctuation.
Not only was there inflation, *but* there was *also* unemployment.

8. Because they link equal grammatical elements, correlative conjunctions should be placed as close as possible to the elements they join.

   misplaced (joining clause and verb phrase)
   Either I must send a telex *or* make a long-distance call.

   repositioned (joining two verb phrases)
   I must *either* send a telex *or* make a long-distance call.

9. The negative counterpart to *either . . . or* is *neither . . . nor*. The conjunction *or* should not be substituted for *nor,* because its substitution will destroy the negative parallelism. However, *or* may occur in combination with *no*.

   not
   He received *neither* a promotion *or* a raise.

   instead
   He received *neither* a promotion *nor* a raise.

   also
   He received *no* promotion *or* raise.

Subordinating conjunction Subordinating conjunctions join a subordinate or dependent clause to a main clause.

10. Subordinating conjunctions are used to express cause, condition or concession, manner, purpose or result, time, place or circumstance, and alternative conditions or possibilities.

    cause
    Because she learns quickly, she is doing well in her new job.

    condition or concession
    Don't call *unless* you have the information.

    manner
    He looks *as though* he is ill.
    We'll do it *however* you tell us to.

    purpose or result
    She routes the mail early *so that* they can read it.

    time
    She kept meetings to a minimum *when* she was president.

    place or circumstance
    I don't know *where* he has gone.
    He tries to help out *wherever* it is possible.

    conditions or possibilities
    It was hard to decide *whether* I should go or stay.

11. The subordinating conjunction *that* introduces several kinds of subordinate clauses, including those used as noun equivalents (such as a subject or an object of a verb or as a predicate nominative).

    Yesterday I learned *that* he has been sick for over a week.

12. In introducing subordinate clauses, subordinating conjunctions deemphasize less important ideas in favor of more important ideas. The writer must take care that the point he or she wishes to emphasize is in the main clause and that the points of less importance are subordinated. Notice how differently these two versions strike the reader.

> We were just coming out of the door *when* the building burst into flames.
> *As* we were just coming out of the door, the building burst into flames.

Conjunctive adverb Conjunctive adverbs are transitional adverbs and adverbial phrases that express relationships between two units of discourse (as two main clauses, two complete sentences, or two or more paragraphs). Conjunctive adverbs are classed as adverbs, but they function as conjunctions when they are used as connectives. Some common conjunctive adverbs are listed below.

accordingly	first	incidentally	on the contrary
also	for example	in conclusion	otherwise
anyhow	for instance	indeed	second
anyway	furthermore	in fact	still
as a result	further on	later	that is (to say)
besides	hence	likewise	then
consequently	however	moreover	therefore
e.g.	i.e.	namely	to be sure
finally	in addition	nevertheless	too

13. Conjunctive adverbs are used to express addition, to add emphasis, to express contrast or discrimination, to introduce illustrations or elaborations, to express or introduce conclusions or results, or to orient elements of discourse as to time or space.

addition
This employee deserves a substantial raise; *furthermore,* she should be promoted.

emphasis
He is brilliant; *indeed,* he is a genius.

contrast or discrimination
The major responsibility lies with the partners; *nevertheless,* associates should be competent in decision-making.

illustrations or elaborations
Losses were due to several negative factors; *namely,* inflation, foreign competition, and restrictive government regulation.

conclusions or results
Government overregulation in that country reached a prohibitive level in the last quarter. *Thus,* we are phasing out all of our operations there.

time or space
First, we can remind them that their account is long overdue; *second,* we can say that we must consider consulting our attorneys if they do not meet their obligation.

14. Conjunctive adverbs are usually placed at the beginning of a clause or sentence. When they are placed later in the clause or sentence, additional emphasis is placed on them.

The overdue shipment arrived this morning; *however,* we must point out that it was incomplete.

The overdue shipment arrived this morning; we must point out, *however,* that it was incomplete.

15. The misuse of conjunctive adverbs can lead to a problem known as *comma fault*. When a conjunctive adverb is used to connect two main clauses, a semicolon should be used; a comma will not suffice. (For more on comma fault and punctuation between main clauses, see paragraphs 1–4 under Comma, pages 55–56 and paragraph 5 under Semicolon, page 83.)

> *comma fault*
> The company had flexible hours, *however* its employees were expected to abide by their selected arrival and departure times.
>
> *repunctuated*
> The company had flexible hours; *however,* its employees were expected to abide by their selected arrival and departure times.

Interjection

Interjections are exclamatory or interrupting words or phrases that express an emotion. Interjections are usually independent clauses that lack grammatical connection with the rest of the sentence. They often stand alone.

1. Interjections may be stressed or ejaculatory words, phrases, or even short sentences.

> Absurd!
> No, no!
> Get out!
> Not now!

2. Interjections may also be so-called "sound" words, such as those representing shouts, hisses, or cries:

> Shh! The meeting has begun.
> Pssst! Come over here.
> Ouch! That hurts.
> Ugh! What a horrible flavor.

3. Emphatic interjections expressing forceful emotions use exclamation points.

> Fire!
> What an awful time we had!

4. Mildly stressed words or sentences may be punctuated with commas and periods.

> *Ah,* that's my idea of a terrific deal.
> *Well, well,* so that's the solution.
> *Oh,* you're probably right.

5. Interjections should be sparingly used in discourse, and then only to signal genuine emotion or for strong emphasis.

Noun

A noun is a word that is the name of something (as a person, animal, place, object, quality, concept, or action). Nouns are used in a sentence as the subject or object of a verb, as the object of a preposition, as a predicate after a linking verb, as an appositive name, or as a name in an absolute construction.

Nouns exhibit these characteristic features: they are inflected for possession; they have number (that is, they are either singular or plural); they are often preceded by determiners (as *a, an, the; this, that, these, those; all, every,* and other such qualifiers; *one, two, three,* and other such numerical quantifiers; *his, her, their,* and other such pronominal adjectives); a few of them still show gender differences (as masculine *host, actor,* feminine *hostess, actress*); and many of them are formed by adding a suffix (such as *-ance, -ist, -ness,* and *-tion*).

1. **Basic uses** Nouns are used as subjects, direct objects, objects of prepositions, indirect objects, retained objects, predicate nominative, objective complements, and appositives and in direct address.

   > *subject*
   > The *office* was quiet.
   >
   > *direct object*
   > He locked the *office.*
   >
   > *object of a preposition*
   > The file is in the *office.*
   >
   > *indirect object*
   > He gave his *client* the papers.
   >
   > *retained object*
   > His client was given the *papers.*
   >
   > *predicate nominative*
   > Mrs. Adams is the managing *partner.*
   >
   > *objective complement*
   > They made Mrs. Adams managing *partner.*
   >
   > *appositive*
   > Mrs. Adams, the managing *partner,* wrote that memorandum.
   >
   > *direct address*
   > *Mrs. Adams,* may I present Mr. Bonkowski.

2. **Compound nouns** Because English is not a static and unchanging entity, many of its words undergo styling variations because of the changing preferences of its users. The styling of compound nouns (whether open, closed, or hyphenated) is especially subject to changing usage. No rigid set of rules can cover every possible variation or combination; however, some consistent patterns of usage can be discerned. For a description of these patterns, see the discussion under Compound Nouns, pages 116–119.

3. **Indefinite articles with nouns** Before a word or abbreviation beginning with a consonant *sound,* the article *a* is used. This is true even if the spelling of the word begins with a vowel.

a BA degree	a COD package	a door
a hat	a human	a union
a one	a U.S. Senator	

4. Before *h-* in an unstressed or lightly stressed first syllable, the article *a* is more frequently used, although *an* is more usual in speech whether or not the *h-* is actually pronounced. Either is acceptable in speech or writing.

a historian   *or*   an historian
a heroic attempt   *or*   an heroic attempt
a hilarious performance   *or*   an hilarious performance

5. Before a word or abbreviation beginning with a vowel *sound,* the article *an* is used. This is true even if the spelling (especially of an abbreviation) begins with a consonant.

an icicle	an orange	an unknown
an hour	an honor	an nth degree
an FCC report	an MIT professor	an Rh factor

6. **Nominals** Nominals are words or groups of words that function as nouns. Adjectives, gerunds, and infinitives act as nominals. An example of an adjective used as a noun is the word *good* in the phrase "the good die young." Examples of gerunds and infinitives used as nouns are *seeing* in the clause "seeing is believing" and *to see* in the clause "to see is to believe." Noun phrases and noun clauses are also considered to be nominals. For more information about gerunds and infinitives, see paragraphs 12–14 under Verb in this section. For information about noun phrases and noun clauses, see pages 35 and 36 respectively.

7. **Nouns used as adjectives** A frequent practice in English is to use a noun as an adjective by placing it before another noun (in the attributive position), as in *school board* or *office management.* When nouns are frequently combined in this way, they become familiar compounds like *profit margin, systems analysis, money market, box lunch.* Such compounds provide useful verbal shortcuts (e.g., office management = the management of an office or offices). However, care should be taken not to pile up so many of these noun modifiers that the reader has difficulty sorting out their meanings.

shorter but unclear
Management review copies of the Division II sales department machine parts file should be indexed.

longer but clear
Copies of the machine parts file from the Division II sales department should be indexed before being sent to management for review.

NOTE: Both of these sentences could be made clearer by hyphenating the compound nouns used as adjectives. For complete information about the treatment of this kind of compound, see the discussion under Compounds That Function as Adjectives, pages 119–122.

> Management-review copies of the Division II sales-department machine-parts file should be indexed.

8. **Plurals** The plurals of nouns are usually indicated by addition of an -*s* or -*es* to the base word, although some nouns (such as those of foreign origin) have irregular plurals. For complete information about the formation of plurals, see the discussion under Plurals, pages 107–111.

9. **Possessives** The possessive case is the only noun case indicated by inflection. Typically, the possessives of nouns are formed by the addition of an apostrophe plus -*s* to singular nouns or just an apostrophe to plural words ending in -*s*. For complete information about the formation of possessives, see the discussion under Possessives, pages 111–114.

10. **Proper nouns** Proper nouns are nouns that name a particular person, place, or thing and distinguish it from other members of the same class. The most obvious feature of proper nouns is that they are almost always capitalized. For complete information about capitalizing proper nouns, see the discussion under Proper Nouns, Pronouns, and Adjectives, pages 88–104.

Preposition

A preposition is a word that combines with a noun, pronoun, or noun equivalent (as a phrase or clause) to form a phrase that usually acts as an adverb, adjective, or noun.

Prepositions are not characterized by inflection, number, case, gender, or identifying suffixes. They can be identified chiefly by their position within sentences and by their grammatical functions. Prepositions may be simple, i.e., composed of only one element (*against, from, near, of, on, out,* or *without);* or they may be compound, i.e., composed of more than one element (*according to, by means of,* or *in spite of).*

1. **Basic uses** Prepositions are chiefly used to link nouns, pronouns, or noun equivalents to the rest of the sentence. A prepositional phrase is usually adverbial or adjectival in function.

   > She expected resistance *on* his part.
   > He sat down *beside* her.

2. **Conjunctions vs. prepositions** The words *after, before, but, for,* and *since* may function as either prepositions or conjunctions. Their position within the sentence identifies them as conjunctions or prepositions. Conjunctions link two words or sentence elements that have the same

grammatical function. Prepositions precede a noun, pronoun, noun phrase, or noun equivalent.

> *conjunction*
> I was a bit concerned *but* not panicky. (*but* links two adjectives)
>
> *preposition*
> I was left with nothing *but* hope. (*but* precedes a noun)
>
> *conjunction*
> The device conserves fuel, *for* it is battery-powered. (*for* links two clauses)
>
> *preposition*
> The device conserves fuel *for* residual heating. (*for* precedes a noun phrase)

3. **Implied prepositions** If two words combine idiomatically with the same preposition, that preposition need not be used after both.

> We were antagonistic [*to*] and opposed *to* the whole idea.
>   *but*
> We are interested *in* and anxious *for* raises.

4. **Position** Prepositions may occur in the following positions: before nouns or pronouns ("*below* the desk," "*beside* them"); after adjectives ("antagonistic *to*," "insufficient *in*," "symbolic *of*"); and after the verbal elements of idiomatically fixed verb + preposition combinations ("take *for*," "get *after*," "come *across*").

5. There is no reason why a preposition cannot terminate a sentence, especially when it is an integral element in an idiomatically fixed verb phrase.

> His lack of organization is only one of the things I put up *with*.
> What does all this add up *to*?

6. **Use of *between* and *among*** Despite an unfounded notion to the contrary, the preposition *between* can be used of more than two items. It is especially appropriate to denote a one-to-one relationship, regardless of the number of items. *Between* can be used when the number is unspecified, when more than two are enumerated, and even when only one item is mentioned (but repetition is implied).

> Treaties established economic cooperation *between* nations.
> This is *between* you and me and the lamppost.
> He paused *between* every sentence to clear his throat.

Among is more appropriate where the emphasis is on overall distribution rather than individual relationships.

> There was discontent *among* the peasants.

NOTE: When *among* is automatically chosen for more than two, the results can sound strained.

> The author alternates *among* quotes, clichés, and street slang.

Pronoun

A pronoun is a word that is used as a substitute for a noun or noun equivalent, takes noun constructions, and refers to persons or things named or understood in the context. The noun or noun equivalent for which it substitutes is called the *antecedent*.

Pronouns exhibit all or some of the following characteristic features: case (nominative, possessive, objective); number (singular, plural); person (first, second, third person); and gender (masculine, feminine, neuter). Pronouns are divided into seven major categories, each with its own function. Each pronoun category is listed and described alphabetically in this section.

Demonstrative pronouns The words *this, that, these,* and *those* are classified as pronouns when they function as nouns (they are classified as demonstrative adjectives when they modify nouns; see the discussion under Adjective in this section).

1. Demonstrative pronouns point out the person or thing referred to and distinguish it from others of the same type.

   These are the best cookies I've ever eaten.

   Those are strong words.

2. They also distinguish between a person or thing nearby and one further away.

   This is my desk; *that* is yours.

3. A potentially troublesome situation occurs when a demonstrative pronoun introduces a sentence referring back to something previously mentioned. The reference should be clear and not cloudy:

   cloudy
   The heir's hemophilia, the influence of an unprincipled faith healer on the royal family, devastating military setbacks, general strikes, mass outbreaks of typhus, and repeated crop failures contributed to the revolution. *This* influenced the course of history.

   clear
   None of the participants in the political scandal kept records of what they said or did. *That* is most unfortunate, and it should be a lesson for the future.

4. When demonstrative pronouns are used with the words *kind, sort,* and *type* + *of* + noun, they should agree in number with both nouns.

   not
   We want *these kind* of *pencils.*

   instead
   We want *this kind* of *pencil.*

   or
   We want *these kinds* of *pencils.*

Indefinite pronouns Indefinite pronouns designate an unidentified or not immediately identifiable person or thing. They are chiefly used as third-person references and do not distinguish gender. Examples of indefinite pronouns are the following: *all, another, any, anybody, anyone, anything, both, each, each one, either, everybody, everyone, everything, few, many, much, neither, nobody, none, no one, other, several, some, somebody, someone, something.*

5. Indefinite pronouns should agree in number with their verb. The following are singular and take singular verbs: *another, anything, each one, everything, much, nobody, no one, one, other, someone, something.*

> *Much is* being done.
> *No one wants* to go.

6. The following indefinite pronouns are plural and take plural verbs: *both, few, many, several.*

> *Many were* called; *few were* chosen.

7. Some indefinite pronouns (such as *all, any, none, some*) present problems because they may be either singular or plural, depending on whether they are used with mass nouns or count nouns (a *mass noun* identifies something not ordinarily thought of in terms of numbered elements; a *count noun* identifies things that can be counted).

> *with mass noun*
> *All* of the *property is* entailed.
> *None* of the *ink was* erasable.
> Not *any* of the *sky was* visible.
>
> *with count noun*
> *All* of our *bases are* covered.
> *None* of the *clerks were* available.
> Not *any* of the *stars were* visible.

8. The following are singular in form, and as such logically take singular verbs. However, because of their plural connotations, informal speech has established the use of plural pronoun references to them: *anybody, anyone, everybody, everyone, somebody.*

> I knew *everybody* by *their* first names.
> Don't tell *anyone; they* might spread the rumor.

Even in more formal contexts, expressions such as the following are used increasingly, especially as a result of attempts to avoid sexism in language:

> We called *everyone* by *their* first *names.*
>
> *instead of*
> We called *everyone* by *his* first *name.*

For more about avoiding sexism in the use of personal pronouns, see paragraph 22 below.

9. In some constructions an apparently singular indefinite pronoun may take a plural verb if the context makes it seem plural. The following two sentences illustrate how a singular indefinite pronoun may take either a singular or plural verb, depending on how the writer interprets *either:*

   Either of these pronunciations *is* acceptable.
   Either of these pronunciations *are* acceptable.

   The conventional choice of verb would be *is,* because the subject of the sentence is the singular pronoun *either.* However, the proximity of the plural word *pronunciations,* together with the possibility of interpreting *either* to mean "one or both," gives the writer or speaker the opportunity to choose either a singular or a plural verb, depending on the interpretation of the subject.

10. The indefinite pronouns *any* and *anyone* are conventionally followed by *other(s)* or *else* when they form part of a comparison of two individuals in the same class.

    not
    Helen has more seniority than *anyone* in the firm.
    instead
    Helen has more seniority than *anyone else* in the firm.
    not
    Our house is older than *any* building on the block.
    instead
    Our house is older than *any other* building on the block.

    The addition of *else* and *other* in the preceding sentences avoids the logical impossibility that Helen has more seniority than herself or that our house is older than itself. Likewise, it prevents the possible misreading that Helen is not a member of the firm or that our house is not on the block.

11. The antecedent of an indefinite pronoun should be clearly stated, not implied. A good check for a clear reference is to see if there is an antecedent in the sentence that could be substituted for the pronoun.

    unclear
    He's the author of a best-selling book on sailing, despite the fact that he's never set foot on *one.*
    clear
    He's the author of a best-selling book on sailing, despite the fact that he's never set foot on a sailboat.

12. **Interrogative pronouns** The interrogative pronouns *what, which, who, whom,* and *whose* as well as combinations of these words with the suffix *-ever* are used to introduce direct and indirect questions.

    Who is she?
    He asked me *who* she was.

Whom did the article accuse?

She asked *whom* the article accused.

Whoever can that be?

We wondered *whoever* that could be.

Personal pronouns Personal pronouns refer to beings and objects and reflect the person, number, and gender of those antecendents. Examples of personal pronouns are: *he, I, it, she, they, we, you.*

13. Most personal pronouns take different forms for the three cases.

	Nominative	Possessive	Objective
first person singular	I	my, mine	me
first person plural	we	our, ours	us
second person singular	you	your, yours	you
second person plural	you	your, yours	you
third person singular	he	his, his	him
	she	her, hers	her
	it	its, its	it
third person plural	they	their, theirs	them

14. A personal pronoun agrees in person, number, and gender with the word it refers to. However, the case of a pronoun is determined by its function within a sentence. The nominative case is used for a pronoun that acts as a subject of a sentence or as a predicate nominative (but see paragraph 15 below). The possessive case is used for pronouns that express possession or a similar relationship. The objective case is used for pronouns that are direct objects, indirect objects, retained objects, objects of prepositions, or objective complements.

You and *I* thought the meeting was useful.

My assistant and *I* attended the seminar.

Our new candidate will be *you.*

We all had *our* own offices.

The vice president informed my assistant and *me* about the seminar.

She gave *me* the papers.

Just between *you* and *me,* the meeting was much too long.

I was given *them* yesterday.

That makes our new candidate *her.*

15. The nominative case after the verb *to be* (as in "It is I" and "This is she") is considered standard English and is preferred by strict grammarians, but the objective case (as in "It's me") also may be used without criticism, especially in spoken English.

The only candidate left for that job may soon be she.
    or
The only candidate left for that job may soon be her.

16. When a personal pronoun follows *than* or *as* and is the subject of an implied verb, it should be in the nominative case:

> He received a bigger bonus than *she* [did].
> She has as much seniority as *I* [do].

17. The suffixes *-self* and *-selves* combine only with the possessive case of the first- and second-person pronouns (*myself, ourselves, yourself, yourselves*) and with the objective case of the third-person pronouns (*himself, herself, itself, themselves*). Other combinations (as "hisself" and "theirselves") are considered nonstandard and should not be used.

18. Personal pronouns in the possessive case (such as *your, their, theirs, its*) do not contain apostrophes and should not be confused with similar-sounding contractions (such as *you're, they're, there's, it's*), which do contain apostrophes.

> *possessive personal pronoun*
> Put the camera in *its* case.
> *Whose* camera is it?
>
> *contraction*
> *It's* an expensive camera.
> *Who's* going to go?

19. When one uses the pronoun *I* or *me* with other pronouns or with other people's names, *I* or *me* should be last in the series:

> Mrs. Smith and *I* were trained together.
> He and *I* were attending the meeting.
> The memorandum was directed to Ms. Montgomery and *me*.

20. Some companies prefer that writers use *we* and not *I* when speaking for their companies in business correspondence. *I* is more often used when a writer is referring only to himself or herself. The following example illustrates use of both within one sentence:

> *We* [i.e., the writer speaks for the company] have reviewed the manuscript that you sent to *me* [i.e., the manuscript was sent only to the writer] on June 1, but *we* [a corporate or group decision] feel that it is too specialized a work to be marketable by *our* company.

21. While the personal pronouns *it, you,* and *they* are often used as indefinite pronouns in spoken English, they can be vague or even redundant in some contexts.

> *vague*
> *They* said at the seminar that the economy would experience a third-quarter upturn. (The question is: Who exactly is *they*?)
>
> *explicit*
> The economists on the panel at the seminar predicted a third-quarter economic upturn.
>
> *redundant*
> In the graph *it* says that production fell off by 50%.
>
> *lean*
> The graph indicates a 50% production drop.

22. Forms of the personal pronoun *he* and the indefinite pronoun *one* are the standard substitutes for antecedents whose genders are mixed or irrelevant:

> Present the letter to the executive for *his* approval.
> Each employee should check *his* W-2 form.
> If *one* really wants to succeed, *one* can.

However, many writers today who are concerned about sexism in language recast such sentences, where possible, to avoid generic use of the masculine pronoun:

> Present the letter to the executive for approval.
> All employees should check *their* W-2 forms.
> Each employee should check *his or her* W-2 form.

The phrase *his or her* should be used sparingly, however, as it seems awkward and could certainly become tiresome if used frequently throughout a text. For more on avoiding the generic use of the masculine pronoun, see paragraph 8 above.

23. **Reciprocal pronouns** The reciprocal pronouns *each other* and *one another* are used in the object position to indicate a mutual action or cross relationship between the members comprised in a plural or compound subject.

> They do not quarrel with *one another*.
> Karen and Rachel spelled *each other* at driving on their trip.

24. Reciprocal pronouns may also be used in the possessive case:

> The two secretaries borrowed *one another's* stationery.
> The president and his vice president depend on *each other's* ideas.

25. **Reflexive pronouns** Reflexive pronouns express reflexive action or add extra emphasis to the subject of the sentence, clause, or verbal phrase in which they occur. Reflexive pronouns are formed by compounding the personal pronouns *him, her, it, my, our, them,* and *your* with *-self* or *-selves.* Reflexive pronouns are used when an object or subjective complement refers to the same thing as the foregoing noun or noun phrase.

> She dressed *herself*.
> The baby isn't *himself* this morning.
> They asked *themselves* if they were being honest.
> I *myself* am not afraid.
> The cook told Jim to help *himself*.

Relative pronouns The relative pronouns are *that, what, which, who, whom,* and *whose,* as well as combinations of these with *-ever*. They introduce subordinate clauses acting as nouns or modifiers. While a relative pronoun itself does not exhibit number, gender, or person, it does determine the number, gender, and person of elements that follow it in the relative clause because of its implicit agreement with its antecedent. Consider, for instance, the following sentence:

People *who are* ready to start *their* jobs should arrive at 8:00 a.m.

In this sentence, the relative pronoun "who" refers to the plural subject "People," and it acts as the subject of the relative clause "who are ready to start their jobs." Because it refers to a plural word it acts like a plural word within its clause and therefore calls for the plural verb "are" and the plural pronoun "their."

26. The relative pronoun *who* typically refers to persons and some animals; *which,* to things and animals; and *that,* to both beings and things.

a man who sought success
a man whom we can trust
Seattle Slew, who won horse racing's Triple Crown
a book which sold well
a dog which barked loudly
a book that sold well
a dog that barked loudly
a man that we can trust

27. Relative pronouns can sometimes be omitted for the sake of brevity.

The man *whom* I was talking to is the president.
    or
The man I was talking to is the president.

28. The relative pronoun *what* may be substituted for the longer and more awkward phrases "that which," "that of which," or "the thing which" in some sentences.

stiff
He was blamed for *that which* he could not have known.

easier
He was blamed for *what* he could not have known.

29. The problem of when to use *who* or *whom* has been blown out of proportion. The situation is very simple: standard written English makes a distinction between the nominative and objective cases of these pronouns when they are used as relatives or interrogatives.

nominative case
Who is she?
Who does she think she is, anyway?
She thinks she is the one *who* ought to be promoted.
Give me a list of the ones *who* you think should be promoted.

objective case
Whom are you referring to?
To *whom* are you referring?

He's a man *whom* everyone should know.
He's a man with *whom* everyone should be acquainted.

In speech, however, case distinctions and boundaries often become blurred, with the result that spoken English favors *who* as a general substitute for all uses of *whom* except in set phrases such as "*To whom it may concern.*" In speech, then, *who* may be used not only as the subject of the clause it introduces but also as the object of a verb in a clause that it introduces or as an interrogative.

Let us select *who* we think will be the best candidate.
See the manager, Mrs. Keats, *who* you should be able to find in her office.
Who should we tell?

30. *Whom* is commonly used as the object of a preposition in a clause that it introduces; however, the form *who* is commonly used to introduce a question even when it is the object of a preposition:

Presiding is a judge *about whom* I know nothing.
He is a man *for whom* I would gladly work.
  but
Who (rarely *whom*) are you going to listen to?
Who (rarely *whom*) do you work for?

31. While in speech the nominative form *who* can be used in the objective case in certain kinds of sentences, the reverse is not true: the objective form *whom* cannot be used in the nominative case, either in spoken or in written English. One should therefore avoid such usages as "*Whom do you suppose is coming to the meeting?*" which result from a mistaken notion that *whom* is somehow always more correct.

32. The relative pronouns *whoever* and *whomever* follow the same principles as *who* and *whom* in formal writing:

nominative
Tell *whoever* is going to research the case that . . . .
He wants to help *whoever* needs it most.
objective
She makes friends with *whomever* she meets.

NOTE: In speech, however, as with *who* and *whom*, case distinctions become blurred, and *whoever* is used without criticism in most sentences:

Whoever did she choose?

Verb

A verb is a word that is characteristically the grammatical center of a predicate and expresses an act, occurrence, or mode of being. Verbs are inflected for agreement with the subject and for mood, voice, or tense. Verbs typically have rather full descriptive meaning and characterizing quality, but they sometimes are almost completely devoid of these especially when they are used as auxiliary or linking verbs.

Verbs exhibit the following characteristic features: inflection *(help, helps, helping, helped)*, person (first, second, third person), number (singular, plural), tense (present, past, future), aspect (time relations other than the simple present, past, and future), voice (active, passive), mood (indicative, subjunctive, imperative), and suffixation (as by the typical suffixal markers *-ate, -en, -ify,* and *-ize*).

Inflection Regular verbs have four inflected forms signaled by the suffixes *-s* or *-es, -ed,* and *-ing*. The verb *help* as shown in the sentence above is regular. Most irregular verbs have four or five forms, as *see, sees, seeing, saw,* and *seen;* and one, the verb *be,* has eight: *be, is, am, are, being, was, were,* and *been*. When one is uncertain about a particular inflected form, one should consult a dictionary that indicates not only the inflections of irregular verbs but also those inflections resulting in changes in base-word spelling.

> blame; blamed; blaming
> spy; spied; spying
> picnic; picnicked; picnicking

A dictionary should also show variant inflected forms.

> bias; biased *or* biassed; biasing *or* biassing
> counsel; counseled *or* counselled; counseling *or* counselling
> diagram; diagramed *or* diagrammed; diagraming *or* diagramming
> travel; traveled *or* travelled; traveling *or* travelling

All of the foregoing forms may be found at their respective main entries in *Webster's Ninth New Collegiate Dictionary*. There are, however, a few rules that will aid one in ascertaining the proper spelling patterns of certain verb forms.

1. Verbs ending in a silent *-e* generally retain the *-e* before consonant suffixes (as *-s*) but drop the *-e* before vowel suffixes (as *-ed* and *-ing*).

   > arrange; arranges; arranged; arranging
   > hope; hopes; hoped; hoping
   > require; requires; required; requiring
   > shape; shapes; shaped; shaping

   NOTE: A few verbs ending in a silent *-e* retain the *-e* before vowel suffixes in order to avoid confusion with other words.

   > dye; dyes; dyed; dyeing (*vs.* dying)
   > singe; singes; singed; singeing (*vs.* singing)

2. Monosyllabic verbs ending in a single consonant preceded by a single vowel double the final consonant before vowel suffixes (as *-ed* and *-ing*).

   > brag; bragged; bragging
   > grip; gripped; gripping
   > pin; pinned; pinning

3. Polysyllabic verbs ending in a single consonant preceded by a single vowel and having an accented last syllable double the final consonant before vowel suffixes (as -*ed* and -*ing*).

> commit; committed; committing
> control; controlled; controlling
> occur; occurred; occurring
> omit; omitted; omitting

NOTE: The final consonant of such verbs is not doubled when two vowels occur before the final consonant or when two consonants form the ending of the verb.

> daub; daubed; daubing
> soil; soiled; soiling
> help; helped; helping
> lurk; lurked; lurking
> peck; pecked; pecking

4. Verbs ending in -*y* preceded by a consonant regularly change the -*y* to -*i* before all suffixes except -*ing*.

> carry; carried; carrying
> marry; married; marrying
> study; studied; studying

NOTE: If the final -*y* is preceded by a vowel, it remains unchanged in suffixation.

> delay; delayed; delaying
> enjoy; enjoyed; enjoying
> obey; obeyed; obeying

5. Verbs ending in -*c* add a -*k* when a suffix beginning with -*e* or -*i* is added.

> mimic; mimics; mimicked; mimicking
> panic; panics; panicked; panicking
> traffic; traffics; trafficked; trafficking

NOTE: Words derived from this type of verb also add a -*k* when such a suffix or the suffix -*y* is added to them.

> panicky
> trafficker

6. **Tense, aspect, voice, and mood** English verbs exhibit their simple present and simple past tenses by use of two single-word grammatical forms.

> simple present=do
> simple past=did

7. The future tense is expressed by *shall* or *will* followed by the base form of the verb or by use of the simple present or present progressive forms in a revealing context.

I *shall do* it.
He *will do* it.
I *leave* shortly for New York.
I *am leaving* shortly for New York.

8. Aspect is a property that allows verbs to indicate time relations other than the simple present, past, or future tenses. Aspect covers these relationships:

action occurring in the past and continuing to the present	has seen	*present perfect*
action completed at a past time or before the immediate past	had seen	*past perfect*
action that will have been completed by a future time	will have seen	*future perfect*
action occurring now	is seeing	*progressive*

In contexts that require it, the perfective and the progressive aspects can be combined to yield special verb forms, such as *had been seeing*.

9. Voice enables a verb to indicate whether the subject of a sentence is acting (he *loves* = active voice) or whether the subject is being acted upon (he *is loved* = passive voice).

10. Mood indicates manner of expression. The indicative mood states a fact or asks a question (He *is* here. *Is* he here?). The subjunctive mood expresses condition contrary to fact (I wish that he *were* here). The imperative mood expresses a command or request (*Come* here. Please *come* here).

11. **Transitive and intransitive verbs** Verbs may be used transitively or intransitively. A *transitive* verb acts upon a direct object.

   She *contributed* money.
   He *ran* the store.

   An *intransitive* verb does not act upon a direct object.

   She *contributed* generously.
   He *ran* down the street.

   NOTE: As in the examples above, many verbs are transitive in one sense and intransitive in another.

Verbals There is another group of words derived from verbs and called *verbals* that deserve added discussion. The members of this group—the gerund, the participle, and the infinitive—exhibit some but not all of the characteristic features of their parent verbs.

12. A gerund is an *-ing* verb form, but it functions mainly as a noun. It has both the active *(seeing)* and the passive *(being seen)* voices. In addi-

tion to voice, a gerund's verbal characteristics are as follows: it conveys the notion of a verb—i.e., action, occurrence, or being; it can take an object; and it can be modified by an adverb. In the following sentences, for instance, "Typing" and "driving" are gerunds, "data" and "cars" are their objects, and "daily" and "fast" are adverbs modifying the gerund.

> *Typing* tabular *data daily* is a boring task.
> He liked *driving cars fast*.

NOTE: Nouns and pronouns occurring before gerunds are expressed by the possessive.

> She is trying to improve *her typing*.
> We objected to *their telling* the story all over town.
> We saw the *boy's whipping*. (i.e., the boy being whipped)
> We expected the *senator's coming*. (i.e., his arrival)

13. Participles, on the other hand, function as adjectives and may occur alone ("a *broken* typewriter") or in phrases that modify other words ("*Having broken the typewriter,* she gave up for the day"). Participles have active and passive forms like gerunds.

> *active-voice participial phrase modifying "he"*
> *Having failed to pass the examination,* he was forced to repeat the course.
> *passive-voice participial phrase modifying "he"*
> *Having been failed* by his instructor, he was forced to repeat the course.

NOTE: Participles, unlike gerunds, are not preceded by possessive nouns or pronouns:

> We saw the *boy whipping* his dog. (i.e., we saw the boy doing the whipping)
> We saw the *senator coming*. (i.e., we saw him arrive)

14. Infinitives may exhibit active *(to do)* and passive *(to be done)* voices, and they may indicate aspect *(to be doing, to have done, to have been doing, to have been done)*. Infinitives may take complements and may be modified by adverbs. In addition, they can function as nouns, adjectives, and adverbs in sentences. Examples:

> *noun use*
> *To be known* is *to be castigated*. (subject and predicate nominative)
> He tried everything except *to bypass his superior*. (object of preposition "except")
> *adjectival use*
> They had found a way *to increase profits greatly*. (modifies the noun "way")
> *adverbial use*
> He was too furious *to speak*. (modifies "furious")

NOTE: Although *to* is the characteristic marker of an infinitive, it is not always stated but may be understood:

> He helped [to] complete the marketing report.

15. **Sequence of tenses** If the main verb in a sentence is in the present tense, any other tense or compound verb form may follow it in subsequent clauses, as:

I *realize* that you *are leaving.* I *realize* that you *will be leaving.*
I *realize* that you *left.* I *realize* that you *will leave.*
I *realize* that you *were leaving.* I *realize* that you *will have been leaving.*
I *realize* that you *have been leaving.* I *realize* that you *can be leaving.*
I *realize* that you *had left.* I *realize* that you *may be leaving.*
I *realize* that you *had been leaving.* I *realize* that you *must be leaving.*

16. If the main verb is in the past tense, that tense imposes time restrictions on any subsequent verbs in the sentence, thus excluding use of the present tense, as:

I *realized* that you *were leaving.* I *realized* that you *would be leaving.*
I *realized* that you *left.* I *realized* that you *could be leaving.*
I *realized* that you *had left.* I *realized* that you *might be leaving.*
I *realized* that you *had been leaving.* I *realized* that you *would leave.*

17. If the main verb is in the future tense, it imposes time restrictions on subsequent verbs in the sentence, thus excluding the possibility of using the simple past tense, as:

He *will see* you because he *is going* to the meeting too.
He *will see* you because he *will be going* to the meeting too.
He *will see* you because he *will go* to the meeting too.
He *will see* you because he *has been going* to the meetings too.
He *will see* you because he *will have been going* to the meetings too.

18. In general, most writers try to maintain an order of tenses throughout their sentences that is consistent with natural or real time, e.g., present tense = present-time matters, past tense = past matters, and future tense = matters that will take place in the future. However, there are two outstanding exceptions to these principles. First, if one is discussing the contents of printed or published material, one conventionally uses the present tense.

In *Etiquette,* Emily Post *discusses* forms of address.
This analysis *gives* market projections for the next two years.
In his latest position paper on the Middle East, the Secretary of State *writes* that . . . .

Second, if one wishes to add the connotation of immediacy to a particular sentence, one may use the present tense instead of the future.

I *leave* for Tel Aviv tonight.

19. The sequence of tenses in sentences which express contrary-to-fact conditions is a special problem frequently encountered in writing. The examples below show the sequence correctly maintained.

If he *were* on time, we *would leave* now.
If he *had been* (not *would have been*) on time, we *would have left* an hour ago.

20. At one time, *shall* was considered the only correct form to use with the first person in simple future tenses *(I shall, we shall)*, while *will* was limited to the second and third persons *(you will, it will, they will)*. Today, however, either of the following forms is considered correct for the first person:

> *more formal*
> We *shall give* your request special attention.
>
> *less formal*
> We *will give* your request special attention.

Subject-verb agreement Verbs agree in number and in person with their grammatical subjects. At times, however, the grammatical subject may be singular in form, but the thought it carries—i.e., the notional subject— may have plural connotations. Here are some general guidelines. For discussion of verb agreement with indefinite-pronoun subjects, see paragraphs 5–9 under Pronoun in this section. For discussion of verb number as affected by a compound subject whose elements are joined by *and/or,* see paragraph 6 under Conjunction in this section.

21. Plural and compound subjects take plural verbs even if the subject is inverted.

> Both dogs and cats *were* tested for the virus.
> Grouped under the heading "fine arts" *are* music, theater, and painting.

22. Compound subjects or plural subjects working as a unit take singular verbs in American English.

> Lord & Taylor *has* stores in the New York area.
> Cauliflower and cheese *is* my favorite vegetable.
> Five hundred dollars *is* a stiff price for a coat.
> *but*
> Twenty-five milligrams of pentazocine *were* administered.

23. Compound subjects expressing mathematical relationships may be either singular or plural.

> One plus one *makes* (or *make*) two.
> Six from eight *leaves* (or *leave*) two.

24. Singular subjects joined by *or* or *nor* take singular verbs; plural subjects so joined take plural verbs.

> A freshman or sophomore *is* eligible for the scholarship.
> Neither freshmen nor sophomores *are* eligible for the scholarship.

NOTE: If one subject is singular and the other plural, the verb agrees with the number of the subject that is closer to it.

> Either the secretaries or the supervisor *has* to do the job.
> Either the supervisor or the secretaries *have* to do the job.

25. Singular subjects introduced by *many a, such a, every, each,* or *no* take singular verbs, even when several such subjects are joined by *and.*

Many an executive *has* gone to the top in that division.

No supervisor and no assembler *is* excused from the time check.

Every chair, table, and desk *has* to be accounted for.

26. The agreement of the verb with its grammatical subject ordinarily should not be skewed by an intervening phrase.

One of my reasons for resigning *involves* purely personal considerations.

The president of the company, as well as members of his staff, *has* arrived.

He, not any of the proxy voters, *has* to be present.

27. The verb *to be* agrees with its grammatical subject and not with its complement.

His mania *was* fast cars and beautiful women.

Women in the work force *constitute* a new field of study.

NOTE: The verb *to be* introduced by the word *there* must agree in number with the subject following it.

There *are* many complications here.

There *is* no reason to worry about him.

28. Collective nouns—such as *orchestra, team, committee, family*—usually take singular verbs but can take plural verbs if the emphasis is on the individual members of the unit rather than on the unit itself.

The committee *has agreed* to extend the deadline.
  but also
The committee *have been* at odds ever since the beginning.

29. The word *number* in the phrase *a number of* usually takes a plural verb, but in the phrase *the number of* it takes a singular verb.

A number of errors *were* (also *was*) made.

The number of errors *was* surprising.

30. A relative clause that follows the expression *one of those/these* + plural noun takes a plural verb in conventional English, but in informal English it may take a singular verb.

He is one of those executives who *worry* (also *worries*) a lot.

This is one of those typewriters that *create* (also *creates*) perfect copies.

31. **Linking and *sense* verbs** Linking verbs (as the various forms of *to be*) and the so-called "sense" verbs (as *feel, look, taste, smell,* as well as particular senses of *appear, become, continue, grow, prove, remain, seem, stand,* and *turn*) connect subjects with predicate nouns or adjectives.

He *is* a vice president.

He *became* vice president.

The temperature *continues* cold.

The future *looks* prosperous.

I *feel* bad.

He *remains* healthy.

NOTE: Sense words often cause confusion, in that writers sometimes mistakenly use adverbs instead of adjectives following these words.

not
This perfume smells nicely.

instead
This perfume smells nice.

not
The meat tastes well.

instead
The meat tastes good.

32. **Split infinitives** A split infinitive is an infinitive that has a modifier between the *to* and the verbal (as in "to really care"). In the past, some grammarians disapproved of this construction, and many people still try to avoid it whenever they can. However, the split infinitive has been around a long time and has been used by a wide variety of distinguished English writers. It can be a useful device if a writer wants to stress the verbal element of an infinitive or express a thought that is most clearly shown with *to* + adverb + infinitive. In some cases where special emphasis on a word or a group of words is desirable, that emphasis cannot be achieved with an undivided infinitive construction. For example, in the phrase "to *thoroughly* complete the financial study" the position of the adverb as close as possible to the verbal element of the whole infinitive phrase strengthens the effect of the adverb on the verbal element. This situation is not necessarily true in the following reworded phrases:

to complete *thoroughly* the financial study
thoroughly to complete the financial study
to complete the financial study *thoroughly*

In other instances, the position of the adverb may actually modify or change the entire meaning.

original
arrived at the office to *unexpectedly* find a new name on the door

recast with new meanings
arrived at the office *unexpectedly* to find a new name on the door
arrived at the office to find a new name on the door *unexpectedly*

NOTE: Very long adverbial modifiers that interrupt an infinitive are clumsy and should be avoided or recast.

clumsy
He wanted to *completely and without mercy* defeat his competitor.

recast
He wanted to defeat his competitor *completely and without mercy*.

33. **Dangling participles** Dangling participles are participles occurring in a sentence without a normally expected syntactic relation to the rest of the sentence. They are best avoided, as they may create confusion for the reader or seem ludicrous.

dangling
Walking through the door, her coat was caught.

recast
While walking through the door, she caught her coat.
Walking through the door, she caught her coat.
She caught her coat while walking through the door.

dangling
Caught in the act, his excuses were unconvincing.

recast
Caught in the act, he could not make his excuses convincing.

dangling
Having been told that he was incompetent and dishonest, the executive fired the man.

recast
Having told the man that he was incompetent and dishonest, the executive fired him.
Having been told by his superior that he was incompetent and dishonest, the man was fired.

NOTE: Participles should not be confused with prepositions that end in *-ing*—like *concerning, considering, providing, regarding, respecting, touching,* etc.

prepositional usage
Concerning your complaint, we can tell you . . . .
Considering all the implications, you have made a dangerous decision.
Touching the matter at hand, we can say that . . . .

Phrases

A phrase is a brief expression that consists of two or more grammatically related words that may contain either a noun or a finite verb (that is, a verb that shows grammatical person and number) but not both, and that often functions as a particular part of speech within a clause or sentence.

Basic Types

There are seven basic types of phrases.

1. An *absolute phrase* consists of a noun followed by a modifier (such as a participle). Absolute phrases act independently within a sentence without modifying a particular element of the sentence. Absolute phrases are also referred to as *nominative absolutes*.

   He stalked out, *his eyes staring straight ahead.*

2. A *gerund phrase* is a verbal phrase that includes a gerund and functions as a noun.

   Sitting on a patient's bed is bad hospital etiquette.

3. An *infinitive phrase* is a verbal phrase that includes an infinitive and that may function as a noun, adjective, or adverb.

> *noun*
> *To do that* would be stupid.
> *adjective*
> This was a performance *to remember.*
> *adverb*
> He struggled *to get free.*

4. A *noun phrase* consists of a noun and its modifiers.

> *The concrete building* is huge.

5. A *participial phrase* is a verbal phrase that includes a participle and that functions as an adjective.

> *Listening all the time with great concentration,* she began to line up her options.

6. A *prepositional phrase* consists of a preposition and its object. It may function as a noun, adjective, or adverb.

> *noun*
> *Out of debt* is where we'd like to be!
> *adjective*
> Here is the desk *with the extra file drawer.*
> *adverb*
> He now walked *without a limp.*

7. A *verb phrase* consists of a verb and any other terms that either modify it or that complete its meaning.

> She *will have arrived too late* for you to talk to her.

Usage Problems

1. Usage problems with phrases occur most often when a modifying phrase is not placed close enough to the word or words that it modifies. The phrase "On December 10" in the following sentence, for example, must be repositioned to clarify just what happened on that date.

> *original*
> We received your letter concerning the shipment of parts on December 10.
> *recast*
> On December 10 we received your letter concerning the shipment of parts.
> *or*
> We received your letter concerning the December 10 shipment of parts.

2. A very common usage problem with phrases involves dangling participial phrases. For a discussion of dangling participles, see paragraph 33 under Verb, pages 33–34.

Clauses

A clause is a group of words containing both a subject and a predicate. A clause functions as an element of a compound or a complex sentence. There are two general types of clauses: the *main* or *independent clause* and the *subordinate* or *dependent clause*. The main clause (such as "it is hot") is an independent grammatical unit and can stand alone. The subordinate clause (such as "because it is hot") cannot stand alone. A subordinate clause is either preceded or followed by a main clause.

Basic Types

Like phrases, clauses can perform as particular parts of speech within the total environment of the sentence. There are three basic types of clauses having part-of-speech functions.

1. The *adjective clause* modifies a noun or pronoun and typically follows the word it modifies.

   > Her administrative assistant, *who was also a speech writer,* was overworked.
   > I can't see the reason *why you're upset.*
   > He is a man *who will succeed.*
   > Anybody *who opts for a career like that* is crazy.

2. The *adverb clause* modifies a verb, an adjective, or another adverb and typically follows the word it modifies.

   > They made a valiant effort, *although the risks were great.*
   > *When it rains,* it pours.
   > I'm certain *that he is guilty.*
   > We accomplished less *than we did before.*

3. The *noun clause* fills a noun slot in a sentence and thus can be a subject, an object, or a complement.

   > *subject*
   > *Whoever is qualified* should apply.
   > *object of a verb*
   > I do not know *what his field is.*
   > *object of a preposition*
   > Route that journal to *whichever department you wish.*
   > *complement*
   > The trouble is *that she has no ambition.*

Elliptical Clauses

Some clause elements may be omitted if the context makes clear the understood elements:

> I remember the first time [that] we met.
> This typewriter is better than that [typewriter is].
> When [she is] on the job, she is always competent and alert.

Placement of Clauses

A modifying clause should be placed as close as possible to the word or words it modifies. This placement will give maximum clarity, and it avoids the possibility that the reader will misinterpret written material. If intervening words muddy the overall meaning of a sentence, it should be rewritten or recast.

muddy
A memorandum is a piece of business writing, less formal than a letter, which serves as a means of interoffice communication.

recast
A memorandum, less formal than a letter, is a means of interoffice communication.

Restrictive and Nonrestrictive Clauses

Clauses that modify are also referred to as *restrictive* or *nonrestrictive*. Whether a clause is restrictive or nonrestrictive has a direct bearing on sentence punctuation. For information about punctuating restrictive and nonrestrictive clauses, see paragraph 10 under Comma, page 57.

1. Restrictive clauses are the so-called "bound" modifiers. They are absolutely essential to the meaning of the word or words they modify, they cannot be omitted without the meaning of the sentences being radically changed, and they are unpunctuated.

   Women who aren't competitive should not aspire to high corporate office.

   In this example, the restrictive clause "who aren't competitive" limits the classification of women, and thus is essential to the total meaning of the sentence. If, on the other hand, the restrictive clause is omitted as shown below, the classification of women is now not limited at all, and the sentence conveys an entirely different idea.

   Women should not aspire to high corporate office.

2. Nonrestrictive clauses are the so-called "free" modifiers. They are not inextricably bound to the word or words they modify but instead convey additional information about them. Nonrestrictive clauses may be omitted altogether without the meaning of the sentence being radically changed, and they are set off by commas; i.e., they are both preceded and followed by commas when they occur in mid-sentence.

   Our guide, who wore a green beret, was an experienced traveler.

   In this example, the nonrestrictive clause "who wore a green beret" does not restrict the classification of the guide; i.e., it does not set him apart from all other guides but merely serves as a bit of incidental detail. Removal of the nonrestrictive clause does not affect the meaning of the sentence:

   Our guide was an experienced traveler.

Tacked-on *Which* Clauses

Tacking a *which* clause onto the end of a sentence when the clause actually refers to the total idea of the sentence is considered to be a usage fault. It can usually be avoided by recasting the sentence.

> *tacked-on*
> The company is retooling, which I personally think is a wise move.
>
> *recast*
> The company's decision to retool is a wise move in my opinion.
>   *or*
> I believe that the company's decision to retool is wise.

Sentences

A sentence is a grammatically self-contained unit that consists of a word or a group of syntactically related words and that (1) expresses a statement (declarative sentence); (2) asks a question (interrogative sentence); (3) expresses a request or command (imperative sentence); or (4) expresses an exclamation (exclamatory sentence). A sentence typically contains both a subject and a predicate, begins with a capital letter, and ends with a punctuation mark.

Basic Types

Sentences are classified into three main types on the basis of their clause structure.

1. The *simple sentence* is a complete grammatical unit having one subject and one predicate (either or both of which may be compound).

    > Paper is costly.
    > Bond and tissue are costly.
    > Bond and tissue are costly and are sometimes scarce.

2. The *compound sentence* is made up of two or more main clauses.

    > I could arrange to arrive late, or I could simply send a proxy.
    > This commute takes at least forty minutes by car, but we can make it in twenty by train.
    > A few of the executives had Ph.D.'s, even more of them had B.A.'s, but the majority of them had both B.A.'s and M.B.A.'s.

3. The *complex sentence* combines a main clause with one or more subordinate clauses (subordinate clauses are italicized in the examples).

    > The committee meeting began *when the business manager and the secretarial staff supervisor walked in.*
    > *Although the city council made some reforms,* the changes came so late *that they could not prevent these abuses.*

Construction

The construction of grammatically sound sentences can be achieved by following some general guidelines.

1. Sentence coordination should be maintained by the use of connectives linking phrases or clauses of equal rank. When a connective is used to link phrases or clauses that are not equal, the resulting sentence is ineffective at best, and can be confusing.

   faulty coordination with improper use of "and"
   I was sitting in on a meeting, and he stood up and started a long rambling discourse on a new pollution-control device.

   recast (one clause subordinated)
   I sat in on a meeting during which he stood up and rambled on about a new pollution-control device.

   recast (two sentences)
   I sat in on that meeting. He stood up and rambled on about a new pollution-control device.

   faulty coordination with improper use of "and"
   This company employs a full-time research staff and was founded in 1945.

   recast (one clause subordinated)
   This company, which employs a full-time research staff, was founded in 1945.

   recast (one clause reworded into a phrase)
   Established in 1945, this company employs a full-time research staff.

2. Parallel, balanced sentence elements are necessary in order to achieve good sentence structure. When clauses having unparallel subjects are linked together, the resulting sentence can be unclear.

   unparallel
   The report gives market statistics, but he does not list his sources for these figures.

   parallel
   The report gives market statistics, but it does not list the sources for these figures.

   unparallel
   We are glad to have you as our client, and please call on us whenever you need help.

   parallel
   We are glad to have you as our client and we hope that you will call on us whenever you need help.

   recast into two sentences
   We are glad to have you as our client. Please do call on us whenever you need help.

3. In order for a sentence to read effectively, its elements should be tightly linked together. When sentence elements are strung together by loose or excessive use of *and,* the sentence as a whole can be too lengthy and lacking in logical flow to be readily understood.

faulty coordination/excessive use of "and"
This company is a Class 1 motor freight common carrier of general commodities and it operates over 10,000 tractors, trailers, and city delivery trucks through 200 terminals, and serves 40 states and the District of Columbia.

recast into three shorter, more effective sentences
This company is a Class 1 motor freight common carrier of general commodities. It operates over 10,000 tractors, trailers, and city delivery trucks through 200 terminals. The company serves 40 states and the District of Columbia.

4. The correct choice of a conjunction to link clauses is important in writing an effective sentence. *And* is a general coordinating conjunction which functions to join sentence elements. If a sentence is expressing more than simple linkage, as when one clause is being contrasted with another, or when a reason or result is being expressed, a more specific conjunction should be used. For more on the specific functions of coordinating and subordinating conjunctions, see paragraphs 1–6 and 10–12 under Conjunction, pages 9–10 and 11–12 respectively.

> *too general*
> The economy was soft *and* we lost a lot of business.
>
> *specific*
> We lost a lot of business *because* the economy was soft.
> The economy was soft, *so* we lost a lot of business.
>
> *specific*
> The soft economy has cost us a lot of business.

5. Unnecessary or unexpected grammatical shifts in a sentence interrupt the reader's thought train and needlessly complicate the material. Some unnecessary grammatical shifts are shown below, along with their improvements:

> *unnecessary shifts in verb voice*
> Any information you *can give* us *will be* greatly *appreciated* and we *assure* you that discretion *will be exercised* in its use.
>
> *rephrased* (note the italicized all-active verb voice)
> We *will appreciate* any information that you *can give* us. We *assure* you that we *will use* it with discretion.
>
> *unnecessary shifts in person*
> *One* can use either erasers or correction fluid to remove typographical errors; however, *you* should make certain that *your* corrections are clean.
>
> *rephrased* (note that the italicized pronouns are consistent)
> *One* can use either erasers or correction fluid to eradicate errors; however, *one* should make certain that *one's* corrections are clean.
>   *or*
> *You* can use either erasers or correction fluid to eradicate errors; however, *you* should make certain that *your* corrections are clean.

unnecessary shift from phrase to clause
Because of the current parts shortage and *we are experiencing a strike*, we cannot fill any orders now.

rephrased
Because of a parts shortage and a strike, we cannot fill any orders now.
  or
Because we are hampered by a parts shortage and we are experiencing a strike, we cannot fill any orders now.

6. A rational, logical ordering of sentence elements is a writer's best guarantee that the material will be understood. Closely related elements, for example, should be placed as close together as possible for the sake of maximum clarity.

   related elements separated
   We would appreciate your sending us the instructions on copy-editing by mail or cable.

   related elements joined
   We would appreciate your sending us by mail or by cable the copy-editing instructions.

   We would appreciate your mailing or cabling us the copy-editing instructions.

   We would appreciate it if you would mail or cable us the copy-editing instructions.

7. Sentences should form complete, independent grammatical units containing both a subject and a predicate. Exceptions are dialogue or specialized copy where fragmentation may be used for particular reasons (as to reflect speech or to attract the reader's attention).

   incomplete grammatical units
   During the last three years, our calculator sales soared. While our conventional office machine sales fell off.

   complete grammatical units
   During the last three years, our calculator sales soared, but our conventional office machine sales fell off.

   While our conventional office machine sales fell off during the last three years, our calculator sales soared.

   sentences fragmented for special effects in advertising
   See it now. The car for the Nineties . . . A car you'll want to own.

Sentence Length

Sentence length is directly related to the writer's purpose: there is no magic number of words that guarantees a good sentence. For example, an executive covering broad and yet complex topics in a long memorandum may choose concise, succinct sentences for the sake of clarity, impact, fast dictation, and readability. On the other hand, a writer who wants the reader to reflect on what is being said may employ longer, more involved sentences. Still another writer may juxtapose long and short sentences to emphasize an important point. The longer sentences may build up to a climactic and forceful short sentence.

Sentence Strategy

1. **Coordination and subordination** Either coordination or subordination or a mixture of both can be used to create a variety of stylistic writing effects. Coordination links independent sentences and sentence elements by means of coordinating conjunctions, while subordination transforms elements into dependent structures by means of subordinating conjunctions. Coordination tends to promote rather loose sentence structure, which can become a fault; subordination tends to tighten the structure and to emphasize a main clause.

   coordination
   During the balance of 1983, this Company expects to issue $100,000,000 of long-term debt and equity securities *and* may guarantee up to $200,000,000 of new corporate bonds.

   subordination
   While this Company expects to issue $100,000,000 of long-term debt and equity securities during the balance of 1983, it may also guarantee up to $200,000,000 of new corporate bonds.

2. **Interrupting elements** Interrupting the normal flow of discourse by inserting comments can be a useful device to call attention to an aside, to emphasize a word or phrase, to convey a particular tone (as forcefulness), or to make the prose a little more informal. Interrupting elements should be used with discretion; too many of them may distract the reader and disrupt his or her train of thought. The following are examples of effective interrupted sentences:

   an aside
   His evidence, if reliable, could send our client to prison.

   emphasis
   These companies—ours as well as theirs—must show more profits.

   forcefulness
   This, gentlemen, is the prime reason for your cost overruns. I trust it will not happen again?

3. **Parallelism and balance** While interruption breaks up the flow of discourse, parallelism and balance work together toward maintaining an even, rhythmic thought flow. Parallelism means a similarity in the grammatical construction of adjacent phrases and clauses that are equivalent, complementary, or antithetical in meaning.

   These ecological problems are of crucial concern *to* scientists, *to* businessmen, *to* government officials, and *to* all citizens.

   Our attorneys have argued *that* the trademark is ours, *that* our rights have been violated, and *that* appropriate compensation is required.

   He was respected not only *for his intelligence* but also *for his integrity*.

Balance is the juxtaposition and equipoise of two or more syntactically parallel constructions (as phrases and clauses) that contain similar, contrasting, or opposing ideas:

> To err is human; to forgive, divine.
>
> —Alexander Pope

> Ask not what your country can do for you—ask what you can do for your country.
>
> —John F. Kennedy

And finally, a series can be an effective way to emphasize a thought and to establish a definite prose rhythm:

> The thing that interested me . . . about New York . . . was the . . . contrast it showed between the dull and the shrewd, the strong and the weak, the rich and the poor, the wise and the ignorant. . . .
>
> —Theodore Dreiser

4. **Periodic and cumulative sentences** Stylistically, there are two basic types of sentences—the periodic and the cumulative or loose. The periodic sentence is structured so that its main idea or its thrust is suspended until the very end, thereby drawing the reader's eye and mind along to an emphatic conclusion. In the example below, the main point follows the final comma.

> While the Commission would wish to give licensees every encouragement to experiment on their own initiative with new and different means of providing access to their stations for the discussion of important public issues, it cannot justify the imposition of a specific right of access by government fiat.
>
> —*Television/Radio Age*

The cumulative sentence, on the other hand, is structured so that its main point appears first, followed by other phrases or clauses expanding on or supporting it. In the following example, the main point precedes the first comma.

> The solution must be finely honed, lest strategists err too much on the side of sophistication only to find that U.S. military forces can be defeated by overwhelming mass.
>
> —William C. Moore

The final phrase or clause in a cumulative sentence theoretically could be deleted without skewing or destroying the essential meaning of the total sentence. A cumulative sentence is therefore more loosely structured than a periodic sentence.

5. **Reversal** A reversal of customary or expected sentence order is another effective stylistic strategy, when used sparingly, because it injects a dash of freshness, unexpectedness, and originality into the prose.

customary or expected order
I find that these realities are indisputable: the economy has taken a drastic downturn, costs on all fronts have soared, and jobs are at a premium.

reversal
That the economy has taken a drastic downturn; that costs on all fronts have soared; that jobs are at a premium—these are the realities that I find indisputable.

6. **Rhetorical questions** The rhetorical question is yet another device to focus the reader's attention on a problem or an issue. The rhetorical question requires no specific response from the reader but often merely sets up the introduction of the writer's own view. In some instances, a rhetorical question works as a topic sentence in a paragraph; in other instances, a whole series of rhetorical questions may spotlight pertinent issues for the reader's consideration.

What can be done to correct the problem? Two things, to begin with: never discuss cases out of the office, and never allow a visitor to see the papers on your desk.

7. **Variety** As a means of keeping the reader's attention, careful writers try to maintain a balance of different kinds of sentences. For example, they may use a combination of simple, compound, and complex sentences in a paragraph, together with a variety of short and long sentences. Writers also vary the beginnings of their sentences so that every sentence in a paragraph does not begin directly with the subject. Any kind of repetitious pattern creates monotony. Through judicious use of combinations of sentence patterns and the sentence strategies discussed in the preceding paragraphs, a writer can attain an interesting, diversified style.

Paragraphs

The underlying structure of any written communication—be it a memorandum, a letter, or a report—must be controlled by the writer if the material is to be clear, coherent, logical in progression, and effective. Since good paragraphing is a means to this end, it is essential that the writer become adept at using techniques of paragraph development and of transition between paragraphs. While the writer is responsible for the paragraphing system, the secretary still should be able to recognize various kinds of paragraphs and their functions as well as the potential problems that might arise in structuring a logical paragraph system. In this way, the secretary can assist the writer, especially by pointing out possible discrepancies that might result in misinterpretation by the reader or that might detract from the total effect of the communication.

A paragraph is a subdivision in writing that consists of one or more sentences, that deals with one or more ideas, or that quotes a speaker or a source. The first line of a paragraph is indented in reports, studies, articles, theses, and books. However, the first line of a paragraph in business letters and memorandums may or may not be indented, depending on the style being followed. See Chapter 4 for business-letter styling.

Paragraphs should not be considered as isolated entities that are self-contained and mechanically lined up without transitions or interrelationship of ideas. Rather, paragraphs should be viewed as components of larger groups or blocks that are tightly interlinked and that interact in the sequential development of a major idea or cluster of ideas. The overall coherence of a communication depends on this interaction.

Individual paragraphs and paragraph blocks are flexible: their length, internal structure, and purpose vary according to the writer's intention and his own style. For example, one writer may be able to express his point in a succinct, one-sentence paragraph, while another may require several sentences to make his point. Writers' concepts of paragraphing also differ. For instance, some writers think of paragraphs as a means of dividing their material into logical segments with each unit developing one particular point in depth and in detail. Others view paragraphs as a means of emphasizing particular points or adding variety to long passages.

Development of Paragraphs

Depending on the writer's intentions, paragraph development may take any of the following directions:

1. The paragraph may move from the general to the specific.

2. The paragraph may move from the specific to the general.

3. The paragraph may exhibit an alternating order of comparison and contrast.

4. The paragraph may chronicle events in a set temporal order—e.g., from the beginning to the end, or from the end to the beginning.

5. The paragraph may describe something (as a group of objects) in a set spatial order—e.g., the items being described may be looked at from near-to-far, or vice versa.

6. The paragraph may follow a climactic sequence with the least important facts or examples described first followed by a buildup of tension leading to the most important facts or examples then followed by a gradual easing of tension. Other material can be so ordered for effectiveness; for example, facts or issues that are easy to comprehend or accept may be set forth first and followed by those that are more difficult to comprehend or accept. In this way the easier material makes the reader receptive and prepares him to comprehend or accept the more difficult points.

7. Anticlimactic order is also useful when the writer's intent is to persuade the reader. With this strategy, the writer sets forth the most

persuasive arguments first so that the reader, having been influenced in a positive way by that persuasion, moves along with the rest of the argument with a growing feeling of assent.

Effective Paragraphing

The following material outlines some ways of building effective paragraphs within a text.

A topic sentence—a key sentence to which the other sentences in the paragraph are related—may be placed either at the beginning or at the end of a paragraph. A lead-in topic sentence should present the main idea in the paragraph and should set the initial tone of the material that follows. A terminal topic sentence should be an analysis, a conclusion, or a summation of what has gone before it.

A single-sentence paragraph can be used to achieve easy transition from a preceding to a subsequent paragraph (especially when the paragraphs are long and complex), if it repeats an important word or phrase from the preceding paragraph, if it contains a pronoun reference to a key individual mentioned in a preceding paragraph, or if it is introduced by an appropriate conjunction or conjunctive adverb that tightly connects the paragraphs.

1. Since the very first paragraph sets initial tone, introduces the subject or topic under discussion, and leads into the main thrust of a communication, it should be worded so as to immediately attract the reader's attention and arouse interest. These openings can be effective:

   A. a succinct statement of purpose or point of view
   B. a concise definition (as of a problem)
   C. a lucid statement of a key issue or fact

2. These openings, by contrast, can blunt the point of the rest of the material:

   A. an apology for the material to be presented
   B. a querulous complaint or a defensive posture
   C. a rehash of ancient history (as a word-for-word recap of previous correspondence)
   D. a presentation of self-evident facts
   E. a group of sentences rendered limp and meaningless because of clichés

3. The last paragraph ties together all of the ideas and points that have been set forth earlier and reemphasizes the main thrust of the communication. These can be effective endings:

   A. a setting forth of the most important conclusion or conclusions drawn from the preceding discussion
   B. a final analysis of the main problem or problems under discussion
   C. a lucid summary of the individual points brought up earlier

D. a final, clear statement of opinion or position
E. concrete suggestions or solutions if applicable
F. specific questions asked of the reader if applicable

4. The following endings, by contrast, can reduce the effectiveness of a communication:

   A. apologies for a poor presentation
   B. qualifying remarks that blunt or negate incisive points made earlier
   C. insertion of minor details or afterthoughts
   D. a meaningless closing couched in clichés

5. The following are tests of good paragraphs:

   A. Does the paragraph have a clear purpose? Is its utility evident, or is it there just to fill up space?
   B. Does the paragraph clarify rather than cloud the writer's ideas?
   C. Is the paragraph adequately developed, or does it merely raise other questions that the writer does not attempt to answer? If a position is being taken, does the writer include supporting information and statistics that are essential to its defense?
   D. Are the length and wording of all the paragraphs sufficiently varied, or does the writer employ the same types of locutions again and again?
   E. Is the sentence structure coherent?
   F. Is each paragraph unified? Do all the sentences really *belong* there; or does the writer digress into areas that would have been better covered in another paragraph or that could have been omitted altogether?
   G. Are the paragraphs coherent so that one sentence leads clearly and logically to another? Is easy, clear transition between paragraphs effected by a wise selection of transitional words and phrases which indicate relationships between ideas and signal the direction in which the writer's presentation is moving?
   H. Does one paragraph simply restate in other terms what has been said before?

CHAPTER 2

The Mechanics of Writing

The English writing system uses certain conventional devices to help clarify the structure and meaning of words and sentences. Punctuation marks, capital letters, italics, and quotation marks are all mechanical devices employed in a variety of ways to help writers express their messages in an unambiguous way. The formation of plurals, possessives, and compounds and the treatment of abbreviations and numbers are aspects of the language in which these mechanical devices are frequently used and often in very specialized ways. This chapter is designed to help writers make effective use of the mechanical devices of the language to convey information in their letter writing.

Punctuation

Punctuation marks are used in the English writing system to help clarify the structure and meaning of sentences. They separate groups of words for meaning and emphasis; they convey an idea of the variations in pitch, volume, pauses, and intonation of the spoken language; and they help avoid contextual ambiguity. In many cases, the relationship between punctuation and grammatical structure is such that the choice of which mark of punctuation to use is clear and unambiguous. In other cases, however, the structure of a sentence may be such that it allows for several patterns of punctuation. In cases like these, varying notions of correctness have grown up, and two writers might, with equal correctness, punctuate the same sentence quite differently. In this section, in situations where more than one pattern of punctuation may be used, each is explained. If there are reasons to prefer one over another, the reasons are presented;

however, in many cases, using punctuation marks requires the exercise of individual judgment and taste.

This section focuses on general uses of punctuation marks. For detailed information about the punctuation of specific elements in a business letter, see Chapter 4, "Style in Business Correspondence," especially the section on General Punctuation Patterns in Business Correspondence, beginning on page 180.

Ampersand

The ampersand represents the word *and,* and its function is to replace the word when a shorter form is desirable. The ampersand is usually not used in regular text in correspondence; however, it is an acceptable substitute for *and* in some situations.

1. The ampersand is used in the names of companies but not in the names of agencies that are part of the federal government.

   American Telephone & Telegraph Co.
   Dow Jones & Company, Inc.
   Occupational Safety and Health Administration
   Securities and Exchange Commission

   NOTE: In styling corporate names, writers often try to reproduce the form of the name preferred by the company (taken from an annual report or company letterhead). However, this information may not be available and, even if it is available, can lead to apparent inconsistencies in the letter if several corporate names are used. If this is the case, choose one styling, preferably the one with the ampersand, and use it in all corporate names that include *and.*

2. When ampersands are used with abbreviations in general correspondence, spaces are often left around the ampersand. Writing which makes extensive use of abbreviations, such as technical writing, more commonly omits the spacing.

   Such loans may be available at your bank or S & L.
   The R&D budget looks adequate for the next fiscal year.

3. When an ampersand is used between the last two elements in a series, the comma is omitted.

   the law firm of Shilliday, Fraser & French

Apostrophe

1. The apostrophe is used to indicate the possessive case of nouns and indefinite pronouns. For details regarding this use, see pages 111–114.

2. Apostrophes are sometimes used to form plurals of letters, numerals, abbreviations, symbols, and words referred to as words. For details regarding this use, see pages 107 and 110–111.

3. Apostrophes mark omissions in contractions made of two or more words that are pronounced as one word.

> didn't   you're   o'clock

4. The apostrophe is used to indicate that letters have been intentionally omitted from the spelling of a word in order to reproduce a perceived pronunciation or to give a highly informal flavor to a piece of writing.

> "Head back to N'Orleans," the man said.
> Get 'em while they're hot.
> dancin' till three

NOTE: Sometimes words are so consistently spelled with an apostrophe that the spelling with the apostrophe becomes an accepted variant.

> fo'c'sle for *forecastle*
> bos'n for *boatswain*
> rock 'n' roll for *rock and roll*

5. Apostrophes mark the omission of numerals.

> class of '88   politics in the '90s

NOTE: Writers who use the apostrophe for styling the plurals of words expressed in numerals usually avoid the use of the apostrophe illustrated in the second example above. Either they omit the apostrophe that stands for the missing figures, or they spell the word out.

> 80's *or* eighties *but not* '80's

6. Apostrophes are used to produce the inflected forms of verbs that are made of numerals or individually pronounced letters. Hyphens are sometimes used for this purpose also.

> 86'ed our proposal
> OK'ing the manuscripts

7. An apostrophe is often used to add an *-er* ending to an abbreviation, especially if some confusion might result from its absence. Hyphens are sometimes used for this purpose also. If no confusion is likely, the apostrophe is usually omitted.

> 4-H'er   AA'er   CBer   DXer

8. The use of apostrophes to form abbreviations (as *ass'n* for *association* or *sec'y* for *secretary*) is avoided in most formal writing.

Brackets

1. Brackets enclose editorial comments, corrections, clarifications, or other material inserted into a text, especially into quoted matter.

> This was the first time since it became law that the Twenty-first Amendment [outlining procedures for the replacement of a dead or incapacitated President or Vice President] had been invoked.

> He wrote, "I am just as cheerful as when you was [sic] here."

2. Brackets set off insertions that supply missing letters.

> "If you can't persuade D[israeli], I'm sure no one can."

3. Brackets enclose insertions that take the place of words or phrases that were used in the original version of a quoted passage.

> The report, entitled "A Decade of Progress," begins with a short message from President Stevens in which she notes that "the loving portraits and revealing accounts of [this report] are not intended to constitute a complete history of the decade. . . . Rather [they] impart the flavor of the events, developments, and achievements of this vibrant period."

4. Brackets enclose insertions that slightly alter the form of a word used in an original text.

> The magazine reported that thousands of the country's children were "go[ing] to bed hungry every night."

5. Brackets are used to indicate that the capitalization or typeface of the original passage has been altered in some way.

> As we point out later, "The length of a quotation usually determines whether it is run into the text or set as a block quotation. . . . [L]ength can be assessed in terms of number of words, the number of typewritten or typeset lines, or the number of sentences in the passage."

> They agreed with and were encouraged by her next point: "In the past, many secretaries have been placed in positions of responsibility *without being delegated enough authority to carry out the responsibility*." [Italics added.]

NOTE: The use of brackets to indicate altered capitalization is optional in most situations. It is required only in cases where meticulous handling of original source material is crucial.

6. Brackets function as parentheses within parentheses.

> The company was incinerating high concentrations of pollutants (such as polychlorinated biphenyls [PCBs]) in a power boiler.

7. Brackets are used in combination with parentheses to indicate units contained within larger units in mathematical copy. They are also used in chemical formulas.

$$x + 5[(x+y)(2x-y)] \qquad\qquad NH_4[Cr(NH_3)_2(SCN)_4] \cdot H_2O$$

8. No punctuation mark (other than a period after an abbreviation) precedes bracketed material within a sentence. If punctuation is required, the mark is placed after the closing bracket.

> The report stated, "If we fail to find additional sources of supply [of oil and gas], our long-term growth will be limited."

9. When brackets enclose a complete sentence, the required punctuation should be placed within the brackets.

> [The results of years of anti-inflation policies are slow growth, a slightly higher unemployment rate, and lower consumer prices.]

10. No space is left between brackets and the material they enclose or between brackets and any mark of punctuation immediately following. In typewritten material, two spaces precede an opening bracket and follow a closing bracket when the brackets enclose a complete sentence.

```
Judging from its economic statistics, the country could
stand a dose of reflation.  [The results of years of
anti-inflation policies are slow growth, a slightly
higher unemployment rate, and lower consumer prices.]
However, its people seem determined to stick with
austerity.
```

Colon

The colon is a mark of introduction. It indicates that what follows it—whether a clause, a phrase, or even a single word—is linked with some element that precedes it. For information on capitalizing the first word following a colon, see paragraphs 7 and 8 under Beginnings, page 87.

1. **With phrases and clauses** A colon introduces a clause or phrase that explains, illustrates, amplifies, or restates what has gone before.

   The sentence was poorly constructed: it lacked both unity and coherence.

   Throughout its history, the organization has combined a tradition of excellence with a dedication to human service: educating the young, caring for the elderly, assisting in community-development programs.

   Disk cartridges provide high-density storage capacity: up to 16 megabytes of information on some cartridges.

   Time was running out: a decision had to be made.

2. A colon directs attention to an appositive.

   The question is this: where will we get the money?

   He had only one pleasure: eating.

3. A colon is used to introduce a series. The introductory statement often includes a phrase such as *the following* or *as follows*.

   The conference was attended by representatives of five nations: England, France, Belgium, Spain, and Portugal.

   Anyone planning to participate should be prepared to do the following: spend all day in a conference session, discuss your company's role in the community, and participate in a conference evaluation.

NOTE: Opinion varies regarding whether a colon should interrupt the grammatical continuity of a clause (as by coming between a verb and its objects). Although many writers avoid this practice and use a full independent clause before the colon, the interrupting colon is common. It is especially likely to be used before a lengthy and complex list, in which case the colon serves to set the list distinctly apart from the normal flow of running text. With shorter or less complex lists, the colon is usually not used.

Our programs to increase profitability include: continued modernization of our manufacturing facilities; consolidation of distribution terminals; discontinuation of unprofitable retail outlets; and reorganization of our personnel structure, along with across-the-board staff reductions.

Our programs to increase profitability include plant modernization, improved distribution and retailing procedures, and staff reductions.

Our programs to increase profitability include the following: continued modernization of our manufacturing facilities; consolidation of distribution terminals; discontinuation of unprofitable retail outlets; and reorganization of our personnel structure, along with across-the-board staff reductions.

4. A colon is used like a dash to introduce a summary statement following a series.

Accounting, home computing, tax laws, investments: she discusses them all.

5. **With quotations** A colon introduces lengthy quoted material that is set off from the rest of a text by indentation but not by quotation marks.

Roy Gaines, executive director of Public Speaking Incorporated, has this to say about speaking to a group:

The best way to get jitters under control is to prepare thoroughly. Get some experience. Get up on stage a few times. Find out what your audience is interested in, know your subject backward and forward, and do research to brighten your talk with anecdotes, jokes, and examples.

Gaines adds that he often mulls over his own speeches late at night while walking the family dog.

6. A colon may be used before a quotation in running text, especially when (1) the quotation is lengthy, (2) the quotation is a formal statement or is being given special emphasis, or (3) the quotation is an appositive.

Said Murdoch: "The key to the success of this project is good planning. We need to know precisely all of the steps that we will need to go through, what kind of staff we will require to accomplish each step, what the entire project will cost, and when we can expect completion."

The inscription reads: "Here lies one whose name was writ in water."

In response, he had this to say: "No one knows better than I do that changes will have to be made soon."

7. **Other uses** A colon separates elements in page references, bibliographical and biblical citations, and fixed formulas used to express ratios and time.

Journal of the American Medical Association 48:356
Springfield, Mass.: Merriam-Webster Inc.
John 4:10
8:30 a.m.
a ratio of 3:5

8. A colon separates titles and subtitles (as of books).

> *The Great Cookie Jar: Taking the Mysteries Out of the Money System*

9. A colon is used to join terms that are being contrasted or compared.

> The budget shows an unfavorable difference in research : advertising dollars.

10. A colon punctuates the salutation in a business letter using the mixed-punctuation pattern. For more on this use of the colon, see pages 191–192.

> Dear Mrs. Wright: Dear Product Manager:
> Dear Laurence: Ladies and Gentlemen:
>   Dear Sir:

11. A colon punctuates memorandum and government correspondence headings and subject lines in general business letters. For more on this use of the colon, see pages 193–195.

> TO: VIA:
> SUBJECT: REFERENCE:

12. A colon separates writer/dictator/typist initials in the identification lines of business letters. For more on this use of the colon, see pages 205–206.

> WAL:jml
> WAL:WEB:jml

13. A colon separates carbon-copy or blind carbon-copy abbreviations from the initials or names of copy recipients in business letters. For more on this use of the colon, see pages 207–208.

> cc:RSP
>   JES
> bcc:MWK
>   FCM

14. **With other marks of punctuation** A colon is placed outside quotation marks and parentheses.

> There's only one thing wrong with "Harold's Indiscretion": it's not funny.
> I quote from the first edition of *Business English* (published in 1985):

15. **Spacing** In typewritten material, two spaces follow a colon used in running text, bibliographical references, publication titles, and letter or memorandum headings.

```
The answer is simple:  don't go.
SUBJECT:  Project X
```

16. No space precedes or follows a colon when it is used between numerals.

> 9:30 a.m.   a ratio of 2:4

17. No space precedes or follows a colon in a business-letter identification line or in a carbon-copy notation that indicates a recipient designated by initials. Two spaces follow a colon in a carbon-copy notation that indicates a recipient designated by a full name.

FCM:hg   cc:FCM

cc: Mr. Johnson

Comma

The comma is the most frequently used punctuation mark in the English writing system. Its most common uses are to separate items in a series and to set off syntactical elements within sentences. This section explains the most common aspects of the comma, listed under the following headings:

Between Main Clauses
With Compound Predicates
With Subordinate Clauses and
    Phrases
With Appositives
With Introductory and
    Interrupting Elements
With Contrasting Expressions
With Items in a Series
With Compound Modifiers

In Quotations, Questions, and
    Indirect Discourse
With Omitted Words
With Addresses, Dates, and
    Numbers
With Names, Degrees, and Titles
In Correspondence
Other Uses
With Other Marks of Punctuation

1. Between main clauses A comma separates main clauses joined by a co-ordinating conjunction (as *and, but, or, nor, for,* and sometimes *so* and *yet*). For use of commas with clauses joined by correlative conjunctions, see paragraph 24 below.

She knew very little about him, and he volunteered nothing.

We will not respond to any more questions on that topic this afternoon, nor will we respond to similar questions at any time in the future.

His face showed disappointment, for he knew that he had failed.

The acoustics in this hall are good, so every note is clear.

We have requested this information many times before, yet we have never gotten a satisfactory reply.

2. When one or both of the clauses are short or when they are closely related in meaning, the comma is often omitted.

We have tested the product and we are pleased.

We hadn't realized it but none of the shipments were arriving on time.

NOTE: In punctuating sentences such as the ones illustrated above, writers have to use their own judgment regarding whether clauses are short enough or closely related enough to warrant omitting the comma. There are no clear-cut rules to follow; however, factors such as the rhythm, parallelism, or logic of the sentence often influence how clearly or smoothly it will read with or without the comma.

3. Commas are sometimes used to separate main clauses that are not joined by conjunctions. This styling is especially likely to be used if the clauses are short and feature obvious parallelism.

> One day you are a successful corporate lawyer, the next day you are out of work.

> The city has suffered terribly in the interim. Bombs have destroyed most of the buildings, disease has ravaged the population.

NOTE: Using a comma to join clauses that are neither short nor obviously parallel is usually called *comma fault* or *comma splice* and it is usually desirable to avoid such a construction. In general, clauses not joined by conjunctions are separated by semicolons.

4. If a sentence is composed of three or more clauses, the clauses may be separated by either commas or semicolons. Clauses that are short and relatively free of commas can be separated by commas even if they are not joined by a conjunction. If the clauses are long or heavily punctuated, they are separated with semicolons, except for the last two clauses which may be separated by either a comma or a semicolon. Usually a comma will be used between the last two clauses only if those clauses are joined by a conjunction. For more examples of clauses separated with commas and semicolons, see paragraph 5 under Semicolon in this section.

> The pace of change seems to have quickened, the economy is uncertain, the technology seems sometimes liberating and sometimes hostile.

> The policy is a complex one to explain; defending it against its critics is not easy, nor is it clear the defense is always necessary.

5. With compound predicates Commas are not usually used to separate the parts of a compound predicate.

> The chairman tried to explain the merger but failed to convince the stockholders.

NOTE: Many writers do use commas to separate the parts of a compound predicate. This is particularly true if the predicate is especially long and complicated, if one part of the predicate is being stressed, or if the absence of a comma could cause even a momentary misreading of the sentence.

> The board helps to develop the financing, new product planning, and marketing strategies for new corporate divisions, and issues periodic reports on expenditures, revenues, and personnel appointments.

> This is an unworkable plan, and has been from the start.

> I try to explain to him what I want him to do, and get nowhere.

6. With subordinate clauses and phrases Adverbial clauses and phrases that precede a main clause are usually set off with commas.

> Having made that decision, we turned our attention to other matters.

> To understand the situation, you must be familiar with the background.

In 1980, the company had its first profitable year.

In addition, staff members respond to queries, take new orders, and initiate billing.

7. If a sentence begins with an adverbial clause or phrase and can be easily read without a comma following it, the comma may be omitted. In most cases where the comma is omitted, the phrase will be short—four words or less. However, the comma can be omitted even after a longer phrase if the sentence can be easily read or seems more forceful that way.

In January the company will introduce a new line of entirely redesigned products.

If the project cannot be done profitably perhaps it should not be done at all.

8. Adverbial clauses and phrases that introduce a main clause other than the first main clause are usually set off with commas. However, if the adverbial clause or phrase follows a conjunction, two commas are usually used: one before the conjunction and one following the clause or phrase. In some cases three commas are used: one before the conjunction and two more to enclose the clause or phrase. Some writers use only one comma to separate the main clauses.

His parents were against the match, and had the couple not eloped, their plans for marriage would have come to nothing.

They have redecorated the entire store, but, to the delight of their customers, the store retains much of its original flavor.

We haven't left Springfield yet, but when we get to Boston we'll call you.

9. A comma is not used after an introductory phrase if the phrase immediately precedes the main verb.

On the filing cabinet lay a bulging portfolio.

10. Subordinate clauses and phrases that follow a main clause or that fall within a main clause are usually not set off by commas if they are restrictive. A clause or phrase is considered restrictive if its removal from the sentence would alter the meaning of the main clause. If the meaning of the main clause would not be altered by removing the subordinate clause or phrase, the clause or phrase is considered nonrestrictive and usually is set off by commas.

We will be delighted if she decides to stay. [restrictive]

Anyone who wants his or her copy of the book autographed by the author should get in line. [restrictive]

Her new book, which was based on a true story, was well received. [nonrestrictive]

That was a good meal, although I didn't particularly like the broccoli in cream sauce. [nonrestrictive]

11. Commas are used to set off an adverbial clause or phrase that falls between the subject and the verb.

> The weather, fluctuating from very hot to downright chilly, necessitated a variety of clothing.

12. Commas set off modifying phrases that do not immediately precede the word or phrase they modify.

> The hunters, tired and discouraged, headed back to camp.
>
> We could see the importance, both long-term and short-term, of her proposal.
>
> The director, burdened with a tight schedule, expanded her staff.

13. Absolute phrases are set off with commas, whether they fall at the beginning, middle, or end of the sentence.

> Our business being concluded, we adjourned for refreshments.
>
> I'm afraid of his reaction, his temper being what it is.

14. **With appositives** Commas are used to set off a word, phrase, or clause that is in apposition to a noun and that is nonrestrictive.

> The sales manager, Mr. Griffith, is in charge of the meeting.
>
> We were most impressed by the third candidate, the one who brought a writing sample and asked so many questions.

NOTE: A nonrestrictive appositive sometimes precedes the word with which it is in apposition. It is set off by commas in this position also.

> A cherished landmark in the city, the Hotel Sandburg has managed once again to escape the wrecking ball.

15. Restrictive appositives are not set off by commas.

> Our account manager Andrea Timmons will be in touch with you.

16. **With introductory and interrupting elements** Commas set off transitional words and phrases (as *finally, meanwhile,* and *after all*).

> Indeed, close coordination between departments can minimize confusion during this period of expansion.
>
> We are eager to begin construction; however, the necessary materials have not yet arrived.
>
> The most recent report, on the other hand, makes clear why the management avoids such agreements.

NOTE: When these words are not used to make a transition, no comma is necessary.

> The materials had finally arrived.

17. Commas set off parenthetical elements, such as authorial asides and supplementary information, that are closely related to the rest of the sentence.

All of us, to tell the truth, were completely amazed by his suggestion.

The president, now in his sixth year with the company, was responsible for the changes in the staff.

NOTE: When the parenthetical element is digressive or otherwise not closely related to the rest of the sentence, it is often set off by dashes or parentheses. For contrasting examples, see paragraph 2 under Dash and paragraph 1 under Parentheses in this section.

18. Commas are used to set off words or phrases that introduce examples or explanations.

He expects to visit three countries this summer, namely, France, Spain, and Germany.

I would like to develop a good, workable plan, i.e., one that would outline our goals and set a timetable for their accomplishment.

NOTE: Words and phrases such as *i.e., e.g., namely, for example,* and *that is* are often preceded by a dash, open parenthesis, or semicolon, depending on the magnitude of the break in continuity created by the examples or explanations. However, regardless of the punctuation that precedes the word or phrase, a comma always follows it. For contrasting examples of dashes, parentheses, and semicolons with these words and phrases, see paragraph 6 under Dash, paragraph 2 under Parentheses, and paragraph 6 under Semicolon in this section.

19. Commas are used to set off words in direct address.

We would like to discuss your account, Mrs. Reid.

The answer, my friends, lies within us.

20. Commas set off mild interjections or exclamations such as *ah* or *oh*.

Ah, weekends—they don't come often enough.

Oh, it was quite a meeting.

21. **With contrasting expressions** A comma is used to set off contrasting expressions within a sentence.

This project will take six months, not six weeks.

22. Style varies regarding use of the comma to set off two or more contrasting phrases used to describe a single word that follows immediately. Some writers put a comma after the first modifier but not between the final modifier and the word modified. Other writers, who treat the contrasting phrase as a nonrestrictive modifier, put a comma both before and after the phrase.

The harsh, although eminently realistic critique is not going to make you popular.

The harsh, although eminently realistic, critique is not going to make you popular.

This street takes you away from, not toward the capitol building.

This street takes you away from, not toward, the capitol building.

23. Adjectives and adverbs that modify the same word or phrase and that are joined by *but* or some other coordinating conjunction are not separated by a comma.

> a bicycle with a light but sturdy frame
> a multicolored but subdued carpet
> errors caused by working carelessly or too quickly

24. A comma does not usually separate elements that are contrasted through the use of a pair of correlative conjunctions (as *either . . . or, neither . . . nor,* and *not only . . . but also*).

> The cost is either $69.95 or $79.95.
>
> Neither my secretary nor I noticed the error.
>
> He was given the post not only because of his diplomatic connections but also because of his great tact and charm.

NOTE: Correlative conjunctions are sometimes used to join main clauses. If the clauses are short, a comma is not added. If the clauses are long, a comma usually separates them.

> Either you do it my way or we don't do it at all.
>
> Not only did she have to see three salesmen and a visiting reporter during the course of the day, but she also had to prepare for the next day's meeting with the president.

25. Long parallel contrasting and comparing clauses are separated by commas; short parallel phrases are not.

> The more I hear about this new computer, the greater is my desire to obtain one for my office.
>
> "The sooner the better," I said.

26. **With items in a series** Words, phrases, and clauses joined in a series are separated by commas. If main clauses are joined in a series, they may be separated by either semicolons or commas. For more on the use of commas and semicolons to separate main clauses, see paragraphs 1, 3, and 4 above and paragraph 5 under Semicolon in this section.

> Pens, pencils, and erasers crowded the drawer.
>
> Her job required her to pack quickly, to travel often, and to have no personal life.
>
> He responded patiently while reporters shouted questions, flashbulbs popped, and the crowd pushed closer.

NOTE: Practice varies regarding the use of the comma between the last two items in a series if those items are also joined by a conjunction. In some cases, as in the example below, omitting the final comma (often called the serial comma) can result in ambiguity. Some writers feel that in most sentences the use of the conjunction makes the comma superfluous, and they favor using the comma only when a misreading could result from omitting it. Others feel that it is easier to include the final comma routinely rather than try to consider each sentence separately to decide whether a misreading is possible without the comma. Most reference books, including this one, and most other book-length works of nonfiction use the serial comma. In most other kinds of writing, however, practice is evenly or nearly evenly divided on the use or omission of this comma.

> We are looking for a house with a big yard, a view of the harbor, and beach and docking privileges. [with serial comma]
>
> We are looking for a house with a big yard, a view of the harbor and beach and docking privileges. [without serial comma]

27. A comma is not used to separate items in a series that are joined with conjunctions.

> I don't understand what this policy covers or doesn't cover or only partially covers.
>
> I have talked to the president and the vice president and three other executives.

28. When the elements in a series are long or complex or consist of clauses that themselves contain commas, the elements are usually separated by semicolons, not commas. For more on this use of the semicolon, see paragraphs 7 and 8 under Semicolon in this section.

29. **With compound modifiers** A comma is used to separate two or more adjectives, adverbs, or phrases that modify the same word or phrase. For the use of commas with contrasting modifiers, see paragraphs 22 and 23 above.

> She wrote in a polished, professional style.
>
> The office was lit with a hard, flickering light.

30. A comma is not used between two adjectives when the first modifies the combination of the second adjective plus the word or phrase it modifies.

> a little brown jug
> a small brick building

31. A comma is not used to separate an adverb from the adjective or adverb that it modifies.

> a truly distinctive manner
> running very quickly down the street

32. **In quotations, questions, and indirect discourse** A comma separates a direct quotation from a phrase identifying its source or speaker. If the quotation is a question or an exclamation and the identifying phrase follows the quotation, the comma is replaced by a question mark or an exclamation point.

> Mary said, "I am leaving."
> "I am leaving," Mary said.

Mary asked, "Where are you going?"

"Where are you going?" Mary asked.

"I am leaving," Mary said, "even if you want me to stay."

"Don't do that!" Mary shouted.

NOTE: In some cases, a colon can replace a comma preceding a quotation. For more on this use of the colon, see paragraph 6 under Colon in this section.

33. A comma does not set off a quotation that is an integral part of the sentence in which it appears.

Throughout the session his only responses were "No comment" and "I don't think so."

Just because he said he was "about to leave this minute" doesn't mean he actually left.

34. Practice varies regarding the use of commas to set off shorter sentences that fall within longer sentences and that do not constitute actual dialogue. These shorter sentences may be mottoes or maxims, unspoken or imaginary dialogue, or sentences referred to as sentences; and they may or may not be enclosed in quotation marks. (For more on the use of quotation marks with sentences like these, see paragraph 6 under Quotation Marks. Double, in this section.) Typically the shorter sentence functions as a subject, object, or complement within the larger sentence and does not require a comma. Sometimes the structure of the larger sentence will be styled like actual quoted dialogue, and in such cases a comma is used to separate the shorter sentence from the text that introduces or identifies it. In some cases, where quotation marks are not used, a comma may be inserted simply to mark the beginning of the shorter sentence clearly.

"The computer is down" was the response she dreaded.

He spoke with a candor that seemed to insist, This actually happened to me and in just this way.

The first rule is, When in doubt, spell it out.

When the shorter sentence functions as an appositive in the larger sentence, it is set off with a comma when nonrestrictive and not when restrictive. (For more on restrictive modifiers and appositives, see paragraphs 10, 14, and 15 above.)

He was fond of the slogan "Every man a king, but no man wears a crown."

We had the club's motto, "We make waves," printed on our T-shirts.

35. A comma introduces a direct question regardless of whether it is enclosed in quotation marks or if its first word is capitalized.

I wondered, what is going on here?

The question is, How do we get out of this situation?

36. The comma is omitted before quotations that are very short exclamations or representations of sounds.

> He jumped up suddenly and cried "Yow!"
> When she was done, she let out a loud "Whew!"

37. A comma is not used to set off indirect discourse or indirect questions introduced by a conjunction (such as *that* or *what*).

> Mary said that she was leaving.
> I wondered what was going on there.
> The clerk told me that the book I had ordered had just come in.

38. **With omitted words** A comma indicates the omission of a word or phrase, especially in parallel constructions where the omitted word or phrase appears earlier in the sentence.

> Common stocks are preferred by some investors; bonds, by others.

39. A comma often replaces the conjunction *that*.

> The road was so steep, we thought surely we would go over the edge.
> The problem is, we don't know how to fix it.

40. **With addresses, dates, and numbers** A comma is used to set off the individual elements of an address except for zip codes. In current practice, no punctuation appears between a state name and the zip code that follows it. If prepositions are used between the elements of the address, commas are not needed.

> Mrs. Bryant may be reached at 52 Kiowa Circle, Mesa, Arizona.
> Mr. Briscoe was born in Liverpool, England.
> The collection will be displayed at the Wilmington, Delaware, Museum of Art.
> Write to the Bureau of the Census, Washington, DC 20233.
> The White House is located at 1600 Pennsylvania Avenue in Washington, D.C.

NOTE: Some writers omit the comma that follows the name of a state when no other element of an address follows it. This is most likely to happen when a city name and state name are being used in combination to modify a noun that follows; however, retaining this comma is still the more common practice.

> We visited their Enid, Oklahoma plant.
> *but more commonly*
> We visited their Enid, Oklahoma, plant.

41. Commas are used to set off the year from the day of the month. When only the month and the year are given, the comma is usually omitted.

> On October 26, 1947, the newly hired employees began work on the project.

In December 1903, the Wright brothers finally succeeded in keeping an airplane aloft for a few seconds.

42. A comma groups numerals into units of three to separate thousands, millions, and so on; however, this comma is generally not used in page numbers, street numbers, or numbers within dates. For more on the styling of numbers, see the section on Numbers, beginning on page 136.

> a population of 350,000   the year 1986
> 4509 South Pleasant Street   page 1419

43. With names, degrees, and titles A comma punctuates an inverted name.

> Sagan, Deborah J.

44. A comma is usually used between a surname and *Junior, Senior,* or their abbreviations.

> Morton A. Williams, Jr.   Douglas Fairbanks, Senior

45. A comma is often used to set off the word *Incorporated* or the abbreviation *Inc.* from the rest of a corporate name; however, many companies elect to omit this comma from their names.

> Leedy Manufacturing Company, Incorporated
> Tektronics, Inc.
> Merz-Fortunata Inc.

46. A comma separates a surname from a following academic, honorary, military, or religious degree or title.

> Amelia P. Artandi, D.V.M.   Robert Menard, M.A., Ph.D.
> John L. Farber, Esq.   Admiral Herman Washington, USN
> Sister Mary Catherine, S.C.

47. In correspondence The comma follows the salutation in informal correspondence and follows the complimentary close in both informal and formal correspondence. In formal correspondence, a colon follows the salutation. For more on this use of the colon, see paragraph 12 under Colon in this section.

> Dear Rachel,   Affectionately,   Very truly yours,

48. Other uses The comma is used to avoid ambiguity when the juxtaposition of two words or expressions could cause confusion.

> Whatever will be, will be.
> To John, Marshall was someone special.
> I repaired the lamp that my brother had broken, and replaced the bulb.

49. A comma often follows a direct object or a predicate nominative or predicate adjective when they precede the subject and verb in the sentence. If the meaning of the sentence is clear without this comma, it is often omitted.

> That we would soon have to raise prices, no one disputed.
>
> Critical about the current state of affairs, we might have been.
>
> A disaster it certainly was.

50. With other marks of punctuation Commas are used in conjunction with brackets, ellipsis points, parentheses, and quotation marks. Commas are not used in conjunction with colons, dashes, exclamation points, question marks, or semicolons. If one of these latter marks falls at the same point in a sentence at which a comma would fall, the comma is dropped and the other mark is retained. For more on the use of commas with other marks of punctuation, see the subheading With Other Marks of Punctuation under the heading for those marks of punctuation.

Dash

The dash can function like a comma, a colon, or a pair of parentheses. Like commas and parentheses, dashes set off parenthetic material such as examples; supplemental facts; or appositional, explanatory, or descriptive phrases. Like colons, dashes introduce clauses that explain or expand upon some element of the material that precedes them. The dash is sometimes considered to be a less formal equivalent of the colon and parenthesis, and it does frequently take their place in advertising and other informal contexts. However, dashes may be found in all kinds of writing, including the most formal, and the choice of which mark to use is usually a matter of personal preference.

The dash exists in a number of different lengths. The dash in most general use is the em dash, which is approximately the width of an uppercase M in typeset material. In typewritten material, it is represented by two hyphens. The en dash and the two- and three-em dashes have more limited uses which are explained in paragraphs 12–15 below.

1. **Abrupt change or suspension** The dash marks an abrupt change or break in the structure of a sentence.

   > The board of directors seem happy with the change, but the shareholders—there is the problem.

2. A dash is used to indicate interrupted speech or a speaker's confusion or hesitation.

   > "The next point I'd like to bring up—" the speaker started to say, "I'm sorry. I'll have to stop you there," the moderator broke in.
   >
   > "Yes," he went on, "yes—that is—I guess I agree."

3. **Parenthetic and amplifying elements** Dashes are used in place of other punctuation (such as commas or parentheses) to emphasize parenthetic or amplifying material or to make such material stand out more clearly from the rest of the sentence.

Mail your subscription—now!

In 1976, they asked for—and received—substantial grants from the federal government.

The privately owned consulting firm—formerly known as Aborjaily and Associates—is now offering many new services.

NOTE: When dashes are used to set off parenthetic elements, they often indicate that the material is more digressive than elements set off with commas but less digressive than elements set off by parentheses. For contrasting examples see paragraph 17 under Comma and paragraph 1 under Parentheses in this section.

4. Dashes are used to set off or to introduce defining and enumerating phrases.

The fund sought to acquire controlling positions—a minimum of 25% of outstanding voting securities—in other companies.

The essay dealt with our problems with waste—cans, bottles, discarded tires, and other trash.

5. A dash is often used in place of a colon or semicolon to link clauses, especially when the clause that follows the dash explains, summarizes, or expands upon the clause that precedes it.

The test results were surprisingly good—none of the tested models displayed serious problems.

6. A dash or a pair of dashes often sets off parenthetic or amplifying material introduced by such phrases as *for example, namely, that is, e.g.,* and *i.e.*

After some discussion the motion was tabled—that is, it was removed indefinitely from the board's consideration.

Sports develop two valuable traits—namely, self-control and the ability to make quick decisions.

Not all "prime" windows—i.e., the ones installed when a house is built—are equal in quality.

NOTE: Commas, parentheses, and semicolons are often used for the same purpose. For contrasting examples, see paragraph 18 under Comma, paragraph 2 under Parentheses, and paragraph 6 under Semicolon in this section.

7. A dash introduces a summary statement that follows a series of words or phrases.

Unemployment, strikes, inflation, stock prices, mortgage rates—all are part of the economy.

Once into bankruptcy, the company would have to pay cash for its supplies, defer maintenance, and lay off workers—moves that could threaten its long-term profitability.

8. **With other marks of punctuation** If a dash appears at a point in a sentence where a comma could also appear, the dash is retained and the comma is dropped.

If we don't succeed—and the critics say we won't—then the whole project is in jeopardy.

Our lawyer has read the transcript—all 1200 pages of it—and he has decided that an appeal would not be useful.

Some of the other departments, however—particularly Accounting, Sales, and Credit Collection—have expanded their computer operations.

9. If the second of a pair of dashes appears at a point in a sentence where a period or semicolon would also appear, the period or semicolon is retained and the dash is dropped.

His conduct has always been exemplary—near-perfect attendance, excellent productivity, a good attitude; nevertheless, his termination cannot be avoided.

10. Dashes are used with exclamation points and question marks. When a pair of dashes sets off parenthetic material calling for either of these marks of punctuation, the exclamation point or the question mark is placed inside the second dash. If the parenthetic material falls at the end of a sentence ending with an exclamation point or question mark, the closing dash is not required.

His hobby was getting on people's nerves—especially mine!—and he was extremely good at it.

When the committee meets next week—are you going to be there?—I will present all of the final figures.

Is there any way to predict the future course of this case—one which we really cannot afford to lose?

11. Dashes and parentheses are used in combination to indicate parenthetic material appearing within parenthetic material. Dashes within parentheses and parentheses within dashes are used with about equal frequency.

We were looking for a narrator (or narrators—sometimes a script calls for more than one) who could handle a variety of assignments.

On our trip south we crossed a number of major rivers—the Hudson, the Delaware, and the Patapsco (which flows through Baltimore)—without paying a single toll.

NOTE: If the inner parenthetic element begins with a dash and its closing dash would fall in the same position as the closing parenthesis, the closing dash is omitted and the parenthesis is retained, as in the first example above. If the inner element begins with a parenthesis and its closing parenthesis would coincide with the closing dash, the closing parenthesis and the closing dash are both retained, as in the second example above.

12. **En dash** En dashes appear only in typeset material, not in typewritten material, and therefore they do not often appear in business correspondence. As a point of information, however, the en dash is shorter

than the em dash but slightly longer than the hyphen. Its most frequent uses include as a replacement for a hyphen following a prefix that is added to an open compound, as an equivalent to "(up) to and including" when used between numbers, dates, or other notations to indicate range, as a replacement for the word *to* between capitalized names, and to indicate linkages, such as boundaries, treaties, or oppositions. In all of these uses, a hyphen can be used in typewritten material.

pre–Civil War architecture	1988–89
the New York–Connecticut area	pages 128–34
Washington–Moscow diplomacy	8:30 a.m.–4:30 p.m.

13. **Long dashes** A two-em dash is used to indicate missing letters in a word and, less frequently, to indicate a missing word. A two-em dash is represented in typewritten material by four hyphens.

> Mr. P—— of Baltimore
> That's b——t and you know it.

14. A three-em dash indicates that a word has been left out or that an unknown word or figure is to be supplied. A three-em dash is represented in typewritten material by six hyphens.

> The study was carried out in ———, a fast-growing Sunbelt city.
> We'll leave New York City on the ——— of August.

15. **Spacing** Practice varies as to spacing around the dash. Some publications and some typists insert a space before and after a dash, others do not. Either practice is acceptable.

Ellipsis Points

Ellipsis points is the name most often given to periods when they are used, usually in groups of three, to signal an omission from quoted material or to indicate a pause or trailing off of speech. Other names for periods used in this way include *ellipses, points of ellipsis,* and *suspension points.* Ellipsis points are often used in conjunction with other marks of punctuation, including periods used to mark the ends of sentences. When ellipsis points are used in this way with a terminal period, the omission is sometimes thought of as being marked by four periods. Most of the conventions described in this section are illustrated with quoted material enclosed in quotation marks. However, the conventions are equally applicable to quoted material set as extracts.

NOTE: The examples given below present passages in which ellipsis points indicate omission of material. In most cases, the full text from which these omissions have been made is some portion of the headnote above.

1. Ellipsis points indicate the omission of one or more words within a quoted sentence.

One book said, "Other names . . . include *ellipses, points of ellipsis,* and *suspension points.*"

2. Ellipsis points are usually not used to indicate the omission of words that precede the quoted portion. However, practice varies on this point, and in some formal contexts, especially those in which the quotation is introduced by a colon, ellipsis points are used.

> The book maintained that "the omission is sometimes thought of as being marked by four periods."
>
> The book maintained: ". . . the omission is sometimes thought of as being marked by four periods."

3. Punctuation used in the original that falls on either side of the ellipsis points is often omitted; however, it may be retained, especially if such retention helps clarify the sentence.

> According to the book, "*Ellipsis points* is the name most often given to periods when they are used . . . to signal an omission from quoted material or to indicate a pause or trailing off of speech."
>
> According to the book, "When ellipsis points are used in this way. . . , the omission is sometimes thought of as being marked by four periods."
>
> According to the book, "*Ellipsis points* is the name most often given to periods when they are used, usually in groups of three, . . . to indicate a pause or trailing off of speech."

4. If an omission comprises an entire sentence within a passage, the last part of a sentence within a passage, or the first part of a sentence other than the first quoted sentence, the end punctuation preceding or following the omission is retained and is followed by three periods.

> That book says, "Other names for periods used in this way include *ellipses, points of ellipsis,* and *suspension points.* . . . When ellipsis points are used in this way with a terminal period, the omission is sometimes thought of as being marked by four periods."
>
> That book says, "*Ellipsis points* is the name given to periods when they are used, usually in groups of three, to signal an omission from quoted material. . . . Other names for periods used in this way include *ellipses, points of ellipsis,* and *suspension points.*"
>
> That book says, "Ellipsis points are often used in conjunction with other marks of punctuation, including periods used to mark ends of sentences. . . . The omission is sometimes thought of as being marked by four periods."

NOTE: The capitalization of the word *The* in the third example is acceptable. When the opening words of a quotation act as a sentence within the quotation, the first word is capitalized, even if that word did not begin a sentence in the original version.

5. If the last words of a quoted sentence are omitted and if the original sentence ends with a period, that period is retained and three ellipsis points follow. However, if the original sentence ends with punctuation

other than a period, the end punctuation often follows the ellipsis points, especially if it helps clarify the quotation.

> Their book said, "Ellipsis points are often used in conjunction with other marks of punctuation. . . ."
>
> He always ends his harangues with some variation on the question, "What could you have been thinking when you . . . ?"

NOTE: Many writers and editors, especially those writing in more informal contexts, choose to ignore the styling considerations presented in paragraphs 4 and 5. They use instead an alternative system in which all omissions are indicated by three periods and all terminal periods that may precede or follow an omission are dropped.

6. Ellipsis points are used to indicate that a quoted sentence has been intentionally left unfinished. In situations such as this the terminal period is not included.

> Read the statement beginning "*Ellipsis points* is the name most often given . . ." and then proceed to the numbered paragraphs.

7. Ellipsis points are used to indicate faltering speech, especially if the faltering involves a long pause between words or a sentence that trails off or is left intentionally unfinished. In these kinds of sentences most writers treat the ellipsis points as terminal punctuation, thus removing the need for any other punctuation; however, practice does vary on this point, and some writers routinely use other punctuation in conjunction with ellipsis points.

> The speaker seemed uncertain how to answer the question. "Well, that's true . . . but even so . . . I think we can do better."
>
> "Despite these uncertainties, we believe we can do it, but . . ."
>
> "I mean . . ." he said, "like . . . How?"

8. Ellipsis points are sometimes used as a stylistic device to catch and hold a reader's attention.

> They think that nothing can go wrong . . . but it does.

9. Each ellipsis point is set off from other ellipsis points, from adjacent punctuation (except for quotation marks, which are closed up to the ellipsis points), and from surrounding text by a space. If a terminal period is used with ellipsis points, it precedes them with no space before it and one space after it.

Exclamation Point

The exclamation point is used to mark a forceful comment. Heavy use can weaken its effect, so it should be used sparingly.

1. An exclamation point can punctuate a sentence, phrase, or interjection.

This is the fourth time in a row he's been late!

No one that I talked to—not even the accounting department!—seemed to know how the figures were calculated.

Ah, those sales figures!

2. The exclamation point replaces the question mark when an ironic or emphatic tone is more important than the actual question.

> Aren't you finished yet!
> Do you realize what you've done!
> Why me!

3. Occasionally the exclamation point is used with a question mark to indicate a very forceful question.

> How much did you say?!
> You did what!?

4. The exclamation point is enclosed within brackets, dashes, parentheses, and quotation marks when it punctuates the material so enclosed rather than the sentence as a whole. It should be placed outside them when it punctuates the entire sentence.

> All of this proves—at long last!—that we were right from the start.
> The dog got the gate open (for the third time!) and ran into the street.
> He shouted, "Wait!" and sprinted toward the train.
> The correct word is "mousse," not "moose"!

5. Exclamatory phrases that occur within a sentence are set off by dashes or parentheses.

> And now our competition—get this!—wants to start sharing secrets.
> The board accepted most of the recommendations, but ours (alas!) was not even considered.

6. If an exclamation point falls at a place in a sentence where a comma or a terminal period could also go, the comma or period is dropped and the exclamation point is retained.

> "Absolutely not!" he snapped.
> She has written about sixty pages so far—and with no help!

NOTE: If the exclamation point is part of a title, as of a play, book, or movie, it may be followed by a comma. If the title falls at the end of a sentence, the terminal period is usually dropped.

> Marshall and Susan went to see the musical *Oklahoma!*, and they enjoyed it very much.
> They enjoyed seeing the muscial *Oklahoma!*

7. In typewritten material, two spaces follow an exclamation point that ends a sentence. If the exclamation point is followed by a closing bracket, closing parenthesis, or closing quotation marks, the two

spaces follow the second mark. In typeset material, only one space follows the exclamation point.

```
The time is now!  Decide what you are going to do.
She said, "The time is now!"  That meant we had to
decide what to do.
```

The time is now! Decide what you are going to do.

She said, "The time is now!" That meant we had to decide what to do.

Hyphen

1. Hyphens are used to link elements in compound words. For more on the styling of compound words, see the section on Compounds, beginning on page 114.

2. A hyphen marks an end-of-line division of a word when part of the word is to be carried down to the next line.

> We visited several showrooms, looked at the prices (it wasn't a pleasant experience; prices in this area have not gone down), and asked all the questions we could think of.

3. A hyphen divides letters or syllables to give the effect of stuttering, sobbing, or halting speech.

S-s-sammy   ah-ah-ah   y-y-es

4. Hyphens indicate a word spelled out letter by letter.

p-r-o-b-a-t-i-o-n

5. A hyphen indicates that a word element is a prefix, suffix, or medial element.

anti-   -ship   -o-

6. A hyphen is used in typewritten material as an equivalent to the phrase "(up) to and including" when placed between numbers and dates. (In typeset material this hyphen is very often replaced by an en dash. For more on the use of the en dash, see paragraph 12 under Dash in this section.)

35-40 years   ages 10-15   1988-89

7. Hyphens are sometimes used to produce inflected forms of verbs that are made of individually pronounced letters or to add an *-er* ending to an abbreviation; however, apostrophes are more commonly used for this purpose. For more on these uses of the apostrophe, see paragraphs 6 and 7 under Apostrophe in this section.

D.H.-ing for the White Sox   a loyal AA-er

Parentheses

Parentheses enclose supplementary elements that are inserted into a main statement but that are not intended to be part of the statement. For some of the cases described below, especially those listed under the heading "Parenthetic Elements," commas and dashes are frequently used instead of parentheses. (For contrasting examples, see paragraph 17 under Comma and paragraph 3 under Dash in this section.) In general, commas tend to be used when the inserted material is closely related, logically or grammatically, to the main clause; parentheses are more often used when the inserted material is incidental or digressive.

1. **Parenthetic elements** Parentheses enclose phrases and clauses that provide examples, explanations, or supplementary facts. Supplementary numerical data may also be enclosed in parentheses.

> Nominations for the association's principal officers (president, vice president, treasurer, and secretary) were heard and approved at the last meeting.
>
> Although we liked the applicant (her background, training, and experience were excellent), we weren't ready to hire anyone at that point.
>
> The company shows good earnings ($3.45 a share vs. $3.05 last year), a strong balance sheet, and a good current yield (7.8%).

2. Parentheses enclose phrases and clauses introduced by expressions such as *namely, that is, e.g.,* and *i.e.* Commas, dashes, and semicolons are also used to perform this function. (For contrasting examples, see paragraph 18 under Comma, paragraph 5 under Dash, and paragraph 6 under Semicolon in this section.)

> In writing to the manufacturer, be as specific as possible (i.e., list the missing or defective parts, describe the nature of the malfunction, and provide the name and address of the store where the unit was purchased).

3. Parentheses set off definitions or translations in the main part of a sentence.

> The company sold off all of its retail outlets and announced plans to sell off its houseware (small appliance) business as well.
>
> The hotel was located just a few blocks from San Antonio's famous Paseo del Rio (river walk).

4. Parentheses enclose abbreviations synonymous with spelled forms and occurring after those forms, or they may enclose the spelled form occurring after the abbreviation.

> She referred to a ruling by the Federal Communications Commission (FCC).
>
> They were involved with a study regarding the manufacture and disposal of PVC (polyvinyl chloride).

5. Parentheses often set off cross-references.

> Telephone ordering service is also provided (refer to the list of stores at the end of this catalog).
>
> The diagram (Fig. 3) illustrates the action of the pump.

6. Parentheses enclose Arabic numerals that confirm a spelled-out number in a general text or in a legal document.

> Delivery will be made in thirty (30) days.
>
> The fee for our services is Four Thousand Dollars ($4,000.00), payable to UNCO, Inc.

7. Parentheses enclose the name of a city or state that is inserted into a proper name for identification.

> the Norristown (Pa.) State Hospital
> the *Tulsa* (Okla.) *Tribune*

8. Some writers use parentheses to set off personal asides.

> It was largely as a result of this conference that the committee was formed (its subsequent growth in influence is another story).

9. Parentheses are used to set off quotations, either attributed or unattributed, that illustrate or support a statement made in the main text.

> After he had had a few brushes with the police, his stepfather had him sent to jail as an incorrigible ("It will do him good").

10. **Other uses** Parentheses enclose unpunctuated numbers or letters separating and heading individual elements or items in a series within running text.

> We must set forth (1) our long-term goals, (2) our immediate objectives, and (3) the means at our disposal.

11. Parentheses indicate alternative terms.

> Please sign and return the enclosed form(s).

12. Parentheses are used in combination with numbers for several other purposes, such as setting off area codes in telephone numbers and indicating losses in accounting.

> (413) 256-7899
>
> Operating Profits (in millions)
>
> | | |
> |---|---|
> | Cosmetics | 26.2 |
> | Food products | 47.7 |
> | Food services | 54.3 |
> | Transportation | (17.7) |
> | Sporting goods | (11.2) |
> | Total | 99.3 |

13. **With other marks of punctuation** If a parenthetic expression is an independent sentence, its first word is capitalized and a period is placed *inside* the last parenthesis. On the other hand, a parenthetic expression that occurs within a sentence—even if it could stand alone as a separate sentence—does not end with a period. It may, however, end with an exclamation point, a question mark, a period after an abbrevi-

ation, or a set of quotation marks. A parenthetic expression within a sentence does not require capitalization unless it is a quoted sentence.

> The discussion was held in the boardroom. (The results are still confidential.)
>
> Although several trade organizations worked actively against the legislation (there were at least three paid lobbyists working on Capitol Hill at any one time), the bill passed easily.
>
> After waiting in line for an hour (why do we do these things?), we finally left.
>
> The conference was held in Vancouver (that's in B.C.).
>
> He was totally confused ("What can we do?") and refused to see anyone.

14. If a parenthetic expression within a sentence is composed of two independent clauses, capitalization and periods are avoided. To separate the clauses within the parentheses, semicolons are usually used. If the parenthetic expression occurs outside of a sentence, normal patterns of capitalization and punctuation prevail.

> We visited several showrooms, looked at the prices (it wasn't a pleasant experience; prices in this area have not gone down), and asked all the questions we could think of.
>
> We visited several showrooms and looked at the prices. (It wasn't a pleasant experience. Prices in this area have not gone down.) If salespeople were available, we asked all of the questions we could think of.

15. No punctuation mark (other than a period after an abbreviation) is placed before parenthetic material within a sentence; if a break is required, the punctuation is placed after the final parenthesis.

> I'll get back to you tomorrow (Friday), when I have more details.

16. Parentheses sometimes appear within parentheses, although the usual practice is to replace the inner pair of parentheses with a pair of brackets. (For an example of brackets within parentheses, see paragraph 6 under Brackets in this section.)

> Checks must be drawn in U.S. dollars, (PLEASE NOTE: In accordance with U.S. Department of Treasury regulations, we cannot accept checks drawn on Canadian banks for amounts less than four U.S. dollars ($4.00). The same regulation applies to Canadian money orders.)

17. Dashes and parentheses are often used together to set off parenthetic material within a larger parenthetic element. For details and examples, see paragraph 11 under Dash in this section.

18. **Spacing** In typewritten material a parenthetic expression that is an independent sentence is followed by two spaces. In typeset material, the sentence is followed by one space. In typewritten or typeset material, a parenthetic expression that falls within a sentence is followed by one space.

```
We visited several showrooms and looked at the prices.
(It wasn't a pleasant experience.  Prices in this area
have not gone down.)  We asked all the questions we
could think of.
```

We visited several showrooms and looked at the prices. (It wasn't a pleasant experience. Prices in this area have not gone down.) We asked all the questions we could think of.

Period

1. A period terminates a sentence or a sentence fragment that is neither interrogative nor exclamatory.

Write the letter.
They wrote the required letters.
Total chaos. Nothing works.

2. A period punctuates some abbreviations. For more on the punctuation of abbreviations, see the section on Abbreviations, beginning on page 126.

a.k.a.	Assn.	Dr.	Jr.	Ph.D.
fig.	in.	No.	e.g.	ibid.
N.W.	U.S.	Inc.	Co.	Corp.

3. A period is used with an individual's initials. If all of the person's initials are used instead of the name, however, the unspaced initials may be written without periods.

F. Scott Fitzgerald   Susan B. Anthony
F.D.R. *or* FDR   T. S. Eliot

4. A period follows Roman and Arabic numerals and also letters when they are used without parentheses in outlines and vertical enumerations.

I. Objectives
  A. Economy
    1. Low initial cost
    2. Low maintenance cost
  B. Ease of operation
Required skills are:
  1. Shorthand
  2. Typing
  3. Transcription

5. A period is placed within quotation marks even when it does not punctuate the quoted material.

The charismatic leader was known to his followers as "the guiding light."

"I said I wanted to fire him," Henry went on, "but she said, 'I don't think you have the contractual privilege to do that.'"

6. When brackets or parentheses enclose a sentence that is independent of surrounding sentences, the period is placed inside the closing parenthesis or bracket. However, when brackets or parentheses enclose a sentence that is part of a surrounding sentence, the period for the enclosed sentence is omitted.

> On Friday the government ordered a 24-hour curfew and told all journalists and photographers to leave the area. (Authorities later confiscated the film of those who did not comply.)
>
> I took a good look at her (she was standing quite close to me at the time).

7. In typewritten material, two spaces follow a period that ends a sentence. If the period is followed by a closing bracket, closing parenthesis, or quotation marks, the two spaces follow the second mark.

> `Here is the car.  Do you want to get in?`
>
> `He said, "Here is the car."  I asked if I should get`
> `in.`

8. One space follows a period that comes after an initial in a name. If a name is composed entirely of initials, no space is required; however, the usual styling for such names is to omit the periods.

> Mr. H. C. Matthews   F.D.R. *or* FDR

9. No space follows an internal period within a punctuated abbreviation.

> f.o.b.   i.e.   Ph.D.   A.D.   p.m.

Question Mark

1. The question mark terminates a direct question.

> What went wrong?
>
> "Who signed the memo?" she asked.

NOTE: The intent of the writer, not the word order of the sentence, determines whether or not the sentence is a question. Polite requests that are worded as questions, for instance, usually take periods, because they are not really questions. Similarly, sentences whose word order is that of a statement but whose force is interrogatory are punctuated with question marks.

> Will you please sit down.
>
> He did that?

2. The question mark terminates an interrogative element that is part of a sentence. An indirect question is not followed by a question mark.

> How did she do it? was the question on everybody's mind.
>
> She wondered, will it work?
>
> She wondered whether it would work.

3. The question mark punctuates each element of an interrogative series that is neither numbered nor lettered. When an interrogative series is

numbered or lettered, only one question mark is used, and it is placed at the end of the series.

> Can you give us a reasonable forecast? back up your predictions? compare them with last year's earnings?

> Can you (1) give us a reasonable forecast, (2) back up your predictions, (3) compare them with last year's earnings?

4. The question mark indicates uncertainty about a fact.

> Susan O'Hara, advertising vice president(?) of the corporation

5. The question mark is placed inside a closing bracket, dash, parenthesis, or pair of quotation marks when it punctuates only the material enclosed by that mark and not the sentence as a whole. It is placed outside that mark when it punctuates the entire sentence.

> What did Andrew mean when he called the project "a fiasco from the start"?

> I had a vacation in 1975 (was it really that long ago?), but I haven't had time for one since.

> He asked, "Do you realize the extent of the problem [the housing shortage]?"

6. In typewritten material, two spaces follow a question mark that ends a sentence. If the question mark is followed by a closing bracket, closing parenthesis, or quotation marks, the two spaces follow the second mark. In typeset material, only one space follows the question mark.

> She wondered, will it work? He said he thought it would.

> She asked, "Will it work?" He said he thought it would.

> She wondered, will it work? He said he thought it would.

7. One space follows a question mark that falls within a sentence.

> Are you coming today? tomorrow? the day after?

Quotation Marks, Double

The following paragraphs describe the use of quotation marks to enclose quoted matter in regular text, to set off translations of words, or to enclose single letters within sentences. For the use of the quotation marks to enclose titles of poems, paintings, or other works, see the section on Capitals, Italics, and Quotation Marks, beginning on page 86.

1. **Basic uses** Quotation marks enclose direct quotations but not indirect quotations.

> She said, "I am leaving."

> "I am leaving," she said, "and I'm not coming back."

> "I am leaving," she said, "This has gone on long enough."

> She said that she was leaving.

2. Quotation marks enclose fragments of quoted matter when they are reproduced exactly as originally stated.

> The agreement makes it clear that he "will be paid only upon receipt of an acceptable manuscript."
>
> As late as 1754, documents refer to him as "yeoman" and "husbandman."

3. Quotation marks enclose words or phrases borrowed from others, words used in a special way, or words of marked informality when they are introduced into formal writing.

> That kind of corporation is referred to as "closed" or "privately held."
>
> Be sure to send a copy of your résumé, or as some folks would say, your "biodata summary."
>
> They were afraid the patient had "stroked out"—had had a cerebrovascular accident.

4. Quotation marks are sometimes used to enclose words referred to as words. Italic type or underlining is also frequently used for this purpose. For more on this use of italics, see paragraph 4 under Other Uses of Italics, pages 105–106.

> He went through the manuscript and changed every "he" to "she."

5. Quotation marks enclose short exclamations or representations of sounds. Representations of sounds are also frequently set in italic type or underlined. For more on this use of italics, see paragraph 7 under Other Uses of Italics, page 106.

> "Ssshh!" she hissed.
>
> They never say anything crude like "shaddap."

6. Quotation marks enclose short sentences that fall within longer sentences, especially when the shorter sentence is meant to suggest spoken dialogue. Kinds of sentences that may be treated in this way include mottoes and maxims, unspoken or imaginary dialogue, or sentences referred to as sentences.

> Throughout the camp, the spirit was "We can do."
>
> She never could get used to his "That's the way it goes" attitude.
>
> In effect, the voters were saying "You blew it, and you don't get another chance."
>
> Their attitude could only be described as "Kill the messenger."
>
> Another example of a palindrome is "Madam, I'm Adam."

NOTE: Style varies regarding the punctuation of sentences such as these. In general, the force of the quotation marks is to set the shorter sentence off more distinctly from the surrounding sentence and to give the shorter sentence more of the feel of spoken dialogue; omitting the quotation marks diminishes the effect. (For a description of the use of commas in sentences like these, see paragraphs 33 and 34 under Comma in this section.)

The first rule is, When in doubt, spell it out.

They weren't happy with the impression she left: "Don't expect favors, because I don't have to give them."

7. Quotation marks are not used to enclose paraphrases.

Build a better mouse trap, Emerson says, and the world will beat a path to your door.

8. Direct questions are usually not enclosed in quotation marks unless they represent quoted dialogue.

The question is, What went wrong?

As we listened to him, we couldn't help wondering, Where's the plan?

She asked, "What went wrong?"

NOTE: As in the sentences presented in paragraph 6 above, style varies regarding the use of quotation marks with direct questions; and in many cases, writers will include the quotation marks.

As we listened to him, we couldn't help wondering, "Where's the plan?"

9. Quotation marks are used to enclose translations of foreign or borrowed terms.

The term *sesquipedalian* comes from the Latin word *sesquipedalis,* meaning "a foot and a half long."

While in Texas, he encountered the armadillo ("little armored one") and developed quite an interest in it.

10. Quotation marks are sometimes used to enclose single letters within a sentence.

The letter "m" is wider than the letter "i."

Put an "x" in the right spot.

The metal rod was shaped into a "V."

NOTE: Practice varies on this point. Letters referred to as letters are commonly set in italic type or underlined. (For more on this use of italics, see paragraphs 4 and 5 under Other Uses of Italics, pages 105–106.) Letters often appear in the same typeface as the surrounding text if no confusion would result from the styling.

a V-shaped blade

He was happy to get a B in the course.

How many e's are in her name?

11. With other marks of punctuation When quotation marks follow a word in a sentence that is also followed by a period or comma, the period or comma is placed within the quotation marks.

He said, "I am leaving."

Her camera was described as "waterproof," but "moisture-resistant" would have been a better description.

NOTE: Some writers draw a distinction between periods and commas that belong logically to the quoted material and those that belong to the whole sentence. If the period or comma belongs to the quoted material, they place it inside the quotation marks; if the period belongs logically to the sentence that surrounds the quoted matter, they place it outside the quotation marks. This distinction was previously observed in a wide range of publications, including U.S. Congressional publications and Merriam-Webster® dictionaries. In current practice, the distinction is made by relatively few writers, although the distinction is routinely made for dashes, exclamation points, and question marks used with quotation marks, as described in paragraph 13 below.

> The package was labeled "Handle with Care".
>
> The act was referred to as the "Army-Navy Medical Services Corps Act of 1947".
>
> Her camera was described as "waterproof", but "moisture-resistant" would have been a better description.
>
> He said, "I am leaving."

12. When quotation marks follow a word in a sentence that is also followed by a colon or semicolon, the colon or semicolon is placed outside the quotation marks.

> There was only one thing to do when he said, "I may not run": promise him a larger campaign contribution.
>
> She spoke of her "little cottage in the country"; she might better have called it a mansion.

13. The dash, question mark, and exclamation point are placed inside quotation marks when they punctuate the quoted matter only. They are placed outside the quotation marks when they punctuate the whole sentence.

> He asked, "When did she leave?"
>
> What is the meaning of "the open door"?
>
> Save us from his "mercy"!
>
> "I can't see how—" he started to say.
>
> He thought he knew where he was going—he remembered her saying, "Take two lefts, then stay to the right"—but the streets didn't look familiar.

14. **Spacing** One space follows a quotation mark that is followed by the rest of a sentence.

> "I am leaving," she said.

15. In typewritten material, two spaces follow a quotation mark that ends a sentence. In typeset material one space follows.

> ```
> He said, "Here is the car."  I asked if I should get
> in.
> ```
>
> He said, "Here is the car," I asked if I should get in.

Quotation Marks, Single

1. Single quotation marks enclose a quotation within a quotation in American (but not British) practice.

> The witness said, "I distinctly heard him say, 'Don't be late,' and then I heard the door close."
>
> The witness said, "I distinctly heard him say, 'Don't be late.' "

NOTE: When both single and double quotation marks occur at the end of a sentence, the period typically falls *within* both sets of marks.

2. Single quotation marks are sometimes used in place of double quotation marks especially in British usage.

> The witness said, 'I distinctly heard him say, "Don't be late," and then I heard the door close.'

3. On rare occasions, authors face the question of how to style a quotation within a quotation within a quotation. Standard styling practice would be to enclose the innermost quotation in double marks; however, this construction can be confusing, and in many cases rewriting the sentence can remove the need for it.

> The witness said, "I distinctly heard him say, 'Don't you say "Shut up" to me.' "
>
> The witness said that she distinctly heard him say, "Don't you say 'Shut up' to me."

Semicolon

The semicolon is used in ways that are similar to those in which periods and commas are used. Like a period, the semicolon marks the end of a complete clause, but it also signals that the clause that follows it is closely related to the one that precedes it. The semicolon is also used to distinguish major sentence divisions from the minor pauses that are represented by commas.

1. Between clauses A semicolon separates independent clauses that are joined together in one sentence without a coordinating conjunction.

> Some people are natural leaders in their willingness to accept responsibility and delegate authority with intelligence; others do not measure up.
>
> He hemmed and hawed for an hour or more; he couldn't make up his mind.

2. Ordinarily a comma separates main clauses joined with a coordinating conjunction. However, if the sentence might be confusing with a comma in this position, a semicolon is used in its place. Potentially confusing sentences include those with other commas in them or with particularly long clauses.

> We fear that this situation may, in fact, occur; but we don't know when.
>
> In a society that seeks to promote social goals, government will play a powerful role; and taxation, once simply a means of raising money, becomes, in addition, a way of furthering those goals.

As recently as 1978 the company felt the operation could be a successful one that would generate significant profits in several different markets; but in 1981 the management changed its mind and began a program of shutting down plants and reducing its product line.

3. A semicolon joins two statements when the grammatical construction of the second clause is elliptical and depends on that of the first.

In many cases the conference sessions, which were designed to allow for full discussions of topics, were much too long and tedious; the breaks between them, much too short.

4. A semicolon joins two clauses when the second begins with a conjunctive adverb, as *accordingly, also, besides, consequently, furthermore, hence, however, indeed, likewise, moreover, namely, nevertheless, otherwise, still, then, therefore,* and *thus.* Phrases such as *by the same token, in that case, as a result, on the other hand,* and *all the same* can also act as conjunctive adverbs.

Most people are covered by insurance of one kind or another; indeed, many people don't even see their medical bills.

It won't be easy to sort out the facts of this confusing situation; however, a decision must be made.

The case could take years to work its way through the court system; as a result, many plaintiffs will accept out-of-court settlements.

NOTE: Practice varies regarding the treatment of clauses introduced by *so* and *yet.* Although many writers continue to treat *so* and *yet* as adverbs, it has become standard to treat these words as coordinating conjunctions that join clauses. In this treatment, a comma precedes *so* and *yet* and no punctuation follows them. (For examples, see paragraph 1 under Comma in this section.)

5. When three or more clauses are separated by semicolons, a coordinating conjunction may or may not precede the final clause. If a coordinating conjunction does precede the final clause, the final semicolon is often replaced with a comma. (For the use of commas to separate three or more clauses without conjunctions, see paragraph 4 under Comma in this section.)

Their report was one-sided and partial; it did not reflect the facts; it distorted them.

They don't understand; they grow bored; and they stop learning.

The report recounted events leading up to the incident; it included observations of eyewitnesses, but it drew no conclusions.

NOTE: The choices of whether to use a conjunction and whether to use a semicolon or comma with the conjunction are matters of personal preference. In general, the force of the semicolon is to make the transition to the final clause more abrupt, which often serves to place more emphasis on that clause. The comma and conjunction ease the transition and make the sentence seem less choppy.

6. **With phrases and clauses introduced by** *for example, i.e.,* **etc.** A semicolon is sometimes used before expressions (as *for example, for instance, that is, namely, e.g.,* or *i.e.*) that introduce expansions or series. Commas, dashes, and parentheses are also used in sentences like these. For contrasting examples, see paragraph 18 under Comma, paragraph 5 under Dash, and paragraph 2 under Parentheses in this section.

> On one point only did everyone agree; namely, that too much money had been spent already.
>
> We were fairly successful on that project; that is, we made our deadlines and met our budget.
>
> Most of the contestants had traveled great distances to participate; for example, three had come from Australia, one from Japan, and two from China.

7. **In a series** A semicolon is used in place of a comma to separate phrases in a series when the phrases themselves contain commas. A comma may replace the semicolon before the last item in a series if the last item is introduced with a conjunction.

> The visitor to Barndale was offered three sources of overnight accommodation: The Rose and Anchor, which housed Barndale's oldest pub; The Crawford, an American-style luxury hotel; and Ellen's Bed and Breakfast on Peabody Lane.
>
> The schedule calls for orientation and planning sessions in the morning; talks on marketing, long-term investments and tax laws directly after lunch, and an introduction to computer terminology in the late afternoon.

8. When the individual items in an enumeration or series are long or are sentences themselves, they are usually separated by semicolons.

> Among the committee's recommendations were the following: more hospital beds in urban areas where there are waiting lists for elective surgery; smaller staff size in half-empty rural hospitals; review procedures for all major purchases.

9. A semicolon separates items in a list in cases where a comma alone would not clearly separate the items or references.

> (Friedlander 1957; Ballas 1962)
> (Genesis 3:1–19; 4:1–16)

10. **With other marks of punctuation** A semicolon is placed outside quotation marks and parentheses.

> They referred to each other as "Mother" and "Father"; they were the archetypal happily married elderly couple.
>
> She accepted the situation with every appearance of equanimity (but with some inward qualms); however, all of that changed the next day.

Virgule

The virgule is known by many names, including *diagonal, solidus, oblique, slant, slash,* and *slash mark.* Most commonly, the virgule is used to represent a word that is not written out or to separate or set off certain adjacent elements of text.

1. **In place of missing words** A virgule represents the word *per* or *to* when used with units of measure or when used to indicate the terms of a ratio.

40,000 tons/year	9 ft./sec.	a 50/50 split
14 gm/100 cc	price/earnings ratio	risk/reward tradeoff

2. A virgule separates alternatives. In this context, the virgule usually represents the words *or* or *and/or*.

alumni/ae	introductory/refresher courses
his/her	oral/written tests

3. A virgule replaces the word *and* in some compound terms.

molybdenum/vanadium steel
in the May/June issue
1973/74
in the Falls Church/McLean, Va., area
an innovative classroom/laboratory

4. A virgule is used, although less commonly, to replace a number of prepositions, such as *at, versus, with,* and *for.*

U.C./Berkeley	parent/child issues
table/mirror	Vice President/Editorial

5. **With abbreviations** A virgule punctuates some abbreviations.

c/o	A/V	d/b/a
A/R	A/1C	S/Sgt
w/	V/STOL	

NOTE: In some cases the virgule may stand for a word that is not represented in the abbreviation (e.g., *in* in *W/O*, the abbreviation for *water in oil*).

6. **To separate elements** The virgule is used in a number of different ways to separate groups of numbers, such as elements in a date, numerators and denominators in fractions, and area codes in telephone numbers. For more on the use of virgules with numbers, see the section on Numbers, beginning on page 136.

7. The virgule serves as a divider between lines of poetry that are run in with the text around them. This method of quoting poetry is usually limited to passages of no more than three or four lines. Longer passages are usually set off from the text as extract quotations.

When Samuel Taylor Coleridge wrote in "Christabel" that "'Tis a month before the month of May,/And the Spring comes slowly up this way," he could have been describing New England.

8. **Spacing** In general, no space is used between the virgule and the words, letters, or figures separated by it; however, some writers do prefer to place spaces around a virgule used to separate lines of poetry.

Capitals, Italics, and Quotation Marks

Words and phrases are capitalized, italicized or underlined, or enclosed in quotation marks in order to indicate that they have a special significance in a particular context. The section that follows is divided into four parts that describe the kinds of contexts in which capitals, italics, and quotation marks are used. The first part explains the use of capitalized words to begin sentences and phrases. The second explains the use of capitals, italics, and quotation marks to indicate that a word or phrase is a proper noun, pronoun, or adjective. The third and fourth parts explain other uses of capital letters and italics. For other uses of quotation marks, see pages 78–82.

Beginnings

1. The first word of a sentence or sentence fragment is capitalized.

> The meeting was postponed.
> No! I cannot do it.
> Will you go?
> Total chaos. Nothing works.

2. The first word of a sentence contained within parentheses is capitalized. However, a parenthetical sentence occurring inside another sentence is not capitalized unless it is a complete quoted sentence.

> The discussion was held in the boardroom. (The results are still confidential.)
> Although we liked the services they could provide (their banquet facilities were especially good), we could not afford to go there often.
> After waiting in line for an hour (why do we do these things?), we finally left.
> He was totally demoralized ("There is just nothing we can do") and was contemplating resignation.

3. The first word of a direct quotation is capitalized. However, if the quotation is interrupted in midsentence, the second part does not begin with a capital.

> The President said, "We have rejected this report entirely."
> "We have rejected this report entirely," the President said, "and we will not comment on it further."

4. When a quotation, whether a sentence fragment or a complete sentence, is syntactically dependent on the sentence in which it occurs, the quotation does not begin with a capital.

> The President made it clear that "there is no room for compromise."

5. The first word of a sentence within a sentence is usually capitalized. Examples of sentences within sentences include mottoes and rules, unspoken or imaginary dialogue, sentences referred to as sentences, and direct questions. For an explanation of the use of commas and quotation marks with sentences such as these, see paragraphs 34 and 35 under Comma, page 62, and paragraph 6 under Quotation Marks, Double, pages 79–80.

> You know the saying, "Honesty is the best policy."
> The first rule is, When in doubt, spell it out.
> The clear message coming back from the audience was "We don't care."
> My question is, When can we go?
> She kept wondering, how did they get here so soon?

6. The first word of a line of poetry is usually capitalized.

> The best lack all conviction, while the worst
> Are full of passionate intensity.
> —W. B. Yeats

7. The first word following a colon may be either lowercased or capitalized if it introduces a complete sentence. While the former is the usual styling, the latter is also quite common, especially when the sentence introduced by the colon is fairly lengthy and distinctly separate from the preceding clause.

> The advantage of this particular system is clear: it's inexpensive.
> The situation is critical: This company cannot hope to recoup the fourth-quarter losses that were sustained in five operating divisions.

8. If a colon introduces a series of sentences, the first word of each sentence is capitalized.

> Consider the following steps that we have taken: A subcommittee has been formed to evaluate our past performance and to report its findings to the full organization. New sources of revenue are being explored, and relevant organizations are being contacted. And several candidates have been interviewed for the new post of executive director.

9. The first words of run-in enumerations that form complete sentences are capitalized, as are the first words of phrasal lists and enumerations arranged vertically beneath running texts. Phrasal enumerations run in with the introductory text, however, are lowercased.

> Do the following tasks at the end of the day: 1. Clean your typewriter. 2. Clear your desktop of papers. 3. Cover office machines. 4. Straighten the contents of your desk drawers, cabinets, and bookcases.

This is the agenda:
    Call to order
    Roll call
    Minutes of the previous meeting
    Treasurer's report
On the agenda will be (1) call to order, (2) roll call, (3) minutes of the previous meeting, (4) treasurer's report . . .

10. The introductory words *Whereas* and *Resolved* are capitalized in minutes and legislation, as is the word *That* or an alternative word or expression which immediately follows either.

Resolved, That . . .
Whereas, Substantial benefits . . .

11. The first word in an outline heading is capitalized.

    I. Editorial tasks
   II. Production responsibilities
       A. Cost estimates
       B. Bids

12. The first word of the salutation of a letter and the first word of a complimentary close are capitalized.

Dear Mary,	Dear Sir or Madam:	Ladies and Gentlemen:
Gentlemen:	Sincerely yours,	Very truly yours,

13. The first word and each subsequent major word following a SUBJECT or TO heading (as in a memorandum) are capitalized.

SUBJECT: Pension Plans
TO: All Department Heads and Editors

Proper Nouns, Pronouns, and Adjectives

The following paragraphs describe the ways in which a broad range of proper nouns, pronouns, and adjectives are styled—with capitals, italics, quotation marks, or some combination of these devices. In almost all cases, proper nouns, pronouns, and adjectives are capitalized. In many cases, proper nouns are italicized (or underlined in typewritten material) or enclosed in quotation marks in addition to being capitalized. No clear distinctions can be drawn between the kinds of words that are capitalized and italicized, capitalized and enclosed in quotation marks, or simply capitalized, as styling on these points is governed almost wholly by tradition.

The paragraphs that follow are grouped under the following alphabetically arranged headings:

Abbreviations	Derivatives of Proper	Historical Periods
Abstractions and	Names	and Events
Personifications	Geographical and	Hyphenated Compounds
Academic Degrees	Topographical	Legal Material
Animals and Plants	References	Medical Terms
Awards, Honors, and	Governmental, Judicial,	Military Terms
Prizes	and Political Bodies	Numerical Designations

Organizations	Religious Terms	Titles
People	Scientific Terms	Trademarks
Pronouns	Time Periods and Zones	Transportation

1. **Abbreviations** Abbreviated forms of proper nouns and adjectives are capitalized, just as the spelled-out forms would be. For more on the capitalization of abbreviations, see the section on Abbreviations, beginning on page 126.

> Dec. for *December*   Wed. for *Wednesday*
> Col. for *Colonel*   Brit. for *British*

2. **Abstractions and personifications** Abstract terms, such as names of concepts or qualities, are usually not capitalized unless the concept or quality is being presented as if it were a person. If the term is simply being used in conjunction with other words that allude to human characteristics or qualities, it is usually not capitalized. For more on the capitalization of abstract terms, see paragraph 2 under Other Uses of Capitals, page 104.

> a time when Peace walked among us
> as Autumn paints each leaf in fiery colors
> an economy gripped by inflation
> hoping that fate would lend a hand

3. Fictitious names used as personifications are capitalized.

> Uncle Sam   Ma Bell   John Bull   Jack Frost
> Big Oil squirmed under the new regulations.

4. **Academic degrees** The names of academic degrees are capitalized when they follow a person's name. The names of specific academic degrees not following a person's name are capitalized or not capitalized according to individual preference. General terms referring to degrees, such as *doctorate, master's degree,* or *bachelor's* are not capitalized. Abbreviations for academic degrees are always capitalized.

> Martin Bonkowski, Doctor of Divinity
> earned her Doctor of Laws degree *or* earned her doctor of laws degree
> working for a bachelor's degree
> Susan Wycliff, M.S.W.
> received her Ph.D.

5. **Animals and plants** The common names of animals and plants are not capitalized unless they contain a proper noun as a separate element, in which case the proper noun is capitalized, but any element of the name following the proper noun is lowercased. Elements of the name preceding the proper noun are usually but not always capitalized. In some cases, the common name of the plant or animal contains a word that was once a proper noun but is no longer thought of as such. In

these cases, the word is usually not capitalized. When in doubt, consult a dictionary. (For an explanation of the capitalization of genus names in binomial nomenclature or of New Latin names for groups above genera in zoology and botany, see paragraphs 67 and 68 below.)

cocker spaniel	lily of the valley	ponderosa pine
great white shark	Hampshire hog	Kentucky bluegrass
Steller's jay	Bengal tiger	Japanese beetle
Rhode Island red	Great Dane	Brown Swiss
black-eyed Susan	wandering Jew	holstein

NOTE: In references to specific breeds, as distinguished from the animals that belong to the breed, all elements of the name are capitalized.

| Gordon Setter | Rhode Island Red | Holstein |

6. **Awards, honors, and prizes** Names of awards, honors, and prizes are capitalized. Descriptive words and phrases that are not actually part of the award's name are lowercased. (For an explanation of capitalizing the names of military decorations, see paragraph 44 below.)

Academy Award	Emmy
Nobel Prize	Nobel Prize in medicine
Nobel Prize winner	Nobel Peace Prize
Rhodes Scholarship	Rhodes scholar
New York Drama Critics' Circle Award	

7. **Derivatives of proper names** Derivatives of proper names are capitalized when they are used in their primary sense. However, if the derived term has taken on a specialized meaning, it is usually not capitalized.

Roman architecture	Victorian customs	Keynesian economics
an Americanism	an Egyptologist	french fries
manila envelope	pasteurized milk	a quixotic undertaking

8. **Geographical and topographical references** Terms that identify divisions of the earth's surface and distinct areas, regions, places, or districts are capitalized, as are derivative nouns and adjectives.

Chicago, Illinois	the Great Plains
the Middle Eastern situation	the Mariana Trench
the Southwest	the Riviera

9. Popular names of localities are capitalized.

| the Big Apple | the Loop | Hell's Kitchen |
| the Village | the Twin Cities | the Valley |

10. Compass points are capitalized when they refer to a geographical region or when they are part of a street name. They are lowercased when they refer to a simple direction.

back East   West Columbus Avenue
out West   down South
east of the Mississippi   traveling north on I-91

11. Nouns and adjectives that are derived from compass points and that designate or refer to a specific geographical region are usually capitalized.

a Southern accent   a Western crop
Northerners   part of the Eastern establishment

12. Words designating global, national, regional, or local political divisions are capitalized when they are essential elements of specific names. However, they are usually lowercased when they precede a proper name or when they are not part of a specific name.

the British Empire   New York City
Washington State   Ward 1
Hampden County   Ohio's Ninth Congressional District
the fall of the empire   the city of New York
the state of Washington   fires in three wards
the county of Hampden   carried her district

NOTE: In legal documents, these words are often capitalized regardless of position.

the State of   the County of   the City of New York
   Washington   Hampden

13. Generic geographical terms (as *lake, mountain, river, valley*) are capitalized if they are part of a specific proper name.

Crater Lake   Lake Como   Rocky Mountains
the Columbia River Ohio Valley   Long Island
Great Barrier Reef Atlantic Ocean   Niagara Falls
Hudson Bay   Strait of Gibraltar   Bering Strait

14. Generic geographical terms preceding names are usually capitalized.

Lakes Mead and Powell   Mounts Whitney and Shasta

NOTE: When *the* precedes the generic term, the generic term is lowercased.

the river Thames

15. Generic geographical terms that are not used as part of a proper name are not capitalized. These include plural generic geographical terms that follow two or more proper names and generic terms that are used descriptively or alone.

the Himalaya and Andes mountains   the Missouri and Platte rivers
the Atlantic coast of Labrador   the Arizona desert
the river valley   the Caribbean islands

16. The names of streets, monuments, parks, landmarks, well-known buildings, and other public places are capitalized. However, generic terms that are part of these names (as *avenue, bridge,* or *tower*) are lowercased when they occur after multiple names or are used alone (but see paragraph 17 below.)

Golden Gate Bridge	The Capitol	Rock Creek Park
Eddystone Lighthouse	the Dorset Hotel	Fanueil Hall
the San Diego Zoo	Coit Tower	the Mall
the Pyramids	the Statue of Liberty	Peachtree Street
the Dorset and Drake hotels		Fifth and Park avenues
on the bridge		walking through the park

17. Well-known informal or shortened forms of place names are capitalized.

the Avenue for *Fifth Avenue*
the Street for *Wall Street*
the Exchange for the *New York Stock Exchange*

18. **Governmental, judicial, and political bodies** Full names of legislative, deliberative, executive, and administrative bodies are capitalized, as are easily recognizable short forms of these names. However, nonspecific noun and adjective references to them are usually lowercased.

United States Congress	the Federal Reserve Board
the Congress	the House
the Federal Bureau of Investigation	the Fed
congressional hearings	a federal agency

NOTE: Practice varies regarding the capitalization of words such as *department, committee,* or *agency* when they are being used in place of the full name of a specific body. They are most often capitalized when the department or agency is referring to itself in print. In most other cases, these words are lowercased.

The Connecticut Department of Transportation is pleased to offer this new booklet on traffic safety. The Department hopes that it will be of use to all drivers.

We received a new booklet from the Connecticut Department of Transportation. This is the second pamphlet the department has issued this month.

19. The U.S. Supreme Court and the short forms *Supreme Court* and *Court* referring to it are capitalized.

The Supreme Court of the United States
the United States Supreme Court
the Supreme Court
the Court

20. Official and full names of higher courts and names of international courts are capitalized. Short forms of official higher court names are often capitalized in legal documents but lowercased in general writing.

The International Court of Arbitration
the United States Court of Appeals for the Second Circuit
the Virginia Supreme Court
the Court of Queen's Bench
a ruling by the court of appeals
the state supreme court

21. Names of city and county courts are usually lowercased.

the Lawton municipal court	police court
the Owensville night court	the county court
small claims court	juvenile court

22. The single designation *court,* when specifically applicable to a judge or a presiding officer, is capitalized.

It is the opinion of this Court that . . .
The Court found that . . .

23. The terms *federal* and *national* are capitalized only when they are essential elements of a name or title.

Federal Trade Commission	National Security Council
federal court	national security

24. The word *administration* is capitalized by some writers when it refers to the administration of a specific United States president. However, the word is more commonly lowercased in this situation. If the word does not refer to a specific presidential administration, it is not capitalized except when it is a part of an official name of a government agency.

the Truman administration   *or*   the Truman Administration
the administration   *or*   the Administration
the Farmers Home Loan Administration
The running of the White House varies considerably from one administration to another.

25. Names of political organizations and their adherents are capitalized, but the word *party* may or may not be capitalized, depending on the writer's preference.

the Democratic National Committee the Republican platform
Tories   Nazis
the Democratic party   *or*   the Democratic Party
the Communist party   *or*   the Communist Party

26. Names of political groups other than parties are usually lowercased, as are their derivative forms.

rightist	right wing	left winger
but usually	the Left	the Right

27. Terms describing political and economic philosophies and their derivative forms are usually capitalized only if they are derived from proper names.

authoritarianism	nationalism	isolationist
democracy	supply-side economics	civil libertarian
fascism *or* Fascism	social Darwinism	Marxist

28. **Historical periods and events** The names of conferences, councils, expositions, and specific sporting, historical, and cultural events are capitalized.

the Yalta Conference	the Games of the XXIII Olympiad
the Minnesota State Fair	the Series
the World Series	the San Francisco Earthquake
the Boston Tea Party	the Philadelphia Folk Festival
the Golden Gate International Exposition	

29. The names of some historical and cultural periods and movements are capitalized. When in doubt, consult a dictionary or encyclopedia.

Augustan Age	Renaissance	Stone Age
Prohibition	the Enlightenment	the Great Depression
fin de siècle	space age	cold war *or* Cold War

30. Numerical designations of historical time periods are capitalized only when they are part of a proper name; otherwise they are lowercased.

the Third Reich	Roaring Twenties
seventeenth century	eighties

31. Full names of treaties, laws, and acts are capitalized.

Treaty of Versailles	The Controlled Substances Act of 1970

32. The full names of wars are capitalized. However, words such as *war, revolution, battle,* and *campaign* are capitalized only when they are part of a proper name. Descriptive terms such as *assault, seige,* and *engagement* are usually lowercased even when used in conjunction with the name of the place where the action occurred.

the French and Indian War	the Spanish-American War
the American Revolution	the War of the Spanish Succession
the Revolution of 1688	the Whiskey Rebellion
the Battle of the Bulge	the Battle of the Coral Sea
the Peninsular Campaign	the naval battle of Guadalcanal
the second battle of Manassas	the American and French revolutions
the Meuse-Argonne offensive	
the assault on Iwo Jima	the seige of Yorktown
was in action throughout most of the war	the winter campaign

33. **Hyphenated compounds** Elements of hyphenated compounds are capitalized if they are proper nouns or adjectives.

Arab-Israeli negotiations
East-West trade agreements
an eighteenth-century poet

Tay-Sachs disease
U.S.-U.S.S.R. détente
American-plan rates

NOTE: If the second element in a two-word compound is not a proper noun or adjective, it is lowercased.

French-speaking peoples
an A-frame house
Thirty-second Street

34. Word elements (as prefixes and combining forms) may or may not be capitalized when joined to a proper noun or adjective. Common prefixes (as *pre-* or *anti-*) are usually not capitalized when so attached. Geographical and ethnic combining forms (as *Anglo-* or *Afro-*) are capitalized; *pan-* is usually capitalized when attached to a proper noun or adjective.

the pro-Soviet faction
un-American activities
Sino-Soviet relations
Pan-Slavic nationalism

post-Civil War politics
Afro-Americans
Greco-Roman architecture
the Pan-African Congress

35. **Legal material** The names of both plaintiff and defendant in legal case titles are italicized (or underlined in typewritten material). The *v.* for *versus* may be roman or italic. Cases that do not involve two opposing parties have titles such as *In re Watson* or *In the matter of John Watson;* these case titles are also italicized. When the person involved rather than the case itself is being discussed, the reference is not italicized.

Jones v. *Massachusetts*
In re Jones
Smith et al. v. *Jones*
She covered the Jones trial for the newspaper.

NOTE: In running text a case name involving two opposing parties may be shortened.

The judge based his ruling on a precedent set in the *Jones* decision.

36. **Medical terms** Proper names that are elements in terms designating diseases, symptoms, syndromes, and tests are capitalized. Common nouns are lowercased.

Duchenne-Erb paralysis
German measles
acquired immunodeficiency
   syndrome
measles

Parkinson's disease
Rorschach test
mumps
herpes simplex

37. Taxonomic names of disease-causing organisms follow the rules established for binomial nonmenclature discussed in paragraph 67 below.

The names of diseases or pathological conditions derived from taxonomic names of organisms are lowercased and not italicized.

a neurotoxin produced by *Clostridium botulinum*
nearly died of botulism

38. Generic names of drugs are lowercased; trade names should be capitalized.

a prescription for chlorpromazine
had been taking Thorazine

39. **Military terms** The full titles of branches of the armed forces are capitalized, as are easily recognized short forms of full branch designations.

U.S. Air Force	the Air Force	U.S. Navy
the Navy	U.S. Army	the Army
U.S. Coast Guard	the Coast Guard	U.S. Marine Corps
the Marine Corps	the Marines	the Corps

40. The terms *air force, army, coast guard, marine(s)*, and *navy* are lowercased unless they form a part of an official name or refer back to a specific branch of the armed forces previously named. They are also lowercased when they are used collectively or in the plural.

the combined air forces of the NATO nations
the navies of the world
the American army

In some countries the duty of the coast guard may include icebreaking in inland waterways.

41. The adjectives *naval* and *marine* are lowercased unless they are part of a proper name.

naval battle   marine barracks   Naval Reserves

42. The full titles of units and organizations of the armed forces are capitalized. Elements of full titles are lowercased when they stand alone.

U.S. Army Corps of Engineers	the corps
the Reserves	a reserve commission
First Battalion	the battalion
4th Marine Regiment	the regiment
Eighth Fleet	the fleet
Cruiser Division	the division
Fifth Army	the army

43. Military ranks are capitalized when they precede the names of their holders, and when they take the place of a person's name (as in direct address). Otherwise they are lowercased.

General Creighton W. Abrams
I can't get this rifle any cleaner, Sergeant.
The major arrived precisely on time.

44. The specific names of decorations, citations, and medals are capitalized.

Medal of Honor	Purple Heart	Silver Star
Navy Cross	Distinguished Service Medal	

45. Numerical designations A noun introducing a reference number is usually capitalized.

Order 704	Flight 409	Form 2E	Policy 118-4-Y

46. Nouns used with numbers or letters to designate major reference headings (as in a literary work) are capitalized. However, nouns designating minor reference headings are typically lowercased.

Book II	Table 3	paragraph 6.1
Volume V	page 101	item 16
Division 4	line 8	question 21

47. Organizations Names of firms, corporations, schools, and organizations and terms derived from those names to designate their members are capitalized. However, common nouns used descriptively or occurring after the names of two or more organizations are lowercased.

Merriam-Webster Inc.	Rotary International
University of Michigan	Kiwanians
Washington Huskies	American and United airlines
played as a Pirate last year	Minnesota North Stars

NOTE: The word *the* at the beginning of such names is capitalized only when the full legal name is used.

48. Words such as *agency, department, division, group,* or *office* that designate corporate and organizational units are capitalized only when they are used with a specific name.

while working for the Criminal Division in the Department of Justice
a notice to all department heads

NOTE: Style varies regarding the capitalization of these words when they are used in place of the full name of a specific body. For more on this aspect of styling, see the note following paragraph 18 above.

49. Nicknames, epithets, or other alternate terms for organizations are capitalized.

referred to IBM as Big Blue
the Big Three automakers
trading stocks on the Big Board

50. People The names and initials of persons are capitalized. If a name is hyphenated, both elements are capitalized. Particles forming the initial elements of surnames (as *de, della, der, du, la, ten, ter, van,* and *von*) may or may not be capitalized, depending on the styling of the indi-

vidual name. However, if a name with a lowercase initial particle begins a sentence, the particle is capitalized.

Thomas De Quincey	E. I. du Pont de Nemours
Sir Arthur Thomas Quiller-Couch	Gerald ter Hoerst
James Van Allen	Heinrich Wilhelm von Kleist
the paintings of de Kooning	De Kooning's paintings are . . .

51. The name of a person or thing can be added to or replaced entirely
by a nickname or epithet, a characterizing word or phrase. Nicknames
and epithets are capitalized.

Calamity Jane	the Golden Bear	Doctor J.
Bubba Smith	Wilt the Stilt	Attila the Hun
Goose Gossage	Murph the Surf	Meadowlark Lemon
Big Mama Thornton	Dusty Rhodes	Lefty Grove

52. Nicknames and epithets are frequently used in conjunction with both
the first and last name of a person. If it is placed between the first and
last name, it will often be enclosed in quotation marks or parentheses.
However, if the nickname is in general use, the quotation marks or
parentheses are often omitted. If the nickname precedes the first
name, it is sometimes enclosed in quotation marks, but more often it
is not.

Earl ("Fatha") Hines	Joanne "Big Mama" Carner
Mary Harris ("Mother") Jones	Dennis (Oil Can) Boyd
Kissin' Jim Folsom	Mother Maybelle Carter

53. Words of family relationship preceding or used in place of a person's
name are capitalized. However, these words are lowercased if they are
part of a noun phrase that is being used in place of a name.

Cousin Mercy	Grandfather Barnes

I know when Mother's birthday is.

I know when my mother's birthday is.

54. Words designating languages, nationalities, peoples, races, religious
groups, and tribes are capitalized. Descriptive terms used to refer to
groups of people are variously capitalized or lowercased. Designations
based on color are usually lowercased.

Latin	Canadians	Ibo	Afro-American
Caucasians	Muslims	Christians	Navajo

Bushman (for a nomadic hunter of southern Africa)

bushman (for an inhabitant of the Australian bush)

the red man in America   black, brown, and white people

55. Corporate, professional, and governmental titles are capitalized when
they immediately precede a person's name, unless the name is being
used as an appositive.

President Roosevelt	Queen Elizabeth	Senator Henry Jackson
Doctor Malatesta	Professor Greenbaum	Pastor Linda Jones

They wanted to meet the new pastor, Linda Jones.

Almost everyone has heard of Chrysler's president, Lee Iacocca.

56. When corporate or governmental titles are used as part of a descriptive phrase to identify a person rather than as a person's official title, the title is lowercased.

Senator Ted Stevens of Alaska   *but*   Ted Stevens, senator from Alaska
Lee Iacocca, president of Chrysler Corporation

NOTE: Style varies when governmental titles are used in descriptive phrases that precede a name.

Alaska senator Ted Stevens   *or*   Alaska Senator Ted Stevens

57. Specific governmental titles may be capitalized when they are used in place of particular individuals' names. In minutes and official records of proceedings, corporate titles are capitalized when they are used in place of individuals' names.

The Secretary of State gave a news conference.
The Judge will respond to questions in her chambers.
The Treasurer then stated his misgivings about the project.

58. Some writers always capitalize the word *president* when it refers to the United States presidency. However, the more common practice is to capitalize the word *president* only when it refers to a specific individual.

It is one of the duties of the President to submit a budget to Congress.
It is one of the duties of the president to submit a budget to Congress.

59. Titles are capitalized when they are used in direct address.

Tell me the truth, Doctor.
Where are we headed, Captain?

60. **Pronouns** The pronoun *I* is capitalized. For pronouns referring to the Deity, see rule 62 below.

He and I will attend the meeting.

61. **Religious terms** Words designating the Deity are capitalized.

Allah   God Almighty   the Creator
Jehovah   Yahweh   the Holy Spirit

62. Personal pronouns referring to the Deity are usually capitalized. Relative pronouns (as *who, whom,* and *whose*) usually are not.

God in His mercy
when God asks us to do His bidding
believing that it was God who created the universe

63. Traditional designations of apostles, prophets, and saints are capitalized.

Our Lady   the Prophet   the Lawgiver

64. Names of religions, denominations, creeds and confessions, and religious orders are capitalized, as are adjectives derived from these names. The word *church* is capitalized only when it is used as part of the name of a specific body or edifice or, in some publications, when it refers to organized Christianity in general.

Judaism   Catholicism
the Church of Christ   the Southern Baptist Convention
Apostles' Creed   the Society of Jesus
the Poor Clares   Franciscans
Hunt Memorial Church   a Buddhist monastery
Islamic   the Baptist church on the corner
the Thirty-nine Articles of the Church of England

65. Names of the Bible or its books, parts, versions, or editions of it and other sacred books are capitalized but not italicized. Adjectives derived from the names of sacred books are variously capitalized and lowercased. When in doubt, consult a dictionary.

Authorized Version   Old Testament   Apocrypha
Talmud   Genesis   Pentateuch
Gospel of Saint Mark   Koran   biblical
talmudic   Koranic   Vedic

66. The names of prayers and well-known passages of the Bible are capitalized.

Ave Maria   the Sermon on the Mount
Ten Commandments   the Beatitudes
the Lord's Prayer   the Our Father

67. **Scientific terms** Genus names in biological binomial nomenclature are capitalized; species names are lowercased, even when derived from a proper name. Both genus and species names are italicized (or underlined in typewritten material).

Both the wolf and the domestic dog are included in the genus *Canis*.

The California condor (*Gymnogyps californianus*) is facing extinction.

NOTE: When used, the names of races, varieties, or subspecies are lowercased. Like genus and species names, they are italicized.

Hyla versicolor chrysoscelis
Otis asio naevius

68. The New Latin names of classes, families, and all groups above the genus level in zoology and botany are capitalized but not italicized. Their derivative adjectives and nouns in English are neither capitalized nor italicized.

Gastropoda   gastropod
Thallophyta   thallophyte

69. The names, both scientific and informal, of planets and their satellites, asteroids, stars, constellations, groups of stars, and other specific celestial objects are capitalized. However, the words *sun, earth,* and *moon* are usually lowercased unless they occur with other astronomical names. Generic terms that are the final element in the name of a celestial object are usually lowercased.

the Milky Way	Sirius	Ursa Major
Pleiades	Big Dipper	Barnard's star
probes heading for the Moon and Mars		

70. Names of meteorological phenomena are lowercased.

aurora borealis	northern lights	parhelic circle

71. Terms that identify geological eras, periods, epochs, and strata are capitalized. The generic terms that follow them are lowercased. The words *upper, middle,* and *lower* are capitalized when they are used to designate an epoch or series within a period; in most other cases, they are lowercased. The word *age* is capitalized in names such as *Age of Reptiles* or *Age of Fishes.*

Mesozoic era	Quaternary period	Oligocene epoch
Upper Cretaceous	Middle Ordovician	Lower Silurian

72. Proper names forming essential elements of scientific laws, theorems, and principles are capitalized. However, the common nouns *law, theorem, theory,* and the like are lowercased.

Boyle's law	Planck's constant
the Pythagorean theorem	Einstein's theory of relativity

NOTE: In terms referring to popular or fanciful theories or observations, descriptive words are usually capitalized as well.

Murphy's Law	the Peter Principle

73. The names of chemical elements and compounds are lowercased.

hydrogen fluoride
ferric ammonium citrate

74. The names of computer services and data bases are usually trademarks and should always be capitalized. The names of computer languages are irregularly styled either with an initial capital letter or with all letters capitalized. The names of some computer languages are commonly written either way. When in doubt, consult a dictionary.

CompuServe	TeleTransfer	PL/1
Atek	PASCAL *or* Pascal	APL
BASIC	COBOL *or* Cobol	FORTRAN *or* Fortran

75. Time periods and zones The names of the days of the week, months of the year, and holidays and holy days are capitalized.

Easter	Independence Day	June
Tuesday	Yom Kippur	Thanksgiving

76. The names of time zones are capitalized when abbreviated but usually lowercased when written out except for words that are themselves proper names.

CST	central standard time
mountain time	Pacific standard time

77. Names of the seasons are lowercased if they simply declare the time of year; however, they are capitalized if they are personified.

> My new book is scheduled to appear this spring.
>
> the sweet breath of Spring

78. Titles Words in titles of books, long poems, magazines, newspapers, plays, movies, novellas that are separately published, and works of art such as paintings and sculpture are capitalized except for internal articles, conjunctions, prepositions, and the *to* of infinitives. The entire title is italicized (or underlined in typewritten material). For the styling of the Bible and other sacred works, see paragraph 65 above.

The Lives of a Cell	*Of Mice and Men*
Saturday Review	*Christian Science Monitor*
Shakespeare's *Othello*	*The Old Man and the Sea*
Gainsborough's *Blue Boy*	the movie *Wait until Dark*

NOTE: Some writers also capitalize prepositions of five or more letters (as *about* or *toward*).

79. An initial article that is part of a title is often omitted if it would be awkward in context. However, when it is included it is capitalized and italicized or underlined. A common exception to this practice regards books that are referred to by an abbreviation. In this case, the initial article is neither capitalized nor italicized.

> *The Oxford English Dictionary*
> the 13-volume *Oxford English Dictionary*
> the *OED*

80. Practice varies widely regarding the capitalization and italicization or underlining of initial articles and city names in the titles of newspapers. One rule that can be followed is to capitalize and italicize any word that is part of the official title of the paper as shown on its masthead. However, this information is not always available, and even if it is available it can lead to apparent inconsistencies in styling. Because of this, many writers choose one way of styling newspaper titles regardless of their official titles. The most common practice is to italicize the city name but not to capitalize or italicize the initial article.

the *New York Times*	the *Wall Street Journal*
the *Des Moines Register*	the *Washington Post*

81. Some writers choose not to use italics or underlining for titles. They either simply capitalize the words or capitalize them and enclose them in quotation marks.

> the Heard on the Street column in the Wall Street Journal
> our review of "The Lives of a Cell" in last week's issue

82. The first word following a colon in a title is capitalized.

> John Crowe Ransom: An Annotated Bibliography

83. The titles of short poems, short stories, essays, lectures, dissertations, chapters of books, articles in periodicals, radio and television programs, and novellas that are published in a collection are capitalized and enclosed in quotation marks. The capitalization of articles, conjunctions, and prepositions is the same as it is for italicized titles, as explained in paragraph 78 above.

> Robert Frost's "Dust of Snow"
> Katherine Anne Porter's "That Tree"
> John Barth's "The Literature of Exhaustion"
> The talk, "Labor's Power: A View for the Nineties," will be given next week.
> the third chapter of *Treasure Island*, entitled "The Black Spot"
> Her article, "Computer Art on a Micro," was in last month's *Popular Computing*.
> listening to "All Things Considered"
> watching "The Tonight Show"
> D. H. Lawrence's "The Woman Who Rode Away"

84. Common titles of book sections (as a preface, introduction, or index) are capitalized but not enclosed in quotation marks when they refer to a section of the same book in which the reference is made. If they refer to another book, they are usually lowercased.

> See the Appendix for further information.
> In the introduction to her book, the author explains her goals.

85. Practice varies regarding the capitalization of the word *chapter* when it is used with a cardinal number to identify a specific chapter in a book. Most writers capitalize the word, but some do not.

> See Chapter 3 for more details.
> is discussed further in Chapter Four
> *but* in the third chapter

86. The titles of long musical compositions such as operas and symphonies are capitalized and italicized (or underlined in typewritten material); the titles of short compositions are capitalized and enclosed in quotation marks. The titles of musical compositions identified by the nature of the musical form in which they were written are capitalized only.

Verdi's *Don Carlos*   "America the Beautiful"
Ravel's "Bolero"   Serenade No. 12 in C Minor

87. Trademarks Registered trademarks, service marks, collective marks, and brand names are capitalized.

Band-Aid   Jacuzzi   Kleenex
College Board   Velcro   Realtor
Kellogg's All-Bran Diet Pepsi   Lay's potato chips

88. Transportation The names of individual ships, submarines, airplanes, satellites, and space vehicles are capitalized and italicized (or underlined in typewritten material). The designations *U.S.S., S.S., M.V.,* and *H.M.S.* are not italicized.

Apollo 11   *Enola Gay*
Mariner 5   *Explorer 10*
Spirit of St. Louis   M.V. *West Star*

Other Uses of Capitals

1. Full capitalization of a word is sometimes used for emphasis or to indicate that a speaker is talking very loudly. Both of these uses of capitals are best used very sparingly or avoided altogether in formal writing. Italicization (or underlining) of words for emphasis is more common. For examples of this use of italics, see paragraph 8 under Other Uses of Italics, page 106.

   Results are not the only criteria for judging performance. HOW we achieve results is important also.

   All applications must be submitted IN WRITING before January 31.

   The waiter rushed by yelling "HOT PLATE! HOT PLATE!"

2. A word is sometimes capitalized to indicate that it is being used as a philosophical concept or to indicate that it stands for an important concept in a discussion.

   Many people seek Truth, but few find it.

   the three M's of advertising, Message, Media, and Management

3. Full capitals or a mixture of capitals and lowercase letters or sometimes even small capitals are used to reproduce the text of signs, labels, or inscriptions.

   a poster reading SPECIAL THRILLS COMING SOON

   a Do Not Disturb sign

   a barn with CHEW MAIL POUCH on the side

4. A letter used to indicate a shape is usually capitalized.

   an A-frame house   a J-bar   V-shaped

Other Uses of Italics

For each of the uses listed below, italic type is used in typeset material (or where it is otherwise available); in typewritten material, underlining is used.

1. Foreign words and phrases that have not been fully adopted into the English language are italicized. The decision whether or not to italicize a word will vary according to the context of the writing and the audience for which the writing is intended. In general, however, any word that appears in the main A–Z vocabulary section of *Webster's Ninth New Collegiate Dictionary* does not need to be italicized.

   > These accomplishments will serve as a monument, *aere perennius,* to the group's skill and dedication.
   >
   > They looked upon this area as a *cordon sanitaire* around the city.
   >
   > After the concert, the crowd headed en masse for the parking lot.
   >
   > The committee meets on an ad hoc basis.

   NOTE: A complete sentence (such as a motto) can also be italicized. However, passages that comprise more than one sentence, or even a single sentence if it is particularly long, are usually treated as quotations; i.e., they are set in roman type and enclosed in quotation marks.

2. Unfamiliar words or words that have a specialized meaning are set in italics, especially when they are accompanied by a short definition. Once these words have been introduced and defined, they do not need to be italicized in subsequent references.

   > *Vitiligo* is a condition in which skin pigment cells stop making pigment.
   >
   > Another method is the *direct-to-consumer* transaction in which the publisher markets directly to the individual by mail or door-to-door.

3. Latin abbreviations are usually not italicized, although the traditional styling has been to italicize them, and some writers still do so.

   > et al.   cf.   e.g.   i.e.   viz.

4. Italic type is used to indicate words referred to as words, letters referred to as letters, or numerals referred to as numerals. However, if the word referred to as a word was actually spoken, it is often enclosed in quotation marks. If the letter is being used to refer to its sound and not its printed form, virgules or brackets can be used instead of italics. And if there is no chance of confusion, numerals referred to as numerals are often not italicized. (For an explanation of the ways in which to form the plurals of words, letters, and numerals referred to as such, see paragraphs 17–19 and 24 under Plurals, pages 110–111.)

   > The panel could not decide whether *data* was a singular or plural noun.
   >
   > *Only* can be an adverb, as in the case of "I *only* tried to help."
   >
   > We heard his warning, but we weren't sure what "other repercussions" meant in that context.

You should dot your *i*'s and cross your *t*'s.
She couldn't pronounce her *s*'s.
He was still having trouble with the /p/ sound.
The first *2* and the last *1* are barely legible.

5. A letter used to indicate a shape is usually capitalized but not set in italics. For more on this use of capital letters, see paragraph 4 under Other Uses of Capitals, page 104.

6. Individual letters are sometimes set in italic type to provide additional typographical contrast. This use of italics is common when letters are used in run-in enumerations or when they are used to identify elements in an illustration.

   providing information about *(a)* typing, *(b)* transcribing, *(c)* formatting, and *(d)* graphics
   located at point *A* on the diagram

7. Italics are used to indicate a word created to suggest a sound.

   We sat listening to the *chat-chat-chat* of the sonar.

8. Italics are used to emphasize or draw attention to a word or words in a sentence.

   Students must notify the dean's office *in writing* of all courses added or dropped from their original list.
   She had become *the* hero, the one everyone else looked up to.

NOTE: Italics serve to draw attention to words in large part because they are used so infrequently. Writers who overuse italics for giving emphasis may find that the italics lose their effectiveness.

Plurals and Possessives

This section describes the ways in which plurals and possessives are most commonly formed. For some of the questions treated here, various solutions have been developed over the years, but no single solution has come to be universally accepted. In these cases, the range of available solutions is described, and writers must use their own personal judgments to choose among them.

   In regard to plurals, consulting a good dictionary will solve many of the problems that are discussed in this chapter. In this regard, the best dictionary to consult is an unabridged dictionary, such as *Webster's Third New International Dictionary.* If such a comprehensive reference book is unavailable the next best thing is a good desk dictionary, such as *Webster's Ninth New Collegiate Dictionary.* Any dictionary that is much smaller than the *Ninth Collegiate* will often be more frustrating in what it fails to show than helpful in what it shows.

In giving examples of plurals and possessives this section uses both *or* and *also* to separate variant forms of the same word. The word *or* is used when both forms of the word are used with approximately equal frequency in standard writing; the form that precedes the *or* is probably slightly more common than the form that follows it. The word *also* is used when one form of the word is much more common than the other; the more common precedes the less common.

Plurals

The plurals of most English words are formed by adding *-s* to the singular. If the noun ends in *-s, -x, -z, -ch* or *-sh*, so that an extra syllable must be added in order to pronounce the plural, *-es* is added to the singular. If the noun ends in a *-y* preceded by a consonant, the *-y* is changed to *-i-* and *-es* is added.

However, many English nouns do not follow this general pattern for forming plurals. Most good dictionaries give thorough coverage to irregular and variant plurals, so they are often the best place to start to answer questions about the plural form of a specific word. The paragraphs that follow describe the ways in which plurals are formed for a number of categories of words whose plural forms are most apt to raise questions.

The symbol → is used throughout this part of this section. In each case, the element that follows the arrow is the plural form of the element that precedes the arrow.

1. **Abbreviations** The plurals of abbreviations are commonly formed by adding *-s* or an apostrophe plus *-s* to the abbreviation; however, there are some significant exceptions to this pattern. For more on the formation of plurals of abbreviations, see paragraphs 1–5 under Plurals, Possessives, and Compounds, page 128.

COLA → COLA's	CPU → CPUs	bldg. → bldgs.
f.o.b. → f.o.b.'s	Ph.D. → Ph.D.'s	p. → pp.

2. **Animals** The names of many fishes, birds, and mammals have both a plural formed with a suffix and one that is identical with the singular. Some have only the *-s* plural; others have only an uninflected plural.

flounder → flounder *or* flounders		mink → mink *or* minks
quail → quail *or* quails		caribou → caribou *or* caribous
cow → cows	hen → hens	rat → rats monkey → monkeys
bison → bison	sheep → sheep	shad → shad moose → moose

3. Many of the animals that have both plural forms are ones that are hunted, fished, or trapped, and those who hunt, fish for, and trap them are most likely to use the uninflected form. The *-s* form is especially likely to be used to emphasize diversity of kinds.

   caught four trout
   but
   trouts of the Rocky Mountains

   a place where fish gather
   but
   the fishes of the Pacific Ocean

4. **Compounds and phrases** Most compounds made up of two nouns, whether they appear as one word, two words, or a hyphenated word, are pluralized by pluralizing the final element.

matchbox → matchboxes   spokeswoman → spokeswomen
judge advocate → judge advocates   tree house → tree houses
city-state → city-states   crow's-foot → crow's-feet

5. The plural form of a compound consisting of an *-er* agent noun and an adverb is made by pluralizing the noun element.

hanger-on → hangers-on   looker-on → lookers-on
onlooker → onlookers   passerby → passersby

6. Nouns made up of words that are not nouns form their plurals on the last element.

also-ran → also-rans   ne'er-do-well → ne'er-do-wells
put-down → put-downs   set-to → set-tos
changeover → changeovers   blowup → blowups

7. Plurals of compounds that are phrases consisting of two nouns separated by a preposition are regularly formed by pluralizing the first noun.

aide-de-camp → aides-de-camp   man-of-war → men-of-war
attorney-at-law → attorneys-at-law lady-in-waiting → ladies-in-waiting
base on balls → bases on balls   coup d'état → coups d'état
power of attorney → powers of attorney

8. Compounds that are phrases consisting of two nouns separated by a preposition and a modifier form their plurals in various ways.

flash in the pan → flashes in the pan
jack-in-the-box → jack-in-the-boxes *or* jacks-in-the-box
jack-of-all-trades → jacks-of-all-trades
son of a gun → sons of guns
stick-in-the-mud → stick-in-the-muds

9. Compounds consisting of a noun followed by an adjective are regularly pluralized by adding a suffix to the noun.

cousin-german → cousins-german
heir apparent → heirs apparent
knight-errant → knights-errant

NOTE: If the adjective in such a compound tends to be construed as a noun, the compound may have more than one plural form.

attorney general → attorneys general   *or*   attorney generals
sergeant major → sergeants major   *or*   sergeant majors
poet laureate → poets laureate   *or*   poet laureates

10. **Foreign words and phrases** Many nouns of foreign origin retain the foreign plural. However, most of them also have a regular English plural.

    alumnus → alumni
    beau → beaux *or* beaus
    crisis → crises
    emporium → emporiums *or* emporia
    index → indexes *or* indices
    larynx → larynges *or* larynxes
    phenomenon → phenomena *or* phenomenons
    schema → schemata *also* schemas
    seraph → seraphim *or* seraphs
    series → series
    tempo → tempi *or* tempos

NOTE: A foreign plural may not be used for all senses of a word or may be more commonly used for some senses than for others.

    antenna (on an insect) → antennae
    antenna (on a radio) → antennas

11. Phrases of foreign origin may have a foreign plural, an English plural, or both.

    beau monde → beau mondes *or* beaux mondes
    carte blanche → cartes blanches
    hors d'oeuvre → hors d'oeuvres

12. **-ful words** A plural *-fuls* can be used for any noun ending in *-ful,* but some of these nouns also have an alternative, usually less common plural with *-s-* preceding the suffix.

    eyeful → eyefuls
    bucketful → bucketfuls *or* bucketsful
    cupful → cupfuls *also* cupsful
    tablespoonful → tablespoonfuls *also* tablespoonsful

13. **Irregular plurals** A small group of English nouns form their plurals by changing one or more of their vowels.

    foot → feet   man → men   woman → women
    goose → geese   mouse → mice   tooth → teeth
    louse → lice

14. A few nouns have *-en* or *-ren* plurals.

    ox → oxen
    child → children
    brother → brethren

15. Some nouns ending in *-f, -fe,* or *-ff* have plurals that end in *-ves.* Some of these also have regularly formed plurals.

elf → elves
knife → knives
life → lives

beef → beefs *or* beeves
staff → staffs *or* staves
wharf → wharves *also* wharfs

16. **Italic elements** Italicized words, phrases, abbreviations, and letters set within a roman context are variously pluralized with either an italic or roman *s*. A roman *s* is the form most commonly used. If the plural is formed with an apostrophe and an *-s*, the *-s* is almost always roman.

> fifteen *Newsweeks* on the shelf
> answered with a series of *uh-huhs*
> a row of *x*'s

17. **Letters** The plurals of letters are usually formed by the addition of an apostrophe and an *-s*, although uppercase letters are sometimes pluralized by the addition of an *-s* alone.

> p's and q's
> V's of geese flying overhead
> dot your *i*'s
> straight As

18. **Numbers** Numerals are pluralized by adding an *-s*, or, less commonly, an apostrophe and an *-s*.

> two par 5s
> 1970s
> in the 80s

> 1960's
> the mid-$20,000s
> DC-10's

19. Spelled-out numbers are usually pluralized without an apostrophe.

> in twos and threes
> scored two sixes

20. **-o words** Most words ending in an *-o* are pluralized by adding an *-s*. However, some words ending in an *-o* preceded by a consonant have *-s* plurals, some have *-es* plurals, and some have both. When in doubt, consult a dictionary.

> alto → altos
> echo → echoes
> motto → mottoes *also* mottos

21. **Proper nouns** The plurals of proper nouns are usually formed with *-s* or *-es*.

> Bruce → Bruces
> Charles → Charleses
> Hastings → Hastingses
> Velasquez → Velasquezes

22. Proper nouns ending in *-y* usually retain the *-y* and add *-s*.

> February → Februarys
> Mary → Marys

Mercury → Mercurys
> *but*
Ptolemy → Ptolemies
Sicily → The Two Sicilies
The Rockies

NOTE: Words that were originally proper nouns and that end in -*y* are usually pluralized by changing -*y*- to -*i*- and adding -*es*, but a few retain the -*y*.

bobby → bobbies   johnny → johnnies
Jerry → Jerries   Tommy → Tommies
Bloody Mary → Bloody Marys

23. **Quoted elements** Practice varies regarding the plural form of words in quotation marks. Some writers form the plural by adding an -*s* or an apostrophe plus -*s* within the quotation marks. Others add an -*s* outside the quotation marks. Both arrangements look awkward, and writers generally try to avoid this construction.

too many "probably's" in the statement
One "you" among millions of "you"s
a response characterized by its "yes, but"s

24. **Symbols** Although symbols are not usually pluralized, when a symbol is being referred to as a character in itself without regard to meaning, the plural is formed by adding an -*s* or an apostrophe plus -*s*.

used &'s instead of *and*'s
his π's are hard to read
printed three *s

25. **Words used as words** Words used as words without regard to meaning usually form their plurals by adding an apostrophe and a roman -*s*.

five *and*'s in one sentence
all those *wherefore*'s and *howsoever*'s

NOTE: When a word used as a word has become part of a fixed phrase, the plural is usually formed by adding a roman -*s* without the apostrophe.

oohs and aahs
dos and don'ts

Possessives

The possessive case of most nouns is formed by adding an apostrophe or an apostrophe plus -*s* to the end of the word.

1. **Common nouns** The possessive case of singular and plural common nouns that do not end in an *s* or *z* sound is formed by adding an apostrophe plus -*s* to the end of the word.

the boy's mother   at her wit's end   the potato's skin
men's clothing   children's books   the symposia's themes

2. The possessive case of singular nouns ending in an *s* or *z* sound is usually formed by adding an apostrophe plus -*s* to the end of the word. An alternate approach, although one less widely accepted, is to add an apostrophe plus -*s* to the word only when the added -*s* is pronounced. If it isn't pronounced, only an apostrophe is added.

the press's books   the index's arrangement
the boss's desk   the horse's saddle

the audience's reaction   *also*   the audience' reaction
the waitress's duties   *also*   the waitress' duties
the conference's outcome *also*   the conference' outcome

NOTE: Even those who follow the pattern of adding an apostrophe plus -*s* to all singular nouns will often make an exception for a multi-syllabic word that ends in an *s* or *z* sound if it is followed by a word beginning with an *s* or *z* sound.

for convenience' sake   for conscience' sake
the illness' symptoms   *or*   the illness's symptoms
to the princess' surprise *or* to the princess's surprise

3. The possessive case of plural nouns ending in an *s* or *z* sound is formed by adding only an apostrophe to the end of the word. One exception to this rule is that the possessive case of one-syllable irregular plurals is usually formed by adding an apostrophe plus -*s*.

horses' stalls   consumers' confidence
geese's calls   mice's habits

4. **Proper names** The possessive forms of proper names are generally made in the same way as they are for common nouns. The possessive form of singular proper names not ending in an *s* or *z* sound is made by adding an apostrophe plus -*s* to the name. The possessive form of plural proper names is made by adding just an apostrophe.

Mrs. Wilson's store   Utah's capital   Canada's rivers
the Wattses' daughter   the Cohens' house   Niagara Falls' location

5. As is the case for the possessive form of singular common nouns (see paragraph 2 above), the possessive form of singular proper names ending in an *s* or *z* sound may be formed either by adding an apostrophe plus -*s* or by adding just an apostrophe to the name. For the sake of consistency, most writers choose one pattern for forming the possessive of all singular names ending in an *s* or *z* sound, regardless of the pronunciation of individual names (for exceptions see paragraphs 6 and 7 below). Adding an apostrophe plus -*s* to all such names is more common than adding just the apostrophe.

Jones's car   *also*   Jones' car
Bliss's statue   *also*   Bliss' statue
Dickens's novels *also*   Dickens' novels

6. The possessive form of classical and biblical names of two or more syllables ending in *-s* or *-es* is usually made by adding an apostrophe without an *-s*. If the name has only one syllable, the possessive form is made by adding an apostrophe and an *-s*.

> Aristophanes' plays Achilles' heel Odysseus' journey
> Judas' betrayal Zeus's anger Mars's help

7. The possessive forms of the names *Jesus* and *Moses* are always formed with just an apostrophe.

> Jesus' time Moses' law

8. The possessive forms of names ending in a silent *-s*, *-z*, or *-x* usually include the apostrophe and the *-s*.

> Arkansas's capital Camus's *The Stranger*
> Delacroix's painting Josquin des Prez's music

9. For the sake of convenience and appearance, some writers will italicize the possessive ending when adding it to a name that is in italics. However, most frequently the possessive ending is in roman.

> the U.S.S. *Constitution*'s cannons the *Mona Lisa*'s somber hues
> *Gone With the Wind*'s ending *High Noon*'s plot

10. **Pronouns** The possessive case of indefinite pronouns such as *anyone, everybody,* and *someone* is formed by adding an apostrophe and an *-s*.

> everyone's anybody's everyone's
> everybody's someone's somebody's

NOTE: Some indefinite pronouns usually require an *of* phrase rather than inflection to indicate possession.

> the rights of each the satisfaction of all
> the inclination of many

11. Possessive pronouns include no apostrophes.

> mine yours his hers
> its ours theirs

12. **Phrases** The possessive form of a phrase is made by adding an apostrophe or an apostrophe plus *-s* to the last word in the phrase.

> board of directors' meeting
> his brother-in-law's sidecar
> from the student of politics' point of view
> a moment or so's thought

NOTE: Constructions such as these can become awkward, and it is often better to rephrase the sentence to eliminate the need for the possessive ending. For instance, the last two examples above could be rephrased as follows:

> from the point of view of the student of politics
> thinking for a moment or so

13. **Words in quotation marks** The possessive form of words in quotation marks can be formed two ways. The apostrophe plus -*s* are placed either inside the quotation marks or outside them. Both arrangements look awkward, and this construction is best avoided.

> the "Today Show"'s cohosts
> the "Grande Dame's" escort
> *but more commonly*
> the cohosts of the "Today Show"
> escort to the "Grande Dame"

14. **Abbreviations** Possessives of abbreviations are formed in the same way as those of nouns that are spelled out. The singular possessive is formed by adding an apostrophe plus -*s* to the abbreviation; the plural possessive, by adding an apostrophe only.

> the AMA's executive committee
> Itek Corp.'s Applied Technology Division
> the Burns Bros.' stores
> the MPs' decisions

15. **Numerals** The possessive form of nouns composed of numerals is made in the same way as for other nouns. The possessive of singular nouns is formed by adding an apostrophe plus -*s;* the possessive form of plural nouns, by adding an apostrophe only.

> 1985's most popular model
> the 1980s' most colorful figure

16. **Individual and joint possession** Individual possession is indicated when an apostrophe plus -*s* is added to each noun in a sequence. Joint possession is most commonly indicated by adding an apostrophe or an apostrophe plus -*s* to the last noun in the sequence. Joint possession may also be indicated by adding a possessive ending to each name.

> Kepler's and Clark's respective clients
> John's, Bill's, and Larry's boats
> Bissell and Hansen's law firm
> Christine and James's vacation home *or* Christine's and James's vacation home

Compounds

A compound is a word or word group that consists of two or more parts that work together as a unit to express a specific concept. Compounds can be formed by combining two or more words (as in *eye shadow, graphic equalizer, farmhouse, cost-effective, blue-pencil, around-the-clock,* or *son of a gun*), by combining word elements (as prefixes or suffixes) with words (as in *ex-president, shoeless, presorted, uninterruptedly,* or *meaningless*), or by combining two or more word elements (as in *supermicro* or *photomicrograph*). Compounds are written in one of three ways: solid (as *cottonmouth*), hyphenated (as *player-manager*), or open (as *field day*).

Some of the explanations that follow make reference to permanent and temporary compounds. Permanent compounds are those that are so commonly used that they have become permanent parts of the language; many of them are entered in dictionaries. Temporary compounds are those created to fit a writer's need at a particular moment. Temporary compounds cannot be found in dictionaries and therefore present particular styling problems.

Self-evident compounds also present styling problems. These are compounds (as *baseball game* or *economic policy*) that are readily understood from the meanings of the words that make them up. Many self-evident compounds, like temporary compounds, are not entered in dictionaries.

In other words, writers faced with having to use compounds cannot rely wholly on dictionaries to guide them in their styling of compounds. They need, in addition, to develop an approach for dealing with compounds that are not in the dictionary.

One approach is simply to leave open any compound that is not in the dictionary. Many writers do this, but there are drawbacks to this approach. A temporary compound may not be as easily recognized as a compound by the reader when it is left open. For instance if you need to use *wide body* as a term for a kind of jet airplane, a phrase like "the operation of wide bodies" may catch the reader unawares. And if you use the open style for a compound modifier, you may create momentary confusion (or even unintended amusement) with a phrase like "the operation of wide body jets."

Another possibility is to hyphenate all compounds that aren't in the dictionary. Hyphenation gives your compound immediate recognition as a compound. But hyphenating all such compounds runs counter to some well-established American practice. Thus you would be calling too much attention to the compound and momentarily distracting the reader.

A third approach is to use analogy to pattern your temporary compound after some other similar compound. This approach is likely to be more complicated than simply picking an open or hyphenated form, and will not free you from the need to make your own decisions in most instances. But it does have the advantage of making your compound less distracting or confusing by making it look as much like other more familiar compounds as possible.

The paragraphs that follow are aimed at helping you to use the analogical approach to styling compounds. You will find compounds listed according to the elements that make them up and the way that they function in a sentence.

This section deals first with compounds formed from whole English words, then compounds formed with word elements, and finally with a small collection of miscellaneous styling conventions relating to compounds. The symbol + in the following paragraphs can be interpreted as "followed immediately by."

Compound Nouns

Compound nouns are combinations of words that function in a sentence as nouns. They may consist of two or more nouns, a noun and a modifier, or two or more elements that are not nouns.

1. **noun + noun** Compounds composed of two nouns that are short, commonly used, and pronounced with falling stress—that is, with the most stress on the first noun and less or no stress on the second—are usually styled solid.

teapot	cottonmouth	birdbath	handmaiden
catfish	sweatband	handsaw	farmyard

2. When a noun + noun compound is short and common but pronounced with equal stress on both nouns, the styling is more likely to be open.

bean sprouts	beach buggy	head louse
fuel oil	duffel bag	dart board

3. Many short noun + noun compounds begin as temporary compounds styled open. As they become more familiar and better established, there is a tendency for them to become solid.

data base	*is becoming*	database
chain saw	*is becoming*	chainsaw
lawn mower	*is becoming*	lawnmower

4. Noun + noun compounds that consist of longer nouns, are self-evident, or are temporary are usually styled open.

wildlife sanctuary	reunion committee
football game	television camera

5. When the nouns in a noun + noun compound describe a double title or double function, the compound is hyphenated.

city-state	dinner-dance	player-manager
decree-law	secretary-treasurer	author-critic

6. Compounds formed from a noun or adjective followed by *man*, *woman*, *person*, or *people* and denoting an occupation are regularly solid.

salesman	saleswoman	salesperson	salespeople
congresswoman	handyman	spokesperson	policewoman

7. Compounds that are units of measurement are hyphenated.

foot-pound	man-hour	light-year
kilowatt-hour	column-inch	board-foot

8. **adjective + noun** Most temporary or self-evident adjective + noun compounds are styled open. Permanent compounds formed from relatively long adjectives or nouns are also open.

automatic weapons	modal auxiliary	modular arithmetic
religious freedom	automatic pilot	graphic equalizer
pancreatic juice	minor seminary	white lightning

9. Adjective + noun compounds consisting of two short words may be styled solid when pronounced with falling stress. Just as often, however, short adjective + noun compounds are styled open; a few are hyphenated.

shortcut	longhand	redline	blueprint
yellowhammer	highland	drywall	wetland
dry run	big deal	high gear	long haul
red tape	yellow jacket	red-eye	red-hot

10. **participle + noun** Most participle + noun compounds are styled open, whether permanent, temporary, or self-evident.

frying pan	furnished apartment	shredded wheat
whipped cream	nagging backache	whipping boy

11. **noun's + noun** Compounds consisting of a possessive noun followed by another noun are usually styled hyphenated or open.

crow's-feet	lion's share	fool's gold
cat's cradle	cat's-eye	cat's-paw
stirred up a hornet's nest		

NOTE: Compounds of this type that have become solid have lost the apostrophe.

foolscap	menswear	sheepshead

12. **noun + verb + -er; noun + verb + -ing** Temporary compounds in which the first noun is the object of the verb to which the suffix has been added are most often styled open. However, a hyphen may be used to make the relationships of the words immediately apparent. Permanent compounds like these are sometimes styled solid as well.

temporary	gene-splicing	opinion maker	cost-cutting
	risk-taking	career planning	English-speakers
permanent	lifesaver	copyediting	flyswatter
	data processing	bird-watcher	fund-raising
	lawn mower	penny-pinching	bookkeeper

13. **object + verb** Noun compounds consisting of a verb preceded by a noun that is its object are variously styled.

clambake	car wash	face-lift	turkey shoot

14. **verb + object** A few compounds are formed from a verb followed by a noun that is its object. These are mostly older words, and they are solid.

tosspot	breakwater	pinchpenny
cutthroat	carryall	pickpocket

15. **noun + adjective** Compounds composed of a noun followed by an adjective are styled open or hyphenated.

battle royal	consul general	secretary-general
governor-designate	heir apparent	letters patent
sum total	mayor-elect	president-elect

16. **particle + noun** Compounds consisting of a particle (usually a preposition or adverb having prepositional, adverbial, or adjectival force in the compound) and a noun are usually styled solid, especially when they are short and pronounced with falling stress.

downpour	inpatient	outpatient	input
output	throughput	aftershock	overskirt
offshoot	undershirt	crossbones	upkeep

17. A few particle + noun compounds, especially when composed of longer elements or having equal stress on both elements, may be hyphenated or open.

off-season	down payment	off year	cross-fertilization

18. **verb + particle; verb + adverb** These compounds may be hyphenated or solid. Compounds with two-letter particles (*by, to, in, up, on*) are most frequently hyphenated, since the hyphen aids quick comprehension. Compounds with three-letter particles (*off, out*) are hyphenated or solid with about equal frequency. Those with longer particles or adverbs are more often but not always solid.

lay-up	lead-in	run-on	set-to
sit-in	flyby	letup	pileup
shoot-out	show-off	dropout	turnoff
breakthrough	gadabout	giveaway	follow-through

19. **verb + -er + particle; verb + -ing + particle** Except for *passerby*, these compounds are hyphenated.

hanger-on	diner-out	falling-out	runner-up
summing-up	talking-to	goings-on	looker-on

20. **Compounds of three or four elements** Compounds of three or four elements are styled either hyphenated or open. Those consisting of noun + prepositional phrase are generally open, although some are hyphenated. Those formed from other combinations are usually hyphenated.

base on balls	justice of the peace	son of a gun
lily of the valley	jack-of-all-trades	lady-in-waiting
know-it-all	pick-me-up	stick-to-itiveness

21. **letter + noun** Compounds formed from a single letter (or sometimes a combination of them) followed by a noun are either open or hyphenated.

A-frame	B-girl	H-bomb	T-shirt
C ration	D day	I beam	T square
ABO system	J-bar lift	Rh factor	H and L hinge

Compounds That Function as Adjectives

Compound adjectives are combinations of words that work together to modify a noun—that is, they work as unit modifiers. As unit modifiers they should be distinguished from other strings of adjectives that may also precede a noun. For instance, in "a low, level tract of land" or "that long, lonesome road" the two adjectives each modify the noun separately. We are talking about a tract of land that is both low and level and about a road that is both long and lonesome. These are coordinate modifiers.

In "a low monthly fee" or "a wrinkled red necktie" the first adjective modifies the noun plus the second adjective. In other words, we mean a monthly fee that is low and a red necktie that is wrinkled. These are non-coordinate modifiers. But in "low-level radiation" we do not mean radiation that is low and level or level radiation that is low; we mean radiation that is at a low level. Both words work as a unit to modify the noun.

Unit modifiers are usually hyphenated. The hyphens not only make it easier for the reader to grasp the relationship of the words but also avoid confusion. The hyphen in "a call for more-specialized controls" removes any ambiguity as to which word *more* modifies. By contrast, the lack of a hyphen in a phrase like "graphic arts exhibition" gives it an undesirable ambiguity.

1. **Before the noun (attributive position)** Most two-word permanent or temporary compound adjectives are hyphenated when placed before the noun.

tree-lined streets	fast-acting medication
an iron-clad guarantee	a tough-minded negotiator
class-conscious persons	Spanish-American relations
well-intended advice	the red-carpet treatment
a profit-and-loss statement	an input-output device
arrested on a trumped-up charge	a risk-free investment

2. Temporary compounds formed of an adverb (as *well, more, less, still*) followed by a participle (or sometimes an adjective) are usually hyphenated when placed before a noun.

more-specialized controls	a just-completed survey
a still-growing company	a well-funded project
these fast-moving times	a now-vulnerable politician

3. Temporary compounds formed from an adverb ending in *-ly* followed by a participle may sometimes be hyphenated but are more commonly open, because adverb + adjective + noun is a normal word order.

a widely-read feature	internationally-known authors
but more often	
generally recognized categories	a beautifully illustrated book
publicly supported universities	our rapidly changing plans

4. The combination of *very* + adjective is not a unit modifier.

> a very satisfied smile

5. Many temporary compound adjectives are formed by using a compound noun—either permanent or temporary—to modify another noun. If the compound noun is an open compound, it is usually hyphenated so that the relationship of the words is more immediately apparent to the reader.

> the farm-bloc vote   a picture-framing shop
> a short-run printing press   a secret-compartment ring
> a tax-law case   ocean-floor hydrophones

6. Some open compound nouns are considered so readily recognizable that they are frequently placed before a noun without a hyphen.

> a high school diploma   *or*   a high-school diploma
> a data processing course   *or*   a data-processing course
> a dry goods store   *or*   a dry-goods store

7. A proper name placed before a noun to modify it is not hyphenated.

> a Thames River marina   a Huck Finn life
> a Korean War veteran   a General Motors car

8. Compound adjectives of three or more words are hyphenated when they precede the noun. Many temporary compounds are formed by hyphenating a phrase and placing it before a noun.

> spur-of-the-moment decisions
> higher-than-anticipated costs

9. Compound adjectives composed of foreign words are not hyphenated when placed before a noun unless they are regularly hyphenated.

> the per capita cost   an a priori argument
> a cordon bleu restaurant   a ci-devant professor

10. Chemical names used as modifiers before a noun are not hyphenated.

> a sodium hypochlorite bleach
> a critic acid solution

11. **Following the noun (as a complement or predicate adjective)** When the words that make up a compound adjective follow the noun they modify, they tend to fall in normal word order and are no longer unit modifiers. They are therefore no longer hyphenated.

> Controls have become more specialized.
> The company is still growing.
> a statement of profit and loss
> arrested on charges that had been trumped up
> decisions made on the spur of the moment
> They were ill prepared for the journey.

12. Many permanent and temporary compounds keep their hyphens after the noun in a sentence if they continue to function as unit modifiers. Compounds consisting of adjective or noun + participle, adjective or noun + noun + -ed (which looks like a participle), or noun + adjective are most likely to remain hyphenated.

> Your ideas are high-minded but impractical.
> streets that are tree-lined
> You were just as nice-looking then.
> metals that are corrosion-resistant
> tends to be accident-prone

13. Permanent compound adjectives are usually styled as they appear in the dictionary whether they precede or follow the noun they modify.

> The group was public-spirited.
> The problems are mind-boggling.
> is well-read in economics

14. Compound adjectives of three or more words are normally not hyphenated when they follow the noun they modify.

> These remarks are off the record.

15. Permanent compounds of three or more words may be entered as hyphenated adjectives in dictionaries. In such cases the hyphens are retained as long as the phrase is being used as a unit modifier.

> the plan is still pay-as-you-go
> *but* a plan in which you pay as you go

16. It is possible that a permanent hyphenated adjective may appear alongside a temporary compound in a position where it would normally be open (as "one who is both ill-humored and ill prepared"). It is best to resolve these inconsistencies, either by hyphenating both compounds or leaving both compounds open.

17. When an adverb modifies another adverb that is the first element of a compound modifier, the compound may lose its hyphen. If the first adverb modifies the whole compound, however, the hyphen should be retained.

> a very well developed idea
> a delightfully well-written book
> a most ill-humored remark

18. Adjective compounds that are names of colors may be styled open or hyphenated. Color names in which each element can function as a noun (as *blue green* or *chrome yellow*) are almost always hyphenated when they precede a noun; they are sometimes open when they follow the noun. Color names in which the first element can only be an adjective are less consistently treated; they are often not hyphenated before a noun and are usually not hyphenated after.

> blue-gray paint
> paint that is blue-gray   *also*   paint that is blue gray
> bluish gray paint   *or*   bluish-gray paint

19. Compound modifiers that include a number followed by a noun are hyphenated when they precede the noun they modify. When the modifier follows the noun, it is usually not hyphenated. For more on the styling of numbers, see the section on Numbers, beginning on page 136.

> five-card stud   ten-foot pole   twelve-year-old girl
> an 18-inch rule   *but*   a 10 percent raise
> a child who is ten years old

20. An adjective that is composed of a number followed by a noun in the possessive is not hyphenated.

> a two weeks' wait   a four blocks' walk

Compounds That Function as Adverbs

1. Adverb compounds consisting of preposition + noun are almost always written solid. However, there are a few well-known exceptions.

> downtown   downwind   onstage   overseas
> upstairs   upfield   offhand   underhand
> *but*
> in-house   off-line   on-line

2. Compound adverbs of more than two words are usually styled open, and they usually follow the words they modify.

> every which way   high and dry   off and on
> little by little   hook, line, and sinker   over and over

3. A few three-word adverbs are homographs of hyphenated adjectives and are therefore styled with hyphens. But many adverbs are styled open even if an adjective formed from the same phrase is hyphenated.

> back-to-back (adverb or adjective)
> face-to-face (adverb or adjective)
> *but*
> hand-to-hand combat   fought hand to hand
> off-the-cuff remarks   spoke off the cuff

Compound Verbs

1. Two-word verbs consisting of a verb followed by an adverb or a preposition are styled open.

> get together   run around   run across
> set to   run wild   put down
> break through   strike out   print out

2. A compound composed of a particle followed by a verb is styled solid.

> upgrade   outflank   overcome   bypass

3. A verb derived from an open or hyphenated compound noun—permanent, temporary, or self-evident—is hyphenated.

blue-pencil	double-check	poor-mouth
sweet-talk	tap-dance	water-ski

4. A verb derived from a solid noun is styled solid.

bankroll	roughhouse	mainstream

Compounds Formed with Word Elements

Many new and temporary compounds are formed by adding word elements to existing words or by combining word elements. There are three basic word elements: prefixes (as *anti-*, *re-*, *non-*, *super-*), suffixes (as *-er*, *-ly*, *-ness*, *-ism*), and combining forms (as *mini-*, *macro-*, *pseud-*, *ortho-*, *-ped*, *-graphy*, *-gamic*, *-plasty*). Prefixes and suffixes are usually attached to existing words; combining forms are usually combined to form new words.

1. **prefix + word** Except as specified below, compounds formed from a prefix and a word are usually styled solid.

precondition	refurnish	suborder	postwar
interagency	misshapen	overfond	unhelpful

2. If the prefix ends with a vowel and the word it is attached to begins with the same vowel, the compound is usually hyphenated.

anti-inflation	co-owner	de-emphasize	multi-institutional

NOTE: There are many exceptions to this styling (as *cooperate* and *reentry*).

3. If the base word to which a prefix is added is capitalized, the compound is hyphenated.

anti-American	post-Victorian	pre-Columbian	inter-Caribbean

NOTE: The prefix is usually not capitalized in such compounds. But if the prefix and the base word together form a new proper name, the compound may be solid with the prefix capitalized (as *Postimpressionist*, *Precambrian*).

4. Compounds made with *self-* and *ex-* meaning "former" are hyphenated.

self-pity	ex-wife

5. If a prefix is added to a hyphenated compound, it may be either followed by a hyphen or closed up solid to the next element. Permanent compounds of this kind should be checked in a dictionary.

unair-conditioned	non-self-governing
ultra-up-to-date	unself-conscious

6. In typewritten material, if a prefix is added to an open compound, the prefix is followed by a hyphen. In typeset material, this hyphen is often represented by an en dash. (For more on this use of the en dash, see paragraph 12 under Dash, on pages 67–68.)

    ex–Boy Scout   post–coup d'état
    ex–Boy Scout   post–coup d'état

7. A compound that would be identical with another word if styled solid is usually hyphenated to prevent misreading.

    a multi-ply fabric   re-collect the money   un-ionized particles

8. A compound that might otherwise be solid may be hyphenated if it could be momentarily puzzling (as from consecutive vowels, doubled consonants, or simply an odd combination of letters.)

    coed *or* co-ed   overreact *or* over-react
    coworker *or* co-worker interrow *or* inter-row

9. Temporary compounds formed from *vice-* are usually hyphenated; however, some permanent compounds (as *vice president* and *vice admiral*) are open.

10. When prefixes are attached to numerals, the compounds are hyphenated.

    pre-1982 expenses   post-1975 vintages   non-20th-century ideas

11. Compounds created from combining forms like *Anglo-*, *Judeo-*, or *Sino-* are hyphenated when the second element is an independent word. They are written solid when it is a combining form.

    Judeo-Christian   Austro-Hungarian   Sino-Soviet
    Italophile   Francophone   Anglophobe

12. Prefixes that are repeated in the same compound are separated by a hyphen.

    sub-subheading

13. Some prefixes and initial combining forms have related independent adjectives or adverbs that may be used where the prefix might be expected. A temporary compound with *quasi(-)* or *pseudo(-)* therefore may be written open as modifier + noun or hyphenated as combining form + noun.

    quasi intellectual *or* quasi-intellectual
    pseudo liberal *or* pseudo-liberal

NOTE: in some cases (as *super, super-*), the independent modifier may not mean quite the same as the prefix.

14. Compounds consisting of different prefixes with the same base word and joined by *and* or *or* are sometimes shortened by pruning the first

compound back to the prefix. The missing base word is indicated by a hyphen on the prefix.

> pre- and postoperative care
> anti- or pro-Revolutionary sympathies

15. **word + suffix** Except as noted below, compounds formed by adding a suffix to a word are styled solid.

> Darwinist   fortyish   landscaper   powerlessness

16. Permanent or temporary compounds formed with a suffix are hyphenated if the addition of the suffix would create a sequence of three identical letters.

> bell-like   will-less   a coffee-er coffee

17. Temporary compounds made with a suffix are often hyphenated if the base word is more than three syllables long, if the base word ends with the same letter the suffix begins with, or if the suffix creates a confusing sequence of letters.

> tunnel-like   American-ness   jaw-wards
> umbrella-like   industry-wide   battle-worthy

18. Compounds made from a number + *odd* are hyphenated whether the number is spelled out or in numerals; a number + *-fold* is solid if the number is spelled out but hyphenated if it is in numerals.

> 20-odd   twenty-odd
> 12-fold   twelvefold

19. Most compounds formed from an open or hyphenated compound + a suffix do not separate the suffix by a hyphen. But such suffixes as *-like, -wide, -worthy,* and *-proof,* all of which are homographs of independent adjectives, are attached by a hyphen.

> good-humoredness   dollar-a-yearism   do-it-yourselfer
> a United Nations-like agency

NOTE: Open compounds often become hyphenated when a suffix is added unless they are proper nouns.

> middle age *but* middle-ager   New Englandism
> tough guy *but* tough-guyese   Wall Streeter

20. **combining form + combining form** Many new terms in technical fields are created by adding combining form to combining form or combining form to a word or word part. Such compounds are generally intended to be permanent, even though many never get into the dictionary. They are regularly styled solid.

Miscellaneous Styling Conventions

1. Compounds that would otherwise be styled solid according to the principles described above are written open or hyphenated to avoid

ambiguity, to ensure rapid comprehension, or to make the pronunciation clearer.

meat-ax *or* meat ax   bi-level   tri-city
re-utter   umbrella-like   un-iced

2. When typographical features such as capitals or italics make word relationships in a sentence clear, it is not necessary to hyphenate an open compound (as when it precedes a noun it modifies).

a *Chicago Tribune* story   an "eyes only" memo
I've been Super Bowled to death.
a *noblesse oblige* attitude

Abbreviations

Abbreviations are used for a variety of reasons: to save space, to avoid repetition of long words and phrases that may distract the reader, and to reduce keystrokes for typists. In addition, abbreviations are used simply to conform to conventional usage.

Unfortunately, the contemporary styling of abbreviations is to a large extent inconsistent and arbitrary. No set of rules can hope to cover all the possible variations, exceptions, and peculiarities encountered in print. The styling of abbreviations—whether capitalized or lowercased, closed up or spaced, punctuated or unpunctuated—depends most often on a writer's preference or an organization's policy. For example, some companies style the abbreviation for *cash on delivery* as *COD;* others prefer *C.O.D.* or *c.o.d.*

All is not complete confusion, however, and general patterns can be discerned. Some abbreviations (as *e.g., etc., i.e., No.,* and *viz.*) are governed by a strong tradition of punctuation, while others (as *NATO, NASA, NOW, OPEC,* and *SALT*) that are pronounced as words tend to be all-capitalized and unpunctuated. Styling problems can be dealt with by consulting a good general dictionary such as *Webster's Ninth New Collegiate Dictionary,* especially for capitalization guidance, and by the following the guidelines of one's own organization or the dictates of one's own preference. An abbreviations dictionary such as *Webster's Guide to Abbreviations* may also be helpful.

Punctuation

The paragraphs that follow describe a few broad principles that apply to abbreviations in general. However, there are many specific situations in which these principles will not apply. The section on Specific Styling Conventions, beginning on page 143, contains information on these specific situations and on particular kinds of abbreviations.

1. A period follows most abbreviations that are formed by omitting all but the first few letters of a word.

bull. for *bulletin*
bro. for *brother*

fig. for *figure*
Fr. for *French*

2. A period follows most abbreviations that are formed by omitting letters from the middle of a word.

secy. for *secretary*
mfg. for *manufacturing*

agcy. for *agency*
Mr. for *Mister*

3. Punctuation is usually omitted from abbreviations that are made up of initial letters of words that constitute a phrase or compound word. However, for some of these abbreviations, especially ones that are not capitalized, the punctuation is retained.

GNP for *gross national product*
EFT for *electronic funds transfer*

PC for *personal computer*
f.o.b. for *free on board*

4. Terms in which a suffix is added to a numeral, such as *1st, 2nd, 3d, 8vo,* and *12mo,* are not abbreviations and do not require a period.

5. Isolated letters of the alphabet used to designate a shape or position in a sequence are not punctuated.

T square   A 1   I beam   V sign

6. Some abbreviations are punctuated with one or more virgules in place of periods.

c/o for *care of*
d/b/a for *doing business as*

w/o for *without*
w/w for *wall to wall*

Capitalization

1. Abbreviations are capitalized if the words they represent are proper nouns or adjectives.

F for *Fahrenheit*
NBC for *National*
   Broadcasting Company

Nov. for *November*
Brit. for *British*

2. Abbreviations are usually capitalized when they represent single letters of words that are normally lowercased. There are, however, some very common abbreviations formed in this way that are not capitalized.

TM for *trademark*
ETA for *estimated time of arrival*
CATV for *community*
   antenna television
a.k.a. for *also known as*

EEG for *electroencephalogram*
FY for *fiscal year*

d/b/a for *doing business as*

3. Most acronyms that are pronounced as words, rather than as a series of letters, are capitalized. If they have been assimilated into the lan-

guage as words in their own right, however, they are most often low-ercased.

OPEC	NATO	MIRV	NOW account
quasar	laser	sonar	scuba

Plurals, Possessives, and Compounds

1. Punctuated abbreviations of single words are pluralized by adding *-s* before the period.

bldgs.	bros.	figs.	mts.

2. Punctuated abbreviations that stand for phrases or compounds are pluralized by adding *-'s* after the last period.

Ph.D.'s	f.o.b.'s	J.P.'s	M.B.A.'s

3. Unpunctuated abbreviations that stand for phrases or compound words are usually pluralized by adding *-s* to the end of the abbreviation.

COLAs	CPUs	PCs	DOSs

NOTE: Some writers pluralize such abbreviations by adding *-'s* to the abbreviation; however, this styling is far less common than the one described above.

4. The plural form of most lowercase single-letter abbreviations is made by repeating the letter. For the plural form of single-letter abbreviations that are abbreviations for units of measure, see paragraph 5 below.

cc. for *copies*	ff. for *and the following ones*
ll. for *lines*	nn. for *notes*
pp. for *pages*	vv. for *verses*

5. The plural form of abbreviations of units of measure is the same as the singular form.

30 sec.	24 ml	20 min.	200 bbl.
30 d.	24 h.	50 m	10 mi.

6. Possessives of abbreviations are formed in the same way as those of spelled-out nouns: the singular possessive is formed by the addition of *-'s*, the plural possessive simply by the addition of an apostrophe.

the CPUs' memory	most CPUs' memories
Brody Corp.'s earnings	Bay Bros.' annual sale

7. Compounds that consist of an abbreviation added to another word are formed in the same way as compounds that consist of spelled-out nouns.

a Kalamazoo, Mich.-based company
an AMA-approved medical school

8. Compounds formed by adding a prefix or suffix to an abbreviation are usually styled with a hyphen.

> an IBM-like organization
> non-DNA molecules
> pre-HEW years

Specific Styling Conventions

The following paragraphs describe styling practices commonly followed for specific kinds of situations involving abbreviations. The paragraphs are arranged under the following alphabetical headings.

A and An	Degrees	Military Ranks and
A.D. and B.C.	Division of	Units
Agencies, Associations,	Abbreviations	Number
and Organizations	Full Forms	Personal Names
Beginning a Sentence	Geographical Names	Saint
Books of the Bible	Latin Words and	Scientific Terms
Company Names	Phrases	Time
Compass Points	Latitude and	Titles
Contractions	Longitude	Units of Measure
Dates	Laws and Bylaws	Versus

1. A and an The choice of the article *a* or *an* before abbreviations depends on the sound with which the abbreviation begins. If an abbreviation begins with a consonant sound, *a* is normally used. If an abbreviation begins with a vowel sound, *an* is used.

a B.A. degree	a YMCA club	a UN agency
an FCC report	an SAT score	an IRS agent

2. A.D. and B.C. The abbreviations A.D. and B.C. are usually styled in typeset matter as punctuated, unspaced small capitals; in typed material they usually appear as punctuated, unspaced capitals.

in printed material	41 B.C.	A.D. 185
in typed material	41 B.C.	A.D. 185

3. The abbreviation A.D. usually precedes the date; the abbreviation B.C. usually follows the date. However, many writers and editors place A.D. after the date, thus making their placement of A.D. consistent with their placement of B.C. In references to whole centuries, the usual practice is to place A.D. after the century. The only alternative is not to use the abbreviation at all in such references.

> A.D. 185   *but also*   185 A.D.
> the fourth century A.D.

4. Agencies, associations, and organizations The names of agencies, associations, and organizations are usually abbreviated after they have been spelled out on their first occurrence in a text. The abbreviations are usually all capitalized and unpunctuated.

> EPA   SEC   NAACP   NCAA   USO   NOW

NOTE: In contexts where the abbreviation will be recognized, it may be used without having its full form spelled out on its first occurrence.

5. **Beginning a sentence** Most writers avoid beginning a sentence with an abbreviation that is ordinarily not capitalized. Abbreviations that are ordinarily capitalized, on the other hand, are commonly used to begin sentences.

> Page 22 contains . . . *not* P. 22 contains . . .
> Doctor Smith believes . . . *or* Dr. Smith believes . . .
> OSHA regulations require . . .

6. **Books of the Bible** Books of the Bible are generally spelled out in running text but abbreviated in references to chapter and verse.

> The minister based the sermon on Genesis.
> In the beginning God created the heavens and the earth.—Gen. 1:1

7. **Company names** The styling of company names varies widely. Many writers avoid abbreviating any part of a company's name unless the abbreviation is part of the company's official name. However, many other writers routinely abbreviate words such as *Company, Corporation,* and *Incorporated.* Words such as *Airlines, Associates, Fabricators* and *Manufacturing,* however, are spelled out.

> Ginn and Company *or* Ginn and Co.
> The Bailey Banks and Biddle Company *or* The Bailey Banks and Biddle Co.

NOTE: An ampersand frequently replaces the word *and* in official company names. For more on this use of the ampersand, see paragraph 1 under Ampersand, page 49.

8. If a company is easily recognizable from its initials, its name is usually spelled out for the first mention and abbreviated in all subsequent references. Some companies have made their initials part of their official name, and in those cases the initials appear in all references.

> *first reference*　　　General Motors Corp. released figures today . . .
> *subsequent reference*　A GM spokesperson said . . .
> MCM Electronics, an Ohio-based electronics company . . .

9. **Compass points** Compass points are abbreviated when occurring after street names, though styling varies regarding whether these abbreviations are punctuated and whether they are preceded by a comma. When compass points form essential internal elements of street names, they are usually spelled out in full.

> 2122 Fourteenth Street, NW *or* 2122 Fourteenth Street NW
> 　*or* 2122 Fourteenth Street, N.W.
> 192 East 49th Street
> 1282 North Avenue

10. **Contractions** Some abbreviations resemble contractions by including an apostrophe in place of omitted letters. These abbreviations are not punctuated with a period.

sec'y for *secretary*   ass'n for *association*   dep't for *department*

NOTE: This style of abbreviation is usually avoided in formal correspondence.

11. **Dates** The names of days and months should not be abbreviated in running text. The names of months are not abbreviated in date lines of business letters, but they may be abbreviated in government or military correspondence.

the December issue of *Scientific American*
a meeting held on August 1, 1985   *not*   a meeting held on Aug. 1, 1985
general business date line   November 1, 1985
military date line   1 Nov 1985

12. **Degrees** Except for a few academic degrees with highly recognizable abbreviations (as *A.B.*, *M.S.*, and *Ph.D.*), the names of degrees and professional ratings are spelled out in full when first mentioned in running text. Often the name of the degree is followed by its abbreviation enclosed in parentheses, so that the abbreviation may be used alone later in running text. When a degree or professional rating follows a person's name it is usually abbreviated.

Special attention is devoted to the master of arts in teaching (M.A.T.) degree.
Julia Ramirez, P.E.

13. Like other abbreviations, abbreviations of degrees and professional ratings are often unpunctuated. In general, punctuated abbreviations are more common for academic degrees, and unpunctuated abbreviations are slightly more common for professional ratings, especially if the latter comprise three or more capitalized letters.

R.Ph.	P.E.	CLA	CMET
Ph.D.	B.Sc.	M.B.A.	BGS

14. The first letter of each element in abbreviations of all degrees and professional ratings is capitalized. Letters other than the first letter are usually not capitalized.

D.Ch.E.	Litt.D.	M.F.A.	D.Th.

15. **Division of abbreviations** Division of abbreviations at the end of lines or between pages is usually avoided.

received an M.B.A.   *not*   received an M.B.-
degree   A. degree

16. **Full forms** When using an abbreviation that may be unfamiliar or confusing to the reader, many writers give the full form first, followed

by the abbreviation in parentheses. In subsequent references just the abbreviation is used.

first reference   At the American Bar Association (ABA) meeting in June . . .

subsequent reference   At that particular ABA meeting . . .

17. **Geographical names** U.S. Postal Service abbreviations for states, possessions, and Canadian provinces are all-capitalized and unpunctuated, as are Postal Service abbreviations for streets and other geographical features when these abbreviations are used on envelopes addressed for automated mass handling.

addressed for automated handling   1234 SMITH BLVD
                                      SMITHVILLE, MN 56789

regular address styling   1234 Smith Blvd.
                                      Smithville, MN 56789

18. Abbreviations of states are often used in running text to identify the location of a city or county. In this context they are set off with commas, and punctuated, upper- and lowercase state abbreviations are usually used. In other situations within running text, the names of states are usually not abbreviated.

John Smith of 15 Chestnut St., Sarasota, Fla., has won . . .
the Louisville, Ky., public library system
Boston, the largest city in Massachusetts, . . .

19. Terms such as *street* and *parkway* are variously abbreviated or unabbreviated in running text. When they are abbreviated, they are usually punctuated.

our office at 1234 Smith Blvd. (*or* Boulevard)
an accident on Windward Road (*or* Rd.)

20. Names of countries are usually spelled in full in running text. The most common exceptions to this pattern are the abbreviations *U.S.S.R.* and *U.S.* (see paragraph 22 below).

Great Britain and the U.S.S.R. announced the agreement.

21. Abbreviations for the names of most countries are punctuated. Abbreviations for countries whose names include more than one word are often not punctuated if the abbreviations are formed from only the initial letters of the individual words.

Mex.	Can.	Scot.
Ger.	Gt. Brit.	U.S. *or* US
U.S.S.R. *or* USSR	U.K. *or* UK	U.A.E. *or* UAE

22. *United States* is often abbreviated when it is being used as an adjective, such as when it modifies the name of a federal agency, policy, or program. When *United States* is used as a noun in running text, it is usu-

ally spelled out, or it is spelled on its initial use and then abbreviated in subsequent references.

U.S. Department of Justice
U.S. foreign policy
The United States has offered to . . .

23. *Saint* is usually abbreviated when it is part of the name of a geographical or topographical feature. *Mount, Point,* and *Fort* are variously spelled out or abbreviated according to individual preference. *Saint, Mount,* and *Point* are routinely abbreviated when space is at a premium. (For more on the abbreviation of *Saint,* see paragraph 35 below.)

St. Louis, Missouri	St. Kitts	Mount McKinley
Mount St. Helens	Fort Sumter	Point Pelee

24. **Latin words and phrases** Words and phrases derived from Latin are commonly abbreviated in contexts where readers can reasonably be expected to recognize them. They are punctuated, lowercased, and usually not italicized.

etc.   i.e.   e.g.   viz.   et al.   pro tem.

25. **Latitude and longitude** Latitude and longitude are abbreviated in tabular data but written out in running text.

in a table   lat. 10°20′N *or* lat. 10-20N

in text   from 10°20′ north latitude to 10°30′ south latitude

26. **Laws and bylaws** Laws and bylaws, when first mentioned, are spelled in full. Subsequent references to them in a text may be abbreviated.

first reference   Article I, Section 1
subsequent reference   Art. I, Sec. 1

27. **Military ranks and units** Military ranks are usually given in full when used with a surname only but are abbreviated when used with a full name.

Colonel Howe   Col. John P. Howe

28. In nonmilitary correspondence, abbreviations for military ranks are punctuated and set in capital and lowercase letters. Within the military (with the exception of the Marine Corps) these abbreviations are all-capitalized and unpunctuated. The Marine Corps follows the punctuated, capital and lowercase styling.

in the military   BG John T. Dow, USA
LCDR Mary I. Lee, USN
Col. S. J. Smith, USMC

outside the military   Brig. Gen. John T. Dow, USA
Lt. Comdr. Mary I. Lee, USN
Col. S. J. Smith, USMC

29. Abbreviations for military units are capitalized and unpunctuated.

USA   USAF   SAC   NORAD

30. Number The word *number,* when used with figures such as *1* or *2* to indicate a rank or rating, is usually abbreviated. When it is, the *N* is capitalized, and the abbreviation is punctuated.

The No. 1 priority is to promote profitability.

31. The word *number* is usually abbreviated when it is part of a set unit (such as a contract number).

Contract No. N-1234-76-57   Publ. Nos. 12 and 13
Policy No. 123-5-X   Index No. 7855

32. Personal names Personal names are not usually abbreviated.

George S. Patterson   *not*   Geo. S. Patterson

33. Unspaced initials of famous persons are sometimes used in place of their full names. The initials may or may not be punctuated.

FDR   *or*   F.D.R.

34. When initials are used with a surname, they are spaced and punctuated.

F. D. Roosevelt

35. Saint The word *Saint* is often abbreviated when used before the name of a saint or when it is the first element of the name of a city or institution named after a saint. However, when it forms part of a surname, it may or may not be abbreviated. In the case of surnames and names of institutions, the styling should be the one used by the person or the institution.

St. Peter   *or*   Saint Peter   St. Cloud, Minnesota
St. John's University   Saint Joseph College
Augustus Saint-Gaudens   Louis St. Laurent

36. Scientific terms In binomial nomenclature, a genus name may be abbreviated with its initial letter after the first reference to it is spelled out. The abbreviation is always punctuated.

first reference   *Escherichia coli*
subsequent reference   *E. coli*

37. Abbreviations for the names of chemical compounds or mechanical or electronic equipment or processes are usually not punctuated.

OCR   PCB   CPU   PBX

38. The symbols for chemical elements are not punctuated.

H   Cl   Pb   Na

39. Time When time is expressed in figures, the abbreviations that follow are most often styled as punctuated lowercase letters; punctuated small capital letters are also common.

8:30 a.m. 10:00 p.m. 8:30 A.M. 10:00 P.M.

40. In transportation schedules *a.m.* and *p.m.* are generally styled in capitalized, unpunctuated, unspaced letters.

8:30 AM 10:00 PM

41. Time zone designations are usually styled in capitalized, unpunctuated, unspaced letters.

EST PST CDT

42. Titles The only courtesy titles that are invariably abbreviated in written references are *Mr., Ms., Mrs.,* and *Messrs.* Other titles, such as *Doctor, Representative,* or *Senator,* may be either written out or abbreviated.

Ms. Lee A. Downs
Messrs. Lake, Mason, and Nambeth
Doctor Howe *or* Dr. Howe

43. Despite some traditional injunctions against the practice, the titles *Honorable* and *Reverend* are often abbreviated.

the Honorable Samuel I. O'Leary *or* the Hon. Samuel I. O'Leary
the Reverend Samuel I. O'Leary *or* the Rev. Samuel I. O'Leary

44. The designations *Jr.* and *Sr.* may be used in conjunction with courtesy titles, with abbreviations for academic degrees, and with professional rating abbreviations. They may or may not be preceded by a comma according to the writer's preference. They are terminated with a period, and they are commonly only used with a full name.

Mr. John K. Walker, Jr.
Dr. John K. Walker, Jr.
General John K. Walker Jr.
The Honorable John K. Walker, Jr.
John K. Walker Jr., M.D.

45. When an abbreviation for an academic degree, professional certification, or association membership follows a name, it is usually preceded by a comma. No courtesy title should precede the name.

Dr. John Smith *or* John Smith, M.D. *but not* Dr. John Smith, M.D.
Katherine Derwinski, CLU
Carol Manning, M.D., FACPS

46. The abbreviation *Esq.* for *Esquire* is used in the United States after the surname of professional persons such as attorneys, architects, consuls, clerks of the court, and justices of the peace. It is not used, however, if a courtesy title such as *Dr., Hon., Miss, Mr., Mrs.,* or *Ms.* precedes the first name. For more on the use of *Esquire,* see pages 250–251.

> Carolyn B. West, Esq.

47. **Units of measure** Measures and weights may be abbreviated in figure plus unit combinations. However, if the numeral is written out, the unit should also be written out.

> 15 cu ft   *or*   15 cu. ft.   *but*   fifteen cubic feet
> How many cubic feet does the refrigerator hold?

48. Abbreviations for metric units are usually not punctuated. Abbreviations for traditional units are usually punctuated.

> 14 ml   12 km   22 mi.   8 ft.   4 sec.   20 min.

49. **Versus** *Versus* is usually abbreviated as the lowercase roman letter *v.* in legal contexts; it is either spelled out or abbreviated as lowercase roman letters *vs.* in general contexts.

> *in a legal context*   Smith v. *Vermont*
> *in a general context*   honesty versus dishonesty
>   *or*
>   honesty vs. dishonesty

Numbers

The styling of numbers presents special difficulties to writers because there are so many conventions to follow, some of which may conflict when applied to particular passages. The writer's major decision is whether to write out numbers or to express them in figures, and usage varies considerably on this point. This chapter explains most of the conventions used in the styling of numbers. A discussion of general principles is followed by detailed information on specific situations involving numbers.

Numbers as Words or Figures

At one extreme of styling, all numbers, sometimes even including dates, are written out. This usage is uncommon and is usually limited to proclamations, legal documents, and some other types of very formal writing. At the other extreme, some types of technical writing, such as statistical reports, contain no written-out numbers except sometimes at the beginning of a sentence.

In general, figures are easier to read than the spelled-out forms of numbers; however, the spelled-out forms are helpful in certain circumstances, such as in distinguishing different categories of numbers or in providing relief from an overwhelming cluster of numerals. Most writers follow one or the other of two common conventions combining numerals and written-out numbers. The conventions are described in this section, along with the situations that provide exceptions to the general rules.

1. **Basic conventions** The first system requires that a writer use figures for exact numbers that are greater than nine and words for numbers nine and below (a variation of this system sets the number ten as the dividing point). In this system, numbers that consist of a whole number between one and nine followed by *hundred, thousand, million,* etc. may be spelled out or expressed in figures.

> She performed in 22 plays on Broadway, seven of which won awards.
>
> The new edition will consist of 25 volumes which will be issued at a rate of approximately four volumes per year.
>
> The cat show attracted an unexpected two thousand entries.
>
> They sold more than 2,000 units in the first year.

2. The second system requires that a writer use figures for all exact numbers 100 and above (or 101 and above) and words for numbers from one to ninety-nine (or one to one hundred) and for numbers that consist of a whole number between one and ninety-nine followed by *hundred, thousand, million,* etc.

> The artist spent nearly twelve years completing these four volumes, which comprise 435 hand-colored engravings.
>
> The 145 seminar participants toured the area's eighteen period houses.
>
> In the course of four hours, the popular author signed twenty-five hundred copies of her new book.

3. **Sentence beginnings** Numbers that begin a sentence are written out, although some writers make an exception for the use of figures for dates that begin a sentence. It is best to avoid spelled-out numbers that are lengthy and awkward by restructuring the sentence so that the number appears elsewhere than at the beginning and may then be styled as a figure.

> Sixty-two new models will be introduced this year.
> *or*
> There will be 62 new models introduced this year.
>
> Nineteen eighty-seven was our best earnings year so far.
> *or*
> 1987 was our best earnings year so far.
>
> One hundred fifty-seven illustrations, including 86 color plates, are contained in the book.
> *or*
> The book contains 157 illustrations, including 86 color plates.

4. **Adjacent numbers and numbers in series** Generally, two separate sets of figures should not be written adjacent to one another in running text unless they form a series. So that the juxtaposition of unrelated figures will not confuse the reader, either the sentence is restructured

or one of the figures is spelled out. Usually the figure with the written form that is shorter and more easily read is converted. When one of two adjacent numbers is an element of a compound modifier, the first of the two numbers is often expressed in words, the second in figures. But if the second number is the shorter, the styling is often reversed.

original	*change to*
16 ½-inch dowels	sixteen ½-inch dowels
25 11-inch platters	twenty-five 11-inch platters
20 100-point games	twenty 100-point games
78 20-point games	78 twenty-point games
By 1997, 300 more of the state's schools will have closed their doors.	By 1997, three hundred more of the state's schools will have closed their doors.

5. Numbers paired at the beginning of a sentence are usually styled alike. If the first word of the sentence is a spelled-out number, the second, related number is also spelled out. However, some writers and editors prefer that each number be styled independently, even if that results in an inconsistent pairing.

> Sixty to seventy-five copies will be required.
> Sixty to 75 copies will be required.

6. Numbers that form a pair or a series referring to comparable quantities within a sentence or a paragraph should be treated consistently. The style of the largest number usually determines the style of the other numbers. Thus, a series of numbers including some which would ordinarily be spelled out might all be styled as figures. Similarly, figures are used to express all the numbers in a series if one of those numbers is a mixed or simple fraction.

> The three jobs took 5, 12, and 4½ hours, respectively.
> We need four desks, three chairs, fourteen typewriters, and six file cabinets.

7. **Round numbers** Approximate or round numbers, particularly those that can be expressed in one or two words, are often written out in general writing; in technical and scientific writing they are more likely to be expressed as numerals.

> seven hundred people
> five thousand years
> four hundred thousand volumes
>
> *but in technical writing*
> 50,000 people per year
> 20,000 species of fish

8. For easier reading, numbers of one million and above may be expressed as figures followed by the word *million, billion,* and so forth. The figure may include a decimal fraction, but the fraction is not usu-

ally carried past the first digit to the right of the decimal point, and it is never carried past the third digit. If a more exact number is required, the whole amount should be written in figures.

about 4.6 billion years old
1.2 million metric tons of grain
the last 600 million years
$7.25 million
$3,456,000,000
   but 200,000 years   *not*   200 thousand years

Ordinal Numbers

1. Ordinal numbers generally follow the styling rules for cardinal numbers. If a figure would be required for the cardinal form of a number, it should also be used from the ordinal form; if the conventions call for a written-out form, it should be used for both cardinal and ordinal numbers. In technical writing, however, ordinal numbers are usually written as figure-plus-suffix combinations. In addition, certain ordinal numbers—for example, those specifying percentiles and latitudinal lines—are conventionally set as figures.

the sixth Robert de Bruce	the 20th century
the ninth grade	the 98th Congress
the 40th parallel	the 12th percentile
the 9th and 14th chapters	the 40th parallel
his twenty-third try	

2. The forms *second* and *third* may be written with figures as *2d* or *2nd, 3d* or *3rd, 22d* or *22nd, 93d* or *93rd, 102d* or *102nd.* A period does not follow the suffix.

Roman Numerals

Roman numerals, which may be written either in capital or lowercase letters, are conventional in the specific situations described below. Roman numerals are formed by adding the numerical values of letters as they are arranged in descending order going from left to right. If a letter with a smaller numerical value is placed to the left of a letter with a greater numerical value, the value of the smaller is subtracted from the value of the larger. A bar placed over a numeral ($\bar{V}$) multiplies its value by one thousand.

1. Roman numerals are traditionally used to differentiate rulers and popes that have identical names.

Elizabeth II	Innocent X
Henry VIII	Louis XIV

2. Roman numerals are used to differentiate related males who have the same name. For more on this use of Roman numerals, see page 85.

James R. Watson II	James R. Watson 2nd *or* 2d

NOTE: Possessive patterns for these names are the following:

singular   James R. Watson III's (*or* 3rd's *or* 3d's) house
plural   the James R. Watson IIIs' (*or* 3rds' *or* 3ds') house

3. Roman numerals are used to differentiate certain vehicles and vessels, such as yachts, that have the same name. If the name is italicized, the numeral is italicized also. Names of American spacecraft formerly bore Roman numerals, but Arabic numerals are now used.

> *Shamrock V*
>
> The U.S. spacecraft *Rangers VII, VIII,* and *IX* took pictures of the moon.
>
> On July 20, 1969, *Apollo 11* landed on the moon.

4. Lowercase Roman numerals are often used to number book pages that precede the regular Arabic sequence, as in a foreword, preface, or introduction.

5. Roman numerals are often used in enumerations to list major headings. An example of an outline with Roman-numeral headings is shown on page 148.

6. Roman numerals are found as part of a few established technical terms such as blood-clotting factors, quadrant numbers, designations of cranial nerves, and virus or organism types. Also, chords in the study of music harmony are designated by capital and lowercase Roman numerals. For the most part, however, technical terms that include numbers express them in Arabic form.

> blood-clotting factor VII   HTLV-III virus
> quadrant III   *but*
> the cranial nerves II and IX   adenosine 3′,5′-monophosphate
> Population II stars   cesium 137
> type I error   PL/1 programming language

Punctuation and Inflection

The paragraphs that follow explain general rules for the use of commas and hyphens in compound and large numbers, as well as the plural forms of numbers. For the styling of specific categories of numbers, such as dates, money, and decimal fractions, see the section on Specific Styling Conventions, beginning on page 143.

1. **Commas in large numbers** In general writing, with the exceptions explained in paragraph 3 below, figures of four digits may be styled with or without a comma; the punctuated form is more common. If the numerals form part of a tabulation, commas are necessary so that four-digit numerals can align with numerals of five or more digits.

> 2,000 case histories   *or less commonly*   1253 people

2. Whole numbers of five digits or more (but not decimal fractions) use a comma to separate three-digit groups, counting from the right.

> a fee of $12,500
> 15,000 units
> a population of 1,500,000

3. Certain types of numbers do not conform to these conventions. Decimal fractions and serial and multidigit numbers in set combinations, such as the numbers of policies, contracts, checks, streets, rooms, suites, telephones, pages, military hours, and years, do not contain commas.

> check 34567   the year 1929
> Room 606   Policy No. 33442
> 1650 hours   page 407

4. **Hyphens** Hyphens are used with written-out numbers between 21 and 99.

> forty-one   forty-first
> four hundred twenty-two
> the twenty-fifth day

5. A hyphen is used between the numerator and the denominator of a fraction that is written out when that fraction is used as a modifier. A written-out fraction consisting of two words only (as *two thirds*) is usually styled open, although the hyphenated form is also common. Multiword numerators and denominators are usually hyphenated. If either the numerator or the denominator is hyphenated, no hyphen is used between them. For more on fractions, see pages 148–149.

> a two-thirds majority   forty-five hundredths
> three fifths of her paycheck   four five-hundredths
> seven and four fifths

6. Numbers that form the first part of a compound modifier expressing measurement are followed by a hyphen. An exception to this practice is that numbers are not followed by a hyphen when the second part of the modifier is the word *percent*.

> a 5-foot board   an eight-pound baby
> a 28-mile trip   a 680-acre ranch
> a 10-pound weight   a 75 percent reduction

7. An adjective or adverb made from a numeral plus the suffix *-fold* contains a hyphen, while a similar term made from a written-out number is styled solid. (For more on the use of suffixes with numbers, see page 125.)

> a fourfold increase
> increased 20-fold

8. Serial numbers, such as social security or engine numbers, often contain hyphens that make lengthy numerals more readable.

   020-42-1691

9. Numbers are usually not divided at the end of a line. If division is unavoidable, the break occurs only after a comma. End-of-line breaks do not occur at decimal points, and a name with a numerical suffix (as Robert F. Walker III) is not divided between the name and the numeral.

10. **Inclusive numbers** Inclusive numbers—those which express a range—are separated either by the word *to* or by a hyphen or en dash, which serves as an arbitrary equivalent of the phrase "(up) to and including" when used between dates and other inclusive numbers. (The en dash is explained in paragraph 12 under Dash, pages 67–68.)

pages 40 to 98	the fiscal year 1987–1988
pages 40–98	spanning the years 1915 to 1941
pp. 40–98	the decade 1920–1930

    NOTE: Inclusive numbers separated by a hyphen or en dash are not used in combination with the words *from* or *between,* as in "from 1955–60" or "between 1970–90." Instead, phrases like these are written as "from 1955 to 1960" or "between 1970 and 1990."

11. Units of measurement expressed in words or abbreviations are usually used only after the second element of an inclusive number. Symbols, however, are repeated.

    an increase in dosage from 200 to 500 mg
    ten to fifteen dollars
    30 to 35 degrees Celsius
      but
    $50 to $60 million
    45° to 48° F

12. Numbers that are part of an inclusive set or range are usually styled alike: figures with figures, spelled-out words with other spelled-out words. Similarly, approximate numbers are usually not paired with exact numbers.

    from 8 to 108 absences
    five to twenty guests
    300,000,000 to 305,000,000   *not*   300 million to 305,000,000

13. Inclusive page numbers and dates may be written in full (1981–1982) or elided (1981–82). However, inclusive dates that appear in titles and other headings are almost never elided. Dates that appear with era designations are also not elided.

467–68 *or* 467–468   1724–27 *or* 1724–1727
203–4 *or* 203–204   1463–1510
552–549 B.C.   1800–1801

NOTE: Elided numbers are used because they save space. The most commonly used style for the elision of inclusive numbers is based on the following rules:

1. Never elide inclusive numbers that have only two digits: 33–37, *not* 33–7.
2. Never elide inclusive numbers when the first number ends in 00: 100–108, *not* 100–08 *and not* 100–8.
3. In other numbers, omit *only* the hundreds digit from the higher number: 232–34, *not* 232–4.
4. Where the next-to-last digit of both numbers is zero, write only one digit for the higher number: 103–4, *not* 103–04.

467–68 *or* 467–468   203–4 *or* 203–204
1724–27 *or* 1724–1727   1800–1801
550–602   552–549 B.C.
1463–1510

14. Plurals The plurals of written-out numbers are formed by the addition of *-s* or *-es*.

Back in the thirties these roads were unpaved.

Christmas shoppers bought the popular toy in twos and threes.

15. The plurals of figures are formed by adding *-s*. Some writers prefer to add an apostrophe before the *-s*. For more on the plurals of figures, see paragraphs 18 and 19 under Plurals, page 110, and paragraph 5 under Apostrophe, page 50.

This ghost town was booming back in the 1840s.

The first two artificial hearts to be implanted in human patients were Jarvik-7s.

but also

1's and *7*'s that looked alike

Specific Styling Conventions

The following paragraphs describe styling practices commonly followed for specific types of situations involving numbers. The paragraphs are arranged under the following alphabetical headings:

Addresses	Fractions and Decimal	Ratios
Dates	Fractions	Serial Numbers and
Degrees of Temperature	Money	Miscellaneous
and Arc	Percentages	Numbers
Enumerations and	Proper Names	Time of Day
Outlines		Units of Measurement

1. Addresses Arabic numerals are used for all building, house, apartment, room, and suite numbers except for *one*, which is written out.

6 Lincoln Road
1436 Fremont Street
but
One Bayside Drive

NOTE: When the address of a building is used as its name, the number in the address is written out.

Fifty Maple Street

2. Numbered streets have their numbers written as ordinals. There are two distinct conventions for the styling of numbered street names. The first, useful where space is limited, calls for Arabic numerals to denote all numbered streets above Twelfth; numbered street names from First through Twelfth are written out. A second, more formal, convention calls for the writing out of all numbered street names up to and including One Hundredth.

19 South 22nd Street   145 East 145th Street
167 West Second Avenue   122 East Forty-second Street
One East Ninth Street   36 East Fiftieth
in the Sixties (streets from 60th to 69th)
in the 120s (streets from 120th to 129th)

NOTE: A disadvantage of the first convention is that the direct juxtaposition of the house or building number and the street number may occur when there is no intervening word such as a compass direction. In these cases, a spaced hyphen may be inserted to distinguish the two numbers, or the second convention may be used and the street number written out.

2018–14th Street
2018 Fourteenth Street

3. Arabic numerals are used to designate interstate, federal, and state highways and, in some states, county roads.

U.S. Route 1   *or*   U.S. 1   Massachusetts 57
Interstate 91 *or*   I-91   County 213

4. **Dates** Year numbers are styled as figures. However, if a number representing a year begins a sentence, it may be written in full or the sentence rewritten to avoid beginning it with a figure. (For additional examples, see paragraph 3 under Numbers as Words or Figures, page 137.)

1988
1888–96
Fifteen eighty-eight marked the end to Spanish ambitions for the control of England.
    or
Spanish ambitions for the control of England ended in 1588 with the destruction of their "Invincible Armada."

5. A year number may be abbreviated, or cut back to its last two digits, in informal writing or when an event is so well-known that it needs no century designation. In these cases an apostrophe precedes the numerals. For more on this use of the apostrophe, see paragraph 5 under Apostrophe, page 50.

> He always maintained that he'd graduated from Korea, Clash of '52.
> the blizzard of '88

6. Full dates (month, day, and year) may be styled in one of two distinct patterns. The traditional styling is the month-day-year sequence, with the year set off by commas that precede and follow it. An alternate styling is the inverted date, or day-month-year sequence, which does not require commas. This sequence is used in U.S. government publications and in the military.

> *traditional style*
> July 8, 1776, was a warm, sunny day in Philadelphia.
> the explosion on July 16, 1945, at Alamaogordo
> *military style*
> the explosion on 16 July 1945 at Alamogordo
> Lee's surrender to Grant on 9 April 1865 at Appomattox

7. Ordinal numbers are not used in expressions of full dates. Even though the numbers may be pronounced as ordinals, they are written as cardinal numbers. Ordinals may be used, however, to express a date without an accompanying year, and they are always used when preceded in a date by the word *the*.

> December 4, 1829
> on December 4th   *or*   on December 4
> on the 4th of December

8. Commas are usually omitted from dates that include the month and year but not the day. Alternatively, writers sometimes insert the word *of* between month and year.

> in November 1805   back in January of 1981

9. Once a numerical date has been given, a reference to a related date may be written out.

> After the meeting on June 6 the conventioneers left for home, and by the seventh the hotel was virtually empty.

10. All-figure dating (as 6-8-85 or 6/8/85) is inappropriate except in the most informal correspondence. It also creates a problem of ambiguity, as it may mean either June 8, 1985, or August 6, 1985.

11. References to specific centuries are often written out, although they may be expressed in figures, especially when they form the first element of a compound modifier.

the nineteenth century
a sixteenth-century painting
but also
20th-century revolutions

12. In general correspondence, the name of a specific decade often takes a short form. Although many writers place an apostrophe before the shortened word and a few capitalize it, both the apostrophe and the capitalization are often omitted when the context clearly indicates that a date is being referred to.

in the turbulent seventies
but also
back in the 'forties
in the early Fifties

13. The name of a specific decade is often expressed in numerals, usually in plural form. (For more on the formation of plural numbers, see paragraphs 14 and 15 under Punctuation and Inflection, page 182.) The figure may be shortened with an apostrophe to indicate the missing numerals, but any sequence of such numbers should be styled consistently. (For more on this use of the apostrophe, see paragraph 5 under Apostrophe, page 50.)

the 1950s and 1960s   *or*   the '50s and '60s
but not
the 1950s and '60s
and not
the '50's and '60's

14. Era designations precede or follow words that specify centuries or numerals that specify years. Era designations are unspaced and are nearly always abbreviated; they are usually printed as small capitals and typed as regular capitals, and they may or may not be punctuated with periods. Any date that is given without an era designation or context is understood to mean A.D. The two most commonly used abbreviations are B.C. (before Christ) and A.D. (*anno Domini*, "in the year of our Lord"). The abbreviation B.C. is placed after the date, while A.D. is usually placed before the date but after a century designation.

1792–1750 B.C.
A.D. 35
the second century A.D.
between 7 B.C. and A.D. 22

15. **Degrees of temperature and arc** In technical writing, figures are generally used for quantities expressed in degrees. In addition, the degree symbol (°) rather than the word *degree* is used with the figure. With the Kelvin scale, however, neither the word *degree* nor the symbol is used with the figure.

a 45° angle
6°40′10″N
32° F
0° C
Absolute zero is zero kelvins or 0 K.

16. In general writing, the quantity expressed in degrees may or may not be written out, depending on the styling conventions being followed. In general, a figure is followed by the degree symbol or the word *degree;* a written-out number is always followed by the word *degree.*

> latitude 43°19″N
> latitude 43 degrees N
> a difference of 43 degrees latitude
> The temperature has risen thirty degrees since this morning.

17. Enumerations and outlines Both run-in and vertical enumerations are often numbered. In run-in enumerations, each item is preceded by a number (or an italicized letter) enclosed in parentheses. The items in the list are separated by commas if the items are brief and have little or no internal punctuation; if the items are complex, they are separated by semicolons. The entire run-in enumeration is introduced by a colon if it is preceded by a full clause.

> We feel that she should (1) increase her administrative skills, (2) pursue additional professional education, and (3) increase her production.
>
> The oldest and most basic word-processing systems consist of the following: (1) a typewriter for keyboarding information, (2) a console to house the storage medium, and (3) the medium itself.
>
> The vendor of your system should (1) instruct you in the care and maintenance of your system; (2) offer regularly scheduled maintenance to ensure that the system is clean, with lubrication and replacement of parts as necessary; and (3) respond promptly to service calls.

18. In vertical enumerations, the numbers are usually not enclosed in parentheses but are followed by a period. Each item in the enumeration begins its own line, which is either flush left or indented. Runover lines are usually aligned with the first word that follows the number, and figures are aligned on the periods that follow them. Each item on the list is usually capitalized if the items on the list are syntactically independent of the words that introduce them. However, style varies on this point, and use of a lowercase style for such items is fairly common. There is no terminal punctuation following the items unless at least one of the items is a complete sentence, in which case a period follows each item. Items that are syntactically dependent on the words that introduce them begin with a lowercase letter and carry the same punctuation marks that they would if they were a run-in series in a sentence.

> Required skills include the following:
> 1. Shorthand

    2. Typing
    3. Transcription

To type a three-column table, follow this procedure:
    1. Clear tab stops.
    2. Remove margin stops.
    3. Determine precise center of the page. Set a tab stop at center.

The vendor of your system should
    1. instruct you in the care and maintenance of your system;
    2. offer regularly scheduled maintenance to ensure that the system is clean, with lubrication and replacement parts as necessary; and
    3. respond promptly to service calls.

19. Outlines make use of Roman numerals, Arabic numerals, and letters.

    I. Editorial tasks
      A. Manuscript editing
      B. Author contact
        1. Authors already under contract
        2. New authors
    II. Production responsibilities
      A. Scheduling
        1. Composition
        2. Printing and binding
      B. Cost estimates and bids
        1. Composition
        2. Printing and binding

20. Fractions and decimal fractions In running text, fractions standing alone are usually written out. Common fractions used as nouns are usually styled as open compounds, but when they are used as modifiers they are usually hyphenated. For more on written-out fractions, see page 141.

    two thirds of the paint
    a two-thirds majority
    three thirty-seconds
    seventy-two hundredths
    one one-hundredth

NOTE: Most writers try to find ways to avoid the necessity of writing out complicated fractions (as *forty-two seventy-fifths*).

21. Mixed fractions (fractions with a whole number, such as $3\frac{1}{2}$) and fractions that form part of a unit modifier are expressed in figures in running text. A *-th* is not added to a figure fraction.

    waiting $2\frac{1}{2}$ hours   a $\frac{7}{8}$-mile course
    $1\frac{1}{4}$ million population   a $2\frac{1}{2}$-kilometer race

NOTE: When mixed fractions are typewritten, the typist leaves a space between the whole number and the fraction. The space is closed up when the number is set in print. Fractions that are not on the typewriter keyboard may be made up by typing the numerator, a virgule, and the denominator in succession without spacing.

22. Fractions used with units of measurement are expressed in figures.

$\frac{1}{10}$ km $\frac{1}{4}$ mile

23. Decimal fractions are always set as figures. In technical writing, a zero is placed to the left of the decimal point when the fraction is less than a whole number. In general writing, the zero is usually omitted.

An example of a pure decimal fraction is 0.375, while 1.402 is classified as a mixed decimal fraction.
0.142857
0.2 gm
received 0.1 mg/kg diazepam i.v.
but
a .40 gauge shotgun

24. A comma is never inserted in the numbers following a decimal point.

25. Fractions and decimal fractions are usually not mixed in a text.

5$\frac{1}{2}$ lb. 2$\frac{1}{5}$ oz.
5.5 lb. 2.2 oz.
but not
5$\frac{1}{2}$ lb. 2.2 oz.

26. Money Sums of money are expressed in words or figures, according to the conventions described under Basic Conventions, page 137. If the sum can be expressed in one or two words, it is usually written out in running text. But if several sums are mentioned in the sentence or paragraph, all are usually expressed as figures. When the amount is written out, the unit of currency is also written out. If the sum is expressed in figures, the symbol of the currency unit is used, with no space between it and the numerals.

We paid $175,000 for the house.
My change came to 87¢.
The shop charged $67.50 for hand-knit sweaters.
The price of a nickel candy bar seems to have risen to more like forty cents.
Fifty dollars was stolen from my wallet.
forty thousand dollars
fifty-two dollars

27. Monetary units of mixed dollars-and-cents amounts are expressed in figures.

$16.75 $307.02 $1.95

28. Even-dollar amounts are often expressed in figures without a decimal point and zeros. But when even-dollar amounts are used in a series with or are near to amounts that include dollars and cents, the decimal point and zeros are usually added for consistency. The dollar sign is repeated before each amount in a series or inclusive range; the word *dollar* may or may not be repeated.

The price of the book rose from $7.95 in 1970 to $8.00 in 1971 and then to $8.50 in 1972.

The bids were eighty, ninety, and one hundred dollars.

or

The bids were eighty dollars, one hundred dollars, and three hundred dollars.

29. Sums of money given in round units of millions or above are usually expressed in a combination of figures and words, either with a dollar sign or with the word *dollars*. For more on the handling of round numbers, see paragraphs 7 and 8 under Numbers as Words or Figures, pages 138–139.

> 60 million dollars
> a $10 million building program
> $4.5 billion

30. In legal documents a sum of money is usually written out fully, with the corresponding figures in parentheses immediately following.

> twenty-five thousand dollars ($25,000)

31. **Percentages** In technical writing, specific percentages are styled as figure plus unspaced percent sign (%). In general correspondence, the percentage number may be expressed as a figure or spelled out, depending on the conventions that apply to it. The word *percent* rather than the symbol is used in nonscientific texts.

technical	*general*
15%	15 percent
13.5%	87.2 percent
	Twenty-five percent of the office staff was out with the flu.
	a four percent increase

32. The word *percentage* or *percent,* used as a noun without an adjacent numeral, should never be replaced by a percent sign.

> Only a small percentage of the staff objected to the smoking ban.

33. In a series or unit combination the percent sign should be included with all numbers, even if one of the numbers is zero.

> a variation of 0% to 10%

34. **Proper names** Numbers in the names of religious organizations and of churches are usually written out in ordinal form. Names of specific governmental bodies may include ordinals, and these are written out if they are one hundred or below.

> Third Congregational Church
> Seventh-Day Adventists
> Third Reich
> First Continental Congress

35. Names of electoral, judicial, and military units may include ordinal numbers that precede the noun. Numbers of one hundred or below are written out.

> First Congressional District
> Twelfth Precinct
> Ninety-eighth Congress *or* 98th Congress
> Circuit Court of Appeals for the Third Circuit
> United States Eighth Army *or* 8th United States Army

36. Specific branches of labor unions and fraternal organizations are conventionally identified by an Arabic numeral usually placed after the name.

> International Brotherhood of Electrical Workers Local 42
> Elks Lodge No. 61
> Local 98 Operating Engineers

37. **Ratios** Ratios expressed in figures use a colon, a hyphen, a virgule, or the word *to* as a means of comparison. Ratios expressed in words use a hyphen, or the word *to*.

> a 3:1 chance
> odds of 100 to 1
> a 6-1 vote
> 22.4 mi/gal
> a ratio of ten to four
> a fifty-fifty chance

38. **Serial numbers and miscellaneous numerals** Figures are used to refer to things that are numbered serially, such as chapter and page numbers, addresses, years, policy and contract numbers, and so forth.

> Serial No. 5274   vol. 5, p. 202
> Permit No. 63709   column 2
> pages 420–515   Table 16

39. Figures are also used to express stock market quotations, mathematical calculations, scores, and tabulations.

> won by a score of 8 to 2 $3\frac{1}{8}$ percent bonds
> the tally: 322 ayes, 80 nays $3 \times 15 = 45$

40. **Time of day** In running text the time of day is usually spelled out when expressed in even, half, or quarter hours.

> Quitting time is four-thirty.
> The meeting should be over by half past eleven.
> We should arrive at a quarter past five.

41. The time of day is also usually spelled out when it is followed by the contraction *o'clock* or when *o'clock* is understood.

> He should be here by four at the latest.

My appointment is at eleven o'clock.
or
My appointment is at 11 o'clock.

42. Figures are used to delineate a precise time.

The meeting is scheduled for 9:15 in the morning.
Her plane is due at 3:05 this afternoon.
The program starts at 8:30 in the evening.

43. Figures are also written when the time of day is used in conjunction with the abbreviations *a.m. (ante meridiem)* and *p.m. (post meridiem).* The punctuated lowercase styling for these abbreviations is most common, but punctuated small capital letters are also frequently used. These abbreviations should not be used in conjunction with the words *morning* or *evening;* and the word *o'clock* should not be combined with either *a.m.* or *p.m.*

8:30 a.m.   *or*   8:30 A.M.
10:30 p.m.   *or*   10:30 P.M.
8 a.m.   *or*   8 A.M.
but
9:15 in the morning
11:00 in the evening
nine o'clock

NOTE: When twelve o'clock is written, it is helpful to add the designation *midnight* or *noon,* as *a.m.* and *p.m.* sometimes cause confusion.

twelve o'clock (midnight)
twelve o'clock (noon)

44. For consistency, even-hour times should be expressed with a colon and two zeros, when used in a series or pairing with any odd-hour times.

He came at 7:00 and left at 9:45.

45. The 24-hour clock system—also called military time—uses no punctuation and is expressed without the use of *a.m., p.m.,* or *o'clock.*

from 0930 to 1100   at 1600 hours

46. Units of measurement Numbers used with units of measurement are treated according to the basic conventions explained in the first part of this section. However, in some cases writers achieve greater clarity by styling all numbers—even those below ten—that express quantities of physical measurement as numerals.

The car was travelling in excess of 80 miles an hour.
The old volume weighed three pounds and was difficult to hold in a reading position.
but also in some general texts

3 hours, 25 minutes
saw 18 eagles in 12 minutes
a 6-pound hammer
weighed 3 pounds, 5 ounces

47. When units of measurement are written as abbreviations or symbols, the adjacent numbers are always figures.

6 cm	67.6 fl oz
1 mm	4′
$4.25	98.6°

48. When two or more quantities are expressed, as in ranges or dimensions or series, an accompanying symbol is usually repeated with each figure.

4″ by 6″ cards
temperature on successive days of 30°, 55°, 43°, and 58°
$400–$500

PROOFREADERS' MARKS

℘ or ૪ or ⁊ delete; take ⁁it out	**lc** set in ⁄Lowercase ⟨lowercase⟩
⊂ close up; print as o͟ne word	***ital*** set in <u>italic</u> ⟨*italic*⟩
ℬ delete and clo⁁se up	**rom** set in <u>roman</u> ⟨roman⟩
∧ or ⟩ or ⋏ caret; insert here ⁁⟨something	**bf** set in <u>boldface</u> ⟨**boldface**⟩
# insert a⁁space	= or -/ or ⹀ or /⊬/ hyphen
eg# space⁁evenly∧where⁁indicated	⅟N or **en** or/N/ en dash ⟨1965–72⟩
stet let marked ~~text~~ stand as set	⅟M or **em** or/M/ em — or long — dash
tr transpo⁁se; change⁀order⁀the⁀	∨ superscript or superior ⟨3∨as in πr^2⟩
/ used to separate two or more marks and often as a concluding stroke at the end of an insertion	∧ subscript or inferior ⟨2∧as in H_2O⟩
⌊ ⌊ set farther to the left	∧̌ or ⅄ centered ⟨⸰ for a centered dot in $p \cdot q$⟩
⌉ set⌉ farther to the right	∿ comma
⁀ set æ or fl as ligatures æ or fl	⸰ apostrophe
= straighten ali⁁gnment	⊙ period
‖ ‖ straighten or align	; or ;/ semicolon
× imperfect or broken character	: or ⊙ colon
⧠ indent or insert em quad space	⹀⹀ or ⹀⹀ quotation marks
¶ begin a new paragraph	(/) parentheses
ⓢⓟ spell out ⟨set⟨5 lbs⟩as five pounds⟩	⌊/⌋ brackets
cap set in <u>capitals</u> ⟨CAPITALS⟩	**ok/?** query to author: has this been set as intended?
sm cap or **s.c.** set in <u>small capitals</u> ⟨SMALL CAPITALS⟩	**wf** wrong font; a character of the wr⁁ong size or esp. st⁁yle

CHAPTER 3

Tone in Writing

The tone of a communication is usually set in the first paragraph. It may be formal or informal, neutral or biased, friendly or critical, or it may reflect any number of other feelings and attitudes. Under ordinary circumstances it is maintained throughout the subsequent paragraphs to the end. What kind of tone a writer wishes to establish will depend on several factors. One important factor is the underlying reason or reasons why the letter is being written. Another important factor is the personal attitude of the writer toward the reader and the subject matter. Finally, the content of the material (for instance, whether it is general or technical) will, to some extent, determine the kind of tone a writer can establish.

The Importance of Tone

The effect of the tone of a communication on its reader cannot be over-emphasized. A letter, for example, may exhibit well-ordered layout, clean typing, attractive stationery, good sentence structure, correct spelling, and smooth flow from one paragraph to another. It may contain complete, logically presented data. Yet if the tone of the letter is abrupt or rude, the effect of the material on the reader will be negative. The reader's response should therefore be kept in mind at all times. Some principles relevant to tone in general business communications are outlined and discussed briefly in the following paragraphs. For further examples of varying tone in business letters, the reader may consult Chapter 6.

A communication should be reader-oriented. The reader's point of view and possible responses should never be forgotten, even when the writer is intent on setting forth his or her objectives. Compare the following two approaches:

abrupt
We have read with interest your article on HDPE pipe in the October 12 issue of *Plastics*. Since our marketing division is preparing a multiclient

study on plastic pipe applications, we will need offprints of the following papers you have written on this subject: . . .

polite
We have read with interest your article on HDPE pipe in the October 12 issue of *Plastics*. Our marketing division is preparing a multiclient study on plastic pipe applications—a study that will not be complete without reference to your outstanding research. We'd therefore be pleased if you'd send us offprints of the following papers you've written on the subject: . . .

A writer's familiarity with the subject matter is not automatically shared by the reader. A writer should neither write down to experts in a given field nor write over the heads of nonexperts. The way information is presented in a communication should be adjusted to the appropriate level of the reader.

Use of the personal pronouns *I, we,* and *you* can go far to personalize a communication, as can common courtesy and tactfulness. An added benefit of all three is that they make the reader feel more involved in the discussion. Passive or impersonal constructions, on the other hand, work against the writer; when overused, they depersonalize a communication and lessen its impact. Compare the following pairs of examples:

impersonal
The enclosed brochure outlining this Company's services may be of interest.

This Company is gratified when its clients offer useful suggestions.

personal
We've enclosed a brochure outlining our services, which we hope will interest you.

We appreciate your taking the time to offer such a useful suggestion.

impersonal
Reference is made to your May 1 letter received by this office yesterday.

Enclosed is the requested material.

It is the understanding of this writer that the contract is in final negotiation stages.

personal
We are referring to your May 1 letter which we received yesterday.

We're enclosing the material you requested.

I understand that the contract is in final negotiation stages.

Originality in Writing Style

The effectiveness and overall output of communications can be markedly increased if one avoids the padding and clichés that can blunt what otherwise might be incisive writing. Unfortunately, these expressions, sometimes called *business static*, have become fixtures in the vocabularies of some writers. Some of the phrases (such as "regret to advise you") are best avoided because they are stale. Others (such as "aforesaid"), while common in legal documents, sound stiff and awkward in general business contexts. Still others (such as "beg to respond") have an antiquated ring. Some expressions (such as "forward on") are redundant, while others (such as "acknowledge receipt of") are too long and unwieldy. One such clumsy phrase, "Enclosed please find," appears all too often in the first line of business letters. True, it is a convenient opener, but it is also stilted and impersonal. An opening such as "We are enclosing" or "Enclosed are" is not only more natural but also more likely to establish a rapport with the customer, client, or other recipient.

These clichéd expressions are all too often used in conspicuous areas of a text: at the very beginning where initial tone is set or at the very end where a summation is made. They are also likely to crop up at the beginning and end of individual sentences and paragraphs where particular ideas and points are being set forth. Their use in these strategic positions works against the writer: a busy reader can become exasperated if it is necessary to wade through superfluous or hackneyed expressions to get at the gist of a communication.

The following is a representative list, in alphabetical order, of expressions that are best avoided by writers seeking more clarity, brevity, and originality in their business communications.

abeyance *hold in abeyance* This expression sounds stilted in most contexts and can usually be avoided. Compare the following sentences:

> *stilted*
> We are holding our final decision in abeyance.
> *easier*
> We are deferring our final decision.
> We are delaying our final decision.
> We are holding up our final decision.

above While the use of this word as a noun ("see the above"), an adjective ("the above figure shows"), and as an adverb ("see above") is indeed acceptable, its overuse within one letter can distract a reader. Alternative expressions include the following:

> See the figure on page 27.
> See the figure at the top of the page.
> This figure shows . . .
> See the material illustrated earlier.

above-mentioned This term is overlong and is often overworked within a single letter.

> *longer*
> The above-mentioned policy . . .
> *shorter*
> This policy . . .

acknowledge receipt of   This expression requires 22 keystrokes, but the alternative expression *have received* is a 13-stroke synonym.

> *longer*
> We acknowledge receipt of your check.
>
> *shorter*
> We have received your check.

advise   This word has been overworked when meaning "to inform." It can be replaced by either of the shorter verbs *say* or *tell.*

> *longer*
> We regret to advise you that Mrs. Mercer is no longer with the firm.
>
> *shorter*
> We must tell you that Mrs. Mercer is no longer with the firm.
> We're sorry to say that Mrs. Mercer is no longer with the firm.

advised and informed   This phrase is redundant, since the two words used here simply repeat each other.

> *redundant*
> He has been advised and informed of our position.
>
> *lean*
> He has been told of our position.
> He knows our position.

affix (one's) signature to   This expression is padding, and can be reduced to *sign.*

> *padded*
> Please affix your signature to the enclosed documents.
>
> *lean*
> Please sign these documents.
> Please sign the enclosed documents.

aforementioned/aforesaid   These words are commonly used in legal documents but sound verbose and pompous in general contexts. The same idea can usually be conveyed by one of the demonstrative adjectives *(this, that, these, those).*

> *verbose*
> The aforementioned company . . .
>
> *natural*
> This company . . .
> The company in question . . .
> The company mentioned earlier . . .
>
> *verbose*
> We must reach a decision regarding the aforesaid dispute.
>
> *natural*
> We must make a decision about this (that) dispute.

amplify to a maximum   This expression may be pared down to *maximize*.

> *padded*
> ... expect all salesmen to amplify to a maximum their sales calls next month.
>
> *lean*
> ... expect all salesmen to maximize their next month's sales calls.

—*see also* REDUCE TO A MINIMUM

and etc.   This phrase is redundant, because *etc.* is the abbreviation of the Latin *et cetera* meaning "and the rest." Omit the *and*.

> *not*
> carbon packs, onionskin, bond, and etc.
>
> *instead*
> carbon packs, onionskin, bond, etc.

and/or   This expression is best restricted to use between two alternatives, where it means "A or B or both." In longer series, such as "A, B and/or C," *and/or* will likely be either vague or unnecessary.

as per   This expression has been overworked when meaning "as," "in accordance with," and "following." It is an unoriginal and formulaic way to begin a letter, paragraph, or sentence.

> *overworked*
> As per your request of ...
> As per our telephone conversation of ...
> As per our agreement ...
>
> *more natural*
> As you requested ...
> According to your request ...
> In accordance with your request ...
> As a follow-up to our telephone conversation ...
> In accordance with our telephone conversation ...
> As we agreed ...
> According to our agreement ...

as regards   This phrase can also be expressed by the terms *concerning* or *regarding*.

> *stiff*
> As regards your complaint ...
> *easier*
> Let's talk about your complaint.

as stated above   This phrase can be more naturally expressed.

> As we have said ...

assuring you that   This is an outmoded participial-phrase ending to a business letter that should not be used.

outmoded
Assuring you that your cooperation will be appreciated, I remain

Sincerely yours

current
I will appreciate your cooperation.

Sincerely yours

as to   This phrase has been as overworked as the phrase *as per*. It can be replaced with *regarding, concerning, about,* or *of.*

overworked
As to your second question . . .

fresher
Regarding your second question . . .
Coming to your second question . . .
Let's look at your second question.

overworked
We have no means of judging as to the wisdom of that decision.

fresher
We cannot (can't) judge the wisdom of that decision.

at all times   This may be shortened to *always*.

longer
We shall be glad to meet with you at all times.

shorter
We'll always be glad to meet with you.
We're always glad to meet with you.

at an early date   This wording is both long and vague. Shorter and clearer alternatives are *immediately* and *by* (date).

at once and by return mail   These terms are repetitious when joined together; either *at once* or *immediately* will suffice.

repetitive
Please send us your check at once and by return mail.

succinct
Please send us your check at once (*or* immediately).

attached hereto/attached herewith   These phrases are quite impersonal and may be expressed in more personal ways.

Attached is/are . . .
We are attaching . . .
We have attached . . .
You'll see attached . . .

—*see also* ENCLOSED HEREWITH

at this point in time/at this time   These phrases may be shortened to *now,* *currently,* or *at (the) present.* Similarly, *at that point in time* and *at that time* may be shortened to *then.*

at this writing   This may be shortened to *now.*

at your earliest convenience   This expression manages to convey nothing more in 28 keystrokes than the alternative *as soon as you can,* which requires only 18 strokes and states the case explicitly. Other alternative expressions include *now, immediately, by* (date), and *within* (number) *days.*

basic fundamentals   This is redundant. Either *the basics* or *the fundamentals* may be substituted.

basis   *on the basis of, on a———basis*   These phrases are somewhat long-winded and can often be avoided.

Longer
On the basis of what we have seen so far, we project a six-month production schedule.

They accepted the project on the basis of the merits of that view.

We will ship parts on an as-needed basis.

Shorter
From what we have seen so far, we project a six-month production schedule.

They accepted the project because of the merits of that view.

We will ship parts as needed.

However, these phrases are sometimes very useful, and there often is no good way to avoid them.

because   Using a clause beginning with *because* as the subject of a sentence is common in speech but is usually avoided in formal writing.

Not
Because you have not received the shipment yet does not mean we did not send it.

Instead
The fact that you have not received the shipment yet does not mean we did not send it.

— *see also* REASON IS BECAUSE

beg   *beg to acknowledge, beg to advise, beg to state*   These and other such *beg* combinations sound antiquated. The following may be used instead:

We acknowledge . . .
We have received . . .

Thank you for . . .
We're pleased to tell you . . .

brought to our notice   This is long and may be recast as follows:

We note . . .
We notice . . .
We see . . .

contents carefully noted   This expression contributes little or no information and should be omitted.

not
Yours of the 1st received and contents carefully noted.
instead
We've read carefully your June 1 letter.
We've read your June 1 letter.
The instructions in your June 1 letter have been followed.

dated   This word is unnecessary when used in phrases like "your letter dated June 1." The word *dated* may simply be omitted.

your June 1 letter
your letter of June 1

deem (it)   This is a stiff way of saying *think* or *believe*.

stiff
We deem it advisable that you . . .
easier
We think you ought to . . .
We think it advisable that you . . .

demand and insist   These words are redundant when joined together; the use of just one of the following at a time will suffice: *demand* or *insist* or *require*.

despite the fact that   This expression may be pared down to *although* or *though*.

due to/due to the fact that   These are both stiff and may be reduced to *because (of)* or *since*.

duly   This word is meaningless in expressions like "Your order has been duly forwarded," and it can almost always be omitted.

Your order has been forwarded.
We've forwarded your order.

earnest endeavor   This phrase can be cloying when used in sentences such as "It will be our earnest endeavor to serve our customers." It should be replaced with more straightforward phrasing, such as "We shall try to serve our customers."

enclosed herewith/enclosed please find   These are impersonal and stilted expressions. The following are better alternatives:

> We enclose . . .
> We are enclosing . . .
> We have enclosed . . .
> Enclosed is/are . . .

—*see also* ATTACHED HERETO/ATTACHED HEREWITH

endeavor   This is an eight-letter verb that can be replaced by the three-letter verb *try,* which is synonymous and not pompous.

> *pompous and longer*
> We shall endeavor to . . .
>
> *direct and shorter*
> We'll (*or* We shall) try to . . .
> We'll make a real effort to . . .
> We'll make every effort to . . .
> We'll do everything we can to . . .
> We'll do our best to . . .

esteemed   This word can seem overly effusive when used in a sentence like "We welcome your esteemed favor of June 9." This sentence can be recast as follows: "Thank you for your letter of June 9."

favor   This word should never be used in the sense of a letter, an order, a check, or other such item.

finalize/prioritize   The suffix *-ize* is frequently added to nouns and adjectives to coin new words, such as *hospitalize, computerize, familiarize,* and *Americanize.* The *-ize* suffix has been applied in this way for hundreds of years, and most words ending in *-ize* are completely acceptable to nearly everyone. However, some 20th-century coinages of this sort, such as *finalize* and *prioritize,* strike some people as being needless neologisms or bureaucratic gobbledygook. To avoid such objections, replace them with "to put in final form," "to give final approval to," and "to rate (or list) in order of priority."

for the purpose of   This expression may be more succinctly worded as *for.*

> *padded*
> necessary for purposes of accounting
> *lean*
> necessary for accounting

forward on   This phrase is redundant, since *forward* alone conveys the meaning adequately.

> *redundant*
> We have forwarded your complaint on to the proper authorities.
> *lean*
> We have forwarded your complaint to the proper authorities.

hand (one) herewith   This expression sounds inflated and can be replaced with leaner alternatives.

> *inflated*
> We are handing you herewith an invoice for the shipment of September 17.
>
> *leaner*
> We are enclosing an invoice for the shipment of September 17.
> Enclosed is an invoice for the shipment of September 17.

have before me   This expression is superfluous. Obviously, the writer has previous correspondence at hand when responding to a letter.

> *not*
> I have before me your letter of June 1 . . .
>
> *but*
> In reply to your June 1 letter . . .

hereto —*see* ATTACHED HERETO/ATTACHED HEREWITH

herewith —*see* ATTACHED HERETO/ATTACHED HEREWITH; ENCLOSED HERE-WITH/ENCLOSED PLEASE FIND

hoping for the favor (*or* to hear)   These and other such participial-phrase endings for business letters are now outmoded and should be omitted.

> *not*
> Hoping for the favor of a reply, I remain
>
> *instead*
> I look forward to hearing from you.
> I look forward to your reply.
> May I hear from you soon?

I am/I remain   These expressions are outmoded when used as lead-ins to complimentary closes and should not be used. Instead, the writer may simply end the body of the letter on a cordial note and let the complimentary close stand on its own.

> *not*
> Looking forward to a speedy reply from you, I am (*or* remain)
>
> *instead*
> I look forward to your immediate reply.
> I am looking forward to a reply from you soon.
> May I please have an immediate reply?
> Will you please reply soon?

immediately and at once   These terms are redundant when joined together; however, each element of the expression may be used separately.

> May we hear from you immediately?
> May we hear from you at once?

incumbent *it is incumbent upon (one)* The thought here is more easily expressed as *I/we must, you must,* or *he/she/they must.*

in re This expression should be avoided in the body of general business letters, although it is often used in the subject line of letters and in legal documents. It may be replaced with *regarding, concerning, in regard to,* or *about.*

> *stiff*
> In re our telephone conversation of . . .
> *easier*
> Concerning our telephone conversation of . . .

institute the necessary inquiries This expression is overlong and overformal, and may be reworded as follows:

> We shall inquire . . .
> We'll find out . . .
> We are inquiring . . .

in the amount of This is a long way of saying *for.*

> *longer*
> We are sending you a check in the amount of $50.95.
> *shorter*
> We are sending you a check for $50.95.
> We are sending you a $50.95 check.

in the course of This phrase may be more concisely expressed by *during* or *while.*

> *longer*
> In the course of the study . . .
> *shorter*
> During the study . . .
> While we were studying . . .

in the event that This phrase may be more concisely expressed by *if* or *in case.*

> *longer*
> In the event that you cannot meet with me next week, we shall . . .
> *shorter*
> If you cannot meet with me next week, we shall . . .

in view of the fact that This expression can be shortened to *because (of)* or *since.*

> *longer*
> In view of the fact that he is now president of . . .
> He was terminated in view of the fact that he had been negligent.
> *shorter*
> Since he is now president of . . .
> He was terminated because of negligence.

in view of the foregoing   This expression can be shortened to *therefore*.

> *longer*
> In view of the foregoing, we cannot accept the terms of the agreement.
> *shorter*
> Therefore, we cannot accept the terms of the agreement.

is because   —*see* REASON IS BECAUSE

it is incumbent upon   —*see* INCUMBENT

it is interesting to note that   This expression often constitutes padding and thus can be dropped or replaced with a transitional word or short phrase.

> *padded*
> It is interesting to note that by this time last year, all orders received in January had been met.
> *lean*
> By this time last year, all orders received in January had been met.
> Moreover, by this time last year, all orders received in January had been met.

it is within (one's) power   —*see* POWER

it may be said that   This phrase often constitutes padding and can be omitted.

> *padded*
> Indeed, it may be said that without the support of this department, this project would not have succeeded.
> *lean*
> Indeed, without the support of this department, this project would not have succeeded.

-ize   —*see* FINALIZE/PRIORITIZE

line   This word is a vague substitute for one of the following more explicit terms: *merchandise, line of goods* (or *merchandise*), *goods, product(s), service(s), system(s)*.

meet with (one's) approval   This is a stiff phrase more easily expressed as *is acceptable, I accept, we approve*.

> *stiff*
> If the plan meets with Mr. Doe's approval . . .
> *easier*
> If the plan is acceptable to Mr. Doe . . .
> If Mr. Doe accepts the plan . . .

note   *we note that, you will note that*   These expressions often constitute padding and thus should be dropped.

padded
We note that your prospectus states . . .
You will note that the amount in the fourth column . . .

lean
Your prospectus states . . .
The amount in the fourth column . . .

NOTE: If a word of this type is required, a more natural substitute is *see:*

We *see* that you have paid the bill in full.

oblige   This word is archaic when used in a sentence such as "Please reply to this letter and oblige." This sentence should be recast to read as follows: "Please reply to this letter immediately."

of the opinion that   This is a stiff way of saying, "We think (*or* believe) that," "Our opinion is that," "Our position is that."

our Mr., Ms., Miss, Mrs.   This phrasing is best avoided.

not
Our Mr. Lee will call on you next Tuesday.

but
Our sales representative, Mr. Lee, will call on you next Tuesday.
Mr. Lee, our sales representative, will call on you next Tuesday.

party   While idiomatic in legal documents, this word is nevertheless awkward in general business contexts when the meaning is "individual" or "person."

awkward
We understand that you are the party who called earlier.

smoother
We understand that you are the person (*or* individual *or* one) who called earlier.

pending receipt of   This phrase is used in legal documents, but in general contexts it is simply a stiff way of saying "until we receive."

stiff
We are holding your order, pending receipt of your check.

easier
We'll ship your order as soon as we receive your check.

permit me to remain   This expression is outmoded and should not be used as part of the last sentence in a business letter.

place an order for   This phrase takes 18 keystrokes, but the verb *order* takes only 5 strokes.

position   *be in a position to*   The phrase "We are not in a position to" is unnecessarily long and may be recast to shorter and more personal phrases, such as "We cannot" or "We are unable."

power *it is (not) within (one's) power to* This is a lengthy way of saying "We can," "We are able to," "We cannot," or "We are unable to."

> *longer*
> It is not within our power to back such an expensive project.
>
> *shorter*
> We cannot back such an expensive project.

prepared to offer This is a set phrase that can be reworded in a number of more original ways.

> *set*
> We are prepared to offer you the following discounts: . . .
>
> *varied*
> We can offer you these discounts: . . .
> We're ready to offer you these discounts: . . .
> We offer the following discounts: . . .

prioritize —*see* FINALIZE/PRIORITIZE

prior to This phrase is a stiff way to say *before*.

> *stiff*
> Prior to receipt of your letter of July 1, we . . .
>
> *easier*
> Before we received your July 1 letter, we . . .
> Before receipt of your July 1 letter, we . . .
> Before receiving your July 1 letter, we . . .

—*see also* SUBSEQUENT TO

pursuant to This is a stiff phrase that unfortunately occurs in the very beginnings of many follow-up letters and memorandums. It can be replaced with *According to, Following up, As a follow-up to,* or *In accordance with.*

> *stiff*
> Pursuant to our telephone conversation of June 1, let me say . . .
>
> *easier*
> Following up our June 1 telephone conversation, I can say . . .

reason is because This expression is often objected to as ungrammatical and redundant, despite the fact that it has been used by some well-known writers. While its use can be defended, it is liable to objection and is best replaced with one of the following: *The reason is, The reason is that, Because.*

receipt —*see* PENDING RECEIPT OF

receipt is acknowledged This is an unnecessarily impersonal passive construction more concisely expressed as *We received* or *We have received.*

recent date *of recent date* This is an unwieldy way to indicate an undated letter; the alternatives *your recent letter* or *your undated letter* are smoother. If the letter is dated, it is best to repeat the exact date.

reduce to a minimum   This phrase may be pared down to *minimize*.

> *wordy*
> This product reduces to a minimum the air pollution in work areas.
>
> *succinct*
> This product minimizes air pollution in work areas.

—*see also* AMPLIFY TO A MAXIMUM

refuse and decline   These words are redundant when used together; the use of one will suffice: *refuse* or *decline*.

> *redundant*
> We must refuse and decline any further dealings with your company.
>
> *lean*
> We must refuse any further dealings . . .
> We must decline to have any further dealings . . .

—*see also* DEMAND AND INSIST

regard   *in regard to, with regard to*   Both of these expressions can often be replaced with *about* for more concise wording.

> *wordy*
> We wrote to them in regard to their unpaid balance several times during this period.
>
> *concise*
> We wrote to them about their unpaid balance several times during this period.

reiterate again   The adverb *again* is redundant in this phrase, because the verb *reiterate* carries the total meaning by itself.

> *redundant*
> Let me reiterate our policy again.
>
> *succinct*
> Let me reiterate our policy.
> Let me restate our policy.
> Let me state our policy again.
> May I state our policy again?

said   This adjective is idiomatic in legal documents; however, it sounds stiff in general contexts.

> *stiff*
> a discussion of said matters
>
> *easier*
> a discussion of those matters

same   This word is an awkward substitute for the pronoun *it* or *them*, or for the applicable noun.

awkward
We have your check and we thank you for same.
Your July 2 inquiry has been received and same is being researched.

easier
Thank you for your check which arrived yesterday.
Your July 2 inquiry has been received and is being researched.

sells at a price of   This is a 19-keystroke phrase more concisely expressed as *costs, sells for,* or *is priced at.*

separate cover   *under separate cover*   This is an overlong and vague phrase. If a specific mailing method (such as Special Delivery) is not to be indicated, the adverb *separately* should be substituted.

subsequent to   This expression is longer than its synonyms *after* or *following.*

> *longer*
> Subsequent to the interview, she . . .
>
> *shorter*
> After the interview, she . . .

—*see also* PRIOR TO

thanking you in advance   This is an outmoded participial-phrase ending that should not be used in modern business letters. Writers who use this phrase are also presumptuous enough to assume that their requests will be honored.

> *not*
> Thanking you in advance for your help, I am
>
>   Sincerely yours
>
> *instead*
> Your help will be appreciated.
> I'll appreciate your help.
> Any help you may give me will be greatly appreciated.
> I'll appreciate any help you may give.
> If you can help me, I'll appreciate it.
> I'll be grateful for your help.

therefor/therein/thereon   These words are commonly used in legal documents, but sound stiff in general business contexts.

> *stiff*
> The order is enclosed herewith with payment therefor.
> The safe is in a secure area with the blueprints kept therein.
> Enclosed please find Forms X, Y, and Z; please affix your signature thereon.
>
> *easier*
> We're enclosing a check with our order.
> The blueprints are kept in the safe, which is located in a secure area.
> Please sign Forms X, Y, and Z, which we have enclosed.

to all intents and purposes   This phrase can usually be shortened to *in effect*.

> *longer*
> Their response was, to all intents and purposes, no response at all.
>
> *shorter*
> Their response was, in effect, no response at all.

trusting you will   This is an outmoded participial-phrase ending that should not be used in business letters. Writers who use this phrase are also presumptuous enough to assume that their requests will be honored.

> *not*
> Trusting that you will inform me of your decision soon, I am
>   Sincerely yours
>
> *but*
> I hope that you'll give me your decision soon.
> Will you please give me your decision soon?

under date of   This is an awkward phrase that should be omitted.

> *not*
> your letter under date of December 31
>
> *instead*
> your December 31 letter
> your letter of December 31

—*see also* DATED

under separate cover   —*see* SEPARATE COVER

(the) undersigned   While common in legal documents, this term is awkward and impersonal in general writing.

> *awkward*
> Please return these photographs to the undersigned.
> The undersigned believes that . . .
>
> *easier*
> Please return these photographs to me.
> I believe that . . .

up to the present writing   This expression is padding and should be omitted.

> *padded*
> Up to the present writing, we do not seem to have received your manuscript.
>
> *lean*
> We have not yet received your manuscript.
> As of now, we have not received your manuscript.
> We still haven't received your manuscript.
> We haven't received your manuscript.

valued This word is redundant when used after the verb *appreciate* which means "to value or admire highly."

> *redundant*
> We appreciate your valued order of . . .
>
> *lean*
> We appreciate your order of . . .
> Your order is, of course, appreciated . . .

with the exception of This phrase can usually be shortened to *except* or *except for*.

> *longer*
> We have completed planning for all of the stages of manufacturing with the exception of packaging.
>
> *shorter*
> We have completed planning for all of the stages of manufacturing except packaging.

would When unnecessarily repeated, this word weakens the impact of a statement.

> *wordy*
> I would think that sales would improve if we hired her.
>
> *lean*
> I think that sales would improve if we hired her.
>
> *leaner*
> Sales would improve if we hired her.

CHAPTER 4

Style in Business Correspondence

The word *style* as applied to business-letter writing encompasses the format of the letter; the punctuation, capitalization, and other mechanical aspects of the writing; grammar and word usage; and the traditional conventions relating to the etiquette of letter-writing, such as proper salutations, closings, and forms of address. This chapter, however, focuses solely on questions of format and general punctuation patterns. For more on punctuation and the details relating to capitalization and other mechanics of writing, see Chapter 2, "The Mechanics of Writing." For a discussion of grammar and word usage, see Chapter 1, "Composition and Grammar" and Chapter 3, "Tone in Writing." For a list of forms of address, see Chapter 5, "Forms of Address."

Style in business correspondence, like language itself, is not a static entity. It has changed over the years to meet the varying needs of its users, and it continues to do so. For example, the open-punctuation pattern and the Simplified Letter have recently gained wide popularity, while the closed-punctuation pattern and the Indented Letter, once considered standard formats, are now little used in the United States. In many cases, this process of change had led to the situation in which writers have a range of alternatives available to them regarding aspects of letter-writing style. This chapter and the ones that follow have been written with these alternative acceptable stylings in mind, and, whenever such alternative stylings exist, they are presented and described. If there are reasons to prefer one over another, the reasons are explained; however, in many cases, the choice will be a question of individual taste, and writers will have to use their own judgment to choose among the acceptable styles.

The Business Letter as Image-Maker

All of the elements of business-letter style come together in a letter to produce a tangible reflection on paper not only of the writer's ability and knowledge and the typist's competence, but also of an organization's total image. For example, well-prepared business letters reflect a firm's pride and its concern for quality. On the other hand, poorly prepared correspondence can create such a negative impression on its recipients that they may have second thoughts about pursuing business relationships with the writer or the writer's organization. This is a special consideration for small businesses. The business letter, then, is actually an indicator of overall organizational style, regardless of the size of the firm. Thus, the impression created by attractively and accurately typed, logically oriented, and clearly written letters can be a crucial factor in the success of any business.

A businessperson may devote as much as 50 percent or more of his or her workday to correspondence. This includes planning and thinking out the directions, tone, and content of outgoing letters or reading and acting on incoming letters. Secretaries spend an even higher proportion of their time on correspondence. And all this time costs money. However, if both writer and typist keep in mind the following simple aids to good letter production, the time and money involved will have been well spent:

1. Stationery should be of high-quality paper having excellent correcting or erasing properties.
2. Typing should be neat and accurate with any corrections or erasures rendered invisible.
3. The essential elements of a letter (such as the date line, inside address, message, and signature block) and any other included parts should conform in page placement and format with one of the generally acceptable, up-to-date business-letter stylings (such as the Simplified Letter, the Block Letter, the Modified Block Letter, the Modified Semi-block Letter, or the Hanging-indented Letter).
4. The language of the letter should be clear, concise, grammatically correct, and devoid of padding and clichés.
5. The ideas in the message should be logically oriented, with the writer always keeping in mind the reader's reaction.
6. All statistical data should be accurate and complete.
7. All names should be checked for accuracy of spelling and style.

Letter Balance and Letterhead Design

It has often been said that an attractive letter should look like a symmetrically framed picture with even margins working as a frame for the typed lines that are balanced under the letterhead. But how many letters really do look like framed pictures? Planning ahead before starting to type is the key to letter symmetry. The following steps will help the writer or typist achieve the desired appearance:

1. Estimate the approximate number of words in the letter or the general length of the message by looking over the writer's rough draft or one's shorthand notes, or by checking the length of a dictated source.
2. Make mental notes of any long quotations, tabular data, long lists or footnotes or of the occurrence of scientific names and formulas that may require margin adjustments, a different typeface, or even handwork within the message.
3. Set the left and right margin stops according to the estimated letter length: about one inch for very long letters (300 words or more, or at least two pages), about one and one-half inches for medium-length ones (about 100–300 words), and about two inches for very short ones (100 words or less).
4. Remember that the closing parts of a letter take 10–12 lines (two inches) or more and that the bottom margin will be at least six lines (one inch). Thus you will want to allow at least three inches from the last line of the message to the bottom of the page.
5. Use the scale on the typewriter's page-end indicator or a guide sheet that numbers each line in the margin as a bottom margin warning; or lightly pencil a warning mark on the paper.
6. Single-space within paragraphs; double-space between paragraphs. Very short letters (up to three sentences) may be double-spaced throughout.
7. Set continuation-sheet margins to match those of the first sheet, and carry over at least three lines of the message to the continuation sheet.

With experience, a secretary can easily estimate the overall length of a letter. An inexperienced secretary should refer to a letter placement table such as Table 4.1 on page 176. As the table suggests, short letters may be typewritten on half-sheets, on Executive-size stationery, or on full-size stationery with wide margins. Some offices, however, use a standard six-inch typing line for all letters on full-size stationery, regardless of length, because it eliminates the need to reset tabs.

Very short letters typed on full-size stationery may create spacing problems. There are three simple ways to handle the extra space involved in these letters:

1. Use the six-inch line but lengthen the space between the date and the inside address, between the complimentary close and the signature, and between the signature and the transcriber's initials or enclosure notations.
2. Use the six-inch line but double-space. Double spacing should be used only in very short letters (about six lines or less, or up to three sentences). If a double-spaced letter contains more than one paragraph,

Table 4.1
Letter Placement Table
Three Sizes of Stationery

Lines in Letter Body	Words in Letter Body	Number of Blank Lines between Date and Inside Address*	Typewriter Marginal Stops Elite/Pica	Length of Typing Line	
				Inches	Spaces Elite/Pica
Half-sheet Stationery: Assume Letterhead takes 7 vertical lines. (Baronial—center No. 33 for Elite; No. 28 for Pica)					
9–10	60–66	7	15–60/10–50	4	48/40
11–12	67–73	6	15–59/10–50	4	48/40
13–14	74–80	5	15–60/10–50	4	48/40
15–16	81–87	4	15–60/10–50	4	48/40
17–18	88–94	3	15–60/10–50	4	48/40
19–20	95–100	2	15–60/10–50	4	48/40
Executive-size Stationery: Assume Letterhead takes 8 lines. (Monarch—center No. 43, Elite; No. 36, Pica)					
13–14	95–115	8	15–75/10–60	5	60/50
15–16	116–135	7	15–75/10–60	5	60/50
17–18	136–155	6	15–75/10–60	5	60/50
19–20	156–175	5	15–75/10–60	5	60/50
Full-size Stationery: Assume Letterhead takes 9 lines. (Standard—center No. 51, Elite; No. 42, Pica)					
3–5	under 100	7–12	25–75/22–62	4	48/40
6–10	100–200	4–8	20–80/17–67	5	60/50
11–14	175–200	7	15–87/12–72	6	72/60
15–18	201–225	6	15–87/12–72	6	72/60
19–22	226–250	5	15–87/12–72	6	72/60
23–26	251–275	4	15–87/12–72	6	72/60
27–30	276–300**	3	15–87/12–72	6	72/60

*Assume that the date is typed three lines below the last line of the letterhead on all letters.
**Letters consisting of more than 300 words should be two-page letters.

an indented-paragraph format should be used to help distinguish the paragraphs.

3. Use a four-inch or five-inch typing line, setting margins as suggested in Table 4.1 above.

Letterhead Design

Letterhead designs vary. Some letterheads are positioned at the center of the top of the page, others are laid out across the top of the page from the left to the right margin, and still others are more heavily balanced right or left of the center. Sometimes a company's name and logo appear at the top of the page, while its address and other data are printed at the bottom.

Regardless of layout and design, a typical business letterhead contains all or some of the following elements, with items 2, 3, 5, and 6 being essential:

1. logo
2. full name of the firm, company, corporation, institution, or group
3. full street address
4. suite, room, or building number, if needed—post office box number, if applicable
5. city, state, and zip code
6. area code and telephone number(s)
7. other data (as telex or cable references, branch offices, or products or services offered)

The names of particular departments, plants, groups, or divisions may be printed on the letterhead of extremely large or diversified companies or institutions. Other organizations such as large law firms may have the full names of their partners and staff attorneys all listed on the letterhead. Elaborate letterhead layouts require especially careful letter planning to avoid an unbalanced look. For example, a letterhead with a long list of names on the left side might be best balanced by use of the Modified Block Letter, where the date, reference numbers, and signature appear on the right side of the page.

High corporate officers frequently use a personalized or executive letterhead. Here the standard company letterhead design is supplemented with the name of the office (as "Office of the President") or with the full name and business title of the officer (as "John M. Jones, Jr., President") printed or engraved in small letters one or two lines beneath the letterhead at or near the left margin. The officer's business title may appear on the same line as his or her name if space permits and if both name and title are short, or it may be blocked directly below the name. Executive stationery is often not printed but instead engraved on a better grade of paper than that of the standard, printed company stationery. Executive stationery is also smaller than the standard, as shown in Table 4.2 on page 179. Envelopes match the paper and are printed with the executive's name and return address.

If you are writing a business letter for an organization that does not have letterhead stationery, you can create a typewritten letterhead. The typewritten letterhead can include all of the elements included in the printed letterhead (listed above) except for the logo; and, as with the printed letterhead, the essential items are (1) the full name of the company, institution, or group; (2) the full street address; (3) the city, state, and zip code; and (4) the area code and telephone number. The elements are centered, each on its own line.

In writing your own personal correspondence, a letterhead, whether printed or typewritten is not required. In this type of correspondence, a three-line heading replaces the letterhead. The correct form for the heading is to put the street address or post-office box number on line 1, the

```
              BEDFORD FALLS HISTORICAL ASSOCIATION

                      324 Sycamore Street

                    Bedford Falls, ST 56789

                      (215)-555-7654


                                            May 9, 1988
```

Figure 4.1.   Typewritten letterhead

city, state, and zip code on line 2, and the date on line 3. The heading may be positioned six lines from the top of the edge of the paper (or higher or lower) to achieve a good balance and with the longest line flush with the right margin (see Figure 4.38).

Choosing the Right Paper

Paper and envelope size, quality, and basis weight vary according to application. Table 4.2 on page 179 lists various paper and envelope sizes along with their uses.

Good-quality paper is an essential element in the production of attractive, effective letters. Paper with rag content is considerably more expensive than sulfite bonds. Nevertheless, many business firms use rag-content paper because it suggests the merit and stature of the company. Since the cost of paper has been estimated at less than five percent of the total cost of the average business letter, it is easy to understand why some companies consider high-quality paper to be worth the added expense—at least for certain types of correspondence. In choosing a good grade of paper, one should look for paper that meets the following standards:

1. The paper withstands corrections and erasures without pitting, buckling, or tearing.
2. The paper accepts even and clear typed characters.
3. The paper permits smooth written signatures.
4. The paper performs well with carbons and in copying machines.
5. The paper withstands storage and repeated handling, and its color wears well over a long time.
6. The paper folds easily without cracking or rippling.
7. The paper holds typeset letterhead without bleed-through.

An important characteristic of paper is its fiber direction or grain. Paper grain should be parallel to the direction of the typewritten lines, thus pro-

Table 4.2
Stationery and Envelope Sizes and Applications

Stationery	Stationery Size	Application	Envelope	Envelope Size
Standard	8½″ × 11″ *also* 8″ × 10½″	general business correspondence	*commercial* No. 6¾ No. 9 No. 10	3⅝″ × 6½″ 3⅞″ × 8⅞″ 4⅛″ × 9½″
			window No. 6¾ No. 9 No. 10	3⅝″ × 6½″ 3⅞″ × 8⅞″ 4⅛″ × 9½″
			airmail No. 6¾ No. 10	3⅝″ × 6½″ 4⅛″ × 9½″
Executive *or* Monarch	7¼″ × 10½″ *or* 7½″ × 10″	high-level corporate officers' correspondence; usually personalized	*regular* *window*	3⅞″ × 7½″ 3⅞″ × 7½″
Half-sheet *or* Baronial	5½″ × 8½″	extremely brief notes	*regular*	3⅝″ × 6½″

viding a smooth surface for clear and even characters, an easy erasing or correcting surface, and a smooth fit of paper against the typewriter platen. Every sheet of paper has a *felt* side, which is the top side of the paper from which a watermark may be read. It is on this side of the sheet that the letterhead should be printed or engraved.

The weight of the paper must also be considered when ordering stationery supplies. *Basis weight,* also called *substance number,* is the weight in pounds of a ream of paper cut to a basic size. Basis 24 is heaviest for stationery; basis 13 is lightest. Table 4.3 on page 180 illustrates various paper weights according to their specific uses in the office.

The paper used for carbon copies is lighter in weight and is available as inexpensive *manifold* paper, a stronger and more expensive *onionskin,* or a lightweight letterhead with the word COPY printed on it.

Continuation sheets, although blank, must match the letterhead sheet in color, basis weight, texture, size, and quality. Envelopes should match both the first and continuation sheets. Therefore, these materials should be ordered along with the letterhead to ensure a good match.

Letterhead and continuation sheets as well as envelopes should be stored in their boxes to prevent soiling. A small supply of these materials may be kept in the typist's stationery drawer, but it should be arranged carefully so as to protect the materials from wear and tear.

Table 4.3
Weights of Letter Papers and Envelopes
For Specific Business Correspondence Applications

Application	Basis Weight
Standard (*i.e., corporate correspondence*)	24 *or* 20
Executive	24 *or* 20
Airmail (*for overseas correspondence*)	13
Branch-office *or* salesmen's stationery	20 *or* 16
Form letters	20 *or* 24
Continuation sheets	match basis weight of first sheet
Half-sheets	24 *or* 20

General Punctuation Patterns in Business Correspondence

Like letterhead designs, the choice of general punctuation patterns in business correspondence is usually determined by the organization. However, it is important that specific punctuation patterns be selected for designated letter stylings and that these patterns be adhered to for the sake of consistency and fast output. The two most common patterns are *open punctuation* and *mixed punctuation*. Their increased popularity in recent years is a reflection of the marked trend toward streamlining correspondence, for these patterns have all but totally replaced the older and more complex *closed punctuation* requiring a terminal mark at the end of each element of a business letter—a pattern that was used most often with the now little-used Indented Letter styling.

Open-Punctuation Pattern

Letters using an open-punctuation pattern exhibit the following characteristics:

1. The end of the date line is unpunctuated, although the comma between day and year is retained.
2. The ends of the lines of the inside address are unpunctuated, unless an abbreviation such as *Inc.* terminates a line, in which case the period after the abbreviation is retained.
3. The salutation if used is unpunctuated.
4. The complimentary close if used is unpunctuated.
5. The ends of the signature block lines are unpunctuated.
6. This pattern is always used with the Simplified Letter (see pages 212–213) and is often used with the Block Letter (see pages 214–215).

Mixed-Punctuation Pattern

Letters using a mixed-punctuation pattern exhibit the following characteristics:

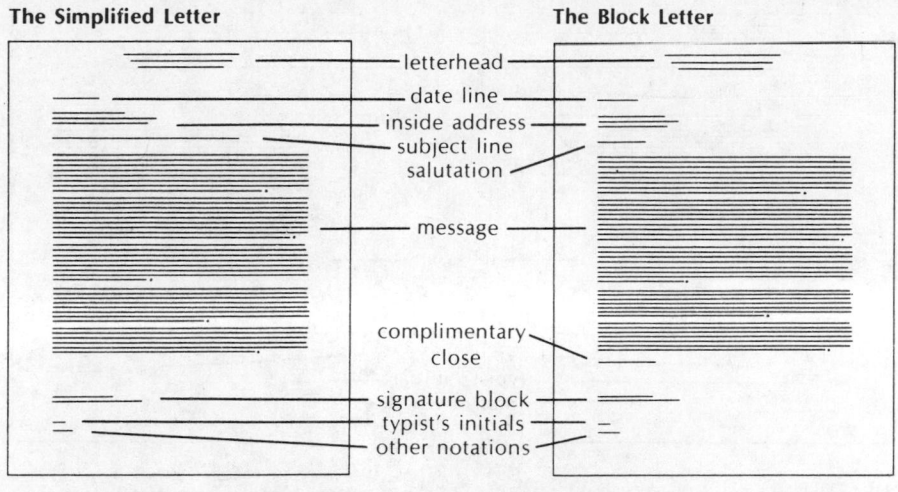

Figure 4.2.   Open-punctuation pattern

1. The end of the date line is unpunctuated, although the comma between the day and year is retained.
2. The ends of the lines of the inside address are unpunctuated unless an abbreviation such as *Inc.* terminates a line, in which case the period after the abbreviation is retained.
3. The salutation is punctuated with a colon.
4. The complimentary close is punctuated with a comma.
5. The end(s) of the signature block line(s) are unpunctuated.
6. This pattern is used with either the Block, the Modified Block, the Modified Semi-block, or the Hanging-indented Letters. (See pages 214–219 and page 211 for facsimiles of these letters.)

As suggested at the beginning of this section, virtually all American business offices today use either the mixed or the open puntuation pattern.

Closed-Punctuation Pattern

Although the closed-punctuation pattern is rarely used in the United States today, it is still employed in some European business correspondence. This pattern exhibits the following characteristics:

1. A period terminates the date line.
2. A comma terminates each line of the inside address except the last, which is ended by a period.

The Block Letter   **The Modified Block Letter**

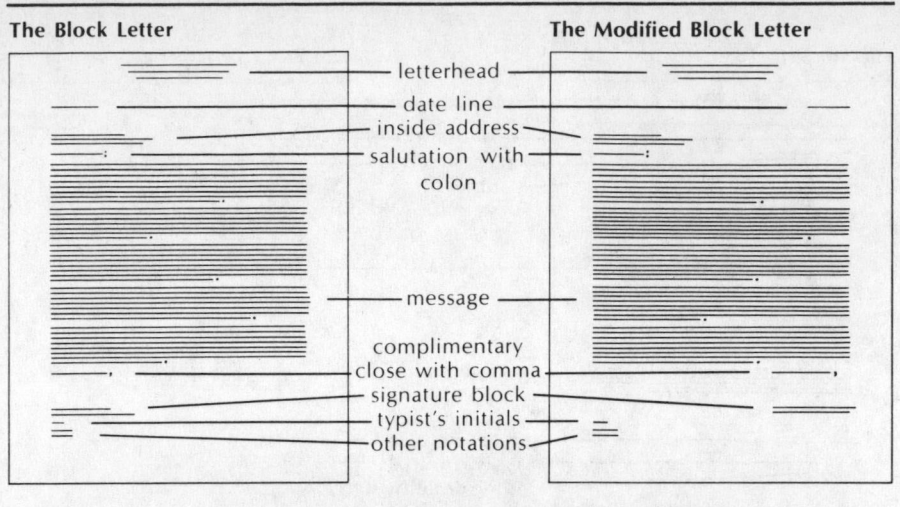

The Modified Semi-block Letter   **The Hanging-indented Letter**

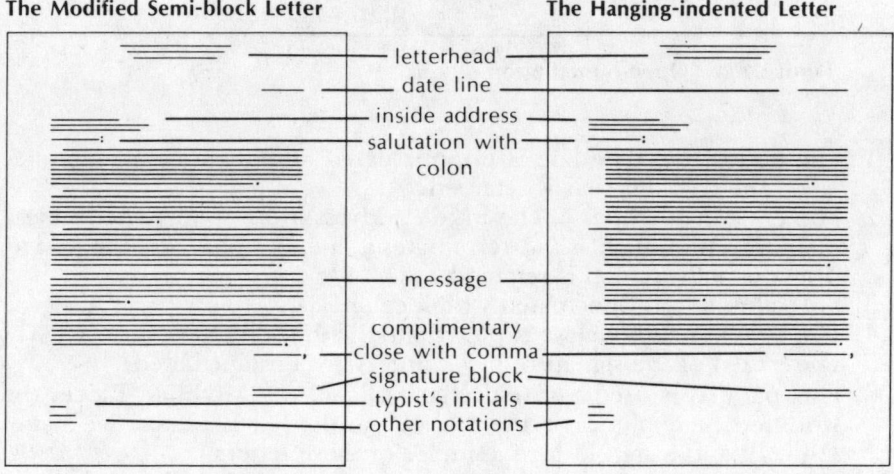

Figure 4.3.   Mixed-punctuation pattern illustrated in four letter stylings

3. A colon punctuates the salutation.
4. A comma punctuates the complimentary close.
5. A comma terminates each line of the signature block except the last, which is terminated by a period.
6. This pattern is used chiefly with the Indented Letter.

It should be pointed out that the illustration of the closed-punctuation pattern is the only description given in this book of the Indented Letter. It is shown here only as a point of information for those who may occasionally encounter it, especially in foreign correspondence.

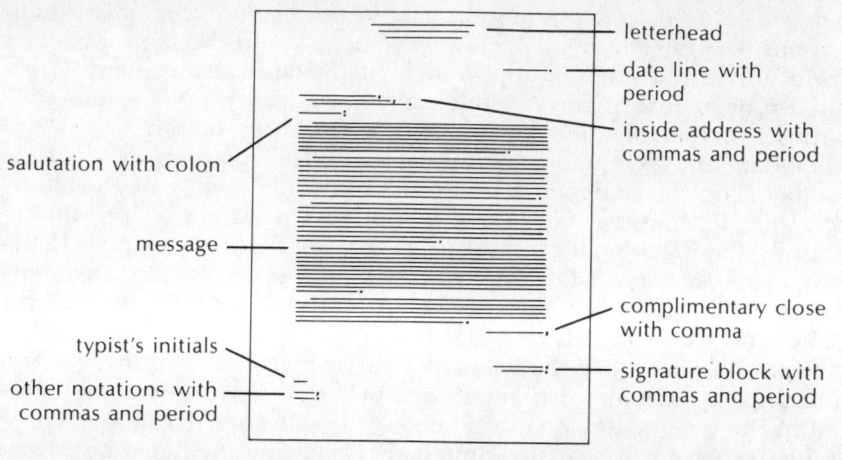

Figure 4.4.   Closed-punctuation pattern with the Indented Letter

The Individual Parts of a Business Letter

The various elements of a business letter are listed below in the order of their occurrence. While asterisked items are essential elements of any letter regardless of its general styling, those items that are unmarked may or may not be included, depending on general styling (as the Simplified Letter or the Block Letter) and on the nature of the letter itself (as general or confidential correspondence):

*date line	attention line	identification initials
reference line	salutation	enclosure notation
special mailing	subject line	carbon copy notation
notations	*message	postscript
on-arrival notations	complimentary close	
*inside address	*signature block	

For a discussion of typewritten letterheads and return addresses, see pages 177–178.

Date Line

The date line may be typed two to six lines below the last line of the printed letterhead; however, three-line spacing is recommended as a standard for most letters. Some office manuals specify a *fixed date line,* positioned three lines below the letterhead in all instances, with extra space added as needed below the date line and elsewhere on the page. Other offices prefer to use a *floating date line,* which may be typed two to six lines below the letterhead, depending on the letter length, space available, and letterhead design. The date line consists of the month, the day, and the year (January 1, 19--), all on one line. Ordinals (such as 1st, 2d, or 24th) should not be used, and the months should not be represented with abbreviations or Arabic numerals. However, the day and the month may be reversed and the comma dropped in United States government correspondence or in British correspondence, where the styling is common (1 January 19--). The date line should never overrun the margin.

The date line is commonly placed in one of four positions, and all are acceptable. The choice depends on the general letter styling or the letterhead layout. Placing the date line *flush with the left margin* is appropriate when using the Block Letter format (see the letter facsimile on pages 214–215 for a full-page view). Placing the date line *flush with the right margin* is appropriate for Hanging-indented, Modified Block, and Modified Semiblock Letters (see pages 211, 216–217, and 218–219). In order to align a date at the right margin, move the typewriter carriage to the right margin and then backspace once for each keystroke (including spaces) that will be required in the typed date. You can then set the tab stops if you are typing several letters that will bear the same date. Centering the date line *directly under the letterhead* or positioning it about *five spaces to the right of center* are other positions that are appropriate when using the Modified Block or Modified Semi-block formats.

Figure 4.5.   Date line blocked flush with the left margin

Figure 4.6.   Date line blocked flush with the right margin

Reference Line

A reference line with file, correspondence, control, order, invoice, or policy numbers is included in a letter when the addressee has specifically requested that correspondence on a subject contain a reference, or when it

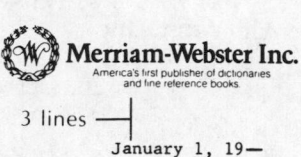

Figure 4.7.   Date line centered directly under the letterhead

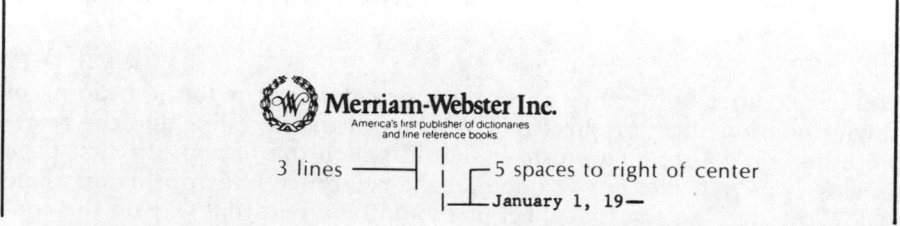

Figure 4.8.   Date line positioned above five spaces to the right of dead center

is needed for filing. It may be centered and typed one to four lines below the date, although some offices require that it be typed and single-spaced directly above or below the date to make it less conspicuous. With the Block Letter, the reference line should be aligned flush left. With the Modified Block and the Modified Semi-block Letters, the reference line may be centered on the page or blocked under or above the date line.

reference line blocked left	*reference line blocked right*
January 1, 19--	January 1, 19--
X-123-4	X-123-4
or	*or*
X-123-4	X-123-4
January 1, 19--	January 1, 19--

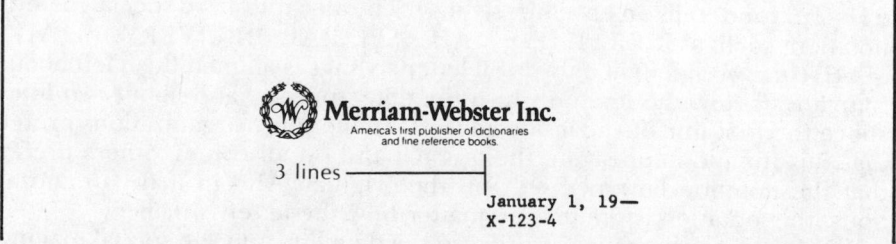

Figure 4.9.   Reference line blocked with date line to right of dead center

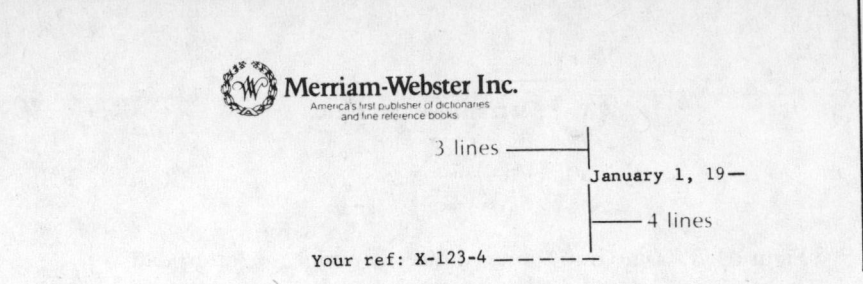

Figure 4.10.   Reference number centered on page, four lines beneath date line

Reference lines on the first sheet must be carried over to the heading of a continuation sheet or sheets. The styling of the date line and the reference line on a continuation sheet should match the one on the first page as closely as possible. For example, if the reference line appears on a line below the date on the first sheet, it should be typed that way on the continuation sheet. The first setup below illustrates a continuation-sheet reference line as used with the Simplified or Block Letter.

      Mr. John B. Jones
      January 1, 19--
      X-123-4
      Page 2

The second example illustrates the positioning of a reference line on the continuation sheet of a Modified Block, a Modified Semi-block, or a Hanging-indented Letter.

      Mr. John B. Jones   -2-   January 1, 19--
                                                                  X-123-4

See Figures 4.18 and 4.19 for continuation-sheet facsimiles.

Special Mailing Notations

If a letter is to be sent by any method other than by regular mail, that fact may be indicated on the letter itself as well as on the envelope (see pages 221–229 for details on envelope styling). The all-capitalized special mailing notation such as CERTIFIED MAIL, SPECIAL DELIVERY, or AIRMAIL (for foreign mail only) in all letter stylings is aligned flush left about four lines below the line on which the date appears, and about two lines above the first line of the inside address. While some organizations prefer that this notation appear on the original and on all copies, others prefer that the notation be typed only on the original. And in many organizations, this notation is omitted no matter how the letter is mailed.

      Vertical spacing (such as between the date line and the special mailing notation) may vary with letter length; i.e., more space may be left for short or medium letter lengths.

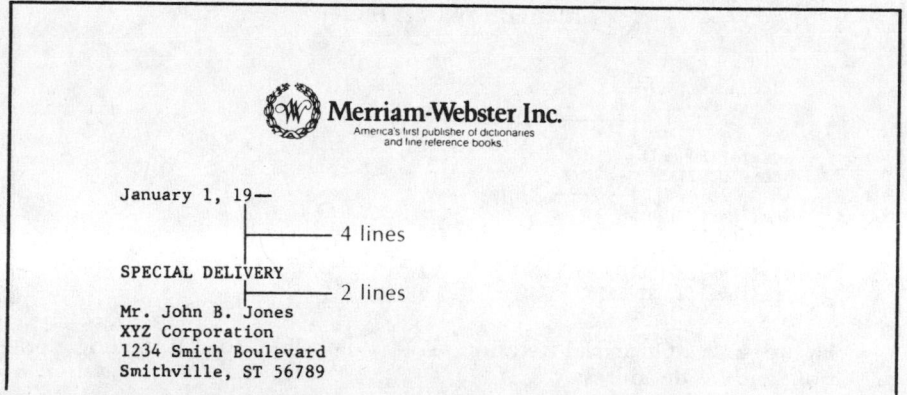

Figure 4.11.   Special mailing notation vis-à-vis inside address and date line

On-arrival Notations

The on-arrival notations that may be included in the letter itself are PERSONAL and CONFIDENTIAL. The first indicates that the letter may be opened and read only by its addressee; the second, that the letter may be opened and read by its addressee and/or any other person or persons authorized to view such material. These all-capitalized notations are usually positioned four lines below the date line and usually two but not more than four lines above the first line of the inside address. They are blocked flush left in all letter stylings. If a special mailing notation has been used, the on-arrival notation is blocked one line beneath it. Spacing between the date line and the on-arrival notation may be increased to as much as six lines if the letter is extremely brief.

If either PERSONAL or CONFIDENTIAL appears in the letter, it must also appear on the envelope (see pages 223–225 for envelope styling).

Inside Address

An inside address typically includes the following elements if it is directed to a particular individual:

1. addressee's courtesy title and full name
2. addressee's business title if required
3. full name of addressee's business affiliation
4. full geographical address

If the letter is addressed to an organization in general, the inside address typically includes the following elements:

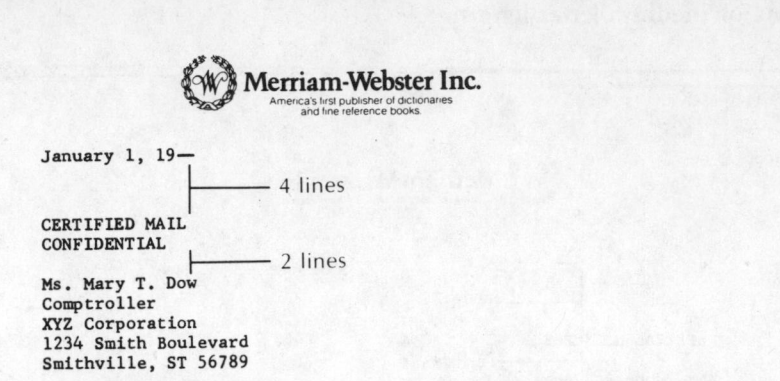

Figure 4.12.   On-arrival notation vis-à-vis date line, special mailing notation, and inside address

1. full name of the firm, company, corporation, or institution
2. individual department name if required
3. full geographical address

The inside address is placed about three to eight but not more than 12 lines below the date. The inside address in the Simplified Letter is typed three lines below the date. Inside-address page placement in relation to the date may be expanded or contracted according to letter length or organization policy. The inside address is always single-spaced internally. In most of the letters discussed in this book, the inside address is blocked flush with the left margin. See pages 209–220 for full-page views.

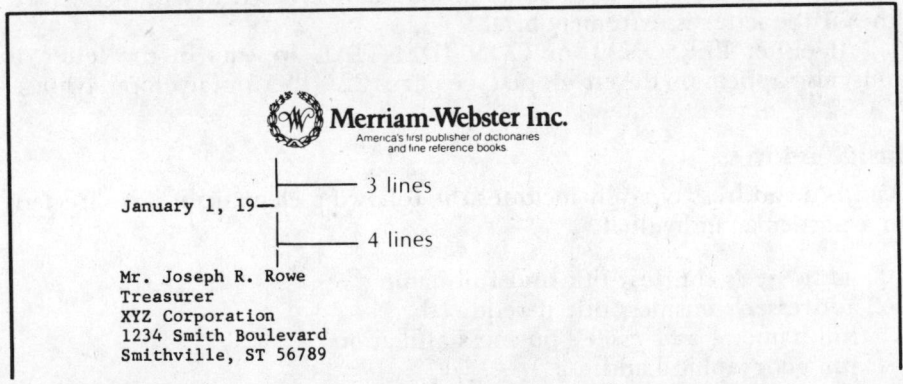

Figure 4.13.   Inside address styling used with the Block Letter

A courtesy title (as *Mr., Ms., Mrs., Miss, Dr.,* or *The Honorable*) should be typed before the addressee's full name, even if a business or professional title (as *Treasurer* or *Chief of Staff*) follows the surname. No courtesy title, however, should ever precede the name when *Esquire* or an abbreviation for a degree follows the name.

Before typing the addressee's full name, the secretary should, if possible, refer to the signature block of previous correspondence from that individual to ascertain the exact spelling and styling of the person's name. This information may also be obtained from printed executive letterhead. A business or professional title, if included, should also match the styling in previous correspondence or in official literature (such as an annual report or a business directory). If an individual holds more than one office (as *Vice President* and *General Manager*) within an organization, the title shown in the signature block of previous correspondence should be copied, or the title of the individual's highest office (in this case, *Vice President*) may be selected. Business and professional titles should not be abbreviated. If a title is so long that it might overrun the center of the page, it may be typed on two lines with the second line indented two spaces.

> Mr. John P. Hemphill, Jr.
> Vice President and Director
>   of Research and Development

Special attention should be paid to the spelling, punctuation, and official abbreviations of company names. Note, for example, whether an ampersand is used for the word *and,* whether series of names are separated by commas, and whether the word *Company* is spelled in full or abbreviated.

The addressee's title may be typed on the same line as the name, separated by a comma. Alternatively, the title may be typed on the second line either by itself or followed by a comma and the name of the organization. Care should be taken, however, to choose a style that will enhance and not detract from the total balance of the letter on the page. The following are acceptable inside-address stylings for business and professional titles:

> Mr. Arthur O. Brown
> News Director
> Radio Station WXYZ
> 1234 Peters Street
> Jonesville, ZZ 56789

> Dr. Joyce A. Cavitt, Dean
> School of Business and Finance
> Stateville University
> Stateville, ST 98765

> Ms. Ann B. Lowe, Director
> Apex Community Theater
> 67 Smith Street
> North Bend, XX 12345

> Mrs. Joyce A. Cavitt
> President, C & A Realty
> Johnson Beach, ZZ 56789

If an individual addressee's name is unknown or irrelevant and the writer wishes to direct a letter to an organization in general or to a unit within that organization, the organization name is typed on line 1 of the inside address, followed on line 2 by the name of a specific department if required. The full address of the organization is then typed on subsequent lines.

XYZ Corporation
Consumer Products Division
1234 Smith Boulevard
Smithville, ST 56789

On the other hand, if an addressee's address is unknown and the writer wishes to send a letter to him or her in care of a third party, the phrase *In care of* (or *c/o*) is used on line 2 before the name of the third party. The percentage sign (%) is a shortcut symbol that can be used, but it is usually not used in formal correspondence.

Street addresses should be typed in full and not abbreviated unless window envelopes are being used (see page 222). Numerals are used for all building, house, apartment, room, and suite numbers except for *One*, which is written out.

One Bayside Drive   6 Link Road   1436 Fremont Avenue

However, when the address of a building is used as its name, the number in the address is written out.

Fifty Maple Street

Numerals are usually used for all numbered street names above *Twelfth*, but numbered street names from *First* through *Twelfth* are usually written out.

19 South 22nd Street   167 West Second   One East Ninth Street
                          Avenue

An alternative, more formal convention calls for writing out all numbered streets up to and including *One Hundredth*.

122 East Forty-second Street   36 East Fiftieth Street

An apartment, building, room, or suite number if required follows the street address on the same line with a comma separating the two.

62 Park Towers, Suite 9   Rosemont Plaza Apartments,
                                    Apartment 117

Note that neither the word *Number* nor its abbreviation *No.* is used between the words *Suite, Apartment,* or *Building* and a following numeral.

Names of cities (except those including the word *Saint*, such as *St. Louis* or *St. Paul*) should be typed out in full, as *Fort Wayne* or *Mount Prospect*. The name of the city is followed by a comma and then by the name of the state and the zip code. Names of states may or may not be abbreviated (the District of Columbia is always styled *DC* or *D.C.*). If a window envelope is being used, the all-capitalized, unpunctuated two-letter Postal Service abbreviation followed by one space and the zip code should be used. If a regular envelope is being used, the name of the state may be typed out in full followed by one space and the zip code, or the two-letter Postal Service abbreviation may be used. Most firms now use the two-letter Postal Service abbreviations on all inside and envelope addresses. See Table 4.5 on page 224 for a list of these abbreviations.

An inside address should comprise no more than five typed lines. No line should overrun the center of the page. Lengthy organizational names, however, like lengthy business titles, may be carried over to a second line and indented two spaces from the left margin.

Sometimes a single letter will have to be sent to two persons at different addresses, both of whom should receive an original. In these cases, the inside address should consist of two complete sets of names and addresses separated by a line of space. The names should be in alphabetical order unless one person is obviously more important than the other. For salutations used in letters to multiple addresses, see pages 249–257.

For information about styling foreign addresses, see pages 225–227.

Attention Line

If the writer wishes to address a letter to an organization in general but at the same time bring it to the attention of a particular individual, an attention line may be typed two lines below the last line of the inside address and two lines above the salutation if there is one. The attention line is usually blocked flush with the left margin; it must be so blocked in the Simplified and Block Letters. On the other hand, some organizations prefer that the attention line be centered on the page. This placement is acceptable with all letters except the Simplified and the Block. This line should be neither underlined nor entirely capitalized; only its main elements are capitalized. The word *Attention* is not abbreviated. Placement of a colon after the word *Attention* is optional unless the open punctuation pattern is being followed throughout the letter, in which case the colon should be omitted:

    Attention Mr. John P. Doe   Attention: Mr. John P. Doe

The salutation appearing beneath the attention line should be "Gentlemen" or "Ladies and Gentlemen" even though the attention line routes the letter to a particular person. Such a letter is actually being written to the organization, so a collective-noun salutation should be used.

Salutation

The salutation—used with all letter stylings except the Simplified—is typed flush with the left margin, two lines beneath the last line of the inside address or two lines below the attention line if there is one. Additional vertical lines of space may be added after the inside address of a short letter which is to be enclosed in a window envelope. The first letter of the first word of the salutation is capitalized, as are the first letters of the addressee's courtesy title and surname. If the mixed-punctuation pattern is being followed in the letter, the salutation is followed by a colon; if open punctuation is being observed, the salutation is unpunctuated.

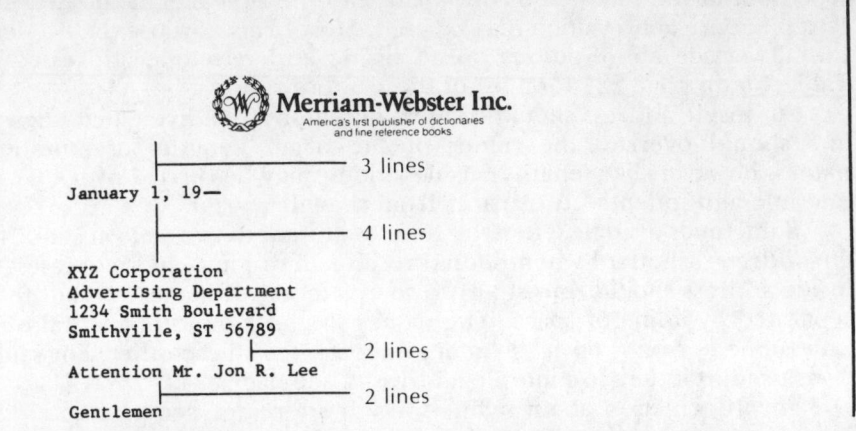

Figure 4.14.   Page placement of an attention line in a Block Letter with open punctuation

Only in informal, personal correspondence is the salutation followed by a comma.

One of the most frequently asked questions today is what salutation to use when addressing an organization or when addressing a person whose name and gender are unknown to the letter-writer. Unfortunately, there are no universally accepted forms to use in these situations. Traditionally the salutation "Dear Sir" has been used when the recipient of the letter is to be a particular individual, and "Gentlemen" has been used when the recipient is to be an organization or a group of people within it. However, as it has become more and more likely that the recipients of these letters may be women, many writers—both male and female—have looked for more appropriate salutations. Most commonly, these writers have adopted "Dear Sir or Madam" and "Ladies and Gentlemen" as substitutes for "Dear Sir" and "Gentlemen" respectively; however, these forms do sound awkward to some people. Some writers have used the salutations "Dear People," "Dear Person," "Gentlepeople," "Gentlepersons," and "Dear Sir, Madam, or Ms."; however, there is little evidence that these forms are catching on.

The salutation "To whom it may concern" is another way to begin such a letter; however, it is extremely impersonal and is usually used only when the writer is unfamiliar with both the person and the organization that is being addressed, as when one is addressing a letter of recommendation. In other instances, when a specific organization is being addressed, most writers try to find an alternate salutation.

A different type of salutation now being used to solve the problem of addressing a company or a company officer whose name and sex are unknown is that which simply names the company ("Dear XYZ Company")

or states the title or department of the intended recipient, as in the following examples:

Dear Personnel Supervisor
Dear Personnel Department
Dear XYZ Engineers

The use of this type of salutation has increased markedly in the past several years and is considered acceptable by most businesspeople.

When a letter is addressed to an all-female organization, the salutations "Ladies" or "Mesdames" may be used.

Occasionally a letter writer is faced with an addressee's name that gives no clue as to the addressee's sex. Traditionally in these uncertain cases, convention has required the writer to use the masculine courtesy title in the salutation, as *Mr. Lee Schmidtke, Mr. T. A. Gagnon.* However, some writers prefer to express their uncertainty by using such forms as the following:

Dear Mr. or Ms. Schmidtke
Dear Lee Schmidtke

The most convenient way of avoiding the problem of sexual semantics is to use the Simplified Letter styling (see the facsimile on pages 212–213), which eliminates the salutation altogether.

The salutation for a married couple may be styled in the following ways:

Dear Mr. and Mrs. Hathaway
Dear Dr. and Mrs. Simpson
Dear Dr. Smith and Mr. Smith

For more information about choosing appropriate salutations, including salutations for two or more persons and for people with specialized titles, see Chapter 5, "Forms of Address."

Subject Line

A subject line gives the gist of a letter. Its phrasing is necessarily succinct and to the point: it should not be so long as to require more than one line. The subject line serves as an immediate point of reference for the reader as well as a convenient filing tool for the secretaries at both ends of the correspondence.

In the Simplified Letter, which does not include a salutation, the subject line (an essential element) is positioned flush left, three lines below the last line of the inside address. The subject line may be entirely capitalized and not underlined. As an alternative, the main words in the subject line may be capitalized and every word underlined.

If a subject line is included in a letter featuring a salutation, it is frequently positioned flush left, two lines beneath the salutation, and may be entirely capitalized. With the Modified Block and Modified Semi-block styles, however, the subject line may be centered or even indented to

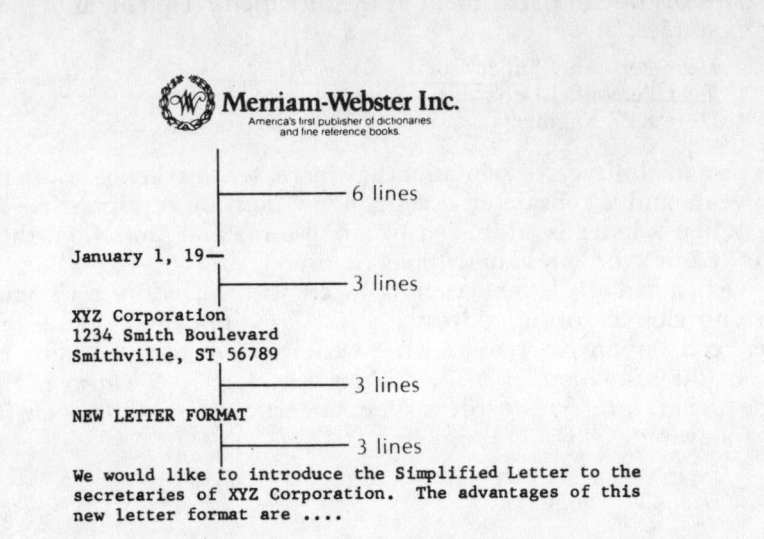

Figure 4.15.   Page placement of the subject line in the Simplified Letter

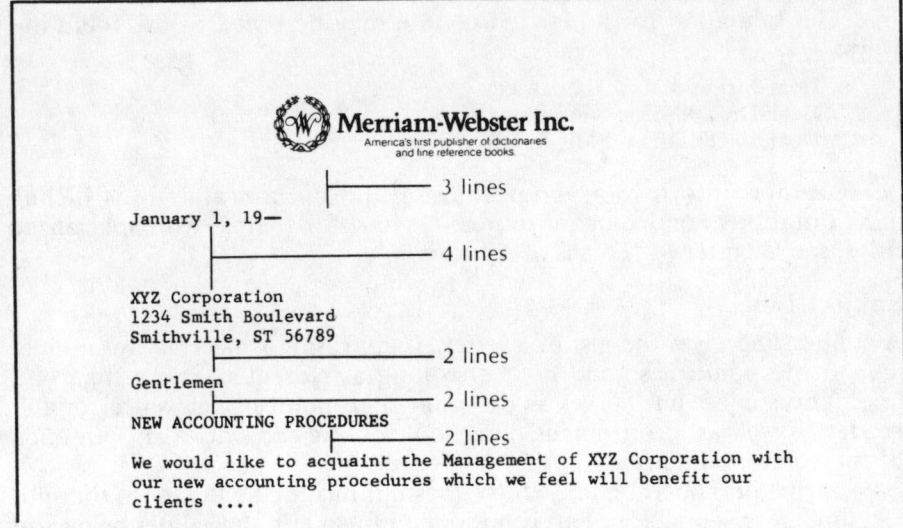

Figure 4.16.   Page placement of the subject line in a Block Letter with open punctuation

match the indention of the paragraphs. Legal correspondence uses the subject line in a variety of positions. Legal correspondence based on letter styles other than the Simplified or Block frequently centers the subject line or positions it at the right. A growing number of law offices prefer to position the subject line two lines above the salutation rather than below it.

The subject line may be entirely capitalized, and the word *subject* may be used to introduce the line. When the word *subject* is used, the subject line may also be capitalized headline-style—that is, with the initial letter of the first word capitalized and with the initial letter of all other words except coordinating conjunctions, articles, and short prepositions also capitalized. The word *reference* is sometimes also used.

SUBJECT: CHANGES IN TRAFFIC ROUTE
Subject: Changes in Traffic Route
Reference: Changes in Traffic Route

The subject-line headings *In re* and *Re* are now seldom used for general office letters; however, they are often used in legal correspondence. Headings should not be used if one is following the Simplified Letter styling.

Care should be taken not to confuse the subject line with the reference line (see pages 184–186). The subject line differs not only in position but also in styling and purpose: the reference line indicates a numerical classification; the subject line identifies the content of the letter.

Message

The body of the letter—the message—should begin two lines below the salutation or two lines below the subject line, if there is one, in all letter stylings except the Simplified Letter, where the message is typed three lines below the subject line.

Paragraphs are single-spaced internally. Double spacing is used to separate paragraphs. If a letter is extremely brief, it may be double-spaced throughout. Paragraphs in such letters should be indented so that they will be readily identifiable.

The first lines of indented paragraphs (as in the Modified Semi-block Letter) should begin five or ten spaces from the left margin; however, the five-space pattern is the most common. With the Hanging-indented Letter, the first lines of the paragraphs are blocked flush left, while subsequent lines are indented five spaces from the left margin. All other letter stylings require flush-left paragraph alignment.

Long quotations should be indented and blocked five to ten spaces from the left and right margins with internal single spacing and top-and-bottom double spacing so that the material will be set off from the rest of the message. Long enumerations should also be indented: enumerations with items requiring more than one line apiece may require single-spacing within each item, followed by double-spacing between items. Tabular data should be centered on the page.

Additional rules for typing letters that have traditionally been observed include the following:

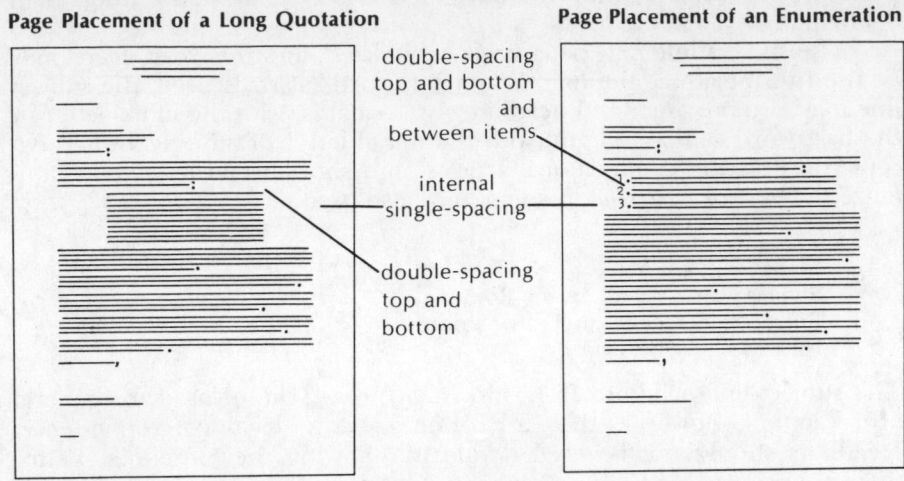

Page Placement of a Long Quotation

double-spacing
top and bottom
and
between items

internal
single-spacing

double-spacing
top and
bottom

Page Placement of an Enumeration

Figure 4.17.   Page placement of items inset within the message

1. Do not divide a word at the end of the first line.
2. Do not divide a word at the end of the last full line of a letter.
3. Do not divide a person's name from his or her courtesy title.

If a letter is long enough to require a continuation sheet or sheets, at least three message lines must be carried over to the next page. The complimentary close and/or typed signature block should never stand alone on a continuation sheet. The last word on a page should not be divided. Continuation-sheet margins should match those of the first sheet. At least six blank lines equaling one inch should be maintained at the top of the continuation sheet.

At the top of every continuation sheet there should be a continuation-sheet heading. The two most common continuation-sheet headings are illustrated in Figures 4.18 and 4.19. The format shown in Figure 4.18 is used with the Simplified and Block Letters. It features a flush-left heading beginning with the page number, followed on the next line by the addressee's courtesy title and full name, and ending with the date on the third line. Some companies prefer that the page number appear as the last line of the continuation-sheet heading, especially if a reference number is included.

Another way to type the heading of a continuation sheet is illustrated in Figure 4.19. In this format, the material is laid out across the page, six lines down from the top edge of the sheet. The addressee's name is typed flush with the left margin, the page number in Arabic numerals is centered on the same line and enclosed with spaced hyphens, and the date is aligned flush with the right margin—all on the same line. This format is often used with the Modified Block, the Modified Semi-block, and the Hanging-indented Letters.

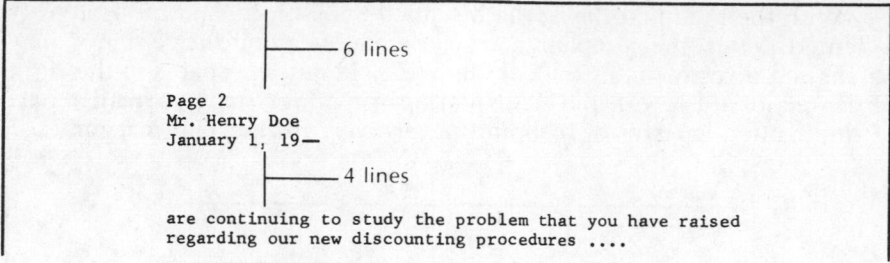

Figure 4.18. Continuation-sheet heading for Simplified and Block Letters

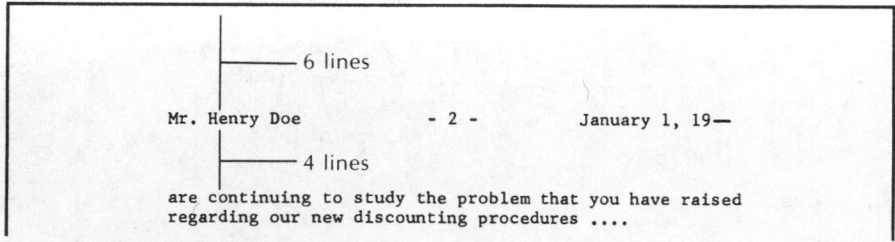

Figure 4.19. Continuation-sheet heading for Modified Block, Modified Semi-block, and Hanging-indented Letters

Complimentary Close

There is no complimentary close in the Simplified Letter. However, a complimentary close is used with all other letter styles. It is typed two lines below the last line of the message. Its page placement depends on the general letter styling being used. With the Block Letter, the complimentary close is blocked flush with the left margin.

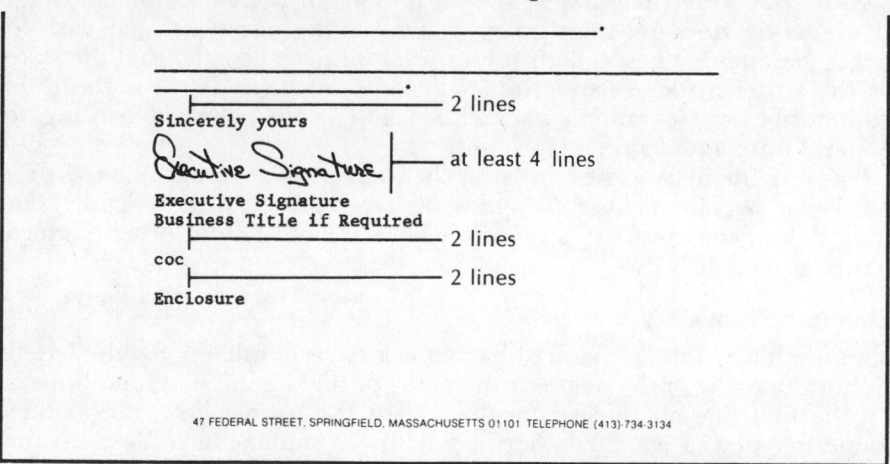

Figure 4.20. Open-punctuation pattern shown in Block Letter format for complimentary close

With the Modified Block, the Modified Semi-block, and the Hanging-indented Letter, the complimentary close may begin at the center or may be aligned directly under the date line (e.g., about five spaces to the right of center, or flush with the right margin) or under some particular part of the printed letterhead. It should never overrun the right margin.

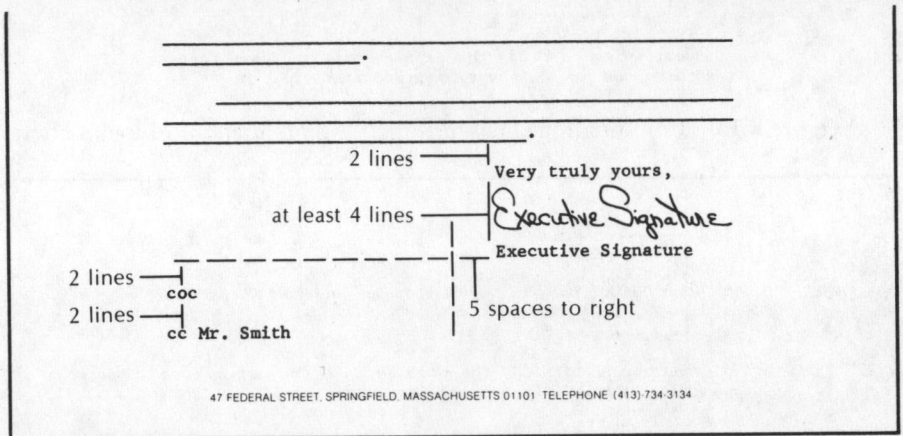

Figure 4.21.   Complimentary close five spaces to right of center as in a Modified Block Letter with mixed punctuation

Only the first word of the complimentary close is capitalized. If the open-punctuation pattern is being followed, the complimentary close is unpunctuated. If the mixed-punctuation pattern is being followed, a comma terminates the complimentary close.

The typist should always use the complimentary close that is dictated, because the writer may have a special reason for the choice of phrasing. If the writer does not specify a particular closing, the typist may wish to select the one that best reflects the general tone of the letter and the state of the writer-reader relationship. Table 4.4 on page 199 lists the most commonly used complimentary closes and groups them according to general tone and degree of formality.

Complimentary closes on letters written over a period of time to a particular person may become gradually more informal and friendly, but they should not revert to a more formal style once an informal pattern has been established.

Signature Block

The first line of the signature block indicates responsibility for the letter. Either the name of the writer or the name of the organization may appear on the first line of the signature block. In the former case, the writer's name is typed at least four lines below the complimentary close; in the latter, the organization name is typed all in capital letters two lines below the complimentary close and the writer's name at least four lines below the organization name.

Table 4.4
Complimentary Closes Common in Business Correspondence

General Tone & Degree of Formality	Complimentary Close
highly formal—usually used in diplomatic, governmental, or ecclesiastical correspondence to show respect and deference to a high-ranking addressee	Respectfully yours Respectfully Very respectfully
politely neutral—usually used in general correspondence	Very truly yours Yours very truly Yours truly
friendly and less formal—usually used in general correspondence	Most sincerely Very sincerely Very sincerely yours Sincerely yours Yours sincerely Sincerely
more friendly and informal—often used when writer and reader are on a first-name basis but also often used in general business correspondence	Most cordially Yours cordially Cordially yours Cordially
most friendly and informal—usually used when writer and reader are on a first-name basis	As ever Best wishes Best regards Kindest regards Kindest personal regards Regards
British	Yours faithfully Yours sincerely

With the Simplified Letter, the name of the writer is typed entirely in capitals flush left at least five lines below the last line of the message. If the writer's business title is not included in the printed letterhead, it may be typed on the same line as the name entirely in capitals and separated from the last element of the name by a spaced hyphen. Some organizations, however, prefer to use a comma in place of the hyphen. A combination of the two may be used if the title is complex.

> JOHN P. HEWETT - DIRECTOR
> JOHN P. HEWETT, DIRECTOR
> JOHN P. HEWETT - DIRECTOR, TECHNICAL INFORMATION
> *or*
> JOHN P. HEWETT - DIRECTOR
> TECHNICAL INFORMATION CENTER

With the Block Letter, the signature block is aligned flush left at least four lines below the complimentary close. Only the first letter of each element of the writer's name is capitalized, and only the first letter of each major element of the writer's business title and department name is capi-

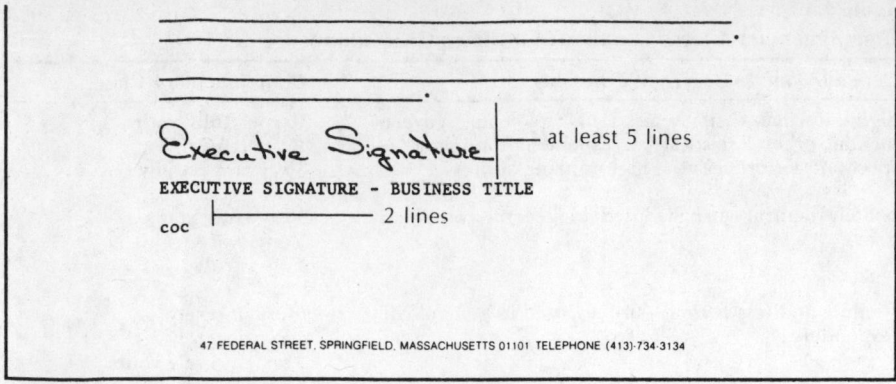

Executive Signature —— at least 5 lines

EXECUTIVE SIGNATURE - BUSINESS TITLE

coc ——— 2 lines

47 FEDERAL STREET, SPRINGFIELD, MASSACHUSETTS 01101 TELEPHONE (413)-734-3134

Figure 4.22.   Page placement of signature block in the Simplified Letter

talized if they are included. The business title and the department name may be omitted if they appear in the printed letterhead:

if title and department name are needed for identification	John D. Russell, Director Consumer Products Division
if department name is already printed on the letterhead	John D. Russell Director
if both title and department name appear in printed letterhead	John D. Russell

——— 2 lines

Very truly yours

Executive's Name —— at least 4 lines

Executive's Name, Ph.D.
Business Title if Required

coc ——— 2 lines

47 FEDERAL STREET, SPRINGFIELD, MASSACHUSETTS 01101 TELEPHONE (413)-734-3134

Figure 4.23.   Signature block in the Block Letter

With the Modified Block, the Modified Semi-block, and the Hanging-indented Letters, the signature block begins with the name of the writer typed at least four lines below the complimentary close. The first letter of the first element of each line in the signature block is aligned directly below the first letter of the first element of the complimentary close, unless this alignment will result in an overrunning of the right margin. In that case the signature block may be centered under the complimentary close, as shown in Figure 4.26. Only the first letter of each of the major elements of the writer's name, title (if used), and department name (if used) is capitalized:

Mrs. Joy L. Tate, Director   Mrs. Joy L. Tate   Mrs. Joy L. Tate
Marketing Division   Director

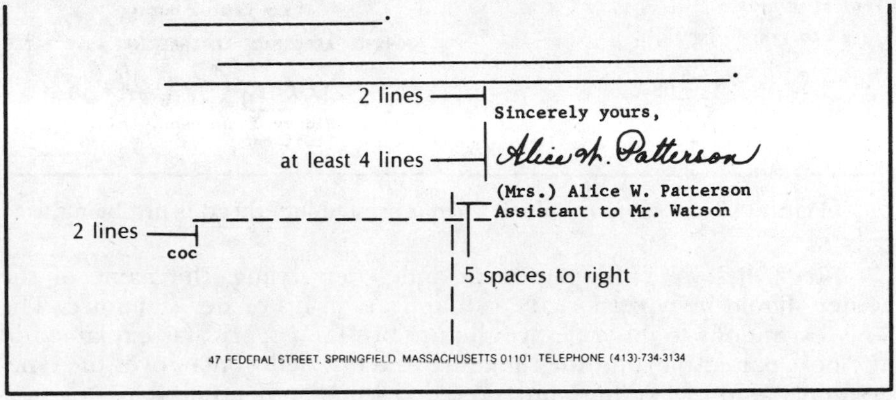

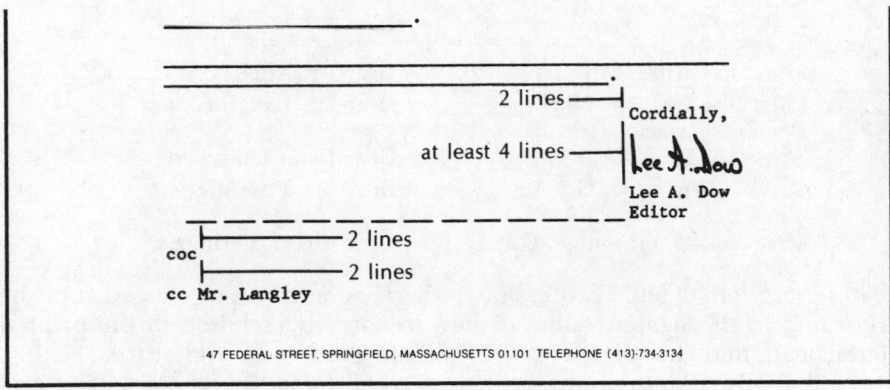

Figure 4.24.   Signature block five spaces to right of center as in a Modified Block Letter with mixed punctuation

Figure 4.25.   Complimentary close and signature block flush right as in the Modified Block Letter

If printed letterhead stationery is being used, the name of the firm should not appear below the complimentary close. If printed letterhead is not being used, the name of the firm may be typed in capitals two lines beneath the complimentary close with the first letter of the firm's name aligned directly underneath and the writer's name typed in capitals and lowercase at least four lines below the firm's name. The writer's title if needed is typed in capitals and lowercase on a line directly underneath the signature line.

If the company name is long enough to overrun the right margin, it may be centered beneath the complimentary close in the Modified Block and the Modified Semi-block Letters.

Very truly yours,   Very truly yours,

AJAX VAN LINES, INC.   JOHNSON AEROSPACE ENGINEERING ASSOCIATES

Samuel O. Lescott   *Sidney C. Johnson*

Samuel O. Lescott   Sidney C. Johnson, Ph.D.
Dispatcher   President

Figure 4.26.   Signature block when a printed letterhead is not being used

Regardless of page placement and letter styling, the name of the writer should be typed exactly as it appears in his or her signature. The only exceptions to this rule are the use of *Ms./Mrs./Miss* (as explained in the next paragraph) and the signature of a married woman over the type-written name of her husband preceded by *Mrs.* If applicable, any academic degrees (as *Ph.D.*) or professional ratings (as *P.E.*) that the writer holds should be included after the surname so that the recipient of the letter will know the proper form of address to use in his or her reply.

Typed Signature	*Salutation in Reply*
Francis E. Atlee, M.D.	Dear Dr. Atlee
Ellen Y. Langford, Ph.D.	Dear Dr. Langford
Dean of Women	*or*
	Dear Dean Langford
Carol I. Etheridge, C.P.A.	Dear Ms. Etheridge
or	
Mrs. Carol I. Etheridge, C.P.A.	Dear Mrs. Etheridge

These academic and professional degrees and ratings need not be repeated in the signature line if they are already included in the printed letterhead, and they are never included in the written signature.

The only titles that may precede a typed signature are *Ms., Mrs.,* and *Miss.* These titles, which may be enclosed in parentheses, are blocked flush left in the Simplified and the Block Letters, and they are aligned with or centered under the complimentary close in the Modified Block, the Modified Semi-block, and the Hanging-indented Letters.

The use of the courtesy title *Ms.* (which usually includes a period even though it is not an abbreviation of any word) has become so widespread that it is now the standard form to use with the name of a woman whose marital status is irrelevant or in doubt. For this reason, there is a marked trend for a woman to omit a courtesy title altogether in the signature line, on the assumption that the recipient will address the reply to "Ms. _____." Only if the writer wishes to show her preference for *Miss* or *Mrs.* will she usually include a courtesy title before her typewritten signature. On the other hand, if the woman's name might be confused with a man's name (as Lee, Lynn, Terry, or Leslie), it is thoughtful to include one of the courtesy titles to help the recipient address a reply. The examples in Figures 4.27 through 4.32 show alternate stylings of the courtesy title with and without the optional parentheses.

Sincerely yours	Sincerely yours	Sincerely yours
Joan Conti	*Joan Conti*	*Joan Conti*
Joan Conti	Miss Joan Conti	Ms. Joan Conti
Vice President	Vice President	Vice President
	Sincerely yours	Sincerely yours
	Joan Conti	*Joan Conti*
	(Miss) Joan Conti	(Ms.) Joan Conti
	Vice President	Vice President

Figure 4.27. Signature stylings for unmarried women

Sincerely yours	Sincerely yours	Sincerely yours
Joan Conti	*Joan Conti*	*Joan Conti*
Joan Conti	Ms. Joan Conti	(Ms.) Joan Conti
Vice President	Vice President	Vice President

Figure 4.28. Signature stylings for women who consider their marital status irrelevant

Sincerely yours	Sincerely yours	Sincerely yours
Joan M. Conti	*Joan M. Conti*	*Joan M. Conti*
Joan M. Conti	Mrs. Joan M. Conti	Ms. Joan M. Conti
	Sincerely yours	Sincerely yours
	Joan M. Conti	*Joan M. Conti*
	(Mrs.) Joan M. Conti	(Ms.) Joan M. Conti

Figure 4.29. Signature stylings for married women using given name + maiden name initial + husband's surname

Sincerely yours   Sincerely yours

Joan Conti   *Joan Conti*

Mrs. Robert A. Conti   (Mrs. Robert A. Conti)
Vice President   Vice President

Figure 4.30. Signature stylings for married women using husband's full name

A widow may use either her first name and her maiden name initial and her late husband's surname with the courtesy title *Mrs.* or *Ms.* enclosed in optional parentheses. She may also use her social signature—her husband's full name with *Mrs.*—although the social signature is not commonly used in business correspondence.

Sincerely yours   Sincerely yours   Sincerely yours

Joan M. Conti   *Joan M. Conti*   *Joan Conti*

Ms. Joan M. Conti   (Ms.) Joan M. Conti   Mrs. Robert A. Conti

---

Figure 4.31. Signature stylings for widows

A divorcée may use her maiden name if it has been legally regained, along with the courtesy title *Ms.* or *Miss* enclosed in optional parentheses or she may omit the title. She may also use her maiden name and her former husband's surname with *Mrs.*

Sincerely yours   Sincerely yours   Sincerely yours

Joan M. Conti   *Joan M. Conti*   *Joan Conti*

Miss Joan M. Conti   Joan M. Conti   Mrs. Matthews Conti

Figure 4.32. Signature stylings for divorcées

Many married women today use both their maiden and married names in hyphenated form, as "Joan Matthews-Dunn" (or "Mrs. Robert Matthews-Dunn"), with the maiden name usually as the first element of the hyphenated compound. In these cases the handwritten signature may not always match the typewritten name. However, the signature should match the hyphenated name when the signer belongs to a Hispanic culture that traditionally combines maternal and paternal family names with a hyphen, as "Carla Monteiro-Lopez."

On rare occasions a letter may be written and signed by two individuals. In these cases, it is generally best to place the names side by side, with the first name flush left in block styles or beginning slightly left of center in other letter styles in order to leave enough room for two horizontally aligned signatures. If horizontal positioning is not feasible, the names may be placed one under the other.

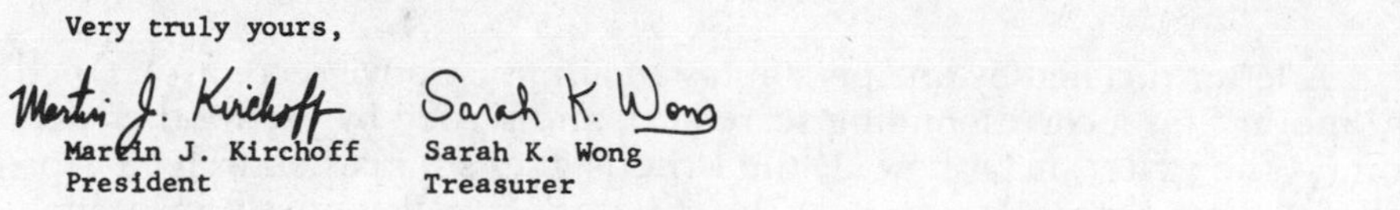

Very truly yours,

Martin J. Kirchoff   *Sarah K. Wong*
Martin J. Kirchoff   Sarah K. Wong
President   Treasurer

Figure 4.33.   Signature block when two people sign a letter

If the secretary signs a letter for the writer, that person's name is followed by the secretary's initials immediately below and to the right of the surname, or centered under the full name. If the secretary signs a letter in his or her own name for someone else, that individual's courtesy title and surname only are typed directly below.

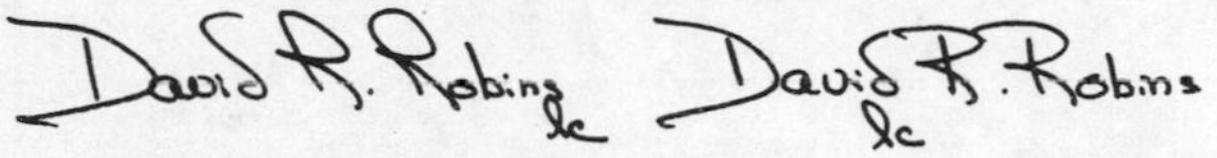

David R. Robins   *David R. Robins*

Figure 4.34.   Signature when secretary signs the writer's name

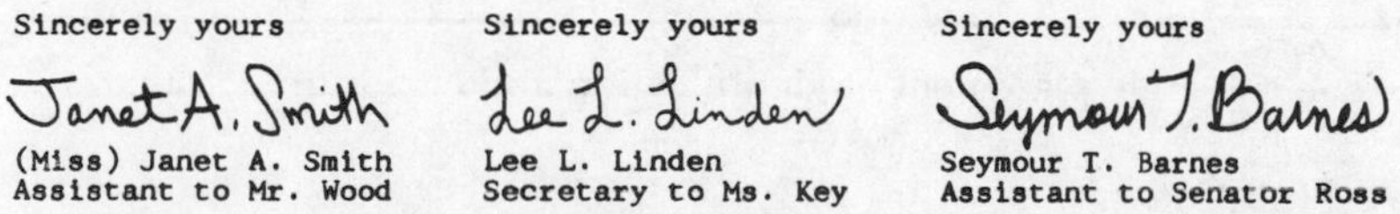

Sincerely yours   Sincerely yours   Sincerely yours

Janet A. Smith   *Lee L. Linden*   *Seymour T. Barnes*
(Miss) Janet A. Smith   Lee L. Linden   Seymour T. Barnes
Assistant to Mr. Wood   Secretary to Ms. Key   Assistant to Senator Ross

---

Figure 4.35.   Signature block when secretary signs as a representative

Identification Initials

The initials of the typist and sometimes those of the writer are placed two lines below the last line of the signature block and are aligned flush left in all letter stylings. Most offices prefer that three capitalized initials be used for the writer's name and two lowercase initials be used for the typist's. There is a marked trend towards complete omission of the writer's initials if the name is already typed in the signature block or if it appears in the printed letterhead. In the Simplified Letter, the writer's initials are usually omitted, and the typist's initials if included on the original are typed in lowercase. Many organizations indicate the typist's initials only on carbons for record-keeping purposes, and they do not show the writer's initials unless another individual signs the letter. The following are common stylings:

FCM/HL	FCM:hl	Franklin C. Mason:
FM/hl	FCM:hol	HL
hol	fcm:hol	
hl	FCM:HL	Franklin C. Mason
	FCM:HOL	HL

A letter dictated by one person (as an administrative secretary), typed by another (as a corresponding secretary), and signed by yet another person (as the writer) may show (1) the writer/signer's initials entirely in capitals followed by a colon and (2) the dictator's initials entirely in capitals followed by a colon and (3) the transcriber/typist's initials in lowercase, as AWM:COC:ds

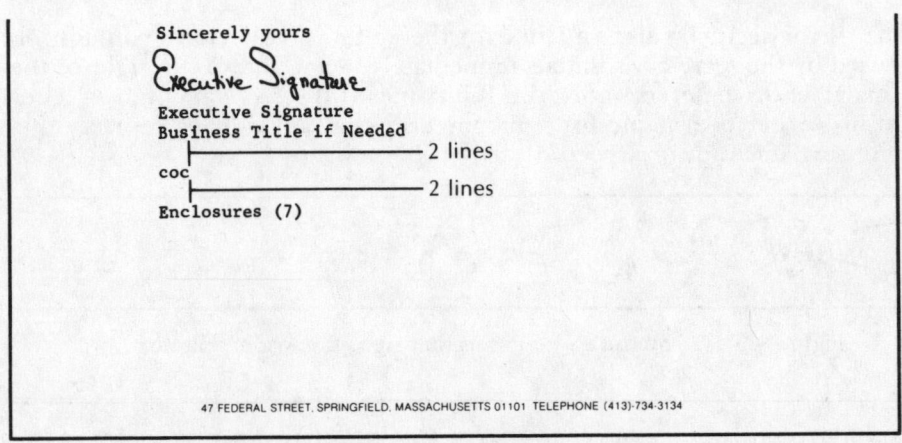

Figure 4.36.   Page placement of identification and enclosure notations

Enclosure Notation

If a letter is to be accompanied by an enclosure or enclosures, one of the following expressions should be aligned flush left and typed one to two lines beneath the identification initials, if there are any, or one to two lines beneath the last line of the signature block, if there is no identification line. The unabbreviated form *Enclosure* is usually preferred.

Enclosure   *or if more than one*   Enclosures (3)
enc.   *or*   encl.   *or if more than one*   3 encs.   *or*   Enc. 3

If the enclosures are of special importance, each of them should be numerically listed and briefly described with single-spacing between each item.

Enclosures: 1. Annual Report (19—), 2 copies
                  2. List of Major Accounts
                  3. Profit and Loss Statement (19—)

The following type of notation then may be typed in the top right corner of each page of each of the enclosures:

Enclosure (1) to Johnson Associates letter No. 1-234-X,
dated January 1, 19—, page 2 of 8

If the enclosure is bound, a single notation attached to its cover sheet will suffice.

When additional material is being mailed separately, a notation such as the following may be used:

Separate mailing: 50th Anniversary Report

Carbon Copy Notation

Carbon copies are now often called *courtesy copies* in view of the widespread use of photocopies; in some offices *c* for *copy* or *pc* for *photocopy* is used instead of the traditional *cc* for *carbon copy*.

A carbon copy notation showing the distribution of courtesy copies to other individuals should be aligned flush left and typed two lines below the signature block if there are no other notations or initials, or two lines below any other notations. If space is very tight, the courtesy copy notation may be single-spaced below the above-mentioned items.

cc   cc: \   Copy to   Copies to

Multiple recipients of copies should be listed alphabetically. Sometimes only their initials are shown.

cc: WPB
     TLC
     CNR

More often, the individuals' names are shown and sometimes also their addresses, especially if the writer feels that such information can be useful to the addressee.

cc: William L. Carton, Esq.   cc   Ms. Lee Jamieson
     45 Park Towers, Suite 1
     Smithville, ST 56789   Copy to Mr. John K. Long

     Dr. Daniel I. Maginnis   Copies to Mr. Houghton
     1300 Dover Drive   Mr. Ott
     Jonesville, ZZ 12345   Mr. Smythe

To save space, the carbon copy notation may group the recipients.

cc Regional Sales Managers

If the recipient of the copy is to receive an enclosure or enclosures as well, that individual's full name and address as well as a description of each enclosure and the total number of enclosed items should be shown in the courtesy copy notation.

cc: Ms. Barbara S. Lee (2 copies, Annual Report)
     123 Jones Street
     Smithville, ST 56789

     Mrs. Sara T. Tufts
     Mrs. Laura E. Yowell

If the first names or initials are given along with the last names, courtesy titles (as *Mr., Mrs., Miss,* and *Ms.*) may be omitted.

cc: William L. Carton   cc: W.L. Carton
      Daniel I. Maginnis   D.I. Maginnis

Typists usually leave either one or two spaces between the *cc:* and the names that follow. However, if only one name follows the *cc:* and it is given in all initials, the space or spaces may be omitted.

cc:JBH

If the writer wishes that copies of the letter be distributed without the list of recipients being shown on the original, the blind carbon copy notation *bcc* or *bcc:* followed by an alphabetical list of the recipients' initials or names may be typed on the copies in the same page position as a regular carbon copy notation. The *bcc* notation may also appear in the upper left-hand corner of the copies.

Carbon or courtesy copies are not usually signed. The secretary may type the signature, preceded by the symbol */S/* or */s/,* to indicate that the writer signed the original copy.

Postscript

A postscript is aligned flush left and is typed two to four lines (depending on space available) below the last notation. If the letter's paragraphs are strict-block, the postscript reflects this format. If the paragraphs within the letter are indented, the first line of the postscript is also indented. If the Hanging-indented Letter styling is used, the first line of the postscript is flush left and all subsequent lines are indented five spaces. All postscripts are single-spaced. Their margins conform with those maintained in the letters themselves. The writer should initial a postscript. While it is not incorrect to head a postscript with the initials *P.S.* (for an initial postscript) and *P.P.S.* (for subsequent ones), these headings are redundant and can be omitted.

Letter Styles for Business Correspondence

The following pages contain full-page letter facsimiles of the five most often used business-letter formats—the Simplified Letter, the Block Letter, the Modified Block Letter, the Modified Semi-block Letter, and the Hanging-indented Letter. In addition, the section contains facsimiles of the following letters: the Official Letter Styling on Executive letterhead, the Official Letter Styling on plain bond, and the Half-sheet. Each facsimile contains a detailed description of letter format and styling. At the end of the section is a discussion of time- and money-saving correspondence methods that have gained acceptance in many of today's business offices.

Office of the President

Merriam-Webster Inc.
America's first publisher of dictionaries
and fine reference books.

January 1, 19—

Dear Ms. Peterson:

This is a facsimile of the Official Letter Styling often used for personal letters
written by an executive, or for letters typed
on his own personalized company stationery.
The paper size is either Executive or Monarch.

The Official Letter Styling is characterized by the page placement of the inside
address: It is typed flush left, two to five
lines below the last line of the signature
block or below the written signature.

The typist's initials if included are
typed two lines below the last line of the
inside address. An enclosure notation if
needed appears two lines below the typist's
initials, or two lines below the last line
of the inside address. These notations are
also flush left.

A typed signature block is not needed
on personalized Executive or Monarch stationery; however, if the writer's signature
is either difficult to decipher or if it
might be unfamiliar to the addressee, it
may be typed four lines below the complimentary close.

Open punctuation and blocked paragraphs
may also be used in this letter.

Sincerely,

Executive Signature

Ms. Martha Peterson
490 Jones Street
Smithville, ST 56789

47 FEDERAL STREET, SPRINGFIELD, MASSACHUSETTS 01101 TELEPHONE (413)-734-3134

Figure 4.37.   The Official Letter Styling with printed Executive letterhead

```
                                    4400 Ambler Boulevard
                                    Smithville, ST 56789
                                    January 1, 19—

        Dear Bob

        This is a facsimile of a letter typed on plain
        Executive or Monarch stationery.  The basic
        format is the same as that of the Official Let-
        ter Styling.  The block paragraphs and the open
        punctuation pattern are illustrated here.

        The heading which includes the writer's full
        address and the date may be positioned six lines
        from the top edge of the page and flush with the
        right margin as shown here.  Approximately six
        vertical lines may be placed after the date line
        down to the salutation.

        The complimentary close is typed two lines be-
        low the last line of the message.  The inside
        address is flush left, two to five lines below
        the last line of the signature block or below
        the written signature.

        Typist's initials, if included, should be posi-
        tioned two lines beneath the last line of the
        inside address.  An enclosure notation or any
        other notation if required should be typed two
        lines below the typist's initials or two lines
        below the last line of the inside address if
        there are no initials.

                                        Sincerely

                                        Executive Signature


        Mr. Robert Y. Owens
        123 East Second Avenue
        Jonesville, ST 45678
```

Figure 4.38.   The Official Letter Styling with plain stationery

Merriam-Webster Inc.
America's first publisher of dictionaries
and fine reference books.

January 1, 19—

Mrs. Althea Nance
Assistant to the President
XYZ Corporation
1234 Smith Boulevard
Smithville, ST 56789

Dear Mrs. Nance:

This is a facsimile of the Hanging-indented Letter which is not ordinarily used
    in general business correspondence but rather in advertising letters as an
    attractive way of catching the reader's eye. Its main feature is the para-
    graph alignment: The first line of each paragraph is aligned flush left,
    but all subsequent lines are indented five spaces from the left margin.
    The paragraphs are single-spaced internally and double-spaced between each
    other. Either the open or the mixed punctuation pattern may be used in the
    Hanging-indented Letter: This facsimile illustrates the mixed pattern.

The date line, usually typed three lines below the last line of the letterhead,
    is aligned flush right. The inside address and salutation are blocked
    flush left. Spacing between these elements parallels that used in the Mod-
    ified Block and the Modified Semi-block Letters.

Continuation sheets must contain at least three message lines, and the last word
    on the first sheet must not be divided. Continuation-sheet headings may be
    blocked left as in the Block Letter or laid out across the top of the page
    as in the Modified Semi-block Letter. Six blank lines are left from the
    top edge of the page to the first line of the heading and four blank lines
    are left before typing the message. Margins and paragraph alignment paral-
    lel those of the first sheet.

The complimentary close and the signature block are aligned under the date.
    Double-spacing is needed between the last message line and the complimenta-
    ry close. At least four lines should be left for the written signature.

Identification initials and enclosure and carbon copy notations are blocked
    flush left at least two lines below the last line of the signature block.
    Postscripts, if needed, are also hanging-indented.

Cordially,

Executive Signature

hg

47 Federal Street, P.O. Box 281, Springfield, MA 01101
Telephone (413) 734-3134

Figure 4.39.   The Hanging-indented Letter

Merriam-Webster Inc.
America's first publisher of dictionaries
and fine reference books.

January 1, 19—

Ms. Sarah H. Smith
Director of Marketing
XYZ Corporation
1234 Smith Boulevard
Smithville, ST 56789

SIMPLIFIED LETTER

Ms. Smith, this is the Simplified Letter recommended by the Administrative Management Society. Its main features—block format,
open punctuation, and fewer internal parts—reduce the number of
keystrokes and typewriter adjustments your secretary must make,
thus cutting costs, saving time, and increasing overall letter
output.

The date line is typed six lines below the last letterhead line.
The inside address, also flush left, appears three lines below the
date line. Since the placement of the inside address is designed
for window envelopes, it is suggested that the all-capitalized,
unpunctuated Postal Service State abbreviation be typed after the
city name, followed by one space and the ZIP Code.

The traditional salutation has been dropped and replaced by an un-
headed, all-capitalized subject line typed flush left, three lines
beneath the last inside-address line. The subject line summarizes
the message.

The first message line begins three lines below the subject line.
The first sentence serves as a greeting to the reader. The addressee's name should appear in the first paragraph, preferably in
the first sentence as shown above. Inclusion of the name adds a
personal touch. All paragraphs are blocked flush left, single-
spaced internally, and double-spaced between each other. Tabular
data and numbered lists are also blocked flush left but are set
off from the rest of the message by double-spacing. Long quotations and unnumbered lists should be indented five to ten spaces
from the left and right margins and set off from the rest of the
message by top and bottom double-spacing.

47 FEDERAL STREET, SPRINGFIELD, MASSACHUSETTS 01101 TELEPHONE (413)-734-3134

Figure 4.40.   The Simplified Letter

Ms. Smith
Page 2
January 1, 19——

If a continuation sheet is required, at least three message lines
must be carried over. Continuation-sheet format and margins match
those of the first sheet. At least six blank lines are left from
the top edge of the page to the first line of the heading which is
blocked flush left, single-spaced internally, and typically composed of the addressee's courtesy title and name, the page number,
and the applicable date. The rest of the message begins four lines
beneath the last heading line.

There is no complimentary close in the Simplified Letter, although
closing sentences such as "You have my best wishes," and "My best
regards are yours" may end the message. The writer's name (and
business title if needed) is aligned flush left and typed all in
capitals at least five lines below the last message line. Although
the Administrative Management Society uses a spaced hyphen between
the writer's surname and his business title, some companies prefer
a comma. The writer's department name may be typed flush left all
in capitals, one line below the signature line.

The identification initials, flush left and two lines below the
last line of the signature block, comprise the typist's initials
only. An enclosure notation may be typed one line below the identification initials and aligned flush left. Carbon copy notations
may be typed one or two lines below the last notation, depending
on available space. If only the signature block and/or typist's
initials appear before it, the carbon copy notation is typed two
lines below.

EXECUTIVE SIGNATURE - BUSINESS TITLE

coc
Enclosures (12)

cc Dr. Alice L. Barnes

Merriam-Webster Inc.
America's first publisher of dictionaries
and fine reference books.

```
January 1, 19—
X-123-4


XYZ Corporation
Sales Department
1234 Smith Boulevard
Smithville, ST 56789

Attention Mr. John Doe

Gentlemen

SUBJECT:  BLOCK LETTER

This is a facsimile of the Block Letter, whose structural parts
are flush left.  It may feature either the open or the mixed punc-
tuation pattern:  The open pattern is shown here.

The date line is typed two to six lines below the last letterhead
line.  Here, it is placed three lines below the letterhead.  Ac-
count or policy numbers if required are single-spaced and blocked
either above or below the date line.

Placement of the inside address varies by letter length.  Here, it
is typed four lines below the date line.  If window envelopes are
used, the all-capitalized, unpunctuated Postal Service state abbre-
viations should be employed.  One space intervenes between the
state abbreviation and the ZIP Code.  If regular envelopes are to
be used, state names may be typed out in full or abbreviated, de-
pending on organization preference.  An attention line if required
is typed two lines below the last inside-address line.

The salutation is typed two lines below the attention line, or two
to four lines below the last inside-address line.  The salutation
is "Gentlemen" if the letter is addressed to an organization, even
if there is an attention line directing the letter to a particular
individual within that organization.  If the letter is addressed
to an individual whose name is on line 1 of the inside address,
the salutation is "Dear Mr. (or Ms. or Mrs. or Miss) + surname" or
"Dear + first name" depending on the writer/reader relationship.
A subject line, typically all in capitals, may be typed two lines
below the salutation.  The subject line is optional.

The first message line is typed two lines below the salutation, or
two lines below the subject line if there is one.  The message is
```

47 FEDERAL STREET, SPRINGFIELD, MASSACHUSETTS 01101 TELEPHONE (413)-734-3134

Figure 4.41.   The Block Letter

XYZ Corporation
Sales Department
January 1, 19—
X-123-4
Page 2

single-spaced internally and double-spaced between paragraphs.
At least three message lines must be carried over to a continuation sheet: At no time should the complimentary close and the
signature block stand alone. The last word on a sheet should not
be divided. The continuation-sheet heading is typed six lines
from the top edge of the page. Account or policy numbers if used
on the first sheet must be included in the continuation-sheet
headings. The message begins four lines below the last line of
the heading.

The complimentary close is typed two lines below the last message
line, followed by at least four blank lines for the written signature, followed by the writer's name in capitals and lowercase.
The writer's business title and/or name of his department may be
included in the typed signature block, if they do not appear in
the printed letterhead.

Identification initials may comprise only the typist's initials if
the same person dictated and signed the letter. These initials
are typed two lines below the last signature-block line. The enclosure notation if used is typed one line below the identification line. The carbon copy notation if needed is placed one or
two lines below any other notations, depending on available space.

Sincerely yours

Executive Signature
Business Title

coc
Enclosures (2)

cc Mr. Howard T. Jansen

Merriam-Webster Inc.

America's first publisher of dictionaries
and fine reference books.

January 1, 19—

REGISTERED MAIL
PERSONAL

Mr. John Z. Teller
Treasurer
XYZ Corporation
1234 Smith Boulevard
Smithville, ST 56789

Dear Mr. Teller:

This is a facsimile of the Modified Block Letter. It differs from the Block
Letter chiefly in the page placement of its date line, its complimentary close,
and its signature block that are aligned at center, toward the right margin, or
at the right margin. Either the open or the mixed punctuation pattern may be
used: The mixed pattern is illustrated here.

While the date line may be positioned from two to six lines below the last line
of the letterhead, its standard position is three lines below the letterhead,
as shown above. In this facsimile, the date line is typed five spaces to the
right of dead center. If an account or policy number is required, it is blocked
and single-spaced on a line above or below the date.

Special mailing notations and on-arrival notations such as the two shown above
are all-capitalized, aligned flush left, and blocked together two lines above
the first line of the inside address. If used singly, either of these notations
appears two lines above the inside address.

The first line of the inside address is typed about four lines below the date
line. This spacing can be expanded or contracted according to the letter length.
The inside address, the salutation, and all paragraphs of the message are aligned
flush left. The salutation, typed two to four lines below the last line of the
inside address, is worded as it would be in the Block Letter. A subject line if
used is typed two lines below the salutation in all-capital letters and is either
blocked flush left or centered on the page. Underscoring the subject line is also acceptable, but in this case, only the first letter of each word would be capitalized.

The message begins two lines below the salutation or the subject line if there is
one. Paragraphs are single-spaced internally and double-spaced between each other; however, in very short letters, the paragraphs may be double-spaced internally and triple-spaced between each other.

47 Federal Street, P.O. Box 281, Springfield, MA 01101
Telephone (413) 734-3134

Figure 4.42.   The Modified Block Letter

Mr. Teller   - 2 -   January 1, 19—

Continuation sheets should contain at least three message lines. The last word on a sheet should not be divided. The continuation-sheet heading may be blocked flush left as in the Block Letter or it may be laid out across the top of the page as shown above. This heading begins six lines from the top edge of the page, and the message is continued four lines beneath it.

The complimentary close is typed two lines below the last line of the message. While the complimentary close may be aligned under some portion of the letterhead, directly under the date line, or even flush with but not overrunning the right margin, it is often typed five spaces to the right of dead center as shown here.

The signature line is typed in capitals and lowercase at least four lines below the complimentary close. The writer's business title and department name may be included if they do not already appear in the printed letterhead. All elements of the signature block must be aligned with each other and with the complimentary close.

Identification initials need include only those of the typist, providing that the writer and the signer are the same person. These initials appear two lines below the last line of the signature block. An enclosure notation is typed one line below the identification line, and the carbon copy notation if required appears one or two lines below any other notations, depending on space available.

                     Sincerely yours,

                     Executive Signature

                     Executive Signature
                     Business Title

hg
Enclosures (5)

cc Dr. Doe
   Dr. Franklin
   Dr. Mason
   Dr. Watson

Merriam-Webster Inc.
America's first publisher of dictionaries
and fine reference books.

January 1, 19—

Mr. Carroll D. Thompson
Sales Manager
XYZ Corporation
1234 Smith Boulevard
Smithville, ST 56789

Dear Mr. Thompson:

MODIFIED SEMI-BLOCK LETTER

This is a facsimile of the Modified Semi-block Letter. It features a date line aligned either slightly to
the right of dead center or flush right (as shown above).
Its inside address and salutation are aligned flush left,
while the paragraphs of the message are indented five or
ten spaces. Its complimentary close and signature block
are aligned under the date, either slightly to the right
or dead center, or flush right. Identification initials,
enclosure notations, and carbon copy notations are aligned
flush left.

A special mailing notation or an on-arrival notation
if required would have been typed flush left and two lines
above the first line of the inside address. An account or
policy number if needed would have been blocked with the
date, one line above or below it. The page placement of
these elements parallels their positioning in the Modified
Block Letter. An attention line if required is aligned
flush left, two lines below the last line of the inside address. A subject line may be typed in all-capitals two
lines below the salutation and is typically centered on the
page.

The paragraphs are single-spaced internally and
double-spaced between each other unless the letter is extremely short, in which case the paragraphs may be double-
spaced internally and triple-spaced between each other.
Continuation sheets should contain at least three message
lines, and the last word on a sheet should never be divided. The heading for a continuation sheet begins at
least six lines from the top edge of the page and follows the format shown in this letter.

Figure 4.43.   The Modified Semi-block Letter

Mr. Thompson   - 2 -   January 1, 19—

    The complimentary close is typed at two lines below
the last line of the message. The signature line, four
lines below the complimentary close, is aligned with it
if possible, or centered under it if the name and title
will be long. In this case, it is better to align both
date and complimentary close about five spaces to the
right of dead center to ensure enough room for the signature block which should never overrun the right margin.
The writer's name, business title and department name (if
not already printed on the stationery) are typed in capitals and lowercase.

    Although open punctuation may be followed, the mixed
punctuation pattern is quite common with the Modified
Semi-block Letter, and it is the latter that is shown
here.

                        Sincerely yours,

                        Executive Signature

                        Executive Signature
                        Business Title

jml

Enclosures: 2

cc: Dr. Bennett P. Oakley
     Addison Engineering Associates
     91011 Jones Street
     Smithville, ST 56789

    A postscript if needed is typically positioned two
to four lines below the last notation. In the Modified
Semi-block Letter, the postscript is indented five to ten
spaces to agree with message paragraphing. It is not
necessary to head the postscript with the abbreviation
P.S. The postscript should be initialed by the writer.

                        ES

Merriam-Webster Inc.
America's first publisher of dictionaries
and fine reference books.

January 1, 19—

Mr. Ken T. Row
123 Key Place
Smithville, ST 56789

Dear Ken:

This is a facsimile of the half
sheet which is used for the briefest
of notes—those containing one or
two sentences or two very short paragraphs.

The Block, Modified Block, or
Modified Semi-block Letters may be
used, and open or mixed punctuation
may be followed.

Sincerely yours,

Executive Signature

jml

Figure 4.44.　The Half-sheet

Time-saving Correspondence Methods

An increasing number of business offices rely on time-saving and cost-cutting measures for sending out and replying to routine correspondence. Among these methods are the use of form letters and form paragraphs, memorandum forms with detachable reply sections, postal cards, and the writing of marginal notations directly on letters received.

Postal cards Brief messages may be typewritten on standard size (5½ by 3½ inches) postal cards. A message can be fitted on the card if you follow these suggestions:

1. Set the margins for a 4½-inch writing line, which allows half-inch margins at each side. Plan to leave a half-inch margin at the bottom.
2. Type the date on the third line from the top.
3. Omit the inside address.
4. Leave one line of space before the salutation.
5. Leave one line of space before the message.
6. Leave one line of space before the complimentary close and the signature.
7. If necessary, omit one or more of the following: salutation, complimentary close, handwritten signature, identification initials.

Pre-addressed postal cards may also be enclosed with a letter of inquiry to encourage and speed an answer back to your office. You may even type various responses so that the recipient can simply check the appropriate response and mail the card.

Marginal notations The procedure described here is used in many business offices to answer routine queries. The answer to an incoming letter is written at the bottom of the letter, a copy is made for the files, and the original is returned to the sender with the reply written directly on it. Frequently a stamped message or sticker is attached explaining that this speedy reply method is for the customer's convenience.

One variation of this procedure is to stamp on your own letter of inquiry, "Reply here to save time. Photocopy for your files." Or you can enclose a photocopy of your original letter with a request that the recipient simply answer in the margin of the copy and return it to you.

Marginal notations save time and cut costs, and they also reduce the number of file copies. However, they should be used only when such informality is appropriate.

Stylings for Envelope Addresses

The following information may appear on any envelope regardless of its size. Asterisked items are essential and those that are unmarked are optional, depending on the requirements of the particular letter:

*1. The addressee's full name and full geographical address typed approximately in the vertical and horizontal center
 2. Special mailing notation or notations typed below the stamp
 3. On-arrival notation or notations typed about nine lines below the top left
*4. Sender's full name and geographical address printed or typed in the upper left corner.

The typeface should be block style. The Postal Service does not recommend unusual or italic typefaces.

The address block on a regular envelope should take up no more than 1½″ × 3¾″ of space. There should be ⅝″ of space from the bottom line of the address block to the bottom edge of the envelope. The entire area from the right and left bottom margins of the address block to the right and left bottom edges of the envelope as well as the area under the center of the address block to the bottom center edge of the envelope should be free of print. With regular envelopes, most address blocks are begun about five spaces to the left of horizontal center to admit room for potentially long lines. The address block should be single-spaced. Block styling should be used throughout.

If a window envelope is being used, all address data must appear within the window space, and at least ¼″ margins must be maintained between the address and the right, left, top, and bottom edges of the window space.

Position of Elements

Address-block elements should be styled and positioned as described in the following paragraphs:

First Line If the addressee is an individual, that person's courtesy title and full name are typed on the first line.

Mr. Lee O. Idlewild

If an individual addressee's business title is included in the inside address, it may be typed either on the first line of the address block with a comma separating it from the addressee's name, or it may be typed alone on the next line, depending on the length of title and name.

Mr. Lee O. Idlewild, President

Mr. Lee O. Idlewild
President

If the addressee is an organization, its full name is typed on the first line. If a particular department within an organization is specified, its name is typed on a line under the name of the organization.

XYZ Corporation
Sales Department

Next line The full street address should be typed out (although it is acceptable to abbreviate such designations as *Street, Avenue, Boulevard,* etc.). In mass mailings that will be presorted for automated handling (see pages 226–229), it is correct to capitalize all elements of the address block and to use the unpunctuated abbreviations for streets and street-designations that are recommended by the U.S. Postal Service. Room, suite, apartment, and building numbers are typed immediately following the last element of the street address and are positioned on the same line with it. Building names, if used, are listed on a separate line just above the street address.

A post-office box number, if used, is typed on the line immediately above the last line in order to assure delivery to this point. (The box number precedes the station name when a station name is included.) Both street address and post-office box number may be written in the address, but the letter will be delivered to the location specified on the next-to-last line.

Last line The last line of the address block contains the city, state, and the zip code number. Only one space intervenes between the last letter of the state abbreviation and the first digit of the zip code. The zip code should never be on a line by itself. The zip code is mandatory, as are the all-capitalized, unpunctuated, two-letter Postal Service abbreviations. It is correct, however, to spell the name of a state in full on the letter while using the Postal Service abbreviation on the envelope.

Mr. John P. Smith
4523 Kendall Place, Apt. 8B
Smithville, ST 56789
       or
Mr. John P. Smith
4523 Kendall Pl., Apt. 8B
Smithville, ST 56789

When both post-office box number and street address are included in an address, the zip code should correctly match the location (usually the post-office box) specified in the line just above the last line of the address.

XYZ Corporation
1234 Smith Boulevard
P. O. Box 600
Smithville, ST 56788

If the addressee has indicated a 9-digit zip code on correspondence to you, use the full number to speed delivery to that address.

Cameron Corporation
765 Bay Street, Room III
Smithville, ST 56789-1234

Other elements On-arrival notations such as PERSONAL or CONFIDENTIAL must be typed entirely in capital letters, about nine lines below the

Table 4.5
Two-letter State Abbreviations for the United States and its Dependencies

Alabama	AL	Kentucky	KY	Oklahoma	OK
Alaska	AK	Louisiana	LA	Oregon	OR
Arizona	AZ	Maine	ME	Pennsylvania	PA
Arkansas	AR	Maryland	MD	Puerto Rico	PR
California	CA	Massachusetts	MA	Rhode Island	RI
Colorado	CO	Michigan	MI	South Carolina	SC
Connecticut	CT	Minnesota	MN	South Dakota	SD
Delaware	DE	Mississippi	MS	Tennessee	TN
District of		Missouri	MO	Texas	TX
Columbia	DC	Montana	MT	Utah	UT
Florida	FL	Nebraska	NE	Vermont	VT
Georgia	GA	Nevada	NV	Virginia	VA
Guam	GU	New Hampshire	NH	Virgin Islands	VI
Hawaii	HI	New Jersey	NJ	Washington	WA
Idaho	ID	New Mexico	NM	West Virginia	WV
Illinois	IL	New York	NY	Wisconsin	WI
Indiana	IN	North Carolina	NC	Wyoming	WY
Iowa	IA	North Dakota	ND		
Kansas	KS	Ohio	OH		

left top edge of the envelope. Any other on-arrival instructions such as *Hold for Arrival* or *Please Forward* may be typed in capitals and lowercase, underlined, and positioned about nine lines from the left top edge of the envelope.

If an attention line is used in the letter itself, it too must appear on the envelope. The attention line must be placed in the address block so that it is directly above the next-to-last line.

> XYZ Corporation
> Sales Department
> Attention Mr. E. R. Bailey
> 1234 Smith Boulevard
> Smithville, ST 56789

A special mailing notation (as CERTIFIED, REGISTERED MAIL, or SPECIAL DELIVERY) is typed entirely in capitals just below the stamp or about nine lines from the right top edge of the envelope. It should not overrun a ½″ margin.

The printed return address (as of a company) may be supplemented by the name of the writer typed in at the top. The return address on a plain envelope should be styled as follows, with the least two blank lines between the return address and the left and top edges of the envelope:

> Stephen P. Lemke
> 123 Ann Street
> Jonesville, XX 12345

See Table 4.2 on page 179 for a chart showing stationery and envelope sizes and applications. See Chapter 12 for detailed treatment of mailing procedures.

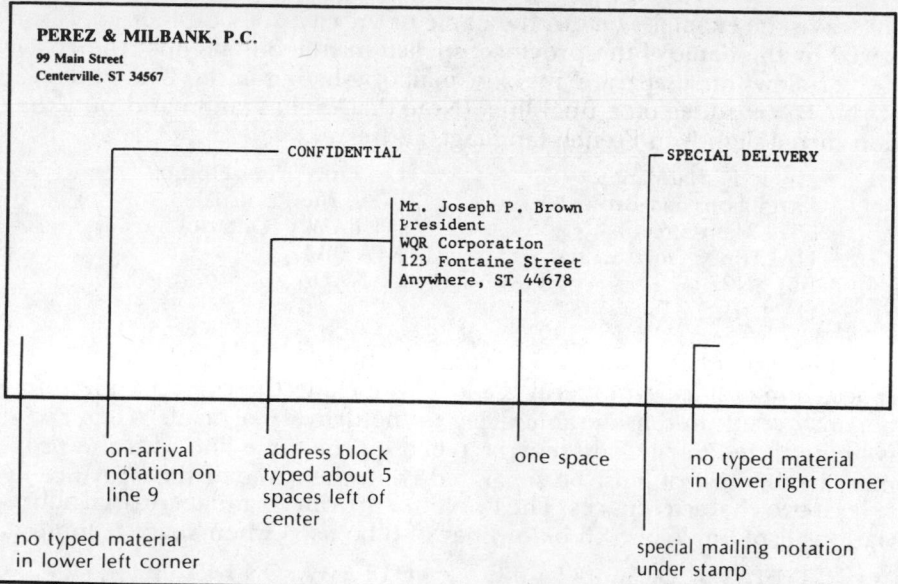

Figure 4.45.   Commercial envelope showing on-arrival and special mailing notations

Foreign Addresses

When typing a foreign address, the secretary should refer first to the return address on the envelope of previous correspondence to ascertain the correct ordering of the essential elements of the address block. Letterhead stationery of previous correspondence may also be checked if an envelope is not available. If neither of these sources is available, the material should be typed as it appears in the inside address of the dictated letter. The following guidelines may be of assistance.

1. All foreign addresses should be typed in English or in English characters. If an address must be in foreign characters (as Russian), an English translation should be inserted between the lines in the address block.
2. Foreign courtesy titles may be substituted for the English, but they are not necessary.
3. The name of the country should be typed in full and in all-capital letters by itself on the last line. Canadian addresses always carry the name CANADA, even though the name of the province is also given.
4. When applicable, foreign postal district numbers should be included. These are positioned either before or after the name of the city, never after the name of the country.

Canadian addresses should adhere to the form requested by the Canada Post for quickest delivery through its automated handling system. As shown in the examples below, the name of the city, fully capitalized, is followed by the name of the province, spelled in full, on one line; the Postal Code follows on a separate line. For mail originating in the United States, CANADA is added on a final line. (Note that capitalization and punctuation differ slightly in French-language addresses.)

Mr. F. F. MacManus	Les Entreprises Optima Ltée
Fitzgibbons and Brown	6789, rue Principale
5678 Main Street	OTTAWA (Ontario)
HALIFAX, Nova Scotia	K1A 0B3
B3J 2N9	CANADA
CANADA	

The Canadian Postal Code consists always of letter-numeral-letter, space, numeral-letter-numeral. Failure to include the correct code number may result in considerable delay in the delivery of mail. When space is limited, the Postal Code may be typed on the same line with the province. In this case, it must be separated from the name of the province by at least two character spaces. The two-letter provincial and territorial abbreviations listed in Table 4.6 below may also be used when space is limited.

OTTAWA, Ontario K1A 0B3   *or*   OTTAWA, ON K1A 0B3

Table 4.6
Two-letter Abbreviations for Canadian Provinces

Alberta	AB	Newfoundland	NF	Quebec	PQ
British Columbia	BC	Northwest Territories	NT	Saskatchewan	SK
Labrador	LB	Nova Scotia	NS	Yukon Territory	YT
Manitoba	MB	Ontario	ON		
New Brunswick	NB	Prince Edward Island	PE		

Some samples of foreign corporate abbreviations are shown in Table 4.7 on page 227.

Addressing for Automation

So that the secretary can take full advantage of the post office's computerized sorting equipment (including new optical character readers that can scan and sort many thousands of pieces of mail an hour), the United States Postal Service recommends that *all* envelopes be addressed properly for automation. All typescript should be clear and easy to read. The basic procedures in addressing envelopes are as follows:

1. Use rectangular envelopes no smaller than $3\frac{1}{2}'' \times 5''$ and no larger than $6\frac{1}{8}'' \times 11\frac{1}{2}''$. There should be good color contrast between the paper and the type impressions.
2. The address should be single-spaced and blocked (straight left margin). The address must be at least 1″ from the left edge of the enve-

Table 4.7
Foreign Corporate Abbreviations

A Brief Sampling of Commonly Used Terms

Language	Type of Business	Abbreviation
Danish	Partnership	I/S
	Limited Partnership	K/S
	Limited-liability Company	A/S
	Private Limited-liability Company	Ap/S
Dutch	Private Company	B.V.
	Public Corporation	N.V.
French	Limited-liability Company	SARL
	Corporation	SA
German	Partnership	OHG
	Limited Partnership	KG
	Limited-liability Company	G.m.b.H.
	Corporation	AG
Italian	Corporation	S.p.A.
	Limited-liability Company	S.r.l.
Portuguese	Corporation	SARL
Spanish	Stock Company	S.A.
	Company	Cía
Swedish	Joint Stock Company	SA

lope and at least ⅝″ up from the bottom. There should be no print to the right of or below the address.

3. Additional data (as the attention line, account number, or date) should be part of the blocked address. These data should be positioned above the second line from bottom. Envelope addresses should be typed entirely in capital letters without punctuation marks. Use type fonts other than script, italic, or proportionally-spaced fonts. Do not type the address at a slant.

```
C REEVES CORP
ATTN MR R C SMITH
XXX XXXX XX XXX XXX
XXXXXXXX XX XXXXX
```

4. If mail is addressed to occupants of multi-unit buildings, the unit number should appear after the street address on the same line.

```
C REEVES CORP
ATTN MR R C SMITH
186 PARK ST ROOM 960
XXXXXXXX XX XXXXX
```

5. The bottom line of the address should contain the city, state, and zip code number (see Table 4.5 on page 224).

    C REEVES CORP
    ATTN MR R C SMITH
    186 PARK ST ROOM 960
    HARTFORD CT 06106

6. A post-office box number is typed on the line above the last to assure delivery to this point. (Use the zip code for the box number, not for the street address.) The box number precedes the station name.

    C REEVES CORP
    186 PARK ST
    PO BOX 210 LINCOLN STA
    HARTFORD CT 06106

7. At least ¼″ should be left between the address and the sides and bottom edges of the opening on window envelopes.

A maximum of 22 strokes or positions is allowed on the last line of an envelope address. The Postal Service suggests the following maximum number of positions:

    13 positions for the city
    1 space between the city and state
    2 positions for the state
    1 space between the state and zip code number
    5 positions for the zip code number

    22 total positions allowed

Many cities exceed the suggested maximum number of 13 positions. The Postal Service suggests that the abbreviations listed in Table 4.8 below be used to facilitate mail processing.

Table 4.8
Abbreviations for Street Designators and for Words that Appear Frequently in Place Names

Academy	ACAD	Bottom	BTM	Churches	CHRS
Agency	AGNCY	Boulevard	BLVD	Circle	CIR
Airport	ARPRT	Branch	BR	City	CY
Alley	ALY	Bridge	BRG	Clear	CLR
Annex	ANX	Brook	BRK	Cliffs	CLFS
Arcade	ARC	Burg	BG	Club	CLB
Arsenal	ARSL	Bypass	BYP	College	CLG
Avenue	AVE	Camp	CP	Corner	COR
Bayou	BYU	Canyon	CYN	Corners	CORS
Beach	BCH	Cape	CPE	Court	CT
Bend	BND	Causeway	CSWY	Courts	CTS
Big	BG	Center	CTR	Cove	CV
Black	BLK	Central	CTL	Creek	CRK
Bluff	BLF	Church	CHR	Crescent	CRES

Crossing	XING	Key	KY	Sainte	ST
Dale	DL	Knolls	KNLS	San	SN
Dam	DM	Lake	LK	Santa	SN
Depot	DPO	Lakes	LKS	Santo	SN
Divide	DIV	Landing	LNDG	School	SCH
Drive	DR	Lane	LN	Seminary	SMNRY
East	E	Light	LGT	Shoal	SHL
Estates	EST	Little	LTL	Shoals	SHLS
Expressway	EXPY	Loaf	LF	Shode	SHD
Extended	EXT	Locks	LCKS	Shore	SHR
Extension	EXT	Lodge	LDG	Shores	SHRS
Fall	FL	Lower	LWR	Siding	SDG
Falls	FLS	Manor	MNR	South	S
Farms	FRMS	Meadows	MDWS	Space Flight	
Ferry	FRY	Meeting	MTG	Center	SFC
Field	FLD	Memorial	MEM	Spring	SPG
Fields	FLDS	Middle	MDL	Springs	SPGS
Flats	FLT	Mile	MLE	Square	SQ
Ford	FRD	Mill	ML	State	ST
Forest	FRST	Mills	MLS	Station	STA
Forge	FRG	Mines	MNS	Stream	STRM
Fork	FRK	Mission	MSN	Street	ST
Forks	FRKS	Mound	MND	Sulphur	SLPHR
Fort	FT	Mount	MT	Summit	SMT
Fountain	FTN	Mountain	MTN	Switch	SWCH
Freeway	FWY	National	NAT	Tannery	TNRY
Furnace	FURN	Neck	NCK	Tavern	TVRN
Gardens	GDNS	New	NW	Terminal	TERM
Gateway	GTWY	North	N	Terrace	TER
Glen	GLN	Orchard	ORCH	Ton	TN
Grand	GRND	Palms	PLMS	Tower	TWR
Great	GR	Park	PK	Town	TWN
Green	GRN	Parkway	PKY	Trail	TRL
Ground	GRD	Pillar	PLR	Trailer	TRLR
Grove	GRV	Pines	PNES	Tunnel	TUNL
Harbor	HBR	Place	PL	Turnpike	TPKE
Haven	HVN	Plain	PLN	Union	UN
Heights	HTS	Plains	PLNS	University	UNIV
High	HI	Plaza	PLZ	Upper	UPR
Highlands	HGLDS	Point	PT	Valley	VLY
Highway	HWY	Port	PRT	Viaduct	VIA
Hill	HL	Prairie	PR	View	VW
Hills	HLS	Ranch	RNCH	Village	VLG
Hollow	HOLW	Ranches	RNCHS	Ville	VL
Hospital	HOSP	Rapids	RPDS	Vista	VIS
Hot	H	Resort	RESRT	Water	WTR
House	HSE	Rest	RST	Wells	WLS
Inlet	INLT	Ridge	RDG	West	W
Institute	INST	River	RIV	White	WHT
Island	IS	Road	RD	Works	WKS
Islands	IS	Rock	RK	Yards	YDS
Isle	IS	Rural	R		
Junction	JCT	Saint	ST		

CHAPTER 5

Forms of Address

It has already been emphasized that the initial impression created by a letter is vital to the letter's ultimate effectiveness. It follows that the proper use of the conventional forms of address is essential, especially since these forms appear in conspicuous areas of the letter: on the envelope, in the inside address, and in the salutation.

Forms of Address Chart

The following pages contain a chart of alphabetically grouped and listed forms of address for individuals where offices, ranks, or professions warrant special courtesy. (For information about choosing complimentary closes, see page 199.) The main categories in the chart are listed below in the order of their appearance.

Clerical and Religious Orders

College and University Faculty and Officials

Consular Officers

Diplomats

Foreign Heads of State

Government Officials—Federal

Government Officials—Local

Government Officials—State

Military Ranks

Miscellaneous Professional Titles

United Nations Officials

A special chart headed "Multiple Addressees" immediately follows the Forms of Address Chart, and a more detailed discussion of special titles and abbreviations (such as *Doctor, Esquire, Honorable,* etc.) begins on page 250. For information about the use of gender-neutral salutations, see pages 192–193.

When two or more stylings are shown in the Forms of Address Chart, it should be understood by the reader that the most formal styling appears first. It should also be understood that if the formal address shown for a man in "Sir," the formal address for a woman is "Madam," and vice versa, and that if the informal address for a man is "Mr.," the informal address for a woman is "Mrs.," "Miss," or "Ms.," and vice versa. In cases where this simple equation does not apply, examples for both male and female addresses are given. In all of the examples for female addresses, the courtesy title *Ms.* has been shown; however, the titles *Mrs.* and *Miss* may be freely substituted in all of these cases according to the preference of the recipient if it is known.

Readers will note that approximately half of the positions and ranks in this chart are illustrated with a man's name and half with a woman's name. This is not meant to suggest that any position or rank in this chart is more likely to be held by a man or a woman. On the contrary, it has been assumed that, except in the category of Clerical and Religious Orders, either a man or woman may hold any position or rank included in this chart; however, space limitations in the chart preclude showing examples of both male and female addresses in every instance.

Lack of space has also resulted in the exclusion from the chart of lower-ranking officials such as city water commissioners. Addressing these minor officials should be no problem, however. An official's title appears in the address only if the official *heads* an agency or department; otherwise, only the name of the agency or department is included.

Mrs. Joan R. White, Chairman Smithville School Board	Mrs. Joan R. White Smithville School Board

Mrs. Joan R. White
Sheriff, Rockland County

Salutations on letters to minor officials consist of courtesy title + surname. The substitution of a professional title (as "Dear Justice Smith") for the courtesy title is correct only for high-ranking officials such as governors and judges; for military officers; and for certain police and fire officers.

Dear Governor Roy Dear Senator Scott Dear Judge Dow Dear Major Smith	Dear Chief Roberts Dear Sheriff Roberts *but also* Dear Mr. Roberts

Military officers retain their highest rank upon retirement and are addressed in the same way as active officers.

Inside Address Styling	Salutation Styling
Clerical and Religious Orders	

abbot
The Right Reverend John R. Smith, O.S.B.   Right Reverend and dear Father
Abbot of _____   Dear Father Abbot
                                            Dear Father

archbishop
The Most Reverend Archbishop of _____   Your Excellency
 or
The Most Reverend John R. Smith   Your Excellency
Archbishop of _____   Dear Archbishop Smith

archdeacon
The Venerable The Archdeacon of _____   Venerable Sir
 or
The Venerable John R. Smith   Venerable Sir
Archdeacon of _____   My dear Archdeacon

bishop, Catholic
The Most Reverend John R. Smith   Your Excellency
Bishop of _____   Dear Bishop Smith

bishop, Episcopal
The Right Reverend The Bishop of _____   Right Reverend Sir
 or
The Right Reverend John R. Smith   Right Reverend Sir
Bishop of _____   Dear Bishop Smith

bishop, Episcopal, Presiding
The Most Reverend John R. Smith   Most Reverend Sir
Presiding Bishop   Dear Bishop
                                            Dear Bishop Smith

bishop, Protestant (excluding Episcopal)
The Reverend John R. Smith   Reverend Sir
                                            Dear Bishop Smith

brotherhood, member of
Brother John, S.J. *(or other initials for the order)*   Dear Brother John

canon
The Reverend John R. Smith   Dear Canon Smith
Canon of _____ Cathedral

cardinal
His Eminence John Cardinal Smith   Your Eminence
                                            Dear Cardinal Smith

 or
His Eminence Cardinal Smith   Your Eminence
                                            Dear Cardinal Smith

 or if also an archbishop
His Eminence John Cardinal Smith   Your Eminence
Archbishop of _____   Dear Cardinal Smith
 or
His Eminence Cardinal Smith   Your Eminence
Archbishop of _____   Dear Cardinal Smith

Inside Address Styling	Salutation Styling
chaplain, college or university—see COLLEGE AND UNIVERSITY FACULTY AND OFFICIALS	

clergyman, Protestant
The Reverend Amelia R. Smith — Dear Ms. Smith
  or if having a doctorate
The Reverend Dr. Amelia R. Smith — Dear Dr. Smith

dean (of a cathedral)
The Very Reverend John R. Smith — Very Reverend Sir
_____ Cathedral — Dear Dean Smith
  or
Dean John R. Smith — Very Reverend Sir
_____ Cathedral — Dear Dean Smith

monsignor, domestic prelate
The Right Reverend Monsignor John R. Smith — Right Reverend and dear Monsignor Smith
  or
The Rt. Rev. Msgr. John R. Smith — Dear Monsignor Smith

monsignor, papal chamberlain
The Very Reverend Monsignor John R. Smith — Very Reverend and dear Monsignor Smith
  or
The Very Rev. Msgr. John R. Smith — Dear Monsignor Smith

mother superior (of a sisterhood)
The Reverend Mother Superior — Reverend Mother
Convent of _____ — Dear Reverend Mother
— My dear Reverend Mother Mary Angelica
  or
Reverend Mother Mary Angelica, O.S.D. — Reverend Mother
  (or other initials of the order) — Dear Reverend Mother
Convent of _____ — My dear Reverend Mother Mary Angelica
  or
Mother Mary Angelica, Superior — Reverend Mother
Convent of _____ — Dear Reverend Mother
— My dear Reverend Mother Mary Angelica

patriarch (of an Eastern Orthodox Church)
His Beatitude the Patriarch of _____ — Most Reverend Lord

pope
His Holiness the Pope — Your Holiness
— Most Holy Father
  or
His Holiness Pope John — Your Holiness
— Most Holy Father

president, Mormon
The President — My dear President
Church of Jesus Christ of Latter-day Saints — Dear President Smith

priest, Catholic
The Reverend Father Smith — Dear Father Smith
  or
The Reverend John R. Smith — Dear Father Smith

Inside Address Styling	Salutation Styling

priest, president (of a college or university)—see COLLEGE AND UNIVERSITY FACULTY AND
   OFFICIALS

rabbi
Rabbi John R. Smith	Dear Rabbi Smith
or if having a doctorate	
Rabbi John R. Smith, D.D.	Dear Dr. Smith

sisterhood, member of
| Sister Mary Angelica, S.C. *(or other initials* | Dear Sister |
| *of the order)* | Dear Sister Mary Angelica |

College and University Faculty and Officials

---

chancellor (of a university)
| Dr. Amelia R. Smith | Dear Dr. Smith |
| Chancellor | |

chaplain (of a college or university)
The Reverend John R. Smith	Dear Chaplain Smith
Chaplain	Dear Mr. Smith
	Dear Father Smith

dean (of a college or university)
Dean Amelia R. Smith	Dear Dr. Smith
	Dear Dean Smith
or	
Dr. Amelia R. Smith	Dear Dr. Smith
Dean	Dear Dean Smith

instructor
| Mr. John R. Smith | Dear Mr. Smith |
| Instructor | |

president
Dr. Amelia R. Smith	Dear Dr. Smith
President	
or	
President Amelia R. Smith	Dear President Smith

president, priest
| The Very Reverend John R. Smith | Dear Father Smith |
| President | |

professor, assistant or associate
Dr. Amelia R. Smith	Dear Dr. Smith
Assistant Professor of _____	Dear Professor Smith
	Dear Ms. Smith
or	
Dr. Amelia R. Smith	Dear Dr. Smith
Associate Professor of _____	Dear Professor Smith
	Dear Ms. Smith

professor, full
Professor John R. Smith	Dear Professor Smith
or	
Dr. John R. Smith	Dear Dr. Smith
Professor of _____	

Inside Address Styling	Salutation Styling

Consular Officers

consulate, American

The American Consulate	Gentlemen
(foreign city, country)	Ladies and Gentlemen
or if in Latin America or Canada	
The Consulate of the United States of America	Gentlemen
	Ladies and Gentlemen

consul, American (covers all consular grades such as *Consul, Consul General, Vice-Consul,* and *Consular Agent*)

The American Consul	Sir
(foreign city, country)	Sir or Madam
or if in Latin America or Canada	
The Consul of the United States of America	Sir
	Sir or Madam
or if individual name is known	
Amelia R. Smith, Esq.	Madam
American Consul	Dear Ms. Smith
or if in Latin America or Canada	
Amelia R. Smith, Esq.	Madam
Consul of the United States of America	Dear Ms. Smith

consulate, foreign

The _____ Consulate	Gentlemen
(U.S. city, state, zip code)	Ladies and Gentlemen
or	
The Consulate of _____	Gentlemen
(U.S. city, state, zip code)	Ladies and Gentlemen

consuls, foreign (covers all consular grades)

The _____ Consul	Sir
(U.S. city, state, zip code)	Sir or Madame
or	
The Consul of _____	Sir
(U.S. city, state, zip code)	Sir or Madame
or if individual name is known	
The Honorable John R. Smith	Sir
_____ Consul	Dear Mr. Smith

Diplomats

ambassador, American

The Honorable Amelia R. Smith	Madam
American Ambassador	Dear Madam Ambassador
or if in Latin America or Canada	
The Honorable Amelia R. Smith	Madam
Ambassador of the United States of America	Dear Madam Ambassador
or	
The Honorable John R. Smith	Sir
American Ambassador	Dear Mr. Ambassador
or if in Latin America or Canada	
The Honorable John R. Smith	Sir
Ambassador of the United States of America	Dear Mr. Ambassador

Inside Address Styling	Salutation Styling

ambassador, foreign

His Excellency John R. Smith   Excellency
Ambassador of _____   Dear Mr. Ambassador
   or
Her Excellency Amelia R. Smith   Excellency
Ambassador of _____   Dear Madame Ambassador

chargé d'affaires ad interim, American

Amelia R. Smith, Esq.   Madam
American Chargé d'Affaires ad Interim   Dear Ms. Smith
   or if in Latin America or Canada
Amelia R. Smith, Esq.   Madam
United States Chargé d'Affaires ad Interim   Dear Ms. Smith

chargé d'affaires ad interim, foreign

Mr. John R. Smith   Sir
Chargé d'Affaires ad Interim of _____   Dear Mr. Smith
   or
Ms. Amelia R. Smith   Madame
Chargé d'Affaires ad Interim of _____   Dear Ms. Smith

chargé d'affaires (de missi), foreign

Ms. Amelia R. Smith   Madame
Chargé d'Affaires of _____   Dear Ms. Smith
   or
Mr. John R. Smith   Sir
Chargé d'Affaires of _____   Dear Mr. Smith

minister, American

The Honorable John R. Smith   Sir
American Minister   Dear Mr. Minister
   or if in Latin America or Canada
The Honorable John R. Smith   Sir
Minister of the United States of America   Dear Mr. Minister
   or
The Honorable Amelia R. Smith   Madam
American Minister   Dear Madam Minister
   or if in Latin America or Canada
The Honorable Amelia R. Smith   Madam
Minister of the United States of America   Dear Madam Minister

minister, foreign

The Honorable Amelia R. Smith   Madame
Minister of _____   Dear Madame Minister
   or
The Honorable John R. Smith   Sir
Minister of _____   Dear Mr. Minister

Foreign Heads of State: A Brief Sampling

---

premier

His Excellency John R. Smith   Excellency
Premier of _____   Dear Mr. Premier
   or
Her Excellency Amelia R. Smith   Excellency
Premier of _____   Dear Madame Premier

Inside Address Styling	Salutation Styling

president of a republic
Her Excellency Amelia R. Smith
President of _____   Excellency
       Dear Madame President
    or
His Excellency John R. Smith   Excellency
President of _____   Dear Mr. President

prime minister
His Excellency John R. Smith   Excellency
       Dear Mr. Prime Minister
    or
Her Excellency Amelia R. Smith   Excellency
       Dear Madame Prime Minister

Government Officials—Federal

attorney general
The Honorable Amelia R. Smith   Dear Madam Attorney General
The Attorney General
    or
The Honorable John R. Smith   Dear Mr. Attorney General
The Attorney General

cabinet officer (other than attorney general)
The Honorable John R. Smith   Sir
Secretary of _____   Dear Mr. Secretary
    or
The Secretary of _____   Sir
    or   Dear Mr. Secretary
The Honorable Amelia R. Smith   Madam
Secretary of _____   Dear Madam Secretary

cabinet officer, former
The Honorable Amelia R. Smith   Dear Ms. Smith

chairman of a (sub) committee, U.S. Congress (stylings shown apply to House of
     Representatives & Senate)
The Honorable John R. Smith   Dear Mr. Chairman
Chairman   Dear Senator Smith
Committee on _____
United States Senate
    or
The Honorable Amelia R. Smith   Dear Madam Chairman
Chairman   Dear Senator Smith
Committee on _____
United States Senate

chief justice—see SUPREME COURT, FEDERAL; STATE

commissioner
  if appointed
The Honorable Amelia R. Smith   Dear Madam Commissioner
Commissioner   Dear Ms. Smith
    or
The Honorable John R. Smith   Dear Mr. Commissioner
Commissioner   Dear Mr. Smith
  if career
Ms. Amelia R. Smith   Dear Ms. Smith
Commissioner

Inside Address Styling	Salutation Styling

congressman—see REPRESENTATIVE, U.S. CONGRESS

director (as of an independent federal agency)
The Honorable John R. Smith   Dear Mr. Smith
Director
———— Agency

district attorney
The Honorable Amelia R. Smith   Dear Ms. Smith
District Attorney

federal judge
The Honorable John R. Smith   Sir
Judge of the United States District   My dear Judge Smith
   Court of the ———— District   Dear Judge Smith
   of ————

justice—see SUPREME COURT, FEDERAL; STATE

librarian of congress
The Honorable Amelia R. Smith   Madam
Librarian of Congress   Dear Ms. Smith

postmaster general
The Honorable John R. Smith   Sir
The Postmaster General   Dear Mr. Postmaster General
   or
The Honorable Amelia R. Smith   Madam
The Postmaster General   Dear Madam Postmaster General

president of the United States
The President   Mr. President
The White House   My dear Mr. President
                                                Dear Mr. President

   or
The Honorable Amelia R. Smith   Madam President
President of the United States   My dear Madam President
The White House   Dear Madam President

president of the United States (former)
The Honorable John R. Smith   Sir
(local address)   Dear Mr. Smith

president-elect of the United States
The Honorable Amelia R. Smith   Dear Madam
President-elect of the United States   Dear Ms. Smith

press secretary to the President of the United States
Mr. John R. Smith   Dear Mr. Smith
Press Secretary to the President
   of the United States

Inside Address Styling	Salutation Styling
representative, United States Congress	
The Honorable Amelia R. Smith	Madam
United States House of Representatives	Dear Representative Smith
or for local address	
The Honorable Amelia R. Smith	Dear Ms. Smith
Representative in Congress	
representative, United States Congress (former)	
The Honorable John R. Smith	Dear Mr. Smith
(local address)	
senator, United States Senate	
The Honorable Amelia R. Smith	Madam
United States Senate	Dear Senator Smith
senator-elect	
The Honorable John R. Smith	Dear Mr. Smith
Senator-elect	
(local address)	
senator (former)	
The Honorable Amelia R. Smith	Dear Senator Smith
(local address)	
speaker, United States House of Representatives	
The Honorable	Sir
The Speaker of the House of Representatives	
or	
The Honorable Speaker of the House	Sir
of Representatives	
or	
The Honorable John R. Smith	Sir
Speaker of the House of Representatives	Dear Mr. Speaker
	Dear Mr. Smith
speaker, United States House of Representatives (former)	
The Honorable Amelia R. Smith	Madam
(local address)	Dear Madam Speaker
special assistant to the President of the United States	
Mr. John R. Smith	Dear Mr. Smith
supreme court, associate justice	
Mr. Justice Smith	Sir
The Supreme Court of the United States	Mr. Justice
	My dear Mr. Justice
	Dear Mr. Justice Smith
or	
Ms. Justice Smith	Madam
The Supreme Court of the United States	Madam Justice
	My dear Madam Justice
	Dear Madam Justice

Inside Address Styling	Salutation Styling
supreme court, chief justice	
The Chief Justice of the United States	Sir
The Supreme Court of the United States	My dear Mr. Chief Justice
	Dear Mr. Chief Justice
	or
	Madam
	My dear Madam Chief Justice
	Dear Madam Chief Justice
or	
The Chief Justice	Sir
The Supreme Court	My dear Mr. Chief Justice
	Dear Mr. Chief Justice
	or
	Madam
	My dear Madam Chief Justice
	Dear Madam Chief Justice
supreme court, retired Justice	
The Honorable Amelia R. Smith	Madam
(local address)	Dear Justice Smith
territorial delegate	
The Honorable Amelia R. Smith	Dear Ms. Smith
Delegate of _____	
House of Representatives	
undersecretary of a department	
The Honorable John R. Smith	Dear Mr. Smith
Undersecretary of _____	
vice president of the United States	
The Vice President of the United States	Madam
United States Senate	My dear Madam Vice President
	Dear Madam Vice President
or	
The Honorable John R. Smith	Sir
Vice President of the United States	My dear Mr. Vice President
Washington, DC (zip code)	Dear Mr. Vice President

Government Officials—Local

alderman	
The Honorable John R. Smith	Dear Mr. Smith
	Dear Alderman Smith
or	
Alderman John R. Smith	Dear Mr. Smith
	Dear Alderman Smith
city attorney (includes city counsel, corporation counsel)	
The Honorable Amelia R. Smith	Dear Ms. Smith
councilman—see ALDERMAN	
county clerk	
The Honorable John R. Smith	Dear Mr. Smith
Clerk of _____ County	

Inside Address Styling	Salutation Styling

county treasurer—see COUNTY CLERK

judge
The Honorable Amelia R. Smith   Dear Judge Smith
Judge of the _____ Court of _____

mayor
The Honorable John R. Smith   Sir
Mayor of _____   Dear Mayor Smith

selectman—see ALDERMAN

Government Officials—State

---

assemblyman—see REPRESENTATIVE, STATE

attorney (as commonwealth's attorney, state's attorney)
The Honorable Amelia R. Smith   Dear Ms. Smith
(title)

attorney general
The Honorable John R. Smith   Sir
Attorney General of the State of _____   Dear Mr. Attorney General
      or
The Honorable Amelia R. Smith   Madam
Attorney General of the State of _____   Dear Madam Attorney General

clerk of a court
Amelia R. Smith, Esq.   Dear Ms. Smith
Clerk of the Court of _____

delegate—see REPRESENTATIVE, STATE

governor
The Honorable John R. Smith   Sir
Governor of _____   Dear Governor Smith
      or in some states
His Excellency, the Governor of _____   Sir
          Dear Governor Smith

governor (acting)
The Honorable Amelia R. Smith   Madam
Acting Governor of _____   Dear Ms. Smith

governor-elect
The Honorable John R. Smith   Dear Mr. Smith
Governor-elect of _____

governor (former)
The Honorable Amelia R. Smith   Dear Ms. Smith

judge, state court
The Honorable John R. Smith   Dear Judge Smith
Judge of the _____ Court

judge/justice, state supreme court—see SUPREME COURT, STATE

Inside Address Styling	Salutation Styling

lieutenant governor

The Honorable Lieutenant Governor of _____ — Madam
or
The Honorable Amelia R. Smith — Madam
Lieutenant Governor of _____ — Dear Ms. Smith

representative, state (includes assemblyman, delegate)

The Honorable John R. Smith — Sir
House of Representatives (or The State — Dear Mr. Smith
   Assembly or The House of Delegates)

secretary of state

The Honorable Secretary of State of _____ — Madam
or
The Honorable Amelia R. Smith — Madam
Secretary of State of _____ — Dear Madam Secretary
or
The Honorable John R. Smith — Sir
Secretary of State of _____ — Dear Mr. Secretary

senate, state, president of

The Honorable John R. Smith — Sir
President of the Senate of the State — Dear Mr. Smith
   (or the Commonwealth) of _____ — Senator

senator, state

The Honorable Amelia R. Smith — Madam
The Senate of _____ — Dear Senator Smith

speaker, state assembly, house of delegates, or house of representatives

The Honorable John R. Smith — Sir
Speaker of _____ — Dear Mr. Smith

supreme court, state, associate justice

The Honorable Amelia R. Smith — Madam
Associate Justice of the Supreme Court — Dear Justice Smith
   of _____

supreme court, state, chief justice

The Honorable John R. Smith — Sir
Chief Justice of the Supreme Court of _____ — Dear Mr. Chief Justice
or
The Honorable Amelia R. Smith — Madam
Chief Justice of the Supreme Court of _____ — Dear Madam Chief Justice

supreme court, state, presiding justice

The Honorable Amelia R. Smith — Madam
Presiding Justice _____ Division — Dear Madam Justice
Supreme Court of _____
or
The Honorable John R. Smith — Sir
Presiding Justice — Dear Mr. Justice
_____ Division
Supreme Court of _____

Inside Address Styling	Salutation Styling

Military Ranks

admiral (coast guard, navy)—see also REAR ADMIRAL, VICE ADMIRAL

Admiral John R. Smith, USCG (or USN)	Dear Admiral Smith
or	
ADM John R. Smith, USCG (or USN)	Dear Admiral Smith

airman

AMN Amelia R. Smith, USAF	Dear Airman Smith

airman basic

AB John R. Smith, USAF	Dear Airman Smith

airman first class

A1C Amelia R. Smith, USAF	Dear Airman Smith

brigadier general (air force, army, marine corps)

Brigadier General John R. Smith, USAF (or USMC)	Dear General Smith
or	
BG John R. Smith, USAF (or USA)	Dear General Smith
or	
Brig. Gen. John R. Smith, USMC	Dear General Smith

cadet (U.S. Air Force Academy, U.S. Military Academy)

Cadet Amelia R. Smith	Dear Cadet Smith

captain (air force, army, coast guard, navy, marine corps)

Captain John R. Smith, USAF (or USA or USCG or USN or USMC)	Dear Captain Smith
or	
CPT John R. Smith, USAF (or USA)	Dear Captain Smith
or	
CAPT John R. Smith, USCG (or USN)	Dear Captain Smith
or	
Capt. John R. Smith, USMC	Dear Captain Smith

chief petty officer (coast guard, navy)

Chief Petty Officer Amelia R. Smith, USCG (or USN)	Dear Petty Officer Smith
or	
CPO Amelia R. Smith, USCG (or USN)	Dear Petty Officer Smith

chief warrant officer W4 (army)

Chief Warrant Officer W4 John R. Smith	Dear Mr. Smith
or	
CWO4 John R. Smith	Dear Mr. Smith

colonel (air force, army, marine corps)

Colonel Amelia R. Smith, USAF (or USA or USMC)	Dear Colonel Smith
or	
COL Amelia R. Smith, USAF (or USA)	Dear Colonel Smith
or	
Col. Amelia R. Smith, USMC	Dear Colonel Smith

Inside Address Styling	Salutation Styling
commander (coast guard or navy)	
Commander John R. Smith, USCG (or USN)	Dear Commander Smith
or	
CDR John R. Smith, USCG (or USN)	Dear Commander Smith
corporal (army)—see also LANCE CORPORAL	
Corporal Amelia R. Smith, USA	Dear Corporal Smith
or	
CPL Amelia R. Smith, USA	Dear Corporal Smith
ensign (coast guard, navy)	
Ensign John R. Smith, USCG (or USN)	Dear Ensign Smith
	Dear Mr. Smith
or	
ENS John R. Smith, USCG (or USN)	Dear Ensign Smith
	Dear Mr. Smith
first lieutenant (air force, army, marine corps)	
First Lieutenant Amelia R. Smith, USAF (or USA or USMC)	Dear Lieutenant Smith
or	
1LT Amelia R. Smith, USAF (or USA)	Dear Lieutenant Smith
or	
1st. Lt. Amelia R. Smith, USMC	Dear Lieutenant Smith
first sergeant (army, marine corps)	
First Sergeant John R. Smith, USA (or USMC)	Dear Sergeant Smith
or	
1SG John R. Smith, USA	Dear Sergeant Smith
or	
1st. Sgt. John R. Smith, USMC	Dear Sergeant Smith
general (air force, army, marine corps)—see also BRIGADIER GENERAL, LIEUTENANT GENERAL, MAJOR GENERAL	
General Amelia R. Smith, USAF (or USA or USMC)	Dear General Smith
or	
GEN Amelia R. Smith, USAF (or USA)	Dear General Smith
or	
Gen. Amelia R. Smith, USMC	Dear General Smith
gunnery sergeant (marine corps)	
Gunnery Sergeant John R. Smith, USMC	Dear Sergeant Smith
or	
Gy. Sgt. John R. Smith, USMC	Dear Sergeant Smith
lance corporal (marine corps)	
Lance Corporal Amelia R. Smith, USMC	Dear Corporal Smith
or	
L/Cpl. Amelia R. Smith, USMC	Dear Corporal Smith
lieutenant (coast guard, navy)—see also FIRST LIEUTENANT, SECOND LIEUTENANT	
Lieutenant John R. Smith, USCG (or USN)	Dear Mr. Smith
or	
LT John R. Smith, USCG (or USN)	Dear Mr. Smith

Inside Address Styling	Salutation Styling
lieutenant colonel (air force, army, marine corps)	
Lieutenant Colonel Amelia R. Smith, USAF (or USA or USMC)	Dear Colonel Smith
or	
LTC Amelia R. Smith, USAF (or USA)	Dear Colonel Smith
or	
Lt. Col. Amelia R. Smith, USMC	Dear Colonel Smith
lieutenant commander (coast guard, navy)	
Lieutenant Commander John R. Smith, USCG (or USN)	Dear Commander Smith
or	
LCDR John R. Smith, USCG (or USN)	Dear Commander Smith
lieutenant general (air force, army, marine corps)	
Lieutenant General Amelia R. Smith, USAF (or USA or USMC)	Dear General Smith
or	
LTG Amelia R. Smith, USAF (or USA)	Dear General Smith
or	
Lt. Gen. Amelia R. Smith, USMC	Dear General Smith
lieutenant junior grade (coast guard, navy)	
Lieutenant (j.g.) John R. Smith, USCG (or USN)	Dear Mr. Smith
or	
LTJG John R. Smith, USCG (or USN)	Dear Mr. Smith
major (air force, army, marine corps)	
Major Amelia R. Smith, USAF (or USA or USMC)	Dear Major Smith
or	
MAJ Amelia R. Smith, USAF (or USA)	Dear Major Smith
or	
Maj. Amelia R. Smith, USMC	Dear Major Smith
major general (air force, army, marine corps)	
Major General John R. Smith, USAF (or USA or USMC)	Dear General Smith
or	
MG John R. Smith, USAF (or USA)	Dear General Smith
or	
Maj. Gen. John R. Smith, USMC	Dear General Smith
master sergeant (air force, army)	
Master Sergeant Amelia R. Smith, USAF (or USA)	Dear Sergeant Smith
or	
MSGT Amelia R. Smith, USAF	Dear Sergeant Smith
or	
MSG Amelia R. Smith, USA	Dear Sergeant Smith
midshipman (coast guard and naval academies)	
Midshipman John R. Smith	Dear Midshipman Smith
petty officer (coast guard, navy)	
Petty Officer Amelia R. Smith, USCG (or USN)	Dear Ms. Smith
or	
PO Amelia R. Smith, USCG (or USN)	Dear Ms. Smith

Inside Address Styling	Salutation Styling

private (army, marine corps)
Private John R. Smith, USA (or USMC) — Dear Private Smith
or
PVT John R. Smith, USA — Dear Private Smith
or
Pvt. John R. Smith, USMC — Dear Private Smith

private first class (army)
Private First Class Amelia R. Smith, USA — Dear Private Smith
or
PFC Amelia R. Smith, USA — Dear Private Smith

seaman (coast guard, navy)
Seaman John R. Smith, USCG (or USN) — Dear Seaman Smith
or
SMN John R. Smith, USCG (or USN) — Dear Seaman Smith

second lieutenant (air force, army, marine corps)
Second Lieutenant John R. Smith, USAF — Dear Lieutenant Smith
  (or USA or USMC)
or
2LT John R. Smith, USAF (or USA) — Dear Lieutenant Smith
or
2nd Lt. John R. Smith, USMC — Dear Lieutenant Smith

senior master sergeant (air force)
Senior Master Sergeant Amelia R. Smith, USAF — Dear Sergeant Smith
or
SMSGT Amelia R. Smith, USAF — Dear Sergeant Smith

sergeant (air force, army)—see also FIRST SERGEANT, GUNNERY SERGEANT, MASTER SERGEANT,
    SENIOR MASTER SERGEANT, SERGEANT MAJOR, STAFF SERGEANT, TECHNICAL SERGEANT
Sergeant John R. Smith, USAF (or USA) — Dear Sergeant Smith
or
SGT John R. Smith, USAF (or USA) — Dear Sergeant Smith

sergeant major (army, marine corps)
Sergeant Major Amelia R. Smith, USA — Dear Sergeant Major Smith
  (or USMC)
or
SGM Amelia R. Smith, USA — Dear Sergeant Major Smith
or
Sgt. Maj. Amelia R. Smith, USMC — Dear Sergeant Major Smith

specialist (army; covers all classes of specialists)
Specialist Fourth Class John R. Smith, USA — Dear Specialist Smith
or
S4 John R. Smith, USA — Dear Specialist Smith

Inside Address Styling	Salutation Styling

staff sergeant (air force, army)
Staff Sergeant Amelia R. Smith, USAF (or USA)   Dear Sergeant Smith
   or
SSGT Amelia R. Smith, USAF   Dear Sergeant Smith
   or
SSG Amelia R. Smith, USA   Dear Sergeant Smith

technical sergeant (air force)
Technical Sergeant John R. Smith, USAF   Dear Sergeant Smith
   or
TSGT John R. Smith, USAF   Dear Sergeant Smith

vice admiral (navy)
Vice Admiral Amelia R. Smith, USN   Dear Admiral Smith
   or
VADM Amelia R. Smith, USN   Dear Admiral Smith

warrant officer (army; covers all classes of warrant officers)
Warrant Officer W1 John R. Smith, USA   Dear Mr. Smith
   or
WO1 John R. Smith, USA   Dear Mr. Smith

any rank not listed
full title + full name + comma + abbreviation of   Dear + rank + surname
   branch of service

Miscellaneous Professional Titles

attorney
Ms. Amelia R. Smith, Attorney-at-Law   Dear Ms. Smith
   or
Amelia R. Smith, Esq.   Dear Ms. Smith

certified public accountant
Amelia R. Smith, C.P.A.   Dear Ms. Smith

dentist
John R. Smith, D.D.S.   Dear Dr. Smith
   or
Dr. John R. Smith   Dear Dr. Smith

physician
Amelia R. Smith, M.D.   Dear Dr. Smith
   or
Dr. Amelia R. Smith   Dear Dr. Smith

veterinarian
John R. Smith, D.V.M.   Dear Dr. Smith
   or
Dr. John R. Smith   Dear Dr. Smith

Inside Address Styling	Salutation Styling

United Nations Officials

representative, American (with ambassadorial rank)

The Honorable Amelia R. Smith
United States Permanent Representative to the
  United Nations

Madam
Dear Madam Ambassador

or

The Honorable John R. Smith
United States Permanent Representative to the
  United Nations

Sir
Dear Mr. Ambassador

representative, foreign (with ambassadorial rank)

His Excellency John R. Smith
Representative of _____ to the United Nations

Excellency
My dear Mr. Ambassador
Dear Mr. Ambassador

or

Her Excellency Amelia R. Smith
Representative of _____ to the United Nations

Excellency
My dear Madame Ambassador
Dear Madame Ambassador

secretary-general

Her Excellency Amelia R. Smith
Secretary-General of the United Nations

Excellency
My dear Madam (*or* Madame) Secretary-
  General
Dear Madam (*or* Madame) Secretary-
  General

or

His Excellency John R. Smith
Secretary-General of the United Nations

Excellency
My dear Mr. Secretary-General
Dear Mr. Secretary-General

undersecretary

The Honorable John R. Smith
Undersecretary of the United Nations

Sir
Dear Mr. Smith

Multiple Addressees (See also discussion on pages 250–257.)

Inside Address Styling	Salutation Styling
two or more men with same surname	
Mr. Arthur W. Jones	Gentlemen
Mr. John H. Jones	
or	*or*
Messrs. A. W. and J. H. Jones	
or	Dear Messrs. Jones
The Messrs. Jones	
two or more men with different surnames	
Mr. Angus D. Langley	Gentlemen *or* Dear Mr. Langley and
Mr. Lionel P. Overton	Mr. Overton
or	*or*
Messrs. A. D. Langley and L. P. Overton	Dear Messrs. Langley and Overton
or	
Messrs. Langley and Overton	
two or more married women with same surname	
Mrs. Arthur W. Jones	Mesdames
Mrs. John H. Jones	
or	*or*
Mesdames A. W. and J. H. Jones	Dear Mesdames Jones
or	
The Mesdames Jones	
two or more unmarried women with same surname	
Miss Alice H. Danvers	Ladies
Miss Margaret T. Danvers	
or	*or*
Misses Alice and Margaret Danvers	
or	Dear Misses Danvers
The Misses Danvers	
two or more women with same surname but whose marital status is unknown or irrelevant	
Ms. Alice H. Danvers	Dear Ms. Alice and Margaret Danvers
Ms. Margaret T. Danvers	
two or more married women with different surnames	
Mrs. Allen Y. Dow	Dear Mrs. Dow and Mrs. Frank
Mrs. Lawrence R. Frank	
or	*or*
Mesdames Dow and Frank	Mesdames *or* Dear Mesdames Dow and Frank
two or more unmarried women with different surnames	
Miss Elizabeth Dudley	Ladies *or* Dear Miss Dudley and
Miss Ann Raymond	Miss Raymond
or	*or*
Misses E. Dudley and A. Raymond	Dear Misses Dudley and Raymond
two or more women with different surnames but whose marital status is unknown or irrelevant	
Ms. Barbara Lee	Dear Ms. Lee and Ms. Key
Ms. Helen Key	

Special Titles, Designations, and Abbreviations

Doctor

If *Doctor* or its abbreviation *Dr.* is used before a person's name, academic degrees (as *D.D.S.*, *D.V.M.*, *M.D.*, or *Ph. D.*) are not included after the surname. The title *Doctor* may be typed out in full or abbreviated in a salutation, but it is usually abbreviated in an envelope address block and in an inside address in order to save space. When *Doctor* appears in a salutation, it must be used in conjunction with the addressee's surname.

> Dear Doctor Smith   *not*   Dear Doctor
> *or*
> Dear Dr. Smith

If a woman holds a doctorate, her title should be used in business-related correspondence even if her husband's name is also included in the letter.

> Dr. Ann R. Smith and Mr. James O. Smith
> Dear Dr. Smith and Mr. Smith

If both husband and wife are doctors, one of the following patterns may be followed.

> Dr. Ann R. Smith and   Ann R. Smith, M.D.
>   Dr. James O. Smith   James O. Smith, M.D.
>
> The Drs. Smith   Drs. Ann R. and James O. Smith
>
> The Doctors Smith
>
> *formal salutation*   *informal salutation*
> My dear Doctors Smith   Dear Drs. Smith
>   Dear Doctors Smith

Address patterns for two or more doctors associated in a joint practice are.

> Drs. Francis X. Sullivan and   Francis X. Sullivan, M.D.
>   Philip K. Ross   Philip K. Ross, M.D.
>
> *formal salutation*   *informal salutation*
> My dear Drs. Sullivan and Ross   Dear Drs. Sullivan and Ross
>   Dear Doctors Sullivan and Ross
>   Dear Dr. Sullivan and Dr. Ross
>   Dear Doctor Sullivan and
>   Doctor Ross

Esquire

The abbreviation *Esq.* for *Esquire* is often used in the United States after the surnames of professional persons such as attorneys, architects, professional engineers, and consuls, and also of court officials such as clerks of court and justices of the peace. *Esquire* may be written in addresses and signature lines but not in salutations. It is used regardless of sex. Some people, however, object to the use of *Esquire* as a title for a woman professional, and one should follow the recipient's wishes, if they are known, in this regard. Alternative forms may then be used, such as "Amy Lutz, Attorney at Law" or "Amy Lutz, P.E."

In Great Britain *Esquire* is generally used after the surnames of people who have distinguished themselves in professional, diplomatic, or social circles. For example, when addressing a letter to a British surgeon or to a high corporate officer of a British firm, one should include *Esq.* after his surname, both on the envelope and in the inside address. Under no circumstances should *Esq.* appear in a salutation. This rule applies to both American and British correspondence. If a courtesy title such as *Dr., Hon., Miss, Mr., Mrs., or Ms.* is used before the addressee's name, *Esquire* or *Esq.* is omitted.

The plural of *Esq.* is *Esqs.* and is used with the surnames of multiple addressees.

Carolyn B. West, Esq. American Consul	Dear Ms. West
Samuel A. Sebert, Esq. Norman D. Langfitt, Esq. *or* Sebert and Langfitt, Esqs. *or* Messrs. Sebert and Langfitt Attorneys-at-Law	Gentlemen Dear Mr. Sebert and Mr. Langfitt Dear Messrs. Sebert and Langfitt
Simpson, Tyler, and Williams, Esqs. *or* Scott A. Simpson, Esq. Annabelle W. Tyler, Esq. David I. Williams, Esq.	Dear Ms. Tyler and Messrs. Simpson and Williams
British Jonathan A. Lyons, Esq. President	Dear Mr. Lyons

Honorable

In the United States, *The Honorable* or its abbreviated form *Hon.* is used as a title of distinction (but not rank) and is accorded elected or appointed (but not career) government officials such as judges, justices, congressmen, and cabinet officers. Neither the full form nor the abbreviation is ever used by its recipient in written signatures, letterhead, business or visiting cards, or in typed signature blocks. While it may be used in an envelope address block and in an inside address of a letter addressed to him or her, it is never used in a salutation. *The Honorable* should never appear before a surname standing alone: there must always be an intervening first name, an initial or initials, or a courtesy title. A courtesy title should not be added, however, when *The Honorable* is used with a full name.

The Honorable John R. Smith	*not* The Honorable Smith
The Honorable J. R. Smith	
The Honorable J. Robert Smith	*and not* The Honorable Mr. John R.
The Honorable Mr. Smith	Smith
The Honorable Dr. Smith	

The Honorable may also precede a woman's name:

The Honorable Jane R. Smith
The Honorable Mrs. Smith

However, if the woman's full name is given, a courtesy title should not be added. When an official and his wife are being addressed, his full name should be typed out.

The Honorable John R. Smith and Mrs. Smith	*or* The Honorable and Mrs. John R. Smith
	Dear Mr. and Mrs. Smith

The stylings "Hon. and Mrs. Smith" and "The Honorable and Mrs. Smith" should *never* be used. If, however, the official's full name is unknown, the styling is:

The Honorable Mr. Smith and Mrs. Smith

If a married woman holds the title and her husband does not, her name appears first on business-related correspondence addressed to both persons. However, if the couple is being addressed socially, the woman's title may be dropped unless she has retained her maiden name for use in personal as well as business correspondence.

business correspondence

The Honorable Harriet M. Johnson and Mr. Johnson	Dear Mrs. (*or* Governor, etc.) Johnson and Mr. Johnson

social correspondence

Mr. and Mrs. Robert Y. Johnson	Dear Mr. and Mrs. Johnson

business correspondence and maiden name retained

The Honorable Harriet A. Ott and Mr. Robert Y. Johnson	Dear Ms. Ott and Mr. Johnson

social correspondence

Ms. Harriet A. Ott Mr. Roger Y. Johnson	Dear Ms. Ott and Mr. Johnson

If space is limited, *The Honorable* may be typed on the first line of an address block, with the recipient's name on the next line.

> The Honorable
> John R. Smith
>   and Mrs. Smith

When *The Honorable* occurs in a running text or in a list of names in such a text, the *T* in *The* is then lowercased.

> A speech by the Honorable Charles H. Patterson, the American Consul in Athens

In informal writing such as newspaper articles, the plural forms *the Honorables* or *Hons.* may be used before a list of persons accorded the distinction. However, in official or formal writing either *the Honorable Messrs.* placed before the entire list of surnames or *the Honorable* or *Hon.* repeated before each full name in the list may be used.

> *formal*
> . . . was supported in the motion by the Honorable Messrs. Clarke, Goodfellow, Thomas, and Harrington.
> . . . met with the Honorable Albert Y. Langley and the Honorable Frances P. Kelley.
> *informal*
> . . . interviewed the Hons. Jacob Y. Stathis, Samuel P. Kenton, William L. Williamson, and Gloria O. Yarnell—all United States Senators.

Jr. and Sr.

The designations *Jr.* and *Sr.* may or may not be preceded by a comma, depending on office policy or writer preference; however, one styling should be selected and adhered to for the sake of uniformity.

> John K. Walker Jr.   *or*   John K. Walker, Jr.

Jr. and *Sr.* may be used in conjunction with courtesy titles, academic degree abbreviations, or professional rating abbreviations.

> Mr. John K. Walker[,] Jr.   John K. Walker[,] Jr., Esq.
> General John K. Walker[,] Jr.   John K. Walker[,] Jr., M.D.
> The Honorable John K. Walker[,]   John K. Walker[,] Jr., C.A.M.
>   Jr.

Madam and Madame

The title *Madam* should be used only in salutations of highly impersonal or high-level governmental and diplomatic correspondence. The title may be used to address women officials in other instances only if the writer is certain that the addressee is married. The French form *Madame* is recommended for salutations in correspondence addressed to foreign diplomats and heads of state. See Forms of Address Chart for examples.

Mesdames

The plural form of *Madam, Madame,* or *Mrs.* is *Mesdames,* which may be used before the names of two or more married women associated together in a professional partnership or in a business. It may appear with their names on an envelope and in the inside address, and it may appear with their names or standing alone in a salutation. (See also the Multiple Addressees Chart, page 249.)

Mesdames T. V. Meade and P. A. Tate Mesdames Meade and Tate	Dear Mesdames Meade and Tate Mesdames
Mesdames V. T. and A. P. Stevens The Mesdames Stevens	Dear Mesdames Stevens Mesdames

Messrs.

The plural abbreviation of *Mr.* is *Messrs.* It is used before the surnames of two or more men associated in a professional partnership or in a business. *Messrs.* may appear on an envelope, in an inside address, and in a salutation when used in conjunction with the surnames of the addressees; however, this abbreviation should never stand alone.

Messrs. Archlake, Smythe, and Dabney Attorneys-at-law	Dear Messrs. Archlake, Smythe, and Dabney Gentlemen
Messrs. K. Y. and P. B. Overton Architects	Dear Messrs. Overton Gentlemen

Messrs. should never be used before a compound corporate name formed from two surnames such as *Lord & Taylor* or *Woodward & Lothrup*, or from a corporate name like *H. L. Jones and Sons.* For correct use of *Messrs. + The Honorable* or *+ The Reverend*, see pages 253 and 256–257, respectively.

Misses

The plural form of *Miss* is *Misses*, and it may be used before the names of two or more unmarried women who are being addressed together. It may appear on an envelope, in an inside address, and in a salutation. Like *Messrs., Misses* should never stand alone but must occur in conjunction with a name or names. (For a complete set of examples in this category, see the Multiple Addressees Chart, page 249.)

Misses Hay and Middleton Misses D. L. Hay and H. K. Middleton	Dear Misses Hay and Middleton Ladies
Misses Tara and Julia Smith The Misses Smith	Dear Misses Smith Ladies

Professor

If used only with a surname, *Professor* should be typed out in full; however, if used with a given name and initial or a set of initials as well as a surname, it may be abbreviated to *Prof.* It is, therefore, usually abbreviated in envelope address blocks and in inside addresses, but typed out in salutations. *Professor* should not stand alone in a salutation.

Prof. Florence C. Marlowe Department of English	Dear Professor Marlowe Dear Dr. Marlowe Dear Miss Marlowe Mrs. Marlowe Ms. Marlowe *but not* Dear Professor

When addressing a letter to a professor and his wife, the title is usually written out in full unless the name is unusually long.

Professor and Mrs. Lee Dow
Prof. and Mrs. Henry Talbott-
  Smythe
	Dear Professor and Mrs. Dow
	Dear Professor and Mrs. Talbott-
	  Smythe

Letters addressed to couples of whom the wife is the professor and the husband is not may follow one of these patterns:

business correspondence
Professor Diana Goode and
  Mr. Goode
	Dear Professor Goode and
	  Mr. Goode

business or social correspondence Mr. and Mrs. Lawrence F. Goode	Dear Mr. and Mrs. Goode
if wife has retained her maiden name Professor Diana Falls Mr. Lawrence F. Goode	Dear Professor (*or* Ms.) Falls and Mr. Goode

When addressing two or more professors—male or female, whether having the same or different surnames—type *Professors* and not *"Profs.":*

Professors A. L. Smith and C. L. Doe	Dear Professors Smith and Doe Dear Drs. Smith and Doe Dear Mr. Smith and Mr. Doe Dear Messrs. Smith and Doe Gentlemen
Professors B. K. Johns and S. T. Yarrell	Dear Professors Johns and Yarrell Dear Drs. Johns and Yarrell Dear Ms. Johns and Mr. Yarrell
Professors G. A. and F. K. Cornett The Professors Cornett	*acceptable for any combination* Dear Professors Cornett Dear Drs. Cornett *if males* Gentlemen *if females* Ladies *or* Mesdames *if married* Dear Mr. and Mrs. Cornett Dear Professors Cornett Dear Drs. Cornett

Reverend

In formal or official writing, *The* should precede *Reverend;* however, *The Reverend* is often abbreviated to *The Rev.* or just *Rev.*, especially in unofficial or informal writing, and particularly in business correspondence where the problem of space on envelopes and in inside addresses is a factor. The typed-out full form *The Reverend* must be used in conjunction with the clergyman's full name, as in the following examples:

> The Reverend Philip D. Asquith
> The Reverend Dr. Philip D. Asquith
> The Reverend P. D. Asquith

The Reverend may appear with just a surname only if another courtesy rule intervenes:

> The Reverend Mr. Asquith
> The Reverend Professor Asquith
> The Reverend Dr. Asquith

The Reverend, The Rev., or *Rev.* should not be used in the salutation, although any one of these titles may be used on the envelope and in the inside address. In salutations, the following titles are acceptable for clergymen: *Mr.* (or *Ms., Miss, Mrs.*), *Father, Chaplain,* or *Dr.* See the Forms of Address Chart under the section entitled "Clerical and Religious Orders" for examples. The only exceptions to this rule are salutations in letters addressed to high prelates of a church (as bishops, monsignors, etc.). See the Forms of Address Chart. When addressing a letter to a clergyman and his wife, the typist should follow one of the following stylings:

> The Rev. and Mrs. P. D. Asquith
> The Rev. and Mrs. Philip D. Asquith
> The Reverend and Mrs. P. D. Asquith
> The Reverend and Mrs. Philip D. Asquith
> Dear Mr. (*or, if having a doctorate,* Dr.) and Mrs. Asquith
> *but never*
> Rev. and Mrs. Asquith

Two clergymen having the same or different surnames should not be addressed in letters as "The Reverends" or "The Revs." or "Revs." They may, however, be addressed as *The Reverend* (or *The Rev.*) *Messrs.* or *The Reverend* (or *The Rev.*) *Drs.*, or the titles *The Reverend, The Rev.*, or *Rev.* may be repeated before each clergyman's name.

> The Reverend Messrs. S. J. and
>   D. V. Smith
> The Rev. Messrs. S. J. and
>   D. V. Smith
> The Reverend Messrs. Smith
> The Rev. Messrs. Smith

> The Rev. S. J. Smith and
>   The Rev. D. V. Smith
> Rev. S. J. Smith and
>   Rev. D. V. Smith

When writing to two or more clergymen having different surnames, the following patterns are acceptable:

The Reverend Messrs. P. A. Francis
and F. L. Beale
The Rev. Messrs. P. A. Francis
and F. L. Beale
The Rev. P. A. Francis
The Rev. F. L. Beale

In either situation, the following salutations are acceptable:

Gentlemen
Dear Mr. and Mrs. Smith
Dear Messrs. Smith
Dear Mr. Francis and Mrs. Beale
Dear Father Francis and Father Beale

In formal texts, "The Reverends," "The Revs.," and "Revs." are not acceptable as collective titles (as in lists of names). *The Reverend* (or *Rev.*) *Messrs.* (or *Drs.* or *Professors*) may be used, or *The Reverend* or *The Rev.* or *Rev.* may be repeated before each clergyman's name. If the term *clergyman* or the expression *the clergy* is mentioned in introducing the list, a single title *the Reverend* or *the Rev.* may be added before the list to serve all of the names. While it is true that "the Revs." is often seen in newspapers and in catalogs, this expression is still not recommended for formal, official writing.

... were the Reverend Messrs. Jones, Smith and Bennett, as well as ...
Among the clergymen present were the Reverend John G. Jones,
    Mr. Smith, and Dr. Doe.
Prayers were offered by the Rev. J. G. Jones, Rev. Mr. Smith,
    and Rev. Dr. Doe.

Second, Third

These designations after surnames may be styled as Roman numerals (I, III, IV) or as ordinals (2nd / 2d, 3rd / 3d, 4th). Such a designation may or may not be separated from a surname by a comma, depending on office policy or writer preference.

Mr. Jason T. Johnson III (*or* 3rd *or* 3d)
Mr. Jason T. Johnson, III (*or* 3rd *or* 3d)

Sequence of Abbreviations and Initials

The proper order of occurrence of initials representing academic degrees, religious orders, and professional ratings that may appear after a name and that are separated from each other by commas is as follows: (1) religious orders (as *S.J.*); (2) theological degrees (as *D.D.*); (3) academic degrees (as *Ph.D.*); (4) honorary degrees (as *Litt.D.*) (5) professional ratings (as *C.P.A.*).

Initials that represent academic degrees (with the exception of *M.D.*, *D.D.S.*, and other medical degrees) are not commonly used in addresses, and two or more sets of such letters appear even more rarely. Only when the initials represent achievements in different fields that are relevant to one's profession should more than one set be used. On the other hand, initials that represent earned professional achievements (such as *C.P.A., C.A.M., C.P.S.,* or *P.E.*) are often used in business addresses. When any of these sets of initials follow a name, however, the courtesy title *(Mr., Mrs., Ms., Miss, Dr.)* is omitted.

Nancy Robinson, P.L.S.
Mary R. Lopez, C.P.A.
John R. Doe, M.D., Ph.D.
Chief of Staff
Smithville Hospital

John R. Doe, J.D., C.M.C.
The Rev. John R. Doe, S.J., D.D.,
 LL.D.
Chaplain, Smithville College

RANKS OF THE UNITED STATES ARMED FORCES

ARMY	MARINES	NAVY	AIR FORCE	COAST GUARD
general of the army		fleet admiral	general of the air force	
general	general	admiral	general	admiral or commandant
lieutenant general	lieutenant general	vice admiral	lieutenant general	vice admiral
major general	major general	rear admiral	major general	rear admiral
brigadier general	brigadier general	commodore	brigadier general	commodore
colonel	colonel	captain	colonel	captain
lieutenant colonel	lieutenant colonel	commander	lieutenant colonel	commander
major	major	lieutenant commander	major	lieutenant commander
captain	captain	lieutenant	captain	lieutenant
first lieutenant	first lieutenant	lieutenant, j.g.	first lieutenant	lieutenant, j.g.
second lieutenant	second lieutenant	ensign	second lieutenant	ensign
chief warrant officer, W-4	chief warrant officer, W-4	chief warrant officer, W-4	chief warrant officer, W-4	chief warrant officer, W-4
chief warrant officer, W-3	chief warrant officer, W-3	warrant officer, W-3	chief warrant officer, W-3	warrant officer, W-3
chief warrant officer, W-2	chief warrant officer, W-2	warrant officer, W-2	chief warrant officer, W-2	warrant officer, W-2
warrant officer, W-1	warrant officer, W-1	warrant officer, W-1	warrant officer, W-1	warrant officer, W-1
sergeant major of the army	sergeant major of the marine corps	master chief petty officer of the navy	chief master sergeant of the air force	master chief petty officer of the coast guard
command sergeant major	sergeant major or master gunnery sergeant	master chief petty officer	chief master sergeant	master chief petty officer
first sergeant or master sergeant	first sergeant or master sergeant	senior chief petty officer	senior master sergeant	senior chief petty officer
platoon sergeant or sergeant first class or specialist 7	gunnery sergeant	chief petty officer	master sergeant	chief petty officer
staff sergeant or specialist 6	staff sergeant	petty officer first class	technical sergeant	petty officer first class
sergeant or specialist 5	sergeant	petty officer second class	staff sergeant	petty officer second class
corporal or specialist 4	corporal	petty officer third class	sergeant	petty officer third class
private first class	lance corporal	seaman	airman first class	seaman
private, E-2	private first class	seaman apprentice	airman	seaman apprentice
private, E-1	private	seaman recruit	airman basic	seaman recruit

CHAPTER 6

Composing Letters

Many of the details concerning business correspondence are routine. The impact that a well-written business letter can have, however, is far from routine. A well-thought-out, precisely expressed letter delivers a positive impression on the reader and encourages cooperation.

The Writing of Letters: General Pointers

Getting Ready to Write

Good, clear business correspondence is not an accident. It is the result of careful planning and usually requires some pre-writing preparations. The following five steps, suggested for preparing a business letter or memorandum, can serve as a checklist for achieving optimum results with maximum efficiency.

1. **Assemble needed materials**   Frequently previous correspondence must be referred to before a meaningful or accurate reply can be sent. Tabular information, reports, printouts, catalogs, reference books, manuals, and other items also may have to be located and arranged for easy reference.

2. **Make marginal notes**   It is helpful to make marginal notes on letters to be answered. Jotting down information such as conference dates, appointments, and titles of brochures in advance will ensure a speedier reply.

3. **Underscore important facts**   It is useful to employ a yellow felt-tip pen or a red auditor's pen to underscore the significant facts in a letter

which are pertinent to the reply. Color will highlight this information and make it easy to identify when the response is later being written.

4. **Outline reply letter content** Before beginning to draft a letter, put all the facts together. Have a clear-cut idea of what you want to say, jot down the major topics that will be treated in the reply letter, and examine examples of previous correspondence for guidance in drafting the reply.

5. **Compose the letter** If careful plans and preparations are made before writing begins, the actual composition of the reply should be easier.

The Makeup of a Good Letter

The construction of good business correspondence is built on three key elements: creating the right opening, sending the right cues to the reader, and devising a friendly close to the letter. Each of these elements is discussed in the following paragraphs.

1. **Creating the opening** Because a corporate image can be enhanced or diminished through word choice in a letter, the writer should make every effort to see that the right words are used. This statement is particularly applicable to the opening paragraph of a letter. The first paragraph should not only set the tone for the entire letter, it should capture the reader's attention. Openings that take into account the reader's point of view will elicit pleasure, satisfaction, and personal involvement in the matters being discussed. The following is an example of a good opening paragraph:

> We feel very fortunate that you have accepted our invitation to appear before a group of new secretaries at our annual "Get-Acquainted Day" on Thursday, October 1. I had the pleasure of hearing you address the CPS meeting last April, and I'm convinced that we couldn't find a better, more interesting speaker.

The reverse is also true. A stilted, cliché-ridden opening such as the following can actually create a negative impression on the recipient of the letter:

> Enclosed please find information regarding details of our annual "Get-Acquainted Day" on Thursday, October 1. We have noted with pleasure your acceptance to deliver a speech at the meeting as per our request.

2. **Cues to the reader** The writer should regard every business-communication reader as a knowledgeable critic of corporate letter production. Thus, each communication to a client or to a potential customer provides an opportunity to epitomize the very best in company service, goodwill, and helpfulness. Here are some ways to create a positive impression on the reader:

A. Use tactful, easy-to-understand language. Short words, clear-cut and direct, are easier to read and to understand than lengthy words. Write as you speak, using natural, everyday expressions.

It is a real pleasure to know that you will lead our Transactional Analysis Seminar on May 14.

B. Organize your language carefully and concisely. Time is a precious commodity, and the busy reader wants to get the gist of the message on the first reading. Interesting messages contain sequences that vary in length and in internal structure. Coherence and continuity are other prime requisites of modern communications. (See also Chapter 1, "Composition and Grammar," pages 1–47, for sentence and paragraph strategy.)

C. Construct sentences correctly. Technical correctness in writing is a worthy goal for any writer. In order to attain it, proofread the material and make sure that none of the following infelicities—among many others—is present: misplaced commas, misspelled words, incorrect word division, numbers written incorrectly, hackneyed and stilted expressions, a lack of agreement between subjects and verbs, and other such grammatical and stylistic pitfalls. (Details concerning these elements of writing may be found in Chapters 1, 2 and 3.)

D. Give accurate, precise information. The omission of one important detail can spell the difference between order and confusion in the reader's mind. The following is an example of a letter written by a guest speaker accepting a speaking engagement for a sales conference (note the questions in paragraph two):

Thank you for your gracious invitation to participate in your secretarial conference on October 19 at Pine Manor. It is thoughtful of you to include me in your program.

Would you please send along a map showing the best driving route to your campus, and also mention the amount of time allotted for my message?

If the writer of the letter had checked the outgoing letter carefully for details, it would not have been necessary for the guest to politely request information on the length of the address and on conference location.

E. Write clearly to avoid any hint of double meaning. It has often been said that if a statement can be misunderstood, it will be! By going over all written messages for unintended hidden meanings, the writer can avoid many problems. Keep the reader's reaction always in mind. For example, the following statement raises several questions:

One and two-page photos are needed for this year's annual report.

The questions raised by this statement include the following: How many photos are actually needed? (The statement doesn't say.) Is the need for one one-page photo and one two-page photo? (The statement is ambiguous.) Is the reader expected to supply all of the photos needed? (The statement doesn't say.) The following rewording of the original statement will prevent any misunderstanding:

> Please prepare one full-page photo and one double-page photo for use in this year's annual report.

F. **Respond to questions raised.** It is frustrating to a correspondent when a question posed in a previous letter goes unanswered. The omission is also poor business practice, as it creates the need for more correspondence. Here is another safeguard that will help to ensure good business writing: double-check to see that no such omissions have been made, by rereading relevant previous correspondence and then comparing it with your response.

G. Introduce an unfavorable comment with a favorable one. It is helpful to present all the positive aspects of a situation first and then to lead into any negative or unfavorable comments. Find points of agreement with the reader and mention them before talking about an unfavorable aspect.

> Your complimentary copy of *Modular Office Units* is on its way to you. Your kind comments about the usefulness of this brochure are greatly appreciated.

> Popular demand for copies of the brochure within recent weeks has depleted our supply, unfortunately. However, please feel free to reproduce temporary copies for use by your staff. When our new shipment arrives, we'll speed a dozen copies to you.

3. **Devising a friendly way to close a letter** Give the reader a pleasant closing thought in the final paragraph of the letter.

> Again, thank you for giving us permission to reprint the article on your company's research in the field of pollution control. This information will provide excellent material for next month's issue of *The Executive*.

Avoid thanking someone for something in advance. It is really rather impertinent to assume beforehand that a request will be honored. Wait until the service is rendered; then, make an appropriate acknowledgment for it. (See also Chapter 3, "Tone in Writing," pages 155–172, for a list of business clichés that should be avoided, especially in letters.)

The recipient of a letter of request should know exactly what is expected of him or her by the end of the letter. If a certain action is expected, it should be stated or restated in a clear and friendly manner in the last paragraph.

Composing Form Letters and Memorandums

Form Letter Construction

An expedient way to handle routine mail is through the use of guide letters or form letters to standardize responses. A ring binder might be used to categorize certain types of letters that are frequently written. By the use of appropriate index tabs on the various divisions of the ring binder, information can be quickly located. Thus, when such letters as those of announcement, acknowledgment, or apology must be written, the writer may refer to similar or prototypical letters—a shortcut that expedites composition. The notebook might also contain a stock of ready-made insertable paragraphs labeled as A, B, C, D, and so on. By referring to these, a writer might delegate to a secretary the responsibility of constructing certain letters. Form letters are often printed in advance. The secretary then adds the date and the inside address; sometimes other data are also added to the body of the form letter. When preprinted form letters are used, try to match the typeface as closely as possible. Automated letter production or word processing is a popular way to reproduce a form letter because it gives the letter the appearance of an original.

The Writing Of Office Memorandums

The office memorandum is another type of routine communication. Written for interoffice circulation only, it may include general messages (as notices, announcements, or inquiries). Memorandums are usually circulated freely among corporate branch offices located in distant cities. Large companies have standardized memorandum forms. There is a wide variety in the printed styling of memorandums; however, the basic parts of most memorandums are the headings (TO, FROM, SUBJECT, DATE) and the body (message). A memorandum has neither salutation nor complimentary close. It is not usually signed but it may be initialed by the author.

Preparing the heading of the memorandum The memorandum is a fast, economical, and efficient way to relay important news that should reach all or a significant fraction of the corporate staff. Today an office copier can, in a few minutes, reproduce multiple copies of a memorandum, thus making it ready for wide distribution to a large readership. On the other hand, a memorandum may also be addressed solely to one person. The TO line may be addressed to one individual, to several individuals, or to a group.

> TO: Frances Rummel, Customer Services Supervisor
> TO: Customer Services Personnel
> TO: Administrative Staff, School of Business

Typically, the other heading components consist of the following: the FROM line, which includes the name of the writer and his or her title or position; the DATE line; the SUBJECT line; and the optional LOCATION (floor, extension, or branch) line.

The subject line of the memorandum The SUBJECT line in the heading of the memorandum is very important, for it gives the reader an overview of the message content. A good SUBJECT line encapsulates the message, which makes it useful for filing purposes. Examples of typical SUBJECT lines are as follows:

>   SUBJECT: April Meeting of the Advisory Council
>   SUBJECT: NEED FOR A NEW ELECTRIC TYPEWRITER
>   SUBJECT: Transportation Rates on Iron or Steel Bars

Composing the message (or body) of the memorandum Brevity, courtesy, factualness, and tact are four requisites of message content in office memorandums. The main idea of the message is usually contained in the first paragraph, while additional or supporting data may be added in succeeding paragraphs. The final part of a memorandum may close with a courteous request for action or further information. In some instances the request for service, action, or specific information may be found in the opening paragraph with supporting data located in subsequent paragraphs.

Editing and Proofreading

Basic editing primarily requires checking a manuscript for grammar, spelling, punctuation, stylistic consistency, and factual accuracy, and may also involve moving or even rewriting entire sentences and paragraphs. Such basic editing is often called *copyediting*. Good editing requires a firm grasp of English style and usage and a strong sense of organizational logic.

Proofreading, in its narrow sense, is the late-stage correcting of material that has already been typeset—that is, professionally set in type by a typesetter. The word means literally the reading and checking of *proofs*—copies of newly typeset material sent back from the typesetter to the editor for correction—against the original manuscript. But the term *proofreading* is generally used today to mean the final checking of *any* written material.

In the era of word processors, laser printers, and desktop publishing systems, the line between editing and proofreading has become blurred. There is, however, still a distinction to be made between the initial critical editing done on any letter or manuscript and the final checking for errors in revised and rekeyboarded material—even when you are simultaneously the author, editor, and proofreader of a given document, and thus communicating only with yourself when you mark it up.

Both editing and proofreading require that you have at hand a good desk dictionary. In addition, it can be very useful to have a style manual (such as Chapter 2 of this book), a thesaurus, and possibly other specialized reference books. If your company has its own style guide, the rules stated there must be followed. See page 154 for a list of proofreaders' marks.

EDITING CHECKLIST

- For the sake of consistency when editing large manuscripts, consider creating a *style sheet*—an alphabetical list of troublesome words that occur in the manuscript, showing their proper spelling, punctuation, or capitalization.

- Check the organization of the document. If there are headings and subheadings, they should by themselves form a coherent outline of the contents.
- Make sure the paragraphing is logical.
- Check the spelling of every word about which you are not absolutely certain.
- Be alert to errors involving similar words (e.g., *it/if/is*) and homophones *(hear/here)*.
- Check all proper names. This can be a sensitive area, and errors can slip through very easily.
- Check that list entries are grammatically parallel.
- Check for noun/verb agreement.
- Check all number sequences, particularly numbered lists and numbered footnotes.
- Check *and recheck* any other numbers that are used—they may be extremely important. It may be wise to check any arithmetic using the computer's calculator function.
- Be sure that all dates are correct.
- Check that all alphabetical lists are in proper alphabetical order.
- Be sure that all punctuation is in place and consistent. Be especially alert to paired punctuation marks—parentheses, quotation marks, dashes, and brackets.
- Be sure that capitalization is consistent, particularly in headings, in unusual terms, and in lists and tables.
- Check any bibliographical references for consistency and accuracy.

PROOFREADING CHECKLIST

- In letters, check especially that the dateline, reference line, initials, enclosure line, and carbon-copy notation have been included.
- Check that all headings and other separate elements are consistent in style and properly positioned.
- Check that any table of contents is accurate as to both titles and page numbers.
- Check all cross-references.
- Check that all margins are proper.
- Check tables for horizontal and vertical alignment.
- Check that no footnotes have been omitted.
- Be alert for unintentional repetition of small words (*and and, the the,* etc.).
- Check that page numbers are correct. Check any running heads (headers) or running feet (footers).
- Check any headings and captions separately.

CHAPTER 7

Computers, Word Processing, and Office Equipment

What we refer to today as word processing is the result of more than a hundred years of technological evolution.

The manual typewriter, which became popular in the late 1800s, was the first major advance in writing technology in centuries and revolutionized the creation of business documents. In the 1930s the first storage mechanism was introduced: a roll of punched paper recorded all the keystrokes used to type a document, and the roll could then be used to produce multiple copies of the same document automatically. Later, it became possible to operate more than one of the paper readers at a time so that text could be merged from different sources. In the 1960s paper tape gave way to the newly developed magnetic tape, which provided much more storage capability and had the added advantage of being reusable. Magnetic tape cartridges (and later magnetic cards) could be erased and reused and were sturdier and easier to handle than paper.

In the 1970s word processing came into its own. The first video-display systems were introduced, allowing the typist to correct or revise material immediately and to view several lines of text on-screen before they were printed. Even with its limited text display, the system increased accuracy and productivity dramatically. At about the same time, magnetic tape and cards were replaced by the floppy diskette, which greatly increased storage capacity and retrieval speed.

Word processing has now evolved into a technologically advanced function that can no longer fairly be called "typing." Word processing is an integral part of almost every office environment, producing print materials ranging from routine memorandums to annual reports. It is performed by managers as well as secretaries, and it exists both as an independent function and as a capability within other computerized tasks such as spreadsheet development. The software advances discussed later in this chapter, coupled with the use of laser printers, have blurred the line between word processing and the newer technology called desktop publishing. (See Chapter 8 for a discussion of desktop publishing.)

267

We can only speculate on what the future of word processing will be. Voice-driven systems that require no keyboard already exist in prototype form, and pen-based computing is another significant new technology. Other input systems will certainly be developed, as will delivery systems that take the word-processed output beyond the printer. The development of word processing is still in its early stages.

The Work Environment

Your desk and the office space immediately adjacent to it are yours to organize for maximum efficiency and attractiveness. Your immediate work area is defined by the arms-length space surrounding your chair in all directions when you are seated at your word processor. This is the area in which you should have all the articles you work with that relate to word processing.

The open landscape design has had a number of positive effects; however, it has also created some problems. The pattern of ceiling lights, which is generally a symmetrical grid for the entire office space, may have no relation to where individual desks and workstations are placed. As a result, you may find that your overhead light is off to the side, while your neighbor may get no direct light at all. To compensate, additional light is often needed, either permanently or just for specific tasks.

Noise is another problem that the open landscape can magnify. Without doors to close, the sound of several impact printers operating all at once can be distracting, if not harmful. If you are sensitive to the noise, there are printer enclosures on the market for virtually every make and model. Laser printers, which are fast replacing impact printers, are almost silent and are ideally suited to the open environment.

In older offices the L-shaped desk arrangement was popular. It consisted of a basic desk and a smaller and somewhat lower typing table attached to the desk at a 90-degree angle. Today, because so many secretaries are working with word processors or computers made up of several component parts, an entire industry has developed to supply customized computer furniture to organize all these parts. The furniture ranges from movable carts, which hold all the devices associated with a computer or word processor, to complete modular systems, which encompass desks, storage shelves, and movable partitions. (In many offices, unfortunately, furnishings have not caught up with technology and the equipment often must be set down wherever it fits.)

For maximum convenience, you should be able to sit at your word-processing equipment and comfortably reach your telephone, your diskettes, and your printer, while still having an accessible flat surface on which to open a manual or other reference book. (If you are connected to a local area network, in which several people share the use of a centralized printer, you will not have to accommodate a printer in your immediate area.)

Keep all foods and liquids far away from word-processing equipment. One spill can result in enormous repair expenses and lost productivity. Avoid placing anything on top of word-processing equipment or adjacent to the many air vents that most devices have. Unblocked ventilation is essential to maintaining the safe operating temperatures required.

Word-processing and computer equipment draws a considerable amount of electricity. Check with your building services department before plugging everything into one outlet. If your screen flickers or the image periodically shrinks while you are working, you may be overloading a circuit.

Ergonomics   As office operations have become increasingly automated, concern for the effects all this automation has on the humans who use it has spawned a new discipline: *ergonomics*, the study of the effects of the physical design of equipment on the physical and emotional well-being of its users. An engineer or designer schooled in ergonomics may be as much concerned with the size and shape of an on/off switch as with whether or not the switch actually works. Can it be reached without the user having to stretch, bend, or risk injury? Is it too large or small to be used conveniently? Is it clearly labeled?

Ergonomics may be thought of as having evolved from the time and motion studies that were popular earlier in the century. However, that movement merely concerned itself with productivity from the employer's standpoint, and we are now looking at office equipment and design from the user's standpoint. Once regarded as an esoteric field, ergonomics has now moved into the mainstream of design. The European Community, for example, established uniform rules in 1992 which made employers responsible for removing health risks from the workplace and required them to be knowledgeable about advances in workstation design.

Specialists in ergonomics have studied the effects of all the various word-processing devices and accessories, examining everything from the color of the components to the shape of the chair. You can profit from the considerable body of knowledge that now exists when selecting or recommending products for your office.

Computer Hardware

Word processing may be performed on either of two types of equipment: a dedicated word processor or a microcomputer, sometimes referred to as a personal computer (PC) even when used only in an office for business purposes.

A *dedicated word processor* is a system designed and sold for one primary application: word processing. A *microcomputer,* on the other hand, is a multifunction system that can be used for a variety of applications depending on the type of software that is installed. Because of their limitations, dedicated word processors are becoming less common; however, the two systems are equally efficient for basic word processing, and in fact they do not differ much in design. For the most part, the description of computer hardware in this chapter applies equally to dedicated word processors and microcomputers.

The computer is a multicomponent system made up of four primary parts:

1. The *computer* itself, which is made up of boards and circuits that process information.
2. The *keyboard,* which is used to enter and format text.
3. The *monitor,* which displays the entered text.
4. The *printer,* which prints the final text on paper.

See the illustration in Fig. 7.1.

Fig. 7.1   Desktop Computer

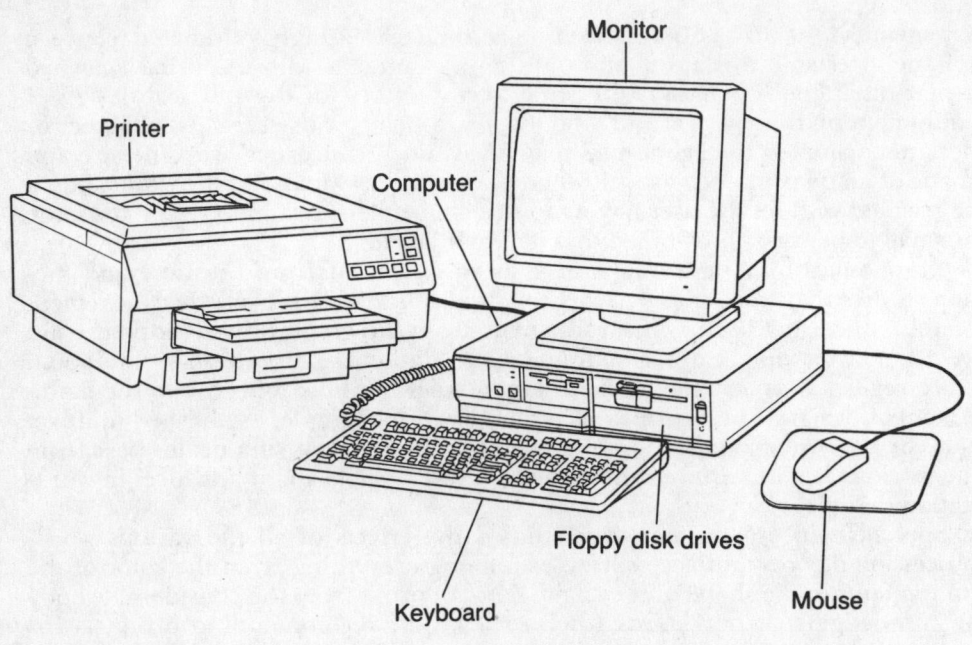

THE COMPUTER

The computer itself depends on a series of *chips,* integrated circuits made from silicon that store and process information. Chips are attached to *boards* inside the computer, which can be removed and replaced only by technicians. The most important board is called the *system board* or *motherboard,* and the most important chip on the system board is the *central processing unit,* or *CPU.* The CPU is the computer's "traffic cop," controlling all the information flowing between the keyboard, the computer itself, the printer, and various other devices you may have connected.

Computer language   A computer does not understand language in the same way that we do. Its language consists of electrical impulses, and it only understands two things: high-voltage impulses and low-voltage impulses. Some people refer to this as "the switch" being "on" or "off." Ultimately, everything must be converted to a pattern of electrical impulses in order for the computer to understand it.

Each electrical impulse is called a *bit,* short for *binary digit.* In the computer's terms, the number 1 represents the switch being on and the number 0 represents the switch being off. Because there are only two possibilities, this is referred to as a *binary system.*

The computer industry has a standardized code in which each keyboard character—every letter, number, and symbol—is represented by a fixed pattern of eight bits, called a *byte.* The code, known as the American Standard Code for Information Interchange, or ASCII (pronounced "as-key"), is recognized and accepted by hardware and software manufacturers. ASCII code actually uses only seven bits to represent a character; the eighth bit may be used for some other purpose by the hardware or software, or it may be ignored. Even so, the code is still described as using eight bits. Here, for example, is the word "HELLO" in ASCII code:

   1001000   1000101   1001100   1001100   1001111

Incidentally, the codes would be different for lowercase letters.

   Each time you press a key on a keyboard, you are sending one byte of electrical impulses to the computer, and the computer is decoding it to display the desired character on the screen.

Computer memory   The computer has two kinds of memory: ROM and RAM. ROM, or *read-only memory,* contains the computer's own internal operating instructions. The computer "reads," or uses, the information in ROM to run itself. The user has no access to anything stored in ROM. RAM, or *random-access memory,* is a temporary work space in which the computer runs your word-processing program and other applications. Unlike ROM, which is permanent memory, anything in RAM is wiped out as soon as you turn off the computer (or experience a power outage). Think of RAM as a desk where you can spread out your work each day but must clean it up at night before leaving.

   Memory, in the computer's terms, is measured in thousands or millions of bytes. A thousand bytes is a *kilobyte,* or K for short. A million bytes is a *megabyte* (Mg). Actually, because of the eight-bit ASCII code, kilobytes and megabytes are multiples of eight, so a kilobyte is really 1,024 bytes, and a megabyte is really 1,048,576 bytes. Here are some common RAM memory capacities. The word equivalents are based on an average of five characters per word.

RAM	Equivalent to approximately:
512K	512,000 characters, or 102,400 words
1Mg	1,024,000 characters, or 204,800 words
4Mg	4,096,000 characters, or 819,200 words
10Mg	10,240,000 characters, or 2,048,000 words

Storage   Your word processor would not be of much use if you could not store the documents that you prepare, and reprint or edit them later on. Information is permanently stored on disks, which are magnetized to record the bits making up your document. Computers use two types of disk: *floppy disks,* which are portable, and *hard disks,* which are usually built into the computer itself.

   Floppy disks, so named because they are generally flexible enough to bend, are thin plastic disks. Originally, all floppy disks were 8″ in diameter; today, the standard sizes are 5¼″ and 3½″. The smaller 3½″ disk is sealed in a thicker casing which does not really bend; however, all portable disks are referred to as floppy disks, floppies, or simply diskettes.

   The floppy disk is inserted through a slot into a device called a *disk drive,* which spins the disk and is able to copy information from it (called "reading" the disk) or record new information on it (called "writing to" the disk).

   Information is stored on the disk in sectors, or rings. The disk drive can access any part of the disk without having to go through it sequentially. This is important because information may be stored on a disk in random locations, and the computer must reassemble the information quickly before displaying it on your screen.

Straight out of the box, a floppy disk will fit into any word processor or computer with the correct size of disk drive (3½" or 5¼"). But it will not work until a simple step, called *formatting,* is carried out. Formatting, which takes only about a minute, customizes the disk for the particular brand of machine in which it will be used. The disk can later be reformatted for use in another computer, but the process erases anything stored on it; be very careful not to reformat a disk unless you are willing to lose all the data on it. Hard disks also need to be formatted, but this is normally done when they are installed in the computer and never again.

Floppy disks require care in handling. They should not be exposed to excessive heat or cold. (Do not leave them in your car, for instance, but they will be safe in the office even if the air-conditioning or heating is turned off over the weekend.) Never touch the surface of the disk, and do not bend it or attach paper clips or anything similar. Use only felt-tip pens when writing on the label. Do not drop it or drop objects on top of it, and avoid forcing it into a disk drive if it will not go in easily. Most important, since the data on the disk is magnetized, keep the disk away from magnets or magnetic fields—for example, telephones—which could scramble the data.

As mentioned, most computers also contain a permanently installed hard disk. The hard disk serves much the same purpose as a floppy disk but stores a great deal more data. Once considered a luxury, hard disks are now generally regarded as essential for storing application programs and the files created with them.

The storage capacity of disks is expressed, as discussed earlier, in kilobytes (K) and megabytes (Mg). Here are some sample storage capacities for the various disks, including the newer high-density (HD) floppy disks:

Disk Type	Storage	Equivalent
3½" floppy	720K	737,280 bytes or 147,456 words
3½" HD floppy	1.44Mg	1,474,560 bytes or 294,912 words
5¼" floppy	360K	368,640 bytes or 73,728 words
5¼" HD floppy	1.2Mg	1,228,800 bytes or 245,760 words
Hard disk	40Mg	40,960,000 bytes or 8,192,000 words
Hard disk	100Mg	102,400,000 bytes or 20,480,000 words

As hard disks fill up, files tend to become fragmented—that is, broken up and stored on different parts of the disk—which may result in a loss of performance. Special defragmenting software will read and rewrite the entire disk, putting the files back together.

THE KEYBOARD

The keyboard can be detached from the computer itself. The cable should be long enough to allow you to position the keyboard for your maximum comfort and convenience.

There are as many keyboard designs as there are manufacturers of word-processing equipment, but they all have some basic things in common.

The central part of the keyboard, containing the alphabet letter keys, is essentially the same as the traditional typewriter keyboard. In addition, most computer keyboards also have the following:

Cursor control keys   These keys, labeled with arrows pointing up, down, left, and right, are used to move the cursor around on the screen. The cursor position represents the precise location where anything you type will appear.

Numeric keypad   Most keyboards include a separate section for typing numbers. The keypad, usually placed at the side of the keyboard, looks like a calculator and may have keys allowing for computation as well as input of numbers.

Function keys   These keys, usually labeled F1 through F10 or higher, are designated to perform different functions for each software program. For example, in one program F3 may be the key that underlines text, while in another program F3 may be used to call up a file from memory. Function keys may appear along the top of the keyboard or at the side.

A typical keyboard is illustrated in Fig. 7.2.

Fig. 7.2   Computer Keyboard

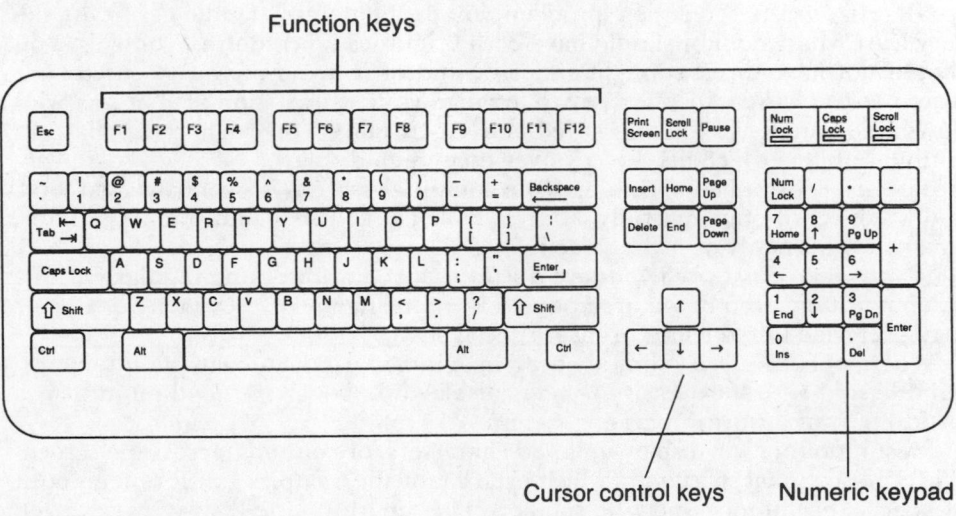

When placed on desktops as they usually are, computer keyboards are generally 3–5″ too high for sustained typing. A special keyboard drawer, which replaces the center drawer of a desk, lowers the keyboard to a more comfortable height and stores it out of the way when not in use.

THE MONITOR

There is much more variation in the types and capabilities of monitors than of keyboards. Your three primary ergonomic concerns about monitors should be ease of positioning adjustment, clarity of image, and absence of glare.

In the early days of word-processing, monitors were fixed in place, and users had to accommodate themselves to the equipment. Today, with an enormous range of monitors available, the user can readily choose a model on which adjustments for convenience and safety can easily be made.

Many monitors have tilt-and-swivel bases that enable you to select the viewing angle you find most comfortable. You may also want a monitor stand to raise the height of the screen so as to avoid neck fatigue.

If space is limited on your desk or if you do not use the monitor all day long, you may want to purchase a monitor arm. A monitor arm suspends the monitor in the air so that it can be raised, lowered, tilted, and swiveled, and pushed out of the way when not in use.

Eyestrain is one of the most common complaints of office workers who spend hours in front of a monitor each day. Monitors vary widely in their ability to deliver a sharp image and to display it without flickering. The screen image is made up of dots, or *pixels,* in much the same way that letters on a dot-matrix printer are made up of dots. The more pixels in the display, the greater clarity you can expect.

Another factor in the screen's comfort level is the color. For example, some people who use a monochrome (one-color) monitor may find that a green or amber display is easier on the eyes than a black-and-white screen. If you have a color monitor, your word-processing program may give you options for text and background display colors. Even if it does not, the program may use different colors to signify different purposes or operations.

Glare from the screen is a problem you can generally handle easily. At the very least, your monitor should have both brightness and contrast controls. You should not have direct sunlight either behind or in front of you when you are seated at the word processor; try to arrange your workstation so that any windows are at angles to you and have blinds or curtains. You can also purchase an anti-glare filter, which fits directly over the screen display.

The effect of radiation coming from computer screens is a controversial topic and a subject of ongoing study. Many people like to use an anti-radiation filter, which also fits easily over the screen.

If you wear glasses, tell your eye doctor that you are working regularly with a video monitor, even if you are not yet experiencing any eyestrain. Your doctor may prescribe tinted lenses or offer special advice about eye care.

When purchasing a monitor, bear in mind that cheap color monitors frequently sold with inexpensive systems display text poorly. A good monitor is a critical part of a word-processing system.

Most monitors will display up to 80 characters, or columns, across the screen. With proportional spacing, in which each character occupies a different amount of space, that number may be smaller. The length of the display varies even more. Most monitors display about half of a standard 11″ page at once; full-page displays are also available, but are more likely to be used for desktop-publishing applications.

Another factor to consider is whether or not the monitor can display graphics. Most word-processing programs allow you to merge graphics and text, but this requires a compatible monitor.

THE PRINTER

The two most common types of printer that can be used with the word processor are impact printers and laser printers. You will probably find both kinds in use in most offices; you may even have both connected to your computer and be able to switch back and forth between them for different purposes.

Impact or dot-matrix printers   The impact or dot-matrix printer prints each character by selecting an arrangement of pins which then strike through an inked ribbon onto the paper. The pin pattern thus resembles the pattern of dots or pixels that makes up each character on your monitor. The greater the number of pins, the higher the quality of the image produced. The most common dot-matrix printers are the 9-pin and 24-pin printers. The better-quality 24-pin printers are sometimes described by their manufacturers as "letter quality" or "near-letter quality." These terms refer to how closely a character produced by the printer resembles one produced by a good electronic typewriter that creates an impression by means of a solid piece of type rather than just a pattern of dots. Printers usually can also be set to produce "draft quality" printing when speed rather than quality is desired.

Dot-matrix printers became popular for a number of reasons. For one thing, they are relatively fast: a dot-matrix printer can print as many as 300 characters per second. And since they work by making impressions, they can print through multilayered forms. They are also flexible enough to handle both standard 8½" paper and 14"-wide computer printouts.

Dot-matrix printers typically use pin-feed paper, which is advanced through the machine by a tractor mechanism. The paper attaches to the tractor by a series of holes along the sides of the sheets; the holes are part of a perforated strip, which can be easily removed after printing. (Cartons of 8½" continuous-form paper are often labeled 9½" because the perforated strip on each side is ½" wide.) Adjusting the paper so that it moves evenly can be tricky, and jams are not unusual, but the dot-matrix printer can be an economical and reliable office workhorse. Many letter quality and near-letter quality printers also offer a single-sheet bypass so that letterhead and envelopes can be fed through without having to remove the continuous-form sheets from the tractor.

Printers do not simply accept one character at a time from the computer and print it; they accept more than they can print at once and store them in temporary memory. As the characters in memory are printed, more are accepted. Dot-matrix printers vary in the amount of memory they have. You may notice that the printer "takes control" of your computer and its memory when printing a document and does not allow it to do anything else.

Laser printers   While a good dot-matrix printer is suitable for most basic office tasks, many companies now rely mainly on the laser printer. Prices have dropped considerably, making the laser printer affordable for small companies and individual business owners.

The laser printer is much like a photocopier. Toner (similar to ink) is housed in a cartridge inside the printer, and electric charges created by the laser beam on the paper attract the toner. Characters are printed in a pattern of dots, but the dots are smaller and in greater density than those produced by a dot-matrix printer—usually 300 dots per inch (DPI). The effect is very close to that of professional typesetting; in fact, many manufacturers talk about "near-typeset quality" when describing the output of their laser printers.

The speed of a laser printer is expressed in the number of pages it can produce per minute. A speed of six to eight pages per minute is common, although expensive lasers can operate much faster. The rated speed of a laser printer describes its performance once it has begun printing multiple copies; the waiting time for the first copy depends to some extent on how full the page is and whether it is straight text or text mixed with graphics.

There are a few drawbacks to laser printers. They can only print one page at a time—no multiple forms—and they cannot accept the oversized paper that a dot-matrix printer can handle. Paper is loaded into cassettes, each of which holds only one size of paper at a time. However, the printer may accommodate two cassettes with a different size in each and may also allow for manual feed of an odd-sized sheet without reloading the cassette. Laser printers also tend to have trouble feeding envelopes smoothly. However, they are becoming more versatile as laser-compatible products flood the market. Adhesive labels that can withstand the heat of the laser are now available, and some manufacturers are offering laser envelopes that feed smoothly through the printer. Other laser products include sheets of rotary address cards, index cards, postcards, and multicolored paper for brochures and mailers.

Some of the most innovative products for the laser printer are directly related to the growth of desktop publishing. In fact, it is the growth of desktop publishing, in which text and graphics are merged, which is largely responsible for the popularity of the laser printer. See Chapter 8 for a discussion of desktop publishing.

The other common type of nonimpact printer is the ink-jet printer, discussed later in this chapter under "Portable Computers."

OTHER HARDWARE

All of the devices that connect to the computer are considered "peripherals." The keyboard, monitor, and printer are the standard peripherals in any word-processing configuration, but there are also a few other devices that may be a part of your system.

The Mouse   The mouse is basically a pointing device. Moving the mouse causes a small, typically arrow- or bar-shaped pointer to make corresponding movements on the computer screen. Using the mouse with appropriate software makes it possible to perform many routine computing tasks more easily and quickly than can be done with just a keyboard. For example, it may be possible to open and close programs and files with a mouse simply by pointing to a small picture (called an *icon*) on the screen and clicking the mouse's button.

Many word-processing programs now allow for at least some use of the mouse, with more and more being adapted to make the mouse useful for almost any task other than typing text. One common use of the mouse is to move the cursor to different places in the text simply by pointing to the desired position and clicking the mouse's button. This is usually much faster than using the arrow keys on the keyboard. The mouse can also be used to select individual words, sentences, and blocks of text to be moved, deleted, or otherwise edited. Many sophisticated programs make it possible to use the mouse for quickly making changes in a document's format—for example, resetting margins and tab stops, choosing a different typeface, or altering the spacing between lines and paragraphs. These are only a few of the functions a mouse can perform.

Some experienced typists find it hard to get used to the mouse because they dislike taking their hands away from the keyboard. Programs designed for use with a mouse do include alternative keyboard methods for the mouse's functions, so it is usually possible to avoid the mouse altogether if you are so inclined. If you spend some time learning to use the mouse, however, you will likely come to feel that it is indispensable for certain tasks.

The modem   A modem enables you to transmit data from one computer to another over ordinary telephone lines. It converts the computer's digital language into the telephone's analog language for transmission. At the other end, a receiving modem converts it back to a digital signal. This is where the modem's name comes from: it is a device that *mo*dulates and *dem*odulates data.

There are two forms of modem: the *internal modem,* a board that fits into a slot in the computer, and the *external modem,* a small box that attaches to the computer cable.

Modems are rated according to the speed at which they transmit data. The measurement is in bits per second, or BPS, sometimes also referred to as the *baud rate*. Here are some common modem speeds:

Modem Speed	Equivalent
1200 BPS	9,000 characters, or 1,800 words per minute
2400 BPS	18,000 characters, or 3,600 words per minute
9600 BPS	72,000 characters, or 14,400 words per minute

In the context of word processing, modems are frequently used to exchange text files between computers. It is not unusual for one person to draft a document, transmit it electronically to someone else who may edit or comment on it, and then return the file to the originator for more work. The electronic transmission may only take seconds, and is far more convenient and economical than exchanging paper, especially across long distances.

There are a number of factors to consider in using modems to exchange files.

1. In addition to word-processing software, both the sender and the receiver must have communications software to drive the modem.
2. The sender and receiver may also need to be using the same word-processing software, so that files loaded at either end preserve the same formatting characteristics (underlines, boldface, type fonts, and so forth). Otherwise, you may have to exchange "text-only" files.
3. Outside third-party vendors, such as electronic mail services, will generally provide for hardware compatibility so that entirely different computers or word processors can exchange files with each other. Differences in software, however, may continue to be a problem. If both parties are transmitting in-house through a local area network (LAN), there should be no problems of hardware or software compatibility.

Every improvement in hardware and software requires a corresponding improvement in transmission capability. If you have a modem, consult your user manual for setup and operating instructions, and do not be surprised or discouraged if you find that you need some technical assistance from the vendor to make it work.

PORTABLE COMPUTERS

Whereas the earliest computers occupied entire rooms, today's word processor or microcomputer is a desktop appliance. With a little effort, you can pick it up and move it around, but it is still hardly portable. Not until the arrival of laptop and notebook computers did true portability become a reality.

The first portable computer was the *laptop computer*—a battery-powered computer, keyboard, and monitor packaged in a briefcase-sized unit that weighed about 20 pounds. The laptop computer soon led to the *notebook computer,* a smaller and lighter version weighing as little as four to six pounds. Advances in the design of chips were responsible for this extraordinary reduction in size. Laptop and notebook computers are available with hard disks, fax modems, and built-in mouse devices, as well as a full range of external devices such as modems, battery chargers, and portable disk drives. They require separate printers, but many vendors offer portable printers as well. The ink-jet printer, which sprays ink on paper, producing a sharper image than those produced by dot-matrix printers, exists in portable as well as nonportable models.

Laptop and notebook computers have tended to be less powerful and more expensive than microcomputers, but with continuing rapid development and cost reduction they can be expected to match the microcomputer soon in both respects.

Computer Supplies and Accessories

SUPPLIES

In many offices, supplies are stored centrally and can only be requisitioned one item at a time as needed. Since word-processing equipment uses a considerable amount of consumable supplies, they should be easily accessible. An adequate supply of blank diskettes is essential, as are labels for them. Extra paper should always be handy for the printer. Individual cut sheets, normally packaged in reams of 500, are easily stored; pin-feed paper for printers with tractors is usually boxed in units of 1000 sheets or more, but the sheets are perforated and any quantity can be easily removed from a large box and stored in a desk drawer. Extra printer ribbons or toner cartridges should also be at hand, especially if your office is given to last-minute rush jobs.

ACCESSORIES

In addition to all the peripheral devices that make up the basic word processor or computer, a range of inexpensive accessories is available to add to your comfort and convenience. Most of these can be purchased at a local computer store or through mail-order catalogs. In a large organization, your purchasing department should be able to help you obtain any of them.

Wrist supports   These useful devices attach to your keyboard and provide a lightweight, comfortable resting place for your hands during prolonged periods of keyboarding. The supports enable you to keep your wrists straight and prevent the fatigue you might otherwise experience when working on long documents. They can also help prevent carpal-tunnel syndrome, an ailment common among long-term users of word processors.

Footrests   Experts on office stress recommend that your knees be higher than your hips when sitting at a keyboard for any length of time. To accomplish this, use a footrest that raises your feet a few inches and lets you adjust the angle of your feet. The footrest reduces the strain on your lower back and aids the circulation in your lower legs.

Copy holder   The tabletop copy stand, familiar in offices for decades, has been improved on by the movable copy holder, which occupies no desk space at all. This device attaches to your desk or to the monitor itself and holds your copy by a clip. It can be raised, lowered, and swiveled so that the copy you are working from is in the most convenient location for you, and can be removed or pushed out of the way when not in use.

Mouse pad   If your word processor or computer uses a mouse, you will want a mouse pad for it. This rubberized pad prevents the mouse from scratching your desk, allows it to move more smoothly, and helps to keep it clean. It also serves to stake out the mouse's territory on the work surface so that it will not tend to be overwhelmed by clutter. Basic mouse pads cost only a few dollars. They can also be purchased with a built-in wrist support.

Power strip   A power strip is basically a heavy-duty extension cord with enough outlets to accommodate all the plugs in your system. The power strip provides two additional features as well. First, it has an on/off switch that controls all the outlets at once, so that you can leave your computer, monitor, and printer permanently switched on and control them through the strip. Some power strips also serve as surge suppressors. Electronic equipment is susceptible to damage from sudden increases in electrical power called "surges" or "spikes," and a surge suppressor will prevent such damage under most circumstances.

Power-backup system   The opposite problem, a loss of power, may be prevented by a power-backup system, which provides emergency power for a period of time ranging from 10 minutes to an hour or more. These systems are considerably more expensive than power strips, and purchasing one may require official approval. Even a momentary power outage can wipe out a considerable amount of work, so if you work in a location where power outages are common you may want to recommend the purchase of a backup system.

Keyboard cover   Word-processing equipment can be susceptible to environmental hazards such as dust particles. The most vulnerable device is your keyboard, because it has so many openings in which dust can accumulate. Fortunately, keyboards tend to be well made, and malfunctions due to dust are not as common as one might assume. Even so, you can contribute to the longevity of these devices by using inexpensive plastic keyboard covers.

Computer tool kit   You may also want to purchase a computer tool kit. These kits include a small vacuum for cleaning keyboards and printers, along with small screwdrivers and other tools for tightening and loosening the cables that connect your devices.

Floor mat   Walking across a carpeted floor, or even just sitting down in an upholstered chair, can cause you to pick up enough static electricity to damage your computer if that is the next thing you touch. Antistatic carpeting is available, but it is costly and not practical if your office is already carpeted. A static-control floor mat under your chair is a convenient and inexpensive alternative. Floor mats also provide a smoother surface for chairs to glide around on, preventing the accidental tipping that can occur if the wheels do not turn smoothly against the carpet.

Chairs   Probably no office furnishing has received as much attention as the chair. Computer stores and catalogs are filled with "ergonomically correct" chairs, some of which look like conventional office chairs while others have strange, futuristic designs. What makes a chair comfortable? According to the experts, it should have these characteristics:

1. It should have an adjustable back support that accomplishes two purposes. First, the lumbar vertebrae at the base of your spine should be supported at all times, no matter how you move around in the chair. Second, your upper back should be supported just below the shoulders.
2. The front edge of the seat should be rounded down (in a so-called waterfall) so that circulation in the thighs is not restricted.
3. The seat height should be adjustable, either manually or by means of a pneumatic cylinder in the post between the seat and the base. Automatic controls should be conveniently accessible from the sitting position. (Chairs on which the seat height is adjusted manually may need to be turned over and the base unscrewed until it extends to the desired height, a cumbersome task that may even require two people.)

4. The chair should both swivel and recline to allow for natural body movements and rest periods, and the angle at which it reclines should be easily adjustable.

5. For safety, the chair base should have five radial legs rather than four. This design makes the chair sturdier and less likely to tip when moved. The casters should turn smoothly.

No matter how comfortable your chair is, do not sit in it all day! Give yourself frequent rest periods, especially if you are working on a long document and find yourself in the same position for extended periods of time.

Cables Because most word processors consist of a collection of components and devices, or "peripherals," you may find yourself with a thick tangle of connecting cables and power cords. Besides being unsightly, they may be safety hazards if not properly stored.

Your office may have modular furniture designed specifically for computers. This type of furniture typically has features that will largely solve the problem. The movable partitions that function as walls for each workstation usually contain channels, called "raceways," at the bottom of each panel. Cables fit into the raceways and are routed to the power source, which may be on the floor, in a wall, or even overhead behind a suspended ceiling. Desk surfaces may have large holes at the back through which connecting cables can be run between the various devices in your office. Together, these features will keep most cables safely stored and out of the way.

If you do not have furniture designed for computers, try to run cables behind equipment where they are less likely to be accidentally pulled or twisted. Avoid kinking or crimping the cables, which may affect the smooth operation of the equipment, and do not put anything down on top of them. You may want to purchase a supply of self-adhesive plastic cable hooks, which attach to any surface and hold a group of cables together neatly.

If you must run cables across the floor to a power source, try to keep them close to a wall and away from foot traffic. Consider covering them with an insulated, adhesive cord-cover which will prevent anyone from tripping on them while guarding the cables from traffic damage.

Computer Software

While some dedicated word processors have their own built-in software, the trend is toward using off-the-shelf, commercially available software packages (often referred to as COTS—Commercial Off-The-Shelf—software). These programs range from the very basic to the highly complex. Most programs offer more features than any one user would ever need. Prices range widely depending on the programs' sophistication. A *site license*—essentially, a discount for multiple purchases—may be available if your organization wants many people to be able to use the same program.

Basically, a word-processing software program consists of one or more disks containing the program itself. When purchasing, you may have to specify whether you need 3½" or 5¼" disks, although some vendors automatically supply both versions. There will also be a user manual that explains how to use the program, and possibly separate installation manuals, reference manuals, or even tutorial manuals as well.

There may also be a licensing agreement that stipulates your responsibilities as a user of the software. Because software files are easily copied from one disk to another, manufacturers are seriously concerned about copyright infringement through the proliferation of "pirated" software. (Recall that software programs are copyrighted in the same way that printed material is.) As a defense, many programs are copy-protected; that is, the files contain an internal program to prevent duplication. Even so, those who would violate the copyright protection of software developers are sometimes able to override those programs and duplicate the files. Protect yourself and your organization from legal problems by avoiding any involvement with pirated software.

The problems related to computer viruses have been well publicized. To minimize the possibility of virus damage, use only commercial software and back up your work systematically. If you think a virus may have penetrated your system, you can use special virus-detection software to locate it.

GETTING STARTED

Some software programs can be run from the original floppy disks, but most programs will need to be installed on the hard disk of a computer. Your manual will contain instructions for installing the program. You may have to copy each individual file, or the program may itself include a built-in installation program that does most of the work for you. Either way, you should not find this a difficult task. You will be instructed to make a set of backup disks first, in case the original disks are lost or damaged. Programs that are copy-protected normally allow you to make one set of backup disks, but no more.

THE WORD-PROCESSING SCREEN

While every program uses different terminology and screen layout, they all share some things in common. In addition to displaying the text that you type, the screen provides certain status information about the document. This information may include any of the following:

- File name
- Length of file, usually in characters
- Page and line on which you are currently working
- Page settings: tabs, margins, etc.
- Current mode (insert or overstrike)

If the program is designed for use with a menu, there may be a menu bar across the top of the screen from which selections can be made by pointing and clicking the mouse's button.

Most full-featured programs make use of the function keys across the top or side of the keyboard to perform certain tasks. Since there are generally more tasks to designate than there are function keys, you may need to use a combination of keys. For example, pressing the Control key (usually labeled "Ctrl") and F6 simultaneously may save a file, while F6 by itself may have an entirely different function. Software programs often include a plastic template that fits on the keyboard and identifies the function of each function key.

STARTING A DOCUMENT

When you begin a new document, the cursor will be in the first position of the document, indicating where the first character you type will appear. The cursor may be a fixed or blinking line positioned either just below or just in front of the next character, or a highlighted box that fully surrounds the character.

The cursor moves with the text as you type. As you progress through the document, you will have occasion to go back and forth making changes; to make those changes, you will need to put the cursor in the right spot. Depending on the program, you may be able to move the cursor in several ways.

1. By using the four arrow keys on the keyboard you can move the cursor up, down, left, or right. Though the cursor normally moves only one position at a time, by holding the key down you may move it rapidly from one end of a line to the other or from the top to the bottom of the page.

2. More sophisticated programs allow you to move the cursor to a specific location with just one or two keystrokes, usually some combination of the Control key and an arrow or function key. You may choose to move to the end of a line (forward or backward), to the start or end of the paragraph, or forward or backward a specified number of characters, words, or pages.

3. The keyboard's Home and End keys, usually located above the arrow keys, can also be used to move the cursor quickly to the beginning ("home") or end of a line and often to make larger movements (such as to the beginning or end of a document) when used in combination with other keys.

4. As mentioned earlier, mouse-driven programs let you move the cursor by simply pointing to the desired location on the screen and clicking the mouse button. This is usually faster than using the keyboard.

Remember that most monitors display somewhat less than a full page at a time. (Word-processing programs generally include a Print Preview feature, however, which allows you to view full pages in a reduced graphics mode before printing.) Full-page monitors are available but are used primarily for desktop publishing. To move around in a lengthy document, you may find it easier to change pages than to move the cursor. Most keyboards contain Page Up and Page Down keys which have the effect of electronically turning the page. Your software may also offer a "scrolling" feature, which lets you move the text continuously up or down until you have located the spot you are looking for, by means of a series of keystrokes or by using the mouse.

BASIC WORD-PROCESSING OPERATIONS

Until you need to add, subtract, or change anything, using a word-processing program is just like typing—you hit a key and the letter or character appears. However, unlike a character typed on paper, the screen display can be changed instantly—and as often as you like—until you are ready to print. Since the finished document is stored on a disk, it can also be kept for editing at a later date and then reprinted.

The word processor performs an automatic carriage return at the end of each line. If you are typing a word with more characters than the line has room for, the program will move the entire word to the beginning of the next line. This feature, called *wordwrap*, is standard with all programs. (What actually happens is that the program looks for a space indicating a break between words. If it runs out of room on a line before the next space is keyed, it treats everything since the last space as a word and moves it to the next line as a unit.) Because of wordwrap, the Return or Enter key on your keyboard is needed only to begin a new line when the previous line ended before reaching the right margin (such as when starting a new paragraph).

The program may also offer an automatic hyphenation feature, in which long words are hyphenated according to standard rules rather than moved in full to the next line.

Word processors generally allow you both to *overstrike*—that is, type over the existing text, automatically deleting it as you do so—and to *insert*—that is, add text *without* losing what is already there. Which of these modes you are in at a given moment may appear at the top or bottom of the screen.

In general, to use any text-editing feature of the program you must perform two steps.

First, identify the text to be affected, usually by *highlighting* it on the screen. Highlighted text will appear either the opposite of its normal color or with a different-colored background surrounding it. Your programs may refer to highlighting as *selecting* or *blocking* the text. There are a number of ways to accomplish it, depending on your software. One method is to use the mouse, holding down one of the buttons and dragging the pointer on the screen across the desired text. Another method requires pressing a function key to start the highlighting process, using the arrow keys to extend it across the desired text, and pressing another key to end the process.

Second, perform the desired operation on the highlighted text, either with a function key, a menu selection, or by typing a special command. Again, the method depends on your program. There is usually a key you can press if you change your mind about an operation you have started. Typically, it is the Escape key (usually labeled "Esc"), but the software program may assign another key instead.

PAGE-SETUP OPTIONS

The following are the most common options available for setting up a page. Others may be available, depending on your program.

Page size   Since the program will automatically paginate for you, it needs to know what size of paper you will be printing on. The standard choices are $8\frac{1}{2}'' \times 11''$ and $8\frac{1}{2}'' \times 14''$.

Page orientation   Most programs will allow you to print either in vertical (sometimes called "portrait") orientation or in horizontal (sometimes called "landscape") orientation. Vertical printing—that is, on an upright page, like the one you are reading—is the normal style, but horizontal is useful for charts, graphics, and other special applications.

Single- and double-spacing   This is another fundamental option available in most programs. The choice between single- and double-spacing can be made for an entire document or for selected sections within a document.

Tabs and margins   There is always an automatic setting for tabs and margins in the program (sometimes called a *default* setting), but you can override the automatic settings for any individual document. This information is generally displayed on the screen.

Page numbering   Most programs provide automatic page numbering, and allow you to specify where the page numbers are to appear. You may also be able to choose between numbering styles, such as Arabic or Roman numerals. (See "Headers and footers," page 285.)

WORD-PROCESSING FEATURES

Some word-processing features affect page setup and appearance, while others affect the arrangement of the text itself. The following features are available in a variety of programs. A few programs may contain all of these features, but most programs will contain only some of them. When selecting a word-processing program or looking to upgrade an existing one, you may want to read through this list and note the features of most use to you, then compare each program you are considering against your list to see how well it will meet your needs.

Append   This feature permits you to take text from one file and add it to another file.

Automatic file backup   Just as you should always back up your files to protect against accidental damage or loss, you should also have a system for saving the previous version of any file you have revised, in case it becomes necessary to have access to the earlier version. Some programs offer a system for automatically saving the previous version.

Boldface   Characters and words can be printed in boldface type for emphasis or to serve as a heading.

Boxes   The ability to create boxes around text, especially when combined with the ability to create horizontal and vertical lines, enables you to design charts, tables, attractive headings, and much else. Boxes can usually be plain, drop-shadowed, or filled with various degrees of shading.

Capitalization   Many programs allow you to select and automatically capitalize any text you have already entered in lowercase. You may also specify that it be set in SMALL CAPITALS.

Centering   Any word, line, or paragraph can be automatically centered between the margins of the document. This is useful for headings, quotations, or any other material that should stand out from the main body of the text.

Columns   This page-layout capability is useful for charts, documentation, and many other applications. It generally permits you to divide your page into a desired number of columns and specify the amount of space between the columns. The most common types of column are newspaper columns, in which the text simply wraps to the top of the next column, and side-by-side columns, in which specific items are lined up directly across from each other.

Copy   Within a file, the Copy feature allows you to select any block of text and duplicate it (see the following "Cut and paste" section). At the directory or menu level of the program, a Copy feature enables you to duplicate an entire file so that an alternative version can be created without losing the original.

Cut and paste   Also called simply *moving copy*, this fundamental feature of all word-processing programs enables you to select any amount of text and move it to another location in the document. The process requires you to "cut" the text after highlighting it, locate the new insertion point with the cursor, and then "paste" it in by using the keys designated by your software. Text that is cut is held in temporary memory until you move it. From temporary memory, it may be pasted into the document multiple times, if desired. If you choose not to paste the text back in—which amounts to deleting it—it will remain in the temporary memory only until you either turn off the computer or displace it by cutting some other text (since there is normally only room for one piece at a time in the temporary memory).

Delete   In the process of editing and correcting, you will probably be deleting text as often as you add it, so this feature is one of the most fundamental capabilities of word processing. Minor deletions are often accomplished by merely backspacing over the last text that was entered. To remove a large block of text, you will have to highlight the entire block and then use whatever method your program requires—function key, Delete key, or a menu choice—to delete it.

Find text   This search feature allows you to specify a word or phrase that occurs anywhere in the document and then have the software locate that spot for you instantly. This is a tremendous time-saver when you are trying to locate something in a long document.

Glossary   This feature enables you to create your own list of frequently used words, phrases, sentences, and paragraphs, and add them to any document with a few keystrokes. Stock sentences and paragraphs, informally known as "boilerplate," can be especially helpful when you need to modify form letters. If your program does not have a glossary function, you can get the same result by storing your boilerplate language as separate files and then loading them into any file as needed.

Graphics   In the early days of word processing, it was a text-only operation. Today, word-processing programs allow you to add, or "import," graphics created through a separate graphics program into your document. Some programs even include a library of useful images that can be placed in a document. This capability has further blurred the lines between word processing and desktop publishing.

Headers and footers   In any document you may need to display repetitive identification at the top or bottom of each page. Typical examples include the name of the document or file, the title of a presentation or proposal, or chapter or section numbers, as well as page numbers. For convenience or attractiveness, you may want these lines to appear as *headers* (that is, lines running across the top of the page, as on the page you are reading) or as *footers* (lines running across the bottom of the page), and your word-processing program should be able to accomplish this for you.

Indexing   This feature automates the job of preparing alphabetical indexes. After you have gone through a lengthy document and highlighted or identified those words or phrases that you want included in the index, the program takes over, pulling together the entire index with appropriate page numbers and formatting.

Justification   This feature controls line width and spacing. Most typed documents have lines of varying length, depending on the number of words in the line. The left margin is flush but the right margin varies, in the style usually called "ragged right." Full justification, also called "right justification," creates equal margins on both sides by inserting extra space as needed between words. Full justification has a more formal look and is desirable for certain kinds of documents, but it is harder to read because of the unequal spacing. Both types of justification are illustrated below.

Ragged right

During the past three years at the Walpole site, Ms. Pestalozzi-Holmes has coordinated the development of CyberWares' systems overview training courses, which were later implemented at our other three plants. She has also coordinated the development of a six-module vendor training program and manual; their success has been a factor in the large retail-sales gains enjoyed by CyberWares' business systems in the last 18 months.

Full justification

During the past three years at the Walpole site, Ms. Pestalozzi-Holmes has coordinated the development of CyberWares' systems overview training courses, which were later implemented at our other three plants. She has also coordinated the development of a six-module vendor training program and manual; their success has been a factor in the large retail-sales gains enjoyed by CyberWares' business systems in the last 18 months.

Kerning   Sometimes the spacing between letters in a word seems too loose or too tight. Increasing or reducing that spacing is called kerning.

Leading   The space between lines on a page is determined by the software and may vary according to the font (that is, the style or design of type) being used and the point size of the letters. The spacing between lines is called leading (pronounced "ledding"). The feature that permits you to increase or decrease the leading is primarily useful for desktop publishing.

Macros   A macro is a miniature computer program you may write by yourself to direct the software to perform one or more repetitive tasks. For example, rather than pressing a series of keys to print, close, and save a file, you could write a macro that would enable you to do all those things with one keystroke. Macros can make word processing much easier, and you should always be alert to the possibility of creating new ones.

Mail merge   The ability to automate large mailings can be one of the great benefits of a word-processing program. This feature allows you to create a document in one file and an address list in another and then merge them to produce personalized letters using each individual's name and address. You will need to embed instructions in the document file telling it where to insert the address and salutation, and you will also have to follow strict rules for formatting the address list so that the information merges correctly.

Pagination   Once you set the page size of a document, the software will automatically begin a new page whenever necessary. If you later edit the document, making it longer or shorter, the system will repaginate for you. You can override this by manually inserting a page break wherever you want one. Page breaks are normally displayed on-screen so that you can always see where they occur.

Password protection   Some programs allow you to establish your own access code so that no one else can get into your files. If this is not part of your word-processing program, you can probably purchase a separate program that does the same thing.

Save   Every program provides a menu choice or function key for saving a file—that is, placing it permanently on a disk for storage. In addition to saving completed files for later use, work in progress should be saved frequently—ideally, every 15 minutes—to avoid loss from power outages or other malfunctions. Some programs offer a timed Save feature, which automatically saves the file you are working on at specified intervals.

Search and replace   This is the advanced version of the Find Text feature described above. In addition to searching for a word or phrase, you can specify another word or phrase to substitute for the original. You can use this feature to make global changes (that is, changes throughout a given document), such as replacing an incorrect name or title wherever it occurs without having to find and retype every instance of it.

Sorting   If you ever need to produce documents with long lists that must appear in either numerical or alphabetical order, look for a sorting feature in your word-processing program. This feature allows you, for example, to select a series of entries and sort them by the first character in the entry to create an alphabetical address file or an index, thus freeing you from having to input the text in the correct order and keep rearranging things when a number or an entry changes.

Spell check   This is one of the great advantages of word-processing technology, available in many software programs. The spell checker will search for every word from a given document in a built-in list of words, notify you when it fails to find it in its present spelling, and suggest alternative spellings based on near matches with other words. Some programs allow you to add words to the list—for example, technical jargon that may be unique to your industry, and proper nouns—so that all those words will be recognized as correct when you use the spell checker on later documents. One caution: Spell checkers cannot identify a word that is correctly spelled but misused. For example, both "there" and "their" would be accepted by a spell checker, although only one would be correct in the context of a particular sentence.

Styles   If you prepare documents containing multiple sections, each with its own characteristics—margins, type font, italics, boldface, or underlining, for example—your word-processing program should offer you the option of creating reusable styles—that is, formats for individual sections. This feature, usually called Styles or Style Sheets, lets you define individual styles, or collections of formatting characteristics, and then apply them to different blocks of text in the document.

Superscript and subscript   Various mathematical formulas and chemical notations employ characters printed slightly above or below the regular line of text, which are termed *superscripts* and *subscripts,* respectively. Trademark and registration symbols are also generally written as superscripts or subscripts. Your word-processing program should provide you with the capability to print characters in this way.

Thesaurus   Similar to the spell checker, the built-in thesaurus will look for synonyms and antonyms of any word you select.

Underline   Underlining is useful for highlighting words or phrases for emphasis or for designating subheadings in a document.

Widow and orphan control   In typesetting terminology, a widow is the last line of a paragraph that spilled over to the top of the next page. An orphan is the opposite: the first line of a paragraph at the bottom of a page, when the rest of the paragraph is on the next page. Both are considered unattractive, and many word-processing programs have a feature to prevent them. An additional line of the paragraph from the previous page is brought over to keep the widow company, and the orphan line is moved to the next page to join the rest of its "family."

WORD-PROCESSING APPLICATIONS

While correspondence is still a major word-processing task, today's secretary is involved in producing a much wider range of documents. The following are some examples.

Contracts   Law firms and legal departments of large companies are involved in producing a wide variety of contracts. Personnel departments may also be involved in preparing contracts of employment.

Financial reports   Since financial reports frequently require normal text combined with spreadsheet data (that is, accounting tables and similar material), an integrated software program that provides both spreadsheet and word-processing capability may be used.

Form letters   The availability of Mail Merge features now allows secretaries to do large mailings that in the past had to be handled by specialized mailing houses. The graphics capability of many programs also allows secretaries to design graphically interesting form letters, even if they require boxes, tear-off coupons, and nontext elements.

Instructional material   To support training programs, a large variety of handouts, quick-reference guides, and procedures manuals may be needed. The production of these materials may overlap with desktop publishing.

Presentations   Support materials and handouts are often required for distribution to participants at meetings and presentations.

Proposals   In manufacturing, marketing, and research environments, sales proposals are a common application. Office workers may also prepare proposals for studies they want to undertake or organizational changes they are recommending.

Reports   Progress reports and status reports may be required as part of a special project.

Slides and overhead transparencies   The ability to import graphics, prepare documents in landscape (horizontal) orientation, and use a variety of type fonts now enables secretaries to produce visual aids that could previously have been created only by a graphic-arts department or an outside vendor. There are also specialized presentation software programs available. This application of word processing overlaps considerably with desktop publishing; see Chapter 10 for a further discussion.

SPECIAL CHARACTER SETS

As the world gets smaller, it is no longer sufficient to be able to communicate only with others who speak the same language. The ASCII character set that represents our language in computer terms allows for either 128 characters (in a seven-bit system) or 256 characters (in an eight-bit system). This leaves enough extra spots for the alphabets of some other languages, though not for every language in which we might want to communicate. For example, the 256-character system is adequate for the Hebrew and Russian alphabets, but not for Japanese, Chinese, or Arabic.

Special software programs enable users to produce documents in many other languages. The requirements are complex. Printers must be able both to reproduce the characters of other alphabets and to follow their conventions. (Hebrew, for example, is printed from right to left.) And there must be an easy way to input those characters on standard keyboards. Some programs now allow the user to switch back and forth between languages just by a series of keystrokes.

In addition to the character sets of other languages, many word-processing programs let you reproduce common symbols, scientific and musical notation, and other graphic elements. These special character sets can be accessed by pressing a series of keys. These keys and the character sets differ from one software program to another, so check your user manual to find out which are available and how to access them. The standard ASCII extended character set is shown in Fig. 7.3.

OPTICAL CHARACTER RECOGNITION (OCR)

Recently developed computer technology enables the user to transfer existing printed material directly into a computer file. This requires a *scanner,* a device that conveys the image of the text from a piece of paper to the monitor; optical character recognition (OCR) software then converts it into a word-processing file. (A scanner's success can vary considerably depending on the size, type, and quality of reproduction of the fonts scanned.) Scanners are also used to reproduce photographs and graphic images. They are most widely used for desktop publishing (see Chapter 8).

MANAGING YOUR FILES

If you are doing high-volume word processing, you may sometimes have difficulty locating individual files unless you have a good system in place. There are several steps you can take to set up an efficient file-management system.

1. *Use a file-naming system that makes it easy to identify the file you are looking for.* If you work with an MS-DOS system, you know that file names can be up to eight characters long, followed by a dot with up to three additional characters as an extension. If you do not specify an extension, most programs will supply one of their own, usually identifying the program itself. If you do most of your work with the same program, this will not be very useful, and you will be better off supplying your own extension.

2. *Use a file-storage system that makes it easy to find files.* On an MS-DOS system, you may create subdirectories in which related files can be stored. On a Macintosh, you may create a "folder"—essentially a subdirectory—for re-

Fig. 7.3   ASCII Extended Character Set

#	Char	#	Char	#	Char	#	Char	#	Char
0		52	4	103	g	154	Ü	205	═
1	☺	53	5	104	h	155	¢	206	╬
2	●	54	6	105	i	156	£	207	╧
3	♥	55	7	106	j	157	¥	208	╨
4	♦	56	8	107	k	158	₧	209	╤
5	♣	57	9	108	l	159	ƒ	210	╥
6	♠	58	:	109	m	160	á	211	╙
7	•	59	;	110	n	161	í	212	╘
8	◘	60	<	111	o	162	ó	213	╒
9	○	61	=	112	p	163	ú	214	╓
10	◙	62	>	113	q	164	ñ	215	╫
11	♂	63	?	114	r	165	Ñ	216	╪
12	♀	64	@	115	s	166	ª	217	┘
13	♪	65	A	116	t	167	º	218	┌
14	♫	66	B	117	u	168	¿	219	█
15	☼	67	C	118	v	169	⌐	220	▄
16	►	68	D	119	w	170	¬	221	▌
17	◄	69	E	120	x	171	½	222	▐
18	↕	70	F	121	y	172	¼	223	▀
19	‼	71	G	122	z	173	¡	224	α
20	¶	72	H	123	{	174	«	225	β
21	§	73	I	124	|	175	»	226	Γ
22	▬	74	J	125	}	176	░	227	π
23	↨	75	K	126	~	177	▒	228	Σ
24	↑	76	L	127	⌂	178	▓	229	σ
25	↓	77	M	128	Ç	179	│	230	µ
26	→	78	N	129	ü	180	┤	231	τ
27	←	79	O	130	é	181	╡	232	Φ
28	∟	80	P	131	â	182	╢	233	θ
29	↔	81	Q	132	ä	183	╖	234	Ω
30	▲	82	R	133	à	184	╕	235	δ
31	▼	83	S	134	å	185	╣	236	∞
32	<space>	84	T	135	ç	186	║	237	ø
33	!	85	U	136	ê	187	╗	238	ε
34	"	86	V	137	ë	188	╝	239	∩
35	#	87	W	138	è	189	╜	240	≡
36	$	88	X	139	ï	190	╛	241	±
37	%	89	Y	140	î	191	┐	242	≥
38	&	90	Z	141	ì	192	└	243	≤
39	'	91	[	142	Ä	193	┴	244	⌠
40	(	92	\	143	Å	194	┬	245	⌡
41	)	93	]	144	É	195	├	246	÷
42	*	94	^	145	æ	196	─	247	≈
43	+	95	_	146	Æ	197	┼	248	°
44	,	96	`	147	ô	198	╞	249	•
45	-	97	a	148	ö	199	╟	250	·
46	.	98	b	149	ò	200	╚	251	√
47	/	99	c	150	û	201	╔	252	η
48	0	100	d	151	ù	202	╩	253	²
49	1	101	e	152	ÿ	203	╦	254	■
50	2	102	f	153	Ö	204	╠	255	
51	3								

lated files. They may be grouped by project, author, department, client, date, or recipient, among other possibilities.

3. *Record the file name on paper copies of the document.* This simple method is often overlooked. At the bottom of the first or last page of the document, type the full file name and subdirectory, if any, in which it is stored. You will save hours of hunting for the file when you need to edit it. One caution: There may be documents on which you would not want this information to appear. For example, if you are sending a personal letter to a customer, you might not want to display codes suggesting that the document is a form letter rather than a personalized one. Instead, handwrite the storage information on your file copy rather than including it on the original.

4. *Print a paper copy of the disk's directory.* Each time you modify anything stored on a floppy disk, print a copy of the directory and store it along with the disk. It is faster than inserting the disk and waiting for the directory to appear on the screen.

5. *Copy the file and edit the copy, not the original.* If you work for people who constantly revise things but do not want the previous versions deleted, be careful to copy the file and edit the copy, not the original. Make sure each version is dated or numbered as part of the file name.

6. *Clean up your files!* On some periodic schedule, go through your files to look for documents that you no longer need to keep. Don't wait until your hard disk is full. Having good records of your files can be especially important here. You may be able to give everyone for whom you do word processing a list of the files you have stored in their names and ask them to identify the ones that are no longer needed. This is an efficient way to handle the task and also takes the responsibility for deleting files off your shoulders.

GETTING HELP

If you use one of the more sophisticated software programs, it probably has features you do not even know about. If you have a problem, here are several resources to consider:

On-line help Most programs have some kind of help system built into the software. A function key or a click of the mouse can display Help messages that may solve your problem. However, Help messages vary in quality from program to program and may or may not be an improvement over looking something up in the user manual.

User manual Every word-processing software program comes with a user manual. Take the time to familiarize yourself with the organization of your manual so that you can easily find explanations when you need them. The installation disks for most software contain so-called "readme" files that contain corrections and last-minute additions to the printed manuals. You should consider marking the corrections, at least, in the manual. If the software includes a guided tutorial for first-time users, take advantage of it even if you are already somewhat familiar with the program.

Staff support In a large organization there may be a software support group staffed by technicians who can help you with the program. If not, ask around to find out who else in the organization uses the same program. Get to know those people and set up your own resource network.

Vendor support Most software vendors offer telephone support and may even list a telephone number in the user manual. Some vendors provide free telephone assistance indefinitely; others provide it only for a limited time after purchase of the program and then charge for it, usually on an annual contract basis.

User groups   A user group is a loose association of individuals who use the same software program. Informal user groups have sprung up around the country, sometimes promoted by individual software vendors but often organized by the users themselves. The function of the groups is to permit members to call each other with questions when help is needed. Sometimes there is a modest membership fee, and there may even be periodic meetings. Check with your software vendor for information about a user group in your area.

Purchasing Hardware and Software

There is more to purchasing hardware and software than selecting a vendor and comparing prices. Your company must assess its needs and be certain that the equipment purchased today will be useful in the future. Since computer technology is constantly advancing, it is important not to overbuy.

A reliable source of information is a computer users' group, described above. Members are constantly discussing new equipment, and you will get honest answers because the members will not be trying to sell you anything. A local computer dealer can recommend users' groups in your area, or you can call the Boston Computer Society (617-252-0600), the Silicon Valley Computer Society (408-286-2969), or the New York PC Users' Group (212-533-6972).

What to Buy for Business is a newsletter that deals with purchasing office equipment such as copiers, computers, printers, and fax machines. It is published 10 times a year, and each issue is devoted to a different type of equipment. You can order one by calling 800-247-2185, or you may be able to find copies at your local library.

If you are new to computer purchasing, support and documentation are especially critical, as is the reputation of the vendor.

Ask to use the hardware and software yourself before buying, rather than relying solely on a demonstration. A demonstration by an experienced vendor can often make a very complex product appear deceptively simple. Be prepared to spend some time discussing many of the questions below with the vendor, since the answers will not always be readily apparent.

When buying printers, bear in mind that, although the dot-matrix printer can be useful for draft copies and forms, the laser printer is becoming the business standard. However, not all laser printers are of equal quality. Ask to see a sample printout from the printer you are considering, and find out how many pages it will print per minute.

The following checklist can guide you in making purchasing decisions:

- Who will use the equipment, and for what purpose? Word processing? Graphics? Desktop publishing? Spreadsheets? Database management? Telecommunications?
- Will the users require their own equipment, or will the equipment be shared?
- Does the equipment come with detailed, understandable setup instructions?
- Will the vendor provide help in installing the equipment?
- Does the equipment come with at least a one-year guarantee?
- Is there a toll-free number I can call for help?

- Is the software documentation easy to understand? Is there a tutorial I can attend? on-line help? a toll-free number for help?
- Is the keyboard comfortable?
- Is the monitor easy on the eyes?
- Does the monitor tilt to eliminate glare? (A flatter screen generally reflects less glare.)
- Is the memory adequate for my purposes?
- Can the computer be upgraded? At what cost?
- Do I want to connect the computer to a network workstation and access a file server?
- Are there expansion slots?
- How many disk drives do I need?
- Will I need one floppy-disk drive for 5.25″ disks and one for 3.5″ disks?
- Will I require high-density or low-density disks?
- Do I require multitasking (running programs simultaneously)?
- Do I need to run the software in a Windows™ environment?
- Is background printing needed for high-volume output?
- Is security an issue?
- Is a site license available?
- Can the software be run on a network?
- Does the software support multipage documents?
- Can spreadsheets be linked together so that a change in one will be reflected in another?
- What is the vendor's reputation?
- How long has the vendor been in business? Will the vendor be there next year if I have a problem?
- Has the vendor kept abreast of the latest technology?
- How do the prices compare to those of other vendors and mail-order houses?
- Will the vendor install the hardware if necessary?
- Is a maintenance contract available?
- Will the vendor provide repair, or will it be contracted to a third party?
- Will a substitute be made available when equipment is out for repair?
- Will the vendor provide training for software?

CHAPTER 8

Desktop Publishing

There have been many important developments in publishing since Gutenberg's movable type in the 1450s began to relieve scribes of the painstaking and tedious task of copying manuscripts by hand. When Benjamin Franklin was setting type manually in the early 1700s, visionaries were thinking to a time when machines could expedite the process, and in 1822 William Church patented a basic typesetting machine. In the 1880s there appeared two inventions, the Linotype and Monotype machines, which cast entire lines of type and individual letters, respectively, from molds that were assembled by using a keyboard. In the mid-1980s, when computers had taken over diverse tasks formerly done manually or mechanically, Paul Brainerd of Aldus Corporation pioneered the concept that publishing could be done from the desktop, beginning another revolution in the publishing industry. Once reserved for the few, publishing is now at everyone's fingertips.

Desktop publishing (DTP) is one of the fastest-growing areas in modern computing. It extends personal computers beyond the realm of word processing and allows the user to produce camera-ready (i.e., ready-for-copying) newsletters, brochures, fliers, advertisements, posters, manuals, and the like, without leaving the office.

In conventional publishing, the author types a manuscript and pastes any necessary artwork in place. The editor then edits it and sends it out for typesetting, and the typeset galleys return for proofreading by the author and editor. These are sent back to the typesetter to be corrected and (usually) pasted up with the artwork into pages. These must again be checked and corrected; errors caught at a late stage can be time-consuming and expensive to correct.

As a desktop publisher, you can be in control of the entire publishing cycle—especially if you are also the author. Most changes that need to be made can be implemented instantly right at your computer, and the endless rounds of mailing manuscript and proofs back and forth and cutting and pasting text and art into pages can be largely eliminated. (There will likely be some projects, however, that are beyond the technical capacities of even an experienced desktop-publishing specialist, and these will probably have to be sent out to a graphic designer.)

Though this chapter will not teach you how to use any particular hardware or software, it will introduce you to the fundamentals of DTP. Refer to the glossary at the end of this chapter for definitions of any unfamiliar terms.

Desktop Publishing Tools

In order to do the job properly, you must have the right tools.

Your desktop publishing system may not include everything you need to complete every assignment. If so, there are outside vendors or service bureaus that will perform particular functions, such as electronic imaging (scanning artwork), laser color copying, and producing 35-mm slides and high-resolution (camera-ready) output from a floppy diskette or data sent from your office by modem. Check under "Computer Graphics," "Desktop Publishing," or "Graphic Designers" in the Yellow Pages.

HARDWARE

Computer. Your primary tool is the computer, which includes the central processing unit, keyboard, disk drive(s), monitor, and mouse. (See Chapter 7 for an extensive discussion of computers.)

Scanner. A scanner converts text and graphic images into a digitized image on your screen, and with the help of OCR software the image is turned into characters that the computer can handle as text. With a scanner you can capture any printed page on your computer for processing. A scanner is not a necessity for most desktop publishing, but for certain tasks it can be extremely useful.

Laser printer. The laser printer lets you produce high-quality printed text; this can either be turned over to a conventional printer (if the job is complex or if large quantities must be printed) or simply duplicated and bound right in the office (for simple jobs and small quantities).

SOFTWARE

Word-processing. Since your text will be created with word-processing software, it will be your first tool. For a detailed discussion of word-processing software, see Chapter 7.

Graphics. There are numerous graphics software packages available to meet almost any DTP need. They vary in sophistication and capabilities, and should be chosen in accordance with your needs. Graphics packages can help you create your own artwork and charts or provide you with public-domain clip art. Fig. 8.1 shows some examples of clip art of the kind available on a typical graphics software package. Though clip art is available in other ways as well, graphics software will help you customize it for your own uses.

Page-layout. This software allows you to take the text you prepared with your word-processing software and the graphics you prepared with your graphics software and turn them into formatted, finished pages. Some word-processing software offers page-layout capabilities.

Communications. This specialized software is necessary only if you will be transmitting your work electronically—to a printer, for example.

Fig. 8.1   Clip Art

Scheduling

Schedule your project to allow ample time for each stage, since there will undoubtedly be delays beyond your control. Give each person involved a copy of the schedule, and be sure that each of them is aware of the due dates. It is essential that all those involved fulfill their obligations if final deadlines are to be met.

To determine how long a project should take, plan the project backwards. Confirm the date on which the project is due and how long the printer needs, and then assign each stage a target date. Certain phases of the project can proceed simultaneously; for example, the artwork can be prepared while the text is being written. See Fig. 8.2 for a sample project schedule.

Contributors often do not realize the effect their delays will have on a schedule. If you find the project is falling behind because of the slowness of others, speak to your supervisor or meet with those involved in order to alter the schedule or determine how time can be made up. Caution your contributors against last-minute changes. Such changes can ripple through an entire document; the addition of one word or phrase can completely alter the page flow, thereby affecting the placement of graphics, the table of contents, and the index.

Get written approval for any revisions that are requested of you, in order to absolve yourself of responsibility. When you submit text or graphics for approval, simply type "Approved by _____" and "Date _____" on the cover of the draft or use a store-bought rubber stamp that provides the same blanks. For more formal and extensive approval routing, see Fig. 8.9.

Typography

Typographic design includes the size and style of type, the length of lines, and the space between lines.

Fig. 8.2 DTP Project Schedule

Due Date		Actual Date
____/____	Text submitted	____/____
____/____	Edited text returned	____/____
____/____	Revised text submitted	____/____
____/____	Text approved	____/____
____/____	Artwork submitted	____/____
____/____	Artwork approved	____/____
____/____	Page layout submitted	____/____
____/____	Page layout approved	____/____
____/____	Final copy completed	____/____
____/____	Final copy approved	____/____
____/____	Final copy/Film to printer	____/____
____/____	Printed copies delivered	____/____

PARTS OF THE LETTER

In Fig. 8.3 the standard parts of typographic letters are labeled. (See the glossary on pages 311–319 for definitions of typographic terms.)

UNITS OF MEASURE

Picas and *points* are fixed units of typographic measure. A pica is equal to approximately ⅙″; picas are commonly used to measure the length of a line of type or the depth of a page. (The page of text you are reading is 30 picas wide and 48 picas deep.) A point is 1/12 of a pica. Your software will often ask you to make typographic and format choices using measurements in points or picas.

Fig. 8.3   Parts and Aspects of Typographic Letters

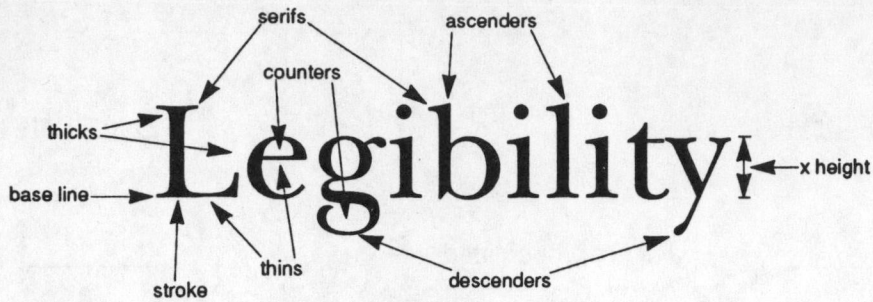

TYPE SIZE

Type size is measured in points. The larger the number of points, the larger the type, as illustrated in the following examples.

Example of 6-point type

Example of 12-point type

Example of 24-point type

Your software will generally allow you to select any size between 4 and 124 points for each available font. The point size of a type font is theoretically measured from the top of the highest ascender to the bottom of the lowest descender. In fact, however, not all typefaces of a given size will actually be the same size. The illustration that follows, in which the two horizontal lines are set 60 points apart, demonstrates the variation among four different "60-point" fonts.

LEADING

All typefaces are designed with enough space above and below so that the descenders on one line do not touch the ascenders on the following line. The amount of space from the base of one line to the base of the next, called leading, can be increased easily using your software. (The text of this book is mostly set in 10-point Baskerville type with 11-point leading, or 10/11—"10 on 11"—Baskerville.)

TYPEFACES

One of the most basic aspects of any typeface is whether it is a serif or sans-serif face.

Serif   Serifs are the tiny trailing lines that finish the strokes of printed letters, as in this text you are reading. Serif typefaces are generally used for normal text because the serifs tend to guide the reader's eye easily (but unnoticeably) across the page. There are many popular serif typefaces, two of which are Times Roman® and Electra®; the roman, italic, and bold fonts of each of these typefaces are shown below.

Times Roman®

abcdefghijklmnopqrstuvwxyz1234567890
ABCDEFGHIJKLMNOPQRSTUVWXYZ

abcdefghijklmnopqrstuvwxyz1234567890
ABCDEFGHIJKLMNOPQRSTUVWXYZ

abcdefghijklmnopqrstuvwxyz1234567890
ABCDEFGHIJKLMNOPQRSTUVWXYZ

Electra®

abcdefghijklmnopqrstuvwxyz1234567890
ABCDEFGHIJKLMNOPQRSTUVWXYZ

abcdefghijklmnopqrstuvwxyz1234567890
ABCDEFGHIJKLMNOPQRSTUVWXYZ

abcdefghijklmnopqrstuvwxyz1234567890
ABCDEFGHIJKLMNOPQRSTUVWXYZ

Sans-Serif *Sans* is French for "without"; therefore, a sans-serif letter lacks serifs. Sans-serif type is clean and crisp, and thus is often used for posters, scientific material, and headings within documents. Of the many sans-serif typefaces, the two most popular are Helvetica® and Optima®; their roman, italic, and bold fonts are shown below.

Helvetica®

abcdefghijklmnopqrstuvwxyz1234567890
ABCDEFGHIJKLMNOPQRSTUVWXYZ

abcdefghijklmnopqrstuvwxyz1234567890
ABCDEFGHIJKLMNOPQRSTUVWXYZ

abcdefghijklmnopqrstuvwxyz1234567890
ABCDEFGHIJKLMNOPQRSTUVWXYZ

Optima®

abcdefghijklmnopqrstuvwxyz1234567890
ABCDEFGHIJKLMNOPQRSTUVWXYZ

abcdefghijklmnopqrstuvwxyz1234567890
ABCDEFGHIJKLMNOPQRSTUVWXYZ

abcdefghijklmnopqrstuvwxyz1234567890
ABCDEFGHIJKLMNOPQRSTUVWXYZ

Mixing typefaces   Try not to mix several typefaces in the same piece. If you stick with one or two, your printed piece will be more attractive. Many publications use a serif typeface for the text and a sans-serif for headings and subheadings. (This book uses serif typefaces for both headings and text.)

Page Layout

When preparing a page layout, remember that your goals are to draw attention to the printed piece and make it pleasing to the eye and easy to read. You might want to prepare a quick hand-drawn sketch like the one in Fig. 8.4 before you attempt to generate your layout on the computer.

Master page layout   The first step in creating a page layout is to prepare a master page. If there is a common design element that will appear throughout the publication (e.g., a designated number of columns or a horizontal bar at the top of each page), including it on the master page will allow the software to generate it automatically.

The software will ask you to make the following selections:

- Page size (standard, legal, etc.).
- Orientation: portrait (vertical) or landscape (horizontal).
- Margins: top, bottom, left, and right (or inside and outside). If your document will be side-bound (e.g., in a ring binder), allow an extra ½″ for the inside margin.
- Number of columns and space between columns (alleys or gutters).
- Number of rows and space between rows.
- Facing pages or single-sided.
- Footers and headers, if any.
- Placement of page number.

Grids   A well-designed piece will have structure, but still offer the flexibility to deviate whenever necessary. Grids, also called *templates,* can provide for structure as well as flexibility.

Grids are invisible rectangular patterns that divide the page area into vertical or horizontal areas. Grids are not rigid and unalterable; they are merely guides. A grid may have as few as two columns or as many as seven or eight. The following are some suggestions for using grids for specific types of design.

Application	*Number of Columns in Grid*
Reports, manuals, and proposals	1, 2, or 3 columns
Tabloid format, two-column layout with substantial artwork	4 columns
Two-column layout with a third narrow column for headings and quotations	5 columns
Two- or three-column newsletters with artwork	6 columns
Creative layouts	7 or 8 columns

Fig. 8.5 shows some design possibilities based on a five-column grid. Notice how the same grid can be used for a number of different layouts, especially

Fig. 8.4   Page-layout Sketch

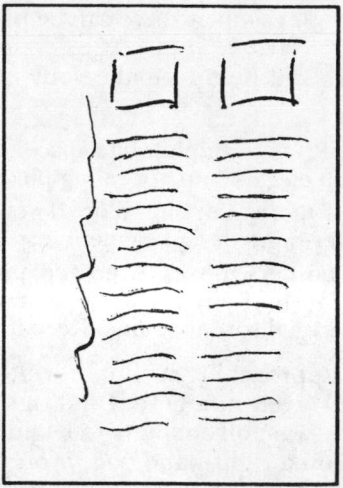

Fig. 8.5   Five-column Grid, with Possible Format Applications

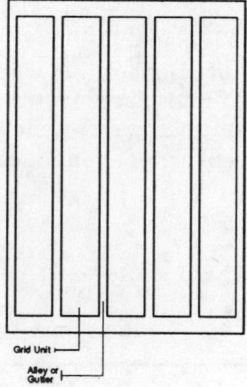

Grid Unit

Alley or
Gutter

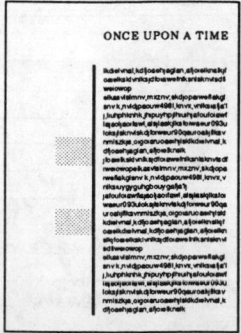

when the text columns are allowed to extend across two or three of the grid columns. Greeking (printed nonsense text) has been used to indicate where the actual text will be placed. Examples such as these can be presented for page-layout approval.

The following suggestions will help to make your layouts eye-catching and easy to follow.

- Never clutter your page. Provide ample white space to shape and frame the content so as to present an elegant and appealing piece.
- If your budget allows, use more than one color. If you are on a limited budget, try shading or an interesting design element instead.
- Consider incorporating borders, boxes, oversized page numbers, and the like, but sparingly. Too much of any single element, or too many different elements, will give the piece a disordered look. Keep it interesting but simple.

When your document is approaching its final form, you should be aware of what will appear on left-hand (even-numbered) and right-hand (odd-numbered) pages. For example, you may want all chapters to begin on right-hand pages; in that case, if Chapter 1 ends on a right-hand page, you must leave the following left-hand page blank so that Chapter 2 will start as a right-hand page.

You can ensure the correct page sequence in several different ways:

1. If your publication has printed page numbers on every page, the printer will not need any further guide. If some pages are blank or unnumbered, their unprinted numbers can be written on the camera copy itself in non-reproducing ("nonrepro") blue ink, or you can indicate that blank pages should be added by means of a note on the last text page preceding them (for example, on page 13 you might simply note "p. 14 is blank").

2. Prepare a *dummy*—that is, a mock-up version of the entire publication, with proofs or photocopies of all text and artwork stripped into place. Most of the dummy pages will often be merely copies of the finished pages generated by your computer, pasted back-to-back, but copies of art not generated on the computer will be pasted in as a guide to the printer.

Fig. 8.6 Production Assembly Sheet

					sheet _1_ of _2_
PRODUCTION ASSEMBLY SHEET					

TITLE: Siddons X-42 Copier: User Manual

no. of pages 32   no. of halftones 5

no. of blanks 4   no. of copy dot

Even (Left)	Odd (Right)	FIGURE	TABLE	HALFTONE	SPECIAL INSTRUCTIONS
	i				title page
ii					c/r
	iii				contents
iv					blank
	1				Chap. 1 opening
2					
	3			1.1	(X-42 copier) Strip as indicated
4		1.2			(exploded diagram)
	5				
6					Chap. 2 opening

3. Prepare an *assembly sheet,* which itemizes each page and any artwork that must be specially provided or printed. For many projects, preparing an assembly sheet (or a dummy) may be laborious and unnecessary, but it can be helpful for complex publications. (See Fig. 8.6.)

When sending camera copy to the printer, it will probably be helpful or necessary to fill out a form such as the one shown in Fig. 8.7, which the printer may provide.

Production and routing forms such as those illustrated in Figs. 8.8 and 8.9 may prove useful for important desktop publishing and design projects.

Fig. 8.7   Printing Specifications Form

```
PRINTING SPECIFICATIONS                          Office Control Number _____
Name:


Title:

Number of Pages:

Format Description:

Quantity:

Trim Size:     text:                                          ☐ plus bleed
               cover:                                         ☐ plus bleed
               other:                                         ☐ plus bleed

Stock:         text:
               cover:
               other:

Ink:           text:
               cover:
               other:

Presswork:     text:      _____ color(s)/_____ side(s);   _____ color(s)/_____ side(s)
               cover:     _____ color(s)/_____ side(s);   _____ color(s)/_____ side(s)
               other:     _____ color(s)/_____ side(s);   _____ color(s)/_____ side(s)

Artwork:       _____ square halftones     _____ line shots     _____ tints
               _____ outline halftones    _____ reverses       _____ strip-ins
               _____ other: _____

Camera Copy:   ☐ camera-ready mechanicals   ☐ existing negatives   ☐ other: _____

Lay Up:        ☐ per mechanicals            ☐ per dummy            ☐ other: _____

Proof:         ☐ blueline      ☐ Color Key      ☐ Cromalin      ☐ other _____

                            — continued next page —
```

Figure 8.7 *Continued*

Finishing:
- ☐ folding:
- ☐ scoring:
- ☐ perforating:
- ☐ punching:
- ☐ die cutting:
- ☐ embossing:
- ☐ other: _____

Binding:
- ☐ saddle stitch, _____ wires on _____-inch side
- ☐ perfect bound on _____-inch side
- ☐ other: _____

Production Schedule:

Special Instructions:

Delivery:

For Further Information, Contact:

Special Conditions:

Courtesy of Promotional Perspectives, Ann Arbor, Michigan.

Fig. 8.8   Creative/Production Checklist

CREATIVE/PRODUCTION
CHECKLIST

MARKETING MATERIALS

Project Name: _____   Deadline: _____

P.O. #: _____

Charge to (Code): _____

Artist/Agency: _____

Telephone: _____

Project Description: _____
_____
_____

Special Instructions: _____
_____
_____

Color/Sides: _____

Mailing List (See Attached) _____

Scans: _____   # Halftones: _____

	Item 1	Item 2	Item 3	Total
Dimensions:	_____	_____	_____	_____
Weight:	_____	_____	_____	_____
Paper Stock:	_____	_____	_____	

Mailing Information:

    Class: _____

    Permit Stat: _____

    Business Reply Mail: Letter/Postcard   Indicia to Artist: _____

Photos:
_____
_____
_____

Graphics/Illustrations:
_____
_____
_____
_____

Final Approval: _____   _____
                           Marketing Dept.   Date

Rec'd by Production Mgr: _____   _____
                                   JBH   Date

Fig. 8.9   Routing Form for Desktop Projects

CONCEPT TO MECHANICALS
MARKETING MATERIALS
Direct Mail/Collateral • Packaging • P.O.P.

PROJECT NAME: _____   DEADLINE: _____

1. Internal [Full Review — Copy/Concept] *   Return by: _____
   (Please route in sequence)

   _____ _____ _____ _____ _____ _____ _____
   LPM   CAA   DFM   TLC   JBH   JMM   SEL

   > Marketing: Submit photocopies simultaneously to JWW & Corporate Legal for
   review and to TES for input/review. To be returned to SEL by: _____

2. Mechanicals [Full Review]   Return by: _____

   _____ _____ _____ _____ _____ _____ _____
   LPM   CAA   DFM   TLC   JBH   JMM   SEL

3. Final Proof [Blues]   Return by: _____

   _____ _____ _____
   DFM   LPM   SEL

Rec'd by Production Mgr: _____ _____
                                 JBH   Date

Please make comments on reverse side of this sheet.

* Areas of responsibility when proofing:
LPM — Copy & content; mail distribution concerns
CAA — Customer Service concerns; ISBNs, style numbers, prices
DFM — Concept; clarity of the sales message
TLC — Operations/fulfillment concerns
JBH — Production/manufacturing concerns
JMM — Copy editing
JWW — Legal concerns
SEL — Concept, copy, content; Final OK

Printing and Binding

PRINTING

There are several possible methods of printing, and your decision should be based on the type of project, the quality needed, and your budget.

Laser printers   Laser printers often represent the least expensive way to generate copy. Most produce only black-and-white copy; color laser printers are more expensive. The toner cartridges, the available fonts, and the low resolution (usually 300 dots per inch) represent limitations of laser printers; other limitations are the size of the paper they can handle and their slowness in producing substantial quantities.

Your selection of paper should be guided by the nature of the material. Laser paper will provide a higher-quality result than copier paper. For internal memos, reports, and manuals, copier paper will probably be adequate; for sales presentations, financial reports, masters, or pre-press proofs, laser paper should be used. White, bright paper makes the type more legible. Opacity—the paper's ability to keep images on one side of the paper from showing through to the other side—is a consideration when printing on both sides. Paper with a smooth finish provides a uniform transfer of toner, so there is less chance that the printed characters will break up.

Quick print shops   These shops offer good-quality printing, generally at affordable prices. However, many quick print shops cannot handle specialty printing with unusual requirements, and they often must send such work to an outside printer. If your graphic material has heavy ink coverage or fine lines, it may lose some of its quality in the printing. Despite their advertised speed, the service provided by these shops is not necessarily faster than that of other printers. Many are equipped with desktop publishing equipment.

Offset printers   Offset printing companies offer excellent quality, large print runs, four-color print processes, and the highest halftone quality available.

BINDINGS

Newsletter-length publications often require no binding at all, being merely folded in two.

Somewhat longer publications can be bound cheaply and efficiently by means of staples along the spine (sometimes called *saddle-wiring*).

Ring binders are particularly appropriate for materials that are to be saved and accumulated. They require only that the sheets be punched.

Portfolio folders with pockets on the inside covers are another possibility, especially when diverse materials must be assembled.

Plastic report covers, often transparent, hold the pages together with a simple clip on the spine.

More elaborate binding methods requiring special equipment are also available to desktop publishers. Thermal binding machines attach the pages to a cover with a preglued spine by means of a heat process in less than a minute. Plastic comb bindings (particularly desirable for publications that must lie flat when open) can also be attached in the office, using a machine that first punches the holes and then inserts the comb binding element. Most of these binding machines are available for a few hundred dollars.

Commercial bookbinding methods such as sewn, perfect, and notch binding are generally more expensive and will be necessary only for major projects with large budgets.

Desktop Publishing Applications

Desktop publishing can be an ideal means of producing a wide variety of publications. Whatever the project, remember that a fancy design cannot make up for inadequate content. Everything you produce should both be well written and incorporate appropriate and attractive—but not ostentatious—visual elements.

Reports   Reports, whether intended for internal distribution or client/customer distribution, can take many forms and will often include graphs, charts, and art. With DTP programs and equipment, you can produce professional-quality reports with well-integrated art of all kinds.

Brochures   Brochures are useful marketing tools that vary widely in length and quality. DTP can produce effective brochures on a limited budget. Though not usually adequate for elaborate brochures, DTP programs can at least be used to prepare layouts for them.

Corporate communications   Corporate communications can take the form of letters, memos, handbooks, employee forms, handouts, and materials to be distributed outside the corporation. Even if distribution is only internal, well-prepared communications are good for morale and present a positive company image to employees.

Advertising and promotional materials   DTP has proved to be a boon in producing promotional material and advertisements for newspapers, magazines, and trade journals at affordable costs.

Catalogs   Catalog information can often be selected from an electronic database and printed using page-layout software.

Newsletters   More than 100,000 different newsletters are published in the United States by individuals, companies, and civic groups, at costs ranging from almost nothing to thousands of dollars. Desktop publishing equipment can produce typeset-quality text on a shoestring budget. Before you enter the newsletter arena, find a book on the subject and gather as many actual newsletters as you can—they are filled with good ideas.

Manuals   Most manuals are substantial or complex enough to require professional printing. However, by producing camera-ready pages for the printer, you can save your company both time and money.

Preparing Presentation Materials

If your organization does not have an in-house art department, the task of planning and creating the visual component of oral presentations may very well fall to you. There is nothing complicated or mysterious about preparing presentation materials, especially if you know how to use the available software packages.

Consider using a presentation software program. Though word-processing software allows you to prepare high-quality charts, presentation software offers much more flexibility, permitting you to design and create 35-mm slides, graphics for overhead projectors, and handouts. Many of these software programs have built-in drawing tools and word-processing components, in addition to a full array of color options and automatic design features. Some programs offer advanced features such as rotating, animation, and resizing. Additionally, such programs may enable you to:

- Write text in the program or import text that was created in a word-processing program.
- Use the internal graphics system to create pie charts, line graphs, bar graphs, and other graphics in black and white or color.
- Use a ready-made template (or automatic format) or create one of your own to give a consistent and professional look to all components of the presentation.
- Integrate transparencies from other presentations so that you do not have to "reinvent the wheel" for each presentation. Many presentations are based on previous ones, and there is obviously a large advantage in being able to integrate and rearrange visual materials that already exist.
- Import data from other programs and other formats. This will let you create slides and transparencies from word processors, spreadsheets, databases, and graphics that have been prepared or scanned.
- Generate your own slides and graphic transparencies. Graphic transparencies for overhead projectors can be produced by placing transparent sheets rather than copy paper in a laser printer and printing them as you would any paper copy. If you have a slide shooter, you can generate your own slides. If not, there are computer graphic services that will produce slides within one or two days after receiving a disk or electronically transmitted data.
- Run your computer as a slide projector. You can create a slide show and set the computer to automatically fade and "wipe" from one slide to another. Synchronized sound is also possible with the proper equipment.

The purpose of a presentation visual is to reinforce and clarify an idea. A presentation can be compared with a magazine article: just as the pictures accompanying the article must be supported by the text, projected images should be used to reinforce the speaker's main points. Visual images can be effectively used to open a presentation, to channel thinking, to emphasize key points, to present numerical or financial information, to show comparisons, and to explain new concepts.

When preparing any visual image, always strive for visibility, clarity, and simplicity. All your charts for a given presentation should have a uniform look. Use both uppercase and lowercase characters for the text; it will be easier to read than all capital letters. Use large type, perhaps 18-point for the text and 24-point for the headings. It is recommended that slide images employ a dark background with light-colored print and that larger transparencies use dark print on a lightly tinted background.

See the sample visuals in Figs. 8.10 and 8.11.

Fig. 8.10 A Sample Overhead Projector Image

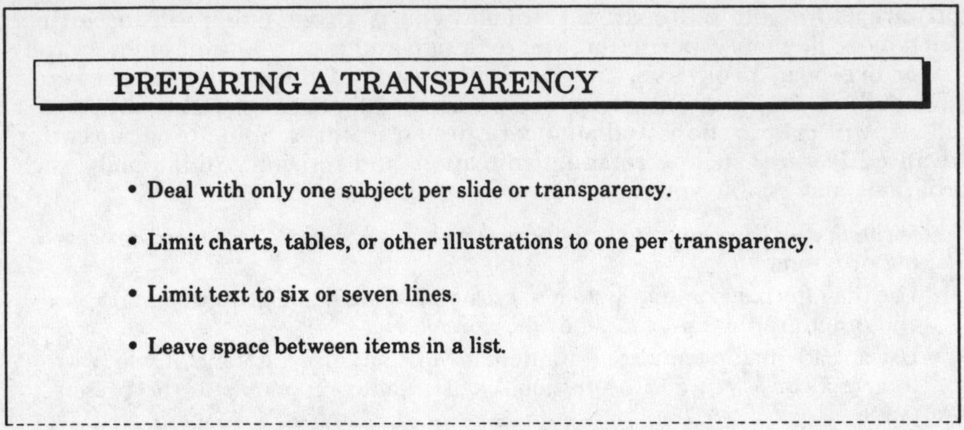

PREPARING A TRANSPARENCY
• Deal with only one subject per slide or transparency.
• Limit charts, tables, or other illustrations to one per transparency.
• Limit text to six or seven lines.
• Leave space between items in a list.

Fig. 8.11 A Sample Slide Image

ABC CORPORATION — SALES ANALYSIS
WESTERN DIVISION
EASTERN DIVISION
CENTRAL DIVISION

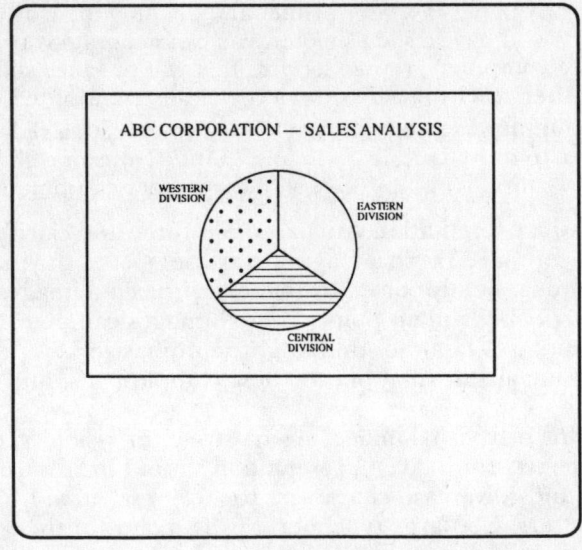

Desktop Publishing Glossary

The following glossary provides concise definitions of terminology that is commonly encountered in desktop publishing.

AA—see AUTHOR'S ALTERATION

air—see WHITE SPACE

alley   The space between two columns of type.—called also *gutter*

alphabet length   The total width of the 26 lowercase unspaced letters in a particular font. The alphabet length is usually given in points and is used as an indicator of the relative width of the typeface.

artwork   Material (such as a drawing or photograph) prepared for reproduction in printed matter.

ascender   1   The part of a lowercase letter (*d, f, k*, etc.) that rises above the x height of the letter.   **2**   A lowercase character that has an ascender.—compare DESCENDER

ascender height   The height of the highest ascender in a typeface.

author's alteration   An alteration made to typeset copy (as at the galley or page-proof stage) that is not caused by a printer's error.—called also *AA;* compare PRINTER'S ERROR

backbone—see SPINE

back margin   The inside margin of a page.—called also *gutter*

back matter   Matter (such as a bibliography or index) that follows the main text of a book.—compare FRONT MATTER

bad break   1   The dividing of a word at the end of a line at an incorrect place within the word.   **2**   The dividing of text between pages in a way that leaves a widow at the top of one page or not enough copy at the bottom of another.

bar graph   A chart showing comparative data by means of vertical rectangles.

base line   An imaginary line on which the body of a typeset letter rests.

binding   Cover and materials that hold a document together.

bleed   Printed image positioned so as to run off the edge of the page after trimming.

block quotation—see EXTRACT

bluelines   Prints in blue ink made from negatives of book pages, used as final proofs.—called also *blues*

blues—see BLUELINES

body   The vertical space that is occupied by a line of type in a given font. The body of a given font is measured from the top of the tallest ascender to the bottom of the deepest descender; however, a line of type can be set on a body that is larger than that actually occupied by the font in order to give the effect of leading between successive lines of type. The 10-point type in this book has a 10-point body, but it is set on an 11-point body.

boldface   1   A heavy-faced type. The entry words in this glossary are in boldface type.   **2**   Printing in boldface.—compare LIGHTFACE

box   A rectangular rule usually enclosing text that is to be set apart from the text around it.

broadside cut   An illustration or table laid on its side to fit the page, the left side being at the bottom of the page.

built-up fraction   A fraction whose numbers are set in the same point size as the surrounding text and occupy more than one line of vertical space. The fraction

$\frac{1}{2}$ is a built-up fraction; the fractions $\frac{1}{2}$. ½, and 1/2 are not.—compare CASE FRACTION

bulk   Degree of thickness (not weight) of paper.

bullet   A large dot used to set off items in a vertical list.

camera copy   Material in final form and ready to be photographed and printed.

camera-ready   Ready to be photographed and printed.

cap   A capital letter.

cap height   The height of a capital letter in a typeface.

caption   **1**   The heading especially of an article or document.   **2**   The identification or explanatory comment accompanying a pictorial illustration.

caret   A wedge-shaped mark made on written or printed matter to indicate the place where something is to be inserted.

case binding   Binding in which sewn signatures with end sheets glued on are fastened to a cover with gauze and glue.

case fraction   A simple fraction whose numbers are set one above the other in a smaller type so as to be contained in one line of type. The term *case fraction* can refer to a fraction that takes the form $\frac{1}{2}$ or ½; however, some people use *case fraction* to refer only to a fraction that takes the form $\frac{1}{2}$. The term *piece fraction* is also used to describe both forms of fractions; however, some people use *piece fraction* to refer only to a fraction that takes the form ½.—compare BUILT-UP FRACTION

castoff   **1**   The process of calculating the number of characters in a given manuscript in order to determine the number of pages it will require when printed.   **2**   The result of making a castoff.

character   A letter, symbol, numeral, or mark of punctuation. For some purposes, the spaces between words are also considered characters.

clip art   Copyright-free art designed for graphic applications. Clip art is available in both book and electronic form.

coated paper   Paper with a coating to give it a particular finish.

color separation   The isolation on separate photographic negatives, by the use of filters and scanners, of the parts of full-color artwork that are to be printed in given colors.

comp   A preliminary design (for a cover, advertisement, etc.) intended for review and approval before being prepared in final form for printing.—short for "composition"

composition   The production of type or typographic characters arranged for printing.

condensed   *of a typeface* Having letters that are narrower than those of a typeface not so characterized.—compare EXPANDED

continuous-tone   *of a piece of artwork* Having gradations of tone from dark to light.

copy   Matter that is to be set or photographed for printing.

copyediting   The usually last editing of a manuscript before it is set in type.

copyright page   A page of a book bearing the copyright notice, including the proprietor's name and the date of copyright.

counter   An area within a letter that is wholly or partly enclosed by strokes.

credit line   A line, note, or name that acknowledges the source of an item (such as an illustration).

crop   To trim a piece of art (photograph, etc.) for printing, often by simply marking for the printer the intended borders of the printed image.

crop marks   Marks indicating where a piece of art is to be cropped.

CRT composition Typesetting in which type images are electronically produced and displayed on a cathode-ray tube's screen, from which they are transferred to film or photosensitive paper.

cyan A greenish blue color, one of the four colors used in four-color process printing.

descender **1** The part of a lowercase letter that descends below the base line. **2** A lowercase character that has a descender.—compare ASCENDER

designer A person who makes decisions about typography, layout, and the physical appearance of a publication.

diacritic A mark used with a letter or group of letters to indicate a change in sound value.

dingbat A typographical symbol or ornament.

display Copy (such as a heading) that is set apart from the text in larger type.

drill To make holes in paper to permit insertion into a ring binder.

drop The vertical distance (as on a page) from one typographic or design element to another.

drop folio A page number that is located at the bottom of a page.

dummy **1** A set of model pages, often consisting of text proofs and copies of illustrations pasted in place on paperboard, and usually intended to serve as a guide for page makeup. **2** A bound, unprinted, or only partially printed sample of a planned publication to show its size, shape, and general appearance.

elite A typewriter type providing 12 characters to the linear inch and 6 lines to the vertical inch.—compare PICA

em dash A dash that is as wide as the point size of the type.

em quad—see EM SPACE

em space A space as wide as the point size of the type.—called also *em quad*

en dash A dash that is shorter than the em dash but slightly longer than the hyphen and is used for the hyphen in some situations.

en quad—see EN SPACE

en space A space that is one-half of an em space.—called also *en quad*

epigraph A quotation set at the beginning of a literary work or a division of it to suggest its theme.

expanded *of a typeface* Having letters that are wider than those of a typeface not so characterized.—called also *extended;* compare CONDENSED

extended—see EXPANDED

extract A long quotation that is set off from the text and set in type that is slightly smaller than that of the text.—called also *block quotation*

F&Gs—see FOLDED AND GATHERED SHEETS

facing pages Two successive pages that face each other as in a book lying open.

final proof A proof made by the compositor from the film, usually a negative, that will be sent to the printer to make printing plates from.

flush-and-hang indention—see HANGING INDENTION

flush left Aligned vertically along the left margin.

flush right Aligned vertically along the right margin.

folded and gathered sheets Printed sheets that have been folded into signatures and collected into the correct order for binding.—called also *F&Gs*

folio A page number.

font A set of type all of the same design (in traditional usage, of the same size as well).

footer—see RUNNING FOOT

foot margin   The bottom margin of a page.

format   The page size, margins, fonts, and general makeup of a document.

four-color process   The standard color printing process, which uses four colors of ink (yellow, magenta [red], cyan [blue], and black) to produce a great variety of other colors.

front margin   The outside margin of a page.

front matter   Matter (such as an introduction or preface) that precedes the main text of a book.—compare BACK MATTER

full measure   The full width of the type page or column.

galley *or* **galley proof**   An early proof of typeset material not yet made into pages. —compare PAGE PROOF

greeking   Nonsense text printed to represent real text when designing page layouts.

grid   Rectangular pattern used to position text and graphics on a page but not intended to appear when the page is printed.

gutter   **1**   The inside margin of a page, or the adjoining inside margins of two facing pages.   **2**   ALLEY.

hair space   A space that is one-fifth of an em, one-sixth of an em, or one-half point in width.—compare THIN SPACE

halftone   A printed image that represents continuous-tone artwork (such as a photograph) through the use of a pattern of dots of varying size.

H & J   Hyphenation and justification.

hanging indention   Indention of all the lines of a passage or index except the first line, which is set flush with the left-hand margin.—called also *flush-and-hang indention*

head *or* **heading**   A word or series of words often in larger letters placed at the beginning of a passage or at the top of a page or column in order to introduce or categorize.

header—see RUNNING HEAD

headline   **1**   A head of a newspaper story or article usually printed in large type and giving the gist of the story or article.   **2**   Words set at the head of a passage or page to introduce or categorize.

head margin   The top margin of a page.

headnote   A note of comment or explanation that prefaces a text.

hickey   A spot or imperfection on a printed page.

horizontal orientation—see LANDSCAPE ORIENTATION

impose   To arrange (pages) in the proper order and orientation for printing.

imposition   The order or arrangement of imposed pages.

inferior   Relating to or being a subscript.—compare SUPERIOR

italic   A type style whose characters slant upward to the right, as in *"these words are italic."*—compare ROMAN

justify   To align the ends of lines of type at the right and left.

kerning   The adjustment of horizontal spacing between letters.

landscape orientation   Orientation of a page whose width is greater than its height.—called also *horizontal orientation;* compare PORTRAIT ORIENTATION

layout   The final page arrangement of text and art to be reproduced especially by printing.

leaders   Dots or sometimes hyphens (as in a table or index) used to lead the eye horizontally across a space to the right word or number.

leading   The distance between lines of type, measured from the base of one line to the base of the next.

legend   An explanatory list of the symbols used on a map or chart or in an illustration, or explanatory remarks that accompany an illustration.

letterpress   The process of printing from an inked, raised surface, expecially when the paper is impressed directly upon the surface.

letterspacing   Insertion of space between the letters of a word.

ligature   A printed character (such as *fi*) consisting of two or more letters or characters joined together.

lightface   **1** A typeface having comparatively light thin lines. **2** Printing in lightface.—compare BOLDFACE

line drawing   A drawing made with a pen or other pointed instrument in solid lines or solid masses.

line graph   A graph in which points representing values of a variable for values of an independent variable are connected by a line.

loose-leaf binding   A style of binding in which pages with holes punched or drilled through them are held together in such a way as to permit removal and replacement of individual pages.

lowercase   Small-letter type used in printing.—compare UPPERCASE

machine-readable   Directly usable by a computer.

magenta   A deep purplish red, one of the four colors used in four-color process printing.

makeup   The arranging of typeset matter, including running heads and illustrations, into pages.

margin   The unprinted area of a page.

margin cut   A small illustration set within a side margin next to the text.

markup   The process of marking on a manuscript all the directions for typesetting.

master proof   A set of proofs bearing all corrections and alterations of both the printer and author.

masthead   The printed matter in a periodical that gives the title, names of editors, pertinent details of ownership, and advertising and subscription rates.

mechanical   A piece of finished copy (representing a page or pages, a book jacket or cover, a brochure, etc.) assembled and mounted, usually on a paperboard sheet, and ready to be photographed for printing.

nut   An en space.

offset printing   A printing process in which an inked impression from a plate is first made on a rubber-blanketed cylinder and then transferred to paper.

opaque   To paint over any translucent areas on a negative that are not wanted on the printing plate.

overlay   A transparent sheet containing graphic matter to be superimposed on another sheet.

overrun   Extra printed copies.

page proof   A proof of typeset material that has been made up into a page.

Pantone Matching System™   An internationally recognized color-matching system. —called also *PMS*

pasteup   Camera-ready copy.—called also *mechanical*

PE—see PRINTER'S ERROR

perfect binding   A binding process in which collated signatures are trimmed at the back and a glue is applied to the cut and roughened edges. A usually paper cover is then wrapped around the book.

photocomposition   The setting of type directly on film or photosensitive paper for reproduction.

photocopy   A photographic reproduction of graphic matter.

pica   **1** 12-point type.   **2** A unit of about ⅙ of an inch used in measuring typographical material.   **3** A typewriter type providing 10 characters to the linear inch and 6 lines to the vertical inch.—compare ELITE

piece fraction—see CASE FRACTION

pie chart   A representation of comparative data by means of a circle divided into wedge-shaped portions.

pixels   Dots on a computer screen that together form the electronic images.

platemaking   The making of printing plates for offset printing.

PMS—see PANTONE MATCHING SYSTEM

point   A unit of typographical measurement that is 1/12 of a pica (about 1/72 of an inch) and that is used especially in measuring the vertical size of type or the amount of space between lines of type.

portrait orientation   Orientation of a page whose height is greater than its width. —called also *vertical orientation;* compare LANDSCAPE ORIENTATION

prepress   The process by which individual page negatives are transferred into a printing plate.

pressrun   The number of copies specified to be printed.

printer's error   An error in typeset copy (such as errors caused by incorrect keyboarding or a program malfunction) that is the responsibility of the typesetter. —called also *PE;* compare AUTHOR'S ALTERATION

production   The processes by which a publication is produced. These extend from the completion of the manuscript to the making of the plates from which the pages will be printed.

proof   A copy of typeset text made for examination or correction.

quad   A space in typesetting that is one en or slightly more in width.

ragged left   Unjustified at the left margin.

ragged right   Unjustified at the right margin.

recto   A right-hand page.—compare VERSO

reference mark   A conventional symbol (such as an asterisk or a dagger) or a superior number or letter placed in a text for directing attention to a footnote.

register   Correct alignment of inks on the printed page.

registration marks   Markings that show a commercial printer how to align color negatives for proper printing.

relief   Projection of letters or images from a flat surface.

repro *or* **reproduction proof**   A high-quality, camera-ready, positive print of typeset matter from which a negative is made for making printing plates.

resolution   Overall clarity of detail in a graphic image.

reverse type   White text printed on a colored or shaded background.

right-reading   Having the correct right-to-left orientation.—compare WRONG-READING

river   An irregular streak running through several lines of close-set printed matter and caused by a series of wide spaces that appear to form a continuous line.

roman   Of or relating to a type style with upright characters.—compare ITALIC

rule   A printed straight line or linear design.

runaround   Type set in lines shorter than full measure in order to fit around an illustration.

run back To transfer text from the beginning of one line to the end of the preceding line.

run down To transfer text from the end of one line to the beginning of the following line.

run in To make (typeset matter) continuous without a paragraph or other break.

running foot A repeated heading (often consisting of the title of the book, chapter, or section) that appears at the bottom of consecutive pages.—called also *footer;* compare RUNNING HEAD

running head A repeated heading (often consisting of the title of the book, chapter, or section) that appears at the top of consecutive pages.—called also *header;* compare RUNNING FOOT

runover Typeset material that exceeds the space estimated or allotted.

saddle-stitched—see SADDLE-WIRED

saddle-wired Secured by a stitch made by driving wire staples through the center fold and clinching them on the inside. This kind of binding is also referred to as being *saddle-stitched,* especially when thread is substituted for the staples.—compare SIDE-STITCHED

sans-serif A letter or typeface with no serifs.

score An impression or dent made during the printing process to permit easier folding.

self-cover **1** A cover made from the same paper stock as the inside pages. **2** A publication having such a cover.

self-mailer A printed piece that meets post-office requirements for mailing without an envelope.

serif **1** Any of the short, trailing lines stemming from and at an angle to the upper and lower ends of the strokes of a printed letter, resembling the beginning or end of a pen stroke. **2** A letter or typeface with serifs.

sheet-fed press A press that prints individual sheets of paper.—compare WEB PRESS

side-stitched Secured by passing a wire or thread from side to side through a complete book or magazine before covering.—called also *side-wired;* compare SADDLE-WIRED

side-wired—see SIDE-STITCHED

signature A printed sheet with usually 8, 16, 24, or 32 pages, which is folded, trimmed, and bound with other signatures.

sinkage The distance from the top of a text page to the first line of text or display type.

small capital A letter having the form of but smaller than a capital letter.

Smyth sewing A method of attaching the signatures of books by means of threads passed through the folds.

spine The back of a bound book that connects the front and back covers.—called also *backbone*

spiral binding Binding in which a continuous spiral wire or plastic strip is passed through holes at the gutter margin.

stet An editorial direction, meaning "let it stand," that is used to indicate that words crossed out in copy or proof are to be restored. "Stet" is written in the margin, and heavy dots are placed under the affected words.

stock Paper to be used for printing, usually identified as to its specific qualities and weight.

strip To arrange (as negatives) in proper position on a flat.

stroke   One of the lines of a letter of the alphabet.

style sheet   A compilation of detailed style rules (as in regard to punctuation, hyphenation, and abbreviations) to be followed consistently throughout a manuscript.

subheading   A heading of a subdivision (as in an outline or index).

subscript   A distinguishing symbol (such as a letter or number) written immediately below or below and to the right or left of another character.—compare SUPERSCRIPT

superior   Relating to or being a superscript.—compare INFERIOR

superscript   A distinguishing symbol (such as a letter or number) written immediately above or above and to the right or left of another character.—compare SUBSCRIPT

tear sheet   A page cut or torn from a publication.

template   A page grid created and intended for repeated use.

text page—see TYPE PAGE

thick   A thick stroke.

thick space   A space that is one-third of an em.—called also *three-to-the-em space*

thin   A thin stroke.

thin space   A space that is one-fourth, or sometimes one-fifth, of an em space. —compare HAIR SPACE

three-to-the-em space—see THICK SPACE

thumbnail   A small sketch of a page.

tint   Percentage of shading on an area of a page (for example, 10 percent black).

title page   A page of a book bearing the title and usually the names of the author and publisher and the place and sometimes the date of publication.

trim marks   Marks placed on a page proof or page negative to show where the edge of the page will be after the printed signatures have been trimmed to their final size.

trim size   The actual size of a book page after excess material required in production has been cut off.

typeface   A particular type design, often including all the standard variants (bold, italic, etc.) of the basic design.

typemark   To specify on the manuscript how type is to be set.

type page *or* **text page**   The area of a page that includes all of the copy measured from the ascender of the top line to the descender of the bottom line. The two terms are usually synonymous; however, the term *type page* is often intended to include the running heads and folios, and the term *text page* to include just the text.

typescript   A typewritten manuscript and especially one that is intended for use as printer's copy.

typesetter   **1**   A person who sets type.   **2**   A device that produces the type from keyboarded instructions.

typesetting   The composing of text for printing, today usually by means of computerized photocomposition.

typography   The style, arrangement, and appearance of typeset matter.

underscore   A line drawn under a word or line to indicate intent to italicize.

uppercase   Capital-letter type used in printing.—compare LOWERCASE

verso   A left-hand page.—compare RECTO

vertical orientation—see PORTRAIT ORIENTATION

web press   A press that prints a continuous roll of paper.—compare SHEET-FED PRESS

weight   Heaviness of paper (20 lb., 50 lb., etc.), as measured for standard 500-sheet reams of 17″ × 22″ sheets.

white space   Intentionally unprinted areas on a printed page.—called also *air*

widow   A single short last line of a paragraph that appears at the top of a printed page or column.

work-and-turn printing   Printing one side of a sheet, turning it over, and printing the other side. Two copies of the pages are produced when the sheet is cut in half.

wrong-reading   Having a reversed right-to-left orientation.—compare RIGHT-READING

WYSIWYG   (pronounced "wizzywig") Literally, "What You See [on the screen] Is What You Get [on paper]"; describes a computer display that exactly reflects the appearance of the document as it will be printed, though at a smaller size.

x height   The height of a lowercase x used to represent the height of the main body of a lowercase letter.

CHAPTER 9

Records Management

If you are an administrative secretary, you must be familiar with all records containing information that the executive may need. This information may take the form of a letter, a memorandum, or a directive; it may be in microform, on cards, on computer tape, or in a reference book. It may be stored in filing cabinets of various types, on open shelves, in a central storage center, in an inactive storage center, in a computer center, or in the company library.

Basic Modes of Storage

Despite the proliferation of computers, it is estimated that paper still accounts for 95 percent of all the filing in the United States. Paper records do have distinct advantages: they are affordable, they are the most acceptable legal form of record, they are reassuring to people who desire to retain physical evidence, and they are difficult to alter.

The need to control the flow of paper is compelling. *Records management* is the broad term that denotes the systematic control over the creation, maintenance, retention, protection, and preservation of records. *Filing* may be defined more narrowly as the arrangement and storage of recorded information according to a simple and logical sequence so as to facilitate future retrieval. *Indexing* refers to systems of classifying items so that they can be retrieved when needed.

In an efficient records-management program, only records of long-term value are kept in storage. A record may have administrative, historical, legal, or research value. Records that are needed for day-to-day or long-term decision making are of administrative value. Financial records must be retained not only for administrative decision making but also for government tax reports. Firms interested in compiling or maintaining corporate history, either for their own needs or for public, university, or private libraries, will wish to preserve those records in which important company-related events have been chronicled. The company legal counsel identifies the records that must be kept for the company's own protection; deeds, long-term contracts, and articles of incorporation or charters are examples of records with long-term legal value. Records that might be of assistance to researchers in various areas of a company's operations are also important and should be kept over the long term. In dealing with this material, the records administrator should be guided by top management.

All other records are of short-term value and are usually kept in an organization's central records center, if there is one, or in an executive office. The dates on which these records should be destroyed are usually officially determined. Guidelines are established by top management, individual executives, legal counsel, and the records manager regarding which records can be destroyed immediately after action has been taken on them, which should be retained for a specified time and then destroyed, and which should be kept indefinitely. Your responsibility is to know the proper storage location of each type of record that is retained and the length of time it is to be kept.

STORAGE OF RECORDS

Your workstation will usually house vertical or lateral filing cabinets. Other means of storage such as open shelves, card files, microfilm, and computer tape are likely to be found in central records. Only the records necessary for day-to-day operations—records used at least once a month—should be kept in the office. All other material is generally considered inactive and should be moved to central storage, from which it can be retrieved by request when needed.

Vertical and lateral cabinets　Vertical storage cabinets may be from two to five drawers in height. Each drawer should be labeled to indicate its contents and should also contain file guides to provide quick reference and adequate physical support for the folders. Each drawer should have from 20 to 25 guides. Letters should be filed left side down in folders, with the most recent letters at the front of each folder. No folder should contain more than 50 sheets of paper.

The order of the guides and folders in a typical drawer is shown in Fig. 9.1: main guide, individual folders, "Out" guides or folders, special name guides, permanent cross-reference guides, and a miscellaneous folder at the end of the section for material not yet considered active. (Some records managers think miscellaneous folders should not be used at all. If they are used, no more than five pieces on a given subject should be allowed to accumulate there before an individual file is set up.)

In vertical cabinets, hanging folders may be used. The sides of hanging folders have hooks which enable the folders to hang from a frame inserted in the file drawer. Hanging folders can hold larger numbers of records than regular folders and the tab may be moved to different positions.

Many information managers are of the opinion that within a few years the vertical filing cabinet will have become passé. Lateral filing cabinets generally permit speedier storage and retrieval. The length of the cabinet lies against the wall and the drawers pull out only about one foot. The fronts of the folders face the left side of the drawer. The back ledge of the cabinet may be moved to accommodate either letter-size or legal-size folders. Like vertical cabinets, lateral cabinets may be from two to five drawers in height.

Open-shelf storage　Open shelves have become popular because of the savings in space over normal cabinets (up to 50 percent) and the quick and easy reference they offer for highly active files. Only where there is neither air-conditioning nor

Fig. 9.1   Guide and Folder Arrangement for Cabinet Files

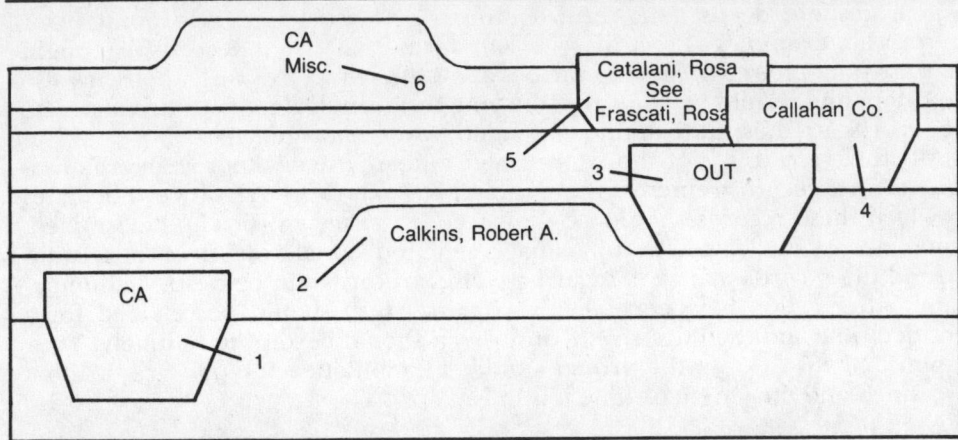

1. *Alphabetical caption guide*   The guide tabs usually are positioned on the left.
2. *Individual account folder*   Most account correspondence and data regarding a company's clients are kept in such folders.
3. *Out guide*   "Out" guides or substitution cards, with tabs at center right, record the identity and location of folders that have been removed.
4. *Special name guide*   Special guides can be inserted at the far right for very active accounts that have more than one folder or that require special handling.
5. *Permanent cross-reference guide*   These guides direct the user to a folder at another location.
6. *Miscellaneous folder*   These folders, placed at the end of each letter-caption category, hold material not yet of sufficient quantity to require an individual folder.

air filtration would the use of open-shelf storage be questionable, since dust and humidity can be harmful to records. Open shelves are sometimes constructed on tracks for movability, requiring less floor space and making filing and retrieving even easier.

Card cabinets   Information for basic reference can be filed in card cabinets of various sizes. The most common card sizes are $3'' \times 5''$, $4'' \times 6''$, $5'' \times 8''$, and $6'' \times 9''$. The most sophisticated card cabinets are those in automatic retrieval units. (See the following section on "Automated systems.")

Visible card cabinets   Visible card cabinets are small desktop cabinets with numerous flat traylike drawers. Racks in these drawers hold cards (usually $6'' \times 4''$ or $8'' \times 5''$) in an overlapping arrangement that permits very rapid access. They are commonly used for indexes to the location and status of other records.

Automated systems   An automated storage and retrieval system offers the advantages of optimum convenience, rapid retrieval, concentration of vast amounts of file material in a small amount of floor space, and superior control over records. Automated units are rotating, electronically driven carriers up to 30 feet high which present the operator with the desired tray at the touch of a button. Some machines can automatically sort and retrieve individual cards or files, thus reducing the handling of cards and files and protecting them against excessive wear. Card index storage and retrieval systems are especially adaptable to mechanized units. Automated storage and retrieval systems also handle microfilm and are adaptable to computer applications. However, mechanized filing operations are extremely expensive and thus are economical only for users with a high daily volume of filing and a minimum amount of space.

Microfilm storage   The use of microfilm has markedly reduced storage space requirements. When hard copy is converted to microfilm, only two percent of the space taken up by the original material is necessary for the microfilm. Microfilm can be filed on 16-mm. and 35-mm. rolls in color or in black and white, and housed in cartridges or magazines. Other microfilm forms, or *microfilms*, include jackets, tab cards, microfiche, and strip holders. Storage cabinets, binders, and small tubs are available for storing microforms.

Computer tape storage   Computer tapes can hold a tremendous amount of information, save large amounts of space, and afford fast information retrieval. A special closed cabinet or a rack kept in a closed area can be used to store these tapes. There are also storage boxes designed so that the tapes slide forward as one is taken out, thus facilitating retrieval. The tapes are indexed, and a record is kept of the location of each tape so that information can be located fast.

Tickler files   Tickler files usually use $3'' \times 5''$ cards and contain reminders for following up projects or meetings. When the tickler file takes the form of a tub file on wheels instead of a card file, guides and folders (12 guides for the months and 31 folders for the days) are arranged in a similar way. Letters that need following up are placed in folders behind the dates or months on which action must be taken. Special folders are also available with sliding tabs that indicate the dates on which action should be taken.

FOLDERS, LABELS, AND GUIDES

Folders   Plain file folders come in a variety of shapes and sizes. A set of folders will normally include equal numbers of folders with tabs at the left, center, and right, permitting the user to stagger them in the file for maximum tab visibility. On "⅓ cut" folders, the tabs are one-third the width of the entire folder; on "⅕ cut" folders, one-fifth the width; and so on.

End- or side-tabbed folders are designed for use in lateral file cabinets or on open shelves. Accordion or expandable file folders (sometimes secured with string) are used to hold a large number of documents; they may have tabs on either the top or the side. Ring folders have two-pronged fasteners that securely attach the records, which must be punched before filing. Folders also may be purchased with several attached inserts, each with its own fastener, or with plain dividers.

Hanging folders, as described earlier, hang from racks inserted in (or built into) the file drawer, by means of hooks at either end of the top of the folder. Since they slide easily along the rack and do not sag even when full, they permit easy access to their contents. They are stronger but more expensive than standard folders.

Folders are commonly made of four types of material:

Manila. The most common and least expensive folder material. Available with wax or Mylar coating for extra durability, and available in various colors (though "manila" frequently refers only to sand-colored folders).

Kraft. Heavier; brown; quite durable; does not soil easily. More expensive than manila; should be used only for folders subjected to much wear and tear.

Pressboard. Expensive, durable material; more suitable for guides than for folders.

Vinyl or other plastic. Very durable, thus suitable for holding papers of permanent value, but quite expensive. Very smooth in texture, hence slippery and not good for stacking. Available in a variety of colors.

Labels　All folders that are not preprinted should be identified with pressure-sensitive (self-adhesive) labels typed neatly and consistently. The caption should be typed as close as possible to the top of the label for greatest visibility. Runovers are usually indented, and sub-captions are blocked with the caption. If the label includes both an index number and a name, adequate space should separate the two. The primary indexing units should precede any secondary units.

6.78　Schwartz, Howard M., Inc.
　　　Footwear Division

Color-coded labels marked with letters or numbers provide an excellent system for files, because one can instantly see if a file is out of sequence by noticing that the colors do not match. A color system may work in one of several ways. A particular color may denote the first two or three letters of a name (e.g., "Co" in Fig. 12.1); labels may be used to indicate each large grouping of files; or a single color may be used for a given year.

Guides　To expedite filing and retrieving, guides should be placed throughout the files to separate the cards or folders into groups. In card files, one guide should be placed after every 25 cards.

When purchasing guides, remember that durability and visibility are the most important considerations. The tab on each guide should project far enough above the folders to be completely visible. In straight numeric files, new guides must be added regularly; in alphabetic files, the guides are usually permanent. Guides should be made of pressboard or vinyl. Pressboard is generally preferable because most records need heavy guides for support; vinyl guides are satisfactory for card files. Since guides are sold in sets based on the size of the files, consider potential growth in your files when purchasing guides.

"Out" guides, special name guides, and permanent cross-reference guides should also be used. Guides may be color-coded like labels to differentiate alphabetic and numeric sections or divisions.

COMPANY LIBRARIES

Many organizations have libraries that house records of historical value as well as reference books and other materials. Be aware of the functions and availability of the types of records and information that are kept in such libraries, including what types of document are *restricted*—that is, available only to authorized persons. For instance, the project notebooks of scientists in an industrial firm may be available only to members of its research and development division, even though they may be stored in the general library. Government contracts, including classified documents and confidential papers, will need to be stored in vaults or cabinets with locks or combinations that meet government security specifications. If you handle this kind of document you will be briefed on the procedures required by the Department of Defense.

Types of Filing Systems

A knowledge of the various commonly used filing systems and their advantages and disadvantages is essential. Each system is designed for specific office requirements, and you need to know not only when to use a particular system but how to use it most effectively.

SELECTING A SYSTEM

The most important questions that must be asked before purchasing a system are these: (1) How is the information to be requested? (2) Under what name, subject, or code number will it be found? (3) What is the means of access to it?

Filing by name is the most obvious and most widely used method. Numbers came into use to accommodate very extensive files and as an aid to securing confidentiality. Today numbers and color codes are widely recognized as useful for speedy filing and retrieving, and the use of numbers has also facilitated the storage and retrieval of information with computer systems.

ALPHABETIC FILING SYSTEMS

Ever since spindles were used for storing and records were simply piled in desk drawers or on desktops, alphabetical filing by surname has been used. When several individuals have the same surname, the alphabetization extends to the first name or initial, and then to the middle name or initial. If a further breakdown is necessary, a city, state, or street name may be used. Fig. 9.2 shows a section of an alphabetic file.

Subject filing   When the name of the individual is less important than the subject of the record, the subject becomes the filing unit for reference. The most important subject name becomes the first unit, and the main guide with that title should have its tab on the far left. Subheadings should have their own guides, with tabs at center left. See Fig. 9.3.

A subject system is difficult to set up because it may require considerable judgment to determine the most important subjects and the proper subject headings. The subject headings can be best selected by producing an outline. After the outline has been approved by those who selected the headings, it must be given to all those using the records center. Subheadings can be cross-referenced back to primary headings for faster reference.

An important element in the subject system is the *relative index*. Because of the difficulty in deciding which subjects should be considered primary, requests may be made for an item under a different heading. For example, you might not know where material relating to employees' annual leave has been filed; however, by looking under *Annual Leave* in a relative index, you could see that the material is filed under *Personnel*. By the same token, if you needed to find a file on office furniture, you could see by looking under *Office Furniture* in the relative index that the material is filed under *Supplies*. An index of this sort also prevents the unnecessary creation of a new heading when an appropriate one is already available. Thus, a relative index—a list of all possible subjects that could be used or sought—is a must in subject filing, as well as a time-saver in some other filing systems.

Fig. 9.2   Guide and Folder Arrangement in an Alphabetic File

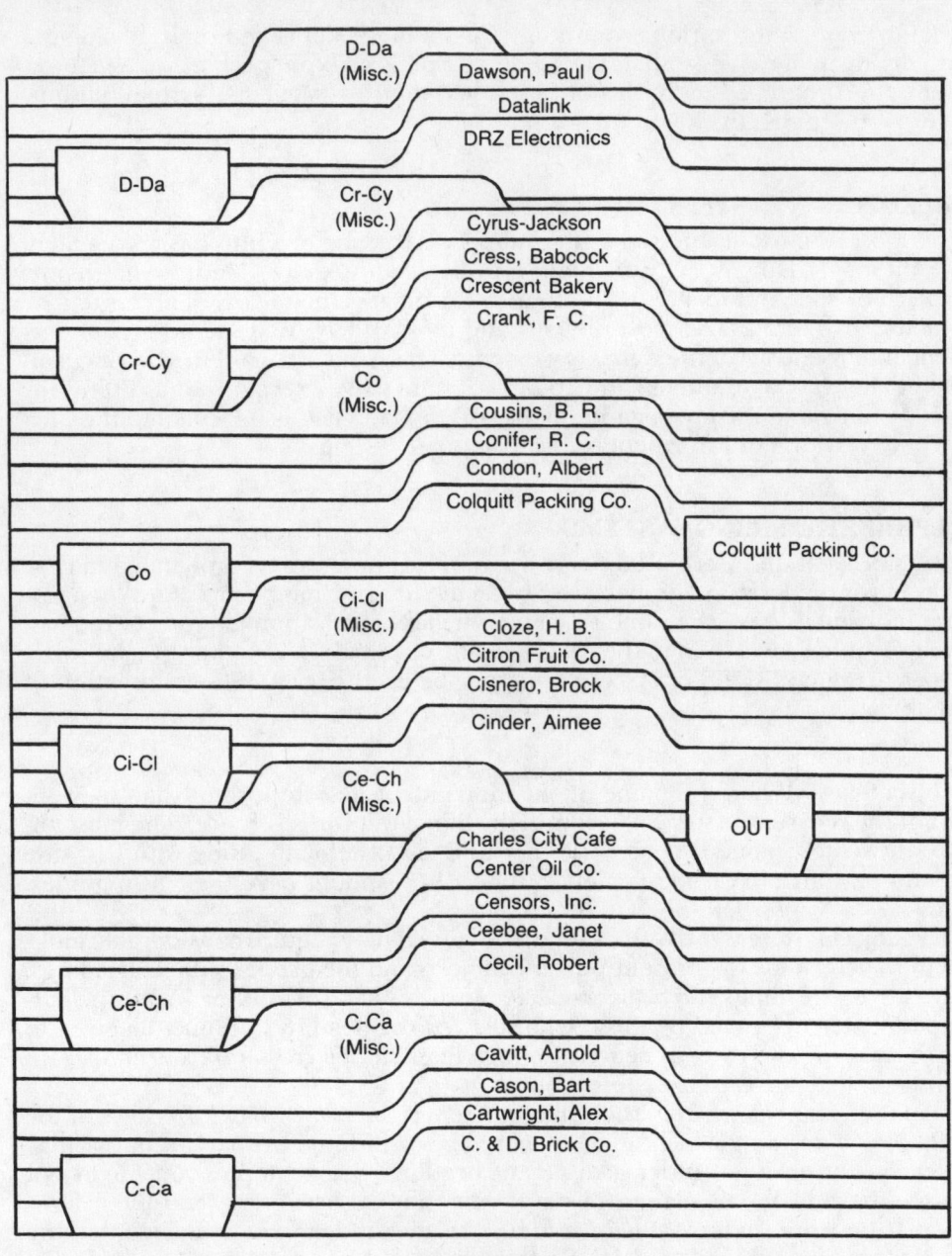

Fig. 9.3 Subject File

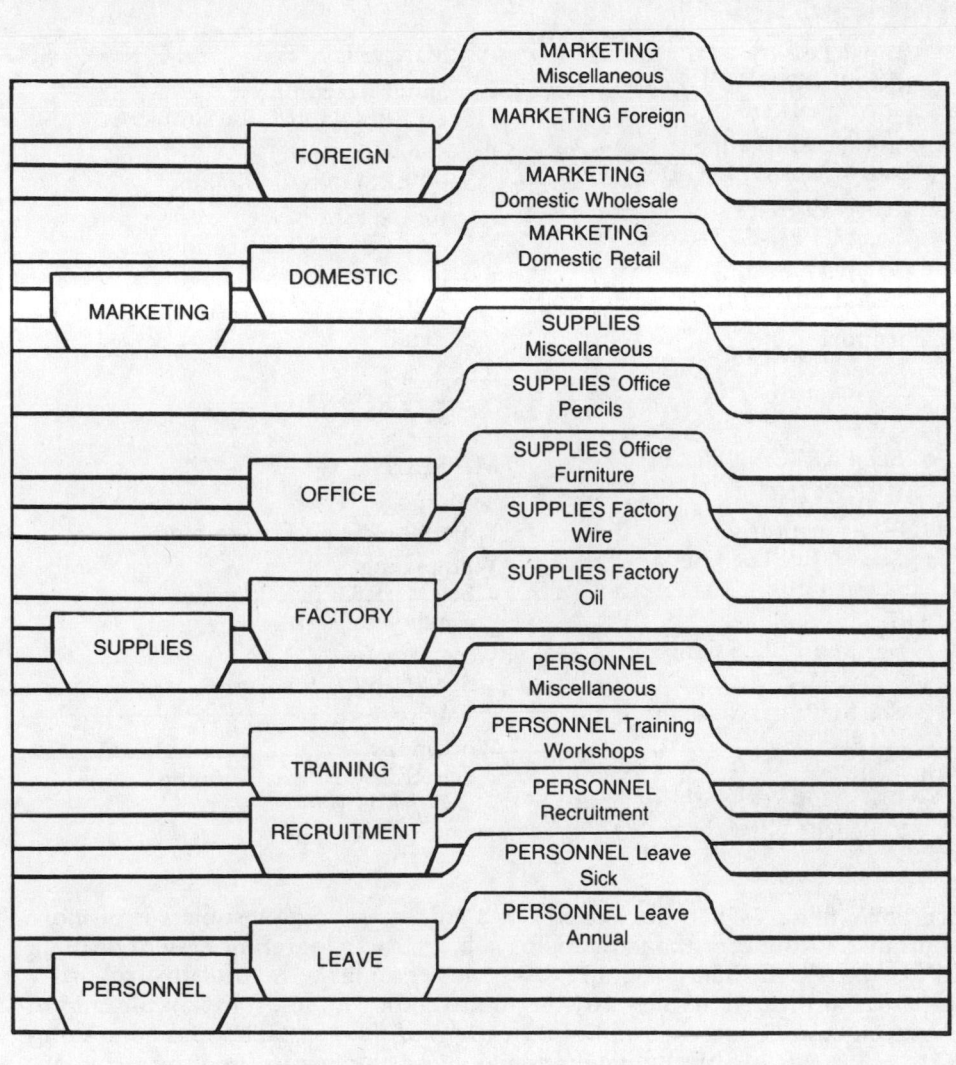

A lengthy relative index may take the form of a card file; a short one may be a simple list such as the following. Whatever form the index takes, it must be kept current to be useful.

Annual Leave
   See PERSONNEL Leave
     Annual

Domestic Marketing
   See MARKETING Domestic

Factory Supplies
   See SUPPLIES Factory

Foreign Marketing
   See MARKETING Foreign

Furniture
   See SUPPLIES Office
     Furniture

Leave
   See PERSONNEL Leave

MARKETING

Office Furniture
   See SUPPLIES Office
     Furniture

Office Supplies
   See SUPPLIES Office

Oil - Factory
   See SUPPLIES Factory
     Oil

Pencils
   See SUPPLIES Office
     Pencils

PERSONNEL

Personnel Recruitment
   See PERSONNEL Recruitment

Personnel Training
   See PERSONNEL Training

Recruitment
   See PERSONNEL Recruitment

Retailing
   See MARKETING Domestic
     Retail

Sick Leave
   See PERSONNEL Leave
     Sick

SUPPLIES

Training
   See PERSONNEL Training

Wholesaling
   See MARKETING Domestic
     Wholesale

Wire - Factory
   See SUPPLIES Factory
     Wire

Workshops
   See PERSONNEL Training
     Workshops

Geographic filing   When the location of a correspondent or subject is of more importance to the user than a name or subject, the geographic system of filing may be preferred. The geographic system is primarily helpful to mail-order companies interested in sales activities in different regions, for example, and to utility companies concerned with the locations of their installations and customers. In such a file, the main guide tabs may show state names, and the secondary guides may indicate cities within each state. When it is evident that a record may be requested under more than one title, a cross-reference procedure is necessary. For example, a company might be operating in more than one city, in which case the main office would be the geographic filing entry. For information about the Hodges Foundry in Lake City, Pennsylvania, a cross-reference might be placed under *Pennsylvania, Lake City, Hodges* to refer the searcher to the main-office location under *Pennsylvania, Pittsburgh, Hodges.*

Combination subject filing   Variations of subject filing are the *subject-numeric system*, in which numbers are assigned to a subject outline; the *duplex numeric system*, in which a combination of numbers is used; the *alphanumeric system*, in which a combination of letters and numbers is used; and the *decimal system*. In all of these variations, an outline is built from the most important subject headings, and numbers or letters are assigned to primary, secondary, third-level, and fourth-level entries. Examples of each of these systems are shown in the following table.

Subject-Numeric System		Duplex Numeric System	
COMMUNICATIONS		1	COMMUNICATIONS
1	Telegraph–Telephone	1-1	Telegraph–Telephone
1-1	Rates–Charges	1-1a	Rates–Charges
2	Mail	1-2	Mail
2-1	Registered–Insured	1-2a	Registered–Insured
2-1-1	Receipts	1-2a-1	Receipts
FORMS		2	FORMS
1	Design–Development	2-1	Design–Development
1-1	Standards	2-1a	Standards
2	Distribution	2-2	Distribution
MEETINGS		3	MEETINGS
1	Local	3-1	Local
1-1	Federal agencies	3-1a	Federal agencies
1-1-1	Bureau of Economics	3-1a-1	Bureau of Economics
2	National	3-2	National
3	International	3-3	International

Alphanumeric System		Decimal System	
A	ADMINISTRATION	100	ADMINISTRATION
A1	COMMUNICATIONS	110	COMMUNICATIONS
A1-1	Telegraph–Telephone	111	Telegraph–Telephone
A1-1-1	Rates–Charges	111.1	Rates–Charges
A1-2	Mail	112	Mail
A1-2-1	Registered–Insured	112.1	Registered–Insured
A1-2-1-1	Receipts	112.11	Receipts
A2	FORMS	120	FORMS
A2-1	Design–Development	121	Design–Development
A2-1-1	Standards	121.1	Standards
A2-2	Distribution	122	Distribution
A3	MEETINGS	130	MEETINGS
A3-1	Local	131	Local
A3-1-1	Federal agencies	131.1	Federal agencies
A3-1-1-1	Bureau of Economics	131.11	Bureau of Economics
A3-2	National	132	National
A3-3	International	133	International

NUMERIC FILING SYSTEMS

A second filing system is the *numeric system*. The straight numeric system is used by attorneys, physicians, and others who require that records be continually added for new customers, patients, or clients. Files are numbered in the order they are created, in strict numeric sequence. New records are first kept in a separate alphabetic file in *Miscellaneous* folders; when five records about an individual or firm have accumulated, an individual folder is made up and a number is assigned to it.

Numeric system components A numeric filing system has the following four parts:

1. An *accession register* that houses a record of the numbers assigned.
2. A *cross-index card file* (relative index) that indicates whether correspondence

is located in miscellaneous or individual numbered files; it is a complete list of correspondents, which could include addresses for a mailing list.

3. The *individual numeric folders* that hold only active records and those to which numbers were sequentially assigned; they are kept separate from the miscellaneous folders.

4. The *miscellaneous alphabetic folders* that hold only those records that are not yet active.

The accession register, in either book form or card form, is a complete list of correspondents in numeric order. If the person desiring a record cannot remember its number, the cross-index card file (relative index), which is arranged alphabetically by correspondent, will furnish the number assigned or indicate that the information is filed in the miscellaneous file.

Terminal-digit system   The *terminal-digit system* is a useful variant of the numeric system which automatically spreads out recent files through the whole system. It is often used by hospitals and insurance companies. The difference between this system and the straight numeric system is that the numbers are read from right to left. The first two numbers at the right are considered primary, the next two numbers (third and fourth from the right) are secondary, and the remaining numbers are tertiary. To find policy no. 61534, therefore, you would look under the 34 section of the file first, then under the 15 portion of that section, and finally under the 6 in the 15 section. A file drawer would thus show the following numbers in this order, from front to back:

61534
41734
17034
98534
30135
10235
20235

The terminal-digit system is easy to work with because filing accuracy is improved and locating folders becomes quicker and easier. Terminal-digit filing is especially convenient when large numbers of recent files are used frequently by more than one person.

PHONETIC FILING SYSTEM

A third system, used only in certain environments, is called the *phonetic system*. It is used in large hospitals, Social Security offices, police departments, and motor-vehicle departments, where a very large number of records (especially in card form) is used, where calls for records come over telephones or intercoms (that is, when names are only heard and not seen), and where retrieval must be quick. The employee translates the name heard into a letter-and-number code without knowing exactly how the name is spelled, and by means of this code the record can be located rapidly.

CHRONOLOGICAL FILING SYSTEMS

The tickler system is an example of a chronologically arranged filing system. Another type is a *chronological* or *reading file,* which consists of copies of every piece of correspondence or other information sent out of the office. This file must be read and culled periodically to ensure that correspondence has been answered or followed up. Chronological files do not replace other filing systems, but they can be a useful supplement.

HINTS FOR LOCATING MISPLACED PAPER FILES

- Look on your employer's desk. If you do not find it there, ask your employer if it may be in his or her briefcase.
- Check inside the file folders in front and in back of where you expected to find the missing one; sometimes folders are inadvertently slipped into one another.
- If you use an alphabetic filing system, check different spellings of the name. If you use a numeric filing system, check different numerical arrangements (e.g., straight numeric instead of terminal-digit). If you use a geographic filing system, look under similar names in other geographic locations. And if you use a subject filing system, check under a related heading.

SUMMARY

Alphabetic files shorten retrieval time because information can be located directly without the use of a separate index. However, misspelled names and errors in alphabetizing can cause retrieval problems. A more serious problem with alphabetic files is the difficulty in planning for expansion; the secretary must leave enough space in the cabinets in the appropriate alphabetic sequences to accommodate future files. Both problems can be solved by use of a numeric filing system. The terminal-digit system has rapidly gained popularity because new folders can be distributed quickly and evenly. However, numeric files are also subject to misfiling, and the maintenance of numeric files is time-consuming because they require an accession register and a cross-index card file. Consult your company's records manager or an outside records expert for assistance in setting up the system that will be most efficient for your office.

Setting up Filing Systems

CENTRALIZED AND DECENTRALIZED FILES

Information storage can be either centralized or decentralized. Centralized storage means that all records of any kind are kept in a central storage area, and authorized personnel charge out records and other resource materials at this location. Certain departmental records may be retained within the department itself for 30–60 days or even a year before being forwarded to the central storage area. Other records are sent on as soon as they are no longer needed by a particular department on a daily or monthly basis. The advantages of a centralized filing system are the following:

- It locates files in a central area accessible to all staff.
- It ensures uniform opening, maintenance, and closing procedures and permits supervision of files.
- It makes optimum use of space.
- It frees the secretary for other assignments.

In a decentralized system, all records are kept in individual departments within an organization. Any records that must be preserved after having served their purpose in the departments are sent to an inactive storage center. In a decentralized system, you have complete control over your own files. Your office or workstation will usually have vertical or lateral file cabinets. The advantages of a decentralized filing system are the following:

- Files are close to the user and more quickly retrieved.
- Familiarity with the files results in fewer misfiled documents.
- Inactive and nonessential materials may be eliminated or transferred by the person most familiar with the file contents.

SELECTING A SYSTEM AND EQUIPMENT

If you know how filed materials will be requested, it will be easy to recommend a filing system appropriate for your office. If records are asked for by name, the alphabetic system should be used. If they are requested by subject, the subject system or a variation of it should be used. If location is the most important factor, the geographic system should be used. If your office requires a filing system in which cases or patients are referred to by number (perhaps for the sake of confidentiality), a numeric system should be used. In organizations where records are usually requested by telephone, the phonetic system may be used.

Before actually setting up the files, you must determine what equipment and supplies will be needed: file cabinets, guides, folders, staplers (no paper clips should be used in storing papers), two-hole punches (if ring folders are used), desk trays (to hold incoming materials and materials to be filed), filing shelves (to attach to a file drawer or an open shelf to hold material to be filed), filing stools, sorters, and so on. (Sorters are racks consisting of open compartments, in which materials to be filed or distributed are sorted temporarily.)

SOURCES OF ASSISTANCE

If your company has a records-management program, the records administrator is the person to consult about establishing a filing system. If a companywide program is not in effect, you may wish to consult secretaries in similar offices elsewhere. However, the most efficient source would be an outside consultant familiar with the particular types of records being analyzed. If you consider the value of an expert's advice and the resultant time savings, you will realize that retaining such a consultant is often well worth the cost. In large cities, records consultants are listed in the Yellow Pages. They may also be sought through office supply and equipment firms that employ consultants.

Steps in Filing

The primary issue in handling records is determining whether they need to be filed at all—that is, whether the record can be destroyed immediately after its information has been disseminated or whether it should be retained for a certain period of time. Retention schedules—set up with the cooperation of the records administrator, top management, legal counsel, and department heads—are a necessity in maintaining control over records. A retention schedule lists categories of records, the department or division responsible for the originals, retention periods, the place where the records are to be stored, microfilming instructions where relevant, and sometimes an indication of the method of destruction.

Documents should be filed daily to reduce the chance of their being misplaced. Procedures to be observed when preparing for the storage of records include the following:

1. Read or scan the document.

2. Be sure that a *release mark* (initials, date, or stamped code), indicating that the document is ready for storage, appears on it.

3. If your system permits it, place a numerical file code or a name or subject code in an upper corner of the document to indicate where the material should be stored. (Some records administrators prefer to do this themselves.)

4. Place on the document another code that will indicate how long it must be retained. (Again, some records administrators prefer to do this themselves.)

5. Check to see whether the record needs cross-referencing. If it might be called for by a title other than the one it is filed under, write "X" in the margin and prepare a cross-reference index card for it. (See "Cross-references," below.)

6. Arrange the material in the order in which it will be stored.

7. Prepare any necessary follow-up notations for a tickler file.

8. Remove paper clips to eliminate bulk and prevent damage to the documents. Mend torn pages and smooth out wrinkles.

9. Place documents in the proper sections of the folder, left side down, with the most recent records toward the front.

10. If certain documents are too large to fit in the folder, insert a cross-reference sheet that refers readers to a special area for oversized documents.

Approximately 25 percent of the records crossing your desk each day can probably be destroyed or recycled immediately or passed on to some other person for disposition.

Reading, scanning, and coding Look for the most important name or subject, and underscore or circle it in pencil, or write or code it onto the letter if it is not mentioned in the text itself. The code will include numbers or letters or both, depending on the filing system being used. (See page 329.) Care should be taken to select the proper code or subject heading. Some records administrators prefer that the secretary not code records that are being sent to central records, as the records personnel will be more familiar with the storage categories. You can, however, always code the records that you will store yourself.

Indicate to the filing personnel that the record is ready to be filed by initialing it or by stamping it "File" or "Release," typically in the upper right corner.

Retention codes As a help to the filing personnel, each document should be marked with a code indicating the retention period of the material (30 days, 60 days, one year, etc.). The retention schedule will indicate whether the records are then to be transferred to inactive storage, microfilmed, or placed in computer storage in accordance with established company policy.

Cross-references Too few offices use any cross-referencing procedure, which can be essential to quick retrieval. When a record might be called for under titles other than the one under which it is filed, a cross-reference sheet should be filed under the possible title, referring searchers to the proper storage location. For example, when correspondence is filed under the legal name of a married woman, a cross-reference sheet should be filed under her husband's name, and vice versa. Cross-reference sheets (or cards) may contain only two lines; for example, "Furst, Mrs. Adam H./*See* Furst, Carrie M." ["Matthews, Carrie"; "Matthews-Furst, Carrie"; etc.] Cross-referencing is also useful when the filing name of departments or government bureaus might not be readily recalled, when a company has offices with different addresses, or when a periodical is filed under its name but a cross-reference under its publisher's name might be helpful. Cross-reference sheets are most easily identifiable in the files if they are of a distinctive color.

When five cross-references have accumulated, a permanent cross-reference guide should be inserted. This should be similar to a regular guide, but the tab should contain the same information as a cross-reference sheet.

In large and complex systems, cross-reference guides may be duplicated in an easily accessible card file. In numeric filing systems, these cross-reference cards for alternative titles would simply be placed in alphabetical order with the cards already in the cross-index file box. In an alphabetic filing system, a special cross-reference card box or a loose-leaf notebook would be required.

Follow-up   If an executive expects to want to see a given record in the near future, you or the executive should indicate on the record the date when it should be returned. If the record is being sent to the records center, you or the records personnel should add a card to the tickler file as a reminder.

Indexing Systems

Indexing systems are used to determine how a record is to be filed so that it can be found when needed. There are many different kinds of indexing systems. Whichever your office chooses, the most important rule is to be consistent by treating each piece of information in the same manner. A respected and authoritative source for indexing rules is *Rules for Alphabetical Filing*, published by the Association of Records Managers and Administrators (ARMA). This publication and others on technical records management may be obtained by writing to ARMA, 4200 Somerset Drive, Suite 215, Prairie Village, KS 66208. ARMA recommends rules for three classifications: (1) names of individuals, (2) names of business establishments, and (3) governmental/political designations.

INDEXING NAMES OF INDIVIDUALS
The following guidelines should be used to alphabetize individual names:

1. Alphabetize the names of individuals by surname + given name or initial + middle name or initial.

    Jones, M. Arthur
    Jones, Mary Ann

2. Alphabetize letter by letter to the end of the surname, then the given names and initials.

    Morison, John A.
    Morison, John Thomas
    Morrison, John Andrew

3. Treat hyphenated or compound names as one word.

    | Fitzgerald, Marcia | Foster-Brown, James | Vandalla, James |
    | Fitz Smith, Patrick | Fosteri, Arnold | van der Meer, Howard |
    | | | Van Dyne, Helen |

4. Disregard titles such as *Dr., Mrs., Captain,* or *Senator* when alphabetizing. However, these designations may be included to provide additional identifying information.

> Nyhus, Lloyd (Dr.)
> Smith, Walter (Senator)

5. Treat religious titles (such as *Reverend* and *Sister*) similarly.

> Raphael, Mary (Sister)
> Smith, John (Reverend)

However, if only one unit of the name is known *(Father Smith, Sister Mary),* the religious title becomes an indexing unit.

6. Alphabetize abbreviated elements (such as *St.*) as if they were spelled out *(Saint).*

> St. Peter, Joanne
> Saint-Simon, Paul
> Sarris, Eleanor

7. Disregard designations such as *Jr., Sr.,* or *2nd* in filing.

> Smith, John T. (Sr.)
> Smith, John Thomas (Jr.)

8. Use the legal signature of a married woman when filing. Her husband's name may be cross-referenced if desired.

> Poulet, Marie Anne (Mrs. Paul Poulet)

9. File "nothing" before "something" if initials are used for a given name.

> Peters, J.
> Peters, J. G.
> Peters, John

10. Arrange surnames having the prefixes *de, La,* and *Mac* just as they are spelled.

> MacDougal, John
> Mbasdeken, John
> McDover, Mary

11. If you are uncertain which name is the surname, file under the last name given and provide a cross-reference for any other possible surname.

> Hop, Chin Sing [with cross-references at *Chin* and *Sing*]
> Hope, Genevieve Carson [with a cross-reference at *Carson*]

INDEXING NAMES OF ORGANIZATIONS OR BUSINESSES

When indexing the names of organizations or businesses, rules similar to those just described are observed. For example, in a company name beginning with the full name of an individual, the name is inverted so that the surname appears first. In the name *Ted Corvair, Inc.,* the first unit becomes *Corvair* and the second unit becomes *Ted.* When no complete name of an individual is used—for example, *Corvair Construction Company*—the company name is indexed as it is ordinarily written. Companies operating under two different names are indexed under the name used most often and cross-referenced under the other name. Compound words and hyphenated names are treated as single units. Compound geographical names are treated differently, however. *The Palo Alto Trust* would be filed under *Palo* as first unit, *Alto* as second unit, and *Trust* as third unit; the initial *The* should be ignored (but any *internal* articles, prepositions, or conjunctions would have been included as elements for alphabetization). Punctuation is also ignored: *Smith's Grocery* would be alphabetized as *Smiths.*

Single letters in names such as those used in radio or television stations are treated as separate units; thus, *KXYZ* would be filed near the beginning of the *K* section. Names of companies beginning with numbers in figure form are filed in numerical order at the front of the entire file. If the numbers are spelled out, however, the name is filed alphabetically. For example, *21st Century Corp.* would be filed in the front section of the complete files, while *One Main Street* would be filed alphabetically under the *O*'s. Names of foreign firms are filed as they are normally written unless elements of them are identifiable as surnames, in which case they are treated like their English counterparts.

Schools named for their geographical location are indexed by the geographical name; for example, *Tulsa, University of*. In an alphabetical listing, *Tulsa Junior College* would follow *Tulsa, University of*. (Since *Tulsa* is the only unit that precedes the comma, the rule of "nothing before something" applies.)

INDEXING GOVERNMENTAL AND POLITICAL ENTITIES

When indexing government correspondence, use the most important word. Many companies file according to the rule that the first three units are always *United States Government*, followed by the name of the department, bureau, or commission. The same approach is taken with states and cities: the official name of the state is used first (e.g., *Texas, State of* or *Virginia, Commonwealth of*), followed by the applicable department, bureau, or division within the state government. Military installations are first filed under *United States Government* and then under the name of the installation (fort, station, base, etc.). Foreign governments are treated like states and cities; a record from a department of the government of South Korea would be filed first under *Korea, Republic of (South Korea)* and then under the department's name.

Although the alphabetization rules provided here are widely observed, you must primarily follow any particular indexing system used by your organization. The records manager should be able to brief you on the company's guidelines.

Controlling Documents in Storage

No matter how or when records are stored, a system for controlling their location and movement must be established and observed by all personnel. If there is no control, records may be missing when they are needed or may fall into the wrong hands. When you have accepted a record for safekeeping, every precaution must be taken to protect that record so that it will be available when needed. A simple method of protecting company records is to permit only authorized personnel to withdraw material from the files.

CHARGE-OUT PROCEDURES

Removal of a record from the files should not be permitted until it has been properly charged out. A record can be charged out to a person who officially requests it for a specific length of time using a special form. This requisition, which should include a description of the record (including whatever information appears on the label or tab), the date of release, and the person's signature, can often also serve as a charge-out form. The form should be inserted into a pocket on the Out guide. If only one record is removed, then an Out guide or substitution card can replace the charged-out record in the file. Consider using an Out folder rather than a guide when an entire folder has been charged out; the Out folder will serve to hold new records that arrive temporarily.

An "On Call" guide may replace the Out folder. The On Call guide directs the filing personnel to send the folder on to the person listed on the guide itself when the folder is returned. Only when the material is back in its place can the Out or On Call guide be removed for reuse.

A control procedure such as this is absolutely essential. Some companies allow records to be kept out for only a few hours; others, for a week or more. In any case, a policy should be determined and adhered to by all members of the organization.

CONFIDENTIAL AND CLASSIFIED MATERIALS

Special precautions must be exercised when confidential or classified documents are in your possession or stored in the records center. In addition to the normal protection just mentioned, an organization can use a safe or a built-in vault large enough for holding storage equipment. Another method of protecting confidential or classified documents is to duplicate or microfilm the material and then give it to an attorney or a bank for safekeeping.

Private firms with government contracts to manufacture, distribute, or store classified government materials or products are required by the Department of Defense to assign special control numbers to any classified documents kept on company premises, as well as communications (such as letters and memorandums) regarding these contracts or projects. Although the responsibility for maintaining records for these classified documents will be in the hands of a special department within the firm, you must be aware of the necessity for control numbers and any other identification that may be placed on classified documents. The Department of Defense typically classifies documents as *Top Secret, Secret,* or *Confidential.* The national-security regulation warning against unauthorized disclosure of classified material is also stamped or typed on the document.

In addition to following special storage procedures for such documents, take care not to leave classified documents uncovered on desks. Be sure that the documents have cover pages and that they are kept in drawers or locked areas when not being used. Classified documents may not be released to a person unless proof has been furnished that the individual is cleared to handle the documents. Other possible precautions include using red-bordered envelopes indicating that classified information is within, hand-carrying documents instead of using interoffice mail, and retaining receipts signed by those charging out the materials.

CHAPTER 10

Basic Accounting and Bookkeeping Systems

This chapter will introduce you to the features of various record-keeping systems in use today. A general understanding of accounting and bookkeeping terminology will help you to assist the executive in managing the operations of the firm. You may be called upon to type financial reports, proofread reports produced by others, or set up systems or documents to record important transactions. These records or reports are maintained and produced using sophisticated computer programs, other data-processing operations, and, particularly in small firms, various manual bookkeeping systems.

This chapter will guide you through some of these systems. An appropriate place to begin is to look at modern automated applications often used today. Once you are familiar with the available equipment and associated technology, you will be prepared to deal with the multitude of reports, statements, and forms that it can generate.

Automated Accounting

The terms *automation* and *data processing* are often used interchangeably. They both refer to the systematic handling of business information with a minimum of manual involvement. You will be involved in the gathering of the data that will enter the system, referred to as *input,* and the processing of the data produced by the system, known as *output.* Once data are retrieved from the system, a variety of facts will be available to present to management for speedy decision making.

DATA PROCESSING

It is likely that you will deal with programmers, computer operators, data-entry specialists, word-processing department personnel, and systems analysts at one time or another. Therefore, you should be familiar with basic computer technology and the various possible types of input and output.

With the help of data-processing equipment, insurance companies can review millions of insurance policies overnight for appropriate billing and updating the next morning, and can process claims and remit appropriate payments to policyholders with minimum loss. Large corporations can handle payrolls for thousands of employees within a matter of hours. Airlines can process passengers with minimal delay, including ticketing, seat selection, and baggage handling. Department stores can track cash collections, inventory merchandise, and generate purchase and sales data for individual departments and units.

Complex automated machinery capable of processing millions of transactions with impressive speed and accuracy is thus available. With so much information available, you must be able to decide how to use it for maximum efficiency.

The use of computers in business today is extremely widespread. However, computer technology is also expensive, and it has taken some time for smaller firms to equip themselves; thus, you may still encounter some older forms of data processing. The most common of the older systems still used today are the following:

1. *Automated data processing (ADP)* Data are processed by automatically operated mechanical or electronic equipment.
2. *Integrated data processing (IDP)* Equipment such as accounting machines and typewriters are provided with special attachments to transfer data to magnetic tape for further processing.
3. *Keypunch machine* Data are processed by the use of punch cards on equipment that can sort, count, merge, select, match, duplicate, perform arithmetic operations, and generate printed reports. It often takes a second machine or group of machines to perform such operations as sorting, verifying, interpreting, and printing.

COMPUTERS

Though computers are discussed at length in Chapter 7, the following review will serve as an introduction to their role in accounting and bookkeeping.

The older forms of data-processing equipment are generally being replaced by electronic data processing (EDP) systems. Such systems involve computers, which offer the most advanced means of processing data. These machines perform arithmetic and decision-making operations at tremendous speeds and with great accuracy and can provide executives with up-to-the-minute reports in attractive formats.

Hardware A computer system has the following capacities:

Input	Converts information from punch cards, magnetic tapes, or disks into a form for computer processing. Terminals containing keyboard equipment are also used as input devices in interactive systems. These are systems in which a terminal located either close to or distant from a computer is used to communicate with that computer. Computer personnel refer to this process as on-line data processing.

Control	Interprets instructions and directs all computer operations.
Storage	Retains instructions and data.
Arithmetic	Adds, subtracts, multiplies, divides, and compares; selects the sequence of processing operations.
Output	Provides results of operations in the form of printed reports and documents or as data on punch cards, magnetic tape, magnetic disks, microfiche, and cathode-ray tubes.

Software   This term is used to describe the instructions that guide a computer. There are four kinds of software:

Disk operating systems	These systems coordinate the interaction between the hardware and other software, including the transfer of information and data between the memory in the system unit (internal memory) and the disk drives (external memory).
Computer program languages	Programs are written in a variety of ways, but computers must convert these forms into their own languages. Examples of program languages are COBOL (Common Business Oriented Language), FORTRAN (Formula Translation), BASIC (Beginner's All-purpose Symbolic Instruction Code), and RPG (Report Program Generator). COBOL and RPG are used widely for business purposes.
Operating environments	Operating environments are programs that change the way an individual interacts with the computer. These programs provide easy-to-use screen displays that allow users to link various programs or work on several projects at one time.
Application programs	Application programs include word processing, spreadsheets, database-management programs, accounting programs, special publishing programs, and programs that provide the user with options to change graphics and special design.

The personal-computer keyboard   In order to use the personal-computer applications just discussed, you need to be able to get the information into the computer. The primary method of doing so is by using a keyboard, which is set up much like a typewriter keyboard. You will see a few familiar keys:

Enter (Return) key	This key may be used to start a new line of text, but is used primarily to enter instructions into the computer.
Shift key	This key works just as it does on the typewriter. You can use it to type capital letters or the upper symbols on dual-use keys (such as $,%,:, and &) and other punctuation and symbols.
Tab key	This key serves the same purpose as it does on the typewriter.

Less familiar may be the 10-key numeric keypad, arrow keys, and function keys:

Number Lock key	When you press this key in the On position, the 10 keys on the right of the keyboard become available to enter numbers and perform calculator functions.

Arrow keys	When the Number Lock key is in the Off position, these keys move the cursor around on the screen.
Cursor	Wherever this blinking mark is positioned is where the next character you type will appear.
Backspace key	You can use this key to correct errors.
Function keys	Function keys change their function for each application and provide a fast way to accomplish various tasks. You will find them to be remarkable in what they can do to save you time.
Control (Ctrl) key and Escape (Esc) key	These keys, like the function keys, serve many purposes depending on the software you are using.

Spreadsheets   A spreadsheet, sometimes called an electronic worksheet, consists of a grid with rows and columns. Spreadsheets are used especially when compiling the potential effect of varying decisions. When you change individual values, the effects of the change are automatically calculated throughout the spreadsheet in each programmed column and row throughout the spreadsheet. A sample spreadsheet is illustrated in Fig. 10.1.

Fig. 10.1   Spreadsheet

	A	B	C	D	E	F	G
1							
2			ABC CORPORATION				
3			SALES ANALYSIS - TOTAL DOLLARS				
4							
5							
6		YEAR 1	YEAR 2	YEAR 3	YEAR 4	YEAR 5	
7							
8	EASTERN DIVISION	646,185	634,324	672,885	381,384	805,629	
9							
10	CENTRAL DIVISION	551,265	452,695	100,258	365,985	258,741	
11							
12	WESTERN DIVISION	652,145	352,147	258,147	265,987	258,965	
13							
14	TOTAL	1,849,595	1,439,166	1,031,290	1,013,356	1,323,335	

There are several factors to consider when selecting a spreadsheet program:

- *Functions*   A spreadsheet program should contain the functions that will match the user's needs.
- *Speed*   The speed of the calculations of a worksheet is an essential consideration.
- *Capacity*   Newer features such as WYSIWYG, which add to the amount of information that can be accessed by a user, are being developed constantly.
- *Output*   The quality of the output from a spreadsheet program is critical to the neatness and presentability of information.
- *Ease of learning/use*   In general, the more recently a spreadsheet program was created, the easier it is to learn. However, the ability to learn a new program depends on the individual, and a prospective user should thoroughly sample a spreadsheet before deciding whether or not to purchase it.

- *Graphics* Since graphs are an excellent way to illustrate a point, the graph features of a spreadsheet program should enable the user to quickly set up a graph in any section of the spreadsheet.
- *Price* The cost of spreadsheet programs do not vary that much, so it should not be the most important consideration. More important than price is efficiency: a spreadsheet that is user-friendly and highly efficient is worth its weight in gold.
- *Hardware and software requirements* The user should investigate how much support is needed for the system to adapt to and handle a new spreadsheet program.

AUTOMATION AS AN AID TO PROFESSIONALS

The ability of computers to retrieve information quickly makes them valuable tools for attorneys, physicians, engineers, educators, and other professionals. Enormous quantities of information can be stored in miniature devices for ready access in printed form. This contrasts sharply with conventional filing systems, which require much space and equipment and expensive clerical time.

SPECIAL EQUIPMENT

Accounting and calculating machines, as well as computer terminals that resemble typewriters and are usually attached to a monitor for viewing, can be provided with attachments to create tapes as by-products of their operations. Teleprinters and teletypewriters are console printers that transmit messages— including handwritten messages—over long distances.

SERVICE BUREAUS

Small and medium-sized firms that do not have computers may contract with service bureaus to process their records. This may be less expensive than owning or renting a computer. Service bureaus provide reports, statements, and documents promptly in whatever form is stipulated.

TIME SHARING

Because computers can be very expensive, some firms purchase time from computer owners instead of purchasing or leasing their own equipment. Other companies may require computer time that their own overburdened computers cannot provide. Time sharing may be desirable for the time seller as well as the time buyer, because it provides income during periods when the computer is not being utilized.

Data Processing with Computers and Calculators

The term *data processing* is not limited to computer programs, expensive equipment, and reports printed on special paper. The daily typewriting and routine arithmetic calculations performed in offices are also forms of data processing. This section describes the calculating machines that you will find in typical offices to process data.

Most desk calculators perform only arithmetic operations: addition, subtraction, multiplication, and division. Other calculating machines may be quite complex: they can perform both arithmetic and logical operations, and they may have the ability to store and retrieve data from machine-readable files. Many of today's calculators are, in fact, nearly indistinguishable from small computers. The major differences between computers and electronic calculators are that computers have larger memories, the ability to make decisions and branch to alternative programs, and the ability to repeat operations a controlled number of times.

ELECTRONIC CALCULATORS

Electronic calculators are much smaller and faster than their predecessors, the manual and electric adding machines. They enable you to perform rapidly all arithmetic functions as well as sequential operations, which are often stored in the calculator's memory. Some calculators print on paper tape while standard models display figures on a digital-readout window.

Electronic printing calculators Printing calculators are useful for accounting purposes when complex addition or multiplication problems must be verified for accuracy. Electronic printing calculators have a 10-key numeric keyboard for entering the values 0 through 9; numbers and totals are printed on a paper tape. Some models have a digital display window as well. Separate keys are available for the four basic arithmetic functions. Many calculators have additional function keys that allow such operations as the automatic calculation of percentages and square roots. A separate key may facilitate chain arithmetic operations, such as repeated multiplications with different multiplicands. An additional key will allow a constant value to be stored in the machine's memory in order that it can be used in separate calculations.

Electronic display calculators The electronic display calculator has a digital-readout window for displaying numbers and totals, but no printing capability. Numbers are displayed as they are entered, and totals are displayed as they are calculated. Since the display calculator provides no audit tape or printed record, the operator can only verify these values one by one on the display window. The display calculator is similar in most other respects to the printing calculator. Display calculators are usually less expensive than printing calculators and have few moving parts, resulting in fewer service calls and lower maintenance costs. The low cost of these machines often makes it more economical to discard a broken one than to have it repaired. While the printing calculator usually draws its power from a standard electrical outlet, most display calculators use standard or rechargeable batteries.

Programmable electronic calculators A programmable calculator can store a complex program in its memory and be directed by a series of instructions to perform sequential calculations automatically. You merely feed the instructions into the calculator, enter any values required, and start the calculation series. These instructions are often called a program. Programs may be recorded on strips of magnetic tape, which are inserted into the calculator whenever the program is required. The use of a program relieves the operator from having to make several repeated calculations in a logical sequence.

Calculator vendors usually have "libraries" containing several routines or programs commonly used in business. In fact, the library often comes with the calculator at no additional cost. Additional programs are available for a small fee. Customized programs designed especially for particular office operations may also be acquired from most vendors. A common arrangement provides for a specific number of customized programs to be delivered with the calculator and additional programs to be prepared at a later date for a specific fee. Some business offices have staff members who are able to write programs for these calculators.

Common features of electronic calculators   In addition to its 10 number keys and its function keys for the four basic arithmetic functions, all electronic calculators contain a number of other keys.

All electronic calculators have a memory, divided into three separate parts: (1) keyboard memory, (2) operating memory, and (3) storage memory. The keyboard memory (sometimes called *keyboard register*) contains the number entered from the keyboard. The operating memory handles addition, subtraction, multiplication, and division. The storage memory retains data that may be recalled in the future.

The following keys, found on most calculators, may be used to make changes in numbers stored in these three memory registers:

Clear Entry (CE)	This key is used to erase a number entered in error. It will erase any number entered into the machine if it is depressed before striking the arithmetic function key.
Clear Memory (CM, MC)	This key erases only the storage memory.
Clear (C)	The Clear key normally erases the keyboard and operating memories but not the storage memory. However, on a calculator that does not have a Clear All key, this key will erase all three sections of memory.
Clear All (CA)	This key will erase the keyboard, operating, and storage memories. It should be depressed before beginning each new calculation in order to clear all previous totals and numbers from the calculator.
Memory Plus (M+)	This key will add the number entered on the keyboard to whatever value is in the storage memory.
Memory Minus (M−)	This key will subtract the number entered on the keyboard from the value in the memory.
Memory Recall (MR, RM)	This function recalls the value in the storage memory in order that it may be displayed or used in an arithmetic calculation, without changing or erasing the value.
Total (T, =, *)	This key will cause the total to be displayed or printed.

The following function keys execute complete calculations:

Round Off (R/O)	This key will round off calculated answers to a selected decimal position. Some calculators have a Round Off switch that may be set to round off all calculations; others have a key for rounding off a given figure.
Constant (K)	The Constant key permits the calculator to use a given value in separate arithmetic operations, usually for repeated multiplication or division. An example is the calculation of a chain of discounts when each discount is identical (5%—5%—5%).
Percent (%)	The Percent key will either give you your answer as a percentage rather than a decimal fraction (e.g., $2 \div 5 = 40\%$, rather than .4) or calculate a percentage relationship and give the answer as a non-percentage (e.g., $60 \times 5\% = 3$).
Percent of Change (% CHG)	This key is usually found only on large calculators. If you enter the base number, depress the Percent-of-Change key, and then enter a second number, the calcu-

lator will automatically show both the amount of change and the percent of change between the base number and the second number.

Some calculator keyboards may have as many as 10 function keys, each of which will automatically perform arithmetic calculations or sequential processing steps that are frequently used in business offices. One example of such a program is the calculation of a number of different chain discounts. A long series of discounts can be recorded as a program, and the entire program can be used by merely pressing one function key. Another example of a program initiated by a function key is the calculation of payroll values. The payroll program can be stored on a cassette tape, and the individual function keys can be used to calculate overtime pay, withholding tax, and Social Security tax. Each deduction requires several arithmetic steps, which the program automatically carries out in the proper sequence.

Verification of arithmetic   Since it is so easy to press the wrong key when entering numbers, you should always verify all your arithmetic. The paper output tape produced by printing calculators makes verification easy by listing each entry as well as the total; many printing calculators will also print a sign representing the arithmetic function applied to each entry. Verifying a calculator's paper tape simply involves comparing each entry on the tape with the number you intended to enter and checking off each correct entry. Verifying arithmetic on a display calculator requires that you repeat the entire input procedure until at least two consecutive final totals are identical.

Hand position for the numeric keyboard   Since you will often have to enter many numbers into a calculator, your operating speed is important. Practice will help anyone develop the skill necessary for touch operation of the keyboard. Like typewriters, calculators have a "home row," with the index, middle, and ring fingers resting on the 4, 5, and 6 keys. The 5 key normally contains a bump or depression to assist in locating the home row by touch. Each of the fingers moves independently from its home-row position straight up to reach the top row of keys and straight down to reach the bottom row. The thumb is used for the zero key.

The numeric keypad on the computer   When you have a computer at your desk, there is little need for a separate calculator. When the Num Lock key is in the On position, you can use the 10-key numeric keypad on the right side of the keyboard to enter numbers and perform all the functions of a calculator. However, if you fail to turn on the Num Lock key, the keys will serve different functions or move the cursor, and you could find yourself typing on the wrong area of your worksheet. Save your data regularly so as to avoid needless destruction of this kind.

Rounding numbers   Most calculators are designed so that any calculated answer completely fills a memory register, often providing an answer with more numbers than are needed by the operator. Thus, an eight-digit-calculator will calculate answers to eight digits, regardless of the operator's need. Some calculators automatically suppress terminal zeros to the right of the decimal point, even though they are calculated and retained in the machine's memory.

When a calculator rounds off numbers through use of the R/O key or switch, it goes through essentially the same process that you can perform without a calculator:

1. Delete all digits beyond four decimal places.
2. When the rightmost, or *test*, digit is 5 or more, add 1 to the digit immediately to its left.
3. Discard the test digit.
4. Repeat steps 2 and 3.

Problem   Round 457.75614 to two decimal places (i.e., two places to the right of the decimal point, or hundredths).

Solution
1. Delete the digits beyond four decimal places.   457.7561
2. Since the test digit (1) is less than 5, do not change the digit to its left.
3. Delete the test digit.   457.756
4. Since the new test digit (6) is larger than 5, add 1 to the digit to its left. Discard the test digit. Your answer is: 457.76

Problem   Round $756.42276 to the nearest cent.

Solution
1. Delete the digits beyond four decimal places.   756.4227
2. Since the test digit (7) is greater than 5, add 1 to the digit to its left.   756.4237
3. Delete the test digit.   756.423
4. Since the new test digit (3) is less than 5, do not change the digit to its left. Discard the test digit. Your answer is: 756.42

CALCULATING PERCENTAGES

Business mathematics employs percentages rather than fractions in expressing relationships between numbers. A percentage is a fraction expressed in hundredths; for example, $1/2 = 50/100 = 50\% = .50$. A few commonly used business fractions with their decimal equivalents are shown in the table on page 347. Invoices typically show a percentage of the total amount due as deductible for prompt payment. Examples of common business discount percentages with their decimal equivalents are shown in the table on page 349. This table also includes the *complement* of each decimal equivalent. The use of complements in calculating chain discounts is explained on pages 348–349.

Calculating a simple percentage   The percentage relationship can be calculated electronically by pressing the % key on your calculator rather than the = key after entering a problem. Percentage can be calculated mentally in the following way:

Percentage Amount = Base Number × Percentage

Problem   What is 9% of $647?

Solution
1. Convert 9% to a decimal by simply placing a decimal point two places from the right (.09).
2. Multiply the base number by the decimal percentage ($647 × .09). Your answer is: $58.23

Table of Common Fractions with Decimal Equivalents

Fraction	Decimal equivalent	Fraction	Decimal equivalent	Fraction	Decimal equivalent
½	.5	1/7	.1429	1/12	.0833
		2/7	.2857	5/12	.4167
⅓	.3333	3/7	.4286	7/12	.5833
⅔	.6667	4/7	.5714	11/12	.9167
		5/7	.7143		
¼	.25	6/7	.8571	1/16	.0625
¾	.75			3/16	.1875
		⅛	.125	5/16	.3125
⅕	.2	⅜	.375	7/16	.4375
⅖	.4	⅝	.625	9/16	.5625
⅗	.6	⅞	.875	11/16	.6875
⅘	.8			13/16	.8125
		1/9	.1111	15/16	.9375
⅙	.1667	2/9	.2222		
⅚	.8333	4/9	.4444		
		5/9	.5556		
		7/9	.7778		
		8/9	.8889		

Calculating the percentage of change   Sometimes it is important to know the percentage that represents the relationship between two amounts. This relationship is called the *change* or *difference* between them. The following formula and examples may help illustrate this calculation, which can also be done by using the % CHG key on your calculator.

Percentage of Change = Amount of Change ÷ Base Amount

Problem	Profits last year were $5000; profits this year were $8500. What is the percentage representing the increase?	
Solution	1. Calculate the *amount* of change by subtracting the smaller from the larger ($8500 − $5000 = $3500).	
	2. Divide the amount of change by the base (first) amount ($3500 ÷ $5000).	.7
	3. Convert this figure into a percentage by moving the decimal point two places to the right. Profits increased by 70%.	70%
Problem	Sales last month were $1500; sales this month were $950. What is the percentage representing the decrease?	
Solution	1. Subtract the smaller figure from the larger ($1500 − $950 = $550).	
	2. Divide by the base amount ($550 ÷ $1500).	.3666
	3. Round off and convert into a percentage. Sales decreased by 37%.	37%

CALCULATING CHAIN DISCOUNTS

Discounts are normally expressed as percentages. A *chain discount* is a series of discounts which are calculated separately. Each discount in the chain (series) is applied to the remaining, reduced amount. The following example illustrates the procedure for calculating the net invoice amount after a chain of discounts has been applied to the beginning invoice amount.

Net Invoice Amount = Invoice Amount − (Invoice Amount × Discount)

Problem	Calculate the net invoice amount for a $1000 invoice with a 5%–3%–2% chain discount.
Solution	1. Calculate 5% of the opening amount ($1000 × .05 = $50), and subtract that figure from the opening amount ($1000 − $50). $950
	2. Calculate 3% of the new figure ($950 × .03 = $28.50) and subtract ($950 − $28.50). $921.50
	3. Calculate 2% of this latest figure ($921.50 × .02 = $18.43) and subtract ($921.50 − $18.43). $903.07
	The net invoice amount is $903.07.

Calculating chain discounts with reciprocals   You may prefer to combine chain discounts into a single value that may be multiplied by the invoice amount to obtain the net invoice amount. Using reciprocals (also called *complements*) can be helpful in this procedure.

A reciprocal is calculated by subtracting the discount percentage from 100 (or in decimal form, 1.00). For example, the reciprocal of 5% is 95% (100 − 5 = 95), and the reciprocal of .15 is .85 (1.00 − .15 = .85). The table below shows the reciprocals of several common discount amounts.

Chain discounts may be combined by multiplying discounts by each other in

Table of Representative Decimal Equivalents with Reciprocals

Percent	Decimal equivalent	Reciprocal
.5 (½ of 1%)	.005	.995
1.0	.01	.99
2.0	.02	.98
2.5	.025	.975
3.0	.03	.97
4.0	.04	.96
5.0	.05	.95
7⅛	.071	.929
7¼	.073	.927
7½	.075	.925
7¾	.0775	.9225
10.0	.10	.90
12.0	.12	.88
12½	.125	.875
15.0	.15	.85
20.0	.20	.80
85.0	.85	.15
90.0	.90	.10

order to obtain a single discount, and then by applying the single discount to the invoice amount. The following example illustrates the use of reciprocals in combining chain discounts:

Net Invoice = (Reciprocal × Reciprocal) × Invoice Amount

Problem	An invoice for $500.00 provides for chain discounts of 10% and 5%. Calculate the net invoice amount.
Solution	1. Calculate, in decimal terms, the reciprocals of 10% (.90) and 5% (.95).
	2. Multiply these two figures (.90 × .95 = .855).
	3. Multiply the result by the invoice figure (.855 × $500). $427.50
	The net invoice amount is $427.50.

CALCULATING MERCHANDISE MARKUP

The basic calculation for retail sales firms is the application of a markup percentage to either the cost or the selling price of merchandise. These two methods of calculating markup are usually designated as (1) calculating selling price with markup based on cost, and (2) calculating selling price with markup based on selling price.

Markup based on cost   This method of calculating the markup involves multiplying the cost of the merchandise by the markup percentage desired and then adding the calculated markup amount to the cost:

Selling price = Cost + (Markup percentage × Cost)

Problem	When an article costs the retailer $20 and the desired markup percentage is 40%, what is the selling price?
Solution	1. Calculate the markup by multiplying the retailer's cost by the decimal percentage ($20 × .40 = $8).
	2. Add this figure to the original cost ($8 + $20). $28
	The selling price is $28.

Markup based on selling price   This method of calculating the markup is somewhat more complicated. Since the selling price is 100% of the amount we wish to calculate, the cost to the retailer plus the markup must equal 100%. For example, if the markup is to be 40% of the selling price, then the cost must be 60% of the selling price: Selling price (100%) = Markup (40%) + Cost (60%). The selling price is determined by dividing the cost by its percentage relationship to the selling price (Selling price = Cost ÷ .60). The following example illustrates.

Selling price = Cost ÷ Cost's percentage of selling price
Markup = Selling price − Cost

Problem	When an article costs the retailer $30 and the desired markup is 20% of the *selling price,* what is the selling price?
Solution	1. Since the markup will be 20% of the selling price, the remaining percentage will represent the cost to the retailer (100% − 20% = 80%).
	2. The selling price equals the cost to the retailer divided by the percentage of the selling price that this cost represents ($30 ÷ .80). $37.50
	The selling price is $37.50.

Banking

Bank services include checking accounts, collection of notes, loans, and money orders. Business activities are so intertwined with banking that you must be aware of how these services are used by their firms. As a secretary, you will often be called on to perform such duties as writing checks, depositing funds, paying bills, and arranging travel finances.

CHECKING ACCOUNTS

A checking account is opened at a commercial bank upon deposit of funds and the completion of bank forms listing the bank's rules and regulations. A signature card must be completed containing the signature(s) of anyone empowered to sign checks for the firm. The depositor is known as the *drawer*, the bank is the *drawee*, and the company or individual to whom a check is made out is the *payee*. A check made out to "Cash" can be cashed by anyone in possession of it.

Ordinarily, banks do not pay interest on checking accounts. However, individuals, sole proprietorships, and partnerships (but not corporations) may open NOW checking accounts. These accounts earn the same interest as passbook savings accounts in most commercial banks. NOW accounts usually require the maintenance of minimum balances to avoid the imposition of service charges.

Deposit slips   Funds deposited in the bank are accompanied by a deposit slip in duplicate listing the types and amounts of money being deposited. This money may include coins, bills, checks, and money orders. Interest coupons may also be included. The duplicate is retained by the depositor after the bank has verified the deposit.

Checkbooks   A company's checkbook usually contains three checks to a page, with prenumbered stubs attached to the perforated prenumbered checks. Information about the check—date, payee, amount, and reason for the disbursement—is written on the stub before filling out the check, thus assuring a permanent record of the payment. In lieu of stubs, some checkbooks contain carbonized paper so that a copy of each check is made automatically when the check is written. In larger companies checks are printed by computers, which store information about the checks internally for quick reference.

Writing checks   Checks may be typed, printed, or written in ink. The signature should be written or printed in facsimile. Erasures and deletions are not permitted. If an error is made, the word "Void" should be written on both the stub and the check. The symbols at the bottom of the check are printed in magnetic ink; through the magnetic ink character recognition (MICR) system, computers process large numbers of checks quickly and efficiently. The MICR system is also used to process deposit slips, loan coupons, and other source documents used in banking. There are now computer software programs that are capable of writing each check and doing all related record-keeping simultaneously.

Voucher checks   Checks may be printed with attached stubs that contain information about the checks. The stubs (vouchers) are used by the payees for recording and reference purposes.

Overdrafts   Despite the best intentions, company checks may occasionally be written for sums greater than the amount on deposit. As a courtesy, the bank may honor an overdrawn check and ask the company to deposit sufficient funds to cover it. On the other hand, it may refuse to honor the check. Since this can cause embarrassment to the company, overdrafts should be treated seriously, and good relations with the bank should be cultivated. A dishonored check may be returned to the depositor with a bank notice indicating the reason for its return—usually "NSF" (Not Sufficient Funds). An overdrawn check may be redeposited if the depositor has accumulated sufficient funds to cover the check.

Stop payments   Should a depositor want to stop payment on an issued check, the bank must be notified immediately. Although a check may be stopped by telephoning the bank, the bank must receive a follow-up written request within 14 days or the stoppage will lapse. The bank cannot stop a check if it has already been cleared. Stop payments are usually requested on stolen or lost checks and on checks that contain errors.

Checkwriters   These machines write check amounts so that they are difficult to change. They also reduce the time it takes to write checks.

Check endorsements   In order to negotiate a check, the payee must endorse it on its reverse side. When endorsed *in blank,* only the payee's name appears as the endorsement. This may be done by a payee who is a private individual, but it is a dangerous practice because the bearer of the endorsed check can cash it or negotiate it further. A *full* or *special* endorsement contains the name of the company or person to whom the check is being given ("Pay to the order of Samuel Howard") followed by the original payee's signature. Only the new payee can negotiate the check further. A *restrictive* endorsement indicates the condition of endorsement and limits the negotiability of the check, such as "For Deposit Only—Jennifer Novatt." The words "For Deposit Only" followed by the payee's signature mean that the check is to be deposited in the payee's bank account and cannot be negotiated again. Checks made out to a business rather than to an individual must be deposited by the payee company and may not be cashed or negotiated. In all cases, it is advisable to write or stamp the depositor's account number below the endorsement. Banks encourage stamped endorsements and often provide signature stamps to their depositors.

BANK STATEMENTS AND BANK RECONCILIATIONS

Depositors receive monthly statements from their banks which indicate the previous month's beginning balance, deposits made and checks paid during that month, other charges or additions, and the ending balance. Because it is likely that certain transactions have not been entered on both the bank's and the depositor's books by the closing date of the statement, their respective end-of-period balances will not coincide. A *bank reconciliation statement* may have to be prepared, indicating the reasons for the disparity. The statement is prepared by the computer, an accountant, or a bookkeeper. Any discrepancies between the bank statement and the depositor's records should be reported to the bank immediately. Banks will send more frequent statements if a depositor requests them and if the volume of checks and deposits is large enough to justify them. For a fee, the bank will help in balancing the depositor's checkbook by providing an accurate record of accounts.

Canceled checks   These are checks that have been paid by the bank and are returned in the envelope containing the bank statement. Many banks are developing systems that eliminate the return of canceled checks, but they will supply them to depositors upon request.

Outstanding checks   If a depositor's check has not cleared the bank by the end of the previous month, it is considered outstanding. After a reasonable time, the depositor should trace the status of any outstanding check.

Deposits-in-transit   Depositors may enter receipt amounts in their records that do not reach the bank as deposits by the closing date of the bank statement and are therefore not included on the bank statement. Such deposits are said to be late or in transit.

Bank service charges   Banks may charge depositors for services such as the collection of notes and stop payments. These charges are listed on the bank statements. Banks also charge for the volume of canceled checks and deposits. However, these charges can be offset by the average balance maintained in the account; consequently, depositors with low average balances sustain charges while those with higher balances generally do not.

Bank memos   Deductions and additions indicated on bank statements are sometimes explained in debit and credit memos sent along with the statement to the bank customer.

OTHER BANK SERVICES AND FEATURES

You should be acquainted with the variety of services offered by banks. Such information is invaluable in helping you assist a busy executive.

Cashier's check   A bank customer who does not have a checking account may purchase a cashier's check—also known as a *treasurer's check* or an *official check*—from the bank by paying the amount of the check plus a service charge. The check is written by the bank on its own funds and is used like an ordinary check, but the payee recognizes that it is guaranteed.

Bank draft   Similar in purpose to a cashier's check, a bank draft is a check written by a bank on funds it has in another bank. The customer pays for the amount of the draft plus a service charge. Bank drafts are used mainly for transactions with foreign banks.

Sight and time drafts   These instruments are often used when a seller is not certain of a buyer's credit rating. The seller gives the bank both the draft and a bill of lading prepared by a transportation company that specifies the nature of the merchandise sold. Upon payment of the draft, the buyer receives the bill of lading from the bank, presents it to the transportation company, and receives the goods. The bank then remits the payment to the seller. If the draft is payable at the end of a certain time period, it is called a *time draft;* if it is payable when presented, it is known as a *sight draft*.

Personal money order   For customers requiring small sums, banks sell money orders similar to those sold by post offices. These bank money orders are negotiable and serve the same purpose as business or personal checks.

Certified check   Should a payee require guaranteed payment, a bank will certify that a depositor's account contains sufficient funds to pay for the check. The amount is subtracted from the depositor's balance when the check is written, and the check is stamped "Certified."

Short-term checking account A depositor can open a temporary checking account for a particular purpose and close it as soon as that purpose has been accomplished.

Bank discounting If a company needs to secure cash in exchange for a draft or note it is holding, it may offer the instrument to a bank for discounting. After deducting a specified percentage, the bank gives the company the remainder and collects on the instrument from the debtor when it comes due.

Foreign payments Firms doing business in foreign countries may send funds through banks in the form of cable money orders, bank drafts, mail payments, and currency.

Safe-deposit box A firm or an individual may rent a safe-deposit box from a bank for the storage of valuable papers and other items.

Transportation bill processing A firm can arrange for the bank to pay its freight bills by having transportation companies send their bills directly to the bank, and the firm will receive monthly statements from the bank showing the amounts paid.

Lockbox For a fee, the bank may handle all steps of a business's accounts-receivable collections: mail pickup, processing, and deposit of payments. The depositor will receive daily reports of the amounts credited to its checking account.

Miscellaneous services Night-drop facilities (which enable businesses to deposit receipts any time of the day or night), automatic tellers (which allow depositors to conduct transactions without the aid of a teller and at times when the bank is closed), and banking by mail are additional conveniences. Banks also provide special payroll processing help, wire transfer of funds to other banks, dividend collections, and other services.

BANK INVESTMENT SERVICES
You should be aware of the proliferation of investment and personal banking opportunities offered by banks to businesses and individuals. The more common ones are listed here.

Certificates of deposit Banks pay interest on short-term deposits (a minimum of 14 days) to customers who do not want cash to lie idle. The bank issues a promissory note to the depositor which is redeemed at the end of the time period.

Commercial paper This consists of short-term promissory notes issued by large corporations for up to six months' duration. Banks act as agents for the sale of the notes, for which they receive a service fee. The notes are in minimum denominations of $25,000.

Treasury bills The federal government sells these obligations through commercial banks and Federal Reserve Banks. They can be purchased in denominations of $10,000 for time periods of up to one year. Most bills are purchased for 30, 60, 90, or 180 days. The bills are discounted at prevailing interest rates at the time of purchase. Banks charge a modest fee for this service, but Federal Reserve Banks do not charge a fee.

Treasury notes These are federal-government obligations of more than one year's duration. They are not discounted at the time of purchase, and interest is paid on them every six months. They may be purchased in $5,000 denominations.

Cash Transaction Records

Accounting for cash is an extremely important part of a firm's financial record-keeping system. Controls must be devised to protect receipts and to account for payments. Responsibilities for handling cash must be assigned to personnel in a way that minimizes the opportunities for theft and collusion.

CASH RECEIPTS AND PAYMENTS

Although specific procedures for the receipt and payment of cash depend on the nature of a company's business, there are fundamental rules to which most enterprises adhere. The rules are devised either by the accounting firm that audits the company's books or by the company's internal accounting department.

Types of cash Most people consider cash as being coins and currency only. From an accounting viewpoint, however, cash also includes checks, money orders, bank drafts, and bank deposits.

Accounting for cash receipts Firms that do business with consumers use cash registers for cash sales. Some registers record sales and sales-tax information on paper tapes. Other registers are tied to computers to provide automatic cash totals, sales distribution information, and inventory updating. Universal Product Code (UPC) markings and optical character recognition (OCR) symbols on merchandise enable retailers to exercise greater control over cash receipts through the use of devices at checkout counters that record sales information automatically.

Cashiers must be trained to operate their registers properly and to make change correctly. Procedures must be devised for periodic daily collections of cash from the registers. Cash received by mail is usually in the form of checks or money orders, but occasionally currency and coins are included. Personnel responsible for opening the mail should prepare lists of the receipts, which are used for making bank deposits and accounting entries. Whether cash is put into a register or received by mail, those who handle the cash should not make the accounting entries in the firm's books. This separation of functions is an effective means of minimizing the chances of collusion and theft. Recording of cash receipts is made in a cash-receipts journal, which may be a book in which entries are made by hand, a form used on an accounting machine, or a magnetic tape on a computer.

Accounting for cash payments Except for very small amounts, firms generally make payments by check. As with cash receipts, personnel responsible for authorizing payments should not sign checks. All checks should be supported by invoices or other documents explaining the disbursements. Cash payments are recorded in a *cash-payments journal,* also called a *cash-disbursements journal* or a *check register.*

Cash short and over Rapid cash-register transactions frequently cause cashiers to make errors in giving change. An end-of-day shortage in cash receipts (as compared with the amount on the register's tape) is considered an expense, while an overage is listed as income.

Cash basis vs. accrual basis of accounting Professionals and many small businesses maintain their accounting records on a cash basis. This involves recording expenses and income only when cash is paid or received. Larger firms use the accrual basis, which provides for charging expenses and listing income during the period in which they occur, regardless of when cash is paid or received. The choice of basis used may, of course, have a significant effect on a firm's reported net income or loss.

PETTY-CASH FUND

Since it is impractical to pay small expenses by check, firms maintain petty-cash funds. Items such as carfare, postage, and small quantities of office supplies are paid from the fund. To start the fund, a check is written and cashed. The cash is kept in a locked office drawer or box and is maintained by a designated person (frequently the secretary). The amount of the fund depends on the size of the business and the frequency of small payments. A disbursement from the fund is recorded on a petty-cash receipt, which indicates the date, receipt number, employee's name, amount, and purpose of the expenditure. It also contains the signature of the person receiving the money. (See Fig. 10.2.) The receipts are kept in the petty-cash box, so that at all times the total of cash and receipts equals the original amount. When a bill has been paid out of petty cash, it is attached to the petty-cash receipt. When the fund is low, a check is cashed to restore it to its starting amount. The petty-cash receipts are given to the accounting department for entry in the financial records.

Fig. 10.2 Petty Cash Receipt

PETTY CASH RECEIPT

Date: __________ No. ___

Paid to: ____________

Amount: _________

Reason: ____________________________

Account Charged: ___________

Received Payment: ________________________

TRAVEL FUNDS

You must be certain that sufficient funds are available to the executive for use on foreign or domestic trips. Your advance preparations may include visits to banks and offices to secure cash substitutes (or foreign money denominations if the trip involves leaving the country) and documents.

Letter of credit   When a business traveler needs funds in a foreign country, he or she presents a letter of credit to a designated bank and the amount received is listed on the document. Letters of credit are available from the firm's bank. They contain the name of the person who will be requesting the funds and the maximum amount (usually quite large) that can be secured. This amount is deducted from the company's bank account. Domestic companies often use letters of credit in transactions with foreign firms.

Traveler's checks   For smaller amounts, traveler's checks can be purchased at banks, Western Union offices, American Express offices, and some travel agencies. They come in denominations of $10, $20, $50, and $100 and cost approximately $1 for each $100 purchased. However, some banks give free traveler's checks to certain depositors and other customers. The checks must be signed at the time of purchase by the person who will use them, and again when they are cashed.

Express money orders   These may be purchased by you and either given or sent to the traveling executive, who is designated as the payee. As with regular checks, the traveler may either cash the money orders or transfer them to other parties.

Foreign currency   Banks sell foreign money in packages for the use of travelers in foreign countries.

Expense record   Since business expenses are deductible for income-tax purposes, the traveler should maintain careful records. The firm's accounting department supplies the proper expense record forms and uses them upon the traveler's return to make appropriate entries in the books.

Voucher system   Although all business organizations require controlled cash accounting systems, the opportunity for fraudulent practices is greater in larger firms. A voucher system, whereby all debts are listed as soon as they arise, is used by some firms to eliminate the possibility of unauthorized payments. Vouchers are numbered forms containing details about each debt and subsequent payment. The bill comes into the purchasing department and is sent out for approval before payment. A voucher controls the entire procedure.

Payroll Procedures

All business organizations are required to conform to federal and state payroll laws and to maintain accurate payroll records. Federal and state tax forms must be filed showing employee names, amounts earned, and payroll deductions. Management frequently requires information about payroll costs and taxes, and employees must be paid promptly and accurately. Since executives are often involved in payroll matters, you must be able to provide them quickly with pertinent data. A knowledge of payroll laws and procedures is therefore essential.

TYPES OF COMPENSATION

An employee is one who works for a business firm and is subject to the company's directions and supervision. An employee is distinguished from an independent contractor who performs services for a company but is not directly under its control. Payroll laws relate to employees only.

Salary This term is generally used to describe compensation for administrative-level employees whose pay is determined on a monthly or annual basis and who are paid in monthly, semimonthly, or biweekly increments.

Wages Employees who work on an hourly or piecework basis are said to receive wages. Such employees may be skilled or unskilled. Many people use the terms *salary* and *wages* interchangeably.

Commissions Salespeople whose compensation is based wholly or in part on their sales totals receive commissions on those sales and are considered employees.

GROSS PAY AND NET PAY

The total salary, wages, or commissions earned is called *gross pay*. For those paid on an hourly basis, gross pay is computed by multiplying the hours worked by the hourly rate. For example, someone who makes $8 an hour and works 30 hours earns gross pay of $240. If an employee works more than 40 hours during a week (overtime), the federal Fair Labor Standards Act requires that payment be made at the rate of time-and-a-half for all hours above 40. The following case illustrates the computation of gross pay where overtime is involved.

Irv Harold earns $10 an hour and worked 42 hours during the week of February 8. The computation is as follows:

Hours Worked		× *Rate of Pay*	=	*Gross Pay*
Total	40 ×	$10.00	=	$400.00
Overtime	2 ×	15.00	=	+ 30.00
				$430.00

Net pay, or *take-home pay*, is determined by subtracting certain payroll deductions from gross pay. If Mr. Harold's deductions came to $100, his net pay would be $330.

PAYROLL DEDUCTIONS

While some types of payroll deductions vary from company to company, there are some that are common to all business organizations. They are:

1. **FICA (Federal Insurance Contributions Act)** This term is used more frequently by accountants and payroll departments than the term *Social Security*. The FICA rate is set by Congress and has been changed several times over the years. FICA deductions support the Old-Age, Survivors, and Disability Insurance (OASDI) program and the Medicare program. The actual deduction for an employee can be determined from FICA tax tables supplied by the government or purchased from stationers, or by multiplying gross pay by the current FICA rate. Each year, Congress sets a tax rate and the maximum amount of gross pay from which FICA taxes are to be deducted. The law also requires employers to match the taxes deducted from employees' pay by remitting a like amount.

2. **Federal Withholding Taxes (FWT)** This term refers to the federal income taxes that employers must withhold from their employees' salaries or wages as the money is earned.
3. **State and City Withholding Taxes (SWT/CWT)** In most states and a few cities, additional taxes are withheld to support local programs.

Federal Unemployment Insurance Tax (FUTA) This tax is used for the administration of unemployment-insurance programs. Employers are required to pay the tax. The employer files an annual Federal Unemployment Tax Return (Form 940) by January 31 of the year following the taxable year. This form lists information about the unemployment-insurance taxes the company has paid to the state and federal government, and also provides for the computation of any additional tax due to the federal government.

State Unemployment Insurance Tax (SUTA) The funds accumulated from this tax are used to pay unemployment-insurance benefits. Merit-rating plans reduce the taxes for employers with stable payrolls. The form is filed quarterly, and its contents vary with the state. Other data that are usually required on this form include employees' names, Social Security numbers, taxable wages, and tax computation. As with federal unemployment insurance, most states tax the employer only.

Workers' compensation insurance Qualifying employers pay an estimated premium for this insurance, which is adjusted upward or downward at the end of the year. The insurance rate depends on the type of work performed by the employees.

Other deductions Further deductions may be made for union dues, U.S. Savings Bonds, health insurance, loans, pension funds, company stock purchase plans, and charitable contributions.

PAYROLL SYSTEMS
You should familiarize yourself with the different methods by which payrolls are processed. The payroll system that a particular company, organization, or institution uses is usually geared to the number of its employees and the complexity of the payroll itself.

Computers High-speed computers can process payrolls in an amazingly short time. The system may also generate printouts (and other media such as magnetic tape) of payroll registers, employee earnings records, employee checks, and payroll tax forms. Computers can also maintain journals, ledgers, schedules, and other records that are essential to the firm's operations.

Service bureaus Your company may have its payroll data processed by a private service bureau.

One-write (pegboard) systems Using this method, payrolls can be processed by hand in such a manner than an employee's earnings record, payroll register line, and check are produced simultaneously. A pegboard aligns the three records and carbon interleaves. When the check and check stub are written, for example, the information transfers itself via carbon or chemically treated carbonless paper onto the earnings record and the payroll register. Since the forms are standard, the user is permitted great flexibility in determining if any additional copies should be made. Each time a payroll check is written, a different earnings record may be inserted between the check and the payroll register.

Since the check, earnings record, and payroll register are all posted at the same time as the check is prepared, the accountant can be satisfied that, once the payroll register is balanced, the check and the earnings record have been posted properly. Pegboard systems thus save a great deal of time and ensure the accurate transfer of information. They are used to record cash, sales, and purchase transactions as well as payroll transactions. A one-write system is illustrated in Fig. 10.3.

TAX FORMS

Employers are required to file certain payroll forms at different times of the year. Information on the forms is derived from the payroll register.

Federal Tax Deposit (Form 501) This form is filed at a commercial bank along with funds withheld for FICA and FWT whenever these amounts plus the employer's FICA contributions amount to more than certain specified amounts.

Employer's Quarterly Federal Tax Return (Form 941) Amounts remitted with Forms 501 plus amounts not yet remitted are summarized on Form 941, which is filed during the month following the payroll quarter. The form also contains a record of the employer's federal tax liabilities and deposits.

Transmittal of Income and Tax Statement (Form W-3) Income taxes withheld and listed on Forms 941 are summarized on Form W-3. The form is accompanied by copies of W-2 forms for all employees.

Wage and Tax Statement (Form W-2) This statement is sent by employers to employees no later than January 31 of each year; it lists the previous year's gross pay, federal income taxes withheld, FICA taxes withheld, and total FICA wages paid. Where state income taxes are deducted, an additional copy is sent. By April 15 employees must file their federal income tax form along with a copy of the W-2 statement. If an employee leaves the firm during the year, a W-2 form must be sent to him or her within 30 days of the last payment of wages, not at the end of the calendar year.

Employee's Withholding Allowance Certificate (Form W-4) This form is completed by the employee and filed with the employer at the time of employment. It lists the number of exemptions to which the employee is entitled and becomes the basis for the employer's use of FWT tables. A new form is filed when the employee's exemptions change.

PAYROLL RECORDS

Some companies design their own payroll forms to conform to computer or accounting-machine specifications. Other firms use standard records that can be purchased from stationery suppliers.

Time cards These cards are used to maintain records of employee arrival and departure times and as an indication of the amount of time spent by employees on specific work assignments.

Fig. 10.3   A One-write (Pegboard) System for Payroll

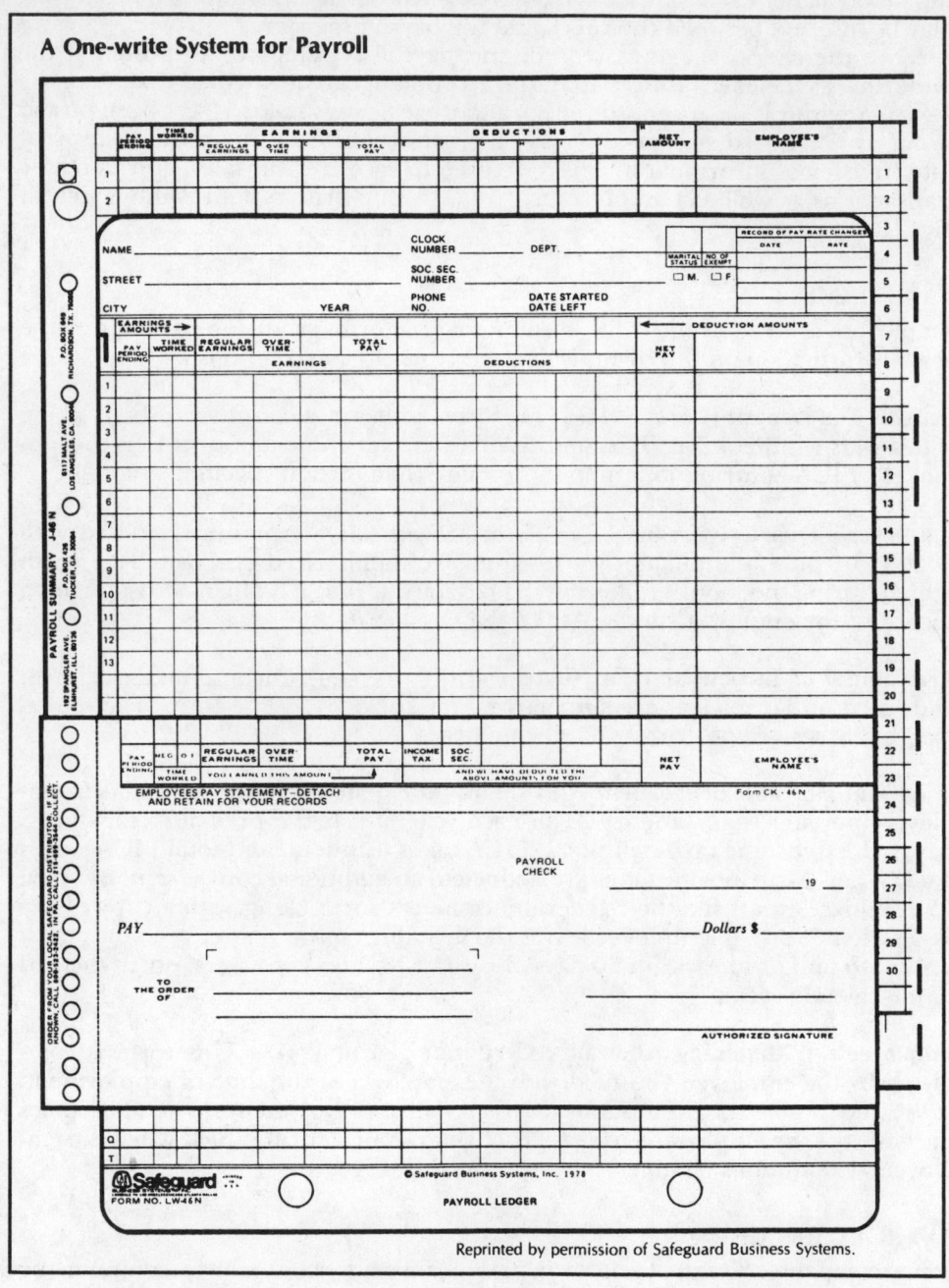

A One-write System for Payroll

Reprinted by permission of Safeguard Business Systems.

Payroll register Information is copied from the time cards onto a payroll register, which also includes employees' names, the number of exemptions claimed, pay rates, gross pay with overtime pay listed separately, taxable earnings for FICA and unemployment-insurance computations, deductions, net pay, and check numbers. The register includes all employees who work during a payroll period. A sample payroll register is shown in Fig. 10.4.

Fig. 10.4 Payroll Register

PAYROLL REGISTER

PAYROLL PERIOD: JANUARY 8-14, 19__

NAME	NO. EX.	HRLY RATE	HRS. WKD	REG.	OVERTIME	TOTAL	FICA	FWT	MED	STATE	CITY	TOTAL	NET PAY	CHK NO.
Gross, Avi	2	11.25	40	$450.00	$0.00	$450.00	$27.90	$44.00	$6.53	$25.51	$9.15	$113.09	$336.92	65
Norris, Neil	1	15.54	40	$621.60	$0.00	$621.60	$38.54	$102.00	$9.01	$40.53	$17.90	$207.98	$413.62	66
Rodriguez, Iris	3	22.00	40	$880.00	$0.00	$880.00	$54.56	$102.00	$12.76	$67.84	$27.10	$264.26	$615.74	67
Van Sant, Nell	2	16.00	36	$576.00	$0.00	$576.00	$35.71	$62.00	$8.35	$35.43	$15.25	$156.74	$419.26	68
Kostos, Arlene	1	15.00	38	$570.00	$0.00	$570.00	$35.34	$85.50	$8.27	$37.05	$15.96	$182.12	$387.89	69
Josephson, Jennifer	1	25.00	28	$700.00	$0.00	$700.00	$43.40	$115.00	$10.15	$77.00	$30.00	$275.55	$424.45	70
TOTAL				$3,797.60	$0.00	$3,797.60	$235.45	$510.50	$55.07	$283.36	$115.36	$1,199.74	$2,597.88	

Employee earnings record The federal Wages and Hours Law requires employees to maintain an individual record for each employee. The employee earnings record contains the employee's name, address, Social Security number, number of exemptions claimed, date of birth, marital status, rate of pay, hours worked, earnings, deductions, net pay, check numbers, and year-to-date earnings. An example is illustrated in Fig. 10.5.

Fig. 10.5 Employee Earnings Record

NAME GROSS, AVI S.S. # 002-45-9011

ADDRESS 106 Minnie Street DATE OF BIRTH 5-Jun-1973

Brooklyn NY 11203 MARITAL STATUS Married

NO. EX. 2 HRLY RATE $11.30

LINE NO.	WEEK ENDED	HOURS WORKED	REG	OVERTIME	TOTAL	TAXABLE EARNINGS FICA	MEDICARE	STATE	CITY	DEDUCTIONS FICA	FWT	MED	STATE	CITY	TOTAL	NET PAY	CHK NO.	YTD
1	7-Jan	41	$450.00	$11.30	$461.25	$461.25	$461.25	$461.25	$461.25	$28.60	$46.00	$6.69	$25.83	$9.60	$116.72	$344.53	22	$461.25
2	14-Jan	40	$450.00	$0.00	$450.00	$450.00	$450.00	$450.00	$450.00	$27.90	$44.00	$6.53	$25.51	$9.15	$113.09	$336.92	65	$450.00
TOTAL			$900.00	$11.30	$911.25	$911.25	$911.25	$911.25	$911.25	$56.50	$90.00	$13.21	$51.34	$18.75	$229.80	$681.45		$911.25

The Employer's Tax Records

Every business organization pays taxes, but not all companies pay the same types of taxes. Taxes are imposed by all levels of government: federal, state, and local. Records must be maintained for information on which tax rates are based, and completed tax forms must be available for ready reference. Accounting journals, ledgers, business papers, and report forms are designed by accountants, office managers, forms design specialists, and systems analysts. Record books and other forms can also be purchased from stationers and printers in preprinted bound or loose-leaf stylings.

The typing of tax-return forms will occasionally be your responsibility. Care must be taken to see that all figures are correct, that all required signatures have been affixed, that payments due are included, and that the forms are mailed on time.

THE FEDERAL INCOME TAX

While corporations and individuals pay federal income taxes and must file annual tax returns, proprietorships and partnerships do not. However, single owners and partners must report business profits on their personal income tax returns. In addition, partnerships are required to file informational returns annually. (Some states require corporations and individuals to pay state income taxes.) You must always maintain confidentiality when dealing with tax returns.

IMPACT OF DECISION MAKING ON TAXES

Business decisions often affect a company's tax liability. For this reason, tax planning is an essential part of a firm's policies. Accountants, tax specialists, and attorneys provide advice to boards of directors, corporate officers, and proprietors on a fee or retainer basis. You will often need to be available to supply necessary information to these consultants.

THE SALES TAX

Most states and many cities impose sales taxes on tangible personal property sold at retail as well as on services furnished at retail. Although this means that consumers are charged the tax, business concerns act as tax collectors by remitting the taxes collected to the government. This tax-collecting responsibility requires companies to maintain sales records that include sales-tax collections. Depending upon the requirements of the particular state or city, sales-tax reports are filed monthly or quarterly along with the remittances.

THE PROPERTY TAX

Local governments impose property taxes on businesses according to the latter's assessed property values. Once its budget needs for the year have been determined, the government establishes a tax rate. The assessed valuation for each business is then multiplied by the tax rate to arrive at its tax liability. Accurate records of business property holdings must be maintained to assure the establishment of fair assessed values.

Financial Statements

Since businesses are organized on a for-profit basis, owners and managers must be able to evaluate their financial operations through the preparation and analysis of statements for varying time periods. The statements are prepared by accountants and may be used by a number of people in the firm for different purposes.

OFFICE BUDGETS

As a key employee, you should be able to provide office cost data. You might even be asked to help in the preparation of the office budget. Budgets are effective only if they are controlled through proper record-keeping. If funds in one category are running low, it may be necessary to shift funds from another category. Situations may arise in which funds are eliminated because of cancellation of an expense category. Periodic statements of budget expenditures will enable you to judge how well the office is adhering to budget allowances.

Office cost elements include personnel, equipment, and supplies. With proper record maintenance and with an awareness of prior years' expenses, a budget can be developed to reflect the new year's plans. Though not every expense can be anticipated, you should attempt to allow for all foreseeable needs, and contingency funds should be included to provide for unexpected expenditures.

THE INCOME STATEMENT

A company determines its profits (or losses) by means of a financial report called an *income statement*. Prepared by an accountant, the income statement provides management with information about its income and expenses. The income statement is also a key document for decision making by stockholders, creditors, and lending institutions.

Time period   Although the income statement can be prepared monthly, quarterly, or semiannually, a formal statement for income-tax purposes and for the corporation's annual report is prepared at the end of the fiscal year.

Components   For a service business, two basic elements appear in the income statement: income and expenses. For a trading concern, the additional element "cost of goods sold" is required. Manufacturing firms also include the element "cost of goods manufactured."

Format   The simple income statement in Fig. 10.6 shows how the profit for the year 19— was calculated for Bert and Meri's Tavern. The heading specifies the type of statement and the time period. The Expenses section lists a variety of expenses normally incurred by a restaurant. The last line indicates the amount of profit for the year.

The next illustration (Fig. 10.7) shows an income statement for a trading company. The "Cost of Goods Sold" section shows the goods on hand on the first day of the year ($422,200), additional purchases of goods made during the year ($435,100), the total amount of goods available for sale during the year ($857,300), the goods on hand on the last day of the year ($376,200), and the cost of goods sold. The gross profit is the profit before deducting expenses.

Analysis   It is more valuable to analyze financial statements using percentages than dollars. For example, it is more useful to say that Bert and Meri's net profit

Fig. 10.6   Income Statement

Bert and Meri's Tavern
Income Statement
for the Year Ended December 31, 19__

Income:		$117,820.
Expenses:		
Salaries	$74,450.	
Rent	8,540.	
Supplies	15,590.	
Utilities	2,210.	
Services	610.	
Miscellaneous	1,150.	
Total Expenses		<u>102,550.</u>
Net Profit:		<u>$15,270.</u>

---

is 13 percent of its income than that the net profit is $15,270 of the $117,820 income. It is easier to compare net profits of different years by using percentages; similarly, we can make better judgments about expense trends by comparing them in percentage terms.

Tax impact   Since corporations pay income taxes on net profits, they constantly analyze their expenses in order to minimize their tax liability. Stockholders receive dividends from net profits and must report the dividends on their personal income tax returns.

THE BALANCE SHEET
This statement shows the financial condition of a business at a particular time. Accountants prepare balance sheets to enable management and stockholders to assess the financial health of their business. Balance sheets are also of interest to creditors and tax agencies.

Components   Three basic elements appear on a balance sheet:

1. *Assets:* items owned by a business.
2. *Liabilities:* amounts owed by a business.
3. *Equity:* the value of the business—that is, the difference between assets and liabilities.

Fig. 10.7   Income Statement for Trading Concern

Susan Hersch Office Supplies
Income Statement
for the Year Ended December 31, 19___

Sales		$710,600.
Cost of Goods Sold:		
Merchandise Inventory —1/1	$422,200.	
Add: Purchases	435,100.	
Goods Available for Sale	857,300.	
Less: Merch. Inv. —12/31	376,200.	
Cost of Goods Sold		481,100.
Gross Profit on Sales		229,500.
Operating Expenses:		
Salaries	$77,500.	
Rent	8,500.	
Supplies	6,200.	
Advertising	4,600.	
Depreciation	8,800.	
Miscellaneous Expenses	3,200.	
Total Expenses		108,800.
Net Profit before income taxes		$120,700.

Format The statement in Fig. 10.8 shows how the components of a balance sheet are presented for convenient reading by those who may not understand accounting. The assets appear on the left. The liabilities and stockholders' equity, representing claims by creditors and stockholders on the firm's assets, are listed on the right. The asset "Cash" includes checks and money orders. The asset "Accounts Receivable" shows how much the company's customers owe; the liability "Accounts Payable" shows how much the firm owes to its creditors.

Fig. 10.8   Balance Sheet

Lady Jeanette Inc.

Balance Sheet

December 31, 19___

Assets		Liabilities	
Cash	$ 4,300.	Accounts Payable	$12,580.
Accounts Receivable	28,250.	Loans Payable	26,000.
Inventory	54,360.	Taxes Payable	3,220.
Office Equipment	17,280.	**Equity**	
Less Accum. Deprec.	(3,420.)	Robin Jeanette, Capital	50,000.
Net Office Equipment	13,860.	Retained Earnings	8,970.
Total Assets	$100,770.	**Total Liabilities and Equity**	$100,770.

Analysis Accountants use ratios to provide management with useful information. For example, Lady Jeanette Inc. has assets in cash, accounts receivable, merchandise, and office supplies totaling $100,770, compared to $41,800 in liabilities, which indicates how well the company is able to meet its current debts: the ratio $100,770 : $41,800 shows that almost $2.50 could be available quickly to pay each $1 of current debt. Other ratios enable management to project future activities.

STATEMENT OF ACCOUNT

A statement of account is sent by a company to its customers monthly to record the transactions for the month and indicate outstanding debt. The next illustration (Fig. 14.9) shows that Harwood Music (the customer) owed $1,512.85 on June 1, paid that balance on June 11, and then incurred additional debt through purchases amounting to $215.12 and $304.81 on June 15 and June 28. The closing balance due on June 30 was $519.93.

Fig. 10.9 Statement of Account

Statement

Sam's Guitar Workshop   To: Harwood Music Co.
67 Main Street   99 Little Town Rd.
Middletown, CT 06457   Jamestown, RI 02835

Date	Explanation	Charges	Credits	Balance
June 1	Opening Bal.			$1,512.85
11	Payment		$1,512.85	00.00
15	Sale	$215.12		215.85
28	Sale	304.81		519.93

Corporations and Securities

A corporation is organized under a charter issued by a state. Although stockholders are the corporation's owners, business policies and decisions are made by a stockholder-elected board of directors. Decisions made by the board of directors are recorded in a minutes book, and accountants rely on these minutes for making entries in the financial records.

Large corporations issue an annual report reviewing the year's activities. In addition to an income statement and balance sheet, the report lists other financial statements and measurements of performance such as earnings per share (of stock), dividends per share, and stockholders' equity per share.

STOCKHOLDERS' RIGHTS

Depending on the class of stock owned, a stockholder may possess the following rights:

1. To vote.
2. To share in the distribution of earnings.
3. To purchase shares of new stock issues so that the same fractional ownership will be maintained (preemptive right).
4. To share in the distribution of assets if the corporation goes out of business.

CAPITAL STOCK

Corporations sell stock to secure operating funds. Ownership of stock is represented by stock certificates, each certificate representing a number of shares owned. An updated record of stockholders' names and number of shares owned is maintained in a stockholders' ledger.

Common stock This class of stock often carries all the four rights just mentioned. Since voting rights are usually provided, those who own a sufficient number of common shares can control the corporation. It is also the class of stock that rises or falls in price most rapidly.

Preferred stock This class of stock receives dividends (distributions) from earnings before common stock does. In the event a corporation is liquidated and goes out of business, it entitles its holders to a share of the assets before holders of common stock. However, a preferred stockholder does not usually have the right to vote.

Dividends These are distributions of corporate profits to stockholders, usually on a quarterly or annual basis. Dividends may be given in the form of cash or additional stock. Only the board of directors has the right to declare dividends.

Market prices of stock Stock is bought and sold through stockbrokers on stock exchanges. Stock prices are affected by corporate earnings, the condition of the nation's economy, government policies, world problems, and other factors. People and institutions trade stock in the hopes of making profits and also in order to receive dividends.

Stock-market tables Information about stock is published in newspapers and financial publications. For each stock shown in the tables, the data usually include (1) the highest and lowest prices at which the stock has sold during the year; (2) dividend information, including amount of annual dividend in dollars per share, percentage of yield, and ratio of price to earnings; (3) daily sales volume; (4) the high, low, and last prices for the day; and (5) the net price change for the day.

BONDS

Corporations may secure additional funds by issuing bonds. A bond is a written promise by a corporation to repay a loan to a creditor at a specific rate of interest at certain time intervals. Most corporate bond interest payments are made semi-annually. Bonds are long-term (e.g., 10-, 20-, 30-year) obligations and sell in minimum denominations of $1,000.

Types of bonds Secured bonds, such as *collateral trust bonds, chattel mortgage bonds,* and *real-estate mortgage bonds,* provide bondholders with claims on specific corporate property in the event of default on bond payments. Unsecured bonds, called *debenture bonds,* are based on the general credit of the corporation. *Registered bonds* provide for bondholders' names to be listed with the corporation, whereas *coupon (bearer) bonds* do not. Bonds that come due at one time are called *term bonds,* while those that mature at different dates are known as *serial bonds. Callable bonds* give the corporation the right to redeem the bonds before maturity, and *convertible bonds* allow bondholders to exchange their bonds for corporate stock.

Bond interest rate The interest rate printed on the bond certificate is called the *contract, nominal,* or *coupon rate.* The actual rate at which a bond is sold is known as the *market* or *effective rate.* Market rates are affected by conditions similar to those that affect stock prices. For a particular bond issue, the contract and market rates may be the same or different, depending on business conditions.

Bond redemption   Bonds may be redeemed by the corporation at maturity or, in the case of callable bonds, as specified in the bond indenture (contract), whenever it is to the corporation's advantage. The corporation may also repurchase its own bonds in the open market.

PROMISSORY NOTES

As defined by the Negotiable Instruments Law, a promissory note is a promise in writing to pay a sum of money to a payee or a bearer of the note upon demand or at a fixed or determinable future time. A note is an important medium of exchange and may be used for short- or long-term purposes. The person who promises the money is called the *maker* of the note, and the one to whom the note is made out is known as the *payee*. To the maker it is a *note payable*, while the payee considers it a *note receivable*. A note is negotiated by delivery when it is made out to "Bearer" rather than to a specific payee. When a payee's name is written on the note, it is negotiated by endorsement. Note forms can be purchased from commercial stationers.

MONEY

NAME	SUBDIVISIONS	COUNTRY
afghani	100 puls	Afghanistan
baht *or* tical	100 satang	Thailand
balboa	100 centesimos	Panama
birr	100 cents	Ethiopia
bolivar	100 centimos	Venezuela
boliviano	100 centavos	Bolivia
cedi	100 pesewas	Ghana
colón	100 centimos	Costa Rica
colón	100 centavos	El Salvador
cordoba	100 centavos	Nicaragua
cruzeiro	100 centavos	Brazil
dalasi	100 bututs	Gambia
deutsche mark	100 pfennig	Germany
dinar	100 centimes	Algeria
dinar	1000 fils	Bahrain
dinar	1000 fils	Iraq
dinar	1000 fils	Jordan
dinar	1000 fils	Kuwait
dinar	1000 dirhams	Libya
dinar	1000 millimes	Tunisia
dinar[1]	1000 fils	Yemen
dinar	100 paras	Yugoslavia
dirham	100 centimes	Morocco
dirham	100 fils	United Arab Emirates
dobra	100 centimos	Sao Tome and Principe
dollar[2]	100 cents	Antigua and Barbuda, Dominica, Grenada, St. Kitts-Nevis, St. Lucia, St. Vincent and the Grenadines
dollar	100 cents	Australia
dollar	100 cents	Bahamas
dollar	100 cents	Barbados
dollar	100 cents	Belize
dollar	100 cents	Bermuda
dollar	100 sen *or* cents	Brunei
dollar	100 cents	Canada
dollar *or* yuan	100 cents	China (Taiwan)
dollar	100 cents	Fiji
dollar	100 cents	Guyana
dollar	100 cents	Hong Kong
dollar	100 cents	Jamaica
dollar	100 cents	Liberia
dollar	100 cents	New Zealand
dollar	100 cents	Singapore
dollar	100 cents	Trinidad and Tobago
dollar	100 cents	United States
dollar	100 cents	Zimbabwe
dollar—see RINGGIT, below		
dong	100 xu	Vietnam
drachma	100 lepta	Greece

NAME	SUBDIVISIONS	COUNTRY
escudo	100 centavos	Cape Verde
escudo	100 centavos	Portugal
escudo—see PESO, below		
florin—see GULDEN, below		
forint	100 filler	Hungary
franc	100 centimes	Belgium
franc[3]	100 centimes	Benin, Burkina Faso, Cameroon, Central African Republic, Chad, Congo, Equatorial Guinea, Gabon, Ivory Coast, Mali, Niger, Senegal, Togo
franc	100 centimes	Burundi
franc	100 centimes	Djibouti
franc	100 centimes	France
franc	100 centimes	Guinea
franc	100 centimes	Luxembourg
franc	100 centimes	Madagascar
franc	100 centimes	Rwanda
franc	100 centimes or rappen	Switzerland
gourde	100 centimes	Haiti
guarani	100 centimos	Paraguay
gulden or guilder or florin	100 cents	Netherlands
gulden or guilder or florin	100 cents	Suriname
kina	100 toea	Papua New Guinea
kip	100 at	Laos
koruna	100 haleru	Czech Republic
krona	100 aurar (sing eyrir)	Iceland
krona	100 ore	Sweden
krone	100 ore	Denmark
krone	100 ore	Norway
kwacha	100 tambala	Malawi
kwacha	100 ngwee	Zambia
kwanza	100 lwei	Angola
kyat	100 pyas	Myanmar
lek	100 qindarka	Albania
lempira	100 centavos	Honduras
leone	100 cents	Sierra Leone
leu	100 bani	Romania
lev	100 stotinki	Bulgaria
lilangeni (pl emalangeni)	100 cents	Swaziland
lira	100 centesimi[4]	Italy
lira or pound	100 cents	Malta
lira	100 kurus	Turkey
livre—see POUND, below		
loti (pl maloti)	100 licente or lisente (sing sente)	Lesotho

NAME	SUBDIVISIONS	COUNTRY
mark—see DEUTSCHE MARK, above		
markka	100 pennia	Finland
metical	100 centavos	Mozambique
naira	100 kobo	Nigeria
ngultrum	100 chetrums	Bhutan
ouguiya	5 khoums	Mauritania
pa'anga	100 seniti	Tonga
pataca	100 avos	Macao
peseta	100 centimos	Spain
peso		Argentina
peso	100 centavos	Chile
peso	100 centavos	Colombia
peso	100 centavos	Cuba
peso	100 centavos	Dominican Republic
peso or escudo	100 centavos	Guinea-Bissau
peso	100 centavos	Mexico
peso or piso	100 sentimos or centavos	Philippines
peso	100 centesimos	Uruguay
pound	100 cents	Cyprus
pound	100 piastres	Egypt
pound	100 pence	Ireland
pound or livre	100 piastres	Lebanon
pound	100 piastres	Sudan
pound	100 piastres	Syria
pound	100 pence	United Kingdom
pound—see LIRA, above		
pula	100 thebe	Botswana
quetzal	100 centavos	Guatemala
rand	100 cents	South Africa
rial	100 dinars	Iran
rial	1000 baiza	Oman
rial[1]	100 fils	Yemen
riel	100 sen	Cambodia
ringgit or dollar	100 sen	Malaysia
riyal	100 dirhams	Qatar
riyal	100 halala	Saudi Arabia
ruble	100 kopecks	Russia
rupee	100 paise	India
rupee	100 cents	Mauritius
rupee	100 paisa	Nepal
rupee	100 paisa	Pakistan
rupee	100 cents	Seychelles
rupee	100 cents	Sri Lanka
rupiah	100 sen	Indonesia
schilling	100 groschen	Austria
shekel or sheqel	100 agorot	Israel
shilling	100 cents	Kenya
shilling	100 cents	Somalia
shilling	100 cents	Tanzania
shilling	100 cents	Uganda
sol	100 centavos	Peru

NAME	SUBDIVISIONS	COUNTRY
sucre	100 centavos	Ecuador
taka	100 paisa *or* poisha	Bangladesh
tala	100 sene	Western Samoa
tical—see BAHT, above		
tugrik	100 mongo	Mongolia
won	100 chon	North Korea
won	100 chon	South Korea
yen	100 sen[4]	Japan
yuan	100 fen	China (mainland)
yuan—see DOLLAR, above		
zaire	100 makuta (*sing* likuta)	Zaire
zloty	100 groszy	Poland

---

[1] The currencies of the formerly separate countries of Southern Yemen and the Yemen Arab Republic are both legal in unified Yemen.

[2] Dollars issued by the Eastern Caribbean Central Bank, established to promote economic cooperation among the member nations.

[3] Francs issued by the African Financial Community, established to promote economic cooperation among the member nations.

[4] No longer minted; a subdivision in name only.

Telephones and Telecommunications

This chapter covers the practical and technical aspects of telephone and telecommunications services commonly found in businesses, including telegraphic services, fax machines, electronic mail, and data networks.

As a secretary you will need to know how to operate some of the telecommunications equipment found in your office. The more you understand about telephones, telecommunications, and computers, the more valuable you will be to your employer. In most businesses, technology is underused because no one really understands the full range of its available practical uses. Consult your user manual, ask the technical staff, or, if necessary, contact the supplier or the account representative who sold the equipment or service to your company.

The field of telecommunications can be confusing today, since it is often hard to distinguish a piece of equipment from a system from a service. For example, telephone companies sell services that provide most of the functions of a PBX system. There will often be several ways to obtain the same function.

As features have multiplied, the design and choice of telephone systems have become important but difficult. You will naturally have to adapt to the system chosen, though you may be able to suggest features that should be included. If some of the features discussed in this chapter are not available in your office today, they probably will be in a few years.

Telephone-Company Services

Telephone-company services have expanded immensely with the thorough computerization of the telephone networks. This has allowed for more flexible direct dialing and the introduction of many new features designed for business use. The dialing methods for basic services are fairly uniform, but the set of available features varies to some extent based on your region and your long-distance carrier.

WHO ARE YOUR PHONE COMPANIES?

Most phone customers today deal with two or three phone companies. Your local company bills you for your basic line charges and all your local calls. That company is usually part of a Regional Bell Operating Company (RBOC). There are seven RBOCs in the United States: NYNEX, Bell Atlantic, Bell South, Ameritech, US WEST, Southwestern Bell, and Pacific Telesis. These companies are sometimes called the "Baby Bells," since they represent the breakup of the domestic-services portion of AT&T. In some areas, the RBOC is also the local telephone provider. (In Minneapolis, for example, US WEST is both the regional and local provider.) In a few areas, there is a regional provider that, for historical reasons, is not considered an RBOC. (Connecticut, for example, is served by SNET, which was never a part of AT&T.)

Local calls are those made within your local calling area. If your local provider is also an RBOC or other regional provider, you will be able to get long-distance service from that provider within a somewhat wider area.

To make most long-distance calls, you must have a long-distance carrier. There are many long-distance carriers, of which the largest are currently AT&T, MCI, and Sprint.

Some businesses have more than one long-distance carrier, usually as a cost-saving measure. Computerized programs can be installed in business phone systems to automatically dial each call out through the carrier that has the least-expensive rates for a given area code. However, since all the long-distance carriers offer volume discount rates, it is often more economical to rely on a single carrier.

For residential customers, long-distance and local charges appear on separate portions of the same phone bill. However, for business accounts, the long-distance bill is usually sent by itself directly from the long-distance carrier.

DOMESTIC LONG-DISTANCE CALLING METHODS

Domestic means primarily the United States, but domestic calling procedures also apply to Canada and most of the Caribbean islands. See Fig. 11.1, which shows time zones and area codes for most of North America.

For domestic long-distance calls, dialing direct is the easiest method. However, you may want to make a charge call if you are out of your office, or an operator-assisted call if you need special assistance.

Domestic direct dialing   If you are making a long-distance call within your area code, dial 1 + seven-digit number. If you are making a long-distance call outside your area code, dial 1 + area code + seven-digit number.

Domestic operator-assisted calls   You will need to use operator assistance if you wish to make a collect call, a person-to-person call, or a bill-to-third-number call. Within your area code, dial 0 + seven-digit number; outside your area code, dial 0 + area code + seven-digit number. The operator will come on the line and ask you what kind of assistance you need. If you simply want to reach your local operator without predialing a number, dial 0; if you wish to reach your long-distance operator, dial 00.

Domestic information   For information within your local calling area, dial 411. For calls within your area code that are not considered local, dial 1 + 411. For long-distance information, dial 1 + area code + 555-1212.

Fig. 11.1   Area Codes and Time Zones in North America

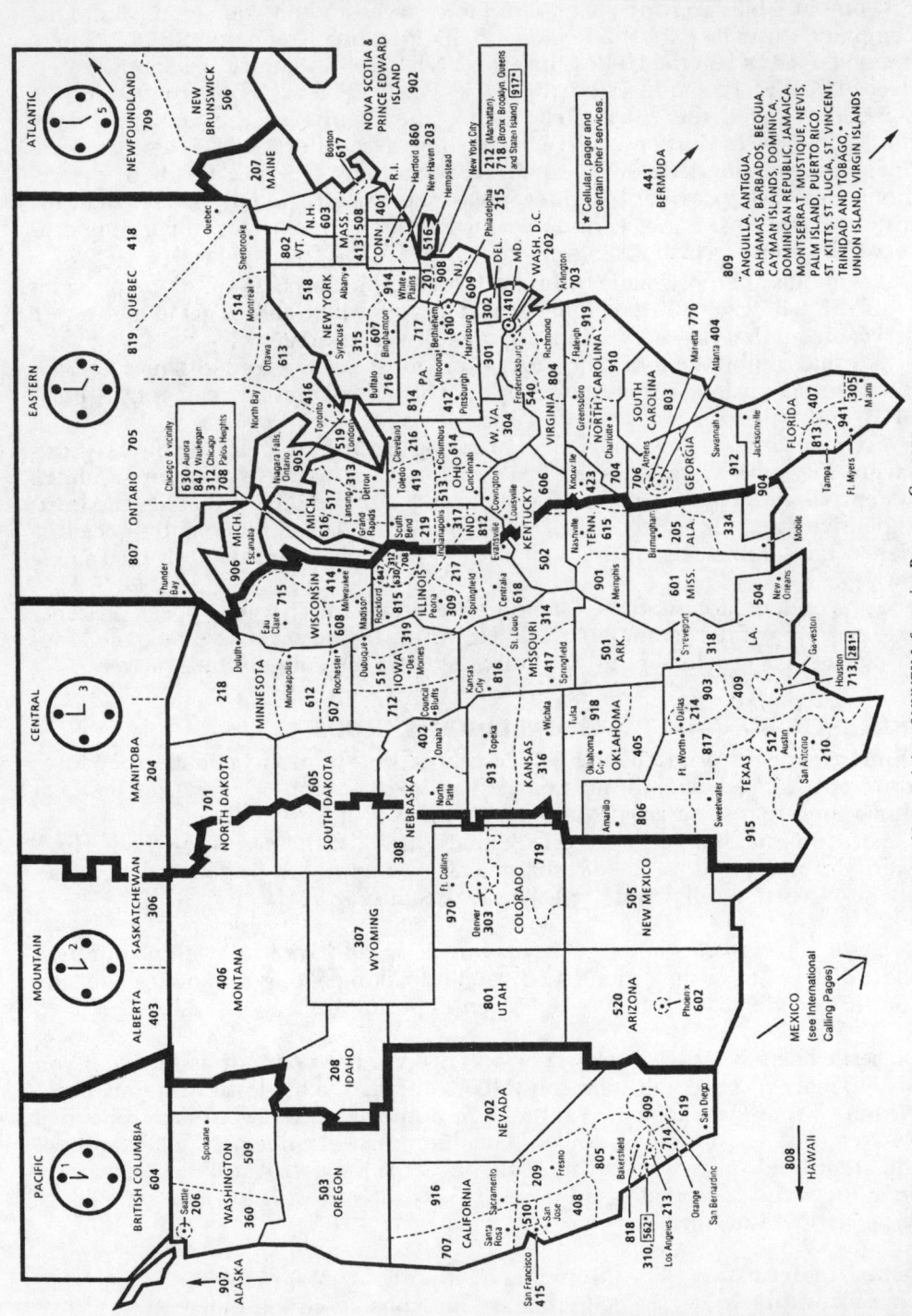

Domestic calling-card calls   Calling cards—that is, credit cards issued to customers by telephone companies for use in making calls from locations other than their home or office—will sometimes be useful. Dial 0 + area code (when needed) + seven-digit number, then wait for the computer tone and enter your calling-card number. For a long-distance call normally billed by your local provider, you will need to enter the calling-card number from that provider. For a long-distance call typically billed by your long-distance carrier, use the calling-card number of your long-distance carrier.

If the phone you are calling from does not use your long-distance carrier, you must first dial the five-digit code of your long-distance carrier, then immediately dial 0 + area code + seven-digit number. The five-digit codes of the major long-distance carriers are:

AT&T   10288
MCI   10222
Sprint 10333

INTERNATIONAL LONG-DISTANCE CALLING METHODS

As mentioned previously, the United States, Canada, Bermuda, Puerto Rico, and most of the Caribbean islands can be reached by domestic dialing. All other countries use international dialing methods. AT&T's annually published *International Telecommunications Guide* lists every country code, city code, and time zone. You can request a free copy by calling 800-874-4000. The international table on pages 435–443 of this book contains much of the same information.

It is becoming increasingly easy to dial international numbers directly. However, if you are unfamiliar with dialing to a particular number or to a particular country, you may wish to use operator assistance. Several less-developed countries are not able to accept direct-dialed calls, so you must always use an operator in those cases.

There can be up to four components in the dialing sequence of an international call, and you should be familiar with each of them.

1. **International Call Dial Prefix**   If you are dialing direct, you must begin by dialing 011.
2. **Country Code**   Every country has a country code that is two or three digits long. (The only exception is the United States, whose country code has only one digit.)
3. **City Code**   Most major cities in the world (except those within the United States and Canada) have city codes that are one to five digits long.
4. **Local Telephone Number**   The local telephone numbers of foreign countries vary in length, sometimes even within the same country.

You should first look up the country code and the city code, if any (see pages 435–443). With this information, you should be able to analyze the number you have been given and better understand how to dial it. Please note that if a 0 appears at the beginning of the phone number, this typically must be dialed only *within* the foreign country.

If you are experienced in dialing international numbers, you may feel comfortable making the call yourself; if not, dial the long-distance operator. Tell the operator the country and city you are dialing and the number as it was given to you. Before the operator places the call, make sure you understand—and write down—exactly what digits will be dialed, and which represent the country code, which represent the city code (if needed), and which represent the local telephone number, so that you will be able to place similar calls yourself the next time. Do not hesitate to ask questions.

When you make an international call, either direct-dialed or operator-assisted, you may have to wait for 30–45 seconds before the receiving phone begins to ring. The tone and spacing of rings varies from country to country; sometimes the ring may sound similar to our busy signal. If you are at all confused by what you hear, make an operator-assisted call and ask the operator to stay on the line and interpret the sound you are hearing.

International direct dialing   To dial an international call directly, dial 011 + country code + city code (if needed) + local number. For example, if you are calling Geneva, you will need the country code for Switzerland (41) and the city code for Geneva (22). You would then dial 011 + 41 + 22 + local number.

International operator-assisted calls   You will need operator assistance to make a collect call, a person-to-person call, or a bill-to-third-number call. Dial 01 + country code + city code (if needed) + local number, and the operator will come on the line. If you want the operator to dial the number for you, dial 00 for your long-distance operator.

International information   To reach an information or directory-assistance operator in a specific country, dial 00 to contact your long-distance operator. Tell the long-distance operator the country, the city, and the name of the party you want to reach. The operator will then contact an English-speaking operator in that country to get the information on your behalf. Make sure you are clear and specific when you give the operator instructions. Unless you are confident you have been given the right number, you should request that the operator place the call for you, so that, if you have been given the wrong number, you can more easily get credit for the call.

International calling-card calls   To place an international calling-card call, dial 01 + country code + city code (if needed) + local number. An operator will then come on the line and ask for your international calling-card number.

Receiving international calls   You may at some time need to give instructions on how to dial your own number to someone in another country. A person in Canada, Bermuda, Puerto Rico, and most of the Caribbean islands can call the United States by simply dialing 1 + area code + seven-digit number. From anywhere else, the person will need to dial the international dialing prefix + 1 + area code + seven-digit number. International dialing to the United States is very similar to domestic dialing, since 1 happens to be our country code and we use area codes instead of city codes.

SPECIAL BILLING NUMBERS

There are many special billing number services, ranging from WATS and 800 number services to the newer 900 services.

WATS services   Wide Area Telecommunications Service, usually known as WATS services, are outbound reduced-rate lines. WATS services can be limited to a given state, the entire United States, or particular countries. The term WATS was originally used by AT&T for specific lines that were billed at less-expensive rates. However, now WATS basically refers to a business-wide volume discount plan for long-distance savings.

800 numbers   Most 800 numbers are used to provide for toll-free calling by customers, prospective customers, and employees outside the office.

Inbound 800 numbers are numbers that are free to the caller; the business that owns the 800 number pays the bills. The 800 number can be a dedicated line (sometimes called an inbound WATS number) or an 800 number that is simply assigned to a regular number. An 800 number may be available only to local callers, to callers within the state, or to callers in several "bands" or areas within the United States, and 800 numbers are also available for international inbound calls.

900 numbers   Most 900 and 976 numbers are used to provide prerecorded messages, for which callers pay at rates often much higher than for regular phone calls. However, many companies also use 900 numbers staffed by operators as a way of charging for customer services. Since these numbers are so widely used for non-company-related personal purposes, most telephone companies offer subscriber companies the option of blocking employee access to 900 numbers.

TELEPHONE SERVICE FEATURES

The following is a list of some of the more common features available directly from your phone company. These features can be obtained as ancillary services to your regular phone subscription.

Call forwarding   This feature lets you program your phone to redirect incoming calls to another phone (and, when desired, to return them to the original phone).

Call waiting   With this feature, a short tone will let you know when someone is trying to call you while you are on the phone. You can quickly press down on the switch hook, putting your original conversation on hold, in order to talk to that person.

Conference calling   Conference or three-way calling is available as an option from your phone company. Even if you do not subscribe to this feature, most local or long-distance carriers can still arrange special conference calls. Consult your local phone book or your long-distance carrier on how to arrange a conference call.

Voice mail   In a voice mail system, calls to an employee's number are recorded if the employee cannot answer the phone. He or she can retrieve the messages from any telephone by dialing a given number and entering a personal identification code. Most larger companies now buy or lease voice mail systems. However, many phone companies offer simple voice mail systems to their customers. These may be preferable to answering machines, since there is less concern over power failures and broken message tapes, and messages can be taken if the caller is busy with another conversation.

TELEPHONE LINES

There are several types of telephone lines and trunks available for business use.

Telephone lines and trunks   Business lines are usually associated with individual telephones. Trunks—that is, channels used as common arteries for communications traffic between switchboards or other switching devices—are associated with PBX telephone systems (see page 382). The term *T-1 line* is often used for what is basically a trunk line.

Foreign exchange service Foreign exchange (FX) service provides you with a telephone number in a service area other than your office, effectively giving you unlimited calling for a flat rate into a specified town, area, or state other than your own. It is also available for international locations. If you call a specific locale frequently, this service may be more economical than toll calls. FX service can also be two-way, allowing incoming calls within a distant area to be answered in your office.

Tie-line service Full-time point-to-point service can be provided by leasing a tie line. Tie lines are used primarily to connect two or more telephone systems that are in constant communication, such as a home office and a plant, or a sales office and a distributor.

In addition to the features and services that have been discussed, a number of new, high-speed services are emerging. These include Integrated Services Digital Network (ISDN), which will allow for high-speed transmission of both data and voice over a standard telephone line. This will make possible expanded features for telephones and a vast increase in transmission capacity.

Telephone Equipment and Systems

There is a vast range of telephone equipment and systems to support today's businesses. As mentioned, it is sometimes hard to differentiate a piece of equipment from a system from a telephone-company service. Some equipment features must be supported by the phone company or the local phone system in order to operate.

You should consult the user manuals for your telephone equipment in order to learn how to use all of the various features. If a manual has been misplaced, you can obtain another from the manufacturer. Do not assume that you need an extensive technical background to understand telecommunications and other office equipment. By consulting user manuals and exercising common sense, you can learn enough about such equipment to be quite comfortable using it day to day.

Telephone systems such as the PBX support numerous features and functions. Take the time to meet the person who selected your company's telephone system and the person who maintains it in order to learn about all its capabilities. If there is no one knowledgeable within your organization, you can call the company that supplied the system and talk to one of their representatives.

TELEPHONE EQUIPMENT FEATURES

The following are brief descriptions of common types of telephone equipment and typical equipment features. You may use some of this equipment in your office, and you may deal with other employees who communicate using devices such as mobile or cellular phones and beepers.

Multi-button telephone The multi-button telephone may have six, 10, 20, or even 30 buttons with which to route calls to other phones in the office. Multi-button telephones are typically used in small business offices to place, answer, transfer, and screen calls.

Electronic telephone   This is a multi-button telephone that incorporates many extra features, such as push-button dialing, electronic tone ringing, and multiple-line pickups. One major advantage of electronic sets is that they can operate with a much smaller telephone wire than the multi-button phone.

Line-status indicator   This device, which is built into most multi-button and electronic telephones, shows which of the lines connected to the telephone are busy.

Automatic call distributor (ACD)   This device is used by mail-order firms, hotels, airlines, and other companies that deal extensively with call-in customers. A taped message informs the caller that he or she is in a queue and that the call will be answered by the next available operator.

Voice-response system   Voice-response systems are used in many customer-service businesses. The caller is usually given a taped message and a menu of choices from which to select to receive further information by pressing various buttons on the telephone. Typically, the caller is given the choice of staying on the line or pressing 0 for an operator if he or she wishes to speak to a live person. A touch-tone phone is usually required to participate in this system. (Most new rotary telephones have a touch-tone function that can be activated when needed.)

Answering machine   Small offices may use answering machines to answer calls during lunch or after hours. Voice mail, however, is becoming increasingly popular as an alternative to answering machines.

Voice mail system   Many companies have installed their own voice mail systems. Some systems are very simple; others offer a large number of features. Most voice mail systems will give the name of the person being called, often with a personal greeting, and then allow the caller to leave a message. Messages can usually be received by the employee from his or her office phone or by calling in from outside the office. Voice mail systems will usually take messages if the individual being called is busy with another call. Frequently they can redirect messages to others within the office. Some systems will even allow for one message to be broadcast to every voice "mailbox" within the office.

If your employer lets you receive calls for him or her directly, you may have the option of taking a message yourself or transferring the caller to the voice mail system to leave a message. You may also wish to leave messages in your employer's voice mailbox if you both find that it is a convenient way to communicate while either of you is away from the office. For example, if your employer is traveling in a different time zone, you could place a call to your employer's voice mailbox to make sure he or she gets an important message before or after work hours. Always identify yourself clearly and speak slowly and distinctly when leaving a message in a voice mail system (or an answering machine).

Speakerphone   A speakerphone is also referred to as a hands-free telephone, since it allows you to talk while leaving both your hands free for other activities. It also permits more than one person in the room to participate in the call. (Be cautious when speaking to someone who uses a speakerphone—there may be other people in the room.)

Prestored telephone numbers   Many phones allow you to prestore frequently dialed numbers, so that you can then push a specific button or a simple code to have the number automatically dialed for you.

Flash button Pushing a flash button is the equivalent of quickly pressing the switch hook. (The switch hook itself can be unreliable.) This feature is useful for such services as call waiting.

Beeper Many business people and professionals now carry beepers. The simplest beepers merely beep or flash a light to tell the individual carrying the beeper to call his or her office. The standard models, however, allow the caller to leave a telephone number, which is then displayed on the beeper. When you call a beeper number, you typically will only hear a short computer tone when the beeper service picks up your call. You should then press in your phone number (or the number you wish the beeper holder to call) and hang up. (You may want to include the area code if you think the beeper holder may be out of your immediate area.) An additional service permits the caller to leave not only a phone number but also a short message. An operator will take the message and it will be printed out on the beeper's display panel.

Cellular or mobile phone Cellular and mobile phones—that is, wireless phones that can be carried anywhere—are increasing in popularity. They are especially valuable to sales and repair people. Some cellular phones can be reached from anywhere in the contiguous United States, others only within a smaller geographic area. When you dial a cellular-phone number, you may receive a recorded message saying that the phone is not within the reach of the cellular base that transmits the calls; if so, you can only keep trying the number until the phone owner returns to the region. Many cellular phone owners also use voice mail so that they can pick up messages that arrived when they were out of range.

TELEPHONE SYSTEMS

A wide variety of telephone systems are offered today by many manufacturers. The range of products extends from small key telephone systems to multi-line, computer-controlled PBX systems for large corporations. Generally, telephone systems can be broken down into three categories: (1) key telephone systems, (2) hybrid telephone systems, and (3) PBX systems.

Key telephone systems These systems provice several line-status indicators. They are usually found in small offices that use multi-button, multi-line telephones with a private interoffice communications arrangement and signaling capability.

Hybrid telephone systems Hybrid systems are basically key systems with extra features similar to those found in PBX systems. For example, specially designed telephones may be used to place and answer calls and perform functions such as transferring and forwarding calls and making conference calls. A central answering switchboard is usually provided with hybrid systems.

PBX systems Private Branch Exchange, or PBX, systems are telephone exchanges serving an individual organization and having direct connections to a public telephone exchange. They are used in offices that require over a hundred telephones. PBX systems include a central console where an operator answers incoming calls. Direct dialing to a specific extension is also available. PBX systems are either analog or digital in design; analog systems are designed primarily for voice transmission, while digital systems also allow for high-speed data and facsimile transmission and teleconferencing services.

SPECIAL FEATURES OF TELEPHONE SYSTEMS

The wide variety of telephone systems on the market and the many special features they offer provide an opportunity for selecting a system that best suits your company's needs. Stored-program electronic switching and the use of computers and detailed message accounting techniques enable these systems to offer a wide range of features and options. Along with the standard inbound and outbound direct dialing, an office telephone system may incorporate any of the following special features:

Abbreviated (speed) dialing   This enables you to program your telephone to accept a short numeric code in place of dialing the full telephone number. Some systems allow systemwide speed dialing for all users.

Automatic call back   With this feature, the caller is informed whenever a certain office phone that was previously busy is now free. On first finding that the line is busy, the caller must dial a code before hanging up the phone; as soon as the called phone is no longer busy the caller's telephone rings, and when the caller picks up the telephone the called party's telephone will automatically ring.

Call detail reporting   This cost and management system automatically records information—the number called and the call's duration—for every call placed through the company's telephone system.

Call forwarding   This feature automatically reroutes incoming calls from one number to another, once you have dialed a forwarding code and the forwarding number.

Call pick-up   This enables you to answer an incoming call directed to another telephone.

Call transfer   With this feature you may transfer an incoming or outgoing call to another party without the assistance of an operator.

Camp on busy   This allows the calling party to be put on hold until the called party hangs up, and then have his or her call automatically placed through. A short tone on the called party's line may notify him or her that a call is waiting.

Centralized attendant service   This system permits PBX systems serving several locations to be answered at a single location.

Conference call   This option allows the telephone user to add a third party in the middle of a conversation without the assistance of an operator.

Least-cost routing   This feature automatically routes outgoing long-distance calls through the PBX to the least-expensive long-distance carrier or trunk group and steps the call up to the second-least-expensive route when the primary routes are busy.

Outgoing trunk queuing   With this queuing feature, a call dialed when all outgoing trunks are busy will automatically be put through as soon as a trunk is free.

Remote access to PBX system   This allows callers to dial a telephone number and authorization code from any telephone outside the PBX system and gain access to designated trunks within the PBX system for outgoing calls.

Traffic analysis This feature automatically gathers trunk loading statistics to assist in determining the number of facilities needed to handle the call load of a company or department.

Telegraphic Services

Telegraphic services are quickly being replaced by fax machines and overnight courier services. However, many of them still may be useful in specific situations. Telegraphic services include telegrams, cablegrams, Mailgrams, Priority Letters, and telex services. Telex services are still used by many international businesses when the telex itself can serve as a document or where phone systems are not modernized enough to handle fax transmissions reliably.

All of these telegraphic services are available through Western Union. If you do not have a telex machine, Western Union will send a telex for you. Many local companies also offer these services; they can be found in the Yellow Pages.

If your company uses telexes frequently, it may have a telex machine. If the company receives telexes only occasionally, you may want to set up your fax machine to receive telexes. The major long-distance companies have telex and electronic-mail services that allow for this capability.

You can also send telegrams, cablegrams, Mailgrams, and Priority Letters from a computer if you have telex and electronic-mail service from a major service provider.

Telegrams, cablegrams, Mailgrams, and Priority Letters Each of these four types of messages can be sent by either going directly to your local Western Union office or phoning in your message.

Telegrams, more commonly used in the past, are still used to some extent today. Telegrams can be sent almost anywhere in the continental United States within a few hours.

Cablegrams Cablegrams are international telegrams, which can be sent to almost every country in the world. If the company you are sending to has a registered cable code, use that code as the cablegram address.

Mailgrams The Mailgram was developed jointly by Western Union and the U.S. Postal Service. A Mailgram can be sent anywhere in the United States, Puerto Rico, Guam, the U.S. Virgin Islands, or Canada. Mailgrams are usually delivered in the next business day's mail. A business reply envelope can be included in a Mailgram to ensure a quick response.

Priority Letters A Priority Letter is a lower-cost alternative to a Mailgram. It can be sent anywhere in the continental United States within two days. There are also services that can deliver hundreds or thousands of Mailgrams or Priority Letters.

Telex There are two kinds of telex services, domestic and international. Domestic telexes, those sent only within the United States, are used very rarely; most telex transmissions today are international.

Most telex numbers include an *answerback,* a code (usually an alphanumeric sequence that repeats the telex number and adds an abbreviation of the country or the company name) that the receiving system sends back when it accepts the telex message. Thus, if you include an answerback as part of the telex address, you can be sure when you have reached the right telex number.

All international telex calls require a country code, which precedes the telex number. These serve the same purpose as telephone country codes but are not identical to them. A list of telex country codes should be available from your telex service company.

If you do not know the telex number of a company you want to reach, call your telex service company.

An international telex or cablegram message may contain uppercase letters, numbers, and the following punctuation only: period, colon, comma, apostrophe or single quotation mark, hyphen, parentheses, and slash.

The Electronic Office

Today's office is steadily acquiring new technologies for high-speed communications. Most offices now have facsimile (fax) machines, and many are using different forms of electronic mail. Local area networks (LANs) are linking office computers, allowing users to share software and data files within an office. Wide area networks (WANs) and other public and private data networks are linking companies over large distances. The electronic office can save time and increase productivity, but it also requires that you keep up with rapidly changing technology.

FACSIMILE (FAX) MACHINES

Facsimile, or fax, machines are almost as common in businesses today as telephones. For certain kinds of material, they have replaced overnight couriers, first-class mail, local messengers, and even the telephone as the means of choice for communicating rapidly.

Fax machines work by scanning your document and creating a digitized "bit map" of the information. That information is then sent over telephone lines, and the receiving fax machine prints a copy of the image by reading the digitized map.

When a fax machine calls up another fax machine, they go through a process called "training" or "handshaking." The sending machine also typically prints out a company identification (if it has been programmed into the machine), along with the time, date, and page number, and these appear as headers on each page.

Here are several suggestions for preparing and sending documents by fax:

1. Prepare a cover sheet. It should include the name of the recipient and the number of pages being sent. (The cover sheet itself will usually be included in the number of pages.) If the recipient is in a large organization, it is useful to include his or her department and personal phone number. You should also include your company's fax number and the sender's name and phone number, so that the recipient can call if the fax is not received clearly or pages are missing. If your company does not have a cover sheet form for sending faxes, it would be very useful to create one. See the sample cover sheet in Fig. 11.2.

Fig. 11.2   Fax Cover Sheet

Facsimile Transmission

Merriam Webster Inc.

47 Federal Street   Fax: 413-731-5979
P.O. Box 281   Telephone: 413-734-3134
Springfield, MA 01102   Telex: 981608 (MWEBSTER)

Company: FAX #:

Attention:

From:

Number of pages (including this page):   Date:

Please let us know if all pages are NOT received

Message:

2. Number the pages you are sending. This will make it easier for the recipient to make sure he or she has received all of the pages. Also, since some fax machines just drop received pages on a table or floor, numbering the pages will help the recipient put the received document in the correct order.

3. If you are concerned about the clarity of the received document—especially if there is small type, pictures, or graphics—you may want to test the transmittal quality by using the machine's copy function before you send your document. Most fax machines allow you to produce a copy of your document that will match the quality of the image that will arrive at the receiving fax machine. If the document you are sending is not clear, you may want to send it in "Fine" mode, available on most fax machines. Documents scanned in finer detail take two to three times longer to transmit.

4. Do not use colored paper or other color on a document without first testing it with the copy function. Even transparent highlighters can block out type.

5. Do not use correction tape or correction fluid, since this may damage your fax machine. If either has been used on the original, photocopy it and use the copy in the fax machine.

6. Make sure you have removed any staples or paper clips before sending your document.

7. If your document is of an irregular size, make a photocopy of it to insert in the machine. The receiving fax machine should, however, be able to accommodate both letter- and legal-size pages.

8. If you have to send more than three to five pages, stay at the fax machine until all the pages are sent. Stack the pages loosely in the machine. You may

carefully add several pages to your stack after the first few pages have been sent; however, never add more pages when the last page is in process. If you are sending a particularly long fax (more than 10–12 pages), you may want to break up the document into more than one transmission. If so, clearly explain what you are doing on the first cover sheet, and include subsequent cover sheets that repeat the explanation.

When you receive a fax, you should check to see that you have received all the pages and that they are readable. If there are pages missing or if some of the document is unreadable, the sender should be notified immediately. You can either place the call yourself or ask the recipient in your organization whether he or she wants to call. Always make sure received faxes are delivered quickly; faxes should be handled with the same urgency as telephone messages.

Faxes printed on thermal paper fade in a few months and become difficult, if not impossible, to read. Thus, if a received fax on thermal paper needs to be filed, you should copy it first. (If your fax machine prints on ordinary paper, you will not need to copy received faxes.)

Many fax machines can prestore commonly used fax numbers, and many will also automatically redial a number if it is busy. (Even when using these features, however, always check the number displayed.)

When sending an international fax, remember that the country you are dialing is probably in a different time zone. Many companies turn off their fax machines at night; thus, if you are having trouble reaching an international fax number, try dialing it during the normal business hours of that country.

You may be able to send faxes from a computer. Some companies have installed "fax boards" in their computers, so that once a document is typed it can be sent directly from the computer.

If you frequently need to send the same fax to many locations, you will want to use the "fax broadcast" feature available on many fax machines.

If you work for an employer who travels frequently, remember that most hotels have a fax machine with which guests can send and receive faxes. You can find out if a hotel offers this service, and the fax phone number, by calling the hotel directly. If you have had trouble reaching your employer by phone, you can even send your own messages to the hotel fax machine.

If you do not have a fax machine, you can use a fax service company. Look in the Yellow Pages under "Facsimile Transmission Service." Most will allow you to both send and receive faxes at their locations. They will typically call you when a fax has arrived for you, and you must then go and pick it up. Make sure that anyone who sends you a fax clearly indicates your name, company, and phone number on the fax.

When the information being sent is confidential, you will need to use your judgment about using a fax machine for delivery, since many fax machines are shared. If you are concerned, you should ask your employer. An alternative means of delivery, such as overnight courier, may be better. One possible method is to ask the recipient to stand by the receiving fax machine as you are sending the document to be sure that it is not seen by others. Some companies have "executive" fax machines or other fax machines that are specially monitored.

ELECTRONIC MAIL

Electronic mail (E-mail) provides a means of data communications between computers. Electronic mail can be on private systems or public networks, or be specialized for a particular function such as Electronic Data Interchange (EDI).

Some of the key characteristics of the various types of electronic-mail systems are explained in the following pages.

Private electronic-mail systems   Many larger companies have electronic-mail systems as part of their computer systems. Some electronic-mail systems are on LANs, while others are on minicomputer or mainframe computer systems.

Electronic-mail systems let users send messages created on their computers to one or more electronic "mailboxes" belonging to other individuals in the company that have access to the mail system. A system administrator is usually responsible for registering system users and for maintaining the system, and he or she should be able to teach new users how to use the system and provide a directory of companywide mailbox addresses.

If you are an electronic-mail user, you will usually have a sign-on identification code as well as a mailbox address. Often the mailbox address will be your name or a code similar to your name. You should check your mailbox periodically to see if you have received an electronic message. When sending a message for your employer, you may need to use his or her sign-on identification. If you use your own sign-on identification to send a message for your employer, be very clear in the message about who it is from, since many mail systems will automatically attach the name of the person whose sign-on identification is being used to the message itself. If someone has asked you to read his or her mailbox, you must sign on as that individual. Make sure you transfer or save the mailbox messages to a computer file or printer.

Many private electronic-mail systems can only be used at one location. However, in large companies the electronic mail systems can usually be networked over a variety of communications avenues so that employees in different parts of the country or the world can communicate with each other. Some private electronic-mail systems are also linked into public electronic-mail systems so that users can have access to individuals outside of their company.

Public electronic-mail systems   There are several major providers of electronic-mail systems in the United States, including AT&T, MCI, Sprint, and CompuServe. These systems provide electronic mail through your office computer. If you are connected through a minicomputer or a mainframe computer to one of these public systems, the technical division within your company will have made all the connections for you.

You will need communications software and a modem to equip a personal computer to use a public electronic-mail system. You can obtain such communications software from your electronic-mail provider or use one of several available brands. A modem is needed to enable your computer to dial up the electronic-mail system so that it can connect with the host computer.

Most public electronic-mail systems can send not only electronic messages but also telexes, messages to fax machines, and computer letters that are delivered through the postal service. Through AT&T you may also send telegrams, cablegrams, Mailgrams, and Priority Letters.

When you send a message through public electronic-mail service, you should be able to obtain notification that the message was delivered. The service should also provide you with a daily summary report of sent messages.

You should not assume that you can send a regular word-processing file through an electronic-mail system, since it could only be read by someone with the same word-processing program. Instead, you must send what are known as *ASCII* ("as-key") or *text files*. You create an ASCII or text file by taking the document you have created in your word-processing program and following the procedures found in your word-processing manual for saving documents as ASCII or text files. (This has the added advantage of eliminating style and formatting from the file.)

However, some electronic-mail systems will let you send word-processing or other computer files such as spreadsheets. This type of service is called File Transfer. File Transfer should only be used when the recipient of the file has the same kind of application program. You would not use this method for sending regular messages, but only for sending a document that another individual needed to work on. This process is the equivalent of giving a file on a disk to another individual to work on.

When you receive messages in a mailbox, you can save them in a computer file or by printing them out. If you want to edit the file in your word-processing program, you will have to consult your word-processing manual on how to edit an ASCII or text file.

There are many private and public electronic-mail systems available, each of which was designed independently. The result is that it may be difficult for these systems to "talk" to each other. During the 1980s, an international committee devised a set of rules to enable electronic-mail systems to interconnect with each other by using the same technical rules or "protocols." As more private and public electronic-mail systems start using these interfaces, electronic mail will become more far-reaching.

The same international committee realized that if a truly universal electronic-mail network was to become a reality, electronic-mail users would need to know who has electronic mailboxes and what their addresses are. Accordingly, it devised a set of rules for creating an automated directory of all electronic-mail addresses.

Unfortunately, a universal directory has not actually been developed yet. For the most part, you still must get mailbox addresses directly from the individuals with whom you want to communicate. Some public electronic-mail users are starting to put their mailbox addresses on their business cards. If your public electronic-mail service does not provide an on-line directory to its subscribers, you may be able to call the service for directory information.

EDI Electronic Data Interchange, or EDI, is a specialized form of electronic mail, most commonly used for orders, order acknowledgments, invoices, and payments. EDI is based on a set of rules created by national and international committees to allow groups doing business together to automate the ordering process.

Without EDI, most manufacturing or distribution and retail companies generate a flow of paperwork that gets input into different computers. There is paperwork involved in creating an order, shipping an order, creating an invoice, and acknowledging payment, and much of the information on these forms—the invoice number, the item being ordered, the recipient of the order, and so on—is repeated. EDI systems allow this information to be input directly into a local computer and then sent to other computers for processing. Since common information does not have to be input again, both time and money are saved. The EDI process relies on special software to handle the EDI electronic forms and a specialized communications carrier to transmit the data over a network.

DATA NETWORKS
There are a variety of public and private networks designed to support the transmission of data. The following are some of the more common data networks used by businesses.

Packet-switching networks Telephone networks are primarily designed for voice transmission, although they are able to carry data as well. Packet-switching, or X.25, networks were designed for data transmission only. These networks divide data into small packets, each consisting of a header (stating the node and connection point to which the packet is to be delviered), the data itself, an error-detection mechanism, and an end-of-packet identifier. Computers connected to packet networks have both a network identifier and a network address.

Wide area networks Wide area networks, or WANs, are set up privately, usually to provide high-speed data transmission within a company that has several locations while bypassing the telephone networks. Most of these networks are based on satellite communications. Telephone companies, however, are beginning to offer switched data channels at very high speeds, using a technology called *wideband* or *broadband switching*.

Local area networks (LANs) LANs, as mentioned earlier, are internal networks that connect personal computers within a company location, usually by means of cables. The LAN systems are installed on centralized personal computers called *servers*. They permit the personal computers that are connected to share a range of resources, including software, high-speed laser printers, high-speed hard disks for storage, and communications links via shared modems to other LANs or mainframe computers. In this way, high-quality and often costly resources can be used by many employees within a company.

Many software companies provide LAN versions of their software; a company can thus buy a single copy for their LAN system, and all users can have access to it. In some cases, users can work on the same database file at the same time, thereby efficiently dividing the work load of updating a large database file. With a LAN, all users within a company can have the advantages of high-quality printers. If more than one user wants to print at the same time, the LAN will create a print queue, whereby the next document waiting in line will automatically start printing when the first is finished. Electronic mail, for easy user-to-user message sending, is also a frequent feature on LANs.

Most organizations with LANs have an LAN administrator, who handles the technical problems involved in installing and operating the system and is also usually responsible for connecting computers to the LAN and registering LAN users.

Simpler systems—sometimes called *peer-to-peer networks*—can be put together on a very small scale to link two, three, or four individuals, and printer-sharing devices are widely used. An employee with an amateur talent for computers can often organize such simple networks.

STANDARD TIME IN 102 PLACES THROUGHOUT THE WORLD WHEN IT IS 12:00 NOON AT NEW YORK

CITY	TIME	CITY	TIME
Adelaide, Australia	2:30 A.M. next day	London, England	5:00 P.M.
Alexandria, Egypt	7:00 P.M.	Los Angeles, California	9:00 A.M.
[1]Amsterdam, Netherlands	6:00 P.M.	[1]Madrid, Spain	6:00 P.M.
Anchorage, Alaska	8:00 A.M.	Manila, Philippines	1:00 A.M. next day
Asunción, Paraguay	1:00 P.M.	Mecca, Saudi Arabia	8:00 P.M.
Athens, Greece	7:00 P.M.	Melbourne, Australia	3:00 A.M. next day
Auckland, New Zealand	5:00 A.M. next day	Mexico City, Mexico	11:00 A.M.
Baghdad, Iraq	8:00 P.M.	Miami, Florida	12:00 NOON
Bangkok, Thailand	12:00 MIDNIGHT	Montevideo, Uruguay	2:00 P.M.
Beijing, China	1:00 A.M. next day	Montreal, Quebec	12:00 NOON
Belgrade, Yugoslavia	6:00 P.M.	[1]Moscow, Russia	8:00 P.M.
Berlin, Germany	6:00 P.M.	Nairobi, Kenya	8:00 P.M.
Bogotá, Colombia	12:00 NOON	New Delhi, India	10:30 P.M.
Bombay, India	10:30 P.M.	Nome, Alaska	8:00 A.M.
Boston, Massachusetts	12:00 NOON	Oslo, Norway	6:00 P.M.
[1]Brussels, Belgium	6:00 P.M.	Ottawa, Ontario	12:00 NOON
Bucharest, Romania	7:00 P.M.	Panama City, Panama	12:00 NOON
Budapest, Hungary	6:00 P.M.	[1]Paris, France	6:00 P.M.
[1]Buenos Aires, Argentina	2:00 P.M.	Perth, Australia	1:00 A.M. next day
Cairo, Egypt	7:00 P.M.	Philadelphia, Pennsylvania	12:00 NOON
Calcutta, India	10:30 P.M.	Prague, Czech Republic	6:00 P.M.
Cape Town, Republic of So. Africa	7:00 P.M.	Quito, Ecuador	12:00 NOON
		Regina, Saskatchewan	11:00 A.M.
Caracas, Venezuela	1:00 P.M.	Reykjavik, Iceland	4:00 P.M.
[1]Casablanca, Morocco	6:00 P.M.	Rio de Janeiro, Brazil	2:00 P.M.
Chicago, Illinois	11:00 A.M.	Rome, Italy	6:00 P.M.
Colombo, Sri Lanka	10:30 P.M.	Saint John's,	1:30 P.M.
Copenhagen, Denmark	6:00 P.M.	Newfoundland	
Denver, Colorado	10:00 A.M.	Saint Louis, Missouri	11:00 A.M.
Detroit, Michigan	12:00 NOON	Saint Petersburg, Russia	8:00 P.M.
Dublin, Ireland	5:00 P.M.	San Francisco, California	9:00 A.M.
Edmonton, Alberta	10:00 A.M.	San Juan, Puerto Rico	1:00 P.M.
Geneva, Switzerland	6:00 P.M.	Santiago, Chile	1:00 P.M.
Glasgow, Scotland	5:00 P.M.	São Paulo, Brazil	2:00 P.M.
Halifax, Nova Scotia	1:00 P.M.	Seattle, Washington	9:00 A.M.
Havana, Cuba	12:00 NOON	Seoul, South Korea	2:00 A.M. next day
Helsinki, Finland	7:00 P.M.	Shanghai, China	1:00 A.M. next day
Ho Chi Minh City, Vietnam	12:00 MIDNIGHT	Singapore	1:00 A.M. next day
		Sofia, Bulgaria	7:00 P.M.
Hong Kong	1:00 A.M. next day	Stockholm, Sweden	6:00 P.M.
Honolulu, Hawaii	7:00 A.M.	Sydney, Australia	3:00 A.M. next day
Houston, Texas	11:00 A.M.	Tehran, Iran	8:30 P.M.
Istanbul, Turkey	7:00 P.M.	Tokyo, Japan	2:00 A.M. next day
Jakarta, Indonesia	12:00 MIDNIGHT	Toronto, Ontario	12:00 NOON
Jerusalem, Israel	7:00 P.M.	Vancouver, British Columbia	9:00 A.M.
Johannesburg, Republic of So. Africa	7:00 P.M.		
		Vienna, Austria	6:00 P.M.
Juneau, Alaska	8:00 A.M.	[1]Vladivostok, Russia	3:00 A.M. next day
Karachi, Pakistan	10:00 P.M.	Warsaw, Poland	6:00 P.M.
Kiev, Ukraine	7:00 P.M.	Washington, D.C.	12:00 NOON
Kuala Lumpur, Malaysia	1:00 A.M. next day	Wellington, New Zealand	5:00 A.M. next day
Lagos, Nigeria	6:00 P.M.	Winnipeg, Manitoba	11:00 A.M.
La Paz, Bolivia	1:00 P.M.	Yangon, Myanmar	11:30 P.M.
Lima, Peru	12:00 NOON		

[1]Time is one hour in advance of the standard meridian.

How to Get Phone Calls and Faxes Through

Here is a real example of a series of phone numbers from the "Italy" section of a directory published by a large, professional, well-funded, multinational organization in the United States:

049/669121
089-871.578
80 5216643
(0923) 869148
055. 217461
(091) 6371830
(396) 6879568
(0344) 40456
(041) 5260130-5261457

Someone uncritical has copied these numbers from information received directly or indirectly from Italy. Apart from failing to standardize their punctuation, the editor has not noticed that two of the contributing Italians have tried to be "helpful": one has taken the zero off the beginning of the number, and the other has changed 06 to 396 to include the country code. This is typical of what happens whenever name and address information has passed through the hands of people who do not understand it.

The Structure of Domestic Numbers

> **Long-Distance Access Code + City Code + Local Number**

MOST COUNTRIES OUTSIDE NORTH AMERICA

In most places outside the North American (Bell) system, each city, with its surrounding area, has a prefix. For consistency, it is always called a *city code* in this book. Inside one city area, the caller just dials the local number, which is usually from four to eight digits long. In some places, the local number does not have a fixed length within one city area. There may very well be both five-digit and six-digit numbers even for lines going into the same office.

To dial from one city area to another within the same country, the caller dials a *long-distance access code*—usually a single 0 (zero), but not always—then the city code for the distant city, and then the local number of the distant phone. In the terminology of this book, the long-distance access code and the city code are two different parts of the number. However, national terminology often has one name for the whole prefix; for example, 071 is often called locally the "dialing code" for central London. City codes are commonly one, two, or three digits long (after the 0 or other long-distance access code), but they can be longer. The following table provides some examples of domestic long-distance dialing.

City	Long-Distance Access Code	City Code	Local Number
Tokyo, Japan	0	3	54217698
Brussels, Belgium	0	2	6490141
Barcelona, Spain	9	3	6362880
Helsinki, Finland	9	0	647920
Hamburg, Germany	0	40	229873
Salzburg, Austria	0	662	975015
Gouda, Netherlands	0	1820	972810

In a few countries, the number for a long-distance call is always the same length. For example, a complete Spanish domestic number is always nine digits long; if the city code is longer, the local number is shorter in order to compensate.

When more numbers are needed in a growing city, most countries will lengthen the local number by adding a one-digit prefix.

There is no standard practice at all for directory information or other services. One country's directory-information service cannot usually be dialed direct from another country.

NATIONAL NUMBERS

Led by France, there is a trend away from city codes and toward national numbering systems, in which the same fixed-length number is used for both local and long-distance calls. Denmark, New Zealand, and Norway have changed to an eight-digit national dialing system, and Israel and undoubtedly other countries intend to change.

NORTH AMERICA

The United States and Canada, along with a number of Caribbean and Pacific islands, use a slightly different system. Local numbers are always seven digits long. The long-distance access code is 1, not 0. It is followed by an *area code*, which is always three digits long. Currently, the second digit of an area code is always 0 or 1. An area code covers a state or province or part of one; area codes never cross state or province boundaries. When more numbers are needed in an area, the phone companies introduce a new area code. For example, in 1991 San Francisco's 415 area-code zone split into two and the city's surrounding areas took the new area code 510. From 1996, area-code splits will not always be strictly geographical. An "overlay" area code can now be allocated to a major city, which will mean that close neighbors, or even a single office, may have phone numbers with different area codes.

SPECIAL PREFIXES

Many countries are introducing prefixes for special purposes, such as business information services and mobile phones. The prefixes sometimes (not in every country) look like city codes but are not geographic in nature. There is no consistency at all between countries.

Until recently, toll-free information services were accessible only within a given country, but they are now starting to open up to international calls, providing that the business offering the service agrees to pay the international call charges. Selected U.S. 800 (toll-free) and 900 (chargeable information) numbers may now be accessed from overseas.

IN-HOUSE DIRECT-DIAL LINES

When a subscriber has multiple lines, an incoming call should be able to "roll over" from one line to another until it finds a free line. This is usually a function of the equipment the subscribers have installed on their own premises. You cannot count on automatic rollovers when calling smaller offices in countries with less-developed telecommunications systems. For example, in some places it may be technically possible to roll calls over only to consecutive numbers.

Some countries allocate a block of numbers to a large office so that all the direct-dial numbers look similar. If all direct-dial numbers begin 264-7———, you can guess that the main switchboard operator is 264-7000. Only in Austria, Finland, Germany, and Italy is there sometimes a systematic way of identifying the operator.

The Structure of International Numbers

> ### IAC + Country Code + City/Area Code + Local Number

The *international access code (IAC)* is a number sequence that warns your national phone system that you are about to dial another country. The system therefore interprets the next few digits as a country code rather than as a city code or a local exchange. The most widely used IAC is 00.

The *country code* is a one-, two-, or three-digit number that uniquely identifies the called country, regardless of where the caller is. From each nation, callers dial their own IAC followed by the unique country code. Thus, since France's country code is always 33, the Germans dial 0033 for France and the Irish dial 1633. After the country code, the caller dials the city code *without* the long-distance access code. "Drop the zero" is a good rule of thumb, but it is not universally true.

The country code of the North American phone system is 1, which is convenient because it makes North American numbers look the same domestically and internationally. An American company will often quote its phone number as, for example, 1-713-222-3131, because that is exactly how you would dial it from out-of-state. From overseas, you would dial your IAC and then that same number. The 1 is thus interpreted as the long-distance access code if you dial in from out-of-state, and as the country code if you dial in from overseas.

All the countries in this book can be dialed from all the other countries, but by no means every country in the world can be dialed *direct* from every other country. When we call Myanmar (Burma) from Houston, we hear an AT&T operations center in Pittsburgh talking to operators in Singapore, whose equipment plays music from *Dr. Zhivago* to soothe us while the operators try to reach Myanmar.

THE + FORMAT

A very sensible convention that is being adopted by businesses all over the world is called in this book the +*(Plus) Format*. By writing a plus sign (+) at the beginning of a number, you announce that you are starting with your country code and are giving the complete international number—except, of course, for the IAC, which will be different for each caller's country. The following four examples illustrate differences between domestic and international dialing.

City	Domestic	International
Tokyo, Japan	(03)5421-7698	+81-3-5421-7698
Houston, Texas	(713) 522-0450	+1-713-522-0450
Helsinki, Finland	(90) 869-0898	+358-0-869-0898
Monterrey, Mexico	(9183) 16 89 01	+52-83-16-89-01

I strongly advocate the use of the + Format, which tells foreigners clearly what they are supposed to dial and removes a whole class of possible misunderstandings.

Signals (Tones)

With a little practice, you can estimate how far your call has progressed. After you finish dialing, there will be complete silence for a few seconds while your local phone system waits to see if you dial any more digits. It probably does not know at this stage how many digits you should dial. (Some equipment lets you press # to show that the number is complete.) Then you will hear a click and a change of sound when it opens an international line for you. There will be a second or two before the foreign phone system reacts, which you may hear as an increase in background noise. In some places, you will hear foreign equipment redialing or connecting the number. If the foreign number does not start to ring within about 15 seconds, something has gone wrong. It is important to pay attention to the normal sequence of sounds, because it will help you to decide what to do when something does go wrong.

There are four basic signals you will hear from most national phone systems. People often have difficulty distinguishing unfamiliar signals from other countries, and do not know whether to wait or hang up. Unfortunately, a certain amount of misinformation is circulated by seemingly authoritative sources. It is best not to completely trust anything one country says about other countries' signals.

A *busy signal* (called an "engaged tone" in British English) tells you the distant phone is in use or unplugged or otherwise unavailable for reasons which are not the phone system's fault. *Almost all busy signals in the world are subsecond beeps, evenly spaced*. The pitch and the speed both vary, but not enough to be confusing. A half-second beep followed by a half-second silence is a common pattern. If the beep is as long as the pause, you are probably not listening to a ringing signal. Exceptions do exist, but are rare; the principal variation among the countries in this book is in Denmark.

There are three *ringing signals* in the world, with minor variations and exceptions. What they have in common is that *the pause between rings is noticeably longer than the ring*. In Europe, the ring is a pure tone lasting about one second, followed by a silence of three or four seconds. In North America and many Asian countries, the ring is a *brrrrr* sound formed by mixing two frequencies; it is meant to imitate a muffled bell. The third system is the British one: each ring is a mixed-frequency *brrrrr* split by a brief pause, and a long pause occurs between complete rings ("brrr-brrr, pause, brrr-brrr").

A *congestion signal* means the phone companies have not been able to reach the line you are dialing, because of equipment overloads or some other reason. Not every country has a distinctive congestion signal. Some prefer to use recorded messages, and some use their busy signal. If a busy signal begins after a delay, it probably means congestion. An extended period of background hiss is also a de facto sign of congestion. A true congestion signal, when one exists, is usually noticeably faster than the country's busy signal.

A *number-unobtainable signal* means that the number you have dialed does not exist or is disconnected. Again, some countries use recorded messages. There is no internationally standardized signal. If you hear a continuous tone or if the tones are much longer than the pauses, you are probably listening to a number-unobtainable signal.

In the individual country chapters I include warnings about unusual signals that could be confusing for foreigners. However, you may come across obsolete or nonstandard equipment that is not described here, particularly when calling rural areas.

One piece of good news is that Group III fax machines sound the same everywhere in the world.

Troubleshooting

Phones are so easy to use that people tend to panic when an international call does not go through immediately. When something goes wrong, ask yourself the classic troubleshooting questions: What was different between this call and all the international calls I have made before? Is my information reliable? Which of the possible explanations can we eliminate?

There are two ways to approach the problem. First, consider the symptoms:

Symptom	Solution
No outside line.	Read "Office Problems" section below.
A recording in your own country, refusing the call.	The IAC, country code, or city code is not correct. Read "Impossible Numbers" section.
A recording in a foreign language that you cannot understand.	Read "Foreign Recordings" section.
A busy signal before you have finished dialing.	Read "Office Problems" and "Impossible Numbers" sections.
A busy signal very quickly after you finish dialing.	Retry a few times over five minutes, then read "Impossible Numbers" section.

Symptom	Solution
A busy signal after a delay.	Retry a few times over five minutes, then read "Failure to Get Through" section.
A foreign signal that you do not understand.	Read "Signals" section above. Retry twice, then place operator-assisted call.
Silence or "white noise."	Retry a few times over five minutes, then read "Impossible Numbers" section.
A congestion signal, your own or the foreign country's.	Keep retrying. Try a different long-distance carrier if you are in a country that offers you a choice.
A continuous or near-continuous tone (or other number-unobtainable signal).	Retry once. Read "Verifying Numbers" section.
A recording after the foreign number has rung.	Read "Foreign Recordings" section.
A human being answering when you expected a fax machine.	Ask clearly for the fax. Read Chapter 5 and "Verifying Numbers" section.
An unexpected person answering in a language you don't understand.	Read Chapter 5 and "Impossible Numbers" and "Verifying Numbers" sections.
A ring that is not answered.	Retry once. Read "Foreign Holidays," "Foreign Business Hours," "Time Differentials," "Verifying Numbers," and "Failure to Get Through" sections.
A person in your own country answering.	Read "Impossible Numbers" section.
A poor-quality line (noise or echo).	Hang up and redial as soon as possible, particularly if you have a long fax, unless you have had a lot of difficulty getting through at all.

Second, examine what mistakes you could be making:

Mistake	Result
Your extension is not authorized for international calls.	You will get an immediate busy signal.
Your call-accounting code is not good.	You will get an immediate busy signal.
You did not dial what you meant to dial.	Anything could happen. Retry all failed calls once, very carefully.
You are dialing too fast (in places with older equipment).	You will get a long silence.
The number you are dialing is too short.	You will get a recording or a busy signal, possibly from your own country's phone system.
The number you are dialing is too long.	The excess digits will be ignored, so the call will probably go through to a wrong number.
The number you are dialing is legitimate, but not the one you want.	There will be no answer, or a stranger will answer.
The foreign company has relocated or changed its number.	You may get a foreign recording, a continuous tone, no answer, or a stranger.

Mistake	Result
Circuits are busy in the foreign country.	You will get a foreign recording or a foreign busy or congestion signal.
They have forwarded their calls to someone else.	An unexpected person will answer.
You are calling outside of office hours.	No answer.
You are calling on a national holiday.	No answer.
You are misunderstanding a foreign ringing signal.	Have patience.

OFFICE PROBLEMS

Consider the possibility that your own office phone system might be the culprit. Is this the first time you have ever dialed an international call from this extension? Has anybody been reconfiguring the phone system in your office? Do you need any special authorization or call-accounting code to make international calls from this extension? If the answer to any of these questions might be yes, try the call on an executive's phone or on a fax machine with a direct outside line.

IMPOSSIBLE NUMBERS

Consider first where you got the phone number from. If the number is from your own address file and you have dialed it many times before, then it is highly reliable. If it has come out of a five-year-old trade directory, it is highly suspect.

The two commonest occurrences of misplaced trust are:

- *You are trusting a phone number that has not come to you directly from its own country.* When such information passes through the hands of nonnatives, mistakes tend to be made. A trade directory that covers multiple countries is unreliable, as is a list of foreign subsidiaries or dealers of a multinational company.

- *You are trusting foreigners to tell you how to call in to them from other countries.* They never do that themselves, so they do not really know whether they are correct or not. However, anyone who gives you a number in the + Format is more likely to be correct. Its use is an encouraging sign that they understand what they are doing.

If the symptoms indicate that you have a number which cannot exist, as opposed to one that is simply disconnected, here are the most likely causes of the problem:

- *You forgot to dial your international access code.* From the United States, 16127359159 is in Minnesota but 01-16127359159 is in Sydney, Australia.

- *You are dialing the wrong country.* Ridiculous? It happens all the time! Which do you want—Northern Ireland or the Republic of Ireland? North Korea or South Korea? the Republic of China or the People's Republic of China? and an American specialty: Austria or Australia?

- *You could be dialing the wrong country code*. It can't happen? You can't look a number up wrong in the phone book? Your boss would never interrupt you between looking up the code and dialing it? The easiest way to get a wrong code is to ask somebody who doesn't want to admit ignorance—"What's Switzerland again?" "39, I think"—and there you are, dialing Italy.

- *You might not have dialed the country code*. Apart from just plain forgetting, this is how it can happen: You are dialing the number 45 59 53 98 in Denmark; the country code for Denmark is 45, so you assume the 45 is the country code, but in fact Denmark has eight-digit domestic numbers.

- *You could have dialed the country code twice*. This may happen because you think the number you are looking at is a domestic number but it actually includes the country code already, as in the example at the beginning of this chapter. The second country code you dial will be taken as the city code, which is probably not valid.

- *You could have dialed the other country's international access code*. Lots of people assume that IACs are the same everywhere. Thus, a "helpful" South African will tell you to dial (092711) 804-1273; you drop the 0, dial your IAC to begin with, as you always do, and it doesn't work!

- *You could have dialed the other country's long-distance access code*. Automatically dialing 0 between the country code and the city code is not only a beginner's mistake. The foreign country's long-distance access code may not be 0! (Watch out for Finland, Spain, and Mexico.) Also, if you are dialing a North American number from overseas, do not dial 1 twice—no area code begins with 1.

- *You could have the wrong city code*. People do know their own city codes. The danger here occurs when you have had to look the code up yourself or get it from an operator. Which Freiburg? Or was it Friedberg? Or Freiberg? Are they in Neukirchen or Neuenkirchen? Which Newcastle? Which San Lorenzo?

- *You could have an out-of-date city code*. The city code for central London is now 71, not 1, and will change again in 1995. In the United States, area codes 312, 415, and 213 have split recently.

- *You could have dropped a 0 that you needed*. A few city codes really do begin with 0, which you need to dial. Helsinki and the Australian state of Tasmania are examples.

- *All local numbers in that city could have changed*. For example, Tokyo numbers have recently increased from seven to eight digits.

VERIFYING NUMBERS

Could you really have a wrong number? Where did you get it from? Was it a clear, recent letterhead or was it an unclear fax or an old trade directory?

Getting foreign directory information is often painful. Many countries are slow to respond. There may be a language barrier. (Spell very slowly; see Chapter 5.) Operators are inclined to tell foreigners there is no listing, in order to get rid of them and move on to an easier customer. You may have better luck calling for directory information in the middle of the foreign country's night, when they are less busy.

Where else can you get foreign numbers? Another difficult source of information is the foreign country's embassy in your capital city, or its associated organizations, such as consulates or trade commissions. They probably have phone books from home, at least old ones, but they may consider it beneath their dignity to look something up for you. Maintain firmly that you want to buy something urgently from the company you are inquiring about, because they are supposed to help their own exporters.

Major business libraries, chambers of commerce, and similar organizations may have foreign phone books that you can consult in person, or may offer to look up foreign numbers if you call them by phone.

You probably deal with a small number of countries regularly. Get their phone books if you can. You may be able to order them from your local phone company, if you have the patience. Another source is listed in the chapter on "Useful Products and Services." You could also ask traveling executives to bring or ship you phone books from overseas. (It will not be the primary task on their minds, so fax their hotel to remind them and suggest that they ask the hotel to take care of it.) All you will generally need is the capital city's phone book. However, Germany is so decentralized that you will need a national trade directory; refer to Chapter 3. The United States is also highly decentralized, but fortunately phone books are less necessary because the phone companies' directory information services work well, provided you know where the business is located. Locating the home of a U.S. business can be quite difficult. However, consolidated U.S. listings on CD-ROM are available off-the-shelf in many U.S. bookstores and software stores.

FOREIGN RECORDINGS

Always listen to a recording to the end; if you are lucky, an English translation will follow. The Norwegians, for example, are aware that few foreigners understand Norwegian messages, so they kindly repeat them in English. However, French and German telecommunications officials never record an English word.

You must pay attention to when the recording starts. Did the number ring or not?

If it rang, you are dealing with an answering machine or voice-mail system, which will beep and wait for your message. Leave your name, country, and number very clearly; leave a fax number too, if appropriate. If you want to send a fax but a recording answers, press START anyway. It may be one of those systems that can recognize a fax tone and connect you to a fax machine. You have incurred a charge already, so do not give up until the line disconnects without the paper moving through your machine.

If the recording is a phone-company recording, it is almost certainly telling you one of three things: (1) circuits are busy, (2) the number is no good, or (3) the number has been changed.

A changed-number recording is usually easy to identify because you will hear a computer-generated voice saying digits slowly in its own language: "incomprehensible (pause) yksi (pause) kaksi (pause) kolme (pause) nelyä." At this point, the official solution is to call your international operators and force them to call an operator in the other country to listen to the recording and interpret for you. Ultimately, the same is true for other recordings. (But see also "Conclusion" below.)

FOREIGN HOLIDAYS

A surprisingly common reason for getting no answer from a foreign number is that you are calling on one of their national or local holidays. Local holidays are impossible to keep track of without an annual world guide. However, the principal holidays observed every year by businesses in the countries in this book are as follows:

FOREIGN HOLIDAYS	
January	1(everywhere), 2(CH,KR,TW), 6(AT,DE,ES,FI,GR,IT,SE), 7(RU), 15(JP), 20(BR), 25(BR), 26(AU,IN)
February	5(MX), 6(NZ), 8(SI), 11(JP), 3d Mon.(US)
March	1(KR), 8(RU), 15(HU), 17(IE), 19(ES,VZ), 21(MX), 25(GR), 29(TW)
April	5(KR,TW), 6(TH,ZA), 9(PH), 12–14(TH), 19(VZ), 21(BR), 23(TR), 25(AU,IT,NZ,PT), 29(JP), 30(NL)
May	1(almost everywhere), 1st Mon.(GB), 3(JP,PO), 5(JP,KR,MX,NL,TH), 8(CS,FR), 9(RU), 17(NO), 19(TR), 21(CL), 25(AR), 28(LU), 29(TR), 31(ZA), penultimate Mon.(CA), last Mon.(GB,US)
June	3(MY), 5(DK), 6(KR), 10(PT), 12(PH,RU), 18(BR), 20(AR), 23(LU), 24(Quebec,VZ), 25(SI)
July	1(CA), 4(US), 5(CS,VZ), 6(CS), 9(AR), 14(FR), 17(KR), 21(BE), 24(VZ), 25(ES)
August	1(CH), 1st Mon.(CA,IE), 8(HU), 9(SC), 12(TH), 15(AT,BE,CH,CL,ES,FR,GR, IN,IT,KR,LU,PO,PT,VZ), 17(AR,ID), 27(PH), 30(TR), 31(MY), last Mon.(GB,HK)
September	1(MX), 1st Mon.(CA,US), 7(BR), 11(CL), 15(JP), 16(MX), 18–19(CL), 23(JP), 28(TW)
October	1(NG), 2(IN), 3(DE,KR), 5(PT), 10(JP,TW,ZA), 12(AR,BR,CL,ES,MX,VZ), 2d Mon.(CA), 23(HU,TH), 25(TW), 26(AT,NZ), 28(CS,GR,TR), 29(TR), 31(TW), last Mon.(IE)
November	1(AT,BE,CH,CL,DE,ES,FR,IT,LU,MX,PO,PT,SI,VZ), 2(BE,BR,LU,MX), 3(JP), 7(RU), 10(TR), 11(BE,CA,FR,PO,US), 12(TW), 15(BR), 3d Wed.(DE), 20(MX), 23(JP), 24–26(CS), 4th Thurs.(US), 30(PH)
December	1(PT), 5(TH), 6(ES,FI), 8(AR,AT,CH,CL,ES,IT,PT), 10(TH), 12(MX), 16(ZA), 23(JP), 24(FI), 25–26(almost everywhere), 30(PH), 31(AR)

There are also international holidays that are not tied to the Western calendar: Chinese New Year (usually February), Good Friday (usually April), Easter Monday (usually April), Ascension (sixth Thursday after Easter), Pentecost (Whit) Monday (eighth Monday after Easter), Corpus Christi (ninth Thursday after Easter), plus numerous movable Chinese, Muslim, and Israeli holidays.

FOREIGN BUSINESS HOURS

Detailed lists of business hours are meaningless. Opening hours and lunch breaks vary more from one company to another than from one country to another. Business hours are typically 8 a.m. to 5 p.m. in smaller towns every-where, and 9 a.m. to 6 p.m. in the largest cities. Executives in all countries often stay in the office later. Lunch is a time-consuming event around the Mediterranean (leave people alone between their noon and 2 p.m.) and in Spanish-speaking countries (try to get them before 2 p.m.). Expect offices in Muslim countries to be closed on Thursday afternoons and Fridays.

TIME DIFFERENTIALS

The following tables, based on Chicago (i.e., Central) time, will help you to identify good times to call during the winter and the summer. Because different countries change to summer time at different dates, there is always doubt about the time differences in the spring and fall; consult the *World Holiday and Time Guide* (see Chapter 3) for precise dates. Obviously, southern-hemisphere countries "spring forward and fall back" on an opposite schedule from northern-hemisphere countries, which creates a double time shift. (In the tables, *tmw* stands for "tomorrow," and *prev.* stands for "previous.")

| Country | TIME DIFFERENCES, NOVEMBER–FEBRUARY | | | |
	Chicago's 8 a.m. is their:	Chicago's 5 p.m. is their:	Their 8 a.m. is Chicago's:	Their 5 p.m. is Chicago's:
Europe:				
Ireland	2 p.m.	11 p.m.	2 a.m.	11 a.m.
Finland	4 p.m.	1 a.m. tmw	midnight prev. night	9 a.m.
Greece	4 p.m.	1 a.m. tmw	midnight prev. night	9 a.m.
Russia (Moscow)	4 p.m.	1 a.m. tmw	midnight prev. night	9 a.m.
Turkey	4 p.m.	1 a.m. tmw	midnight prev. night	9 a.m.
United Kingdom	2 p.m.	11 p.m.	2 a.m.	11 a.m.
Other Europe	3 p.m.	midnight	1 a.m.	10 a.m.
Middle East:				
Israel	4 p.m.	1 a.m. tmw	midnight prev. night	9 a.m.
Saudi Arabia	5 p.m.	2 a.m. tmw	11 p.m. prev. night	8 a.m.
Southern-Hemisphere America:				
Argentina	noon	9 p.m.	4 a.m.	1 p.m.
Brazil (Rio, São Paulo)	noon	9 p.m.	4 a.m.	1 p.m.
Chile	11 a.m.	8 p.m.	5 a.m.	2 p.m.
Northern-Hemisphere America:				
Mexico (Mexico City)	8 a.m.	5 p.m.	8 a.m.	5 p.m.
Venezuela	10 a.m.	7 p.m.	6 a.m.	3 p.m.
Northern-Hemisphere Pacific:				
China	10 p.m.	7 a.m. tmw	6 p.m. prev. day	3 a.m.
Hong Kong	10 p.m.	7 a.m. tmw	6 p.m. prev. day	3 a.m.
Indonesia (Jakarta)	9 p.m.	6 a.m. tmw	7 p.m. prev. day	4 a.m.
Japan	11 p.m.	8 a.m. tmw	5 p.m. prev. day	2 a.m.
Korea	11 p.m.	8 a.m. tmw	5 p.m. prev. day	2 a.m.

Country	Chicago's 8 a.m. is their:	Chicago's 5 p.m. is their:	Their 8 a.m. is Chicago's:	Their 5 p.m. is Chicago's:
Malaysia	10 p.m.	7 a.m. tmw	6 p.m. prev. day	3 a.m.
Philippines	10 p.m.	7 a.m. tmw	6 p.m. prev. day	3 a.m.
Singapore	10 p.m.	7 a.m. tmw	6 p.m. prev. day	3 a.m.
Taiwan	10 p.m.	7 a.m. tmw	6 p.m. prev. day	3 a.m.
Thailand	9 p.m.	6 a.m. tmw	7 p.m. prev. day	4 a.m.
Other:				
Australia (Sydney)	1 a.m. tmw	10 a.m. tmw	3 p.m. prev. day	midnight prev. night
India	7:30 p.m.	4:30 a.m. tmw	8:30 p.m. prev. day	5:30 a.m.
New Zealand	3 a.m. tmw	noon tmw	1 p.m. prev. day	10 p.m. prev. day
Nigeria	3 p.m.	midnight	1 a.m.	10 a.m.
South Africa	4 p.m.	1 a.m. tmw	midnight prev. night	9 a.m.

TIME DIFFERENCES, MAY–AUGUST

Country	Chicago's 8 a.m. is their:	Chicago's 5 p.m. is their:	Their 8 a.m. is Chicago's:	Their 5 p.m. is Chicago's:
Europe:				
Ireland	2 p.m.	11 p.m.	2 a.m.	11 a.m.
Finland	4 p.m.	1 a.m. tmw	midnight prev. night	9 a.m.
Greece	4 p.m.	1 a.m. tmw	midnight prev. night	9 a.m.
Russia (Moscow)	4 p.m.	1 a.m. tmw	midnight prev. night	9 a.m.
Turkey	4 p.m.	1 a.m. tmw	midnight prev. night	9 a.m.
United Kingdom	2 p.m.	11 p.m.	2 a.m.	11 a.m.
Other Europe	3 p.m.	midnight	1 a.m.	10 a.m.
Middle East:				
Israel	4 p.m.	1 a.m. tmw	midnight prev. night	9 a.m.
Saudi Arabia	4 p.m.	1 a.m. tmw	midnight prev. night	9 a.m.
Southern-Hemisphere America:				
Argentina	10 a.m.	7 p.m.	6 a.m.	3 p.m.
Brazil (Rio, São Paulo)	10 a.m.	7 p.m.	6 a.m.	3 p.m.
Chile	9 a.m.	6 p.m.	7 a.m.	4 p.m.
Northern-Hemisphere America:				
Mexico (Mexico City)	7 a.m.	4 p.m.	9 a.m.	6 p.m.
Venezuela	9 a.m.	6 p.m.	7 a.m.	4 p.m.
Northern-Hemisphere Pacific:				
China	10 p.m.	7 a.m. tmw	6 p.m. prev. day	3 a.m.
Hong Kong	9 p.m.	6 a.m. tmw	7 p.m. prev. day	4 a.m.
Indonesia (Jakarta)	8 p.m.	5 a.m. tmw	8 p.m. prev. day	5 a.m.
Japan	10 p.m.	7 a.m. tmw	6 p.m. prev. day	3 a.m.
Korea	10 p.m.	7 a.m. tmw	6 p.m. prev. day	3 a.m.
Malaysia	9 p.m.	6 a.m. tmw	7 p.m. prev. day	4 a.m.

Country	Chicago's 8 a.m. is their:	Chicago's 5 p.m. is their:	Their 8 a.m. is Chicago's:	Their 5 p.m. is Chicago's:
Philippines	9 p.m.	6 a.m. tmw	7 p.m. prev. day	4 a.m.
Singapore	9 p.m.	6 a.m. tmw	7 p.m. prev. day	4 a.m.
Taiwan	9 p.m.	6 a.m. tn.	7 p.m. prev. day	4 a.m.
Thailand	8 p.m.	5 a.m. tmw	8 p.m. prev. day	5 a.m.
Other:				
Australia (Sydney)	11 p.m.	8 a.m. tmw	5 p.m. prev. day	2 a.m.
India	6:30 p.m.	3:30 a.m. tmw	9:30 p.m. prev. day	6:30 a.m.
New Zealand	1 a.m. tmw	10 a.m. tmw	3 p.m. prev. day	midnight prev. night
Nigeria	2 p.m.	11 p.m.	2 a.m.	11 a.m.
South Africa	3 p.m.	midnight	1 a.m.	10 a.m.

An obvious error is to call from the Americas to Asia or Australia on Friday evening, or back from there on Monday morning; crossing the International Date Line, your call will reach an empty office on the weekend.

FAILURE TO GET THROUGH

Maybe you really cannot get through. Any of several problems on the other end could cause a foreign busy signal: All their lines could really be busy. Their fax could be out of paper. Their phone could be switched off. Their power could be out. Their phone could be off the hook. Their switchboard could be down.

Before you give up on an important call, try any other number you know in the same company. If you do not know one, try another office of the same company and ask whether they are having any problems, and whether they have any internal way of communicating (such as an electronic mail system). Also, do not forget that telexes and telegrams still exist.

Conclusion

Failing to reach someone by phone or fax can be discouraging and frustrating. There are two ways you can try to prepare to overcome telecommunications problems. One way is to find any cooperative company, institution, or library in your town that has a good collection of foreign phone books and trade directories. The second way is to cultivate people you deal with in other countries, regardless of what their official relationship to your company is. You need a personal network of people you can trade favors with. It is *much* easier for friends in the other country to track down a relocated company or fight their way through their local phone system. A business-card collection is an important personal asset for anyone who wants to make a career in international business.

CHAPTER 12

Postal Services and Classes of Mail

Domestic Mail Classification

If your office does not have a mail room, it will be your responsibility to send the mail out efficiently and economically. Since postal rates change frequently, you will need to write or call the post office for a brochure of current rates as well as brochures describing all the various classes of mail, the special services, and the rates for each class or service. The brochures are offered at no charge and contain a wealth of information on mail preparation, wrapping instructions, weight, zones, and rates. Another useful reference is the *Domestic Mail Manual* (DMM), which can be purchased at most post offices. The DMM provides detailed information on every aspect of domestic mail and special postal services, some of which are discussed here.

First-class mail   This category includes handwritten and typewritten messages, bills and statements of account, postcards and postal cards (postal cards are the ones printed by the Postal Service), canceled and uncanceled checks, and business reply mail with a weight of 11 ounces or less. First-class mail is sealed and may not be opened for postal inspection. Within a local area, overnight delivery can ordinarily be expected. Your post office will designate what constitutes your local area. To qualify for overnight delivery, you must deposit letters at a post office by 5 p.m., or at a mail processing facility by 6 p.m. Second-day delivery is standard for other points within specified local states. Third-day delivery is standard for other points within the 48 contiguous states.

Mailable envelopes, cards, and self-mailers can be no smaller than 3½″ × 5″

and should be at least .007 inches thick (about the thickness of a postal card). To avoid a surcharge on first-class mail weighing less than one ounce, the envelope should not exceed $11\frac{1}{2}'' \times 6\frac{1}{8}'' \times \frac{1}{4}''$. First-class postage is required for cards exceeding $4\frac{1}{4}'' \times 6''$. Large envelopes or packages sent as first-class mail should be stamped "FIRST CLASS" just below the postage area to avoid confusion with third-class mail at the post office. Envelopes with green diamond edging are useful because they immediately identify the contents as first-class mail.

First-class zone-rated (priority) mail   All first-class mail exceeding 11 ounces is rated as priority mail and receives the same treatment as regular first-class mail. Rates are determined by weight and by distance to the delivery zone. The maximum weight for priority mail is 70 pounds, and the maximum size is 108″ in combined girth and length.

Second-class mail   This category includes magazines, newspapers, and other periodicals issued at least four times a year. A permit is required to mail such material at the second-class rate.

Third-class mail   This category includes items not required to be mailed first-class, not having a permit as second-class, and weighing less than 16 ounces. It generally consists of circulars, books, catalogs, and other printed materials (such as newsletters, or corrected proof sheets with manuscript copy). Merchandise, farm and factory products, photographs, keys, and printed drawings may all be sent third-class. Much of what constitutes third-class mail is sometimes referred to as "advertising mail" or "direct mail." The two categories of third-class mail are *single-piece* and *bulk*. Bulk mail costs less than single-piece but it requires a permit, a minimum number of separately addressed pieces (more than 200 pieces or more than 50 pounds), and presorted bundling. Third-class mail is usually not sealed, so that it can be opened easily for postal inspection. It is generally slower than other types of mail, including fourth-class.

Fourth-class mail (parcel post)   This category consists mainly of domestic parcel post. Also included in it are special catalog mailings, special fourth-class mailings, and library mailings. It is mostly used to send packages or parcels weighing 16 ounces or more. Parcels may not weigh more than 70 pounds or exceed 108″ in combined length and girth. Parcel-post rates are based on weight and delivery distance. Parcels under 16 ounces are usually mailed as third-class, first-class, or priority mail.

Overnight delivery can be expected within the local area if parcels are mailed by 5 p.m. at post offices or receiving platforms. Second-day service can be expected for distances up to 150 miles. Service time depends on the distance the parcel must travel; for example, delivery may require as much as eight days for distances beyond 1,800 miles.

A written message in an envelope may be taped to the outside of a parcel if first-class postage is affixed to the envelope. Another way to include a letter with a package is to enclose the letter in the package, mark "First-Class Mail Enclosed" on the package, and affix first-class letter postage in addition to the fourth-class mailing charge.

It is extremely important to wrap parcels securely—in a strong container with the contents thoroughly cushioned—and to write or type the address legibly. The Postal Service prefers that packages be secured with strong tape rather than twine, which can jam the machines that handle the parcels.

International Mail

This category includes all material destined for foreign countries except over-seas military mail—that is, APO (Army Post Office) and FPO (Fleet Post Office) mail.

Since the subject of international mail is too large to cover adequately in this book, you should obtain a copy of the *International Mail Manual* (IMM), which is available for purchase from many post offices, or by mailing an application that can be obtained from your post office, or by calling the Government Printing Office at 202-783-3238. This publication is a valuable reference source for those who must handle large amounts of outgoing mail of this type. It contains detailed instructions for sending mail abroad, including specific information for each country. The Postal Service will also provide, without charge, *International Postage Rates and Fees* in booklet or poster form. This publication includes both an overview of international mail services and specific information about rates and fees.

International mail consists of three categories: postal union mail, parcel post, and Express Mail International Service.

Postal union mail is divided into two classes: *letter* or *LC mail* (from the French, "Lettres et Cartes"), which includes letters, letter packages, aerogrammes, and postcards; and *AO mail* (from the French, "Autres Objets"), which includes printed materials, materials for the blind, books, sheet music, periodicals, and small packets. Aerogrammes, a convenient form of stationery for international correspondence, are discussed under "Special Services." Postal union articles should be addressed legibly and completely. The bottom line of the address must show only the country name, written in full (no abbreviations) and in capital letters. Be sure to use the ZIP code or postal delivery zone if available. It is permissible to use a foreign-language address, provided that the names of the post office, province, and country are in English. The envelopes or wrappers of postal union mail should be marked with the mail classification: "Letter," "Printed Matter," "Printed Matter—Books," "Printed Matter—Sheet Music," and so on. Clearly mark "PAR AVION" (that is, "Airmail") on the front and back of any letter or package for which the airmail rate has been paid. The maximum permissible size for envelopes and packages is 36″ in combined length, width, and thickness, with a maximum length of 24″. For tubes or rolls, the maximum length is 36″, and the length plus twice the diameter must add up to no more than 42″.

Registered-mail service and daily airmail service are available to almost all countries. Registered letters and registered letter packages must be sealed. Neither insurance nor certified-mail service is available for postal union mail. Special-delivery service is available to most countries. It is also possible to obtain a return receipt.

Special customs forms for postal union mail must be used for dutiable letter packages, printed material, and all small packets. These are not the same forms that are used for parcel post.

All articles should be correctly prepaid in order to avoid delays. If an article is returned for additional postage, the proper amount should be affixed and the "Returned for postage" notation should be crossed out. Postal union mail is generally returned to the sender if delivery cannot be made.

Parcel post, sometimes known as *CP mail* (from the French, "Colis Postaux"), is available to most countries. It is similar to domestic fourth-class mail. The maximum combined length and girth generally allowed is 79″, with a maximum length of 42″. Parcels should be packed very securely in strong containers made of good-quality material that will withstand often radical climatic changes and repeated and rough handling. Insurance is available to most countries. Insured parcels must be sealed. Customs declarations describing the contents must be attached to all parcel-post packages. The forms used for parcel post are not the same as those used for postal-union mail.

Express Mail International Service provides fast, reliable mail service to certain countries. Insurance is provided against loss or damage at no extra charge. However, there is no guarantee that the mail will be delivered without delay.

There are private companies licensed by the U.S. government, called *custom-house brokers,* that help importers prepare the customs documents required for imported packages and articles. Other services rendered by brokers include export crating, reforwarding, delivery to and from airports and ocean ports, and bonded warehouse marking and distribution. Through these services, brokers offer savings on import/export charges and expedite delivery.

Special Services

The special services provided by the Postal Service are listed alphabetically and discussed briefly here.

Aerogramme   This is a combined letter and envelope with imprinted postage which provides an economical means of communicating abroad. An aerogramme can be purchased at any post office and can be registered. It should not contain any sort of enclosure; if it does, it will be subject to the higher airmail letter rate. It should not be sealed with stickers or tape.

Business reply mail   A business may wish to pay the postage for those responding to its mail—an important factor when selling by mail. To use the business reply service, submit an application on Form 3614-A (obtainable from your local post office), along with the annual permit fee. The mailer guarantees that the first-class postage and handling charge will be paid for each reply. Postage may be collected when the reply is delivered, although an advance deposit may be required under certain conditions. Above the addressee's name and address should appear the following on three lines: "BUSINESS REPLY MAIL," in capital letters at least 3/16″ high; "FIRST-CLASS MAIL PERMIT NO. _____, [CITY], [STATE]," in capital letters; and "Postage Will Be Paid By Addressee." The upper right corner, where postage is usually affixed, must contain the words "No Postage Necessary if Mailed in the United States."

Certificate of Mailing   A Certificate of Mailing is used by a mailer to prove that an item was actually mailed. Certificates for individual pieces of mail can be issued for a fee. The post office keeps no record of such certificates.

Certified mail   This service provides an initial receipt to the mailer, followed by a record of delivery. The carrier obtains a signature from the addressee on a receipt form, which is kept by the delivering post office for two years. A return receipt will be provided for an additional fee. A sample receipt is shown in Fig. 12.1.

Fig. 12.1
Certified Mail Receipt

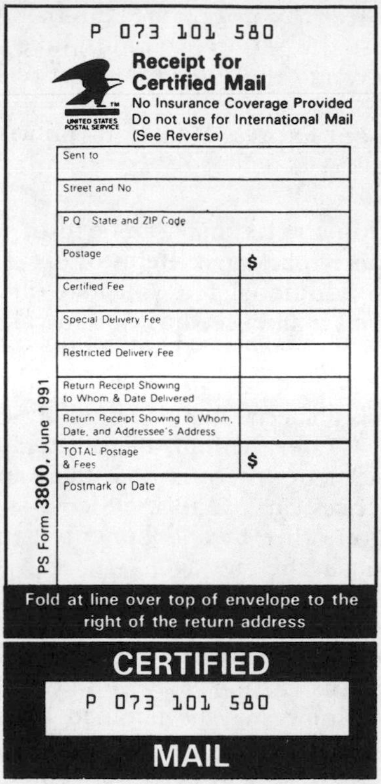

P 073 101 580

Receipt for
Certified Mail

UNITED STATES
POSTAL SERVICE

No Insurance Coverage Provided
Do not use for International Mail
(See Reverse)

Sent to	
Street and No	
P O State and ZIP Code	
Postage	$
Certified Fee	
Special Delivery Fee	
Restricted Delivery Fee	
Return Receipt Showing to Whom & Date Delivered	
Return Receipt Showing to Whom, Date, and Addressee's Address	
TOTAL Postage & Fees	$
Postmark or Date	

PS Form 3800, June 1991

Fold at line over top of envelope to the
right of the return address

CERTIFIED

P 073 101 580

MAIL

Collect on Delivery With Collect on Delivery (COD), both the postage and the price of the contents of a parcel or letter are collected from the addressee. The maximum amount that can be collected is $600. The fee charged for COD includes insurance against loss or damage and failure to receive payment. First-, third-, and fourth-class mail and Express Mail can be sent COD, the regular postage being paid in addition to the COD fee. The addressee may not examine the contents of the letter or parcel before paying the charges. Parcels sent must be based upon bona fide orders or on agreement between the mailer and addressee. For an additional fee, the mailer of COD letters or parcels will be notified of nondelivery. First-class mail sent domestic COD may be registered at an additional charge.

Express mail Express Mail is a fast intercity delivery system linking metropolitan areas in the United States. It is used for the reliable delivery of mail weighing up to 70 pounds and measuring up to 108″ in combined length and girth.

Express Mail Next Day Service requires that your shipment be taken to a post office by the time specified by the postmaster. The post office supplies special packets and address labels for your use. The package will be delivered to the addressee by 12 noon or 3 p.m. the following day, or it may be picked up at the post office as early as 10 a.m. on the next business day. Rates include insurance, a mailing receipt, and a record of delivery at the destination post office. If you are too late for next-day service, you can be assured of Express Mail Second Day Service provided that you post your shipment by 5 p.m. or such later time as your postmaster authorizes. Express Mail shipments can be picked up at your office for an additional charge.

The Postal Service also offers Express Mail Same Day Airport Service between many major airports. To use this service, you must take the shipment to the airport mail-processing facility, and the addressee must pick it up on arrival at the destination airport.

If you have questions about Express Mail, or if you wish to schedule a pickup, call 800-222-1811.

Insured mail   Third- and fourth-class mail can be insured against loss and damage up to $600 if it is properly packaged. Items of greater value should be sent by registered mail. For an additional fee, you may obtain a return receipt as proof of delivery for insured mail exceeding $50 in value. Payment of another fee provides that the mail will be delivered only to the addressee.

Mailgram   The Mailgram is a special mail-via-satellite service offered jointly by the U.S. Postal Service and Western Union. These letter-telegrams are delivered the next business day by U.S. letter carriers to virtually any address within the 48 contiguous states. Small offices can use this service by supplying the Mailgram message to a Western Union office by telephone (toll-free) or in person. Rates are based on 100-word units in the message.

Within larger firms, up to 50 common or variable-text messages can be typed directly from the company's teleprinter into the Western Union computer on a single connection. A basic fee is charged for each message, in addition to the telex/TWX usage charges. (Instructions may be found in the firm's telex/TWX directory.) Mailgrams in volume may be handled by putting mailing lists on computer tape, which can hold up to 10,000 address lines on a single tape. There is a basic fee for each message of 600 characters or less and a fee for each additional 600 characters, plus a minimum charge for each tape. The most economical way to input a Mailgram is from the company's computer directly into Western Union's computer. In this case, a basic fee is charged for each message, in addition to a minimum fee for each tape.

An additional electronic-mail system allows companies to transmit messages from their computers directly to post-office computers, which will then print and deliver as many copies as are requested.

Money orders   Money can be sent through the mail by purchasing postal money orders worth up to $700 each that are redeemable at any post office. International money orders can also be purchased.

Post-office boxes   Boxes and drawers in post offices may be rented. These facilitate the receiving of mail, since mail can be picked up whenever the post-office lobby is open.

Registered mail   Material that has been posted at first-class rates may be registered to protect valuable and important items. Registered mail is kept separate from other mail and is monitored throughout the delivery process. It is therefore the most secure method of mailing. The fee for this service is based on the declared value of the mail, with an indemnity limit of $25,000. The customer is given a receipt at the time of mailing; therefore, registered mail cannot be dropped into a regular collection box. The post office keeps a record of the mailing through the number it has been assigned. Insurance coverage may be purchased to protect against loss or damage. For an additional fee, a return receipt can be sent to the mailer after delivery.

Return receipts   A mailer may request a return receipt that shows to whom and when a piece of COD, express, certified, insured, or registered mail is delivered. If the request is made at the time of mailing, the fee is considerably lower than if the request is made later. The information is mailed to the sender on a card like that shown in Fig. 12.2.

Fig. 12.2   Domestic Return Receipt

● **SENDER:** Complete items 1 and 2 when additional services are desired, and complete items 3 and 4.
Put your address in the "RETURN TO" Space on the reverse side. Failure to do this will prevent this card from being returned to you. The return receipt fee will provide you the name of the person delivered to and the date of delivery. For additional fees the following services are available. Consult postmaster for fees and check box(es) for additional service(s) requested.

1. ☐ Show to whom delivered, date, and addressee's address.   2. ☐ Restricted Delivery
        (Extra charge)   *(Extra charge)*

3. Article Addressed to:

4. Article Number

Type of Service:
☐ Registered   ☐ Insured
☐ Certified   ☐ COD
☐ Express Mail   ☐ Return Receipt for Merchandise

Always obtain signature of addressee or agent and <u>DATE DELIVERED</u>.

5. Signature — Address
X

6. Signature — Agent
X

7. Date of Delivery

8. Addressee's Address *(ONLY if requested and fee paid)*

Is your RETURN ADDRESS completed on the reverse side?

Thank you for using Return Receipt Service.

PS Form **3811**, Mar. 1988   ★ U.S.G.P.O. 1988-212-865   **DOMESTIC RETURN RECEIPT**

Self-service postal centers   Self-service postal centers are located in convenient places such as post-office lobbies, shopping centers, and automobile drive-ups. They supplement existing postal services by providing around-the-clock service seven days a week. Automatic vending machines dispense stamps, postal cards, stamped envelopes, and minimum parcel insurance. These stamps are sold at face value, unlike those from private vending machines.

Special delivery   This designation virtually assures delivery on the day mail is received at the destination post office, including Sundays and holidays. As soon as the mail is received there, it is delivered by messenger. Special delivery may be used for all classes of mail. Although special delivery does not speed mail transportation from the post office of origin to the destination post office, it does assure rapid delivery from the destination post office to the intended addressee. The mailer must remember that mail cannot be delivered to post-office boxes or on weekends to offices that are closed. Also, some small post offices provide special-delivery service only during post-office hours.

Special handling   This designation assures preferential, separate handling for third- and fourth-class mail and normally speeds its delivery between post offices. It does not ensure speedy delivery after arrival at the destination post office.

FORWARDING, RECALLING, AND TRACING MAIL

All first-class mail is forwarded without charge when the addressee's new address is known. To forward a piece of mail, change the address on the original wrapper and add any required postage. Undeliverable first-class mail will be returned to the sender without charge. To ensure the return of other classes of mail, you must endorse the envelope "Return Postage Guaranteed" and be willing to pay extra postage when the mail is returned to you.

It is wise to purge your mailing lists occasionally to avoid paying consistently for mail that cannot be delivered. To do this, you should print "Forwarding and Address Correction Requested" on each envelope you send out. If the addressee has moved to a known address, the post office will forward the mail and send you the new address. If the mail is undeliverable for any known reason, the post office will tell you the reason. There is a fee for each address correction returned to the sender.

If you ever wish to recall a piece of mail already delivered to the post office, you must fill out a request form at the post office as soon as possible and be prepared to pay all costs of the recall, including telegrams and long-distance telephone calls. You will be notified if the mail has already been delivered. Other post-office forms are available that allow either the sender or the addressee to request lost mail to be traced within a year of the mailing date.

Other Delivery Methods

Shipments to and from business offices are often made by means other than the post office. Shipments are made by air, rail, ship, bus, and truck. Delivery services such as United Parcel Service use all of these methods. Check your local Yellow Pages under "Delivery Services" or "Courier Services" for the names of other parcel delivery services in your area. Before preparing the package, be sure to find out the carrier's regulations concerning size, weight, wrapping, and sealing.

Messenger services may also be called upon to make local, same-day deliveries (as to banks) when the need occurs. Some companies have their own messengers; many others prefer to use the commercial messenger services. These services are also listed in the Yellow Pages.

EXPRESS SERVICE

Air express   Air express is a fast-growing industry. While it is expensive, it is the fastest means of door-to-door pickup and delivery of letters and parcels to most cities in the United States. Air express companies also offer international delivery service. There are many occasions in a business office when quick delivery is essential and it is worthwhile to bear the extra cost.

Bus express   Most bus lines offer a shipping service. This method of delivery is speedy and is especially suitable for delivery to small towns that are not served by airlines. Many items are insurable. The weight limit is 100 pounds per package, and the size limit is $33'' \times 33'' \times 48''$. There is an extra charge for pickup and delivery service.

Railway express   To use rail express service, you must drop off your package for shipping and arrange for someone to pick it up when it reaches its destination station.

FREIGHT SERVICES

Freight, although slower than express, is the most economical way to ship large quantities of material in bulky packages. The various types of freight are railroad, motor, air, and water freight.

INTERNATIONAL SHIPMENTS

As the international business dealings of corporations increase, there is a steadily greater need for international deliveries. Shipments may be made by sea or by air. Since foreign shipments involve special forms and packaging, you must contact international airlines and steamship companies for instructions. They have personnel to assist in preparing the necessary forms and to furnish packing and shipping instructions.

FULL-SERVICE COMPANIES

There are two companies offering several services, including domestic and international air express, that deserve further discussion: United Parcel Service and Federal Express.

United Parcel Service   United Parcel Service (UPS) provides ground and air service within the United States and to over 180 countries worldwide for delivery of letters and packages weighing up to 70 pounds and measuring up to 130″ in combined length and girth, with a maximum length of 108″. You may not use string, cellophane tape, or masking tape. All packages are automatically insured against loss or damage up to $100. Higher insurance protection may be obtained for an additional charge, up to a maximum of $25,000. For information on service, rates, and restrictions, and to order the service guides, contact your local UPS office.

Domestic ground and air service is available to any address in the United States and Puerto Rico. There are two types of air service.

UPS Next Day Air® Service guarantees delivery of letters and packages on the next business day to all addresses in the 48 contiguous states, Puerto Rico, the island of Oahu in Hawaii, and some locations in Alaska. Most of these deliveries, including those to major metropolitan areas, are made by 10:30 a.m., and many others by noon. Other Hawaiian islands may require an extra day; rural Alaska may require one or more additional days. Saturday deliveries can also be scheduled for an additional charge.

UPS 2nd Day Air® Service guarantees delivery of packages on the second business day, except in rural Alaska, which may require one or more extra days.

Special services include address correction, COD service, delivery confirmation service (which provides proof of delivery), and Call Tag service (which allows for return of merchandise previously delivered by UPS from anywhere in the 48 contiguous states). Hazardous materials may not be shipped anywhere by air, nor by ground service to Canada. Some such materials may be shipped by domestic ground service.

UPS service to Canada includes ground service to any address in the 10 provinces, and Air Express service to all of Canada, including the Yukon and the Northwest Territories.

Export documentation is required for shipments to Puerto Rico and Canada, except for UPS Next Day Air letters to Puerto Rico and UPS Air Express letters to Canada.

International service consists of two door-to-door service levels: UPS Worldwide Express service, which serves more than 180 countries and generally provides delivery of letters and packages in two business days, and UPS Worldwide Expedited service, which provides precisely scheduled delivery of packages to major cities in Europe and Asia within four business days. Export documentation is required for all packages. For information on international shipments, including customs brokerage information, call the UPS International Information Center at 800-782-7892.

Federal Express   Federal Express provides fast delivery of letters and packages up to 150 pounds, and measuring up to 130″ in combined length and girth, with a maximum length of 108″, within the United States and to more than 170 countries worldwide. Freight service is also available for larger and heavier packages. Automatic insurance against loss or damage is provided up to $100, with additional coverage available up to a maximum of $25,000. For information regarding domestic shipping, call 800-238-5355. For international shipping, call 800-247-4747.

The *Federal Express Service Guide,* in two volumes, provides details of services, packaging requirements, customs clearance, and related matters. Volume 1 deals with domestic service, Volume 2, with international deliveries. An overview of some Federal Express services follows.

Domestic services include FedEx® Priority Overnight Service, which provides delivery of letters and packages by 10:30 a.m. or by noon to most locations in the United States. FedEx® Standard Overnight Service offers delivery by 3 p.m. or 4:30 p.m. to most areas. Economy Two-Day℠ Service provides delivery of packages by 4:30 p.m. (5 p.m. within Alaska and Hawaii) on the second business day. With FedEx® Overnight Freight Service, packages weighing from 150 to 500 pounds per piece can be delivered by the next business day within the 48 contiguous states. FedEx® Two-Day Freight Service provides delivery by 4:30 p.m. on the second business day to the 48 states and Anchorage, Alaska. Approval must be obtained in advance for freight shipments exceeding 500 pounds. Dangerous-goods delivery is offered anywhere in the United States, with some restrictions. Other special services include COD service, proof of performance, and volume discounts.

International services include International Priority® Service, which provides scheduled door-to-door delivery, including customs clearance, on one to three days. Export documentation is required for international shipments. Dangerous goods can be shipped to some locations. Consult the *Service Guide* for further information on international service, including extensive freight and cargo services.

ELECTRONIC MAIL

Electronic mail (E-mail) refers to computer-based message systems that send digitally encoded documents directly from terminal to terminal and whose messages are displayed on a cathode-ray tube (CRT) terminal, with the option of a printed hard copy. Through electronic-mail systems, urgent correspondence can be transmitted in a matter of seconds to most major cities around the world.

CHAPTER 13

Travel Arrangements and International Business

A large increase in business-related travel, especially international travel, has been one of the results of the intensely competitive global market. Consequently, the secretary's role has been extended in yet another direction. But no longer is it enough just to make plane reservations and prepare itineraries. You now must have a fairly broad understanding of what types of trade and travel information are needed for various kinds of business trips, know where to obtain current information quickly, and be able to extract the essential data for the executive. In short, you must be able to expedite a business trip from the initial planning stages through the post-trip follow-up. Good secretarial support during all stages of a trip can sometimes mean the difference between success and failure.

Executives must be kept informed of developments in the countries with which they may be dealing. They must also have an understanding of foreign cultures and social structures in order to establish and maintain friendly working relationships with their foreign counterparts. A secretary who can supply in-depth information about the society and customs of these countries can be of great value to the executive and the company. An awareness of the economic relationships between the U.S. government and other governments is also desirable. Finally, knowledge of at least one foreign language could be one of your most important qualifications.

This chapter provides an overview of domestic and multinational travel and business and the secretary's expanded role in facilitating and supporting them.

Setting Up a Trip

A successful foreign business trip requires careful preparations carried out methodically. Even if your firm has an in-house travel department, you yourself should know what information will be needed and where it may be obtained. You should know *in advance* the following:

1. *Office policies and procedure*
   - Whether travel arrangements are to be made by an in-house travel department, a travel agent, or you and the executive.
   - The procedure for making a formal travel request.

- The procedure for requesting cash advances and/or prepayment or reimbursement of expenses.
- How to coordinate office schedules in the executive's absence.

2. *The executive's personal preferences and needs*
   - Means of transportation—specific carrier, class, time of day, meal service, and special services.
   - Hotel accommodations—chain affiliation, required facilities, smoking or nonsmoking room, and special arrangements.
   - Entertainment and sightseeing.
   - Ground transportation services.
   - Amount of leisure time.
   - Personal interests.
   - Medical problems.

3. *Methods for keeping records of the trip*
   - Portable dictation equipment, telephone communication, secretary's attendance, outside clerical assistance, or dictation upon return.

Although gathering and organizing this information may involve a great deal of time, the result will make the investment worthwhile.

In addition, you must determine the following:

- Purpose of the trip, departure and return dates, and number of people traveling.
- Most convenient and expedient means of transportation, mileage, and estimated travel time.
- Hotel most completely equipped and closest to trip activities.
- Arrangements and facilities for meetings.
- Forms to be completed before departure.
- Availability of necessary supplies (dictation equipment, reference books or research facilities, files, handout materials, etc.) and services (clerical, reproduction, etc.).
- Allocation of free time and designated activities.
- Additional arrangements for family and traveling companions.
- Notes on climate, time zones, and accepted modes of dress.

COMMERCIAL TRAVEL AGENCIES

Reputable travel agencies are staffed with skilled employees who can assist international and domestic travelers at no additional cost to the traveler. A call to a travel agent will save time and assure a minimum of confusion from the beginning to the end of the trip. Travel agents make travel reservations, issue tickets, recommend hotels and make hotel reservations, arrange for car rentals, and assist in obtaining passports and visas. They sometimes give additional help with incidentals such as tickets for the theater or sporting events. They have at their fingertips data about airline flight schedules and prices, air distances and travel times to principal cities around the globe, luggage limitations, and air freight.

The selection of a travel agent may be based on personal recommendations, established reputation, or spot usage. Once an agent has been chosen, try to use the same agent to arrange all trips, so that he or she can become familiar with the traveler's habits and a rapport can develop between you.

Names of accredited travel agencies are available from the American Society of Travel Agents (ASTA), 1101 King Street, Alexandria, VA 22314. You can also get a list of Certified Travel Agencies in your area by sending a self-addressed, stamped envelope to the Institute of Certified Travel Agents, 148 Linden Street,

P.O. Box 56, Wellesley, MA 02181. Once you have determined the names of a few agencies you may be interested in using, consider asking the following questions: Do you specialize in business travel? What businesses in the area are using your services? Are you associated with ASTA and are your agents certified?

Have all necessary information at hand before calling the agent, and be courteous and friendly yet completely candid about the executive's desires. Be ready to supply the following information:

1. The executive's name, office address, and home and office telephone numbers.
2. The desired dates and times of departure and return.
3. The executive's travel preferences—first-class or coach, smoking or non-smoking, etc.

The agent will provide confirmation, suggest an acceptable method of payment, tell you the check-in time and the estimated time of arrival, and arrange either to send the tickets to you or have you pick them up.

IN-HOUSE TRAVEL DEPARTMENTS

Many companies have in-house travel departments that monitor travel requests and provide a detailed tracking system of monies spent. Some companies have special policies regarding returning frequent-flyer awards to the company, and this too can be monitored by an in-house travel department.

ELECTRONIC RESERVATION SYSTEMS

Regardless of whether you are making reservations through a commercial travel agency or an in-house travel department or on your own, there are computer services such as Prodigy and CompuServe through which you can make reservations and obtain tickets. The *Official Airline Guide* (Official Airline Guides, 2000 Clearwater Dr., Oak Brook, IL 60521; 800-323-3537) has an Electronic Edition (OAGEE). The following services are literally at your fingertips by means of a computerized travel service: latest flight information, ticketing arrangements, credit-card arrangements, meal selections, seating preferences, hotel and motel reservations, restaurant information, banquet and conference facilities, weather conditions in cities throughout the world, and travel tips.

MAKING TRAVEL ARRANGEMENTS DIRECTLY

If you make travel reservations without the help of an agent, preparation is more complex. It involves obtaining and keeping current the appropriate schedules and brochures from airlines, bus lines, railroads, travel clubs, motor clubs, and various travel agencies. If you make extensive arrangements directly with airlines, keep the current copy of the *Official Airline Guide,* available by subscription at the address above. The guides are published in both domestic and international editions.

Know the full particulars of the trip before making any reservations. Contact the chamber of commerce, convention bureau, or tourism office of the destination city for brochures and special information. Another source of information is the local newspaper of the destination city, where you can find special-events calendars, weather reports, and service and facility advertisements.

Most of the major airlines, hotels, and car-rental agencies have toll-free numbers. If you do not have access to a directory of toll-free 800 numbers, call the toll-free information number, 800-555-1212, for the listing you need.

Airline reservations   If you do not rely on an agent for airline reservations, a call to the airline will provide information about its schedules and rates. Reservations and even seat assignments may be made instantly. You can confirm flights and sometimes make hotel reservations through the airline, but you should always confirm hotel reservations yourself. Clip the special service announcements and schedules that are often published in newspapers. Allot enough time between connecting flights. Inquire specifically as to (1) methods of payment, (2) how to pick up the ticket, (3) check-in time at the airport, and (4) space available for carry-on luggage.

Most major airlines have private clubroom facilities in the larger airports. An annual membership charge enables the club member to avoid the turmoil of a busy airport, find a quiet place to work during layovers, change reservations if necessary, and obtain seat assignments well in advance of the gate's opening. Information about such facilities is available from ticket agents and flight attendants.

Railroad travel   Rail travel is limited to certain cities at certain times of the day and is feasible only when time and access to Amtrak terminals are available. Rail travel generally requires more time than the executive is likely to have, but some people prefer to travel by train. You can obtain a schedule for Amtrak trains as well as for connecting or commuter lines from the nearest Amtrak station. A call to a ticket agent will answer any additional questions. If the executive will be driving to the station, provisions for parking must be made. The National Railway Publications Co., 424 West 33 Street, New York, NY 10001, and the Thomas Cook Travel, 4435 Main Street, Suite 150, Kansas City, MO 64111, offer timetables, fares, and a host of other information regarding railroad travel.

Automobile travel   In some instances the executive may choose to travel by automobile. Membership in an automobile or oil-company travel club provides guides and maps, towing and repair service, and detailed road trip plans. If the executive prefers to rent a car, the type of car and rate should be guaranteed with the agency. You should determine the method of payment, special discounts available, insurance requirements, and driver's-license stipulations. The executive's arrival time should be relayed to the rental agency so that no unnecessary delays are encountered at the destination. Some car-rental agencies use the term "unlimited mileage" to indicate that the driver pays a set amount for a designated period of time, regardless of the number of miles the car is driven. The term "drop-off charges" refers to the fee the driver must pay when the car is rented at one location but returned to another.

Hotel reservations   It is essential to make hotel reservations as soon as the dates of the trip are definite, since hotels in major cities may be fully booked several weeks in advance. *The Hotel & Motel Red Book,* published by the American Hotel and Motel Association, 1201 New York Avenue, NW, Washington, DC 20005, provides descriptions of selected hotels and motels throughout the United States. Reservations are normally made by telephone and confirmed in writing. When making hotel reservations, you should provide the name, address, and telephone number of the guest and your own name for reference. You should also specify whether the traveler will desire a smoking or nonsmoking room. Many hotels hold reservations only until a certain hour, usually 6 p.m. You may frequently hold a reservation beyond that hour by guaranteeing payment whether or not the guest arrives. To guarantee a room, you will need to give the name and address of the firm or the number and expiration date of a major credit card.

Advise the hotel by telephone as to the executive's preference and inquire about a guarantee that such accommodations will be available. Find out about valet and laundry services, barber/hairdressers, masseurs, health clubs, and shoe shining and repair facilities, and make notes of these services on the itinerary. It may be desirable to make advance appointments for certain services. Request written confirmation of all hotel reservations, including arrival and departure dates, guarantee, room rates, and tax. In addition, ask about check-out times, payment procedures, credit and check-cashing privileges, fax machine availability, meeting facilities, and other needed services.

An understanding of hotel meal plans is helpful when making reservations. The American Plan (AP) includes all meals; the Modified Plan (MP) includes breakfast and dinner; the Breakfast Plan (BP) includes breakfast only; the Continental Plan (CP) includes a breakfast of coffee, tea, juice, muffins, and rolls; and the European Plan (EP) includes no meals.

Ask about complimentary limousine service from the airport or railway station and the comparative rates and times of other means of ground transportation. The clerk should also be able to tell you how to find ground transportation upon arrival if arrangements cannot be made beforehand. There may be a direct telephone line to the hotel from the baggage-claim area of the airport, for example, or an agent at a desk or curbside, or posted notices of available transportation.

SPECIAL ARRANGEMENTS

The executive with health problems may have to wear appropriate identification, carry medication, and arrange for access to a local physician. Provision for special diets or storage facilities may also have to be made.

THE TRAVEL FOLDER

File all notes on the various arrangements in one folder to facilitate the preparation of an itinerary and appointment schedule. When the arrangements are completed, mark a deadline on the calendar for receipt of confirmations. If confirmations are not received by that date, a follow-up phone call must be made.

The itinerary   An itinerary is invaluable in guiding an executive through a hectic day in a distant city. The itinerary should be logically and neatly arranged so that he or she can review it at a glance and accomplish the trip's purpose as easily as possible. It should include a brief description of activities, with dates and times; departure and arrival times, with airports or train stations specified; hotel names and addresses, and confirmed reservations (official confirmations are usually attached); and social engagements, with comments as to dress. A detailed itinerary may also contain pertinent information about individuals, reference to files or reports and correspondence, reminders to reconfirm flight reservations and meeting arrangements, and comments on climate and social amenities.

In preparing the itinerary, confer with the executive and make careful notes about desired dates and times of departure and return, the time needed for each meeting or appointment, and any need for free time to relax or attend to personal matters. The traveler should be told the details of any flight—what meals will be served, whether the flight is nonstop, the distance between terminals if a change of planes is involved, and the approximate distance between the airport and the hotel. Errors in planning can result in costly delays and needless confusion.

Travel agents also provide itineraries, but these are usually in the form of a printout from a computerized reservation service and thus should be carefully reviewed and supplemented with additional appointments and information. In some cases a separate appointment schedule is advisable, with notes for each meeting—participants, papers needed, and so on. After the draft itinerary is approved by the executive, the final itinerary is typed and filed in the travel folder, and copies may be distributed as needed within the office.

The travel checklist   The final step is to assemble all the necessary materials and equipment. The following checklist may be helpful:

_____ tickets
_____ frequent-flyer number
_____ hotel/motel information
_____ car-rental confirmation
_____ traveler's checks
_____ passport, visa, international driving permit
_____ medical prescriptions
_____ vaccination certificate
_____ itinerary
_____ names, addresses, and phone numbers of business associates at destination
_____ agenda and advance publicity for conferences/meetings
_____ all necessary files
_____ speeches, reports
_____ slides or transparencies
_____ business cards
_____ company letterhead and envelopes
_____ gummed note tags, paper clips, manila folders, etc.
_____ laptop computer
_____ portable fax machine
_____ portable dictating equipment, extra tapes
_____ reference books for destination city and country

CANCELING A PLANNED TRIP

When a planned trip is canceled, you must notify all parties as quickly as possible. Transportation and hotel arrangements should be canceled promptly by telephone, and a follow-up letter should confirm the cancellation. Meeting arrangements should be canceled with the concierge, catering manager, or meeting coordinator.

If the tickets have been prepaid, application for a refund (accompanied by the unused tickets if you have them) is made directly to the carrier or travel agent. If hotel accommodations have been paid for in advance, apply for a refund to the hotel by letter promptly after telephoning the cancellation. If hotel reservations are guaranteed, *prompt* cancellation is crucial to avoid charges. If any payment has been made by charge card, application for credit should be made through the carrier, the hotel reservations clerk, or the travel agent. Be sure that the correct credit has been allowed on the monthly statement.

INTERNATIONAL TRAVEL

Passports and Visas   To find information about passports, look in the telephone directory under "United States Government," or contact Passport Services, Bureau of Consular Affairs, 1425 K Street, NW, Washington, DC 20524 (202-647-0518). If a passport is required, a person can apply at a passport agent's office or through a clerk of a federal court, a clerk of a state court of record, a judge or clerk of a probate court, or a designated postal clerk. Passport agencies are located in Boston, Chicago, Honolulu, Houston, Los Angeles, Miami, New Orleans, New York, Philadelphia, San Francisco, Seattle, Stamford (Connecticut), and Washington, D.C.

All U.S. citizens generally need passports to leave and reenter the United States and to enter most foreign countries. Even though a passport is not required by U.S. law for travel to North, South, and Central America or adjacent islands except for Cuba, it is still recommended. Travelers who visit countries in these areas without a passport should carry personal identification (such as a driver's license or an employee ID card) and a birth certificate or some other documentary evidence showing U.S. citizenship. Information about passport requirements for travel to and from specific countries can be obtained from the embassies or consulates of these countries. The pamphlet *Your Trip Abroad* is available from the Superintendent of Documents, P.O. Box 371954, Pittsburgh, PA 15250-7954. Another pamphlet, *Foreign Entry Requirements,* is available from Consumer Information Center, Pueblo, CO 81009.

The traveler should apply early for a passport, preferably several weeks before the planned departure. To apply for a first passport, the traveler should present a completed passport application at one of the issuing offices. A second passport can be applied for by mail if the conditions stated on the application are met. Several items are needed for filing an application for a passport:

1. **Evidence of citizenship**   A previously issued passport provides this evidence. A first-time applicant must provide an original birth certificate with an embossed seal, a certificate of naturalization, a baptismal certificate, voter-registration certification, or if all these are lacking, other evidence such as insurance papers.

2. **Two passport photos taken within six months of the date of application** Photos should be $2'' \times 2''$, front view and full-faced. Color shots are acceptable.

3. **Proof of identity**   Personal identity must be established to the satisfaction of the person executing the application. If the applicant is personally known by the executor, no further identification is required. Items generally accepted for identification are a previously issued U.S. passport, a driver's license, a certificate of naturalization or citizenship, or a government (federal, state, or municipal) card or pass. Social Security cards and credit cards are not acceptable.

Business firms contracting with U.S. government agencies to carry out missions abroad should check with the contracting agency about special requirements for passports.

New passport applications may be made by mail if the applicant has held a U.S. passport for not more than eight years before the date of application. Passports are valid for five years from the date of issuance unless they are specifically limited by the Secretary of State. Lost or stolen passports should be reported immediately to the Passport Services office or to the nearest American consular office. Stolen passports should also be reported to local police authorities. Every precaution should be taken to prevent loss or theft of passports, for there may be considerable delay before a new passport can be issued.

A visa is permission granted by the government of a country for an alien to enter that country and remain there for a specified period of time. Visas are usually stamped in passports. Visas should, when possible, be obtained well in advance from the nearest embassy or consular office of the country or countries to which one is going. The addresses of foreign consular offices in the United States may be obtained by consulting *The Congressional Directory* or telephone directories for larger cities.

Because visa policies change, up-to-date information should be obtained before each trip. Even in countries not requiring visas, the traveler should carry evidence of U.S. citizenship and personal identification.

International driving permits   Some countries will not honor U.S. driver's licenses and require local licenses in the native language. The American Automobile Association (AAA) recommends that anyone renting a car in a foreign country inquire about an international driving permit. For more information, you can call the AAA collect at 407-444-7883.

Vaccinations and required immunizations   Up-to-date information about required immunizations must be obtained before any trip to a foreign country. Details concerning the immunizations and other disease-prevention measures recommended or required for travel to all areas of the world can be obtained from local, county, or state health departments. The countries that the executive intends to visit should be determined well in advance of the trip, since entry into and exit from some countries require special immunizations. The World Health Organization now recommends that most countries no longer require from travelers a certificate of vaccination against smallpox. Several countries require certificates showing that travelers have been vaccinated against cholera and yellow fever. For return to the United States, a smallpox certificate is required only if in the preceding days the traveler has visited a country in which smallpox has broken out. Required immunizations must be recorded on approved forms— International Certificates of Vaccination—available through most local health department offices. Exemptions from immunizations can be obtained if a physician thinks certain immunizations should not be given on medical grounds, in which case the traveler should be given a signed and dated statement of these reasons written on the physician's stationery. If smallpox and cholera shots are given by a private physician, the physician must give the traveler an official written statement confirming that the shots have been given. Yellow-fever shots can be given only by a local, county, or state health department. Allowing ample time for a traveler to complete all necessary shots before departure is of the utmost importance. You should call the health department to arrange for the executive's shots, since certain shots may be given only on specific days of the week.

The publication *Health Information for International Travel,* which contains information about required immunizations for different countries as well as many useful suggestions for coping with travel conditions, can be obtained from the Superintendent of Documents, P.O. Box 371954, Pittsburgh, PA 15250-7954.

Medical help overseas   It is wise for the traveler to take a few emergency items such as aspirin, decongestants, bandages, first-aid cream, and antidiarrheal medication. In some countries there are problems with water or disease that the traveler should be aware of. Most major hotels have a doctor on call and have arrangements with a nearby hospital or clinic, but before traveling overseas it might be wise to contact (1) your personal physician; (2) the International Association for Medical Assistance to Travelers (IAMAT), 417 Center Street, Lewiston, NY 14092 (716-754-4883), a nonprofit organization that accepts donations; or (3) International SOS Assistance, Inc., P.O. Box 11568, Philadelphia, PA 19116 (215-244-1500).

Legal help overseas If a legal problem should arise during foreign travel, the traveler should contact a law firm that is experienced in such matters as customs or immigration violations and driving infractions. International Legal Defense Counsel, 111 S. 15th Street, 24th floor, Philadelphia, PA 19102, is staffed with attorneys experienced in overseas legal matters.

Luggage For international travel, check about luggage requirements and excess-weight charges with the airline on which the passenger will be traveling. Passengers are generally allowed two checked bags and one carry-on piece; however, size limits and the amount of under-seat space available for carry-on luggage vary with the airline.

Unless an excess valuation is declared before departure, the airline's maximum liability for baggage and claims on such baggage will be strictly limited; the passenger should inquire about liability limitations. Claims for damage must be filed in writing within seven days, and claims for loss or delay must be filed within 21 days.

Customs declarations Travelers should pay special attention to duty-free imports and items that must be declared. Articles acquired abroad and brought into the United States are subject to duty and internal revenue tax; however, as a returning resident, a traveler is allowed certain exemptions from duties on items obtained abroad. Articles totaling $400 (based on fair retail value in the country where they were purchased) may be entered duty-free; this may include only small amounts of liquor, cigarettes, and cigars. Failure to declare an article may lead to its seizure and forfeiture, and to an additional liability equal in amount to the value of the article in the United States. If in doubt about whether an article is dutiable, the article should be declared and the customs inspector should be asked about it. The understatement of an article's value or the misrepresentation of its nature may lead to seizure and forfeiture. Duty must be paid even if an article is seized. The original invoice or bill of sale must reflect the true value of the article.

Detailed pamphlets on customs regulations, including *Customs Hints for Returning U.S. Residents,* are available from the Office of Public Information, U.S. Customs Service, 1301 Constitution Ave., NW, Washington, DC 20229 (202-927-5580), as well as from the Superintendent of Documents.

Film and recordings Before departure, the traveler should register cameras, tape recorders, computers, and other articles that can be readily identified by serial numbers or other markings. All foreign-made articles are subject to duty each time they are brought into the United States unless the traveler has acceptable proof of prior possession. Certificates of registration can be obtained at the nearest customs office. If such certificates for any reason cannot be obtained, one can use bills of sale, insurance policies, or purchase receipts as proof of prior possession.

Exposed film that a traveler has purchased abroad may be released without examination by customs if it is not to be used for commercial purposes and if it does not contain objectionable matter. Developed or undeveloped U.S. film exposed abroad is duty-free and need not be listed in customs exemptions. Motion-picture film to be used for commercial purposes is, however, dutiable when returned to the United States. Foreign film purchased abroad as well as prints developed there are subject to duty, but they may be included in customs exemptions. U.S.-manufactured film may be mailed to the United States in the mailing envelopes obtainable from film manufacturers or processing laboratories. The outside wrapper should be marked "Undeveloped photographic film of U.S. manufacture—Examine with care."

International customs and amenities The American executive who conducts business abroad should be familiar with the business and social customs of the host countries so as not to risk offending those with whom he or she confers or negotiates. Acceptable behavior is often based more on experience, instinct, and a feel for good manners than on written protocol. Although social practices and behavior in homes and restaurants do vary from country to country, tact, subtlety, courtesy, and geniality are always in order. Foreign business executives, and particularly those whose educational ties are European, are impressed if a visitor understands the cultural heritage and language of their country. The American executive going abroad should therefore take the time and make the effort to become well informed about the countries that will be visited and to brush up on the languages of these countries.

The American who is invited to a foreign business associate's home for an evening should take the invitation seriously, even though such an occasion is likely to be strictly social. The American executive who can talk intelligently about the arts and world affairs will make a favorable impression. If an executive is a guest in a foreign colleague's home, a small present might be given to the host or hostess. The guest should be discreet about choosing gifts; certainly the selection should not be ostentatious. Flowers are generally appropriate. No gift should be taken if one is a guest at a private club; however, if the entertainment is a golf game, the guest might present the host with golf balls imprinted with the company name and its logo.

Business behavior is as important and as varied as social behavior in different countries; for example, Austrians are formal in their business associations, but less so than Germans. Shaking hands is a polite gesture when greeting or leaving throughout Europe. In some countries, visiting cards are exchanged among executives. In some, business is conducted during lunch; in others, it is not. Business hours differ from country to country, and from summer to winter. For example, office hours in Italy are customarily from 8:00 a.m. to 1:00 p.m. and from 4:00 p.m. to 7:00 p.m.; in Denmark, summer hours are from 8:30 a.m. to 3:00 p.m., but winter hours are from 9:00 a.m. to 5:00 p.m. Banking hours also vary from country to country. Punctuality is important in many countries; in fact, delays of more than five minutes in some countries might be considered rude. In other countries, meetings customarily begin late.

Local customs for making appointments and for dress also should be adhered to. The American practice of making spur-of-the-moment appointments by telephone is looked upon with disapproval in many countries. Foreign business people are accustomed to receiving requests for appointments by letter well in advance; such a letter should contain the visitor's corporate title and specify the reason for the meeting. While Americans make a habit of working lunches, European luncheons are more frequently a time for building personal relationships than for discussing business.

Executives should be familiar with the dress conventions of the countries they visit. A dark business suit may be the masculine uniform in one country, but more casual attire may be acceptable in another. Some countries have strong notions about female attire; for example, pants are considered inappropriate in many countries. It is the traveler's responsibility to be informed on social and business customs before embarking on a trip. You should try to provide background material for the executive so that he or she will be an exemplary representative of both company and country abroad.

For more about cultural and business customs in individual countries, contact their embassies or consulates, many of which have brochures or booklets on the subject. Almost all travel guides deal with these issues as well.

Worldwide holidays   Holidays in foreign countries can affect the American executive's travel and appointment schedule. You can help the executive by supplying a list of holidays observed in the countries that will be visited. Holidays should also be included in the itinerary. For instance, Muslim, Christian, and Jewish holidays all might affect the schedule of an executive traveling in the Middle East. Indeed, there are very few days in the year when there is no holiday somewhere in the world. American travelers also must consider U.S. holidays when scheduling appointments with U.S. government representatives and American business people stationed overseas.

In the Western nations, New Year's (Jan. 1) and Christmas (Dec. 25) are always observed, Easter Monday and Boxing Day (Dec. 26) are almost always observed, and Labor Day (May 1) and Good Friday are widely observed.

Holiday schedules for a given country may vary from year to year, dates may be changed by law, new holidays may be added, and established holidays may be renamed, curtailed, or dropped altogether. When in doubt about a holiday in a particular country, telephone the consulate or embassy of that country. You may also consult the international division of a large bank or call the U.S. Department of State. A very useful booklet is the *World Holiday and Time Guide,* published annually by J.P. Morgan & Co., 60 Wall Street, New York, NY 10260; every firm engaged in international business should keep the current edition on hand.

Holidays occurring on Saturdays and especially Sundays are often celebrated on the preceding Friday or the following Monday. Avoid scheduling appointments on days which may be affected.

The celebration of some holidays often begins at noon or 1 p.m. on the day preceding. Sometimes stores, banks, and offices will remain closed until about noon of the day following the holiday.

In Israel, banks, government offices, and businesses are closed on Saturday. Most Israeli holidays follow the Jewish religious calendar.

Countries in which the Muslim religion is predominant (Saudi Arabia, Egypt, Indonesia, Jordan, Tunisia, Morocco, Pakistan, etc.) observe religious holidays which are based on the lunar calendar and are therefore variable. Banks and other offices are usually closed on Friday but are open on Saturday and Sunday. Some other countries (such as Guyana and Nigeria) observe both Muslim and non-Muslim holidays. Some Asian countries observe holidays based on the Buddhist and other Eastern religious calendars.

In some countries such as France and Italy, business activity is sharply curtailed in July and August when people go on vacation. It is therefore wise to avoid traveling in these countries on business during the summer months unless one is sure that one's business colleagues will not be on vacation. The practice of taking long weekends is also customary in many countries; you may have to inquire if foreign business associates will be in their offices on Friday. In Muslim countries, business is generally conducted on Saturday and Sunday but not on Friday.

Time differences The world is divided into 24 standard time zones (some of these are further divided into half-zones), beginning at the International Date Line. This line approximates the 180° meridian in the Pacific Ocean between Asia and Hawaii. It is here that one day officially ends and another begins: for example, when it is Monday morning in Tokyo, it is still Sunday in the United States. On the opposite side of the globe is the prime or zero meridian, which passes through Greenwich, England, and marks Greenwich Mean Time, the standard by which other times are reckoned.

The United States lies within seven of the 24 standard time zones, from the westernmost point of Alaska to the East Coast. The standard time-zone numbers increase from west to east, starting at the International Date Line. Remember that the earth turns toward the east and that the sun rises earlier in the east than in the west. Thus, the farther east from the United States, the later in the day it is. When it is 8 a.m. Monday on the West Coast, it is 11 a.m. on the East Coast. It is even later (5 p.m.) in much of Europe, and still later—Monday evening— in India. Even farther east, in Siberia, it is already early Tuesday morning—all while it is still Monday morning on the West Coast of the United States.

The chart on pages 435–443 shows the comparative standard times of major countries of the world.

Many countries observe daylight saving time during the spring and summer. The dates of change from standard time differ from those in the United States, however, and the traveler should check with foreign embassies or consulates or see the *World Holiday and Time Guide* to find out what these dates are.

Expense account records Reimbursable and tax-deductible items are key listings in any record of business expenses. Forms for recording expense records can be prepared by the forms designers and analysts in corporations, and must comply with Internal Revenue Service requirements. Conditions and record-keeping rules underlying deductions on federal income-tax returns for travel, entertainment, and gifts are set forth in the Internal Revenue Service's pamphlet *Travel, Entertainment, and Gift Expenses*. Copies can be obtained from the Superintendent of Documents, P.O. Box 371954, Pittsburgh, PA 15250-7954.

Business people bringing home gifts from abroad must be able to substantiate the following information: cost, date of purchase, description, reason for giving it, and information about the recipient including name, title, and occupation.

Metric equivalents Many secretaries in multinational firms must work with metric measures. A table of metric measures with their U.S. equivalents is shown on page 464. In the first part of the table, nonmetric units are listed on the left and their metric equivalents on the right. In the second part, metric units are listed on the left, with their nonmetric equivalents on the right. (In the "Weight" portion of the table, *Avoirdupois* refers to standard American measure, *Troy* refers to the measure commonly used for precious metals, and *Apothecaries'* is the measure traditionally used for drugs.)

Background Research

Executives who travel and work in foreign countries frequently need a great deal of background information before going abroad, as do executives in the United States who work with those in other countries. Economics, marketing, management, language, culture, politics, history, and geography are all important facets of this background. A knowledge of the changing international policies of the United States and other nations is also vital, because foreign relations can affect the operations of multinational firms.

Company, city, and university libraries house source materials (such as federal government publications) on these subjects. A description of especially useful reference works appears on the following pages.

INDEXES

Using indexes is a practical way to identify periodicals in print and to research topics discussed in them. Finding the headings under which articles are listed can be difficult until one becomes comfortable with the system of topical indexing that these books employ. Librarians can assist researchers in finding the required headings in these indexes. Some of the most useful indexes are listed here, together with brief descriptions of their scope and utility.

Business Periodicals Index (Bronx, N.Y.: H. W. Wilson).   This monthly publication indexes English-language periodicals in the fields of accounting, banking, labor, and management; it also includes listings for specific businesses, industries, and trades. The heading "Multinational" will direct the researcher to more specific subheadings.

International Executive (Glendale, Ariz.: American Graduate School of International Management).   This index contains references to over 200 periodicals and highlights material that is basic to international business operations. Books and articles are listed with descriptive notes. *International Executive* is published three times a year.

Monthly Catalog of United States Government Publications (Washington, D.C.: Government Printing Office).   This catalog lists current publications (particularly those originating in the Commerce Department), many of which are of interest to executives in multinational firms. Instructions for ordering publications are included.

New York Times Index (New York: New York Times Co.).   This index covers only articles from the *New York Times*. Refer to "Economic Conditions and Trends (General)" for general material on world conditions and especially conditions in underdeveloped areas and for information on private foreign investments. See "Foreign Aid" for general material on government. Refer to "Commerce" for news about continents, groups of countries, or specific countries. Other headings that may prove helpful are "United Nations," "Agriculture," and "Labor."

Predicasts F&S Index Europe (Cleveland, Ohio: Predicasts).   This monthly index covers company, product, and industry information from over 750 financial publications, business-oriented newspapers, trade magazines, and special reports. It is divided into three sections: Industries and Products, Countries, and Companies.

Reader's Guide to Periodical Literature (Bronx, N.Y.: H. W. Wilson).   This index covers virtually all the major periodicals in the United States. The "Multinational" heading is followed by subheadings such as "Corporations—International." Relatively few are strictly business-oriented; however, many general periodicals carry articles of interest to business people.

Social Sciences Index (Bronx, N.Y.: H. W. Wilson).   This publication, though not primarily oriented to business, does index some periodicals (such as *Asia, Business History Review, Far Eastern Economic Review, Foreign Affairs,* and *The Journal of Economic History*) that are important to the internationally-minded executive.

Ulrich's International Periodicals Directory (New York: R. R. Bowker).   This is a yearly index of the names of over 100,000 periodicals in print throughout the world. Under the heading "Business and Economics" are the headings "Chamber of Commerce Publications," "International Commerce," and other pertinent topics.

Wall Street Journal Index (New York: Dow Jones).   This index covers only articles in the *Wall Street Journal,* separating corporate news from general information. The researcher interested in a foreign country should look under its name. The International Monetary Fund and the World Bank are specifically indexed.

TRAVEL GUIDES

Travel guides—also important sources of information because of their frequent updating—are likely to be especially valuable to those who travel on a regular basis. The following annotated list is a representative sampling of these books.

Fielding's Europe, by Joseph Raff (New York: William Morrow).   This annual guide contains information on travel preparations, money and prices, food, hotels, tipping, and the attitudes of Europeans toward tourists.

Fodor's Europe (New York: David McKay).   This guide, updated annually, contains historical sketches of each country as well as information about its people, art, food and drink, and weather. A tourist's vocabulary in 12 European languages is included.

Michelin Red Guides (Greenville, S.C.: Michelin Travel Publications).   These guides rate hotels, motels, and dining service in various European countries. They include maps, tables of distances between cities, and points of interest.

South American Handbook (New York: Prentice Hall Press).   Updated annually, this is an extensive guide to South America including Mexico, Central America, and the Caribbean countries. It includes detailed information on weather, government, roads, and other matters beyond the normal tourist information.

The Wall Street Journal Guides to Business Travel, by Eugene Fodor (New York: David McKay).   These four guides—*Europe, The Pacific Rim, USA and Canada,* and *International Cities*—written solely for the business traveler are updated annually. They cover topics ranging from import/export regulations and the location of major banks to tipping customs.

ENCYCLOPEDIAS AND ATLASES

Encyclopedias can be helpful to the researcher, particularly the *Encyclopaedia Britannica,* which contains articles the length of short books on many of the world's nations.

Atlases may also be helpful. The major atlases, all of which offer an enormous amount of textual information in addition to finely detailed maps, are the *Times Atlas of the World,* 9th ed. (New York: Times Books, 1992), the *Britannica Atlas* (Chicago: Encyclopaedia Britannica, 1991), the *National Geographic Atlas of the World,* 6th ed. (Washington, D.C.: National Geographic, 1990), and the *New International Atlas,* Anniversary Ed. (Chicago: Rand McNally, 1991). However,

Rand McNally and other publishers also publish numerous small, portable atlases with good-quality maps.

STATISTICAL REFERENCES

Three useful statistical sources of interest to executives in multinational firms are:

Commodity Year Book (New York: Commodity Research Bureau). This annual publication includes an appraisal of trends in supply, demand, and prices for the 110 basic commodities. For example, the treatment of copper includes information on world copper production starting with 1961 and world smelter production for the major copper-producing countries, U.S. imports from and exports to selected countries, and refined copper stocks outside the United States. The statistical data are preceded by a brief discussion of the particular commodity market for the year. Both agricultural and mineral commodities are included.

Direction of Trade Statistics (Washington, D.C.: International Monetary Fund). This monthly volume reports statistics on exports and imports. Values of trade are given in U.S. dollars. Not all countries of the world are included in each issue.

Foreign Trade Reports: Highlights of U.S. Export and Import Trade (Washington, D.C.: U.S. Bureau of the Census). This is a monthly compilation of statistical data on U.S. exports and imports, prepared by the Bureau of the Census and the Department of Commerce. Statistics are grouped under headings such as individual commodities by unit of quantity, for all methods of transportation collectively, as well as separately for water and air shipments. Data concerning each commodity for the current year and month and for the previous year and month are included. Cumulative amounts for prior years and months are also shown.

PAMPHLETS

Background Notes A series of pamphlets published by the Bureau of Public Affairs of the U.S. Department of State (available from the Superintendent of Documents, Government Printing Office, Washington, DC 20402). These periodically updated pamphlets offer the reader a quick look at various countries and territories. Each pamphlet contains information on a country's land, people, history, government, political situation, economy, and foreign relations, as well as a map and a brief bibliography.

PERIODICALS

Secretaries who do research for executives can find information pertinent to multinational business in a variety of periodicals. Some of the periodicals that will assist executives in keeping up-to-date with international business and economics are listed here. For other periodicals devoted to foreign business, and for information about ordering any of these periodicals, consult *Ulrich's International Periodicals Directory* (available in the reference section of most city libraries).

Business America (Washington, D.C.: International Trade Administration, U.S. Department of Commerce). This biweekly publication is the principal news publication of the Department of Commerce. It includes current reports from the Foreign Service, listings of worldwide business opportunities, and articles on topics such as the economies of foreign countries.

Business International (New York: Business International Corp.). This weekly report is addressed to managers of worldwide business and industrial operations. Topics such as personnel and labor, foreign trade, government and politics, the European Community, and economic conditions in specific countries are covered in short articles.

Business Week (New York: McGraw-Hill Publications).   This important weekly business-news magazine discusses current business topics and related subjects.

The Commercial and Financial Chronicle (Arlington, Mass.: National News Service).   This is a weekly newspaper which, in addition to articles on business topics, features a digest of market letters, offering its readers a digest of financial news from these financial publications, a list of sales and purchases of stock by officers of firms, stock-exchange records, and listings of securities offered by the U.S. government and its agencies.

The Economist (London: Economist Newspaper).   *The Economist* is a weekly magazine that not only deals with business and economics but also contains thorough coverage of world events. Its primary function, however, is to provide its readers with current economic and business news of Europe and America.

Finance and Development (Washington, D.C.: International Monetary Fund and International Bank for Reconstruction and Development).   This quarterly journal is published in English, French, Chinese, Spanish, German, and Portuguese. Its articles reflect the changing global economic scene, explain the workings and the policies of the Fund and the Bank, and discuss activities of the Fund such as assistance to countries in short-term balance-of-trade difficulties. Another section of the journal offers reviews of books on topics such as exchange and trade controls, international trade policies, and international monetary reform.

Financial Times (London: Financial Times).   This daily British equivalent of *The Wall Street Journal* typically contains coverage of bank base rates, company news, foreign-exchange quotations and rates, international company news, labor news, mining news, the state of the money market, overseas markets and news, stock-exchange reports, and world trade news.

Forbes (New York: Forbes, Inc.).   This magazine, published biweekly, carries articles on domestic and foreign business and presents its viewpoint on investments, discussing past performance of and outlook for specific firms.

Fortune (New York: Time, Inc.).   This biweekly magazine typically carries articles related to domestic and foreign business operations, firms, and executives. The "Fortune Directory" of the largest industrial corporations, commercial-banking companies and life-insurance companies, and utilities companies are useful features.

IMF Survey (Washington, D.C.: International Monetary Fund).   This weekly briefly summarizes articles pertaining to organizations such as the European Community, the Inter-American Development Bank, and the International Monetary Fund. It also contains articles on individual countries of the world and on commodities.

Nation's Business (Washington, D.C.: Chamber of Commerce of the United States).   Articles in this monthly relate strictly to the domestic business scene.

Survey of Current Business (Washington, D.C.: Bureau of Economic Analysis, U.S. Department of Commerce).   This monthly publishes current business statistics (monthly and annual) under headings such as "General Business Indicators," "Commodities," "Prices," "Labor Force," "Employment," and "Earnings," and articles on topics such as balance of foreign payments and foreign trade.

The Wall Street Journal (New York: Dow Jones).   This daily (except Saturday and Sunday) newspaper primarily covers current financial and business news in areas such as foreign trade, investments, stocks, bonds, and commodity markets. Coverage of foreign business news is limited.

UN Chronicle (New York: United Nations Publications). This periodical, issued 11 times a year, summarizes the activities of the United Nations and its specialized agencies, including the Economic Commission, which concerns itself with Latin America, Western Asia, and other areas of the world. It contains articles on monetary systems, multinational corporations, and the International Monetary Fund (IMF).

International Trade

To increase its awareness of expanding foreign markets and to obtain assistance in developing these markets, private enterprise can look to the U.S. Department of Commerce, the U.S. Department of State, and the Chamber of Commerce of the United States as well as to commercial banking institutions. For American firms, the international scene involves more than just exports: it also includes cooperative ventures, consulting agreements, and joint developmental projects with foreign corporations and foreign governments. Government assistance programs are varied and specialized, but taken together they represent a planned program of great importance to American business.

The concept of international trade has broadened to encompass international service industries. The problems related to the sale of services are similar to those encountered in exporting products. The most important service industries are accounting, advertising, banking, construction and engineering, franchising, health services, insurance, shipping, and tourism.

Secretaries in firms that have never exported their services or products can play an important role in helping to develop foreign markets for their firms by collecting information on procedures for conducting business abroad and on sources of assistance, development of overseas markets, and ways of financing exports. This material can be invaluable to executives interested in penetrating foreign markets. Secretaries in firms already active in these markets can lend valuable assistance by keeping up-to-date on developments related to world trade.

The secretary who is involved in the international business of a company should be able to find answers to questions about the markets and products of the countries that the company does business with, including such questions as the following:

Is the country industrialized? evolving into an industrialized nation?

What is its standard of living?

What is its level of education?

What is its official language? What other languages are used?

How tolerant is the country of foreign products?

Are there religious and social influences to be considered regarding particular products?

What types of customer reside in this country?

How big is the market for our type of product?

How many of this type of product are now sold?

Who sells these products?

What share of the market do they control?

How do our competitors' products differ from our own?

What kind of service for specific products will be needed?
How can marketing strategies be developed?

The discussion that follows provides basic information on international trade and suggestions on how to obtain further information.

U.S. DEPARTMENT OF COMMERCE

The Department of Commerce offers assistance to multinational corporations and to firms desiring to compete in foreign markets. Through the Department's many district offices, aid is available to companies that are launching new programs abroad or expanding their existing programs. You should turn to these offices for more detailed information and assistance.

The International Trade Administration (ITA) of the Department of Commerce works in several ways to help Americans benefit from world trade. First, it strengthens and promotes America's international trade, investment, and sales with the following services:

Counseling the business community on the benefits of exporting, how to get started, how to find buyers and distributors, and how to compete for foreign government contracts.

Staging overseas commercial exhibitions of U.S. products and conducting trade missions, catalog exhibitions, and sales seminars abroad to introduce U.S. manufacturers to foreign buyers.

Maintaining a corps of Foreign Commercial Service Officers around the world to gather information on commercial and industrial trends for the benefit of the U.S. business community.

Publishing commercial and marketing information on the world's regions and countries.

Providing local business communities with information and assistance on exporting and investing abroad.

Operating the Worldwide Information and Trade System (WITS), a computerized international marketing system that links U.S. and foreign commercial services with the Washington headquarters.

Second, the ITA helps to develop and maintain an effective U.S. trade policy through activities such as the following:

Identifying key issues affecting America's international commerce and trade.

Implementing and monitoring tariff and nontariff agreements with our trading partners.

Analyzing international regulations and practices affecting foreign investment.

Third, the ITA tries to control certain export or import practices that adversely affect the United States by doing the following:

Investigating complaints of dumping to determine their validity.

Determining if foreign governments are subsidizing their exports to us.

Administering our export control laws and statutory programs involving exports of certain items.

The Foreign Commercial Service (FCS) of the Department of Commerce is a component of the Foreign Service. Promoting U.S. trade and facilitating U.S. investment are its primary responsibilities. To pursue its mission, the FCS has about 130 offices in almost 70 countries, some of them in foreign-trade centers and some in U.S. embassies and consulates. Foreign Commercial Service officers work directly with foreign governments, business representatives, and individuals interested in increasing and continuing trade.

Export Development Offices (EDOs), maintained by the Department of Commerce, are the principal export promotion facilities abroad. These offices, found in major commercial cities worldwide, cooperate with the Foreign Commercial Service and the Department of State, including consulates. Some of their important services are initial market research, assistance with shipping and customs, and the mounting of exhibits. Export Development Offices organize trade fairs, solo exhibitions, trade seminars, and special promotions. To help the exporter participate in such trade promotions, EDOs will provide office space, design and construct exhibits, advise on shipments to the site, unpack and set up displays, and provide basic utilities and housekeeping services, lounges and meeting rooms, appropriate hospitality, and market counseling.

A Basic Guide to Exporting, published by the International Trade Administration, is sold by the Superintendent of Documents. This guide should be in the library of any secretary involved in international trade. It tells the potential exporter what is needed to establish a profitable international trade and how to get assistance in doing so. In addition to explaining the basics of establishing export programs, it directs readers to additional sources of information in the government and the private sector. It includes an extensive glossary of terms used in international trade and a bibliography of export reference publications.

U.S. DEPARTMENT OF STATE

The Department of State plays an important part in developing international trade. It negotiates treaties and agreements that affect commerce and trade. It also handles commercial and economic functions in countries with little commercial activity. In all countries that have U.S. embassies, American businesspeople can get assistance from the Economic/Commercial Officers who brief them and introduce them to firms, individuals, and government officials. Those who are anticipating such assistance should write to foreign service posts at least two weeks before leaving the United States.

Assistance within the United States is available from Country Desk Officers in the Department of State. These officers brief representatives of American firms on the political and economic climate in the countries they represent. Write to [country] Desk Officer, Department of State, Washington, DC 20520, for assistance.

U.S. FOREIGN SERVICE POSTS

American consulates are located around the world. Americans traveling and working abroad can go to them for assistance in business and personal matters. The table on pages 524–32 shows the sites of all U.S. embassies, legations, and consulates, along with other important cities. The addresses of these embassies, consulates, and legations may be found in the current edition of *Key Officers of Foreign Service Posts: Guide for Business Representatives,* available from the Superintendent of Documents.

THE U.S. CHAMBER OF COMMERCE

The Chamber of Commerce of the United States, a private organization, perceives private enterprise as a key contributor to world economic development. It believes that U.S. businesspeople abroad have a dual role, as unofficial ambassadors and as corporate representatives. The Chamber helps business executives adapt to the demands of this dual role, and it cooperates with the government agencies responsible for international policies and programs. It advocates a freer international flow of goods, services, and capital. The International Group of the Chamber of Commerce contributes to the Chamber's formulation of policies in major international trade, investment, energy, and monetary issues. Other activities of the International Group are the following:

Analyzing legislation that affects American business abroad and preparing testimony on bills before Congress.

Maintaining close contact with key congressional staff and Executive Branch officials on matters that affect international business.

Providing active support for an improved and expanded national export promotion program.

Producing a variety of reports, surveys, and other publications (including audiovisual materials) on important international economic questions.

Inquiries related to multinational corporations and global business should be sent to the Chamber of Commerce of the United States, Washington, DC 20062.

FINANCING EXPORTS

In addition to developing foreign trade for American firms, U.S. government agencies facilitate the financing of the sale of goods and services to foreign buyers. Such financing is accomplished in cooperation with commercial banks. To reduce the risk for American exporters, credit insurance is available through the U.S. government in association with the insurance industry. Many exporters, however, obtain direct financing through the numerous U.S. banks that have qualified international banking departments, with experts in different kinds of commodities and transactions. Through correspondent relationships with foreign banks, they provide direct channels to overseas customers of American companies.

The Export-Import Bank of the United States   This organization is an independent agency of the U.S. government that participates in financing America's exports by offering direct loans to overseas purchasers of American goods and services. It cooperates with commercial banks in the United States and abroad in providing financial arrangements that help U.S. exporters offer credit to their overseas buyers, provides export credit guarantees to commercial banks which in turn finance export sales, and offers export credit insurance.

INTERNATIONAL TABLE

The following table lists every nation in the world (in 1993), along with a number of colonies, territories, and other possessions.

Each entry includes the languages predominantly spoken in the country (the official language or languages are listed first) and the name of the country's currency.

The time differential between the United States and each country listed, based on eastern standard time, appears in a separate column. To obtain the time in a given country, add the figure opposite the country's name in the time-differential column to the hour where you are, always remembering to allow for any time-zone difference between your office and eastern standard time. Thus, if it is 4:00 p.m. in your office in Los Angeles, it will be 4:30 a.m. in Afghanistan, since the total differential will be 12½ (that is, 9½ + 3) hours. At the same time, it will be 6:00 p.m. in Costa Rica, since the total differential will be only two hours (that is, the −1 in the time-differential column indicates that the difference will be one hour less than Los Angeles's normal differential with eastern standard time).

Daylight saving time—which in America prevails basically from April through October—effectively moves a country one time zone eastward, thus diminishing the positive time-differential figures by an hour and increasing the negative figures by an hour with respect to countries that do not observe daylight saving time. Daylight saving time is observed by most of the temperate-zone nations in the Northern Hemisphere (though it rarely extends past September). It is generally not observed by countries in the tropical zone. In the temperate-zone nations of the Southern Hemisphere, it is generally observed in reverse. Daylight saving time may thus account for additional differences of an hour, or even two hours, especially when calling countries outside of Europe.

In the right-hand column are listed some of the countries' principal cities. The cities in normal roman type represent the sites of *all* the U.S. embassies and consulates worldwide (1993). The first city listed is always the capital; except when printed in italics, it is also the site of the U.S. embassy or chief consular office. All the other cities listed, except those in italics, have U.S. consular offices.

The dialing code for each country appears in parentheses after its name. If the initials "A.C." (for "Area Code") precede the code, it may be dialed exactly like an area code within the United States. If no code appears after the country's name, the country cannot be dialed direct. Each city's dialing code, if any, appears after the city's name; where no number appears, no code is needed. For instructions on international dialing, see pages 377–378.

Several currency names—in particular, *franc, peso, dinar, pound, rupee, shilling,* and *dollar*—are each used in more than one country for currencies that are not in fact identical in value. Except where indicated, the currency is that of the individual country only. However, the CFA franc (CFA stands for Communauté Financière Africaine, or African Financial Community) and the East Caribbean dollar are genuinely international currencies.

Country and dialing code	Languages	Currency	Time diff.	Cities and dialing codes
Afghanistan	Pashto, Dari Persian	Afghani	9½	*Kabul*
Albania (355)	Albanian	Lek	7	Tirana (42)
Algeria (213)	Arabic, French, Berber	Dinar	6	Algiers (2), Oran (6)
American Samoa [U.S.] (684)	English	U.S. dollar	−6	Pago Pago
Andorra (33)	Catalan, Spanish, French	French franc, Spanish peseta	6	*Andorra la Vella* (628); embassy: Barcelona, Spain
Angola (244)	Portuguese	Kwanza	6	*Luanda* (2)
Antigua and Barbuda (A.C. 809)	English	East Caribbean dollar	1	St. Johns
Argentina (54)	Spanish	Peso	2	Buenos Aires (1), *Córdoba* (51), *Rosario* (41)
Armenia (7)	Armenian, Russian	Dram	9	Yerevan (885)

Country and dialing code	Languages	Currency	Time diff.	Cities and dialing codes
Aruba [Neth.] (297)	Dutch	Guilder	1	*Oranjestad* (8)
Australia (61)	English	Dollar	13, 14½, 15	Canberra (6), Adelaide (8), Brisbane (7), Melbourne (3), Perth (9), Sydney (2)
Austria (43)	German	Schilling	6	Vienna (1), Salzburg (662)
Azerbaijan (7)	Azerbaijani, Russian	Manat	9	Baku (8922)
Azores [Port.] (351)	Portuguese	Portuguese escudo	4	Ponta Delgada (96), *Madalena* (92)
Bahamas (A.C. 809)	English	Dollar	0	Nassau
Bahrain (973)	Arabic, English	Dinar	8	Manama
Bangladesh (880)	Bengali [Bangla], English	Taka	11	Dhaka (2)
Barbados (A.C. 809)	English	Dollar	1	Bridgetown
Belarus (7)	Belorussian, Russian	Ruble	8	Minsk (0172)
Belgium (32)	Flemish, French, German	Franc	6	Brussels (2), Antwerp (3)
Belize (501)	English, Spanish	Dollar	− 1	Belize City (2)
Benin (229)	French	CFA franc	6	Cotonou
Bermuda [U.K.] (A.C. 809)	English	British pound	1	Hamilton
Bhutan (975)	Dzongkha, Nepali, English	Ngultrum	10½	*Thimbu;* consulate: New Delhi, India
Bolivia (591)	Spanish, Quechua, Aymara	Boliviano	1	La Paz (2), *Santa Cruz* (33), *Cochabamba* (42)
Bosnia and Herzegovina (387)	Serbo-Croatian	Dinar	6	*Sarajevo* (71)
Botswana (267)	English, Tswana	Pula	7	Gaborone (31)
Brazil (55)	Portuguese	Cruzeiro	1,2	Brasília (61), Belém [Pará] (91), Belo Horizonte (31), Manaus (92), Porto Alegre (512), Recife (81), Rio de Janeiro (21), Salvador [Bahía] (71), São Paulo (11)
Brunei (673)	Malay, English, Chinese	Dollar	13	Bandar Seri Begawan (2)
Bulgaria (359)	Bulgarian	Lev	7	Sofia (2)
Burkina Faso (226)	French	CFA franc	5	Ouagadougou
Burma—see Myanmar				
Burundi (257)	French, Kirundi	Franc	7	Bujumbura
Cambodia (855)	Khmer, French	Riel	12	Phnom Penh (23)

Country and dialing code	Languages	Currency	Time diff.	Cities and dialing codes
Cameroon (237)	English, French	CFA franc	6	Yaoundé, Douala
Canada (no code needed when dialing from United States)	English, French	Dollar	−3, −2, −1, 0,1, 1½	Ottawa (613), Calgary (403), *Edmonton* (403), Halifax (902), *Hamilton* (519), Montreal (514), Québec (418), Toronto (416), Vancouver (604), *Winnipeg* (204)
Cape Verde (238)	Portuguese	Escudo	4	Praia
Central African Republic (236)	French	CFA franc	6	Bangui
Chad (235)	French, Arabic	CFA franc	6	N'Djamena (51)
Chile (56)	Spanish	Peso	1	Santiago (2)
China (86)	Mandarin Chinese	Yuan	13	Beijing (1), Chengdu (28), Guangzhou [Canton] (20), Shanghai (21), Shenyang [Mukden] (24), *Tianjin [Tientsin]* (22)
Colombia (57)	Spanish	Peso	0	Bogotá (1), Barranquilla (58)
Commonwealth of Independent States—see individual countries				
Comoros (269)	Arabic, French	CFA franc	8	Moroni
Congo (242)	French	CFA franc	6	Brazzaville
Costa Rica (506)	Spanish	Colón	−1	San José
Côte d'Ivoire (225)	French	CFA franc	5	Abidjan or *Yamoussoukro*
Croatia (385)	Serbo-Croatian	Kuna	6	Zagreb (41)
Cuba	Spanish	Peso	0	Havana
Cyprus (357)	Greek, Turkish, English	Pound	7	Nicosia (2)
Czech Rep. (42)	Czech	Koruna	6	Prague (2)
Denmark (45)	Danish	Krone	6	Copenhagen
Djibouti (253)	French, Arabic	Franc	8	Djibouti
Dominica (A.C. 809)	English	East Caribbean dollar	1	*Roseau;* embassy: Bridgetown, Barbados
Dominican Republic (A.C. 809)	Spanish	Peso	0	Santo Domingo
Ecuador (593)	Spanish, Quechua	Sucre	0	Quito (2), Guayaquil (4)
Egypt (20)	Arabic	Pound	7	Cairo (2), Alexandria (3)
El Salvador (503)	Spanish	Colón	−1	San Salvador
England—see United Kingdom				
Equatorial Guinea (240)	Spanish	CFA franc	6	Malabo (9)

Country and dialing code	Languages	Currency	Time diff.	Cities and dialing codes
Eritrea (291)	Amharic	Birr	8	Asmara (4)
Estonia (372)	Estonian, Russian	Kroon	7	Tallinn (2)
Ethiopia (251)	Amharic	Birr	8	Addis Ababa (1)
Fiji (679)	English, Fijian	Dollar	17	Suva
Finland (358)	Finnish, Swedish	Markka	7	Helsinki (0)
France (33)	French	Franc	6	Paris (1), Bordeaux (56), *Lyon* (7), Marseilles (91), Strasbourg (88)
French Guiana [Fr.] (596)	French	French franc	1	*Cayenne;* consulate: Fort-de-France, Martinique
Gabon (241)	French	CFA franc	6	Libreville
Gambia (220)	English	Dalasi	5	Banjul
Georgia (7)	Georgian, Russian	Ruble	9	Tbilisi (8832)
Germany (49)	German	Deutsche Mark	6	Berlin (30), Bonn (228), *Cologne [Köln]* (221), *Essen* (201), Frankfurt (69), Hamburg (40), Leipzig (341), Munich [München] (89), Stuttgart (711)
Ghana (233)	English	Cedi	5	Accra (21)
Gibraltar [U.K.] (350)	English	British pound	6	*Gibraltar*
Greece (30)	Greek	Drachma	7	Athens (1), Thessaloniki [Salonika] (31)
Greenland [Denm.] (299)	Danish	Danish krone	1,2,4	*Godthaab* (2)
Grenada (A.C. 809)	English	East Caribbean dollar	1	St. George's
Guadeloupe [Fr.] (590)	French	French franc	1	*Basse-Terre*
Guam [U.S.] (671)	English, Chamorro	U.S. dollar	15	Agaña
Guatemala (502)	Spanish	Quetzal	−1	Guatemala City (2)
Guinea (224)	French	Franc	5	Conakry (4)
Guinea-Bissau (245)	Portuguese	Peso	5	Bissau
Guyana (592)	English	Dollar	2	Georgetown (2)
Haiti (509)	French, Creole	Gourde	0	Port-au-Prince
Honduras (504)	Spanish	Lempira	−1	Tegucigalpa
Hong Kong [U.K.] (852)	English, Chinese	British pound	13	Hong Kong
Hungary (36)	Hungarian [Magyar]	Forint	6	Budapest (1)
Iceland (354)	Icelandic	Króna	5	Reykjavik (1)
India (91)	Hindi, English	Rupee	10½	New Delhi (11), Bombay (22), Calcutta (33), Madras (44)

Country and dialing code	Languages	Currency	Time diff.	Cities and dialing codes
Indonesia (62)	Bahasa Indonesia	Rupiah	12	Djakarta (21), Medan (61), Surabaya (31)
Iran (98)	Persian [Farsi]	Rial	8½	*Teheran (21)*
Iraq (964)	Arabic	Dinar	8	*Baghdad (1)*
Ireland (353)	Irish, English	Pound	5	Dublin (1)
Israel (972)	Hebrew, Arabic	Shekel	7	Tel Aviv (3) or Jerusalem (2), *Haifa (4)*
Italy (39)	Italian	Lira	6	Rome (6), Florence (55), Genoa (10), Milan (2), Naples (81), Palermo (91), *Turin (11)*, *Venice (41)*

Ivory Coast—see Côte d'Ivoire

Country and dialing code	Languages	Currency	Time diff.	Cities and dialing codes
Jamaica (A.C. 809)	English	Dollar	0	Kingston
Japan (81)	Japanese	Yen	14	Tokyo (3), Fukuoka (92), Kyoto (75), Nagoya (52), Naha (988), Osaka (6), Sapporo (11), *Yokohama (45)*
Jordan (962)	Arabic, English	Dinar	7	Amman (6)
Kazakhstan (7)	Russian, Kazakh	Ruble	10,11	Alma-Ata (3272)
Kenya (254)	Swahili, English	Shilling	8	Nairobi (2), Mombasa (11)
Kiribati (686)	English, Gilbertese	Australian dollar	17	*Tarawa*
Kuwait (965)	Arabic, English	Dinar	8	Kuwait
Kyrgyzstan (7)	Kirghiz	Som	11	Bishkek (3312)
Laos (856)	Lao, French, English	Kip	12	Vientiane (21)
Latvia (371)	Latvian, Russian	Ruble	7	Riga (2)
Lebanon (961)	Arabic, French	Pound	7	Beirut (1)
Lesotho (266)	English, Sesotho	Loti	7	Maseru
Liberia (231)	English	Dollar	5	Monrovia
Libya (218)	Arabic	Dinar	7	*Tripoli (21)*
Liechtenstein (41)	German	Swiss franc	6	*Vaduz (75)*; embassy: Zurich, Switzerland
Lithuania (370)	Lithuanian, Russian	Litas	7	Vilnius (2)
Luxembourg (352)	French, German	Franc	6	Luxembourg
Macao [Port.] (853)	Portuguese, Chinese	Patacá	13	*Macao;*
Macedonia (389)	Macedonian	Denar	6	*Skopje (91)*
Madagascar (261)	Malagasy, French	Franc	8	Antananarivo (2)
Malawi (265)	English, Chichewa	Kwacha	7	Lilongwe, *Blantyre*
Malaysia (60)	Malay, Chinese, English	Ringgit	13	Kuala Lumpur (3)

Country and dialing code	Languages	Currency	Time diff.	Cities and dialing codes
Maldives (960)	Dhivehi	Rufiyaa	10	*Malé;* embassy: Colombo, Sri Lanka
Mali (223)	French, Bambara	CFA franc	5	Bamako
Malta (356)	Maltese, English, Italian	Lira, Pound	6	Valletta/Floriana
Marshall Islands (692)	Marshallese, English	U.S. dollar	17	Majuro (9)
Martinique [Fr.] (596)	French	French franc	1	Fort-de-France
Mauritania (222)	Arabic, French	Ouguiya	5	Nouakchott
Mauritius (230)	English, French, Creole, Hindi	Rupee	9	Port Louis
Mexico (52)	Spanish	Peso	−1, −2, −3	Mexico City (5), Ciudad Juárez (16), Guadalajara (3), Hermosillo (62), Matamoros (891), Mazatlán (69), Mérida (99), Monterrey (83), Nuevo Laredo (871), Tijuana (66)
Micronesia, Federated States of (691)	English	U.S. dollar	16	Kolonia
Moldova (7)	Romanian, Russian	Leu	8	Kishinev [Chisinau] (2)
Monaco (33)	French	French franc	6	*Monaco* (93); consulate: Marseille, France
Mongolia (976)	Mongolian	Tugrik	12,13, 14	Ulan Bator (1)
Morocco (212)	Arabic, French	Dirham	5	Rabat (7), Casablanca (2)
Mozambique (258)	Portuguese	Metical	7	Maputo (1)
Myanmar (95)	Burmese	Kyat	11½	Yangon [Rangoon] (1)
Namibia (264)	English, Afrikaans, German	Dollar	7	Windhoek (61)
Nauru (674)	Nauruan, English	Australian dollar	17	*Yaren;* embassy: Canberra, Australia
Nepal (977)	Nepali	Rupee	10½	Kathmandu (1)
Netherlands (31)	Dutch	Gulden	6	The Hague ['s Gravenhage] (70), Amsterdam (20), *Rotterdam* (10)
Netherlands Antilles [Neth.] (599)	Dutch	Dutch gulden	1	Willemstad (9)

Country and dialing code	Languages	Currency	Time diff.	Cities and dialing codes
New Zealand (64)	English, Maori	Dollar	17	Wellington (4), Auckland (9), *Christchurch* (3)
Nicaragua (505)	Spanish	Córdoba	−1	Managua (2)
Niger (227)	French, Hausa	CFA franc	6	Niamey
Nigeria (234)	English, Hausa	Naira	6	Lagos (1), Kaduna (62)
Northern Ireland—see United Kingdom				
Northern Mariana Islands [U.S.]	English	U.S. dollar	14	
North Korea	Korean	Won	14	*Pyongyang*
Norway (47)	Norwegian	Krone	6	Oslo (22)
Oman (968)	Arabic, English	Rial	9	Muscat
Pakistan (92)	English, Urdu	Rupee	10	Islamabad (51), Karachi (21), Lahore (42), Peshawar (521)
Palau [U.S.] (680)	English	U.S. dollar	14	Koror
Panama (507)	Spanish, English	Balboa	0	Panama City
Papua New Guinea (675)	English, Pidgin English, Motu	Kina	15	Port Moresby
Paraguay (595)	Spanish, Guaraní	Guaraní	2	Asunción (21)
Peru (51)	Spanish, Quechua	Sol	0	Lima (14)
Philippines (63)	Pilipino, English	Peso	13	Manila (2), Cebu (32), *Quezon City* (2)
Poland (48)	Polish	Zloty	6	Warsaw (22), Krakow (12), Poznan (61)
Portugal (351)	Portuguese	Escudo	5	Lisbon (1), *Oporto* (2)
Puerto Rico [U.S.] (A.C. 809)	Spanish, English	U.S. dollar	0	San Juan
Qatar (974)	Arabic, English	Riyal	8	Doha
Réunion [Fr.] (262)	French, Creole	French franc	9	*Saint-Denis*
Romania (40)	Romanian, Hungarian [Magyar], German	Leu	7	Bucharest (1)
Russia (7)	Russian	Ruble	8,9,10, 11	Moscow (095), St. Petersburg (812), Vladivostok
Rwanda (250)	French, Kinyarwandu	Franc	7	Kigali
St. Kitts and Nevis (A.C. 809)	English	East Caribbean dollar	1	*Basseterre;* embassy: St. Johns, Antigua
St. Lucia (A.C. 809)	English	East Caribbean dollar	1	*Castries;* embassy: Bridgetown, Barbados
St. Vincent and the Grenadines (A.C. 809)	English	East Caribbean dollar	1	*Kingstown*

Country and dialing code	Languages	Currency	Time diff.	Cities and dialing codes
San Marino (39)	Italian	Italian lira	6	*San Marino* (549); embassy: Florence, Italy
São Tomé and Principe (239)	Portuguese	Dobra	5	*São Tomé;* embassy: Libreville, Gabon
Saudi Arabia (966)	Arabic	Riyal	8	Riyadh (1), Dhahran (3), Jidda (2)
Scotland—see United Kingdom				
Senegal (221)	French	CFA franc	5	Dakar
Serbia-Montenegro (381)	Serbo-Croatian	Dinar	6	Belgrade (11)
Seychelles (248)	Creole, English, French	Rupee	9	Victoria
Sierra Leone (232)	English	Leone	5	Freetown (22)
Singapore (65)	Chinese, Malay, Tamil, English	Dollar	13	Singapore
Slovakia (42)	Slovak	Koruna	6	Bratislava (7)
Slovenia (386)	Slovene	Tolar	6	Ljubljana (61)
Solomon Islands (677)	English	Dollar	16	Honiara
Somalia	Somali, Arabic	Shilling	8	*Mogadishu*
South Africa (27)	Afrikaans, English	Rand	7	Pretoria (12), Cape Town (21), Durban (31), Johannesburg (11)
South Korea (82)	Korean	Won	14	Seoul (2), *Inchon* (32), Pusan (51), *Taegu* (53)
Spain (34)	Spanish	Peseta	6	Madrid (1), Barcelona (3), Bilbao (4), *Valencia* (6)
Sri Lanka (94)	Sinhalese, Tamil, English	Rupee	10½	Colombo (1)
Sudan	Arabic, English	Dinar	7	Khartoum
Suriname (597)	Dutch, Sranan Tongo, English	Gulden	1½	Paramaribo
Swaziland (268)	Swazi, English	Lilangeni	7	Mbabane
Sweden (46)	Swedish	Krona	6	Stockholm (8)
Switzerland (41)	German, French, Italian	Franc	6	Bern (31), *Basel* (61), *Geneva* (22), Zurich (1)
Syria (963)	Arabic	Pound	8	Damascus (11)
Taiwan (886)	Mandarin Chinese	Dollar	13	*Taipei* (2), *Kaohsiung* (7)
Tajikistan (7)	Tajiki, Russian	Ruble	11	Dushanbe (3772)
Tanzania (255)	Swahili, English	Shilling	8	Dar es Salaam (51)
Thailand (66)	Thai, Chinese, English	Baht (Tical)	12	Bangkok (2), Chiang Mai (53), Songkhla (74), Udorn (42)
Togo (228)	French, Ewé	CFA franc	5	Lomé

Country and dialing code	Languages	Currency	Time diff.	Cities and dialing codes
Tonga (676)	Tongan, English	Pa'anga	18	*Nuku'alofa;* embassy: Suva, Fiji
Trinidad and Tobago (A.C. 809)	English	Dollar	1	Port-of-Spain
Tunisia (216)	Arabic, French	Dinar	6	Tunis (1)
Turkey (90)	Turkish	Lira	7	Ankara (4), Adana (71), Istambul (1), Izmir (51)
Turkmenistan (7)	Turkmenian, Russian	Manat	10	Ashkhabad (3632)
Tuvalu (688)	Tuvaluan, English	Australian dollar	17	*Funafuti*
Uganda (256)	English, Swahili	Shilling	8	Kampala (41)
Ukraine (7)	Ukrainian, Russian	Karbovanets	8	Kiev (044)
United Arab Emirates (971)	Arabic, Persian [Farsi], English	Dirham	9	Abu Dhabi (2), Dubai (4)
United Kingdom (44)	English	Pound	5	London (71, 81), Belfast, Northern Ireland (232), *Birmingham* (21), Edinburgh, Scotland (31), *Glasgow, Scotland* (41), *Manchester* (61)
Upper Volta—see Burkina Faso				
Uruguay (598)	Spanish	Peso	2	Montevideo (2)
U.S. Virgin Islands [U.S.] (A.C. 809)	English	U.S. dollar	1	*Charlotte Amalie*
Uzbekistan (7)	Uzbek, Russian	Ruble	10,11	Tashkent (3712)
Vanuatu (678)	Bislama, French, English	Vatu	16	*Vila;* embassy: Port Moresby, Papua New Guinea
Vatican City (39)	Italian, Latin	Italian lira	6	All points: (6)
Venezuela (58)	Spanish	Bolivar	1	Caracas (2), Maracaibo (61)
Vietnam (84)	Vietnamese, French, English	Dong	12	*Hanoi* (4), *Ho Chi Minh City* (8)
Virgin Islands—see U.S. Virgin Islands				
Western Samoa (685)	Samoan, English	Tala	−6	*Apia;* embassy: Wellington, New Zealand
Yemen (967)	Arabic	Dinar, Rial	8	San'a (1)
Yugoslavia—see Serbia-Montenegro				
Zaire (243)	French	Zaire	6,7	Kinshasa (12), Lubumbashi (222)
Zambia (260)	English	Kwacha	7	Lusaka (1)
Zimbabwe (263)	English	Dollar	7	Harare (4)

CHAPTER 14

Useful Products
and Services

This chapter will attempt to identify a variety of books, services, and other resources ranging from the merely convenient to the indispensable.

Bibliography

Your bookshelf should contain the following:

Any *world atlas*.

A *map of Europe* with a multinational list of places, such as the *Europa Strassenatlas mit Orts- und Namenverzeichnis* ("Europe Road Atlas with Index of Places and Names"), published by Hallwag, Bern, Switzerland. Local maps can be obtained from specialized bookstores, such as:

Traveller's Bookstore
75 Rockefeller Plaza
22 West 52nd Street
NEW YORK NY 10019
Tel.: 800/755-8728
Fax: 212/397-3984

Stanfords
12-14 Long Acre
LONDON WC2E 9LP
U.K.
Tel.: +44-1-71-836-1321
Fax: +44-1-71-836-0189

A *road atlas of the United States*, such as the *Rand McNally Road Atlas*.

The *postal regulations of your own country*. In the United States, the *Domestic Mail Manual* and the *International Mail Manual* are published every six months and are available on subscription (allow plenty of lead time) from:

Superintendent of Documents
P. O. Box 371954
PITTSBURGH PA 15250-7954
Tel.: 202/512-1800
Fax: 202/512-2250

The *national postcode directory* of any country that you deal with extensively, if you can understand it. In the United States, the USPS book is republished as the *National Five-Digit ZIP Code and Post Office Directory* by:

National Information Data Center
P. O. Box 96523
WASHINGTON DC 20090-6523
Tel.: 301/816-8950
Fax: 301/816-8945

In other countries, you will need to activate your local contacts to get post-office publications. Requesting them by mail is a long and frustrating process in most cases.

The *AT&T International Dialing Guide*, which provides a listing of country and city codes for U.S. callers to every country in the world. It is available free of charge from AT&T by calling 800/428-8468.

Phone books for at least the capital cities of any countries you deal with regularly. Most foreign phone books are obtainable from:

M. Arman Publishing Inc.
P. O. Box 785
ORMOND BEACH FL 32175
Tel.: 904/673-5576
Fax: 904/673-6560

A *national trade directory* for any country that you are interested in. For most countries in this book, the most readily available directory is the one published by Kompass AG, Zürich, Switzerland, and its international associates. For the United States, industry-specific directories (such as *Data Sources*, published by Ziff-Davis, for the computer industry) are more useful and accurate than general directories. One informative general reference work for the United States is the *Directory of Corporate Affiliations*, available from:

National Register Publishing Co./Reed Reference
121 Chanlon Rd.
NEW PROVIDENCE NJ 07974
Tel.: 908/464-6800
Fax: 908/665-6688

The *Japan Company Handbook*, an English-language book on Japanese corporations, is published by:

Toyo Keizai America Inc.
380 Lexington Ave., Suite 4505
NEW YORK NY 10168
Tel.: 212/949-6737
Fax: 212/949-6648

Stock-exchange directories, in particular the *NASDAQ Fact Book and Company Directory* in the United States, available from the National Association of Securities Dealers (202/728-8000); and the (London) *Stock Exchange Official Yearbook* in the United Kingdom, available from the London Stock Exchange by phone (+44-71-797-3306) or fax (+44-71-410-6861).

An *international airline guide,* of which there are two in English: the *Official Airline Guide* (Oak Brook, Ill.: Official Airline Guides) in the United States, and the *ABC World Airways Guide* (Dunstable, Beds.: Reed Travel Group) in the United Kingdom.

A *schedule for European railroads,* such as the *Thomas Cook European Railway Timetable,* which is available from certain offices of the Thomas Cook travel agency chain, or more easily in the United States from:

Forsyth Travel Library
P. O. Box 2975
SHAWNEE MISSION KS 66201-1375
Tel.: 800/FORSYTH
Fax: 913/384-3553

A *guide to holidays and time differences,* such as the *World Holiday and Time Guide*, published by:

Corporate Communication Dept.
J. P. Morgan & Co.
60 Wall Street, 45th floor
NEW YORK NY 10260
Tel.: 212/648-9607

A *guide to shipping documentation,* such as Alan E. Branch's *Import and Export Documentation* (New York: Chapman & Hall, 1989).

A *guide to international business etiquette,* such as Roger Axtell's *Do's and Taboos around the World,* 3d ed. (New York: John Wiley, 1993). *Do's and Taboos of International Trade: A Small Business Primer,* by the same author (Wiley, 1994), is another helpful guide.

Cost-of-Living Information

You can spend a small fortune on specialized research services and personnel consultants to advise your organization about costs of business travel and expatriate living in foreign countries. There are also the following excellent sources of less detailed information.

A free booklet called *Prices and Earnings around the Globe* is intermittently available from the Union Bank of Switzerland, which has offices in major cities everywhere, including:

444 S. Flower St., Suite 4500
LOS ANGELES CA 90071
Tel.: 213/489-0600
Fax: 213/489-0637

Information compiled by the U.S. government for its own overseas personnel policy is available to the public. There are two particularly useful documents entitled *Maximum Travel Per Diem Allowances for Foreign Areas* and *U.S. Dept. of State Indexes of Living Costs Abroad.* Copies are available from:

Superintendent of Documents
P. O. Box 371954
PITTSBURGH PA 15250-7954
Tel.: 202/512-1800
Fax: 202/512-2250

Prices in these publications are a very good guide to comparative costs and are themselves good budget figures for professional staff who are traveling to countries they are unfamiliar with. Someone with local knowledge, or who speaks the local language, or who is on a tight budget can travel a little more cheaply, at maybe 75 percent of the cost. On the other hand, a senior executive using the major international hotel chains can easily spend double the government allowances.

A source of detailed practical information for business travelers is the *Multinational Executive Travel Companion,* published by:

Suburban Publishing of Connecticut
P.O. Box 1293
STAMFORD CT 06904-1293
Tel.: 203/324-3007
Fax: 203/967-8404

and republished by other organizations, including the Union Bank of Finland. Be aware that information on "Local Customs" in publications of this type is apt to be very subjective.

Associations

Someone in your organization may be interested in belonging to one of the following associations, which all publish interesting newsletters, even if you are not able to play an active part:

International Telecommunications
  Users Group
31 Westminster Palace Gardens
Artillery Row
LONDON SW1P 1RR
U.K.
Tel.: +44-1-71-799-2446
Fax: +44-71-799-2445

International Communications
  Association
2735 Villa Creek Drive, Ste. 200
DALLAS TX 75234-7419
Tel.: 214/233-3889
Fax: 214/488-9985

International Facsimile Association/
  International Facsimile
  Consultative Council
4019 Lakeview Drive
LAKE HAVASU CITY AZ 86406
Tel.: 520/453-3850
Fax: 520/453-9234

Foreign-Language Correspondence

If you intend to try and write in another language, you should equip yourself with the best local dictionary you can afford, the best bilingual dictionary you can afford, and, if there is one available, a commercial dictionary. A good test of a bilingual dictionary is to see whether it translates accounting terminology. Look up *receivables, payables, ledger, journal entry.* If it passes that test, try some warehouse terminology: *skid, gantry, lift truck.*

You will also need a secretarial handbook and a book of sample letters from the foreign country.

Most multilingual (as opposed to bilingual) dictionaries and phrase books contain an inadequate level of detail. However, two books worth knowing about are the *Handbook for Multilingual Business Writing,* 2d ed., distributed in the United States by NTC Business Books, and a series in several volumes called the *Bilingual Guides to Business and Professional Correspondence,* distributed in the United States by Franklin Book Co. Neither is perfect, but the idea behind them—to provide a structured vocabulary of phrases that you can assemble into a routine letter with a very limited knowledge of the foreign language—is very good. Microsoft publishes a technical glossary which is useful for anyone localizing computer programs or manuals.

Translators

When should you have outgoing material translated, and who should do the work?

In most business situations, all sales and promotional literature should be translated, unless the market is highly technical. Instruction books should also be translated unless you are sure that the users are professionals who will be fluent in English. All safety warnings should be translated.

It is always difficult to decide whether to have internal documentation or detailed maintenance instructions and product specifications translated. Often, engineers in your foreign affiliates, distributors, and major clients would rather have up-to-date documentation in English than out-of-date or poorly translated versions in their own language. Maintaining a long description of an evolving product in several languages over a period of years represents a significant cost and effort which is not to be underestimated. You should consult the readers before committing resources to it; they might tell you that they only want an index or a glossary in their own languages.

Advertising, unless it is extremely factual, should never be translated, for a different reason. Advertising styles differ greatly from country to country. A design or an idea that catches the eye of an American may not work at all in other countries, including Britain. Advertising generally needs to be rethought by local specialists.

Promotional literature presents a similar problem. A translator is unlikely to be a competent direct-mail copywriter. At worst, you may find translators whose real interests are literary and cultural and who are mildly antibusiness. Your carefully worded letter expressing enthusiastically the advantages of your product or service and detailing the immense benefits of placing an immediate order may return from the translation agency with a distinct loss of color and persuasiveness. A marketing person with a limited knowledge of the foreign language can negotiate with the translator to restore the sales pitch to the letter. If nobody understands the foreign language well enough to do this, you should plan on a two-stage process in which the translator produces a literal translation and then a foreign copywriter (even a distributor's sales representative) improves it. Again, it may help the translator if you can collect some samples of direct-mail letters in the foreign language.

Technical material should really be translated by people who understand the subject matter. Nobody will know how to translate "twisted-pair" unless he or she is familiar with the terminology of the telecommunications industry. To keep up to date, a professional will subscribe to foreign-language trade publications and search them carefully for terms that are not yet accepted into dictionaries. Specialized translators for a particular subject and language may be difficult or impossible to find. You should plan for a joint effort between your engineers, your own technical writers, and the translators; you cannot expect good results if you just unload material onto a translator without an explanation of your specialized vocabulary.

Translation agencies and individual professional translators can be found in all major cities through the Yellow Pages. Amateurs, such as immigrants and students, can also be useful, especially for rarer languages, and for incoming translations at less than publication-quality. You can find amateurs through associations, such as a Swedish-American Chamber of Commerce or a Chinese-American Voter Registration Project. Organizations like these often are not listed in the phone book, but consulates, universities, immigrant churches, ethnic restaurants, and often local newspapers and politicians will know them. You can also look overseas for translators, particularly if you need an industry specialist or a press watch.

AT&T can set up a conference call with an interpreter while you wait. The AT&T Language Line can be reached at 800/752-6096 or, from outside the United States, at +1-408-648-5861. You will need a credit card.

CompuServe (800/848-8199) offers both automatic and manual translation services for electronic mail. Other e-mail services are likely to appear during the currency of this book.

Further information and guidance is published by

American Translators Association
1800 Diagonal Road, Suite 220
ALEXANDRIA VA 22314
Tel.: 703/683-6100

Computer Products

NON-ROMAN FONTS

The following companies offer fonts and word-processing programs in a wide variety of alphabets.

Timeworks
625 Academy Dr.
NORTHBROOK IL 60062
Tel.: 708/559-1300

Data-Cal Corporation
531 East Elliot Rd., Suite 145
CHANDLER AZ 85225-1118
Tel.: 602/813-3100
Fax: 602/545-8090

Linguist's Software
P. O. Box 580
EDMONDS WA 98020-0580
Tel.: 206/775-1130
Fax: 206/771-5911

CIMOS
73, avenue Gambetta
75020 PARIS
FRANCE
Tel.: +33-1-43.66.88.48
Fax: +33-1-43.66.51.13

Wright & Associates
P. O. Box 994
KENT OH 44240-0994
Tel.: 330/673-0043
Fax: 330/673-0738

Diplomat Software
P. O. Box 9878
NEWPORT BEACH CA 92658
Tel.: 714/775-1229
Fax: 714/448-0895

Gamma Productions Inc.
12625 High Bluff Drive, Suite 218
SAN DIEGO CA 92130
Tel.: 619/794-6399
Fax: 619/794-7294

TRANSLATION SOFTWARE

Translation software originated as a productivity aid for professional translators. At the time of writing, PC translation products are not suitable for ordinary office use. They can be valuable for an organization that translates large volumes of rather uniform material. But to work well, they need to be specialized very carefully over a long period of time with the technical vocabulary of their users, and the output needs to be reviewed manually. It is not currently realistic to expect to produce automatic translations of average business correspondence, especially marketing materials. However, it would be worth evaluating translation products if you are interested in scanning foreign-language text just to see what you want to have professionally translated. Products of this type are likely to improve over the next few years. The following are specialist companies:

Globalink, Inc.
9302 Lee Highway, 12th floor
FAIRFAX VA 22031
Tel.: 800/255-5660
Fax: 703/273-3866

Polygon Industries, Inc.
P. O. Box 24096
NEW ORLEANS LA 70184
Tel.: 504/451-5721
Fax: 504/486-2371

Linguistic Products, Inc.
P. O. Box 8263
THE WOODLANDS TX 77387
Tel.: 713/298-2565
Fax: 713/298-1911

Microtak Software
4375 Jutland Drive, Suite 110
SAN DIEGO CA 92117
Tel.: 619/272-5700
Fax: 619/272-9734

To test a product of this type, do two things. Take an article from the foreign trade press, scan it, transfer it to the translation package by whatever means the producer recommends, translate it, and see if you can understand it. Then take a standard business letter—for example, a cover letter that accompanies brochures you send out—and use the product to translate it into a foreign language and back again. Do not accept translations of text prepared by the vendors as a valid test—they are usually carefully written to be easy to translate.

A magazine called *Multilingual Computing* is a source of information about new products and services in this field. For information call 208/263-8178, fax 208/263-6310, or e-mail info@multilingual.com. Expect it to support vendors' optimism about who can realistically use their products.

Address Hygiene

"Address hygiene" and "(mailing) list hygiene" are the computer industry's jargon for the level of accuracy and standardization of postal addresses. The U.S. Postal Service operates an Address List Correction Service based on its Carrier Route Information System (CRIS), and also licenses its National Change of Address (NCOA) system information to a variety of private vendors. More and more U.S. software products incorporate NCOA address correctors. One reseller with a personal-computer *Address Corrector* based on this system is Alpha Software Corporation (800/622-7105), vendors of the Alpha Five database.

A prominent mainframe vendor is Group One Corporation (800/368-5806 or +1-301-731-2300). Products of this kind greatly assist the elimination of duplicate addresses as well as economizing on postage for bulk mailings.

In 1996, the correction of addresses in other countries is still far more difficult. National software is available from the post offices of the United Kingdom, Germany, and Japan (though not for Roman-alphabet Japanese addresses), and others will probably follow suit during the currency of this book. Two independent software vendors providing national address hygiene software are AFD Ltd. (at +44-1924-823221, fax +44-1924-822905) for the United Kingdom, and Corradress S.A. (at +33-1-40.77.54.67, fax +33-1-40.77.54.68) for France.

A multinational address corection software product is Global-Z, created by Dasgar Systems Inc. (at 802/447-3978, fax 802/442-3473).

Government Information Services

Most countries' governments make at least a show of providing assistance to their taxpaying exporters. But the taxpaying exporters often have an unrealistic idea of what they can expect in the way of assistance.

The inexperienced exporter will usually be looking at a number of likely countries, wanting market research, information about local regulatory requirements, general information about market opportunities, specific contacts with major customers, and specific information about distribution channels and individual distributors.

A typical *embassy* is located in a capital city and consists, at the lower levels, of consular, commercial, and information departments. *Consular officers* issue (or refuse to issue) passports, visas, birth certificates, death certificates, and the like. *Commercial officers* are there to assist exporters from their own country. *Information officers* report home about the foreign political situation, distribute positive information about their own country, and arrange cultural exchanges of various kinds. Any of these officers may have the title of consul or vice-consul. A *consulate-general* is a branch of an embassy, usually located outside the capital city, and also performs the above functions. A *consulate* is a sub-office with a limited set of functions and may well not have a commercial department. (Spell these words correctly: if you confuse consuls and councils and counsels, you will look ignorant to diplomats.) Embassies may also have military and technical specialists on loan from various government departments, who may be valuable contacts on regulatory and procurement matters. Some countries (not the United States) call their commercial organization a *trade commission* and keep it physically separate from embassies and consulates-general, but all the same comments apply to it. Individual provinces and regions of some countries, including many states of the United States, have established their own overseas commercial representative offices because of dissatisfaction with their national organizations. For simplicity, all these functions will be referred to below collectively as a *Foreign Service*.

Exporters can theoretically get information about foreign market conditions and opportunities from the commercial departments of their own Foreign Service. The entry point into the system in the United States is through the International Trade Administration of the Department of Commerce, which has offices all around the country. In case of difficulty, call 202/482-3809 in Washington, D.C., for the location of the regional office responsible for your area. The corresponding organizations for U.K. exporters are the British Overseas Trade Board (071-215 5000) and the Department of Trade and Industry. If your interest is in a specific country or two, you can bypass the ITA (or BOTB) by writing to your embassy in those foreign capitals. The U.S. embassies usually have special domestic addresses you can use (for example, "AmEmbassy Moscow, PSC 77-FCS, APO AE 09721"), which you can obtain from the U.S. State Department (202/647-4000).

The Japanese External Trade Relations Organization (JETRO) is the one foreign trade commission that may assist you to export. Generally, Foreign Services of other countries have no mandate to promote U.S. exports, and ours does not encourage imports.

What can an exporter expect? You will be able to obtain basic factual information from the Foreign Service about the economy of the country, business hours, the most popular trade shows, and addresses of national regulatory agencies. It may have specific information about retail trade distribution channels. The Foreign Service may sponsor occasional exhibitions or participate in trade shows. It may have lists of the names of some local translators, lawyers, accountants, and consultants of various kinds. Their standard information may or may not be up-to-date, depending on the trading importance of the country. Whether they can do more for you will depend on the individuals; if you are lucky, local staff with business backgrounds may have useful suggestions and contacts. But the official systems for finding trading partners for you produce very haphazard results.

If you are an importer, on the other hand, you must turn to the Foreign Service of the country that you want to buy from. Write politely to their commercial department, explaining what you want, and expect to make an appointment. Someone is quite likely to visit you if you appear serious. They will write a report on you, and the information is supposed to circulate to exporters in their home country. Do not hold your breath waiting for the official system to work. However, again, individuals may be knowledgeable and may provide useful background information.

If you want standard information about a foreign country, any of the above sources (commercial and information departments of your Foreign Service or theirs) will probably be willing to look it up for you in Yellow Pages, almanacs, or trade directories. Their information may not be very recent. You must have precise questions; it is not reasonable to ask these people to study your business and make recommendations.

Contact with consular departments is usually frustrating for businesspeople. Regulations are constructed to control immigration, without making many allowances for the legitimate needs of international business visitors. Visas, residence permits, and work permits are processed at a pace that may have been appropriate in the nineteenth century. Many business executives therefore travel around as tourists on the borderline of illegality, because it is just impractical to comply with official requirements, particularly when executives are relocating for overseas assignments. If you do research for relocations, be particularly careful to find out about permits for spouses and live-in companions. Regulations are invariably written with the assumption that an accompanying companion is a nonworking female, legally married to the principal male applicant.

There is another category of government organizations whose object is to encourage you to establish manufacturing and similar facilities in their country. This is often a regional or local function with varying degrees of central government coordination. Commercial departments will be able to tell you who to contact concerning their own regions. Well-known examples of economic development organizations active in the United States are Locate in Scotland (formerly the Scottish Development Agency) and the French DATAR.

In other countries, financial information published by large public companies is less carefully controlled than it is in the United States by the SEC. However, private companies in most countries have to file annual financial statements with their governments, and these are generally public records. Getting access to them may be difficult and time-consuming, particularly if there is a language barrier, but local intermediaries can obtain them for a fee. Local Foreign Service people should know how you can obtain financial information about individual companies.

Nongovernment Information Services

If you have a precise target market, the local *chamber of commerce* can usually provide lists of local companies. Do not underestimate them as sources of information. In many European countries membership is mandatory, and therefore their information about local businesses is the most comprehensive.

Controlled by or cooperating with chambers of commerce are some 250 *World Trade Centers* in principal cities around the world, which largely duplicate the functions described in the previous section. They have libraries and databases, provide office space and hotel discounts for visitors, organize trade missions, and help to find trading partners. Your local WTC probably has reciprocal membership facilities with its counterparts overseas.

The *national trade association* for your industry may have an international business department, or it may belong to some international federation that can supply market information. Always request lists of publications from organizations like these.

Call the *trade journals* of your industry. Many of them have sister publications overseas or links with similar publications in other countries, or at least staff members who cover international news.

Specialized consultants can be extremely valuable, but are hard to find. Someone who is really familiar with your market or activity can give you advice in a few days that would otherwise take you months or years to discover. An example in the computer industry is EMS (111 Pine Street, San Francisco CA 94111; tel.: 415/433-4344). Find such consultants through the trade press or through major manufacturers in your industry.

The *Big Six accounting firms* are an excellent source of information about overseas business matters of all kinds. In the United States, the Big Six are known as Arthur Andersen, Coopers & Lybrand, Deloitte & Touche, Ernst & Young, Peat Marwick, and Price Waterhouse. Each one has related firms, usually with similar names, all over the world, and each one publishes information about tax and other business matters in dozens of countries. You can take all kinds of business problems to their international management consulting partners. (Finding the right people to deal with can be a little difficult outside of major cities—insist on seeing an internal directory if necessary.) These organizations combine a multinational perspective with the detailed local business knowledge and the local contacts to solve the typical problems of the inexperienced exporter. Of course, their services are not free by any means.

Banks possess some of the same capabilities but are less organized internationally to give general business advice, and it is not what they sell. Their in-house knowledge of your sector of industry may be very good, but it may be hard to locate and benefit from. *Law firms* with international connections may have access to excellent knowledge of major companies overseas, but are likely to be specialized in strictly professional matters.

Credit information about overseas companies is offered by the principal U.S. companies in the business, but it is expensive and at least as erratic as it is in the United States. Basically, you are not going to trust anybody, anyway, because of the difficulty of enforcement.

In summary: If you are a newcomer to international business and cannot find an international specialist who knows your exact business, the Big Six are the most effective place to commission practical help. Commercial services organized by governments are apt to be of limited usefulness, although many individual officers will do their best to be helpful.

CHAPTER 15
Math and Science Basics

PLANETS				
NAME	SYMBOL	MEAN DISTANCE FROM THE SUN		PERIOD OF REVOLUTION IN DAYS OR YEARS	EQUATORIAL DIAMETER IN MILES
		astronomical units	million miles		
Mercury	☿	0.387	36.0	87.97 d.	3,032
Venus	♀	0.723	67.2	224.70 d.	7,523
Earth	⊕	1.000	92.9	365.26 d.	7,928
Mars	♂	1.524	141.5	686.98 d.	4,218
Jupiter	♃	5.203	483.4	11.86 y.	88,900
Saturn	♄	9.522	884.6	29.46 y.	74,900
Uranus	♅	19.201	1783.8	84.01 y.	31,800
Neptune	♆	30.074	2793.9	164.79 y.	30,800
Pluto	♇	39.725	3690.5	247.69 y.	1,400

TABLE OF CONSTELLATIONS

NAME AND MEANING	DECLINATION
[1]Andromeda \an-'dräm-əd-ə\ *Andromeda, the Chained Lady*	40° N
Antlia (Antlia Pneumatica) \'ant-lē-ə-n(y)ü-'mat-i-kə\ *Pump (Air Pump)*	35° S
[1]Apus \'ā-pəs\ *Bird of Paradise*	75° S
[1]Aquarius \ə-'kwar-ē-əs\ *Water Carrier*	10° S
[1]Aquila \ə-'kwil-ə\ *Eagle*	5° N
[1]Ara \'ar-ə\ *Altar*	55° S
[1]Aries \'ar-ˌēz\ *Ram*	20° N
[1]Auriga \ȯ-'rī-gə\ *Charioteer*	40° N
[1]Boötes \bō-'ōt-ēz\ *Herdsman*	30° N
Caelum (Caela Sculptoris) \'sē-ləm, 'sē-lə-ˌskəlp-'tōr-əs\ *Graving Tool*	40° S
Camelopardalis \kə-ˌmel-ə-'pär-də-ləs, kam-ə-lō-\ *Giraffe*	70° N
[1]Cancer \'kan-sər\ *Crab*	20° N
Canes Venatici \'kā-ˌnēz-və-'nat-ə-ˌsī\ *Hunting Dogs*	40° N
[1]Canis Major \'kā-nəs-'mā-jər, 'kan-əs-\ *Larger Dog*	20° S
[1]Canis Minor \'kā-nəs-'mī-nər, 'kan-əs-\ *Lesser Dog*	5° N
[1]Capricornis \ˌkap-rə-'kȯr-nəs\ *Horned Goat*	20° S
[2]Carina \kə-'rī-nə\ *Keel*	60° S
[1]Cassiopeia \ˌkas-ē-ə-'pē-ə\ *Cassiopeia, the Lady in the Chair*	60° N
[1]Centaurus \sen-'tȯr-əs\ *Centaur*	45° S
[1]Cepheus \'sē-ˌfyüs, -fē-əs\ *Cepheus, the Monarch*	70° N
[1]Cetus \'sē-təs\ *Whale*	5° S
Chamaeleon \kə-'mēl-yən\ *Chameleon*	80° S
[1]Circinus \'sərs-ᵊn-əs\ *Pair of Compasses*	65° S
Columba (Columba Noae) \kə-'ləm-bə-'nō-ˌē\ *Dove (Noah's Dove)*	35° S
Coma Berenices \'kō-mə-ˌber-ə-'nī-(ˌ)sēz\ *Berenice's Hair*	25° N
[1]Corona Australis \kə-'rō-nə-ȯ-'strā-ləs\ *Southern Crown*	40° S
[1]Corona Borealis \kə-'rō-nə-ˌbōr-ē-'al-əs, -'ā-ləs\ *Northern Crown*	30° N
[1]Corvus \'kȯr-vəs\ *Crow*	20° S
[1]Crater \'krāt-ər\ *Cup*	15° S
Crux \'krəks\ *Southern Cross*	60° S
[1]Cygnus \'sig-nəs\ *Swan*	40° N
[1]Delphinus \del-'fī-nəs\ *Dolphin*	15° N
Dorado \də-'rä-(ˌ)dō\ *Dorado [a fish]*	60° S
[1]Draco \'drā-ˌkō\ *Dragon*	65° N
[1]Equuleus \e-'kwü-lē-əs\ *Colt*	5° N
[1]Eridanus \ə-'rid-ᵊn-əs\ *Eridanus, the River Po*	20° S
Fornax \'fōr-ˌnaks\ *Furnace*	30° S
[1]Gemini \'jem-ə-ˌnī\ *Twins*	25° N
Grus \'grəs, 'grüs\ *Crane*	45° S
[1]Hercules \'hər-kyə-ˌlēz\ *Hercules*	30° N

NAME AND MEANING	DECLINATION
Horologium \ˌhȯr-ə-'lō-jē-əm\ *Clock*	50° S
[1]Hydra \'hī-drə\ *Water Monster*	10° S
Hydrus \'hī-drəs\ *Water Snake*	70° S
Indus \'in-dəs\ *Indian*	55° S
Lacerta \lə-'sert-ə\ *Lizard*	45° N
[1]Leo \'lē-(ˌ)ō\ *Lion*	15° N
Leo Minor \'lē-(ˌ)ō-'mī-nər\ *Smaller Lion*	25° N
[1]Lepus \'lē-pəs, 'lep-əs\ *Hare*	20° S
[1]Libra \'lī-brə, 'lē-\ *Balance*	15° S
[1]Lupus \'lü-pəs\ *Wolf*	40° S
Lynx \'liŋks\ *Lynx*	45° N
[1]Lyra \'lī-rə\ *Lyre*	35° N
Mensa (Mons Mensae) \'men-sə, 'mänz-'men-ˌsē\ *Table (Table Mountain)*	75° S
Microscopium \ˌmī-krə-'skō-pē-əm\ *Microscope*	35° S
Monoceros \mə-'näs-ə-rəs\ *Unicorn*	5° S
Musca \'məs-kə\ *Fly*	70° S
Norma \'nȯr-mə\ *Square (and Rule)*	50° S
Octans \'äk-ˌtanz\ *Octant*	85° S
[1]Ophiuchus \ˌō-fē-'yü-kəs\ *Serpent Holder*	0°
[1]Orion \ȯ-'rī-ən\ *Orion, the Hunter*	0°
Pavo \'pā-(ˌ)vō, 'pä-\ *Peacock*	65° S
[1]Pegasus \'peg-ə-səs\ *Pegasus, the Winged Horse*	20° N
[1]Perseus \'pər-ˌsüs, -sē-əs\ *Perseus, the Rescuer or Champion*	45° N
Phoenix \'fē-niks\ *Phoenix*	50° S
Pictor \'pik-tər\ *Painter's Easel*	55° S
[1]Pisces \'pī-ˌsēz, 'pis-ˌēz\ *Fishes*	10° N
[1]Piscis Austrinus \'pis-əs-ȯ-'strī-nəs\ *Southern Fish*	30° S
[2]Puppis \'pəp-əs\ *Stern*	30° S
[2]Pyxis \'pik-səs\ *Mariner's Compass*	30° S
Reticulum \rə-'tik-yə-ləm\ *Net*	60° S
[1]Sagitta \sə-'jit-ə\ *Arrow*	20° N
[1]Sagittarius \ˌsaj-ə-'tar-ē-əs\ *Archer*	30° S
[1]Scorpius \'skȯr-pē-əs\ *Scorpion*	30° S
Sculptor \'skəlp-tər\ *Sculptor's Workshop*	30° S
Scutum \'sk(y)üt-əm\ *Shield*	10° S
[1]Serpens \'sər-pənz, -ˌpenz\ *Serpent*	0°
Sextans \'sek-ˌstanz\ *Sextant*	5° S
[1]Taurus \'tȯr-əs\ *Bull*	20° N
Telescopium \ˌtel-ə-'skō-pē-əm\ *Telescope*	50° S
[1]Triangulum \trī-'aŋ-gyə-ləm\ *Triangle*	30° N
Triangulum Australe \trī-'aŋ-gyə-ləm-ȯ-'strä-(ˌ)lē\ *Southern Triangle*	65° S
Tucana \tü-'kan-ə, -'kän-\ *Toucan*	65° S
[1]Ursa Major \'ər-sə-'mā-jər\ *Larger Bear*	50° N
[1]Ursa Minor \'ər-sə-'mī-nər\ *Smaller Bear*	80° N
[2]Vela \'vē-lə\ *Sails*	45° S
[1]Virgo \'vər-ˌgō\ *Virgin*	0°
Volans (Piscis Volans) \'pis-əs-'vō-ˌlanz\ *Flying Fish*	70° S
[1]Vulpecula \ˌvəl-'pek-yə-lə\ *Little Fox*	25° N

[1]One of the 48 constellations of Ptolemy.

[2]One of the subdivisions of the Ptolemaic constellation Argo Navis \'är-(ˌ)gō-'nā-vəs\ the Ship Argo, which included Carina, Puppis, Pyxis, and Vela.

CONSTELLATIONS AND STARS

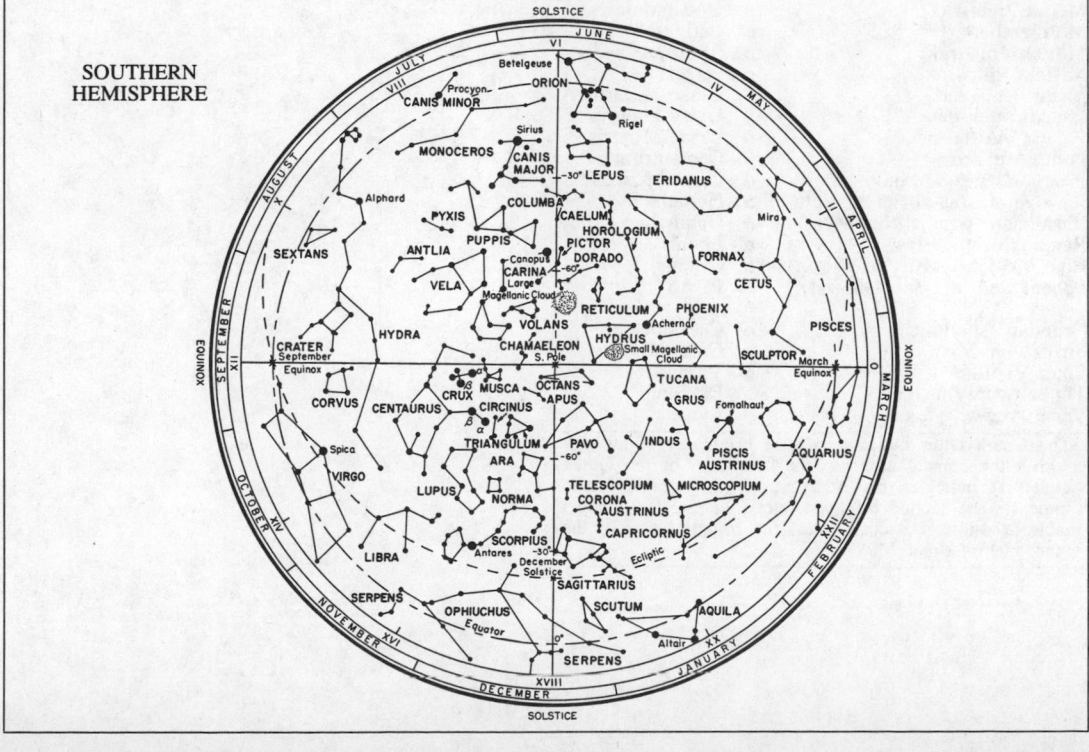

NORTHERN HEMISPHERE

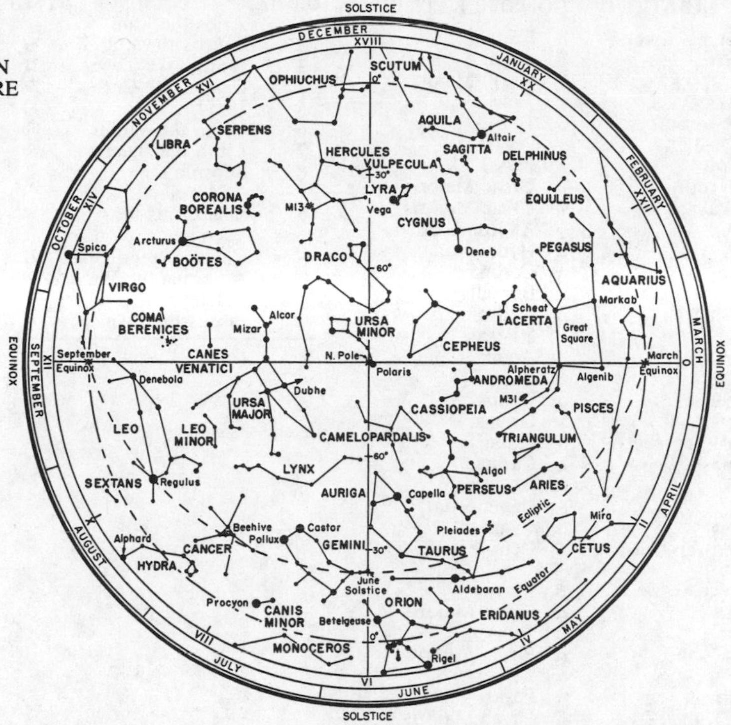

SOUTHERN HEMISPHERE

FIFTY IMPORTANT STARS

NAME & PRONUNCIATION	CONSTELLATION[1]	
Achernar \'ak-ər-ˌnär, 'ā-kər-\	α	Eridani
Albireo \al-'bir-ē-ˌō\	β	Cygni
Alcor \'al-ˌkȯr\	80	Ursae Majoris
Alcyone \al-'sī-ə-(ˌ)nē\	η	Tauri
Aldebaran \al-'deb-ə-rən\	α	Tauri
Algenib \al-'jen-əb, -'jēn-\	γ	Pegasi
Algol \'al-ˌgäl, -ˌgȯl\	β	Persei
Alioth \'al-ē-ˌäth, -ˌȯth\	ε	Ursae Majoris
Alkaid \'al-'kïd, -'kād\	η	Ursae Majoris
Almach \'al-ˌmak\	γ	Andromedae
Alphard \'al-ˌfärd\	α	Hydrae
Alphecca \al-'fek-ə\	α	Corona Borealis
Alpheratz \al-'fer-əts\	α	Andromedae or δ Pegasi
Altair \al-'tïr, -'tar\	α	Aquilae
Antares \an-'tar-ēz\	α	Scorpii
Arcturus \ärk-'t(y)ür-əs\	α	Boötis
Bellatrix \bə-'lā-triks\	γ	Orionis
Betelgeuse \'bet-əl-ˌjüz, 'bēt-\	α	Orionis
Canopus \kə-'nō-pəs\	α	Carinae
Capella \kə-'pel-ə\	α	Aurigae
Castor \'kas-tər\	α	Geminorum
Deneb \'den-ˌeb, -əb\	α	Cygni
Deneb Kaitos \'den-ˌeb-'kït-əs, -əb-, -'kāt-, -ˌäs\	β	Ceti
Denebola \də-'neb-ə-lə\	β	Leonis
Dubhe \'dü-bə, 'də-\	α	Ursae Majoris
Elnath \'el-ˌnath\	β	Tauri
Fomalhaut \'fō-məl-ˌhȯt\	α	Piscis Austrni
Hamal \'ham-əl\	α	Arietis
Markab \'mär-ˌkab\	α	Pegasi
Megrez \'mē-ˌgrez, 'meg-ˌrez\	δ	Ursae Majoris
Menkar \'men-ˌkär\	α	Ceti
Merak \'mē-ˌrak\	β	Ursae Majoris
Mira \'mī-rə\	o	Ceti
Mirach \'mī-ˌrak\	β	Andromedae
Mirfak \'mir-ˌfak\	α	Persei
Mizar \'mī-ˌzär\	ζ	Ursae Majoris
Phecda \'fek-də\	γ	Ursae Majoris
Polaris \pō-'lar-əs\	α	Ursae Minoris
Pollux \'päl-əks\	β	Geminorum
Procyon \'prō-sē-ˌän\	α	Canis Minoris
Rasalgethi \ˌras-əl-'jet-ē, -'jeth-\	α	Herculis
Rasalhague \ˌras-əl-'häg-wē\	α	Ophiuchi
Regulus \'reg-yə-ləs\	α	Leonis
Rigel \'rī-jel, -gəl\	β	Orionis
Scheat \shē-ˌat, -'ät; 'shē-ˌat, -ˌät\	β	Pegasi
Schedar \'shed-ər\	α	Cassiopeiae
Sirius \'sir-ē-əs\	α	Canis Majoris
Spica \'spī-kə\	α	Virginis
Thuban \'th(y)ü-ˌban\	α	Draconis
Vega \'veg-ə, 'vā-gə\	α	Lyrae

[1] The Greek letter indicates relative brightness of the star within the constellation: α (the first letter of the Greek alphabet) indicates the brightest; β (the second letter) indicates the second brightest, etc. (See Greek Alphabet table at GREEK.) Alcor is the 80th brightest star in the constellation Ursae Majoris.

SIGNS OF THE ZODIAC

NUMBER	NAME	SYMBOL	SUN ENTERS	
1	Aries the Ram	♈	March	21
2	Taurus the Bull	♉	April	20
3	Gemini the Twins	♊	May	21
4	Cancer the Crab	♋	June	22
5	Leo the Lion	♌	July	23
6	Virgo the Virgin	♍	August	23
7	Libra the Balance	♎	September	23
8	Scorpio the Scorpion	♏	October	24
9	Sagittarius the Archer	♐	November	22
10	Capricorn the Goat	♑	December	22
11	Aquarius the Water Bearer	♒	January	20
12	Pisces the Fishes	♓	February	19

GEOLOGIC TIME

EON	ERA	PERIOD	EPOCH	BEGINNING OF INTERVAL*	BIOLOGICAL FORMS
Phanerozoic	Cenozoic	Quaternary	Holocene	0.01	
			Pleistocene	1.6	Earliest humans
		Tertiary	Pliocene	5	
			Miocene	24	Earliest hominids
			Oligocene	37	
			Eocene	58	Earliest grasses
			Paleocene	65	Earliest large mammals
		Cretaceous-Tertiary boundary (65 million years ago): extinction of dinosaurs			
	Mesozoic	Cretaceous	Upper	98	
			Lower	144	Earliest flowering plants; dinosaurs in ascendancy
		Jurassic		208	Earliest birds & mammals
		Triassic		245	Age of Dinosaurs begins
	Paleozoic	Permian		286	
		Carboniferous			
		Pennsylvanian		320	Earliest reptiles
		Mississippian		360	Earliest winged insects
		Devonian		408	Earliest vascular plants (as ferns & mosses) & amphibians
		Silurian		438	Earliest land plants & insects
		Ordovician		505	Earliest corals
		Cambrian		570	Earliest fish
Proterozoic	Precambrian			2500	Earliest colonial algae & soft-bodied invertebrates
Archean				4000	Life appears: earliest algae & primitive bacteria

*In millions of years before the present

PERIODIC TABLE

This is a common long form of the table. Roman numerals and letters heading the vertical columns indicate the groups (there are differences of opinion regarding the letter designations, those given here being probably the most generally used). The horizontal rows represent the periods, with two series removed from the two very long periods and represented below the main table. Atomic numbers are given above the symbols for the elements. Compare ELEMENT table.

IA[1]																VIIA[3]	Zero[4]
1 H	IIA[2]											IIIA	IVA	VA	VIA	1 H	2 He
3 Li	4 Be											5 B	6 C	7 N	8 O	9 F	10 Ne
11 Na	12 Mg	IIIB	IVB	VB	VIB	VIIB		VIII		IB	IIB	13 Al	14 Si	15 P	16 S	17 Cl	18 Ar
19 K	20 Ca	21 Sc	22 Ti	23 V	24 Cr	25 Mn	26 Fe	27 Co	28 Ni	29 Cu	30 Zn	31 Ga	32 Ge	33 As	34 Se	35 Br	36 Kr
37 Rb	38 Sr	39 Y	40 Zr	41 Nb	42 Mo	43 Tc	44 Ru	45 Rh	46 Pd	47 Ag	48 Cd	49 In	50 Sn	51 Sb	52 Te	53 I	54 Xe
55 Cs	56 Ba	57 *La	72 Hf	73 Ta	74 W	75 Re	76 Os	77 Ir	78 Pt	79 Au	80 Hg	81 Tl	82 Pb	83 Bi	84 Po	85 At	86 Rn
87 Fr	88 Ra	89 #Ac	104 Unq	105 Unp	106 Unh												

*LANTHANIDE SERIES	58 Ce	59 Pr	60 Nd	61 Pm	62 Sm	63 Eu	64 Gd	65 Tb	66 Dy	67 Ho	68 Er	69 Tm	70 Yb	71 Lu
#ACTINIDE SERIES	90 Th	91 Pa	92 U	93 Np	94 Pu	95 Am	96 Cm	97 Bk	98 Cf	99 Es	100 Fm	101 Md	102 No	103 Lr

[1]Group IA (excluding hydrogen) comprises the alkali metals.   [3]Group VIIA (excluding hydrogen) comprises the halogens.
[2]Group IIA comprises the alkaline-earth metals.   [4]Group Zero comprises the noble gases.

CHEMICAL ELEMENTS

ELEMENT	SYMBOL	ATOMIC NUMBER	ATOMIC WEIGHT (C = 12)
actinium	Ac	89	227.0278
aluminum	Al	13	26.98154
americium	Am	95	
antimony	Sb	51	121.75
argon	Ar	18	39.948
arsenic	As	33	74.9216
astatine	At	85	
barium	Ba	56	137.33
berkelium	Bk	97	
beryllium	Be	4	9.01218
bismuth	Bi	83	208.9804
boron	B	5	10.81
bromine	Br	35	79.904
cadmium	Cd	48	112.41
calcium	Ca	20	40.08
californium	Cf	98	
carbon	C	6	12.011

ELEMENT	SYMBOL	ATOMIC NUMBER	ATOMIC WEIGHT (C = 12)
cerium	Ce	58	140.12
cesium	Cs	55	132.9054
chlorine	Cl	17	35.453
chromium	Cr	24	51.996
cobalt	Co	27	58.9332
copper	Cu	29	63.546
curium	Cm	96	
dysprosium	Dy	66	162.50
einsteinium	Es	99	
erbium	Er	68	167.26
europium	Eu	63	151.96
fermium	Fm	100	
fluorine	F	9	18.998403
francium	Fr	87	
gadolinium	Gd	64	157.25
gallium	Ga	31	69.72
germanium	Ge	32	72.59
gold	Au	79	196.9665
hafnium	Hf	72	178.49
helium	He	2	4.00260
holmium	Ho	67	164.9304
hydrogen	H	1	1.0079
indium	In	49	114.82
iodine	I	53	126.9045
iridium	Ir	77	192.22
iron	Fe	26	55.847
krypton	Kr	36	83.80
lanthanum	La	57	138.9055
lawrencium	Lr	103	
lead	Pb	82	207.2
lithium	Li	3	6.941
lutetium	Lu	71	174.967

ELEMENT	SYMBOL	ATOMIC NUMBER	ATOMIC WEIGHT (C = 12)
magnesium	Mg	12	24.305
manganese	Mn	25	54.9380
mendelevium	Md	101	
mercury	Hg	80	200.59
molybdenum	Mo	42	95.94
neodymium	Nd	60	144.24
neon	Ne	10	20.179
neptunium	Np	93	237.0482
nickel	Ni	28	58.69
niobium	Nb	41	92.9064
nitrogen	N	7	14.0067
nobelium	No	102	
osmium	Os	76	190.2
oxygen	O	8	15.9994
palladium	Pd	46	106.42
phosphorus	P	15	30.97376
platinum	Pt	78	195.08
plutonium	Pu	94	
polonium	Po	84	
potassium	K	19	39.0983
praseodymium	Pr	59	140.9077
promethium	Pm	61	
protactinium	Pa	91	231.0359
radium	Ra	88	226.0254
radon	Rn	86	
rhenium	Re	75	186.207
rhodium	Rh	45	102.9055
rubidium	Rb	37	85.4678
ruthenium	Ru	44	101.07
samarium	Sm	62	150.36
scandium	Sc	21	44.9559
selenium	Se	34	78.96
silicon	Si	14	28.0855
silver	Ag	47	107.868
sodium	Na	11	22.98977
strontium	Sr	38	87.62
sulfur	S	16	32.06
tantalum	Ta	73	180.9479
technetium	Tc	43	
tellurium	Te	52	127.60
terbium	Tb	65	158.9254
thallium	Tl	81	204.383
thorium	Th	90	232.0381
thulium	Tm	69	168.9342
tin	Sn	50	118.69
titanium	Ti	22	47.88
tungsten	W	74	183.85
unnilhexium	Unh	106	
unnilpentium	Unp	105	
unnilquadium	Unq	104	
uranium	U	92	238.0289
vanadium	V	23	50.9415
xenon	Xe	54	131.29
ytterbium	Yb	70	173.04
yttrium	Y	39	88.9059
zinc	Zn	30	65.38
zirconium	Zr	40	91.22

COMMON AREA FORMULAS

FIGURE	FORMULA	MEANING OF LETTERS
rectangle	$A = ab$	a = base; b = height
square	$A = a^2$	a = a side
triangle	$A = \frac{ab}{2}$	a = base; b = height
trapezoid	$A = \frac{h(a+b)}{2}$	h = height; a = the longer parallel side; b = the shorter side
parallelogram	$A = ab$	a = base; b = height
regular pentagon	$A = 1.720a^2$	a = a side
regular octagon	$A = 4.828a^2$	a = a side
circle	$A = \pi r^2$	r = radius; $\pi = 3.1416$

VOLUME FORMULAS

FIGURE	FORMULA	MEANING OF LETTERS
cube	$V = a^3$	a = length of one edge
rectangular solid	$V = lwh$	l = length of base; w = width of base; h = height
pyramid	$V = \frac{Ah}{3}$	A = area of base; h = height
cylinder	$V = \pi r^2 h$	$\pi = 3.1416$; r = radius of the base; h = height
cone	$V = \frac{\pi r^2 h}{3}$	$\pi = 3.1416$; r = radius of the base; h = height
sphere	$V = \frac{4\pi r^3}{3}$	$\pi = 3.1416$; r = radius

WEIGHTS AND MEASURES[1]

UNIT	ABBREVIATION OR SYMBOL	EQUIVALENT IN OTHER U.S. UNITS	METRIC EQUIVALENT
WEIGHT			
avoirdupois (ordinary commodities)			
ton			
short ton		20 short hundredweight, 2000 pounds	0.907 metric ton
long ton		20 long hundredweight, 2240 pounds	1.016 metric tons
hundredweight	cwt		
short hundredweight		100 pounds, 0.05 short ton	45.359 kilograms
long hundredweight		112 pounds, 0.05 long ton	50.802 kilograms
pound	lb *or* lb avdp *also* #	16 ounces, 7000 grains (1.215 apothecaries' or troy pound)	0.454 kilogram
ounce	oz *or* oz avdp	16 drams, 437.5 grains (0.911 apothecaries' or troy ounce)	28.350 grams
dram	dr *or* dr avdp	27.344 grains, 0.0625 ounce	1.772 grams
grain	gr	0.037 dram, 0.002286 ounce (1.0 apothecaries' or troy grain)	0.0648 gram
troy (precious metals, jewels)			
pound	lb t	12 ounces, 240 pennyweight, 5760 grains (0.823 avoirdupois pound, 1.0 apothecaries' pound)	0.373 kilogram
ounce	oz t	20 pennyweight, 480 grains (1.097 avoirdupois ounce, 1.0 apothecaries' ounce)	31.103 grams
pennyweight	dwt *also* pwt	24 grains, 0.05 ounce	1.555 grams
grain	gr	0.042 pennyweight, 0.002083 ounce (1.0 avoirdupois or apothecaries' grain)	0.0648 gram
apothecaries' (drugs)			
pound	lb ap	12 ounces, 5760 grains (0.822 avoirdupois pound, 1.0 troy pound)	0.373 kilogram
ounce	oz ap *or* ℥	8 drams, 480 grains (1.097 avoirdupois ounce, 1.0 troy ounce)	31.103 grams
dram	dr ap *or* ʒ	0.125 ounce, 60 grains	3.888 grams
grain	gr	0.0166 dram, 0.002083 ounce (1.0 avoirdupois or troy grain)	0.0648 gram
CAPACITY			
U.S. liquid measure			
gallon	gal	4 quarts (231 cubic inches)	3.785 liters
quart	qt	2 pints (57.75 cubic inches)	0.946 liter
pint	pt	4 gills (28.875 cubic inches)	0.473 liter
gill	gi	4 fluid ounces (7.219 cubic inches)	118.294 milliliters
fluid ounce	fl oz *or* f℥	8 fluid drams (1.805 cubic inches)	29.573 milliliters
fluid dram	fl dr *or* fʒ	60 minims (0.226 cubic inch)	3.697 milliliters
minim	min *or* ♍	1/60 fluid dram (0.003760 cubic inch)	0.061610 milliliter
U.S. dry measure			
bushel	bu	4 pecks (2150.42 cubic inches)	35.239 liters
peck	pk	8 quarts (537.605 cubic inches)	8.810 liters
quart	qt	2 pints (67.201 cubic inches)	1.101 liters
pint	pt	1/2 quart (33.600 cubic inches)	0.551 liter
LENGTH			
mile	mi	5280 feet, 320 rods, 1760 yards	1.609 kilometers
rod	rd	5.50 yards, 16.5 feet	5.029 meters
yard	yd	3 feet, 36 inches	0.9144 meter
foot	ft *or* '	12 inches, 0.333 yard	30.48 centimeters
inch	in *or* "	0.083 foot, 0.028 yard	2.54 centimeters
AREA			
square mile	sq mi *or* mi^2	640 acre, 102,400 square rods	2.590 square kilometers
acre		4840 square yards, 43,560 square feet	4047 square meters
square rod	sq rd *or* rd^2	30.25 square yards, 0.00625 acre	25.293 square meters
square yard	sq yd *or* yd^2	1296 square inches, 9 square feet	0.836 square meter
square foot	sq ft *or* ft^2	144 square inches, 0.111 square yard	0.093 square meter
square inch	sq in *or* in^2	0.0069 square foot, 0.00077 square yard	6.452 square centimeters
VOLUME			
cubic yard	cu yd *or* yd^3	27 cubic feet, 46,656 cubic inches	0.765 cubic meter
cubic foot	cu ft *or* ft^3	1728 cubic inches, 0.0370 cubic yard	0.028 cubic meter
cubic inch	cu in *or* in^3	0.00058 cubic foot, 0.000021 cubic yard	16.387 cubic centimeters

[1]For U.S. equivalents of metric units see Metric System table

METRIC SYSTEM[1]

LENGTH

unit	abbreviation	number of meters	approximate U.S. equivalent
kilometer	km	1,000	0.62 mile
hectometer	hm	100	328.08 feet
dekameter	dam	10	32.81 feet
meter	m	1	39.37 inches
decimeter	dm	0.1	3.94 inches
centimeter	cm	0.01	0.39 inch
millimeter	mm	0.001	0.039 inch

AREA

unit	abbreviation	number of square meters	approximate U.S. equivalent
square kilometer	sq km *or* km²	1,000,000	0.3861 square mile
hectare	ha	10,000	2.47 acres
are	a	100	119.60 square yards
square centimeter	sq cm *or* cm²	0.0001	0.155 square inch

VOLUME

unit	abbreviation	number of cubic meters	approximate U.S. equivalent
cubic meter	m³	1	1.307 cubic yards
cubic decimeter	dm³	0.001	61.023 cubic inches
cubic centimeter	cu cm *or* cm³ *also* cc	0.000001	0.061 cubic inch

CAPACITY

unit	abbreviation	number of liters	approximate U.S. equivalent cubic	dry	liquid
kiloliter	kl	1,000	1.31 cubic yards		
hectoliter	hl	100	3.53 cubic feet	2.84 bushels	
dekaliter	dal	10	0.35 cubic foot	1.14 pecks	2.64 gallons
liter	l	1	61.02 cubic inches	0.908 quart	1.057 quarts
deciliter	dl	0.1	6.1 cubic inches	0.18 pint	0.21 pint
centiliter	cl	0.01	0.61 cubic inch		0.338 fluid ounce
milliliter	ml	0.001	0.061 cubic inch		0.27 fluid dram

MASS AND WEIGHT

unit	abbreviation	number of grams	approximate U.S. equivalent
metric ton	t	1,000,000	1.102 short tons
kilogram	kg	1,000	2.2046 pounds
hectogram	hg	100	3.527 ounces
dekagram	dag	10	0.353 ounce
gram	g	1	0.035 ounce
decigram	dg	0.1	1.543 grains
centigram	cg	0.01	0.154 grain
milligram	mg	0.001	0.015 grain

[1]For metric equivalents of U.S. units see Weights and Measures table

NONMETRIC-TO-METRIC WEIGHTS AND MEASURES

WEIGHT
Avoirdupois

ton		
short ton	20 short hundredweight, 2000 pounds	0.907 metric ton
long ton	20 long hundredweight, 2240 pounds	1.016 metric tons
hundredweight (cwt)		
short hundredweight	100 pounds, 0.05 short ton	45.359 kilograms
long hundredweight	112 pounds, 0.05 long ton	50.802 kilograms
pound (lb, lb avdp *also* #)	16 ounces, 7000 grains	0.454 kilogram
ounce (oz, oz avdp)	16 drams, 437.5 grains, 0.0625 pound	28.350 grams
dram (dr, dr avdp)	27.344 grains, 0.0625 ounce	1.772 grams
grain (gr)	0.037 dram, 0.002286 ounce	0.0648 gram

Troy

pound (lb t)	12 ounces, 240 pennyweight, 5760 grains	0.373 kilogram
ounce (oz t)	20 pennyweight, 480 grains, 0.083 pound	31.103 grams
pennyweight (dwt *also* pwt)	24 grains, 0.05 ounce	1.555 grams
grain (gr)	0.042 pennyweight, 0.002083 ounce	0.0648 gram

Apothecaries'

pound (lb ap)	12 ounces, 5760 grains	0.373 kilogram
ounce (oz ap)	8 drams, 480 grains, 0.083 pound	31.103 grams
dram (dr ap)	3 scruples, 60 grains	3.888 grams
scruple (s ap)	20 grains, 0.333 dram	1.296 grams
grain (gr)	0.05 scruple, 0.002083 ounce, 0.0166 dram	0.0648 gram

CAPACITY
U.S. liquid measure

gallon (gal)	4 quarts (231 cubic inches)	3.785 liters
quart (qt)	2 pints (57.75 cubic inches)	0.946 liter
pint (pt)	4 gills (28.875 cubic inches)	0.473 liter
gill (gi)	4 fluid ounces (7.219 cubic inches)	118.294 milliliters
fluid ounce (fl oz)	8 fluid drams (1.805 cubic inches)	29.573 milliliters
fluid dram (fl dr)	60 minims (0.226 cubic inch)	3.697 milliliters

U.S. dry measure

bushel (bu)	4 pecks (2150.42 cubic inches)	35.239 liters
peck (pk)	8 quarts (537.605 cubic inches)	8.810 liters
quart (qt)	2 pints (67.201 cubic inches)	1.101 liters
pint (pt)	½ quart (33.600 cubic inches)	0.551 liter

British imperial liquid and dry measure

bushel (bu)	4 pecks (2219.36 cubic inches)	0.036 cubic meter
peck (pk)	2 gallons (554.84 cubic inches)	0.0091 cubic meter
gallon (gal)	4 quarts (277.420 cubic inches)	4.546 liters
quart (qt)	2 pints (69.355 cubic inches)	1.136 liters
pint (pt)	4 gills (34.678 cubic inches)	568.26 cubic centimeters
gill (gi)	5 fluid ounces (8.669 cubic inches)	142.066 cubic centimeters
fluid ounce (fl oz)	8 fluid drams (1.7339 cubic inches)	28.412 cubic centimeters
fluid dram (fl dr)	60 minims (0.216734 cubic inch)	3.5516 cubic centimeters

LENGTH

mile (mi)	5280 feet, 1760 yards, 320 rods	1.609 kilometers
yard (yd)	3 feet, 36 inches	0.9144 meter
foot (ft, ')	12 inches, 0.333 yard	30.48 centimeters
inch (in, ")	0.083 foot, 0.028 yard	2.54 centimeters

AREA

square mile (sq mi, mi²)	640 acres, 102,400 square rods	2.590 square kilometers
acre	4840 square yards, 43,560 square feet	0.405 hectare, 4047 square meters
square yard (sq yd, yd²)	1296 square inches, 9 square feet	0.836 square meter
square foot (sq ft, ft²)	144 square inches, 0.111 square yard	0.093 square meter
square inch (sq in, in²)	0.0069 square foot, 0.00077 square yard	6.452 square centimeters

VOLUME

cubic yard (cu yd, yd³)	27 cubic feet, 46.656 cubic inches	0.765 cubic meter
cubic foot (cu ft, ft³)	1728 cubic inches, 0.0370 cubic yard	0.028 cubic meter
cubic inch (cu in, in³)	0.00058 cubic foot, 0.000021 cubic yard	16.387 cubic centimeters

TABLE OF NUMBERS

CARDINAL NUMBERS[1]			ORDINAL NUMBERS[4]	
NAME[2]	SYMBOL		NAME[5]	SYMBOL
	Hindu-Arabic	Roman[3]		
zero or naught or cipher	0		first	1st
one	1	I	second	2d or 2nd
two	2	II	third	3d or 3rd
three	3	III	fourth	4th
four	4	IV	fifth	5th
five	5	V	sixth	6th
six	6	VI	seventh	7th
seven	7	VII	eighth	8th
eight	8	VIII	ninth	9th
nine	9	IX	tenth	10th
ten	10	X	eleventh	11th
eleven	11	XI	twelfth	12th
twelve	12	XII	thirteenth	13th
thirteen	13	XIII	fourteenth	14th
fourteen	14	XIV	fifteenth	15th
fifteen	15	XV	sixteenth	16th
sixteen	16	XVI	seventeenth	17th
seventeen	17	XVII	eighteenth	18th
eighteen	18	XVIII	nineteenth	19th
nineteen	19	XIX	twentieth	20th
twenty	20	XX	twenty-first	21st
twenty-one	21	XXI	twenty-second	22d or 22nd
twenty-two	22	XXII	twenty-third	23d or 23rd
twenty-three	23	XXIII	twenty-fourth	24th
twenty-four	24	XXIV	twenty-fifth	25th
twenty-five	25	XXV	twenty-sixth	26th
twenty-six	26	XXVI	twenty-seventh	27th
twenty-seven	27	XXVII	twenty-eighth	28th
twenty-eight	28	XXVIII	twenty-ninth	29th
twenty-nine	29	XXIX	thirtieth	30th
thirty	30	XXX	thirty-first etc	31st
thirty-one etc	31	XXXI	fortieth	40th
forty	40	XL	fiftieth	50th
fifty	50	L	sixtieth	60th
sixty	60	LX	seventieth	70th
seventy	70	LXX	eightieth	80th
eighty	80	LXXX	ninetieth	90th
ninety	90	XC	hundredth or one hundredth	100th
one hundred	100	C		
one hundred one or one hundred and one etc	101	CI	hundred and first or one hundred and first etc	101st
two hundred	200	CC	two hundredth	200th
three hundred	300	CCC	three hundredth	300th
four hundred	400	CD	four hundredth	400th
five hundred	500	D	five hundredth	500th
six hundred	600	DC	six hundredth	600th
seven hundred	700	DCC	seven hundredth	700th
eight hundred	800	DCCC	eight hundredth	800th
nine hundred	900	CM	nine hundredth	900th
one thousand or ten hundred etc	1,000	M	thousandth or one thousandth	1,000th
			two thousandth etc	2,000th
two thousand etc	2,000	MM	five thousandth	5,000th
five thousand	5,000	$\overline{\text{V}}$	ten thousandth	10,000th
ten thousand	10,000	$\overline{\text{X}}$	hundred thousandth or one hundred thousandth	100,000th
one hundred thousand	100,000	$\overline{\text{C}}$		
one million	1,000,000	$\overline{\text{M}}$	millionth or one millionth	1,000,000th

[1]The cardinal numbers are used in simple counting or in answer to "how many?" The words for these numbers may be used as nouns (I counted to *ten*), as pronouns (*ten* were found), or as adjectives (*ten* cows).

[2]In formal writing the numbers one to one hundred and in less formal writing the numbers one to nine are commonly written out, while larger numbers are given in numerals. A number occurring at the beginning of a sentence is usually written out. Except in very formal writing numerals are used for dates. Hindu-Arabic numerals from 1,000 to 9,999 are often written without commas (1000; 9999). Year numbers are always written without commas (1783).

[3]The Roman numerals are written either in capitals or in lowercase letters.

[4]The ordinal numbers are used to show the order in which such items as names, objects, and periods of time are considered (the *twelfth* month; the *fourth* row of seats; the *18th* century).

[5]Each of the names of the ordinal numbers except *first* and *second* is used for one of the equal parts into which a whole may be divided (a *fourth*; a *sixth*; a *tenth*) and also as the denominator in fractions (*one fourth*; *three fifths*). Fractions used as nouns are usually written as two words, but fractions used as adjectives are usually hyphenated (a *two-thirds* majority). When a two-word ordinal number is used as a noun to name a denominator, a hyphen is usually used to make sure that there is only one meaning (*six hundred ten-thousandths* means only 600/10,000 and not 610/1000). When fractions are written in numerals, the cardinal symbols are used (¼, ⅓, ⅙).

BEAUFORT SCALE

BEAUFORT NUMBER	NAME	WIND SPEED		DESCRIPTION
		MPH	KPH	
0	calm	<1	<1	calm; smoke rises vertically
1	light air	1-3	1-5	direction of wind shown by smoke but not by wind vanes
2	light breeze	4-7	6-11	wind felt on face; leaves rustle; wind vane moves
3	gentle breeze	8-12	12-19	leaves and small twigs in constant motion; wind extends light flag
4	moderate breeze	13-18	20-28	wind raises dust and loose paper; small branches move
5	fresh breeze	19-24	29-38	small-leaved trees begin to sway; crested wavelets form on inland waters
6	strong breeze	25-31	39-49	large branches move; overhead wires whistle; umbrellas difficult to control
7	moderate gale	32-38	50-61	whole trees sway; walking against wind is difficult
8	fresh gale or gale	39-46	62-74	twigs break off trees; moving cars veer
9	strong gale	47-54	75-88	slight structural damage occurs; shingles may blow away
10	whole gale or storm	55-63	89-102	trees uprooted; considerable structural damage occurs
11	storm or violent storm	64-72	103-117	widespread damage occurs
12	hurricane*	>72	>117	widespread damage occurs

*The U.S. uses 74 statute mph as the speed criterion for hurricane.

CHAPTER 16

Names

Geographical Names

This section contains definitions of current and historical place names likely to be of interest to the student. It adds to the general vocabulary by entering many adjectives and nouns formed from geographical names, such as **Florentine** at **Florence** and **Libyan** at **Libya.** In the entries the letters N, E, S, and W singly or in combination indicate direction and are not part of a place name. They may represent either the name of the direction (as *north*) or the adjective derived from it (as *northern*); thus, west-northwest of Santiago appears as WNW of Santiago and southern California appears as S California. The only other special abbreviations used in this section are U.S. for United States, and U.S.S.R. for Union of Soviet Socialist Republics. All heights and distances are given in metric units.

Ab·er·deen \ab-ər-'dēn\ city NE Scotland in Grampian region — **Ab·er·do·ni·an** \-'dō-nē-ən\ *adj or n*

Ab·i·djan \ab-i-'jän\ city, capital of Ivory Coast

Abu Dha·bi \äb-ü-'däb-ē\ city, capital of United Arab Emirates

Abu·ja \ä-'bü-jä\ city, official capital of Nigeria

Ab·ys·sin·ia \ab-ə-'sin-ē-ə, -'sin-yə\ — see ETHIOPIA — **Ab·ys·sin·i·an** \-ē-ən, -yən\ *adj or n*

Aca·dia \ə-'kād-ē-ə\ *or French* **Aca·die** \à-kà-dē\ NOVA SCOTIA — an early name — **Aca·di·an** \-ē-ən\ *adj or n*

Aca·pul·co \äk-ə-'pül-kō, ak-\ city S Mexico on the Pacific

Ac·cra \ə-'krä\ city, capital of Ghana

Acon·ca·gua \ak-ən-'käg-wə, äk-, -əŋ-\ mountain 6960 meters W Argentina; highest in the Andes & in North America & South America

Ad·dis Aba·ba \ad-ə-'sab-ə-bə\ city, capital of Ethiopia

Ad·e·laide \'ad-ᵊl-ād\ city, capital of South Australia

Aden \'äd-ᵊn, 'äd-, 'ad-\ city S Yemen; formerly capital of People's Democratic Republic of Yemen

Aden, Gulf of arm of Indian ocean between Yemen (Arabia) & Somalia (Africa)

Ad·i·ron·dack \ad-ə-'rän-dak\ mountains NE New York; highest Mount Marcy 1629 meters

Ad·mi·ral·ty \'ad-m(ə-)rəl-tē\ **1** island SE Alaska in N Alexander island group **2** islands W Pacific N of New Guinea; belong to Papua New Guinea

Adri·at·ic \ā-drē-'at-ik, ad-rē-\ sea arm of Mediterranean between Italy & Balkan peninsula

Ae·ge·an \i-'jē-ən\ sea arm of Mediterranean between Asia Minor & Greece

Af·ghan·i·stan \af-'gan-ə-stan\ country W Asia E of Iran; capital, Kabul

Af·ri·ca \'af-ri-kə\ continent S of Mediterranean

Aga·na \ə-'gän-yə\ town, capital of Guam

Ag·as·siz Lake \'ag-ə-sē-\ prehistoric lake 1130 kilometers long in region consisting of present S Manitoba, E Saskatchewan, NW Minnesota, & E North Dakota

Agra \'äg-rə\ city N India

Aguas·ca·lien·tes \äg-wə-skäl-'yen-tās\ city central Mexico, NE of Guadalajara

Agul·has, Cape \-ə-'gəl-əs\ cape Republic of South Africa in S Cape Province; most southerly point of Africa, at 34°50′ S latitude

Ahag·gar \ə-'häg-ər, ä-hə-'gär\ mountains S Algeria in W central Sahara

Ah·mad·abad *or* **Ah·med·abad** \'äm-əd-ə-bäd\ city W India

Ak·ron \'ak-rən\ city NE Ohio

Al·a·bama \al-ə-'bam-ə\ state SE U.S.; capital, Montgomery — **Al·a·bam·i·an** \-'bam-ē-ən\ *or* **Al·a·bam·an** \-'bam-ən\ *adj or n*

Alas·ka \ə-'las-kə\ **1** peninsula SW Alaska SW of Cook inlet **2** state of U.S. in NW North America; capital, Juneau **3** mountain range S Alaska extending from Alaska peninsula to Yukon boundary —**Alas·kan** \-kən\ *adj or n*

Alaska, Gulf of inlet of Pacific off S Alaska between Alaska peninsula on W & Alexander island group on E

Al·ba·nia \al-'bā-nē-ə, -nyə\ country S Europe in Balkan peninsula on Adriatic; capital, Tirane

Al·ba·ny \'ȯl-bə-nē\ city, capital of New York

Al·be·marle \'al-bə-märl\ inlet of Atlantic in NE North Carolina

Al·bert, Lake \-'al-bərt\ lake E Africa between Uganda & Zaire in course of Nile

Al·ber·ta \al-'bərt-ə\ province W Canada; capital, Edmonton — **Al·ber·tan** \-'bərt-ᵊn\ *adj or n*

Al·bu·quer·que \'al-b(y)ə-kər-kē\ city central New Mexico

Al·ca·traz \'al-kə-traz\ island California in San Francisco Bay

Al·da·bra \'al-də-brə\ island NW Indian ocean N of Madagascar; belongs to Seychelles

Al·der·ney \'ȯl-dər-nē\ island in English channel — see CHANNEL

Alep·po \ə-'lep-ō\ city N Syria

Aleu·tian \ə-'lü-shən\ islands SW Alaska extending 1930 kilometers W from Alaska peninsula

Al·ex·an·der \al-ig-'zan-dər, el-\ island group SE Alaska

Al·ex·an·dria \al-ig-'zan-drē-ə, el-\ **1** city N Virginia **2** city N Egypt on Mediterranean — **Al·ex·an·dri·an** \-drē-ən\ *adj or n*

Al·ge·ria \al-'jir-ē-ə\ country NW Africa on Mediterranean; capital, Algiers — **Al·ge·ri·an** \-ē-ən\ *adj or n*

Al·giers \al-'ji(ə)rz\ city, capital of Algeria — **Al·ge·rine** \al-jə-'rēn\ *adj or n*

Al·lah·abad \'al-ə-hə-bad, -bäd\ city N India

Al·le·ghe·ny \al-ə-'gā-nē\ **1** river 523 kilometers long W Pennsylvania & SW New York **2** mountains of Appalachian system E U.S. in Pennsylvania, Maryland, Virginia, & West Virginia

Al·len·town \'al-ən-taȯn\ city E Pennsylvania

Al·ma-Ata \al-mə-ə-'tä\ city, capital of Kazakhstan

Alps \'alps\ mountain system central Europe — see MONT BLANC

Al·tai \\'al-₁tī\\ mountain system central Asia between Mongolia & W China & between Kazakhstan & Russia; highest peak Tabun Bogdo 4653 meters

Ama·ga·sa·ki \\₁am-ə-gə-'säk-ē\\ city Japan in W central Honshu

Am·a·ril·lo \\₁am-ə-'ril-ō, -'ril-ə\\ city NW Texas

Am·a·zon \\'am-ə-₁zän, -zən\\ river about 6275 kilometers long N South America flowing from Peruvian Andes into Atlantic in N Brazil

Amer·i·ca \\ə-'mer-ə-kə\\ **1** either continent (North America or South America) of western hemisphere **2** *or the* **Amer·i·cas** \\-kəz\\ lands of western hemisphere including North, Central, & South America & West Indies **3** UNITED STATES OF AMERICA

American Falls — see NIAGARA FALLS

American Samoa *or* **Eastern Samoa** islands SW central Pacific; capital, Pago Pago (on Tutuila island)

Am·man \\ə-'män, -'man\\ city, capital of Jordan

Am·ster·dam \\'am(p)-stər-₁dam\\ city; official capital of the Netherlands

Amur \\ä-'mü(ə)r\\ river 2865 kilometers long E Asia flowing into the Pacific & forming part of boundary between China & Russia

An·a·heim \\'an-ə-₁hīm\\ city SW California E of Long Beach

An·a·to·lia \\₁an-ə-'tō-lē-ə, -'tōl-yə\\ — see ASIA MINOR — **An·a·to·li·an** \\-'tō-lē-ən, -'tōl-yən\\ *adj or n*

An·chor·age \\'aŋ-k(ə-)rij\\ city S central Alaska

An·da·man \\'an-də-mən, -₁man\\ **1** islands India in Bay of Bengal S of Myanmar & N of Nicobar islands **2** sea arm of Bay of Bengal S of Myanmar — **An·da·man·ese** \\₁an-də-mə-'nēz, -'nēs\\ *adj or n*

An·des \\'an-dēz\\ mountain system W South America extending from Panama to Tierra del Fuego — see ACONCAGUA — **An·de·an** \\'an-(₁)dē-ən, an-'dē-\\ *adj* — **An·dine** \\'an-₁dēn, -₁dīn\\ *adj*

An·dor·ra \\an-'dȯr-ə, -där-ə\\ country SW Europe in E Pyrenees between France & Spain; capital, Andorra la Vella — **An·dor·ran** \\-ən\\ *adj or n*

An·dros \\'an-drəs\\ island, largest of Bahamas

An·gel Falls \\ān-jəl-\\ waterfall 979 meters SE Venezuela; world's highest waterfall

Ang·kor \\'aŋ-₁kȯ(ə)r\\ ruins of ancient city NW Cambodia

An·gle·sey \\'aŋ-gəl-sē\\ island NW Wales

An·go·la \\aŋ-'gō-lə, an-\\ country SW Africa S of mouth of Congo river; until 1975 a dependency of Portugal; capital, Luanda — **An·go·lan** \\-lən\\ *adj or n*

An·i·ak·chak Crater \\₁an-ē-'ak-₁chak-\\ volcano 1347 meters SW Alaska on Alaska peninsula; crater 10 kilometers in diameter

An·ka·ra \\'aŋ-kə-rə, äŋ-\\ city, capital of Turkey in N central Anatolia

An·nap·o·lis \\ə-'nap-(ə-)ləs\\ city, capital of Maryland

Ann Ar·bor \\a-'när-bər\\ city SE Michigan

An·shan \\'än-'shän\\ city NE China

An·ta·nan·a·ri·vo \\₁an-tə-₁nan-ə-'rē-vō\\ city, capital of Madagascar

Ant·arc·ti·ca \\(')ant-'ärk-ti-kə, -'ärt-i-\\ *or* **Ant·arc·tic continent** \\-'ärk-tik-, -'ärt-ik-\\ body of land around the South Pole; plateau covered by great ice cap

An·ti·gua \\an-'tē-gə\\ island West Indies in the Leewards E of Nevis; capital, Saint Johns; part of independent Antigua and Barbuda

Antigua and Barbuda country West Indies in the Leewards; capital, St. Johns

An·til·les \\an-'til-ēz\\ the West Indies except for the Bahamas — see GREATER ANTILLES, LESSER ANTILLES — **An·til·le·an** \\-'til-ē-ən\\ *adj*

An·trim \\'an-trəm\\ **1** district E Northern Ireland **2** town in Antrim district

Aorangi — see COOK, MOUNT

Ap·en·nines \\'ap-ə-₁nīnz\\ mountain chain Italy extending length of the peninsula; highest point Monte Corno (NE of Rome) 2914 meters — **Ap·en·nine** \\-₁nīn\\ *adj*

Apia \\ə-'pē-ə\\ town, capital of Western Samoa

Apo, Mount \\-'äp-ō\\ volcano Philippines in SE Mindanao 2594 meters; highest peak in the Philippines

Ap·pa·la·chia \\₁ap-ə-'lā-chə, -'lach-ə, -'lā-shə\\ region E U.S. including Appalachian mountains from S central New York to central Alabama

Ap·pa·la·chian \\₁ap-ə-'lā-ch(ē-)ən, -'lach(-ē)-ən, -'lā-sh(ē-)ən\\ mountain system E North America extending from S Quebec to central Alabama — see MITCHELL, MOUNT

'Aqa·ba, Gulf of \\-'äk-ə-bə, -'ak-\\ arm of Red sea E of Sinai peninsula

Aquid·neck Island \\ə-'kwid-₁nek-\\ *or* **Rhode Island** island SE Rhode Island in Narragansett Bay

Ara·bia \\ə-'rā-bē-ə\\ peninsula of SW Asia including Saudi Arabia, Yemen, Oman, & Persian Gulf States

Ara·bi·an \\ə-'rā-bē-ən\\ sea NW section of Indian ocean between Arabia & India

Ar·a·fu·ra \\₁ar-ə-'für-ə\\ sea between N Australia & W New Guinea

Ar·al sea \\'ar-əl-\\ *or formerly* **Lake Aral** lake W Asia between Kazakhstan & Uzbekistan

Ar·a·rat \\'ar-ə-₁rat\\ mountain 5165 meters E Turkey near border of Iran

Arc·tic \\'ärk-tik, 'ärt-ik\\ **1** ocean N of Arctic circle **2** Arctic regions **3** island group N Canada in N & E Northwest Territories

Ar·da·bil *or* **Ar·de·bil** \\₁är-də-'bē(ə)l\\ city NW Iran

Ards \\'ärdz\\ district E Northern Ireland

Ar·gen·ti·na \\₁är-jən-'tē-nə\\ country S South America between the Andes & the Atlantic; capital, Buenos Aires — **Argentine** \\'är-jən-₁tēn, -₁tīn\\ *adj or n* — **Ar·gen·tin·ean** *or* **Ar·gen·tin·i·an** \\₁är-jən-'tin-ē-ən\\ *adj or n*

Ar·gos \\'är-₁gäs, -gəs\\ ancient Greek city & state S Greece

Ar·i·zo·na \\₁ar-ə-'zō-nə\\ state SW U.S.; capital, Phoenix — **Ar·i·zo·nan** \\-nən\\ *or* **Ar·i·zo·nian** \\-nē-ən, -nyən\\ *adj or n*

Ar·kan·sas \\'är-kən-₁sȯ; *1 is also* är-'kan-zəs\\ **1** river 2335 kilometers long SW central U.S. flowing SE into the Mississippi **2** state S central U.S.; capital, Little Rock — **Ar·kan·san** \\är-'kan-zən\\ *adj or n*

Ar·ling·ton \\'är-liŋ-tən\\ city N Texas

Ar·magh \\är-'mä, 'är-₁mä\\ **1** district S Northern Ireland **2** town in Armagh district

Ar·me·nia \\är-'mē-nē-ə, -nyə\\ **1** region W Asia in mountainous area SE of Black sea & SW of Caspian sea divided between Iran, Turkey, & Armenia (country) **2** country E Europe; capital, Yerevan; a republic of U.S.S.R. 1936–91 — **Ar·me·ni·an** \\-nē-ən, -nyən\\ *adj or n*

Arn·hem Land \\'är-nəm-\\ region N Australia on N coast of Northern Territory

Ar·no \\'är-nō\\ river 225 kilometers long central Italy flowing through Florence

Aru·ba \\ə-'rü-bə\\ island Netherlands Antilles off coast of NW Venezuela

Ashkh·a·bad \\'ash-kə-₁bad, -₁bäd\\ city, capital of Turkmenistan

Asia \\'ā-zhə, -shə\\ continent of eastern hemisphere N of equator — see EURASIA

Asia Mi·nor \\-'mī-nər\\ *or* **Anatolia** peninsula in modern Turkey between Black sea on N & the Mediterranean on S

Asmara \\az-'mär-ə, -'mar-ə\\ city, capital of Eritrea

As·syr·ia \\ə-'sir-ē-ə\\ ancient empire W Asia extending along the middle Tigris & over foothills to the E — **As·syr·i·an** \\-ən\\ *adj or n*

Asun·ción \ə-ˌsün(t)-sē-ˈōn, (ˌ)ä-\ city, capital of Paraguay

As·wân \a-ˈswän, ä-\ city S Egypt on the Nile near site of **Aswân High Dam**

Ata·ca·ma \ˌat-ə-ˈkäm-ə\ desert N Chile

Atchaf·a·laya \(ə-)ˌchaf-ə-ˈlī-ə\ river 362 kilometers long S Louisiana flowing S into Gulf of Mexico

Ath·a·bas·ca or **Ath·a·bas·ka** \ˌath-ə-ˈbas-kə\ river 1231 kilometers long NE Alberta flowing into Lake Athabasca

Athabasca, Lake lake W central Canada on Alberta–Saskatchewan border

Ath·ens \ˈath-ənz\ city, capital of Greece — **Athe·nian** \ə-ˈthē-nē-ən, -nyən\ adj or n

At·lan·ta \ət-ˈlant-ə, at-\ city, capital of Georgia

At·lan·tic \ət-ˈlant-ik, at-\ ocean separating North America & South America from Europe & Africa — **Atlantic** adj

At·las \ˈat-ləs\ mountains NW Africa extending from SW Morocco to N Tunisia

At·ti·ca \ˈat-i-kə\ ancient division & state E Greece; chief city Athens — **At·tic** \ˈat-ik\ adj

Auck·land \ˈȯ-klənd\ city N New Zealand on NW North island

Au·gus·ta \ȯ-ˈgəst-ə, ə-\ city, capital of Maine

Au·ro·ra \ə-ˈrȯr-ə, ȯ-, -ˈrȯr-\ city NE central Colorado

Aus·tin \ˈȯs-tən, ˈäs-\ city, capital of Texas

Aus·tral·asia \ˌȯs-trə-ˈlā-zhə, ˌäs-, -ˈlā-shə\ Australia, Tasmania, New Zealand, & Melanesia — **Aus·tral·asian** \-zhən, -shən\ adj or n

Aus·tra·lia \ȯ-ˈstrāl-yə, ä-, ə-\ **1** continent of eastern hemisphere SE of Asia **2** independent country in the Commonwealth including continent of Australia & island of Tasmania; capital, Canberra — **Aus·tra·lian** \-yən\ adj or n

Australian Alps mountain range SE Australia in E Victoria & SE New South Wales; part of Great Dividing range

Australian Capital Territory district SE Australia including two areas, one containing Canberra (capital of Australia) & the other on Jervis Bay; surrounded by New South Wales

Aus·tria \ˈȯs-trē-ə, ˈäs-\ country central Europe; capital, Vienna — **Aus·tri·an** \-ən\ adj or n

Aus·tria–Hun·ga·ry \-ˈhəŋ-gə-rē\ country 1867–1918 central Europe including Bohemia, Moravia, Bukovina, Transylvania, Galicia, and what are now Austria, Hungary, Slovenia, Croatia, & part of NE Italy — **Aus·tro–Hun·gar·i·an** \ˈȯs-(ˌ)trō-ˌhəŋ-ˈgar-ē-ən, ˈäs-, -ˈger-\ adj or n

Aus·tro·ne·sia \ˌȯs-trə-ˈnē-zhə, ˌäs-, -ˈnē-shə\ **1** islands of the S Pacific **2** area extending from Madagascar through Malay peninsula & island group to Hawaii & Easter island — **Aus·tro·ne·sian** \-zhən, -shən\ adj or n

Avon \ˈā-vən, ˈav-ən, in the U.S. also ˈā-ˌvän\ **1** river 155 kilometers long central England flowing WSW into the Severn **2** county SW England

Ayles·bury \ˈā(ə)lz-b(ə-)rē, in the U.S. also -ˌber-ē\ borough SE central England in Buckinghamshire

Ayr \ˈa(ə)r, ˈe(ə)r\ or **Ayr·shire** \-ˌshi(ə)r, -shər\ former county SW Scotland

Az·ca·po·tzal·co \ˌäs-kə-pət-ˈsäl-(ˌ)kō, ˌäz-gə-\ city central Mexico, NW of Mexico City

Azer·bai·jan \ˌaz-ər-ˌbī-ˈjän, ˌäz-\ country SE Europe bordering on Caspian sea; capital, Baku; a republic of U.S.S.R. 1936–91

Azores \ˈā-ˌzō(ə)rz, -ˌzȯ(ə)rz; ə-ˈzō(ə)rz, -ˈzȯ(ə)rz\ islands N Atlantic belonging to Portugal & lying 1290 kilometers W of Portuguese coast — **Azor·e·an** or **Azor·i·an** \ā-ˈzȯr-ē-ən, ə-, -ˈzȯr-\ adj or n

Bab·y·lon \ˈbab-ə-lən, -ˌlän\ ancient city, capital of Babylonia; site about 80 kilometers S of Baghdad near the

Euphrates — **Bab·y·lo·nian** \ˌbab-ə-ˈlō-nyən, -nē-ən\ adj or n

Bab·y·lo·nia \ˌbab-ə-ˈlō-nyə, -nē-ə\ ancient country W Asia in valley of lower Euphrates and Tigris rivers; capital, Babylon — **Bab·y·lo·nian** \-nyən, -nē-ən\ adj or n

Bac·tria \ˈbak-trē-ə\ ancient country W Asia in present NE Afghanistan — **Bac·tri·an** \-ən\ adj or n

Bad Lands barren region SW South Dakota & NW Nebraska

Baf·fin \ˈbaf-ən\ island NE Canada in Arctic island group N of Hudson strait

Baffin Bay inlet of the Atlantic between W Greenland & E Baffin island

Bagh·dad \ˈbag-ˌdad\ city, capital of Iraq on the Tigris

Ba·guio \ˌbäg-ē-ˈō\ city, summer capital of the Philippines in NW central Luzon

Ba·ha·mas \bə-ˈhäm-əz, by outsiders also -ˈhā-məz\ islands in N Atlantic SE of Florida; an independent member of the Commonwealth; capital, Nassau — **Ba·ha·mi·an** \-ˈhā-mē-ən, -ˈhäm-ē-ən\ or **Ba·ha·man** \-ˈhä-mən, -ˈhäm-ən\ adj or n

Bahia — see SALVADOR

Bah·rain \bä-ˈrān\ islands in Persian gulf off coast of Arabia; an independent country; capital, Manama

Bai·kal, Lake \-bī-ˈkȯl, -ˈkäl\ lake Russia, in mountains N of Mongolia

Ba·ja California \ˌbä-(ˌ)hä-\ peninsula NW Mexico W of Gulf of California

Ba·kers·field \ˈbā-kərz-ˌfēld\ city S California

Ba·ku \bä-ˈkü\ city, capital of Azerbaijan on W coast of Caspian sea

Bal·a·ton \ˈbal-ə-ˌtän, ˈbȯl-ə-ˌtōn\ lake W Hungary

Bal·boa Heights \(ˌ)bal-ˌbō-ə-\ town Panama; formerly the center of administration for Canal Zone

Ba·li \ˈbäl-ē\ island Indonesia off E end of Java — **Ba·li·nese** \ˌbäl-i-ˈnēz, ˌbal-, -ˈnēs\ adj or n

Bal·kan \ˈbȯl-kən\ **1** mountains N Bulgaria extending from Yugoslavia border to Black sea; highest about 2380 meters **2** peninsula SE Europe between Adriatic & Ionian seas on the W & Aegean & Black seas on the E

Bal·kans \ˈbȯl-kənz\ or **Balkan States** countries occupying the Balkan peninsula: Slovenia, Croatia, Bosnia and Herzegovina, Macedonia, Yugoslavia, Romania, Bulgaria, Albania, Greece, Turkey (in Europe)

Bal·ly·cas·tle \ˌbal-ē-ˈkas-əl\ town N Northern Ireland in Moyledistrict

Bal·ly·me·na \ˌbal-ē-ˈmē-nə\ district NE central Northern Ireland

Bal·ly·mon·ey \ˌbal-ē-ˈmən-ē\ district N central Northern Ireland

Bal·tic \ˈbȯl-tik\ sea arm of the Atlantic N Europe E of Scandinavian peninsula

Bal·ti·more \ˈbȯl-tə-ˌmō(ə)r, -ˌmȯ(ə)r; ˈbȯl-(tə-)mər\ city N central Maryland

Ba·ma·ko \ˌbäm-ə-ˈkō\ city, capital of Mali on the Niger

Ba·na·ras \bə-ˈnär-əs, -ēz\ or **Va·ra·na·si** \və-ˈrän-ə-(ˌ)sē\ city N India

Ban·bridge \ban-ˈbrij\ district SE central Northern Ireland

Ban·dar Se·ri Be·ga·wan \ˌbən-dər-ˌser-ē-bə-ˈgä-wən\ town, capital of Brunei

Ban·dung \ˈbän-ˌdüŋ\ city Indonesia in W Java SE of Djakarta

Ban·ga·lore \ˈbaŋ-gə-ˌlō(ə)r, -ˌlȯ(ə)r\ city S India W of Madras

Bang·kok \ˈbaŋ-ˌkäk, baŋ-ˈkäk\ city, capital of Thailand

Ban·gla·desh \ˌbäŋ-gle-ˈdesh, ˌbaŋ-, -ˈdäsh\ country S Asia E of India; formerly part of Pakistan; an independent state since 1971; capital, Dacca — see EAST PAKISTAN

Ban·gor \ˈbaŋ-ˌgȯ(ə)r, ˈban-ˌgȯ(ə)r, ˈbaŋ-gər\ city area E Northern Ireland in North Down district

Ban·gui \bäŋ-ˈgē\ city, capital of Central African Republic

Ban·jul \ˈbän-ˌjül\ or formerly **Bath·urst** \ˈbath-(ˌ)ərst\ city, capital of Gambia

Bao·tou or **Pao–t'ou** \ˈbaù-ˈtō\ city N China

Bar·ba·dos \bär-ˈbād-əs, -ōz, -äs, -ōs\ island West Indies in Lesser Antilles E of Windward Islands; an independent country in the Commonwealth since 1966; capital, Bridgetown — **Bar·ba·di·an** \-ˈbād-ē-ən\ adj or n

Bar·bu·da \bär-ˈbüd-ə\ island West Indies; part of independent Antigua and Barbuda

Bar·ce·lo·na \ˌbär-sə-ˈlō-nə\ city NE Spain on the Mediterranean; chief city of Catalonia

Bar·king \ˈbär-kiŋ\ city area of E Greater London county, England

Bar·na·ul \ˌbär-nə-ˈül\ city S Russia

Bar·net \ˈbär-nət\ city area of N Greater London county, England

Bar·ran·qui·lla \ˌbar-ən-ˈkē-(y)ə\ city N Colombia

Barren Grounds treeless plains N Canada W of Hudson bay

Bar·row, Point \-ˈbar-ō\ most northerly point of Alaska & of United States at about 71°25′N latitude

Ba·si·lan \bä-ˈsē-ˌlän\ island S Philippines

Bas·il·don \ˈbaz-əl-dən\ town SE England in Essex county

Bass \ˈbas\ strait separating Tasmania & continent of Australia

Basse·terre \bas-ˈte(ə)r, bäs-\ seaport St. Kitts, capital of Saint Kitts-Nevis

Basutoland — see LESOTHO

Batavia — see JAKARTA

Bathurst — see BANJUL

Bat·on Rouge \ˌbat-ᵊn-ˈrüzh\ city, capital of Louisiana

Ba·var·ia \bə-ˈver-ē-ə, -ˈvar-\ or German **Bay·ern** \ˈbī-ərn\ state SE Germany bordering on Czech Republic & Austria — **Ba·var·i·an** \bə-ˈver-ē-ən, -ˈvar-\ adj or n

Ba·ya·mon \ˌbī-ə-ˈmōn\ city NE central Puerto Rico

Beau·fort \ˈbō-fərt\ sea consisting of part of Arctic ocean NE of Alaska & NW of Canada

Beau·mont \ˈbō-ˌmänt, bō-ˈmänt\ city SE Texas

Bech·u·a·na·land \ˌbech-(ə-)ˈwän-ə-ˌland\ **1** region S Africa N of Orange river **2** — see BOTSWANA — **Bech·u·a·na** \ˌbech-(ə-)ˈwän-ə\ adj or n

Bed·ford·shire \ˈbed-fərd-ˌshi(ə)r, -shər\ or **Bedford** county SE England

Bedloe's or **Bedloe** — see LIBERTY

Bei·jing \ˈbā-ˈjiŋ\ or **Pe·king** \ˈpē-ˈkiŋ, ˈpā-\ city, capital of China

Bei·rut \bā-ˈrüt\ city, capital of Lebanon

Be·la·rus \ˌbē-lə-ˈrüs, ˌbyel-ə-\ or **Bye·la·rus** \ˌbē-el-ə-, ˌbyel-ə-\ country central Europe; capital, Minsk

Be·lau \bə-ˈlaù\ or formerly **Pa·lau** \pə-ˈlaù\ island group W Pacific in the W Carolines

Be·lém \bə-ˈlem\ city N Brazil

Bel·fast \ˈbel-ˌfast, bel-ˈfast\ **1** district E Northern Ireland **2** city, capital of Northern Ireland in Antrim district

Belgian Congo — see ZAIRE

Bel·gium \ˈbel-jəm\ or French **Bel·gique** \bel-zhēk\ or Flemish **Bel·gië** \ˈbel-gē-ə\ county W Europe; capital, Brussels — **Bel·gian** \ˈbel-jən\ adj or n

Bel·grade \ˈbel-ˌgrād, -ˌgräd, -ˌgrad\ or **Beo·grad** \ˈbeù-ˌgräd\ city, capital of Yugoslavia on the Danube

Be·lize \bə-ˈlēz\ or formerly **British Honduras** country Central America on the Caribbean; capital, Belmopan

Bel·mo·pan \ˌbel-mō-ˈpan\ city, capital of Belize

Be·lo Ho·ri·zon·te \ˈbā-lō-ˌhȯr-ə-ˈzänt-ē, ˈbel-ō-, -ˌhär-\ city E Brazil N of Rio de Janeiro

Be·lo·rus·sia \ˌbel-ō-ˈrəsh-ə, ˌbyel-\ or **Bye·lo·rus·sia** \ˌbē-el-ō-, ˌbyel-ō-\ former republic of U.S.S.R.; became independent Belarus in 1991 — **Belorussian** adj or n

Benares — see BANARAS

Ben·gal \ben-ˈgȯl, beŋ-\ region S Asia including delta of Ganges & Brahmaputra rivers; divided between Bangladesh & India — **Ben·gal·ese** \ˌbeŋ-gə-ˈlēz, ˌben-, -ˈlēs\ adj or n

Bengal, Bay of arm of Indian ocean between India & Myanmar

Be·nin \bə-ˈnin, -ˈnēn; ˈben-ən\ or formerly **Da·ho·mey** \də-ˈhō-mē\ country W Africa on Gulf of Guinea; capital, Porto-Novo — **Ben·i·nese** \bə-ˌnin-ˈēz, -ˌnēn-; ˌben-i-ˈnēz, -ˈnēs\ adj or n

Ben Nev·is \ben-ˈnev-əs\ mountain 1343 meters W Scotland in the Grampians; highest in Great Britain

Ber·gen \ˈbər-gən, ˈbe(ə)r-\ city SW Norway

Be·ring \ˈbi(ə)r-iŋ, ˈbe(ə)r-\ **1** sea arm of the N Pacific between Alaska & NE Siberia **2** strait about 90 kilometers wide between North America (Alaska) and Asia (Russia)

Berke·ley \ˈbər-klē\ city W California on San Francisco Bay N of Oakland

Berk·shire \ˈbərk-ˌshi(ə)r, -shər, for 2 British usually ˈbärk-\ **1** hills W Massachusetts; highest point Mount Greylock 1064 meters **2** county S England W of London

Ber·lin \(ˌ)bər-ˈlin\ city, official capital of Germany; divided 1945–90 into **East Berlin** (capital of East Germany) & **West Berlin** (city of West Germany lying within East Germany) — **Ber·lin·er** \-ˈlin-ər\ n

Ber·mu·da \(ˌ)bər-ˈmyüd-ə\ islands W Atlantic ESE of Cape Hatteras; a British colony; capital, Hamilton — **Ber·mu·dan** \-ˈmyüd-ᵊn\ or **Ber·mu·di·an** \-ˈmyüd-ē-ən\ adj or n

Bern or **Berne** \ˈbərn, ˈbe(ə)rn\ city, capital of Switzerland — **Ber·nese** \(ˌ)bər-ˈnēz, -ˈnēs\ adj or n

Bes·sa·ra·bia \ˌbes-ə-ˈrä-bē-ə\ region SE Europe now chiefly in Moldova — **Bes·sa·ra·bi·an** \-bē-ən\ adj or n

Beth·le·hem \ˈbeth-li-ˌhem, -lē-həm, -lē-əm\ town of ancient Palestine in Judea SW of Jerusalem in area occupied by Israel since 1967

Bev·er·ly Hills \ˌbev-ər-lē-ˈhilz\ city SW California within city of Los Angeles

Bex·ley \ˈbek-slē\ city area of E Greater London county, England

Bho·pal \bō-ˈpäl\ city N central India

Bhu·tan \bü-ˈtan, -ˈtän\ country S Asia in the Himalayas on NE border of India; capital, Thimbu — **Bhu·ta·nese** \ˌbüt-ᵊn-ˈēz, -ˈēs\ adj or n

Bi·ki·ni \bə-ˈkē-nē\ island W Pacific in Marshall islands

Bil·lings \ˈbil-iŋz\ city S central Montana; largest in state

Bi·loxi \bə-ˈlək-sē, -ˈläk-\ city SE Mississippi on Gulf of Mexico

Bi·o·ko \bē-ˈō-kō\ or formerly **Fer·nan·do Po** \fər-ˌnan-(ˌ)dō-ˈpō\ or 1973–79 **Ma·cí·as Ngue·ma Bi·yo·go** \ˈmä-thē-ə-ˌsəŋ-ˈ(g)wä-mə-bi-ˈyō-(ˌ)gō\ island portion of Equatorial Guinea in Gulf of Guinea

Bir·ken·head \ˈbər-kən-ˌhed, ˌbər-kən-ˈhed\ city area NW England in Merseyside county

Bir·ming·ham \ˈbər-miŋ-ˌham, British usually -miŋ-əm\ **1** city N central Alabama **2** city W central England in West Midlands county

Bisayas — see VISAYAN

Bis·cay, Bay of \-ˈbis-ˌkā, -kē\ inlet of the Atlantic between W coast of France & N coast of Spain

Bish·kek \bish-ˈkek\ or 1926–91 **Frunze** \ˈfrün-zə\ city, capital of Kyrgyzstan

Bis·marck \ˈbiz-ˌmärk\ **1** city, capital of North Dakota

2 island group W Pacific N of E end of New Guinea

Bis·sau \bis-ˈaù\ city, capital of Guinea-Bissau

Bi·thyn·ia \bə-ˈthin-ē-ə\ ancient country NW Asia Minor bordering on Sea of Marmara and Black sea — **Bithyn·i·an** \-ē-ən\ adj or n

Bit·ter·root Range \ˈbit-ə(r)-ˌrüt-, -ˌrùt-\ range of the Rockies along Idaho-Montana boundary

Black·burn \ˈblak-(ˌ)bərn\ city area NW England in Lancashire

Black Forest forested mountain region SW Germany along E bank of the upper Rhine

Black hills mountains W South Dakota & NE Wyoming; highest Harney Peak 2207 meters

Black·pool \ˈblak-ˌpül\ city area NW England in Lancashire

Black sea or ancient **Pon·tus Eux·i·nus** \ˈpänt-əs-ˌyük-ˈsī-nəs\ or **Pon·tus** sea between Europe & Asia connected with Aegean sea through the Bosporus, Sea of Marmara, & Dardanelles

Blanc, Mont — see MONT BLANC

Bloem·fon·tein \ˈblüm-fən-ˌtān, -ˌfān-\ city Republic of South Africa, capital of Orange Free State & judicial capital of the country

Blue Ridge E range of the Applachians E U.S. extending from S Pennsylvania to N Georgia

Boe·o·tia \bē-ˈō-sh(ē-)ə\ ancient state E central Greece NW of Attica; chief ancient city, Thebes — **Boe·o·tian** \bē-ˈō-shən\ adj or n

Bo·go·tá \ˌbō-gə-ˈtó, -ˈtä\ city, capital of Colombia

Bo Hai or **Po Hai** \ˈbō-ˈhī\ or **Gulf of Chih·li** \ˈchē-lē, ˈjir-\ arm of Yellow Sea NE China

Bo·he·mia \bō-ˈhē-mē-ə\ region W Czech Republic; once a kingdom; chief city, Prague

Bo·hol \bō-ˈhól\ island S central Philippines

Boi·se \ˈbói-sē, -zē\ city, capital of Idaho

Bo·liv·ia \bə-ˈliv-ē-ə\ country W central South America; administrative capital, La Paz; constitutional capital, Sucre — **Bo·liv·i·an** \-ē-ən\ adj or n

Bol·ton \ˈbōlt-ᵊn\ or in full **Bolton–le–Moors** \-lə-ˌmù(ə)rz\ city area NW England in Greater Manchester county

Bom·bay \bäm-ˈbā\ city W India

Bonn \ˈbän, ˈbòn\ city, seat of government of Germany; formerly capital of West Germany

Boo·thia \ˈbü-thē-ə\ peninsula N Canada W of Baffin island; its N tip is most northerly point in North America except for islands

Bor·ders \ˈbórd-ərz\ region SE Scotland; established 1975

Bor·neo \ˈbór-nē-ˌō\ island Malay group SW of the Philippines; divided between Brunei, Indonesia, and Malaysia

Bos·nia \ˈbäz-nē-ə\ region S Europe; with Herzegovina forms independent **Bosnia and Her·ze·go·vi·na** \ˌhert-sə-gō-ˈvē-nə, ˌhərt-, -ˈgō-və-nə\; capital, Sarajevo — **Bos·ni·an** \-nē-ən\ adj or n

Bos·po·rus \ˈbäs-p(ə-)rəs\ or ancient **Bosporus Thra·ci·us** \-ˈthrā-sh(ē-)əs\ strait about 29 kilometers long between Turkey in Europe & Turkey in Asia connecting Sea of Marmara & Black sea

Bos·ton \ˈbó-stən\ city, capital of Massachusetts — **Bos·to·nian** \bó-ˈstō-nē-ən, -nyən\ adj or n

Bot·a·ny Bay \ˈbät-ᵊn-ē-, ˈbät-nē-\ inlet of S Pacific SE Australia in New South Wales S of Sydney

Both·nia, Gulf of \-ˈbäth-nē-ə\ arm of Baltic sea between Sweden & Finland

Bo·tswa·na \bät-ˈswän-ə\ country S Africa; formerly (as Bechuanaland) dependent on Britain; now an independent state; capital, Gaborone

Boul·der \ˈbōl-dər\ city N central Colorado

Boulder Dam — see HOOVER DAM

Bourne·mouth \ˈbō(ə)rn-məth, ˈbò(ə)rn-, ˈbù(ə)rn-\ town S England in Dorset county on English channel

Brad·ford \ˈbrad-fərd\ city N England in West Yorkshire

Brah·ma·pu·tra \ˌbräm-ə-ˈp(y)ü-trə\ river 2705 kilometers long S Asia flowing from the Himalayas in Tibet to Ganges delta

Bra·sí·lia \brə-ˈzil-yə\ city, capital of Brazil

Bra·ti·sla·va \ˌbrat-ə-ˈsläv-ə, ˌbrät-\ city on the Danube; capital of Slovakia

Bra·zil \brə-ˈzil\ country E & central South America; capital, Brasília — **Bra·zil·ian** \brə-ˈzil-yən\ adj or n

Braz·za·ville \ˈbraz-ə-ˌvil, ˈbräz-ə-ˌvēl\ city, capital of Congo on W bank of lower Congo river

Bre·men \ˈbrem-ən, ˈbrā-mən\ city NW Germany

Bren·ner \ˈbren-ər\ pass 1397 meters in the Alps between Austria & Italy

Brent \ˈbrent\ city area of W Greater London county, England

Bret·on, Cape \kăp-ˈbret-ᵊn, kə-ˈbret-, -ˈbrit-\ cape Canada; most easterly point of Cape Breton Island & of Nova Scotia

Bridge·port \ˈbrij-ˌpō(ə)rt, -ˌpò(ə)rt\ city SW Connecticut

Bridge·town \ˈbrij-ˌtaùn\ city, capital of Barbados

Brigh·ton \ˈbrīt-ᵊn\ city area S England in East Sussex county on English channel

Bris·bane \ˈbriz-bən, -ˌbān\ city E Australia, capital of Queensland

Bris·tol \ˈbris-tᵊl\ 1 city SW England in Avon 2 channel between S Wales & SW England

Brit·ain \ˈbrit-ᵊn\ 1 the island of Great Britain 2 UNITED KINGDOM

British Columbia province W Canada on Pacific coast; capital, Victoria

British Commonwealth of Nations — see COMMONWEALTH, THE

British Guiana — see GUYANA

British Honduras — see BELIZE

British India the part of India formerly under direct British administration

British Indian Ocean Territory British colony in Indian ocean consisting of Chagos island group

British Isles island group W Europe consisting of Great Britain, Ireland, & nearby islands

British Virgin Islands E islands of Virgin islands group; a British possession

British West Indies islands of the West Indies belonging to the Commonwealth & including Jamaica, Trinidad and Tobago, & the Bahama & Cayman islands, Windward Islands, Leeward Islands, & British Virgin Islands

Brit·ta·ny \ˈbrit-ᵊn-ē\ region NW France SW of Normandy

Brom·ley \ˈbräm-lē\ city area of SE Greater London county, England

Bronx \ˈbräŋ(k)s\ or **The Bronx** section of New York City NE of Manhattan island

Brook·lyn \ˈbrùk-lən\ section of New York City at SW end of Long Island

Brooks Range \ˈbrùks-\ mountains N Alaska

Browns·ville \ˈbraùnz-ˌvil, -vəl\ city S Texas on the Rio Grande

Bru·nei \brù-ˈnī, ˈbrü-ˌnī\ country NE Borneo; formerly under British authority; capital, Bandar Seri Begawan

Brus·sels \ˈbrəs-əlz\ city, capital of Belgium

Bu·cha·rest \ˈb(y)ü-kə-ˌrest\ city, capital of Romania

Buck·ing·ham·shire \ˈbək-iŋ-əm-ˌshi(ə)r, -shər, in the U.S. also -iŋ-ˌham-\ or **Buckingham** county SE central England

Bu·da·pest \\'büd-ə-ˌpest *also* 'byüd-, 'büd-, -ˌpesht\ city, capital of Hungary

Bue·nos Ai·res \ˌbwā-nə-'sa(ə)r-ēz, ˌbō-nə-, -'se(ə)r-, -'sī(ə)r-\ city, capital of Argentina

Buf·fa·lo \'bəf-ə-ˌlō\ city W New York on Lake Erie

Bu·jum·bu·ra \ˌbü-jəm-'bùr-ə\ city, capital of Burundi

Bu·ko·vi·na \ˌbü-kə-'vē-nə\ region E central Europe in foothills of E Carpathians

Bul·gar·ia \ˌbəl-'gar-ē-ə, bùl-, -'ger-\ country SE Europe on Black sea; capital, Sofia

Bull Run \'bùl-'rən\ stream NE Virginia

Bun·ker Hill \ˌbəŋ-kər-\ height in Boston, Massachusetts

Bur·gun·dy \'bər-gən-dē\ region E France — **Bur·gun·di·an** \(ˌ)bər-'gən-dē-ən\ *adj or n*

Bur·ki·na Fa·so \bùr-'kē-nə-'fä-sō\ *or formerly* **Upper Volta** \-'vōl-tə, -'vòl-\ country W Africa N of Ivory Coast, Ghana, & Togo; capital, Ouagadougou

Bur·ling·ton \'bər-liŋ-tən\ city NW Vermont; largest in state

Bur·ma \'bər-mə\ — see MYANMAR

Bu·run·di \bù-'rün-dē\ country E central Africa; capital, Bujumbura — see RUANDA-URUNDI

Bute \'byüt\ island SW Scotland in Firth of Clyde

Butte \'byüt\ city SW Montana

Byelarus — see BELARUS

Byelorussia — see BELORUSSIA

By·zan·tine Empire \'biz-ᵊn-ˌtēn, 'bīz-, -ˌtīn; bə-'zan-ˌtēn, -tīn, bī-\ empire of SE and S Europe and W Asia from 4th to 15th century

By·zan·ti·um \bə-'zan-sh(ē-)əm, -'zant-ē-əm\ ancient city on site of modern Istanbul

Caer·nar·von \kär-'när-vən, kə(r)-\ city area NW Wales in Gwynedd county

Cai·ro \'kī-rō\ city, capital of Egypt — **Cai·rene** \kī-'rēn\ *adj or n*

Ca·la·bria \kə-'lä-brē-ə, -'läb-rē-\ district of ancient Italy consisting of area forming heel of Italian peninsula — **Ca·la·bri·an** \kə-'lä-brē-ən, -'läb-rē-\ *adj or n*

Cal·cut·ta \kal-'kət-ə\ city E India on Hooghly river — **Cal·cut·tan** \-'kət-ᵊn\ *adj or n*

Cal·e·do·nia \ˌkal-ə-'dō-nyə, -nē-ə\ — see SCOTLAND — **Cal·e·do·nian** \-nyən, -nē-ən\ *adj or n*

Cal·ga·ry \'kal-gə-rē\ city SW Alberta, Canada

Ca·li \'käl-ē\ city W Colombia

Cal·i·for·nia \ˌkal-ə-'fòr-nyə\ state SW U.S.; capital, Sacramento — **Cal·i·for·nian** \-nyən\ *adj or n*

California, Gulf of arm of the Pacific NW Mexico

Cal·va·ry \'kalv-(ə-)rē\ place outside ancient Jerusalem where Christ was crucified

Cam·bay, Gulf of \-kam-'bā\ inlet of Arabian sea India N of Bombay

Cam·bo·dia \kam-'bōd-ē-ə\ *or* **Kam·pu·chea** \ˌkam-pə-'chē-ə\ *or 1970–75* **Khmer Republic** \kə-'me(ə)r-\ country SE Asia in S Indochina; capital, Phnom Penh

Cam·bria \'kam-brē-ə\ WALES — an old name

Cam·bridge \'kām-brij\ city E England in Cambridgeshire

Cam·bridge·shire \'kām-brij-ˌshi(ə)r, -shər\ *or* **Cambridge** county E England

Cam·den \'kam-dən\ city area of N Greater London county, England

Cam·er·oon *or French* **Cam·er·oun** \ˌkam-ə-'rün\ country W Africa; capital, Yaoundé — **Cam·er·oo·nian** \-'rü-nē-ən, -rü-nyən\ *adj or n*

Ca·mi·guin \ˌkam-ə-'gēn\ island Philippines, off N coast of Mindanao

Ca·naan \'kā-nən\ ancient region SW Asia; approximately the area later called Palestine — **Ca·naan·ite** \'kā-nə-ˌnīt\ *adj or n*

Can·a·da \'kan-ə-də\ country N North America; independent state in the Commonwealth; capital, Ottawa — **Ca·na·di·an** \kə-'nād-ē-ən\ *adj or n*

Canadian Falls — see NIAGARA FALLS

Canadian Shield — see LAURENTIAN HIGHLANDS

Canal Zone *or* **Panama Canal Zone** former strip of territory Panama leased to U.S. for Panama canal

Ca·nary \kə-'ne(ə)r-ē\ islands in the Atlantic off NW coast of Africa belonging to Spain

Ca·nav·er·al, Cape \-kə-'nav-(ə-)rəl\ *or 1963–1973* **Cape Ken·ne·dy** \-'ken-ə-dē\ cape E Florida in the Atlantic on Canaveral peninsula E of Indian river

Can·ber·ra \'kan-b(ə-)rə, -ˌber-ə\ city, capital of Australia in Australian Capital Territory

Can·on City \ˌkan-yən-\ city S central Colorado on Arkansas river

Can·ter·bury \'kant-ə(r)-ˌber-ē, -b(ə-)rē\ **1** city SE Australia in E New South Wales **2** city SE England in Kent county

Canton — see GUANGZHOU

Cape Bret·on Island \ˌkāp-'bret-ᵊn-, kə-'bret-, -'brit-\ island NE Nova Scotia

Cape Horn — see HORN, CAPE

Cape of Good Hope 1 — see GOOD HOPE, CAPE OF **2** — see CAPE PROVINCE

Cape Province *or* **Cape of Good Hope** *or formerly* **Cape Colony** province S Republic of South Africa; capital, Cape Town

Cape Town \'kāp-ˌtaùn\ city Republic of South Africa, capital of Cape Province & legislative capital of the country

Cape Verde \-'vərd\ islands in the N Atlantic off W Africa; an independent country; capital, Praia; until 1975 belonged to Portugal

Cape York peninsula \-'yò(ə)rk-\ peninsula NE Australia in N Queensland

Ca·pri \ka-'prē, kə-; 'käp-rē, 'kap-\ island Italy S of Bay of Naples

Ca·ra·cas \kə-'rak-əs, -'räk-\ city, capital of Venezuela

Car·diff \'kärd-əf\ city, capital of Wales in South Glamorgan county

Ca·rib·be·an \ˌkar-ə-'bē-ən, kə-'rib-ē-\ sea arm of the Atlantic; on N & E are the West Indies, on S is South America, & on W is Central America — **Caribbean** *adj*

Car·lisle \kär-'lī(ə)l, kər-, 'kär-ˌlī(ə)l\ city NW England in Cumbria county

Carls·bad Caverns \'kärlz-ˌbad-\ series of caves SE New Mexico

Car·mar·then \kär-'mär-t͟hən, kə(r)-\ port S Wales in Dyfed county

Car·o·li·na \ˌkar-ə-'lī-nə\ English colony on E coast of North America founded 1663 & divided 1729 into North Carolina & South Carolina (the **Carolinas**) — **Car·o·lin·i·an** \-'lin-e-ən\ *adj or n*

Ca·ro·li·na \ˌkär-ə-'lē-nə\ city NE Puerto Rico

Car·o·line \'kar-ə-ˌlīn, -lən\ islands W Pacific E of S Philippines; formerly part of Trust Territory of the Pacific Islands

Car·pa·thi·an \kär-'pā-thē-ən\ mountains E central Europe along boundary between Slovakia & Poland & in N & central Romania; highest Gerlachovka 2663 meters

Car·pen·tar·ia, Gulf of \-ˌkär-pən-'ter-ē-ə, -tar-\ inlet of Arafura sea N of Australia

Car·rick·fer·gus \ˌkar-ik-'fər-gəs\ district E Northern Ireland

Car·son City \'kärs-ᵊn-\ city, capital of Nevada

Car·thage \'kär-thij\ ancient city N Africa NE of modern Tunis; capital of an empire that once included much of NW Africa, E Spain, & Sicily — **Car·tha·gin·ian** \ˌkär-thə-'jin-yən, -'jin-ē-ən\ *adj or n*

Ca·sa·blan·ca \ˌkas-ə-'blaŋ-kə, ˌkaz-\ city W Morocco on the Atlantic

Cas·cade Range \(ˈ)kas-'kād-\ mountains NW U.S. in Washington, Oregon, & N California — see RAINIER, MOUNT

Cas·per \'kas-pər\ city central Wyoming; largest in state

Cas·pi·an sea \\'kas-pē-ən-\ salt lake between Europe and Asia about 27 meters below sea level

Cas·tile \kas-'tē(ə)l\ *or in full* **Cas·ti·lla** \kä-'stē-yä\ region & ancient kingdom central & N Spain

Cast·le·reagh \\'kas-əl-rā\ district E Northern Ireland

Cas·tries \\'kas-ˌtrēz, -ˌtrēs\ seaport, capital of Saint Lucia

Cat·a·lo·nia \ˌkat-əl-'ō-nyə, -nē-ə\ region NE Spain bordering on France & the Mediterranean; chief city, Barcelona — **Cat·a·lo·nian** \-'ō-nyən, -nē-ən\ *adj or n*

Ca·tan·dua·nes \ˌkät-ən-'dwän-əs\ island E Philippines

Ca·thay \'kath-'ā\ an old name for China

Cats·kill \\'kat-ˌskil\ mountains in Appalachian system SE New York W of the Hudson

Cau·ca·sus \\'ko-kə-səs\ mountain system SE Europe between Black and Caspian seas in Russia, Georgia, Azerbaijan, & Armenia

Cay·enne \kī-'en, kā-\ city, capital of French Guiana

Cay·man \(ˈ)kā-'man, 'kā-mən\ islands West Indies NW of Jamaica; a British colony

Ce·bu \sā-'bü\ island E central Philippines

Ce·dar Rapids \\'sēd-ər-\ city E Iowa

Celebes — see SULAWESI

Cel·tic \\'kel-tik, 'sel-\ sea inlet of the Atlantic in British Isles SE of Ireland, SW of Wales, & W of Cornwall and Isles of Scilly county, England

Central region central Scotland; established 1975

Central African Republic country N central Africa; capital, Bangui

Central America narrow portion of North America from S border of Mexico to South America — **Central American** *adj or n*

Central Valley valley of Sacramento & San Joaquin rivers in California between Sierra Nevada & Coast ranges

Cey·lon \si-'län, sā-\ **1** island in Indian ocean off S India **2** — see SRI LANKA — **Cey·lon·ese** \ˌsā-lə-'nēz, ˌsē-lə-, ˌsel-ə-, -'nēs\ *adj or n*

Chad \'chad\ country N central Africa; capital, N'Djamena — **Chad·ian** \\'chad-ē-ən\ *adj or n*

Chad, Lake shallow lake N central Africa at junction of boundaries of Chad, Niger, & Nigeria

Cha·gos \\'chä-gəs\ island group central Indian ocean; forms British Indian Ocean Territory — see DIEGO GARCIA

Chal·dea \kal-'dē-ə\ ancient region SW Asia on Euphrates river & Persian gulf — **Chal·de·an** \-'dē-ən\ *adj or n* — **Chal·dee** \\'kal-ˌdē\ *n*

Cham·pagne \sham-'pān\ region NE France

Champlain, Lake \sham-'plān\ lake between New York & Vermont extending N into Quebec

Chan·di·garh \\'chən-dē-gər\ city N India N of Delhi

Chang \'chäŋ\ *or* **Yang·tze** \'yaŋ-'sē, 'yaŋ(k)t-'sē\ river 4990 kilometers long central China flowing into East China sea

Chang·chun \\'chäŋ-'chùn\ city NE China

Chang·sha \\'chäŋ-'shä\ city SE central China

Channel 1 — see SANTA BARBARA **2** islands in English channel including Jersey, Guernsey, & Alderney & belonging to United Kingdom

Charles \\'chär(ə)lz\ river 76 kilometers long E Massachusetts flowing into Boston harbor

Charles, Cape cape E Virginia N of entrance to Chesapeake Bay

Charles·ton \\'chärl-stən\ **1** seaport SE South Carolina **2** city, capital of West Virginia

Char·lotte \\'shär-lət\ city S North Carolina

Charlotte Ama·lie \-'am-ə-lē\ city, capital of Virgin Islands of the U.S.; on Saint Thomas island

Char·lottes·ville \\'shär-ləts-ˌvil, -vəl\ city central Virginia

Char·lotte·town \\'shär-lət-ˌtaùn\ city, capital of Prince Edward Island, Canada

Chat·ta·noo·ga \ˌchat-ə-'nü-gə, ˌchat-ᵊn-'ü-\ city SE Tennessee

Chelms·ford \\'chelm-sfərd, 'chem-\ city area SE England in Essex county

Che·lya·binsk \chel-'yä-bən(t)sk\ city W Russia, S of Sverdlovsk

Cheng–chou — see ZHENGZHOU

Cheng·du *or* **Ch'eng–tu** \\'chəŋ-'dü\ city SW central China

Ches·a·peake \\'ches-(ə-)ˌpēk\ city SE Virginia

Chesapeake Bay inlet of the Atlantic in Virginia & Maryland

Chesh·ire \\'chesh-ər, 'chesh-ˌi(ə)r\ *or* **Ches·ter** \\'chestər\ county W England bordering on Wales

Ches·ter \\'ches-tər\ city NW England in Cheshire

Chev·i·ot \\'chev-ē-ət, 'chē-vē-ət\ hills along English–Scottish border

Chey·enne \shī-'an, -'en\ city, capital of Wyoming

Chi·ba \\'chē-bə\ city E Japan in Honshu on Tokyo Bay E of Tokyo

Chi·ca·go \shə-'käg-ō, -'kòg-\ city NE Illinois — **Chi·ca·go·an** \-'käg-ə-wən, -'kòg-\ *n*

Chi·chén It·zá \chə-ˌchen-ət-'sä\ ruined Mayan city SE Mexico in Yucatán

Chich·es·ter \\'chich-ə-stər\ city S England in West Sussex county

Ch'i–ch'i–ha–erh — see QIQIHAR

Chihli, Gulf of — see BO HAI

Chi·le \\'chil-ē\ country SW South America; capital, Santiago — **Chil·ean** \\'chil-ē-ən, chə-'lā-ən\ *adj or n*

Chim·bo·ra·zo \ˌchim-bə-'räz-ō, ˌshim-\ mountain 6267 meters W central Ecuador

Chi·na \\'chī-nə\ **1** *or in full* **People's Republic of China** country E Asia; capital, Beijing **2** *or officially* **Republic of China** — see TAIWAN **3** sea section of the W Pacific; divided at Taiwan strait into East China & South China seas

Chin–chou *or* **Chinchow** — see JINZHOU

Chit·ta·gong \\'chit-ə-ˌgäŋ, -ˌgòŋ\ city SE Bangladesh on Bay of Bengal

Chong·qing *or* **Ch'ung–ch'ing** \\'chùŋ-'chiŋ\ *or* **Chungking** \\'chùŋ-'kiŋ\ city SW central China

Christ·church \\'krīs(t)-ˌchərch\ city New Zealand on E coast of South island

Christ·mas \\'kris-məs\ island E Indian ocean SW of Java; governed by Australia

Cin·cin·na·ti \ˌsin(t)-sə-'nat-ē, -'nat-ə\ city SW Ohio

Ciudad Trujillo — see SANTO DOMINGO

Cleve·land \\'klēv-lənd\ **1** city NE Ohio **2** county N England N of North Yorkshire

Clwyd \\'klüid\ county NE Wales; established 1974

Clyde \\'klīd\ river 171 kilometers long SW Scotland flowing into **Firth of Clyde** (estuary)

Coast mountains mountain range W British Columbia, Canada; the N continuation of Cascade range

Coast ranges chain of mountain ranges W North America extending along Pacific coast W of Sierra Nevada & Cascade range & through Vancouver island into S Alaska to Kenai peninsula & Kodiak island

Cod, Cape \-'käd\ peninsula SE Massachusetts

Coim·ba·tore \ˌkòim-bə-'tō(ə)r, -'tò(ə)r\ city S India

Cole·raine \kōl-'rān, 'kōl-ˌran\ **1** county N Northern Ireland **2** port in Coleraine county

Co·logne \kə-'lōn\ city W Germany on the Rhine

Co·lom·bia \kə-'ləm-bē-ə\ country NW South America; capital, Bogotá — **Co·lom·bi·an** \-bē-ən\ *adj or n*

Co·lom·bo \kə-'ləm-bō\ city, capital of Sri Lanka

Col·o·ra·do \ˌkäl-ə-'rad-ō, -'räd-\ **1** river 2335 kilome-

\ə\abut \ᵊ\kitten \ər\further \a\ash \ā\ace \ä\mop, mar
\aù\out \ch\chin \e\bet \ē\easy \g\go \i\hit \ī\ice \j\job
\ŋ\sing \ō\go \ò\law \òi\boy \th\thin \<u>th</u>\the \ü\loot \ù\foot
\y\yet \zh\vision *see also* Pronunciation Symbols page

ters long SW U.S. & NW Mexico flowing from N Colorado into Gulf of California **2** desert SE California **3** plateau region SW U.S. W of Rocky mountains **4** state W U.S.; capital, Denver — **Col·o·rad·an** \-ˈrad-ən, -ˈräd-\ *or* **Co·lo·ra·do·an** \-ˈrad-ə-wən, -ˈräd-\ *adj or n*

Colorado Springs city central Colorado

Co·lum·bia \kə-ˈləm-bē-ə\ **1** river 2045 kilometers long SW Canada & NW U.S. flowing S & W from SE British Columbia into the Pacific **2** plateau in Columbia river basin in E Washington, E Oregon, & SW Idaho **3** city, capital of South Carolina **4** — see UNITED STATES OF AMERICA

Co·lum·bus \kə-ˈləm-bəs\ **1** city W Georgia **2** city, capital of Ohio

Com·mon·wealth, the \ˈkäm-ən-ˌwel(t)th\ *or* **Commonwealth of Nations** *or formerly* **British Commonwealth of Nations** the United Kingdom & most of the countries formerly dependent on it

Com·o·ro \ˈkäm-ə-ˌrō\ islands off SE Africa NW of Madagascar; formerly a French possession; an independent country (except for Mayotte Island remaining French) since 1975; capital, Moroni

Con·a·kry \ˈkän-ə-krē\ city, capital of Guinea

Con·cord \ˈkäŋ-kərd\ **1** city W California **2** city, capital of New Hampshire **3** town E Massachusetts NW of Boston

Con·go \ˈkäŋ-gō\ **1** *or* **Zaire** \ˈzī(ə)r, zä-ˈi(ə)r\ river 4830 kilometers long W Africa flowing into the Atlantic **2** — see ZAIRE **3** country W central Africa W of lower Congo river; capital, Brazzaville — **Con·go·lese** \ˌkäŋ-gə-ˈlēz, -ˈlēs\ *adj or n*

Con·nacht \ˈkän-ˌȯt\ province W Ireland

Con·nect·i·cut \kə-ˈnet-i-kət\ **1** river 655 kilometers long NE U.S. flowing S from N New Hampshire into Long Island Sound **2** state NE U.S.; capital, Hartford

Constantinople — see ISTANBUL

Con·ti·nen·tal Di·vide \ˌkänt-ᵊn-ˌent-ᵊl-di-ˈvīd\ line of highest points of land separating the waters flowing W from those flowing N or E and extending SSE from NW Canada across W U.S. through Mexico & Central America to South America where it joins the Andes mountains

Cook \ˈku̇k\ **1** inlet of the Pacific S Alaska W of Kenai peninsula **2** islands S Pacific SW of Society islands belonging to New Zealand **3** strait New Zealand between North island & South island

Cook, Mount *or formerly* **Ao·rangi** \au̇-ˈräŋ-ē\ mountain 3764 meters New Zealand in W central South island in Southern Alps; highest in New Zealand

Cooks·town \ˈku̇k-ˌstau̇n\ district central Northern Ireland

Co·pen·ha·gen \ˌkō-pən-ˈhā-gən, -ˈhäg-ən\ city, capital of Denmark

Cor·al \ˈkȯr-əl, ˈkär-\ sea arm of the W Pacific NE of Australia

Cór·do·ba \ˈkȯrd-ə-bə, -ə-və\ city N central Argentina

Cor·inth \ˈkȯr-ən(t)th, ˈkär-\ **1** region of ancient Greece **2** ancient city, its capital; site SW of present city of Corinth — **Co·rin·thi·an** \kə-ˈrin(t)-thē-ən\ *adj or n*

Corinth, Gulf of inlet of Ionian sea central Greece N of the Peloponnisos

Cork \ˈkȯ(ə)rk\ city S Ireland in Munster

Corn·wall \ˈkȯrn-ˌwȯl, -wəl\ area and once a county SW England

Cornwall and Isles of Scilly county SW England

Cor·pus Chris·ti \ˌkȯr-pə-ˈskris-tē\ city S Texas

Cor·reg·i·dor \kə-ˈreg-ə-ˌdȯ(ə)r\ island Philippines at entrance to Manila Bay

Cor·si·ca \ˈkȯr-si-kə\ island France in the Mediterranean N of Sardinia — **Cor·si·can** \ˈkȯr-si-kən\ *adj or n*

Cos·ta Ri·ca \ˌkäs-tə-ˈrē-kə, ˌkȯs-, ˌkōs-\ country Central America between Nicaragua & Panama; capital, San José — **Cos·ta Ri·can** \-ˈrē-kən\ *adj or n*

Cots·wold \ˈkät-ˌswōld\ hills SW central England

Cov·en·try \ˈkäv-ən-trē, ˈkəv-\ city central England in West Midlands county

Cow·pens \ˈkau̇-ˌpenz\ town NW South Carolina

Craig·av·on \krā-ˈgav-ən\ district central Northern Ireland

Cra·ter \ˈkrāt-ər\ lake 589 meters deep SW Oregon in Cascade range — see MAZAMA, MOUNT

Crete \ˈkrēt\ island Greece in E Mediterranean — **Cre·tan** \ˈkrēt-ᵊn\ *adj or n*

Cri·mea \krī-ˈmē-ə, krə-\ peninsula SE Europe, extending into Black sea — **Cri·me·an** \krī-ˈmē-ən, krə-\ *adj*

Cro·atia \krō-ˈā-sh(ē-)ə\ country SE Europe; capital, Zagreb; a republic of Yugoslavia 1946-91

Croy·don \ˈkrȯid-ᵊn\ city area of S Greater London county, England

Cu·ba \ˈkyü-bə\ island in the West Indies; an independent country; capital, Havana — **Cu·ban** \-bən\ *adj or n*

Cum·ber·land \ˈkəm-bər-lənd\ river 1106 kilometers long S Kentucky & N Tennessee

Cumberland Gap pass through Cumberland plateau NE Tennessee

Cumberland plateau *or* **Cumberland mountains** mountain region E U.S.; part of S Appalachian mountains extending from S West Virginia to NE Alabama

Cum·bria \ˈkəm-brē-ə\ county NW England — **Cum·bri·an** \-ən\ *adj or n*

Cumbrian mountains NW England chiefly in Cumbria county

Cu·par \ˈkü-pər\ town E Scotland in Fife region

Cu·ri·ti·ba \ˌku̇r-ə-ˈtē-bə\ city S Brazil SW of São Paulo

Cush \ˈkəsh, ˈku̇sh\ ancient country NE Africa in upper Nile valley S of Egypt — **Cush·ite** \-ˌīt\ *n* — **Cush·it·ic** \kəsh-ˈit-ik, ku̇sh-\ *adj*

Cuz·co \ˈkü-skō\ city S central Peru

Cymru — see WALES

Cy·prus \ˈsī-prəs\ island E Mediterranean S of Turkey; an independent country in the Commonwealth; capital, Nicosia — **Cyp·ri·ot** \ˈsip-rē-ət, -rē-ˌät\ *or* **Cyp·ri·ote** \-ˌōt, -ət\ *adj or n*

Cy·re·na·ica \ˌsir-ə-ˈnā-ə-kə, ˌsī-rə-\ ancient region N Africa on coast W of Egypt; capital, Cyrene — **Cy·re·na·i·can** \-kən\ *adj or n*

Czecho·slo·va·kia \ˌchek-ə-slō-ˈväk-ē-ə, -ˈvak-\ former country central Europe; capital, Prague; since January 1, 1993 divided into the independent states of the **Czech Republic** (capital, Prague) & **Slovakia** (capital, Bratislava) — **Czecho·slo·vak** \-ˈslō-ˌväk, -ˌvak\ *adj or n* — **Czecho·slo·va·ki·an** \-slō-ˈväk-ē-ən, -ˈvak-\ *adj or n*

Dac·ca *or* **Dha·ka** \ˈdak-ə, ˈdäk-ə\ city, capital of Bangladesh

Dahomey — see BENIN

Dairen — see LÜDA

Da·kar \ˈdak-ˌär, də-ˈkär\ city, capital of Senegal

Da·ko·ta Territory \də-ˈkōt-ə-\ territory 1861–89 NW U.S. divided 1889 into states of North Dakota & South Dakota (the **Da·ko·tas** \-əz\)

Dal·las \ˈdal-əs, -is\ city NE Texas

Dal·ma·tia \dal-ˈmā-sh(ē-)ə\ region W Balkan peninsula on the Adriatic — **Dal·ma·tian** \-shən\ *adj or n*

Da·mas·cus \də-ˈmas-kəs\ city, capital of Syria

Dan·ube \ˈdan-yüb\ river 2776 kilometers long S Europe flowing from SW Germany into Black sea — **Da·nu·bi·an** \da-ˈnyü-bē-ən\ *adj*

Dar·da·nelles \ˌdärd-ᵊn-ˈelz\ *or* **Hel·les·pont** \ˈhel-ə-ˌspänt\ strait NW Turkey connecting Sea of Marmara & the Aegean

Dar es Sa·laam \ˌdär-es-sə-ˈläm\ city, capital of Tanzania

Dar·ling \ˈdär-liŋ\ river 1865 kilometers long SE Australia in Queensland & New South Wales flowing SW into the Murray

Dar·win \'där-wən\ city Australia, capital of Northern Territory

Da·vao \'däv-ˌaů,dä-'vaů\ city S Philippines in E Mindanao on Davao Gulf

Dav·en·port \'dav-ən-ˌpō(ə)rt, -ˌpȯ(ə)rt\ city E Iowa

Da·vis \'dā-vəs\ strait between SW Greenland & E Baffin island connecting Baffin Bay & the Atlantic

Day·ton \'dāt-ᵊn\ city SW Ohio

Dead sea \'ded-\ salt lake between Israel & Jordan; 397 meters below sea level

Death Valley \'deth-\ dry valley E California & S Nevada containing lowest point in U.S. (86 meters below sea level)

Dec·can \'dek-ən, -ˌan\ plateau region S India

Del·a·ware \'del-ə-ˌwa(ə)r, -ˌwe(ə)r, -wər\ 1 river 476 kilometers long E U.S. flowing S from S New York into Delaware Bay 2 state E U.S.; capital, Dover — **Del·a·war·ean** or **Del·a·war·ian** \ˌdel-ə-'war-ē-ən, -'wer-\ adj or n

Delaware Bay inlet of the Atlantic between SW New Jersey & E Delaware

Del·hi \'del-ē\ city N India — see NEW DELHI

De·los \'dē-ˌläs\ island Greece — **De·lian** \'dē-lē-ən, 'dēl-yən\ adj or n

Del·phi \'del-ˌfī\ ancient town central Greece on S slope of Parnassus

Democratic Republic of the Congo — see ZAIRE

Denali — see MCKINLEY, MOUNT

Den·mark \'den-ˌmärk\ country N Europe occupying most of Jutland & neighboring islands; capital, Copenhagen

Den·ver \'den-vər\ city, capital of Colorado

Der·by \'där-bē, chiefly in the U.S. 'dər-bē\ city area N central England in Derbyshire

Der·by·shire \'där-bē-ˌshi(ə)r, -shər, U.S. also 'dər-\ **Derby** county N central England

Der·ry \'der-ē\ or **Lon·don·der·ry** \ˌlən-dən-'der-ē; 'lən-dən-ˌder-ē, -d(ə-)rē\ 1 district NW Northern Ireland 2 seaport in Londonderry district

Des Moines \di-'mȯin\ city, capital of Iowa

De·troit \di-'trȯit\ 1 river 50 kilometers long between SE Michigan & Ontario connecting Lake Saint Clair & Lake Erie 2 city SE Michigan

Dev·on \'dev-ən\ or **De·von·shire** \-ˌshi(ə)r, -shər\ county SW England

Dhaka — see DACCA

Die·go Gar·cia \dē-ˌā-gō-ˌgär-'sē-ə\ island in Indian ocean; chief island of Chagos island group

Di·nar·ic Alps \də-ˌnar-ik-\ range of the E Alps in W Slovenia, W Croatia, Bosnia and Herzegovina, & Montenegro

District of Co·lum·bia \-kə-'ləm-bē-ə\ federal district E U.S. coextensive with city of Washington

Djakarta — see JAKARTA

Dji·bou·ti \jə-'büt-ē\ 1 country E Africa on Gulf of Aden 2 city, its capital

Dne·pro·pe·trovsk \'nep-(ˌ)rō-pə-'trȯfsk\ city E central Ukraine

Dodge City \'däj-\ city S Kansas on Arkansas river

Do·ha \'dō-hä\ city & port, capital of Qatar on Persian gulf

Dom·i·ni·ca \ˌdäm-ə-'nē-kə, də-'min-ə-kə\ island West Indies in the Leeward Islands; an independent country; capital, Roseau

Do·min·i·can Republic \də-ˌmin-i-kən-\ country West Indies in E Hispaniola; capital, Santo Domingo — **Do·min·i·can** \də-'min-i-kən\ adj or n

Don \'dän\ river 1930 kilometers long SW Russia

Do·netsk \də-'netsk\ city E Ukraine

Dor·ches·ter \'dȯr-chə-stər, -ˌches-tər\ city area S England in Dorset county

Dor·set \'dȯr-sət\ or **Dor·set·shire** \-ˌshi(ə)r, -shər\ county S England on English channel

Dort·mund \'dȯ(ə)rt-ˌmůnt, -mənd\ city W Germany in the Ruhr

Dou·ro \'dōr-ü, 'dȯr-\ or Spanish **Due·ro** \'dwe(ə)r-ō\ or ancient **Du·ri·us** \'d(y)ůr-ē-əs\ river 780 kilometers long N Spain & N Portugal flowing into the Atlantic

Do·ver \'dō-vər\ city, capital of Delaware

Dover, Strait of channel between SE England & N France; the most easterly section of English channel

Down \'daůn\ district SE Northern Ireland

Down·pat·rick \daůn-'pa-trik\ city district E Northern Ireland in Down district

Dra·kens·berg \'dräk-ənz-ˌbərg\ mountain range E Republic of South Africa & Lesotho; highest peak Thabana Ntlenyana 3482 meters

Dres·den \'drez-dən\ city E Germany

Dub·lin \'dəb-lən\ or ancient **Eb·la·na** \'eb-lə-nə\ city, capital of Ireland in Leinster

Dud·ley \'dəd-lē\ city area W central England in West Midlands county

Duis·burg \'dü-əs-ˌbərg; 'd(y)üz-ˌbərg\ city W Germany at junction of Rhine & Ruhr rivers

Du·luth \də-'lüth\ city NE Minnesota

Dum·fries \ˌdəm-'frēs\ town S Scotland in Dumfries and Galloway region

Dumfries and Gal·lo·way \-'gal-ə-ˌwā\ region S Scotland; established 1975

Dun·dee \ˌdən-'dē\ city E Scotland in Tayside region

Dun·gan·non \ˌdən-'gan-ən\ district W Northern Ireland

Dur·ban \'dər-bən\ city E Republic of South Africa in E Natal

Dur·ham \'dər-əm, 'də-rəm, 'důr-əm\ 1 city N central North Carolina 2 county N England on North sea 3 city area in Durham county

Du·shan·be \d(y)ü-'sham-bə, -'shäm-\ city, capital of Tajikistan

Düs·sel·dorf \'d(y)üs-əl-ˌdȯrf\ city W Germany on the Rhine

Dutch East Indies — see NETHERLANDS EAST INDIES

Dy·fed \'dəv-ed, -əd\ county SW Wales; established 1974

Ea·ling \'ē-liŋ\ city area of W Greater London county, England

East An·glia \-aŋ-glē-ə\ region E England including Norfolk & Suffolk counties

East China sea — see CHINA

Eas·ter \'ē-stər\ island SE Pacific 3220 kilometers W of Chilean coast; belongs to Chile

Eastern Ghats \-'gȯts\ chain of low mountains SE India along coast

Eastern Roman Empire the Byzantine Empire from 395 to 474

Eastern Samoa — see AMERICAN SAMOA

East Germany the German Democratic Republic — see GERMANY

East Indies the Malay island group — **East Indian** adj or n

East London city S republic of south africa in SE Cape Province

East Pakistan the former E division of Pakistan consisting of E portion of Bengal; now the independent country of Bangladesh

East river strait SE New York connecting upper New York Bay & Long Island Sound & separating Manhattan island and Long Island

East Sus·sex \-'səs-iks, U.S. also -eks\ county SE England

Eblana — see DUBLIN

\ə\abut \ᵊ\kitten \ər\further \a\ash \ā\ace \ä\mop, mar \aů\out \ch\chin \e\bet \ē\easy \g\go \i\hit \ī\ice \j\job \ŋ\sing \ō\go \ȯ\law \ȯi\boy \th\thin \t̲h̲\the \ü\loot \ů\foot \y\yet \zh\vision see also Pronunciation Symbols page

Ebro \'ā-brō\ river 775 kilometers long NE Spain flowing into the Mediterranean

Ec·ua·dor \'ek-wə-ˌdȯ(ə)r\ country W South America; capital, Quito — **Ec·ua·dor·an** \ek-wə-ˈdȯr-ən, -ˈdōr-\ or **Ec·ua·dor·ean** or **Ec·ua·dor·ian** \-ē-ən\ adj or n

Ed·in·burgh \'ed-ᵊn-ˌbər-ə, -ˌbə-rə, -b(ə)rə\ city, capital of Scotland, in Lothian region

Ed·mon·ton \'ed-mən-tən\ city, capital of Alberta, Canada

Edom \'ēd-əm\ ancient country SW Asia S of Judea & Dead sea — **Edom·ite** \'ēd-ə-ˌmīt\ n

Egypt \'ē-jəpt\ country NE Africa & Sinai peninsula of SW Asia bordering on Mediterranean & Red seas; capital, Cairo

Eire — see IRELAND

Elam \'ē-ləm\ ancient country SW Asia at head of Persian gulf E of Babylonia — **Elam·ite** \'ē-lə-ˌmīt\ n

Elbe \'el-bə, 'elb\ river 1160 kilometers long N Czech Republic & NE Germany flowing NW into North sea

El·bert, Mount \-'el-bərt\ mountain 4399 meters W central Colorado; highest in Colorado & the Rocky mountains

El·burz \el-ˈbu̇(ə)rz\ mountains N Iran

Eliz·a·beth \i-ˈliz-ə-bəth\ city NE New Jersey

Elles·mere \'elz-ˌmi(ə)r\ island N Canada in Northwest Territories

Ellice — see TUVALU

El Paso \el-ˈpas-ō\ city W Texas on Rio Grande

El Sal·va·dor \el-ˈsal-və-ˌdȯ(ə)r, -ˌsal-və-ˈdȯ(ə)r\ country Central America bordering on the Pacific; capital, San Salvador

Ely, Isle of \-ˈē-lē\ district E England in Cambridgeshire

En·field \'en-ˌfēld\ city area of N Greater London county, England

En·gland \'iŋ-glənd also 'iŋ-lənd\ country S Great Britain; a division of United Kingdom; capital, London

English channel arm of the Atlantic between S England & N France

En·nis·kil·len \ˌen-ə-ˈskil-ən\ city district SW Northern Ireland in Fermanagh district

Ephra·im \'ē-frē-əm\ 1 hilly region N Jordan E of Jordan river 2 — see ISRAEL — **Ephra·im·ite** \'ē-frē-ə-ˌmīt\ n

Equatorial Guinea or formerly **Spanish Guinea** country W Africa including Río Muni & Bioko; capital, Malabo

Erie \'i(ə)r-ē\ 1 city NW Pennsylvania 2 canal New York between Hudson river at Albany & Lake Erie at Buffalo; built 1817–25; now superseded by New York State Barge Canal

Erie, Lake lake E central North America in U.S. & Canada; one of the Great Lakes

Er·in \'er-ən\ poetic name of Ireland

Er·i·trea \ˌer-ə-ˈtrē-ə, -ˈtrā-\ country NE Africa; capital, Asmara — **Er·i·tre·an** \-ən\ adj or n

Española — see HISPANIOLA

Es·sen \'es-ᵊn\ city W Germany in the Ruhr

Es·sex \'es-iks\ county SE England on North sea

Es·to·nia \e-ˈstō-nē-ə, -nyə\ country E Europe on Baltic sea; capital, Tallinn; a republic of U.S.S.R. 1940–91

Ethi·o·pia \ˌē-thē-ˈō-pē-ə\ or **Ab·ys·sin·ia** \ˌab-ə-ˈsin-yə, -ˈsin-ē-ə\ country E Africa; capital, Addis Ababa — **Ethi·o·pi·an** \-pē-ən\ adj or n

Et·na \'et-nə\ volcano 3323 meters Italy in NE Sicily

Eto·bi·coke \et-ˈō-bi-ˌkō\ city Canada in SE Ontario

Etru·ria \i-ˈtru̇r-ē-ə\ ancient country central Italy

Eu·gene \yu̇-ˈjēn\ city W Oregon

Eu·phra·tes \yu̇-ˈfrāt-ēz\ river 2735 kilometers long SW Asia flowing from E Turkey & uniting with the Tigris to form the Shatt-al-Arab

Eur·asia \yu̇-ˈrā-zhə, -shə\ landmass consisting of Europe & Asia — **Eur·asian** \-zhən, -shən\ adj or n

Eu·rope \'yu̇r-əp\ continent of the eastern hemisphere between Asia & the Atlantic

Ev·ans·ville \'ev-ənz-ˌvil\ city SW Indiana

Ev·er·est, Mount \-'ev-(ə-)rəst\ mountain 8848 meters S Asia in the Himalayas on border between Nepal & Tibet; highest in the world

Ev·er·glades \'ev-ər-ˌglādz\ swamp region S Florida now partly drained

Ex·e·ter \'ek-sət-ər\ 1 town SE New Hampshire 2 city SW England in Devon county

Faer·oe or **Far·oe** \'fa(ə)r-ō, 'fe(ə)r-\ islands NE Atlantic NW of the Shetlands belonging to Denmark — **Faero·ese** \ˌfar-ə-ˈwēz, ˌfer-, -ˈwēs\ adj or n

Fair·field \'fa(ə)r-ˌfēld, 'fe(ə)r-\ city SE Australia in E New South Wales

Fai·sa·la·bad \ˌfī-ˌsäl-ə-ˈbäd, -ˌsal-ə-ˈbad\ or formerly **Ly·all·pur** \lē-ˌäl-ˈpu̇(ə)r\ city NE Pakistan W of Lahore

Falk·land \'fȯ(l)-klənd\ or Spanish **Is·las Mal·vi·nas** \ˌēz-läz-mäl-ˈvē-näs\ islands SW Atlantic E of S end of Argentina; a British colony; capital, Stanley

Far East the countries of E Asia & the Malay island group — usually thought to consist of the Asian countries bordering on the Pacific but sometimes including also India, Sri Lanka, Bangladesh, Tibet, & Myanmar — **Far Eastern** adj

Far·go \'fär-gō\ city E North Dakota; largest in state

Fear, Cape \-'fi(ə)r\ cape SE North Carolina at mouth of Cape Fear river

Fer·man·agh \fər-ˈman-ə\ district SW Northern Ireland

Fernando Po — see BIOKO

Fez \'fez\ city N central Morocco

Fife \'fīf\ or **Fife·shire** \-ˌshi(ə)r, -shər\ region E Scotland

Fi·ji \'fē-jē\ islands SW Pacific; an independent country in the Commonwealth; capital, Suva — **Fi·ji·an** \-jē-ən\ adj or n

Fin·land \'fin-lənd\ country NE Europe; capital, Helsinki — **Fin·land·er** n

Flan·ders \'flan-dərz\ region W Belgium & N France on North sea

Flat·tery, Cape \-'flat-ə-rē\ cape NW Washington at entrance to Strait of Juan de Fuca

Flint \'flint\ city SE Michigan

Flor·ence \'flȯr-ən(t)s, 'flär-\ or Italian **Fi·ren·ze** \fē-ˈrent-sä\ or ancient **Flo·ren·tia** \flə-ˈren-chə, -chē-ə\ city central Italy — **Flor·en·tine** \'flȯr-ən-ˌtēn, 'flär-, -ˌtīn\ adj or n

Flor·i·da \'flȯr-əd-ə, 'flär-\ state SE U.S.; capital, Tallahassee — **Flo·rid·i·an** \flə-ˈrid-ē-ən\ or **Flor·i·dan** \'flȯr-əd-ᵊn, 'flär-\ adj or n

Florida, Straits of channel between Florida Keys on NW & Cuba & Bahamas on S & E connecting Gulf of Mexico & the Atlantic

Florida Keys chain of islands off S tip of Florida

Foochow — see FUZHOU

For·a·ker, Mount \-'fȯr-i-kər, -'fär-\ mountain 5304 meters S central Alaska in Alaska range

For·mo·sa \fȯr-ˈmō-sə, fər-, -zə\ — see TAIWAN — **For·mo·san** \-ˈmōs-ᵊn, -ˈmōz-\ adj or n

For·ta·le·za \ˌfȯrt-ᵊl-ˈā-zə\ city NE Brazil

Fort–de–France \ˌfȯrd-ə-ˈfräns\ city West Indies, capital of Martinique on W coast

Forth \'fȯ(ə)rth, 'fȯ(ə)rth\ river 183 kilometers long S central Scotland flowing E into North sea through **Firth of Forth**

Fort Knox \-'näks\ military reservation N central Kentucky SSW of Louisville; location of U.S. Gold Bullion Depository

Fort Lau·der·dale \-'lȯd-ər-ˌdāl\ city SE Florida

Fort Wayne \-'wān\ city NE Indiana

Fort Worth \-'wərth\ city NE Texas

Fox \'fäks\ islands SW Alaska in the E Aleutians

Foxe Basin \'fäks-\ inlet of the Atlantic N Canada in E Northwest Territories W of Baffin island

France \\'fran(t)s\\ country W Europe between the English channel & the Mediterranean; capital, Paris

Frank·fort \\'fraŋk-fərt\\ city, capital of Kentucky

Frank·furt \\'fraŋk-fərt, 'fräŋ-ˌfu̇(ə)rt\\ *or in full* **Frankfurt am Main** \\-(ˌ)äm-'mīn\\ *or* **Frankfort on the Main** city W Germany on Main river

Frank·lin \\'fraŋ-klən\\ former district N Canada in Northwest Territories including Arctic islands & Boothia & Melville peninsulas

Fra·ser \\'frā-zər, -zhər\\ river 1370 kilometers long Canada in S central British Columbia flowing into the Pacific

Fred·er·ic·ton \\'fred-(ə-)rik-tən\\ city, capital of New Brunswick, Canada

Free·town \\'frē-ˌtau̇n\\ city, capital of Sierra Leone

Fre·mont \\'frē-mänt\\ city W California

French Guiana country N South America on the Atlantic; an overseas division of France; capital, Cayenne

French Indochina — see INDOCHINA

Fres·no \\'frez-nō\\ city S central California

Frunze — see BISHKEK

Fu·ji \\'f(y)ü-jē\\ *or* **Fu·ji·ya·ma** \\ˌf(y)ü-jē-'(y)äm-ə\\ mountain 3776 meters Japan in S central Honshu; highest in Japan

Fu·ku·o·ka \\ˌfü-kə-'wō-kə\\ city Japan in N Kyushu

Ful·ler·ton \\'fu̇l-ərt-ᵊn\\ city SW California

Fu·na·fu·ti \\ˌf(y)ü-nə-'f(y)üt-ē\\ city, capital of Tuvalu

Fun·dy, Bay of \\-'fən-dē\\ inlet of the Atlantic SE Canada between New Brunswick & Nova Scotia

Fu·shun \\'fü-'shùn\\ city NE China E of Shenyang

Fu·zhou \\'fü-'jō\\ *or* **Foo·chow** \\'fü-'jō, -'chau̇\\ city SE China

Ga·bon \\ga-'bōn\\ country W Africa on the equator; capital, Libreville — **Gab·o·nese** \\ˌgab-ə-'nēz, -'nēs\\ *adj or n*

Ga·bo·rone \\ˌgäb-ə-'rōn\\ city, capital of Botswana

Gads·den Purchase \\'gadz-dən-\\ area of land S of Gila river in present Arizona & New Mexico purchased 1853 by the U.S. from Mexico

Ga·la·pa·gos islands \\gə-'läp-ə-gəs-, -'lap-\\ island group Ecuador in the Pacific 965 kilometers W of South America

Ga·la·tia \\gə-'lā-sh(ē-)ə\\ ancient country central Asia Minor in region around modern Ankara, Turkey — **Ga·la·tian** \\-shən\\ *adj or n*

Ga·li·cia \\gə-'lish-(ē-)ə\\ **1** region E central Europe now divided between Poland & Ukraine **2** region NW Spain on the Atlantic — **Ga·li·cian** \\-'lish-ən\\ *adj or n*

Gal·i·lee \\'gal-ə-ˌlē\\ hilly region N Israel — **Gal·i·le·an** \\ˌgal-ə-'lē-ən\\ *adj or n*

Galilee, Sea of *or* **Lake of Gen·nes·a·ret** \\-gə-'nəs-ə-ˌret, -rət\\ lake N Israel on Syrian border; crossed by Jordan river

Gal·lo·way \\'gal-ə-ˌwā\\ district SW Scotland — see DUMFRIES AND GALLOWAY

Gam·bia \\'gam-bē-ə\\ country W Africa; capital, Banjul — **Gam·bi·an** \\-bē-ən\\ *adj or n*

Gan·ges \\'gan-ˌjēz\\ river 2495 kilometers long N India flowing from the Himalayas SE & E to unite with the Brahmaputra & empty into Bay of Bengal through a vast delta — **Gan·get·ic** \\gan-'jet-ik\\ *adj*

Garden Grove city SW California

Gar·land \\'gär-lənd\\ city NE Texas

Ga·ronne \\gə-'rän, -'rōn\\ river 571 kilometers long SE France flowing NW

Gary \\'ga(ə)r-ē, 'ge(ə)r-ē\\ city NW Indiana on Lake Michigan

Gas·co·ny \\'gas-kə-nē\\ region SW France — **Gas·con** \\'gas-kən\\ *adj or n*

Gas·pé \\gas-'pā, 'gas-ˌpā\\ peninsula SE Quebec E of mouth of the Saint Lawrence — **Gas·pe·sian** \\ga-'spē-zhən\\ *adj or n*

Gaul \\'gȯl\\ *or Latin* **Gal·lia** \\'gal-ē-ə\\ ancient country W Europe chiefly consisting of region occupied by modern France & Belgium but at one time including also Po valley in N Italy

Ga·za Strip \\'gäz-ə-\\ district NE Sinai Peninsula on the Mediterranean

Gee·long \\jə-'lȯŋ\\ city SE Australia in S Victoria

Ge·ne·va \\jə-'nē-və\\ city SW Switzerland on Lake of Geneva — **Ge·ne·van** \\-vən\\ *adj or n* — **Gen·e·vese** \\ˌjen-ə-'vēz, -'vēs\\ *adj or n*

Geneva, Lake of lake on border between SW Switzerland & E France; crossed by the Rhone

Gen·oa \\'jen-ə-wə\\ *or Italian* **Ge·no·va** \\'je-nō-vä\\ city NW Italy — **Gen·o·ese** \\ˌjen-ə-'wēz, -'wēs\\ *or* **Gen·o·vese** \\-ə-'vēz, -'vēs\\ *adj or n*

George·town \\'jȯ(ə)rj-ˌtau̇n\\ **1** a W section of Washington, District of Columbia **2** city, capital of Guyana

Geor·gia \\'jȯr-jə\\ **1** state SE U.S.; capital, Atlanta **2** *or* **Republic of Georgia** country SE Europe on Black sea S of Caucasus mountains; capital, Tiflis; a republic of U.S.S.R. 1936–91 — **Georgian** *adj or n*

Georgia, Strait of channel Canada & U.S. between Vancouver Island & main part of British Columbia NW of Puget Sound

Georgian Bay inlet of Lake Huron in S Ontario

Ger·man·town \\'jər-mən-ˌtau̇n\\ a NW section of Philadelphia, Pennsylvania

Ger·ma·ny \\'jərm-(ə-)nē\\ country central Europe bordering on North & Baltic seas; official capital, Berlin; divided 1946–90 into two independent states: the Federal Republic of Germany (capital, Bonn) & the German Democratic Republic (capital, East Berlin)

Get·tys·burg \\'get-ēz-ˌbərg\\ town S Pennsylvania

Gha·na \\'gän-ə, 'gan-ə\\ *or formerly* **Gold Coast** country W Africa on Gulf of Guinea; an independent state in the Commonwealth; capital, Accra — **Gha·na·ian** \\gä-'nā-ən, ga-, -yən; -'nī-ən\\ *or* **Gha·ni·an** \\'gän-ē-ən, 'gän-yən, 'gan-\\ *adj or n*

Ghats \\'gȯts\\ two mountain chains S India — see EASTERN GHATS, WESTERN GHATS

Ghent \\'gent\\ city NW central Belgium

Gi·bral·tar \\jə-'brȯl-tər\\ British colony on S coast of Spain including Rock of Gibraltar

Gibraltar, Rock of cape on S coast of Spain in Gibraltar colony at E end of Strait of Gibraltar; highest point 426 meters

Gibraltar, Strait of passage between Spain & Africa connecting the Atlantic & the Mediterranean

Gi·la \\'hē-lə\\ river 1015 kilometers long SW New Mexico and S Arizona flowing W into the Colorado

Gil·bert and El·lice Islands \\'gil-bərt-ən(d)-'el-əs-\\ island group W Pacific; until 1976 a British colony; now divided into the independent states of Kiribati and Tuvalu

Gil·e·ad \\'gil-ē-əd\\ mountain region NE Palestine E of Jordan river; now in NW Jordan — **Gil·e·ad·ite** \\-ē-ə-ˌdīt\\ *n*

Gi·za \\'gē-zə\\ city N Egypt on the Nile SW of Cairo

Gla·cier Bay \\ˌglā-shər-\\ inlet SE Alaska at S end of Saint Elias range

Glas·gow \\'glas-kō, 'glas-gō, 'glaz-gō\\ city S central Scotland in Strathclyde region on the Clyde — **Glas·we·gian** \\glas-'wē-jən\\ *adj or n*

Glen·dale \\'glen-ˌdāl\\ city S California NE of Los Angeles

Glouces·ter \\'gläs-tər, 'glȯs-\\ city area SW central England in Gloucestershire

Glouces·ter·shire \\'gläs-tər-ˌshi(ə)r, 'glȯs-, -shər\\ *or* **Gloucester** county SW central England

---

\\ə\\abut \\ᵊ\\kitten \\ər\\further \\a\\ash \\ā\\ace \\ä\\mop, mar \\au̇\\out \\ch\\chin \\e\\bet \\ē\\easy \\g\\go \\i\\hit \\ī\\ice \\j\\job \\ŋ\\sing \\ō\\go \\ȯ\\law \\ȯi\\boy \\th\\thin \\th̲\\the \\ü\\loot \\u̇\\foot \\y\\yet \\zh\\vision *see also* Pronunciation Symbols page

Goa \ˈgō-ə\ district W India on Malabar coast belonging to Portugal before 1962

Goat Island island W New York in Niagara river — see NIAGARA FALLS

Go·bi \ˈgō-bē\ desert E central Asia in Mongolia & N China

Godt·haab \ˈgȯt-ˌhȯb, ˈgät-\ town, capital of Greenland on SW coast

Godwin Austen — see K2

Go·lan Heights \ˌgō-ˌlän-, -lən-\ hilly region NE of Sea of Galilee

Gol·con·da \gäl-ˈkän-də\ ruined city central India W of Hyderabad

Gold Coast 1 — see GHANA **2** coast region W Africa on N shore of Gulf of Guinea E of Ivory Coast

Golden Gate strait W California

Good Hope, Cape of \-ˌgu̇d-ˈhōp\ cape S Republic of South Africa in SW Cape Province

Gor'kiy or **Gorky** — see NIZHNI NOVGOROD

Gram·pi·an \ˈgram-pē-ən\ **1** hills N central Scotland **2** region NE central Scotland; established 1975

Grand Banks shallow area in the W Atlantic SE of Newfoundland

Grand Canyon gorge of Colorado river NW Arizona

Grand Canyon of the Snake — see HELLS CANYON

Grande, Rio — see RIO GRANDE

Grand Rapids city SW Michigan

Great Australian Bight wide bay on S coast of Australia

Great Barrier Reef coral reef Australia off NE coast of Queensland

Great Basin region W U.S. between Sierra Nevada & Wasatch mountains including most of Nevada & parts of California, Idaho, Utah, Wyoming, and Oregon; has no drainage to ocean

Great Bear lake Canada in W Northwest Territories draining through Great Bear river into Mackenzie river

Great Brit·ain \-ˈbrit-ᵊn\ **1** island W Europe NW of France consisting of England, Scotland, & Wales **2** UNITED KINGDOM

Great Dividing range mountain system E Australia & Tasmania extending S from Cape York peninsula — see KOSCIUSKO, MOUNT

Greater An·til·les \-an-ˈtil-ēz\ group of islands of the West Indies including Cuba, Hispaniola, Jamaica, & Puerto Rico — see LESSER ANTILLES

Greater London county SE England consisting of City of London & 32 surrounding city areas

Greater Manchester county NW England including city of Manchester

Great Lakes chain of five lakes (Superior, Michigan, Huron, Erie, & Ontario) central North America in U.S. & Canada

Great Plains elevated plains region W central U.S. & W Canada E of the Rockies; extending from W Texas to NE British Columbia & NW Alberta

Great Rift valley \-ˈrift-\ basin SW Asia & E Africa extending with several breaks from valley of the Jordan S to central Mozambique

Great Salt lake N Utah having salty waters & no outlet

Great Slave lake NW Canada in S Northwest Territories drained by Mackenzie river

Great Smoky mountains between W North Carolina & E Tennessee; highest Clingmans Dome 2024 meters

Greece \ˈgrēs\ country S Europe at S end of Balkan peninsula; capital, Athens

Green \ˈgrēn\ **1** mountains E North America in the Appalachians extending from S Quebec S through Vermont into W Massachusetts **2** river 1175 kilometers long W U.S. flowing from W Wyoming S into the Colorado in SE Utah

Green Bay inlet of NW Lake Michigan 193 kilometers long in NW Michigan & NE Wisconsin

Green·land \ˈgrēn-lənd, -ˌland\ island in the N Atlantic off NE North America belonging to Denmark; capital, Godthaab

Greens·boro \ˈgrēnz-ˌbər-ə, -ˌbə-rə\ city N central North Carolina

Green·wich \ˈgrin-ij, ˈgren-, -ich\ city area of SE Greater London county, England

Green·wich Village \ˌgren-ich-, ˌgrin-, -ij-\ section of New York City in Manhattan on lower W side

Gre·na·da \grə-ˈnād-ə\ island West Indies in S Windward Islands; an independent country; capital, Saint George's

Gua·da·la·ja·ra \ˌgwäd-ə-lə-ˈhär-ə\ city W central Mexico

Gua·dal·ca·nal \ˌgwäd-ᵊl-kə-ˈnal, ˌgwäd-ə-kə-\ island W Pacific in the SE Solomons

Gua·dal·qui·vir \ˌgwäd-ᵊl-ˈkwiv-ər, -ki-ˈvi(ə)r\ river 602 kilometers long S Spain flowing into the Atlantic

Gua·de·loupe \ˈgwäd-ᵊl-ˌüp\ two islands separated by a narrow channel in West Indies in central Leeward Islands; an overseas division of France

Gua·lla·ti·ri \ˌgwä-yə-ˈtir-ē, ˌgwī-ə-\ volcano 6060 meters N Chile; highest volcano in world

Guam \ˈgwäm\ island W Pacific in S Marianas belonging to U.S.; capital, Agana — **Gua·ma·ni·an** \gwä-ˈmä-nē-ən\ adj or n

Gua·na·ba·ra Bay \ˌgwän-ə-ˈbar-ə, -ˈbär-\ inlet of the Atlantic SE Brazil on which city of Rio de Janeiro is located

Guang·zhou \ˈgwäŋ-ˈjō\ or **Can·ton** \ˈkan-ˌtän, kan-ˈ\ city SE China

Guan·tá·na·mo Bay \gwän-ˈtän-ə-ˌmō\ inlet of the Caribbean in SE Cuba; site of U.S. naval station

Gua·te·ma·la \ˌgwät-ə-ˈmäl-ə\ **1** country Central America **2** or **Guatemala City** city, its capital — **Gua·te·ma·lan** \-ˈmäl-ən\ adj or n

Gua·ya·quil \ˌgwī-ə-ˈkē(ə)l, -ˈkil\ city W Ecuador

Guern·sey \ˈgərn-zē\ island in English channel — see CHANNEL

Gui·a·na \gē-ˈan-ə, -ˈän-ə; gī-ˈan-ə\ region N South America on the Atlantic; includes Guyana, French Guiana, Suriname, & nearby parts of Brazil & Venezuela — **Gui·a·nan** \-ən\ adj or n

Guin·ea \ˈgin-ē\ **1** region W Africa on the Atlantic extending along coast from Gambia to Angola **2** country W Africa N of Sierra Leone & Liberia; capital, Conakry — **Guin·ean** \ˈgin-ē-ən\ adj or n

Guinea, Gulf of arm of the Atlantic W central Africa

Guin·ea–Bis·sau \ˌgin-ē-bis-ˈau̇\ country W Africa; an independent state since 1974; capital, Bissau

Gui·yang \ˈgwē-ˈyäŋ\ or **Kuei–yang** \ˈgwā-ˈyäŋ\ city S China

Gulf States states of U.S. bordering on Gulf of Mexico: Florida, Alabama, Mississippi, Louisiana, and Texas

Gulf Stream warm current of the Atlantic ocean flowing from Gulf of Mexico NE along coast of U.S. to Nantucket island and from there eastward

Guy·ana \gī-ˈan-ə\ or formerly **British Guiana** country N South America on the Atlantic; an independent state in the Commonwealth since 1970; capital, Georgetown

Gwent \ˈgwent\ county SE Wales; established 1974

Gwyn·edd \ˈgwin-eth\ county NW Wales; established 1974

Hack·ney \ˈhak-nē\ city area of N Greater London county, England

Hague, The \thə-ˈhäg\ city SW Netherlands; a capital of the Netherlands

Haidarabad — see HYDERABAD

Hai·kou \ˈhī-ˈkō\ city SE China

Hai·ti \ˈhāt-ē\ **1** — see HISPANIOLA **2** country West Indies in W Hispaniola; capital, Port-au-Prince — **Hai·tian** \ˈhā-shən\ adj or n

Ha·le·a·ka·la Crater \ˌhäl-ē-ˌäk-ə-ˈlä\ crater 829 meters deep & 32 kilometers in circumference Hawaii in E Maui Island

Hal·i·fax \'hal-ə-ˌfaks\ city, capital of Nova Scotia, Canada

Ham·burg \'ham-ˌbərg, 'häm-ˌbù(ə)rg\ city N Germany on the Elbe — **Ham·burg·er** \-ˌbər-gər, -ˌbùr-\ *n*

Ham·il·ton \'ham-əl-tən, -əlt-ᵊn\ **1** city S Ontario, Canada **2** town, capital of Bermuda

Ham·mer·smith \'ham-ər-ˌsmith\ city area of SW Greater London county, England

Hamp·shire \'ham(p)-ˌshi(ə)r, -shər\ county S England on English channel

Hamp·ton \'ham(p)-tən\ city SE Virginia

Hampton Roads channel SE Virginia through which James river flows into Chesapeake Bay

Hang·zhou \'häŋ-'jō\ *or* **Hang·chow** \'haŋ-'chaù, 'häŋ-'jō\ *or* **Hang–chou** \'häŋ-'jō\ city E China

Han·ni·bal \'han-ə-bəl\ city NE Missouri on the Mississippi river

Han·no·ver *or* **Han·o·ver** \'han-ˌō-vər, 'han-ə-vər; *German* hä-'nō-vər\ city N central Germany

Ha·noi \ha-'nói, hə-, hä-\ city, capital of Vietnam

Ha·ra·re \hə-'rä-rä\ *or formerly* **Salis·bury** \'sólz-ˌber-ē, -b(ə)rē\ city, capital of Zimbabwe

Har·bin \'här-bən, här-'bin\ *or* **Ha–erh–pin** \'hä-'er-'bin\ city NE China

Har·in·gey \'har-iŋ-ˌgā\ city area of N Greater London county, England

Har·lem \'här-ləm\ section of New York City in N Manhattan

Har·ris·burg \'har-əs-ˌbərg\ city, capital of Pennsylvania

Har·row \'har-ō\ city area of NW Greater London county, England

Hart·ford \'härt-fərd\ city, capital of Connecticut

Hat·ter·as, Cape \-'hat-ə-rəs, -'ha-trəs\ cape, North Carolina on Cape Hatteras Island

Ha·vana \hə-'van-ə\ city, capital of Cuba

Hav·ant and Wa·ter·loo \'hav-ənt-ᵊn-ˌwòt-ər-'lü, -ˌwät-\ town S England in Hampshire

Ha·ver·ing \'hāv-(ə-)riŋ\ city area of NE Greater London county, England

Ha·waii \hə-'wä-(y)ē, -'wī-, -'wò-\ **1** *or* **Ha·wai·ian Islands** *or formerly* **Sand·wich islands** \ˌsan-(d)wich-\ group of islands central Pacific belonging to U.S. **2** island, largest of the group **3** state of U.S. consisting of Hawaiian Islands except Midway; capital, Honolulu

Heb·ri·des \'heb-rə-ˌdēz\ islands W Scotland in the Atlantic consisting of **Outer Hebrides** (to W) and **Inner Hebrides** (to E) — see WESTERN ISLES — **Heb·ri·de·an** \ˌheb-rə-'dē-ən\ *adj or n*

Hel·e·na \'hel-ə-nə\ city, capital of Montana

Hellespont — see DARDANELLES

Hells Canyon \'helz-\ *or* **Grand Canyon of the Snake** canyon of Snake river on Idaho-Oregon boundary

Hel·sin·ki \'hel-ˌsiŋ-kē, hel-'siŋ-\ city, capital of Finland

Henry, Cape \-'hen-rē\ cape E Virginia S of entrance to Chesapeake Bay

Her·e·ford and Wor·ces·ter \'her-ə-fərd-ᵊn-'wùs-tər, *in the U.S. also* 'hər-fərd-\ county W England bordering on Wales

Hert·ford·shire \'här-fərd-ˌshi(ə)r, -shər, *also* 'härt-, *in the U.S. also* 'hərt-\ *or* **Hertford** county SE England

Hi·a·le·ah \ˌhī-ə-'lē-ə\ city SE Florida

Hi·ber·nia \hī-'bər-nē-ə\ — see IRELAND — **Hi·ber·ni·an** \-ən\ *adj or n*

Hi·ga·shi·ōsa·ka \hē-ˌgä-shē-ō-'säk-ə\ city Japan in S Honshu E of Osaka

High·land \'hī-lənd\ region NW Scotland

High·lands \'hī-lən(d)z\ the mountainous N part of Scotland lying N & W of the Lowlands

High Plains the Great Plains especially from Nebraska southward

Hil·ling·don \'hil-iŋ-dən\ city area of W Greater London county, England

Hi·ma·la·ya \ˌhim-ə-'lā-ə, hə-'mäl-(ə-)yə\ mountain system S Asia on border between India & Tibet & in Kashmir, Nepal, & Bhutan — see EVEREST, MOUNT — **Hi·ma·la·yan** \ˌhim-ə-'lā-ən, hə-'mäl-(ə-)yən\ *adj*

Hin·du Kush \ˌhin-(ˌ)dü-'kùsh, -'kəsh\ mountain range central Asia SW of the Pamirs on border of Kashmir & in Afghanistan

Hin·du·stan \ˌhin-(ˌ)dü-'stan, -də-, -'stän\ **1** region N India **2** the subcontinent of India **3** the country of India

Hi·ro·shi·ma \ˌhir-ə-'shē-mə, hə-'rō-shə-mə\ city Japan in SW Honshu on Inland sea

His·pan·io·la \ˌhis-pən-'yō-lə\ *or Spanish* **Es·pa·ño·la** \ˌes-ˌpañ-'yō-lə\ *or formerly* **Hai·ti** \'hāt-ē\ island West Indies in Greater Antilles divided between Haiti on W & Dominican Republic on E

Ho·bart \'hō-ˌbärt\ city Australia, capital of Tasmania

Ho Chi Minh City \ˌhō-chē-ˌmin-, -ˌshē-\ *or formerly* **Sai·gon** \sī-'gän, 'sī-ˌgän\ city S Vietnam

Hoh·hot \'hō-ˌhōt\ *or* **Hu·he·hot** \'hü-ˌhä-'hōt\ city N China, capital of Inner Mongolia

Hok·kai·do \hä-'kīd-ō\ island N Japan N of Honshu

Hol·land \'häl-ənd\ **1** county of Holy Roman Empire bordering on North sea & consisting of area now forming part of W Netherlands **2** — see NETHERLANDS — **Hol·land·er** \-ən-dər\ *n*

Hol·ly·wood \'häl-ē-ˌwùd\ **1** section of Los Angeles, California, NW of downtown district **2** city SE Florida

Holy Land PALESTINE

Holy Roman Empire empire consisting mainly of German and Italian territories and existing from the 9th or 10th century to 1806

Hon·du·ras \hän-'d(y)ùr-əs\ country Central America; capital, Tegucigalpa — **Hon·du·ran** \-ən\ *or* **Hon·du·ra·ne·an** *or* **Hon·du·ra·ni·an** \ˌhän-d(y)ù-'rä-nē-ən\ *adj or n*

Hong Kong \'häŋ-ˌkäŋ, -'käŋ; 'hòŋ-ˌkòŋ, -'kòŋ\ British colony on coast of SE China including Hong Kong Island & Kowloon peninsula; capital, Victoria

Ho·ni·a·ra \ˌhō-nē-'är-ə\ town, capital of Solomon Islands

Ho·no·lu·lu \ˌhän-ᵊl-'ü-lü, ˌhōn-ᵊl-\ city, capital of Hawaii on Oahu Island

Hon·shu \'hän-shü\ *or* **Hon·do** \'hän-dō\ island Japan; largest of the four chief islands

Hood, Mount \-'hùd\ mountain 3424 meters NW Oregon in Cascade Range

Hoo·ghly *or* **Hu·gli** \'hü-glē\ river 193 kilometers long E India flowing S into Bay of Bengal; most westerly channel of the Ganges in its delta

Hoo·ver Dam \ˌhü-vər-\ *or* **Boul·der Dam** \ˌbōl-dər-\ dam 221 meters high in Colorado river between Arizona & Nevada — see MEAD, LAKE

Horn, Cape \-'hó(ə)rn\ cape S Chile on an island in Tierra del Fuego; the most southerly point of South America at 55°59′ S latitude

Horseshoe Falls — see NIAGARA FALLS

Houns·low \'haùnz-ˌlō\ city area of SW Greater London county, England

Hous·ton \'(h)yü-stən\ city SE Texas

How·rah \'haù-rə\ city E India on Hooghly river opposite Calcutta

Huang *or* **Hwang** \'hwäŋ\ *or* **Yellow** river 4830 kilometers long N China flowing into Bo Hai

Hud·ders·field \'həd-ərz-ˌfēld\ city area N England in West Yorkshire NE of Manchester

Hud·son \'həd-sən\ **1** river 492 kilometers long E New

\ə\abut \ᵊ\kitten \ər\further \a\ash \ā\ace \ä\mop, mar
\aù\out \ch\chin \e\bet \ē\easy \g\go \i\hit \ī\ice \j\job
\ŋ\sing \ō\go \ò\law \ói\boy \th\thin \th̲\the \ü\loot \ù\foot
\y\yet \zh\vision *see also* Pronunciation Symbols page

York flowing S **2** bay inlet of the Atlantic in N Canada **3** strait NE Canada connecting Hudson bay & the Atlantic

Huhehot — see HOHHOT

Hull \'həl\ *or* **Kings·ton upon Hull** \'kiŋ(k)-stən-\ city N England in Humberside county

Hum·ber·side \'həm-bər-ˌsīd\ county E England

Hun·ga·ry \'həŋ-g(ə-)rē\ country central Europe; capital, Budapest

Hunt·ing·ton Beach \'hənt-iŋ-tən-\ city SW California

Hunts·ville \'hən(t)s-ˌvil, -vəl\ city N Alabama

Hu·ron, Lake \-'(h)yùr-ən, -'(h)yü(ə)r-ˌän\ lake E central North America in U.S. & Canada; one of the Great Lakes

Hy·der·abad \'hīd-(ə-)rə-ˌbad, -ˌbäd\ **1** *or* **Hai·dar·abad** city S central India **2** city SE Pakistan on the Indus

Iba·dan \i-'bäd-ᵊn, -'bad-\ city SW Nigeria

Ibe·ri·an \ī-'bir-ē-ən\ peninsula SW Europe occupied by Spain & Portugal

Ice·land \'ī-slənd, -ˌsland\ island SE of Greenland between Arctic & Atlantic oceans; capital, Reykjavik — **Ice·land·er** \-ˌslan-dər, -slən-dər\ *n*

Ida·ho \'īd-ə-ˌhō\ state NW U.S.; capital, Boise — **Ida·ho·an** \ˌīd-ə-'hō-ən\ *adj or n*

Igua·çu *or Spanish* **Igua·zú** \ˌē-gwə-'sü\ river 612 kilometers long S Brazil flowing W

IJs·sel *or* **Ijs·sel** \'ī-səl\ river 113 kilometers long E Netherlands flowing out of Rhine N into IJsselmeer

IJs·sel·meer \'ī-səl-ˌme(ə)r\ *or* **Lake Ijs·sel** freshwater lake N Netherlands separated from North sea by a dike; part of former Zuider Zee (inlet of North sea)

Ilium *or* **Ilion** — see TROY

Il·li·nois \ˌil-ə-'nòi *also* -'nòiz\ state N central U.S.; capital, Springfield — **Il·li·nois·an** \-'nòi-ən, -'nòiz-ᵊn\ *adj or n*

Il·lyr·ia \il-'ir-ē-ə\ ancient country S Europe and Balkan peninsula on the Adriatic — **Il·lyr·i·an** \-ē-ən\ *adj or n*

Im·pe·ri·al Valley \im-'pir-ē-əl-\ valley SE corner of California & partly in Baja California, Mexico

In·chon \'in-ˌchän\ city South Korea on Yellow sea

In·de·pen·dence \ˌin-də-'pen-dən(t)s\ city W Missouri E of Kansas City

In·dia \'in-dē-ə\ **1** subcontinent S Asia S of the Himalayas between Bay of Bengal & Arabian sea **2** *or* **Bharat** \'bər-ət, 'bə-rət\ country consisting of major portion of the subcontinent; an independent state in the Commonwealth; capital, New Delhi **3** *or* **Indian Empire** before 1947 those parts of the Indian subcontinent under British rule or protection

In·di·an \'in-dē-ən\ ocean E of Africa, S of Asia, W of Australia, & N of Antarctica

In·di·ana \ˌin-dē-'an-ə\ state E central U.S.; capital, Indianapolis — **In·di·an·an** \-'an-ən\ *or* **In·di·an·i·an** \-'an-ē-ən\ *adj or n*

In·di·a·nap·o·lis \ˌin-dē-ə-'nap-(ə-)ləs\ city, capital of Indiana

Indian river lagoon 266 kilometers long E Florida between main part of the state & coastal islands

Indian Territory former territory S U.S. in present state of Oklahoma

In·dies \'in-dēz\ **1** EAST INDIES **2** WEST INDIES

In·do·chi·na \'in-(ˌ)dō-'chī-nə\ **1** peninsula SE Asia including Myanmar, Malay peninsula, Thailand, Cambodia, Laos, & Vietnam **2** *or* **French Indochina** former country SE Asia consisting of area now forming Cambodia, Laos, & Vietnam — **In·do–Chi·nese** \-chī-'nēz, -'nēs\ *adj or n*

In·do·ne·sia \ˌin-də-'nē-zhə, -shə\ country SE Asia in Malay island group consisting of Sumatra, Java, S & E Borneo, Sulawesi, W New Guinea, & many smaller islands; capital, Jakarta — see NETHERLANDS EAST INDIES — **In·do·ne·sian** \-zhən, -shən\ *adj or n*

In·dore \in-'dō(ə)r, -'dò(ə)r\ city W central India

In·dus \'in-dəs\ river 2900 kilometers long S Asia flowing from Tibet NW & SSW through Pakistan into Arabian sea

In·gle·wood \'iŋ-gəl-ˌwùd\ city SW California

In·land \'in-ˌland, -lənd\ sea inlet of the Pacific in SW Japan between Honshu on N and Shikoku and Kyushu on S

Inner Hebrides — see HEBRIDES

Inner Mon·go·lia \-män-'gōl-yə, mäŋ-, -'gō-lē-ə\ region N China

Inside Passage *or* **Inland Passage** protected shipping route between Puget Sound, Washington, & Skagway, Alaska

In·ver·ness \ˌin-vər-'nes\ town NW Scotland in Highland region

Io·ni·an \ī-'ō-nē-ən\ **1** sea arm of the Mediterranean between SE Italy & W Greece **2** islands W Greece in Ionian sea

Io·wa \'ī-ə-wə\ state N central U.S.; capital, Des Moines — **Io·wan** \-wən\ *adj or n*

Ips·wich \'ip-(ˌ)swich\ city area SE England in Suffolk county

Iran \i-'rän, -'ran; ī-'ran\ *or formerly* **Per·sia** \'pər-zhə\ country SW Asia; capital, Tehran — **Irani** \i-'rän-ē, -'ran-\ *adj or n* — **Ira·nian** \ir-'ā-nē-ən, -'an-ē-, -'än-ē-\ *adj or n*

Iraq \i-'räk, -'rak\ country SW Asia in Mesopotamia; capital, Baghdad — **Iraqi** \-'räk-ē, -'rak-\ *adj or n*

Ire·land \'ī(ə)r-lənd\ **1** *or Latin* **Hi·ber·nia** \hī-'bər-nē-ə\ island W Europe in the Atlantic; one of the British Isles **2** *or* **Irish Republic** *or* **Ei·re** \'ar-ə, 'ar-ē, 'er-, 'är-, 'īr-\ country occupying major portion of the island; capital, Dublin

Irish sea \'īr-ish-\ arm of the Atlantic between Great Britain & Ireland

Ir·kutsk \i(ə)r-'kütsk, ˌər-\ city S Russia near Lake Baikal

Ir·ra·wad·dy \ˌir-ə-'wäd-ē\ river 2175 kilometers long Myanmar flowing S into Bay of Bengal

Ir·tysh \i(ə)r-'tish, ˌər-\ river 3540 kilometers long central Asia flowing NW & N from Altai mountains in China, through Kazakhstan, and into W central Russia

Ir·ving \'ər-viŋ\ city NE Texas NW of Dallas

Is·fa·han \ˌis-fə-'hän, -'han\ *or formerly* **Is·pa·han** \ˌis-pə-\ city W central Iran

Is·lam·abad \is-'läm-ə-ˌbäd, iz-'lam-ə-ˌbad\ city, capital of Pakistan

Isle of Man — see MAN, ISLE OF

Isle of Wight \-'wīt\ island and county S England in English channel

Isle Roy·ale \(ˌ)ī(ə)l-'rói(-ə)l\ island Michigan in Lake Superior

Isles of Scilly — see CORNWALL AND ISLES OF SCILLY; SCILLY

Is·ling·ton \'iz-liŋ-tən\ city area of N Greater London county, England

Is·ra·el \'iz-rē-əl, -rā-əl, -rəl\ **1** ancient kingdom Palestine consisting of lands occupied by the Hebrew people **2** *or* **Ephra·im** \'ē-frē-əm\ the N part of the Hebrew kingdom after about 933 B.C. **3** country SW Asia in Palestine; established 1948; capital, Jerusalem — **Is·rae·li** \iz-'rā-lē\ *adj or n*

Is·tan·bul \ˌis-təm-'bül, -ˌtäm-, -tam-, -ˌtän-\ *or formerly* **Con·stan·ti·no·ple** \ˌkän-ˌstant-ᵊn-'ō-pəl\ city NW Turkey on the Bosporus & Sea of Marmara; former capital of Turkey

Is·tria \'is-trē-ə\ peninsula in Croatia & Slovenia extending into the N Adriatic — **Is·tri·an** \-trē-ən\ *adj or n*

It·a·ly \'it-ᵊl-ē\ **1** peninsula 1225 kilometers long S Europe extending into the Mediterranean between Adriatic & Tyrrhenian seas **2** country including the peninsula of Italy, Sicily, & Sardinia; capital, Rome

Itas·ca, Lake \-ī-'tas-kə\ lake NW central Minnesota; source of the Mississippi

Ivory Coast country W Africa on Gulf of Guinea; capital, Abidjan

Iwo Ji·ma \ē-(ˌ)wō-ˈjē-mə\ island Japan in W Pacific about 1130 kilometers SSE of Tokyo

Ix·ta·pa·la·pa \ē-stə-pə-ˈläp-ə\ city S central Mexico SE of Mexico City

Izhevsk \ē-ˌzhefsk\ *or 1985-87* **Usti·nov** \ˈüs-ti-ˌnȯf, -ˌnȯv\ city W Russia

Iz·mir \iz-ˈmi(ə)r\ *or formerly* **Smyr·na** \ˈsmər-nə\ city W Turkey

Jack·son \ˈjak-sən\ city, capital of Mississippi

Jack·son·ville \ˈjak-sən-ˌvil\ city NE Florida

Jai·pur \ˈjī-ˌpu̇(ə)r\ city NW India

Jakarta *or* **Dja·kar·ta** \jə-ˈkärt-ə\ city, capital of Indonesia in NW Java

Ja·mai·ca \jə-ˈmā-kə\ island West Indies in Greater Antilles; an independent country in the Commonwealth; capital, Kingston — **Ja·mai·can** \-kən\ *adj or n*

James \ˈjāmz\ **1** river 1145 kilometers long North Dakota and South Dakota flowing S into the Missouri **2** river 550 kilometers long Virginia flowing E into Chesapeake Bay

James Bay the S extension of Hudson bay between NE Ontario & W Quebec

James·town \ˈjām-ˌstau̇n\ ruined village E Virginia on James river; first permanent English settlement in America (1607)

Jam·shed·pur \ˈjäm-ˌshed-ˌpu̇(ə)r\ city E India

Ja·pan \jə-ˈpan, ji-, ja-\ *or Japanese* **Nip·pon** \nip-ˈän\ country E Asia consisting of Honshu, Hokkaido, Kyushu, Shikoku, & other islands in the W Pacific; capital, Tokyo

Japan, Sea of arm of the Pacific between Japan & main part of Asia

Ja·va \ˈjäv-ə, ˈjav-ə\ island Indonesia SW of Borneo; chief city, Jakarta — **Ja·van** \-ən\ *adj or n*

Jef·fer·son City \ˈjef-ər-sən-\ city, capital of Missouri

Jer·sey \ˈjər-zē\ island in English channel — see CHANNEL — **Jer·sey·ite** \-zē-ˌīt\ *n*

Jersey City city NE New Jersey on Hudson river

Je·ru·sa·lem \jə-ˈrü-s(ə-)ləm, -ˈrüz-(ə-)ləm\ city NW of Dead sea divided 1948–67 between Israel & Jordan; capital of Israel since 1950 & formerly of ancient kingdom of Israel

Jid·da \ˈjid-ə\ city W Saudi Arabia on Red sea

Ji·lin \ˈjē-ˈlin\ *or* **Ki·rin** \ˈkē-ˈrin\ city NE China

Ji·nan *or* **Tsi·nan** \ˈjē-ˈnän\ city E China

Jin·zhou *or* **Chin–chou** *or* **Chin–chow** \ˈjin-ˈjō\ city NE China

Jo·han·nes·burg \jō-ˈhan-əs-ˌbərg, -ˈhän-\ city NE Republic of South Africa in S Transvaal province

Jor·dan \ˈjȯrd-ᵊn\ **1** river 320 kilometers long Israel & Jordan flowing S from Syria into Dead sea **2** country SW Asia in NW Arabia; capital, Amman — **Jor·da·ni·an** \jȯr-ˈdā-nē-ən\ *adj or n*

Juan de Fu·ca, Strait of \-ˌ(h)wän-də-ˈfyü-kə\ strait 160 kilometers long between Vancouver Island, British Columbia, & Olympic peninsula, Washington

Ju·dea *or* **Ju·daea** \jü-ˈdē-ə, -ˈdā-\ ancient region Palestine forming the S division (Judah) of the country under Persian, Greek, & Roman rule — **Ju·dean** \-ən\ *adj or n*

Ju·go·sla·via \ˌyü-gō-ˈsläv-ē-ə\ — see YUGOSLAVIA — **Ju·go·slav** \ˌyü-gō-ˈsläv, -ˈslav\ *or* **Ju·go·sla·vi·an** \-ˈsläv-ē-ən\ *adj or n*

Ju·neau \ˈjü-nō, jü-ˈnō\ city, capital of Alaska

Ju·ra \ˈju̇r-ə\ mountain range extending along boundary between France & Switzerland N of Lake of Geneva

Jut·land \ˈjət-lənd\ **1** peninsula N Europe extending into North sea & consisting of main part of Denmark & N portion of Germany **2** the main part of Denmark

Ka·bul \ˈkäb-əl, kä-ˈbül\ city, capital of Afghanistan

Ka Lae \kä-ˈlä-ä\ *or* **South Cape** *or* **South Point** most southerly point of Hawaii & of U.S.

Kal·a·ha·ri \ˌkal-ə-ˈhär-ē\ desert region S Africa N of Orange river in S Botswana & NW Republic of South Africa

Kalgan — see ZHANGJIAKOU

Ka·li·man·tan \ˌkal-ə-ˈman-ˌtan, ˌkäl-ə-ˈmän-ˌtän\ **1** BORNEO — its Indonesian name **2** the S & E portion of Borneo belonging to Indonesia; formerly part of Netherlands East Indies

Kam·chat·ka \kam-ˈchat-kə\ peninsula 1205 kilometers long E Russia

Kam·pa·la \käm-ˈpäl-ə\ city, capital of Uganda

Kampuchea — see CAMBODIA

Ka·no \ˈkän-ō\ city N central Nigeria

Kan·pur \ˈkän-ˌpu̇(ə)r\ city N India on the Ganges

Kan·sas \ˈkan-zəs\ state W central U.S.; capital, Topeka — **Kan·san** \-zən\ *adj or n*

Kansas City 1 city NE Kansas bordering on Kansas City, Missouri **2** city W Missouri

Kao·hsiung \ˈkau̇-shē-ˈu̇ŋ, ˈgau̇-\ city China in SW Taiwan

Ka·ra·chi \kə-ˈräch-ē\ city S Pakistan on Arabian sea

Ka·ra·gan·da \ˌkar-ə-gən-ˈdä\ city central Kazakhstan

Ka·re·lia \kə-ˈrē-lē-ə, -ˈrēl-yə\ region NE Europe in Finland & Russia — **Ka·re·lian** \-ˈrē-lē-ən, -ˈrēl-yən\ *adj or n*

Kar·roo \kə-ˈrü\ plateau region W Republic of South Africa W of Drakensberg mountains

Kash·mir \ˈkash-ˌmi(ə)r, ˈkazh-, kash-ˈmi(ə)r, kazh-ˈmi(ə)r\ region and former state N Indian subcontinent — **Kash·miri** \kash-ˈmi(ə)r-ē, kazh-\ *adj or n*

Ka·thi·a·war \ˌkät-ē-ə-ˈwär\ peninsula W India N of Gulf of Cambay

Kath·man·du *or* **Kat·man·du** \ˌkat-ˌman-ˈdü\ city, capital of Nepal

Kat·mai, Mount \-ˈkat-ˌmī\ volcano 2047 meters S Alaska on Alaska peninsula

Kat·te·gat \ˈkat-i-ˌgat\ arm of North sea between Sweden & E coast of Jutland peninsula of Denmark

Kau·ai \ˈkau̇-ˌī\ island Hawaii NW of Oahu

Ka·wa·sa·ki \ˌkä-wə-ˈsäk-ē\ city Japan in E Honshu S of Tokyo

Ka·zakh·stan \kə-ˌzak-ˈstan; kə-ˌzäk-ˈstän, ˌkä-\ country NW central Asia; capital, Alma-Ata; a republic (**Ka·zakh Soviet Socialist Republic** \kə-ˌzak-, -ˌzäk-\) of U.S.S.R. 1936–91

Ka·zan \kə-ˈzan, -ˈzän-(yə)\ city W Russia

Kee·wa·tin \kē-ˈwät-ᵊn\ former district N Canada in E Northwest Territories NW of Hudson bay

Ke·me·ro·vo \ˈkem-ə-rə-və, -ˌrō-və, -rə-ˌvȯ\ city S central Russia

Ke·nai \ˈkē-ˌnī\ peninsula S Alaska E of Cook inlet

Kennedy, Cape — see CANAVERAL, CAPE

Ken·sing·ton and Chel·sea \ˈken-ziŋ-tən-ən-ˈchel-sē, ˈken(t)-siŋ-\ city area of W Greater London county, England

Kent \ˈkent\ county SE England — **Kent·ish** \ˈkent-ish\ *adj*

Ken·tucky \kən-ˈtək-ē\ state E central U.S.; capital, Frankfort — **Ken·tuck·i·an** \-ē-ən\ *adj or n*

Ken·ya \ˈken-yə, ˈkēn-\ **1** mountain 5194 meters central Kenya **2** country E Africa S of Ethiopia; capital, Nairobi — **Ken·yan** \-yən\ *adj or n*

Key West \ˈkē-ˈwest\ city SW Florida on Key West island

Kha·ba·rovsk \kə-ˈbär-əfsk\ city SE Russia

Khar·kov \ˈkär-ˌkȯf, -ˌkȯv, -kəf\ city NE Ukraine

\ə\abut \ᵊ\kitten \ər\further \a\ash \ā\ace \ä\mop, mar \au̇\out \ch\chin \e\bet \ē\easy \g\go \i\hit \ī\ice \j\job \ŋ\sing \ō\go \ȯ\law \ȯi\boy \th\thin \th\the \ü\loot \u̇\foot \y\yet \zh\vision *see also* Pronunciation Symbols page

Khar·toum \kär-'tüm\ city, capital of Sudan

Khmer Republic — see CAMBODIA

Khy·ber \'kī-bər\ pass 53 kilometers long on border between Afghanistan & Pakistan

Ki·bo \'kē-bō\ mountain peak 5888 meters NE Tanzania; highest peak of Kilimanjaro & highest point in Africa

Kiel \'kē(ə)l\ canal 98 kilometers long N Germany across base of Jutland peninsula connecting Baltic sea & North sea

Ki·ev or Russian **Ki·yev** \'kē-ˌ(y)ef, -(y)ev, -(y)əf\ city, capital of Ukraine

Ki·ga·li \ki-'gäl-ē\ city, capital of Rwanda

Ki·lau·ea \ˌkē-ˌlaù-'ā-ə\ volcanic crater Hawaii on Hawaii island on E slope of Mauna Loa

Kil·i·man·ja·ro \ˌkil-ə-mən-'jär-ō, -'jar-\ mountain NE Tanzania; highest in Africa — see KIBO

Kil·lar·ney, Lakes of \-kil-'är-nē\ three lakes SW Ireland

Kings·ton \'kiŋ-stən\ city, capital of Jamaica

Kingston upon Hull — see HULL

Kingston upon Thames \-'temz\ city area of SW Greater London county, England

Kings·town \'kiŋ-ˌstaùn\ seaport, capital of Saint Vincent and the Grenadines

Kin·sha·sa \kin-'shäs-ə\ city, capital of Zaire

Kirgiz Republic or **Kirghiz Republic** or **Kirghizia** — see KYRGYZSTAN

Ki·ri·bati \'kir-ə-ˌbas\ island group W Pacific; an independent country; capital, Tarawa

Kirin — see JILIN

Kirk·wall \'kər-ˌkwòl\ town and port N Scotland in Orkney region

Ki·shi·nev \'kish-ə-ˌnef, -nev\ city central Moldova; its capital

Ki·ta·kyu·shu \kē-'tä-kē-'ü-shü\ city Japan in N Kyushu

Kitch·e·ner \'kich-(ə-)nər\ city SE Ontario, Canada

Kit·ty Hawk \'kit-ē-ˌhòk\ village E North Carolina

Klon·dike \'klän-ˌdīk\ region NW Canada in central Yukon Territory in valley of Klondike river

Knox·ville \'näks-ˌvil, -vəl\ city E Tennessee

Ko·be \'kō-bē, -ˌbā\ city Japan in S Honshu

Ko·di·ak \'kōd-ē-ˌak\ island S Alaska E of Alaska peninsula

Ko·la \'kō-lə\ peninsula NW Russia

Ko·rea \kə-'rē-ə, especially South kō-\ country E Asia between Yellow sea & Sea of Japan; capital, Seoul; divided after World War II at 38th parallel of latitude into independent countries of **North Korea** (capital, Pyongyang) & **South Korea** (capital, Seoul)

Kos·ci·us·ko, Mount \-ˌkäz-ē-'əs-kō\ mountain 2230 meters SE Australia in SE New South Wales; highest in Greater Dividing range & in Australia

Kow·loon \'kaù-'lün\ **1** peninsula SE China in Hong Kong colony opposite Hong Kong island **2** city on Kowloon peninsula

Krak·a·toa \ˌkrak-ə-'tō-ə\ or **Krak·a·tau** \-'taù\ island & volcano Indonesia between Sumatra & Java

Kra·kow \'kräk-ˌaù, 'krak-, 'kräk-, -ō, Polish 'kräk-ˌüf\ city S Poland

Kras·no·dar \'kras-nə-ˌdär\ city SW Russia

Kras·no·yarsk \ˌkras-nə-'yärsk\ city S central Russia

Kri·voy Rog \ˌkriv-ˌòi-'ròg, -'ròk\ city SE central Ukraine

K2 \'kā-'tü\ or **God·win Aus·ten** \ˌgäd-wə-'nòs-tən, -'näs-tən\ mountain 8611 meters N Kashmir in Karakoram range; second highest in the world

Kua·la Lum·pur \ˌkwäl-ə-'lùm-ˌpù(ə)r, -'ləm-\ city, capital of Malaysia

Kuei–yang — see GUIYANG

Kun·lun \'kün-lün\ mountain system W China extending E from the Pamirs; highest peak Ulugh Muztagh 7724 meters

Kun·ming \'kùn-'miŋ\ city S China

Kur·di·stan \ˌkùr-də-'stan, ˌkər-, -'stän; 'kər-də-ˌ\ region SW Asia chiefly in E Turkey, NW Iran, & N Iraq

Ku·ril or **Ku·rile** \'kyùr-ˌēl, 'kùr-; kyù-'rē(ə)l, kù-\ islands Russia in W Pacific between Kamchatka peninsula & Hokkaido island

Ku·wait \kə-'wāt\ **1** country SW Asia in Arabia at head of Persian gulf **2** city, its capital — **Ku·waiti** \-'wāt-ē\ adj or n

Kuybyshev — see SAMARA

Kuz·netsk basin \kùz-'netsk-\ or **Kuz·bass** or **Kuzbas** \'kùz-ˌbas\ basin S central Russia

Kwa·ja·lein \'kwäj-ə-lən, -ˌlān\ island W Pacific in Marshall islands

Kwang·ju \'gwäŋ-jü, 'kwäŋ-\ city SW South Korea

Kyo·to \kē-'ōt-ō\ city Japan in W central Honshu; formerly capital of Japan

Kyr·gyz·stan \ˌkir-gi-'stan, -'stän; 'kir-gi-ˌ\ country W central Asia; capital, Bishkek; a republic (**Kir·giz Republic** or **Kir·ghiz Republic** \(ˌ)kir-'gēz-\ or **Kir·ghizia** \kir-'gē-zh(ē-)ə, -zē-ə\ of U.S.S.R. 1936–91

Kyu·shu \kē-'ü-shü\ island Japan S of W end of Honshu

Lab·ra·dor \'lab-rə-ˌdò(ə)r\ **1** peninsula E Canada between Hudson bay & the Atlantic divided between Quebec & Newfoundland **2** the part of the peninsula belonging to Newfoundland — **Lab·ra·dor·ean** or **Lab·ra·dor·ian** \ˌlab-rə-'dòr-ē-ən, -'dòr-\ adj or n

Lac·ca·dive \'lak-ə-ˌdēv, -ˌdīv\ islands India in Arabian sea N of Maldive islands

Lac·e·dae·mon \ˌlas-ə-'dē-mən\ — see SPARTA — **Lac·e·dae·mo·nian** \ˌlas-əd-i-'mō-nē-ən, -nyən\ adj or n

La·co·nia \lə-'kō-nē-ə, -nyə\ ancient country S Greece in SE Peloponnisos; capital, Sparta — **La·co·nian** \-nē-ən, -nyən\ adj or n

La·gos \'lā-ˌgäs\ city, former capital of Nigeria

La·hore \lə-'hō(ə)r, -'hò(ə)r\ city E Pakistan

Lake District region NW England in Cumbria county & NW Lancashire containing many lakes & mountains

Lake·hurst \'lāk-(ˌ)hərst\ town E New Jersey

Lake·wood \'lā-ˌkwùd\ city central Colorado

Lam·beth \'lam-bəth, -ˌbeth\ city area of S Greater London county, England

La·nai \lə-'nī\ island Hawaii W of Maui

Lan·ca·shire \'laŋ-kə-ˌshi(ə)r, -shər\ or **Lan·cas·ter** \'laŋ-kə-stər\ county NW England — **Lan·cas·tri·an** \laŋ-'kas-trē-ən, lan-\ adj or n

Lan·cas·ter \'laŋ-kə-stər; 'lan-ˌkas-tər, 'laŋ-\ city area, capital of Lancashire, England

Land's End \'lan(d)-'zend\ cape SW England; most westerly point of England, at 5°41′ W longitude

Lan·sing \'lan(t)-siŋ\ city, capital of Michigan

Lan·zhou or **Lan–chou** \'län-'jō\ city W China

Laos \'laùs, 'lā-ˌäs, 'lä-ōs\ country SE Asia in Indochina NE of Thailand; capital, Vientiane

La Paz \lə-'paz, -'päz, -'päs\ city, administrative capital of Bolivia

Lap·land \'lap-ˌland, -lənd\ region N Europe above the arctic circle in N Norway, N Sweden, N Finland, & Kola peninsula of Russia — **Lap·land·er** \-ˌlan-dər, -lən-\ n

La·re·do \lə-'rā-(ˌ)dō\ city S Texas on the Rio Grande

Larne \'lärn\ district NE Northern Ireland

Las·sen Peak \'las-ᵊn-\ volcano 3187 meters N California at S end of Cascade Range

Las Ve·gas \läs-'vā-gəs\ city SE Nevada

Latin America 1 Spanish America and Brazil **2** all of the Americas S of the U.S. — **Latin–American** adj — **Latin American** n

Latin Quarter section of Paris, France S of the Seine

Lat·via \'lat-vē-ə\ country E Europe on Baltic sea; capital, Riga; a republic of U.S.S.R. 1940–91

Lau·ren·tian \lò-'ren-chən\ hills E Canada in S Quebec N of the Saint Lawrence on S edge of Laurentian Highlands

Lau·ren·tian Highlands *or* **Canadian Shield** plateau region E Canada & NE U.S. extending from Mackenzie basin E to Davis strait & S to S Quebec, S central Ontario, NE Minnesota, N Wisconsin, NW Michigan, and NE New York including the Adirondacks

La·val \lə-'val\ city S Quebec NW of Montreal

Law·rence \'lȯr-ən(t)s, 'lär-\ city NE corner of Massachusetts

Leb·a·non \'leb-ə-nən, -ˌnän\ **1** mountains Lebanon running parallel to coast; highest Dahr el Qadib 3088 meters **2** country SW Asia on the Mediterranean; capital, Beirut — **Leb·a·nese** \ˌleb-ə-'nēz, -'nēs\ *adj or n*

Leeds \'lēdz\ city N England in West Yorkshire

Lee·ward Islands \'lē-wərd-\ **1** islands Hawaii extending WNW from main islands of the group **2** islands S Pacific in W Society islands **3** islands West Indies in N Lesser Antilles extending from Virgin islands (on N) to Dominica (on S)

Le Ha·vre \lə-'hävrᵊ\ city N France on English channel

Leh·man Caves \'lē-mən-\ limestone caverns E Nevada

Leices·ter \'les-tər\ city central England in Leicestershire ENE of Birmingham

Leices·ter·shire \'les-tər-ˌshi(ə)r, -shər\ *or* **Leicester** county central England

Lein·ster \'len(t)-stər\ province E Ireland

Leip·zig \'līp-sig, -sik\ city E Germany

Le·na \'lē-nə, 'lā-\ river 4830 kilometers long E Russia, flowing NE & N from mountains W of Lake Baikal into Arctic ocean

Leningrad — see SAINT PETERSBURG

Le·ón \lā-'ōn\ city central Mexico

Ler·wick \'lər-(ˌ)wik, 'le(ə)r-\ town and port N Scotland in Shetland region

Le·so·tho \lə-'sō-tō, -'sü-(ˌ)tü\ country S Africa surrounded by Republic of South Africa; formerly British territory of **Ba·su·to·land** \bə-'süt-ə-ˌland\, now an independent country in the Commonwealth; capital, Maseru

Lesser An·til·les \-an-'til-ēz\ islands in the West Indies including Virgin Islands, Leeward Islands, & Windward Islands, Barbados, Trinidad, Tobago, & islands in the S Caribbean N of Venezuela — see GREATER ANTILLES

Le·vant \lə-'vant\ the countries bordering on the E Mediterranean — **Lev·an·tine** \'lev-ən-ˌtīn, -ˌtēn, lə-'van-\ *adj or n*

Lew·es \'lü-əs\ city area S England in East Sussex county

Lew·i·sham \'lü-ə-shəm\ city area of SE Greater London county, England

Lew·is with Har·ris \ˌlü-ə-swəth-'har-əs, -swəth-\ island NW Scotland in Outer Hebrides

Lex·ing·ton \'lek-siŋ-tən\ town NE Massachusetts

Lexington–Fayette \'lek-siŋ-tən-fā-'et\ city N central Kentucky

Ley·te \'lāt-ē\ island Philippines S of Samar

Lha·sa \'läs-ə, 'las-\ city SW China, capital of Tibet

Li·be·ria \lī-'bir-ē-ə\ country W Africa on the Atlantic; capital, Monrovia — **Li·be·ri·an** \-ē-ən\ *adj or n*

Lib·er·ty \'lib-ərt-ē\ *or formerly* **Bed·loe's** \'bed-ˌlōz\ *or* **Bed·loe** \-ˌlō\ island SE New York; the Statue of Liberty is on it

Li·bre·ville \'lē-brə-ˌvil, -ˌvē(ə)l\ city, capital of Gabon

Lib·ya \'lib-ē-ə\ **1** the part of Africa N of the Sahara and just W of Egypt — an ancient name **2** northern Africa W of Egypt — an ancient name **3** country N Africa on the Mediterranean W of Egypt; capital, Tripoli — **Lib·y·an** \'lib-ē-ən\ *adj or n*

Libyan desert N Africa W of the Nile in Libya, Egypt, & Sudan

Liech·ten·stein \'lik-tən-ˌstīn, -ˌshtīn\ country W Europe between Austria & Switzerland; capital, Vaduz — **Liech·ten·stein·er** \-ˌstī-nər, -ˌshtī-\ *n*

Lif·fey \'lif-ē\ river 80 kilometers long E Ireland

Li·gu·ria \lə-'gyur-ē-ə\ ancient region SW Europe — **Li·gu·ri·an** \-ē-ən\ *adj or n*

Ligurian sea arm of the Mediterranean N of Corsica

Li·lon·gwe \li-'lȯŋ-wā\ city, capital of Malawi

Li·ma \'lē-mə\ city, capital of Peru

Lim·a·vady \ˌlim-ə-'vad-ē\ district NW Northern Ireland

Lim·po·po \lim-'pō-pō\ river 1610 kilometers long Africa flowing from Transvaal into Indian ocean in Mozambique

Lin·coln \'liŋ-kən\ **1** city, capital of Nebraska **2** city E England in Lincolnshire

Lin·coln·shire \'liŋ-kən-ˌshi(ə)r, -shər\ *or* **Lincoln** county E England

Line \'līn\ islands Kiribati S of Hawaii; formerly divided between U.S. & United Kingdom

Lis·bon \'liz-bən\ *or Portuguese* **Lis·boa** \lēzh-'vō-ə\ city, capital of Portugal

Lis·burn \'liz-(ˌ)bərn\ district E Northern Ireland

Lith·u·a·nia \ˌlith-(y)ə-'wā-nē-ə, -nyə\ country E Europe; capital, Vilnius; a republic of U.S.S.R. 1940–91

Lit·tle Rock \'lit-ᵊl-ˌräk\ city, capital of Arkansas

Liv·er·pool \'liv-ər-ˌpül\ city NW England in Merseyside county

Li·vo·nia \lə-'vō-nē-ə, -nyə\ city SE Michigan

Lju·blja·na \lē-ü-blē-'än-ə\ city, capital of Slovenia

Llan·drin·dod Wells \hlan-'drin-ˌdȯd-, lan-\ town E Wales in Powys county

Lla·no Es·ta·ca·do \'lan-(ˌ)ō-ˌes-ta-'käd-ō, 'län-\ *or* **Staked Plain** \'stāk(t)-\ plateau region SE New Mexico & NW Texas

Lodz \'lüj, 'lädz\ city central Poland WSW of Warsaw

Lo·fo·ten \'lō-ˌfōt-ᵊn\ islands NW Norway

Lo·gan, Mount \-'lō-gən\ mountain 6050 meters NW Canada in Saint Elias range; highest in Canada & second highest in North America

Loire \lə-'wär\ river 1005 kilometers long central France flowing NW & W into Bay of Biscay

Lo·mé \lō-'mā\ city, capital of Togo

Lo·mond, Loch \-'lō-mənd\ lake S central Scotland

Lon·don \'lən-dən\ **1** city S Ontario, Canada **2** city, capital of England & of United Kingdom on the Thames; consists of **City of London** & Greater London county — **Lon·don·er** \-də-nər\ *n*

Londonderry — see DERRY

Long Beach city SW California S of Los Angeles

Long Island island 190 kilometers long SE New York S of Connecticut

Long Island Sound inlet of the Atlantic between Connecticut & Long Island, New York

Lon·gueuil \lȯŋ-'gā(ə)l\ city Canada in S Quebec E of Montreal

Lor·raine \lə-'rān, lȯ-\ region NE France

Los An·ge·les \lȯ-'san-jə-ləs *also* -'saŋ-g(ə-)ləs\ city SW California

Lo·thi·an \'lō-thē-ən\ region SE Scotland S of Firth of Forth; established 1975; includes Edinburgh

Lou·ise, Lake \-lü-'ēz\ lake SW Alberta, Canada

Lou·i·si·ana \lü-ˌē-zē-'an-ə, ˌlü-ə-zē-, ˌlü-zē-\ state S U.S.; capital, Baton Rouge — **Lou·i·si·an·ian** \-'an-ē-ən, -'an-yən\ *or* **Lou·i·si·an·an** \-'an-ən\ *adj or n*

Louisiana Purchase area W central U.S. between Rocky mountains & the Mississippi purchased 1803 from France

Lou·is·ville \'lü-i-ˌvil, -vəl\ city N Kentucky on the Ohio river

---

\ə\abut \ᵊ\kitten \ər\further \a\ash \ā\ace \ä\mop, mar \au̇\out \ch\chin \e\bet \ē\easy \g\go \i\hit \ī\ice \j\job \ŋ\sing \ō\go \ȯ\law \ȯi\boy \th\thin \ṯh\the \ü\loot \u̇\foot \y\yet \zh\vision *see also* Pronunciation Symbols page

Low Countries region W Europe consisting of modern Belgium, Luxembourg, & the Netherlands

Lower 48 the continental states of the U.S. excluding Alaska

Low·lands \'lō-lən(d)z, -ˌlan(d)z\ the central & E part of Scotland

Lu·an·da \lù-'an-də\ city, capital of Angola

Lub·bock \'ləb-ək\ city NW Texas

Luck·now \'lək-ˌnaù\ city N India

Lü·da or **Lü–ta** \'lü-'dä\ or **Dai·ren** \'dī-'ren\ city NE China

Lu·ray Caverns \'lü-ˌrā-, lü-'rā-\ series of caves N Virginia

Lu·sa·ka \lü-'säk-ə\ city, capital of Zambia

Lü·shun \'lü-'shùn\ or **Port Ar·thur** \-'är-thər\ city NE China

Lu·ton \'lüt-ᵊn\ city area SE central England in Bedfordshire

Lux·em·bourg or **Lux·em·burg** \'lək-səm-ˌbərg, 'lùk-səm-ˌbù(ə)rg\ 1 country W Europe bordered by Belgium, France, & Germany 2 city, its capital — **Lux·em·bourg·er** \-ˌbər-gər, -ˌbùr-\ n — **Lux·em·bourg·ian** \ˌlək-səm-'bər-gē-ən, ˌlùk-səm-'bùr-\ adj

Lu·zon \lü-'zän\ island N Philippines

Lvov \lə-'vȯf, -'vòv\ or Polish **Lwów** \lə-'vüf, -'vüv\ or Ukrainian **Lwiw** \lə-'vēf\ city W Ukraine

Lyallpur — see FAISALABAD

Lyd·ia \'lid-ē-ə\ ancient country W Asia Minor on the Aegean — **Lyd·i·an** \-ē-ən\ adj or n

Lynn \'lin\ city NE corner of Massachusetts

Ma·cao or Portuguese **Ma·cau** \mə-'kaù\ 1 Portuguese territory on coast of SE China W of Hong Kong 2 city, its capital — **Mac·a·nese** \ˌmak-ə-'nēz, -'nēs\ n

Mac·e·do·nia \ˌmas-ə-'dō-nyə, -nē-ə\ 1 region S Europe in Balkan peninsula in NE Greece, the country of Macedonia, and SW Bulgaria including territory of ancient kingdom of Macedonia (**Mac·e·don** \'mas-əd-ən, -əˌdän\) 2 country S central Balkan peninsula; capital, Skopje; a former republic of Yugoslavia — **Mac·e·do·nian** \ˌmas-ə-'dō-nyən, -nē-ən\ adj or n

Mac·gil·li·cud·dy's Reeks \mə-ˌgil-ə-ˌkəd-ēz-'rēks\ mountains SW Ireland; highest Carrantuo hill 1041 meters

Ma·chu Pic·chu \ˌmäch-ü-'pēk-chü\ site SE Peru of ancient Inca city

Macías Nguema Biyogo — see BIOKO

Mac·ken·zie \mə-'ken-zē\ 1 river 1800 kilometers long NW Canada flowing from Great Slave lake NW into Beaufort sea 2 former district NW Canada in W Northwest Territories in basin of Mackenzie river

Mack·i·nac, Straits of \-'mak-ə-ˌnak, -ˌnȯ\ channel N Michigan connecting Lake Huron & Lake Michigan

Mc·Kin·ley, Mount \-mə-'kin-lē\ or **De·na·li** \də-'näl-ē\ mountain 6194 meters S central Alaska in Alaska range; highest in U.S. & North America

Ma·con \'mā-kən\ city central Georgia

Mad·a·gas·car \ˌmad-ə-'gas-kər\ or formerly **Mal·a·gasy Republic** \ˌmal-ə-ˌgas-ē-\ island W Indian ocean off SE Africa; an independent country; capital, Antananarivo — **Mad·a·gas·can** \ˌmad-ə-'gas-kən\ adj or n

Ma·dei·ra \mə-'dir-ə, -'der-\ 1 river 3380 kilometers long W Brazil flowing NE into the Amazon 2 islands in the N Atlantic N of the Canary islands belonging to Portugal 3 island; chief of the Madeira group — **Ma·dei·ran** \-ən\ adj or n

Ma·di·nat ash Sha'b \mə-'dē-ˌnət-ash-'shab\ town S Yemen

Mad·i·son \'mad-ə-sən\ city, capital of Wisconsin

Ma·dras \mə-'dras, -'dräs\ city SE India

Ma·drid \mə-'drid\ city, capital of Spain

Ma·du·rai \ˌmäd-ə-'rī\ city S India

Magh·er·a·felt \'mär-ə-ˌfelt, 'maﹾ-ə-rə-ˌfelt\ district central Northern Ireland

Maid·stone \'mād-stən, -ˌstōn\ city district SE England in Kent county

Main \'mīn, 'mān\ river 490 kilometers long S central Germany flowing W into the Rhine

Maine \'mān\ state NE U.S.; capital, Augusta

Ma·jor·ca \mə-'jȯr-kə, -'yȯr-\ or Spanish **Ma·llor·ca** \mə-'yȯr-kə\ island Spain in W Mediterranean — **Ma·jor·can** \-'jȯr-kən, -'yȯr-\ adj or n

Mal·a·bar \'mal-ə-ˌbär\ coast region SW India on Arabian sea

Ma·la·bo \mä-'lä-bō\ city, capital of Equatorial Guinea

Ma·lac·ca, Strait of \-mə-'lak-ə, -'läk-\ channel between S Malay peninsula & island of Sumatra

Ma·la·wi \mə-'lä-wē, -'laù-ē\ or formerly **Ny·asa·land** \nī-'as-ə-ˌland, nē-\ country SE Africa on Lake Nyasa; an independent state since 1964; capital, Lilongwe

Ma·lay \mə-'lā, 'mā-lā\ 1 island group SE Asia including Sumatra, Java, Borneo, Sulawesi, Moluccas, & Timor; usually thought to include the Philippines & sometimes New Guinea 2 peninsula about 1100 kilometers long SE Asia divided between Thailand and Malaysia (country)

Ma·laya \mə-'lā-ə, mä-\ 1 the Malay peninsula 2 former country SE Asia on Malay peninsula; since 1963 part of Malaysia — see MALAYSIA

Ma·lay·sia \mə-'lā-zh(ē-)ə, -sh(ē-)ə\ 1 the Malay island group 2 the Malay peninsula & Malay island group 3 country SE Asia, a union of Malaya, Sabah, Sarawak, & (until 1965) Singapore; capital, Kuala Lumpur — **Ma·lay·sian** \mə-'lā-zhən, -shən\ adj or n

Mal·dives \'mal-ˌdīvz, 'mȯl-\ islands in Indian ocean S of the Laccadives; formerly under British protection; since 1965 an independent country; capital, Male — **Mal·div·i·an** \mȯl-'div-ē-ən\ adj or n

Ma·li \'mäl-ē, 'mal-ē\ country W Africa; capital, Bamako — **Ma·li·an** \-ē-ən\ adj or n

Mal·ta \'mȯl-tə\ islands in the Mediterranean S of Sicily; a former British colony; an independent country since 1964; capital, Valletta

Malvinas, Islas — see FALKLAND

Mam·moth Cave \ˌmam-əth-\ limestone caverns SW central Kentucky

Man, Isle of \-'man\ island British Isles in Irish sea; has own legislature & laws

Ma·na·gua \mə-'näg-wə\ city, capital of Nicaragua

Ma·na·ma \mə-'nam-ə\ city, capital of Bahrain

Man·ches·ter \'man-ˌches-tər, -chə-stər\ 1 city S central New Hampshire; largest in state 2 city NW England in Greater Manchester county

Man·chu·ria \man-'chùr-ē-ə\ region NE China S of the Amur — **Man·chu·ri·an** \man-'chùr-ē-ən\ adj or n

Man·hat·tan \man-'hat-ᵊn, mən-\ 1 island SE New York in New York City 2 section of New York City consisting chiefly of Manhattan island

Ma·nila \mə-'nil-ə\ city, capital of Philippines in W Luzon

Man·i·to·ba \ˌman-ə-'tō-bə\ province central Canada; capital, Winnipeg — **Man·i·to·ban** \-'tō-bən\ adj or n

Man·i·tou·lin \ˌman-ə-'tü-lən\ island 130 kilometers long S Ontario in Lake Huron

Ma·pu·to \mä-'pü-tō\ city, capital of Mozambique

Mar·a·cai·bo \ˌmar-ə-'kī-bō\ city NW Venezuela

Maracaibo, Lake extension of a gulf NW Venezuela

Mar·a·thon \'mar-ə-ˌthän, -thən\ plain E Greece NE of Athens

Mar·i·ana \ˌmar-ē-'an-ə, ˌmer-\ islands W Pacific N of Caroline islands; comprise Commonwealth of Northern Mariana Islands & Guam

Mariana Trench ocean trench W Pacific extending from SE of Guam to NW of Mariana islands; deepest in world

Ma·rin·du·que \ˌmar-ən-'dü-kā, ˌmär-\ island central Philippines

Maritime Provinces the Canadian provinces of New

Brunswick, Nova Scotia, & Prince Edward Island & sometimes thought to include Newfoundland

Ma·ri·u·pol \mar-ē-'ü-ˌpȯl\ *or 1949–89* **Zhda·nov** \zhə-'dän-əf\ city E Ukraine

Mar·ma·ra, Sea of \-'mär-mə-rə\ sea NW Turkey connected with Black sea by the Bosporus & with Aegean sea by the Dardanelles

Marne \'märn\ river 523 kilometers long NE France flowing W into the Seine

Mar·que·sas \mär-'kā-zəz, -zəs, -səz, -səs\ islands S Pacific — **Mar·que·san** \-zən, -sən\ *adj or n*

Mar·seilles \mär-'sā, -'sā(ə)lz\ *or* **Mar·seille** \mär-'sā\ *or ancient* **Mas·sil·ia** \mə-'sil-ē-ə\ city SE France

Mar·shall \'mär-shəl\ islands W Pacific E of the Carolines; formerly part of Trust Territory of the Pacific Islands

Mar·tha's Vineyard \ˌmär-thəz-\ island SE Massachusetts off SW coast of Cape Cod WNW of Nantucket

Mar·ti·nique \ˌmärt-ᵊn-'ēk\ island West Indies in the Windward Islands; an overseas division of France; capital, Fort-de-France

Mary·land \'mer-ə-lənd\ state E U.S.; capital, Annapolis — **Mary·land·er** \-lən-dər, -ˌlan-\ *n*

Mas·ba·te \ˌmäz-'bät-ē\ island central Philippines

Mas·e·ru \'maz-ə-ˌrü\ city, capital of Lesotho

Mash·had \mə-'shad\ city NE Iran

Ma·son–Dix·on line \ˌmās-ᵊn-'dik-sən-\ boundary between Maryland & Pennsylvania; was in part boundary between free & slave states

Mas·sa·chu·setts \ˌmas(-ə)-'chü-səts, -zəts\ state NE U.S.; capital, Boston

Mat·a·be·le·land \ˌmat-ə-'bē-lē-ˌland\ region SW Zimbabwe

Mat·lock \'mat-ˌläk\ town N England in Derbyshire

Mat·ter·horn \'mat-ər-ˌhȯ(ə)rn, 'mät-\ mountain 4478 meters on border between Switzerland & Italy

Maui \'maủ-ē\ island Hawaii NW of Hawaii island

Mau·na Kea \ˌmaủ-nə-'kā-ə\ extinct volcano 4205 meters Hawaii in N central Hawaii island

Mau·na Loa \ˌmaủ-nə-'lō-ə\ volcano 4170 meters Hawaii in S central Hawaii island

Mau·re·ta·nia *or* **Mau·ri·ta·nia** \ˌmȯr-ə-'tā-nē-ə, ˌmär-, -nyə\ ancient country NW Africa in modern Morocco & W Algeria — **Mau·re·ta·ni·an** \-nē-ən, -nyən\ *adj or n*

Mauritania country NW Africa on the Atlantic N of Senegal river; capital, Nouakchott — **Mauritanian** *adj or n*

Mau·ri·tius \mȯ-'rish-(ē-)əs\ island in Indian ocean E of Madagascar; an independent country in the Commonwealth; capital, Port Louis — **Mau·ri·tian** \-'rish-ən\ *adj or n*

May, Cape \-'mā\ cape S New Jersey at entrance to Delaware Bay

Ma·yon, Mount \-mä-'yōn\ volcano 2525 meters Philippines in SE Luzon

Ma·yotte Island \mä-'yät-\ island Comoro group — see COMORO

Ma·za·ma, Mount \-mə-'zäm-ə\ prehistoric mountain SW Oregon the collapse of whose top formed Crater lake

Mba·bane \ˌem-bə-'bän\ city, capital of Swaziland

Mbi·ni \em-'bē-nē\ *or formerly* **Río Mu·ni** \ˌrē-ō-'mü-nē\ mainland portion of Equatorial Guinea

Mead, Lake \-'mēd\ reservoir NW Arizona & SE Nevada formed by Hoover Dam in Colorado river

Mec·ca \'mek-ə\ city W Saudi Arabia containing the Great Mosque of Islam

Me·dan \mā-'dän\ city Indonesia in N Sumatra

Me·de·llín \ˌmed-ᵊl-'ēn, ˌmā-thə-'yēn\ city NW Colombia

Med·i·ter·ra·nean \ˌmed-ə-tə-'rā-nē-ən, -nyən\ sea 3750 kilometers long between Europe & Africa connecting with the Atlantic through Strait of Gibraltar

Me·kong \'mā-'kȯŋ, -'käŋ\ river 4185 kilometers long SE Asia flowing from E Tibet S & SE into South China sea in S Vietnam

Mel·a·ne·sia \ˌmel-ə-'nē-zhə, -shə\ islands of the Pacific NE of Australia & S of Micronesia including Bismarck, the Solomons, Vanuatu, New Caledonia, & the Fijis

Mel·bourne \'mel-bərn\ city SE Australia, capital of Victoria

Me·los \'mē-ˌläs\ island Greece — **Me·li·an** \'mē-lē-ən\ *adj or n*

Mel·ville \'mel-ˌvil\ 1 island N Canada in N Northwest Territories 2 peninsula E Northwest Territories, Canada

Mem·phis \'mem(p)-fəs\ 1 city SW Tennessee 2 ancient city N Egypt S of modern Cairo

Men·do·ci·no, Cape \-ˌmen-də-'sē-nō\ cape NW California

Mer·cia \'mər-sh(ē-)ə\ ancient Anglo-Saxon kingdom central England — **Mer·cian** \'mər-shən\ *adj or n*

Mer·sey \'mər-zē\ river 110 kilometers long NW England flowing NW & W into Irish sea

Mer·sey·side \'mər-zē-ˌsīd\ county NW England; includes Liverpool

Mer·ton \'mərt-ᵊn\ city area of SW Greater London county, England

Me·sa \'mā-sə\ city S central Arizona

Me·sa·bi range \mə-'säb-ē\ region NE Minnesota that contains iron ore

Mes·o·po·ta·mia \ˌmes-(ə-)pə-'tā-mē-ə, -myə\ 1 region SW Asia between Euphrates & Tigris rivers 2 the entire Tigris-Euphrates valley — **Mes·o·po·ta·mian** \-mē-ən, -myən\ *adj or n*

Meuse \'myüz, 'mə(r)z\ river 925 kilometers long W Europe flowing from NE France into North sea in the Netherlands

Mex·i·co \'mek-si-ˌkō\ 1 country S North America 2 *or* **Mexico City** city, its capital

Mexico, Gulf of inlet of the Atlantic SE North America

Mi·ami \mī-'am-ē, -'am-ə\ city SE Florida

Miami Beach city SE Florida

Mich·i·gan \'mish-i-gən\ state N central U.S.; capital, Lansing — **Mich·i·gan·der** \ˌmish-i-'gan-dər\ *n* — **Mich·i·gan·ite** \'mish-i-gə-ˌnīt\ *n*

Michigan, Lake lake N central U.S.; one of the Great Lakes

Mi·cro·ne·sia \ˌmī-krə-'nē-zhə, -shə\ islands of the W Pacific E of the Philippines & N of Melanesia including Caroline, Kiribati, Mariana, & Marshall groups — **Mi·cro·ne·sian** \-zhən, -shən\ *adj or n*

Middle East the countries of SW Asia & N Africa — usually thought to include the countries extending from Libya on the W to Afghanistan on the E — **Middle Eastern** *or* **Mid·east·ern** \'mid-'ē-stərn\ *adj*

Mid·dles·brough \'mid-ᵊlz-brə\ town N England in Cleveland county

Mid Gla·mor·gan \'mid-glə-'mȯr-gən\ county SE Wales; established 1974

Mid·i·an \'mid-ē-ən\ ancient region NW Arabia E of Gulf of 'Aqaba — **Mid·i·an·ite** \-ē-ə-ˌnīt\ *n*

Mid·lands \'mid-lən(d)z\ the central counties of England usually thought to consist of Bedfordshire, Buckinghamshire, Cambridgeshire, Derbyshire, Leicestershire, Lincolnshire, Northamptonshire, Nottinghamshire, Oxfordshire, Staffordshire, Warwickshire, West Midlands, & part of Hereford and Worcester

Mid·way \'mid-ˌwā\ islands central Pacific in Hawaiian group 2090 kilometers WNW of Honolulu belonging to U.S.; not included in state of Hawaii

---

\ə\abut \ᵊ\kitten \ər\further \a\ash \ā\ace \ä\mop, mar \aủ\out \ch\chin \e\bet \ē\easy \g\go \i\hit \ī\ice \j\job \ŋ\sing \ō\go \ȯ\law \ȯi\boy \th\thin \t͟h\the \ü\loot \ủ\foot \y\yet \zh\vision *see also* Pronunciation Symbols page

Mid·west \\,mid-'west\\ *or* **Middle West** region N central U.S. including area around Great Lakes & in upper Mississippi valley from Ohio on the E to North Dakota, South Dakota, Nebraska, & Kansas on the W — **Mid·wes·tern** \\,mid-'wes-tərn\\ *or* **Middle Western** *adj* — **Mid·wes·tern·er** \\,mid-'wes-tə(r)-nər\\ *or* **Middle Westerner** *n*

Mi·lan \\mə-'lan, -'län\\ *or Italian* **Mi·la·no** \\mi-'län-ō\\ city NW Italy — **Mil·a·nese** \\,mil-ə-'nēz, -'nēs\\ *adj or n*

Mil·wau·kee \\mil-'wò-kē\\ city SE Wisconsin

Mi·nas Basin \\,mī-nəs-\\ bay central Nova Scotia; NE extension of Bay of Fundy

Min·da·nao \\,min-də-'nä-ō, -'naù\\ island S Philippines

Min·do·ro \\min-'dōr-ō, -'dòr-\\ island central Philippines

Min·ne·ap·o·lis \\,min-ē-'ap-(ə-)ləs\\ city SE Minnesota

Min·ne·so·ta \\,min-ə-'sōt-ə\\ state N central U.S.; capital, Saint Paul — **Min·ne·so·tan** \\-'sōt-ᵊn\\ *adj or n*

Mi·nor·ca \\mə-'nòr-kə\\ island Spain in W Mediterranean — **Mi·nor·can** \\mə-'nòr-kən\\ *adj or n*

Minsk \\'min(t)sk\\ city, capital of Belarus

Mis·sis·sip·pi \\,mis-(ə-)'sip-ē\\ **1** river 3975 kilometers long central U.S. flowing into Gulf of Mexico — see ITASCA, LAKE **2** state S U.S.; capital, Jackson

Mis·sou·ri \\mə-'zù(ə)r-ē, -'zùr-ə\\ **1** river 4345 kilometers long W U.S. flowing from SW Montana to the Mississippi in E Missouri **2** state central U.S.; capital, Jefferson City — **Mis·sou·ri·an** \\-'zùr-ē-ən\\ *adj or n*

Mitch·ell, Mount \\-'mich-əl\\ mountain 2037 meters W North Carolina in the Appalachians; highest in U.S. E of the Mississippi

Mo·bile \\mō-'bē(ə)l, 'mō-,bēl\\ city SW Alabama on Mobile Bay

Mo·des·to \\mə-'des-tō\\ city central California

Mog·a·di·shu \\,mäg-ə-'dish-ü, -'dēsh-\\ *or* **Mog·a·di·scio** \\-ō\\ city, capital of Somalia

Mo·hawk \\'mō-,hòk\\ river E central New York flowing into the Hudson

Mo·ja·ve *or* **Mo·ha·ve** \\mə-'häv-ē\\ desert S California SE of S end of Sierra Nevada

Mold \\'mōld\\ town NE Wales in Clwyd county

Mol·da·via \\mäl-'dā-vē-ə, -vyə\\ **1** region E Europe in NE Romania & Moldova **2** former republic of U.S.S.R. bordered by Ukraine, Black sea, & Romania; became independent (as Moldova) 1991 — **Mol·da·vian** \\-vē-ən, -vyən\\ *adj or n*

Mol·do·va \\mäl-'dō-və, mòl-\\ country E Europe in E Moldavia region; capital, Kishinev

Mol·o·kai \\,mäl-ə-'kī, ,mō-lə-\\ island Hawaii ESE of Oahu

Mo·luc·cas \\mə-'lək-əz\\ islands Indonesia E of Sulawesi — **Mo·luc·ca** \\mə-'lək-ə\\ *adj* — **Mo·luc·can** \\-ən\\ *adj or n*

Mo·na·co \\'män-ə-,kō *also* mə-'näk-ō\\ country W Europe on Mediterranean coast of France; capital, Monaco — **Mo·na·can** \\'män-ə-kən, mə-'näk-ən\\ *adj or n* — **Mon·e·gasque** \\,män-i-'gask\\ *n*

Mon·go·lia \\män-'gōl-yə, mäŋ-, -'gō-lē-ə\\ **1** region E Asia E of Altai mountains; includes Gobi desert **2** country E Asia consisting of major portion of Mongolia region; capital Ulan Bator

Mo·non·ga·he·la \\mə-,nän-gə-'hē-lə, -,näŋ-gə-, -'hā-lə\\ river N West Virginia & SW Pennsylvania

Mon·ro·via \\(,)mən-'rō-vē-ə\\ city, capital of Liberia

Mon·tana \\män-'tan-ə\\ state NW U.S.; capital, Helena — **Mon·tan·an** \\-ən\\ *adj or n*

Mont Blanc \\'mōn-'bläŋ(k)\\ mountain 4807 meters SE France on Italian border; highest in the Alps

Mon·te·ne·gro \\,män-tə-'nē-(,)grō, -'nā-\\ region SW Yugoslavia on the Adriatic sea

Mon·ter·rey \\,mänt-ə-'rā\\ city NE Mexico

Mon·te·vi·deo \\,mänt-ə-və-'dā-ō, -'vid-ē-,ō\\ city, capital of Uruguay

Mont·gom·ery \\(,)mən(t)-'gəm-(ə-)rē, män(t)-, -'gäm-\\ city, capital of Alabama

Mont·pe·lier \\mänt-'pēl-yər, -'pil-\\ city, capital of Vermont

Mont·re·al \\,män-trē-'òl, ,mən-\\ city S Quebec, Canada on Montreal Island in the Saint Lawrence

Mont·ser·rat \\,män(t)-sə-'rat\\ island West Indies in the Leeward Islands

Mo·ra·via \\mə-'rā-vē-ə\\ region E Czech Republic — **Mo·ra·vi·an** \\mə-'rā-vē-ən\\ *adj or n*

Mo·rea \\mə-'rē-ə\\ PELOPONNISOS — an old name — **Mo·re·an** \\-'rē-ən\\ *adj or n*

Mo·roc·co \\mə-'räk-ō\\ country NW Africa; a kingdom; capital, Rabat — **Mo·roc·can** \\-'räk-ən\\ *adj or n*

Mo·ro·ni \\mò-'rō-nē\\ city, capital of Comoro

Mos·cow \\'mäs-,kaù, -kō\\ *or Russian* **Mos·kva** \\mäsk-'vä\\ city, capital of Russia and formerly of U.S.S.R. and of Russian Soviet Federated Socialist Republic

Mourne \\'mō(ə)rn, 'mò(ə)rn\\ district S Northern Ireland

Moyle \\'mòi(ə)l\\ district N Northern Ireland

Mo·zam·bique \\,mō-zam-'bēk\\ **1** channel SE Africa between Mozambique & Madagascar **2** country SE Africa; capital, Maputo

Mukden — see SHENYANG

Mul·tan \\mùl-'tän\\ city NE Pakistan SW of Lahore

Mu·nich \\'myü-nik\\ *or German* **Mün·chen** \\'m(y)ün-kən\\ city S Germany in Bavaria

Mun·ster \\'mən(t)-stər\\ province S Ireland

Mur·cia \\'mər-sh(ē-)ə\\ region & ancient kingdom SE Spain — **Mur·cian** \\-shən\\ *adj or n*

Mur·ray \\'mər-ē, 'mə-rē\\ river 1930 kilometers long SE Australia flowing W from E Victoria into Indian ocean in South Australia — see DARLING

Mur·rum·bidg·ee \\,mər-əm-'bij-ē, ,mə-rəm-\\ river 1610 kilometers long SE Australia in New South Wales flowing W into the Murray

Mus·cat \\'məs-,kat, -kət\\ town E Arabia, capital of Oman

Muscovy \\'məs-kə-vē\\ principality from about 1280 to 15th century consisting of Moscow, Russia

Myan·mar \\'myän-,mär\\ *or* **Myan·ma** \\-,mä\\ *or formerly* **Bur·ma** \\'bər-mə\\ country SE Asia; capital, Yangon

My·ce·nae \\mī-'sē-nē\\ ancient city S Greece in NE Peloponnisos

My·sore \\mī-'sō(ə)r, -'sò(ə)r\\ city S India

Nab·a·taea *or* **Nab·a·tea** \\,nab-ə-'tē-ə\\ ancient Arab kingdom SE of Palestine — **Nab·a·tae·an** *or* **Nab·a·te·an** \\-'tē-ən\\ *adj or n*

Na·goya \\nə-'gòi-ə, 'näg-ə-,yä\\ city Japan in S central Honshu

Nag·pur \\'näg-,pù(ə)r\\ city E central India

Nai·ro·bi \\nī-'rō-bē\\ city, capital of Kenya

Na·mib·ia \\nə-'mib-ē-ə\\ *or formerly* **South–West Africa** country SW Africa on the Atlantic; capital, Windhoek

Nan·chang \\'nän-'jäŋ\\ city SE China

Nan·jing \\'nän-'jiŋ\\ *or* **Nan·king** \\'nan-'kiŋ, 'nän-\\ city E China

Nan·tuck·et \\nan-'tək-ət\\ island SE Massachusetts S of Cape Cod

Na·ples \\'nā-pəlz\\ *or Italian* **Na·po·li** \\'näp-ə-lē\\ *or ancient* **Ne·ap·o·lis** \\nē-'ap-ə-ləs\\ city S Italy on Bay of Naples — **Ne·a·pol·i·tan** \\,nē-ə-'päl-ət-ᵊn\\ *adj or n*

Nar·ra·gan·sett Bay \\,nar-ə-'gan(t)-sət\\ inlet of the Atlantic SE Rhode Island

Nash·ville \\'nash-,vil, -vəl\\ city, capital of Tennessee

Nas·sau \\'nas-ò\\ city, capital of Bahamas on New Providence island

Na·tal \\nə-'tal, -'täl\\ province E Republic of South Africa; capital, Pietermaritzburg

Na·u·ru \\nä-'ü-rü\\ island W Pacific 42 kilometers S of the equator; formerly a shared British, New Zealand,

& Australian trust territory; an independent country in the Commonwealth since 1968

Naz·a·reth \\\'naz-(ə-)rəth\ town of ancient Palestine in central Galilee; now a city of N Israel

N'Dja·me·na \en-\'jäm-ə-nə\ city, capital of Chad

Neagh, Lough \läk-\'nā\ lake Northern Ireland; largest in British Isles

Near East the countries of NE Africa & SW Asia — **Near Eastern** *adj*

Ne·bras·ka \nə-\'bras-kə\ state central U.S.; capital, Lincoln — **Ne·bras·kan** \-kən\ *adj or n*

Neg·ev \\\'neg-\ˌev\ desert region S Israel

Ne·gros \\\'nā-(ˌ)grōs\ island central Philippines

Ne·pal \nə-\'pȯl, -\'päl, -\'pal\ country Asia on NE border of India in the Himalayas; a kingdom; capital, Kathmandu — **Nep·a·lese** \ˌnep-ə-\'lēz, -\'lēs\ *adj or n* — **Ne·pali** \nə-\'pȯl-ē, -\'päl-, -\'pal-\ *adj or n*

Ness, Loch \\\'nes\ lake NW Scotland

Neth·er·lands \\\'neth-ər-lən(d)z\ **1** *or Dutch* **Ne·der·land** \\\'nād-ər-ˌlänt\ *also* **Holland** country NW Europe on North sea; a kingdom; capitals, Amsterdam and The Hague **2** LOW COUNTRIES — an historical usage — **Neth·er·land** \\\'neth-ər-lənd\ *adj* — **Neth·er·land·er** \-ˌlan-dər, -lən-\ *n* — **Neth·er·land·ish** \-dish\ *adj*

Netherlands An·til·les \-an-\'til-ēz\ islands of the West Indies belonging to the Netherlands

Netherlands East Indies *or* **Netherlands India** *or* **Dutch East Indies** former Dutch possessions in the East Indies including Indonesia

Ne·va \\\'nē-və, \'nā-\ river 65 kilometers long W Russia; flows through Saint Petersburg

Ne·vada \nə-\'vad-ə, -\'väd-ə\ state W U.S.; capital, Carson City — **Ne·vad·an** \-\'vad-ᵊn, -\'väd-ᵊn\ *or* **Ne·vadi·an** \-\'vad-ē-ən, -\'väd-\ *adj or n*

Ne·vis \\\'nē-vəs\ island West Indies in the Leeward Islands — see SAINT KITTS

New Am·ster·dam \-\'am(p)-stər-ˌdam\ town founded 1625 on Manhattan island by the Dutch; renamed New York 1664 by the British

New·ark \\\'n(y)ü-ərk, \'n(y)ù-(ə-)rk\ city NE New Jersey

New Brit·ain \-\'brit-ᵊn\ island W Pacific

New Bruns·wick \-\'brənz-(ˌ)wik\ province SE Canada; capital, Fredericton

New Cal·e·do·nia \-ˌkal-ə-\'dō-nyə, -nē-ə\ island SW Pacific SW of Vanuatu; an overseas department of France; capital, Nouméa

New·cas·tle \\\'n(y)ü-ˌkas-əl\ city SE Australia in E New South Wales

Newcastle *or* **New·cas·tle up·on Tyne** \n(y)ü-\'kas-əl-ə-ˌpȯn-\'tīn\ city N England in Tyne and Wear county

New Del·hi \-\'del-ē\ city, capital of India S of Delhi

New England section of U.S. consisting of states of Maine, New Hampshire, Vermont, Massachusetts, Rhode Island, & Connecticut — **New En·gland·er** \-\'iŋ-glən-dər *also* -\'iŋ-lən-\ *n*

New·found·land \\\'n(y)ü-fən-(d)lənd, -ˌ(d)land; ˌn(y)ü-fən-\'(d)land\ **1** island Canada in the Atlantic **2** province E Canada consisting of Newfoundland island & Labrador; capital, Saint John's — **New·found·land·er** \-(d)lən-dər, -\'(d)lan-dər\ *n*

New France the possessions of France in North America before 1763

New Guin·ea \-\'gin-ē\ **1** island W Pacific N of E Australia divided between West Irian & Papua New Guinea **2** the NE portion of the island of New Guinea together with some nearby islands; now part of Papua New Guinea — **New Guin·e·an** \-\'gin-ē-ən\ *adj or n*

New·ham \\\'n(y)ü-əm\ city area of E Greater London county, England

New Hamp·shire \-\'ham(p)-shər, -ˌshi(ə)r\ state NE U.S.; capital, Concord — **New Hamp·shire·man** \-mən\ *n* — **New Hamp·shir·ite** \-ˌīt\ *n*

New Ha·ven \-\'hā-vən\ city S Connecticut

New Hebrides — see VANUATU

New Jer·sey \-\'jər-zē\ state E U.S.; capital, Trenton — **New Jer·sey·ite** \-ˌīt\ *n*

New Mex·i·co \-\'mek-si-ˌkō\ state SW U.S.; capital, Santa Fe — **New Mex·i·can** \-si-kən\ *adj or n*

New Neth·er·land \-\'neth-ər-lənd\ former Dutch colony (1613–64) North America along Hudson & lower Delaware rivers; capital, New Amsterdam

New Or·leans \-\'ȯr-lē-ənz, -\'ȯrl-(y)ənz, -(ˌ)ȯr-\'lēnz\ city SE Louisiana

New·port \\\'n(y)ü-ˌpō(ə)rt, -ˌpȯ(ə)rt\ **1** city area S England in Isle of Wight **2** city SE Wales in Gwent county

Newport News \ˌn(y)ü-ˌpȯrt-\'n(y)üz, -ˌpȯrt-, -pərt-\ city SE Virginia

New Prov·i·dence \-\'präv-əd-ən(t)s, -ə-ˌden(t)s\ island NW central Bahamas; chief town, Nassau

New·ry \\\'n(y)ù(ə)r-ē\ city district S Northern Ireland in Mourne district

New South Wales state SE Australia; capital, Sydney

New Spain former Spanish possessions in North America, Central America, West Indies, & the Philippines; capital, Mexico City

New Sweden former Swedish colony (1638–55) North America on W bank of Delaware river

New·town·ab·bey \ˌn(y)üt-ᵊn-\'ab-ē\ district E Northern Ireland

New·town·ards \ˌn(y)üt-ᵊn-\'ärdz\ city area E Northern Ireland in Ards district

Newtown Saint Bos·wells \-sənt-\'bäz-wəlz, -sänt-\ village S Scotland in Borders region

New World the western hemisphere including North America and South America

New York \-\'yȯ(ə)rk\ **1** state NE U.S.; capital, Albany **2** *or* **New York City** city SE New York — **New York·er** \-\'yȯr-kər\ *n*

New York State Barge Canal — see ERIE

New Zea·land \-\'zē-lənd\ country SW Pacific ESE of Australia; an independent country in the Commonwealth; capital, Wellington — **New Zea·land·er** \-lən-dər\ *n*

Ni·ag·a·ra Falls \(ˌ)nī-\'ag-(ə-)rə-\ falls New York & Ontario in **Niagara river** (58 kilometers long flowing N from Lake Erie into Lake Ontario); divided by Goat Island into Horseshoe Falls, or Canadian Falls (48 meters high, 917 meters wide) & American Falls (51 meters high, 323 meters wide)

Nia·mey \nē-\'äm-ā, nyä-\'mā\ city, capital of Niger

Ni·caea \nī-\'sē-ə\ *or* **Nice** \\\'nīs\ ancient city W Bithynia; site at modern village in NW Turkey — **Ni·cae·an** \nī-\'sē-ən\ *adj or n* — **Ni·cene** \nī-\'sēn, nī-\'sēn\ *adj*

Ni·ca·ra·gua \ˌnik-ə-\'räg-wə\ **1** lake 160 kilometers long S Nicaragua **2** country Central America; capital, Managua — **Ni·ca·ra·guan** \-wən\ *adj or n*

Nic·o·bar \\\'nik-ə-ˌbär\ islands India in Bay of Bengal S of the Andamans — see ANDAMAN

Nic·o·sia \ˌnik-ə-\'sē-ə\ city, capital of Cyprus

Ni·ger \\\'nī-jər\ **1** river 4185 kilometers long W Africa flowing into Gulf of Guinea **2** country W Africa N of Nigeria; capital, Niamey

Ni·ge·ria \nī-\'jir-ē-ə\ country W Africa on Gulf of Guinea; an independent state in the Commonwealth; official capital, Abuja — **Ni·ge·ri·an** \-ē-ən\ *adj or n*

Nii·hau \\\'nē-ˌhaù\ island Hawaii WSW of Kauai

Nile \\\'nī(ə)l\ river 6497 kilometers long E Africa flowing from Lake Victoria in Uganda N into the Mediterranean in Egypt

Nil·gi·ri \\\'nil-gə-rē\ hills S India

\ə\abut \ᵊ\kitten \ər\further \a\ash \ā\ace \ä\mop, mar
\aù\out \ch\chin \e\bet \ē\easy \g\go \i\hit \ī\ice \j\job
\ŋ\sing \ō\go \ȯ\law \ȯi\boy \th\thin \t̲h̲\the \ü\loot \ù\foot
\y\yet \zh\vision *see also* Pronunciation Symbols page

Nin·e·veh \'nin-ə-və\ ancient city, capital of Assyria; ruins in Iraq on the Tigris

Nip·i·gon, Lake \-'nip-ə-ˌgän\ lake Canada in W Ontario N of Lake Superior

Nip·pon \nip-'än\ — see JAPAN — **Nip·pon·ese** \ˌnip-ə-'nēz, -'nēs\ adj or n

Nizh·ni Nov·go·rod \ˌnizh-nē-'näv-gə-ˌräd, -'nȯv-gə-rət\ or 1932-89 Gor'·kiy or Gor·ki \'gȯr-kē\ city W Russia

Nome \'nōm\ city W Alaska

Nor·folk\'nȯr-fək, in the U.S. also -ˌfȯk\ **1** city SE Virginia **2** county E England on North sea

Nor·man·dy \'nȯr-mən-dē\ region NW France NE of Brittany

North 1 river estuary of the Hudson between NE New Jersey & SE New York **2** sea arm of the Atlantic E of Great Britain **3** island N New Zealand

North·al·ler·ton \nȯr-'thal-ərt-ᵊn\ town N England in North Yorkshire

North America continent of western hemisphere NW of South America & N of the equator — **North American** adj or n

North·amp·ton \nȯrth-'(h)am(p)-tən\ city area central England in Northamptonshire

North·amp·ton·shire \nȯrth-'(h)am(p)-tən-ˌshi(ə)r, -shər\ or **Northampton** county central England

North Cape cape New Zealand at N end of North island

North Car·o·li·na \-ˌkar-ə-'lī-nə\ state E U.S.; capital, Raleigh — **North Car·o·lin·ian** \-'lin-ē-ən, -'lin-yən\ adj or n

North Da·ko·ta \-də-'kōt-ə\ state N U.S.; capital, Bismarck — **North Da·ko·tan** \-'kōt-ᵊn\ adj or n

North Down district E Northern Ireland

Northern Cook \-'kùk\ islands S central Pacific N of Cook islands

Northern Ireland region N Ireland comprising 26 districts of Ulster; a division of United Kingdom; capital, Belfast

Northern Mar·i·ana Islands \-ˌmar-ē-'an-ə-, -ˌmer-\ islands W Pacific; a U.S. commonwealth since 1986

Northern Rhodesia — see ZAMBIA

Northern Territory territory N & central Australia; capital, Darwin

North Korea — see KOREA

North Slope region N Alaska between Brooks Range & Arctic ocean

North·um·ber·land \nȯr-'thəm-bər-lənd\ county England — **North·um·bri·an** \-'thəm-brē-ən\ adj or n

North·um·bria \nȯr-'thəm-brē-ə\ ancient country Great Britain in what is now N England and S Scotland — **North·um·bri·an** \-brē-ən\ adj or n

North Vietnam — see VIETNAM

Northwest Territories territory N Canada consisting of the arctic islands, the mainland N of 60° between Yukon Territory & Hudson bay, & the islands in Hudson bay

North Yorkshire county N England

Nor·way \'nȯ(ə)r-ˌwā\ country N Europe in Scandinavia; a kingdom; capital, Oslo

Nor·wich \'nȯ(ə)r-(ˌ)wich; 'nȯr-ich, 'när-\ city E England in Norfolk county

Not·ting·ham \'nät-iŋ-əm, in the U.S. also -ˌham\ city N central England in Nottinghamshire

Not·ting·ham·shire \'nät-iŋ-əm-ˌshi(ə)r, -shər, in the U.S. also -ˌham-\ or **Nottingham** county N central England

Nouak·chott \nù-'äk-ˌshät\ city, capital of Mauritania

Nou·méa \nü-'mā-ə\ city, capital of New Caledonia

No·va Sco·tia \ˌnō-və-'skō-shə\ province SE Canada; capital, Halifax — **No·va Sco·tian** \-'skō-shən\ adj or n

No·vo·kuz·netsk \ˌnō-(ˌ)vō-kúz-'netsk\ city S Russia

No·vo·si·birsk \ˌnō-(ˌ)vō-sə-'bi(ə)rsk\ city S Russia

Nu·bia \'n(y)ü-bē-ə\ region NE Africa in Nile valley in S Egypt & N Sudan — **Nu·bi·an** \-bē-ən\ adj or n

Nu·ku·a·lo·fa \ˌnü-kə-wə-'lȯ-fə\ seaport, capital of Tonga

Nu·mid·ia \n(y)ù-'mid-ē-ə\ ancient country N Africa E of Mauretania in modern Algeria — **Nu·mid·i·an** \-ē-ən\ adj or n

Ny·asa, Lake \-nī-'as-ə, -nē-\ lake SE Africa in Malawi, Mozambique, & Tanzania

Nyasaland — see MALAWI

Oa·hu \ə-'wä-hü\ island Hawaii; site of Honolulu

Oak·land \'ō-klənd\ city W California on San Francisco Bay E of San Francisco

Oce·a·nia \ˌō-shē-'an-ē-ə, -'ä-nē-ə\ lands of the central & S Pacific: Micronesia, Melanesia, Polynesia including New Zealand, & sometimes Australia & Malay island group — **Oce·a·ni·an** \-'an-ē-ən, -'ä-nē-\ adj or n

Oder \'ōd-ər\ or **Odra** \'ȯ-drə\ river 906 kilometers long central Europe flowing from Silesia NW into Baltic sea; forms part of boundary between Poland & Germany

Odes·sa \ō-'des-ə\ city & port S Ukraine on Black sea

Ohio \ō-'hī-ō\ **1** river 1579 kilometers long E U.S. flowing from W Pennsylvania into the Mississippi **2** state E central U.S.; capital, Columbus — **Ohio·an** \ō-'hī-ə-wən\ adj or n

Oka·ya·ma \ˌō-kə-'yäm-ə\ city Japan in W Honshu on Inland sea

Okee·cho·bee, Lake \ˌō-kə-'chō-bē\ lake S central Florida

Oke·fe·no·kee \ˌō-kə-fə-'nō-kē\ swamp SE Georgia & NE Florida

Oki·na·wa \ˌō-kə-'nä-wə, -'naù-ə\ **1** islands Japan in central Ryukyus **2** island, chief of group — **Oki·na·wan** \-'nä-wən, -'naù-ən\ adj or n

Okla·ho·ma \ˌō-klə-'hō-mə\ state S U.S.; capital, Oklahoma City — **Okla·ho·man** \-mən\ adj or n

Oklahoma City city, capital of Oklahoma

Old·ham \'ōl-dəm\ city NW England in Greater Manchester county

Old Point Comfort cape SE Virginia N of entrance to Hampton Roads

Ol·du·vai Gorge \'ōl-də-ˌvī-\ canyon N Tanzania SE of Serengeti Plain; site of fossil beds

Old World the half of the earth to the east of the Atlantic ocean including Europe, Asia, and Africa; esp : the continent of Europe

Olym·pia \ə-'lim-pē-ə, ō-\ **1** city, capital of Washington **2** plain S Greece in NW Peloponnisos

Olym·pic \ə-'lim-pik, ō-\ mountains NW Washington on Olympic peninsula; highest Mt. Olympus 2428 meters

Olym·pus \ə-'lim-pəs, ō-\ mountains NE Greece

Omagh \'ō-mə\ **1** district W Northern Ireland **2** town in Omagh district

Oma·ha \'ō-mə-ˌhȯ, -ˌhä\ city E Nebraska

Oman \ō-'män, -'man\ country SW Asia in SE Arabia; a sultanate; capital, Muscat

Oman, Gulf of arm of Arabian sea between Oman & SE Iran

Omsk \'ȯm(p)sk, 'äm(p)sk\ city S Russia

On·tar·io \än-'ter-ē-ō, -'tar-\ province E Canada; capital, Toronto — **On·tar·i·an** \-ē-ən\ adj or n

Ontario, Lake lake E central North America in U.S. & Canada; one of the Great Lakes

Or·ange \'ȯr-inj, 'är-, -ənj\ river 2090 kilometers long S Africa flowing W from Drakensberg mountains into the Atlantic

Orange Free State province E central Republic of South Africa; capital, Bloemfontein

Or·e·gon \'ȯr-i-gən, 'är-, -ˌgän\ state NW U.S.; capital, Salem — **Or·e·go·nian** \ˌȯr-i-'gō-nē-ən, ˌär-, -nyən\ adj or n

Oregon Trail pioneer route to the Pacific Northwest about 3220 kilometers long from Missouri to Washington

Ori·no·co \ˌōr-ə-ˈnō-kō, ˌór-\ river 2575 kilometers long Venezuela flowing into the Atlantic

Ork·ney \ˈórk-nē\ islands N Scotland forming a region

Or·lan·do \ór-ˈlan-dō\ city central Florida

Osa·ka \ō-ˈsäk-ə\ city Japan in S Honshu

Osh·a·wa \ˈäsh-ə-ˌwä\ city SE Ontario, Canada on Lake Ontario ENE of Toronto

Os·lo \ˈäz-lō, ˈäs-\ city, capital of Norway

Ot·ta·wa \ˈät-ə-ˌwä, -wə, -ˌwó\ city, capital of Canada in SE Ontario on Ottawa river

Ottoman Empire \ˌät-ə-mən-\ former Turkish sultanate in SE Europe, W Asia, & N Africa

Oua·ga·dou·gou \ˌwäg-ə-ˈdü-ˌgü\ city, capital of Burkina Faso

Outer Hebrides — see HEBRIDES

Ox·ford \ˈäks-fərd\ city central England in Oxfordshire

Ox·ford·shire \ˈäks-fərd-ˌshi(ə)r, -shər\ *or* **Oxford** county central England

Ox·nard \ˈäk-ˌsnärd\ city SW California

Ozark plateau \ˈō-ˌzärk-\ *or* **Ozark mountains** eroded plateau N Arkansas, S Missouri, & NE Oklahoma with E extension into S Illinois

Pa·cif·ic \pə-ˈsif-ik\ ocean extending from arctic circle to the equator (North Pacific) and from the equator to the antarctic regions (South Pacific) & from W North America & W South America to E Asia & Australia — **Pacific** *adj*

Pacific Islands, Trust Territory of the grouping of islands in W Pacific formerly under U.S. administration: the Carolines & the Marshalls

Pa·dang \ˈpä-ˌdäŋ\ city Indonesia in W Sumatra

Pa·dre \ˈpäd-rē, ˈpad-\ island about 160 kilometers long S Texas in Gulf of Mexico

Pa·go Pa·go \ˈpäŋ-(g)ō-ˈpäŋ-(g)ō, ˌpäg-ō-ˈpäg-ō\ town, capital of American Samoa on Tutuila island

Painted Desert region N central Arizona

Pak·i·stan \ˈpak-i-ˌstan, ˌpäk-i-ˈstän\ country S Asia NW of India; until 1971 included also an eastern division E of India; capital, Islamabad — see EAST PAKISTAN — **Pak·i·stani** \-ˈstan-ē, -ˈstän-ē\ *adj or n*

Palau — see BELAU

Pa·la·wan \pə-ˈlä-wən, -ˌwän\ island W Philippines between South China & Sulu seas

Pa·lem·bang \ˌpäl-əm-ˈbäŋ\ city Indonesia in SE Sumatra

Pa·ler·mo \pə-ˈlər-mō, -ˈle(ə)r-\ city Italy, capital of Sicily

Pal·es·tine \ˈpal-ə-ˌstīn, -ˌstēn\ region SW Asia between Syrian Desert & the Mediterranean now divided between Israel & Jordan — **Pal·es·tin·ian** \ˌpal-ə-ˈstin-ē-ən, -ˈstin-yən\ *adj or n*

Pal·i·sades \ˌpal-ə-ˈsādz\ line of high cliffs 24 kilometers long on W bank of the Hudson in SE New York & NE New Jersey

Pa·mirs \pə-ˈmi(ə)rz\ *or* **Pa·mir** \pə-ˈmi(ə)r\ elevated mountainous region central Asia in E Tajikistan & on borders of China, India, Pakistan, & Afghanistan; many peaks over 6000 meters

Pam·li·co \ˈpam-li-ˌkō\ inlet of the Atlantic E North Carolina between main part of the state & offshore islands

Pam·pa \ˈpam-pə\ city NW Texas

Pan·a·ma \ˈpan-ə-ˌmä, -ˌmó, ˌpan-ə-ˈmä, -ˈmó\ **1** country S Central America **2** *or* **Panama City** city, its capital on the Pacific **3** canal 82 kilometers long Panama connecting Atlantic & Pacific oceans — **Pan·a·ma·ni·an** \ˌpan-ə-ˈmä-nē-ən\ *adj or n*

Panama, Isthmus of *or formerly* **Isthmus of Dar·i·en** \-ˌdar-ē-ˈen\ strip of land central Panama connecting North America & South America

Panama Canal Zone — see CANAL ZONE

Pa·nay \pə-ˈnī\ island central Philippines

Pao-t'ou — see BAOTOU

Pap·ua, Territory of \-ˈpap-yə-wə, -ˈpäp-ə-wə\ former British territory consisting of SE New Guinea & offshore islands; now part of Papua New Guinea

Papua New Guinea country combining former territories of Papua & New Guinea; formerly a United Nations trust territory governed by Australia; independent since 1975; capital, Port Moresby

Par·a·guay \ˈpar-ə-ˌgwī, -ˌgwä\ **1** river 2415 kilometers long central South America flowing from Brazil S into the Paraná in Paraguay **2** country central South America; capital, Asunción — **Par·a·guay·an** \ˌpar-ə-ˈgwī-ən, -ˈgwä-\ *adj or n*

Par·a·mar·i·bo \ˌpar-ə-ˈmar-ə-ˌbō\ city, capital of Suriname

Pa·ra·ná \ˌpar-ə-ˈnä\ river 3285 kilometers long central South America flowing S from Brazil into Argentina

Pa·ri·cu·tin \pə-ˈrē-kə-ˌtēn\ **1** former village Mexico **2** volcano on site of former village of Paricutin

Par·is \ˈpar-əs\ city, capital of France — **Pa·ri·sian** \pə-ˈrizh-ən, -ˈrēzh-\ *adj or n*

Par·nas·sus \pär-ˈnas-əs\ mountain central Greece

Par·os \ˈpar-ˌäs, ˈper-\ island Greece — **Par·i·an** \ˈpar-ē-ən, ˈper-\ *adj*

Par·ra·mat·ta \ˌpar-ə-ˈmat-ə\ city SE Australia in New South Wales NW of Sydney

Par·thia \ˈpär-thē-ə\ ancient country SW Asia in NE modern Iran — **Par·thi·an** \-thē-ən\ *adj or n*

Pas·a·de·na \ˌpas-ə-ˈdē-nə\ **1** city SW California E of Glendale **2** city SE Texas

Pat·a·go·nia \ˌpat-ə-ˈgō-nyə, -nē-ə\ region South America S of about 40° S latitude in S Argentina & S tip of Chile; sometimes thought to include Tierra del Fuego — **Pat·a·go·nian** \-nyən, -nē-ən\ *adj or n*

Pat·er·son \ˈpat-ər-sən\ city NE New Jersey

Pat·mos \ˈpat-məs\ island Greece SSW of Samos

Pat·na \ˈpət-nə\ city NE India on the Ganges

Pearl Harbor inlet Hawaii on S coast of Oahu W of Honolulu

Peking — see BEIJING

Pe·li·on \ˈpē-lē-ən\ mountain 1618 meters NE Greece

Pel·o·pon·ni·sos \ˌpel-ə-pə-ˈnē-səs\ peninsula forming S part of mainland of Greece

Pen·nine Chain \ˈpen-ˌīn-\ mountains N England; highest Cross Fell 893 meters

Penn·syl·va·nia \ˌpen(t)-səl-ˈvā-nyə, -nē-ə\ state E U.S.; capital, Harrisburg

People's Democratic Republic of Yemen — see YEMEN

People's Republic of China — see CHINA

Pe·o·ria \pē-ˈór-ē-ə, -ˈōr-\ city N central Illinois

Per·ga·mum \ˈpər-gə-məm\ *or* **Per·ga·mus** \-məs\ ancient Greek kingdom including most of Asia Minor; at its height 263–133 B.C.; capital, Pergamum (in what is now W Turkey)

Perm \ˈpərm, ˈpe(ə)rm\ city W Russia

Pernambuco — see RECIFE

Persia — see IRAN

Per·sian \ˈpər-zhən\ gulf arm of Arabian sea between Iran & Arabia

Perth \ˈpərth\ city, capital of Western Australia

Pe·ru \pə-ˈrü\ country W South America; capital, Lima — **Pe·ru·vi·an** \pə-ˈrü-vē-ən\ *adj or n*

Pe·ter·bor·ough \ˈpēt-ər-ˌbər-ə, -ˌbə-rə, -b(ə-)rə\ city area central England in Cambridgeshire

Pe·tra \ˈpē-trə, ˈpe-trə\ ancient city NW Arabia; site in SW Jordan

Petrograd — see SAINT PETERSBURG

Phil·a·del·phia \ˌfil-ə-ˈdel-fyə, -fē-ə\ city SE Pennsylvania — **Phil·a·del·phian** \-fyən, -fē-ən\ *adj or n*

Phil·ip·pines \ˌfil-ə-ˌpēnz, ˈfil-ə-ˌpēnz\ island group ap-

\ə\abut \ᵊ\kitten \ər\further \a\ash \ā\ace \ä\mop, mar \aú\out \ch\chin \e\bet \ē\easy \g\go \i\hit \ī\ice \j\job \ŋ\sing \ō\go \ó\law \ói\boy \th\thin \t͟h\the \ü\loot \ú\foot \y\yet \zh\vision *see also* Pronunciation Symbols page

proximately 800 kilometers off SE coast of Asia; an independent country; capital, Manila — **Phil·ip·pine** \-ˈpēn, -ˌpēn\ *adj*

Phnom Penh \(pə-)ˈnóm-ˈpen, (pə-)ˈnäm-\ city, capital of Cambodia

Phoe·ni·cia \fi-ˈnish-(ē-)ə, -ˈnēsh-\ ancient country SW Asia on the Mediterranean in modern Syria & Lebanon

Phoe·nix \ˈfē-niks\ city, capital of Arizona

Phry·gia \ˈfrij-(ē-)ə\ ancient country W central Asia Minor

Pied·mont \ˈpēd-ˌmänt\ plateau region E U.S. E of the Appalachians between SE New York & NE Alabama — **Pied·mon·tese** \ˌpēd-mən-ˈtēz, -(ˌ)män-, -ˈtēs\ *adj or n*

Pierre \ˈpi(ə)r\ city, capital of South Dakota

Pie·ter·mar·itz·burg \ˈpēt-ər-ˈmar-əts-ˌbərg\ city E Republic of South Africa, capital of Natal

Pikes Peak \ˈpīks-\ mountain 4301 meters E central Colorado in a range of the Rockies

Pin·dus \ˈpin-dəs\ mountains W Greece; highest point 2480 meters

Pi·sa \ˈpē-zə\ city W central Italy W of Florence

Pit·cairn \ˈpit-ˌka(ə)rn, -ˌke(ə)rn\ island S Pacific; a British colony

Pitts·burgh \ˈpits-ˌbərg\ city SW Pennsylvania

Plac·id, Lake \-ˈplas-əd\ lake NE New York

Plym·outh \ˈplim-əth\ 1 town SE Massachusetts 2 city SW England in Devon county

Po \ˈpō\ river 673 kilometers N Italy flowing into the Adriatic

Po Hai — see BO HAI

Po·land \ˈpō-lənd\ country central Europe on Baltic sea; capital, Warsaw

Pol·y·ne·sia \ˌpäl-ə-ˈnē-zhə, -shə\ islands of the central & S Pacific including Hawaii, the Line, Tonga, Cook, & Samoa islands, & often New Zealand among others

Pom·er·a·nia \ˌpäm-ə-ˈrā-nē-ə, -nyə\ region N Europe on Baltic sea; formerly in Germany, now mostly in Poland

Pom·peii \päm-ˈpā, -ˈpā-ˌē\ ancient city S Italy SE of Naples destroyed 79 A.D. by eruption of Vesuvius — **Pom·pe·ian** \-ˈpā-ən\ *adj or n*

Po·na·pe \ˈpō-nə-ˌpā\ island W Pacific in the E Carolines

Pon·ce \ˈpón(t)-sā\ city S Puerto Rico

Pon·do·land \ˈpän-(ˌ)dō-ˌland\ territory E Republic of South Africa

Pon·ta Del·ga·da \ˌpän-tə-del-ˈgäd-ə, -ˈgad-\ city & port Portugal, largest in the Azores

Pont·char·train, Lake \-ˈpän-chər-ˌtrān, -ˌpän-chər-ˈtrān\ lake SE Louisiana E of the Mississippi & N of New Orleans

Pon·tus \ˈpänt-əs\ 1 ancient country NE Asia Minor 2 or **Pontus Euxinus** — see BLACK SEA — **Pon·tic** \ˈpänt-ik\ *adj or n*

Poole \ˈpül\ city area S England in Dorset county on English Channel

Poo·na \ˈpü-nə\ city W India, ESE of Bombay

Po·po·ca·te·petl \ˌpō-pə-kat-ə-ˈpet-ᵊl\ volcano 5452 meters SE central Mexico

Port Arthur — see LÜSHUN

Port–au–Prince \ˌpōrt-ō-ˈprin(t)s, ˌport-\ city, capital of Haiti

Port Jack·son \-ˈjak-sən\ inlet of S Pacific SE Australia in New South Wales; harbor of Sydney

Port·land \ˈpōrt-lənd, ˈport-\ 1 city SW Maine; largest in state 2 city NW Oregon

Port Lou·is \-ˈlü-əs, -ˈlü-ē, -lü-ˈē\ city, capital of Mauritius

Port Mores·by \-ˈmō(ə)rz-bē, -ˈmó(ə)rz-\ city, capital of Papua New Guinea

Pôr·to Ale·gre \ˌpōrt-ō-ə-ˈleg-rə, ˌport-\ city S Brazil

Port of Spain city NW Trinidad, capital of Trinidad and Tobago

Por·to–No·vo \ˌpōrt-ə-ˈnō-vō, ˌport-\ city, capital of Benin

Port Phil·lip Bay \-ˈfil-əp-\ inlet of S Pacific SE Australia in Victoria; harbor of Melbourne

Ports·mouth \ˈpōrt-sməth, ˈport-\ 1 city SE Virginia 2 city S England in Hampshire

Por·tu·gal \ˈpōr-chi-gəl, ˈpór-\ country SW Europe; capital, Lisbon

Portuguese India former Portuguese possession on W coast of India; became part of India 1962

Po·to·mac \pə-ˈtō-mək, -mik\ river 462 kilometers long flowing from West Virginia into Chesapeake Bay & forming boundary between Maryland & Virginia

Pough·keep·sie \pə-ˈkip-sē, pō-\ city and river port SE New York on the Hudson

Po·wys \ˈpō-əs\ county E central Wales; established 1974

Prague \ˈpräg\ or Czech **Pra·ha** \ˈprä-hä\ city, capital of Czech Republic & formerly of Czechoslovakia

Praia \ˈprī-ə\ town, capital of Cape Verde

Prairie Provinces the Canadian provinces of Alberta, Manitoba, & Saskatchewan

Pres·ton \ˈpres-tən\ city area NW England in Lancashire

Pre·to·ria \pri-ˈtōr-ē-ə, -ˈtór-\ city Republic of South Africa, capital of Transvaal & administrative capital of the country

Prib·i·lof \ˈprib-ə-ˌlóf\ islands Alaska in Bering sea

Prince Ed·ward Island \-ˌed-wərd-\ island SE Canada in Gulf of Saint Lawrence; a province; capital, Charlottetown

Prince Ru·pert's Land \-ˈrü-pərts-\ historical region N & W Canada consisting of drainage basin of Hudson bay granted 1670 by King Charles II to Hudson's Bay Company

Prince·ton \ˈprin(t)-stən\ town W central New Jersey

Prin·ci·pe \ˈprin(t)-sə-pə\ island W Africa in Gulf of Guinea — see SAO TOME AND PRINCIPE

Prom·on·to·ry \ˈpräm-ən-ˌtōr-ē, -ˌtór-\ locality NW Utah

Pro·vence \prə-ˈvän(t)s\ region SE France on the Mediterranean

Prov·i·dence \ˈpräv-əd-ən(t)s, -ə-ˌden(t)s\ city, capital of Rhode Island

Prus·sia \ˈprəsh-ə\ former kingdom &, later, state Germany; capital, Berlin — **Prus·sian** \-ən\ *adj or n*

Pueb·lo \pü-ˈeb-lō, ˈpweb-, pyü-ˈeb-\ city SE central Colorado SSE of Colorado Springs

Puer·to Ri·co \ˌpōrt-ə-ˈrē-kō, ˌpórt-, ˌpwert-\ island West Indies E of Hispaniola; a self-governing commonwealth associated with U.S.; capital, San Juan — **Puer·to Ri·can** \-ˈrē-kən\ *adj or n*

Pu·get Sound \ˌpyü-jət-\ arm of the Pacific W Washington

Pun·jab \ˌpən-ˈjäb, -ˈjab, ˈpen-ˌjäb, -ˌjab\ region in Pakistan & NW India in valley of the Indus

Pu·san \ˈpü-ˌsän\ city SE South Korea

Pyong·yang \pē-ˈóŋ-ˌyäŋ, pē-ˈəŋ-, -ˌyaŋ\ city, capital of North Korea

Pyr·e·nees \ˈpir-ə-ˌnēz\ mountains on French-Spanish border extending from Bay of Biscay to the Mediterranean; highest Pico de Aneto 3404 meters

Qa·tar \ˈkät-ər, ˈgät-, ˈgət-\ independent country E Arabia on peninsula extending into Persian gulf; capital, Doha

Qing·dao \ˈchiŋ-ˈdaù\ or **Tsing·tao** \ˈchiŋ-ˈdaù, ˈ(t)siŋ-\ city & port E China

Qi·qi·har \ˈchē-chē-ˈhär\ or **Ch'i·ch'i·ha·erh** \ˈchē-ˈchē-ˈhä-ˈər\ city NE China

Que·bec \kwi-ˈbek, ki-\ or French **Qué·bec** \kā-bek\ 1 province E Canada 2 city, its capital, on the Saint Lawrence

Queens \ˈkwēnz\ section of New York City on Long Island E of Brooklyn

Queens·land \\'kwĕnz-ˌland, -lənd\\ state NE Australia; capital, Brisbane — **Queens·land·er** \\-ər\\ *n*

Que·zon City \\'kā-ˌsòn-\\ city Philippines in Luzon; formerly capital of the country

Qui·to \\'kē-tò\\ city, capital of Ecuador

Ra·bat \\rə-'bät\\ city, capital of Morocco

Rai·nier, Mount \\-rə-'ni(ə)r, -rā-\\ mountain 4392 meters W central Washington; highest in Cascade Range

Rajasthan — see RAJPUTANA

Raj·pu·ta·na \\ˌräj-pə-'tän-ə\\ *or* **Ra·ja·sthan** \\'räj-ə-ˌstän\\ region NW India S of Punjab

Ra·leigh \\'rò-lē, 'räl-ē\\ city, capital of North Carolina

Rand — see WITWATERSRAND

Rand·wick \\'ran-(ˌ)dwik\\ city SE Australia in E New South Wales

Rangoon — see YANGON

Ra·wal·pin·di \\rä-wəl-'pin-dē, raùl-'pin-, ròl-'pin-\\ city NE Pakistan NNW of Lahore

Read·ing \\'red-iŋ\\ city area S England in Berkshire

Re·ci·fe \\rə-'sē-fə\\ *or formerly* **Per·nam·bu·co** \\ˌpər-nəm-'b(y)ü-kō, ˌper-nəm-'bü-\\ city NE Brazil

Red \\'red\\ **1** river 1638 kilometers long flowing E on Oklahoma-Texas boundary & into the Atchafalaya & the Mississippi in Louisiana **2** sea between Arabia & NE Africa

Red·bridge \\'red-(ˌ)brij\\ city area of NE Greater London county, England

Re·gi·na \\ri-'jī-nə\\ city, capital of Saskatchewan, Canada

Re·no \\'rē-nō\\ city NW Nevada

Republic of China — see CHINA

Ré·union \\rē-'yün-yən\\ island W Indian ocean; an overseas division of France; capital Saint-Denis

Reyk·ja·vik \\'rāk-(y)ə-ˌvik, -ˌvēk\\ city, capital of Iceland

Rhine \\'rīn\\ river 1320 kilometers long W Europe flowing from SE Switzerland to North sea in the Netherlands — **Rhen·ish** \\'ren-ish, 'rē-nish\\ *adj or n*

Rhine·land \\'rīn-ˌland, -lənd\\ *or German* **Rhein·land** \\'rīn-ˌlänt\\ the part of Germany W of the Rhine — **Rhine·land·er** \\'rīn-ˌlan-dər, -lən-\\ *n*

Rhode Is·land \\rō-'dī-lənd\\ **1** *or officially* **Rhode Island and Providence Plantations** state NE U.S.; capital, Providence **2** — see AQUIDNECK ISLAND — **Rhode Is·land·er** \\-lən-dər\\ *n*

Rho·de·sia \\rō-'dē-zh(ē-)ə\\ — see ZIMBABWE — **Rho·de·sian** \\-zh(ē-)ən\\ *adj or n*

Rhone *or French* **Rhône** \\'rōn\\ *or ancient* **Rhod·a·nus** \\'räd-ə-n-əs\\ river 800 kilometers long Switzerland & SE France

Rich·mond \\'rich-mənd\\ **1** — see STATEN ISLAND **2** city, capital of Virginia

Richmond upon Thames \\-'temz\\ city area of SW Greater London county, England

Ri·ga \\'rē-gə\\ city, capital of Latvia

Rio \\'rē-ò\\ RIO DE JANEIRO

Rio de Ja·nei·ro \\'rē-ō-ˌdā-zhə-'ne(ə)r-ō, -ˌdē-, -də-, -jə-'ne(ə)r-\\ city SE Brazil on Guanabara Bay

Rio Grande \\ˌrē-(ˌ)ō-'grand(-ē)\\ *or Mexican* **Rio Bra·vo** \\-'bräv-ō\\ river 3035 kilometers long SW U.S. forming part of U.S.-Mexico boundary & flowing into Gulf of Mexico

Río Muni — see MBINI

Riv·er·side \\'riv-ər-ˌsīd\\ city S California

Riv·i·era \\ˌriv-ē-'er-ə\\ coast region SE France & NW Italy

Ri·yadh \\rē-'(y)äd\\ city, capital of Saudi Arabia

Ro·a·noke \\'rō-(ə-)ˌnōk\\ city W Virginia

Roanoke Island island North Carolina S of entrance to Albemarle sound

Rob·son, Mount \\-'räb-sən\\ mountain 3954 meters W Canada in E British Columbia; highest in the Canadian Rockies

Roch·es·ter \\'räch-ə-stər, 'räch-ˌes-tər\\ city W New York

Rock·ford \\'räk-fərd\\ city N Illinois

Rocky \\'räk-ē\\ mountains W North America extending SE from N Alaska to central New Mexico — see ELBERT, MOUNT; ROBSON, MOUNT

Roman Empire the empire of ancient Rome

Ro·ma·nia \\rō-'mä-nē-ə, -nyə\\ *or* **Ru·ma·nia** \\rù-\\ country SE Europe on Black sea; capital, Bucharest

Rom·blon \\räm-'blōn\\ island group central Philippines

Rome \\'rōm\\ **1** *or Italian* **Ro·ma** \\'rō-mä\\ city, capital of Italy **2** the Roman Empire

Ro·sa·rio \\rō-'zär-ē-ˌō, -'sär-\\ city E central Argentina

Ro·seau \\rō-'zō\\ seaport, capital of Dominica

Ros·tov \\rə-'stóf, -'stòv\\ city SW Russia, on the Don

Ros·well \\'räz-ˌwel, -wəl\\ city SE New Mexico

Ro·ta \\'rōt-ə\\ island W Pacific in Marianas

Rot·ter·dam \\'rät-ər-ˌdam\\ city SW Netherlands

Ru·an·da–Urun·di \\rù-ˌän-də-ù-'rün-dē\\ former territory E central Africa bordering on Lake Tanganyika & administered by Belgium; divided into Burundi & Rwanda 1962

Ru·dolf, Lake \\-'rü-ˌdälf\\ lake N Kenya in Great Rift valley

Ruhr \\'rù(ə)r\\ industrial district W Germany E of the Rhine in valley of Ruhr river

Rupert's Land PRINCE RUPERT'S LAND

Rush·more, Mount \\-'rəsh-ˌmō(ə)r, -ˌmò(ə)r\\ mountain 1890 meters W South Dakota in Black hills

Rus·sia \\'rəsh-ə\\ **1** former empire largely having the same boundaries as U.S.S.R.; capital, Petrograd (Saint Petersburg) **2** : UNION OF SOVIET SOCIALIST REPUBLICS **3** country E Europe & N Asia; capital, Moscow; a republic (**Russian Soviet Federated Socialist Republic** *or* **Soviet Russia**) of U.S.S.R. 1922-91

Ru·the·nia \\rü-'thē-nyə, -nē-ə\\ region W Ukraine W of the N Carpathians — **Ru·the·nian** \\rü-'thē-nyən, -nē-ən\\ *adj or n*

Ru·wen·zo·ri \\ˌrü-(w)ən-'zōr-ē, -'zòr-\\ mountain group E central Africa between Uganda & Zaire; highest Mount Margherita 5019 meters

Rwan·da *or formerly* **Ru·an·da** \\rù-'än-də\\ country E central Africa, until 1962 part of Ruanda-Urundi trust territory; capital, Kigali — **Rwan·dan** \\-dən\\ *adj or n*

Ryu·kyu \\rē-'(y)ü-k(y)ü\\ islands W Pacific extending in an arc from Kyushu, Japan, to Taiwan, China; belong to Japan — **Ryu·kyu·an** \\-ˌ(y)ü-'k(y)ü-ən\\ *adj or n*

Saar \\'sär, 'zär\\ **1** river 135 kilometers long Europe flowing from E France to W Germany **2** *or* **Saar·land** \\'sär-ˌland, 'zär-\\ district W Europe in valley of Saar river between France and Germany

Sa·bah \\'säb-ə\\ part of Malaysia in NE Borneo

Sac·ra·men·to \\ˌsak-rə-'ment-ō\\ **1** river 615 kilometers long N California flowing S into Suisun Bay **2** city, capital of California

Sag·ue·nay \\'sag-ə-ˌnā, ˌsag-ə-'nā\\ river 200 kilometers long Canada in S Quebec flowing E into the Saint Lawrence

Sa·ha·ra \\sə-'har-ə, -'her-, -'här-\\ desert region N Africa N of Sudan region extending from Atlantic coast to Red sea or, as sometimes thought, to the Nile — **Sa·ha·ran** \\-ən\\ *adj*

Sa·hel \\'sa-hil, sə-'hil\\ the S fringe of the Sahara

Saigon — see HO CHI MINH CITY

Saint Al·bans \\-'ól-bənz\\ city area SE England in Hertfordshire

Saint Cath·a·rines \\-'kath-(ə-)rənz\\ city Canada in SE Ontario

---

\\ə\\abut \\ᵊ\\kitten \\ər\\further \\a\\ash \\ā\\ace \\ä\\mop, mar \\aù\\out \\ch\\chin \\e\\bet \\ē\\easy \\g\\go \\i\\hit \\ī\\ice \\j\\job \\ŋ\\sing \\ō\\go \\ò\\law \\òi\\boy \\th\\thin \\t̲h̲\\the \\ü\\loot \\ù\\foot \\y\\yet \\zh\\vision *see also* Pronunciation Symbols page

Saint Clair, Lake \\-ʼkla(ə)r, -ʼkle(ə)r\ lake SE Michigan & SE Ontario connected by **Saint Clair river** (64 kilometers long) with Lake Huron & draining by Detroit river into Lake Erie

Saint Croix \sānt-ʼkroi, sənt-\ **1** river 120 kilometers long Canada & U.S. on border between New Brunswick & Maine **2** island West Indies; largest of Virgin Islands of the U.S.

Saint Eli·as, Mount \-ˌsānt-ᵊl-ʼī-əs\ mountain 5489 meters on Alaska-Canada boundary in **Saint Elias range**

Saint George's \-ʼjȯr-jəz\ town, capital of Grenada

Saint George's Channel channel British Isles between SW Wales & Ireland

Saint Gott·hard \sānt-ʼgät-ərd, -ʼgäth-, sənt-\ **1** pass S central Switzerland in Saint Gotthard range of the Alps **2** tunnel 15 kilometers long near the pass

Saint He·le·na \ˌsānt-ᵊl-ʼē-nə, ˌsānt-hə-ʼlē-\ island S Atlantic; a British colony

Saint Hel·ens \sānt-ʼhel-ənz, sənt-\ city area NW England in Merseyside county ENE of Liverpool

Saint Helens, Mount volcano S Washington

Saint John \sānt-ʼjän, sənt-\ city Canada in New Brunswick

Saint Johns \sānt-ʼjänz, sənt-\ city, capital of Antigua and Barbuda

Saint John's \sānt-ʼjänz, sənt-\ city, capital of Newfoundland, Canada

Saint Kitts \sānt-ʼkits\ or **Saint Chris·to·pher** \-ʼkris-tə-fər\ island West Indies in the Leeward Islands; with Nevis forms independent **Saint Kitts-Nevis**; capital Basseterre (on Saint Kitts)

Saint Law·rence \sānt-ʼlȯr-ən(t)s, sənt-, -ʼlär-\ **1** river 1225 kilometers long E Canada in Ontario & Quebec bordering on U.S. in New York & flowing from Lake Ontario NE into the **Gulf of Saint Lawrence** (inlet of the Atlantic) **2** seaway Canada &U.S. in & along the Saint Lawrence between Lake Ontario & Montreal

Saint Lou·is \sānt-ʼlü-əs, sənt-\ city E Missouri on the Mississippi

Saint Lu·cia \sānt-ʼlü-shə, sənt-\ island West Indies in the Windwards S of Martinique; an independent country; capital, Castries

Saint Paul \-ʼpȯl\ city, capital of Minnesota

Saint Pe·ters·burg \-ʼpēt-ərz-ˌbərg\ **1** city W Florida **2** or 1914–24 **Pet·ro·grad** \ʼpe-trə-ˌgrad, -ˌgräd\ or 1924–91 **Le·nin·grad** \ʼlen-ən-ˌgrad, -ˌgräd\ city W Russia

Saint Thom·as \-ʼtäm-əs\ island West Indies, one of Virgin Islands of the U.S.; chief town, Charlotte Amalie

Saint Vin·cent \sānt-ʼvin(t)-sənt, sənt-\ island West Indies in the central Windward Islands; with N Grenadines forms independent **Saint Vincent and the Grenadines**; capital, Kingstown (on Saint Vincent)

Sai·pan \sī-ʼpan, -ʼpän; ʼsī-ˌpan, -ˌpän\ island W Pacific in S central Marianas

Sa·kai \(ʼ)sä-ʼki\ city Japanin S Honshu

Sa·kha·lin \ʼsak-ə-ˌlēn, -lən; ˌsak-ə-ʼlēn\ island SE Russia W Pacific N of Hokkaido, Japan; until 1945 divided between Japan & U.S.S.R.

Sal·a·mis \ʼsal-ə-məs\ **1** ancient city Cyprus on E coast **2** island Greece off Attica

Sa·lem \ʼsā-ləm\ city, capital of Oregon

Sal·ford \ʼsȯl-fərd\ city area NW England in Greater Manchester county

Salisbury — SEE HARARE

Sa·lo·ni·ka \sə-ʼlän-i-kə, ˌsal-ə-ʼnē-kə\ or **Thes·sa·lo·ni·ca** \ˌthes-ə-lə-ʼnī-kə, -ʼlän-i-kə\ city N Greece in Macedonia

Sal·op \ʼsal-əp\ or **Shrop·shire** \ʼshräp-ˌshi(ə)r, -shər\ county W England bordering on Wales

Salt Lake City city, capital of Utah

Sal·va·dor \ʼsal-və-ˌdȯ(ə)r, ˌsal-və-ʼdȯ(ə)r\ or **Ba·hia** \bä-ʼē-ə\ city NE Brazil on the Atlantic — **Sal·va·dor·an** \ˌsal-və-ʼdȯr-ən, -ʼdȯr-\ or **Sal·va·dor·ian** \-ē-ən\ adj or n

Sal·ween \ʼsal-ˌwēn\ river 2815 kilometers long SE Asia flowing S

Sa·mar \ʼsäm-ˌär\ island central Philippines

Sa·ma·ra \sə-ʼmär-ə\ or 1935–91 **Kuy·by·shev** \ʼkwē-bə-ˌshef, -ˌshev\ city W Russia, on the Volga

Sam·ni·um \ʼsam-nē-əm\ ancient country S central Italy — **Sam·nite** \ʼsam-ˌnīt\ adj or n

Sa·moa \sə-ʼmō-ə\ islands SW central Pacific N of Tonga islands; divided at longitude 171° W into American Samoa or Eastern Samoa & Western Samoa — **Sa·mo·an** \-ən\ adj or n

Sa·mos \ʼsā-ˌmäs\ island Greece in the Aegean off coast of Turkey — **Sa·mi·an** \-mē-ən\ adj or n

San·'a \ʼsan-ˌä, san-ʼä\ city SW Arabia, capital of Yemen & formerly of Yemen Arab Republic

San An·to·nio \ˌsan-ən-ʼtō-nē-ˌō\ city S Texas

San Ber·nar·di·no \ˌsan-bər-nə(r)-ʼdē-nō\ city S California

San Di·ego \ˌsan-dē-ʼā-gō\ city SW California

Sand·wich \ʼsan-(ˌ)(d)wich\ town SE England

Sandwich islands — see HAWAII

San Fran·cis·co \ˌsan-frən-ʼsis-kō\ city W California on San Francisco Bay & Pacific ocean

San Joa·quin \ˌsan-wä-ʼkēn, -wȯ-\ river 563 kilometers long central California flowing NW into the Sacramento

San Jo·se \ˌsan-ə-ʼzā\ city W California SE of San Francisco

San Jo·sé \ˌsan-ə-ʼzā, -ō-ʼzā, -hō-ʼzā\ city, capital of Costa Rica

San Juan \san-ʼhwän, -ʼwän\ city, capital of Puerto Rico

San Ma·ri·no \ˌsan-mə-ʼrē-nō\ **1** country S Europe on Italian peninsula ENE of Florence near Adriatic sea **2** town, its capital

San Sal·va·dor \san-ʼsal-və-ˌdȯ(ə)r\ **1** island central Bahama islands **2** city, capital of El Salvador

San·ta Ana \ˌsant-ə-ʼan-ə\ city SW California ESE of Long Beach

San·ta Bar·ba·ra \-ʼbär-b(ə-)rə\ or **Channel** islands California in the Pacific off SW coast

San·ta Fe \ˌsant-ə-ʼfā\ city, capital of New Mexico

Santa Fe Trail pioneer route to the Southwest 1290 kilometers long used especially 1821–80 from vicinity of Kansas City, Missouri, to Santa Fe, New Mexico

San·ti·a·go \ˌsant-ē-ʼäg-ō, ˌsänt-\ city, capital of Chile

San·to Do·min·go \ˌsant-əd-ə-ʼmiŋ-gō\ or formerly **Ci·u·dad Tru·ji·llo** \sē-ù-ˌthä-trü-ʼhē-(y)ō, ˌsē-ù-ˌdad-\ city, capital of Dominican Republic

São Pau·lo \ˌsä-ō-ʼpaù-lō\ city SE Brazil

São To·mé \ˌsä-ō-tō-ʼmā\ town, capital of Sao Tome and Principe

Sao Tome and Principe country W Africa; formerly a Portuguese colony; became independent 1975; capital São Tomé

Sap·po·ro \ʼsäp-ə-ˌrō; sə-ʼpōr-ō, -ʼpȯr-\ city Japan on W Hokkaido

Sa·ra·tov \sə-ʼrät-əf\ city W Russia, on the Volga

Sa·ra·wak \sə-ʼrä-(ˌ)wä(k), -ˌwak\ part of Malaysia in N Borneo

Sar·din·ia \sär-ʼdin-ē-ə, -ʼdin-yə\ island Italy in the Mediterranean S of Corsica — **Sar·din·ian** \-ʼdin-ē-ən, -ʼdin-yən\ adj or n

Sar·gas·so sea \sär-ˌgas-ō-\ area of nearly still water in the N Atlantic lying chiefly between 25°& 35° N latitude & 40°& 70° W longitude

Sas·katch·e·wan \sə-ʼskach-ə-wən, sa-, -ˌwän\ province W Canada; capital, Regina

Sas·ka·toon \ˌsas-kə-ʼtün\ city central Saskatchewan, Canada

Sau·di Ara·bia \ˌsaùd-ē-ə-ʼrä-bē-ə, ˌsȯd-ē-, sä-ˌüd-ē-\ country SW Asia occupying largest part of Arabian peninsula; a kingdom; capital, Riyadh — **Saudi** *adj or n* — **Saudi Arabian** *adj or n*

Sault Sainte Ma·rie canals \ˌsü-(ˌ)sänt-mə-ˈrē-\ *or* **Soo canals** \ˌsü-\ three ship canals, two in U.S. (Michigan) & one in Canada (Ontario), at rapids in river connecting Lake Superior & Lake Huron

Sa·vaii \sə-ˈvī-ˌē\ island, largest in Western Samoa

Sa·van·nah \sə-ˈvan-ə\ city E Georgia

Sa·voy \sə-ˈvȯi\ *or French* **Sa·voie** \sȧ-vwȧ\ region SE France SW of Switzerland bordering on Italy — **Sa·voy·ard** \sə-ˈvȯi-ˌärd, ˌsav-ˌȯi-ˈärd; ˌsav-wä-ˈyär(d)\ *adj or n*

Sca·fell Pike \ˈskȯ-ˈfel-\ mountain 978 meters NW England in Cumbria county; highest in Cumbrian mountains & in England

Scan·di·na·via \ˌskan-də-ˈnā-vē-ə, -vyə\ **1** peninsula N Europe occupied by Norway & Sweden **2** Denmark, Norway, Sweden, & sometimes also Iceland & Finland — **Scan·di·na·vian** \-vē-ən, -vyən\ *adj or n*

Scar·bor·ough \ˈskär-ˌbər-ə, -b(ə-)rə\ city Canada in SE Ontario near Toronto

Scheldt \ˈskelt\ *or* **Schel·de** \ˈskel-də\ *or ancient* **Scaldis** \ˈskal-dəs\ river 435 kilometers long W Europe flowing from N France through Belgium into North sea in Netherlands

Scil·ly \ˈsil-ē\ islands SW England off Land's End in Cornwall and Isles of Scilly county

Sco·tia \ˈskō-shə\ SCOTLAND — the Medieval Latin name

Scot·land \ˈskät-lənd\ *or Latin* **Cal·e·do·nia** \ˌkal-ə-ˈdō-nyə, -nē-ə\ country N Great Britain; a division of United Kingdom of Great Britain and Northern Ireland; capital, Edinburgh

Scyth·ia \ˈsith-ē-ə, ˈsith-\ ancient area of Europe & Asia N & NE of Black sea & E of Aral sea — **Scyth·i·an** \-ē-ən\ *adj or n*

Se·at·tle \sē-ˈat-ᵊl\ city W Washington

Seine \ˈsān, ˈsen\ river 773 kilometers long N France flowing NW into English channel

Sel·kirk \ˈsel-ˌkərk\ range of the Rocky mountains SE British Columbia, Canada; highest peak, Mount Sir Donald 3390 meters

Se·ma·rang \sə-ˈmär-ˌäŋ\ city Indonesia in central Java

Sen·dai \(ˈ)sen-ˈdī\ city Japan in NE Honshu

Sen·e·ca Falls \ˈsen-i-kə-\ village W central New York

Sen·e·gal \ˌsen-i-ˈgȯl\ **1** river 1690 kilometers long W Africa flowing W into the Atlantic **2** country W Africa; capital, Dakar — **Sen·e·ga·lese** \ˌsen-i-gə-ˈlēz, -ˈlēs\ *adj or n*

Seoul \ˈsōl\ city, capital of South Korea

Ser·bia \ˈsər-bē-ə\ region in the Balkans comprising the largest part of Yugoslavia

Ser·en·ge·ti Plain \ˌser-ən-ˈget-ē\ area N Tanzania

Seven Hills the seven hills upon and about which was built the city of Rome

Sev·ern \ˈsev-ərn\ river 338 kilometers long Wales & England flowing from E central Wales into Bristol channel

Se·ville \sə-ˈvil\ *or Spanish* **Se·vi·lla** \sā-ˈvē-(y)ä\ city SW Spain

Sey·chelles \sā-ˈshel(z)\ islands W Indian ocean NE of Madagascar; formerly a British colony; became independent 1976; capital, Victoria

Shang·hai \shaŋ-ˈhī\ city E China

Shan·non \ˈshan-ən\ river 386 kilometers long W Ireland flowing S & W into the Atlantic

Shas·ta, Mount \-ˈshas-tə\ mountain 4317 meters N California in Cascade Range

Shatt–al–Ar·ab \ˌshat-ˌal-ˈar-əb\ river 193 kilometers long SE Iraq formed by flowing together of Euphrates & Tigris rivers & flowing SE into Persian gulf

Shef·field \ˈshef-ˌēld\ city N England in South Yorkshire

Shen·an·do·ah Valley \ˌshen-ən-ˈdō-ə-, ˌshan-ə-ˈdō-ə-\

valley Virginia between the Allegheney & Blue Ridge mountains

Shen·yang \ˈshən-ˈyäŋ\ *or* **Muk·den** \ˈmuk-dən, ˈmək-; ˌmuk-ˈden\ city NE China; chief city of Manchuria

Sher·brooke \ˈshər-ˌbrük\ city Quebec, Canada E of Montreal

Sher·wood Forest \ˌshər-ˌwud-\ ancient royal forest central England chiefly in Nottinghamshire

Shet·land \ˈshet-lənd\ **1** islands N Scotland NE of the Orkneys **2** *or* **Zet·land** \ˈzet-\ region consisting of the Shetland islands

Shi·jia·zhuang *or* **Shih·kia·chwang** \ˈshi(ə)r-jē-ˈäj-ˈwäŋ, ˈshē-jē-\ city NE China

Shi·ko·ku \shi-ˈkō-kü\ island S Japan E of Kyushu

Shreve·port \ˈshrēv-ˌpō(ə)rt, -ˌpȯ(ə)rt\ city NW Louisiana

Shrews·bury \ˈsh(r)üz-ˌber-ē, ˈshrōz-\ city area W England in Salop county

Shropshire — see SALOP

Siam — see THAILAND

Siam, Gulf of *or* **Gulf of Thailand** arm of South China sea between Indochina and Malay peninsula

Sian — see XI'AN

Si·be·ria \sī-ˈbir-ē-ə\ region N Asia in Russia between the Urals & the Pacific — **Si·be·ri·an** \-ē-ən\ *adj or n*

Sic·i·ly \ˈsis-(ə-)lē\ *or Italian* **Si·ci·lia** \sē-ˈchēl-yä\ island S Italy SW of toe of Italian peninsula; capital, Palermo — **Si·cil·ian** \sə-ˈsil-yən\ *adj or n*

Si·er·ra Le·one \sē-ˌer-ə-lē-ˈōn, ˌsir-ə-\ country W Africa on the Atlantic; capital, Freetown — **Si·er·ra Le·on·ean** \-ˈō-nē-ən\ *adj or n*

Si·er·ra Ma·dre \sē-ˌer-ə-ˈmäd-rē\ mountain system Mexico including **Sierra Madre Oc·ci·den·tal** \-ˌäk-sə-ˌden-ˈtäl\ range W of the central plateau, **Sierra Madre Ori·en·tal** \-ˌȯr-ē-ˌen-ˈtäl, -ˌȯr-\ range E of the plateau, & **Sierra del Sur** \sē-ˌer-ə-ˌdel-ˈsù(ə)r\ range to the S

Sierra Ne·va·da \-nə-ˈvad-ə, -ˈväd-\ **1** mountain range E California & W Nevada — see WHITNEY, MOUNT **2** mountain range S Spain; highest peak Mulhacén 3477 meters, highest in Spain

Sik·kim \ˈsik-əm, -ˌim\ former country SE Asia on S slope of the Himalayas between Nepal & Bhutan; part of India (country) since 1975; capital, Gangtok

Si·le·sia \sī-ˈlē-zh(ē-)ə, -sh(ē-)ə, sə-\ region E central Europe in valley of the upper Oder; formerly chiefly in Germany now chiefly in E Czech Republic & SW Poland — **Si·le·sian** \-zh(ē-)ən, -sh(ē-)ən\ *adj or n*

Sim·coe, Lake \-ˈsim-kō\ lake Canada in SE Ontario

Si·nai \ˈsī-ˌnī\ **1** mountain on Sinai peninsula where according to the Bible the Law was given to Moses **2** peninsula extension of continent of Asia NE Egypt between Red sea & the Mediterranean

Sin·ga·pore \ˈsiŋ-(g)ə-ˌpō(ə)r, -ˌpȯ(ə)r\ **1** island off S end of Malay peninsula; an independent country in the Commonwealth **2** city, its capital — **Sin·ga·por·ean** \ˌsiŋ-(g)ə-ˈpōr-ē-ən, -ˈpȯr-\ *adj or n*

Sinkiang Uighur — see XINJIANG UYGUR

Sioux Falls \ˈsü-\ city SE South Dakota; largest in state

Skag·ge·rak \ˈskag-ə-ˌrak\ arm of North sea between S Norway & N Denmark

Skag·way \ˈskag-wā\ city SE Alaska

Sla·vo·nia \slə-ˈvō-nē-ə, -nyə\ region E Croatia — **Sla·vo·ni·an** \-nē-ən, -nyən\ *adj or n*

Slo·va·kia \slō-ˈväk-ē-ə, -ˈvak-\ country central Europe; capital, Bratislava; formerly part of Czechoslovakia

Slo·ve·nia \slō-ˈvē-nē-ə, -nyə\ country S Europe; capital, Ljubljana; a republic of Yugoslavia 1946–91

Smyrna — see IZMIR

\ə\abut \ᵊ\kitten \ər\further \a\ash \ā\ace \ä\mop, mar
\aù\out \ch\chin \e\bet \ē\easy \g\go \i\hit \ī\ice \j\job
\ŋ\sing \ō\go \ȯ\law \ȯi\boy \th\thin \t͟h\the \ü\loot \ù\foot
\y\yet \zh\vision *see also* Pronunciation Symbols page

Snake \\'snāk\ river NW U.S. flowing from NW Wyoming into the Columbia in SE Washington

Snow·don \\'snōd-ᵊn\ massif 1085 meters NW Wales; highest point in Wales

Snow·do·nia \snō-'dō-nē-ə, -nyə\ mountainous district NW Wales in area around Snowdon

So·ci·e·ty \sə-'sī-ət-ē\ islands S Pacific; belong to France; chief island, Tahiti

So·fia \\'sō-fē-ə, 'sò-, sō-'fē-\ city, capital of Bulgaria

So·ho \\'sō-ˌhō\ district of central London, England, in Westminster

So·li·hull \ˌsō-li-'həl\ city area central England in West Midlands county

Sol·o·mon \\'säl-ə-mən\ **1** islands W Pacific E of New Guinea divided between Papua New Guinea & independent Solomon Islands (capital, Honiara) **2** sea arm of Coral sea W of the Solomons

So·ma·lia \sō-'mäl-ē-ə, sə-, -'mäl-yə\ country E Africa on Gulf of Aden & Indian ocean; capital, Mogadishu — **So·ma·li·an** \-'mäl-ē-ən, -'mäl-yən\ adj or n

So·ma·li·land \sō-'mäl-ē-ˌland, sə-\ region E Africa consisting of Somalia, Djibouti, & part of E Ethiopia — **So·ma·li** \sō-'mäl-ē\ n

Som·er·set \\'səm-ər-ˌset, -sət\ or **Som·er·set·shire** \-ˌshi(ə)r, -shər\ county SW England

So·nor·an \sə-'nōr-ən, -'nòr-\ or **Sonora** desert SW U.S. & NW Mexico

Soo canals — see SAULT SAINTE MARIE CANALS

South island S New Zealand

South Africa, Republic of country S Africa; formerly (as **Union of South Africa**) a British dominion; became independent 1961; administrative capital, Pretoria; legislative capital, Cape Town; judicial capital, Bloemfontein — **South African** adj or n

South America continent of western hemisphere SE of North America & chiefly S of the equator — **South American** adj or n

South·amp·ton \saùth-'(h)am(p)-tən\ city S England in Hampshire

South Australia state S Australia; capital, Adelaide — **South Australian** adj or n

South Bend \-'bend\ city N Indiana

South Cape or **South Point** — see KA LAE

South Car·o·li·na \-ˌkar-ə-'lī-nə\ state SE U.S.; capital, Columbia — **South Car·o·lin·i·an** \-'lin-ē-ən, -'lin-yən\ adj or n

South China sea — see CHINA

South Da·ko·ta \-də-'kōt-ə\ state NW central U.S.; capital, Pierre — **South Da·ko·tan** \-'kōt-ᵊn\ adj or n

South·end on Sea \ˌsaù-ˌthend-\ city area SE England in Essex county E of London

Southern Alps mountain range New Zealand in W South island extending almost the length of the island

Southern Rhodesia — see ZIMBABWE

South Gla·mor·gan \-glə-'mòr-gən\ county SE Wales; established 1974; includes Cardiff

South Korea — see KOREA

South seas the areas of the Atlantic, Indian, & Pacific oceans in the southern hemisphere

South Shields \-'shē(ə)l(d)z\ city N England in Tyne and Wear county

South Vietnam — see VIETNAM

South·wark \\'səth-ərk, 'saùth-wərk\ city area of S Greater London county, England

South–West Africa territory SW Africa; under administration of Union (later Republic) of South Africa 1919–90 — see NAMIBIA

South Yorkshire county N England; includes Barnsley

Soviet Central Asia portion of central & SW Asia formerly belonging to U.S.S.R. & including Kirghiz Soviet Socialist Republic, Tadzhik Soviet Socialist Republic, Turkmen Soviet Socialist Republic, Uzbek Soviet Socialist Republic & sometimes Kazakhstan

Soviet Russia 1 — see RUSSIA **2** — see UNION OF SOVIET SOCIALIST REPUBLICS

Soviet Union — see UNION OF SOVIET SOCIALIST REPUBLICS

Spain \\'spān\ country SW Europe in Iberian peninsula; a kingdom; capital, Madrid

Spanish America 1 the Spanish-speaking countries of America **2** the parts of America settled & formerly governed by the Spanish

Spanish Guinea — see EQUATORIAL GUINEA

Spanish Sahara — see WESTERN SAHARA

Spar·ta \\'spärt-ə\ or **Lac·e·dae·mon** \ˌlas-ə-'dē-mən\ ancient city S Greece in Peloponnisos; capital of Laconia

Spo·kane \spō-'kan\ city E Washington

Spring·field \\'spriŋ-ˌfēld\ **1** city, capital of Illinois **2** city SW Massachusetts **3** city SW Missouri

Sri Lan·ka \(')srē-'läŋ-kə, (')shrē-\ or formerly **Cey·lon** \si-'län, sā-\ country having the same boundaries as island of Ceylon; an independent state in the Commonwealth; capital, Colombo

Sri·na·gar \sri-'nəg-ər\ city N India

Staked Plain — see LLANO ESTACADO

Staf·ford \\'staf-ərd\ city area W central England in Staffordshire

Staf·ford·shire \\'staf-ərd-ˌshi(ə)r, -shər\ or **Stafford** county W central England

Stam·ford \\'stam(p)-fərd\ city SW Connecticut

Stan·ley \\'stan-lē\ town, capital of Falkland islands

Stat·en Island \ˌstat-ᵊn-\ **1** island SE New York SW of mouth of the Hudson **2** or formerly **Rich·mond** \\'rich-mənd\ section of New York City including Staten Island

Sterling Heights city SE Michigan

Stir·ling \\'stər-liŋ\ town central Scotland in Central region

Stock·holm \\'stäk-ˌhō(l)m\ city, capital of Sweden

Stock·port \\'stäk-ˌpō(ə)rt, -ˌpò(ə)rt\ city area NW England in Greater Manchester county

Stock·ton \\'stäk-tən\ city central California

Stoke on Trent \ˌstō-ˌkòn-'trent, -ˌkän-\ city central England in Staffordshire

Stone Mountain mountain 514 meters NW Georgia E of Atlanta

Stor·no·way \\'stòr-nə-ˌwā\ town NW Scotland in Western Isles region

Stra·bane \strə-'ban\ district W Northern Ireland

Strath·clyde \strath-'klīd\ region SW Scotland; established 1975; includes Glasgow

Strom·bo·li \\'sträm-bə-lē\ volcano 927 meters Italy on Stromboli Island

Stutt·gart \\'shtùt-ˌgärt, 'stùt-, 'stət-\ city SW Germany

Styx \\'stiks\ chief river of the underworld in Greek mythology

Süchow — see XUZHOU

Su·cre \\'sü-krā\ city, constitutional capital of Bolivia

Su·dan \sü-'dan, -'dän\ **1** region N Africa S of the Sahara between the Atlantic & the upper Nile **2** country NE Africa S of Egypt; capital, Khartoum — **Su·da·nese** \ˌsüd-ᵊn-'ēz, -'ēs\ adj or n

Sud·bury \\'səd-ˌber-ē, -b(ə-)rē\ city SE Ontario, Canada

Su·ez \sü-'ez, 'sü-ˌez\ canal 148 kilometers long NE Egypt across Isthmus of Suez

Suez, Gulf of arm of Red sea

Suez, Isthmus of isthmus NE Egypt between Mediterranean & Red seas connecting Africa & Asia

Suf·folk \\'səf-ək\ county E England on North sea

Sui·sun Bay \sə-'sün-\ inlet of San Francisco Bay, W central California

Su·la·we·si \ˌsü-lə-'wā-sē\ or **Ce·le·bes** \\'sel-ə-ˌbēz, sə-'lē-bēz\ island Indonesia E of Borneo

Su·lu \\'sü-lü\ **1** island group SW Philippines SW of Mindanao **2** sea W Philippines

Su·ma·tra \sù-ˈmä-trə\ island W Indonesia S of Malay peninsula — **Su·ma·tran** \-trən\ *adj or n*

Su·mer \ˈsü-mər\ the S division of ancient Babylonia — **Su·me·ri·an** \sü-ˈmer-ē-ən, -ˈmir-\ *adj or n*

Sun·da \ˈsün-də\ strait between Java & Sumatra

Sun·der·land \ˈsən-dər-lənd\ city area N England in Tyne and Wear county

Sun·ny·vale \ˈsən-ē-ˌvāl\ city W California

Sun Valley resort center central Idaho

Su·pe·ri·or, Lake \-sù-ˈpir-ē-ər\ lake E central North America in U.S. & Canada; largest of the Great Lakes

Su·ra·ba·ja \ˌsùr-ə-ˈbī-ə\ city Indonesia in NE Java

Su·ri·na·me \ˌsùr-ə-ˈnäm-ə\ or **Su·ri·nam** \ˈsùr-ə-ˌnam, ˌsùr-ə-ˈnäm\ country N South America between Guyana & French Guiana; formerly a territory of the Netherlands; became independent 1975; capital, Paramaribo

Sur·rey \ˈsər-ē, ˈsə-rē\ **1** county SE England SW of London **2** city Canada in SW British Columbia

Sut·ton \ˈsət-ᵊn\ city area of S Greater London county, England

Su·va \ˈsü-və\ city, capital of Fiji on Viti Levu island

Sverdlovsk — se YEKATERINBURG

Swan·sea \ˈswän-zē\ city SE Wales in West Glamorgan county

Swa·zi·land \ˈswäz-ē-ˌland\ country SE Africa between Transvaal & Mozambique; an independent kingdom; capital, Mbabane — **Swa·zi** \ˈswäz-ē\ *adj or n*

Swe·den \ˈswēd-ᵊn\ country N Europe on Scandinavian peninsula bordering on Baltic sea; a kingdom; capital, Stockholm

Swit·zer·land \ˈswit-sər-lənd\ country W Europe in the Alps; capital, Bern

Syd·ney \ˈsid-nē\ city SE Australia, capital of New South Wales

Syr·a·cuse \ˈsir-ə-ˌkyüs, -ˌkyüz\ city central New York

Syr·ia \ˈsir-ē-ə\ **1** ancient region SW Asia bordering on the Mediterranean **2** former area under administration of France (1920–44) including present Syria & Lebanon **3** country S of Turkey; capital, Damascus — **Syr·i·an** \ˈsir-ē-ən\ *adj or n*

Syrian Desert desert region between Mediterranean coast & the Euphrates in N Saudi Arabia, SE Syria, W Iraq, & NE Jordan

Ta·ble Bay harbor of Cape Town, Republic of South Africa

Ta·briz \tə-ˈbrēz\ city NW Iran

Ta·co·ma \tə-ˈkō-mə\ city W Washington

Tae·gu \ta-ˈgü, tī-\ city South Korea NNW of Pusan

Tae·jon \ta-ˈjön, tī-\ city South Korea NW of Taegu

Ta·gus \ˈtā-gəs\ or *Spanish* **Ta·jo** \ˈtä-hō\ or *Portuguese* **Te·jo** \ˈtä-zhü\ river 911 kilometers long Spain & Portugal flowing W into the Atlantic

Ta·hi·ti \tə-ˈhēt-ē\ island S Pacific in Society islands — **Ta·hi·tian** \-ˈhē-shən\ *adj or n*

Tai·chung \ˈtī-ˈchùŋ\ city China in W Taiwan

Tai·nan \ˈtī-ˈnän\ city China in SW Taiwan

Tai·pei \ˈtī-ˈpā, -ˈbā\ or *formerly* **Tai·ho·ku** \ˈtī-ˈhō-ˌkü\ city, capital of (Nationalist) China in N Taiwan

Tai·wan \ˈtī-ˈwän\ or **For·mo·sa** \fòr-ˈmō-sə, fər-, -zə\ **1** island China off SE coast; since 1949 seat of government of (Nationalist) Republic of China; capital, Taipei **2** strait between Taiwan & main part of China connecting East China & South China seas — **Tai·wan·ese** \ˌtī-wə-ˈnēz, -ˈnēs\ *adj or n*

Tai·yuan \ˈtī-yü-ˈän\ city N China

Ta·jik·i·stan \tä-ˌjik-i-ˈstan, -ˈstän, -ˌjik-i-ˌ, -ˈjēk-\ country W central Asia bordering on China & Afghanistan; capital, Dushanbe; a republic (**Ta·dzhik Soviet Socialist Republic** \tä-ˈjik-, -ˈjēk-\ or **Ta·dzhik·i·stan** *same as* TAJIKISTAN\) of U.S.S.R. 1929–91

Ta·kli·ma·kan or **Ta·kla Ma·kan** \ˌtäk-lə-mə-ˈkän\ desert W China

Tal·la·has·see \ˌtal-ə-ˈhas-ē\ city, capital of Florida

Tal·linn \ˈtal-ən, ˈtäl-\ city, capital of Estonia

Tam·pa \ˈtam-pə\ city W Florida on Tampa Bay

Tan·gan·yi·ka \ˌtan-gən-ˈyē-kə, ˌtaŋ-gən-, -gə-ˈnē-\ former country E Africa S of Kenya; became part of Tanzania 1964

Tanganyika, Lake lake E Africa between Tanzania & Zaire

Tang·shan \ˈdäŋ-ˈshän, ˈtäŋ-\ city NE China

Tan·za·nia \ˌtan-zə-ˈnē-ə, ˌtän-\ country E Africa on Indian ocean; formed 1964 by union of Tanganyika & Zanzibar; capital, Dar es Salaam — **Tan·za·ni·an** \-ˈnē-ən\ *adj or n*

Ta·ra·wa \tə-ˈrä-wə, ˈtar-ə-ˌwä\ island central Pacific, capital of Kiribati

Tar·lac \ˈtär-ˌläk\ city Philippines in central Luzon

Tar·ry·town \ˈtar-ē-ˌtaùn\ village SE New York

Tar·sus \ˈtär-səs\ ancient city of S Asia Minor; now a city in S Turkey

Tash·kent \tash-ˈkent\ city, capital of Uzbekistan

Tas·man \ˈtaz-mən\ sea consisting of the part of the S Pacific between SE Australia & New Zealand

Tas·ma·nia \taz-ˈmā-nē-ə, -nyə\ or *earlier* **Van Diemen's Land** \van-ˈdē-mənz-\ island SE Australia S of Victoria; a state; capital, Hobart — **Tas·ma·nian** \-nē-ən, -nyən\ *adj or n*

Ta·try \ˈtä-trē\ or **Ta·tra** \ˈtä-trə\ mountains N Slovakia & S Poland in central Carpathian mountains

Taun·ton \ˈtònt-ᵊn, ˈtänt-, ˈtant-\ city area SW England in Somerset county

Tay·side \ˈtā-ˌsīd\ region E central Scotland; established 1975

Tbi·li·si \tə-ˈbil-ə-sē\ or **Tif·lis** \ˈtif-ləs, tə-ˈflēs\ city, capital of Republic of Georgia

Te·gu·ci·gal·pa \tə-ˌgü-sə-ˈgal-pə\ city, capital of Honduras

Teh·ran \ˌtā-ˈran, -ˈrän\ city, capital of Iran; at foot of S slope of Elburz mountains

Tel Aviv \ˌtel-ə-ˈvēv\ city W Israel

Tem·pe \tem-ˈpē\ city S central Arizona

Ten·nes·see \ˌten-ə-ˈsē, ˈten-ə-ˌsē\ **1** river 1049 kilometers long in Tennessee, N Alabama, & W Kentucky **2** state E central U.S.; capital, Nashville

Te·noch·ti·tlan \tā-ˌnòch-tē-ˈtlän\ ancient name of Mexico City

Tex·as \ˈtek-səs, -siz\ state S U.S.; capital, Austin — **Tex·an** \-sən\ *adj or n*

Thai·land \ˈtī-ˌland, -lənd\ or *formerly* **Si·am** \sī-ˈam\ country SE Asia on Gulf of Siam; capital, Bangkok — **Thai·land·er** \ˈtī-ˌlan-dər, -lən-dər\ *n*

Thames \ˈtemz\ river 338 kilometers long S England flowing E from the Cotswolds in Gloucestershire into the North sea

Thar \ˈtär\ desert E Pakistan & NW India (country) E of Indus river

Thebes \ˈthēbz\ **1** or *ancient* **The·bae** \ˈthē-bē\ ancient city S Egypt on the Nile **2** ancient city E Greece NNW of Athens on site of modern village of Thivai — **Theban** \ˈthē-bən\ *adj or n*

Thes·sa·lo·ni·ca \ˌthes-ə-lə-ˈnī-kə, -ˈlän-i-kə\ — see SALONIKA — **Thes·sa·lo·nian** \-ˈlō-nē-ən, -ˈlō-nyən\ *adj or n*

Thim·bu \ˈthim-bü\ city, capital of Bhutan

Thousand islands Canada & U.S. in the Saint Lawrence in Ontario & New York

Thrace \ˈthrās\ or *ancient* **Thra·cia** \ˈthrā-sh(ē-)ə\ region SE Europe in Balkan peninsula N of the Aegean now divided between Greece & Turkey; in ancient

---

\ə\abut \ᵊ\kitten \ər\further \a\ash \ā\ace \ä\mop, mar \aù\out \ch\chin \e\bet \ē\easy \g\go \i\hit \ī\ice \j\job \ŋ\sing \ō\go \ò\law \òi\boy \th\thin \th\the \ü\loot \ù\foot \y\yet \zh\vision *see also* Pronunciation Symbols page

times extended N to the Danube — **Thra·cian** \\'thrā-shən\ *adj or n*

Three Rivers *or* **Trois–Ri·vieres** \\t(r)wä-riv-'ye(ə)r\ city S Quebec, Canada

Thunder Bay city SW Ontario, Canada

Thur·rock \\'thər-ək, 'thə-rək\ district SE England in Essex county

Tian·jin \tē-'än-'jin\ *or* **Tien·tsin** \tē-'en(t)-'sin\ city NE China SE of Beijing

Tian Shan *or* **Tien Shan** \tē-'en-'shän, tē-'än-\ mountain system central Asia extending NE from Pamirs

Ti·ber \\'tī-bər\ *or Italian* **Te·ve·re** \\'tā-vā-rā\ *or ancient* **Ti·ber·is** \\'tī-bə-rəs\ river 360 kilometers long central Italy flowing through Rome into Tyrrhenian sea

Ti·bes·ti \tə-'bes-tē\ mountains N central Africa in central Sahara in NW Chad; highest 3415 meters

Ti·bet \tə-'bet\ region SW China on high plateau (average altitude 4875 meters) N of the Himalayas; capital, Lhasa

Tier·ra del Fue·go \tē-'er-ə-₁del-f(y)ù-'ā-gō\ **1** island group off S South America **2** chief island of the group; divided between Argentina & Chile

Tiflis — see TBILISI

Ti·gris \\'tī-grəs\ river 1850 kilometers long Turkey & Iraq flowing SSE & uniting with the Euphrates to form the Shatt-al-Arab

Ti·mor \\'tē-₁mò(ə)r, tē-'mò(ə)r\ island Indonesia SE of Sulawesi; W half formerly belonged to Netherlands, E half to Portugal

Ti·ra·ne *or* **Ti·ra·na** \ti-'rän-ə\ city, capital of Albania

Ti·rol *or* **Ty·rol** \tə-'rōl; 'tī-₁rōl, tī-'rōl; 'tir-əl\ *or Italian* **Ti·ro·lo** \tē-'rò-lō\ region in E Alps in W Austria & NE Italy — **Ti·ro·le·an** \tə-'rō-lē-ən, tī-; ₁tir-ə-'lē-, ₁tī-rə-'lē-\ *or* **Tir·o·lese** \₁tir-ə-'lēz, ₁tī-rə-, -'lēs\ *adj or n*

Ti·ti·ca·ca, Lake \-₁tit-i-'käk-ə\ lake on Bolivia-Peru boundary at altitude of 3810 meters

To·ba·go \tə-'bā-gō\ island West Indies NE of Trinidad; part of independent Trinidad and Tobago

To·go \\'tō-gō\ country W Africa on Gulf of Guinea; capital, Lomé — **To·go·lese** \₁tō-gə-'lēz, -'lēs\ *adj or n*

To·kyo \\'tō-kē-₁ō\ city, capital of Japan in SE Honshu on Tokyo Bay — **To·kyo·ite** \\'tō-kē-(₁)ō-₁īt\ *n*

To·le·do \tə-'lēd-ō, -'lēd-ə\ city NW Ohio

Tol'·yat·ti \tól-'yät-ē\ city W Russia; NW of Samara

Ton·ga \\'täŋ-(g)ə\ islands SW Pacific E of Fiji islands; a kingdom in the Commonwealth; capital, Nukualofa — **Ton·gan** \-(g)ən\ *adj or n*

To·pe·ka \tə-'pē-kə\ city, capital of Kansas

Tor·bay \(')tòr-'bā\ town SW England in Devon county

To·ron·to \tə-'ränt-ō, -'ränt-ə\ city, capital of Ontario, Canada

Tor·rance \\'tòr-ən(t)s, 'tär-\ city SW California

Tor·res \\'tòr-əs\ strait between New Guinea & Cape York peninsula, Australia

Tower Hamlets city area of E Greater London county, England

To·yo·na·ka \₁tòi-ə-'näk-ə\ city Japan on Honshu; a suburb of Osaka

Trans·vaal \tran(t)s-'väl, tranz-\ province NE Republic of South Africa; capital, Pretoria

Tran·syl·va·nia \₁tran(t)s-əl-'vā-nyə, -nē-ə\ region W Romania — **Tran·syl·va·nian** \-nyən, -nē-ən\ *adj or n*

Transylvanian Alps a S extension of Carpathian mountains in central Romania

Tren·ton \\'trent-ᵊn\ city, capital of New Jersey

Trin·i·dad \\'trin-ə-₁dad\ island West Indies off NE coast of Venezuela; with Tobago forms (since 1962) the independent country of **Trinidad and Tobago**; capital, Port of Spain — **Trin·i·da·di·an** \₁trin-ə-'dād-ē-ən, -'dad-\ *adj or n*

Trip·o·li \\'trip-ə-lē\ city, capital of Libya

Tris·tan da Cu·nha \₁tris-tən-də-'kü-nə, -nyə\ island S Atlantic, chief of the Tristan da Cunha islands belonging to British colony of Saint Helena

Tri·van·drum \triv-'an-drəm\ city S India

Tro·bri·and \\'trō-brē-₁änd\ islands SW Pacific in Solomon sea belonging to Papua New Guinea

Trois–Rivieres — see THREE RIVERS

Trow·bridge \\'trō-(₁)brij\ town S England in Wiltshire

Troy \\'tròi\ *or* **Il·i·um** \\'il-ē-əm\ *or* **Il·i·on** \\'il-ē-₁än, -ē-ən\ *or ancient* **Troia** \\'tròi-ə, 'trō-yə\ *or* **Tro·ja** \\'trō-jə, -yə\ ancient city NW Asia Minor SW of the Dardanelles

Truk \\'trək, 'trùk\ islands W Pacific in central Carolines

Tru·ro \\'trù(ə)r-ō\ city SW England in Cornwall and Isles of Scilly county

Trust Territory of the Pacific Islands — see PACIFIC ISLANDS, TRUST TERRITORY OF THE

Tsinan — see JINAN

Tsingtao — see QINGDAO

Tuc·son \\'tü-₁sän, tü-'sän\ city SE Arizona

Tu·la \\'tü-lə\ city W Russia S of Moscow

Tul·sa \\'təl-sə\ city NE Oklahoma

Tu·nis \\'t(y)ü-nəs\ city, capital of Tunisia

Tu·ni·sia \t(y)ü-'nē-zh(ē-)ə, -'nizh-(ē-)ə\ country N Africa on the Mediterranean E of Algeria; capital, Tunis — **Tu·ni·sian** \-'nē-zh(ē-)ən, -'nizh-(ē-)ən\ *adj or n*

Tu·rin \\'t(y)ùr-ən, t(y)ù-'rin\ city NW Italy on the Po

Tur·key \\'tər-kē\ country W Asia & SE Europe between Mediterranean & Black seas; capital, Ankara

Turk·men·i·stan \(₁)tərk-₁men-ə-'stan, -'stän; -'mcn-ə-₁\ country central Asia; capital, Ashkhabad; a republic (**Turk·men Soviet Socialist Republic** \\'tərk-mən-\) of U.S.S.R. 1925–91 — **Turk·me·ni·an** \₁tərk-'mē-nē-ən\ *adj*

Turks and Cai·cos \₁tərk-sən-'kā-kəs\ two groups of islands West Indies at SE end of the Bahamas; a British colony

Tu·tu·ila \₁tüt-ə-'wē-lə\ island S Pacific, chief of American Samoa group

Tu·va·lu \tü-'väl-ü, -'vär-\ *or formerly* **El·lice** \\'el-əs\ islands W Pacific N of Fiji; an independent country in the Commonwealth; capital, Funafuti — see GILBERT AND ELLICE ISLANDS

Tyne and Wear \\'tī-nən-'(d)wi(ə)r\ county N England; includes Newcastle

Tyre \\'tī(ə)r\ ancient city, capital of Phoenicia; now a town of S Lebanon — **Tyr·i·an** \\'tir-ē-ən\ *adj or n*

Tyrol — see TIROL — **Tyrolean** *adj or n* — **Tyrolese** *adj or n*

Tyr·rhe·ni·an \tə-'rē-nē-ən\ sea, part of the Mediterranean SW of Italy, N of Sicily, & E of Sardinia & Corsica

Ufa \ü-'fä\ city W Russia NE of Samara

Ugan·da \yü-'gan-də, -'gän-, -'gän-\ country E Africa N of Lake Victoria; an independent state in the Commonwealth; capital, Kampala — **Ugan·dan** \-dən\ *adj or n*

Ukraine \yü-'krān, 'yü-₁krān\ *or* **the Ukraine** country E Europe on N coast of Black sea; capital, Kiev; a republic of U.S.S.R. 1923–91

Ulan Ba·tor \ü-₁län-'bä-₁tò(ə)r\ city, capital of Mongolia

Ul·ster \\'əl-stər\ **1** region N Ireland (island) consisting of Northern Ireland & N Ireland (country) **2** province N Ireland (country) **3** NORTHERN IRELAND

Um·bria \\'əm-brē-ə\ region central Italy in the Apennines

Un·ga·va \₁ən-'gav-ə\ **1** bay inlet of Hudson strait NE Canada **2** peninsula region NE Canada in N Quebec

Union of South Africa — see SOUTH AFRICA, REPUBLIC OF

Union of Soviet Socialist Republics *or* **Soviet Union** *or* **Soviet Russia** country 1922–91 E Europe & N Asia; a union of 15 now independent republics; capital, Moscow

United Arab Emir·ates \-i-'mi(ə)r-əts, -₁āts\ country E Arabia on Persian Gulf; composed of seven emirates; capital, Abu Dhabi

United Kingdom *or in full* **United Kingdom of Great Britain and Northern Ireland** country W Europe in British Isles consisting of England, Scotland, Wales, Northern Ireland, Channel islands, & Isle of Man; capital, London

United Nations international territory; a small area in New York City in E central Manhattan; seat of permanent headquarters of the United Nations

United States of America *or* **United States** country North America bordering on Atlantic, Pacific, & Arctic oceans & including Hawaii; capital, Washington

Upper Volta — see BURKINA FASO — **Upper Vol·tan** \-ˈvält-ᵊn, -ˈvōlt-, -ˈvȯlt-\ *adj or n*

Ural \ˈyu̇r-əl\ **1** mountains Russia & Kazakhstan extending about 2575 kilometers; usually thought of as dividing line between Europe & Asia; highest about 1830 meters **2** river 2255 kilometers long Russia & Kazakhstan flowing from S end of Ural mountains into Caspian sea

Uru·guay \ˈ(y)u̇r-ə-ˌgwī, ˈyu̇r-ə-ˌgwä\ **1** river 1577 kilometers long SE South America **2** country SE South America; capital, Montevideo — **Uru·guay·an** \ˌ(y)u̇r-ə-ˈgwī-ən, ˌyu̇r-ə-ˈgwä-\ *adj or n*

Ürüm·qi \ˈœ̄-ˈrœ̄m-ˈchē\ *or* **Urum·chi** \u̇-ˈru̇m-chē, ˌu̇r-əm-ˈchē\ city NW China

Us·pa·lla·ta \ˌu̇-spə-ˈyät-ə, -ˈzhät-\ mountain pass 3840 meters S South America in the Andes between Argentina & Chile

Ustinov — see IZHEVSK

Utah \ˈyü-ˌtȯ, -ˌtä\ state W U.S.; capital, Salt Lake City — **Utah·an** \-ˌtȯ(-ə)n, -ˌtä(-ə)n\ *adj or n* — **Utahn** \-ˌtȯ(-ə)n, -ˌtä(-ə)n\ *n*

Uz·bek·i·stan \(ˌ)u̇z-ˌbek-i-ˈstan, -ˈstän; -ˈbek-i-ˌ\ country W central Asia between Aral sea & Afghanistan; capital, Tashkent; a republic (**Uz·bek Soviet Socialist Republic** \ˈu̇z-ˌbek, ˈəz-; u̇z-ˈ\) of U.S.S.R. 1924–91

Va·duz \vä-ˈdüts\ town, capital of Liechtenstein

Val·dez \val-ˈdēz\ town and port S Alaska

Va·len·cia \və-ˈlen-ch(ē-)ə, -ˈlen(t)-sē-ə\ **1** region & ancient kingdom E Spain **2** city, its capital, on the Mediterranean

Valley Forge locality SE Pennsylvania

Val·let·ta \və-ˈlet-ə\ city, capital of Malta

Van·cou·ver \van-ˈkü-vər\ **1** island W Canada in SW British Columbia **2** city SW British Columbia, Canada

Van Diemen's Land — see TASMANIA

Van·u·atu \ˌvan-ˌwä-ˈtü, ˌvän-, -ˈwä-ˌtü\ *or formerly* **New Heb·ri·des** \-ˈheb-rə-ˌdēz\ islands SW Pacific W of Fiji; formerly under shared British and French administration; became independent 1980; capital, Vila

Varanasi — see BANARAS

Vat·i·can City \ˌvat-i-kən-\ independent state within Rome, Italy; created 1929 as headquarters for the Pope

Ven·e·zu·e·la \ˌven-əz(-ə)-ˈwā-lə, -ˈwē-\ country N South America; capital, Caracas — **Ven·e·zu·e·lan** \-lən\ *adj or n*

Ven·ice \ˈven-əs\ *or Italian* **Ve·ne·zia** \və-ˈnet-sē-ə\ city N Italy on islands in Lagoon of Venice

Ve·ra·cruz \ˌver-ə-ˈkrüz, -ˈkrüs\ city E Mexico

Ver·mont \vər-ˈmänt\ state NE U.S.; capital, Montpelier — **Ver·mont·er** \-ər\ *n*

Ve·ro·na \və-ˈrō-nə\ city N Italy W of Venice

Ve·su·vi·us \və-ˈsü-vē-əs\ volcano about 1220 meters S Italy near Bay of Naples

Vicks·burg \ˈviks-ˌbərg\ city W Mississippi

Vic·to·ria \vik-ˈtōr-ē-ə, -ˈtȯr-\ **1** city, capital of British Columbia, Canada on Vancouver island **2** island N Canada in Arctic island group **3** state SE Australia; capital, Melbourne **4** city, capital of Hong Kong **5** seaport, capital of Seychelles — **Vic·to·ri·an** \-ē-ən\ *adj or n*

Victoria, Lake lake E Africa in Tanzania, Kenya, & Uganda

Vi·en·na \vē-ˈen-ə\ *or ancient* **Vin·dob·o·na** \vin-ˈdäb-

ə-nə\ *or* **Vin·dob·na** \-ˈdäb-nə\ city, capital of Austria on the Danube — **Vi·en·nese** \ˌvē-ə-ˈnēz, -ˈnēs\ *adj or n*

Vien·tiane \(ˈ)vyen-ˈtyän\ city, capital of Laos

Viet·nam \vē-ˈet-ˈnäm, vyet-, ˌvē-ət-, -ˈnam\ country SE Asia in Indochina; capital, Hanoi; established 1945–46 & divided 1954–75 at 17th parallel into the independent states of **North Vietnam** (capital, Hanoi) & **South Vietnam** (capital, Saigon)

Vi·la \ˈvē-lə\ city, capital of Vanuatu

Vil·ni·us \ˈvil-nē-əs\ *or Russian* **Vil·na** \ˈvil-nə\ *or* **Vil·no** \-nō\ city, capital of Lithuania

Vin·land \ˈvin-lənd\ a portion of the coast of North America visited and so called by Norse voyagers about 1000 A.D.; perhaps Newfoundland

Vir·gin·ia \vər-ˈjin-yə, -ˈjin-ē-ə\ state E U.S.; capital, Richmond — **Vir·gin·ian** \-yən, -ē-ən\ *adj or n*

Virginia Beach city SE Virginia

Virginia City village W Nevada

Vir·gin Islands \ˌvər-jən-\ island group West Indies E of Puerto Rico — see BRITISH VIRGIN ISLANDS; VIRGIN ISLANDS OF THE UNITED STATES

Virgin Islands of the United States the W islands of the Virgin Islands group; capital, Charlotte Amalie (on Saint Thomas)

Vi·sa·yan \və-ˈsī-ən\ *or* **Bi·sa·yas** \bə-ˈsī-əz\ islands central Philippines

Vish·a·kha·pat·nam \vi-ˌshäk-ə-ˈpət-nəm\ *or* **Vis·a·kha·pat·nam** \-ˌsä-\ city E India

Vis·tu·la \ˈvis(h)-tə-lə, ˈvis-tə-lə\ river 1015 kilometers long Poland flowing N from the Carpathians

Vi·ti Le·vu \ˌvēt-ē-ˈlev-ü\ island SW Pacific; largest of the Fiji group

Vlad·i·vos·tok \ˌvlad-ə-və-ˈstäk, -ˈväs-ˌtäk\ city & port SE Russia on Sea of Japan

Vol·ga \ˈväl-gə, ˈvȯl-, ˈvōl-\ river 3742 kilometers long W Russia; longest river in Europe

Vol·go·grad \ˈväl-gə-ˌgrad, ˈvȯl-, ˈvōl-\ city SW Russia, on the Volga

Vol·ta \ˈväl-tə, ˈvȯl-\ river 160 kilometers long Ghana flowing from Lake Volta (reservoir) into Gulf of Guinea

Vo·ro·nezh \və-ˈrō-nish\ city SW Russia

Vosges \ˈvōzh\ mountains NE France on W side of Rhine valley; highest 1423 meters

Wa·co \ˈwā-kō\ city central Texas

Wake \ˈwāk\ island N Pacific N of Marshall islands; belongs to U.S.

Wake·field \ˈwāk-ˌfēld\ city N England in West Yorkshire

Wa·la·chia *or* **Wal·la·chia** \wä-ˈlā-kē-ə\ region S Romania between Transylvanian Alps & the Danube

Wales \ˈwā(ə)lz\ *or Welsh* **Cym·ru** \ˈkəm-ˌrē\ principality SW Great Britain; a division of United Kingdom; capital, Cardiff

Wal·sall \ˈwȯl-ˌsȯl, -səl\ city area W central England in West Midlands county

Wal·tham Forest \ˌwȯl-thəm-\ city area of NE Greater London county, England

Wands·worth \ˈwän(d)z-(ˌ)wərth\ city area of SW Greater London county, England

War·ley \ˈwȯr-lē\ city area W central England in West Midlands county

War·ren \ˈwȯr-ən, ˈwär-\ city SE Michigan

War·saw \ˈwȯr-ˌsȯ\ *or Polish* **War·sza·wa** \vär-ˈshäv-ə\ city, capital of Poland

War·wick \ˈwär-ik\ city area central England in Warwickshire

War·wick·shire \ˈwär-ik-ˌshi(ə)r, -shər\ *or* **Warwick-** county central England

Wa·satch \'wȯ-ˌsach\ range of the Rockies SE Idaho & N central Utah; highest Mount Timpanogos 3660 meters (in Utah)

Wash·ing·ton \'wȯsh-iŋ-tən, 'wäsh-\ **1** state NW U.S.; capital, Olympia **2** city, capital of U.S.; having the same boundaries as District of Columbia — **Wash·ing·to·nian** \ˌwȯsh-iŋ-ˈtō-nē-ən, ˌwäsh-, -nyən\ *adj or n*

Washington, Mount mountain 1917 meters N New Hampshire; highest in White mountains

Wa·ter·bury \'wȯt-ə(r)-ˌber-ē, 'wät-\ city W central Connecticut

Wa·ver·ley \'wā-vər-lē\ city SE Australia in E New South Wales

Wei·mar Republic \'vī-ˌmär-\ the German republic 1919–33

Wel·land \'wel-ənd\ canal 45 kilometers long SE Ontario connecting Lake Erie & Lake Ontario

Wel·ling·ton \'wel-iŋ-tən\ city, capital of New Zealand

Wes·sex \'wes-iks\ ancient kingdom S England; capital, Winchester

West Bank area Palestine W of Jordan river; occupied by Israel since 1967

West Brom·wich \-'brəm-ij, -'bräm-, -ich\ city area W central England in West Midlands county

Western Australia state W Australia; capital, Perth — **Western Australian** *adj or n*

Western Ghats \-'gȯts\ chain of low mountains SW India

Western Isles region W Scotland consisting of the Outer Hebrides; established 1975

Western Sahara *or* **Spanish Sahara** region NW Africa; occupied by Morocco

Western Samoa islands Samoa W of 171° W; an independent country in the Commonwealth since 1962; capital, Apia

West Germany the Federal Republic of Germany — see GERMANY

West Gla·mor·gan \-glə-'mȯr-gən\ county S Wales; established 1974

West Indies islands lying between SE North America & N South America & consisting of the Greater Antilles, Lesser Antilles, & Bahamas — **West Indian** *adj or n*

West Iri·an \-ˌir-ē-'än\ *or* **West New Guinea** territory of Indonesia consisting of W half of New Guinea

West Midlands county W central England; includes Birmingham

West·min·ster \'wes(t)-ˌmint(s)-stər\ *or* **City of Westminster** city area of W central Greater London county, England

West Pakistan the former W division of Pakistan now having the same boundaries as Pakistan

West·pha·lia \wes(t)-'fāl-yə, -'fā-lē-ə\ region W Germany E of the Rhine — **West·pha·lian** \-'fāl-yən, -'fā-lē-ən\ *adj or n*

West Point U.S. military post SE New York

West Quod·dy Head \-ˌkwäd-ē-\ cape; most easterly point of Maine & of the Lower 48 states

West Sus·sex \-'səs-iks\ county SE England

West Virginia state E U.S.; capital, Charleston — **West Virginian** *adj or n*

West York·shire \-'yȯrk-ˌshi(ə)r, -shər\ county NW England; includes Wakefield

White mountains N New Hampshire in the Appalachians — see WASHINGTON, MOUNT

White·horse \'hwīt-ˌhȯ(ə)rs, 'wīt-\ city, capital of Yukon Territory, Canada

White sea sea inlet NW Russia

Whit·ney, Mount \-'hwit-nē, -'wit-\ mountain 4418 meters SE central California in Sierra Nevada; highest in U.S. outside of Alaska

Wich·i·ta \'wich-ə-ˌtȯ\ city S Kansas

Wight, Isle of \-'wīt\ — see ISLE OF WIGHT

Wil·lem·stad \'vil-əm-ˌstät\ city, capital of Netherlands Antilles

Wil·liams·burg \'wil-yəmz-ˌbərg\ city SE Virginia

Wil·ming·ton \'wil-miŋ-tən\ city N Delaware; largest in state

Wilt·shire \'wilt-ˌshi(ə)r, 'wil-chər, 'wilt-shər\ county S England

Win·ches·ter \'win-ˌches-tər, -chə-stər\ city area S England in Hampshire

Win·der·mere \'win-də(r)-ˌmi(ə)r\ lake NW England·in Lake District

Wind·hoek \'vint-ˌhùk\ city, capital of Namibia

Wind·sor \'win-zər\ city S Ontario, Canada on Detroit river

Wind·ward Islands \'win-dwərd-\ islands West Indies in the S Lesser Antilles extending S from Martinique but not including Barbados, Tobago, or Trinidad

Win·ni·peg \'win-ə-ˌpeg\ city, capital of Manitoba, Canada

Winnipeg, Lake lake S central Manitoba, Canada

Win·ni·pe·sau·kee, Lake \-ˌwin-ə-pə-'sȯ-kē\ lake central New Hampshire

Win·ston–Sa·lem \ˌwin(t)-stən-'sā-ləm\ city N central North Carolina

Wis·con·sin \wis-'kän(t)-sən\ state N central U.S.; capital, Madison — **Wis·con·sin·ite** \-sə-ˌnīt\ *n*

Wit·wa·ters·rand \'wit-ˌwȯt-ərz-ˌrand, -ˌwät-, -ˌränd, -ˌränt\ *or* **Rand** \'rand, 'ränd, 'ränt\ ridge of gold-bearing rock NE Republic of South Africa in S Transvaal

Wol·lon·gong \'wùl-ən-ˌgäŋ, -ˌgȯŋ\ city SE Australia in E New South Wales S of Sydney

Wol·ver·hamp·ton \'wùl-vər-ˌham(p)-tən\ city area W central England in West Midlands county NW of Birmingham

Worces·ter \'wùs-tər\ **1** city E central Massachusetts **2** city W central England in Hereford and Worcester county

Wran·gell, Mount \'raŋ-gəl\ volcano 4317 meters S Alaska in Wrangell range

Wro·claw \'vrȯt-ˌsläf, -ˌsläv\ city SW Poland in Silesia

Wu·han \'wü-'hän\ city S China

Wu·sih *or* **Wu–hsi** \'wü-'shē\ city E China

Wy·o·ming \wī-'ō-miŋ\ state NW U.S.; capital, Cheyenne — **Wy·o·ming·ite** \-miŋ-ˌīt\ *n*

Xi'an *or* **Si·an** \'shē-'än\ city E central China

Xin·jiang Uy·gur *or* **Sin·kiang Ui·ghur** \'shin-jē-'äŋ-'wē-gər\ region W China

Xu·zhou \'shü-'jō\ *or* **Sü·chow** \'shü-'jō, 'sü-; 'sü-'chaù\ city E China

Yak·i·ma \'yak-ə-ˌmȯ\ city S central Washington

Ya·lu \'yäl-ü\ river 480 kilometers long SE Manchuria & North Korea

Yan·gon \ˌyän-'gōn\ *or formerly* **Ran·goon** \ran-'gün, raŋ-\ city, capital of Myanmar

Yangtze — see CHANG

Yaoun·dé \yaùn-'dā\ city, capital of Cameroon

Yap \'yap, 'yäp\ island W Pacific in the W Carolines

Ya·ro·slavl \ˌyär-ə-'släv-əl\ city W Russia, NE of Moscow

Yaz·oo \ya-'zü, 'yaz-ü\ river W central Mississippi

Ye·ka·te·rin·burg \yi-'kat-ə-rən-ˌbərg, -'kät-, -ˌbərk\ *or* **1924–91 Sverd·lovsk** \sverd-'lȯfsk\ city W Russia, in central Ural mountains

Yellow 1 — see HUANG **2** sea section of East China sea between N China, North Korea, & South Korea

Yel·low·knife \'yel-ə-ˌnīf\ town, capital of Northwest Territories, Canada

Ye·men \'yem-ən\ country S Arabia bordering on Red sea & Gulf of Aden; capital, San'a; before 1990 divided into the independent states of **Yemen Arab Republic** (capital, San'a) & **People's Democratic Republic of Yemen** (capital, Aden) — **Ye·me·ni** \'yem-ə-nē\ *adj or n* — **Ye·men·ite** \-ə-ˌnīt\ *n*

Yen·i·sey \ˌyen-ə-ˈsā\ river 4505 kilometers long central Russia, flowing N into Arctic ocean

Ye·re·van \ˌyer-ə-ˈvän\ city, capital of Armenia

Yo·ko·ha·ma \ˌyō-kə-ˈhäm-ə\ city Japan in SE Honshu on Tokyo Bay S of Tokyo

Yon·kers \ˈyäŋ-kərz\ city SE New York N of New York City

York \ˈyȯ(ə)rk\ city N England in North Yorkshire

York, Cape cape NE Australia in Queensland at N tip of Cape York peninsula

York·shire \ˈyȯrk-ˌshi(ə)r, -shər\ former county N England

Yo·sem·i·te Falls \yō-ˌsem-ət-ē-\ waterfall E California in Yosemite valley; includes two falls, the upper 436 meters & the lower 98 meters

Youngs·town \ˈyəŋ-ˌstaůn\ city NE Ohio

Yu·ca·tán \ˌyü-kə-ˈtan, -ˈtän\ peninsula SE Mexico & N Central America including Belize& N Guatemala

Yu·go·sla·via *or* **Ju·go·sla·via** \ˌyü-gō-ˈsläv-ē-ə\ country S Europe including Serbia & Montenegro and formerly also Slovenia, Croatia, Bosnia and Herzegovina, & Macedonia; capital, Belgrade — **Yu·go·slav** \ˌyü-gō-ˈsläv, -ˈslav\ *or* **Yu·go·sla·vi·an** \-ˈsläv-ē-ən\ *adj or n*

Yu·kon \ˈyü-ˌkän\ **1** river 3185 kilometers long NW Canada & Alaska flowing into Bering sea **2** *or* **Yukon Territory** territory NW Canada; capital, Whitehorse

Yu·ma \ˈyü-mə\ city SW corner of Arizona on the Colorado

Za·greb \ˈzäg-ˌreb\ city, capital of Croatia

Zaire \zä-ˈi(ə)r *also* ˈzī(ə)r\ **1** river in Africa — see CONGO **2** *or formerly* **Democratic Republic of the Congo** *or earlier* **Belgian Congo** country central Africa consisting of most of Congo river basin E of lower Congo river; capital, Kinshasa

Zam·be·zi *or* **Zam·be·si** \zam-ˈbē-zē\ river 2655 kilometers long SE Africa flowing from NW Zambia into Mozambique channel

Zam·bia \ˈzam-bē-ə\ country S Africa N of the Zambezi; formerly (as **Northern Rhodesia**) dependent on Britain; became independent 1964; capital, Lusaka

Zan·zi·bar \ˈzan-zə-ˌbär\ island Tanzania off NE Tanganyika coast; formerly a sultanate; became independent 1963; united 1964 with Tanganyika forming Tanzania

Za·po·ro·zhye \ˌzäp-ə-ˈrȯ-zhə\ city SE Ukraine

Zetland — see SHETLAND

Zhang·jia·kou \ˈjäŋ-jē-ˈä-ˈkō\ *or* **Kal·gan** \ˈkal-ˈgan\ city NE China NW of Beijing

Zhdanov — see MARIUPOL

Zheng·zhou *or* **Cheng–chcu** \ˈjəŋ-ˈjō\ city NE central China

Zim·ba·bwe \zim-ˈbäb-wē, -wä\ *or formerly* **Rhodesia** country S Africa S of Zambezi river; an independent state in the Commonwealth; capital, Harare

Zui·der Zee \ˌzīd-ər-ˈzā, -ˈzē\ former inlet of North sea N Netherlands — see IJSSELMEER

Zu·lu·land \ˈzü-(ˌ)lü-ˌland\ territory E Republic of South Africa in NE Natal on Indian ocean

Zu·rich \ˈzů(ə)r-ik\ city N Switzerland

Biographical, Biblical, and Mythological Names

This section is a listing of the names of important figures from recorded history, biblical tradition, classical mythology, popular legend, and current events. Figures from the Bible, myth, or legend are clearly identified as such. In cases where figures have alternate names, they are entered under the name by which they are best known. The part of the name shown in boldface type is either the family name or the common shorter name for that figure. The dates following the name or pronunciation are the birth and death dates. Other dates in the entry refer to the dates of a particular office, honor, or achievement. Italicized names within an entry refer to a person's nickname, original name, title, or other name.

Aar·on \\'ar-ən, 'er-\\ brother of Moses and first high priest of the Hebrews in the Bible

Abel \\'ā-bəl\\ son of Adam and Eve and brother of Cain in the Bible

Abra·ham \\'ā-brə-ˌham\\ patriarch and founder of the Hebrew people in the Bible

Achil·les \\ə-'kil-ēz\\ Greek hero in the Trojan War in mythology

Ad·am \\'ad-əm\\ the first man in the Bible

Ad·ams \\'ad-əmz\\ Abigail 1744–1818 American writer; wife of John Adams

Adams John 1735–1826 2d president of the U.S. (1797–1801)

Adams John Quin·cy \\'kwin-zē, 'kwin(t)-sē\\ 1767–1848 6th president of the U.S. (1825–29); son of John and Abigail Adams

Adams Samuel 1722–1803 patriot in the American Revolutionary War

Ad·dams \\'ad-əmz\\ Jane 1860–1935 American social worker; Nobel Prize winner (1931)

Ado·nis \\ə-'dän-əs, -'dō-nəs\\ beautiful youth in Greek mythology who is loved by Aphrodite

Ae·ne·as \\i-'nē-əs\\ Trojan hero in Greek and Roman mythology

Ae·o·lus \\'ē-ə-ləs\\ god of the winds in Greek mythology

Aes·chy·lus \\'es-kə-ləs, 'ēs-\\ 525–456 B.C. Greek dramatist

Aes·cu·la·pi·us \\ˌes-kyə-'lā-pē-əs\\ god of medicine in Roman mythology — compare ASCLEPIUS

Ae·sop \\'ē-ˌsäp, -səp\\ legendary Greek writer of fables

Ag·a·mem·non \\ˌag-ə-'mem-ˌnän, -nən\\ leader of the Greeks during the Trojan War in Greek mythology

Ag·nes \\'ag-nəs\\ Saint *died* 304 A.D. Christian martyr

Ahab \\'ā-ˌhab\\ king of Israel in the 9th century B.C. and husband of Jezebel

Ajax \\'ā-ˌjaks\\ hero in Greek mythology who kills himself because the armor of Achilles is awarded to Odysseus during the Trojan War

Alad·din \\ə-'lad-ᵊn\\ youth in the *Arabian Nights' Entertainments* who comes into possession of a magic lamp and ring

Al·cott \\'ȯl-kət, 'al-, -ˌkät\\ Louisa May 1832–1888 American author

Al·ex·an·der \\ˌal-ig-'zan-der, ˌel-\\ name of eight popes: especially **VI** (Rodrigo Lanzol y Borja) 1431–1503 (pope 1492–1503)

Alexander III of Macedon 356–323 B.C. *the Great* king (336–323)

Al·fred \\'al-frəd, -fərd\\ 849–899 *the Great* king of the West Saxons (871–899)

Ali Ba·ba \\ˌal-ē-'bäb-ə\\ a woodcutter in the *Arabian Nights' Entertainments* who enters the cave of the Forty Thieves by using the password *Sesame*

Al·len \\'al-ən\\ Ethan 1738–1789 American Revolutionary soldier

Amerigo Vespucci — see VESPUCCI

Am·herst \\'am-(ˌ)ərst\\ Jeffrey 1717–1797 *Baron Amherst* British general in America

Amund·sen \\'äm-ən-sən\\ Roald 1872–1928 Norwegian explorer and discoverer of the South Pole (1911)

An·a·ni·as \\ˌan-ə-'nī-əs\\ early Christian struck dead for lying

An·der·sen \\'an-dər-sən\\ Hans Christian 1805–1875 Danish writer of fairy tales

An·der·son \\'an-dər-sən\\ Marian 1897–1993 American contralto

Anne \\'an\\ 1665–1714 queen of Great Britain (1702–14)

An·tho·ny \\'an(t)-thə-nē\\ Susan Brownell 1820–1906 American suffragist

An·tig·o·ne \\an-'tig-ə-nē\\ daughter of Oedipus and Jocasta in Greek mythology

An·to·ni·us \\an-'tō-nē-əs\\ Marcus *about* 82–30 B.C. *Mark* or *Marc An·to·ny* or *An·tho·ny* \\'an(t)-thə-nē, *chiefly British* 'an-tə-nē\\ Roman general

Aph·ro·di·te \\ˌaf-rə-'dīt-ē\\ goddess of love and beauty in Greek mythology — compare VENUS

Apol·lo \\ə-'päl-ō\\ god of sunlight, prophecy, music, and poetry in Greek and Roman mythology

Aqui·nas \\ə-'kwī-nəs\\ Saint Thomas 1224 (or 1225)–1274 Italian theologian

Ar·chi·me·des \\ˌär-kə-'mēd-ēz\\ *about* 287–212 B.C. Greek mathematician

Ares \\'a(ə)r-ēz, 'e(ə)r-\\ god of war in Greek mythology — compare MARS

Ar·is·toph·a·nes \\ˌar-ə-'stäf-ə-ˌnēz\\ *about* 450– *about* 388 B.C. Greek dramatist

Ar·is·tot·le \\'ar-ə-ˌstät-ᵊl\\ 384–322 B.C. Greek philosopher

Arm·strong \\'ärm-ˌstrȯŋ\\ Louis 1901–1971 *Satch·mo* \\'sach-ˌmō\\ American jazz musician

Armstrong Neil Alden 1930– American astronaut and first man on the moon (1969)

Ar·nold \\'ärn-ᵊld\\ Benedict 1741–1801 American Revolutionary general and traitor

Ar·te·mis \\'ärt-ə-məs\\ goddess of the moon, wild animals, and hunting in Greek mythology — compare DI-ANA

Ar·thur \\'är-thər\\ legendary king of the Britons whose story is based on traditions of a 6th century military leader — **Ar·thu·ri·an** \\är-'th(y)ùr-ē-ən\\ *adj*

Arthur Chester Alan 1829–1886 21st president of the U.S. (1881–85)

As·cle·pi·us \\ə-'sklē-pē-əs\\ god of medicine in Greek mythology — compare AESCULAPIUS

As·tor \\'as-tər\\ John Jacob 1763–1848 American (German-born) fur trader and capitalist

Athe·na \\ə-'thē-nə\\ *or* **Athe·ne** \\-nē\\ goddess of wisdom in Greek mythology — compare MINERVA

At·las \\'at-ləs\\ Titan in Greek mythology forced to bear the heavens on his shoulders

At·ti·la \\ə-'til-ə, 'at-°l-ə\\ 406?–453 A.D. *the Scourge of God* king of the Huns

At·tucks \\'at-əks\\ Crispus 1723?–1770 American patriot; one of five men killed in Boston Massacre

Au·du·bon \\'ȯd-ə-ˌbän, -bən\\ John James 1785–1851 American (Haitian-born) artist and naturalist

Au·gus·tine \\'ȯ-gə-ˌstēn; ȯ-'gəs-tən, ə-\\ Saint 354–430 A.D. church father; bishop of Hippo (396–430)

Au·gus·tus \\ȯ-'gəs-təs, ə-\\ *or* **Augustus Caesar** *or* **Oc·ta·vi·an** \\äk-'tā-vē-ən\\ 63 B.C.–14 A.D. 1st Roman emperor (27 B.C.–14 A.D.)

Aus·ten \\'ȯs-tən, 'äs-\\ Jane 1775–1817 English author

Bac·chus \\'bak-əs\\ — see DIONYSUS

Bach \\'bäk, 'bäḵ\\ Johann Sebastian 1685–1750 German composer and organist

Ba·con \\'bā-kən\\ Francis 1561–1626 English philosopher and author

Ba·den–Pow·ell \\ˌbād-°n-'pō-əl\\ Robert Stephenson Smyth 1857–1941 English founder of Boy Scout movement

Baf·fin \\'baf-ən\\ William *about* 1584–1622 English navigator

Bal·boa, de \\bal-'bō-ə\\ Vasco Núñez 1475–1519 Spanish explorer and discoverer of Pacific Ocean (1513)

Bal·ti·more \\'bȯl-tə-ˌmō(ə)r, -ˌmȯ(ə)r\\ Lord — see George CALVERT

Bal·zac, de \\'bȯl-ˌzak, 'bal-\\ Honoré 1799–1850 French author

Ba·rab·bas \\bə-'rab-əs\\ prisoner released in preference to Jesus at the demand of the multitude

Bar·num \\'bär-nəm\\ Phineas Taylor 1810–1891 American show-business manager

Bar·rie \\'bar-ē\\ Sir James Matthew 1860–1937 Scottish author

Bar·thol·di \\bär-'täl-dē, -'tȯl-, -'thäl-, -'thȯl-\\ Frédéric= Auguste 1834–1904 French sculptor who designed the Statue of Liberty

Bar·ton \\'bärt-°n\\ Clara 1821–1912 founder of American Red Cross Society

Beau·re·gard \\'bōr-ə-ˌgärd, 'bȯr-\\ Pierre Gustave Toutant 1818–1893 American Confederate general

Beck·et, à \\ə-'bek-ət, ä-\\ Saint Thomas *about* 1118–1170 archbishop of Canterbury (1162–1170)

Bee·tho·ven \\'bā-ˌtō-vən\\ Ludwig van 1770–1827 German composer

Bell \\'bel\\ Alexander Graham 1847–1922 American (Scottish-born) inventor of the telephone

Ben·e·dict \\'ben-ə-ˌdikt\\ name of 15 popes: especially **XIV** (*Prospero Lambertini*) 1675–1758 (pope 1740–58); **XV** (*Giacomo della Chiesa*) 1854–1922 (pope 1914–22)

Be·nét \\bə-'nā\\ Stephen Vincent 1898–1943 American author

Ben·ja·min \\'benj-(ə-)mən\\ youngest son of Jacob and ancestor of one of the 12 tribes of Israel in the Bible

Ben·ton \\'bent-°n\\ Thomas Hart 1889–1975 American painter

Be·o·wulf \\'bā-ə-ˌwùlf\\ legendary warrior and hero of the Old English poem *Beowulf*

Be·ring \\'bi(ə)r-iŋ, 'be(ə)r-\\ Vitus 1681–1741 Danish navigator; discovered Bering strait and Bering sea

Ber·lin \\(ˌ)bər-'lin\\ Irving 1888–1989 American (Russian-born) composer

Ber·ni·ni \\bər-'nē-nē\\ Gian Lorenzo 1598–1680 Italian sculptor, architect, and painter

Bes·se·mer \\'bes-ə-mər\\ Sir Henry 1813–1898 English engineer and inventor

Be·thune \\bə-'th(y)ün\\ Mary 1875–1955 née *McLeod* American educator

Bi·zet \\bē-'zā\\ Alexandre-César-Léopold 1838–1875 called *Georges* French composer

Black Hawk \\'blak-ˌhȯk\\ 1767–1838 American Indian chief

Black·well \\'blak-ˌwel, -wəl\\ Elizabeth 1821–1910 American (English-born) physician

Blake \\'blāk\\ William 1757–1827 English poet and artist

Bloom·er \\'blü-mər\\ Amelia Jenks 1818–1894 American social reformer

Boc·cac·cio \\bō-'käch-(ē-ˌ)ō\\ Giovanni 1313–1375 Italian author

Bohr \\'bō(ə)r, 'bȯ(ə)r\\ Niels 1885–1962 Danish physicist

Bo·leyn \\bù-'lin, 'bùl-ən\\ Anne 1507?–1536 2d wife of Henry VIII and mother of Elizabeth I of England

Bo·lí·var Si·món \\si-ˌmōn-bə-'lē-ˌvär, ˌsī-mən-'bäl-ə-vər\\ 1783–1830 South American liberator

Bon·i·face \\'bän-ə-fəs, -ˌfās\\ name of nine popes: especially **VIII** (*Benedetto Caetani*) *about* 1235 (or 1240)–1303 (pope 1294–1303)

Boone \\'bün\\ Daniel 1734–1820 American pioneer

Booth \\'büth\\ John Wilkes 1838–1865 assassin of Abraham Lincoln

Bo·re·as \\'bōr-ē-əs, 'bȯr-\\ god of the north wind in Greek mythology

Bot·ti·cel·li \\ˌbät-ə-'chel-ē\\ Sandro 1445–1510 Italian painter

Bow·ie \\'bü-ē, 'bō-\\ James 1796–1836 hero of Texas revolution

Boyle \\'bȯi(ə)l\\ Robert 1627–1691 English physicist and chemist

Brad·bury \\'brad-ˌber-ē, -b(ə-)rē\\ Ray Douglas 1920– American author

Brad·dock \\'brad-ək\\ Edward 1695–1755 British general in America

Brad·ford \\'brad-fərd\\ William 1590–1657 Pilgrim leader

Brad·street \\'brad-ˌstrēt\\ Anne *about* 1612–1672 American poet

Bra·dy \\'brād-ē\\ Mathew B. 1823?–1896 American photographer

Brah·ma \\'bräm-ə\\ creator god of the Hindu sacred triad — compare SIVA, VISHNU

Brahms \\'brämz\\ Johannes 1833–1897 German composer

Braille \\'brā(ə)l, 'brī\\ Louis 1809–1852 French blind teacher of the blind

Braun \\'braùn\\ Wernher von 1912–1977 American (German-born) engineer

Brezh·nev \\'brezh-ˌnef\\ Leonid Ilyich 1906–1982 Russian politician; 1st secretary of Communist party (1964–82); president of the U.S.S.R. (1960–64; 1977–82)

Brid·ger \\'brij-ər\\ James 1804–1881 American pioneer and scout

Bron·të \\'bränt-ē, 'brän-ˌtā\\ family of English writers: Charlotte 1816–1855 and her sisters Emily 1818–1848 and Anne 1820–1849

Brooks \\'brùks\\ Gwendolyn Elizabeth 1917– American poet

Brown \\'braùn\\ John *Old Brown of Osa·wat·o·mie* \\ˌō-sə-'wät- ə-mē\\ 1800–1859 American abolitionist

Brow·ning \\'braù-niŋ\\ Elizabeth Barrett 1806–1861 English poet; wife of Robert

Browning Robert 1812–1889 English poet; husband of Elizabeth

Bru·tus \\'brüt-əs\\ Marcus Junius 85–42 B.C. Roman politician; one of Julius Caesar's assassins

Bry·an \\'brī-ən\\ William Jennings 1860–1925 American lawyer and politician

Bu·chan·an \\byü-'kan-ən, bə-\\ James 1791–1868 15th president of the U.S. (1857–61)

Buck \\'bək\\ Pearl 1892–1973 American author; Nobel Prize winner (1938)

Buddha — see GAUTAMA BUDDHA

Buffalo Bill — see William Frederick CODY

Bun·yan \\'bən-yən\\ John 1628–1688 English preacher and author

Bur·bank \\'bər-ˌbaŋk\\ Luther 1849–1926 American horticulturist

Bur·goyne \\(ˌ)bər-'gȯin, 'bər-ˌgȯin\\ John 1722–1792 British general in America

Burns \\'bərnz\\ Robert 1759–1796 Scottish poet

Burn·side \\'bərn-ˌsīd\\ Ambrose Everett 1824–1881 American general

Burr \\'bər\\ Aaron 1756–1836 vice president of the U.S. (1801–05)

Bush \\'bush\\ George Herbert Walker 1924–   41st president of the U.S. (1989–93)

By·ron \\'bī-rən\\ Lord 1788–1824 *George Gordon Byron* English poet

Cab·ot \\'kab-ət\\ John *about* 1450–*about* 1499 Italian navigator; explored coast of North America for England

Cabot Sebastian 1476?–1557 English navigator; son of John Cabot

Ca·bri·ni \\kə-'brē-nē\\ Saint Frances Xavier 1850–1917 *Mother Cabrini* first American (Italian-born) saint (1946)

Cae·sar \\'sē-zər\\ Gaius Julius 100–44 B.C. Roman general, political leader, and writer

Cain \\'kān\\ brother of Abel in the Bible

Cal·houn \\kal-'hün\\ John Caldwell 1782–1850 vice president of the U.S. (1825–32)

Ca·lig·u·la \\kə-'lig-yə-lə\\ 12–41 A.D. *Gaius Caesar* Roman emperor (37–41)

Cal·li·ope \\kə-'lī-ə-ˌpē\\ muse of heroic poetry in Greek mythology

Cal·vert \\'kal-vərt\\ George 1580?–1632 1st Baron *Baltimore* English colonist in America

Cal·vin \\'kal-vən\\ John 1509–1564 French theologian and reformer

Ca·nute \\kə-'n(y)üt\\ *died* 1035 *the Great* king of England (1016–35); of Denmark (1018–35); of Norway (1028–35)

Car·ne·gie \\'kär-nə-gē, kär-'neg-ē\\ Andrew 1835–1919 American (Scottish-born) industrialist and philanthropist

Carroll Lewis — see Charles Lutwidge DODGSON

Car·son \\'kärs-ᵊn\\ Christopher 1809–1868 *Kit* American soldier and guide

Carson Rachel Louise 1907–1964 American scientist

Car·ter \\'kärt-ər\\ James Earl, Jr. 1924–   *Jimmy* 39th president of the U.S. (1977–81)

Car·tier \\kär-'tyā, 'kärt-ē-ˌā\\ Jacques 1491–1557 French navigator; discovered Saint Lawrence river

Ca·ru·so \\kə-'rü-sō, -zō\\ En·ri·co \\en-'rē-kō\\ 1873–1921 Italian tenor

Car·ver \\'kär-vər\\ George Washington *about* 1864–1943 American botanist

Ca·sa·no·va \\ˌkaz-ə-'nō-və, ˌkas-\\ Giovanni Giacomo 1725–1798 Italian adventurer

Cas·san·dra \\kə-'san-drə\\ daughter of Priam in Greek mythology who is endowed with the gift of prophecy but fated never to be believed

Cas·satt \\kə-'sat\\ Mary 1845–1926 American painter

Cas·tro \\'kas-trō, 'käs-\\ **(Ruz)** \\'rüs\\ Fi·del \\fē-'del\\ 1926–   Cuban premier (1959–   )

Cath·er \\'kath-ər\\ Willa Sibert 1873–1947 American author

Cath·er·ine \\'kath-(ə-)rən\\ name of 1st, 5th, and 6th wives of Henry VIII of England: Catherine of Aragon 1485–1536; Catherine Howard 1520?–1542; Catherine Parr 1512–1548

Catherine I 1684–1727 wife of Peter the Great; empress of Russia (1725–27)

Catherine II 1729–1796 *the Great* empress of Russia (1762–96)

Cav·en·dish \\'kav-ən-(ˌ)dish\\ Henry 1731–1810 English scientist

Ce·ci·lia \\sə-'sēl-yə, -'sil-\\ Saint 2d or 3d century A.D. Roman martyr; patron saint of music

Ce·res \\'si(ə)r-ˌēz\\ the goddess of agriculture in Roman mythology — compare DEMETER

Cer·van·tes \\sər-'van-ˌtēz\\ Miguel de 1547–1616 Spanish author

Cé·zanne \\sā-'zan\\ Paul 1839–1906 French painter

Cha·gall \\shə-'gäl, -'gal\\ Marc 1887–1985 Russian painter

Cham·plain \\(ˈ)sham-'plān\\ Samuel de *about* 1567–1635 French explorer in America; founder of Quebec

Chap·lin \\'chap-lən\\ Sir Charles Spencer 1889–1977 British actor and producer

Chap·man \\'chap-mən\\ John 1774–1845 *Johnny Appleseed* \\'ap-əl-ˌsēd\\ American pioneer

Char·le·magne \\'shär-lə-ˌmän\\ 742–814 A.D. *Charles the Great* or *Charles I* Frankish king (768–814); emperor of the West (800–814)

Charles \\'chär(-ə)lz\\ name of 10 kings of France: especially **I** 823–877 A.D. (reigned 840–77) *the Bald*; Holy Roman emperor as *Charles II* (875–77); **IV** 1294–1328 (reigned 1322–28) *the Fair*; **V** 1337–1380 (reigned 1364–80) *the Wise*; **VI** 1368–1422 (reigned 1380–1422) *the Mad* or *the Beloved*; **VII** 1403–1461 (reigned 1422–61) *the Victorious*; **IX** 1550–1574 (reigned 1560–74); **X** 1757–1836 (reigned 1824–30)

Charles name of two kings of Great Britain: **I** 1600–1649 (reigned 1625–49) *Charles Stuart*; **II** 1630–1685 (reigned 1660–85) son of Charles I

Charles V 1500–1558 Holy Roman emperor (1519–56); king of Spain as *Charles I* (1516–56)

Charles Edward Stuart 1720–1788 *the Young Pretender*; *(Bonnie) Prince Charlie* English prince

Charles Mar·tel \\mär-'tel\\ *about* 688–741 A.D. Frankish ruler (719–41); grandfather of Charlemagne

Cha·ryb·dis \\kə-'rib-dəs, shə-, chə-\\ a whirlpool off the coast of Sicily personified in Greek mythology as a female monster

Chau·cer \\'chȯ-sər\\ Geoffrey *about* 1342–1400 English poet

Che·khov \\'chek-ˌȯf, -ˌȯv\\ Anton Pavlovich 1860–1904 Russian author

Cheops — see KHUFU

Ches·ter·ton \\'ches-tərt-ᵊn\\ Gilbert Keith 1874–1936 English author

Cho·pin \\'shō-ˌpan\\ Frédéric François 1810–1849 Polish pianist and composer

Chou En-lai \\'jō-'en-'lī\\ 1898–1976 Chinese Communist politician; premier (1949–76)

Christ Jesus — see JESUS

Chris·tie \\'kris-tē\\ Agatha 1890–1976 English author

Chur·chill \\'chər-chil, 'chərch-ˌhil\\ Sir Winston Leonard Spencer 1874–1965 British prime minister (1940–45; 1951–55)

Clark \\'klärk\\ George Rogers 1752–1818 American soldier and pioneer

---

\\ə\\abut \\ᵊ\\kitten \\ər\\further \\a\\ash \\ā\\ace \\ä\\mop, mar
\\aú\\out \\ch\\chin \\e\\bet \\ē\\easy \\g\\go \\i\\hit \\ī\\ice \\j\\job
\\ŋ\\sing \\ō\\go \\ȯ\\law \\ȯi\\boy \\th\\thin \\t̲h̲\\the \\ü\\loot \\ù\\foot
\\y\\yet \\zh\\vision *see also* Pronunciation Symbols page

Clark William 1770–1838 American explorer

Clay \\'klā\ Henry 1777–1852 American politician and orator

Clem·ens \\'klem-ənz\ Samuel Langhorne 1835–1910 pseudonym *Mark Twain* \\'twān\ American author

Cle·o·pa·tra \\ˌklē-ə-'pa-trə, -'pä-, -'pä-\ 69–30 B.C. queen of Egypt (51–30)

Cleve·land \\'klēv-lənd\ (Stephen) Grover 1837–1908 22d and 24th president of the U.S. (1885–89; 1893–97)

Clin·ton \\'klin-t°n\ William Jefferson 1946– 42d president of the U.S.(1993–)

Cly·tem·nes·tra \\ˌklīt-əm-'nes- trə\ wife of Agamemnon in Greek mythology

Cobb \\'käb\ Tyrus Raymond 1886–1961 *Ty* American baseball player

Co·chise \kō-'chēs\ 1812?–1874 Apache Indian chief

Co·dy \\'kōd-ē\ William Frederick 1846–1917 *Buffalo Bill* American hunter, guide, and entertainer

Co·han \\'kō-ˌhan\ George Michael 1878–1942 American actor and composer

Cole·ridge \\'kōl-rij, 'kō-lə-rij\ Samuel Taylor 1772–1834 English poet

Co·lette \kȯ-'let\ Sidonie-Gabrielle 1873–1954 French author

Co·lum·bus \kə-'ləm-bəs\ Christopher 1451–1506 Italian navigator; discovered America for Spain (1492)

Con·fu·cius \kən-'fyü-shəs\ 551–479 B.C. Chinese philosopher

Con·rad \\'kän-ˌrad\ Joseph 1857–1924 British (Ukrainian-born of Polish parents) author

Con·sta·ble \\'kən(t)-stə-bəl, 'kän(t)-\ John 1776–1837 English painter

Con·stan·tine \\'kän(t)-stən-ˌtēn, -ˌtīn\ *died* 337 A.D. *the Great* Roman emperor (306–37)

Cook \\'kùk\ Captain James 1728–1779 English navigator

Coo·lidge \\'kü-lij\ (John) Calvin 1872–1933 30th president of the U.S. (1923–29)

Coo·per \\'kü-pər, 'kùp-ər\ James Fen·i·more \\'fen-ə-ˌmō(ə)r, -ˌmȯ(ə)r\ 1789–1851 American author

Co·per·ni·cus \kō-'pər-ni-kəs\ Nicolaus 1473–1543 Polish astronomer

Cop·land \\'kō-plənd\ Aaron 1900–1990 American composer

Cop·ley \\'käp-lē\ John Sin·gle·ton \\'siŋ-gəl-tən\ 1738–1815 American portrait painter

Corn·wal·lis \kȯrn-'wäl-əs\ 1st Marquis 1738–1805 *Charles Cornwallis* British general in America

Co·ro·na·do \ˌkȯr-ə-'näd-ō, ˌkär-\ Francisco Vásquez de *about* 1510–1554 Spanish explorer of southwestern U.S.

Cor·tés \kȯr-'tez, 'kȯr-ˌtez\ Hernán *or* Hernando 1485–1547 Spanish conqueror of Mexico

Cous·teau \kü-'stō\ Jacques-Yves 1910– French marine explorer

Crane \\'krān\ Stephen 1871–1900 American author

Crazy Horse \\'krā-zē-ˌhȯrs\ 1842–1877 Sioux Indian chief

Crock·ett \\'kräk-ət\ David 1786–1836 *Davy* American pioneer

Crom·well \\'kräm-ˌwel, 'krəm-, -wəl\ Oliver 1599–1658 English general and political leader; lord protector of England (1653–58)

Cro·nus \\'krō-nəs, 'krän-əs\ a Titan in Greek mythology overthrown by his son Zeus

Cum·mings \\'kəm-iŋz\ Edward Estlin 1894–1962 known as *e. e. cummings* American poet

Cu·pid \\'kyü-pəd\ god of love in Roman mythology — compare EROS

Cu·rie \kyü-'rē, 'kyü(ə)r-ē\ Marie 1867–1934 French (Polish-born) chemist; Nobel Prize winner (1903–1911)

Curie Pierre 1859–1906 French chemist; Nobel Prize winner (1903)

Cus·ter \\'kəs-tər\ George Armstrong 1839–1876 American general

Cy·ra·no de Ber·ge·rac \ˌsir-ə-ˌnō-də-'ber-zhə-ˌrak\ Savinien de 1619–1655 French poet and soldier

Dae·da·lus \\'ded-°l-əs, 'dēd-\ builder in Greek mythology of the Cretan labyrinth and inventor of wings by which he and his son Icarus escape from it

Dal·ton \\'dȯlt-°n\ John 1766–1844 English chemist and physicist

Da·na \\'dā-nə\ Richard Henry 1815–1882 American author

Dan·iel \\'dan-yəl\ a prophet in the Bible who is held captive in Babylon and delivered by God from a den of lions

Dan·te \\'dän-tā, 'dan-, -tē\ 1265–1321 Italian poet

Dare \\'da(ə)r, 'de(ə)r\ Virginia 1587–? first child born in America of English parents

Da·ri·us I \də-'rī-əs\ 550–486 B.C. *the Great* king of Persia (522–486)

Dar·row \\'dar-ō\ Clarence Seward 1857–1938 American lawyer

Dar·win \\'där-wən\ Charles Robert 1809–1882 English naturalist

Da·vid \\'dā-vəd\ a youth in the Bible who slays Goliath and succeeds Saul as king of Israel

Da·vis \\'dā-vəs\ Jefferson 1808–1889 president of the Confederate States of America (1861–65)

Dawes \\'dȯz\ William 1745–1799 American patriot

Debs \\'debz\ Eugene Victor 1855–1926 American socialist

De·bus·sy \ˌdeb-yü-'sē, ˌdäb-; də-'byü-sē\ (Achille-) Claude 1862–1918 French composer

De·ca·tur \di-'kāt-ər\ Stephen 1779–1820 American naval officer

De·foe \di-'fō\ Daniel 1660–1731 English author

De·gas \də-'gä\ (Hilaire-Germain-) Edgar 1834–1917 French painter

de Gaulle \di-'gōl, -'gȯl\ Charles-André-Joseph-Marie 1890–1970 French general; president of Fifth Republic (1958–69)

De·li·lah \di-'lī-lə\ mistress and betrayer of Samson in the Bible

De·me·ter \di-'mēt-ər\ goddess of agriculture in Greek mythology — compare CERES

de Mille \də-'mil\ Agnes George 1909?–1993 American dancer and choreographer

Des·cartes \dā-'kärt\ René 1596–1650 French mathematician and philosopher

de So·to \di-'sōt-ō\ Hernando 1496 (or 1499 or 1500)–1542 Spanish explorer in America

Dew·ey \\'d(y)ü-ē\ George 1837–1917 American admiral

Dewey John 1859–1952 American philosopher and educator

Dewey Melvil 1851–1931 American librarian

Di·ana \dī-'an-ə\ goddess of the forest and of childbirth in ancient Italian mythology who was identified with Artemis by the Romans

Dick·ens \\'dik-ənz\ Charles John Huffam 1812–1870 pseudonym *Boz* \\'bäz, 'bōz\ English author

Dick·in·son \\'dik-ən-sən\ Emily Elizabeth 1830–1886 American poet

Di·do \\'dīd-ō\ legendary queen of Carthage who falls in love with Aeneas and kills herself when he leaves her

Di·o·ny·sus \ˌdī-ə-'nī -səs, -'nē-\ god of wine and ecstasy in Greek mythology — **Di·o·ny·sian** \ˌdī-ə-'nizh-ē-ən\ *adj*

Dis·ney \\'diz-nē\ Walter Elias 1901–1966 American film producer

Dis·rae·li \diz-'rā-lē\ Benjamin 1804–1881 1st Earl of *Bea·cons·field* \\'bē-kənz-ˌfēld\ British prime minister (1868; 1874–80)

Dix \\'diks\ Dorothea Lynde 1802–1887 American social reformer

Dodg·son \'däj-sən, 'däd-\ Charles Lut·widge \'lət-wij\ 1832–1898 pseudonym *Lewis Car·roll* \'kar-əl\ English author and mathematician

Donne \'dən\ John 1572–1631 English poet and minister

Don Qui·xote \ˌdän-kē-'(h)ōt-ē, ˌdäŋ-; dän-'kwik-sət\ the idealistic and impractical hero of Cervantes' *Don Quixote*

Dos·to·yev·ski \ˌdäs-tə-'yef-skē, -'yev-\ Fyodor Mikhaylovich 1821–1881 Russian novelist

Doug·las \'dəg-ləs\ Stephen Arnold 1813–1861 American politician

Doug·lass \'dəg-ləs\ Frederick 1817–1895 American abolitionist

Doyle \'dȯi(ə)l\ Sir Arthur Co·nan \'kō-nən\ 1859–1930 British physician, novelist, and detective-story writer

Drake \'drāk\ Sir Francis 1540 (or 1543)–1596 English navigator and admiral

Drei·ser \'drī-sər, -zər\ Theodore 1871–1945 American author

Du Bois \d(y)ü-'bȯis\ William Edward Burghardt 1868–1963 American educator and writer

Du·mas \d(y)ü-'mä, 'd(y)ü-ˌmä\ Alexandre 1802–1870 *Dumas père* \'pe(ə)r\ French author

Dumas Alexandre 1824–1895 *Dumas fils* \'fēs\ French author

Dun·can \'dəŋ-kən\ Isadora 1877–1927 American dancer

Dü·rer \'d(y)ùr-ər\ Albrecht 1471–1528 German painter and engraver

Ea·kins \'ā-kənz\ Thomas 1844–1916 American artist

Ear·hart \'e(ə)r-ˌhärt, 'i(ə)r-\ Amelia 1897–1937 American aviator

Ed·dy \'ed-ē\ Mary Baker 1821–1910 American founder of the Christian Science Church

Ed·i·son \'ed-ə-sən\ Thomas Alva 1847–1931 American inventor

Ed·ward \'ed-wərd\ name of eight post-Norman kings of England: **I** 1239–1307 (reigned 1272–1307) *Longshanks*; **II** 1284–1327 (reigned 1307–27); **III** 1312–1377 (reigned 1327–77); **IV** 1442–1483 (reigned 1461–70; 1471–83); **V** 1470–1483 (reigned 1483); **VI** 1537–1553 (reigned 1547–53) son of Henry VIII and Jane Seymour; **VII** 1841–1910 (reigned 1901–10) *Albert Edward* son of Queen Victoria; **VIII** 1894–1972 (reigned 1936; abdicated) *Duke of Windsor* son of George V

Ein·stein \'īn-ˌstīn\ Albert 1879–1955 American (German-born) physicist; Nobel Prize winner (1921)

Ei·sen·how·er \'īz-ᵊn-ˌhaů(-ə)r\ Dwight David 1890–1969 American general; 34th president of the U.S. (1953–61)

Elec·tra \i-'lek-trə\ sister of Orestes in Greek mythology who with her brother avenges their father's murder

Eli·jah \i-'lī-jə\ Hebrew prophet of the 9th century B.C.

El·iot \'el-ē-ət, 'el-yət\ George 1819–1880 pseudonym of *Mary Ann Evans* English author

Eliot Thomas Stearns 1888–1965 British (American-born) poet and critic

Eliz·a·beth I \i-'liz-ə-bəth\ 1533–1603 daughter of Henry VIII and Anne Boleyn; queen of England (1558–1603)

Elizabeth II 1926–   queen of the United Kingdom (1952–)

Em·er·son \'em-ər-sən\ Ralph Waldo 1803–1882 American essayist and poet

En·dym·i·on \en-'dim-ē-ən\ beautiful youth in Greek mythology loved by the goddess of the moon

Ep·i·cu·rus \ˌep-i-'kyùr-əs\ 341–270 B.C. Greek philosopher

Er·ik \'er-ik\ *the Red* 10th century Norwegian navigator; explored Greenland coast

Eriksson Leif — see LEIF ERIKSSON

Eros \'e(ə)r-ˌäs, 'i(ə)r-\ god of love in Greek mythology — compare CUPID

Esau \'ē-(ˌ)sȯ\ son of Isaac and Rebekah and elder twin brother of Jacob in the Bible

Es·ther \'es-tər\ Hebrew woman in the Bible who as the queen of Persia delivers her people from destruction

Eu·clid \'yü-kləd\ *flourished about* 300 B.C. Greek mathematician

Eu·rip·i·des \yù-'rip-ə-ˌdēz\ *about* 484–406 B.C. Greek dramatist

Eu·ro·pa \yù-'rō-pə\ a princess in Greek mythology who was carried off by Zeus disguised as a white bull

Eu·ryd·i·ce \yù-'rid-ə-sē\ the wife of Orpheus whom he attempts to bring back from Hades

Eve \'ēv\ the first woman in the Bible

Eze·kiel \i-'zē-kyəl, -kē-əl\ Hebrew prophet of the 6th century B.C.

Fahr·en·heit \'far-ən-ˌhīt, 'fär-\ Daniel Gabriel 1686–1736 German physicist

Far·a·day \'far-ə-ˌdā, -əd-ē\ Michael 1791–1867 English chemist and physicist

Far·ra·gut \'far-ə-gət\ David Glasgow 1801–1870 American admiral

Faulk·ner \'fȯk-nər\ William 1897–1962 American author; Nobel Prize winner (1949)

Faust \'faůst\ *or* **Fau·stus** \'faů-stəs, 'fȯ-\ a legendary German magician who sells his soul to the devil

Fawkes \'fȯks\ Guy 1570–1606 English conspirator

Fer·di·nand \'fərd-ᵊn-ˌand\ II of Aragon *or* V of Castile 1452–1516 *the Catholic* king of Castile (1474–1504); of Aragon (1479–1516); of Naples (1504–16); founder of the Spanish monarchy

Fer·mi \'fe(ə)r-mē\ Enrico 1901–1954 American (Italian-born) physicist; Nobel Prize winner (1938)

Field·ing \'fē(ə)l-diŋ\ Henry 1707–1754 English author

Fill·more \'fil-ˌmō(ə)r, -ˌmȯ(ə)r\ Millard 1800–1874 13th president of the U.S. (1850–53)

Fitz·ger·ald \fits-'jer-əld\ Francis Scott Key 1896–1940 American author

Flem·ing \'flem-iŋ\ Sir Alexander 1881–1955 British bacteriologist; Nobel Prize winner (1945)

Flo·ra \'flōr-ə, 'flȯr-\ goddess of flowers in Roman mythology

Flying Dutchman legendary Dutch mariner condemned to sail the seas until Judgment Day

Ford \'fō(ə)rd, 'fȯ(ə)rd\ Gerald Rudolph 1913–   38th president of the U.S. (1974–77)

Ford Henry 1863–1947 American automobile manufacturer

Fos·ter \'fȯs-tər, 'fäs-\ Stephen Collins 1826–1864 American songwriter

Francis \'fran(t)-səs\ **of As·si·si** \ə-'sis-ē, -'sē-zē, -'sē-sē, -'siz-ē\ Saint 1181 (or 1182)–1226 Italian friar; founder of Franciscan order

Frank·lin \'fraŋ-klən\ Benjamin 1706–1790 American patriot, author, and inventor

Fred·er·ick I \'fred-(ə-)rik\ *about* 1123–1190 *Frederick Bar·ba·ros·sa* \ˌbär-bə-'räs-ə, -'rȯs-\ Holy Roman emperor (1152–90)

Frederick II 1712–1786 *the Great* king of Prussia (1740–86)

Fré·mont \'frē-ˌmänt\ John Charles 1813–1890 American general and explorer

French \'french\ Daniel Chester 1850–1931 American sculptor

Freud \'frȯid\ Sigmund 1856–1939 Austrian neurologist; founder of psychoanalysis

Frig·ga \'frig-ə\ wife of Odin and goddess of married love and the hearth in Norse mythology

Frost \'frȯst\ Robert Lee 1874–1963 American poet

\ə\abut \ᵊ\kitten \ər\further \a\ash \ā\ace \ä\mop, mar
\aů\out \ch\chin \e\bet \ē\easy \g\go \i\hit \ī\ice \j\job
\ŋ\sing \ō\go \ȯ\law \ȯi\boy \th\thin \t̲h̲\the \ü\loot \ù\foot
\y\yet \zh\vision *see also* Pronunciation Symbols page

Ful·ler \\'ful-ər\ (Richard) Buckminster 1895–1983 American engineer

Fuller (Sarah) Margaret 1810–1850 American author and reformer

Ful·ton \\'fult-ᵊn\ Robert 1765–1815 American inventor

Ga·bri·el \\'gā-brē-əl\ one of the four archangels named in Hebrew tradition — compare MICHAEL, RAPHAEL, URIEL

Ga·ga·rin \gə-'gär-ən\ Yu·ry \\'yu̇(ə)r-ē\ Alekseyevich 1934–1968 Russian astronaut; first man in space

Gage \\'gāj\ Thomas 1721–1787 British general in America

Gal·a·had \\'gal-ə-ˌhad\ knight of the Round Table who finds the Holy Grail

Gal·a·tea \ˌgal-ə-'tē-ə\ a female figure sculpted by Pygmalion in Greek mythology and given life by Aphrodite in answer to the sculptor's prayer

Ga·len \\'gā-lən\ 129–*about* 199 A.D. Greek physician and writer

Ga·li·lei \ˌgal-ə-'lā-ē\ Ga·li·leo \ˌgal-ə-'lē-ō, -'lā-\ 1564–1642 usually called *Galileo* Italian astronomer and physicist — **Gal·i·le·an** \ˌgal-ə-'lē-ən\ *adj*

Gall \\'gȯl\ 1840?–1894 Sioux Indian leader

Ga·ma, da \\'gam-ə, 'gäm-\ Vasco *about* 1460–1524 Portuguese navigator

Gan·dhi \\'gän-dē, 'gan-\ Mohandas Karamchand 1869–1948 *Ma·hat·ma* \mə-'hät-mə, -'hat-\ Indian leader

Gar·field \\'gär-ˌfēld\ James Abram 1831–1881 20th president of the U.S. (1881)

Gar·i·bal·di \ˌgar-ə-'bȯl-dē\ Giuseppe 1807–1882 Italian patriot

Gar·ri·son \\'gar-ə-sən\ William Lloyd 1805–1879 American abolitionist

Gau·guin \gō-gan\ (Eugène-Henri-) Paul 1848–1903 French painter

Gau·ta·ma Bud·dha \ˌgau̇t-ə-mə-'büd-ə, -'bu̇d-\ *about* 563–*about* 483 B.C. *The Buddha* Indian philosopher; founder of Buddhism

Gen·ghis Khan \ˌjeŋ-gə-'skän, ˌgeŋ-\ *about* 1162–1227 Mongol conqueror

George \\'jȯ(ə)rj\ name of six kings of Great Britain: **I** 1660–1727 (reigned 1714–27); **II** 1683–1760 (reigned 1727–60); **III** 1738–1820 (reigned 1760–1820); **IV** 1762–1830 (reigned 1820–30); **V** 1865–1936 (reigned 1910–36); **VI** 1895–1952 (reigned 1936–52)

Ge·ron·i·mo \jə-'rän-ə-ˌmō\ 1829–1909 Apache Indian leader

Gersh·win \\'gərsh-wən\ George 1898–1937 American composer

Gid·e·on \\'gid-ē-ən\ Hebrew hero in the Bible

Gil·bert \\'gil-bərt\ Sir William Schwenck 1836–1911 English librettist and poet; collaborator with Sir Arthur Sullivan

Glad·stone \\'glad-ˌstōn, *chiefly British* -stən\ William Ewart 1809–1898 British prime minister (1868–74; 1880–85; 1886; 1892–94)

Glenn \\'glen\ John Herschel 1921– American astronaut and politician; first American to orbit the earth (1962)

Go·di·va \gə-'dī-və\ an English gentlewoman who in legend rode naked through Coventry to save its citizens from a tax

Goe·thals \\'gō-thəlz\ George Washington 1858–1928 American general and engineer

Goe·the \\'gə(r)-tə\ Johann Wolfgang von 1749–1832 German author

Gogh, van \van-'gō, -'gäk̲, -'k̲ȯk̲\ Vincent Willem 1853–1890 Dutch painter

Go·li·ath \gə-'lī-əth\ Philistine giant who is killed by David in the Bible

Gom·pers \\'gäm-pərz\ Samuel 1850–1924 American (British-born) labor leader

Good·year \\'gu̇d-ˌyi(ə)r, 'gu̇j-ˌi(ə)r\ Charles 1800–1860 American inventor

Gor·gas \\'gȯr-gəs\ William Crawford 1854–1920 American army surgeon

Gra·ham \\'grā-əm, 'gra(-ə)m\ Martha 1893–1991 American dancer and choreographer

Grant \\'grant\ Ulysses 1822–1885 originally *Hiram Ulysses Grant* American general; 18th president of the U.S. (1869–77)

Gre·co, El \el-'grek-ō\ 1541–1614 *Doménikos Theotokópoulos* Spanish (Cretan-born) painter

Gree·ley \\'grē-lē\ Horace 1811–1872 American journalist and politician

Greene \\'grēn\ Graham 1904–1991 British novelist

Greene Nathanael 1742–1786 American Revolutionary general

Greg·o·ry \\'greg-(ə-)rē\ name of 16 popes: especially **I** Saint *about* 540–604 *the Great* (pope 590–604); **VII** Saint *about* 1020–1085 (pope 1073–85); **XIII** 1502–1585 (pope 1572–85)

Grey \\'grā\ Lady Jane 1537–1554 English noblewoman beheaded as a possible rival for the throne of Mary I

Grey Zane 1875–1939 American novelist

Grimm \\'grim\ Jacob 1785–1863 and his brother Wilhelm 1786–1859 German philologists and folklorists

Guin·e·vere \\'gwin-ə-ˌvi(ə)r\ wife of King Arthur and lover of Lancelot

Gu·ten·berg \\'güt-ᵊn-ˌbərg\ Johannes *about* 1390–1468 German inventor of printing from movable type

Ha·des \\'hād-ˌēz\ — see PLUTO

Ha·dri·an \\'hā-drē-ən\ 76–138 A.D. Roman emperor (117–138)

Ha·gar \\'hā-ˌgär, -gər\ mistress of Abraham and mother of Ishmael in the Bible

Hai·le Se·las·sie \ˌhī-lē-sə-'las-ē, -'läs-\ 1892–1975 emperor of Ethiopia (1930–36; 1941–74)

Hale \\'hā(ə)l\ Edward Everett 1822–1909 American minister and author

Hale Nathan 1755–1776 American Revolutionary hero

Hal·ley \\'hal-ē, 'hā-lē\ Edmond *or* Edmund 1656–1742 English astronomer

Hal·sey \\'hȯl-sē, -zē\ William Frederick 1882–1959 American admiral

Ham·il·ton \\'ham-əl-tən\ Alexander 1755–1804 American political leader

Ham·mu·ra·bi \ˌham-ə-'räb-ē\ *or* **Ham·mu·ra·pi** \-'räp-ē\ *died* 1750 B.C. king of Babylon (1792–50)

Han·cock \\'han-ˌkäk\ John 1737–1793 American Revolutionary patriot

Han·del \\'han-dᵊl\ George Frideric 1685–1759 British (German-born) composer

Han·dy \\'han-dē\ William Christopher 1873–1958 American blues musician

Han·ni·bal \\'han-ə-bəl\ 247–183 B.C. Carthaginian general

Har·ding \\'härd-iŋ\ Warren Gamaliel 1865–1923 29th president of the U.S. (1921–23)

Har·dy \\'härd-ē\ Thomas 1840–1928 English author

Har·ri·son \\'har-ə-sən\ Benjamin 1833–1901 23d president of the U.S. (1889–93); grandson of William Henry Harrison

Harte \\'härt\ Francis Brett 1836–1902 known as *Bret* American author

Har·vey \\'här-vē\ William 1578–1657 English physician and anatomist

Haw·thorne \\'hȯ-ˌthȯ(ə)rn\ Nathaniel 1804–1864 American author

Hayes \\'hāz\ Rutherford Birchard 1822–1893 19th president of the U.S. (1877–81)

Hearst \\'hərst\ William Randolph 1863–1951 American newspaper publisher

Hec·tor \\'hek-tər\ son of Priam and Trojan hero slain by Achilles in Greek mythology

Hec·u·ba \'hek-yə-bə\ wife of Priam in Greek mythology

Hel·en of Troy \'hel-ə-nəv-'tròi\ wife of Menelaus whose abduction by Paris in Greek mythology caused the Trojan War

He·li·os \'hē-lē-əs, -ōs\ god of the sun in Greek mythology

Hem·ing·way \'hem-iŋ-ˌwā\ Ernest Miller 1899–1961 American author; Nobel Prize winner (1954)

Hen·ry \'hen-rē\ name of eight kings of England: **I** 1068–1135 (reigned 1100–35); **II** 1133–1189 (reigned 1154–89); **III** 1207–1272 (reigned 1216–72); **IV** 1367–1413 (reigned 1399–1413); **V** 1387–1422 (reigned 1413–22); **VI** 1421–1471 (reigned 1422–61; 1470–71); **VII** 1457–1509 (reigned 1485–1509); **VIII** 1491–1547 (reigned 1509–47)

Henry name of 4 kings of France: **I** 1008–1060 (reigned 1031–60); **II** 1519–1559 (reigned 1547–59); **III** 1551–1589 (reigned 1574–89); **IV** 1553–1610 *Henry of Navarre* (reigned 1589–1610)

Henry O. — see William Sydney PORTER

Henry Patrick 1736–1799 American patriot and orator

He·phaes·tus \hi-'fes-təs, -'fēs-\ god of fire and of metalworking in Greek mythology — compare VULCAN

He·ra \'hir-ə, 'hē-rə\ sister and wife of Zeus and goddess of women and marriage in Greek mythology — compare JUNO

Her·cu·les \'hər-kyə-ˌlēz\ *or* **Her·a·cles** \'her-ə-ˌklēz\ hero in Greek mythology noted for his strength and for performing 12 labors imposed on him by Hera

Her·maph·ro·di·tus \(ˌ)hər-ˌmaf-rə-'dīt-əs\ son of Hermes and Aphrodite who in Greek mythology is joined with a nymph into one body

Her·mes \'hər-mēz\ god of commerce, eloquence, invention, travel, and theft who serves as herald and messenger of the other gods in Greek mythology

Her·od \'her-əd\ 73–4 B.C. *the Great* Roman king of Judea (37–4)

Herod An·ti·pas \'ant-ə-ˌpas, -pəs\ 21 B.C.–39 A.D. Roman governor of Galilee (4 B.C.–39 A.D.); son of Herod the Great

Hey·er·dahl \'hā-ər-ˌdäl, 'hī-\ Thor 1914– Norwegian explorer and author

Hi·a·wa·tha \ˌhī-ə-'wò-thə, ˌhē-ə-, -'wäth-ə\ legendary Indian chief

Hick·ok \'hik-ˌäk\ James Butler 1837–1876 *Wild Bill* American scout and United States marshal

Hil·ton \'hilt-ᵊn\ James 1900–1954 English novelist

Hip·poc·ra·tes \hip-'äk-rə-ˌtēz\ *about* 460–*about* 377 B.C. *founder of medicine* Greek physician

Hi·ro·hi·to \ˌhir-ō-'hē-tō\ 1901–1989 emperor of Japan (1926–89)

Hit·ler \'hit-lər\ Adolf 1889–1945 German (Austrian-born) chancellor (1933–45)

Holmes \'hōmz, 'hōlmz\ Oliver Wendell 1809–1894 American physician and author

Holmes Oliver Wendell 1841–1935 American jurist; son of the preceding

Ho·mer \'hō-mər\ 9th–8th? century B.C. Greek epic poet — **Ho·mer·ic** \hō-'mer-ik\ *adj*

Homer Winslow 1836–1910 American painter

Hooke \'hùk\ Robert 1635–1703 English scientist

Hook·er \'hùk-ər\ Thomas 1586?–1647 English colonist; a founder of Connecticut

Hoo·ver \'hü-vər\ Herbert Clark 1874–1964 31st president of the U.S. (1929–33)

Hoover John Edgar 1895–1972 American criminologist; director of the Federal Bureau of Investigation (1924–72)

Hou·di·ni \hü-'dē-nē\ Harry 1874–1926 originally *Ehrich Weiss* American magician

Hous·ton \'(h)yü-stən\ Samuel 1793–1863 *Sam* American general; president of the Republic of Texas (1836–38; 1841–44)

Howe \'haù\ Elias 1819–1867 American inventor

Howe Julia 1819–1910 née *Ward* American suffragist and reformer

Hud·son \'həd-sən\ Henry *died* 1611 English navigator and explorer

Hughes \'hyüz *also* 'yüz\ (James) Langston 1902–1967 American author

Hus·sein I \hü-'sān\ 1935– king of Jordan (1952–)

Hutch·in·son \'həch-ə(n)-sən\ Anne 1591–1643 religious leader in America

Hutchinson Thomas 1711–1780 American colonial administrator

Hux·ley \'hək-slē\ Aldous Leonard 1894–1963 English author

Hy·men \'hī-mən\ god of marriage in Greek mythology

Ib·sen \'ib-sən, 'ip-\ Henrik 1828–1906 Norwegian dramatist and poet

Ic·a·rus \'ik-ə-rəs\ son of Daedalus who in Greek mythology falls into the sea when the wax of his artificial wings melts as he flies too near the sun

Ig·na·tius \ig-'nā-sh(ē-)əs\ *Saint Ignatius of Loy·o·la* \ˌlòi-'ō-lə\ 1491–1556 Spanish soldier and priest; founded the Society of Jesus

In·no·cent \'in-ə-sənt\ name of 13 popes: especially **II** *died* 1143 (pope 1130–43); **III** 1160 (or 1161)–1216 (pope 1198–1216); **IV** *died* 1254 (pope 1243–54); **XI** 1611–1689 (pope 1676–89)

Ir·ving \'ər-viŋ\ Washington 1783–1859 American author

Isaac \'ī-zik, -zək\ son of Abraham and father of Jacob in the Bible

Is·a·bel·la I \ˌiz-ə-'bel-ə\ 1451–1504 queen of Castile (1474–1504) and of Aragon (1479–1504); wife of Ferdinand V of Castile

Isa·iah \ī-'zā-ə\ Hebrew prophet of the 8th century B.C.

Ish·ma·el \'ish-(ˌ)mā-əl, -mē-\ outcast son of Abraham and Hagar in the Bible

Ives \'īvz\ Charles Edward 1874–1954 American composer

Jack·son \'jak-sən\ Andrew 1767–1845 American general; 7th president of the U.S. (1829–37)

Jackson Thomas Jonathan 1824–1863 *Stonewall* American Confederate general

Ja·cob \'jā-kəb\ son of Isaac and Rebekah and younger twin brother of Esau in the Bible

James \'jāmz\ one of the 12 apostles in the Bible

James *the Less* one of the 12 apostles in the Bible

James name of two kings of Great Britain: **I** 1566–1625 (reigned 1603–25); king of Scotland as *James VI* (reigned 1567–1603); **II** 1633–1701 (reigned 1685–88)

James Henry 1843–1916 British (American-born) author

Ja·nus \'jā-nəs\ god of gates and doors and of beginnings and endings in Roman mythology who is usually pictured as having two opposite faces

Ja·son \'jās-ᵊn\ hero in Greek mythology noted for his successful quest of the Golden Fleece

Jay \'jā\ John 1745–1829 American jurist and political leader; 1st chief justice of the U.S. Supreme Court (1789–95)

Jef·fer·son \'jef-ər-sən\ Thomas 1743–1826 3d president of the U.S. (1801–09) — **Jef·fer·so·nian** \ˌjef-ər-'sō-nē-ən, -nyən\ *adj*

Jer·e·mi·ah \ˌjer-ə-'mī-ə\ Hebrew prophet of the 6th and 7th centuries B.C.

Je·sus \'jē-zəs, -zəz\ *or* **Jesus Christ** \'krīst\ *or* **Christ** Jesus *about* 6 B.C.–*about* 30 A.D. source of the Christian religion and Savior in the Christian faith

Jez·e·bel \'jez-ə-ˌbel\ queen of Israel and wife of Ahab who was noted for her wickedness

---

\ə\abut \ᵊ\kitten \ər\further \a\ash \ā\ace \ä\mop, mar
\aù\out \ch\chin \e\bet \ē\easy \g\go \i\hit \ī\ice \j\job
\ŋ\sing \ō\go \ò\law \òi\boy \th\thin \t̲h̲\the \ü\loot \ù\foot
\y\yet \zh\vision *see also* Pronunciation Symbols page

Joan of Arc \ˌjō-nə-ˈvärk\ Saint *about* 1412–1431 *the Maid of Orleans* French national heroine

Job \ˈjōb\ man in the Bible who has many sufferings but keeps his faith

Jo·cas·ta \jō-ˈkas-tə\ queen of Thebes in Greek mythology who unknowingly marries her son Oedipus

John \ˈjän\ *the Baptist* prophet and baptizer of Jesus in the Bible

John one of the 12 apostles believed to be the author of the fourth Gospel, three Epistles, and the Book of Revelation

John name of 21 popes: especially **XXIII** 1881–1963 (pope 1958–63)

John 1167–1216 *John Lack·land* \ˈlak-ˌland\ king of England (1199–1216)

John·son \ˈjän(t)-sən\ Andrew 1808–1875 17th president of the U.S. (1865–69)

Johnson Lyndon Baines 1908–1973 36th president of the U.S. (1963–69)

Johnson Samuel 1709–1784 *Dr. Johnson* English lexicographer and author

Jol·liet *or* **Jo·liet** \zhȯl-ˈyā, ˌjō-lē-ˈet\ Louis 1645–1700 French explorer in America

Jo·nah \ˈjō-nə\ Hebrew prophet who in the Bible spends three days in the belly of a great fish

Jones \ˈjōnz\ John Paul 1747–1792 American (Scottish-born) naval officer

Jop·lin \ˈjäp-lən\ Scott 1868–1917 American pianist and composer

Jo·seph \ˈjō-zəf *also* -səf\ a son of Jacob in the Bible who rose to high office in Egypt after being sold into slavery by his brothers

Joseph *about* 1840–1904 Nez Percé Indian chief

Joseph *Saint* husband of Mary, the mother of Jesus, in the Bible

Josh·ua \ˈjäsh-(ə-)wə\ Hebrew leader in the Bible who succeeds Moses during the settlement of the Israelites in Canaan

Ju·dah \ˈjüd-ə\ son of Jacob and ancestor of one of the 12 tribes of Israel in the Bible

Ju·das \ˈjüd-əs\ *or* **Judas Is·car·i·ot** \-is-ˈkar-ē-ət\ one of the 12 apostles and the betrayer of Jesus in the Bible

Ju·no \ˈjü-nō\ the queen of heaven in Roman mythology, wife of Jupiter, and goddess of light, birth, women, and marriage — compare HERA

Ju·pi·ter \ˈjü-pət-ər\ the chief god in Roman mythology, husband of Juno, and the god of light, of the sky and weather, and of the state

Kalb \ˈkälp, ˈkalb\ Johann 1721–1780 Baron *de Kalb* \di-ˈkalb\ German general in American Revolutionary army

Keats \ˈkēts\ John 1795–1821 English poet

Kel·ler \ˈkel-ər\ Helen Adams 1880–1968 American deaf and blind lecturer

Kel·vin \ˈkel-vən\ 1st Baron 1824–1907 *William Thomson* British mathematician and physicist

Ken·ne·dy \ˈken-əd-ē\ John Fitzgerald 1917–1963 35th president of the U.S. (1961–63)

Kennedy Robert Francis 1925–1968 American politician; attorney general of the U.S. (1961–64); brother of John F. Kennedy

Ke·o·kuk \ˈkē-ə-ˌkək\ 1788?–?1848 American Indian chief

Key \ˈkē\ Francis Scott 1779–1843 American lawyer; author of "The Star-Spangled Banner"

Khayyám Omar — see OMAR KHAYYÁM

Khru·shchev \krüsh-ˈ(ch)ȯf, -ˈ(ch)ȯv, -ˈ(ch)ef\ Ni·ki·ta \nə-ˈkēt-ə\ Sergeyevich 1894–1971 premier of U.S.S.R. (1958–64)

Khu·fu \ˈkü-fü\ *or Greek* **Che·ops** \ˈkē-ˌäps\ 26th century B.C. king of Egypt and pyramid builder

Kidd \ˈkid\ William *about* 1645–1701 *Captain Kidd* Scottish pirate

King \ˈkiŋ\ Martin Luther, Jr. 1929–1968 American minister and civil rights leader; Nobel Prize winner (1964)

Kip·ling \ˈkip-liŋ\ Rud·yard \ˈrəd-yərd, ˈrəj-ərd\ 1865–1936 English author

Kis·sin·ger \ˈkis-ᵊn-jər\ Henry Alfred 1923– American (German-born) scholar and government official; U.S. secretary of state (1973–77); Nobel Prize winner (1973)

Knox \ˈnäks\ John *about* 1514–1572 Scottish religious reformer

Koch \ˈkȯk, ˈkȯk͟h\ Robert 1843–1910 German bacteriologist; Nobel Prize winner (1905)

Koś·ciusz·ko \ˌkäs-ē-ˈəs-ˌkō, kȯsh-ˈchùsh-kō\ Tadeusz 1746–1817 Polish patriot and general in American Revolutionary army

Krish·na \ˈkrish-nə\ god worshipped in later Hinduism

Kriss Kringle — see SANTA CLAUS

Ku·blai Khan \ˌkü-blə-ˈkän, -ˌblī-\ 1215–1294 founder of Mongol dynasty in China

La·fa·yette \ˌläf-ē-ˈet, ˌlaf-\ Marquis de 1757–1834 French general in American Revolutionary army

La·ius \ˈlā-(y)əs, ˈlī-əs\ king of Thebes who in Greek mythology is killed by his son Oedipus

Lan·ce·lot \ˈlan(t)-sə-ˌlät\ legendary knight of the Round Table and lover of Queen Guinevere

La Salle \lə-ˈsal\ Sieur de 1643–1687 French explorer in America

La·voi·sier \ləv-ˈwäz-ē-ˌā\ Antoine-Laurent 1743–1794 French chemist

Law·rence \ˈlȯr-ən(t)s, ˈlär-\ Thomas Edward 1888–1935 *Lawrence of Arabia* later surnamed *Shaw* British archaeologist, soldier, and author

Laz·a·rus \ˈlaz-(ə-)rəs\ brother of Mary and Martha who in the Bible is raised by Jesus from the dead

Lazarus beggar in the biblical parable of the rich man and the beggar

Le·da \ˈlēd-ə\ a queen of Sparta in Greek mythology who is courted by Zeus in the form of a swan

Lee \ˈlē\ Ann 1736–1784 English mystic; founder of Shaker society in the U.S.

Lee Henry 1756–1818 *Light-Horse Harry* American general

Lee Robert Edward 1807–1870 American Confederate general

Leeu·wen·hoek \ˈlā-vən-ˌhùk\ Antonie van 1632–1723 Dutch naturalist

Leif Er·iks·son \ˌlā-ˈver-ik-sən, ˌlē-ˈfer-\ *or* **Er·ics·son** *flourished* 1000 Norwegian explorer; son of Erik the Red

Le·nin \ˈlen-ən\ 1870–1924 originally *Vladimir Ilyich Ul·ya·nov* \ül-ˈyän-əf, -ȯf, -ȯv\ Russian Communist leader

Leo \ˈlē-ō\ name of 13 popes: especially **I** Saint *died* 461 (pope 440–61); **III** Saint *died* 816 (pope 795–816); **XIII** 1810–1903 (pope 1878–1903)

Le·o·nar·do da Vin·ci \ˌlē-ə-ˈnärd-ˌōd-ə-ˈvin-chē, ˌlä-, -ˈvēn-\ 1452–1519 Italian painter, sculptor, architect, and engineer

Lew·is \ˈlü-əs\ John Llewellyn 1880–1969 American labor leader

Lewis Meriwether 1774–1809 American explorer (with William Clark)

Lewis (Harry) Sinclair 1885–1951 American author; Nobel Prize winner (1930)

Lin·coln \ˈliŋ-kən\ Abraham 1809–1865 16th president of the U.S. (1861–65)

Lind·bergh \ˈlin(d)-ˌbərg\ Charles Augustus 1902–1974 American aviator

Lin·nae·us \lə-ˈnē-əs, -ˈnā-\ Carolus 1707–1778 Swedish *Carl von Lin·né* \lə-ˈnā\ Swedish botanist

Lis·ter \ˈlis-tər\ Joseph 1827–1912 English surgeon

Liszt \ˈlist\ Franz 1811–1886 Hungarian pianist and composer

NAMES

Liv·ing·stone \\'liv-iŋ-stən\ David 1813–1873 Scottish explorer in Africa

Long·fel·low \\'lȯŋ-ˌfel-ō\ Henry Wads·worth \\'wädz-(ˌ)wərth\ 1807–1882 American poet

Lou·is \\'lü-ē, 'lü-əs\ name of 18 kings of France: especially **IX** Saint 1214–1270 (reigned 1226–70); **XI** 1423–1483 (reigned 1461–83); **XII** 1462–1515 (reigned 1498–1515); **XIII** 1601–1643 (reigned 1610–43); **XIV** 1638–1715 (reigned 1643–1715); **XV** 1710–1774 (reigned 1715–74); **XVI** 1754–1793 (reigned 1774–92; guillotined); **XVII** 1785–1795 (reigned in name 1793–95); **XVIII** 1755–1824 (reigned 1814–15; 1815–24)

Low \\'lō\ Juliette Gordon 1860–1927 American founder of the Girl Scouts

Low·ell \\'lō-əl\ Amy 1874–1925 American poet

Lowell James Russell 1819–1891 American author

Luke \\'lük\ physician and companion of the apostle Paul believed to be the author of the third Gospel and the Book of Acts

Lu·ther \\'lü-thər\ Martin 1483–1546 German Reformation leader

Ly·on \\'lī-ən\ Mary 1797–1849 American educator

Mac·Ar·thur \mə-'kär-thər\ Douglas 1880–1964 American general

Mc·Car·thy \mə-'kär-thē\ Joseph Raymond 1908–1957 American politician

Mc·Clel·lan \mə-'klel-ən\ George Brinton 1826–1885 American general

Mc·Cor·mick \mə-'kȯr-mik\ Cyrus Hall 1809–1884 American inventor

Mc·Kin·ley \mə-'kin-lē\ William 1843–1901 25th president of the U.S. (1897–1901)

Ma·cy \\'mā-sē\ Anne Sullivan 1866–1936 American educator; teacher of Helen Keller

Mad·i·son \\'mad-ə-sən\ James 1751–1836 4th president of the U.S. (1809–17)

Ma·gel·lan \mə-'jel-ən\ Ferdinand *about* 1480–1521 Portuguese navigator

Mal·colm X \ˌmal-kə-'meks\ 1925–1965 American civil rights leader

Ma·net \ma-'nā, mä-\ Édouard 1832–1883 French painter

Mann \\'man\ Horace 1796–1859 American educator

Mao Tse-tung \ˌmaú(d)-zə-'dúŋ, ˌmaút-sə-\ 1893–1976 Chinese Communist; leader of People's Republic of China (1949–76)

Mar·co·ni \mär-'kō-nē\ Guglielmo 1874–1937 Italian physicist and inventor; Nobel Prize winner (1909)

Ma·rie An·toi·nette \mə-'rē-ˌan-t(w)ə-'net\ 1755–1793 wife of Louis XVI

Mar·i·on \\'mer-ē-ən, 'mar-ē-\ Francis 1732?–1795 *the Swamp Fox* American commander in Revolution

Mark \\'märk\ evangelist believed to be the author of the second Gospel

Mar·quette \mär-'ket\ Jacques 1637–1675 French-born Jesuit missionary and explorer in America

Mars \\'märz\ the god of war in Roman mythology

Mar·shall \\'mär-shəl\ George Catlett 1880–1959 American general and diplomat

Marshall John 1755–1835 American jurist; chief justice of the U.S. Supreme Court (1801–35)

Mar·tha \\'mär-thə\ sister of Lazarus and Mary and friend of Jesus in the Bible

Mar·tin \\'märt-ᵊn\ Saint *about* 316–397 *Martin of Tours* \-'tù(ə)r\ patron saint of France

Marx \\'märks\ Karl 1818–1883 German political philosopher and socialist

Mary \\'me(ə)r-ē, 'ma(ə)r-ē, 'mā-rē\ mother of Jesus

Mary sister of Lazarus and Martha in the Bible

Mary I 1516–1558 *Mary Tudor*; *Bloody Mary* queen of England (1553–58)

Mary II 1662–1694 joint British sovereign with William III (1689–94)

Mary Mag·da·lene \-'mag-də-ˌlən, -ˌlēn\ woman in the Bible who was healed of evil spirits by Jesus and who later saw the risen Christ

Mary Stuart 1542–1587 *Mary, Queen of Scots* queen of Scotland (1542–87)

Mas·sa·soit \ˌmas-ə-'sȯit\ *died* 1661 Indian chief in eastern Massachusetts

Math·er \\'math-ər, 'math-\ Cotton 1663–1728 American religious leader and author

Mather Increase 1639–1723 American minister and author; father of Cotton Mather

Mat·thew \\'math-yü\ apostle believed to be the author of the first Gospel

Mau·pas·sant \ˌmō-pə-'sänt\ (Henri-René-Albert-) Guy de 1850–1893 French short-story writer

Mead \\'mēd\ Margaret 1901–1978 American anthropologist

Meade \\'mēd\ George Gordon 1815–1872 American general

Mea·ny \\'mē-nē\ George 1894–1980 American labor leader

Me·dea \mə-'dē-ə\ woman with magic powers in Greek mythology who helps Jason to win the Golden Fleece and who kills her children when he leaves her

Me·di·ci, de' \\'med-ə-chē\ Catherine 1519–1589 French *Catherine de Médicis* \ˌmäd-ə-'sē(s)\ queen of Henry II of France

Me·ir \me-'i(ə)r\ Golda 1898–1978 prime minister of Israel (1969–74)

Mel·ville \\'mel-ˌvil\ Herman 1819–1891 American author

Men·del \\'men-dᵊl\ Gregor Johann 1822–1884 Austrian botanist

Men·e·la·us \ˌmen-ᵊl-'ā-əs\ king of Sparta, brother of Agamemnon, and husband of Helen of Troy in Greek mythology

Meph·is·toph·e·les \ˌmef-ə-'stäf-ə-ˌlēz\ chief devil in the Faust legend

Mer·ca·tor \(ˌ)mər-'kāt-ər\ Gerardus 1512–1594 Flemish mapmaker

Mer·cu·ry \\'mər-kyə-rē, -k(ə-)rē\ god of commerce, eloquence, travel, and theft who serves as herald and messenger of the other gods in Roman mythology

Mer·lin \\'mər-lən\ prophet and magician in the legend of King Arthur

Mi·chael \\'mī-kəl\ one of the four archangels named in Hebrew tradition — compare GABRIEL, RAPHAEL, URIEL

Mi·chel·an·ge·lo \ˌmī-kə-'lan-jə-ˌlō, ˌmik-ə-'lan-, ˌmē-kə-'län-\ 1475–1564 Italian sculptor, painter, architect, and poet

Mi·das \\'mīd-əs\ legendary king who was given the power to turn everything he touched into gold

Mil·lay \mil-'ā\ Edna St. Vincent 1892–1950 American poet

Mil·ler \\'mil-ər\ Arthur 1915–   American author

Mil·ton \\'milt-ᵊn\ John 1608–1674 English poet

Mi·ner·va \mə-'nər-və\ goddess of wisdom in Roman mythology — compare ATHENA

Mi·no·taur \\'min-ə-ˌtȯ(ə)r, 'mī-nə-\ monster in Greek mythology shaped half like a man and half like a bull

Min·u·it \\'min-yə-wət\ Peter 1580–1638 Dutch colonial administrator in America

Mitch·ell \\'mich-əl\ Maria 1818–1889 American astronomer

Mo·lière \mōl-'ye(ə)r, 'mōl-ˌye(ə)r\ 1622–1673 originally *Jean-Baptiste Poquelin* French actor and dramatist

Mo·net \mō-'nā\ Claude 1840–1926 French painter

\ə\abut \ᵊ\kitten \ər\further \a\ash \ā\ace \ä\mop, mar \aú\out \ch\chin \e\bet \ē\easy \g\go \i\hit \ī\ice \j\job \ŋ\sing \ō\go \ȯ\law \ȯi\boy \th\thin \t̶h̶\the \ü\loot \ú\foot \y\yet \zh\vision *see also* Pronunciation Symbols page

Mon·roe \mən-ˈrō\ James 1758–1831 5th president of the U.S. (1817–25)

Mont·calm de Saint-Vé·ran \mänt-ˈkäm-də-ˌsan-vä-ˈrän, -ˈkälm-\ Marquis de 1712–1759 French field marshal in Canada

Mon·tes·so·ri \ˌmänt-ə-ˈsōr-ē, -ˈsȯr-\ Maria 1870–1952 Italian physician and educator

Mon·te·zu·ma II \ˌmänt-ə-ˈzü-mə\ 1466–1520 last Aztec emperor of Mexico (1502–20)

Moore \ˈmō(ə)r, ˈmȯ(ə)r, ˈmu̇(ə)r\ Marianne Craig 1887–1972 American poet

More \ˈmō(ə)r, ˈmȯ(ə)r\ Sir Thomas 1478–1535 *Saint* English public official and author

Mor·gan \ˈmȯr-gən\ John Pierpont 1837–1913 American financier

Morse \ˈmȯ(ə)rs\ Samuel Finley Breese 1791–1872 American artist and inventor

Mo·ses \ˈmō-zəz *also* -zəs\ Hebrew prophet and lawgiver who in the Bible freed the Israelites from slavery in Egypt

Mott \ˈmät\ Lucretia 1793–1880 American reformer

Mo·zart \ˈmōt-ˌsärt\ Wolfgang Amadeus 1756–1791 Austrian composer

Mu·h·am·mad \mō-ˈham-əd, -ˈhäm- *also* mü-\ *about* 570–632 Arab prophet and founder of Islam

Mus·so·li·ni \ˌmü-sə-ˈlē-nē, ˌmu̇s-ə-\ Be·ni·to \bə-ˈnēt-ō\ 1883–1945 *Il Du·ce* \ēl-ˈdü-chā\ Italian fascist premier (1922–43)

Na·po·léon I \nə-ˈpōl-yən, -ˈpō-lē-ən\ *or* Napoléon Bo·na·parte \ˈbō-nə-ˌpärt\ 1769–1821 emperor of the French (1804–15) — **Na·po·le·on·ic** \nə-ˌpō-lē-ˈän-ik\ *adj*

Nar·cis·sus \när-ˈsis-əs\ a beautiful youth in Greek mythology who pines away for love of his own reflection and is then turned into the narcissus flower

Nash \ˈnash\ Ogden 1902–1971 American poet

Na·tion \ˈnā-shən\ Car·ry \ˈkar-ē\ Amelia 1846–1911 American social reformer

Neb·u·cha·drez·zar II \ˌneb-(y)ə-kə-ˈdrez-ər\ *also* **Neb·u·chad·nez·zar** \-kəd-ˈnez-\ *about* 630–562 B.C. Chaldean king of Babylon (605–562)

Neh·ru \ˈne(ə)r-ü, ˈnā-rü\ Ja·wa·har·lal \jə-ˈwä-hər-ˌläl\ 1889–1964 Indian nationalist; 1st prime minister (1947–64)

Nel·son \ˈnel-sən\ Horatio 1758–1805 Viscount *Nelson* British admiral

Nem·e·sis \ˈnem-ə-səs\ the goddess of reward and punishment in Greek mythology

Nep·tune \ˈnep-ˌt(y)ün\ the god of the sea in Roman mythology

Ne·ro \ˈnē-ˌrō, ˈni(ə)r-ō\ 37–68 A.D. Roman emperor (54–68)

New·ton \ˈn(y)üt-ᵊn\ Sir Isaac 1642–1727 English mathematician and physicist

Nich·o·las \ˈnik-(ə-)ləs\ Saint 4th century Christian bishop

Nicholas I 1796–1855 czar of Russia (1825–55)

Nicholas II 1868–1918 czar of Russia (1894–1917)

Night·in·gale \ˈnīt-ᵊn-ˌgāl, -iŋ-\ Florence 1820–1910 English nurse and philanthropist

Ni·ke \ˈnī-kē\ the goddess of victory in Greek mythology

Ni·o·be \ˈnī-ə-bē\ a daughter of Tantalus in Greek mythology who while weeping for her slain children is turned into a stone from which her tears continue to flow

Nix·on \ˈnik-sən\ Richard Mil·hous \ˈmil-ˌhau̇s\ 1913–1994 37th president of the U.S. (1969–74)

No·ah \ˈnō-ə\ Old Testament builder of the ark in which he, his family, and living creatures of every kind survived the Flood

No·bel \nō-ˈbel\ Alfred Bernhard 1833–1896 Swedish manufacturer, inventor, and philanthropist

Oce·anus \ō-ˈsē-ə-nəs\ a Titan who rules over a great river encircling the earth in Greek mythology

Odin \ˈōd-ᵊn\ *or* **Wo·den** \ˈwōd-ᵊn\ god of war and patron of heroes in Norse mythology

Odys·seus \ō-ˈdis-ē-əs, -ˈdis-yəs, -ˈdish-əs, -ˈdish-ˌüs\ *or* **Ulys·ses** \yu̇-ˈlis-ēz\ king of Ithaca and hero in Greek mythology who after the Trojan war wanders for 10 years before reaching home

Oe·di·pus \ˈed-ə-pəs, ˈēd-\ son of Laius and Jocasta who in Greek mythology kills his father and marries his mother not knowing their identity

Ogle·thorpe \ˈō-gəl-ˌthȯrp\ James Edward 1696–1785 English general and philanthropist; founder of Georgia

O'·Keeffe \ō-ˈkēf\ Georgia 1887–1986 American painter

Omar Khay·yám \ˌō-mär-ˌkī-ˈ(y)äm, ˌō-mər-, -ˈ(y)am\ 1048?–1122 Persian poet and astronomer

O'·Neill \ō-ˈnē(ə)l\ Eugene Gladstone 1888–1953 American dramatist; Nobel Prize winner (1936)

Or·pheus \ˈȯr-ˌfyüs, -fē-əs\ poet and musician in Greek mythology who almost rescues his wife Eurydice from Hades by charming Pluto and Persephone with his lyre

Or·well \ˈȯr-ˌwel, -wəl\ George 1903–1950 pseudonym of *Eric Blair* English author — **Or·well·ian** \ȯr-ˈwel-ē-ən\ *adj*

Osce·o·la \ˌäs-ē-ˈō-lə, ˌō-sē-\ *about* 1800–1838 Seminole Indian chief

Otis \ˈōt-əs\ James 1725–1783 American Revolutionary patriot

Ov·id \ˈäv-əd\ 43 B.C.–17A.D.? Roman poet

Ow·en \ˈō-ən\ Robert 1771–1858 Welsh social reformer

Ow·ens \ˈō-ənz\ Jesse 1913–1980 originally *James Cleveland* American athlete

Paine \ˈpān\ Thomas 1737–1809 American (English-born) political philosopher and author

Pan \ˈpan\ god of forests, pastures, flocks, and shepherds in Greek mythology who is represented as having the legs, ears, and horns of a goat

Pan·do·ra \pan-ˈdōr-ə, -ˈdȯr-\ woman in Greek mythology who out of curiosity opened a box and let loose all of the evils that trouble humans

Par·is \ˈpar-əs\ son of Priam whose abduction of Helen of Troy in Greek mythology led to the Trojan War

Park·man \ˈpärk-mən\ Francis 1823–1893 American historian

Pas·cal \pas-ˈkal\ Blaise 1623–1662 French mathematician and philosopher

Pas·ter·nak \ˈpas-tər-ˌnak\ Boris Leonidovich 1890–1960 Russian author; Nobel Prize winner (1958)

Pas·teur \pas-ˈtər\ Louis 1822–1895 French chemist and microbiologist

Pat·rick \ˈpa-trik\ Saint 5th century apostle and patron saint of Ireland

Pat·ton \ˈpat-ᵊn\ George Smith 1885–1945 American general

Paul \ˈpȯl\ Saint *died between* 62 *and* 68 A.D. author of several New Testament epistles — **Pau·line** \ˈpȯ-ˌlīn\ *adj*

Paul name of six popes: especially **III** 1468–1549 (pope 1534–49); **V** 1552–1621 (pope 1605–21); **VI** 1897–1978 (pope 1963–78)

Paul Bun·yan \ˈpȯl-ˈbən-yən\ giant lumberjack in American folklore

Pau·ling \ˈpȯ-liŋ\ Linus Carl 1901–   American chemist; Nobel Prize winner (1954, 1962)

Pav·lov \ˈpäv-ˌlȯf, ˈpav-, -ˌlȯv\ Ivan Petrovich 1849–1936 Russian physiologist; Nobel Prize winner (1904)

Pa·vlo·va \ˈpav-lə-və, pav-ˈlō-və\ Anna 1882–1931 Russian ballerina

Pea·ry \ˈpi(ə)r-ē\ Robert Edwin 1856–1920 American arctic explorer

Pe·cos Bill \ˌpā-kəs-ˈbil\ a cowboy in American folklore known for his extraordinary feats

Peg·a·sus \ˈpeg-ə-səs\ winged horse in Greek mythology

Penn \\'pen\\ William 1644–1718 English Quaker; founder of Pennsylvania

Per·i·cles \\'per-ə-ˌklēz\\ *about* 495–429 B.C. Athenian political leader

Per·ry \\'per-ē\\ Matthew Calbraith 1794–1858 American commodore

Perry Oliver Hazard 1785–1819 American naval officer

Per·seph·o·ne \\pər-'sef-ə-nē\\ daughter of Zeus and Demeter who in Greek mythology is abducted by Pluto to rule with him over the underworld

Per·shing \\'pər-shiŋ, -zhiŋ\\ John Joseph 1860–1948 American general

Pe·ter \\'pēt-ər\\ Saint *died about* 64 A.D. *Si·mon Peter* \\'sī-mən-\\ one of the 12 apostles in the Bible

Peter I 1672–1725 *the Great* czar of Russia (1682–1725)

Phil·ip \\'fil-əp\\ one of the 12 apostles in the Bible

Philip 1639?–1676 American Indian chief

Philip name of six kings of France: espcially **II** *or* **Philip Augustus** 1165–1223 (reigned 1179–1223); **IV** 1268–1314 (reigned 1285–1314) *the Fair*; **VI** 1293–1350 (reigned 1328–50)

Philip name of five kings of Spain: especially **II** 1527–1598 (reigned 1556–98); **V** 1683–1746 (reigned 1700–46)

Philip II 382–336 B.C. king of Macedon (359–336); father of Alexander the Great

Pi·cas·so \\pi-'käs-ō, -'kas-\\ Pablo 1881–1973 Spanish painter and sculptor in France

Pick·ett \\'pik-ət\\ George Edward 1825–1875 American Confederate general

Pierce \\'pi(ə)rs\\ Franklin 1804–1869 14th president of the U.S. (1853–57)

Pi·late \\'pī-lət\\ Pon·tius \\'pän-chəs, 'pən-chəs\\ *died* after 36 A.D. Roman governor of Judea

Pitt \\'pit\\ William 1759–1806 English prime minister (1783–1801; 1804–6)

Pi·us \\'pī-əs\\ name of 12 popes: especially **VII** 1742–1823 (pope 1800–23); **IX** 1792–1878 (pope 1846–78); **X** 1835–1914 (pope 1903–14); **XI** 1857–1939 (pope 1922–39); **XII** 1876–1958 (pope 1939–58)

Pi·zar·ro \\pə-'zär-ō\\ Francisco *about* 1475–1541 Spanish conqueror of Peru

Pla·to \\'plāt-ō\\ *about* 428–348 (*or* 347) B.C. Greek philosopher

Plu·to \\'plüt-ō\\ god of the dead and the underworld in Greek mythology

Po·ca·hon·tas \\ˌpō-kə-'hänt-əs\\ *about* 1595–1617 American Indian princess

Poe \\'pō\\ Edgar Allan 1809–1849 American author

Polk \\'pōk\\ James Knox 1795–1849 11th president of the U.S. (1845–49)

Po·lo \\'pō-lō\\ Mar·co \\'mär-kō\\ 1254–1324 Venetian traveler

Poly·phe·mus \\ˌpäl-ə-'fē-məs\\ a Cyclops in Greek mythology who is blinded by Odysseus

Ponce de Le·ón \\ˌpän(t)s-sə-ˌdā-lē-'ōn, ˌpän(t)s-də-'lē-ən\\ Juan 1460–1521 Spanish explorer and discoverer of Florida (1513)

Pon·ti·ac \\'pänt-ē-ˌak\\ *about* 1720–1769 American Indian chief

Por·ter \\'pōrt-ər, 'pòrt-\\ Cole Albert 1891–1964 American composer and songwriter

Porter David Dixon 1813–1891 American admiral

Porter Katherine Anne 1890–1980 American author

Porter William Sydney 1862–1910 pseudonym *O. Henry* \\(')ō-'hen-rē\\ American author

Po·sei·don \\pə-'sīd-ᵊn\\ god of the sea in Greek mythology — compare NEPTUNE

Pot·ter \\'pät-ər\\ Beatrix 1866–1943 British author and illustrator

Pow·ha·tan \\ˌpaù-ə-'tan, paù-'hat-ᵊn\\ 1550?–1618 American Indian chief

Pri·am \\'prī-əm, -ˌam\\ king of Troy during the Trojan War in Greek mythology

Pro·me·theus \\prə-'mē-th(y)üs, -thē-əs\\ a Titan in Greek mythology who is punished by Zeus for stealing fire from heaven and giving it to human beings

Pro·teus \\'prō-ˌt(y)üs, 'prōt-ē-əs\\ sea god in Greek mythology who is capable of assuming different forms

Puc·ci·ni \\pü-'chē-nē\\ Giacomo 1858–1924 Italian composer

Pu·las·ki \\pə-'las-kē, pyü-\\ Kazimierz 1747–1779 Polish soldier in American Revolutionary army

Pu·lit·zer \\'pùl-ət-sər, 'pyü-lət-sər\\ Joseph 1847–1911 American (Hungarian-born) journalist

Pyg·ma·lion \\pig-'māl-yən, -'mā-lē-ən\\ a sculptor in Greek mythology who falls in love with a statue which is then brought to life

Py·thag·o·ras \\pə-'thag-ə-rəs, pī-\\ *about* 580–*about* 500 B.C. Greek philosopher and mathematician

Ra \\'rä, 'rò\\ god of the sun and chief deity of ancient Egypt

Ra·leigh *or* **Ra·legh** \\'ròl-ē, 'räl- *also* 'ral-\\ Sir Walter 1554–1618 English navigator and historian

Ram·ses \\'ram-ˌsēz\\ *or* **Ram·e·ses** \\'ram-ə-ˌsēz\\ name of 12 kings of Egypt: especially **II** (reigned 1304–1237 B.C.); **III** (reigned 1198–66 B.C.)

Ran·dolph \\'ran-ˌdälf\\ Asa Philip 1889–1979 American labor leader

Ra·pha·el \\'raf-ē-əl, 'rā-fē-\\ one of the four archangels named in Hebrew tradition — compare GABRIEL, MICHAEL, URIEL

Ra·pha·el \\'raf-ē-əl, 'rā-fē-, 'räf-ē-\\ 1483–1520 Italian painter

Ras·pu·tin \\ra-'sp(y)üt-ᵊn, -'spùt-\\ Grigory Yefimovich 1872–1916 Russian mystic

Rea·gan \\'rā-gən *also* 'rē-\\ Ronald Wilson 1911– 40th president of the U.S. (1981–89)

Re·bek·ah *or* **Re·bec·ca** \\ri-'bek-ə\\ wife of Isaac in the Bible

Red Cloud \\'red-ˌklaùd\\ 1822–1909 American Indian chief

Reed \\'rēd\\ Walter 1851–1902 American army surgeon

Rem·brandt \\'rem-ˌbrant *also* -ˌbränt\\ 1606–1669 Dutch painter

Re·mus \\'rē-məs\\ son of Mars who in Roman mythology is killed by his twin brother Romulus

Re·noir \\'ren-ˌwär, rən-'wär\\ Pierre-Auguste 1841–1919 French painter

Re·vere \\ri-'vi(ə)r\\ Paul 1735–1818 American patriot and silversmith

Rich·ard \\'rich-ərd\\ name of three kings of England: **I** 1157–1199 (reigned 1189–99) *the Lion-Hearted*; **II** 1367–1400 (reigned 1377–99); **III** 1452–1485 (reigned 1483–85)

Rob·in Good·fel·low \\ˌräb-ən-'gùd-ˌfel-ō\\ mischievous elf in English folklore

Rob·in·son \\'räb-ən-sən\\ Edwin Arlington 1869–1935 American poet

Rob·in·son Cru·soe \\ˌräb-ə(n)-sən-'krü-sō\\ a shipwrecked sailor in Daniel Defoe's *Robinson Crusoe* who lives for many years on a desert island

Ro·cham·beau \\ˌrō-ˌsham-'bō\\ Comte de 1725–1807 French general in American Revolution

Rocke·fel·ler \\'räk-i-ˌfel-ər, 'räk-ˌfel-\\ John Davison father 1839–1937 and son 1874–1960 American oil magnates and philanthropists

Ro·ma·nov *or* **Ro·ma·noff** \\rō-'män-əf, 'rō-mə-ˌnäf\\ Michael 1596–1645 1st czar (1613–45) of Russian Romanov dynasty (1613–1917)

Rom·u·lus \\'räm-yə-ləs\\ son of Mars in Roman mythol-

\\ə\\abut \\ᵊ\\kitten \\ər\\further \\a\\ash \\ā\\ace \\ä\\mop, mar
\\aù\\out \\ch\\chin \\e\\bet \\ē\\easy \\g\\go \\i\\hit \\ī\\ice \\j\\job
\\ŋ\\sing \\ō\\go \\ò\\law \\òi\\boy \\th\\thin \\t̲h̲\\the \\ü\\loot \\ù\\foot
\\y\\yet \\zh\\vision *see also* Pronunciation Symbols page

ogy who was the twin brother of Remus and the founder of Rome

Rönt·gen *or* **Roent·gen** \\'rent-gən, 'rənt-, -jən\\ Wilhelm Conrad 1845–1923 German physicist; Nobel Prize winner (1901)

Roo·se·velt \\'rō-zə-vəlt (*Roosevelts' usual pronunciation*), -ˌvelt *also* 'rü-\\ (Anna) Eleanor 1884–1962 American lecturer and writer; wife of Franklin Delano Roosevelt

Roosevelt Franklin Del·a·no \\'del-ə-ˌnō\\ 1882–1945 32d president of the U.S. (1933–45)

Roosevelt Theodore 1858–1919 26th president of the U.S. (1901–09); Nobel Prize winner (1906)

Ross \\'rós\\ Betsy 1752–1836 reputed maker of first American flag

Ros·si·ni \\rȯ-'sē-nē, rə-\\ Gioacchino Antonio 1792–1868 Italian composer

Ru·bens \\'rü-bənz\\ Peter Paul 1577–1640 Flemish painter

Rus·sell \\'rəs-əl\\ Bertrand Arthur William 1872–1970 English mathematician and philosopher; Nobel Prize winner (1950)

Ruth \\'rüth\\ woman in the Bible who was one of the ancestors of King David

Ruth George Herman 1895–1948 *Babe* American baseball player

Ruth·er·ford \\'rəth̲-ə(r)-fərd, 'rəth̲-\\ Ernest 1871–1937 1st Baron *Rutherford of Nelson* British physicist

Sa·bin \\'sā-bin\\ Albert Bruce 1906–1993 American physician

Sac·a·ga·wea \\ˌsak-ə-jə-'wē-ə, -'wä-ə\\ 1786?–1812 American Indian guide to Lewis and Clark

Sa·dat \\sə-'dat, -'dät\\ Anwar as- 1918–1981 president of Egypt (1970–81)

Saint Nicholas — see NICHOLAS, SANTA CLAUS

Sal·in·ger \\'sal-ən-jər\\ Jerome David 1919–   American author

Salk \\'sȯk, 'sȯlk\\ Jonas Edward 1914–   American physician

Sa·lo·me \\sə-'lō-mē\\ niece of Herod Antipas who in the Bible is given the head of John the Baptist as a reward for her dancing

Sa·mo·set \\'sam-ə-ˌset, sə-'mäs-ət\\ *died about* 1653 American Indian leader

Sam·son \\'sam(p)-sən\\ powerful Hebrew hero in the Bible who fought against the Philistines

Sam·u·el \\'sam-yə(-wə)l\\ Hebrew judge in the Bible who appointed Saul and then David king

Sand·burg \\'san(d)-ˌbərg\\ Carl 1878–1967 American author

San·ta Claus \\'sant-ē-ˌklȯz, 'sant-ə-\\ *or* **Saint Nich·o·las** \\ˌsänt-'nik-(ə-)ləs, sənt-\\ *or* **Kriss Krin·gle** \\'kris-ˌkrin-gəl\\ a fat jolly old man in modern folklore who delivers presents to good children at Christmastime

Sap·pho \\'saf-ō\\ *flourished about* 610–*about* 580 B.C. Greek poet

Sa·rah \\'ser-ə, 'sar-ə, 'sā-rə\\ wife of Abraham and mother of Isaac in the Bible

Sar·gent \\'sär-jənt\\ John Singer 1856–1925 American painter

Sat·urn \\'sat-ərn\\ a god of agriculture in Roman mythology

Saul \\'sȯl\\ first king of Israel in the Bible

Saul *or* **Saul of Tar·sus** \\-'tär-səs\\ the apostle Paul

Sche·her·a·zade \\shə-ˌher-ə-'zäd(-ə), -'zäd(-ē)\\ fictional oriental queen and narrator of the tales in the *Arabian Nights' Entertainments*

Schu·bert \\'shü-bərt, -ˌbərt\\ Franz Peter 1797–1828 Austrian composer

Schweit·zer \\'shwīt-sər, 'swīt-, 'shvīt-\\ Albert 1875–1965 French Protestant minister, philosopher, physician, and music scholar; Nobel Prize winner (1952)

Scott \\'skät\\ Dred \\'dred\\ 1795?–1858 American slave

Scott Sir Walter 1771–1832 Scottish author

Scott Winfield 1786–1866 American general

Scyl·la \\'sil-ə\\ a nymph in Greek mythology who is changed into a monster and inhabits a cave opposite the whirlpool Charybdis off the coast of Sicily

Se·quoya \\si-'kwȯi-ə\\ *about* 1760–1843 Cherokee Indian leader

Ser·ra \\'ser-ə\\ Junípero 1713–1784 Spanish missionary in Mexico and California

Se·ton \\'sēt-ᵊn\\ Saint Elizabeth Ann Bayley 1774–1821 *Mother Seton* American religious leader

Sew·ard \\'sü-ərd, 'sü-(ə)rd\\ William Henry 1801–1872 American politician; secretary of state (1861–69)

Shake·speare \\'shāk-ˌspi(ə)r\\ William 1564–1616 English dramatist and poet

Shaw \\'shȯ\\ George Bernard 1856–1950 British author

Shel·ley \\'shel-ē\\ Mary Woll·stone·craft \\'wùl-stən-ˌkraft\\ 1797–1851 English novelist; wife of Percy Bysshe Shelley

Shelley Percy Bysshe \\'bish\\ 1792–1822 English poet

Shep·ard \\'shep-ərd\\ Alan Bartlett 1923–   American astronaut; first American in space (1961)

Sher·i·dan \\'sher-əd-ᵊn\\ Philip Henry 1831–1888 American general

Sher·lock Holmes \\'shər-ˌläk-'hōmz, -'hōlmz\\ detective in stories by Sir Arthur Conan Doyle

Sher·man \\'shər-mən\\ John 1823–1900 American politician

Sherman William Tecumseh 1820–1891 American general

Sieg·fried \\'sig-ˌfrēd, 'sēg-\\ hero in Germanic legend who kills a dragon guarding a gold hoard

Si·mon \\'sī-mən\\ *or* **Simon the Zealot** one of the 12 apostles

Sind·bad the Sailor \\'sin-ˌbad-\\ citizen of Baghdad whose adventures are narrated in the *Arabian Nights' Entertainments*

Sis·y·phus \\'sis-ə-fəs\\ king of Corinth who in Greek mythology is condemned to roll a heavy stone up a hill in Hades only to have it roll down again as it nears the top

Sit·ting Bull \\ˌsit-iŋ-'bùl\\ *about* 1831–90 Sioux Indian leader

Si·va \\'shiv-ə, 'siv-; 'shē-və, 'sē-\\ god of destruction in the Hindu sacred triad — compare BRAHMA, VISHNU

Smith \\'smith\\ Bessie 1894 (or 1898)–1937 American blues singer

Smith John *about* 1580–1631 English colonist in America

Smith Joseph 1805–1844 American founder of the Mormon Church

Soc·ra·tes \\'säk-rə-ˌtēz\\ *about* 470–399 B.C. Greek philosopher

Sol·o·mon \\'säl-ə-mən\\ son of David and 10th-century B.C. king of Israel noted for his wisdom

Soph·o·cles \\'säf-ə-ˌklēz\\ *about* 496–406 B.C. Greek dramatist

Sou·sa \\'sü-zə, 'sü-sə\\ John Philip 1854–1932 American bandmaster and composer

Spar·ta·cus \\'spärt-ə-kəs\\ *died* 71 B.C. Roman slave and gladiator; leader of a slave rebellion

Sphinx \\'sfiŋ(k)s\\ monster in Greek mythology having a lion's body, wings, and the head and bust of a woman

Squan·to \\'skwän-tō\\ *died* 1622 Indian friend of the Pilgrims

Sta·lin \\'stäl-ən, 'stal-, -ˌēn\\ Joseph 1879–1953 Soviet leader

Stan·dish \\'stan-dish\\ Myles *or* Miles 1584?–1656 American colonist

Stan·ley \\'stan-lē\\ Sir Henry Morton 1841–1904 British explorer in Africa

Stan·ton \\'stant-ᵊn\\ Elizabeth Cady 1815–1902 American suffragist

Stein \\'stīn\\ Gertrude 1874–1946 American author

Stein·beck \'stīn-ˌbek\ John Ernst 1902–1968 American author; Nobel Prize winner (1962)

Steu·ben, von \'st(y)ü-bən, 'shtöi-\ Baron Friedrich Wilhelm Ludolf Gerhard Augustin 1730–1794 Prussian-born general in American Revolution

Ste·ven·son \'stē-vən-sən\ Adlai Ewing 1900–1965 American politician

Stevenson Robert Louis Balfour 1850–1894 Scottish author

Stowe \'stō\ Harriet Elizabeth Beecher 1811–1896 American author

Stra·di·va·ri \ˌstrad-ə-'vär-ē, -'var-, -'ver-\ Antonio 1644–1737 Latin *Antonius Strad·i·var·i·us* \ˌstrad-ə-'var-ē-əs, -'ver-\ Italian violin maker

Strauss \'straùs, 'shtraùs\ Johann father 1804–1849 and his sons Johann 1825–1899 and Josef 1827–1870 Austrian composers

Stu·art \'st(y)ü-ərt, 'st(y)ù(-ə)rt\ — see CHARLES I, MARY STUART

Stuart Charles—CHARLES EDWARD STUART

Stuart Gilbert Charles 1755–1828 American painter

Stuart James Ewell Brown 1833–1864 *Jeb* American Confederate general

Stuy·ve·sant \'stī-və-sənt\ Peter *about* 1610–1672 Dutch colonial administrator in America

Sul·li·van \'səl-ə-vən\ Sir Arthur Seymour 1842–1900 English composer; collaborator with Sir William Gilbert

Sullivan Louis Henri 1856–1924 American architect

Sum·ner \'səm-nər\ Charles 1811–1874 American politician

Swift \'swift\ Jonathan 1667–1745 English author

Taft \'taft\ William Howard 1857–1930 27th president of the U.S. (1909–13); chief justice of the U.S. Supreme Court (1921–30)

Ta·ney \'tȯ-nē\ Roger Brooke 1777–1864 American jurist; chief justice of the U.S. Supreme Court (1836–64)

Tan·ta·lus \'tant-ᵊl-əs\ king in Greek mythology who is condemned to stand up to his chin in a pool of water in Hades and beneath fruit-laden boughs only to have the water or fruit go out of reach at each attempt to drink or eat

Tay·lor \'tā-lər\ Zachary 1784–1850 12th president of the U.S. (1849–50)

Tchai·kov·sky \chī-'kȯf-skē, chə-, -'kȯv-\ Pyotr Ilich 1840–1893 Russian composer

Te·cum·seh \tə-'kəm(p)-sə, -sē\ 1768–1813 Shawnee Indian chief

Ten·ny·son \'ten-ə-sən\ Alfred 1809–1892 known as *Alfred, Lord Tennyson* English poet

Te·re·sa \tə-'rā-zə, -'rē-sə\ **of Ávi·la** \'äv-i-lə\ Saint 1515–1582 Spanish nun and mystic

The·seus \'thē-ˌsüs, -sē-əs\ hero in Greek mythology who kills the Minotaur and conquers the Amazons

Thom·as \'täm-əs\ apostle in the Bible who demanded proof of Christ's resurrection

Thomas à Becket — see BECKET, À

Thor \'thȯ(ə)r\ god of thunder, weather, and crops in Norse mythology

Tho·reau \thə-'rō, thȯ-; 'thȯr-ō\ Henry David 1817–1862 American author

Thur·ber \'thər-bər\ James Grover 1894–1961 American author

Ti·be·ri·us \tī-'bir-ē-əs\ 42 B.C.–37 A.D. Roman emperor (14–37)

Tocque·ville \'tōk-ˌvil, 'tȯk-, 'täk-, -ˌvēl, -vəl\ Alexis-Charles-Henri Clérel de 1805–1859 French politician and author

Tol·kien \'tȯl-ˌkēn, 'tōl-, 'täl-\ John Ronald Reuel 1892–1973 English author

Tol·stoy \tȯl-'stȯi, tōl-'stȯi, täl-'stȯi, 'tȯl-ˌstȯi, 'tōl-ˌstȯi, 'täl-ˌstȯi\ Count Lev Nikolayevich 1828–1910 Russian author

Tri·ton \'trīt-ᵊn\ sea god in Greek mythology who is half man and half fish

Trots·ky \'trät-skē, 'trȯt-\ Leon 1879–1940 originally *Lev Davidovich Bronstein* Russian Communist

Tru·man \'trü-mən\ Harry S 1884–1972 33d president of the U.S. (1945–53)

Truth \'trüth\ Sojourner 1797?–1883 American abolitionist

Tub·man \'təb-mən\ Harriet *about* 1820–1913 American abolitionist

Tut·ankh·a·men \ˌtü-ˌtaŋ-'käm-ən, -ˌtäŋ-\ *or* **Tut·ankh·a·ten** \-'kät-ᵊn\ *about* 1370–1352 B.C. king of Egypt (1361–1352 B.C.)

Twain Mark — see CLEMENS

Tweed \'twēd\ William Marcy 1823–1878 *Boss Tweed* American politician

Ty·ler \'tī-lər\ John 1790–1862 10th president of the U.S. (1841–45)

Ulysses — see ODYSSEUS

Ura·nus \'yùr-ə-nəs, yù-'rā-\ the sky personified as a god and father of the Titans in Greek mythology

Ur·ban \'ər-bən\ name of eight popes: especially **II** *about* 1035–1099 (pope 1088–99)

Uri·el \'yùr-ē-əl\ one of the four archangels named in Hebrew tradition — compare GABRIEL, MICHAEL, RAPHAEL

Val·en·tine \'val-ən-ˌtīn\ Saint 3d century Christian martyr

Van Bu·ren \van-'byùr-ən, vən-\ Martin 1782–1862 8th president of the U.S.(1837–41)

Van Dyck *or* **Van·dyke** \van-'dīk, vən-\ Sir Anthony 1599–1641 Flemish painter

Ve·láz·quez \və-'las-kəs\ Diego Rodríguez de Silva 1599–1660 Spanish painter

Ve·nus \'vē-nəs\ the goddess of love and beauty in Roman mythology — compare APHRODITE

Ver·di \'ve(ə)rd-ē\ Giuseppe Fortunio Francesco 1813–1901 Italian composer

Ver·meer \vər-'me(ə)r, -'mi(ə)r\ Jan 1632–1675 also called *Jan van der Meer van Delft* Dutch painter

Verne Jules \'jülz-'vərn\ 1828–1905 French author

Ves·puc·ci \ve-'spü-chē\ Ame·ri·go \ˌäm-ə-'rē-gō\ 1454–1512 Latin *Amer·i·cus Ves·pu·cius* \ə-'mer-ə-kəs-ˌves-'pyü-sh(ē-)əs\ Italian navigator for whom America was named

Vic·to·ria \vik-'tōr-ē-ə, -'tȯr-\ 1819–1901 *Alexandrina Victoria* queen of Great Britain (1837–1901)

Vinci, da Leonardo — see LEONARDO DA VINCI

Vir·gil *also* **Ver·gil** \'vər-jəl\ 70–19 B.C. Roman poet

Vish·nu \'vish-nü\ god of preservation in the Hindu sacred triad — compare BRAHMA, SIVA

Vol·ta \'vōl-tə, 'väl-, 'vȯl-\ Count Alessandro Giuseppe Antonio Anastasio 1745–1827 Italian physicist

Vol·taire \vōl-'ta(ə)r, vȯl-, väl-, -'te(ə)r\ 1694–1778 originally *François-Marie Arouet* French author

Vul·can \'vəl-kən\ the god of fire and metalworking in Roman mythology — compare HEPHAESTUS

Wag·ner \'väg-nər\ (Wilhelm) Ri·chard \'rik-ärt, 'rik-\ 1813–1883 German composer

War·ren \'wȯr-ən, 'wär-\ Earl 1891–1974 American jurist; chief justice of the U.S. Supreme Court (1953–69)

Wash·ing·ton \'wȯsh-iŋ-tən, 'wäsh-\ Book·er \'bùk-ər\ Tal·ia·ferro \'täl-ə-vər\ 1856–1915 American educator

Washington George 1732–1799 American general; 1st president of the U.S. (1789–97)

Watt \'wät\ James 1736–1819 Scottish inventor

Wayne \'wān\ Anthony 1745–1796 *Mad Anthony* American general

---

\ə\abut \ᵊ\kitten \ər\further \a\ash \ā\ace \ä\mop, mar
\aù\out \ch\chin \e\bet \ē\easy \g\go \i\hit \ī\ice \j\job
\ŋ\sing \ō\go \ȯ\law \ȯi\boy \th\thin \th\the \ü\loot \ù\foot
\y\yet \zh\vision *see also* Pronunciation Symbols page

Web·ster \'web-stər\ Daniel 1782–1852 American politician

Webster Noah 1758–1843 American lexicographer

Wel·ling·ton \'wel-iŋ-tən\ 1st Duke of 1769–1852 *Arthur Wellesley*; *the Iron Duke* British general and politician

Wells \'welz\ Herbert George 1866–1946 English author and historian

Wes·ley \'wes-lē, 'wez-\ John 1703–1791 English founder of Methodism

Wes·ting·house \'wes-tiŋ-ˌhaùs\ George 1846–1914 American inventor

Whar·ton \'hwȯrt-ᵊn, 'wȯrt-\ Edith Newbold 1862–1937 American author

Whis·tler \'hwis-lər, 'wis-\ James Abbott McNeill 1834–1903 American artist

Whit·man \'hwit-mən, 'wit-\ Walt 1819–1892 American poet

Whit·ney \'hwit-nē, 'wit-\ Eli 1765–1825 American inventor

Whit·ti·er \'hwit-ē-ər, 'wit-\ John Greenleaf 1807–1892 American poet

Wilde \'wī(ə)ld\ Oscar Fingal O'Flahertie Wills 1854–1900 Irish author

Wil·der \'wīl-dər\ Thornton Niven 1897–1975 American author

Wil·liam \'wil-yəm\ name of four kings of England: **I** *(the Conqueror) about* 1028–1087 (reigned 1066–87); **II** *(Rufus* \'rü-fəs\ *about* 1056–1100 (reigned 1087–1100); **III** 1650–1702 (reigned 1689–1702); **IV** 1765–1837 (reigned 1830–37)

Wil·liam Tell \ˌwil-yəm-'tel\ legendary Swiss patriot commanded to shoot an apple from his son's head

Wil·liams \'wil-yəmz\ Roger 1603?–1683 English colonist; founder of Rhode Island

Williams Tennessee 1911–1983 originally *Thomas Lanier Williams* American dramatist

Wil·son \'wil-sən\ (Thomas) Wood·row \'wùd-ˌrō\ 1856–1924 28th president of the U.S. (1913–21); Nobel Prize winner (1919)

Win·throp \'win(t)-thrəp\ John 1588–1649 1st governor of Massachusetts Bay Colony

Woden — see ODIN

Woolf \'wùlf\ Virginia 1882–1941 English author

Words·worth \'wərdz-(ˌ)wərth\ William 1770–1850 English poet

Wren \'ren\ Sir Christopher 1632–1723 English architect

Wright \'rīt\ Frank Lloyd 1867–1959 American architect

Wright Or·ville \'ȯr-vəl\ 1871–1948 and his brother Wilbur 1867–1912 American pioneers in aviation

Wright Richard 1908–1960 American author

Wy·eth \'wī-əth\ Andrew Newell 1917–   American painter

Yeats \'yāts\ William Butler 1865–1939 Irish author

Young \'yəŋ\ Brig·ham \'brig-əm\ 1801–1877 American Mormon leader

Zech·a·ri·ah \ˌzek-ə-'rī-ə\ Hebrew prophet of the 6th century B.C.

Zeng·er \'zeŋ-(g)ər\ John Peter 1697–1746 American (German-born) journalist and printer

Zeph·y·rus \'zef-ə-rəs\ god of the west wind in Greek mythology

Zeus \'züs\ chief god, ruler of the sky and weather (as lightning and rain), and husband of Hera in Greek mythology

Common English Given Names

The following vocabulary presents given names that are most frequent in English use. The list is not exhaustive either of the names themselves or the variant spellings of those names which are entered. Compound or double names and surnames used as given names are not entered except in cases where long-continued or common use gives them an independent character.

Besides the pronunciations of the names, the list usually provides at least one of the following kinds of information at each entry: (1) etymology, indicating the language source but not the original form of the name, and (2) meaning where known or ascertainable with reasonable certainty.

Names of Men

Aar·on \\'ar-ən, 'er-\ [Heb]
Abra·ham \\'ā-brə-ˌham\ [Heb]
Ad·am \\'ad-əm\ [Heb] man
Ad·di·son \\'ad-ə-sən\ [fr. a surname]
Adolph \\'ad-ˌälf, 'ā-ˌdälf\ [Gmc] noble wolf, *i.e.,* noble hero
Adri·an \\'ā-drē-ən\ [L] of Hadria, ancient town in central Italy
Al \al\ *dim of* ALAN, ALBERT, etc.
Al·an \\'al-ən\ [Celt]
Al·bert \\'al-bərt\ [Gmc] illustrious through nobility
Al·den \\'ȯl-dən\ [OE] old friend
Al·ex \\'al-iks\ *or* **Al·ec** \\'al-ik\ *dim of* ALEXANDER
Al·ex·an·der \\'al-ig-'zan-dər\ [Gk] a defender of men
Al·fred \\'al-frəd, -fərd\ [OE] elf counsel, *i.e.,* good counsel
Al·len *or* **Al·lan** *or* **Al·lyn** \\'al-ən\ *var of* ALAN
Al·ton \\'ȯlt-ᵊn, 'alt-\ [prob. fr. a surname]
Al·va *or* **Al·vah** \\'al-və\ [Heb]
Al·vin \\'al-vən\ [Gmc]
Amos \\'ā-məs\ [Heb]
An·dre \\'än-(ˌ)drā\ [F] *var of* ANDREW
An·drew \\'an-(ˌ)drü\ [Gk] manly
An·dy \\'an-dē\ *dim of* ANDREW
An·ge·lo \\'an-jə-ˌlō\ [It, fr. Gk] angel, messenger
An·gus \\'aŋ-gəs\ [Celt]
An·tho·ny \\'an(t)-thə-nē, *chiefly Brit* 'an-tə-\ [L]
An·ton \\'ant-ᵊn, 'an-ˌtän\ [G & Slav] *var of* ANTHONY
An·to·nio \an-'tō-nē-ˌō\ [It] *var of* ANTHONY
Ar·chi·bald \\'är-chə-ˌbȯld, -bəld\ [Gmc]
Ar·chie \\'är-chē\ *dim of* ARCHIBALD
Ar·den \\'ärd-ᵊn\ [prob. fr. a surname]
Ar·len *or* **Ar·lin** \\'är-lən\ [prob. fr. a surname]
Ar·lo \\'är-(ˌ)lō\
Ar·mand \\'är-ˌmänd, -mənd\ [F] *var of* HERMAN
Arne \\'ärn\ [Scand] eagle
Ar·nold \\'ärn-ᵊld\ [Gmc] power of an eagle
Art \\'ärt\ *dim of* ARTHUR
Ar·thur \\'är-thər\ [prob. L]
Au·brey \\'ȯ-brē\ [Gmc] elf ruler
Au·gust \\'ȯ-gəst\ [L] August, majestic
Aus·tin \\'ȯs-tən, 'äs-\ *alter of* Augustine

Bai·ley \\'bā-lē\ [fr. a surname]
Bar·clay \\'bär-klē\ [fr. a surname]
Bar·net *or* **Bar·nett** \bär-'net\ [fr. a surname]
Bar·ney \\'bär-nē\ *dim of* BERNARD
Bar·rett \\'bar-ət\ [fr. a surname]
Bar·ry *or* **Bar·rie** \\'bar-ē\ [Ir]
Bart \\'bärt\ *dim of* Bartholomew
Bar·ton \\'bärt-ᵊn\ [fr. a surname]

Ba·sil \\'baz-əl, 'bäs-, 'bās-, 'bāz-\ [Gk] kingly, royal
Ben \\'ben\ *or* **Ben·nie** *or* **Ben·ny** \\'ben-ē\ *dim of* BENJAMIN
Ben·e·dict \\'ben-ə-ˌdikt\ [L] blessed
Ben·ja·min \\'benj-(ə-)mən\ [Heb] son of the right hand
Ben·nett \\'ben-ət\ [OF] *var of* BENEDICT
Ben·ton \\'bent-ᵊn\ [fr. a surname]
Ber·nard \\'bər-nərd, (ˌ)bər-'närd\ *or* **Bern·hard** \\'bərn-ˌhärd\ [Gmc] bold as a bear
Ber·nie \\'bər-nē\ *dim of* BERNARD
Bert *or* **Burt** \\'bərt\ *dim of* BERTRAM, ALBERT, etc.
Ber·tram \\'bər-trəm\ [Gmc] bright raven
Bill \\'bil\ *or* **Bil·ly** *or* **Bil·lie** \\'bil-ē\ *dim of* WILLIAM
Blaine \\'blān\ [fr. a surname]
Blair \\'bla(ə)r, 'ble(ə)r\ [fr. a surname]
Bob·by \\'bäb-ē\ *or* **Bob** \\'bäb\ *dim of* ROBERT
Bo·ris \\'bȯr-əs, 'bȯr-, 'bär-\ [Russ]
Boyd \\'bȯid\ [fr. a surname]
Brad·ford \\'brad-fərd\ [fr. a surname]
Brad·ley \\'brad-lē\ [fr. a surname]
Bran·don \\'bran-dən\ [fr. a surname]
Bren·dan \\'bren-dən\ [Celt]
Brent \\'brent\ [fr. a surname]
Brett *or* **Bret** \\'bret\ [IrGael]
Bri·an *or* **Bry·an** \\'brī-ən\ [Celt]
Brooks \\'brŭks\ [fr. a surname]
Bruce \\'brüs\ [fr. a surname]
Bru·no \\'brü-(ˌ)nō\ [It, fr. Gmc] brown
Bryce *or* **Brice** \\'brīs\ [fr. a surname]
Bud·dy \\'bəd-ē\ [prob. alter. of *brother*]
Bu·ford \\'byü-fərd\ [fr. a surname]
Burke \\'bərk\ [fr. a surname]
Bur·ton \\'bərt-ᵊn\ [fr. a surname]
By·ron \\'bī-rən\ [fr. a surname]

Cal·vin \\'kal-vən\ [fr. a surname]
Cam·er·on \\'kam-(ə-)rən\ [fr. a surname]
Carl \\'kär(-ə)l\ *var of* KARL
Car·los \\'kär-ləs, -ˌlōs\ [Sp] *var of* CHARLES
Carl·ton *or* **Carle·ton** \\'kär(-ə)l-tən, 'kärlt-ᵊn\ [fr. a surname]
Car·lyle \kär-'lī(ə)l, 'kär-ˌ\ [fr. a surname]
Car·men \\'kär-mən\ [Sp, fr. L] song
Car·roll \\'kar-əl\ [fr. a surname]
Car·son \\'kärs-ᵊn\ [fr. a surname]
Car·ter \\'kärt-ər\ [fr. a surname]
Cary *or* **Car·ey** \\'ka(ə)r-ē, 'ke(ə)r-ē\ [fr. a surname]
Ce·cil \\'sē-səl, 'ses-əl\ [L]
Chad \\'chad\ [Gmc]

Charles \\'chär(-ə)lz\\ [Gmc] man of the common people
Ches·ter \\'ches-tər\\ [fr. a surname]
Chris \\'kris\\ *dim of* CHRISTOPHER
Chris·tian \\'kris(h)-chən\\ [Gk] Christian (the believer)
Chris·to·pher \\'kris-tə-fər\\ [Gk] Christ bearer
Clar·ence \\'klar-ən(t)s\\ [fr. the English dukedom]
Clark *or* **Clarke** \\'klärk\\ [fr. a surname]
Claude *or* **Claud** \\'klȯd\\ [L]
Clay \\'klā\\ *dim of* CLAYTON
Clay·ton \\'klāt-ᵊn\\ [fr. a surname]
Clem \\'klem\\ *dim of* CLEMENT
Clem·ent \\'klem-ənt\\ [L] mild, merciful
Clif·ford \\'klif-ərd\\ [fr. a surname]
Clif·ton \\'klif-tən\\ [fr. a surname]
Clint \\'klint\\ *dim of* CLINTON
Clin·ton \\'klint-ᵊn\\ [fr. a surname]
Clyde \\'klīd\\ [fr. a surname]
Cole \\'kōl\\ [fr. a surname]
Co·lin \\'käl-ən, 'kō-lən\\ *or* **Col·lin** \\'käl-ən\\ *dim of* NICH-OLAS
Con·rad \\'kän-ˌrad, -rəd\\ [Gmc] bold counsel
Con·stan·tine \\'kän(t)-stən-ˌtēn, -ˌtīn\\ [L]
Cor·ey \\'kȯr-ē\\ [fr. a surname]
Cor·ne·lius \\kȯr-'nēl-yəs\\ [L]
Craig \\'krāg\\ [fr. a surname]
Cur·tis \\'kərt-əs\\ [OF] courteous
Cyr·il \\'sir-əl\\ [Gk] lordly
Cy·rus \\'sī-rəs\\ [OPer]

Dale \\'dā(ə)l\\ [fr. a surname]
Dal·las \\'dal-əs\\ [fr. a surname]
Dal·ton \\'dȯlt-ᵊn\\ [fr. a surname]
Dan \\'dan\\ [Heb] judge
Da·na \\'dā-nə\\ [fr. a surname]
Dan·iel \\'dan-yəl *also* 'dan-ᵊl\\ [Heb] God has judged
Dan·ny \\'dan-ē\\ *dim of* DANIEL
Dar·old \\'dar-əld\\ *perh alter of* DARRELL
Dar·rell *or* **Dar·rel** *or* **Dar·ryl** *or* **Dar·yl** \\'dar-əl\\ [fr. a surname]
Dar·win \\'där-wən\\ [fr. a surname]
Dave \\'dāv\\ *dim of* DAVID
Da·vid \\'dā-vəd\\ [Heb] beloved
Da·vis \\'dā-vəs\\ [fr. a surname]
Dean *or* **Deane** \\'dēn\\ [fr. a surname]
Del·a·no \\'del-ə-ˌnō\\ [fr. a surname]
Del·bert \\'del-bərt\\ *dim of* Adalbert
Del·mar \\'del-mər, -ˌmär\\ *or* **Del·mer** \\-mər\\ [fr. a surname]
Den·nis *or* **Den·is** \\'den-əs\\ [OF, fr. Gk] belonging to Dionysus, god of wine
Den·ny \\'den-ē\\ *dim of* DENNIS
Den·ton \\'dent-ᵊn\\ [fr. a surname]
Der·ek \\'der-ik\\ [Middle Dutch, fr. Gmc] ruler of the people
Dew·ey \\'d(y)ü-ē\\ [fr. a surname]
De·witt \\di-'wit\\ [fr. a surname]
Dex·ter \\'dek-stər\\ [L] on the right hand, fortunate
Dick \\'dik\\ *dim of* RICHARD
Dirk \\'dərk\\ [Dutch] *var of* DEREK
Dom·i·nic *or* **Dom·i·nick** \\'däm-ə-(ˌ)nik\\ [L] belonging to the Lord
Don *or* **Donn** \\'dän\\ *dim of* DONALD
Don·al \\'dän-ᵊl\\ *var of* DONALD
Don·ald \\'dän-ᵊld\\ [ScGael] world ruler
Don·nie \\'dän-ē\\ *dim of* DON
Don·o·van \\'dän-ə-vən, 'dən-\\ [fr. a surname]
Doug \\'dəg\\ *dim of* DOUGLAS
Doug·las *or* **Doug·lass** \\'dəg-ləs\\ [fr. a surname]
Duane \\dü-'ān, 'dwān\\ [fr. a surname]
Dud·ley \\'dəd-lē\\ [fr. a surname]
Dun·can \\'dən-kən\\ [ScGael] brown head
Dur·ward \\'dər-wərd\\ [fr. a surname]
Dwayne *or* **Dwaine** \\'dwān\\ [fr. a surname]

Dwight \\'dwīt\\ [fr. a surname]
Dy·lan \\'dil-ən\\ [W]

Earl *or* **Earle** \\'ər(-ə)l\\ [OE] warrior, noble
Ed \\'ed\\ *dim of* EDWARD, EDGAR, etc.
Ed·die *or* **Ed·dy** \\'ed-ē\\ *dim of* ED
Ed·gar \\'ed-gər\\ [OE] spear of wealth
Ed·mund *or* **Ed·mond** \\'ed-mənd\\ [OE] protector of wealth
Ed·son \\'ed-sən\\ [fr. a surname]
Ed·ward \\'ed-wərd\\ [OE] guardian of wealth
Ed·win \\'ed-wən\\ [OE] friend of wealth
El·bert \\'el-bərt\\ *var of* ALBERT
Eli \\'ē-ˌlī\\ [Heb] high
E·li·as \\i-'lī-əs\\ [Gk] *var of* Elijah
El·liott *or* **El·liot** *or* **El·iot** \\'el-ē-ət, 'el-yət\\ [fr. a surname]
El·lis \\'el-əs\\ *var of* ELIAS
Ells·worth \\'elz-(ˌ)wərth\\ [fr. a surname]
El·mer \\'el-mər\\ [fr. a surname]
El·mo \\'el-(ˌ)mō\\ [It, fr. Gk] lovable
El·ton \\'elt-ᵊn\\ [fr. a surname]
El·vin \\'el-vən\\ [fr. a surname]
El·wood *or* **Ell·wood** \\'el-ˌwüd\\ [fr. a surname]
Em·man·u·el *or* **Eman·u·el** \\i-'man-yə(-wə)l\\ [Heb] God with us
Em·er·son \\'em-ər-sən\\ [fr. a surname]
Emil \\'ā-məl\\ *or* **Emile** \\ā-'mē(ə)l\\ [L]
Em·mett \\'em-ət\\ [fr. a surname]
Em·o·ry *or* **Em·ery** \\'em-(ə-)rē\\ [Gmc]
Er·ic *or* **Er·ich** *or* **Er·ik** \\'er-ik\\ [Scand]
Er·nest *or* **Ear·nest** \\'ər-nəst\\ [G] earnestness
Er·nie \\'ər-nē\\ *dim of* ERNEST
Ernst \\'ərn(t)st, 'e(ə)rn(t)st\\ [G] *var of* ERNEST
Er·rol \\'er-əl\\ [prob. fr. a surname]
Ethan \\'ē-thən\\ [Heb] strength
Eu·gene \\yu̇-'jēn, 'yü-ˌ\\ [Gk] wellborn
Ev·an \\'ev-ən\\ [W] *var of* JOHN
Ev·er·ett \\'ev-(ə-)rət\\ [fr. a surname]

Fe·lix \\'fē-liks\\ [L] happy, prosperous
Fer·di·nand \\'fərd-ᵊn-ˌand\\ [Gmc]
Fer·nan·do \\fər-'nan-(ˌ)dō\\ [Sp] *var of* FERDINAND
Fletch·er \\'flech-ər\\ [fr. a surname]
Floyd \\'flȯid\\ [fr. a surname]
For·rest *or* **For·est** \\'fȯr-əst, 'fär-\\ [fr. a surname]
Fos·ter \\'fȯs-tər, 'fäs-\\ [fr. a surname]
Fran·cis \\'fran(t)-səs\\ [OIt & OF] Frenchman
Fran·cis·co \\fran-'sis-(ˌ)kō\\ [Sp] *var of* FRANCIS
Frank \\'fraŋk\\ [Gmc] freeman, Frank
Frank·lin *or* **Frank·lyn** \\'fraŋ-klən\\ [fr. a surname]
Fred \\'fred\\ *dim of* FREDERICK, ALFRED
Fred·die \\'fred-ē\\ *dim of* FREDERICK
Fred·er·ick *or* **Fred·er·ic** *or* **Fred·rick** *or* **Fred·ric** \\'fred-(ə-)rik\\ [Gmc] peaceful ruler
Free·man \\'frē-mən\\ [fr. a surname]
Fritz \\'frits\\ [G] *dim of* Friedrich

Ga·bri·el \\'gā-brē-əl\\ [Heb] man of God
Gar·land \\'gär-lənd\\ [fr. a surname]
Gar·rett \\'gar-ət\\ [fr. a surname]
Garth \\'gärth\\ [fr. a surname]
Gary \\'gar-ē, 'ger-ē\\ *or* **Gar·ry** \\'gar-\\ [prob. fr. a surname]
Gay·lord \\'gā-ˌlȯ(ə)rd\\ [fr. a surname]
Gene \\'jēn\\ *dim of* EUGENE
Geof·frey \\'jef-rē\\ [OF, fr. Gmc]
George \\'jȯ(ə)rj\\ [Gk] of or relating to a farmer
Ger·ald \\'jer-əld\\ [Gmc] spear dominion
Ge·rard \\jə-'rärd, *chiefly Brit* 'jer-ˌärd, -ərd\\ *or* **Ger·hard** \\'ge(ə)r-ˌhärd\\ [Gmc] strong with the spear
Ger·ry \\'jer-ē\\ *var of* JERRY

Gil·bert \'gil-bərt\ [Gmc] *prob* illustrious through hostages

Giles \'jī(ə)lz\ [OF, fr. LL]

Glenn *or* **Glen** \'glen\ [fr. a surname]

Gor·don \'gȯrd-ᵊn\ [fr. a surname]

Gra·ham \'grā-əm, 'gra(-ə)m\ [fr. a surname]

Grant \'grant\ [fr. a surname]

Gran·ville \'gran-ˌvil\ [fr. a surname]

Gray \'grā\ [fr. a surname]

Gregg *or* **Greg** \'greg\ *dim of* GREGORY

Greg·o·ry \'greg-(ə-)rē\ [LGk] vigilant

Gro·ver \'grō-vər\ [fr. a surname]

Gus \'gəs\ *dim of* Gustav *or* Augustus

Guy \'gī\ [OF, fr. Gmc]

Hal \'hal\ *dim of* HENRY

Hall \'hȯl\ [fr. a surname]

Ham·il·ton \'ham-əl-tən, -əlt-ᵊn\ [fr. a surname]

Hans \'hanz, 'hän(t)s\ [G] *dim of* Johannes

Har·lan \'här-lən\ *or* **Har·land** \-lənd\ [fr. a surname]

Har·ley \'här-lē\ [fr. a surname]

Har·low \'här-(ˌ)lō\ [fr. a surname]

Har·mon \'här-mən\ [fr. a surname]

Har·old \'har-əld\ [OE] army dominion

Har·ris \'har-əs\ [fr. a surname]

Har·ri·son \'har-ə-sən\ [fr. a surname]

Har·ry \'har-ē\ *dim of* HENRY

Har·vey \'här-vē\ [fr. a surname]

Hec·tor \'hek-tər\ [Gk] holding fast

Hel·mut \'hel-mət, -ˌmüt\ [G] helmet courage

Hen·ry \'hen-rē\ [Gmc] ruler of the home

Her·bert \'hər-bərt\ [Gmc] illustrious by reason of an army

Her·man *or* **Her·mann** \'hər-mən\ [Gmc] warrior

Her·schel *or* **Her·shel** \'hər-shəl\ [fr. a surname]

Hi·ram \'hī-rəm\ [Phoenician]

Ho·bart \'hō-bərt, -ˌbärt\ [fr. a surname]

Hol·lis \'häl-əs\ [fr. a surname]

Ho·mer \'hō-mər\ [Gk]

Hor·ace \'hȯr-əs, 'här-\ [L]

How·ard \'haủ(-ə)rd\ [fr. a surname]

How·ell \'haủ(-ə)l\ [W]

Hu·bert \'hyü-bərt\ [Gmc] bright in spirit

Hud·son \'həd-sən\ [fr. a surname]

Hugh \'hyü\ *or* **Hu·go** \'hyü-(ˌ)gō\ [Gmc] *prob* mind, spirit

Ian \'ē-ən\ [ScGael] *var of* JOHN

Ira \'ī-rə\ [Heb]

Ir·ving \'ər-viŋ\ *or* **Ir·vin** \-vən\ [fr. a surname]

Ir·win \'ər-wən\ [fr. a surname]

Isaac \'ī-zik, -zək\ [Heb] he laughs

Ivan \'ī-vən\ [Russ] *var of* JOHN

Jack \'jak\ *dim of* JOHN

Jack·son \'jak-sən\ [fr. a surname]

Ja·cob \'jā-kəb, -kəp\ [Heb] one who supplants

Jacques *or* **Jacque** \'zhäk\ [F] *var of* JAMES

Jake \'jāk\ *dim of* JACOB

James \'jāmz\ [OF, fr. LL *Jacobus*] *var of* JACOB

Ja·mie \'jā-mē\ *dim of* JAMES

Jan \'jan\ [Dutch & LG] *var of* JOHN

Jar·ed \'jar-əd, 'jer-\ [Heb] descent

Ja·son \'jäs-ᵊn\ [Gk]

Jay \'jā\ [prob. fr. a surname]

Jed \'jed\ *dim of* Jedidiah

Jef·frey *or* **Jeff·ery** *or* **Jef·fry** \'jef-(ə-)rē\ *var of* GEOFFREY

Jer·ald *or* **Jer·old** *or* **Jer·rold** \'jer-əld\ *var of* GERALD

Jer·e·my \'jer-ə-mē\ *or* **Jer·e·mi·ah** \ˌjer-ə-'mī-ə\ [Heb] *prob* Yahweh exalts

Je·rome \jə-'rōm, *Brit also* 'jer-əm\ [Gk] bearing a holy name

Jer·ry *or* **Jere** \'jer-ē\ *dim of* GERALD

Jes·se \'jes-ē\ [Heb]

Jim \'jim\ *or* **Jim·my** *or* **Jim·mie** \'jim-ē\ *dim of* JAMES

Jo·dy \'jō-dē\ *perh alter of* JOSEPH

Joe \'jō\ *dim of* JOSEPH

Jo·el \'jō-əl\ [Heb] Yahweh is God

John \'jän\ [Heb] Yahweh is gracious

Jon \'jän\ *var of* JOHN

Jo·nah \'jō-nə\ [Heb]

Jon·a·than \'jän-ə-thən\ [Heb] Yahweh has given

Jor·dan \'jȯrd-ᵊn\ [fr. a surname]

Jo·seph *or* **Josef** \'jō-zəf *also* -səf\ [Heb] he shall add

Josh·u·a \'jäsh-(ə-)wə\ [Heb] Yahweh saves

Judd \'jəd\ [fr. a surname]

Jud·son \'jəd-sən\ [fr. a surname]

Jules \'jülz\ [F] *var of* JULIUS

Ju·lian *or* **Ju·lien** \'jül-yən\ [L] sprung from or belonging to Julius

Ju·lius \'jül-yəs\ *or* **Ju·lio** \-(ˌ)yō\ [L]

Jus·tin \'jəs-tən\ *or* **Jus·tus** \-təs\ [L] just

Karl \'kär(-ə)l\ [G & Scand] *var of* CHARLES

Keith \'kēth\ [fr. a surname]

Kel·ly \'kel-ē\ [fr. a surname]

Ken \'ken\ *dim of* KENNETH

Ken·dall \'ken-dᵊl\ [fr. a surname]

Ken·neth \'ken-əth\ [ScGael]

Kent \'kent\ [prob. fr. a surname]

Ken·ton \'kent-ᵊn\ [fr. a surname]

Ker·mit \'kər-mət\ [prob. fr. a surname]

Ker·ry \'ker-ē\ [prob. fr. the county of Ireland]

Kev·in \'kev-ən\ [OIr]

Kir·by \'kər-bē\ [fr. a surname]

Kirk \'kərk\ [fr. a surname]

Klaus \'klaủs, 'klȯs\ [G] *dim of* Nikolaus

Kurt \'kərt, 'kủ(ə)rt\ [G] *dim of* CONRAD

Kyle \'kī(ə)l\ [Celt]

La·mar \lə-'mär\ [fr. a surname]

Lance \'lan(t)s\ *dim of* Lancelot

Lane \'lān\ [fr. a surname]

Lan·ny \'lan-ē\ *prob dim of* LAWRENCE

Lar·ry \'lar-ē\ *dim of* LAWRENCE

Lars \'lärz\ [Sw] *var of* LAWRENCE

Law·rence *or* **Lau·rence** \'lȯr-ən(t)s, 'lär-\ [L] of Laurentum, ancient city in central Italy

Lee *or* **Leigh** \'lē\ [fr. a surname]

Leigh·ton *or* **Lay·ton** \'lāt-ᵊn\ [fr. a surname]

Le·land \'lē-lənd\ [fr. a surname]

Len \'len\ *dim of* LEONARD

Leo \'lē-(ˌ)ō\ [L] lion

Le·on \'lē-ˌän, -ən\ [Sp] *var of* LEO

Leon·ard \'len-ərd\ [G] strong or brave as a lion

Le·roy \li-'rȯi, 'lē-ˌ\ [OF] royal

Les·lie \'les-lē, 'lez-\ [fr. a surname]

Les·ter \'les-tər\ [fr. a surname]

Lew·is \'lü-əs\ *var of* LOUIS

Li·am \'lē-əm\ [Ir]

Lin·coln \'liŋ-kən\ [fr. a surname]

Li·o·nel \'lī-ən-ᵊl, -ə-ˌnel\ [OF] young lion

Lloyd *or* **Loyd** \'lȯid\ [W] gray

Lo·gan \'lō-gən\ [fr. a surname]

Lon \'län\ *dim of* Alonzo

Lon·nie *or* **Lon·ny** \'län-ē\ *dim of* LON

Lo·ren \'lȯr-ən, 'lȯr-\ *dim of* Lorenzo

Lou·ie \'lü-ē\ *var of* LOUIS

Lou·is *or* **Lu·is** \'lü-əs, 'lü-ē\ [Gmc] famous warrior

Low·ell \'lō-əl\ [fr. a surname]

Lu·cian \'lü-shən\ [Gk]

\ə\abut \ᵊ\kitten \ər\further \a\ash \ā\ace \ä\mop, mar
\aủ\out \ch\chin \e\bet \ē\easy \g\go \i\hit \ī\ice \j\job
\ŋ\sing \ō\go \ȯ\law \ȯi\boy \th\thin \t͟h\the \ü\loot \ủ\foot
\y\yet \zh\vision *see also* Pronunciation Symbols page

Lud·wig \ˈləd-(ˌ)wig, ˈlüd-\ [G] *var of* LOUIS
Luke \ˈlük\ [Gk] *prob dim of* LUCIUS
Lu·ther \ˈlü-thər\ [fr. a surname]
Lyle \ˈlī(ə)l\ [fr. a surname]
Ly·man \ˈlī-mən\ [fr. a surname]
Lynn \ˈlin\ [fr. a surname]

Mack *or* **Mac** \ˈmak\ [fr. surnames beginning with *Mc* or *Mac*, fr. Gael *mac* son]
Mal·colm \ˈmal-kəm\ [ScGael] servant of (St.) Columba (6th cent. Irish missionary)
Man·fred \ˈman-frəd\ [Gmc] peace among men
Man·u·el \ˈman-yə(-wə)l\ [Sp & Pg] *var of* EMMANUEL
Mar·cus \ˈmär-kəs\ [L]
Ma·rio \ˈmär-ē-ˌō\ [It] *var of* MARIUS
Mar·i·on \ˈmer-ē-ən, ˈmar-\ [fr. a surname]
Mark *or* **Marc** \ˈmärk\ *var of* MARCUS
Mar·lin \ˈmär-lən\ [prob. fr. a surname]
Mar·shall *or* **Mar·shal** \ˈmär-shəl\ [fr. a surname]
Mar·tin \ˈmärt-ᵊn\ [LL] of Mars
Mar·vin \ˈmär-vən\ [prob. fr. a surname]
Ma·son \ˈmās-ᵊn\ [fr. a surname]
Matt \ˈmat\ *dim of* MATTHEW
Mat·thew \ˈmath-(ˌ)yü *also* ˈmath-(ˌ)ü\ [Heb] gift of Yahweh
Mau·rice \ˈmȯr-əs, ˈmär-; mȯ-ˈrēs\ [LL] *prob* Moorish
Max \ˈmaks\ *dim of* MAXIMILIAN
Max·well \ˈmak-ˌswel, -swəl\ [fr. a surname]
May·nard \ˈmā-nərd\ [Gmc] bold in strength
Mel·ville \ˈmel-ˌvil\ [fr. a surname]
Mel·vin *or* **Mel·vyn** \ˈmel-vən\ [prob. fr. a surname]
Mer·e·dith \ˈmer-əd-əth\ [W]
Merle \ˈmər(-ə)l\ [F] blackbird
Mer·lin *or* **Mer·lyn** \ˈmər-lən\ [Celt]
Mer·rill \ˈmer-əl\ [fr. a surname]
Mi·chael \ˈmī-kəl\ [Heb] who is like God?
Mick·ey \ˈmik-ē\ *dim of* MICHAEL
Mike \ˈmīk\ *dim of* MICHAEL
Mi·lan \ˈmī-lən\ [prob. fr. the city in Italy]
Miles *or* **Myles** \ˈmī(ə)lz\ [Gmc]
Mil·ford \ˈmil-fərd\ [fr. a surname]
Mil·lard \ˈmil-ərd, mil-ˈärd\ [fr. a surname]
Mi·lo \ˈmī-(ˌ)lō\ [prob. L]
Mil·ton \ˈmilt-ᵊn\ [fr. a surname]
Mitch·ell \ˈmich-əl\ [fr. a surname]
Mon·roe \mən-ˈrō, ˈmən-ˌ\ [fr. a surname]
Mon·te *or* **Mon·ty** \ˈmänt-ē\ *dim of* MONTAGUE
Mor·gan \ˈmȯr-gən\ [W] *prob* dweller on the sea
Mor·ris \ˈmȯr-əs, ˈmär-\ *var of* MAURICE
Mor·ton \ˈmȯrt-ᵊn\ [fr. a surname]
Mur·ray \ˈmər-ē, ˈmə-rē\ [fr. a surname]
My·ron \ˈmī-rən\ [Gk]

Na·than \ˈnā-thən\ [Heb] given, gift
Na·than·iel \nə-ˈthan-yəl\ [Heb] gift of God
Ned \ˈned\ *dim of* EDWARD, EDWIN
Neil *or* **Neal** \ˈnē(ə)l\ [Celt]
Nel·son \ˈnel-sən\ [fr. a surname]
Nev·ille \ˈnev-əl\ [fr. a surname]
Nev·in \ˈnev-ən\ [fr. a surname]
New·ell \ˈn(y)ü-əl\ [fr. a surname]
New·ton \ˈn(y)üt-ᵊn\ [fr. a surname]
Nich·o·las \ˈnik-(ə-)ləs\ [Gk] victorious among the people
Nick \ˈnik\ *dim of* NICHOLAS
Niles \ˈnī(ə)lz\ [fr. a surname]
Nils \ˈnils, ˈnē(ə)ls\ [Scand]
No·ah \ˈnō-ə\ [Heb] rest
No·el \ˈnō-əl\ [F, fr. L] Christmas
No·lan \ˈnō-lən\ [fr. a surname]
Nor·man \ˈnȯr-mən\ [Gmc] Norseman, Norman
Nor·ris \ˈnȯr-əs, ˈnär-\ [fr. a surname]
Nor·ton \ˈnȯrt-ᵊn\ [fr. a surname]

Ol·i·ver \ˈäl-ə-vər\ [OF]
Ol·lie \ˈäl-ē\ *dim of* OLIVER
Or·lan·do \ȯr-ˈlan-(ˌ)dō\ [It] *var of* ROLAND
Or·rin \ˈȯr-ən, ˈär-\ *or* **Orin** *or* **Oren** \ˈȯr-, ˈär-, ˈōr-\ [prob. fr. a surname]
Or·ville *or* **Or·val** \ˈȯr-vəl\ [prob. fr. a surname]
Os·car \ˈäs-kər\ [OE] spear of a deity
Otis \ˈōt-əs\ [fr. a surname]
Ot·to \ˈät-(ˌ)ō\ [Gmc]
Ow·en \ˈō-ən\ [OW]

Palm·er \ˈpäm-ər, ˈpäl-mər\ [fr. a surname]
Par·ker \ˈpär-kər\ [fr. a surname]
Pat \ˈpat\ *dim of* PATRICK
Pat·rick \ˈpa-trik\ [L] patrician
Paul \ˈpȯl\ [L] little
Pe·dro \ˈpē-(ˌ)drō, ˈpā-\ [Sp] *var of* PETER
Per·cy \ˈpər-sē\ [fr. a surname]
Per·ry \ˈper-ē\ [fr. a surname]
Pete \ˈpēt\ *dim of* PETER
Pe·ter \ˈpēt-ər\ [Gk] rock
Phil \ˈfil\ *dim of* PHILIP
Phil·ip *or* **Phil·lip** \ˈfil-əp\ [Gk] lover of horses
Pierre \pē-ˈe(ə)r\ [F] *var of* PETER
Por·ter \ˈpōrt-ər, ˈpȯrt-\ [fr. a surname]
Pres·ton \ˈpres-tən\ [fr. a surname]

Quen·tin \ˈkwent-ᵊn\ [LL] of or relating to the fifth

Ra·fa·el *or* **Ra·pha·el** \ˈraf-ē-əl, ˈrä-fē-\ [Heb] God has healed
Ra·leigh \ˈrȯl-ē, ˈräl-\ [fr. a surname]
Ralph \ˈralf, *Brit also* ˈrāf\ [Gmc] wolf in counsel
Ra·mon \rə-ˈmōn, ˈrä-mən\ [Sp] *var of* RAYMOND
Ran·dall *or* **Ran·dal** \ˈran-dᵊl\ *var of* RANDOLPH
Ran·dolph \ˈran-ˌdälf\ [Gmc] shield wolf
Ran·dy \ˈran-dē\ *dim of* RANDOLPH
Ray \ˈrā\ *dim of* RAYMOND
Ray·mond \ˈrā-mənd\ [Gmc] wise protection
Reed *or* **Reid** \ˈrēd\ [fr. a surname]
Reg·gie \ˈrej-ē\ *dim of* REGINALD
Reg·i·nald \ˈrej-ən-ᵊld\ [Gmc] wise dominion
Re·gis \ˈrē-jəs\ [fr. a proper name]
Re·ne \ˈren-(ˌ)ā, rə-ˈnā, ˈrä-nē, ˈrē-nē\ [F, fr. L] reborn
Reu·ben *or* **Ru·ben** \ˈrü-bən\ [Heb]
Rex \ˈreks\ [L] king
Reyn·old \ˈren-ᵊld\ *var of* REGINALD
Rich·ard \ˈrich-ərd\ [Gmc] strong in rule
Rob·ert \ˈräb-ərt\ [Gmc] bright in fame
Ro·ber·to \rə-ˈbərt-(ˌ)ō, rō-, -ˈbert-\ [Sp & It] *var of* ROBERT
Rob·in \ˈräb-ən\ *dim of* ROBERT
Rod·er·ick \ˈräd-(ə-)rik\ [Gmc] famous ruler
Rod·ney \ˈräd-nē\ [fr. a surname]
Rog·er *or* **Rod·ger** \ˈräj-ər\ [Gmc] famous spear
Rog·ers \ˈräj-ərz\ [fr. a surname]
Ro·land \ˈrō-lənd\ *or* **Rol·land** \ˈräl-ənd\ *or* **Row·land** \ˈrō-lənd\ [Gmc] famous land
Rolf \ˈrälf\ *var of* RUDOLPH
Rol·lin \ˈräl-ən\ *var of* ROLAND
Ron \ˈrän\ *dim of* RONALD
Ron·al \ˈrän-ᵊl\ *var of* RONALD
Ron·ald \ˈrän-ᵊld\ [ON] *var of* REGINALD
Ron·nie *or* **Ron·ny** \ˈrän-ē\ *dim of* RONALD
Ros·coe \ˈräs-(ˌ)kō, ˈrȯs-\ [fr. a surname]
Ross \ˈrȯs\ [fr. a surname]
Roy \ˈrȯi\ [ScGael]
Roy·al \ˈrȯi(-ə)l\ [prob. fr. a surname]
Royce \ˈrȯis\ [fr. a surname]
Ru·dolph *or* **Ru·dolf** \ˈrü-ˌdälf\ [Gmc] famous wolf
Ru·dy \ˈrüd-ē\ *dim of* RUDOLPH
Ru·fus \ˈrü-fəs\ [L] red, red-haired
Ru·pert \ˈrü-pərt\ *var of* ROBERT

Rus·sell or Rus·sel \'rəs-əl\ [fr. a surname]
Ry·an \'rī-ən\ [IrGael]

Sal·va·tore \'sal-və-ˌtō(ə)r, -ˌtȯ(ə)r; ˌsal-və-'tōr-ē, -'tȯr-\ [It] savior
Sam \'sam\ dim of SAMUEL
Sam·my or Sam·mie \'sam-ē\ dim of SAM
Sam·u·el \'sam-yə(-wə)l\ [Heb] name of God
San·ford \'san-fərd\ [fr. a surname]
Saul \'sȯl\ [Heb] asked for
Scott \'skät\ [fr. a surname]
Sean \'shȯn\ [Ir] var of JOHN
Seth \'seth\ [Heb]
Sey·mour \'sē-ˌmō(ə)r, -ˌmȯ(ə)r\ [fr. a surname]
Shel·by \'shel-bē\ [fr. a surname]
Shel·don \'shel-dən\ [fr. a surname]
Sher·i·dan \'sher-əd-ᵊn\ [fr. a surname]
Sher·man \'shər-mən\ [fr. a surname]
Sher·win \'shər-wən\ [fr. a surname]
Sher·wood \'shər-ˌwủd, 'she(ə)r-\ [fr. a surname]
Sid·ney or Syd·ney \'sid-nē\ [fr. a surname]
Sieg·fried \'sig-ˌfrēd, 'sēg-\ [Gmc] victorious peace
Sig·mund \'sig-mənd\ [Gmc] victorious protection
Si·mon \'sī-mən\ [Heb]
Sol·o·mon \'säl-ə-mən\ [Heb] peaceable
Spen·cer \'spen(t)-sər\ [fr. a surname]
Sta·cy or Sta·cey \'stā-sē\ [ML]
Stan \'stan\ dim of STANLEY
Stan·ford \'stan-fərd\ [fr. a surname]
Stan·ley \'stan-lē\ [fr. a surname]
Stan·ton \'stant-ᵊn\ [fr. a surname]
Ste·fan \'stef-ən, -ˌän\ [Pol] var of STEPHEN
Ste·phen or Ste·ven or Ste·phan \'stē-vən\ [Gk] crown
Ster·ling \'stər-liŋ\ [fr. a surname]
Steve \'stēv\ dim of STEVEN
Stu·art or Stew·art \'st(y)ü-ərt, 'st(y)ü(-ə)rt\ [fr. a surname]
Syl·ves·ter \sil-'ves-tər\ [L] woodsy, of the woods

Tay·lor \'tā-lər\ [fr. a surname]
Ted \'ted\ or Ted·dy \'ted-ē\ dim of EDWARD, THEODORE
Ter·ence or Ter·rance or Ter·rence \'ter-ən(t)s\ [L]
Ter·rell or Ter·rill \'tcr-əl\ [fr. a surname]
Ter·ry \'ter-ē\ dim of TERENCE
Thad \'thad\ dim of THADDEUS
Thad·de·us \'thad-ē-əs\ [Gk]
The·o·dore \'thē-ə-ˌdō(ə)r, -ˌdȯ(ə)r, -əd-ər\ [Gk] gift of God
Thom·as \'täm-əs\ [Aram] twin
Thur·man \'thər-mən\ [fr. a surname]
Tim \'tim\ dim of TIMOTHY
Tim·o·thy \'tim-ə-thē\ [Gk] revering God
To·by \'tō-bē\ dim of TOBIAS
Todd \'täd\ [prob. fr. a surname]
Tom \'täm\ or Tom·my or Tom·mie \'täm-ē\ dim of THOMAS
To·ny \'tō-nē\ dim of ANTHONY
Tra·cy \'trā-sē\ [fr. a surname]
Trav·is \'trav-əs\ [fr. a surname]
Trent \'trent\ [fr. a surname]
Tre·vor \'trev-ər\ [Celt]
Troy \'trȯi\ [prob. fr. a surname]
Tru·man \'trü-mən\ [fr. a surname]
Ty·ler \'tī-lər\ [fr. a surname]
Ty·rone \'tī-ˌrōn, tī-'; tir-'ōn\ [prob. fr. the county in Ireland]

Val \'val\ dim of VALENTINE
Van \'van\ [fr. surnames beginning with Van, fr. Dutch van of]
Vance \'van(t)s\ [fr. a surname]
Vaughn \'vȯn, 'vän\ [fr. a surname]
Verne or Vern \'vərn\ prob alter of VERNON

Ver·non \'vər-nən\ [prob. fr. a surname]
Vic·tor \'vik-tər\ [L] conqueror
Vin·cent \'vin(t)-sənt\ [LL] of or relating to the conquering one
Vir·gil \'vər-jəl\ [L]

Wade \'wād\ [fr. a surname]
Wal·lace or Wal·lis \'wäl-əs\ [fr. a surname]
Walt \'wȯlt\ dim of WALTER
Wal·ter \'wȯl-tər\ [Gmc] army of dominion
Wal·ton \'wȯlt-ᵊn\ [fr. a surname]
Ward \'wȯ(ə)rd\ [fr. a surname]
War·ner \'wȯr-nər\ [fr. a surname]
War·ren \'wȯr-ən, 'wär-\ [fr. a surname]
Wayne \'wān\ [fr. a surname]
Wel·don \'wel-dən\ [fr. a surname]
Wen·dell \'wen-dᵊl\ [fr. a surname]
Wer·ner \'wər-nər, 'we(ə)r-\ [Gmc] army of the Varini, a Germanic people
Wes·ley \'wes-lē also 'wez-\ [fr. a surname]
Wil·bur or Wil·ber \'wil-bər\ [fr. a surname]
Wi·ley or Wy·lie \'wī-lē\ [fr. a surname]
Wil·ford \'wil-fərd\ [fr. a surname]
Wil·fred \'wil-frəd\ [OE] desired peace
Will \'wil\ or Wil·lie \-ē\ dim of WILLIAM
Wil·lard \'wil-ərd\ [fr. a surname]
Wil·liam \'wil-yəm\ [Gmc] desired helmet
Wil·lis \'wil-əs\ [fr. a surname]
Wil·mer \'wil-mər\ [fr. a surname]
Wil·son \'wil-sən\ [fr. a surname]
Wil·ton \'wilt-ᵊn\ [fr. a surname]
Win·field \'win-ˌfēld\ [fr. a surname]
Win·fred \'win-frəd\ [OE] prob joyous peace
Win·ston \'win(t)-stən\ [fr. a surname]
Win·ton \'wint-ᵊn\ [fr. a surname]
Wood·row \'wủd-(ˌ)rō\ [fr. a surname]
Wy·att \'wī-ət\ [fr. a surname]

Yale \'yā(ə)l\ [fr. a surname]

Zach·a·ry \'zak-ə-rē\ dim of ZACHARIAH
Zane \'zān\ [fr. a surname]

Names of Women

Ab·by \'ab-ē\ dim of ABIGAIL
Ab·i·gail \'ab-ə-ˌgāl\ [Heb] prob source of joy
Ada \'ād-ə\ [Heb] prob ornament
Ad·di·son \'ad-ə-sən\ [fr. a surname]
Ad·e·laide \'ad-ᵊl-ˌād\ [Gmc] of noble rank
Adele \ə-'del\ [Gmc] noble
Adri·enne \'ā-drē-ˌen, -ən\ [F] fem of ADRIEN
Ag·nes \'ag-nəs\ [LL]
Ai·leen \ī-'lēn\ [IrGael] var of HELEN
Al·ber·ta \al-'bərt-ə\ fem of ALBERT
Al·ex·an·dra \ˌal-ig-'zan-drə\ [Gk] fem of ALEXANDER
Alex·is \ə-'lek-səs\ [Gk]
Al·ice or Al·yce \'al-əs\ [OF] var of ADELAIDE
Ali·cia \ə-'lish-ə\ [ML] var of ADELAIDE
Al·i·son or Al·li·son \'al-ə-sən\ [OF] dim of ALICE
Al·ma \'al-mə\ [L] nourishing, cherishing
Al·va \'al-və\ [Sp, fr. L] white
Aman·da \ə-'man-də\ [L] worthy to be loved
Am·ber \'am-bər\ [E]
Ame·lia \ə-'mēl-yə\ [Gmc]

\ə\abut \ᵊ\kitten \ər\further \a\ash \ā\ace \ä\mop, mar
\aủ\out \ch\chin \e\bet \ē\easy \g\go \i\hit \ī\ice \j\job
\ŋ\sing \ō\go \ȯ\law \ȯi\boy \th\thin \t̶h̶\the \ü\loot \ủ\foot
\y\yet \zh\vision see also Pronunciation Symbols page

Amy \'ā-mē\ [L] beloved
An·as·ta·sia \ˌan-ə-'stā-zh(ē-)ə\ [LGk] of the Resurrection
An·drea \'an-drē-ə, an-'drā-ə\ *fem of* ANDREW
An·ge·la \'an-jə-lə\ [It, fr. Gk] angel
An·gel·i·ca \an-'jel-i-kə\ *var of* ANGELA
An·ge·line \'an-jə-ˌlīn, -ˌlēn\ *dim of* ANGELA
Ani·ta \ə-'nēt-ə\ [Sp] *dim of* ANN
Ann *or* **Anne** \'an\ *or* **An·na** \'an-ə\ [Heb] grace
An·na·belle \'an-ə-ˌbel\ *prob var of* MABEL
An·nette \a-'net, ə-\ *or* **An·net·ta** \-'net-ə\ [F] *dim of* ANN
An·nie \'an-ē\ *dim of* ANN
An·toi·nette \ˌan-t(w)ə-'net\ [F] *dim of* ANTONIA
April \'ā-prəl\ [E] April (the month)
Ar·dell *or* **Ar·delle** \är-'del\ *var of* ADELE
Ar·lene *or* **Ar·leen** *or* **Ar·line** \är-'lēn\
Ash·ley \'ash-lē\ [OE] ash-tree meadow
As·trid \'as-trəd\ [Scand] beautiful as a deity
Au·dra \'o-drə\ *var of* AUDREY
Au·drey \'o-drē\ [OE] noble strength

Ba·bette \ba-'bet\ [F] *dim of* ELIZABETH
Bar·ba·ra \'bär-b(ə-)rə\ [Gk] foreign
Be·atrice \'bē-ə-trəs\ [It, fr. ML] she that makes happy
Becky \'bek-ē\ *dim of* REBECCA
Ber·na·dette \ˌbər-nə-'det\ [F] *fem of* BERNARD
Ber·na·dine \'bər-nə-ˌdēn\ *fem of* BERNARD
Ber·nice \(ˌ)bər-'nēs, 'bər-nəs\ [Gk] bringing victory
Ber·tha \'bər-thə\ [Gmc] bright
Ber·yl \'ber-əl\ [Gk] beryl (the mineral)
Bes·sie \'bes-ē\ *dim of* ELIZABETH
Beth \'beth\ *dim of* ELIZABETH
Bet·sy *or* **Bet·sey** \'bet-sē\ *dim of* ELIZABETH
Bet·ty *or* **Bet·te** *or* **Bet·tye** *or* **Bet·tie** \'bet-ē\ *dim of* ELIZABETH
Beu·lah \'byü-lə\ [Heb] married
Bev·er·ly *or* **Bev·er·ley** \'bev-ər-lē\ [prob. fr. a surname]
Bil·lie \'bil-ē\ *fem of* BILLY
Blair \'ble(ə)r\ [fr. a surname]
Blake \'blāk\ [fr. a surname]
Blanche \'blanch\ [OF, fr. Gmc] white
Bob·bie \'bäb-ē\ *dim of* ROBERTA
Bo·ni·ta \bə-'nēt-ə\ [Sp] pretty
Bon·nie \'bän-ē\ [ME] pretty
Bran·dy \'bran-dē\ [E]
Bren·da \'bren-də\ [Scand]
Bri·gitte \'brij-ət, brə-'jit\ [G] *var of* BRIDGET
Brit·tany \'brit-ᵊn-ē\ [E]
Brooke \'brŭk\ [OE] brook

Cait·lin \'kāt-lin\ [Ir] *var of* CATHERINE
Ca·mil·la \kə-'mil-ə\ [L] freeborn girl attendant at a sacrifice
Ca·mille \kə-'mē(ə)l\ [F] *var of* CAMILLA
Can·da·ce \'kan-dəs, kan-'dā-sē\ [Gk]
Car·la \'kär-lə\ [It] *fem of* Carlo
Car·lene \kär-'lēn\ *var of* CARLA
Car·lot·ta \kär-'lät-ə\ [It] *var of* CHARLOTTE
Car·men \'kär-mən\ *or* **Car·mine** \kär-'mēn, 'kär-mən\ [Sp, fr. L] song
Car·ol *or* **Car·ole** *or* **Car·yl** \'kar-əl\ *dim of* CAROLYN
Car·o·lyn \'kar-ə-lən\ *or* **Car·o·line** \-lən, -ˌlīn\ [It] *fem of* CHARLES
Car·rie \'kar-ē\ *dim of* CAROLINE
Cath·er·ine *or* **Cath·a·rine** \'kath-(ə-)rən\ [LGk]
Cath·leen \kath-'lēn\ [IrGael] *var of* CATHERINE
Cath·ryn \'kath-rən\ *var of* CATHERINE
Cathy *or* **Cath·ie** \'kath-ē\ *dim of* CATHERINE
Ce·cile \sə-'sē(ə)l\ *var of* CECILIA
Ce·ci·lia \sə-'sēl-yə, -'sil-\ *or* **Ce·ce·lia** \-'sēl-\ [L] *fem of* CECIL
Ce·leste \sə-'lest\ [L] heavenly
Ce·lia \'sēl-yə\ *dim of* CECILIA

Char·lene \shär-'lēn\ *fem of* CHARLES
Char·lotte \'shär-lət\ [F] *fem dim of* CHARLES
Cher·ie \'sher-ē\ [F] dear
Cher·ry \'cher-ē\ [E] cherry
Cher·yl \'cher-əl, 'sher-\ *prob var of* CHERRY
Chloe \'klō-ē\ [Gk] young verdure
Chris·tie \'kris-tē\ *dim of* CHRISTINE
Chris·tine \kris-'tēn\ *or* **Chris·ti·na** \-'tē-nə\ [Gk] Christian
Cin·dy \'sin-dē\ *dim of* LUCINDA
Claire *or* **Clare** \'kla(ə)r, 'kle(ə)r\ *var of* CLARA
Clara \'klar-ə\ [L] bright
Cla·rice \'klar-əs, klə-'rēs\ *dim of* CLARA
Clau·dette \klò-'det\ [F] *fem of* CLAUDE
Clau·dia \'klòd-ē-ə\ [L] *fem of* CLAUDE
Clau·dine \klò-'dēn\ [F] *fem of* CLAUDE
Cleo \'klē-(ˌ)ō\ *dim of* Cleopatra
Co·lette \kä-'let\ [OF] *fem dim of* NICHOLAS
Col·leen \kä-'lēn\ [IrGael] girl
Con·nie \'kän-ē\ *dim of* CONSTANCE
Con·stance \'kän(t)-stən(t)s\ [L] constancy
Co·ra \'kōr-ə, 'kòr-\ [Gk] maiden
Cor·ey \'kòr-ē\ [Ir]
Co·rinne *or* **Cor·rine** \kə-'rin, -'rēn\ [Gk] *dim of* CORA
Cor·ne·lia \kòr-'nēl-yə\ [L] *fem of* CORNELIUS
Court·ney \'kō(ə)rt-nē, 'kò(ə)rt-\ [OE] of the court
Crys·tal \'kris-tᵊl\ [E]
Cyn·thia \'sin(t)-thē-ə\ [Gk] she of Mount Cynthus on the island of Delos

Dai·sy \'dā-zē\ [E] daisy
Dale \'dā(ə)l\ [E] valley
Da·na \'dā-nə\ [fr. a surname]
Dan·ielle \dăn-'yel\ [F] *fem of* DANIEL
Daph·ne \'daf-nē\ [Gk] laurel
Dar·la \'där-lə\ [deriv. of *darling*]
Dar·lene \där-'lēn\ [deriv. of *darling*]
Dawn \'dòn, 'dän\ [E] dawn
De·an·na \dē-'an-ə\ *or* **De·anne** \-'an\ *var of* DIANA
Deb·bie *or* **Deb·by** \'deb-ē\ *dim of* DEBORAH
Deb·o·rah *or* **Deb·o·ra** \'deb-(ə-)rə\ [Heb] bee
Deb·ra \'deb-rə\ *var of* DEBORAH
Dee \'dē\ *prob dim of* EDITH
Deir·dre \'di(ə)r-drē, 'de(ə)r-\ [IrGael]
De·lia \'dēl-yə\ [Gk] she of Delos (i.e. the goddess Artemis)
Del·la \'del-ə\ *dim of* ADELAIDE, DELIA
De·lo·res \də-'lòr-əs, -'lòr-\ *var of* DOLORES
De·na *or* **Dee·na** \'dē-nə\ *dim of* GERALDINE
De·nise \də-'nēz, -'nēs\ [F] *fem of* DENIS
Di·ana *or* **Di·an·na** \dī-'an-ə\ [L]
Di·ane *or* **Di·anne** *or* **Di·an** *or* **Di·ann** \dī-'an\ [F] *var of* DIANA
Di·na *or* **Di·nah** \'dī-nə\ [Heb] judged
Dix·ie \'dik-sē\ [E] *prob* Dixie (nickname for the southern states of the U.S.)
Do·lo·res \də-'lòr-əs, -'lòr-\ [Sp, fr. L] sorrows (i.e. those of the Virgin Mary)
Don·na \'dän-ə\ *or* **Do·na** \'dän-ə, 'dō-nə\ [It, fr. L] lady
Do·ra \'dōr-ə, 'dòr-\ *dim of* THEODORA, Eudora
Do·reen \dò-'rēn, də-\ [IrGael]
Dor·is \'dòr-əs, 'där-\ [Gk] *prob* Dorian (a member of an ancient Hellenic race)
Dor·o·thy \'dòr-ə-thē, 'där-\ *or* **Dor·o·thea** \ˌdòr-ə-'thē-ə, ˌdär-\ [LGk] goddess of gifts
Dot·tie *or* **Dot·ty** \'dät-ē\ *dim of* DOROTHY

Edith *or* **Edythe** \'ēd-əth\ [OE]
Ed·na \'ed-nə\ [Aram]
Ed·wi·na \e-'dwē-nə, -'dwin-ə\ *fem of* EDWIN
Ef·fie \'ef-ē\ *dim of* Euphemia
Ei·leen \ī-'lēn\ [IrGael] *var of* HELEN
Elaine \i-'lān\ [OF] *var of* HELEN

El·ea·nor or El·i·nor or El·ea·nore \'el-ə-nər, -ˌnȯ(ə)r, -ˌnō(ə)r\ [OProv] var of HELEN
Ele·na \'el-ə-nə, ə-'lē-nə\ [It] var of HELEN
Elise \ə-'lēz, -'lēs\ [F] var of ELIZABETH
Eliz·a·beth or Elis·a·beth \i-'liz-ə-bəth\ [Heb] God has sworn
El·la \'el-ə\ [OF]
El·len or El·lyn \'el-ən\ var of HELEN
El·o·ise \'el-ə-ˌwēz, ˌel-ə-'\ [OF, fr. Gmc]
El·sa \'el-sə\ [G] dim of ELIZABETH
El·sie \'el-sē\ dim of ELIZABETH
El·va \'el-və\ [Gmc] elf
Em·i·ly or Em·i·lie \'em-(ə-)lē\ [L] fem of EMIL
Em·ma \'em-ə\ [Gmc] var of ERMA
Enid \'ē-nəd\ [W]
Er·i·ka \'er-i-kə\ fem of ERIC
Er·in \'er-ən\ [IrGael]
Er·ma \'ər-mə\ [Gmc]
Er·nes·tine \'ər-nə-ˌstēn\ fem of ERNEST
Es·telle \e-'stel\ or Es·tel·la \e-'stel-ə\ [OProv, fr. L] star
Es·ther \'es-tər\ [prob. fr. Per] prob star
Eth·el \'eth-əl\ [OE] noble
Et·ta \'et-ə\ dim of HENRIETTA
Eu·ge·nia \yu̇-'jēn-yə\ or Eu·ge·nie \-'jē-nē\ fem of EUGENE
Eu·nice \'yü-nəs\ [Gk] having (i.e. bringing) happy victory
Eva \'ē-və\ var of EVE
Evan·ge·line \i-'van-jə-lən, -ˌlēn, -ˌlīn\ [Gk] bringing good news
Eve \'ēv\ [Heb] life, living
Ev·e·lyn \'ev-(ə-)lən, chiefly Brit 'ēv-\ [OF, fr. Gmc]

Faith \'fāth\ [E] faith
Faye or Fay \'fā\ dim of FAITH
Fe·lice \fə-'lēs\ [L] happiness
Fern or Ferne \'fərn\ [E] fern
Flo·ra \'flōr-ə, 'flȯr-\ [L] goddess of flowers
Flor·ence \'flōr-ən(t)s, 'flär-\ [L] bloom, prosperity
Fran·ces \'fran(t)-səs, -ˌsəz\ fem of FRANCIS
Fran·cine \fran-'sēn\ [F] prob dim of FRANCES
Fre·da or Frie·da \'frēd-ə\ dim of WINIFRED
Fred·er·ic·ka or Fred·er·i·ca \ˌfred-(ə-)'rē-kə, -'rik-ə\ fem of FREDERICK

Gail or Gayle or Gale \'gā(ə)l\ dim of ABIGAIL
Gay \'gā\ [E] gay
Ge·ne·va \jə-'nē-və\ var of GENEVIEVE
Gen·e·vieve \'jen-ə-ˌvēv\ [prob. fr. Celt]
George·ann \ˌjȯr-'jan\ [George + Ann]
Geor·gette \jȯr-'jet\ fem of GEORGE
Geor·gia \'jȯr-jə\ fem of GEORGE
Geor·gi·na \jȯr-'jē-nə\ fem of GEORGE
Ger·al·dine \'jer-əl-ˌdēn\ fem of GERALD
Ger·trude \'gər-ˌtrüd\ [Gmc] spear strength
Gil·li·an \'jil-ē-ən\ var of JULIANA
Gin·ger \'jin-jər\ [E] ginger
Gi·sela \jə-'sel-ə, -'zel-\ [Gmc] pledge
Gi·selle \jə-'zel\ var of GISELA
Glad·ys \'glad-əs\ [W]
Glen·da \'glen-də\ prob var of GLENNA
Glen·na \'glen-ə\ fem of GLENN
Glo·ria \'glōr-ē-ə, 'glȯr-\ [L] glory
Grace \'grās\ [L] favor, grace
Gre·ta \'grēt-ə, 'gret-\ dim of MARGARET
Gretch·en \'grech-ən\ [G] dim of MARGARET
Gwen \'gwen\ dim of GWENDOLYN
Gwen·do·lyn \'gwen-də-lən\ [W]

Han·nah \'han-ə\ [Heb] var of ANN
Har·ri·et or Har·ri·ett or Har·ri·ette \'har-ē-ət\ var of HENRIETTA
Hat·tie \'hat-ē\ dim of HARRIET

Ha·zel \'hā-zəl\ [E] hazel
Heath·er \'heth-ər\ [ME] heather (the shrub)
Hei·di \'hīd-ē\ [G] dim of ADELAIDE
He·laine \hə-'lān\ var of HELEN
Hel·en \'hel-ən\ or He·le·na \'hel-ə-nə, hə-'lē-nə\ [Gk]
He·lene \hə-'lēn\ [F] var of HELEN
Hel·ga \'hel-gə\ [Scand] holy
Hen·ri·et·ta \ˌhen-rē-'et-ə\ [MF] fem of HENRY
Her·mine \'hər-ˌmēn\ [G] prob fem of HERMAN
Hes·ter \'hes-tər\ var of ESTHER
Hil·ary or Hil·la·ry \'hil-ə-rē\ [L] cheerful
Hil·da \'hil-də\ [OE] battle
Hil·de·gard or Hil·de·garde \'hil-də-ˌgärd\ [Gmc] prob battle enclosure
Hol·ly \'häl-ē\ [E] holly
Hope \'hōp\ [E] hope

Ida \'īd-ə\ [Gmc]
Ilene \ī-'lēn\ var of EILEEN
Imo·gene \'im-ə-ˌjēn, 'ī-mə-\
Ina \'ī-nə\
Inez \ī-'nez, 'ī-nəz\ [Sp] var of AGNES
In·grid \'iŋ-grəd\ [Scand] beautiful as Ing (an ancient Germanic god)
Irene \ī-'rēn\ [Gk] peace
Iris \'ī-rəs\ [Gk] rainbow
Ir·ma \'ər-mə\ var of ERMA
Is·a·bel or Is·a·belle \'iz-ə-bel\ [OProv] var of ELIZABETH

Jack·ie or Jacky \'jak-ē\ dim of JACQUELINE
Jac·que·line or Jac·que·lyn or Jac·que·lin \'jak-(w)ə-lən, -ˌlēn\ [OF] fem of JACOB
Ja·mie \'jā-mē\ fem of JAMES
Jan \'jan\ dim of JANET
Jane or Jayne \'jān\ [OF] var of JOAN
Ja·net or Ja·nette \'jan-ət, jə-'net\ dim of JANE
Ja·nice \'jan-əs, jə-'nēs\ or Jan·is \'jan-əs\ prob dim of JANE
Ja·nie \'jā-nē\ dim of JANE
Jean or Jeanne \'jēn\ [OF] var of JOAN
Jea·nette or Jean·nette \jə-'net\ [F] dim of JEANNE
Jean·nie or Jean·ie \'jē-nē\ dim of JEAN
Jean·nine or Jea·nine \jə-'nēn\ [F] dim of JEANNE
Jen·nie or Jen·ny \'jen-ē\ dim of JANE
Jen·ni·fer \'jen-ə-fər\ [Celt]
Jer·al·dine \'jer-əl-ˌdēn\ var of GERALDINE
Jer·i·lyn \'jer-ə-lən\ var of GERALDINE
Jer·ry or Jeri or Jer·rie \'jer-ē\ dim of GERALDINE
Jes·si·ca \'jes-i-kə\ [prob. Heb]
Jes·sie \'jes-ē\ [Sc] dim of JANET
Jew·el or Jew·ell \'jü(-ə)l, 'jü(-ə)l\ [E] jewel
Jill \'jil\ dim of JULIANA
Jo \'jō\ dim of JOSEPHINE
Joan or Joann or Joanne \'jō(-ə)n, jō-'an\ [Gk] fem of JOHN
Jo·an·na \jō-'an-ə\ or Jo·han·na \-'(h)an-ə\ var of JOAN
Joc·e·lyn \'jäs-(ə-)lən\ [OF, fr. Gmc]
Jo·dy or Jo·die \'jō-dē\ alter of JUDITH
Jo·lene \jō-'lēn\ prob dim of JO
Jo·se·phine \'jō-zə-ˌfēn also 'jō-sə-\ fem of JOSEPH
Joy \'jȯi\ [E] joy
Joyce \'jȯis\ [OF]
Jua·ni·ta \wä-'nēt-ə\ [Sp] fem dim of JOHN
Ju·dith \'jüd-əth\ [Heb] Jewess
Ju·dy or Ju·di or Ju·die \'jüd-ē\ dim of JUDITH
Ju·lia \'jül-yə\ [L] fem of JULIUS
Ju·li·ana \ˌjü-lē-'an-ə\ [LL] fem of JULIAN

Ju·li·anne *or* Ju·li·ann \ˌjü-lē-'an, jül-'yan\ *var of* JULI-ANA

Ju·lie \'jü-lē\ [MF] *var of* JULIA

Ju·liet \'jül-yət, -ē-ˌet, -ē-ət; ˌjül-ē-'et, jül-'yet, 'jül-ˌyet\ [It] *dim of* JULIA

June \'jün\ [E] June (the month)

Jus·tine \ˌjəs-'tēn\ [F] *fem of* JUSTIN

Ka·ra \'kär-ə, 'kar-ə\ *var of* CATHERINE

Kar·en *or* Kar·in *or* Kaa·ren \'kar-ən, 'kär-\ [Scand] *var of* CATHERINE

Kar·la \'kär-lə\ *var of* CARLA

Kar·ol \'kar-əl\ *var of* CAROL

Kar·o·lyn \'kar-ə-lən\ *var of* CAROLYN

Kate \'kāt\ *dim of* CATHERINE

Kath·er·ine *or* Kath·a·rine *or* Kath·ryn \'kath-(ə-)rən\ *var of* CATHERINE

Kath·leen \kath-'lēn\ [IrGael] *var of* CATHERINE

Kathy \'kath-ē\ *dim of* CATHERINE

Ka·tie \'kāt-ē\ *dim of* KATE

Kay *or* Kaye \'kā\ *dim of* CATHERINE

Kel·ly \'kel-ē\ [fr. a surname]

Ker·ry \'ker-ē\ [prob. fr. the county of Ireland]

Kim \'kim\ *prob dim of* KIMBERLY

Kim·ber·ly \'kim-bər-lē\ [OE]

Kit·ty \'kit-ē\ *dim of* CATHERINE

Kris·tin \'kris-tən\ [Scand] *var of* CHRISTINE

Kris·tine \kris-'tēn\ *var of* CHRISTINE

La·na \'lan-ə, 'län-ə, 'lä-nə\

Lau·ra \'lȯr-ə, 'lär-\ [ML] *prob fem dim of* LAWRENCE

Lau·rel \'lȯr-əl, 'lär-\ [E] laurel

Lau·ren \'lȯr-ən, 'lär-\ *var of* LAURA

Lau·rie \'lȯr-ē, 'lär-\ *dim of* LAURA

La·verne *or* La·vern \lə-'vərn\

Le·ah \'lē-ə\ [Heb] *prob* wild cow

Le·anne \lē-'an\ [prob. fr. *Lee* + *Ann*]

Lee \'lē\ [fr. a surname]

Leigh \'lē\ *var of* LEE

Lei·la *or* Le·la \'lē-lə\ [Per] dark as night

Le·lia \'lēl-yə\ [L]

Le·na \'lē-nə\ [G] *dim of* HELENA, Magdalena

Le·nore \lə-'nō(ə)r, -'nȯ(ə)r\ *or* Le·no·ra \lə-'nōr-ə, -'nȯr-\ *var of* LEONORA

Le·o·na \lē-'ō-nə\ *fem of* LEON

Le·o·no·ra \ˌlē-ə-'nōr-ə, -'nȯr-\ *var of* ELEANOR

Les·lie *or* Les·ley \'les-lē *also* 'lez-\ [fr. a surname]

Le·ti·tia \li-'tish-ə, -'tē-shə\ [L] gladness

Lib·by \'lib-ē\ *dim of* ELIZABETH

Li·la \'lī-lə\ *var of* LEILA

Lil·lian \'lil-yən, 'lil-ē-ən\ *prob dim of* ELIZABETH

Lil·lie \'lil-ē\ *dim of* LILLIAN

Lily \'lil-ē\ [E] lily

Lin·da *or* Lyn·da \'lin-də\ *dim of* MELINDA, Belinda

Lind·sey *or* Lind·say \'lin-zē\ [OE] linden isle

Li·sa \'lī-zə, 'lē-\ *dim of* ELIZABETH

Lo·is \'lō-əs\ [Gk]

Lo·la \'lō-lə\ [Sp] *dim of* DOLORES

Lon·na \'län-ə\ *fem of* LON

Lo·ra \'lōr-ə, 'lȯr-\ *var of* LAURA

Lo·re·lei \'lōr-ə-ˌlī, 'lȯr-\ [G]

Lo·rene \lō-'rēn\ *dim of* LORA

Lo·ret·ta \lə-'ret-ə, lȯ-\ [ML] *var of* Lauretta

Lo·ri \'lōr-ē, 'lȯr-\ *var of* LAURA

Lor·na \'lȯr-nə\

Lor·raine *or* Lo·raine \lə-'rān, lȯ-\ [prob. fr. *Lorraine*, region in northeast France]

Lou \'lü\ *dim of* LOUISE

Lou·ise \lü-'ēz\ *or* Lou·i·sa \-'ē-zə\ *fem of* LOUIS

Lu·anne \lü-'an\ [*Lu-* + *Anne*]

Lu·cille *or* Lu·cile \lü-'sē(ə)l\ [L] *prob dim of* LUCIA

Lu·cin·da \lü-'sin-də\ [L] *var of* LUCY

Lu·cre·tia \lü-'krē-shə\ [L]

Lu·cy \'lü-sē\ *or* Lu·cia \'lü-shə\ [L] *fem of* Lucius

Lu·el·la \lü-'el-ə\ [prob. fr. *Lou* (dim. of *Louise*) + *Ella*]

Lyd·ia \'lid-ē-ə\ [Gk] woman of Lydia, ancient country in Asia Minor

Ly·nette \lə-'net\ [W]

Lynne *or* Lynn \'lin\ *dim of* CAROLYN, JACQUELYN, etc.

Ma·bel \'mā-bəl\ [L] lovable

Mac·ken·zie \mə-'ken-zē\ [fr. a surname]

Mad·e·line *or* Mad·e·leine *or* Mad·e·lyn \'mad-ᵊl-ən\ [Gk] woman of Magdala, ancient town in northern Palestine

Madge \'maj\ *dim of* MARGARET

Mal·lory \'mal-(ə-)rē\ [fr. a surname]

Ma·mie \'mā-mē\ *dim of* MARGARET

Ma·ra \'mär-ə\ *var of* MARY

Mar·cel·la \mär-'sel-ə\ [L] *fem of* Marcellus

Mar·cia \'mär-shə\ [L] *fem of* MARCUS

Mar·ga·ret \'mär-g(ə-)rət\ [Gk] pearl

Mar·gery \'märj-(ə-)rē\ [OF] *var of* MARGARET

Mar·gie \'mär-jē\ *dim of* MARGARET

Mar·go \'mär-(ˌ)gō\ *var of* MARGOT

Mar·got \'mär-(ˌ)gō, -gət\ *dim of* MARGARET

Mar·gue·rite \ˌmär-g(y)ə-'rēt\ [OF] *var of* MARGARET

Ma·ria \mə-'rē-ə *also* -'rī-\ *var of* MARY

Mar·i·an \'mer-ē-ən, 'mar-\ *var of* MARIANNE

Mar·i·anne \ˌmer-ē-'an, ˌmar-\ *or* Mar·i·an·na \-'an-ə\ [F] *dim of* MARY

Ma·rie \mə-'rē\ [OF] *var of* MARY

Mar·i·et·ta \ˌmer-ē-'et-ə, ˌmar-\ *dim of* MARY

Mar·i·lee \'mer-ə-(ˌ)lē, 'mar-\ [prob. fr. *Mary* + *Lee*]

Mar·i·lyn *or* Mar·i·lynn *or* Mar·y·lyn \'mer-ə-lən, 'mar-\ [prob. fr. *Mary* + *-lyn*]

Ma·ri·na \mə-'rē-nə\ [LGk]

Mar·i·on \'mer-ē-ən, 'mar-\ *dim of* MARY

Mar·jo·rie *or* Mar·jo·ry \'märj-(ə-)rē\ *var of* MARGERY

Mar·la \'mär-lə\ *prob dim of* MARLENE

Mar·lene \mär-'lēn(-ə), -'lā-nə\ [G] *dim of* Magdalene

Mar·lyn \'mär-lən\ *prob var of* MARLENE

Mar·sha \'mär-shə\ *var of* MARCIA

Mar·ta \'märt-ə\ [It] *var of* MARTHA

Mar·tha \'mär-thə\ [Aram] lady

Mar·va \'mär-və\ *prob fem of* MARVIN

Mary \'me(ə)r-ē, 'mā-rē\ [Gk, fr. Heb]

Mary·ann *or* Mary·anne \ˌmer-ē-'an, ˌmā-rē-\ [*Mary* + *Ann*]

Mary·el·len \ˌmer-ē-'el-ən, ˌmā-rē-\ [*Mary* + *Ellen*]

Mar·y·lon \'mer-ə-lən, 'mar-\ *var of* MARILYN

Maude \'mȯd\ [OF] *var of* Matilda

Mau·reen *or* Mau·rine \mȯ-'rēn\ [Ir] *dim of* MARY

Max·ine \mak-'sēn\ [F] *fem dim of* Maximilian

May *or* Mae \'mā\ *dim of* MARY

Me·gan \'meg-ən, 'mē-gən\ [Ir]

Mel·a·nie \'mel-ə-nē\ [Gk] blackness

Mel·ba \'mel-bə\ [E] woman of Melbourne, Australia

Me·lin·da \mə-'lin-də\ *prob alter of* Belinda

Me·lis·sa \mə-'lis-ə\ [Gk] bee

Mel·va \'mel-və\ *prob fem of* MELVIN

Mer·e·dith \'mer-əd-əth\ [W]

Merle \'mər(-ə)l\ [F] blackbird

Mer·ri·ly \'mer-ə-lē\ *alter of* MARILEE

Mer·ry \'mer-ē\ [E] merry

Mia \'mē-ə\ [It]

Mi·chele *or* Mi·chelle \mi-'shel\ [F] *fem of* MICHAEL

Mil·dred \'mil-drəd\ [OE] gentle strength

Mil·li·cent \'mil-ə-sənt\ [Gmc]

Mil·lie \'mil-ē\ *dim of* MILDRED

Min·nie \'min-ē\ [Sc] *dim of* MARY

Mir·an·da \mə-'ran-də\ [L] admirable

Mir·i·am \'mir-ē-əm\ [Heb] *var of* MARY

Mit·zi \'mit-sē\ *prob dim of* MARGARET

Mol·ly *or* Mol·lie \'mäl-ē\ *dim of* MARY

Mo·na \'mō-nə\ [IrGael]

Mon·i·ca \'män-i-kə\ [LL]
Mu·ri·el \'myŭr-ē-əl\ [prob. Celt]
My·ra \'mī-rə\
Myr·na \'mər-nə\
Myr·tle \'mərt-ᵊl\ [Gk] myrtle

Na·dine \nā-'dēn, nə-\ [F, fr. Russ] hope
Nan \'nan\ dim of ANN
Nan·cy \'nan(t)-sē\ dim of ANN
Nan·nette or Na·nette \na-'net, nə-\ [F] dim of ANN
Na·o·mi \nā-'ō-mē\ [Heb] pleasant
Nat·a·lie \'nat-ᵊl-ē\ [LL] of or relating to Christmas
Nel·lie \'nel-ē\ or Nell \'nel\ dim of ELLEN, HELEN, ELEANOR
Net·tie \'net-ē\ [Sc] dim of JANET
Ni·cole \nē-'kōl\ [F] fem of NICHOLAS
Ni·na \'nē-nə\ [Russ] dim of ANN
Ni·ta \'nēt-ə\ [Sp] dim of JUANITA
No·na \'nō-nə\ [L] ninth
No·ra \'nōr-ə, 'nȯr-\ dim of LEONORA, ELEANOR, Honora
No·reen \nȯ-'rēn\ [IrGael] dim of NORA
Nor·ma \'nȯr-mə\ [It]

Ol·ga \'äl-gə, 'ōl-\ [Russ] var of HELGA
Ol·ive \'äl-iv, -əv\ or O·liv·ia \ə-'liv-ē-ə, ō-\ [L] olive
Opal \'ō-pəl\ [E] opal

Pam \'pam\ dim of PAMELA
Pa·me·la \'pam-ə-lə; pə-'mē-lə, pa-\
Pa·tri·cia \pə-'trish-ə, -'trē-shə\ [L] fem of PATRICK
Pat·sy \'pat-sē\ dim of PATRICIA
Pat·ty or Pat·ti or Pat·tie \'pat-ē\ dim of PATRICIA
Pau·la \'pȯ-lə\ [L] fem of PAUL
Pau·lette \pȯ-'let\ fem dim of PAUL
Pau·line \pȯ-'lēn\ fem dim of PAUL
Pearl \'pər(-ə)l\ [E] pearl
Peg·gy \'peg-ē\ dim of MARGARET
Pe·nel·o·pe \pə-'nel-ə-pē\ [Gk]
Pen·ny \'pen-ē\ dim of PENELOPE
Phoe·be \'fē-bē\ [Gk] shining
Phyl·lis \'fil-əs\ [Gk] green leaf
Pol·ly \'päl-ē\ dim of MARY
Por·tia \'pōr-shə, 'pȯr-\ [L]
Pris·cil·la \prə-'sil-ə\ [L]
Pru·dence \'prüd-ᵊn(t)s\ [E] prudence

Ra·chel \'rā-chəl\ [Heb] ewe
Rae \'rā\ dim of RACHEL
Ra·mo·na \rə-'mō-nə\ [Sp] fem of RAMON
Re·ba \'rē-bə\ dim of REBECCA
Re·bec·ca \ri-'bek-ə\ [Heb]
Re·gi·na \ri-'jē-nə, -'jī-\ [L] queen
Re·nee \rə-'nā, 'ren-(ˌ)ā, 'rā-nē, 'rē-nē\ [F] reborn
Rhea \'rē-ə\ [Gk]
Rho·da \'rōd-ə\ [Gk] rose
Ri·ta \'rēt-ə\ [It] dim of MARGARET
Ro·ber·ta \rə-'bərt-ə, rō-\ fem of ROBERT
Rob·in or Rob·yn \'räb-ən\ [E] robin
Ro·chelle \rō-'shel\ [prob. fr. a surname]
Ro·na or Rho·na \'rō-nə\
Ron·da \'rän-də\ var of Rhonda
Ron·nie \'rän-ē\ dim of VERONICA
Ro·sa·lie \'rō-zə-(ˌ)lē, 'räz-ə-\ [L] festival of roses
Ro·sa·lind \'räz-(ə-)lənd, 'rō-zə-lənd\ [Sp]
Rose \'rōz\ or Ro·sa \'rō-zə\ [L] rose
Rose·anne \rō-'zan\ [Rose + Anne]
Rose·mary \'rōz-ˌmer-ē\ or Rose·ma·rie \ˌrōz-mə-'rē\ [E] rosemary
Ro·set·ta \rō-'zet-ə\ dim of ROSE
Ros·lyn \'räz-lən\ or Ro·sa·lyn or Ro·se·lyn \'räz-(ə-)lən, 'rō-zə-lən\ var of ROSALIND
Ro·we·na \rə-'wē-nə\ [perh. fr. OE]
Rox·anne \räk-'san\ [OPer]
Ru·by \'rü-bē\ [E] ruby
Ruth \'rüth\ [Heb]

Ruth·ann \rü-'than\ [Ruth + Ann]

Sa·bra \'sā-brə\ dim of Sabrina
Sa·die \'sād-ē\ dim of SARA
Sal·ly or Sal·lie \'sal-ē\ dim of SARA
Sa·man·tha \sə-'man-thə\ [Aram]
San·dra \'san-drə, 'sän-\ dim of ALEXANDRA
San·dy \'san-dē\ dim of ALEXANDRA
Sar·ah or Sara \'ser-ə, 'sar-ə, 'sä-rə\ [Heb] princess
Sara·lee \'ser-ə-(ˌ)lē\ [prob. fr. Sara + Lee]
Saun·dra \'sȯn-drə, 'sän-\ var of SANDRA
Sel·ma \'sel-mə\ [Sw] fem dim of Anselm
Shari \'sha(ə)r-ē, 'she(ə)r-\ dim of SHARON
Shar·lene \shär-'lēn\ var of CHARLENE
Shar·on or Shar·ron \'shar-ən, 'sher-\ [Heb]
Shei·la \'shē-lə\ [IrGael] var of CECILIA
She·lia \'shēl-yə\ var of SHEILA
Shel·ley \'shel-ē\ [fr. a surname]
Sher·rill or Sher·yl \'sher-əl\ [prob. fr. a surname]
Sher·ry or Sher·rie or Sheri \'sher-ē\
Shir·ley \'shər-lē\ [fr. a surname]
Sig·rid \'sig-rəd\ [Scand] beautiful as victory
Son·dra \'sän-drə\ var of SANDRA
So·nia or So·nya or So·nja \'sō-nyə, 'sȯ-\ [Russ] dim of SOPHIA
So·phia \sə-'fē-ə, -'fī-\ or So·phie \'sō-fē\ [Gk] wisdom
Sta·cy or Sta·cey \'stā-sē\ dim of ANASTASIA
Stel·la \'stel-ə\ [L] star
Steph·a·nie \'stef-ə-nē\ fem of STEPHEN
Sue \'sü\ or Su·sie \'sü-zē\ dim of SUSAN
Su·el·len \sü-'el-ən\ [Sue + Ellen]
Su·san or Su·zan \'süz-ᵊn\ dim of SUSANNA
Su·san·na or Su·san·nah \sü-'zan-ə\ [Heb] lily
Su·zanne or Su·sanne or Su·zann \sü-'zan\ [F] var of SUSAN
Syb·il \'sib-əl\ [Gk] sibyl
Syl·via \'sil-vē-ə\ [L] she of the forest

Ta·mara \tə-'mar-ə\ [prob. fr. Georgian (language of the Republic of Georgia)]
Tan·ya \'tan-yə\ [Russ] dim of TATIANA
Ta·ra \'tär-ə\ [IrGael]
Tat·i·ana \ˌtät-ē-'än-ə\ [Russ]
Te·re·sa \tə-'rē-sə\ var of THERESA
Ter·ry or Ter·ri \'ter-ē\ dim of THERESA
Thel·ma \'thel-mə\
The·o·do·ra \ˌthē-ə-'dōr-ə, -'dȯr-\ [LGk] fem of THEODORE
The·re·sa or Te·re·sa \tə-'rē-sə\ [LL]
The·rese \tə-'rēs\ var of THERESA
Tif·fa·ny \'tif-ə-nē\ [Gk]
Ti·na \'tē-nə\ dim of CHRISTINA
To·by \'tō-bē\
To·ni \'tō-nē\ dim of Antonia
Tra·cy \'trā-sē\ [fr. a surname]
Tru·dy \'trüd-ē\ dim of GERTRUDE

Ur·su·la \'ər-sə-lə\ [LL] little she-bear

Val·er·ie \'val-ə-rē\ [L] prob strong
Van·es·sa \və-'nes-ə\
Vel·ma \'vel-mə\
Ve·ra \'vir-ə\ [Russ] faith
Ver·na \'vər-nə\ prob fem of VERNON
Ve·ron·i·ca \və-'rän-i-kə\ [LL]
Vicki or Vicky or Vick·ie \'vik-ē\ dim of VICTORIA
Vic·to·ria \vik-'tōr-ē-ə, -'tȯr-\ [L] victory
Vi·da \'vēd-ə, 'vīd-\ fem dim of DAVID
Vi·o·la \vī-'ō-lə, vē-'ō-, 'vī-ə-, 'vē-ə-\ [L] violet

\ə\abut \ᵊ\kitten \ər\further \a\ash \ā\ace \ä\mop, mar
\aŭ\out \ch\chin \e\bet \ē\easy \g\go \i\hit \ī\ice \j\job
\ŋ\sing \ō\go \ȯ\law \ȯi\boy \th\thin \th\the \ü\loot \ŭ\foot
\y\yet \zh\vision see also Pronunciation Symbols page

Vi·o·let \\'vī-ə-lət\ [OF, fr. L] violet
Vir·gin·ia \vər-'jin-yə, -'jin-ē-ə\ [L]
Viv·i·an \\'viv-ē-ən\ [LL]

Wan·da \\'wän-də\ [Pol]
Wen·dy \\'wen-dē\
Whit·ney \\'hwit-nē, 'wit-\ [OE]
Wil·da \\'wil-də\ *var of* WILLA

Wil·la \\'wil-ə\ *or* **Wil·lie** \\'wil-ē\ *prob fem dim of* WILLIAM
Wil·ma \\'wil-mə\ *prob fem dim of* WILLIAM
Win·i·fred \\'win-ə-frəd\ [W]

Yvette \i-'vet\ [F]
Yvonne \i-'vän\ [F]

Zel·da \\'zel-də\ *dim of* Griselda

CHAPTER 17

United States Facts

STATES

NAME, U.S. P.O. ABBR., and NICKNAME	AREA[1] sq.mi. (sq. km.)	rank	POPULATION 1990 census	rank	ADMITTED TO UNION[2] date	rank	CAPITAL	MOTTO
Alabama (AL) *Heart of Dixie*	51,705 (133,916)	29th	4,040,587	22d	1819	22d	Montgomery	We Dare Defend Our Rights
Alaska[3] (AK) *The Last Frontier*	591,004 (1,530,700)	1st	550,043	49th	1959	49th	Juneau	North to the Future
Arizona (AZ) *Grand Canyon State*	114,000 (295,260)	6th	3,665,228	24th	1912	48th	Phoenix	Ditat Deus (God Enriches)
Arkansas (AR) *Land of Opportunity*	53,187 (137,754)	27th	2,350,725	33d	1836	25th	Little Rock	Regnat Populus (The People Rule)
California (CA) *Golden State*	158,706 (411,048)	3d	29,760,020	1st	1850	31st	Sacramento	Eureka (I Have Found It)
Colorado (CO) *Centennial State*	104,247 (270,000)	8th	3,294,394	26th	1876	38th	Denver	Nil Sine Numine (Nothing Without the Divine Will)
Connecticut[2] (CT) *Constitution State, Nutmeg State*	5,018 (12,997)	48th	3,287,116	27th	1788	5th	Hartford	Qui Transtulit Sustinet (He Who Transplanted Sustains)
Delaware[2] (DE) *First State, Diamond State*	2,057 (5,328)	49th	666,168	46th	1787	1st	Dover	Liberty and Independence
Florida (FL) *Sunshine State*	58,664 (151,940)	22d	12,937,926	4th	1845	27th	Tallahassee	In God We Trust
Georgia[2] (GA) *Empire State of the South, Peach State*	58,910 (152,577)	21st	6,478,216	11th	1788	4th	Atlanta	Wisdom, Justice, Moderation
Hawaii[3] (HI) *Aloha State*	6,471 (16,760)	47th	1,108,229	41st	1959	50th	Honolulu	Ua Mau Ke Ea O Ka Aina I Ka Pono (The Life of the Land is Established in Righteousness)
Idaho (ID) *Gem State*	83,557 (216,413)	13th	1,006,749	42d	1890	43d	Boise	Esto Perpetua (May She Endure Forever)
Illinois (IL) *Prairie State*	56,400 (146,076)	24th	11,430,602	6th	1818	21st	Springfield	State Sovereignty–National Union

NAME, U.S. P.O. ABBR., and NICKNAME	AREA[1] sq.mi. (sq. km.)	rank	POPULATION 1990 census	rank	ADMITTED TO UNION[2] date	rank	CAPITAL	MOTTO
Indiana (IN) *Hoosier State*	36,291 (93,994)	38th	5,544,159	14th	1816	19th	Indianapolis	The Crossroads of America
Iowa (IA) *Hawkeye State*	56,275 (145,752)	25th	2,776,755	30th	1846	29th	Des Moines	Our Liberties We Prize and Our Rights We Will Maintain
Kansas (KS) *Sunflower State*	82,277 (213,097)	14th	2,477,574	32d	1861	34th	Topeka	Ad Astra per Aspera (To the Stars by Hard Ways)
Kentucky (KY) *Bluegrass State*	40,395 (104,623)	37th	3,685,296	23d	1792	15th	Frankfort	United We Stand, Divided We Fall
Louisiana (LA) *Pelican State*	48,523 (125,674)	31st	4,219,973	21st	1812	18th	Baton Rouge	Union, Justice, Confidence
Maine (ME) *Pine Tree State*	33,265 (86,156)	39th	1,227,928	38th	1820	23d	Augusta	Dirigo (I Direct)
Maryland[2] (MD) *Old Line State*	10,460 (27,091)	42d	4,781,468	19th	1788	7th	Annapolis	Fatti Maschii, Parole Femine (Manly Deeds, Womanly Words)
Massachusetts[2] (MA) *Bay State*	8,284 (21,456)	45th	6,016,425	13th	1788	6th	Boston	Ense Petit Placidam Sub Libertate Quietem (By the Sword We Seek Peace, but Peace Only Under Liberty)
Michigan (MI) *Wolverine State, Great Lakes State*	58,216 (150,779)	23d	9,295,297	8th	1837	26th	Lansing	Si Quaeris Peninsulam Amoenam Circumspice (If You Seek a Beautiful Peninsula, Look Around)
Minnesota (MN) *Gopher State, North Star State*	84,068 (217,736)	12th	4,375,099	20th	1858	32d	St. Paul	L'étoile du Nord (Star of the North)
Mississippi (MS) *Magnolia State*	47,689 (123,514)	32d	2,573,216	31st	1817	20th	Jackson	Virtute et Armis (By Valor and Arms)
Missouri (MO) *Show Me State*	69,697 (180,515)	19th	5,117,073	15th	1821	24th	Jefferson City	Salus Populi Suprema Lex Esto (Let the Welfare of the People Be the Supreme Law)
Montana (MT) *Treasure State*	147,046 (380,849)	4th	799,065	44th	1889	41st	Helena	Oro y Plata (Gold and Silver)
Nebraska (NE) *Cornhusker State*	77,355 (200,349)	15th	1,578,385	36th	1867	37th	Lincoln	Equality Before the Law
Nevada (NV) *Silver State*	110,561 (286,353)	7th	1,201,833	39th	1864	36th	Carson City	All For Our Country

NAME, U.S. P.O. ABBR., and NICKNAME	AREA[1]		POPULATION		ADMITTED TO UNION[2]		CAPITAL	MOTTO
	sq.mi. (sq. km.)	rank	1990 census	rank	date	rank		
New Hampshire[2] (NH) *Granite State*	9,279 (24,033)	44th	1,109,252	40th	1788	9th	Concord	Live Free Or Die
New Jersey[2] (NJ) *Garden State*	7,787 (20,168)	46th	7,730,188	9th	1787	3d	Trenton	Liberty and Prosperity
New Mexico (NM) *Land of Enchantment*	121,593 (314,926)	5th	1,515,069	37th	1912	47th	Santa Fe	Crescit Eundo (It Grows As It Goes)
New York[2] (NY) *Empire State*	49,576 (128,402)	30th	17,990,456	2d	1788	11th	Albany	Excelsior (Still Higher)
North Carolina[2] (NC) *Tar Heel State, Old North State*	52,669 (136,413)	28th	6,628,637	10th	1789	12th	Raleigh	To Be Rather Than To Seem
North Dakota (ND) *Flicker-tail State*	70,665 (183,022)	17th	638,800	47th	1889	39th	Bismarck	Liberty and Union, Now and Forever, One and Inseparable
Ohio (OH) *Buckeye State*	41,222 (106,765)	35th	10,847,115	7th	1803	17th	Columbus	
Oklahoma (OK) *Sooner State*	69,956 (181,186)	18th	3,145,585	28th	1907	46th	Oklahoma City	Labor Omnia Vin-cit (Labor Con-quers All Things)
Oregon (OR) *Beaver State*	97,073 (251,419)	10th	2,842,321	29th	1859	33d	Salem	Alis Volat Propriis (She Flies With Her Own Wings)
Pennsylvania[2] (PA) *Keystone State*	45,333 (117,412)	33d	11,881,643	5th	1787	2d	Harrisburg	Virtue, Liberty, and Independence
Rhode Island[2] (RI) *Ocean State, Little Rhody*	1,212 (3,139)	50th	1,003,464	43d	1790	13th	Providence	Hope
South Carolina[2] (SC) *Palmetto State*	31,113 (80,583)	40th	3,486,703	25th	1788	8th	Columbia	Dum Spiro, Spero (While I Breathe, I Hope)
South Dakota (SD) *Mount Rushmore State*	77,116 (199,730)	16th	696,004	45th	1889	40th	Pierre	Under God the People Rule
Tennessee (TN) *Volunteer State*	42,144 (109,153)	34th	4,877,185	17th	1796	16th	Nashville	Agriculture and Commerce
Texas (TX) *Lone Star State*	266,807 (691,030)	2d	16,986,510	3d	1845	28th	Austin	Friendship
Utah (UT) *Beehive State*	84,899 (219,888)	11th	1,722,850	35th	1896	45th	Salt Lake City	Industry
Vermont (VT) *Green Mountain State*	9,609 (24,887)	43d	562,758	48th	1791	14th	Montpelier	Freedom and Unity

NAME, U.S. P.O. ABBR., and NICKNAME	AREA[1] sq.mi. (sq. km.)	rank	POPULATION 1990 census	rank	ADMITTED TO UNION[2] date	rank	CAPITAL	MOTTO
Virginia[2] (VA) *Old Dominion*	40,767 (105,586)	36th	6,187,358	12th	1788	10th	Richmond	Sic Semper Tyran- nis (Thus Ever to Tyrants)
Washington (WA) *Evergreen State*	68,192 (176,617)	20th	4,866,692	18th	1889	42d	Olympia	Alki (By and By)
West Virginia (WV) *Moun- tain State*	24,181 (62,629)	41st	1,793,477	34th	1863	35th	Charleston	Montani Semper Liberi (Mountaineers Are Always Free)
Wisconsin (WI) *Badger State*	56,154 (145,439)	26th	4,891,769	16th	1848	30th	Madison	Forward
Wyoming (WY) *Equality State, Cowboy State*	97,914 (253,597)	9th	453,588	50th	1890	44th	Cheyenne	Equal Rights
District of Columbia[4] (DC)	69 (179)		609,909				Washington	E Pluribus Unum (One Out of Many)

TERRITORIES AND POSSESSIONS

NAME and U.S. P.O. ABBR.	TOTAL AREA sq. mi.	sq. km.	POPULATION 1990 census	CAPITAL
American Samoa (AS)	77	199	46,773	Pago Pago
Guam (GU)	209	541	133,152	Agana
Puerto Rico[6] (PR)	3435	8897	3,522,037	San Juan
Virgin Islands of the United States (VI)	133	345	101,809	Charlotte Amalie
Other (Belau, Northern Mariana Islands, etc.)	367	951	63,982	

[1]Total land and inland water.
[2]Date of admission of the 13 original colonies is that of ratification of the Constitution.
[3]The Alaska Statehood Act was signed by the President July 7, 1958; the Hawaii Statehood Act, Mar. 18, 1959.
[4]Coextensive with the city of Washington.
[5]Total land and inland water; does not include 74,364 sq. mi. (192,603 sq. km.) of Great Lakes and other
 primary bodies of water, of which total the state of Michigan has 38,575 sq. mi. (99,909 sq. km.).
[6]Adopted constitution 1952 establishing it as a commonwealth with autonomy in internal affairs.

EXECUTIVE DEPARTMENTS OF THE UNITED STATES

DEPARTMENT	TITLE OF CHIEF	DATE OF CREATION	FUNCTIONS
Department of State	Secretary of State	July 27, 1789, as Dept. of Foreign Affairs; Sept. 15, 1789, under present name	conduct of foreign relations
Department of the Treasury	Secretary of the Treasury	Sept. 2, 1789	administration of national fiscal policies
*Department of Defense	Secretary of Defense	July 26, 1947, as National Military Establishment; Aug. 10, 1949, under present name	responsibility for national defense and security
Department of Justice	Attorney General (office created Sept. 24, 1789)	June 22, 1870	enforcement of federal laws; provision of legal counsel in federal cases; interpretation of laws for other departments
Department of the Interior	Secretary of the Interior	March 3, 1849	conservation and development of natural resources of U.S. and territories; guardianship of American Indians
Department of Agriculture	Secretary of Agriculture	May 15, 1862; made executive department Feb. 9, 1889	acquisition and diffusion of useful information on agricultural subjects; supervision of national forests; administration of price support programs
Department of Commerce	Secretary of Commerce	Feb. 14, 1903, as the Dept. of Commerce and Labor; reorganized Mar. 4, 1913, under present name	promotion and development of foreign and domestic commerce
Department of Labor	Secretary of Labor	Mar. 4, 1913	administration and enforcement of statutes designed to promote welfare of wage earners
Department of Housing and Urban Development	Secretary of Housing and Urban Development	Sept. 9, 1965	supervision and coordination of federal programs relating to housing and urban renewal
Department of Transportation	Secretary of Transportation	Oct. 15, 1966	administration and coordination of federal agencies and programs dealing with transportation
Department of Energy	Secretary of Energy	August 4, 1977	administration of agencies promoting energy conservation and development
Department of Education	Secretary of Education	October 17, 1979; upon abolition of Dept. of Health, Education, and Welfare (created April 11, 1953), assumed education functions	administration of agencies promoting educational programs and policies
Department of Health and Human Services	Secretary of Health and Human Services	October 17, 1979; upon abolition of Dept. of Health, Education, and Welfare (created April 11, 1953), assumed health and welfare functions	administration of welfare, social security, and health agencies

*The Department of the Army, created Aug. 7, 1789, as the Department of War and the Department of the Navy, created April 30, 1789, lost executive status July 26, 1947, on merger under their present names in the newly created National Military Establishment. The Department of the Air Force was created Sept. 18, 1947, as a third subordinate department of the National Military Establishment.

Population of Places in the United States

Having 19,000 or More Inhabitants in 1990

A

Aberdeen, S. Dak.	24,927
Abilene, Tex.	106,654
Addison, Ill.	32,058
Adrian, Mich.	22,097
Agawam, Mass.	27,323
Agoura Hills, Calif.	20,390
Aiken, S.C.	19,872
Akron, Ohio	223,019
Alameda, Calif.	76,459
Alamogordo, N. Mex.	27,596
Albany, Ga.	78,122
Albany, N.Y.	101,082
Albany, Oreg.	29,462
Albuquerque, N. Mex.	384,736
Alexandria, La.	49,188
Alexandria, Va.	111,183
Alhambra, Calif.	82,106
Alice, Tex.	19,788
Allen Park, Mich.	31,092
Allentown, Pa.	105,090
Alliance, Ohio	23,376
Altamonte Springs, Fla.	34,879
Alton, Ill.	32,905
Altoona, Pa.	51,881
Altus, Okla.	21,910
Alvin, Tex.	19,220
Amarillo, Tex.	157,615
Ames, Iowa	47,198
Amherst, Mass.	35,228
Amsterdam, N.Y.	20,714
Anaheim, Calif.	266,406
Anchorage, Alaska	226,338
Anderson, Ind.	59,459
Anderson, S.C.	26,184
Andover, Mass.	29,151
Annapolis, Md.	33,187
Ann Arbor, Mich.	109,592
Anniston, Ala.	26,623
Antioch, Calif.	62,195
Appleton, Wis.	65,695
Apple Valley, Calif.	46,079
Apple Valley, Minn.	34,598
Arcadia, Calif.	48,290
Ardmore, Okla.	23,079
Arlington, Mass.	44,630
Arlington, Tex.	261,721
Arlington Heights, Ill.	75,460
Arvada, Colo.	89,235
Asheville, N.C.	61,607
Ashland, Ky.	23,622
Ashland, Ohio	20,079
Ashtabula, Ohio	21,633
Atascadero, Calif.	23,138
Athens, Ga.	45,734
Athens, Ohio	21,265
Atlanta, Ga.	394,017
Atlantic City, N.J.	37,986

Attleboro, Mass.	38,383
Atwater, Calif.	22,282
Auburn, Ala.	33,830
Auburn, Me.	24,309
Auburn, N.Y.	31,258
Auburn, Wash.	33,102
Augusta, Ga.	44,639
Augusta, Me.	21,325
Aurora, Colo.	222,103
Aurora, Ill.	99,581
Austin, Minn.	21,907
Austin, Tex.	465,622
Azusa, Calif.	41,333

B

Bakersfield, Calif.	174,820
Baldwin, Pa.	21,923
Baldwin Park, Calif.	69,330
Ballwin, Mo.	21,816
Baltimore, Md.	736,014
Bangor, Me.	33,181
Banning, Calif.	20,570
Barberton, Ohio	27,623
Barnstable, Mass.	40,949
Barstow, Calif.	21,472
Bartlesville, Okla.	34,256
Bartlett, Ill.	19,373
Bartlett, Tenn.	26,989
Baton Rouge, La.	219,531
Battle Creek, Mich.	53,540
Bay City, Mich.	38,936
Bayonne, N.J.	61,444
Baytown, Tex.	63,850
Beaumont, Tex.	114,323
Beavercreek, Ohio	33,626
Beaverton, Oreg.	53,310
Bedford, Tex.	43,762
Bell, Calif.	34,365
Belleville, Ill.	42,785
Belleville, N.J.	34,213
Bellevue, Nebr.	30,982
Bellevue, Wash.	86,874
Bellflower, Calif.	61,815
Bell Gardens, Calif.	42,355
Bellingham, Wash.	52,179
Bellwood, Ill.	20,241
Belmont, Calif.	24,127
Belmont, Mass.	24,720
Beloit, Wis.	35,573
Benbrook, Tex.	19,564
Bend, Oreg.	20,469
Benicia, Calif.	24,437
Berea, Ohio	19,051
Bergenfield, N.J.	24,458
Berkeley, Calif.	102,724
Berwyn, Ill.	45,426
Bessemer, Ala.	33,497
Bethany, Okla.	20,075

Bethel Park, Pa.	33,823
Bethesda, Md.	62,936
Bethlehem, Pa.	71,428
Bettendorf, Iowa	28,132
Beverly, Mass.	38,195
Beverly Hills, Calif.	31,971
Biddeford, Me.	20,710
Big Spring, Tex.	23,093
Billerica, Mass.	37,609
Billings, Mont.	81,151
Biloxi, Miss.	46,319
Binghamton, N.Y.	53,008
Birmingham, Ala.	265,968
Birmingham, Mich.	19,997
Bismarck, N. Dak.	49,256
Blacksburg, Va.	34,590
Blaine, Minn.	38,975
Bloomfield, N.J.	45,061
Bloomington, Ill.	51,972
Bloomington, Ind.	60,633
Bloomington, Minn.	86,335
Blue Island, Ill.	21,203
Blue Springs, Mo.	40,153
Blytheville, Ark.	22,906
Boca Raton, Fla.	61,492
Boise, Idaho	125,738
Bolingbrook, Ill.	40,843
Bossier City, La.	52,721
Boston, Mass.	574,283
Boulder, Colo.	83,312
Bountiful, Utah	36,659
Bowie, Md.	37,589
Bowling Green, Ky.	40,641
Bowling Green, Ohio	28,176
Boynton Beach, Fla.	46,194
Bozeman, Mont.	22,660
Bradenton, Fla.	43,779
Braintree, Mass.	33,836
Branford, Conn.	27,603
Brea, Calif.	32,873
Bremerton, Wash.	38,142
Bridgeport, Conn.	141,686
Bristol, Conn.	60,640
Bristol, R.I.	21,625
Bristol, Tenn.	23,421
Brockton, Mass.	92,788
Broken Arrow, Okla.	58,043
Brookfield, Wis.	35,184
Brookline, Mass.	54,718
Brooklyn Center, Minn.	28,887
Brooklyn Park, Minn.	56,381
Brook Park, Ohio	22,865
Broomfield, Colo.	24,638
Brownsville, Tex.	98,962
Brunswick, Me.	20,906
Brunswick, Ohio	28,230
Bryan, Tex.	55,002
Buena Park, Calif.	68,784
Buffalo, N.Y.	328,123
Buffalo Grove, Ill.	36,427
Bullhead City, Ariz.	21,951
Burbank, Calif.	93,643
Burbank, Ill.	27,600
Burlingame, Calif.	26,801
Burlington, Iowa	27,208
Burlington, Mass.	23,302
Burlington, N.C.	39,498
Burlington, Vt.	39,127
Burnsville, Minn.	51,288
Burton, Mich.	27,617
Butte, Mont.	33,336

C

Calumet City, Ill.	37,840
Camarillo, Calif.	52,303
Cambridge, Mass.	95,802
Camden, N.J.	87,492
Campbell, Calif.	36,048
Canton, Ohio	84,161
Cape Coral, Fla.	74,991
Cape Girardeau, Mo.	34,438
Carbondale, Ill.	27,033
Carlsbad, Calif.	63,126
Carlsbad, N. Mex.	24,952
Carmel, Ind.	25,380
Carol Stream, Ill.	31,716
Carpentersville, Ill.	23,049
Carrollton, Tex.	82,169
Carson, Calif.	83,995
Carson City, Nev.	40,443
Carteret, N.J.	19,025
Cary, N.C.	43,858
Casa Grande, Ariz.	19,082
Casper, Wyo.	46,742
Cathedral City, Calif.	30,085
Cedar Falls, Iowa	34,298
Cedar Hill, Tex.	19,976
Cedar Rapids, Iowa	108,751
Centerville, Ohio	21,082
Ceres, Calif.	26,314
Cerritos, Calif.	53,240
Champaign, Ill.	63,502
Chandler, Ariz.	90,533
Chapel Hill, N.C.	38,719
Charleston, Ill.	20,398
Charleston, S.C.	80,414
Charleston, W. Va.	57,287
Charlotte, N.C.	395,934
Charlottesville, Va.	40,341
Chattanooga, Tenn.	152,466
Chelmsford, Mass.	32,383
Chelsea, Mass.	28,710
Chesapeake, Va.	151,976
Cheshire, Conn.	25,684
Chester, Pa.	41,856
Chesterfield, Mo.	37,991
Cheyenne, Wyo.	50,008
Chicago, Ill.	2,783,726
Chicago Heights, Ill.	33,072
Chico, Calif.	40,079
Chicopee, Mass.	56,632
Chillicothe, Ohio	21,923
Chino, Calif.	59,682
Chula Vista, Calif.	135,163
Cicero, Ill.	67,436
Cincinnati, Ohio	364,040
Claremont, Calif.	32,503
Clarksdale, Miss.	19,717
Clarksville, Ind.	19,833
Clarksville, Tenn.	75,494
Clearfield, Utah	21,435
Clearwater, Fla.	98,784
Cleburne, Tex.	22,205
Cleveland, Ohio	505,616
Cleveland, Tenn.	30,354
Cleveland Heights, Ohio	54,052
Cliffside Park, N.J.	20,393
Clifton, N.J.	71,742
Clinton, Iowa	29,201
Clinton, Miss.	21,847
Clovis, Calif.	50,323
Clovis, N. Mex.	30,954
Coconut Creek, Fla.	27,485
Coeur d'Alene, Idaho	24,563

College Park, Ga.	20,457
College Park, Md.	21,927
College Station, Tex.	52,456
Collinsville, Ill.	22,446
Colorado Springs, Colo.	281,140
Colton, Calif.	40,213
Columbia, Mo.	69,101
Columbia, S.C.	98,052
Columbia, Tenn.	28,583
Columbus, Ga.	179,278
Columbus, Ind.	31,802
Columbus, Miss.	23,799
Columbus, Nebr.	19,480
Columbus, Ohio	632,910
Compton, Calif.	90,454
Concord, Calif.	111,348
Concord, N.H.	36,006
Concord, N.C.	27,347
Conroe, Tex.	27,610
Conway, Ark.	26,481
Cookeville, Tenn.	21,744
Coon Rapids, Minn.	52,978
Cooper City, Fla.	20,791
Copperas Cove, Tex.	24,079
Coral Gables, Fla.	40,091
Coral Springs, Fla.	79,443
Corona, Calif.	76,095
Coronado, Calif.	26,540
Corpus Christi, Tex.	257,453
Corsicana, Tex.	22,911
Cortland, N.Y.	19,801
Corvallis, Oreg.	44,757
Costa Mesa, Calif.	96,357
Cottage Grove, Minn.	22,935
Council Bluffs, Iowa	54,315
Coventry, R.I.	31,083
Covina, Calif.	43,207
Covington, Ky.	43,264
Cranston, R.I.	76,060
Crystal, Minn.	23,788
Crystal Lake, Ill.	24,512
Cudahy, Calif.	22,817
Culver City, Calif.	38,793
Cumberland, Md.	23,706
Cumberland, R.I.	29,038
Cupertino, Calif.	40,263
Cuyahoga Falls, Ohio	48,950
Cypress, Calif.	42,655

D

Dallas, Tex.	1,006,877
Dalton, Ga.	21,761
Daly City, Calif.	92,311
Dana Point, Calif.	31,896
Danbury, Conn.	65,585
Danvers, Mass.	24,174
Danville, Calif.	31,306
Danville, Ill.	33,828
Danville, Va.	53,056
Dartmouth, Mass.	27,244
Davenport, Iowa	95,333
Davie, Fla.	47,217
Davis, Calif.	46,209
Dayton, Ohio	182,044
Daytona Beach, Fla.	61,921
Dearborn, Mich.	89,286
Dearborn Heights, Mich.	60,838
Decatur, Ala.	48,761
Decatur, Ill.	83,885
Dedham, Mass.	23,782
Deerfield Beach, Fla.	46,325
Deer Park, Tex.	27,652
De Kalb, Ill.	34,925

Delano, Calif.	22,762
Delaware, Ohio	20,030
Del City, Okla.	23,928
Delray Beach, Fla.	47,181
Del Rio, Tex.	30,705
Denison, Tex.	21,505
Denton, Tex.	66,270
Denver, Colo.	467,610
Derry, N.H.	29,603
Des Moines, Iowa	193,187
De Soto, Tex.	30,544
Des Plaines, Ill.	53,223
Detroit, Mich.	1,027,974
Diamond Bar, Calif.	53,672
Dodge City, Kans.	21,129
Dolton, Ill.	23,930
Dothan, Ala.	53,589
Dover, Del.	27,630
Dover, N.H.	25,042
Downers Grove, Ill.	46,858
Downey, Calif.	91,444
Dracut, Mass.	25,594
Duarte, Calif.	20,688
Dublin, Calif.	23,229
Dubuque, Iowa	57,546
Duluth, Minn.	85,493
Duncan, Okla.	21,732
Duncanville, Tex.	35,748
Dunedin, Fla.	34,012
Durham, N.C.	136,611

E

Eagan, Minn.	47,409
Eagle Pass, Tex.	20,651
East Chicago, Ind.	33,892
East Cleveland, Ohio	33,096
East Detroit, Mich.	35,283
East Hartford, Conn.	50,452
East Haven, Conn.	26,144
Eastlake, Ohio	21,161
East Lansing, Mich.	50,677
East Moline, Ill.	20,147
Easton, Mass.	19,807
Easton, Pa.	26,276
East Orange, N.J.	73,552
East Palo Alto, Calif.	23,451
East Peoria, Ill.	21,378
East Point, Ga.	34,402
East Providence, R.I.	50,380
East Ridge, Tenn.	21,101
East St. Louis, Ill.	40,944
Eau Claire, Wis.	56,856
Eden Prairie, Minn.	39,311
Edina, Minn.	46,070
Edinburg, Tex.	29,885
Edmond, Okla.	52,315
Edmonds, Wash.	30,744
El Cajon, Calif.	88,693
El Centro, Calif.	31,384
El Cerrito, Calif.	22,869
El Dorado, Ark.	23,146
Elgin, Ill.	77,010
Elizabeth, N.J.	110,002
Elk Grove Village, Ill.	33,429
Elkhart, Ind.	43,627
Elmhurst, Ill.	42,029
Elmira, N.Y.	33,724
El Monte, Calif.	106,209
Elmwood Park, Ill.	23,206
El Paso, Tex.	515,342
Elyria, Ohio	56,746
Emporia, Kans.	25,512
Encinitas, Calif.	55,386

Enfield, Conn.	45,532
Englewood, Colo.	29,387
Englewood, N.J.	24,850
Enid, Okla.	45,309
Enterprise, Ala.	20,123
Erie, Pa.	108,718
Escondido, Calif.	108,635
Euclid, Ohio	54,875
Eugene, Oreg.	112,669
Euless, Tex.	38,149
Eureka, Calif.	27,025
Evanston, Ill.	73,233
Evansville, Ind.	126,272
Everett, Mass.	35,701
Everett, Wash.	69,961
Evergreen Park, Ill.	20,874

F

Fairbanks, Alaska	30,843
Fairborn, Ohio	31,300
Fairfax, Va.	19,622
Fairfield, Calif.	77,211
Fairfield, Conn.	53,418
Fairfield, Ohio	39,729
Fair Lawn, N.J.	30,548
Fairmont, W. Va.	20,210
Fall River, Mass.	92,703
Falmouth, Mass.	27,960
Fargo, N. Dak.	74,111
Farmers Branch, Tex.	24,250
Farmington, N. Mex.	33,997
Farmington Hills, Mich.	74,652
Fayetteville, Ark.	42,099
Fayetteville, N.C.	75,695
Ferguson, Mo.	22,286
Ferndale, Mich.	25,084
Findlay, Ohio	35,703
Fitchburg, Mass.	41,194
Flagstaff, Ariz.	45,857
Flint, Mich.	140,761
Florence, Ala.	36,426
Florence, S.C.	29,813
Florissant, Mo.	51,206
Folsom, Calif.	29,802
Fond du Lac, Wis.	37,757
Fontana, Calif.	87,535
Fort Collins, Colo.	87,758
Fort Dodge, Iowa	25,894
Fort Lauderdale, Fla.	149,377
Fort Lee, N.J.	31,997
Fort Myers, Fla.	45,206
Fort Pierce, Fla.	36,830
Fort Smith, Ark.	72,798
Fort Walton Beach, Fla.	21,471
Fort Wayne, Ind.	173,072
Fort Worth, Tex.	447,619
Foster City, Calif.	28,176
Fountain Valley, Calif.	53,691
Framingham, Mass.	64,989
Frankfort, Ky.	25,968
Franklin, Mass.	22,095
Franklin, Tenn.	20,098
Franklin, Wis.	21,855
Frederick, Md.	40,148
Fredericksburg, Va.	19,027
Freeport, Ill.	25,840
Freeport, N.Y.	39,894
Fremont, Calif.	173,339
Fremont, Nebr.	23,680
Fresno, Calif.	354,202
Fridley, Minn.	28,335
Friendswood, Tex.	22,814
Fullerton, Calif.	114,144

G

Gadsden, Ala.	42,523
Gahanna, Ohio	27,791
Gainesville, Fla.	84,770
Gaithersburg, Md.	39,542
Galesburg, Ill.	33,530
Gallup, N. Mex.	19,154
Galveston, Tex.	59,070
Gardena, Calif.	49,847
Garden City, Kans.	24,097
Garden City, Mich.	31,846
Garden City, N.Y.	21,686
Garden Grove, Calif.	143,050
Gardner, Mass.	20,125
Garfield, N.J.	26,727
Garfield Heights, Ohio	31,739
Garland, Tex.	180,650
Gary, Ind.	116,646
Gastonia, N.C.	54,732
Germantown, Tenn.	32,893
Gilbert, Ariz.	29,188
Gilroy, Calif.	31,487
Gladstone, Mo.	26,243
Glastonbury, Conn.	27,901
Glen Cove, N.Y.	24,149
Glendale, Ariz.	148,134
Glendale, Calif.	180,038
Glendale Heights, Ill.	27,973
Glendora, Calif.	47,828
Glen Ellyn, Ill.	24,944
Glenview, Ill.	37,093
Gloucester, Mass.	28,716
Golden Valley, Minn.	20,971
Goldsboro, N.C.	40,709
Goose Creek, S.C.	24,692
Goshen, Ind.	23,797
Grand Forks, N. Dak.	49,425
Grand Island, Nebr.	39,386
Grand Junction, Colo.	29,034
Grand Prairie, Tex.	99,616
Grand Rapids, Mich.	189,126
Grandview, Mo.	24,967
Granite City, Ill.	32,862
Grapevine, Tex.	29,202
Great Falls, Mont.	55,097
Greeley, Colo.	60,536
Green Bay, Wis.	96,466
Greenbelt, Md.	21,096
Greenfield, Wis.	33,403
Greensboro, N.C.	183,521
Greenville, Miss.	45,226
Greenville, N.C.	44,972
Greenville, S.C.	58,282
Greenville, Tex.	23,071
Greenwich, Conn.	58,441
Greenwood, Ind.	26,265
Greenwood, S.C.	20,807
Gresham, Oreg.	68,235
Griffin, Ga.	21,347
Groton, Conn.	45,144
Grove City, Ohio	19,661
Guilford, Conn.	19,848
Gulfport, Miss.	40,775

H

Hackensack, N.J.	37,049
Hagerstown, Md.	35,445
Hallandale, Fla.	30,996
Haltom City, Tex.	32,856
Hamden, Conn.	52,434
Hamilton, Ohio	61,368
Hammond, Ind.	84,236

Hampton, Va.	133,793	Irvine, Calif.	110,330
Hanford, Calif.	30,897	Irving, Tex.	155,037
Hanover Park, Ill.	32,895	Ithaca, N.Y.	29,541
Harlingen, Tex.	48,735		
Harrisburg, Pa.	52,376	**J**	
Harrison, N.Y.	23,308		
Harrisonburg, Va.	30,707	Jackson, Mich.	37,446
Hartford, Conn.	139,739	Jackson, Miss.	196,637
Harvey, Ill.	29,771	Jackson, Tenn.	48,949
Hastings, Nebr.	22,837	Jacksonville, Ark.	29,101
Hattiesburg, Miss.	41,882	Jacksonville, Fla.	672,971
Havelock, N.C.	20,268	Jacksonville, Ill.	19,324
Haverhill, Mass.	51,418	Jacksonville, N.C.	30,013
Hawthorne, Calif.	71,349	Jamestown, N.Y.	34,681
Hayward, Calif.	111,498	Janesville, Wis.	52,133
Hazel Park, Mich.	20,051	Jefferson City, Mo.	35,481
Hazleton, Pa.	24,730	Jeffersontown, Ky.	23,221
Helena, Mont.	24,569	Jeffersonville, Ind.	21,841
Hemet, Calif.	36,094	Jersey City, N.J.	228,537
Hempstead, N.Y.	49,453	Johnson City, Tenn.	49,381
Henderson, Ky.	25,945	Johnston, R.I.	26,542
Henderson, Nev.	64,942	Johnstown, Pa.	28,134
Hendersonville, Tenn.	32,188	Joliet, Ill.	76,836
Hesperia, Calif.	50,418	Jonesboro, Ark.	46,535
Hialeah, Fla.	188,004	Joplin, Mo.	40,961
Hickory, N.C.	28,301	Junction City, Kans.	20,604
Highland, Calif.	34,439	Juneau, Alaska	26,751
Highland, Ind.	23,696	Jupiter, Fla.	24,986
Highland Park, Ill.	30,575		
Highland Park, Mich.	20,121	**K**	
High Point, N.C.	69,496		
Hillsboro, Oreg.	37,520	Kailua, Hawaii	36,818
Hilo, Hawaii	37,808	Kalamazoo, Mich.	80,277
Hilton Head Island, S.C.	23,694	Kaneohe, Hawaii	35,448
Hinesville, Ga.	21,603	Kankakee, Ill.	27,575
Hingham, Mass.	19,821	Kannapolis, N.C.	29,696
Hobart, Ind.	21,822	Kansas City, Kans.	149,767
Hobbs, N. Mex.	29,115	Kansas City, Mo.	435,146
Hoboken, N.J.	33,397	Kearney, Nebr.	24,396
Hoffman Estates, Ill.	46,561	Kearny, N.J.	34,874
Holland, Mich.	30,745	Keene, N.H.	22,430
Hollister, Calif.	19,212	Keizer, Oreg.	21,884
Hollywood, Fla.	121,697	Kenner, La.	72,033
Holyoke, Mass.	43,704	Kennewick, Wash.	42,155
Homestead, Fla.	26,866	Kenosha, Wis.	80,352
Homewood, Ala.	22,922	Kent, Ohio	28,835
Homewood, Ill.	19,278	Kent, Wash.	37,960
Honolulu, Hawaii	365,272	Kentwood, Mich.	37,826
Hoover, Ala.	39,788	Kettering, Ohio	60,569
Hopewell, Va.	23,101	Key West, Fla.	24,832
Hopkinsville, Ky.	29,809	Killeen, Tex.	63,535
Hot Springs, Ark.	32,462	Kingsport, Tenn.	36,365
Houma, La.	30,495	Kingston, N.Y.	23,095
Houston, Tex.	1,630,553	Kingsville, Tex.	25,276
Huber Heights, Ohio	38,696	Kinston, N.C.	25,295
Huntington, W. Va.	54,844	Kirkland, Wash.	40,052
Huntington Beach, Calif.	181,519	Kirkwood, Mo.	27,291
Huntington Park, Calif.	56,065	Kissimmee, Fla.	30,050
Huntsville, Ala.	159,789	Knoxville, Tenn.	165,121
Huntsville, Tex.	27,925	Kokomo, Ind.	44,962
Hurst, Tex.	33,574		
Hutchinson, Kans.	39,308	**L**	
		La Cañada Flintridge, Calif.	19,378
I		Lacey, Wash.	19,279
		Lackawanna, N.Y.	20,585
Idaho Falls, Idaho	43,929	La Crosse, Wis.	51,003
Imperial Beach, Calif.	26,512	Lafayette, Calif.	23,501
Independence, Mo.	112,301	Lafayette, Ind.	43,764
Indianapolis, Ind.	741,952	Lafayette, La.	94,440
Indio, Calif.	36,793	La Grange, Ga.	25,597
Inglewood, Calif.	109,602	Laguna Beach, Calif.	23,170
Inkster, Mich.	30,772	Laguna Niguel, Calif.	44,400
Inver Grove Heights, Minn.	22,477	La Habra, Calif.	51,266
Iowa City, Iowa	59,738	Lake Charles, La.	70,580
		Lake Havasu City, Ariz.	24,363

Lake Jackson, Tex.	22,776
Lakeland, Fla.	70,576
Lake Oswego, Oreg.	30,576
Lakeville, Minn.	24,854
Lakewood, Calif.	73,557
Lakewood, Colo.	126,481
Lakewood, Ohio	59,718
Lake Worth, Fla.	28,564
La Mesa, Calif.	52,931
La Mirada, Calif.	40,452
Lancaster, Calif.	97,291
Lancaster, Ohio	34,507
Lancaster, Pa.	55,551
Lancaster, Tex.	22,117
Lansing, Ill.	28,086
Lansing, Mich.	127,321
La Porte, Ind.	21,507
La Porte, Tex.	27,910
La Puente, Calif.	36,955
Laramie, Wyo.	26,687
Laredo, Tex.	122,899
Largo, Fla.	65,674
Las Cruces, N. Mex.	62,126
Las Vegas, Nev.	258,295
Lauderdale Lakes, Fla.	27,341
Lauderhill, Fla.	49,708
Laurel, Md.	19,438
La Verne, Calif.	30,897
Lawndale, Calif.	27,331
Lawrence, Ind.	26,763
Lawrence, Kans.	65,608
Lawrence, Mass.	70,207
Lawton, Okla.	80,561
Layton, Utah	41,784
League City, Tex.	30,159
Leavenworth, Kans.	38,495
Leawood, Kans.	19,693
Lebanon, Pa.	24,800
Lee's Summit, Mo.	46,418
Lemon Grove, Calif.	23,984
Lenexa, Kans.	34,034
Leominster, Mass.	38,145
Lewiston, Idaho	28,082
Lewiston, Me.	39,757
Lewisville, Tex.	46,521
Lexington, Ky.	225,366
Lexington, Mass.	28,974
Liberty, Mo.	20,459
Libertyville, Ill.	19,174
Lima, Ohio	45,549
Lincoln, Nebr.	191,972
Lincoln Park, Mich.	41,832
Linden, N.J.	36,701
Lindenhurst, N.Y.	26,879
Lisle, Ill.	19,512
Little Rock, Ark.	175,795
Littleton, Colo.	33,685
Livermore, Calif.	56,741
Livonia, Mich.	100,850
Lockport, N.Y.	24,426
Lodi, Calif.	51,874
Lodi, N.J.	22,355
Logan, Utah	32,762
Lombard, Ill.	39,408
Lomita, Calif.	19,382
Lompoc, Calif.	37,649
Long Beach, Calif.	429,433
Long Beach, N.Y.	33,510
Long Branch, N.J.	28,658
Longmont, Colo.	51,555
Longview, Tex.	70,311
Longview, Wash.	31,499
Lorain, Ohio	71,245

Los Altos, Calif.	26,303
Los Angeles, Calif.	3,485,398
Los Gatos, Calif.	27,357
Louisville, Ky.	269,063
Loveland, Colo.	37,352
Lowell, Mass.	103,439
Lubbock, Tex.	186,206
Lufkin, Tex.	30,206
Lynbrook, N.Y.	19,208
Lynchburg, Va.	66,049
Lynn, Mass.	81,245
Lynnwood, Wash.	28,695
Lynwood, Calif.	61,945

M

McAllen, Tex.	84,021
Machesney Park, Ill.	19,033
McKeesport, Pa.	26,016
McKinney, Tex.	21,283
Macomb, Ill.	19,952
Macon, Ga.	106,612
Madera, Calif.	29,281
Madison, Wis.	191,262
Madison Heights, Mich.	32,196
Malden, Mass.	53,884
Manassas, Va.	27,957
Manchester, Conn.	51,618
Manchester, N.H.	99,567
Manhattan, Kans.	37,712
Manhattan Beach, Calif.	32,063
Manitowoc, Wis.	32,520
Mankato, Minn.	31,477
Mansfield, Conn.	21,103
Mansfield, Ohio	50,627
Manteca, Calif.	40,773
Maple Grove, Minn.	38,736
Maple Heights, Ohio	27,089
Maplewood, Minn.	30,954
Marblehead, Mass.	19,971
Margate, Fla.	42,985
Marietta, Ga.	44,129
Marina, Calif.	26,436
Marion, Ind.	32,618
Marion, Iowa	20,403
Marion, Ohio	34,075
Marlborough, Mass.	31,813
Marquette, Mich.	21,977
Marshall, Tex.	23,682
Marshalltown, Iowa	25,178
Marshfield, Mass.	21,531
Marshfield, Wis.	19,291
Martinez, Calif.	31,808
Maryland Heights, Mo.	25,407
Maryville, Tenn.	19,208
Mason City, Iowa	29,040
Massillon, Ohio	31,007
Mayfield Heights, Ohio	19,847
Maywood, Calif.	27,850
Maywood, Ill.	27,139
Medford, Mass.	57,407
Medford, Oreg.	46,951
Melbourne, Fla.	59,646
Melrose, Mass.	28,150
Melrose Park, Ill.	20,859
Memphis, Tenn.	610,337
Menlo Park, Calif.	28,040
Menomonee Falls, Wis.	26,840
Mentor, Ohio	47,358
Merced, Calif.	56,216
Mercer Island, Wash.	20,816
Meriden, Conn.	59,479
Meridian, Miss.	41,036
Merrillville, Ind.	27,257

Mesa, Ariz.	288,091	Naples, Fla.	19,505
Mesquite, Tex.	101,484	Nashua, N.H.	79,662
Methuen, Mass.	39,990	Nashville, Tenn.	510,784
Miami, Fla.	358,548	Natchez, Miss.	19,460
Miami Beach, Fla.	92,639	Natick, Mass.	30,510
Michigan City, Ind.	33,822	National City, Calif.	54,249
Middletown, Conn.	42,762	Naugatuck, Conn.	30,625
Middletown, N.Y.	24,160	Needham, Mass.	27,557
Middletown, Ohio	46,022	Neenah, Wis.	23,219
Middletown, R.I.	19,460	New Albany, Ind.	36,322
Midland, Mich.	38,053	Newark, Calif.	37,861
Midland, Tex.	89,443	Newark, Del.	25,098
Midwest City, Okla.	52,267	Newark, N.J.	275,221
Milford, Conn.	49,938	Newark, Ohio	44,389
Milford, Mass.	25,355	New Bedford, Mass.	99,922
Mililani Town, Hawaii	29,359	New Berlin, Wis.	33,592
Millbrae, Calif.	20,412	New Braunfels, Tex.	27,334
Millville, N.J.	25,992	New Brighton, Minn.	22,207
Milpitas, Calif.	50,686	New Britain, Conn.	75,491
Milton, Mass.	25,725	New Brunswick, N.J.	41,711
Milwaukee, Wis.	628,088	Newburgh, N.Y.	26,454
Minneapolis, Minn.	368,383	New Castle, Pa.	28,334
Minnetonka, Minn.	48,370	New Haven, Conn.	130,474
Minot, N. Dak.	34,544	New Hope, Minn.	21,853
Miramar, Fla.	40,663	New Iberia, La.	31,828
Mishawaka, Ind.	42,608	Newington, Conn.	29,208
Mission, Tex.	28,653	New London, Conn.	28,540
Mission Viejo, Calif.	72,820	New Milford, Conn.	23,629
Missoula, Mont.	42,918	New Orleans, La.	496,938
Missouri City, Tex.	36,176	Newport, R.I.	28,227
Mobile, Ala.	196,278	Newport Beach, Calif.	66,643
Modesto, Calif.	164,730	Newport News, Va.	170,045
Moline, Ill.	43,202	New Rochelle, N.Y.	67,265
Monroe, La.	54,909	Newton, Mass.	82,585
Monroe, Mich.	22,902	Newtown, Conn.	20,779
Monroeville, Pa.	29,169	New York City, N.Y.	7,322,564
Monrovia, Calif.	35,761	Bronx	1,203,789
Montclair, Calif.	28,434	Brooklyn	2,300,664
Montclair, N.J.	37,729	Manhattan	1,487,536
Montebello, Calif.	59,564	Queens	1,951,598
Monterey, Calif.	31,954	Richmond	378,977
Monterey Park, Calif.	60,738	Niagara Falls, N.Y.	61,840
Montgomery, Ala.	187,106	Niles, Ill.	28,284
Moore, Okla.	40,318	Niles, Ohio	21,128
Moorhead, Minn.	32,295	Nogales, Ariz.	19,489
Moorpark, Calif.	25,494	Norco, Calif.	28,302
Moreno Valley, Calif.	118,779	Norfolk, Nebr.	21,476
Morgan Hill, Calif.	23,928	Norfolk, Va.	261,229
Morgantown, W. Va.	25,879	Normal, Ill.	40,023
Morristown, Tenn.	21,385	Norman, Okla.	80,071
Morton Grove, Ill.	22,408	Norristown, Pa.	30,749
Mountain Brook, Ala.	19,810	Northampton, Mass.	29,289
Mountain View, Calif.	67,460	North Andover, Mass.	22,792
Mountlake Terrace, Wash.	19,320	North Attleboro, Mass.	25,038
Mount Pleasant, Mich.	23,285	Northbrook, Ill.	32,308
Mount Pleasant, S.C.	30,108	North Charleston, S.C.	70,218
Mount Prospect, Ill.	53,170	North Chicago, Ill.	34,978
Mount Vernon, N.Y.	67,153	Northglenn, Colo.	27,195
Muncie, Ind.	71,035	North Haven, Conn.	22,247
Mundelein, Ill.	21,215	North Kingstown, R.I.	23,786
Munster, Ind.	19,949	North Las Vegas, Nev.	47,707
Murfreesboro, Tenn.	44,922	North Lauderdale, Fla.	26,506
Murray, Utah	31,282	North Little Rock, Ark.	61,741
Muscatine, Iowa	22,881	North Miami, Fla.	49,998
Muskegon, Mich.	40,283	North Miami Beach, Fla.	35,359
Muskogee, Okla.	37,708	North Olmsted, Ohio	34,204
Myrtle Beach, S.C.	24,848	North Platte, Nebr.	22,605
		North Providence, R.I.	32,090
N		North Richland Hills, Tex.	45,895
Nacogdoches, Tex.	30,872	North Ridgeville, Ohio	21,564
Nampa, Idaho	28,365	North Royalton, Ohio	23,197
Napa, Calif.	61,842	North Tonawanda, N.Y.	34,989
Naperville, Ill.	85,351	Norton Shores, Mich.	21,755

Norwalk, Calif.	94,279
Norwalk, Conn.	78,331
Norwich, Conn.	37,391
Norwood, Mass.	28,700
Norwood, Ohio	23,674
Novato, Calif.	47,585
Novi, Mich.	32,998
Nutley, N.J.	27,099

O

Oak Creek, Wis.	19,513
Oak Forest, Ill.	26,203
Oakland, Calif.	372,242
Oakland Park, Fla.	26,326
Oak Lawn, Ill.	56,182
Oak Park, Ill.	53,648
Oak Park, Mich.	30,462
Oak Ridge, Tenn.	27,310
Ocala, Fla.	42,045
Oceanside, Calif.	128,398
Odessa, Tex.	89,699
Ogden, Utah	63,909
Oklahoma City, Okla.	444,719
Olathe, Kans.	63,352
Olympia, Wash.	33,840
Omaha, Nebr.	335,795
Ontario, Calif.	133,179
Opelika, Ala.	22,122
Orange, Calif.	110,658
Orange, N.J.	29,925
Orange, Tex.	19,381
Orem, Utah	67,561
Orlando, Fla.	164,693
Orland Park, Ill.	35,720
Ormond Beach, Fla.	29,721
Oshkosh, Wis.	55,006
Ossining, N.Y.	22,582
Oswego, N.Y.	19,195
Ottumwa, Iowa	24,488
Overland Park, Kans.	111,790
Owatonna, Minn.	19,386
Owensboro, Ky.	53,549
Oxnard, Calif.	142,216

P

Pacifica, Calif.	37,670
Paducah, Ky.	27,256
Palatine, Ill.	39,253
Palm Bay, Fla.	62,632
Palm Springs, Calif.	40,181
Palo Alto, Calif.	55,900
Pampa, Tex.	19,959
Panama City, Fla.	34,378
Paradise, Calif.	25,408
Paramount, Calif.	47,669
Paramus, N.J.	25,067
Paris, Tex.	24,699
Parkersburg, W. Va.	33,862
Park Forest, Ill.	24,646
Park Ridge, Ill.	36,175
Parma, Ohio	87,876
Parma Heights, Ohio	21,448
Pasadena, Calif.	119,363
Pasadena, Tex.	131,591
Pascagoula, Miss.	25,899
Pasco, Wash.	20,337
Passaic, N.J.	58,041
Paterson, N.J.	140,891
Pawtucket, R.I.	72,644
Peabody, Mass.	47,039
Peachtree City, Ga.	19,027
Pearl, Miss.	19,588
Pearl City, Hawaii	30,993

Peekskill, N.Y.	19,536
Pekin, Ill.	32,254
Pembroke Pines, Fla.	65,452
Pensacola, Fla.	58,165
Peoria, Ariz.	50,618
Peoria, Ill.	113,504
Perris, Calif.	21,460
Perth Amboy, N.J.	41,967
Petaluma, Calif.	43,184
Petersburg, Va.	38,386
Pharr, Tex.	32,921
Phenix City, Ala.	25,312
Philadelphia, Pa.	1,585,577
Phoenix, Ariz.	983,403
Pico Rivera, Calif.	59,177
Pine Bluff, Ark.	57,140
Pinellas Park, Fla.	43,426
Piqua, Ohio	20,612
Pittsburg, Calif.	47,564
Pittsburgh, Pa.	369,879
Pittsfield, Mass.	48,622
Placentia, Calif.	41,259
Plainfield, N.J.	46,567
Plainview, Tex.	21,700
Plano, Tex.	128,713
Plantation, Fla.	66,692
Plant City, Fla.	22,754
Plattsburgh, N.Y.	21,255
Pleasant Hill, Calif.	31,585
Pleasanton, Calif.	50,553
Plum, Pa.	25,609
Plymouth, Mass.	45,608
Plymouth, Minn.	50,889
Pocatello, Idaho	46,080
Pomona, Calif.	131,723
Pompano Beach, Fla.	72,411
Ponca City, Okla.	26,359
Pontiac, Mich.	71,166
Portage, Ind.	29,060
Portage, Mich.	41,042
Port Arthur, Tex.	58,724
Port Chester, N.Y.	24,728
Porterville, Calif.	29,563
Port Hueneme, Calif.	20,319
Port Huron, Mich.	33,694
Portland, Me.	64,358
Portland, Oreg.	437,319
Port Orange, Fla.	35,317
Port St. Lucie, Fla.	55,866
Portsmouth, N.H.	25,925
Portsmouth, Ohio	22,676
Portsmouth, Va.	103,907
Pottstown, Pa.	21,831
Poughkeepsie, N.Y.	28,844
Poway, Calif.	43,516
Prairie Village, Kans.	23,186
Prattville, Ala.	19,587
Prescott, Ariz.	26,455
Prichard, Ala.	34,311
Providence, R.I.	160,728
Provo, Utah	86,835
Pueblo, Colo.	98,640
Pullman, Wash.	23,478
Puyallup, Wash.	23,875

Q

Quincy, Ill.	39,681
Quincy, Mass.	84,985

R

Racine, Wis.	84,298
Radcliff, Ky.	19,772
Rahway, N.J.	25,325

538

Raleigh, N.C.	207,951
Rancho Cucamonga, Calif.	101,409
Rancho Palos Verdes, Calif.	41,659
Randolph, Mass.	30,093
Rapid City, S. Dak.	54,523
Raytown, Mo.	30,601
Reading, Mass.	22,539
Reading, Pa.	78,380
Redding, Calif.	66,462
Redlands, Calif.	60,394
Redmond, Wash.	35,800
Redondo Beach, Calif.	60,167
Redwood City, Calif.	66,072
Reno, Nev.	133,850
Renton, Wash.	41,688
Revere, Mass.	42,786
Reynoldsburg, Ohio	25,748
Rialto, Calif.	72,388
Richardson, Tex.	74,840
Richfield, Minn.	35,710
Richland, Wash.	32,315
Richmond, Calif.	87,425
Richmond, Ind.	38,705
Richmond, Ky.	21,155
Richmond, Va.	203,056
Ridgecrest, Calif.	27,725
Ridgefield, Conn.	20,919
Ridgewood, N.J.	24,152
Rio Rancho, N. Mex.	32,505
Riverside, Calif.	226,505
Riviera Beach, Fla.	27,639
Roanoke, Va.	96,397
Rochester, Minn.	70,745
Rochester, N.H.	26,630
Rochester, N.Y.	231,636
Rochester Hills, Mich.	61,766
Rockford, Ill.	139,426
Rock Hill, S.C.	41,643
Rock Island, Ill.	40,552
Rocklin, Calif.	19,033
Rock Springs, Wyo.	19,050
Rockville, Md.	44,835
Rockville Centre, N.Y.	24,727
Rocky Mount, N.C.	48,997
Rocky River, Ohio	20,410
Rogers, Ark.	24,692
Rohnert Park, Calif.	36,326
Rolling Meadows, Ill.	22,591
Rome, Ga.	30,326
Rome, N.Y.	44,350
Romulus, Mich.	22,897
Roselle, Ill.	20,819
Roselle, N.J.	20,314
Rosemead, Calif.	51,638
Rosenberg, Tex.	20,183
Roseville, Calif.	44,685
Roseville, Mich.	51,412
Roseville, Minn.	33,485
Roswell, Ga.	47,923
Roswell, N. Mex.	44,654
Round Rock, Tex.	30,923
Rowlett, Tex.	23,260
Roy, Utah	24,603
Royal Oak, Mich.	65,410
Russellville, Ark.	21,260
Ruston, La.	20,027

S

Sacramento, Calif.	369,365
Saginaw, Mich.	69,512
St. Charles, Ill.	22,501
St. Charles, Mo.	54,555
St. Clair Shores, Mich.	68,107

St. Cloud, Minn.	48,812
St. George, Utah	28,502
St. Joseph, Mo.	71,852
St. Louis, Mo.	396,685
St. Louis Park, Minn.	43,787
St. Paul, Minn.	272,235
St. Peters, Mo.	45,779
St. Petersburg, Fla.	238,629
Salem, Mass.	38,091
Salem, N.H.	25,746
Salem, Oreg.	107,786
Salem, Va.	23,756
Salina, Kans.	42,303
Salinas, Calif.	108,777
Salisbury, Md.	20,592
Salisbury, N.C.	23,087
Salt Lake City, Utah	159,936
San Angelo, Tex.	84,474
San Antonio, Tex.	935,933
San Benito, Tex.	20,125
San Bernardino, Calif.	164,164
San Bruno, Calif.	38,961
San Carlos, Calif.	26,167
San Clemente, Calif.	41,100
San Diego, Calif.	1,110,549
San Dimas, Calif.	32,397
Sandusky, Ohio	29,764
Sandy, Utah	75,058
San Fernando, Calif.	22,580
Sanford, Fla.	32,387
Sanford, Me.	20,463
San Francisco, Calif.	723,959
San Gabriel, Calif.	37,120
San Jose, Calif.	782,248
San Juan Capistrano, Calif.	26,183
San Leandro, Calif.	68,223
San Luis Obispo, Calif.	41,958
San Marcos, Calif.	38,974
San Marcos, Tex.	28,743
San Mateo, Calif.	85,486
San Pablo, Calif.	25,158
San Rafael, Calif.	48,404
San Ramon, Calif.	35,303
Santa Ana, Calif.	293,742
Santa Barbara, Calif.	85,571
Santa Clara, Calif.	93,613
Santa Clarita, Calif.	110,642
Santa Cruz, Calif.	49,040
Santa Fe, N. Mex.	55,859
Santa Maria, Calif.	61,284
Santa Monica, Calif.	86,905
Santa Paula, Calif.	25,062
Santa Rosa, Calif.	113,313
Santee, Calif.	52,902
Sarasota, Fla.	50,961
Saratoga, Calif.	28,061
Saratoga Springs, N.Y.	25,001
Saugus, Mass.	25,549
Savannah, Ga.	137,560
Sayreville, N.J.	34,986
Schaumburg, Ill.	68,586
Schenectady, N.Y.	65,566
Schererville, Ind.	19,926
Schofield Barracks, Hawaii	19,597
Scottsdale, Ariz.	130,069
Scranton, Pa.	81,805
Seal Beach, Calif.	25,098
Seaside, Calif.	38,901
Seattle, Wash.	516,259
Sedalia, Mo.	19,800
Selma, Ala.	23,755
Shaker Heights, Ohio	30,831
Shawnee, Kans.	37,993

Shawnee, Okla.	26,017
Sheboygan, Wis.	49,676
Shelton, Conn.	35,418
Sherman, Tex.	31,601
Shoreview, Minn.	24,587
Shreveport, La.	198,525
Shrewsbury, Mass.	24,146
Sierra Vista, Ariz.	32,983
Simi Valley, Calif.	100,217
Simsbury, Conn.	22,023
Sioux City, Iowa	80,505
Sioux Falls, S. Dak.	100,814
Skokie, Ill.	59,432
Slidell, La.	24,124
Smithfield, R.I.	19,163
Smyrna, Ga.	30,981
Socorro, Tex.	22,995
Somerville, Mass.	76,210
South Bend, Ind.	105,511
South El Monte, Calif.	20,850
South Euclid, Ohio	23,866
Southfield, Mich.	75,728
South Gate, Calif.	86,284
Southgate, Mich.	30,771
South Holland, Ill.	22,105
Southington, Conn.	38,518
South Kingstown, R.I.	24,631
South Lake Tahoe, Calif.	21,586
South Milwaukee, Wis.	20,958
South Pasadena, Calif.	23,936
South Plainfield, N.J.	20,489
South Portland, Me.	23,163
South St. Paul, Minn.	20,197
South San Francisco, Calif.	54,312
South Windsor, Conn.	22,090
Sparks, Nev.	53,367
Spartanburg, S.C.	43,467
Spokane, Wash.	177,196
Springdale, Ark.	29,941
Springfield, Ill.	105,227
Springfield, Mass.	156,983
Springfield, Mo.	140,494
Springfield, Ohio	70,487
Springfield, Oreg.	44,683
Spring Valley, N.Y.	21,802
Stamford, Conn.	108,056
Stanton, Calif.	30,491
State College, Pa.	38,923
Staunton, Va.	24,461
Sterling Heights, Mich.	117,810
Steubenville, Ohio	22,125
Stevens Point, Wis.	23,006
Stillwater, Okla.	36,676
Stockton, Calif.	210,943
Stoneham, Mass.	22,203
Stoughton, Mass.	26,777
Stow, Ohio	27,702
Stratford, Conn.	49,389
Streamwood, Ill.	30,987
Strongsville, Ohio	35,308
Suffolk, Va.	52,141
Sugar Land, Tex.	24,529
Suisun City, Calif.	22,686
Sulphur, La.	20,125
Summerville, S.C.	22,519
Summit, N.J.	19,757
Sumter, S.C.	41,943
Sunnyvale, Calif.	117,229
Sunrise, Fla.	64,407
Superior, Wis.	27,134
Syracuse, N.Y.	163,860

T

Tacoma, Wash.	176,664
Tallahassee, Fla.	124,773
Tamarac, Fla.	44,822
Tampa, Fla.	280,015
Taunton, Mass.	49,832
Taylor, Mich.	70,811
Temecula, Calif.	27,099
Tempe, Ariz.	141,865
Temple, Tex.	46,109
Temple City, Calif.	31,100
Terre Haute, Ind.	57,483
Tewksbury, Mass.	27,266
Texarkana, Ark.	22,631
Texarkana, Tex.	31,656
Texas City, Tex.	40,822
The Colony, Tex.	22,113
Thornton, Colo.	55,031
Thousand Oaks, Calif.	104,352
Tigard, Oreg.	29,344
Tinley Park, Ill.	37,121
Titusville, Fla.	39,394
Toledo, Ohio	332,943
Topeka, Kans.	119,883
Torrance, Calif.	133,107
Torrington, Conn.	33,687
Tracy, Calif.	33,558
Trenton, Mich.	20,586
Trenton, N.J.	88,675
Troy, Mich.	72,884
Troy, N.Y.	54,269
Troy, Ohio	19,478
Trumbull, Conn.	32,016
Tucson, Ariz.	405,390
Tulare, Calif.	33,249
Tulsa, Okla.	367,302
Tupelo, Miss.	30,685
Turlock, Calif.	42,198
Tuscaloosa, Ala.	77,759
Tustin, Calif.	50,689
Twin Falls, Idaho	27,591
Tyler, Tex.	75,450

U

Union City, Calif.	53,762
Union City, N.J.	58,012
University City, Mo.	40,087
University Park, Tex.	22,259
Upland, Calif.	63,374
Upper Arlington, Ohio	34,128
Urbana, Ill.	36,344
Urbandale, Iowa	23,500
Utica, N.Y.	68,637

V

Vacaville, Calif.	71,479
Valdosta, Ga.	39,806
Vallejo, Calif.	109,199
Valley Stream, N.Y.	33,946
Valparaiso, Ind.	24,414
Vancouver, Wash.	46,380
Ventura (San Buenaventura), Calif.	92,575
Vernon, Conn.	29,841
Vestavia Hills, Ala.	19,749
Vicksburg, Miss.	20,908
Victoria, Tex.	55,076
Victorville, Calif.	40,674
Villa Park, Ill.	22,253
Vincennes, Ind.	19,859
Vineland, N.J.	54,870
Virginia Beach, Va.	393,069
Visalia, Calif.	75,636

Vista, Calif.	71,872	West Springfield, Mass.	27,537
		West Valley City, Utah	86,976
W		West Warwick, R.I.	29,268
Waco, Tex.	103,590	Wethersfield, Conn.	25,651
Waipahu, Hawaii	31,435	Weymouth, Mass.	54,063
Wakefield, Mass.	24,825	Wheaton, Ill.	51,464
Walla Walla, Wash.	26,478	Wheat Ridge, Colo.	29,419
Wallingford, Conn.	40,822	Wheeling, Ill.	29,911
Walnut, Calif.	29,105	Wheeling, W. Va.	34,882
Walnut Creek, Calif.	60,569	White Bear Lake, Minn.	24,704
Walpole, Mass.	20,212	Whitehall, Ohio	20,572
Waltham, Mass.	57,878	White Plains, N.Y.	48,718
Wareham, Mass.	19,232	Whittier, Calif.	77,671
Warner Robins, Ga.	43,726	Wichita, Kans.	304,011
Warren, Mich.	144,864	Wichita Falls, Tex.	96,259
Warren, Ohio	50,793	Wilkes-Barre, Pa.	47,523
Warwick, R.I.	85,427	Wilkinsburg, Pa.	21,080
Washington, D.C.	609,909	Williamsport, Pa.	31,933
Watauga, Tex.	20,009	Willoughby, Ohio	20,510
Waterbury, Conn.	108,961	Wilmette, Ill.	26,690
Waterloo, Iowa	66,467	Wilmington, Del.	71,529
Watertown, Conn.	20,456	Wilmington, N.C.	55,530
Watertown, Mass.	33,284	Wilson, N.C.	36,930
Watertown, N.Y.	29,429	Winchester, Mass.	20,267
Watertown, Wis.	19,142	Winchester, Va.	21,947
Watsonville, Calif.	31,099	Windham, Conn.	22,039
Waukegan, Ill.	69,392	Windsor, Conn.	27,817
Waukesha, Wis.	56,958	Winona, Minn.	25,399
Wausau, Wis.	37,060	Winston-Salem, N.C.	143,485
Wauwatosa, Wis.	49,366	Winter Haven, Fla.	24,725
Wayne, Mich.	19,899	Winter Park, Fla.	22,242
Webster Groves, Mo.	22,987	Winter Springs, Fla.	22,151
Weirton, W. Va.	22,124	Woburn, Mass.	35,943
Wellesley, Mass.	26,615	Woodbury, Minn.	20,075
Wenatchee, Wash.	21,756	Woodland, Calif.	39,802
Weslaco, Tex.	21,877	Woodridge, Ill.	26,256
West Allis, Wis.	63,221	Woonsocket, R.I.	43,877
West Bend, Wis.	23,916	Wooster, Ohio	22,191
West Covina, Calif.	96,086	Worcester, Mass.	169,759
West Des Moines, Iowa	31,702	Wyandotte, Mich.	30,938
Westerly, R.I.	21,605	Wyoming, Mich.	63,891
Westerville, Ohio	30,269		
Westfield, Mass.	38,372	**X**	
Westfield, N.J.	28,870	Xenia, Ohio	24,664
West Hartford, Conn.	60,110		
West Haven, Conn.	54,021	**Y**	
West Hollywood, Calif.	36,118	Yakima, Wash.	54,827
West Jordan, Utah	42,892	Yarmouth, Mass.	21,174
West Lafayette, Ind.	25,907	Yonkers, N.Y.	188,082
Westlake, Ohio	27,018	Yorba Linda, Calif.	52,422
Westland, Mich.	84,724	York, Pa.	42,192
West Memphis, Ark.	28,259	Youngstown, Ohio	95,732
West Mifflin, Pa.	23,644	Ypsilanti, Mich.	24,846
Westminster, Calif.	78,118	Yuba City, Calif.	27,437
Westminster, Colo.	74,625	Yucaipa, Calif.	32,824
Westmont, Ill.	21,228	Yukon, Okla.	20,935
West New York, N.J.	38,125	Yuma, Ariz.	54,923
West Orange, N.J.	39,103		
West Palm Beach, Fla.	67,643	**Z**	
Westport, Conn.	24,410	Zanesville, Ohio	26,778
West Sacramento, Calif.	28,898	Zion, Ill.	19,775
West St. Paul, Minn.	19,248		

CHAPTER 18
Nations of the World

Name and Pronunciation	Population
Afghanistan \af-'ga-nə-ˌstan\	20,269,000
Albania \al-'bā-nē-ə\	3,422,000
Algeria \al-'jir-ē-ə\	27,029,000
Andorra \an-'dor-ə\	61,900
Angola \aŋ-'gō-lə, an-\	10,916,000
Antigua and Barbuda	
\an-'tē-gə...bär-'bü-də\	66,000
Argentina \ˌär-jen-'tē-nə\	33,507,000
Armenia \är-'mē-nē-ə\	3,550,000
Australia \o-'strāl-yə\	17,729,000
Austria \'os-trē-ə\	7,938,000
Azerbaijan \ˌä-zər-bī-'jän\	7,398,000
Bahamas \bə-'hä-məz\	266,000
Bahrain \bä-'rān\	486,000
Bangladesh \ˌbäŋ-glə-'desh, -'däsh\	115,075,000
Barbados \bär-'bā-dəs, -(ˌ)dōz,	
-(ˌ)däs\	260,000
Belarus \ˌbye-lə-'rüs\	10,353,000
Belgium \'bel-jəm\	10,072,000
Belize \bə-'lēz\	204,000
Benin \bə-'nin\	5,091,000
Bhutan \bü-'tan, -'tän\	1,546,000
Bolivia \bə-'li-vē-ə\	7,715,000
Bosnia and Herzegovina	
\'bäz-nē-ə...hert-sə-gō-'vē-nə,	
-'gō-və-nə\	4,422,000
Botswana \bät-'swä-nə\	1,406,000
Brazil \brə-'zil\	156,493,000
Brunei \brü-'nī\	275,000
Bulgaria \ˌbəl-'gar-ē-ə, bùl-\	8,466,000
Burkina Faso \bùr-ˌkē-nə-'fä-sō\	9,780,000
Burundi \bù-'rün-dē\	5,665,000
Cambodia \kam-'bō-dē-ə\	9,287,000
Cameroon \ˌka-mə-'rün\	13,103,000
Canada \'ka-nə-də\	27,296,859
Cape Verde \ˌkāp-'vərd\	350,000
Central African Republic	2,998,000
Chad \'chad\	6,118,000
Chile \'chi-lē\	13,542,000
China, People's Republic of \-'chī-nə\ ..	1,179,467,000
Colombia \kə-'ləm-bē-ə\	33,951,000
Comoro Islands \'kä-mə-ˌrō-\	516,000
Congo \'käŋ-go\	2,775,000
Costa Rica \ˌkäs-tə-'rē-kə\	3,199,000
Croatia \krō-'ā-shə\	4,821,000
Cuba \'kyü-bə\	10,892,000
Cyprus \'sī-prəs\	764,000
Czech Republic \'chek-\	10,332,000
Denmark \'den-ˌmärk\	5,187,000
Djibouti \jə-'bü-tē\	565,000
Dominica \ˌdä-mə-'nē-kə\	74,000
Dominican Republic \də-'mi-ni-kən-\ ...	7,634,000
Ecuador \'e-kwə-ˌdor\	10,985,000
Egypt \'ē-jəpt\	57,109,000
El Salvador \el-'sal-və-ˌdor\	5,517,000
Equatorial Guinea \-'gi-nē\	377,000
Eritrea \ˌer-ə-'trā-ə\	3,317,611
Estonia \e-'stō-nē-ə\	1,536,000

Name and Pronunciation	Population
Ethiopia \ˌē-thē-'ō-pē-ə\	52,078,000
Fiji \'fē-(ˌ)jē\	762,000
Finland \'fin-lənd\	5,058,000
France \'frans\	57,690,000
Gabon \ga-'bōn\	1,280,000
Gambia \'gam-bē-ə\	1,033,000
Georgia \'jor-jə\	5,493,000
Germany \'jər-mə-nē\	81,187,000
Ghana \'gä-nə\	15,636,000
Greece \'grēs\	10,310,000
Grenada \grə-'nā-də\	91,000
Guatemala \ˌgwä-tə-'mä-lə\	9,713,000
Guinea \'gi-nē\	7,418,000
Guinea-Bissau \-bi-'saù\	1,036,000
Guyana \gī-'a-nə\	755,000
Haiti \'hā-tē\	6,902,000
Honduras \hän-'dùr-əs\	5,148,000
Hungary \'həŋ-gə-rē\	10,296,000
Iceland \'īs-lənd, -ˌland\	264,000
India \'in-dē-ə\	896,567,000
Indonesia \ˌin-də-'nē-zhə\	188,216,000
Iran \i-'ran, -'rän\	60,768,000
Iraq \i-'räk, -'rak\	19,435,000
Ireland \'īr-lənd\	3,516,000
Israel \'iz-rē-əl\	5,451,000
Italy \'i-tə-lē\	57,235,000
Ivory Coast	13,459,000
Jamaica \jə-'mā-kə\	2,472,000
Japan \jə-'pan\	124,670,000
Jordan \'jor-dən\	3,764,000
Kazakhstan \ˌkä-zäk-'stän\	17,186,000
Kenya \'ken-yə, 'kēn-\	28,113,000
Kiribati \'kir-ə-ˌbas\	76,900
Kuwait \kə-'wāt\	1,433,000
Kyrgyzstan \ˌkir-gi-'stän\	4,526,000
Laos \'laùs, 'lä-ōs\	4,533,000
Latvia \'lat-vē-ə\	2,596,000
Lebanon \'le-bə-nən\	2,909,000
Lesotho \lə-'sü-ˌtü\	1,903,000
Liberia \lī-'bir-ē-ə\	2,844,000
Libya \'li-bē-ə\	4,573,000
Liechtenstein \'lik-tən-ˌshtīn\	30,100
Lithuania \ˌli-thə-'wā-nē-ə\	3,753,000
Luxembourg \'lək-səm-ˌbərg,	
'lùk-səm-ˌbùrg\	392,000
Macedonia \ˌma-sə-'dō-nē-ə\	2,063,000
Madagascar \ˌma-də-'gas-kər\	13,255,000
Malawi \mə-'lä-wē\	10,581,000
Malaysia \mə-'lā-zhə\	19,077,000
Maldives \'mol-ˌdēvz, -ˌdīvz\	237,000
Mali \'mä-lē\	8,646,000
Malta \'mol-tə\	363,000
Mauritania \ˌmor-ə-'tā-nē-ə\	2,171,000

\ə\abut \ᵊ\kitten \ər\further \a\ash \ā\ace \ä\mop, mar \aù\out \ch\chin \e\bet \ē\easy \g\go \i\hit \ī\ice \j\job \ŋ\sing \ō\go \ò\law \òi\boy \th\thin \t͟h\the \ü\loot \ù\foot \y\yet \zh\vision *see also* Pronunciation Symbols page

Name and Pronunciation	Population
Mauritius \mȯ-'ri-shē-əs\	1,103,000
Mexico \'mek-si-ˌkō\	89,955,000
Moldova \mäl-'dō-və\	4,362,000
Monaco \'mä-nə-ˌkō\	30,500
Mongolia \män-'gōl-yə\	2,256,000
Morocco \mə-'rä-kō\	26,494,000
Mozambique \ˌmō-zəm-'bēk\	15,243,000
Myanmar \'myän-ˌmär\	44,613,000
Namibia \na-'mi-bē-ə\	1,537,000
Nauru \nä-'ü-(ˌ)rü\	10,000
Nepal \nə-'pȯl\	19,264,000
Netherlands \'ne-thər-ləndz\	15,302,000
New Zealand \-'zē-lənd\	3,520,000
Nicaragua \ˌni-kə-'rä-gwə\	4,265,000
Niger \'nī-jər\	8,516,000
Nigeria \nī-'jir-ē-ə\	91,549,000
North Korea \-kə-'rē-ə\	22,646,000
Norway \'nȯr-ˌwā\	4,308,000
Oman \ō-'män\	1,698,000
Pakistan \'pa-ki-ˌstan, ˌpä-ki-'stän\	127,962,000
Panama \'pa-nə-ˌmä\	2,563,000
Papua New Guinea \'pä-pə-wə-\	3,918,000
Paraguay \'par-ə-ˌgwī, -ˌgwä\	4,613,000
Peru \pə-'rü\	22,916,000
Philippines \ˌfi-lə-'pēnz, 'fi-lə-ˌpēnz\	64,954,000
Poland \'pō-lənd\	38,521,000
Portugal \'pȯr-chi-gəl\	9,823,000
Qatar \'kä-tər\	539,000
Romania \rù-'mā-nē-ə\	22,789,000
Russia \'rə-shə\	148,000,000
Rwanda \rù-'än-də\	7,584,000
St. Kitts-Nevis \-'kits-'nē-vəs\	41,800
St. Lucia \-'lü-shə\	136,000
St. Vincent and the Grenadines \-'vin-sənt...ˌgre-nə-'dēnz\	109,000
San Marino \ˌsan-mə-'rē-nō\	24,100
Sao Tome and Principe \ˌsaù-tə-'mä...'prin-sə-pə\	125,000
Saudi Arabia \ˌsaù-dē-ə-'rä-bē-ə, sä-ü-dē-\	17,419,000
Senegal \ˌse-ni-'gȯl\	7,899,000
Seychelles \sā-'chelz\	71,000
Sierra Leone \sē-ˌer-ə-lē-'ōn\	4,491,000
Singapore \'siŋ-ə-ˌpȯr\	2,876,000
Slovakia \slō-'vä-kē-ə\	5,329,000
Slovenia \slō-'vē-nē-ə\	1,997,000
Solomon Islands \'sä-lə-mən-\	349,000

Name and Pronunciation	Population
Somalia \sō-'mä-lē-ə\	8,050,000
South Africa, Republic of	33,071,000
South Korea \-kə-'rē-ə\	44,042,000
Spain \'spān\	39,141,000
Sri Lanka \srē-'läŋ-kə, shrē-\	17,616,000
Sudan \sü-'dan\	25,000,000
Suriname \ˌsùr-ə-'nä-mə\	405,000
Swaziland \'swä-zē-ˌland\	814,000
Sweden \'swē-dən\	8,727,000
Switzerland \'swit-sər-lənd\	6,996,000
Syria \'sir-ē-ə\	13,398,000
Taiwan (Republic of China) \tī-'wän\	20,926,000
Tajikistan \tä-ˌji-ki-'stän\	5,705,000
Tanzania \ˌtan-zə-'nē-ə\	26,542,000
Thailand \'tī-ˌland, -lənd\	57,829,000
Togo \'tō-gō\	3,810,000
Tonga \'täŋ-gə\	99,100
Trinidad and Tobago \'trin-ə-ˌdad...tə-'bā-gō\	1,249,000
Tunisia \tü-'nē-zhə\	8,530,000
Turkey \'tər-kē\	59,869,000
Turkmenistan \ˌtərk-ˌme-nə-'stän\	4,294,000
Tuvalu \tü-'vä-lü\	9,500
Uganda \yü-'gan-də\	17,741,000
Ukraine \'yü-ˌkrān, yü-'krān\	52,344,000
United Arab Emirates	1,986,000
United Kingdom of Great Britain and Northern Ireland \-'bri-tən...'īr-lənd\	55,500,000
England \'iŋ-glənd\	46,161,000
Northern Ireland	1,583,000
Scotland \'skät-lənd\	4,957,000
Wales \'wālz\	2,799,000
United States of America \-ə-'mer-i-kə\	249,632,692
Uruguay \'ür-ə-ˌgwī, 'yùr-ə-ˌgwä\	3,149,000
Uzbekistan \ˌùz-ˌbe-ki-'stän\	21,901,000
Vanuatu \ˌvan-ˌwä-'tü\	160,000
Vatican City State \'va-ti-kən-\	1,800
Venezuela \ˌve-nə-'zwā-lə\	20,609,000
Vietnam \vē-'et-'näm\	70,902,000
Western Samoa \-sə-'mō-ə\	163,000
Yemen \'ye-mən\	12,519,000
Yugoslavia \ˌyü-gō-'slä-vē-ə\	10,561,000
Zaire \zä-'ir\	42,473,000
Zambia \'zam-bē-ə\	8,504,000
Zimbabwe \zim-'bäb-wā\	10,123,000

Population of Places in Canada

Having 21,500 or More Inhabitants in 1991

Ajax, Ont.	57,350	Lachine, Que.	35,266
Alma, Que.	25,910	Langley, B.C.	66,040
Ancaster, Ont.	21,988	LaSalle, Que.	73,804
Anjou, Que.	37,210	Laval, Que.	314,398
Aurora, Ont.	29,454	Lethbridge, Alta.	60,974
Aylmer, Que.	32,244	Lévis-Lauzon, Que.	39,452
Baie-Comeau, Que.	26,012	London, Ont.	303,165
Barrie, Ont.	62,728	Longueuil, Que.	129,874
Beauport, Que.	69,158	Lunenburg, N.S.	25,720
Belleville, Ont.	37,243	Maple Ridge, B.C.	48,422
Blainville, Que.	22,679	Markham, Ont.	153,811
Boucherville, Que.	33,796	Mascouche, Que.	25,828
Brampton, Ont.	234,445	Matsqui, B.C.	68,064
Brandon, Man.	38,567	Medicine Hat, Alta.	43,625
Brantford, Ont.	81,997	Milton, Ont.	32,075
Brockville, Ont.	21,582	Mission, B.C.	26,202
Brossard, Que.	64,793	Mississauga, Ont.	463,388
Burlington, Ont.	129,575	Moncton, N.B.	57,010
Burnaby, B.C.	158,858	Montreal, Que.	1,017,666
Caledon, Ont.	34,965	Montreal North, Que.	85,516
Calgary, Alta.	710,677	Moose Jaw, Sask.	33,593
Cambridge, Ont.	92,772	Mount Pearl, Nfld.	23,689
Cap-de-la-Madeleine, Que.	33,716	Nanaimo, B.C.	60,129
Charlesbourg, Que.	70,788	Nanticoke, Ont.	22,727
Châteauguay, Que.	39,833	Nepean, Ont.	107,627
Chatham, Ont.	43,557	Newcastle, Ont.	49,479
Chicoutimi, Que.	62,670	Newmarket, Ont.	45,474
Chilliwack, B.C.	49,531	New Westminster, B.C.	43,585
Coquitlam, B.C.	84,021	Niagara Falls, Ont.	75,399
Corner Brook, Nfld.	22,410	North Bay, Ont.	55,405
Cornwall, Ont.	47,137	North Vancouver, B.C.	38,436
Côte-St-Luc, Que.	28,700	North York, Ont.	562,564
Cumberland, Ont.	40,697	Oakville, Ont.	114,670
Dartmouth, N.S.	67,798	Orillia, Ont.	25,925
Delta, B.C.	88,978	Oshawa, Ont.	129,344
Dollard-des-Ormeaux, Que.	46,922	Ottawa, Ont.	313,987
Drummondville, Que.	35,462	Outremont, Que.	22,935
Dundas, Ont.	21,868	Owen Sound, Ont.	21,674
East York, Ont.	102,696	Penticton, B.C.	27,258
Edmonton, Alta.	616,741	Peterborough, Ont.	68,371
Etobicoke, Ont.	309,993	Pickering, Ont.	68,631
Flamborough, Ont.	29,616	Pierrefonds, Que.	48,735
Fort Erie, Ont.	26,006	Pointe-Claire, Que.	27,647
Fort McMurray, Alta.	34,706	Port Coquitlam, B.C.	36,773
Fredericton, N.B.	46,466	Prince Albert, Sask.	34,181
Gatineau, Que.	92,284	Prince George, B.C.	69,653
Georgina, Ont.	29,746	Quebec, Que.	167,517
Gloucester, Ont.	101,677	Red Deer, Alta.	58,134
Granby, Que.	42,804	Regina, Sask.	179,178
Grande Prairie, Alta.	28,271	Repentigny, Que.	49,630
Guelph, Ont.	87,976	Richmond Hill, Ont.	80,142
Halifax, N.S.	114,455	Rimouski, Que.	30,873
Halton Hills, Ont.	36,816	Rouyn-Noranda, Que.	26,448
Hamilton, Ont.	318,499	Saanich, B.C.	95,577
Hull, Que.	60,707	St. Albert, Alta.	42,146
Innisfil, Ont.	21,667	St-Bruno-de-Montarville, Que.	23,849
Jonquière, Que.	57,933	St. Catharines, Ont.	129,300
Kamloops, B.C.	67,057	Ste-Foy, Que.	71,133
Kanata, Ont.	37,344	Ste-Thérèse, Que.	24,158
Kelowna, B.C.	75,950	St. Eustache, Que.	37,278
Kingston, Ont.	56,597	St-Hubert, Que.	74,027
Kitchener, Ont.	168,282	St-Hyacinthe, Que.	39,292

St-Jean-sur-Richelieu, Que.	37,607	Thunder Bay, Ont.	113,946
St-Jerôme, Que.	23,384	Timmins, Ont.	47,461
Saint John, N.B.	74,969	Toronto, Ont.	635,395
St. John's, Nfld.	95,770	Trois-Rivières, Que.	49,426
St-Laurent, Que.	72,402	Val-d'Or, Que.	23,842
St-Léonard, Que.	73,120	Valley East, Ont.	21,939
St. Thomas, Ont.	29,990	Vancouver, B.C.	471,844
Salaberry-de-Valleyfield, Que.	27,598	Vaughan, Ont.	111,359
Sarnia-Clearwater, Ont.	74,376	Verdun, Que.	61,307
Saskatoon, Sask.	186,058	Vernon, B.C.	23,514
Sault Ste. Marie, Ont.	81,476	Victoria, B.C.	71,228
Scarborough, Ont.	524,598	Waterloo, Ont.	71,181
Sept-Iles, Que.	24,848	Welland, Ont.	47,914
Sherbrooke, Que.	76,429	West Vancouver, B.C.	38,783
Stoney Creek, Ont.	49,968	Whitby, Ont.	61,281
Stratford, Ont.	27,666	Windsor, Ont.	191,435
Sudbury, Ont.	92,884	Winnipeg, Man.	616,790
Surrey, B.C.	245,173	Woodstock, Ont.	30,075
Sydney, N.S.	26,063	York, Ont.	140,525
Terrebonne, Que.	39,678		

Population of Canada in 1991

Summary by Provinces and Territories

Alberta	2,545,553	Prince Edward Island	129,765
British Columbia	3,282,061	Quebec	6,895,963
Manitoba	1,091,942	Saskatchewan	988,928
New Brunswick	723,900	Yukon Territory	27,797
Newfoundland	568,474	Northwest Territories	57,649
Nova Scotia	899,942	TOTAL	27,296,859
Ontario	10,084,885		

CHAPTER 19
Signs and Symbols

Astronomy

☉	the sun; Sunday	⊕, ⊖, or ♁	the earth
◑, ☾, or ☽	the moon; Monday	♂	Mars; Tuesday
●	new moon	♃	Jupiter; Thursday
☽, ◑, ☽, ☾	first quarter	♄ or ♄	Saturn; Saturday
○ or ☺	full moon	♁, ♅, or ♅	Uranus
☾, ◑, ☾, ☾	last quarter	♆, ♆, or ♆	Neptune
☿	Mercury; Wednesday	♇	Pluto
		☄	comet
♀	Venus; Friday	✳ or ✶	fixed star

Business

a/c	account ⟨in a/c with⟩	%	percent
@	at; each ⟨4 apples @ 5¢ = 20¢⟩	‰	per thousand
/ or ℔	per	$	dollars
c/o	care of	¢	cents
#	number if it precedes a numeral ⟨track #3⟩; pounds if it follows ⟨a 5# sack of sugar⟩	£	pounds
		/	shillings
		©	copyrighted
℔	pound; pounds	®	registered trademark

Mathematics

+ plus; positive ⟨a + b=c⟩—used also to indicate omitted figures or an approximation

− minus; negative

± plus or minus ⟨the square root of 4a² is ± 2a⟩

× multiplied by; times ⟨6×4=24⟩—also indicated by placing a dot between the factors ⟨6·4=24⟩ or by writing the factors one after the other, often enclosed in parentheses, without explicitly indicating multiplication ⟨(4)(5)(3) =60⟩ ⟨−4abc⟩

÷ or : divided by ⟨24÷6=4⟩—also indicated by writing the divisor under the dividend with a line between ⟨$\frac{24}{6}$=4⟩ or by writing the divisor after the dividend with an oblique line between ⟨3/8⟩

= equals ⟨6+2=8⟩

≠ or ≠ is not equal to

> is greater than ⟨6>5⟩

< is less than ⟨3<4⟩

≧ or ≥ is greater than or equal to

≦ or ≤ is less than or equal to

∝ varies directly as; is proportional to

: is to; the ratio of

∴ therefore

∞ infinity

∠ angle; the angle ⟨∠ABC⟩

∟ right angle ⟨∟ABC⟩

⊥ the perpendicular; is perpendicular to ⟨AB⊥CD⟩

∥ parallel; is parallel to ⟨AB ∥ CD⟩

⊙ or ○ circle

⌒ arc of a circle

△ triangle

□ square

▭ rectangle

√ or √ root—used without a figure to indicate a square root (as in $\sqrt{4}$=2) or with an index above the sign to indicate a higher degree (as in $\sqrt[3]{3}, \sqrt[3]{7}$);

also denoted by a fractional index at the right of a number whose denominator expresses the degree of the root $\langle 3^{1/3} = \sqrt[3]{3} \rangle$

( ) parentheses ⎫

[ ] brackets ⎬ indicate that the quantities enclosed by them are to be taken together

{ } braces ⎭

s standard deviation of a sample taken from a population

σ standard deviation of a population

$\bar{x}$ arithmetic mean of a sample of a variable x

μ arithmetic mean of a population

μ_2 or σ^2 variance

π pi; the number 3.14159265 + ; the ratio of the circumference of a circle to its diameter

° degree $\langle 60° \rangle$

′ minute; foot $\langle 30' \rangle$—used also to distinguish between different values of the same variable or between different variables (as a', a'', a''', usually read a prime, a double prime, a triple prime)

″ second; inch $\langle 30'' \rangle$

^{0}, ^{1}, ^{2}, ^{3}, etc. —used as exponents placed above and at the right of an expression to indicate that it is raised to a power whose degree is indicated by the figure $\langle a^0$ equals 1$\rangle$ $\langle a^1$ equals $a \rangle$ $\langle a^2$ is the square of $a \rangle$

$^{-1}$, $^{-2}$, $^{-3}$, etc. —used as exponents placed above and at the right of an expression to indicate that the reciprocal of the expression is raised to the power whose degree is indicated by the figure $\langle a^{-1}$ equals $1/a \rangle$ $\langle a^{-2}$ equals $1/a^2 \rangle$

! factorial $\langle n! = n\,(n-1)(n-2) \ldots 1 \rangle$

n an unspecified number esp. when an integer

⊂ is included in, is a subset of

⊃ contains as a subset

∈ or ϵ is an element of

∉ is not an element of

Medicine

$\overline{AA}$, $\overline{A}$, or āā of each

℞ take—used on prescriptions; prescription; treatment

☠ poison

Miscellaneous

& and

&c et cetera; and so forth

" or " ditto marks

/ virgule; used to mean "or" (as in *and/or*), "and/or" (as in *dead/wounded*), "per" (as in *feet/second*), indicates end of a line of verse; separates the figures of a date (4/8/74)

☞ index *or* fist

< derived from ⎫

> whence derived ⎬ used in linguistics

+ and ⎭

* hypothetical, ungrammatical

† died—used esp. in genealogies

✚ cross

✳ monogram from Greek XP signifying Christ

卐 swastika

✡ Judaism

† ankh

℣ versicle

℟ response

✳ —used in Roman Catholic and Anglican service books to divide each verse of a psalm, indicating where the response begins

✠ or + —used in some service books to indicate where the sign of the cross is to be made; also used by certain Roman Catholic and Anglican prelates as a sign of the cross preceding their signatures

LXX Septuagint

fl or *f*: relative aperture of a photographic lens

civil defense

peace

Reference marks

*	asterisk *or* star		§	section *or* numbered clause
†	dagger		‖	parallels
‡	double dagger		¶ *or* ℙ	paragraph

Stamps and stamp collecting

★ *or* *   unused
★★ *or* **   unused with original gum intact and never mounted with a stamp hinge
⊙ *or* ◯ *or* 0   used
⊞   block of four or more
⊠   entire cover or card

Weather

H *or* Ⓗ	high pressure region		∞	haze
L *or* Ⓛ	low pressure region			hurricane
◎	calm			tropical storm
◯	clear		•	rain
◖	cloudy (partly)			rain and snow
●	cloudy (completely overcast)			frost
⇥	drifting or blowing snow			sandstorm or dust storm
	drizzle		▽	shower(s)
≡	fog			shower of rain
∿	freezing rain			shower of hail
▲▲▲▲	cold front		△	sleet
▃▃▃	warm front		✳	snow
∿●	stationary front		℞	thunderstorm
)(	funnel clouds		⌢∿	visibility reduced by smoke

CHAPTER 20

Calendar Facts

MONTHS OF THE PRINCIPAL CALENDARS

GREGORIAN[1]		JEWISH		ISLAMIC	
Name	Days	Name	Days	Name	Days
January begins 10 days after the winter solstice	31	Tishri in year 5755 began Sept. 6, 1994	30	Muharram[4] in A.H. 1415 began June 10, 1994	30
February	28	Heshvan	29 or 30	Safar	29
in leap years	29	Kislev	29 or 30	Rabi I	30
March	31	Tebet	29	Rabi II	29
April	30	Shebat	30	Jumada I	30
May	31	Adar[2]	29 or 30	Jumada II	29
June	30	Nisan[3]	30	Rajab	30
July	31	Iyar	29	Sha'ban	29
August	31	Sivan	30	Ramadan	30
September	30	Tammuz	29	Shawwal	29
October	31	Ab	30	Dhu'l-Qa'dah	30
November	30	Elul	29	Dhu'l-Hijja	29
December	31			in leap years	30

[1] The equinoxes occur about March 21 and September 23, the solstices about June 22 and December 22.

[2] In leap years an intercalary month of 30 days takes the place of Adar, and is sometimes called Adar I. Adar then becomes the 29-day Veadar or Adar Sheni (sometimes called Adar II), and retains the usual festivals and holidays of Adar.

[3] The first month of the ecclesiastical year; anciently called Abib.

[4] Retrogresses through the seasons; the Islamic year is lunar and each month begins at the approximate new moon; the year 1 A.H. began on Friday, July 16, A.D. 622.

YEARS OF THREE OF THE PRINCIPAL CALENDARS

CALENDAR	GREGORIAN	JEWISH	MUSLIM
YEAR CHRONOLOGY	From Roman year 754, the year immediately following the birth of Christ as placed by Dionysus Exiguus in the 753d year of Rome	From the Creation as fixed at 3761 B.C.	From the year of the Hegira, A.D. 622
YEAR BEGINS	Ten days after the winter solstice	First new moon after the autumnal equinox. The postexilic year began in the spring with the month Nisan, this now being sometimes called the ecclesiastical year	Retrogresses through the seasons; the year 1 began on Friday, July 16
NUMBER OF DAYS	365 (common years) 366 (leap years)	defective 353 (common years) 383 (leap years) regular 354 (common years) 384 (leap years) perfect or abundant 355 (common years) 385 (leap years) (There is no regular pattern for defective, regular, and perfect years; adjustments are made so that certain holidays will fall on proper days of the week)	354 (common years) 355 (leap years)
LEAP YEARS	Every fourth year but only those centesimal years divisible by 400	The 3d, 6th, 8th, 11th, 14th, 17th, and 19th years of each 19-year cycle	The 2d, 5th, 7th, 10th, 13th, 16th, 18th, 21st, 24th, 26th, and 29th years of each 30-year cycle

EASTER DATES

YEAR	ASH WEDNESDAY		EASTER	
1995	March	1	April	16
1996	February	21	April	7
1997	February	12	March	30
1998	February	25	April	12
1999	February	17	April	4
2000	March	8	April	23
2001	February	28	April	15
2002	February	13	March	31
2003	March	5	April	20
2004	February	25	April	11
2005	February	9	March	27
2006	March	1	April	16
2007	February	21	April	8
2008	February	6	March	23
2009	February	25	April	12
2010	February	17	April	4
2011	March	9	April	24
2012	February	22	April	8
2013	February	13	March	31
2014	March	5	April	20

JEWISH YEARS 5754–5773

JEWISH YEAR		A.D.
5754	begins	Sept. 16, 1993
5755	begins	Sept. 6, 1994
5756	begins	Sept. 25, 1995
5757	begins	Sept. 14, 1996
5758	begins	Oct. 2, 1997
5759	begins	Sept. 21, 1998
5760	begins	Sept. 11, 1999
5761	begins	Sept. 30, 2000
5762	begins	Sept. 18, 2001
5763	begins	Sept. 7, 2002
5764	begins	Sept. 27, 2003
5765	begins	Sept. 16, 2004
5766	begins	Oct. 4, 2005
5767	begins	Sept. 23, 2006
5768	begins	Sept. 13, 2007
5769	begins	Sept. 30, 2008
5770	begins	Sept. 19, 2009
5771	begins	Sept. 9, 2010
5772	begins	Sept. 29, 2011
5773	begins	Sept. 17, 2012

PERPETUAL CALENDAR (1753–2050)

DAY OF THE MONTH					Jan. Oct.	Apr. July *Jan.*	Sept. Dec.	June	Feb. Mar. Nov.	Aug. *Feb.*	May	DAY OF THE WEEK
1	8	15	22	29	a	b	c	d	e	f	g	Monday
2	9	16	23	30	g	a	b	c	d	e	f	Tuesday
3	10	17	24	31	f	g	a	b	c	d	e	Wednesday
4	11	18	25		e	f	g	a	b	c	d	Thursday
5	12	19	26		d	e	f	g	a	b	c	Friday
6	13	20	27		c	d	e	f	g	a	b	Saturday
7	14	21	28		b	c	d	e	f	g	a	Sunday

Jan. Oct.	Apr. July *Jan.*	Sept. Dec.	June	Feb. Mar. Nov.	Aug. *Feb.*	May
1753	1754	1755	1761	*1756*	1757	1758
1759	1765	*1760*	1767	1762	1763	1769
1764	1771	1766	*1772*	1773	*1768*	1775
1770	*1776*	1777	1778	1779	1774	*1780*
1781	1782	1783	1789	*1784*	1785	1786
1787	1793	*1788*	1795	1790	1791	1797
1792	1799	1794	1801	1802	*1796*	1809
1798	1805	1800	1807	1813	1803	1815
1804	1811	1806	*1812*	1819	*1808*	*1820*
1810	*1816*	1817	1818	*1824*	1814	1826
1821	1822	1823	1829	1830	1825	1837
1827	1833	*1828*	1835	1841	1831	1843
1832	1839	1834	*1840*	1847	*1836*	*1848*
1838	*1844*	1845	1846	*1852*	1842	1854
1849	1850	1851	1857	1858	1853	1865
1855	1861	*1856*	1863	1869	1859	1871
1860	1867	1862	*1868*	1875	*1864*	*1876*
1866	*1872*	1873	1874	*1880*	1870	1882
1877	1878	1879	1885	1886	1881	1893
1883	1889	*1884*	1891	1897	1887	1899
1888	1895	1890	*1896*	1909	*1892*	1905
1894	1901	1902	1903	1915	1898	1911
1900	1907	1913	*1908*	*1920*	*1904*	*1916*
1906	*1912*	1919	1914	1926	1910	1922
1917	1918	*1924*	1925	1937	1921	1933
1923	1929	1930	1931	1943	1927	1939
1928	1935	1941	*1936*	*1948*	*1932*	*1944*
1934	*1940*	1947	1942	1954	1938	1950
1945	1946	*1952*	1953	1965	1949	1961
1951	1957	1958	1959	1971	1955	1967
1956	1963	1969	*1964*	1976	*1960*	*1972*
1962	*1968*	1975	1970	1982	1966	1978
1973	1974	*1980*	1981	1993	1977	1989
1979	1985	1986	1987	1999	1983	1995
1984	1991	1997	*1992*	*2004*	*1988*	*2000*
1990	*1996*	2003	1998	2010	1994	2006
2001	2002	*2008*	2009	2021	2005	2017
2007	2013	2014	2015	2027	2011	2023
2012	2019	2025	*2020*	*2032*	*2016*	*2028*
2018	*2024*	2031	2026	2038	2022	2034
2029	2030	*2036*	2037	2049	2033	2045
2035	2041	2042	2043		2039	
2040	2047		*2048*		*2044*	
2046					2050	

To find the day of the week corresponding to any date:

1. Find the small letter directly under the name of the month* and opposite the number of the day of the month.
2. Next, find the year in the year columns and follow the column up to where that same letter appears.
3. Follow the row out to the right to find the day of the week that the date occurred in that year.

For example, to find the day of the week on which July 20, 1969 fell, find the row in which number 20 appears and the column in which July appears. Follow the row across and the column down to find that they converge on the letter *d*. Next, find the year 1969 in the third year column and follow the column up to where the letter *d* appears. Follow that row out to the right to find that July 20, 1969 was a Sunday.

*Leap years are shown in *italics*. For dates occurring in January or February of a leap year, use *italic* names of months, above.

CHAPTER 21

Dictionary of the English Language

A

¹**a** *n, pl* **a's** *or* **as** : 1st letter of the alphabet

²**a** *indefinite article* : one or some — used to indicate an unspecified or unidentified individual

aard·vark *n* : ant-eating African mammal

aback *adv* : by surprise

aba·cus *n, pl* **aba·ci** *or* **aba·cus·es** : calculating instrument using rows of beads

abaft *adv* : toward or at the stern

ab·a·lo·ne *n* : large edible shellfish

¹**aban·don** *vb* : give up without intent to reclaim — **aban·don·ment** *n*

²**abandon** *n* : thorough yielding to impulses

aban·doned *adj* : morally unrestrained

abase *vb* **abased; abas·ing** : lower in dignity — **abase·ment** *n*

abash *vb* : embarrass — **abashment** *n*

abate *vb* **abat·ed; abat·ing** : decrease or lessen

abate·ment *n* : tax reduction

ab·at·toir *n* : slaughterhouse

ab·bess *n* : head of a convent

ab·bey *n, pl* **-beys** : monastery or convent

ab·bot *n* : head of a monastery

ab·bre·vi·ate *vb* **-at·ed; -at·ing** : shorten — **ab·bre·vi·a·tion** *n*

ab·di·cate *vb* **-cat·ed; -cat·ing** : renounce — **ab·di·ca·tion** *n*

ab·do·men *n* 1 : body area between chest and pelvis 2 : hindmost part of an insect — **ab·dom·i·nal** *adj* — **ab·dom·i·nal·ly** *adv*

ab·duct *vb* : kidnap — **ab·duc·tion** *n* — **ab·duc·tor** *n*

abed *adv or adj* : in bed

ab·er·ra·tion *n* : deviation or distortion — **ab·er·rant** *adj*

abet *vb* **-tt-** : incite or encourage — **abet·tor, abet·ter** *n*

abey·ance *n* : state of inactivity

ab·hor *vb* **-rr-** : hate — **ab·hor·rence** *n* — **ab·hor·rent** *adj*

abide *vb* **abode** *or* **abid·ed; abid·ing** 1 : endure 2 : remain, last, or reside

ab·ject *adj* : low in spirit or hope — **ab·jec·tion** *n* — **ab·ject·ly** *adv* — **ab·ject·ness** *n*

ab·jure *vb* 1 : renounce 2 : abstain from — **ab·ju·ra·tion** *n*

ablaze *adj or adv* : on fire

able *adj* **abler; ablest** 1 : having sufficient power, skill, or resources 2 : skilled or efficient — **abil·i·ty** *n* — **ably** *adv*

-able, -ible *adj suffix* 1 : capable of, fit for, or worthy of 2 : tending, given, or liable to

ab·lu·tion *n* : washing of one's body

ab·ne·gate *vb* **-gat·ed; -gat·ing** 1 : relinquish 2 : renounce — **ab·ne·ga·tion** *n*

ab·nor·mal *adj* : deviating from the normal or average — **ab·nor·mal·i·ty** *n* — **ab·nor·mal·ly** *adv*

aboard *adv* : on, onto, or within a car, ship, or aircraft ~ *prep* : on or within

abode *n* : residence

abol·ish *vb* : do away with — **ab·o·li·tion** *n*

abom·i·na·ble *adj* : thoroughly unpleasant or revolting

abom·i·nate *vb* **-nat·ed; -nat·ing** : hate — **abom·i·na·tion** *n*

ab·orig·i·nal *adj* 1 : original 2 : primitive

ab·orig·i·ne *n* : original inhabitant

abort *vb* : terminate prematurely — **abor·tive** *adj*

abor·tion *n* : spontaneous or induced termination of pregnancy

abound *vb* : be plentiful

about *adv* : around ~ *prep* 1 : on every side of 2 : on the verge of 3 : having as a subject

above *adv* : in or to a higher place ~ *prep* 1 : in or to a higher place than 2 : more than

above·board *adv or adj* : without deception

abrade *vb* **abrad·ed; abrad·ing** : wear away by rubbing — **abra·sion** *n*

abra·sive *n* : substance for grinding, smoothing, or polishing ~ *adj* 1 : tending to abrade 2 : causing irritation — **abra·sive·ly** *adv* — **abra·sive·ness** *n*

abreast *adv or adj* 1 : side by side 2 : up to a standard or level

abridge *vb* **abridged; abridg·ing** : shorten or condense — **abridg·ment, abridge·ment** *n*

abroad *adv or adj* 1 : over a wide area 2 : outside one's country

ab·ro·gate *vb* **-gat·ed; -gat·ing** : annul or revoke — **ab·ro·ga·tion** *n*

abrupt *adj* 1 : sudden 2 : so quick as to seem rude — **abrupt·ly** *adv*

ab·scess *n* : collection of pus surrounded by inflamed tissue — **abscessed** *adj*

ab·scond *vb* : run away and hide

ab·sent *adj* : not present ~ **ab·sent** *vb* : keep oneself away — **ab·sence** *n* — **ab·sen·tee** *n*

ab·sent·mind·ed *adj* : unaware of one's surroundings or action — **ab·sent·mind·ed·ly** *adv* — **ab·sent·mind·ed·ness** *n*

ab·so·lute *adj* 1 : pure 2 : free from restriction 3 : definite — **ab·so·lute·ly** *adv*

ab·so·lu·tion *n* : remission of sins

ab·solve *vb* **-solved; -solv·ing** : set free of the consequences of guilt

ab·sorb *vb* 1 : suck up or take in as a sponge does 2 : engage (one's attention) — **ab·sor·ben·cy** *n* — **ab·sor·bent** *adj or n* — **ab·sorb·ing** *adj* — **ab·sorb·ing·ly** *adv*

ab·sorp·tion *n* : process of absorbing — **ab·sorp·tive** *adj*

ab·stain *vb* : refrain from doing something — **ab·stain·er** *n* — **ab·sten·tion** *n* — **ab·sti·nence** *n*

ab·ste·mi·ous *adj* : sparing in use of food or drink — **ab·ste·mi·ous·ly** *adv* — **ab·ste·mi·ous·ness** *n*

ab·stract *adj* 1 : expressing a quality apart from an object 2 : not representing something specific ~ *n* : summary ~ *vb* 1 : remove or separate 2 : make an abstract of — **ab·stract·ly** *adv* — **ab·stract·ness** *n*

ab·strac·tion *n* 1 : act of abstracting 2 : abstract idea or work of art

ab·struse *adj* : hard to understand — **ab·struse·ly** *adv* — **ab·struse·ness** *n*

ab·surd *adj* : ridiculous or unreasonable — **ab·sur·di·ty** *n* — **ab·surd·ly** *adv*

abun·dant *adj* : more than enough — **abun·dance** *n* — **abun·dant·ly** *adv*

abuse *vb* **abused; abus·ing** 1 : misuse 2 : mistreat 3 : attack with words ~ *n* 1 : corrupt practice 2 : improper use 3 : mistreatment 4 : coarse and insulting speech — **abus·er** *n* — **abu·sive** *adj* — **abu·sive·ly** *adv* — **abu·sive·ness** *n*

abut *vb* **-tt-** : touch along a border — **abut·ter** *n*

abut·ment *n* : part of a bridge that supports weight

abys·mal *adj* 1 : immeasurably deep 2 : wretched — **abys·mal·ly** *adv*

abyss *n* : immeasurably deep gulf

-ac *n suffix* : one affected with

aca·cia *n* : leguminous tree or shrub

ac·a·dem·ic *adj* 1 : relating to schools or colleges 2 : theoretical — **academic** *n* — **ac·a·dem·i·cal·ly** *adv*

acad•e•my *n, pl* **-mies 1** : private high school **2** : society of scholars or artists

acan•thus *n, pl* **acanthus 1** : prickly Mediterranean herb **2** : ornament representing acanthus leaves

ac•cede *vb* **-ced•ed; -ced•ing 1** : become a party to an agreement **2** : express approval **3** : enter upon an office

ac•cel•er•ate *vb* **-at•ed; -at•ing 1** : bring about earlier **2** : speed up — **ac•cel•er•a•tion** *n*

ac•cel•er•a•tor *n* : pedal for controlling the speed of a motor vehicle

ac•cent *n* **1** : distinctive manner of pronunciation **2** : prominence given to one syllable of a word **3** : mark (as ´, ` , ^) over a vowel in writing or printing to indicate pronunciation ~ *vb* : emphasize — **ac•cen•tu•al** *adj*

ac•cen•tu•ate *vb* **-at•ed; -at•ing** : stress or show off by a contrast — **ac•cen•tu•a•tion** *n*

ac•cept *vb* **1** : receive willingly **2** : agree to — **ac•cept•abil•i•ty** *n* — **ac•cept•able** *adj* — **ac•cep•tance** *n*

ac•cess *n* : capability or way of approaching — **ac•ces•si•bil•i•ty** *n* — **ac•ces•si•ble** *adj*

ac•ces•sion *n* **1** : something added **2** : act of taking office

ac•ces•so•ry *n, pl* **-ries 1** : nonessential addition **2** : one guilty of aiding a criminal — **accessory** *adj*

ac•ci•dent *n* **1** : event occurring by chance or unintentionally **2** : chance — **ac•ci•den•tal** *adj* — **ac•ci•den•tal•ly** *adv*

ac•claim *vb or n* : praise

ac•cla•ma•tion *n* **1** : eager applause **2** : unanimous vote

ac•cli•mate *vb* **-mat•ed; -mat•ing** : acclimatize — **ac•cli•ma•tion** *n*

ac•cli•ma•tize *vb* **-tized; -tiz•ing** : accustom to a new climate or situation — **ac•cli•ma•ti•za•tion** *n*

ac•co•lade *n* : expression of praise

ac•com•mo•date *vb* **-dated; -dat•ing 1** : adapt **2** : provide with something needed **3** : hold without crowding

ac•com•mo•da•tion *n* **1** : quarters — usu. pl. **2** : act of accommodating

ac•com•pa•ny *vb* **-nied; -ny•ing 1** : go or occur with **2** : play supporting music — **ac•com•pa•ni•ment** *n* — **ac•com•pa•nist** *n*

ac•com•plice *n* : associate in crime

ac•com•plish *vb* : do, fulfill, or bring about — **ac•com•plished** *adj* — **ac•com•plish•er** *n* — **ac•com•plish•ment** *n*

ac•cord *vb* **1** : grant **2** : agree ~ *n* **1** : agreement **2** : willingness to act — **ac•cor•dance** *n* — **ac•cor•dant** *adj*

ac•cord•ing•ly *adv* : consequently

according to *prep* **1** : in conformity with **2** : as stated by

ac•cor•di•on *n* : keyboard instrument with a bellows and reeds ~ *adj* : folding like an accordion bellows — **ac•cor•di•on•ist** *n*

ac•cost *vb* : approach and speak to esp. aggressively

ac•count *n* **1** : statement of business transactions **2** : credit arrangement with a vendor **3** : report **4** : worth **5** : sum deposited in a bank ~ *vb* : give an explanation

ac•count•able *adj* : responsible — **ac•count•abil•i•ty** *n*

ac•coun•tant *n* : one skilled in accounting — **ac•coun•tan•cy** *n*

ac•count•ing *n* : financial record keeping

ac•cou•tre, ac•cou•ter *vb* **-tred** *or* **-tered; -tring** *or* **-ter•ing** : equip

ac•cou•tre•ment, ac•cou•ter•ment *n* **1** : accessory item — usu. pl. **2** : identifying characteristic

ac•cred•it *vb* **1** : approve officially **2** : attribute — **ac•cred•i•ta•tion** *n*

ac•crue *vb* **-crued; -cru•ing** : be added by periodic growth — **ac•cru•al** *n*

ac•cu•mu•late *vb* **-lat•ed; -lat•ing** : collect or pile up — **ac•cu•mu•la•tion** *n* — **ac•cu•mu•la•tor** *n*

ac•cu•rate *adj* : free from error — **ac•cu•ra•cy** *n* — **ac•cu•rate•ly** *adv* — **ac•cu•rate•ness** *n*

ac•cursed, ac•curst *adj* **1** : being under a curse **2** : damnable

ac•cuse *vb* **-cused; -cus•ing** : charge with an offense — **ac•cu•sa•tion** *n* — **ac•cus•er** *n*

ac•cused *n, pl* **-cused** : defendant in a criminal case

ac•cus•tom *vb* : make familiar through use or experience

ace *n* : one that excels

acer•bic *adj* : sour or biting in temper, mood, or tone

acet•amin•o•phen *n* : pain reliever

ac•e•tate *n* : fabric or plastic derived from acetic acid

ace•tic acid *n* : acid found in vinegar

acet•y•lene *n* : colorless gas used as a fuel in welding

ache *vb* **ached; ach•ing 1** : suffer a dull persistent pain **2** : yearn — **ache** *n*

achieve *vb* **achieved; achiev•ing** : gain by work or effort — **achieve•ment** *n* — **achiev•er** *n*

ac•id *adj* **1** : sour or biting to the taste **2** : sharp in manner **3** : of or relating to an acid ~ *n* : sour water-soluble chemical compound that reacts with a base to form a salt — **acid•ic** *adj* — **acid•i•fy** *vb* — **acid•i•ty** *n* **acid•ly** *adv*

ac•knowl•edge *vb* **-edged; -edg•ing 1** : admit as true **2** : admit the authority of **3** : express thanks for — **ac•knowl•edg•ment** *n*

ac•me *n* : highest point

ac•ne *n* : skin disorder marked esp. by pimples

ac•o•lyte *n* : assistant to a member of clergy in a religious service

acorn *n* : nut of the oak

acous•tic *adj* : relating to hearing or sound — **acous•ti•cal** *adj* — **acous•ti•cal•ly** *adv*

acous•tics *n sing or pl* **1** : science of sound **2** : qualities in a room that affect how sound is heard

ac•quaint *vb* **1** : inform **2** : make familiar

ac•quain•tance *n* **1** : personal knowledge **2** : person with whom one is acquainted — **ac•quain•tance•ship** *n*

ac•qui•esce *vb* **-esced; -esc•ing** : consent or submit — **ac•qui•es•cence** *n* — **ac•qui•es•cent** *adj* — **ac•qui•es•cent•ly** *adv*

ac•quire *vb* **-quired; -quir•ing** : gain

ac•qui•si•tion *n* : a gaining or something gained — **acqui•si•tive** *adj*

ac•quit *vb* **-tt- 1** : pronounce not guilty **2** : conduct (oneself) usu. well — **ac•quit•tal** *n*

acre *n* **1** : lands **2** : 4840 square yards

acre•age *n* : area in acres

ac•rid *adj* : sharp and biting — **acrid•i•ty** *n* — **ac•rid•ly** *adv* — **ac•rid•ness** *n*

ac•ri•mo•ny *n, pl* **-nies** : harshness of language or feeling — **ac•ri•mo•ni•ous** *adj* — **ac•ri•mo•ni•ous•ly** *adv*

ac•ro•bat *n* : performer of tumbling feats — **ac•ro•bat•ic** *adj*

across *adv* : to or on the opposite side ~ *prep* **1** : to or on the opposite side of **2** : on so as to cross

acryl•ic *n* **1** : plastic used for molded parts or in paints **2** : synthetic textile fiber

act *n* **1** : thing done **2** : law **3** : main division of a play ~ *vb* **1** : perform in a play **2** : conduct oneself **3** : operate **4** : produce an effect

ac•tion *n* **1** : legal proceeding **2** : manner or method of performing **3** : activity **4** : thing done over a period of time or in stages **5** : combat **6** : events of a literary plot **7** : operating mechanism

ac•ti•vate *vb* **-vat•ed; -vat•ing** : make active or reactive — **ac•ti•va•tion** *n*

ac•tive *adj* **1** : causing action or change **2** : lively, vigorous, or energetic **3** : erupting or likely to erupt **4** : now in operation — **active** *n* — **ac•tive•ly** *adv*

ac•tiv•i•ty *n, pl* **-ties 1** : quality or state of being active **2** : what one is actively doing

ac•tor *n* : one that acts

ac•tress *n* : woman who acts in plays

ac•tu•al *adj* : really existing — **ac•tu•al•i•ty** *n* — **ac•tu•al•iza•tion** *n* — **ac•tu•al•ize** *vb* — **ac•tu•al•ly** *adv*

ac•tu•ary *n, pl* **-ar•ies** : one who calculates insurance risks and premiums — **ac•tu•ar•i•al** *adj*

ac•tu•ate *vb* **-at•ed; -at•ing** : put into action — **ac•tu•a•tor** *n*

acu•men *n* : mental keenness

acu•punc•ture *n* : treatment by puncturing the body with needles — **acu•punc•tur•ist** *n*

acute *adj* **acut•er; acut•est 1** : sharp **2** : containing less than 90 degrees **3** : mentally alert **4** : severe — **acute•ly** *adv* — **acute•ness** *n*

ad *n* : advertisement

ad•age *n* : old familiar saying

ad•a•mant *adj* : insistent — **ad•a•mant•ly** *adv*

adapt *vb* : adjust to be suitable for a new use or condition — **adapt•abil•i•ty** *n* — **adapt•able** *adj* — **ad•ap•ta•tion** *n* — **adap•ter** *n* — **adap•tive** *adj*

add *vb* **1** : join to something else so as to increase in amount **2** : say further **3** : find a sum — **ad•di•tion** *n*

ad•der *n* **1** : poisonous European snake **2** : No. American snake

ad•dict *n* : one who is psychologically or physiologically dependent (as on a drug) ~ *vb* : cause to become an addict — **ad•dic•tion** *n* — **ad•dic•tive** *adj*

ad•di•tion•al *adj* : existing as a result of adding — **ad•di•tion•al•ly** *adv*

ad•di•tive *n* : substance added to another

ad•dle *vb* **-dled; -dling** : confuse

ad•dress *vb* **1** : direct one's remarks to **2** : mark an address on ~ *n* **1** : formal speech **2** : place where a person may be reached or mail may be delivered

ad•duce *vb* **-duced; -duc•ing** : offer as proof

ad•e•noid *n* : enlarged tissue near the opening of the nose into the throat — usu. pl. — **adenoid, ad•e•noi•dal** *adj*

adept *adj* : highly skilled — **adept•ly** *adv* — **adept•ness** *n*

ad•e•quate *adj* : good or plentiful enough — **ad•e•qua•cy** *n* — **ad•e•quate•ly** *adv*

ad•here *vb* **-hered; -her•ing 1** : remain loyal **2** : stick fast — **ad•her•ence** *n* — **ad•her•ent** *adj or n*

ad•he•sion *n* : act or state of adhering

ad•he•sive *adj* : tending to adhere ~ *n* : adhesive substance

adieu *n, pl* **adieus** *or* **adieux** : farewell

ad•ja•cent *adj* : situated near or next

ad•jec•tive *n* : word that serves as a modifier of a noun — **ad•jec•ti•val** *adj* — **ad•jec•ti•val•ly** *adv*

ad•join *vb* : be next to

ad•journ *vb* : end a meeting — **ad•journ•ment** *n*

ad•judge *vb* **-judged; -judg•ing 1** : think or pronounce to be **2** : award by judicial decision

ad•ju•di•cate *vb* **-cat•ed; -cat•ing** : settle judicially — **ad•ju•di•ca•tion** *n*

ad•junct *n* : something joined or added but not essential

ad•just *vb* : fix, adapt, or set right — **ad•just•able** *adj* — **ad•just•er, ad•jus•tor** *n* — **ad•just•ment** *n*

ad•ju•tant *n* : aide esp. to a commanding officer

ad-lib *vb* **-bb-** : speak without preparation — **ad-lib** *n or adj*

ad-min-is-ter *vb* 1 : manage 2 : give out esp. in doses — **ad-min-is-tra-ble** *adj* — **ad-min-is-trant** *n*

ad-min-is-tra-tion *n* 1 : process of managing 2 : persons responsible for managing — **ad-min-is-tra-tive** *adj* — **ad-min-is-tra-tive-ly** *adv*

ad-min-is-tra-tor *n* : one that manages

ad-mi-ra-ble *adj* : worthy of admiration — **ad-mi-ra-bly** *adv*

ad-mi-ral *n* : commissioned officer in the navy ranking next below a fleet admiral

ad-mire *vb* **-mired; -mir-ing** : have high regard for — **ad-mi-ra-tion** *n* — **ad-mir-er** *n* — **ad-mir-ing-ly** *adv*

ad-mis-si-ble *adj* : that can be permitted — **ad-mis-si-bil-i-ty** *n*

ad-mis-sion *n* 1 : act of admitting 2 : admittance or a fee paid for this 3 : acknowledgment of a fact

ad-mit *vb* **-tt-** 1 : allow to enter 2 : permit 3 : recognize as genuine — **ad-mit-ted-ly** *adv*

ad-mit-tance *n* : permission to enter

ad-mix-ture *n* 1 : thing added in mixing 2 : mixture

ad-mon-ish *vb* : rebuke — **ad-mon-ish-ment** *n* — **ad-mo-ni-tion** *n* — **ad-mon-i-to-ry** *adj*

ado *n* 1 : fuss 2 : trouble

ado-be *n* : sun-dried building brick

ad-o-les-cence *n* : period of growth between childhood and maturity — **ad-o-les-cent** *adj or n*

adopt *vb* 1 : take (a child of other parents) as one's own child 2 : take up and practice as one's own — **adop-tion** *n*

adore *vb* **adored; ador-ing** 1 : worship 2 : be extremely fond of — **ador-able** *adj* — **ador-ably** *adv* — **ad-o-ra-tion** *n*

adorn *vb* : decorate with ornaments — **adorn-ment** *n*

adrift *adv or adj* 1 : afloat without motive power or moorings 2 : without guidance or purpose

adroit *adj* : dexterous or shrewd — **adroit-ly** *adv* — **adroit-ness** *n*

adult *adj* : fully developed and mature ~ *n* : grown-up person — **adult-hood** *n*

adul-ter-ate *vb* **-at-ed; -at-ing** : make impure by mixture — **adul-ter-a-tion** *n*

adul-tery *n, pl* **-ter-ies** : sexual unfaithfulness of a married person — **adul-ter-er** *n* — **adul-ter-ess** *n* — **adul-ter-ous** *adj*

ad-vance *vb* **-vanced; -vanc-ing** 1 : bring or move forward 2 : promote 3 : lend ~ *n* 1 : forward movement 2 : improvement 3 : offer ~ *adj* : being ahead of time — **ad-vance-ment** *n*

ad-van-tage *n* 1 : superiority of position 2 : benefit or gain — **ad-van-ta-geous** *adj* — **ad-van-ta-geous-ly** *adv*

ad-vent *n* 1 *cap* : period before Christmas 2 : a coming into being or use

ad-ven-ti-tious *adj* : accidental — **ad-ven-ti-tious-ly** *adv*

ad-ven-ture *n* 1 : risky undertaking 2 : exciting experience — **ad-ven-tur-er** *n* — **ad-ven-ture-some** *adj* — **ad-ven-tur-ous** *adj*

ad-verb *n* : word that modifies a verb, an adjective, or another adverb — **ad-ver-bi-al** *adj* — **ad-ver-bi-al-ly** *adv*

ad-ver-sary *n, pl* **-sar-ies** : enemy or rival — **adversary** *adj*

ad-verse *adj* : opposing or unfavorable — **ad-verse-ly** *adv*

ad-ver-si-ty *n, pl* **-ties** : hard times

ad-vert *vb* : refer

ad-ver-tise *vb* **-tised; -tis-ing** : call public attention to — **ad-ver-tise-ment** *n* — **ad-ver-tis-er** *n*

ad-ver-tis-ing *n* : business of preparing advertisements

ad-vice *n* : recommendation with regard to a course of action

ad-vis-able *adj* : wise or prudent — **ad-vis-abil-i-ty** *n*

ad-vise *vb* **-vised; -vis-ing** : give advice to — **ad-vis-er, ad-vis-or** *n*

ad-vise-ment *n* : careful consideration

ad-vi-so-ry *adj* : having power to advise

ad-vo-cate *n* : one who argues or pleads for a cause or proposal ~ *vb* **-cat-ed; -cat-ing** : recommend — **ad-vo-ca-cy** *n*

adze *n* : tool for shaping wood

ae-gis *n* : protection or sponsorship

ae-on *n* : indefinitely long time

aer-ate *vb* **-at-ed; -at-ing** : supply or impregnate with air — **aer-a-tion** *n* — **aer-a-tor** *n*

ae-ri-al *adj* : inhabiting, occurring in, or done in the air ~ *n* : antenna

ae-rie *n* : eagle's nest

aer-o-bic *adj* : using or needing oxygen

aer-o-bics *n sing or pl* : exercises that produce a marked increase in respiration and heart rate

aero-dy-nam-ics *n* : science of bodies in motion in a gas — **aero-dy-nam-ic** *adj* — **aero-dy-nam-i-cal-ly** *adv*

aero-nau-tics *n* : science dealing with aircraft — **aero-nau-ti-cal** *adj*

aero-sol *n* 1 : liquid or solid particles suspended in a gas 2 : substance sprayed as an aerosol

aero-space *n* : earth's atmosphere and the space beyond — **aerospace** *adj*

aes-thet-ic *adj* : relating to beauty — **aes-thet-i-cal-ly** *adv*

aes-thet-ics *n* : branch of philosophy dealing with beauty

afar *adv* : from, at, or to a great distance — **afar** *n*

af-fa-ble *adj* : easy to talk to — **af-fa-bil-i-ty** *n* — **af-fa-bly** *adv*

af-fair *n* : something that relates to or involves one

¹**af-fect** *vb* : assume for effect — **af-fec-ta-tion** *n*

²**affect** *vb* : produce an effect on

af-fect-ed *adj* 1 : pretending to some trait 2 : artificially assumed to impress — **af-fect-ed-ly** *adv*

af-fect-ing *adj* : arousing pity or sorrow — **af-fect-ing-ly** *adv*

af-fec-tion *n* : kind or loving feeling — **af-fec-tion-ate** *adj* — **af-fec-tion-ate-ly** *adv*

af-fi-da-vit *n* : sworn statement

af-fil-i-ate *vb* **-at-ed; -at-ing** : become a member or branch — **affiliate** *n* — **af-fil-i-a-tion** *n*

af-fin-i-ty *n, pl* **-ties** : close attraction or relationship

af-firm *vb* : assert positively — **af-fir-ma-tion** *n*

af-fir-ma-tive *adj* : asserting the truth or existence of something ~ *n* : statement of affirmation or agreement

af-fix *vb* : attach

af-flict *vb* : cause pain and distress to — **af-flic-tion** *n*

af-flu-ence *n* : wealth — **af-flu-ent** *adj*

af-ford *vb* 1 : manage to bear the cost of 2 : provide

af-fray *n* : fight

af-front *vb or n* : insult

af-ghan *n* : crocheted or knitted blanket

afire *adj or adv* : being on fire

aflame *adj or adv* : flaming

afloat *adj or adv* : floating

afoot *adv or adj* 1 : on foot 2 : in progress

afore-said *adj* : said or named before

afraid *adj* : filled with fear

afresh *adv* : anew

aft *adv* : to or toward the stern or tail

af-ter *adv* : at a later time ~ *prep* 1 : behind in place or time 2 : in pursuit of ~ *conj* : following

the time when ~ *adj* 1 : later 2 : located toward the back

af-ter-life *n* : existence after death

af-ter-math *n* : results

af-ter-noon *n* : time between noon and evening

af-ter-thought *n* : later thought

af-ter-ward, af-ter-wards *adv* : at a later time

again *adv* 1 : once more 2 : on the other hand 3 : in addition

against *prep* 1 : directly opposite to 2 : in opposition to 3 : so as to touch or strike

agape *adj or adv* : having the mouth open in astonishment

ag-ate *n* : quartz with bands or masses of various colors

age *n* 1 : length of time of life or existence 2 : particular time in life (as majority or the latter part) 3 : quality of being old 4 : long time 5 : period in history ~ *vb* : become old or mature

-age *n suffix* 1 : aggregate 2 : action or process 3 : result of 4 : rate of 5 : place of 6 : state or rank 7 : fee

aged *adj* 1 : old 2 : allowed to mature

age-less *adj* : eternal

agen-cy *n, pl* **-cies** 1 : one through which something is accomplished 2 : office or function of an agent 3 : government administrative division

agen-da *n* : list of things to be done

agent *n* 1 : means 2 : person acting or doing business for another

ag-gran-dize *vb* **-dized; -diz-ing** : make great or greater — **ag-gran-dize-ment** *n*

ag-gra-vate *vb* **-vat-ed; -vat-ing** 1 : make more severe 2 : irritate — **ag-gra-va-tion** *n*

ag-gre-gate *adj* : formed into a mass ~ *vb* **-gat-ed; -gat-ing** : collect into a mass ~ *n* 1 : mass 2 : whole amount

ag-gres-sion *n* 1 : unprovoked attack 2 : hostile behavior — **ag-gres-sor** *n*

ag-gres-sive *adj* 1 : easily provoked to fight 2 : hard working and enterprising — **ag-gres-sive-ly** *adv* — **ag-gres-sive-ness** *n*

ag-grieve *vb* **-grieved; -griev-ing** 1 : cause grief to 2 : inflict injury on

aghast *adj* : struck with amazement or horror

ag-ile *adj* : able to move quickly and easily — **agil-i-ty** *n*

ag-i-tate *vb* **-tat-ed; -tat-ing** 1 : shake or stir back and forth 2 : excite or trouble the mind of 3 : try to arouse public feeling — **ag-i-ta-tion** *n* — **ag-i-ta-tor** *n*

ag-nos-tic *n* : one who doubts the existence of God

ago *adj or adv* : earlier than the present

agog *adj* : full of excitement

ag-o-nize *vb* **-nized; -niz-ing** : suffer mental agony — **ag-o-niz-ing-ly** *adv*

ag-o-ny *n, pl* **-nies** : extreme pain or mental distress

agrar-i-an *adj* : relating to land ownership or farming interests — **agrarian** *n* — **agrar-i-an-ism** *n*

agree *vb* **agreed; agree-ing** 1 : be of the same opinion 2 : express willingness 3 : get along together 4 : be similar 5 : be appropriate, suitable, or healthful

agree-able *adj* 1 : pleasing 2 : willing to give approval — **agree-able-ness** *n* — **agree-ably** *adv*

agree-ment *n* 1 : harmony of opinion or purpose 2 : mutual understanding or arrangement

ag-ri-cul-ture *n* : farming — **ag-ri-cul-tur-al** *adj* — **ag-ri-cul-tur-ist, ag-ri-cul-tur-al-ist** *n*

aground *adv or adj* : on or onto the bottom or shore

ague *n* 1 : fever with recurrent chills and sweating 2 : malaria

ahead *adv or adj* 1 : in or toward the front 2

: into or for the future **3** : in a more advantageous position

ahead of *prep* **1** : in front or advance of **2** : in excess of

ahoy *interj* — used in hailing

aid *vb* : provide help or support ~ *n* : help

aide *n* : helper

AIDS *n* : serious disease of the human immune system

ail *vb* **1** : trouble **2** : be ill

ai·le·ron *n* : movable part of an airplane wing

ail·ment *n* : bodily disorder

aim *vb* **1** : point or direct (as a weapon) **2** : direct one's efforts ~ *n* **1** : an aiming or the direction of aiming **2** : object or purpose — **aim·less** *adj* — **aim·less·ly** *adv* — **aim·less·ness** *n*

air *n* **1** : mixture of gases surrounding the earth **2** : melody **3** : outward appearance **4** : artificial manner **5** : compressed air **6** : travel by or use of aircraft **7** : medium of transmission of radio waves ~ *vb* **1** : expose to the air **2** : broadcast — **air·borne** *adj*

air–condition *vb* : equip with an apparatus (**air conditioner**) for filtering and cooling the air

air·craft *n, pl* **aircraft** : craft that flies

Aire·dale terrier *n* : large terrier with a hard wiry coat

air·field *n* : airport or its landing field

air force *n* : military organization for conducting warfare by air

air·lift *n* : a transporting of esp. emergency supplies by aircraft — **airlift** *vb*

air·line *n* : air transportation system — **air·lin·er** *n*

air·mail *n* : system of transporting mail by airplane — **airmail** *vb*

air·man *n* **1** : aviator **2** : enlisted man in the air force in one of the 3 ranks below sergeant **3** : enlisted man in the air force ranking just below airman first class

airman basic *n* : enlisted man of the lowest rank in the air force

airman first class *n* : enlisted man in the air force ranking just below sergeant

air·plane *n* : fixed-wing aircraft heavier than air

air·port *n* : place for landing aircraft and usu. for receiving passengers

air·ship *n* : powered lighter-than-air aircraft

air·strip *n* : airfield runway

air·tight *adj* : tightly sealed to prevent flow of air

air·waves *n pl* : medium of transmission of radio waves

airy *adj* **air·i·er; -est** **1** : delicate **2** : breezy

aisle *n* : passage between sections of seats

ajar *adj or adv* : partly open

akim·bo *adj or adv* : having the hand on the hip and the elbow turned outward

akin *adj* **1** : related by blood **2** : similar in kind

-al *adj suffix* : of, relating to, or characterized by

al·a·bas·ter *n* : white or translucent mineral

alac·ri·ty *n* : cheerful readiness

alarm *n* **1** : warning signal or device **2** : fear at sudden danger ~ *vb* **1** : warn **2** : frighten

alas *interj* — used to express unhappiness, pity, or concern

al·ba·tross *n, pl* **-tross** *or* **-trosses** : large seabird

al·be·it *conj* : even though

al·bi·no *n, pl* **-nos** : person or animal with abnormally white skin — **al·bi·nism** *n*

al·bum *n* **1** : book for displaying a collection (as of photographs) **2** : collection of recordings

al·bu·men *n* **1** : white of an egg **2** : albumin

al·bu·min *n* : protein found in blood, milk, egg white, and tissues

al·che·my *n* : medieval chemistry — **al·che·mist** *n*

al·co·hol *n* **1** : intoxicating agent in liquor **2** : liquor — **alcoholic** *adj*

al·co·hol·ic *n* : person affected with alcoholism

al·co·hol·ism *n* : addiction to alcoholic beverages

al·cove *n* : recess in a room or wall

al·der·man *n* : city official

ale *n* : beerlike beverage — **alehouse** *n*

alert *adj* **1** : watchful **2** : quick to perceive and act ~ *n* : alarm ~ *vb* : warn — **alert·ly** *adv* — **alert·ness** *n*

ale·wife *n* : fish of the herring family

al·fal·fa *n* : cloverlike forage plant

al·ga *n, pl* **-gae** : any of a group of lower plants that includes seaweed — **al·gal** *adj*

al·ge·bra *n* : branch of mathematics using symbols — **al·ge·bra·ic** *adj* — **al·ge·bra·i·cal·ly** *adv*

alias *adv* : otherwise called ~ *n* : assumed name

al·i·bi *n* **1** : defense of having been elsewhere when a crime was committed **2** : justification ~ *vb* **-bied; -bi·ing** : offer an excuse

alien *adj* : foreign ~ *n* **1** : foreign-born resident **2** : extraterrestrial

alien·ate *vb* **-at·ed; -at·ing** : cause to be no longer friendly — **alien·ation** *n*

alight *vb* : dismount

align *vb* : bring into line — **align·er** *n* — **align·ment** *n*

alike *adj* : identical or very similar ~ *adv* : equally

al·i·men·ta·ry *adj* : relating to or functioning in nutrition

al·i·mo·ny *n, pl* **-nies** : money paid to a separated or divorced spouse

alive *adj* **1** : having life **2** : lively or animated

al·ka·li *n, pl* **-lies** *or* **-lis** : strong chemical base — **al·ka·line** *adj* — **al·ka·lin·i·ty** *n*

all *adj* **1** : the whole of **2** : greatest possible **3** : every one of ~ *adv* **1** : wholly **2** : so much **3** : for each side ~ *pron* **1** : whole number or amount **2** : everything or everyone

Al·lah *n* : God of Islam

all–around *adj* : versatile

al·lay *vb* **1** : alleviate **2** : calm

al·lege *vb* **-leged; -leg·ing** : assert without proof — **al·le·ga·tion** *n* — **al·leg·ed·ly** *adv*

al·le·giance *n* : loyalty

al·le·go·ry *n, pl* **-ries** : story in which figures and actions are symbols of general truths — **al·le·gor·i·cal** *adj*

al·le·lu·ia *interj* : hallelujah

al·ler·gen *n* : something that causes allergy — **al·ler·gen·ic** *adj*

al·ler·gy *n, pl* **-gies** : abnormal reaction to a substance — **al·ler·gic** *adj* — **al·ler·gist** *n*

al·le·vi·ate *vb* **-at·ed; -at·ing** : relieve or lessen — **al·le·vi·a·tion** *n*

al·ley *n, pl* **-leys** **1** : place for bowling **2** : narrow passage between buildings

al·li·ance *n* : association

al·li·ga·tor *n* : large aquatic reptile related to the crocodiles

al·lit·er·a·tion *n* : repetition of initial sounds of words — **al·lit·er·a·tive** *adj*

al·lo·cate *vb* **-cat·ed; -cat·ing** : assign — **al·lo·ca·tion** *n*

al·lot *vb* **-tt-** : distribute as a share — **al·lot·ment** *n*

al·low *vb* **1** : admit or concede **2** : permit — **al·low·able** *adj*

al·low·ance *n* **1** : allotted share **2** : money given regularly for expenses

al·loy *n* : metals melted together — **al·loy** *vb*

all right *adv or adj* **1** : satisfactorily **2** : yes **3** : certainly

all·spice *n* : berry of a West Indian tree made into a spice

al·lude *vb* **-lud·ed; -lud·ing** : refer indirectly — **al·lu·sion** *n* — **al·lu·sive** *adj* — **al·lu·sive·ly** *adv* — **al·lu·sive·ness** *n*

al·lure *vb* **-lured; -lur·ing** : entice ~ *n* : attractive power

al·ly *vb* **-lied; -ly·ing** : enter into an alliance — **al·ly** *n*

-al·ly *adv suffix* : -ly

al·ma·nac *n* : annual information book

al·mighty *adj* : having absolute power

al·mond *n* : tree with nutlike fruit kernels

al·most *adv* : very nearly

alms *n, pl* **alms** : charitable gift

aloft *adv* : high in the air

alo·ha *interj* — used to greet or bid farewell

alone *adj* **1** : separated from others **2** : not including anyone or anything else — **alone** *adv*

along *prep* **1** : in line with the direction of **2** : at a point on or during ~ *adv* **1** : forward **2** : as a companion **3** : all the time

along·side *adv or prep* : along or by the side

alongside of *prep* : alongside

aloof *adj* : indifferent and reserved — **aloof·ness** *n*

aloud *adv* : so as to be heard

al·paca *n* **1** : So. American mammal related to the llama **2** : alpaca wool or cloth made of this

al·pha·bet *n* : ordered set of letters of a language — **al·pha·bet·i·cal, al·pha·bet·ic** *adj* — **al·pha·bet·i·cal·ly** *adv*

al·pha·bet·ize *vb* **-ized; -iz·ing** : arrange in alphabetical order — **al·pha·bet·iz·er** *n*

al·ready *adv* : by a given time

al·so *adv* : in addition

al·tar *n* : structure for rituals

al·ter *vb* : make different — **al·ter·a·tion** *n*

al·ter·ca·tion *n* : dispute

al·ter·nate *adj* **1** : arranged or succeeding by turns **2** : every other ~ *vb* **-nat·ed; -nat·ing** : occur or cause to occur by turns ~ *n* : substitute — **al·ter·nate·ly** *adv* — **al·ter·na·tion** *n*

alternating current *n* : electric current that regularly reverses direction

al·ter·na·tive *adj* : offering a choice — **alternative** *n*

al·ter·na·tor *n* : alternating-current generator

al·though *conj* : even though

al·tim·e·ter *n* : instrument for measuring altitude

al·ti·tude *n* **1** : distance up from the ground **2** : angular distance above the horizon

al·to *n, pl* **-tos** : lower female choral voice

al·to·geth·er *adv* **1** : wholly **2** : on the whole

al·tru·ism *n* : concern for others — **al·tru·ist** *n* — **al·tru·is·tic** *adj* — **al·tru·is·ti·cal·ly** *adv*

al·um *n* : crystalline compound containing aluminum

alu·mi·num *n* : silver-white malleable ductile light metallic element

alum·na *n, pl* **-nae** : woman graduate

alum·nus *n, pl* **-ni** : graduate

al·ways *adv* **1** : at all times **2** : forever

am *pres 1st sing of* BE

amal·gam *n* **1** : mercury alloy **2** : mixture

amal·gam·ate *vb* **-at·ed; -at·ing** : unite — **amal·ga·ma·tion** *n*

am·a·ryl·lis *n* : bulbous herb with clusters of large colored flowers like lilies

amass *vb* : gather

am·a·teur *n* **1** : person who does something for pleasure rather than for pay **2** : person who is not expert — **am·a·teur·ish** *adj* — **ama·teur·ism** *n*

am·a·to·ry *adj* : of or expressing sexual love

amaze *vb* **amazed; amaz·ing** : fill with wonder — **amaze·ment** *n* — **amaz·ing·ly** *adv*

am·a·zon *n* : tall strong woman — **am·a·zo·ni·an** *adj*

am·bas·sa·dor *n* : representative esp. of a government — **am·bas·sa·do·ri·al** *adj* — **ambas·sa·dor·ship** *n*

am·ber *n* : yellowish fossil resin or its color

am·ber·gris *n* : waxy substance from certain whales used in making perfumes

am·bi·dex·trous *adj* : equally skilled with both hands — **am·bi·dex·trous·ly** *adv*

am·bi·ence, am·bi·ance *n* : pervading atmosphere

am·big·u·ous *adj* : having more than one interpretation — **am·bi·gu·i·ty** *n*

am·bi·tion *n* : eager desire for success or power — **am·bi·tious** *adj* — **am·bi·tious·ly** *adv*

am·biv·a·lence *n* : simultaneous attraction and repulsion — **am·biv·a·lent** *adj*

am·ble *vb* **-bled; -bling** : go at a leisurely gait — **amble** *n*

am·bu·lance *n* : vehicle for carrying injured or sick persons

am·bu·la·to·ry *adj* 1 : relating to or adapted to walking 2 : able to walk about

am·bush *n* : trap by which a surprise attack is made from a place of hiding — **ambush** *vb*

ame·lio·rate *vb* **-rat·ed; -rat·ing** : make or grow better — **ame·lio·ra·tion** *n*

amen *interj* — used for affirmation esp. at the end of prayers

ame·na·ble *adj* : ready to yield or be influenced

amend *vb* 1 : improve 2 : alter in writing

amend·ment *n* : change made in a formal document (as a law)

amends *n sing or pl* : compensation for injury or loss

ame·ni·ty *n, pl* **-ties** 1 : agreeableness 2 *pl* : social conventions 3 : something serving to comfort or accommodate

am·e·thyst *n* : purple gemstone

ami·a·ble *adj* : easy to get along with — **ami·a·bil·i·ty** *n* — **ami·a·bly** *adv*

am·i·ca·ble *adj* : friendly — **am·i·ca·bly** *adv*

amid, amidst *prep* : in or into the middle of

amino acid *n* : nitrogen-containing acid

amiss *adv* : in the wrong way ~ *adj* : wrong

am·me·ter *n* : instrument for measuring electric current

am·mo·nia *n* 1 : colorless gaseous compound of nitrogen and hydrogen 2 : solution of ammonia in water

am·mu·ni·tion *n* 1 : projectiles fired from guns 2 : explosive items used in war

am·ne·sia *n* : sudden loss of memory — **am·ne·si·ac, am·ne·sic** *adj or n*

am·nes·ty *n, pl* **-ties** : a pardon for a group — **amnesty** *vb*

amoe·ba *n, pl* **-bas** *or* **-bae** : tiny one-celled animal that occurs esp. in water — **amoe·bic** *adj*

amok *adv* : in a violent or uncontrolled way

among *prep* 1 : in or through 2 : in the number or class of 3 : in shares to each of

am·o·rous *adj* 1 : inclined to love 2 : being in love 3 : indicative of love — **am·o·rous·ly** *adv* — **am·o·rous·ness** *n*

amor·phous *adj* : shapeless

am·or·tize *vb* **-tized; -tiz·ing** : get rid of (as a debt) gradually with periodic payments — **amor·ti·za·tion** *n*

amount *vb* 1 : be equivalent 2 : reach a total ~ *n* : total number or quantity

amour *n* 1 : love affair 2 : lover

am·pere *n* : unit of electric current

am·per·sand *n* : character & used for the word *and*

am·phib·i·ous *adj* 1 : able to live both on land and in water 2 : adapted for both land and water — **am·phib·i·an** *n*

am·phi·the·ater *n* : oval or circular structure with rising tiers of seats around an arena

am·ple *adj* **-pler ; -plest** 1 : large 2 : sufficient — **am·ply** *adv*

am·pli·fy *vb* **-fied; -fy·ing** : make louder, stronger, or more thorough — **am·pli·fi·ca·tion** *n* — **am·pli·fi·er** *n*

am·pli·tude *n* 1 : fullness 2 : extent of a vibratory movement

am·pu·tate *vb* **-tat·ed; -tat·ing** : cut off (a body part) — **am·pu·ta·tion** *n* — **am·pu·tee** *n*

amuck *var of* AMOK

am·u·let *n* : ornament worn as a charm against evil

amuse *vb* **amused; amus·ing** 1 : engage the attention of in an interesting and pleasant way 2 : make laugh — **amuse·ment** *n*

an *indefinite article* : a — used before words beginning with a vowel sound

-an, -ian , -ean *n suffix* 1 : one that belongs to 2 : one skilled in ~ *adj suffix* 1 : of or belonging to 2 : characteristic of or resembling

anach·ro·nism *n* : one that is chronologically out of place — **anach·ro·nis·tic** *adj*

an·a·con·da *n* : large So. American snake

ana·gram *n* : word or phrase made by transposing the letters of another word or phrase

anal *adj* : relating to the anus

an·al·ge·sic *n* : pain reliever

anal·o·gy *n, pl* **-gies** 1 : similarity between unlike things 2 : example of something similar — **an·a·log·i·cal** *adj* — **an·a·log·i·cal·ly** *adv* — **anal·o·gous** *adj*

anal·y·sis *n, pl* **-y·ses** 1 : examination of a thing to determine its parts 2 : psychoanalysis — **an·a·lyst** *n* — **an·a·lyt·ic, an·a·lyt·i·cal** *adj* — **an·a·lyt·i·cal·ly** *adv*

an·a·lyze *vb* **-lyzed; -lyz·ing** : make an analysis of

an·ar·chism *n* : theory that all government is undesirable — **an·ar·chist** *n or adj* — **an·ar·chis·tic** *adj*

an·ar·chy *n* : lack of government or order — **an·ar·chic** *adj* — **an·ar·chi·cal·ly** *adv*

anath·e·ma *n* 1 : solemn curse 2 : person or thing accursed or intensely disliked

anat·o·my *n, pl* **-mies** : science dealing with the structure of organisms — **an·a·tom·ic, ana·tom·i·cal** *adj* — **an·a·tom·i·cal·ly** *adv* — **anat·o·mist** *n*

-ance *n suffix* 1 : action or process 2 : quality or state 3 : amount or degree

an·ces·tor *n* : one from whom an individual is descended

an·ces·tress *n* : female ancestor

an·ces·try *n* 1 : line of descent 2 : ancestors — **an·ces·tral** *adj*

an·chor *n* : heavy device that catches in the sea bottom to hold a ship in place ~ *vb* : hold or become held in place by or as if by an anchor — **an·chor·age** *n*

an·chor·man *n* : news broadcast coordinator

an·cho·vy *n, pl* **-vies** *or* **-vy** : small herringlike fish

an·cient *adj* 1 : having existed for many years 2 : belonging to times long past — **ancient** *n*

-ancy *n suffix* : quality or state

and *conj* — used to indicate connection or addition

and·iron *n* : one of 2 metal supports for wood in a fireplace

an·drog·y·nous *adj* 1 : having characteristics of both male and female 2 : suitable for either sex

an·ec·dote *n* : brief story — **an·ec·dot·al** *adj*

ane·mia *n* : blood deficiency — **ane·mic** *adj*

anem·o·ne *n* : small herb with showy usu. white flowers

an·es·the·sia *n* : loss of bodily sensation

an·es·thet·ic *n* : agent that produces anesthesia — **anesthetic** *adj* — **anes·the·tist** *n* — **anes·the·tize** *vb*

anew *adv* : over again

an·gel *n* : spiritual being superior to humans — **an·gel·ic, an·gel·i·cal** *adj* — **an·gel·i·cal·ly** *adv*

an·ger *n* : strong feeling of displeasure ~ *vb* : make angry

an·gi·na *n* : painful disorder of heart muscles — **an·gi·nal** *adj*

¹an·gle *n* 1 : figure formed by the meeting of 2 lines in a point 2 : sharp corner 3 : point of view ~ *vb* **-gled; -gling** : turn or direct at an angle

²angle *vb* **an·gled; an·gling** : fish with a hook and line — **an·gler** *n* — **an·gle·worm** *n* — **an·gling** *n*

an·go·ra *n* : yarn or cloth made from the hair of an Angora goat or rabbit

an·gry *adj* **-gri·er; -est** : feeling or showing anger — **an·gri·ly** *adv*

an·guish *n* : extreme pain or distress of mind — **an·guished** *adj*

an·gu·lar *adj* 1 : having many or sharp angles 2 : thin and bony — **an·gu·lar·i·ty** *n*

an·i·mal *n* 1 : living being capable of feeling and voluntary motion 2 : lower animal as distinguished from humans

an·i·mate *adj* : having life ~ *vb* **-mat·ed; -mat·ing** 1 : give life or vigor to 2 : make appear to move — **an·i·mat·ed** *adj*

an·i·ma·tion *n* 1 : liveliness 2 : animated cartoon

an·i·mos·i·ty *n, pl* **-ties** : resentment

an·i·mus *n* : deep-seated hostility

an·ise *n* : herb related to the carrot with aromatic seeds (**ani·seed**) used in flavoring

an·kle *n* : joint or region between the foot and the leg — **an·kle·bone** *n*

an·nals *n pl* : chronological record of history — **an·nal·ist** *n*

an·neal *vb* 1 : make less brittle by heating and then cooling 2 : strengthen or toughen

an·nex *vb* : assume political control over (a territory) ~ *n* : added building — **an·nex·a·tion** *n*

an·ni·hi·late *vb* **-lat·ed; -lat·ing** : destroy — **an·ni·hi·la·tion** *n*

an·ni·ver·sa·ry *n, pl* **-ries** : annual return of the date of a notable event or its celebration

an·no·tate *vb* **-tat·ed; -tat·ing** : furnish with notes — **an·no·ta·tion** *n* — **an·no·ta·tor** *n*

an·nounce *vb* **-nounced; -nounc·ing** : make known publicly — **an·nounce·ment** *n* — **an·nounc·er** *n*

an·noy *vb* : disturb or irritate — **an·noy·ance** *n* — **an·noy·ing·ly** *adv*

an·nu·al *adj* 1 : occurring once a year 2 : living only one year — **annual** *n* — **an·nu·al·ly** *adv*

an·nu·i·ty *n, pl* **-ties** : amount payable annually or the right to such a payment

an·nul *vb* **-ll-** : make legally void — **an·nul·ment** *n*

an·ode *n* 1 : positive electrode 2 : negative battery terminal — **an·od·ic** *adj*

anoint *vb* : apply oil to as a rite — **anoint·ment** *n*

anom·a·ly *n, pl* **-lies** : something abnormal or unusual — **anom·a·lous** *adj*

anon·y·mous *adj* : of unknown origin — **an·o·nym·i·ty** *n* — **anon·y·mous·ly** *adv*

an·oth·er *adj* 1 : any or some other 2 : one more ~ *pron* 1 : one more 2 : one different

an·swer *n* 1 : something spoken or written in reply to a question 2 : solution to a problem ~ *vb* 1 : reply to 2 : be responsible 3 : be adequate — **an·swer·er** *n*

an·swer·able *adj* : responsible

ant *n* : small social insect — **ant·hill** *n*

-ant *n suffix* 1 : one that performs or causes an action 2 : thing that is acted upon ~ *adj suffix* 1 : performing an action or being in a condition 2 : causing an action or process

an·tag·o·nism *n* : active opposition or hostility — **an·tag·o·nist** *n* — **an·tag·o·nis·tic** *adj*

an·tag·o·nize *vb* **-nized; -niz·ing** : cause to be hostile

ant•arc•tic *adj* : relating to the region near the south pole

antarctic circle *n* : circle parallel to the equator approximately 23°27' from the south pole

an•te•bel•lum *adj* : existing before the U.S. Civil War

an•te•ced•ent *n* : one that comes before — **antecedent** *adj*

an•te•lope *n, pl* **-lope** *or* **-lopes** : deerlike mammal related to the ox

an•ten•na *n, pl* **-nae** *or* **-nas 1** : one of the long slender paired sensory organs on the head of an arthropod **2** *pl* **-nas** : metallic device for sending or receiving radio waves

an•te•ri•or *adj* : located before in place or time

an•them *n* : song or hymn of praise or gladness

an•ther *n* : part of a seed plant that contains pollen

an•thol•o•gy *n, pl* **-gies** : literary collection

an•thra•cite *n* : hard coal

an•thro•poid *n* : large ape — **anthropoid** *adj*

an•thro•pol•o•gy *n* : science dealing with humans — **an•thro•po•log•i•cal** *adj* — **an•thro•pol•o•gist** *n*

anti-, ant-, anth- *prefix* **1** : opposite in kind, position, or action **2** : opposing or hostile toward **3** : defending against **4** : curing or treating

antiabortion	antievolution
antiacademic	antievolutionary
antiadministration	antifamily
antiaggression	antifascism
antiaircraft	antifascist
antialien	antifatigue
antiapartheid	antifemale
antiaristocratic	antifeminine
antiart	antifeminism
antiauthoritarian	antifeminist
antiauthority	antifertility
antibacterial	antiforeign
antibias	antiforeigner
antiblack	antifraud
antibourgeois	antigambling
antiboycott	antiglare
antibureaucratic	antigovernment
antiburglar	antiguerrilla
antiburglary	antigun
antibusiness	antihijack
anticancer	antihomosexual
anticapitalism	antihuman
anticapitalist	antihumanism
anti-Catholic	antihumanistic
anticensorship	antihunting
anti-Christian	anti-imperialism
anti-Christianity	anti-imperialist
antichurch	anti-inflation
anticigarette	anti-inflationary
anticlerical	anti-institutional
anticollision	anti-integration
anticolonial	anti-intellectual
anticommunism	anti-intellectualism
anticommunist	antijamming
anticonservation	anti-Jewish
anticonservationist	antilabor
anticonsumer	antiliberal
anticonventional	antiliberalism
anticorrosion	antilitter
anticorrosive	antilittering
anticorruption	antilynching
anticrime	antimale
anticruelty	antimanagement
anticult	antimaterialism
anticultural	antimaterialist
antidandruff	antimicrobial
antidemocratic	antimilitarism
antidiscrimination	antimilitarist
antidrug	antimilitary
antidumping	antimiscegenation
antiestablishment	antimonopolist

antimonopoly	antispending
antimosquito	antistrike
antinoise	antistudent
antiobesity	antisubmarine
antiobscenity	antisubversion
antipapal	antisubversive
antipersonnel	antisuicide
antipolice	antitank
antipollution	antitax
antipornographic	antitechnological
antipornography	antitechnology
antipoverty	antiterrorism
antiprofiteering	antiterrorist
antiprogressive	antitheft
antiprostitution	antitobacco
antirabies	antitotalitarian
antiracketeering	antitoxin
antiradical	antitraditional
antirape	antitrust
antirealism	antituberculosis
antirecession	antitumor
antireform	antityphoid
antireligious	antiulcer
antirevolutionary	antiunemployment
antiriot	antiunion
antiromantic	antiuniversity
antirust	antiurban
antisegregation	antiviolence
antisex	antiviral
antisexist	antivivisection
antisexual	antiwar
antishoplifting	anti-West
antislavery	anti-Western
antismoking	antiwhite
antismuggling	antiwoman
antismut	

an•ti•bi•ot•ic *n* : substance that inhibits harmful microorganisms — **antibiotic** *adj*

an•ti•body *n* : bodily substance that counteracts the effects of a foreign substance or organism

an•tic *n* : playful act ~ *adj* : playful

an•tic•i•pate *vb* **-pat•ed; -pat•ing 1** : be prepared for **2** : look forward to — **an•tic•i•pa•tion** *n* — **an•tic•i•pa•to•ry** *adj*

an•ti•cli•max *n* : something strikingly less important than what has preceded it — **an•ti•cli•mac•tic** *adj*

an•ti•dote *n* : remedy for poison

an•ti•freeze *n* : substance to prevent a liquid from freezing

an•ti•mo•ny *n* : brittle white metallic chemical element

an•tip•a•thy *n, pl* **-thies** : strong dislike

an•ti•quar•i•an *adj* : relating to antiquities or old books — **antiquarian** *n* — **an•ti•quar•i•an•ism** *n*

an•ti•quary *n, pl* **-quar•ies** : one who collects or studies antiquities

an•ti•quat•ed *adj* : out-of-date

an•tique *adj* : very old or out-of-date — **antique** *n*

an•tiq•ui•ty *n, pl* **-ties 1** : ancient times **2** *pl* : relics of ancient times

an•ti•sep•tic *adj* : killing or checking the growth of germs — **antiseptic** *n* — **an•ti•sep•ti•cal•ly** *adv*

an•tith•e•sis *n, pl* **-e•ses** : direct opposite

ant•ler *n* : solid branched horn of a deer — **ant•lered** *adj*

ant•onym *n* : word of opposite meaning

anus *n* : the rear opening of the alimentary canal

an•vil *n* : heavy iron block on which metal is shaped

anx•i•ety *n, pl* **-eties** : uneasiness usu. over an expected misfortune

anx•ious *adj* **1** : uneasy **2** : earnestly wishing — **anx•ious•ly** *adv*

any *adj* **1** : one chosen at random **2** : of whatever number or quantity ~ *pron* **1** : any one or ones **2** : any amount ~ *adv* : to any extent or degree

any•body *pron* : anyone

any•how *adv* **1** : in any way **2** : nevertheless

any•more *adv* : at the present time

any•one *pron* : any person

any•place *adv* : anywhere

any•thing *pron* : any thing whatever

any•time *adv* : at any time whatever

any•way *adv* : anyhow

any•where *adv* : in or to any place

aor•ta *n, pl* **-tas** *or* **-tae** : main artery from the heart — **aor•tic** *adj*

apart *adv* **1** : separately in place or time **2** : aside **3** : to pieces

apart•heid *n* : racial segregation

apart•ment *n* : set of usu. rented rooms

ap•a•thy *n* : lack of emotion or interest — **ap•a•thet•ic** *adj* — **ap•a•thet•i•cal•ly** *adv*

ape *n* : large tailless primate ~ *vb* **aped; ap•ing** : imitate

ap•er•ture *n* : opening

apex *n, pl* **apex•es** *or* **api•ces** : highest point

aphid *n* : small insect that sucks plant juices

aph•o•rism *n* : short saying stating a general truth — **aph•oris•tic** *adj*

aph•ro•di•si•ac *n* : substance that excites sexual desire

api•a•rist *n* : beekeeper — **api•ary** *n*

apiece *adv* : for each one

aplen•ty *adj* : plentiful or abundant

aplomb *n* : complete calmness or self-assurance

apoc•a•lypse *n* : writing prophesying a cataclysm in which evil forces are destroyed — **apoc•alyp•tic** *adj*

apoc•ry•pha *n* : writings of dubious authenticity — **apoc•ry•phal** *adj*

apol•o•get•ic *adj* : expressing apology — **apol•o•get•i•cal•ly** *adv*

apol•o•gize *vb* **-gized; -giz•ing** : make an apology — **apol•o•gist** *n*

apol•o•gy *n, pl* **-gies 1** : formal justification **2** : expression of regret for a wrong

ap•o•plexy *n* : sudden loss of consciousness caused by rupture or obstruction of an artery of the brain — **ap•o•plec•tic** *adj*

apos•ta•sy *n, pl* **-sies** : abandonment of a former loyalty — **apos•tate** *adj or n*

apos•tle *n* : disciple or advocate — **apos•tle•ship** *n* — **ap•os•tolic** *adj*

apos•tro•phe *n* : punctuation mark ' to indicate the possessive case or the omission of a letter or figure

apoth•e•cary *n, pl* **-car•ies** : druggist

ap•pall *vb* : fill with horror or dismay

ap•pa•ra•tus *n, pl* **-tus•es** *or* **-tus 1** : equipment **2** : complex machine or device

ap•par•el *n* : clothing

ap•par•ent *adj* **1** : visible **2** : obvious **3** : seeming — **ap•par•ent•ly** *adv*

ap•pa•ri•tion *n* : ghost

ap•peal *vb* **1** : try to have a court case reheard **2** : ask earnestly **3** : have an attraction — **appeal** *n*

ap•pear *vb* **1** : become visible or evident **2** : come into the presence of someone **3** : seem

ap•pear•ance *n* **1** : act of appearing **2** : outward aspect

ap•pease *vb* **-peased; -peas•ing** : pacify with concessions — **ap•pease•ment** *n*

ap•pel•late *adj* : having power to review decisions

ap•pend *vb* : attach

ap•pend•age *n* : something attached

ap•pen•dec•to•my *n, pl* **-mies** : surgical removal of the appendix

ap•pen•di•ci•tis *n* : inflammation of the appendix

ap•pen•dix *n, pl* **-dix•es** *or* **-di•ces 1** : supplementary matter **2** : narrow closed tube extending from lower right intestine

ap•pe•tite *n* **1** : natural desire esp. for food **2** : preference

ap•pe•tiz•er *n* : food or drink to stimulate the appetite

ap•pe•tiz•ing *adj* : tempting to the appetite — **ap•pe•tiz•ing•ly** *adv*

ap•plaud *vb* : show approval esp. by clapping

ap•plause *n* : a clapping in approval

ap•ple *n* : rounded fruit with firm white flesh

ap•ple•jack *n* : brandy made from cider

ap•pli•ance *n* : household machine or device

ap•pli•ca•ble *adj* : capable of being applied — **ap•pli•ca•bil•i•ty** *n*

ap•pli•cant *n* : one who applies

ap•pli•ca•tion *n* **1** : act of applying or thing applied **2** : constant attention **3** : request

ap•pli•ca•tor *n* : device for applying a substance

ap•pli•qué *n* : cut-out fabric decoration — **appliqué** *vb*

ap•ply *vb* **-plied; -ply•ing 1** : place in contact **2** : put to practical use **3** : devote (one's) attention or efforts to something **4** : submit a request **5** : have reference or a connection

ap•point *vb* **1** : set or assign officially **2** : equip or furnish — **ap•poin•tee** *n*

ap•point•ment *n* **1** : act of appointing **2** : nonelective political job **3** : arrangement for a meeting

ap•por•tion *vb* : distribute proportionately — **ap•por•tion•ment** *n*

ap•po•site *adj* : suitable — **ap•po•site•ly** *adv* — **ap•po•site•ness** *n*

ap•praise *vb* **-praised; -prais•ing** : set value on — **ap•prais•al** *n* — **ap•prais•er** *n*

ap•pre•cia•ble *adj* : considerable — **ap•pre•cia•bly** *adv*

ap•pre•ci•ate *vb* **-ated; -at•ing 1** : value justly **2** : be grateful for **3** : increase in value — **ap•pre•cia•tion** *n*

ap•pre•cia•tive *adj* : showing appreciation

ap•pre•hend *vb* **1** : arrest **2** : look forward to in dread **3** : understand — **ap•pre•hen•sion** *n*

ap•pre•hen•sive *adj* : fearful — **ap•pre•hen•sive•ly** *adv* — **ap•pre•hen•sive•ness** *n*

ap•pren•tice *n* : person learning a craft ~ *vb* **-ticed; -tic•ing** : employ or work as an apprentice — **ap•pren•tice•ship** *n*

ap•prise *vb* **-prised; -pris•ing** : inform

ap•proach *vb* **1** : move nearer or be close to **2** : make initial advances or efforts toward — **approach** *n* — **ap•proach•able** *adj*

ap•pro•ba•tion *n* : approval

ap•pro•pri•ate *vb* **-at•ed; -at•ing 1** : take possession of **2** : set apart for a particular use ~ *adj* : suitable — **ap•pro•pri•ate•ly** *adv* — **ap•pro•pri•ate•ness** *n* — **ap•pro•pri•a•tion** *n*

ap•prov•al *n* : act of approving

ap•prove *vb* **-proved; -prov•ing** : accept as satisfactory

ap•prox•i•mate *adj* : nearly correct or exact ~ *vb* **-mat•ed; -mat•ing** : come near — **ap•prox•i•mate•ly** *adv* — **ap•prox•i•ma•tion** *n*

ap•pur•te•nance *n* : accessory — **ap•pur•te•nant** *adj*

apri•cot *n* : peachlike fruit

April *n* : 4th month of the year having 30 days

apron *n* : protective garment

ap•ro•pos *adv* : suitably ~ *adj* : being to the point

apropos of *prep* : with regard to

apt *adj* **1** : suitable **2** : likely **3** : quick to learn — **apt•ly** *adv* — **apt•ness** *n*

ap•ti•tude *n* **1** : capacity for learning **2** : natural ability

aqua *n* : light greenish blue color

aquar•i•um *n, pl* **-iums** *or* **-ia** : glass container for aquatic animals and plants

aquat•ic *adj* : of or relating to water — **aquatic** *n*

aq•ue•duct *n* : conduit for carrying running water

aq•ui•line *adj* : curved like an eagle's beak

-ar *adj suffix* **1** : of, relating to, or being **2** : resembling

ar•a•besque *n* : intricate design

ar•a•ble *adj* : fit for crops

ar•bi•ter *n* : final authority

ar•bi•trary *adj* **1** : selected at random **2** : autocratic — **ar•bi•trari•ly** *adv* — **ar•bi•trari•ness** *n*

ar•bi•trate *vb* **-trat•ed; -trat•ing** : settle a dispute as arbitrator — **ar•bi•tra•tion** *n*

ar•bi•tra•tor *n* : one chosen to settle a dispute

ar•bor *n* : shelter under branches or vines

ar•bo•re•al *adj* : living in trees

arc *n* **1** : part of a circle **2** : bright sustained electrical discharge ~ *vb* **arced; arc•ing** : form an arc

ar•cade *n* : arched passageway between shops

ar•cane *adj* : mysterious or secret

¹arch *n* : curved structure spanning an opening ~ *vb* : cover with or form into an arch

²arch *adj* **1** : chief — usu. in combination **2** : mischievous — **arch•ly** *adv* — **arch•ness** *n*

ar•chae•ol•o•gy, ar•che•ol•o•gy *n* : study of past human life — **ar•chae•o•log•i•cal** *adj* — **ar•chae•ol•o•gist** *n*

ar•cha•ic *adj* : belonging to an earlier time — **ar•cha•i•cal•ly** *adv*

arch•an•gel *n* : angel of high rank

arch•bish•op *n* : chief bishop — **arch•bish•op•ric** *n*

arch•di•o•cese *n* : diocese of an archbishop

ar•chery *n* : shooting with bow and arrows — **ar•cher** *n*

ar•che•type *n* : original pattern or model

ar•chi•pel•a•go *n, pl* **-goes** *or* **-gos** : group of islands

ar•chi•tect *n* : building designer

ar•chi•tec•ture *n* **1** : building design **2** : style of building **3** : manner of organizing elements — **ar•chi•tec•tur•al** *adj* — **ar•chi•tec•tur•al•ly** *adv*

ar•chives *n pl* : public records or their storage place — **archi•vist** *n*

arch•way *n* : passageway under an arch

arc•tic *adj* **1** : relating to the region near the north pole **2** : frigid

arctic circle *n* : circle parallel to the equator approximately 23°27′ from the north pole

-ard *suffix* : one that is

ar•dent *adj* : characterized by warmth of feeling — **ar•dent•ly** *adv*

ar•dor *n* : warmth of feeling

ar•du•ous *adj* : difficult — **ar•du•ous•ly** *adv* — **ar•du•ous•ness** *n*

are *pres 2d sing or pres pl of* BE

ar•ea *n* **1** : space for something **2** : amount of surface included **3** : region **4** : range covered by a thing or concept

area code *n* : 3-digit area-identifying telephone number

are•na *n* **1** : enclosed exhibition area **2** : sphere of activity

ar•gon *n* : colorless odorless gaseous chemical element

ar•got *n* : special language (as of the underworld)

argu•able *adj* : open to dispute

ar•gue *vb* **-gued; -gu•ing 1** : give reasons for or against something **2** : disagree in words

ar•gu•ment *n* **1** : reasons given to persuade **2** : dispute with words

ar•gu•men•ta•tive *adj* : inclined to argue

ar•gyle *n* : colorful diamond pattern in knitting

aria *n* : opera solo

ar•id *adj* : very dry — **arid•i•ty** *n*

arise *vb* **arose ; aris•en ; aris•ing 1** : get up **2** : originate

ar•is•toc•ra•cy *n, pl* **-cies** : upper class — **aris•to•crat** *n* — **aris•to•crat•ic** *adj*

arith•me•tic *n* : mathematics that deals with numbers — **ar•ith•met•ic, ar•ith•met•i•cal** *adj*

ark *n* : big boat

¹arm *n* **1** : upper limb **2** : branch — **armed** *adj* — **arm•less** *adj*

²arm *vb* : furnish with weapons ~ *n* **1** : weapon **2** : branch of the military forces **3** *pl* : family's heraldic designs

ar•ma•da *n* : naval fleet

ar•ma•dil•lo *n, pl* **-los** : burrowing mammal covered with bony plates

ar•ma•ment *n* : military arms and equipment

ar•ma•ture *n* : rotating part of an electric generator or motor

armed forces *n pl* : military

ar•mi•stice *n* : truce

ar•mor *n* : protective covering — **ar•mored** *adj*

ar•mory *n, pl* **-mor•ies** : factory or storehouse for arms

arm•pit *n* : hollow under the junction of the arm and shoulder

ar•my *n, pl* **-mies 1** : body of men organized for war esp. on land **2** : great number

aro•ma *n* : usu. pleasing odor — **ar•o•mat•ic** *adj*

around *adv* **1** : in or along a circuit **2** : on all sides **3** : near **4** : in an opposite direction ~ *prep* **1** : surrounding **2** : along the circuit of **3** : to or on the other side of **4** : near

arouse *vb* **aroused; arous•ing 1** : awaken from sleep **2** : stir up — **arous•al** *n*

ar•raign *vb* **1** : call before a court to answer to an indictment **2** : accuse — **ar•raign•ment** *n*

ar•range *vb* **-ranged; -rang•ing 1** : put in order **2** : settle or agree on **3** : adapt (a musical composition) for voices or instruments — **ar•range•ment** *n* — **ar•rang•er** *n*

ar•ray *vb* **1** : arrange in order **2** : dress esp. splendidly ~ *n* **1** : arrangement **2** : rich clothing **3** : imposing group

ar•rears *n pl* : state of being behind in paying debts

ar•rest *vb* **1** : stop **2** : take into legal custody — **arrest** *n*

ar•rive *vb* **-rived; -riv•ing 1** : reach a destination, point, or stage **2** : come near in time — **ar•riv•al** *n*

ar•ro•gant *adj* : showing an offensive sense of superiority — **ar•ro•gance** *n* — **ar•ro•gant•ly** *adv*

ar•ro•gate *vb* **-gat•ed; -gat•ing** : to claim without justification

ar•row *n* : slender missile shot from a bow — **ar•row•head** *n*

ar•royo *n, pl* **-royos 1** : watercourse **2** : gully

ar•se•nal *n* **1** : place where arms are made or stored **2** : store

ar•se•nic *n* : solid grayish poisonous chemical element

ar•son *n* : willful or malicious burning of property — **ar•son•ist** *n*

art *n* **1** : skill **2** : branch of learning **3** : creation of things of beauty or works so produced **4** : ingenuity

ar•te•rio•scle•ro•sis *n* : hardening of the arteries — **ar•te•rio•scle•rot•ic** *adj or n*

ar•tery *n, pl* **-ter•ies 1** : tubular vessel carrying blood from the heart **2** : thoroughfare — **ar•te•ri•al** *adj*

art•ful *adj* **1** : ingenious **2** : crafty — **art•ful•ly** *adv* — **art•ful•ness** *n*

ar•thri•tis *n, pl* **-ti•des** : inflammation of the joints — **ar•thrit•ic** *adj or n*

ar•thro•pod *n* : invertebrate animal (as an insect or crab) with segmented body and jointed limbs — **arthropod** *adj*

ar•ti•choke *n* : tall thistlelike herb or its edible flower head

ar•ti•cle *n* **1** : distinct part of a written document **2** : nonfictional published piece of writing **3** : word (as *an, the*) used to limit a noun **4** : item or piece

ar•tic•u•late *adj* : able to speak effectively ~ *vb* **-lated; -lat•ing 1** : utter distinctly **2** : unite by joints — **ar•tic•u•late•ly** *adv* — **ar•tic•u•late•ness** *n* — **ar•tic•u•la•tion** *n*

ar•ti•fact *n* : object of esp. prehistoric human workmanship

ar•ti•fice *n* **1** : trick or trickery **2** : ingenious device or ingenuity

ar•ti•fi•cial *adj* **1** : man-made **2** : not genuine — **ar•ti•fi•ci•al•i•ty** *n* — **ar•ti•fi•cial•ly** *adv* — **ar•ti•fi•cial•ness** *n*

ar•til•lery *n, pl* **-ler•ies** : large caliber firearms

ar•ti•san *n* : skilled craftsman

art•ist *n* : one who creates art — **ar•tis•tic** *adj* — **ar•tis•ti•cal•ly** *adv* — **ar•tis•try** *n*

art•less *adj* : sincere or natural — **art•less•ly** *adv* — **art•less•ness** *n*

arty *adj* **art•i•er; -est** : pretentiously artistic — **art•i•ly** *adv* — **art•i•ness** *n*

-ary *adj suffix* : of, relating to, or connected with

as *adv* **1** : to the same degree **2** : for example ~ *conj* **1** : in the same way or degree as **2** : while **3** : because **4** : though — *pron* — used after *same* or *such* ~ *prep* : in the capacity of

as•bes•tos *n* : fibrous incombustible mineral

as•cend *vb* : move upward — **as•cen•sion** *n*

as•cen•dan•cy *n* : domination

as•cen•dant *n* : dominant position ~ *adj* **1** : moving upward **2** : dominant

as•cent *n* **1** : act of moving upward **2** : degree of upward slope

as•cer•tain *vb* : determine — **as•cer•tain•able** *adj*

as•cet•ic *adj* : self-denying — **ascetic** *n* — **as•cet•i•cism** *n*

as•cribe *vb* **-cribed; -crib•ing** : attribute — **as•crib•able** *adj* — **as•crip•tion** *n*

asep•tic *adj* : free of disease germs

¹ash *n* : tree related to the olives

²ash *n* : matter left when something is burned — **ash•tray** *n*

ashamed *adj* : feeling shame — **asham•ed•ly** *adv*

ash•en *adj* : deadly pale

ashore *adv* : on or to the shore

aside *adv* **1** : toward the side **2** : out of the way

aside from *prep* **1** : besides **2** : except for

as•i•nine *adj* : foolish — **asi•nin•i•ty** *n*

ask *vb* **1** : call on for an answer or help **2** : utter (a question or request) **3** : invite

askance *adv* **1** : with a side glance **2** : with mistrust

askew *adv or adj* : out of line

asleep *adv or adj* **1** : sleeping **2** : numbed **3** : inactive

as long as *conj* **1** : on condition that **2** : because

as of *prep* : from the time of

as•par•a•gus *n* : tall herb related to the lilies or its edible stalks

as•pect *n* **1** : way something looks to the eye or mind **2** : phase

as•pen *n* : poplar

as•per•i•ty *n, pl* **-ties 1** : roughness **2** : harshness

as•per•sion *n* : remark that hurts someone's reputation

as•phalt *n* : dark tarlike substance used in paving

as•phyx•ia *n* : lack of oxygen causing unconsciousness

as•phyx•i•ate *vb* **-at•ed; -at•ing** : suffocate — **as•phyx•i•a•tion** *n*

as•pi•ra•tion *n* : strong desire to achieve a goal

as•pire *vb* **-pired; -pir•ing** : have an ambition — **as•pir•ant** *n*

as•pi•rin *n, pl* **aspirin** *or* **aspirins** : pain reliever

ass *n* **1** : long-eared animal related to the horse **2** : stupid person

as•sail *vb* : attack violently — **as•sail•able** *adj* — **as•sail•ant** *n*

as•sas•si•nate *vb* **-nat•ed; -nat•ing** : murder esp. for political reasons — **as•sas•sin** *n* — **as•sas•si•na•tion** *n*

as•sault *n or vb* : attack

as•say *n* : analysis (as of an ore) to determine quality or properties — **as•say** *vb*

as•sem•ble *vb* **-bled; -bling 1** : collect into one place **2** : fit together the parts of

as•sem•bly *n, pl* **-blies 1** : meeting **2** *cap* : legislative body **3** : a fitting together of parts

as•sem•bly•man *n* : member of a legislative assembly

as•sem•bly•wom•an *n* : woman who is a member of a legislative assembly

as•sent *vb or n* : consent

as•sert *vb* **1** : declare **2** : defend — **as•ser•tion** *n* — **as•sert•ive** *adj* — **as•sert•ive•ness** *n*

as•sess *vb* **1** : impose (as a tax) **2** : evaluate for taxation — **as•sess•ment** *n* — **as•ses•sor** *n*

as•set *n* **1** *pl* : individually owned property **2** : advantage or resource

as•sid•u•ous *adj* : diligent — **as•si•du•i•ty** *n* — **as•sid•u•ous•ly** *adv* — **as•sid•u•ous•ness** *n*

as•sign *vb* **1** : transfer to another **2** : appoint to a duty **3** : designate as a task **4** : attribute — **assign•able** *adj* — **as•sign•ment** *n*

as•sim•i•late *vb* **-lat•ed; -lat•ing 1** : absorb as nourishment **2** : understand — **as•sim•i•la•tion** *n*

as•sist *vb* : help — **assist** *n* — **assis•tance** *n* — **as•sis•tant** *n*

as•so•ci•ate *vb* **-at•ed; -at•ing 1** : join in companionship or partnership **2** : connect in thought — **as•so•ci•ate** *n* — **as•so•ci•a•tion** *n*

as soon as *conj* : when

as•sort•ed *adj* : consisting of various kinds

as•sort•ment *n* : assorted collection

as•suage *vb* **-suaged; -suag•ing** : ease or satisfy

as•sume *vb* **-sumed; -sum•ing 1** : take upon oneself **2** : pretend to have or be **3** : take as true

as•sump•tion *n* : something assumed

as•sure *vb* **-sured; -sur•ing 1** : give confidence or conviction to **2** : guarantee — **as•sur•ance** *n*

as•ter *n* : herb with daisylike flowers

as•ter•isk *n* : a character ° used as a reference mark or as an indication of omission of words

astern *adv or adj* **1** : behind **2** : at or toward the stern

as•ter•oid *n* : small planet between Mars and Jupiter

asth•ma *n* : disorder marked by difficulty in breathing — **asth•mat•ic** *adj or n*

astig•ma•tism *n* : visual defect — **as•tig•mat•ic** *adj*

as to *prep* **1** : concerning **2** : according to

as•ton•ish *vb* : amaze — **as•ton•ish•ing•ly** *adv* — **as•ton•ish•ment** *n*

as•tound *vb* : fill with confused wonder — **as•tound•ing•ly** *adv*

astrad•dle *adv or prep* : so as to straddle

as•tral *adj* : relating to or coming from the stars

astray *adv or adj* : off the right path

astride *adv* : with legs apart or one on each side ~ *prep* : with one leg on each side of

as•trin•gent *adj* : causing shrinking or puckering of tissues — **as•trin•gen•cy** *n* — **astringent** *n*

as•trol•o•gy *n* : prediction of events by the stars — **as•trol•o•ger** *n* — **as•tro•log•i•cal** *adj*

as•tro•naut *n* : space traveler

as•tro•nau•tics *n* : construction and operation of spacecraft — **as•tro•nau•tic, as•tro•nau•ti•cal** *adj*

as•tro•nom•i•cal *adj* **1** : relating to astronomy **2** : extremely large

as•tron•o•my *n, pl* **-mies** : study of the celestial bodies — **as•tron•o•mer** *n*

as•tute *adj* : shrewd — **as•tute•ly** *adv* — **as•tute•ness** *n*

asun•der *adv or adj* **1** : into separate pieces **2** : separated

asy•lum *n* **1** : refuge **2** : institution for care esp. of the insane

asym•met•ri•cal, asym•met•ric *adj* : not symmetrical — **asym•me•try** *n*

at *prep* **1** — used to indicate a point in time or space **2** — used to indicate a goal **3** — used to indicate condition, means, cause, or manner

at all *adv* : without restriction or under any circumstances

ate *past of* EAT

-ate *n suffix* **1** : office or rank **2** : group of persons holding an office or rank ~ *adj suffix* **1** : brought into or being in a state **2** : marked by having

athe•ist *n* : one who denies the existence of God — **athe•ism** *n* — **athe•is•tic** *adj*

ath•ero•scle•ro•sis *n* : arteriosclerosis with deposition of fatty substances in the arteries — **ath•ero•scle•rot•ic** *adj*

ath•lete *n* : one trained to compete in athletics

ath•let•ics *n sing or pl* : exercises and games requiring physical skill — **ath•let•ic** *adj*

-ation *n suffix* : action or process

-ative *adj suffix* **1** : of, relating to, or connected with **2** : tending to

atlas *n* : book of maps

at•mo•sphere *n* **1** : mass of air surrounding the earth **2** : surrounding influence — **at•mo•spher•ic** *adj* — **at•mo•spher•i•cal•ly** *adv*

atoll *n* : ring-shaped coral island

at•om *n* **1** : tiny bit **2** : smallest particle of a chemical element that can exist alone or in combination

atom•ic *adj* **1** : relating to atoms **2** : nuclear

atomic bomb *n* : bomb utilizing the energy released by splitting the atom

at•om•iz•er *n* : device for dispersing a liquid as a very fine spray

atone *vb* **atoned; aton•ing** : make amends — **atone•ment** *n*

atop *prep* : on top of ~ *adv or adj* : on, to, or at the top

atri•um *n, pl* **atria** *or* **atriums 1** : open central room or court **2** : heart chamber that receives blood from the veins

atro•cious *adj* : appalling or abominable — **atro•cious•ly** *adv* — **atro•cious•ness** *n*

atroc•i•ty *n, pl* **-ties** : savage act

at•ro•phy *n, pl* **-phies** : wasting away of a bodily part or tissue — **at•ro•phy** *vb*

at•ro•pine *n* : drug used esp. to relieve spasms

at•tach *vb* **1** : seize legally **2** : bind by personalities **3** : join — **at•tach•ment** *n*

at•ta•ché *n* : technical expert on a diplomatic staff

at•tack *vb* **1** : try to hurt or destroy with violence or words **2** : set to work on ~ *n* **1** : act of attacking **2** : fit of sickness

at•tain *vb* **1** : achieve or accomplish **2** : reach — **at•tain•abil•i•ty** *n* — **at•tain•able** *adj* — **at•tain•ment** *n*

at•tempt *vb* : make an effort toward — **attempt** *n*

at•tend *vb* **1** : handle or provide for the care of something **2** : accompany **3** : be present at **4** : pay attention — **at•ten•dance** *n* — **at•ten•dant** *adj or n*

at•ten•tion *n* **1** : concentration of the mind on something **2** : notice or awareness — **at•ten•tive** *adj* — **at•ten•tive•ly** *adv* — **at•ten•tive•ness** *n*

at•ten•u•ate *vb* **-at•ed; -at•ing 1** : make or become thin **2** : weaken — **at•ten•u•a•tion** *n*

at•test *vb* : certify or bear witness — **at•tes•ta•tion** *n*

at•tic *n* : space just below the roof

at•tire *vb* **-tired; -tir•ing** : dress — **attire** *vb*

at•ti•tude *n* **1** : posture or relative position **2** : feeling, opinion, or mood

at•tor•ney *n, pl* **-neys** : legal agent

at•tract *vb* **1** : draw to oneself **2** : have emotional or aesthetic appeal for — **at•trac•tion** *n* — **at•trac•tive** *adj* — **at•trac•tive•ly** *adv* — **at•trac•tive•ness** *n*

at•tri•bute *n* : inherent characteristic ~ *vb* **-trib•ut•ed; -trib•ut•ing 1** : regard as having a specific cause or origin **2** : regard as a characteristic — **at•trib•ut•able** *adj* — **at•tri•bu•tion** *n*

at•tune *vb* : bring into harmony

au•burn *adj* : reddish brown

auc•tion *n* : public sale of property to the highest bidder — **auction** *vb* — **auc•tion•eer** *n*

au•dac•i•ty *n* : boldness or insolence — **au•da•cious** *adj*

au•di•ble *adj* : capable of being heard — **au•di•bly** *adv*

au•di•ence *n* **1** : formal interview **2** : group of listeners or spectators

au•dio *adj* : relating to sound or its reproduction ~ *n* : television sound

au•dio•vi•su•al *adj* : relating to both hearing and sight

au•dit *vb* : examine financial accounts — **audit** *n* — **au•di•tor** *n*

au•di•tion *n* : tryout performance — **audition** *vb*

au•di•to•ri•um *n, pl* **-ri•ums** *or* **-ria** : room or building used for public performances

au•di•to•ry *adj* : relating to hearing

au•ger *n* : tool for boring

aug•ment *vb* : enlarge or increase — **aug•men•ta•tion** *n*

au•gur *n* : prophet ~ *vb* : predict — **au•gu•ry** *n*

au•gust *adj* : majestic

Au•gust *n* : 8th month of the year having 31 days

auk *n* : stocky diving seabird

aunt *n* **1** : sister of one's father or mother **2** : wife of one's uncle

au•ra *n* **1** : distinctive atmosphere **2** : luminous radiation

au•ral *adj* : relating to the ear or to hearing

au•ri•cle *n* : atrium or ear-shaped pouch in the atrium of the heart

au•ro•ra bo•re•al•is *n* : display of light in the night sky of northern latitudes

aus•pic•es *n pl* : patronage and protection

aus•pi•cious *adj* : favorable

aus•tere *adj* : severe — **aus•tere•ly** *adv* — **aus•ter•i•ty** *n*

au•then•tic *adj* : genuine — **au•then•ti•cal•ly** *adv* — **au•then•tic•i•ty** *n*

au•then•ti•cate *vb* **-cat•ed; -cat•ing** : prove genuine — **au•then•ti•ca•tion** *n*

au•thor *n* **1** : writer **2** : creator — **au•thor•ship** *n*

au•thor•i•tar•i•an *adj* : marked by blind obedience to authority

au•thor•i•ta•tive *adj* : being an authority — **au•thor•i•ta•tive•ly** *adv* **au•thor•i•ta•tive•ness** *n*

au•thor•i•ty *n, pl* **-ties 1** : expert **2** : right, responsibility, or power to influence **3** *pl* : persons in official positions

au•tho•rize *vb* **-rized; -riz•ing** : permit or give official approval for — **au•tho•ri•za•tion** *n*

au•to *n, pl* **autos** : automobile

au•to•bi•og•ra•phy *n* : writer's own life story — **au•to•bi•og•ra•pher** *n* — **au•to•bio•graph•i•cal** *adj*

au•toc•ra•cy *n, pl* **-cies** : government by one person having unlimited power — **au•to•crat** *n* — **au•to•crat•ic** *adj* — **au•to•crat•i•cal•ly** *adv*

au•to•graph *n* : signature ~ *vb* : write one's name on

au•to•mate *vb* **-mat•ed; -mat•ing** : make automatic — **au•to•ma•tion** *n*

au•to•mat•ic *adj* **1** : involuntary **2** : designed to function without human intervention ~ *n* : automatic device (as a firearm) — **au•to•mat•i•cal•ly** *adv*

au•tom•a•ton *n, pl* **-a•tons** *or* **-a•ta** : robot

au•to•mo•bile *n* : 4-wheeled passenger vehicle with its own power source

au•to•mo•tive *adj* : relating to automobiles

au•ton•o•mous *adj* : self-governing — **au•ton•o•mous•ly** *adv* — **au•ton•o•my** *n*

au•top•sy *n, pl* **-sies** : medical examination of a corpse

au•tumn *n* : season between summer and winter — **au•tum•nal** *adj*

aux•il•ia•ry *adj* **1** : being a supplement or reserve **2** : accompanying a main verb form to express person, number, mood, or tense — **auxiliary** *n*

avail *vb* : be of use or make use ~ *n* : use

avail•able *adj* **1** : usable **2** : accessible — **avail•abil•i•ty** *n*

av•a•lanche *n* : mass of sliding or falling snow or rock

av•a•rice *n* : greed — **av•a•ri•cious** *adj*

avenge *vb* **avenged; aveng•ing** : take vengeance for — **aveng•er** *n*

av•e•nue *n* **1** : way of approach **2** : broad street

av•er•age *adj* **1** : being about midway between

extremes **2** : ordinary ~ *vb* **1** : be usually **2** : find the mean of ~ *n* : mean

averse *adj* : feeling dislike or reluctance — **aver•sion** *n*

avert *vb* : turn away

avi•ary *n, pl* **-ar•ies** : place where birds are kept

avi•a•tion *n* : operation or manufacture of airplanes — **avi•a•tor** *n*

av•id *adj* **1** : greedy **2** : enthusiastic — **avid•i•ty** *n* — **av•id•ly** *adv*

av•o•ca•do *n, pl* **-dos** : tropical fruit with green pulp

av•o•ca•tion *n* : hobby

avoid *vb* **1** : keep away from **2** : prevent the occurrence of **3** : refrain from — **avoid•able** *adj* — **avoid•ance** *n*

av•oir•du•pois *n* : system of weight based on the pound of 16 ounces

avow *vb* : declare openly — **avow•al** *n*

await *vb* : wait for

awake *vb* **awoke; awok•en** *or* **awaked; awak•ing** : wake up — **awake** *adj*

awak•en *vb* **-ened; -en•ing** : wake up

award *vb* : give (something won or deserved) ~ *n* **1** : judgment **2** : prize

aware *adj* : having realization or consciousness — **aware•ness** *n*

awash *adv or adj* : flooded

away *adv* **1** : from this or that place or time **2** : out of the way **3** : in another direction **4** : from one's possession ~ *adj* **1** : absent **2** : distant

awe *n* : respectful fear or wonder ~ *vb* **awed; aw•ing** : fill with awe — **awe•some** *adj* — **awe•struck** *adj*

aw•ful *adj* **1** : inspiring awe **2** : extremely disagreeable **3** : very great — **aw•ful•ly** *adv*

awhile *adv* : for a while

awk•ward *adj* **1** : clumsy **2** : embarrassing — **awk•ward•ly** *adv* — **awk•ward•ness** *n*

awl *n* : hole-making tool

aw•ning *n* : window cover

awry *adv or adj* : wrong

ax, axe *n* : chopping tool

ax•i•om *n* : generally accepted truth — **ax•i•om•at•ic** *adj*

ax•is *n, pl* **ax•es** : center of rotation — **ax•i•al** *adj* — **ax•i•al•ly** *adv*

ax•le *n* : shaft on which a wheel revolves

aye *adv* : yes ~ *n* : a vote of yes

aza•lea *n* : rhododendron with funnel-shaped blossoms

az•i•muth *n* : horizontal direction expressed as an angle

azure *n* : blue of the sky — **azure** *adj*

B

b *n, pl* **b's** *or* **bs** : 2d letter of the alphabet

bab•ble *vb* **-bled; -bling 1** : utter meaningless sounds **2** : talk foolishly or too much — **babble** *n* — **bab•bler** *n*

babe *n* : baby

ba•bel *n* : noisy confusion

ba•boon *n* : large Asian or African ape with a doglike muzzle

ba•by *n, pl* **-bies** : very young child ~ *vb* **-bied; -by•ing** : pamper — **baby** *adj* — **ba•by•hood** *n* — **ba•by•ish** *adj*

ba•by–sit *vb* **-sat; -sit•ting** : care for children while parents are away — **baby–sit•ter** *n*

bac•ca•lau•re•ate *n* : bachelor's degree

bac•cha•na•lia *n, pl* **-lia** : drunken orgy — **bac•cha•na•lian** *adj or n*

bach•e•lor *n* **1** : holder of lowest 4-year college degree **2** : unmarried man — **bach•e•lor•hood** *n*

ba•cil•lus *n, pl* **-li** : rod-shaped bacterium — **bac•il•lary** *adj*

back *n* **1** : part of a human or animal body nearest the spine **2** : part opposite the front **3** : player farthest from the opponent's goal ~ *adv* **1** : to or at the back **2** : ago **3** : to or in a former place or state **4** : in reply ~ *adj* **1** : located at the back **2** : not paid on time **3** : moving or working backward **4** : not current ~ *vb* **1** : support **2** : go or cause to go back **3** : form the back of — **back•ache** *n* — **back•er** *n* — **back•ing** *n* — **back•less** *adj* — **back•rest** *n*

back•bite *vb* **-bit; -bit•ten; -bit•ing** : say spiteful things about someone absent — **back•bit•er** *n*

back•bone *n* **1** : bony column in the back that encloses the spinal cord **2** : firm character

back•drop *n* : painted cloth hung across the rear of a stage

back•fire *n* : loud noise from the wrongly timed explosion of fuel in an engine ~ *vb* **1** : make or undergo a backfire **2** : have a result opposite of that intended

back•gam•mon *n* : board game

back•ground *n* **1** : scenery behind something **2** : sum of a person's experience or training

back•hand *n* : stroke (as in tennis) made with the back of the hand turned forward — **backhand** *adj or vb* — **back•hand•ed** *adj*

back•lash *n* : adverse reaction

back•log *n* : accumulation of things to be done — **backlog** *vb*

back·pack *n* : camping pack carried on the back ~ *vb* : hike with a backpack — **back·pack·er** *n*

back·slide *vb* **-slid; -slid** *or* **-slid·den ; -slid·ing** : lapse in morals or religious practice — **back·slid·er** *n*

back·stage *adv or adj* : in or to an area behind a stage

back·up *n* : substitute

back·ward, back·wards *adv* 1 : toward the back 2 : with the back foremost 3 : in a reverse direction 4 : toward an earlier or worse state ~ *adj* 1 : directed, turned, or done backward 2 : retarded in development — **back·ward·ness** *n*

back·woods *n pl* : remote or isolated place

ba·con *n* : salted and smoked meat from a pig

bac·te·ri·um *n, pl* **-ria** : microscopic plant — **bac·te·ri·al** *adj* — **bac·te·ri·o·log·ic, bac·te·ri·o·log·i·cal** *adj* — **bac·te·ri·ol·o·gist** *n* — **bac·te·ri·ol·o·gy** *n*

bad *adj* **worse; worst** 1 : not good 2 : naughty 3 : faulty 4 : spoiled — **bad** *n or adv* — **bad·ly** *adv* — **bad·ness** *n*

bade *past of* BID

badge *n* : symbol of status

bad·ger *n* : burrowing mammal ~ *vb* : harass

bad·min·ton *n* : tennislike game played with a shuttlecock

baf·fle *vb* **-fled; -fling** : perplex ~ *n* : device to alter flow (as of liquid or sound) — **baf·fle·ment** *n*

bag *n* : flexible usu. closable container ~ *vb* **-gg-** 1 : bulge out 2 : put in a bag 3 : catch in hunting

bag·a·telle *n* : trifle

ba·gel *n* : hard doughnut-shaped roll

bag·gage *n* : traveler's bags and belongings

bag·gy *adj* **-gi·er; -est** : puffed out like a bag — **bag·gi·ly** *adv* — **bag·gi·ness** *n*

bag·pipe *n* : musical instrument with a bag, a tube with valves, and sounding pipes — often pl.

¹**bail** *n* : container for scooping water out of a boat — **bail** *vb* — **bail·er** *n*

²**bail** *n* 1 : security given to guarantee a prisoner's appearance in court 2 : release secured by bail ~ *vb* : bring about the release of by giving bail

bai·liff *n* 1 : British sheriff's aide 2 : minor officer of a U.S. court

bai·li·wick *n* : one's special field or domain

bail·out *n* : rescue from financial distress

bait *vb* 1 : harass with dogs usu. for sport 2 : furnish (a hook or trap) with bait ~ *n* : lure esp. for catching animals

bake *vb* **baked; bak·ing** : cook in dry heat esp. in an oven ~ *n* : party featuring baked food — **baker** *n* — **bak·ery** *n* — **bake·shop** *n*

bal·ance *n* 1 : weighing device 2 : counteracting weight, force, or influence 3 : equilibrium 4 : that which remains ~ *vb* **-anced; -anc·ing** 1 : compute the balance 2 : equalize 3 : bring into harmony or proportion — **bal·anced** *adj*

bal·co·ny *n, pl* **-nies** : platform projecting from a wall

bald *adj* 1 : lacking a natural or usual covering (as of hair) 2 : plain — **bald·ing** *adj* — **bald·ly** *adv* — **bald·ness** *n*

bal·der·dash *n* : nonsense

bale *n* : large bundle ~ *vb* **baled; bal·ing** : pack in a bale — **bal·er** *n*

bale·ful *adj* 1 : deadly 2 : ominous

balk *n* : hindrance ~ *vb* 1 : thwart 2 : stop short and refuse to go on — **balky** *adj*

¹**ball** *n* 1 : rounded mass 2 : game played with a ball ~ *vb* : form into a ball

²**ball** *n* : large formal dance — **ball·room** *n*

bal·lad *n* 1 : narrative poem 2 : slow romantic song — **bal·lad·eer** *n*

bal·last *n* : heavy material to steady a ship or balloon ~ *vb* : provide with ballast

bal·le·ri·na *n* : female ballet dancer

bal·let *n* : theatrical dancing

bal·lis·tics *n sing or pl* : science of projectile motion — **ballistic** *adj*

bal·loon *n* : inflated bag ~ *vb* 1 : travel in a balloon 2 : swell out — **bal·loon·ist** *n*

bal·lot *n* 1 : paper used to cast a vote 2 : system of voting ~ *vb* : vote

bal·ly·hoo *n* : publicity — **ballyhoo** *vb*

balm *n* 1 : fragrant healing or soothing preparation 2 : spicy fragrant herb

balmy *adj* **balm·i·er; -est** : gently soothing — **balm·i·ness** *n*

ba·lo·ney *n* : nonsense

bal·sa *n* : very light wood of a tropical tree

bal·sam *n* 1 : aromatic resinous plant substance 2 : balsam-yielding plant — **bal·sam·ic** *adj*

bal·us·ter *n* : upright support for a rail

bal·us·trade *n* : row of balusters topped by a rail

bam·boo *n* : tall tropical grass with strong hollow stems

bam·boo·zle *vb* **-zled; -zling** : deceive

ban *vb* **-nn-** : prohibit ~ *n* : legal prohibition

ba·nal *adj* : ordinary and uninteresting — **ba·nal·i·ty** *n*

ba·nana *n* : elongated fruit of a treelike tropical plant

¹**band** *n* 1 : something that ties or binds 2 : strip or stripe different (as in color) from nearby matter 3 : range of radio wavelengths ~ *vb* 1 : enclose with a band 2 : unite for a common end — **band·ed** *adj* — **band·er** *n*

²**band** *n* 1 : group 2 : musicians playing together

ban·dage *n* : material used esp. in dressing wounds ~ *vb* : dress or cover with a bandage

ban·dan·na, ban·dana *n* : large colored figured handkerchief

ban·dit *n* : outlaw or robber — **ban·dit·ry** *n*

band·stand *n* : stage for band concerts

band·wag·on *n* : candidate, side, or movement gaining support

¹**ban·dy** *vb* **-died; -dy·ing** : exchange in rapid succession

²**bandy** *adj* : curved outward

bane *n* 1 : poison 2 : cause of woe — **bane·ful** *adj*

¹**bang** *vb* : strike, thrust, or move usu. with a loud noise ~ *n* 1 : blow 2 : sudden loud noise ~ *adv* : directly

²**bang** *n* : fringe of short hair over the forehead — usu. pl. ~ *vb* : cut in bangs

ban·gle *n* : bracelet

ban·ish *vb* 1 : force by authority to leave a country 2 : expel — **ban·ish·ment** *n*

ban·is·ter *n* 1 : baluster 2 : handrail

ban·jo *n, pl* **-jos** : stringed instrument with a drumlike body — **banjo·ist** *n*

¹**bank** *n* 1 : piled-up mass 2 : rising ground along a body of water 3 : sideways slope along a curve ~ *vb* 1 : form a bank 2 : cover (as a fire) to keep inactive 3 : incline (an airplane) laterally

²**bank** *n* : tier of objects

³**bank** *n* 1 : money institution 2 : reserve supply ~ *vb* : conduct business in a bank — **bank·book** *n* — **bank·er** *n* — **bank·ing** *n*

bank·rupt *n* : one required by law to forfeit assets to pay off debts — *adj* 1 : legally a bankrupt 2 : lacking something essential — **bankrupt** *vb* — **bank·rupt·cy** *n*

ban·ner *n* : flag — *adj* : excellent

banns *n pl* : announcement in church of a proposed marriage

ban·quet *n* : ceremonial dinner — **bánquet** *vb*

ban·shee *n* : wailing female spirit that foretells death

ban·tam *n* : miniature domestic fowl

ban·ter *n* : good-natured joking — **banter** *vb*

ban·yan *n* : large tree that grows new trunks from the limbs

bap·tism *n* : Christian rite signifying spiritual cleansing — **bap·tis·mal** *adj*

bap·tize *vb* **-tized; -tiz·ing** : administer baptism to

bar *n* 1 : long narrow object used esp. as a lever, fastening, or support 2 : barrier 3 : body of practicing lawyers 4 : wide stripe 5 : food counter 6 : place where liquor is served 7 : vertical line across the musical staff ~ *vb* **-rr-** 1 : obstruct with a bar 2 : shut out 3 : prohibit ~ *prep* : excluding — **barred** *adj* — **bar·room** *n* — **bar·tend·er** *n*

barb *n* : sharp projection pointing backward — **barbed** *adj*

bar·bar·ian *adj* 1 : relating to people considered backward 2 : not refined — **barbarian** *n*

bar·bar·ic *adj* : barbarian

bar·ba·rous *adj* 1 : lacking refinement 2 : mercilessly cruel — **bar·bar·ism** *n* — **bar·bar·i·ty** *n* — **bar·ba·rous·ly** *adv*

bar·be·cue *n* : gathering at which barbecued food is served ~ *vb* **-cued; -cu·ing** : cook over hot coals or on a spit often with a highly seasoned sauce

bar·ber *n* : one who cuts hair

bar·bi·tu·rate *n* : sedative or hypnotic drug

bard *n* : poet

bare *adj* **bar·er; bar·est** 1 : naked 2 : not concealed 3 : empty 4 : leaving nothing to spare 5 : plain ~ *vb* **bared; bar·ing** : make or lay bare — **bare·foot, bare·foot·ed** *adv or adj* — **bare·hand·ed** *adv or adj* — **bare·head·ed** *adv or adj* — **bare·ly** *adv* — **bare·ness** *n*

bare·back, bare·backed *adv or adj* : without a saddle

bare·faced *adj* : open and esp. brazen

bar·gain *n* 1 : agreement 2 : something bought for less than its value ~ *vb* 1 : negotiate 2 : barter

barge *n* : broad flat-bottomed boat ~ *vb* **barged; barg·ing** : move rudely or clumsily — **barge·man** *n*

bari·tone *n* : male voice between bass and tenor

bar·i·um *n* : silver-white metallic chemical element

¹**bark** *vb* 1 : make the sound of a dog 2 : speak in a loud curt tone ~ *n* : sound of a barking dog

²**bark** *n* : tough corky outer covering of a woody stem or root ~ *vb* : remove bark or skin from

³**bark** *n* : sailing ship with a fore-and-aft rear sail

bark·er *n* : one who calls out to attract people to a show

bar·ley *n* : cereal grass or its seeds

barn *n* : building for keeping hay or livestock — **barn·yard** *n*

bar·na·cle *n* : marine crustacean

barn·storm *vb* : tour through rural districts giving performances

ba·rom·e·ter *n* : instrument for measuring atmospheric pressure — **baro·met·ric** *adj*

bar·on *n* : British peer — **bar·on·age** *n* — **ba·ro·ni·al** *adj* — **bar·ony** *n*

bar·on·ess *n* 1 : baron's wife 2 : woman holding a baronial title

bar·on·et *n* : man holding a rank between a baron and a knight — **bar·on·et·cy** *n*

ba·roque *adj* : elaborately ornamented

bar·racks *n sing or pl* : soldiers' housing

bar·ra·cu·da *n, pl* **-da** *or* **-das** : large predatory sea fish

bar·rage *n* : heavy artillery fire

bar·rel *n* 1 : closed cylindrical container 2 : amount held by a barrel 3 : cylindrical part ~ *vb* **-reled** *or* **-relled; -rel·ing** *or* **-rel·ling** 1 : pack in a barrel 2 : move at high speed — **bar·reled** *adj*

bar·ren *adj* 1 : unproductive of life 2 : uninteresting — **bar·ren·ness** *n*

bar·rette *n* : clasp for a woman's hair

bar·ri·cade *n* : barrier — **barricade** *vb*

bar•ri•er *n* : something that separates or obstructs

bar•ring *prep* : omitting

bar•ris•ter *n* : British trial lawyer

bar•row *n* : wheelbarrow

bar•ter *vb* : trade by exchange of goods — **barter** *n*

ba•salt *n* : dark fine-grained igneous rock — **ba•sal•tic** *adj*

¹base *n, pl* **bas•es** **1** : bottom **2** : fundamental part **3** : beginning point **4** : supply source of a force **5** : compound that reacts with an acid to form a salt ~ *vb* **based; bas•ing** : establish — **base•less** *adj*

²base *adj* **bas•er; bas•est** **1** : inferior **2** : contemptible — **base•ly** *adv* — **base•ness** *n*

base•ball *n* : game played with a bat and ball by 2 teams

base•ment *n* : part of a building below ground level

bash *vb* : strike violently ~ *n* : heavy blow

bash•ful *adj* : self-conscious — **bash•ful•ness** *n*

ba•sic *adj* **1** : relating to or forming the base or essence **2** : relating to a chemical base — **ba•si•cally** *adv* — **ba•sic•i•ty** *n*

ba•sil *n* : aromatic mint

ba•sil•i•ca *n* : important church or cathedral

ba•sin *n* **1** : large bowl or pan **2** : region drained by a river

ba•sis *n, pl* **ba•ses** **1** : something that supports **2** : fundamental principle

bask *vb* : enjoy pleasant warmth

bas•ket *n* : woven container — **bas•ket•ful** *n*

bas•ket•ball *n* : game played with a ball on a court by 2 teams

bas—re•lief *n* : flat sculpture with slightly raised design

¹bass *n, pl* **bass** *or* **bass•es** : spiny-finned sport and food fish

²bass *n* **1** : deep tone **2** : lowest choral voice

bas•set hound *n* : short-legged dog with long ears

bas•si•net *n* : baby's bed

bas•soon *n* : low-pitched wind instrument

bas•tard *n* **1** : illegitimate child **2** : offensive person ~ *adj* **1** : illegitimate **2** : inferior — **bas•tard•ize** *vb* — **bas•tardy** *n*

¹baste *vb* **bast•ed; bast•ing** : sew temporarily with long stitches

²baste *vb* **bast•ed; bast•ing** : moisten at intervals while cooking

bas•tion *n* : fortified position

¹bat *n* **1** : stick or club **2** : sharp blow ~ *vb* **-tt-** : hit with a bat

²bat *n* : small flying mammal

³bat *vb* **-tt-** : wink or blink

batch *n* : quantity used or produced at one time

bate *vb* **bat•ed; bat•ing** : moderate or reduce

bath *n, pl* **baths** **1** : a washing of the body **2** : water for washing the body **3** : liquid in which something is immersed **4** : bathroom **5** : large financial loss — **bath•tub** *n*

bathe *vb* **bathed; bath•ing** **1** : wash in liquid **2** : flow against so as to wet **3** : shine light over **4** : take a bath or a swim — **bath•er** *n*

bath•robe *n* : robe worn around the house

bath•room *n* : room with a bathtub or shower and usu. a sink and toilet

ba•tiste *n* : fine sheer fabric

ba•ton *n* : musical conductor's stick

bat•tal•ion *n* : military unit composed of a headquarters and two or more companies

bat•ten *n* : strip of wood used to seal or reinforce ~ *vb* : furnish or fasten with battens

¹bat•ter *vb* : beat or damage with repeated blows

²batter *n* : mixture of flour and liquid

³batter *n* : player who bats

bat•tery *n, pl* **-ter•ies** **1** : illegal beating of a person **2** : group of artillery guns **3** : group of electric cells

bat•ting *n* : layers of cotton or wool for stuffing

bat•tle *n* : military fighting ~ *vb* **-tled; -tling** : engage in battle — **battle•field** *n*

bat•tle—ax *n* : long-handled ax formerly used as a weapon

bat•tle•ment *n* : parapet on top of a wall

bat•tle•ship *n* : heavily armed warship

bat•ty *adj* **-ti•er; -est** : crazy

bau•ble *n* : trinket

bawdy *adj* **bawd•i•er; -est** : obscene or lewd — **bawd•i•ly** *adv* — **bawd•i•ness** *n*

bawl *vb* : cry loudly ~ *n* : long loud cry

¹bay *adj* : reddish brown ~ *n* : bay-colored animal

²bay *n* : European laurel

³bay *n* **1** : compartment **2** : area projecting out from a building and containing a window (**bay window**)

⁴bay *vb* : bark with deep long tones ~ *n* **1** : position of one unable to escape danger **2** : baying of dogs

⁵bay *n* : body of water smaller than a gulf and nearly surrounded by land

bay•ber•ry *n* : shrub bearing small waxy berries

bay•o•net *n* : dagger that fits on the end of a rifle ~ *vb* **-net•ed; -net•ing** : stab with a bayonet

bay•ou *n* : creek flowing through marshy land

ba•zaar *n* **1** : market **2** : fair for charity

ba•zoo•ka *n* : weapon that shoots armor-piercing rockets

BB *n* : small shot pellet

be *vb* **was, were; been; be•ing; am, is, are** **1** : equal **2** : exist **3** : occupy a certain place **4** : occur ~ *verbal auxiliary* — used to show continuous action or to form the passive voice

beach *n* : sandy shore of a sea, lake, or river ~ *vb* : drive ashore

beach•comb•er *n* : one who searches the shore for useful objects

beach•head *n* : shore area held by an attacking force in an invasion

bea•con *n* : guiding or warning light or signal

bead *n* : small round body esp. strung on a thread ~ *vb* : form into a bead — **bead•ing** *n* — **beady** *adj*

bea•gle *n* : small short-legged hound

beak *n* : bill of a bird — **beaked** *adj*

bea•ker *n* **1** : large drinking cup **2** : laboratory vessel

beam *n* **1** : large long piece of timber or metal **2** : ray of light **3** : directed radio signals for the guidance of pilots ~ *vb* **1** : send out light **2** : smile **3** : aim a radio broadcast

bean *n* : edible plant seed borne in pods

¹bear *n, pl* **bears** **1** *or pl* **bear** : large heavy mammal with shaggy hair **2** : gruff or sullen person — **bear•ish** *adj*

²bear *vb* **bore; borne; bear•ing** **1** : carry **2** : give birth to or produce **3** : endure **4** : press **5** : go in an indicated direction — **bear•able** *adj* — **bear•er** *n*

beard *n* **1** : facial hair on a man **2** : tuft like a beard ~ *vb* : confront boldly — **beard•ed** *adj* — **beard•less** *adj*

bear•ing *n* **1** : way of carrying oneself **2** : supporting object or purpose **3** : significance **4** : machine part in which another part turns **5** : direction with respect esp. to compass points

beast *n* **1** : animal **2** : brutal person — **beast•li•ness** *n* — **beast•ly** *adj*

beat *vb* **beat; beat•en** *or* **beat; beat•ing** **1** : strike repeatedly **2** : defeat **3** : act or arrive before **4** : throb ~ *n* **1** : single stroke or pulsation **2** : rhythmic stress in poetry or music ~ *adj* : exhausted — **beat•er** *n*

be•atif•ic *adj* : blissful

be•at•i•fy *vb* **-fied; -fy•ing** : make happy or blessed — **be•at•i•fi•ca•tion** *n*

be•at•i•tude *n* : saying in the Sermon on the

Mount (Matthew 5:3-12) beginning "Blessed are"

beau *n, pl* **beaux** *or* **beaus** : suitor

beau•ty *n, pl* **-ties** : qualities that please the senses or mind — **beau•te•ous** *adj* — **beau•te•ous•ly** *adv* — **beau•ti•fi•ca•tion** *n* — **beau•ti•fi•er** *n* — **beau•ti•ful** *adj* — **beau•ti•ful•ly** *adv* — **beau•ti•fy** *vb*

bea•ver *n* : large fur-bearing rodent

be•cause *conj* : for the reason that

because of *prep* : by reason of

beck *n* : summons

beck•on *vb* : summon esp. by a nod or gesture

be•come *vb* **-came; -come; -com•ing** **1** : come to be **2** : be suitable — **be•com•ing** *adj* — **be•com•ing•ly** *adv*

bed *n* **1** : piece of furniture to sleep on **2** : flat or level surface ~ *vb* **-dd-** : put or go to bed — **bed•spread** *n*

bed•bug *n* : wingless bloodsucking insect

bed•clothes *n pl* : bedding

bed•ding *n* **1** : sheets and blankets for a bed **2** : soft material (as hay) for an animal's bed

be•deck *vb* : adorn

be•dev•il *vb* : harass

bed•lam *n* : uproar and confusion

be•drag•gled *adj* : dirty and disordered

bed•rid•den *adj* : kept in bed by illness

bed•rock *n* : solid subsurface rock — **bedrock** *adj*

¹bee *n* : 4-winged honey-producing insect — **bee•hive** *n* — **bee•keep•er** *n* — **bees•wax** *n*

²bee *n* : neighborly work session

beech *n, pl* **beech•es** *or* **beech** : tree with smooth gray bark and edible nuts (**beech•nuts**) — **beech•en** *adj*

beef *n, pl* **beefs** *or* **beeves** : flesh of a steer, cow, or bull ~ *vb* : strengthen — used with *up* — **beef•steak** *n*

bee•line *n* : straight course

been *past part of* BE

beep *n* : short usu. high-pitched warning sound — **beep** *vb* — **beep•er** *n*

beer *n* : alcoholic drink brewed from malt and hops — **beery** *adj*

beet *n* : garden root vegetable

bee•tle *n* : 4-winged insect

be•fall *vb* **-fell; -fall•en** : happen to

be•fit *vb* : be suitable to

be•fore *adv* **1** : in front **2** : earlier ~ *prep* **1** : in front of **2** : earlier than ~ *conj* : earlier than

be•fore•hand *adv or adj* : in advance

be•friend *vb* : act as friend to

be•fud•dle *vb* : confuse

beg *vb* **-gg-** : ask earnestly

be•get *vb* **-got; -got•ten** *or* **-got; -get•ting** : become the father of

beg•gar *n* : one that begs ~ *vb* : make poor — **beg•gar•ly** *adj* — **beg•gary** *n*

be•gin *vb* **-gan; -gun; -gin•ning** **1** : start **2** : come into being — **be•gin•ner** *n*

be•gone *vb* : go away

be•go•nia *n* : tropical herb with waxy flowers

be•grudge *vb* **1** : concede reluctantly **2** : look upon disapprovingly

be•guile *vb* **-guiled; -guil•ing** **1** : deceive **2** : amuse

be•half *n* : benefit

be•have *vb* **-haved; -hav•ing** : act in a certain way

be•hav•ior *n* : way of behaving — **be•hav•ior•al** *adj*

be•head *vb* : cut off the head of

be•hest *n* : command

be•hind *adv* : at the back ~ *prep* **1** : in back of **2** : less than **3** : supporting

be•hold *vb* **-held; -hold•ing** : see — **be•hold•er** *n*

be•hold•en *adj* : indebted

be·hoove *vb* **-hooved; -hoov·ing** : be necessary for

beige *n* : yellowish brown — **beige** *adj*

be·ing *n* 1 : existence 2 : living thing

be·la·bor *vb* : carry on to absurd lengths

be·lat·ed *adj* : delayed

belch *vb* 1 : expel stomach gas orally 2 : emit forcefully — **belch** *n*

be·lea·guer *vb* 1 : besiege 2 : harass

bel·fry *n, pl* **-fries** : bell tower

be·lie *vb* **-lied; -ly·ing** 1 : misrepresent 2 : prove false

be·lief *n* 1 : trust 2 : something believed

be·lieve *vb* **-lieved; -liev·ing** 1 : trust in 2 : accept as true 3 : hold as an opinion — **be·liev·able** *adj* — **be·liev·ably** *adv* — **be·liev·er** *n*

be·lit·tle *vb* **-lit·tled; -lit·tling** 1 : disparage 2 : make seem less

bell *n* : hollow metallic device that rings when struck ~ *vb* : provide with a bell

bel·la·don·na *n* : poisonous herb yielding a drug

belle *n* : beautiful woman

bel·li·cose *adj* : pugnacious — **bel·li·cos·i·ty** *n*

bel·lig·er·ent *adj* 1 : waging war 2 : truculent — **bel·lig·er·ence** *n* — **bel·lig·er·en·cy** *n* — **belligerent** *n*

bel·low *vb* : make a loud deep roar or shout — **bellow** *n*

bel·lows *n sing or pl* : device with sides that can be compressed to expel air

bell·weth·er *n* : leader

bel·ly *n, pl* **-lies** : abdomen ~ *vb* **-lied; -ly·ing** : bulge

be·long *vb* 1 : be suitable 2 : be owned 3 : be a part of

be·long·ings *n pl* : possessions

be·loved *adj* : dearly loved — **beloved** *n*

be·low *adv* : in or to a lower place ~ *prep* : lower than

belt *n* 1 : strip (as of leather) worn about the waist 2 : endless band to impart motion 3 : distinct region ~ *vb* 1 : put a belt around 2 : thrash

be·moan *vb* : lament

be·muse *vb* : confuse

bench *n* 1 : long seat 2 : judge's seat 3 : court

bend *vb* **bent; bending** 1 : curve or cause a change of shape in 2 : turn in a certain direction ~ *n* 1 : act of bending 2 : curve

be·neath *adv or prep* : below

bene·dic·tion *n* : closing blessing

bene·fac·tor *n* : one who gives esp. charitable aid

be·nef·i·cence *n* : quality of doing good — **be·nef·i·cent** *adj*

ben·e·fi·cial *adj* : being of benefit — **ben·e·fi·cial·ly** *adv*

ben·e·fi·cia·ry *n, pl* **-ries** : one who receives benefits

ben·e·fit *n* 1 : something that does good 2 : help 3 : fund-raising event — **benefit** *vb*

be·nev·o·lence *n* 1 : charitable nature 2 : act of kindness — **be·nev·o·lent** *adj* — **be·nev·o·lent·ly** *adv*

be·night·ed *adj* : ignorant

be·nign *adj* 1 : gentle or kindly 2 : not malignant — **be·nig·ni·ty** *n*

be·nig·nant *adj* : benign

bent *n* : aptitude or interest

be·numb *vb* : make numb esp. by cold

ben·zene *n* : colorless flammable liquid

be·queath *vb* 1 : give by will 2 : hand down

be·quest *n* : something bequeathed

be·rate *vb* : scold harshly

be·reaved *adj* : suffering the death of a loved one ~ *n, pl* **bereaved** : one who is bereaved — **be·reave·ment** *n*

be·reft *adj* : deprived of or lacking something

be·ret *n* : round soft visorless cap

beri·beri *n* : thiamine-deficiency disease

berm *n* : bank of earth

ber·ry *n, pl* **-ries** : small pulpy fruit

ber·serk *adj* : crazed — **berserk** *adv*

berth *n* 1 : place where a ship is anchored 2 : place to sit or sleep esp. on a ship 3 : job ~ *vb* : to bring or come into a berth

ber·yl *n* : light-colored silicate mineral

be·seech *vb* **-sought** *or* **-seeched; -seech·ing** : entreat

be·set *vb* 1 : harass 2 : hem in

be·side *prep* 1 : by the side of 2 : besides

be·sides *adv* 1 : in addition 2 : moreover ~ *prep* 1 : other than 2 : in addition to

be·siege *vb* : lay siege to — **be·sieg·er** *n*

be·smirch *vb* : soil

be·sot *vb* **-tt-** : become drunk

be·speak *vb* **-spoke; -spo·ken; -speak·ing** 1 : address 2 : indicate

best *adj, superlative of* GOOD 1 : excelling all others 2 : most productive 3 : largest ~ *adv, superlative of* WELL 1 : in the best way 2 : most ~ *n* : one that is best ~ *vb* : outdo

bes·tial *adj* 1 : relating to beasts 2 : brutish — **bes·ti·al·i·ty** *n*

be·stir *vb* : rouse to action

best man *n* : chief male attendant at a wedding

be·stow *vb* : give — **be·stow·al** *n*

bet *n* 1 : something risked or pledged on the outcome of a contest 2 : the making of a bet ~ *vb* **het; bet·ting** 1 : risk (as money) on an outcome 2 : make a bet with

be·tide *vb* : happen to

be·to·ken *vb* : give an indication of

be·tray *vb* 1 : seduce 2 : report or reveal to an enemy by treachery 3 : abandon 4 : prove unfaithful to 5 : reveal unintentionally — **be·tray·al** *n* — **be·tray·er** *n*

be·troth *vb* : promise to marry — **be·troth·al** *n* — **be·trothed** *n*

bet·ter *adj, comparative of* GOOD 1 : more than half 2 : improved in health 3 : of higher quality ~ *adv, comparative of* WELL 1 : in a superior manner 2 : more ~ *n* 1 : one that is better 2 : advantage ~ *vb* 1 : improve 2 : surpass — **bet·ter·ment** *n*

bet·tor, bet·ter *n* : one who bets

be·tween *prep* 1 — used to show two things considered together 2 : in the space separating 3 — used to indicate a comparison or choice ~ *adv* : in an intervening space or interval

bev·el *n* : slant on an edge ~ *vb* **-eled** *or* **-elled; -el·ing** *or* **-el·ling** 1 : cut or shape to a bevel 2 : incline

bev·er·age *n* : drink

bevy *n, pl* **bev·ies** : large group

be·wail *vb* : lament

be·ware *vb* : be cautious

be·wil·der *vb* : confuse — **be·wil·der·ment** *n*

be·witch *vb* 1 : affect by witchcraft 2 : charm — **be·witch·ment** *n*

be·yond *adv* 1 : farther 2 : besides ~ *prep* 1 : on or to the farther side of 2 : out of the reach of 3 : besides

bi- *prefix* 1 : two 2 : coming or occurring every two 3 : twice, doubly, or on both sides

bicolored	bifunctional
biconcave	bimetal
biconcavity	bimetallic
biconvex	binational
biconvexity	biparental
bicultural	bipolar
bidirectional	biracial

bi·an·nu·al *adj* : occurring twice a year — **bi·an·nu·al·ly** *adv*

bi·as *n* 1 : line diagonal to the grain of a fabric 2 : prejudice ~ *vb* **-ased** *or* **-assed; -as·ing** *or* **-as·sing** : prejudice

bib *n* : shield tied under the chin to protect the clothes while eating

Bi·ble *n* 1 : sacred scriptures of Christians 2 : sacred scriptures of Judaism or of some other religion — **bib·li·cal** *adj*

bib·li·og·ra·phy *n, pl* **-phies** : list of writings on a subject or of an author — **bib·li·og·ra·pher** *n* — **bib·li·o·graph·ic** *adj*

bi·cam·er·al *adj* : having 2 legislative chambers

bi·car·bon·ate *n* : acid carbonate

bi·cen·ten·ni·al *n* : 200th anniversary — **bicentennial** *adj*

bi·ceps *n* : large muscle of the upper arm

bick·er *vb or n* : squabble

bi·cus·pid *n* : double-pointed tooth

bi·cy·cle *n* : 2-wheeled vehicle moved by pedaling ~ *vb* **-cled; -cling** : ride a bicycle — **bi·cy·cler** *n* **bi·cy·clist** *n*

bid *vb* **bade** *or* **bid; bid·den** *or* **bid; bid·ding** 1 : order 2 : invite 3 : express 4 : make a bid ~ *n* 1 : act of bidding 2 : buyer's proposed price — **bid·da·ble** *adj* — **bid·der** *n*

bide *vb* **bode** *or* **bid·ed; bided; bid·ing** 1 : wait 2 : dwell

bi·en·ni·al *adj* 1 : occurring once in 2 years 2 : lasting 2 years — **biennial** *n* — **bi·en·ni·al·ly** *adv*

bier *n* : stand for a coffin

bi·fo·cals *n pl* : eyeglasses that correct for near and distant vision

big *adj* **-gg-** : large in size, amount, or scope — **big·ness** *n*

big·a·my *n* : marrying one person while still married to another — **big·a·mist** *n* — **big·a·mous** *adj*

big·horn *n, pl* **-horn** *or* **-horns** : wild mountain sheep

bight *n* 1 : loop of a rope 2 : bay

big·ot *n* : one who is intolerant of others — **big·ot·ed** *adj* — **big·ot·ry** *n*

big shot *n* : important person

big·wig *n* : big shot

bike *n* : bicycle or motorcycle

bi·ki·ni *n* : woman's brief 2-piece bathing suit

bi·lat·er·al *adj* : involving 2 sides — **bi·lat·er·al·ly** *adv*

bile *n* 1 : greenish liver secretion that aids digestion 2 : bad temper

bi·lin·gual *adj* : using 2 languages

bil·ious *adj* : irritable — **bil·ious·ness** *n*

bilk *vb* : cheat

¹bill *n* : jaws of a bird together with their horny covering ~ *vb* : caress fondly — **billed** *adj*

²bill *n* 1 : draft of a law 2 : list of things to be paid for 3 : printed advertisement 4 : piece of paper money ~ *vb* : submit a bill or account to

bill·board *n* : surface for displaying advertising bills

bil·let *n* : soldiers' quarters ~ *vb* : lodge in a billet

bill·fold *n* : wallet

bil·liards *n* : game of driving balls into one another or into pockets on a table

bil·lion *n, pl* **billions** *or* **billion** : 1000 millions — **billion** *adj* — **bil·lionth** *adj or n*

bil·low *n* 1 : great wave 2 : rolling mass ~ *vb* : swell out — **bil·lowy** *adj*

billy goat *n* : male goat

bin *n* : storage box

bi·na·ry *adj* : consisting of 2 things — **binary** *n*

bind *vb* **bound; bind·ing** 1 : tie 2 : obligate 3 : unite into a mass 4 : bandage — **bind·er** *n* — **binding** *n*

binge *n* : spree

bin·go *n, pl* **-gos** : game of covering numbers on a card

bin·oc·u·lar *adj* : of or relating to both eyes ~ *n* : binocular optical instrument — usu. pl.

bio·chem·is·try *n* : chemistry dealing with

organisms — **bio•chemi•cal** *adj or n* — **bio•chem•ist** *n*

bio•de•grad•able *adj* : able to be reduced to harmless products by organisms — **bio•de•grad•abil•i•ty** *n* — **bio•deg•ra•da•tion** *n* — **bio•de•grade** *vb*

bi•og•ra•phy *n, pl* **-phies** : written history of a person's life — **bi•og•ra•pher** *n* — **bio•graph•i•cal** *adj*

bi•ol•o•gy *n* : science of living beings and life processes — **bi•o•log•ic , bi•o•log•i•cal** *adj* — **bi•ol•o•gist** *n*

bio•phys•ics *n* : application of physics to biological problems — **bio•phys•i•cal** *adj* — **bio•phys•i•cist** *n*

bi•op•sy *n, pl* **-sies** : removal of live bodily tissue for examination

bio•tech•nol•o•gy *n* : manufacture of products using techniques involving the manipulation of DNA

bi•par•ti•san *adj* : involving members of 2 parties

bi•ped *n* : 2-footed animal

birch *n* : deciduous tree with close-grained wood — **birch, birch•en** *adj*

bird *n* : warm-blooded egg-laying vertebrate with wings and feathers — **bird•bath** *n* — **bird•house** *n* — **bird•seed** *n*

bird's–eye *adj* 1 : seen from above 2 : cursory

birth *n* 1 : act or fact of being born or of producing young 2 : origin — **birth•day** *n* — **birth•place** *n* — **birth•rate** *n*

birth•mark *n* :.unusual blemish on the skin at birth

birth•right *n* : something one is entitled to by birth

bis•cuit *n* : small bread made with leavening other than yeast

bi•sect *vb* : divide into 2 parts — **bi•sec•tion** *n* — **bi•sec•tor** *n*

bish•op *n* : clergy member higher than a priest

bish•op•ric *n* 1 : diocese 2 : office of bishop

bis•muth *n* : heavy brittle metallic chemical element

bi•son *n, pl* **-son** : large shaggy wild ox of central U.S.

bis•tro *n, pl* **-tros** : small restaurant or bar

¹**bit** *n* 1 : part of a bridle that goes in a horse's mouth 2 : drilling tool

²**bit** *n* 1 : small piece or quantity 2 : small degree

bitch *n* : female dog ~ *vb* : complain

bite *vb* **bit; bit•ten; bit•ing** 1 : to grip or cut with teeth or jaws 2 : dig in or grab and hold 3 : sting 4 : take bait ~ *n* 1 : act of biting 2 : bit of food 3 : wound made by biting — **biting** *adj*

bit•ter *adj* 1 : having an acrid lingering taste 2 : intense or severe 3 : extremely harsh or resentful — **bit•ter•ly** *adv* — **bit•ter•ness** *n*

bit•tern *n* : small heron

bi•tu•mi•nous coal *n* : coal that yields volatile waste matter when heated

bi•valve *n* : animal (as a clam) with a shell of 2 parts — **bivalve** *adj*

biv•ouac *n* : temporary camp ~ *vb* **-ouacked; -ouack•ing** : camp

bi•zarre *adj* : very strange — **bi•zarre•ly** *adv*

blab *vb* **-bb-** : talk too much

black *adj* 1 : of the color black 2 : Negro 3 : soiled 4 : lacking light 5 : wicked or evil 6 : gloomy ~ *n* 1 : black pigment or dye 2 : something black 3 : color of least lightness 4 : person of a dark-skinned race ~ *vb* : blacken — **black•ing** *n* — **black•ish** *adj* — **black•ly** *adv* — **black•ness** *n*

black–and–blue *adj* : darkly discolored from bruising

black•ball *vb* 1 : ostracize 2 : boycott — **black•ball** *n*

black•ber•ry *n* : black or purple fruit of a bramble

black•bird *n* : bird of which the male is largely or wholly black

black•board *n* : dark surface for writing on with chalk

black•en *vb* 1 : make or become black 2 : defame

black•guard *n* : scoundrel

black•head *n* : small dark oily mass plugging the outlet of a skin gland

black hole *n* : invisible extremely massive celestial object

black•jack *n* 1 : flexible leather-covered club 2 : card game ~ *vb* : hit with a blackjack

black•list *n* : list of persons to be punished or boycotted — **blacklist** *vb*

black•mail *n* 1 : extortion by threat of exposure 2 : something extorted by blackmail — **blackmail** *vb* — **black•mail•er** *n*

black•out *n* 1 : darkness due to electrical failure 2 : brief fainting spell — **black out** *vb*

black•smith *n* : one who forges iron

black•top *n* : dark tarry material for surfacing roads — **blacktop** *vb*

blad•der *n* : sac into which urine passes from the kidneys

blade *n* 1 : leaf esp. of grass 2 : something resembling the flat part of a leaf 3 : cutting part of an instrument or tool — **blad•ed** *adj*

blame *vb* **blamed; blam•ing** 1 : find fault with 2 : hold responsible or responsible for — **blam•able** *adj* — **blame** *n* — **blame•less** *adj* — **blame•less•ly** *adv* — **blame•wor•thi•ness** *n* — **blame•worthy** *adj*

blanch *vb* : make or become white or pale

bland *adj* 1 : smooth in manner 2 : soothing 3 : tasteless — **bland•ly** *adv* — **bland•ness** *n*

blan•dish•ment *n* : flattering or coaxing speech or act

blank *adj* 1 : showing or causing a dazed look 2 : lacking expression 3 : empty 4 : free from writing 5 : downright ~ *n* 1 : an empty space 2 : form with spaces to write in 3 : unfinished form (as of a key) 4 : cartridge with no bullet ~ *vb* : cover or close up — **blank•ly** *adv* — **blank•ness** *n*

blan•ket *n* 1 : heavy covering for a bed 2 : covering layer ~ *vb* : cover ~ *adj* : applying to a group

blare *vb* **blared; blar•ing** : make a loud harsh sound — **blare** *n*

blar•ney *n* : skillful flattery

bla•sé *adj* : indifferent to pleasure or excitement

blas•pheme *vb* **-phemed; -phem•ing** : speak blasphemy — **blas•phem•er** *n*

blas•phe•my *n, pl* **-mies** : irreverence toward God or anything sacred — **blas•phe•mous** *adj*

blast *n* 1 : violent gust of wind 2 : explosion ~ *vb* : shatter by or as if by explosive — **blast off** *vb* : take off esp. in a rocket

bla•tant *adj* : offensively showy — **bla•tan•cy** *n* — **bla•tant•ly** *adv*

¹**blaze** *n* 1 : fire 2 : intense direct light 3 : strong display ~ *vb* **blazed; blaz•ing** : burn or shine brightly

²**blaze** *n* 1 : white stripe on an animal's face 2 : trail marker esp. on a tree ~ *vb* **blazed; blaz•ing** : mark with blazes

blaz•er *n* : sports jacket

bleach *vb* : whiten — **bleach** *n*

bleach•ers *n sing or pl* : uncovered stand for spectators

bleak *adj* 1 : desolately barren 2 : lacking cheering qualities — **bleak•ish** *adj* — **bleak•ly** *adv* — **bleak•ness** *n*

blear *adj* : dim with water or tears

bleary *adj* : dull or dimmed esp. from fatigue

bleat *n* : cry of a sheep or goat or a sound like it — **bleat** *vb*

bleed *vb* **bled; bleed•ing** 1 : lose or shed blood 2 : feel distress 3 : flow from a wound 4 : draw fluid from 5 : extort money from — **bleed•er** *n*

blem•ish *vb* : spoil by a flaw ~ *n* : noticeable flaw

¹**blench** *vb* : flinch

²**blench** *vb* : grow or make pale

blend *vb* 1 : mix thoroughly 2 : combine into an integrated whole — **blend** *n* — **blend•er** *n*

bless *vb* **blessed; bless•ing** 1 : consecrate by religious rite 2 : invoke divine care for 3 : make happy — **bless•ed, blest** *adj* — **bless•ed•ly** *adv* — **bless•ed•ness** *n* — **bless•ing** *n*

blew *past of* BLOW

blight *n* 1 : plant disorder marked by withering or an organism causing it 2 : harmful influence 3 : deteriorated condition ~ *vb* : affect with or suffer from blight

blimp *n* : airship holding form by pressure of contained gas

blind *adj* 1 : lacking or quite deficient in ability to see 2 : not intelligently controlled 3 : having no way out ~ *vb* 1 : to make blind 2 : dazzle ~ *n* 1 : something to conceal or darken 2 : place of concealment — **blind•ly** *adv* — **blind•ness** *n*

blind•fold *vb* : cover the eyes of — **blindfold** *n*

blink *vb* 1 : wink 2 : shine intermittently ~ *n* : wink

blink•er *n* : a blinking light

bliss *n* 1 : complete happiness 2 : heaven or paradise — **bliss•ful** *adj* — **bliss•ful•ly** *adv*

blis•ter *n* 1 : raised area of skin containing watery fluid 2 : raised or swollen spot ~ *vb* : develop or cause blisters

blithe *adj* **blith•er; blith•est** : cheerful — **blithe•ly** *adv* — **blithe•some** *adj*

blitz *n* 1 : series of air raids 2 : fast intensive campaign — **blitz** *vb*

bliz•zard *n* : severe snowstorm

bloat *vb* : swell

blob *n* : small lump or drop

bloc *n* : group working together

block *n* 1 : solid piece 2 : frame enclosing a pulley 3 : quantity considered together 4 : large building divided into separate units 5 : a city square or the distance along one of its sides 6 : obstruction 7 : interruption of a bodily or mental function ~ *vb* : obstruct or hinder

block•ade *n* : isolation of a place usu. by troops or ships — **block•ade** *vb* — **block•ad•er** *n*

block•head *n* : stupid person

blond, blonde *adj* 1 : fair in complexion 2 : of a light color — **blond, blonde** *n*

blood *n* 1 : red liquid that circulates in the heart, arteries, and veins of animals 2 : lifeblood 3 : lineage — **blood•ed** *adj* — **blood•less** *adj* — **blood•stain** *n* — **blood•stained** *adj* — **blood•suck•er** *n* — **blood•suck•ing** *n* — **bloody** *adj*

blood•cur•dling *adj* : terrifying

blood•hound *n* : large hound with a keen sense of smell

blood•mo•bile *n* : truck for collecting blood from donors

blood•shed *n* : slaughter

blood•shot *adj* : inflamed to redness

blood•stream *n* : blood in a circulatory system

blood•thirsty *adj* : eager to shed blood — **blood•thirst•i•ly** *adv* — **blood•thirst•i•ness** *n*

bloom *n* 1 : flower 2 : period of flowering 3 : fresh or healthy look ~ *vb* 1 : yield flowers 2 : mature — **bloomy** *adj*

bloo•mers *n pl* : woman's underwear of short loose trousers

bloop•er *n* : public blunder

blos•som *n or vb* : flower

blot *n* 1 : stain 2 : blemish ~ *vb* **-tt-** 1 : spot 2 : dry with absorbent paper — **blot•ter** *n*

blotch *n* : large spot — **blotch** *vb* — **blotchy** *adj*

blouse *n* : loose garment reaching from the neck to the waist

¹**blow** *vb* **blew; blown; blow•ing** 1 : move for-

cibly **2** : send forth a current of air **3** : sound **4** : shape by blowing **5** : explode **6** : bungle ~ *n* **1** : gale **2** : act of blowing — **blow·er** *n* — **blowy** *adj*

²blow *n* **1** : forcible stroke **2** *pl* : fighting **3** : calamity

blow·out *n* : bursting of a tire

blow·torch *n* : small torch that uses a blast of air

¹blub·ber *n* : fat of whales

²blubber *vb* : cry noisily

blud·geon *n* : short club ~ *vb* : hit with a bludgeon

blue *adj* **blu·er**; **blu·est 1** : of the color blue **2** : melancholy ~ *n* : color of the clear sky — **blu·ish** *adj*

blue·bell *n* : plant with blue bell-shaped flowers

blue·ber·ry *n* : edible blue or blackish berry

blue·bird *n* : small bluish songbird

blue·fish *n* : bluish marine food fish

blue jay *n* : American crested jay

blue·print *n* **1** : photographic print in white on blue of a mechanical drawing **2** : plan of action — **blueprint** *vb*

blues *n pl* **1** : depression **2** : music in a melancholy style

¹bluff *adj* **1** : rising steeply with a broad flat front **2** : frank ~ *n* : cliff

²bluff *vb* : deceive by pretense ~ *n* : act of bluffing — **bluff·er** *n*

blu·ing, blue·ing *n* : laundry preparation to keep fabrics white

blun·der *vb* **1** : move clumsily **2** : make a stupid mistake ~ *n* : bad mistake

blun·der·buss *n* : obsolete short-barreled firearm

blunt *adj* **1** : not sharp **2** : tactless ~ *vb* : make dull — **blunt·ly** *adv* — **blunt·ness** *n*

blur *n* **1** : smear **2** : something perceived indistinctly ~ *vb* -**rr**- : cloud or obscure — **blur·ry** *adj*

blurb *n* : short publicity notice

blurt *vb* : utter suddenly

blush *n* : reddening of the face — **blush** *vb* — **blush·ful** *adj*

blus·ter *vb* **1** : blow violently **2** : talk or act with boasts or threats — **blus·ter** *n* — **blus·tery** *adj*

boa *n* **1** : a large snake (as the **boa con·stric·tor**) that crushes its prey **2** : fluffy scarf

boar *n* : male swine

board *n* **1** : long thin piece of sawed lumber **2** : flat thin sheet esp. for games **3** : daily meals furnished for pay **4** : official body ~ *vb* **1** : go aboard **2** : cover with boards **3** : supply meals to — **board·er** *n*

board·walk *n* : wooden walk along a beach

boast *vb* : praise oneself or one's possessions — **boast** *n* — **boast·er** *n* — **boast·ful** *adj* — **boast·ful·ly** *adv*

boat *n* : small vessel for traveling on water — **boat** *vb* — **boat·man** *n*

boat·swain *n* : ship's officer in charge of the hull

¹bob *vb* -**bb**- **1** : move up and down **2** : appear suddenly

²bob *n* **1** : float **2** : woman's short haircut ~ *vb* : cut hair in a bob

bob·bin *n* : spindle for holding thread

bob·ble *vb* -**bled**; -**bling** : fumble — **bobble** *n*

bob·cat *n* : small American lynx

bob·o·link *n* : American songbird

bob·sled *n* : racing sled — **bobsled** *vb*

bob·white *n* : quail

bock *n* : dark beer

¹bode *vb* **bod·ed; bod·ing** : indicate by signs

²bode *past of* BIDE

bod·ice *n* : close-fitting top of dress

bodi·ly *adj* : relating to the body ~ *adv* **1** : in the flesh **2** : as a whole

body *n, pl* **bod·ies 1** : the physical whole of an organism **2** : human being **3** : main part **4** : mass

of matter **5** : group — **bod·ied** *adj* — **bodi·less** *adj* — **body·guard** *n*

bog *n* : swamp ~ *vb* -**gg**- : sink in or as if in a bog — **bog·gy** *adj*

bo·gey *n, pl* -**geys** : someone or something frightening

bog·gle *vb* -**gled**; -**gling** : overwhelm with amazement

bo·gus *adj* : fake

bo·he·mi·an *n* : one living unconventionally — **bohemian** *adj*

¹boil *n* : inflamed swelling

²boil *vb* **1** : heat to a temperature (**boiling point**) at which vapor forms **2** : cook in boiling liquid **3** : be agitated — **boil** *n*

boil·er *n* : tank holding hot water or steam

bois·ter·ous *adj* : noisily turbulent — **bois·ter·ous·ly** *adv*

bold *adj* **1** : courageous **2** : insolent **3** : daring — **bold·ly** *adv* — **bold·ness** *n*

bo·le·ro *n, pl* -**ros 1** : Spanish dance **2** : short open jacket

boll *n* : seed pod

boll weevil *n* : small grayish weevil that infests the cotton plant

bo·lo·gna *n* : large smoked sausage

bol·ster *n* : long pillow ~ *vb* -**stered**; -**ster·ing** : support

bolt *n* **1** : flash of lightning **2** : sliding bar used to fasten a door **3** : roll of cloth **4** : threaded pin used with a nut ~ *vb* **1** : move suddenly **2** : fasten with a bolt **3** : swallow hastily

bomb *n* : explosive device ~ *vb* : attack with bombs — **bomb·proof** *adj*

bom·bard *vb* : attack with or as if with artillery — **bom·bard·ment** *n*

bom·bar·dier *n* : one who releases the bombs from a bomber

bom·bast *n* : pretentious language — **bom·bas·tic** *adj*

bomb·er *n* **1** : one that bombs **2** : airplane for dropping bombs

bomb·shell *n* **1** : bomb **2** : great surprise

bona fide *adj* **1** : made in good faith **2** : genuine

bo·nan·za *n* : something yielding a rich return

bon·bon *n* : piece of candy

bond *n* **1** *pl* : fetters **2** : uniting force **3** : obligation made binding by money **4** : interest-bearing certificate ~ *vb* **1** : insure **2** : cause to adhere — **bond·hold·er** *n*

bond·age *n* : slavery — **bond·man** *n* — **bond·wom·an** *n*

¹bonds·man *n* : slave

²bondsman *n* : surety

bone *n* : skeletal material ~ *vb* **boned; bon·ing** : to free from bones — **bone·less** *adj* — **bony** *adj*

bon·er *n* : blunder

bon·fire *n* : outdoor fire

bo·ni·to *n, pl* -**tos** *or* -**to** : medium-sized tuna

bon·net *n* : hat for a woman or infant

bo·nus *n* : extra payment

boo *n, pl* **boos** : shout of disapproval — **boo** *vb*

boo·by *n, pl* -**bies** : dunce

book *n* **1** : paper sheets bound into a volume **2** : long literary work or a subdivision of one ~ *vb* : reserve — **book·case** *n* — **book·let** *n* — **book·mark** *n* — **book·sell·er** *n* — **book·shelf** *n*

book·end *n* : support to hold up a row of books

book·ie *n* : bookmaker

book·ish *adj* : fond of books and reading

book·keep·er *n* : one who keeps business accounts — **book·keep·ing** *n*

book·mak·er *n* : one who takes bets — **book·mak·ing** *n*

book·worm *n* : one devoted to reading

¹boom *n* **1** : long spar to extend the bottom of a sail **2** : beam projecting from the pole of a derrick

²boom *vb* **1** : make a deep hollow sound **2** : grow rapidly esp. in value ~ *n* **1** : booming sound **2** : rapid growth

boo·mer·ang *n* : angular club that returns to the thrower

¹boon *n* : benefit

²boon *adj* : congenial

boon·docks *n pl* : rural area

boor *n* : rude person — **boor·ish** *adj*

boost *vb* **1** : raise **2** : promote — **boost** *n* — **boost·er** *n*

boot *n* **1** : covering for the foot and leg **2** : kick ~ *vb* : kick

boo·tee, boo·tie *n* : infant's knitted sock

booth *n, pl* **booths** : small enclosed stall or seating area

boot·leg *vb* : make or sell liquor illegally — **bootleg** *adj or n* — **boot·leg·ger** *n*

boo·ty *n, pl* -**ties** : plunder

booze *vb* **boozed; booz·ing** : drink liquor to excess ~ *n* : liquor — **booz·er** *n* — **boozy** *adj*

bo·rax *n* : crystalline compound of boron

bor·der *n* **1** : edge **2** : boundary ~ *vb* **1** : put a border on **2** : be close

¹bore *vb* **bored; bor·ing 1** : pierce **2** : make by piercing ~ *n* : cylindrical hole or its diameter — **bor·er** *n*

²bore *past of* BEAR

³bore *n* : one that is dull ~ *vb* **bored; bor·ing** : tire with dullness — **bore·dom** *n*

born *adj* **1** : brought into life **2** : being such by birth

borne *past part of* BEAR

bo·ron *n* : dark-colored chemical element

bor·ough *n* : incorporated town or village

bor·row *vb* **1** : take as a loan **2** : take into use

bo·som *n* : breast ~ *adj* : intimate — **bo·somed** *adj*

boss *n* : employer or supervisor ~ *vb* : supervise — **bossy** *adj*

bot·a·ny *n* : plant biology — **bo·tan·i·cal** *adj* — **bot·a·nist** *n* — **bot·a·nize** *vb*

botch *vb* : do clumsily — **botch** *n*

both *adj or pron* : the one and the other ~ *conj* — used to show each of two is included

both·er *vb* **1** : annoy or worry **2** : take the trouble — **bother** *n* — **both·er·some** *adj*

bot·tle *n* : container with a narrow neck and no handles ~ *vb* **bot·tled; bot·tling** : put into a bottle

bot·tle·neck *n* : place or cause of congestion

bot·tom *n* **1** : supporting surface **2** : lowest part or place — **bottom** *adj* — **bot·tomed** *adj* — **bot·tom·less** *adj*

bot·u·lism *n* : acute food poisoning

bou·doir *n* : woman's private room

bough *n* : large tree branch

bought *past of* BUY

bouil·lon *n* : clear soup

boul·der *n* : large rounded rock — **boul·dered** *adj*

bou·le·vard *n* : broad thoroughfare

bounce *vb* **bounced; bounc·ing 1** : spring back **2** : make bounce — **bounce** *n* — **bouncy** *adj*

¹bound *adj* : intending to go

²bound *n* : limit or boundary ~ *vb* : be a boundary of — **bound·less** *adj* — **bound·less·ness** *n*

³bound *adj* **1** : obliged **2** : having a binding **3** : determined **4** : incapable of failing

⁴bound *n* : leap ~ *vb* : move by springing

bound·ary *n, pl* -**aries** : line marking extent or separation

boun·ty *n, pl* -**ties 1** : generosity **2** : reward — **boun·te·ous** *adj* — **boun·te·ous·ly** *adv* — **boun·ti·ful** *adj* — **boun·ti·ful·ly** *adv*

bou·quet *n* **1** : bunch of flowers **2** : fragrance

bour·bon *n* : corn whiskey

bour·geoi·sie *n* : middle class of society — **bour·geois** *n or adj*

bout *n* 1 : contest 2 : outbreak

bou·tique *n* : specialty shop

bo·vine *adj* : relating to cattle — **bovine** *n*

¹bow *vb* 1 : submit 2 : bend the head or body ~ *n* : act of bowing

²bow *n* 1 : bend or arch 2 : weapon for shooting arrows 3 : knot with loops 4 : rod with stretched horsehairs for playing a stringed instrument ~ *vb* : curve or bend — **bow·man** *n* — **bow·string** *n*

³bow *n* : forward part of a ship — **bow** *adj*

bow·els *n pl* 1 : intestines 2 : inmost parts

bow·er *n* : arbor

¹bowl *n* : concave vessel or part — **bowl·ful** *n*

²bowl *n* : round ball for bowling ~ *vb* : roll a ball in bowling — **bowl·er** *n*

bowl·ing *n* : game in which balls are rolled to knock down pins

¹box *n, pl* **box** *or* **box·es** : evergreen shrub — **box·wood** *n*

²box *n* 1 : container usu. with 4 sides and a cover 2 : small compartment ~ *vb* : put in a box

³box *n* : slap ~ *vb* 1 : slap 2 : fight with the fists — **box·er** *n* — **box·ing** *n*

box·car *n* : roofed freight car

box office *n* : theater ticket office

boy *n* : male child — **boy·hood** *n* — **boy·ish** *adj* — **boy·ish·ly** *adv* — **boy·ish·ness** *n*

boy·cott *vb* : refrain from dealing with — **boycott** *n*

boy·friend *n* 1 : male friend 2 : woman's regular male companion

brace *n* 1 : crank for turning a bit 2 : something that resists weight or supports 3 : punctuation mark { or } ~ *vb* **braced; brac·ing** 1 : make taut or steady 2 : invigorate 3 : strengthen

brace·let *n* : ornamental band for the wrist or arm

brack·et *n* 1 : projecting support 2 : punctuation mark [or] 3 : class ~ *vb* 1 : furnish or fasten with brackets 2 : place within brackets 3 : group

brack·ish *adj* : salty

brad *n* : nail with a small head

brag *vb* **-gg-** : boast — **brag** *n*

brag·gart *n* : boaster

braid *vb* : interweave ~ *n* : something braided

braille *n* : system of writing for the blind using raised dots

brain *n* 1 : organ of thought and nervous coordination enclosed in the skull 2 : intelligence ~ *vb* : smash the skull of — **brained** *adj* — **brain·less** *adj* — **brainy** *adj*

braise *vb* **braised; brais·ing** : cook (meat) slowly in a covered dish

brake *n* : device for slowing or stopping ~ *vb* **braked; brak·ing** : slow or stop by a brake

bram·ble *n* : prickly shrub

bran *n* : edible cracked grain husks

branch *n* 1 : division of a plant stem 2 : part ~ *vb* 1 : develop branches 2 : diverge — **branched** *adj*

brand *n* 1 : identifying mark made by burning 2 : stigma 3 : distinctive kind (as of goods from one firm) ~ *vb* : mark with a brand

bran·dish *vb* : wave

brand–new *adj* : unused

bran·dy *n, pl* **-dies** : liquor distilled from wine

brash *adj* 1 : impulsive 2 : aggressively self-assertive

brass *n* 1 : alloy of copper and zinc 2 : brazen self-assurance 3 : high-ranking military officers — **brassy** *adj*

bras·siere *n* : woman's undergarment to support the breasts

brat *n* : ill-behaved child — **brat·ti·ness** *n* — **brat·ty** *adj*

bra·va·do *n, pl* **-does** *or* **-dos** : false bravery

¹brave *adj* **brav·er; brav·est** : showing courage ~ *vb* **braved; brav·ing** : face with courage — **brave·ly** *adv* — **brav·ery** *n*

²brave *n* : American Indian warrior

bra·vo *n, pl* **-vos** : shout of approval

brawl *n* : noisy quarrel or violent fight — **brawl** *vb* — **brawl·er** *n*

brawn *n* : muscular strength — **brawny** *adj* — **brawn·i·ness** *n*

bray *n* : harsh cry of a donkey — **bray** *vb*

bra·zen *adj* 1 : made of brass 2 : bold — **bra·zen·ly** *adv* — **bra·zen·ness** *n*

bra·zier *n* : charcoal grill

breach *n* 1 : breaking of a law, obligation, or standard 2 : gap ~ *vb* : make a breach in

bread *n* : baked food made of flour ~ *vb* : cover with bread crumbs

breadth *n* : width

bread·win·ner *n* : wage earner

break *vb* **broke; bro·ken; break·ing** 1 : knock into pieces 2 : transgress 3 : force a way into or out of 4 : exceed 5 : interrupt 6 : fail ~ *n* 1 : act or result of breaking 2 : stroke of good luck — **break·able** *adj or n* — **break·age** *n* — **break·er** *n* — **break in** *vb* 1 : enter by force 2 : interrupt 3 : train — **break out** *vb* 1 : erupt with force 2 : develop a rash

break·down *n* : physical or mental failure — **break down** *vb*

break·fast *n* : first meal of the day — **break·fast** *vb*

breast *n* 1 : milk-producing gland esp. of a woman 2 : front part of the chest

breast·bone *n* : sternum

breath *n* 1 : slight breeze 2 : air breathed in or out — **breath·less** *adj* — **breath·less·ly** *adv* — **breath·less·ness** *n* — **breathy** *adj*

breathe *vb* **breathed; breath·ing** 1 : draw air into the lungs and expel it 2 : live 3 : utter

breath·tak·ing *adj* : exciting

breech·es *n pl* : trousers ending near the knee

breed *vb* **bred; breed·ing** 1 : give birth to 2 : propagate 3 : raise ~ *n* 1 : kind of plant or animal usu. developed by humans 2 : class — **breed·er** *n*

breeze *n* : light wind ~ *vb* **breezed; breez·ing** : move fast — **breezy** *adj*

breth·ren *pl of* BROTHER

bre·via·ry *n, pl* **-ries** : prayer book used by Roman Catholic priests

brev·i·ty *n, pl* **-ties** : shortness or conciseness

brew *vb* : make by fermenting or steeping — **brew** *n* — **brew·er** *n* — **brew·ery** *n*

bri·ar *var of* BRIER

bribe *vb* **bribed; brib·ing** : corrupt or influence by gifts ~ *n* : something offered or given in bribing — **brib·able** *adj* — **brib·ery** *n*

bric–a–brac *n pl* : small ornamental articles

brick *n* : building block of baked clay — **brick** *vb* — **brick·lay·er** *n* — **brick·lay·ing** *n*

bride *n* : woman just married or about to be married — **brid·al** *adj*

bride·groom *n* : man just married or about to be married

brides·maid *n* : woman who attends a bride at her wedding

¹bridge *n* 1 : structure built for passage over a depression or obstacle 2 : upper part of the nose 3 : compartment from which a ship is navigated 4 : artificial replacement for missing teeth ~ *vb* : build a bridge over — **bridge·able** *adj*

²bridge *n* : card game for 4 players

bri·dle *n* : headgear to control a horse ~ *vb* **-dled; -dling** 1 : put a bridle on 2 : restrain 3 : show hostility or scorn

brief *adj* : short or concise ~ *n* : concise summary (as of a legal case) ~ *vb* : give final instruc-

tions or essential information to — **brief·ly** *adv* — **brief·ness** *n*

brief·case *n* : case for papers

¹bri·er *n* : thorny plant

²brier *n* : heath of southern Europe

¹brig *n* : 2-masted ship

²brig *n* : jail on a naval ship

bri·gade *n* 1 : large military unit 2 : group organized for a special activity

brig·a·dier general *n* : officer ranking next below a major general

brig·and *n* : bandit — **brig·and·age** *n*

bright *adj* 1 : radiating or reflecting light 2 : cheerful 3 : intelligent — **bright·en** *vb* — **bright·en·er** *n* — **bright·ly** *adv* — **bright·ness** *n*

bril·liant *adj* 1 : very bright 2 : splendid 3 : very intelligent — **bril·liance** *n* — **bril·lian·cy** *n* — **bril·liant·ly** *adv*

brim *n* : edge or rim ~ *vb* : be or become full — **brim·less** *adj* — **brimmed** *adj*

brim·ful *adj* : full to the brim

brim·stone *n* : sulfur

brin·dled *adj* : gray or tawny with dark streaks or flecks

brine *n* 1 : salt water 2 : ocean — **brin·i·ness** *n* — **briny** *adj*

bring *vb* **brought; bring·ing** 1 : cause to come with one 2 : persuade 3 : produce 4 : sell for — **bring·er** *n* — **bring about** *vb* : make happen — **bring up** *vb* 1 : care for and educate 2 : cause to be noticed

brink *n* : edge

bri·quette, bri·quet *n* : pressed mass (as of charcoal)

brisk *adj* 1 : lively 2 : invigorating — **brisk·ly** *adv* — **brisk·ness** *n*

bris·ket *n* : breast or lower chest of a quadruped

bris·tle *n* : short stiff hair ~ *vb* **-tled; -tling** 1 : stand erect 2 : show angry defiance 3 : appear as if covered with bristles — **bris·tly** *adj*

brit·tle *adj* **-tler; -tlest** : easily broken — **brit·tle·ness** *n*

broach *n* : pointed tool (as for opening casks) ~ *vb* 1 : pierce (as a cask) to open 2 : introduce for discussion

broad *adj* 1 : wide 2 : spacious 3 : clear or open 4 : obvious 5 : tolerant in outlook 6 : widely applicable 7 : dealing with essential points — **broad·en** *vb* — **broad·ly** *adv* — **broad·ness** *n*

broad·cast *n* 1 : transmission by radio waves 2 : radio or television program ~ *vb* **-cast; -cast·ing** 1 : scatter or sow in all directions 2 : make widely known 3 : send out on a broadcast — **broad·cast·er** *n*

broad·cloth *n* : fine cloth

broad·loom *adj* : woven on a wide loom esp. in solid color

broad–mind·ed *adj* : tolerant of varied opinions — **broad–mind·ed·ly** *adv* — **broad–mind·ed·ness** *n*

broad·side *n* 1 : simultaneous firing of all guns on one side of a ship 2 : verbal attack

bro·cade *n* : usu. silk fabric with a raised design

broc·co·li *n* : green vegetable akin to cauliflower

bro·chure *n* : pamphlet

brogue *n* : Irish accent

broil *vb* : cook by radiant heat — **broil** *n*

broil·er *n* 1 : utensil for broiling 2 : chicken fit for broiling

¹broke *past of* BREAK

²broke *adj* : out of money

bro·ken *adj* : imperfectly spoken — **bro·ken·ly** *adv*

bro·ken·heart·ed *adj* : overcome by grief or despair

bro·ker *n* : agent who buys and sells for a fee — **broker** *vb* — **bro·ker·age** *n*

bro•mine *n* : deep red liquid corrosive chemical element

bron•chi•tis *n* : inflammation of the bronchi

bron•chus *n, pl* **-chi** : division of the windpipe leading to a lung — **bron•chi•al** *adj*

bronze *vb* **bronzed; bronz•ing** : make bronze in color ~ *n* **1** : alloy of copper and tin **2** : yellowish brown — **bronzy** *adj*

brooch *n* : ornamental clasp or pin

brood *n* : family of young ~ *vb* **1** : sit on eggs to hatch them **2** : ponder ~ *adj* : kept for breeding — **brood•er** *n* — **brood•ing•ly** *adv*

¹**brook** *vb* : tolerate

²**brook** *n* : small stream

broom *n* **1** : flowering shrub **2** : implement for sweeping — **broom•stick** *n*

broth *n, pl* **broths** : liquid in which meat has been cooked

broth•el *n* : house of prostitutes

broth•er *n, pl* **brothers** *also* **breth•ren 1** : male sharing one or both parents with another person **2** : kinsman — **broth•er•hood** *n* — **broth•er•li•ness** *n* — **broth•er•ly** *adj*

broth•er–in–law *n, pl* **brothers–in–law** : brother of one's spouse or husband of one's sister or of one's spouse's sister

brought *past of* BRING

brow *n* **1** : eyebrow **2** : forehead **3** : edge of a steep place

brow•beat *vb* **-beat; -beat•en** *or* **-beat; -beat•ing** : intimidate

brown *adj* **1** : of the color brown **2** : of dark or tanned complexion ~ *n* : a color like that of coffee ~ *vb* : make or become brown — **brown•ish** *adj*

browse *vb* **browsed; brows•ing 1** : graze **2** : look over casually — **brows•er** *n*

bru•in *n* : bear

bruise *vb* **bruised; bruis•ing 1** : make a bruise on **2** : become bruised ~ *n* : surface injury to flesh

brunch *n* : late breakfast, early lunch, or combination of both

bru•net, bru•nette *adj* : having dark hair and usu. dark skin — **bru•net, brunette** *n*

brunt *n* : main impact

¹**brush** *n* **1** : small cut branches **2** : coarse shrubby vegetation

²**brush** *n* **1** : bristles set in a handle used esp. for cleaning or painting **2** : light touch ~ *vb* **1** : apply a brush to **2** : remove with or as if with a brush **3** : dismiss in an offhand way **4** : touch lightly — **brush up** *vb* : renew one's skill

³**brush** *n* : skirmish

brush–off *n* : curt dismissal

brusque *adj* : curt or blunt in manner — **brusque•ly** *adv*

bru•tal *adj* : like a brute and esp. cruel — **bru•tal•i•ty** *n* — **bru•tal•ize** *vb* — **bru•tal•ly** *adv*

brute *adj* **1** : relating to beasts **2** : unreasoning **3** : purely physical ~ *n* **1** : beast **2** : brutal person — **brut•ish** *adj*

bub•ble *vb* **-bled; -bling** : form, rise in, or give off bubbles ~ *n* : globule of gas in or covered with a liquid — **bub•bly** *adj*

bu•bo *n, pl* **buboes** : inflammatory swelling of a lymph gland — **bu•bon•ic** *adj*

buc•ca•neer *n* : pirate

buck *n, pl* **buck** *or* **bucks 1** : male animal (as a deer) **2** : dollar ~ *vb* **1** : jerk forward **2** : oppose

buck•et *n* : pail — **buck•et•ful** *n*

buck•le *n* **1** : clasp (as on a belt) for two loose ends **2** : bend or fold ~ *vb* **-led; -ling 1** : fasten with a buckle **2** : apply oneself **3** : bend or crumple

buck•ler *n* : shield

buck•shot *n* : coarse lead shot

buck•skin *n* : soft leather (as from the skin of a buck) — **buckskin** *adj*

buck•tooth *n* : large projecting front tooth — **buck–toothed** *adj*

buck•wheat *n* : herb whose seeds are used as a cereal grain or the seeds themselves

bu•col•ic *adj* : pastoral

bud *n* **1** : undeveloped plant shoot **2** : partly opened flower ~ *vb* **-dd- 1** : form or put forth buds **2** : be or develop like a bud

Bud•dhism *n* : religion of eastern and central Asia — **Bud•dhist** *n or adj*

bud•dy *n, pl* **-dies** : friend

budge *vb* **budged; budg•ing** : move from a place

bud•get *n* **1** : estimate of income and expenses **2** : plan for coordinating income and expenses **3** : money available for a particular use — **budget** *vb or adj* — **bud•get•ary** *adj*

buff *n* **1** : yellow to orange yellow color **2** : enthusiast ~ *adj* : of the color buff ~ *vb* : polish

buf•fa•lo *n, pl* **-lo** *or* **-loes** : wild ox (as a bison)

¹**buff•er** *n* : shield or protector

²**buffer** *n* : one that buffs

¹**buf•fet** *n* : blow or slap ~ *vb* : hit esp. repeatedly

²**buf•fet** *n* **1** : sideboard **2** : meal at which people serve themselves

buf•foon *n* : clown — **buf•foon•ery** *n*

bug *n* **1** : small usu. obnoxious crawling creature **2** : 4-winged sucking insect **3** : unexpected imperfection **4** : disease-producing germ **5** : hidden microphone ~ *vb* **-gg- 1** : pester **2** : conceal a microphone in

bug•a•boo *n, pl* **-boos** : bogey

bug•bear *n* : source of dread

bug•gy *n, pl* **-gies** : light carriage

bu•gle *n* : trumpetlike brass instrument — **bu•gler** *n*

build *vb* **built; build•ing 1** : put together **2** : establish **3** : increase ~ *n* : physique — **build•er** *n*

build•ing *n* **1** : roofed and walled structure **2** : art or business of constructing buildings

bulb *n* **1** : large underground plant bud **2** : rounded or pear-shaped object — **bul•bous** *adj*

bulge *n* : swelling projecting part ~ *vb* **bulged; bulg•ing** : swell out

bulk *n* **1** : magnitude **2** : indigestible food material **3** : large mass **4** : major portion ~ *vb* : cause to swell or bulge — **bulky** *adj*

bulk•head *n* : ship's partition

¹**bull** *n* : large adult male animal (as of cattle) ~ *adj* : male

²**bull** *n* **1** : papal letter **2** : decree

bull•dog *n* : compact short-haired dog

bull•doze *vb* **1** : move or level with a tractor (**bull•doz•er**) having a broad blade **2** : force

bul•let *n* : missile to be shot from a gun — **bul•let•proof** *adj*

bul•le•tin *n* **1** : brief public report **2** : periodical

bull•fight *n* : sport of taunting and killing bulls — **bull•fight•er** *n*

bull•frog *n* : large deep-voiced frog

bull•head•ed *adj* : stupidly stubborn

bul•lion *n* : gold or silver esp. in bars

bull•ock *n* **1** : young bull **2** : steer

bull's–eye *n, pl* **bull's–eyes** : center of a target

bul•ly *n, pl* **-lies** : one who hurts or intimidates others ~ *vb* **-lied; -ly•ing** : act like a bully toward

bul•rush *n* : tall coarse rush or sedge

bul•wark *n* **1** : wall-like defense **2** : strong support or protection

bum *vb* **-mm- 1** : wander as a tramp **2** : get by begging ~ *n* : idle worthless person ~ *adj* : bad

bum•ble•bee *n* : large hairy bee

bump *vb* : strike or knock forcibly ~ *n* **1** : sudden blow **2** : small bulge or swelling — **bumpy** *adj*

¹**bum•per** *adj* : unusually large

²**bump•er** *n* : shock-absorbing bar at either end of a car

bump•kin *n* : awkward country person

bun *n* : sweet biscuit or roll

bunch *n* : group ~ *vb* : form into a group — **bunchy** *adj*

bun•dle *n* **1** : several items bunched together **2** : something wrapped for carrying **3** : large amount ~ *vb* **-dled; -dling** : gather into a bundle

bun•ga•low *n* : one-story house

bun•gle *vb* **-gled; -gling** : do badly — **bungle** — **bun•gler** *n*

bun•ion *n* : inflamed swelling of the first joint of the big toe

¹**bunk** *n* : built-in bed that is often one of a tier ~ *vb* : sleep

²**bunk** *n* : nonsense

bun•ker *n* **1** : storage compartment **2** : protective embankment

bun•kum, bun•combe *n* : nonsense

bun•ny *n, pl* **-nies** : rabbit

¹**bun•ting** *n* : small finch

²**bunting** *n* : flag material

buoy *n* : floating marker anchored in water ~ *vb* **1** : keep afloat **2** : raise the spirits of — **buoy•an•cy** *n* — **buoy•ant** *adj*

bur, burr *n* : rough or prickly covering of a fruit — **bur•ry** *adj*

bur•den *n* **1** : something carried **2** : something oppressive **3** : cargo ~ *vb* : load or oppress — **bur•den•some** *adj*

bur•dock *n* : tall coarse herb with prickly flower heads

bu•reau *n* **1** : chest of drawers **2** : administrative unit **3** : business office

bu•reau•cra•cy *n, pl* **-cies 1** : body of government officials **2** : unwieldy administrative system — **bu•reau•crat** *n* — **bu•reau•crat•ic** *adj*

bur•geon *vb* : grow

bur•glary *n, pl* **-glar•ies** : forcible entry into a building to steal — **bur•glar** *n* — **bur•glar•ize** *vb*

bur•gle *vb* **-gled; -gling** : commit burglary on or in

Bur•gun•dy *n, pl* **-dies** : kind of table wine

buri•al *n* : act of burying

bur•lap *n* : coarse fabric usu. of jute or hemp

bur•lesque *n* **1** : witty or derisive imitation **2** : broadly humorous variety show ~ *vb* **-lesqued; -lesqu•ing** : mock

bur•ly *adj* **-li•er; -est** : strongly and heavily built

burn *vb* **burned** *or* **burnt; burn•ing 1** : be on fire **2** : feel or look as if on fire **3** : alter or become altered by or as if by fire or heat **4** : cause or make by fire ~ *n* : injury or effect produced by burning — **burn•er** *n*

bur•nish *vb* : polish

burp *n or vb* : belch

bur•ro *n, pl* **-os** : small donkey

bur•row *n* : hole in the ground made by an animal ~ *vb* : make a burrow — **bur•row•er** *n*

bur•sar *n* : treasurer esp. of a college

bur•si•tis *n* : inflammation of a sac (**bur•sa**) in a joint

burst *vb* **burst** *or* **burst•ed; burst•ing 1** : fly apart or into pieces **2** : enter or emerge suddenly ~ *n* : sudden outbreak or effort

bury *vb* **bur•ied; bury•ing 1** : deposit in the earth **2** : hide

bus *n, pl* **bus•es** *or* **bus•ses** : large motor-driven passenger vehicle ~ *vb* **bused** *or* **bussed; bus•ing** *or* **bus•sing** : travel or transport by bus

bus•boy *n* : waiter's helper

bush *n* **1** : shrub **2** : rough uncleared country **3** : a thick tuft or mat — **bushy** *adj*

bush•el *n* : 4 pecks

bush•ing *n* : metal lining used as a guide or bearing

busi•ness *n* 1 : vocation 2 : commercial or industrial enterprise 3 : personal concerns — **business•man** *n* — **busi•ness•wom•an** *n*

¹bust *n* 1 : sculpture of the head and upper torso 2 : breasts of a woman

²bust *vb* 1 : burst or break 2 : tame ~ *n* 1 : punch 2 : failure

¹bus•tle *vb* **-tled; -tling** : move or work briskly ~ *n* : energetic activity

²bustle *n* : pad or frame formerly worn under a woman's skirt

busy *adj* **busi•er; -est** 1 : engaged in action 2 : being in use 3 : full of activity ~ *vb* **busied; busy•ing** : make or keep busy — **busi•ly** *adv*

busy•body *n* : meddler

but *conj* 1 : if not for the fact 2 : that 3 : without the certainty that 4 : rather 5 : yet ~ *prep* : other than

butch•er *n* 1 : one who slaughters animals or dresses their flesh 2 : brutal killer 3 : bungler — **butcher** *vb* — **butch•ery** *n*

but•ler *n* : chief male household servant

¹butt *vb* : strike with a butt ~ *n* : blow with the head or horns

²butt *n* 1 : target 2 : victim

³butt *vb* : join edge to edge

⁴butt *n* : large end or bottom

⁵butt *n* : large cask

butte *n* : isolated steep hill

but•ter *n* : solid edible fat churned from cream ~ *vb* : spread with butter — **but•tery** *adj*

but•ter•cup *n* : yellow-flowered herb

but•ter•fat *n* : natural fat of milk and of butter

but•ter•fly *n* : insect with 4 broad wings

but•ter•milk *n* : liquid remaining after butter is churned

but•ter•nut *n* : edible nut of a tree related to the walnut or this tree

but•ter•scotch *n* : candy made from sugar, corn syrup, and water

but•tocks *n pl* : rear part of the hips

but•ton *n* 1 : small knob for fastening clothing 2 : buttonlike object ~ *vb* : fasten with buttons

but•ton•hole *n* : hole or slit for a button ~ *vb* : hold in talk

but•tress *n* 1 : projecting structure to support a wall 2 : support — **buttress** *vb*

bux•om *adj* : full-bosomed

buy *vb* **bought; buy•ing** : purchase ~ *n* : bargain — **buy•er** *n*

buzz *vb* : make a low humming sound ~ *n* : act or sound of buzzing

buz•zard *n* : large bird of prey

buzz•er *n* : signaling device that buzzes

buzz•word *n* : word or phrase in vogue

by *prep* 1 : near 2 : through 3 : beyond 4 : throughout 5 : no later than ~ *adv* 1 : near 2 : farther

by•gone *adj* : past — **bygone** *n*

by•law, bye•law *n* : organization's rule

by–line *n* : writer's name on an article

by•pass *n* : alternate route ~ *vb* : go around

by–prod•uct *n* : product in addition to the main product

by•stand•er *n* : spectator

by•way *n* : side road

by•word *n* : proverb

C

c *n*, *pl* **c's** *or* **cs** : 3d letter of the alphabet

cab *n* 1 : light closed horse-drawn carriage 2 : taxicab 3 : compartment for a driver — **cab•bie, cabby** *n* — **cab•stand** *n*

ca•bal *n* : group of conspirators

ca•bana *n* : shelter at a beach or pool

cab•a•ret *n* : nightclub

cab•bage *n* : vegetable with a dense head of leaves

cab•in *n* 1 : private room on a ship 2 : small house 3 : airplane compartment

cab•i•net *n* 1 : display case or cupboard 2 : advisory council of a head of state — **cab•i•net•mak•er** *n* — **cab•i•net•mak•ing** *n* — **cab•i•net•work** *n*

ca•ble *n* 1 : strong rope, wire, or chain 2 : cablegram 3 : bundle of electrical wires ~ *vb* **-bled; -bling** : send a cablegram to

ca•ble•gram *n* : message sent by a submarine telegraph cable

ca•boose *n* : crew car on a train

ca•cao *n*, *pl* **cacaos** : So. American tree whose seeds (**cacao beans**) yield cocoa and chocolate

cache *n* 1 : hiding place 2 : something hidden — **cache** *vb*

ca•chet *n* : prestige or a feature conferring this

cack•le *vb* **-led; -ling** : make a cry or laugh like the sound of a hen — **cackle** *n* — **cack•ler** *n*

ca•coph•o•ny *n*, *pl* **-nies** : harsh noise — **ca•coph•o•nous** *adj*

cac•tus *n*, *pl* **cac•ti** *or* **-tus•es** : drought-resistant flowering plant with scales or prickles

cad *n* : ungentlemanly person — **cad•dish** *adj* — **cad•dish•ly** *adv* — **cad•dish•ness** *n*

ca•dav•er *n* : dead body — **ca•dav•er•ous** *adj*

cad•die, cad•dy *n*, *pl* **-dies** : golfer's helper — **caddie, caddy** *vb*

cad•dy *n*, *pl* **-dies** : small tea chest

ca•dence *n* : measure of a rhythmical flow — **ca•denced** *adj*

ca•det *n* : student in a military academy

cadge *vb* **cadged; cadg•ing** : beg — **cadg•er** *n*

cad•mi•um *n* : grayish metallic chemical element

cad•re *n* : nucleus of highly trained people

ca•fé *n* : restaurant

caf•e•te•ria *n* : self-service restaurant

caf•feine *n* : stimulating alkaloid in coffee and tea

cage *n* : box of wire or bars for confining an animal ~ *vb* **caged; cag•ing** : put or keep in a cage

ca•gey *adj* **-gi•er; -est** : shrewd — **ca•gi•ly** *adv* — **ca•gi•ness** *n*

cais•son *n* 1 : ammunition carriage 2 : watertight chamber for underwater construction

ca•jole *vb* **-joled; -jol•ing** : persuade or coax — **ca•jol•ery** *n*

cake *n* 1 : food of baked or fried usu. sweet batter 2 : compacted mass ~ *vb* **caked; cak•ing** 1 : form into a cake 2 : encrust

cal•a•bash *n* : gourd

cal•a•mine *n* : lotion of oxides of zinc and iron

ca•lam•i•ty *n*, *pl* **-ties** : disaster — **ca•lam•i•tous** *adj* — **ca•lam•i•tous•ly** *adv* — **ca•lam•i•tous•ness** *n*

cal•ci•fy *vb* **-fied; -fy•ing** : harden — **cal•ci•fi•ca•tion** *n*

cal•ci•um *n* : silver-white soft metallic chemical element

cal•cu•late *vb* **-lat•ed; -lat•ing** 1 : determine by mathematical processes 2 : judge — **cal•cu•la•ble** *adj* — **cal•cu•la•tion** *n* — **cal•cu•la•tor** *n*

cal•cu•lat•ing *adj* : shrewd

cal•cu•lus *n*, *pl* **-li** : higher mathematics dealing with rates of change

cal•dron *var of* CAULDRON

cal•en•dar *n* : list of days, weeks, and months

¹calf *n*, *pl* **calves** : young cow or related mammal — **calf•skin** *n*

²calf *n*, *pl* **calves** : back part of the leg below the knee

cal•i•ber, cal•i•bre *n* 1 : diameter of a bullet or shell or of a gun bore 2 : degree of mental or moral excellence

cal•i•brate *vb* **-brat•ed; -brat•ing** : adjust precisely — **cal•i•bra•tion** *n*

cal•i•co *n*, *pl* **-coes** *or* **-cos** 1 : printed cotton fabric 2 : animal with fur having patches of different colors

cal•i•pers *n* : measuring instrument with two adjustable legs

ca•liph *n* : title of head of Islam — **ca•liph•ate** *n*

cal•is•then•ics *n sing or pl* : stretching and jumping exercises — **cal•is•then•ic** *adj*

calk *var of* CAULK

call *vb* 1 : shout 2 : summon 3 : demand 4 : telephone 5 : make a visit 6 : name — **call** *n* — **call•er** *n* — **call down** *vb* : reprimand — **call off** *vb* : cancel

call•ing *n* : vocation

cal•li•ope *n* : musical instrument of steam whistles

cal•lous *adj* 1 : thickened and hardened 2 : unfeeling ~ *vb* : make callous — **cal•los•i•ty** *n* — **cal•lous•ly** *adv* — **cal•lous•ness** *n*

cal•low *adj* : inexperienced or innocent — **cal•low•ness** *n*

cal•lus *n* : callous area on skin or bark ~ *vb* : form a callus

calm *n* 1 : period or condition of peacefulness or stillness ~ *adj* : still or tranquil ~ *vb* : make calm — **calm•ly** *adv* — **calm•ness** *n*

ca•lor•ic *adj* : relating to heat or calories

cal•o•rie *n* : unit for measuring heat and energy value of food

ca•lum•ni•ate *vb* **-at•ed; -at•ing** : slander — **ca•lum•ni•a•tion** *n*

cal•um•ny *n*, *pl* **-nies** : false and malicious charge — **ca•lum•ni•ous** *adj*

calve *vb* **calved; calv•ing** : give birth to a calf

calves *pl of* CALF

ca•lyp•so *n*, *pl* **-sos** : West Indian style of music

ca•lyx *n*, *pl* **-lyx•es** *or* **-ly•ces** : sepals of a flower

cam *n* : machine part that slides or rotates irregularly to transmit linear motion

ca•ma•ra•de•rie *n* : fellowship

cam•bric *n* : fine thin linen or cotton fabric

came *past of* COME

cam•el *n* : large hoofed mammal of desert areas

ca•mel•lia *n* : shrub or tree grown for its showy roselike flowers or the flower itself

cam•eo *n*, *pl* **-eos** : gem carved in relief

cam•era *n* : box with a lens for taking pictures — **cam•era•man** *n*

cam•ou•flage *vb* : hide by disguising — **camouflage** *n*

camp *n* 1 : place to stay temporarily esp. in a tent 2 : group living in a camp ~ *vb* : make or live in a camp — **camp•er** *n* — **camp•ground** *n* — **camp•site** *n*

cam•paign *n* : series of military operations or of activities meant to gain a result — **campaign** *vb*

cam•pa•ni•le *n*, *pl* **-ni•les** *or* **-ni•li** : bell tower

cam•phor *n* : gummy volatile aromatic compound from an evergreen tree (**cam•phor tree**)

cam•pus *n* : grounds and buildings of a college or school

¹can *vb, past* **could** ; *pres sing & pl* **can 1** : be able to **2** : be permitted to by conscience or feeling **3** : have permission or liberty to

²can *n* : metal container ~ *vb* **-nn-** : preserve by sealing in airtight cans or jars — **can·ner** *n* — **can·nery** *n*

ca·nal *n* **1** : tubular passage in the body **2** : channel filled with water

can·a·pé *n* : appetizer

ca·nard *n* : false report

ca·nary *n, pl* **-nar·ies** : yellow or greenish finch often kept as a pet

can·cel *vb* **-celed** *or* **-celled; -cel·ing** *or* **-cel·ling 1** : cross out **2** : destroy, neutralize, or match the force or effect of — **cancel** *n* — **can·cel·la·tion** *n* — **can·cel·er, can·cel·ler** *n*

can·cer *n* **1** : malignant tumor that tends to spread **2** : slowly destructive evil — **can·cer·ous** *adj* — **can·cer·ous·ly** *adv*

can·de·la·bra *n* : candelabrum

can·de·la·brum *n, pl* **-bra** : ornamental branched candlestick

can·did *adj* **1** : frank **2** : unposed — **can·did·ly** *adv* — **can·did·ness** *n*

can·di·date *n* : one who seeks an office or membership — **can·di·da·cy** *n*

can·dle *n* : tallow or wax molded around a wick and burned to give light — **can·dle·light** *n* — **can·dle·stick** *n*

can·dor *n* : frankness

can·dy *n, pl* **-dies** : food made from sugar ~ *vb* **-died; -dy·ing** : encrust in sugar

cane *n* **1** : slender plant stem **2** : a tall woody grass or reed **3** : stick for walking or beating ~ *vb* **caned; can·ing 1** : beat with a cane **2** : weave or make with cane — **can·er** *n*

ca·nine *adj* : relating to dogs ~ *n* **1** : pointed tooth next to the incisors **2** : dog

can·is·ter *rr* : cylindrical container

can·ker *n* : mouth ulcer — **can·ker·ous** *adj*

can·na·bis *n* : preparation derived from hemp

can·ni·bal *n* : human or animal that eats its own kind — **can·ni·bal·ism** *n* — **can·ni·bal·is·tic** *adj*

can·ni·bal·ize *vb* **-ized; -iz·ing 1** : take usable parts from **2** : practice cannibalism

can·non *n, pl* **-nons** *or* **-non** : large heavy gun — **can·non·ball** *n* — **can·non·eer** *n*

can·non·ade *n* : heavy artillery fire ~ *vb* **-ad·ed; -ad·ing** : bombard

can·not : can not — **cannot but** : be bound to

can·ny *adj* **-ni·er; -est** : shrewd — **can·ni·ly** *adv* — **can·ni·ness** *n*

ca·noe *n* : narrow sharp-ended boat propelled by paddles — **canoe** *vb* — **ca·noe·ist** *n*

¹can·on *n* **1** : regulation governing a church **2** : authoritative list **3** : an accepted principle

²canon *n* : clergy member in a cathedral

ca·non·i·cal *adj* **1** : relating to or conforming to a canon **2** : orthodox — **ca·non·i·cal·ly** *adv*

can·on·ize *vb* **-ized; -iz·ing** : recognize as a saint — **can·on·iza·tion** *n*

can·o·py *n, pl* **-pies** : overhanging cover — **can·opy** *vb*

¹cant *n* **1** : slanting surface **2** : slant ~ *vb* **1** : tip up **2** : lean to one side

²cant *vb* : talk hypocritically ~ *n* **1** : jargon **2** : insincere talk

can't : can not

can·ta·loupe *n* : muskmelon with orange flesh

can·tan·ker·ous *adj* : hard to deal with — **can·tan·ker·ous·ly** *adv* — **can·tan·ker·ous·ness** *n*

can·ta·ta *n* : choral work

can·teen *n* **1** : place of recreation for service personnel **2** : water container

can·ter *n* : slow gallop — **canter** *vb*

can·ti·cle *n* : liturgical song

can·ti·le·ver *n* : beam or structure supported only at one end

can·to *n, pl* **-tos** : major division of a long poem

can·tor *n* : synagogue official who sings liturgical music

can·vas *n* **1** : strong cloth orig. used for making tents and sails **2** : set of sails **3** : oil painting

can·vass *vb* : solicit votes, orders, or opinions from ~ *n* : act of canvassing — **can·vass·er** *n*

can·yon *n* : deep valley with steep sides

cap *n* **1** : covering for the head **2** : top or cover like a cap **3** : upper limit ~ *vb* **-pp- 1** : provide or protect with a cap **2** : climax — **cap·ful** *n*

ca·pa·ble *adj* : able to do something — **ca·pa·bil·i·ty** *n* — **ca·pa·bly** *adv*

ca·pa·cious *adj* : able to contain much

ca·pac·i·tance *n* : ability to store electrical energy

ca·pac·i·tor *n* : device for storing electrical energy

ca·pac·i·ty *n, pl* **-ties 1** : ability to contain **2** : volume **3** : ability **4** : role or job ~ *adj* : equaling maximum capacity

¹cape *n* : point of land jutting out into water

²cape *n* : garment that drapes over the shoulders

¹ca·per *n* : flower bud of a shrub pickled for use as a relish

²caper *vb* : leap or prance about ~ *n* **1** : frolicsome leap **2** : escapade

cap·il·lary *adj* **1** : resembling a hair **2** : having a very small bore ~ *n, pl* **-lar·ies** : tiny thin-walled blood vessel

¹cap·i·tal *adj* **1** : punishable by death **2** : being in the series A, B, C rather than a, b, c **3** : relating to capital **4** : excellent ~ *n* **1** : capital letter **2** : seat of government **3** : wealth **4** : total face value of a company's stock **5** : investors as a group

²capital *n* : top part of a column

cap·i·tal·ism *n* : economic system of private ownership of capital

cap·i·tal·ist *n* **1** : person with capital invested in business **2** : believer in capitalism ~ *adj* **1** : owning capital **2** : practicing, advocating, or marked by capitalism — **cap·i·tal·is·tic** *adj* — **cap·i·tal·is·ti·cal·ly** *adv*

cap·i·tal·ize *vb* **-ized; -iz·ing 1** : write or print with a capital letter **2** : use as capital **3** : supply capital for **4** : turn something to advantage — **cap·i·tal·i·za·tion** *n*

cap·i·tol *n* : building in which a legislature sits

ca·pit·u·late *vb* **-lat·ed; -lat·ing** : surrender — **ca·pit·u·la·tion** *n*

ca·pon *n* : castrated male chicken

ca·price *n* : whim — **ca·pri·cious** *adj* — **ca·pri·cious·ly** *adv* — **ca·pri·cious·ness** *n*

cap·size *vb* **-sized; -siz·ing** : overturn

cap·stan *n* : upright winch

cap·sule *n* **1** : enveloping cover (as for medicine) **2** : small pressurized compartment for astronauts ~ *adj* : very brief or compact — **cap·su·lar** *adj* — **cap·su·lat·ed** *adj*

cap·tain *n* **1** : commander of a body of troops **2** : officer in charge of a ship **3** : commissioned officer in the navy ranking next below a rear admiral or a commodore **4** : commissioned officer (as in the army) ranking next below a major **5** : leader ~ *vb* : be captain of — **cap·tain·cy** *n*

cap·tion *n* **1** : title **2** : explanation with an illustration — **caption** *vb*

cap·tious *adj* : tending to find fault — **cap·tious·ly** *adv*

cap·ti·vate *vb* **-vat·ed; -vat·ing** : attract and charm — **cap·ti·va·tion** *n* — **cap·ti·va·tor** *n*

cap·tive *adj* **1** : made prisoner **2** : confined or under control — **captive** *n* — **cap·tiv·i·ty** *n*

cap·tor *n* : one that captures

cap·ture *n* : seizure by force or trickery ~ *vb* **-tured; -tur·ing** : take captive

car *n* **1** : vehicle moved on wheels **2** : cage of an elevator

ca·rafe *n* : decanter

car·a·mel *n* **1** : burnt sugar used for flavoring and coloring **2** : firm chewy candy

¹carat *var of* KARAT

²car·at *n* : unit of weight for precious stones

car·a·van *n* : travelers journeying together (as in a line)

car·a·way *n* : aromatic herb with seeds used in seasoning

car·bine *n* : short-barreled rifle

car·bo·hy·drate *n* : compound of carbon, hydrogen, and oxygen

car·bon *n* **1** : chemical element occurring in nature esp. as diamond and graphite **2** : piece of carbon paper or a copy made with it

¹car·bon·ate *n* : salt or ester of a carbon-containing acid

²car·bon·ate *vb* **-at·ed; -at·ing** : impregnate with carbon dioxide — **car·bon·ation** *n*

carbon paper *n* : thin paper coated with a pigment for making copies

car·bun·cle *n* : painful inflammation of the skin and underlying tissue

car·bu·re·tor *n* : device for mixing fuel and air

car·cass *n* : dead body

car·cin·o·gen *n* : agent causing cancer — **car·ci·no·gen·ic** *adj*

car·ci·no·ma *n, pl* **-mas** *or* **-ma·ta** : malignant tumor — **car·ci·no·ma·tous** *adj*

¹card *vb* : comb (fibers) before spinning ~ *n* : device for carding fibers — **card·er** *n*

²card *n* **1** : playing card **2** *pl* : game played with playing cards **3** : small flat piece of paper

card·board *n* : stiff material like paper

car·di·ac *adj* : relating to the heart

car·di·gan *n* : sweater with an opening in the front

¹car·di·nal *n* **1** : official of the Roman Catholic Church **2** : bright red songbird

²cardinal *adj* : of basic importance

cardinal number *n* : number (as 1, 82, 357) used in counting

car·di·ol·o·gy *n* : study of the heart — **car·di·ol·o·gist** *n*

car·dio·vas·cu·lar *adj* : relating to the heart and blood vessels

care *n* **1** : anxiety **2** : watchful attention **3** : supervision ~ *vb* **cared; car·ing 1** : feel anxiety or concern **2** : like **3** : provide care — **care·free** *adj* — **care·ful** *adj* — **care·ful·ly** *adv* — **care·ful·ness** *n* — **care·giv·er** *n* — **care·less** *adj* — **care·less·ly** *adv* — **care·less·ness** *n*

ca·reen *vb* **1** : sway from side to side **2** : career

ca·reer *n* : vocation ~ *vb* : go at top speed

ca·ress *n* : tender touch ~ *vb* : touch lovingly or tenderly

car·et *n* : mark ^showing where something is to be inserted

care·tak·er *n* : one in charge for another or temporarily

car·go *n, pl* **-goes** *or* **-gos** : transported goods

car·i·bou *n, pl* **-bou** *or* **-bous** : large No. American deer

car·i·ca·ture *n* : distorted representation for humor or ridicule — **caricature** *vb* — **car·i·ca·tur·ist** *n*

car·ies *n, pl* **caries** : tooth decay

car·il·lon *n* : set of tuned bells

car·mine *n* : vivid red

car·nage *n* : slaughter

car·nal *adj* : sensual — **car·nal·i·ty** *n* — **car·nal·ly** *adv*

car·na·tion *n* : showy flower

car·ni·val *n* **1** : festival **2** : traveling enterprise offering amusements

car·ni·vore n : flesh-eating animal — **car·niv·o·rous** adj — **car·niv·o·rous·ly** adv — **car·niv·o·rous·ness** n

car·ol n : song of joy — **carol** vb — **car·ol·er**, **car·ol·ler** n

car·om n or vb : rebound

ca·rouse vb **-roused**; **-rous·ing** : drink and be boisterous — **carouse** n — **ca·rous·er** n

car·ou·sel, car·rou·sel n : merry-go-round

¹**carp** vb : find fault

²**carp** n, pl **carp** or **carps** : freshwater fish

car·pel n : modified leaf forming part of the ovary of a flower

car·pen·ter n : one who builds with wood — **carpenter** vb — **car·pen·try** n

car·pet n : fabric floor covering ~ vb : cover with a carpet — **car·pet·ing** n

car·port n : open-sided automobile shelter

car·riage n 1 : conveyance 2 : manner of holding oneself 3 : wheeled vehicle

car·ri·on n : dead and decaying flesh

car·rot n : orange root vegetable

car·ry vb **-ried**; **-ry·ing** 1 : move while supporting 2 : hold (oneself) in a specified way 3 : support 4 : keep in stock 5 : reach to a distance 6 : win — **car·ri·er** n — **carry on** 1 : conduct 2 : behave excitedly — **carry out** vb : put into effect

cart n : wheeled vehicle ~ vb : carry in a cart — **cart·age** n — **cart·er** n

car·tel n : business combination designed to limit competition

car·ti·lage n : elastic skeletal tissue — **car·ti·lag·i·nous** adj

car·tog·ra·phy n : making of maps — **car·tog·ra·pher** n

car·ton n : cardboard box

car·toon n 1 : humorous drawing 2 : comic strip — **cartoon** vb — **car·toon·ist** n

car·tridge n 1 : tube containing powder and a bullet or shot for a firearm 2 : container of material for insertion into an apparatus

carve vb **carved**; **carv·ing** 1 : cut with care 2 : cut into pieces or slices — **carv·er** n

cas·cade n : small steep waterfall ~ vb **-cad·ed**; **-cad·ing** : fall in a cascade

¹**case** n 1 : particular instance 2 : convincing argument 3 : inflectional form esp. of a noun or pronoun 4 : fact 5 : lawsuit 6 : instance of disease — **in case** : as a precaution — **in case of** : in the event of

²**case** n 1 : box 2 : outer covering ~ vb **cased**; **cas·ing** 1 : enclose 2 : inspect

case·ment n : window that opens like a door

cash n 1 : ready money 2 : money paid at the time of purchase ~ vb : give or get cash for

ca·shew n : tropical American tree or its nut

¹**ca·shier** vb : dismiss in disgrace

²**cash·ier** n : person who receives and records payments

cash·mere n : fine goat's wool or a fabric of this

ca·si·no n, pl **-nos** : place for gambling

cask n : barrel-shaped container for liquids

cas·ket n : coffin

cas·se·role n : baking dish or the food cooked in this

cas·sette n : case containing magnetic tape

cas·sock n : long clerical garment

cast vb **cast**; **cast·ing** 1 : throw 2 : deposit (a ballot) 3 : assign parts in a play 4 : mold ~ n 1 : throw 2 : appearance 3 : rigid surgical dressing 4 : actors in a play

cas·ta·nets n pl : shells clicked together in the hand

cast·away n : survivor of a shipwreck — **cast·away** adj

caste n : social class or rank

cast·er n : small wheel on furniture

cas·ti·gate vb **-gat·ed**; **-gat·ing** : chastise severely — **cas·ti·ga·tion** n — **cas·ti·ga·tor** n

cast iron n : hard brittle alloy of iron

cas·tle n : fortified building

cast–off adj : thrown away — **cast·off** n

cas·trate vb **-trat·ed**; **-trat·ing** : remove the testes of — **cas·tra·tion** n

ca·su·al adj 1 : happening by chance 2 : showing little concern 3 : informal — **ca·su·al·ly** adv — **ca·su·al·ness** n

ca·su·al·ty n, pl **-ties** 1 : serious or fatal accident 2 : one injured, lost, or destroyed

ca·su·ist·ry n, pl **-ries** : rationalization — **ca·su·ist** n

cat n 1 : small domestic mammal 2 : related animal (as a lion) — **cat·like** adj

cat·a·clysm n : violent change — **cat·a·clys·mal, cat·a·clys·mic** adj

cat·a·comb n : underground burial place

cat·a·log, cat·a·logue n 1 : list 2 : book containing a description of items ~ vb **-loged** or **-logued**; **-log·ing** or **-logu·ing** 1 : make a catalog of 2 : enter in a catalog — **cat·a·log·er, cat·a·logu·er** n

ca·tal·pa n : tree with broad leaves and long pods

ca·tal·y·sis n, pl **-y·ses** : increase in the rate of chemical reaction caused by a substance (**cat·a·lyst**) that is itself unchanged — **cat·a·lyt·ic** adj

cat·a·ma·ran n : boat with twin hulls

cat·a·mount n : cougar

cat·a·pult n : device for hurling or launching — **catapult** vb

cat·a·ract n 1 : large waterfall 2 : cloudiness of the lens of the eye

ca·tarrh n : inflammation of the nose and throat

ca·tas·tro·phe n 1 : great disaster or misfortune 2 : utter failure — **cat·a·stroph·ic** adj — **cat·a·stroph·i·cal·ly** adv

cat·bird n : American songbird

cat·call n : noise of disapproval

catch vb **caught**; **catch·ing** 1 : capture esp. after pursuit 2 : trap 3 : detect esp. by surprise 4 : grasp 5 : get entangled 6 : become affected with or by 7 : seize and hold firmly ~ n 1 : act of catching 2 : something caught 3 : something that fastens 4 : hidden difficulty — **catch·er** n

catch·ing adj : infectious

catch·up var of KETCHUP

catch·word n : slogan

catchy adj **catch·i·er**; **-est** : likely to catch interest

cat·e·chism n : set of questions and answers esp. to teach religious doctrine

cat·e·gor·i·cal adj : absolute — **cat·e·gor·i·cal·ly** adv

cat·e·go·ry n, pl **-ries** : group or class — **cat·e·go·ri·za·tion** n — **cat·e·go·rize** vb

ca·ter vb 1 : provide food for 2 : supply what is wanted — **ca·ter·er** n

cat·er–cor·ner, cat·er–cor·nered adv or adj : in a diagonal position

cat·er·pil·lar n : butterfly or moth larva

cat·er·waul vb : make the harsh cry of a cat — **caterwaul** n

cat·fish n : big-headed fish with feelers about the mouth

cat·gut n : tough cord made usu. from sheep intestines

ca·thar·sis n, pl **ca·thar·ses** : a purging — **ca·thar·tic** adj or n

ca·the·dral n : principal church of a diocese

cath·e·ter n : tube for insertion into a body cavity

cath·ode n 1 : negative electrode 2 : positive battery terminal — **ca·thod·ic** adj

cath·o·lic adj 1 : universal 2 cap : relating to Roman Catholics

Cath·o·lic n : member of the Roman Catholic Church — **Ca·thol·i·cism** n

cat·kin n : long dense flower cluster

cat·nap n : short light nap — **catnap** vb

cat·nip n : aromatic mint rel- ished by cats

cat's–paw n, pl **cat's–paws** : person used as if a tool

cat·sup var of KETCHUP

cat·tail n : marsh herb with furry brown spikes

cat·tle n pl : domestic bovines — **cat·tle·man** n

cat·ty adj **-ti·er**; **-est** : mean or spiteful — **cat·ti·ly** adv — **cat·ti·ness** n

cat·walk n : high narrow walk

Cau·ca·sian adj : relating to the white race — **Caucasian** n

cau·cus n : political meeting — **caucus** vb

caught past of CATCH

cauldron n : large kettle

cau·li·flow·er n : vegetable having a compact head of usu. white undeveloped flowers

caulk vb : make seams watertight — **caulk** n — **caulk·er** n

caus·al adj : relating to or being a cause — **cau·sal·i·ty** n — **caus·al·ly** adv

cause n 1 : something that brings about a result 2 : reason 3 : lawsuit 4 : principle or movement to support ~ vb **caused**; **caus·ing** : be the cause of — **cau·sa·tion** n — **caus·ative** adj — **cause·less** adj — **caus·er** n

cause·way n : raised road esp. over water

caus·tic adj 1 : corrosive 2 : sharp or biting — **caustic** n

cau·ter·ize vb **-ized**; **-iz·ing** : burn to prevent infection or bleeding — **cau·ter·i·za·tion** n

cau·tion n 1 : warning 2 : care or prudence ~ vb : warn — **cau·tion·ary** adj

cau·tious adj : taking caution — **cau·tious·ly** adv — **cau·tious·ness** n

cav·al·cade n 1 : procession on horseback 2 : series

cav·a·lier n : mounted soldier ~ adj : disdainful or arrogant — **cav·a·lier·ly** adv

cav·al·ry n, pl **-ries** : troops on horseback or in vehicles — **cav·al·ry·man** n

cave n : natural underground chamber — **cave in** vb : collapse

cav·ern n : large cave — **cav·ern·ous** adj — **cav·ern·ous·ly** adv

cav·i·ar, cav·i·are n : salted fish roe

cav·il vb **-iled** or **-illed**; **-il·ing** or **-il·ling** : raise trivial objections — **cavil** n — **cav·il·er, cav·il·ler** n

cav·i·ty n, pl **-ties** 1 : unfilled place within a mass 2 : decay in a tooth

ca·vort vb : prance or caper

caw vb : utter the harsh call of the crow — **caw** n

cay·enne pepper n : ground dried fruits of a hot pepper

CD n : compact disc

cease vb **ceased**; **ceas·ing** : stop

cease·less adj : continuous

ce·dar n : cone-bearing tree with fragrant durable wood

cede vb **ced·ed**; **ced·ing** : surrender — **ced·er** n

ceil·ing n 1 : overhead surface of a room 2 : upper limit

cel·e·brate vb **-brat·ed**; **-brat·ing** 1 : perform with appropriate rites 2 : honor with ceremonies 3 : extol — **cel·e·brant** n — **cel·e·bra·tion** n — **cel·e·bra·tor** n

cel·e·brat·ed adj : renowned

ce·leb·ri·ty n, pl **-ties** 1 : renown 2 : well-known person

ce·ler·i·ty n : speed

cel·ery n, pl **-er·ies** : herb grown for crisp edible stalks

ce·les·ta , ce·leste n : keyboard musical instrument

ce·les·tial adj 1 : relating to the sky 2 : heavenly

cel·i·ba·cy n 1 : state of being unmarried 2 : abstention from sexual intercourse — **cel•i•bate** *n or adj*

cell *n* 1 : small room 2 : tiny mass of protoplasm that forms the fundamental unit of living matter 3 : container holding an electrolyte for generating electricity — **celled** *adj*

cel•lar *n* : room or area below ground

cel•lo *n, pl* **-los** : bass member of the violin family — **cel•list** *n*

cel•lo•phane *n* : thin transparent cellulose wrapping

cel•lu•lar *adj* : relating to or consisting of cells

cel•lu•lose *n* : complex plant carbohydrate

Cel•sius *adj* : relating to a thermometer scale on which the freezing point of water is 0° and the boiling point is 100°

ce•ment *n* 1 : powdery mixture of clay and limestone that hardens when wetted 2 : binding agent ~ *vb* : unite or cover with cement — **ce•ment•er** *n*

cem•e•tery *n, pl* **-ter•ies** : burial ground

cen•ser *n* : vessel for burning incense

cen•sor *n* : one with power to suppress anything objectionable (as in printed matter) ~ *vb* : be a censor of — **cen•so•ri•al** *adj* — **cen•sor•ship** *n*

cen•so•ri•ous *adj* : critical — **cen•so•ri•ous•ly** *adv* — **cen•so•ri•ous•ness** *n*

cen•sure *n* : official reprimand ~ *vb* **-sured; -sur•ing** : find blameworthy — **cen•sur•able** *adj*

cen•sus *n* : periodic population count — **cen•sus** *vb*

cent *n* : monetary unit equal to ¹⁄₁₀₀ of a basic unit of value

cen•taur *n* : mythological creature that is half man and half horse

cen•ten•ni•al *n* : 100th anniversary — **centennial** *adj*

cen•ter *n* 1 : middle point 2 : point of origin or greatest concentration 3 : region of concentrated population 4 : player near the middle of the team ~ *vb* 1 : place, fix, or concentrate at or around a center 2 : have a center — **cen•ter•piece** *n*

cen•ti•grade *adj* : Celsius

cen•ti•me•ter *n* : 1/100 meter

cen•ti•pede *n* : long flat many-legged arthropod

cen•tral *adj* 1 : constituting or being near a center 2 : essential or principal — **cen•tral•ly** *adv*

cen•tral•ize *vb* **-ized; -iz•ing** : bring to a central point or under central control — **cen•tral•i•za•tion** *n* — **cen•tral•iz•er** *n*

cen•tre *chiefly Brit var of* CENTER

cen•trif•u•gal *adj* : acting in a direction away from a center or axis

cen•tri•fuge *n* : machine that separates substances by spinning

cen•trip•e•tal *adj* : acting in a direction toward a center or axis

cen•tu•ri•on *n* : Roman military officer

cen•tu•ry *n, pl* **-ries** : 100 years

ce•ram•ic *n* 1 : art or process of shaping and hardening articles from clay 2 : product of ceramics — **ceramic** *adj*

ce•re•al *adj* : made of or relating to grain or to the plants that produce it ~ *n* 1 : grass yielding edible grain 2 : food prepared from a cereal grain

cer•e•bel•lum *n, pl* **-bel•lums** *or* **-bel•la** : part of the brain controlling muscular coordination — **cer•e•bel•lar** *adj*

ce•re•bral *adj* 1 : relating to the brain, intellect, or cerebrum 2 : appealing to the intellect

cerebral palsy *n* : disorder caused by brain damage and marked esp. by defective muscle control

cer•e•brate *vb* **-brat•ed; -brat•ing** : think — **cer•e•bra•tion** *n*

ce•re•brum *n, pl* **-brums** *or* **-bra** : part of the brain that contains the higher nervous centers

cer•e•mo•ny *n, pl* **-nies** 1 : formal act prescribed by law, ritual, or convention 2 : prescribed procedures — **cer•e•mo•ni•al** *adj or n* — **cer•e•mo•ni•ous** *adj*

ce•rise *n* : moderate red

cer•tain *adj* 1 : settled 2 : true 3 : specific but not named 4 : bound 5 : assured ~ *pron* : certain ones — **cer•tain•ly** *adv* — **cer•tain•ty** *n*

cer•tif•i•cate *n* : document establishing truth or fulfillment

cer•ti•fy *vb* **-fied; -fy•ing** 1 : verify 2 : endorse — **cer•ti•fi•able** *adj* — **cer•ti•fi•ably** *adv* — **cer•ti•fi•ca•tion** *n* — **cer•ti•fi•er** *n*

cer•ti•tude *n* : state of being certain

cer•vix *n, pl* **-vi•ces** *or* **-vix•es** 1 : neck 2 : narrow end of the uterus — **cer•vi•cal** *adj*

ce•sar•e•an *n* : surgical operation to deliver a baby — **cesarean** *adj*

ce•si•um *n* : silver-white soft ductile chemical element

ces•sa•tion *n* : a halting

ces•sion *n* : a yielding

cess•pool *n* : underground sewage pit

Cha•blis *n, pl* **Cha•blis** : dry white wine

chafe *vb* **chafed; chaf•ing** 1 : fret 2 : make sore by rubbing

chaff *n* 1 : debris separated from grain 2 : something worthless

chaf•ing dish *n* : utensil for cooking at the table

cha•grin *n* : embarrassment or humiliation ~ *vb* : cause to feel chagrin

chain *n* 1 : flexible series of connected links 2 *pl* : fetters 3 : linked series ~ *vb* : bind or connect with a chain

chair *n* 1 : seat with a back 2 : position of authority or dignity 3 : chairman ~ *vb* : act as chairman of

chair•man *n* : presiding officer — **chair•man•ship** *n*

chair•wom•an *n* : woman who acts as a presiding officer

chaise longue *n, pl* **chaise longues** : long chair for reclining

cha•let *n* : Swiss mountain cottage with overhanging roof

chal•ice *n* : eucharistic cup

chalk *n* 1 : soft limestone 2 : chalky material used as a crayon ~ *vb* : mark with chalk — **chalky** *adj* — **chalk up** *vb* 1 : credit 2 : achieve

chalk•board *n* : blackboard

chal•lenge *vb* **-lenged; -leng•ing** 1 : dispute 2 : invite or dare to act or compete — **challenge** *n* — **chal•leng•er** *n*

cham•ber *n* 1 : room 2 : enclosed space 3 : legislative meeting place or body 4 *pl* : judge's consultation room — **cham•bered** *adj*

cham•ber•maid *n* : bedroom maid

chamber music *n* : music by a small group for a small audience

cha•me•leon *n* : small lizard whose skin changes color

cham•ois *n, pl* **cham•ois** 1 : goatlike antelope 2 : soft leather

¹champ *vb* : chew noisily

²champ *n* : champion

cham•pagne *n* : sparkling white wine

cham•pi•on *n* 1 : advocate or defender 2 : winning contestant ~ *vb* : protect or fight for

cham•pi•on•ship *n* 1 : title of a champion 2 : contest to pick a champion

chance *n* 1 : unpredictable element of existence 2 : opportunity 3 : probability 4 : risk 5 : raffle ticket ~ *vb* **chanced; chanc•ing** 1 : happen 2 : encounter unexpectedly 3 : risk — **chance** *adj*

chan•cel *n* : part of a church around the altar

chan•cel•lery, chan•cel•lory *n, pl* **-ler•ies** *or* **-lor•ies** 1 : position of a chancellor 2 : chancellor's office

chan•cel•lor *n* 1 : chief or high state official 2 : head of a university — **chan•cel•lor•ship** *n*

chan•cre *n* : skin ulcer esp. from syphilis

chancy *adj* **chanc•i•er; -est** : risky

chan•de•lier *n* : hanging lighting fixture

chan•dler *n* : provisions dealer — **chan•dlery** *n*

change *vb* **changed; chang•ing** 1 : make or become different 2 : exchange 3 : give or receive change for ~ *n* 1 : a changing 2 : excess from a payment 3 : money in smaller denominations 4 : coins — **change•able** *adj* — **change•less** *adj* — **chang•er** *n*

chan•nel *n* 1 : deeper part of a waterway 2 : means of passage or communication 3 : strait 4 : broadcast frequency ~ *vb* **-neled** *or* **-nelled; -nel•ing** *or* **-nel•ling** : make or direct through a channel

chant *vb* : sing or speak in one tone — **chant** *n* — **chant•er** *n*

chan•tey, chan•ty *n, pl* **-teys** *or* **-ties** : sailors' work song

Cha•nu•kah *var of* HANUKKAH

cha•os *n* : complete disorder — **cha•ot•ic** *adj* — **cha•ot•i•cal•ly** *adv*

¹chap *n* : fellow

²chap *vb* **-pp-** : dry and crack open usu. from wind and cold

cha•pel *n* : private or small place of worship

chap•er•on, chap•er•one *n* : older person who accompanies young people at a social gathering ~ *vb* **-oned; -on•ing** : act as chaperon at or for — **chap•er•on•age** *n*

chap•lain *n* : clergy member in a military unit or a prison — **chap•lain•cy** *n*

chap•ter *n* 1 : main book division 2 : branch of a society

char *vb* **-rr-** 1 : burn to charcoal 2 : scorch

char•ac•ter *n* 1 : letter or graphic mark 2 : trait or distinctive combination of traits 3 : peculiar person 4 : fictional person — **char•ac•ter•i•za•tion** *n* — **char•ac•ter•ize** *vb*

char•ac•ter•is•tic *adj* : typical ~ *n* : distinguishing quality — **char•ac•ter•is•ti•cal•ly** *adv*

cha•rades *n sing or pl* : pantomime guessing game

char•coal *n* : porous carbon prepared by partial combustion

chard *n* : leafy vegetable

charge *vb* **charged; charg•ing** 1 : give an electric charge to 2 : impose a task or responsibility on 3 : command 4 : accuse 5 : rush forward in assault 6 : assume a debt for 7 : fix as a price ~ *n* 1 : excess or deficiency of electrons in a body 2 : tax 3 : responsibility 4 : accusation 5 : cost 6 : attack — **charge•able** *adj*

charg•er *n* : horse ridden in battle

char•i•ot *n* : ancient 2-wheeled vehicle — **char•i•o•teer** *n*

cha•ris•ma *n* : special ability to lead — **char•is•mat•ic** *adj*

char•i•ty *n, pl* **-ties** 1 : love for mankind 2 : generosity or leniency 3 : alms 4 : institution for relief of the needy — **char•i•ta•ble** *adj* — **char•i•ta•ble•ness** *n* — **char•i•ta•bly** *adv*

char•la•tan *n* : impostor

charm *n* 1 : something with magic power 2 : appealing trait 3 : small ornament ~ *vb* : fascinate — **charm•er** *n* — **charm•ing** *adj* — **charm•ing•ly** *adv*

char•nel house *n* : place for dead bodies

chart *n* 1 : map 2 : diagram ~ *vb* 1 : make a chart of 2 : plan

char•ter *n* 1 : document granting rights 2 : constitution ~ *vb* 1 : establish by charter 2 : rent — **char•ter•er** *n*

char•treuse *n* : brilliant yellow green

char•wom•an *n* : cleaning woman

chary *adj* **chari•er; -est** : cautious — **char•i•ly** *adv*

¹chase *vb* **chased; chas•ing** 1 : follow trying to catch 2 : drive away — **chase** *n* — **chas•er** *n*

²**chase** *vb* **chased; chas•ing** : decorate (metal) by embossing or engraving

chasm *n* : gorge

chas•sis *n, pl* **chas•sis** : supporting structural frame

chaste *adj* **chast•er; chast•est** 1 : abstaining from all or unlawful sexual relations 2 : modest or decent 3 : severely simple — **chaste•ly** *adv* — **chaste•ness** *n* — **chas•ti•ty** *n*

chas•ten *vb* : discipline

chas•tise *vb* **-tised; -tis•ing** 1 : punish 2 : censure — **chas•tise•ment** *n*

chat *n* : informal talk — **chat** *vb* — **chat•ty** *adj*

châ•teau *n, pl* **-teaus** *or* **-teaux** 1 : large country house 2 : French vineyard estate

chat•tel *n* : item of tangible property other than real estate

chat•ter *vb* 1 : utter rapidly succeeding sounds 2 : talk fast or too much — **chatter** *n* — **chat•ter•er** *n*

chat•ter•box *n* : incessant talker

chauf•feur *n* : hired car driver ~ *vb* : work as a chauffeur

chau•vin•ism *n* : excessive patriotism — **chau•vin•ist** *n* — **chau•vin•is•tic** *adj*

cheap *adj* 1 : inexpensive 2 : shoddy — **cheap** *adv* — **cheap•en** *vb* — **cheap•ly** *adv* — **cheap•ness** *n*

cheap•skate *n* : stingy person

cheat *n* 1 : act of deceiving 2 : one that cheats ~ *vb* 1 : deprive through fraud or deceit 2 : violate rules dishonestly — **cheat•er** *n*

check *n* 1 : sudden stoppage 2 : restraint 3 : test or standard for testing 4 : written order to a bank to pay money 5 : ticket showing ownership 6 : slip showing an amount due 7 : pattern in squares or fabric in such a pattern 8 : mark placed beside an item noted ~ *vb* 1 : slow down or stop 2 : restrain 3 : compare or correspond with a source or original 4 : inspect or test for condition 5 : mark with a check 6 : leave or accept for safekeeping or shipment 7 : checker — **check in** *vb* : report one's arrival — **check out** *vb* : settle one's account and leave

¹**check•er** *n* : piece in checkers ~ *vb* : mark with different colors or into squares

²**checker** *n* : one that checks

check•er•board *n* : board of 64 squares of alternate colors

check•ers *n* : game for 2 played on a checkerboard

check•mate *vb* : thwart completely — **check•mate** *n*

check•point *n* : place where traffic is checked

check•up *n* : physical examination

ched•dar *n* : hard smooth cheese

cheek *n* 1 : fleshy side part of the face 2 : impudence — **cheeked** *adj* — **cheeky** *adj*

cheep *vb* : utter faint shrill sounds — **cheep** *n*

cheer *n* 1 : good spirits 2 : food and drink for a feast 3 : shout of applause or encouragement ~ *vb* 1 : give hope or courage to 2 : make or become glad 3 : urge on or applaud with shouts — **cheer•er** *n* — **cheer•ful** *adj* — **cheer•ful•ly** *adv* — **cheer•ful•ness** *n* — **cheer•lead•er** *n* — **cheer•less** *adj* — **cheer•less•ly** *adv* — **cheer•less•ness** *n*

cheery *adj* **cheer•i•er; -est** : cheerful — **cheer•i•ly** *adv* — **cheer•i•ness** *n*

cheese *n* : curd of milk usu. pressed and cured — **cheesy** *adj*

cheese•cloth *n* : lightweight coarse cotton gauze

chee•tah *n* : spotted swift-moving African cat

chef *n* : chief cook

chem•i•cal *adj* 1 : relating to chemistry 2 : working or produced by chemicals ~ *n* : substance obtained by chemistry — **chem•i•cal•ly** *adv*

che•mise *n* 1 : woman's one-piece undergarment 2 : loose dress

chem•ist *n* 1 : one trained in chemistry 2 *Brit* : pharmacist

chem•is•try *n, pl* **-tries** : science that deals with the composition and properties of substances

che•mo•ther•a•py *n* : use of chemicals in the treatment of disease — **che•mo•ther•a•peu•tic** *adj*

che•nille *n* : yarn with protruding pile or fabric of such yarn

cheque *chiefly Brit var of* CHECK 4

cher•ish *vb* : hold dear

cher•ry *n, pl* **-ries** : small fleshy fruit of a tree related to the roses or the tree or its wood

cher•ub *n* 1 *pl* **-u•bim** : angel 2 *pl* **-ubs** : chubby child — **che•ru•bic** *adj*

chess *n* : game for 2 played on a checkerboard — **chess•board** *n* — **chess•man** *n*

chest *n* 1 : boxlike container 2 : part of the body enclosed by the ribs and breastbone — **chest•ed** *adj*

chest•nut *n* : nut of a tree related to the beech or the tree

chev•i•ot *n* 1 : heavy rough wool fabric 2 : soft-finished cotton fabric

chev•ron *n* : V-shaped insignia

chew *vb* : crush or grind with the teeth ~ *n* : something to chew — **chew•able** *adj* — **chew•er** *n* — **chewy** *adj*

chic *n* : smart elegance of dress or manner ~ *adj* 1 : stylish 2 : currently fashionable

chi•ca•nery *n, pl* **-ner•ies** : trickery

chick *n* : young chicken or bird

chick•a•dee *n* : small grayish American bird

chick•en *n* 1 : common domestic fowl or its flesh used as food 2 : coward

chicken pox *n* : acute contagious virus disease esp. of children

chi•cle *n* : gum from a tropical evergreen tree

chic•o•ry *n, pl* **-ries** : herb used in salad or its dried ground root used to adulterate coffee

chide *vb* **chid** *or* **chid•ed; chid** *or* **chid•den** *or* **chided; chid•ing** : scold

chief *n* : leader ~ *adj* 1 : highest in rank 2 : most important — **chief•dom** *n* — **chief•ly** *adv*

chief•tain *n* : chief

chif•fon *n* : sheer fabric

chig•ger *n* : bloodsucking mite

chi•gnon *n* : knot of hair

chil•blain *n* : sore or inflamed swelling caused by cold

child *n, pl* **chil•dren** 1 : unborn or recently born person 2 : son or daughter — **child•bear•ing** *n or adj* — **child•birth** *n* — **child•hood** *n* — **child•ish** *adj* — **child•ish•ly** *adv* — **child•ish•ness** *n* — **child•less** *adj* — **child•less•ness** *n* — **child•like** *adj* — **child•proof** *adj*

chili, chile, chil•li *n, pl* **chil•ies** *or* **chil•es** *or* **chil•lies** 1 : hot pepper 2 : spicy stew of ground beef, chilies, and beans

chill *vb* : make or become cold or chilly ~ *adj* : moderately cold ~ *n* 1 : feeling of coldness with shivering 2 : moderate coldness

chilly *adj* **chill•i•er; -est** : noticeably cold — **chill•i•ness** *n*

chime *n* : set of tuned bells or their sound ~ *vb* : make bell-like sounds — **chime in** *vb* : break into or join in a conversation

chi•me•ra, chi•mae•ra *n* 1 : imaginary monster 2 : illusion — **chi•me•ri•cal** *adj*

chim•ney *n, pl* **-neys** 1 : passage for smoke 2 : glass tube around a lamp flame

chimp *n* : chimpanzee

chim•pan•zee *n* : small ape

chin *n* : part of the face below the mouth — **chin•less** *adj*

chi•na *n* 1 : porcelain ware 2 : domestic pottery

chin•chil•la *n* : small So. American rodent with soft pearl-gray fur or this fur

chink *n* : small crack ~ *vb* : fill chinks of

chintz *n* : printed cotton cloth

chip *n* 1 : small thin flat piece cut or broken off 2 : thin crisp morsel of food 3 : counter used in games 4 : flaw where a chip came off 5 : small slice of semiconductor containing electronic circuits ~ *vb* **-pp-** : cut or break chips from — **chip in** *vb* : contribute

chip•munk *n* : small striped ground-dwelling rodent

chip•per *adj* : lively and cheerful

chi•rop•o•dy *n* : podiatry — **chi•rop•o•dist** *n*

chi•ro•prac•tic *n* : system of healing based esp. on manipulation of body structures — **chi•ro•prac•tor** *n*

chirp *n* : short sharp sound like that of a bird or cricket — **chirp** *vb*

chis•el *n* : sharp-edged metal tool ~ *vb* **-eled** *or* **-elled; -el•ing** *or* **-el•ling** 1 : work with a chisel 2 : cheat — **chis•el•er** *n*

chit *n* : signed voucher for a small debt

chit•chat *n* : casual conversation — **chitchat** *vb*

chiv•al•rous *adj* 1 : relating to chivalry 2 : honest, courteous, or generous — **chiv•al•rous•ly** *adv* — **chiv•al•rous•ness** *n*

chiv•al•ry *n, pl* **-ries** 1 : system or practices of knighthood 2 : spirit or character of the ideal knight — **chi•val•ric** *adj*

chive *n* : herb related to the onion

chlo•ride *n* : compound of chlorine

chlo•ri•nate *vb* **-nat•ed; -nat•ing** : treat or combine with chlorine — **chlo•ri•na•tion** *n*

chlo•rine *n* : chemical element that is a heavy strong-smelling greenish yellow irritating gas

chlo•ro•form *n* : etherlike colorless heavy fluid ~ *vb* : anesthetize or kill with chloroform

chlo•ro•phyll *n* : green coloring matter of plants

chock *n* : wedge for blocking the movement of a wheel — **chock** *vb*

chock–full *adj* : full to the limit

choc•o•late *n* 1 : ground roasted cacao beans or a beverage made from them 2 : candy made of or with chocolate 3 : dark brown

choice *n* 1 : act or power of choosing 2 : one selected 3 : variety offered for selection ~ *adj* **choic•er; choic•est** 1 : worthy of being chosen 2 : selected with care 3 : of high quality

choir *n* : group of singers esp. in church — **choir•boy** *n* — **choir•mas•ter** *n*

choke *vb* **choked; chok•ing** 1 : hinder breathing 2 : clog or obstruct ~ *n* 1 : a choking or sound of choking 2 : valve for controlling air intake in a gasoline engine

chok•er *n* : tight necklace

chol•er *n* : bad temper — **cho•ler•ic** *adj*

chol•era *n* : disease marked by severe vomiting and dysentery

cho•les•ter•ol *n* : waxy substance in animal tissues

choose *vb* **chose ; cho•sen ; choos•ing** 1 : select after consideration 2 : decide 3 : prefer — **choos•er** *n*

choosy, choos•ey *adj* **choos•i•er; -est** : fussy in making choices

chop *vb* **-pp-** 1 : cut by repeated blows 2 : cut into small pieces ~ *n* 1 : sharp downward blow 2 : small cut of meat often with part of a rib

chop•per *n* 1 : one that chops 2 : helicopter

chop•py *adj* **-pi•er; -est** 1 : rough with small waves 2 : jerky or disconnected — **chop•pi•ly** *adv* — **chop•pi•ness** *n*

chops *n pl* : fleshy covering of the jaws

chop•sticks *n pl* : pair of sticks used in eating in oriental countries

cho•ral *adj* : relating to or sung by a choir or chorus or in chorus — **cho•ral•ly** *adv*

cho•rale *n* 1 : hymn tune or harmonization of a traditional melody 2 : chorus or choir

¹chord n : harmonious tones sounded together

²chord n 1 : cordlike anatomical structure 2 : straight line joining 2 points on a curve

chore n 1 pl : daily household or farm work 2 : routine or disagreeable task

cho•re•og•ra•phy n, pl **-phies** : art of composing and arranging dances — **cho•reo•graph** vb — **cho•re•og•ra•pher** n — **cho•reo•graph•ic** adj

cho•ris•ter n : choir singer

chor•tle vb **-tled; -tling** : laugh or chuckle — **chortle** n

cho•rus n 1 : group of singers or dancers 2 : part of a song repeated at intervals 3 : composition for a chorus ~ vb : sing or utter together

chose past of CHOOSE

cho•sen adj : favored

¹chow n : food

²chow n : thick-coated muscular dog

chow•der n : thick soup usu. of seafood and milk

chow mein n : thick stew of shredded vegetables and meat

chris•ten vb 1 : baptize 2 : name — **chris•ten•ing** n

Chris•ten•dom n : areas where Christianity prevails

Chris•tian n : adherent of Christianity ~ adj : relating to or professing a belief in Christianity or Jesus Christ — **Chris•tian•ize** vb

Chris•ti•an•i•ty n : religion derived from the teachings of Jesus Christ

Christian name n : first name

Christ•mas n : December 25 celebrated as the birthday of Christ

chro•mat•ic adj 1 : relating to color 2 : proceeding by half steps of the musical scale

chrome n : chromium or something plated with it

chro•mi•um n : a bluish white metallic element used esp. in alloys

chro•mo•some n : part of a cell nucleus that contains the genes — **chro•mo•som•al** adj

chron•ic adj : frequent or persistent — **chron•i•cal•ly** adv

chron•i•cle n : history ~ vb **-cled; -cling** : record — **chron•i•cler** n

chro•nol•o•gy n, pl **-gies** : list of events in order of their occurrence — **chron•o•log•i•cal** adj — **chron•o•log•i•cal•ly** adv

chro•nom•e•ter n : very accurate timepiece

chrys•a•lis n, pl **chry•sal•i•des** or **chrys•a•lis•es** : insect pupa enclosed in a shell

chry•san•the•mum n : plant with showy flowers

chub•by adj **-bi•er; -est** : fat — **chub•bi•ness** n

¹chuck vb 1 : tap 2 : toss ~ n 1 : light pat under the chin 2 : toss

²chuck n 1 : cut of beef 2 : machine part that holds work or another part

chuck•le vb **-led; -ling** : laugh quietly — **chuckle** n

chug n : sound of a laboring engine ~ vb **-gg-** : work or move with chugs

chum n : close friend ~ vb **-mm-** : be chums — **chum•my** adj

chump n : fool

chunk n 1 : short thick piece 2 : sizable amount

chunky adj **chunk•i•er; -est** 1 : stocky 2 : containing chunks

church n 1 : building esp. for Christian public worship 2 : whole body of Christians 3 : denomination 4 : congregation — **church•go•er** n — **church•go•ing** adj or n

church•yard n : cemetery beside a church

churl n : rude ill-bred person — **churl•ish** adj

churn n : container in which butter is made ~ vb 1 : agitate in a churn 2 : shake violently

chute n : trough or passage

chut•ney n, pl **-neys** : sweet and sour relish

chutz•pah n : nerve or insolence

ci•ca•da n : stout-bodied insect with transparent wings

ci•der n : apple juice

ci•gar n : roll of leaf tobacco for smoking

cig•a•rette n : cut tobacco rolled in paper for smoking

cinch n 1 : strap holding a saddle or pack in place 2 : sure thing — **cinch** vb

cin•cho•na n : So. American tree that yields quinine

cinc•ture n : belt or sash

cin•der n 1 pl : ashes 2 : piece of partly burned wood or coal

cin•e•ma n : movies or a movie theater — **cin•e•mat•ic** adj

cin•na•mon n : spice from an aromatic tree bark

ci•pher n 1 : zero 2 : code

cir•ca prep : about

cir•cle n 1 : closed symmetrical curve 2 : cycle 3 : group with a common tie ~ vb **-cled; -cling** 1 : enclose in a circle 2 : move or revolve around

cir•cuit n 1 : boundary 2 : regular tour of a territory 3 : complete path of an electric current 4 : group of electronic components

cir•cu•itous adj : circular or winding

cir•cuit•ry n, pl **-ries** : arrangement of an electric circuit

cir•cu•lar adj 1 : round 2 : moving in a circle ~ n : advertising leaflet — **cir•cu•lar•i•ty** n

cir•cu•late vb **-lat•ed; -lat•ing** : move or cause to move in a circle or from place to place or person to person — **cir•cu•la•tion** n — **cir•cu•la•to•ry** adj

cir•cum•cise vb **-cised; -cis•ing** : cut off the foreskin of — **cir•cum•ci•sion** n

cir•cum•fer•ence n : perimeter of a circle

cir•cum•flex n : phonetic mark (as ^)

cir•cum•lo•cu•tion n : excessive use of words

cir•cum•nav•i•gate vb : sail completely around — **cir•cum•nav•i•ga•tion** n

cir•cum•scribe vb 1 : draw a line around 2 : limit

cir•cum•spect adj : careful — **cir•cum•spec•tion** n

cir•cum•stance n 1 : fact or event 2 pl : surrounding conditions 3 pl : financial situation — **cir•cum•stan•tial** adj

cir•cum•vent vb : get around esp. by trickery — **cir•cum•ven•tion** n

cir•cus n : show with feats of skill, animal acts, and clowns

cir•rho•sis n, pl **-rho•ses** : fibrosis of the liver — **cir•rhot•ic** adj or n

cir•rus n, pl **-ri** : wispy white cloud

cis•tern n : underground water tank

cit•a•del n : fortress

cite vb **cit•ed; cit•ing** 1 : summon before a court 2 : quote 3 : refer to esp. in commendation — **ci•ta•tion** n

cit•i•zen n : member of a country — **cit•i•zen•ry** n — **cit•i•zen•ship** n

cit•ron n : lemonlike fruit

cit•rus n, pl **-rus** or **-rus•es** : evergreen tree or shrub grown for its fruit (as the orange or lemon)

city n, pl **cit•ies** : place larger or more important than a town

civ•ic adj : relating to citizenship or civil affairs

civ•ics n : study of citizenship

civ•il adj 1 : relating to citizens 2 : polite 3 : relating to or being a lawsuit — **civ•il•ly** adv

ci•vil•ian n : person not in a military, police, or fire-fighting force

ci•vil•i•ty n, pl **-ties** : courtesy

civ•i•li•za•tion n 1 : high level of cultural development 2 : culture of a time or place

civ•i•lize vb **-lized; -liz•ing** : raise from a primitive stage of cultural development — **civ•i•lized** adj

civil liberty n : freedom from arbitrary governmental interference — usu. pl.

civil rights n pl : nonpolitical rights of a citizen

civil service n : government service

civil war n : war among citizens of one country

clack vb : make or cause a clatter — **clack** n

clad adj : covered

claim vb 1 : demand or take as the rightful owner 2 : maintain ~ n 1 : demand of right or ownership 2 : declaration 3 : something claimed — **claim•ant** n

clair•voy•ant adj : able to perceive things beyond the senses — **clair•voy•ance** n — **clairvoy•ant** n

clam n : bivalve mollusk

clam•ber vb : climb awkwardly

clam•my adj **-mi•er; -est** : being damp, soft, and usu. cool — **clam•mi•ness** n

clam•or n 1 : uproar 2 : protest — **clamor** vb — **clam•or•ous** adj

clamp n : device for holding things together — **clamp** vb

clan n : group of related families — **clan•nish** adj — **clan•nish•ness** n

clan•des•tine adj : secret

clang n : loud metallic ringing — **clang** vb

clan•gor n : jumble of clangs

clank n : brief sound of struck metal — **clank** vb

clap vb **-pp-** 1 : strike noisily 2 : applaud ~ n 1 : loud crash 2 : noise made by clapping the hands

clap•board n : narrow tapered board used for siding

clap•per n : tongue of a bell

claque n 1 : group hired to applaud at a performance 2 : group of sycophants

clar•et n : dry red wine

clar•i•fy vb **-fied; -fy•ing** : make or become clear — **clar•i•fi•ca•tion** n

clar•i•net n : woodwind instrument shaped like a tube — **clar•i•net•ist, clar•i•net•tist** n

clar•i•on adj : loud and clear

clar•i•ty n : clearness

clash vb 1 : make or cause a clash 2 : be in opposition or disharmony ~ n 1 : crashing sound 2 : hostile encounter

clasp n 1 : device for holding things together 2 : embrace or grasp ~ vb 1 : fasten 2 : embrace or grasp

class n 1 : group of the same status or nature 2 : social rank 3 : course of instruction 4 : group of students ~ vb : classify — **class•less** adj — **class•mate** n — **class•room** n

clas•sic adj 1 : serving as a standard of excellence 2 : classical ~ n : work of enduring excellence and esp. of ancient Greece or Rome — **clas•si•cal** adj — **clas•si•cal•ly** adv — **clas•si•cism** n — **clas•si•cist** n

clas•si•fied adj : restricted for security reasons

clas•si•fy vb **-fied; -fy•ing** : arrange in or assign to classes — **clas•si•fi•ca•tion** n — **clas•si•fi•er** n

clat•ter n : rattling sound — **clatter** vb

clause n 1 : separate part of a document 2 : part of a sentence with a subject and predicate

claus•tro•pho•bia n : fear of closed or narrow spaces — **claus•tro•pho•bic** adj

clav•i•chord n : early keyboard instrument

clav•i•cle n : collarbone

claw n : sharp curved nail or process (as on the toe of an animal) ~ vb : scratch or dig — **clawed** adj

clay n : plastic earthy material — **clay•ey** adj

clean adj 1 : free from dirt or disease 2 : pure or honorable 3 : thorough ~ vb : make or become clean — **clean** adv — **clean•er** n — **clean•ly** adv — **clean•ness** n

clean•ly adj **-li•er; -est** : clean — **clean•li•ness** n

cleanse vb **cleansed; cleans•ing** : make clean — **cleans•er** n

clear adj 1 : bright 2 : free from clouds 3 : transparent 4 : easily heard, seen or understood 5 : free from doubt 6 : free from restriction or obstruction ~ *vb* 1 : make or become clear 2 : go away 3 : free from accusation or blame 4 : explain or settle 5 : net 6 : jump or pass without touching ~ *n* : clear space or part — **clear** *adv* — **clear·ance** *n*

clear·ing *n* : land cleared of wood

clear·ly *adv* 1 : in a clear manner 2 : it is obvious that

cleat *n* : projection that strengthens or prevents slipping

cleav·age *n* 1 : a splitting apart 2 : depression between a woman's breasts

¹cleave *vb* **cleaved** *or* **clove** ; **cleav·ing** : adhere

²cleave *vb* **cleaved** ; **cleav·ing** : split apart

cleav·er *n* : heavy chopping knife

clef *n* : sign on the staff in music to show pitch

cleft *n* : crack

clem·ent *adj* 1 : merciful 2 : temperate or mild — **clem·en·cy** *n*

clench *vb* 1 : hold fast 2 : close tightly

cler·gy *n* : body of religious officials — **cler·gy·man** *n*

cler·ic *n* : member of the clergy

cler·i·cal *adj* 1 : relating to the clergy 2 : relating to a clerk or office worker

clerk *n* 1 : official responsible for record-keeping 2 : person doing general office work 3 : salesperson in a store — **clerk** *vb* — **clerk·ship** *n*

clev·er *adj* 1 : resourceful 2 : marked by wit or ingenuity — **clev·er·ly** *adv* — **clev·er·ness** *n*

clew *var of* CLUE

cli·ché *n* : trite phrase — **cli·chéd** *adj*

click *n* : slight sharp noise ~ *vb* : make or cause to make a click

cli·ent *n* 1 : person who engages professional services 2 : customer

cli·en·tele *n* : body of customers

cliff *n* : high steep face of rock

cli·mate *n* : average weather conditions over a period of years — **cli·mat·ic** *adj*

cli·max *n* : the highest point ~ *vb* : come to a climax — **cli·mac·tic** *adj*

climb *vb* 1 : go up or down by use of hands and feet 2 : rise ~ *n* : a climbing — **climb·er** *n*

clinch *vb* 1 : fasten securely 2 : settle 3 : hold fast or firmly — **clinch** *n* — **clinch·er** *n*

cling *vb* **clung** ; **cling·ing** 1 : adhere firmly 2 : hold on tightly

clin·ic *n* : facility for diagnosis and treatment of outpatients — **clin·i·cal** *adj* — **clin·i·cal·ly** *adv*

clink *vb* : make a slight metallic sound — **clink** *n*

clin·ker *n* : fused stony matter esp. in a furnace

¹clip *vb* **-pp-** : fasten with a clip ~ *n* : device to hold things together

²clip *vb* **-pp-** 1 : cut or cut off 2 : hit ~ *n* 1 : clippers 2 : sharp blow 3 : rapid pace

clip·per *n* 1 *pl* : implement for clipping 2 : fast sailing ship

clique *n* : small exclusive group of people

cli·to·ris *n*, *pl* **cli·to·ri·des** : small organ at the front of the vulva

cloak *n* 1 : loose outer garment 2 : something that conceals ~ *vb* : cover or hide with a cloak

clob·ber *vb* : hit hard

clock *n* : timepiece not carried on the person ~ *vb* : record the time of

clock·wise *adv or adj* : in the same direction as a clock's hands move

clod *n* 1 : lump esp. of earth 2 : dull insensitive person

clog *n* 1 : restraining weight 2 : thick-soled shoe ~ *vb* **-gg-** 1 : impede with a clog 2 : obstruct passage through 3 : become plugged up

clois·ter *n* 1 : monastic establishment 2 : covered passage ~ *vb* : shut away from the world

clone *n* 1 : offspring produced from a single organism 2 : copy

¹close *vb* **closed** ; **clos·ing** 1 : shut 2 : cease operation 3 : terminate 4 : bring or come together ~ *n* : conclusion or end

²close *adj* **clos·er** ; **clos·est** 1 : confining 2 : secretive 3 : strict 4 : stuffy 5 : having little space between items 6 : fitting tightly 7 : near 8 : intimate 9 : accurate 10 : nearly even — **close** *adv* — **close·ly** *adv* — **close·ness** *n*

clos·et *n* : small compartment for household utensils or clothing ~ *vb* : take into a private room for a talk

clo·sure *n* 1 : act of closing 2 : something that closes

clot *n* : dried mass of a liquid — **clot** *vb*

cloth *n*, *pl* **cloths** 1 : fabric 2 : tablecloth

clothe *vb* **clothed** *or* **clad** ; **cloth·ing** : dress

clothes *n pl* 1 : clothing 2 : bedclothes

cloth·ier *n* : maker or seller of clothing

cloth·ing *n* : covering for the human body

cloud *n* 1 : visible mass of particles in the air 2 : something that darkens, hides, or threatens ~ *vb* : darken or hide — **cloud·i·ness** *n* — **cloud·less** *adj* — **cloudy** *adj*

cloud·burst *n* : sudden heavy rain

clout *n* 1 : blow 2 : influence ~ *vb* : hit forcefully

¹clove *n* : section of a bulb

²clove *past of* CLEAVE

³clove *n* : dried flower bud of an East Indian tree used as a spice

clo·ver *n* : leguminous herb with usu. 3-part leaves

clo·ver·leaf *n*, *pl* **-leafs** *or* **-leaves** : highway interchange

clown *n* : funny costumed entertainer esp. in a circus ~ *vb* : act like a clown — **clown·ish** *adj* — **clown·ish·ly** *adv* — **clown·ish·ness** *n*

cloy *vb* : disgust with excess **cloy·ing·ly** *adv*

club *n* 1 : heavy wooden stick 2 : playing card of a suit marked with a black figure like a clover leaf 3 : group associated for a common purpose ~ *vb* **-bb-** : hit with a club

club·foot *n* : misshapen foot twisted out of position from birth — **club·foot·ed** *adj*

cluck *n* : sound made by a hen — **cluck** *vb*

clue *n* : piece of evidence that helps solve a problem — *vb* **clued** ; **clue·ing** *or* **clu·ing** : provide with a clue

clump *n* 1 : cluster 2 : heavy tramping sound ~ *vb* : tread heavily

clum·sy *adj* **-si·er** ; **-est** 1 : lacking dexterity, nimbleness, or grace 2 : tactless — **clum·si·ly** *adv* — **clum·si·ness** *n*

clung *past of* CLING

clunk·er *n* : old automobile

clus·ter *n* : group ~ *vb* : grow or gather in a cluster

clutch *vb* : grasp ~ *n* 1 : grasping hand or claws 2 : control or power 3 : coupling for connecting two working parts in machinery

clut·ter *vb* : fill with things that get in the way — **clutter** *n*

co- *prefix* : with, together, joint, or jointly

coact	codirector
coactor	codiscoverer
coauthor	codrive
coauthorship	codriver
cocaptain	coedit
cochairman	coeditor
cochampion	coexecutor
cocomposer	coexist
coconspirator	coexistence
cocreator	coexistent
codefendant	cofeature
codesign	cofinance
codevelop	cofound
codeveloper	cofounder
codirect	coheir

coheiress	coproduce
cohost	coproducer
cohostess	coproduction
coinvent	copromoter
coinventor	coproprietor
coinvestigator	copublish
coleader	copublisher
comanagement	corecipient
comanager	coresident
co-organizer	cosignatory
co-own	cosigner
co-owner	cosponsor
copartner	costar
copartnership	cowinner
copresident	coworker
coprincipal	cowrite
coprisoner	

coach *n* 1 : closed 2-door 4-wheeled carriage 2 : railroad passenger car 3 : bus 4 : 2d-class air travel 5 : one who instructs or trains performers ~ *vb* : instruct or direct as a coach

co·ag·u·late *vb* **-lat·ed** ; **-lat·ing** : clot — **co·ag·u·lant** *n* — **co·ag·u·la·tion** *n*

coal *n* 1 : ember 2 : black solid mineral used as fuel — **coal·field** *n*

co·alesce *vb* **-alesced** ; **-alesc·ing** : grow together — **co·ales·cence** *n*

co·ali·tion *n* : temporary alliance

coarse *adj* **coars·er** ; **coars·est** 1 : composed of large particles 2 : rough or crude — **coarse·ly** *adv* — **coars·en** *vb* — **coarse·ness** *n*

coast *n* : seashore ~ *vb* : move without effort — **coast·al** *adj*

coast·er *n* 1 : one that coasts 2 : plate or mat to protect a surface

coast guard *n* : military force that guards or patrols a coast — **coast·guards·man** *n*

coast·line *n* : shape of a coast

coat *n* 1 : outer garment for the upper body 2 : external growth of fur or feathers 3 : covering layer ~ *vb* : cover with a coat — **coat·ed** *adj* — **coat·ing** *n*

coax *vb* : move to action or achieve by gentle urging or flattery

cob *n* : corncob

co·balt *n* : shiny silver-white magnetic metallic chemical element

cob·ble *vb* **cob·bled** ; **cob·bling** : make or put together hastily

cob·bler *n* 1 : shoemaker 2 : deep-dish fruit pie

cob·ble·stone *n* : small round paving stone

co·bra *n* : venomous snake

cob·web *n* : network spun by a spider or a similar filament

co·caine *n* : drug obtained from the leaves of a So. American shrub (**co·ca**)

co·chlea *n*, *pl* **-chle·as** *or* **-chle·ae** : the usu. spiral part of the inner ear — **coch·le·ar** *adj*

cock *n* 1 : male fowl 2 : valve or faucet ~ *vb* 1 : draw back the hammer of a firearm 2 : tilt to one side — **cock·fight** *n*

cock·ade *n* : badge on a hat

cock·a·too *n*, *pl* **-toos** : large Australian crested parrot

cock·eyed *adj* 1 : tilted to one side 2 : slightly crazy

cock·le *n* : edible shellfish

cock·pit *n* : place for a pilot, driver, or helmsman

cock·roach *n* : nocturnal insect often infesting houses

cock·tail *n* 1 : iced drink of liquor and flavorings 2 : appetizer

cocky *adj* **cock·i·er** ; **-est** : overconfident — **cock·i·ly** *adv* — **cock·i·ness** *n*

co·coa *n* 1 : cacao 2 : powdered chocolate or a drink made from this

co•co•nut *n* : large nutlike fruit of a tropical palm (**coconut palm**)

co•coon *n* : case protecting an insect pupa

cod *n, pl* **cod** : food fish of the No. Atlantic

cod•dle *vb* **-dled; -dling** : pamper

code *n* **1** : system of laws or rules **2** : system of signals

co•deine *n* : narcotic drug used in cough remedies

cod•ger *n* : odd fellow

cod•i•cil *n* : postscript to a will

cod•i•fy *vb* **-fied; -fy•ing** : arrange systematically — **cod•i•fi•ca•tion** *n*

co•ed *n* : female student in a coeducational institution — **coed** *adj*

co•ed•u•ca•tion *n* : education of the sexes together — **co•ed•u•ca•tion•al** *adj*

co•ef•fi•cient *n* **1** : number that is a multiplier of another **2** : number that serves as a measure of some property

co•erce *vb* **-erced; -erc•ing** : force — **co•er•cion** *n* — **co•er•cive** *adj*

cof•fee *n* : drink made from the roasted and ground seeds (**coffee beans**) of a tropical shrub — **cof•fee•house** *n* — **cof•fee•pot** *n*

cof•fer *n* : box for valuables

cof•fin *n* : box for burial

cog *n* : tooth on the rim of a gear — **cogged** *adj* — **cog•wheel** *n*

co•gent *adj* : compelling or convincing — **co•gen•cy** *n*

cog•i•tate *vb* **-tat•ed; -tat•ing** : think over — **cog•i•ta•tion** *n* — **cog•i•ta•tive** *adj*

co•gnac *n* : French brandy

cog•nate *adj* : related — **cog•nate** *n*

cog•ni•tion *n* : act or process of knowing — **cog•ni•tive** *adj*

cog•ni•zance *n* : notice or awareness — **cog•ni•zant** *adj*

co•hab•it *vb* : live together as husband and wife — **co•hab•i•ta•tion** *n*

co•here *vb* **-hered; -her•ing** : stick together

co•her•ent *adj* **1** : able to stick together **2** : logically consistent — **co•her•ence** *n* — **co•her•ent•ly** *adv*

co•he•sion *n* : a sticking together — **co•he•sive** *adj* — **co•he•sive•ly** *adv* — **co•he•sive•ness** *n*

co•hort *n* **1** : group of soldiers **2** : companion

coif•fure *n* : hair style

coil *vb* : wind in a spiral ~ *n* : series of loops (as of rope)

coin *n* : piece of metal used as money ~ *vb* **1** : make (a coin) by stamping **2** : create — **coin•age** *n* — **coin•er** *n*

co•in•cide *vb* **-cid•ed; -cid•ing 1** : be in the same place **2** : happen at the same time **3** : be alike — **co•in•ci•dence** *n* — **co•in•ci•dent** *adj* — **co•in•ci•den•tal** *adj*

co•itus *n* : sexual intercourse — **co•ital** *adj*

coke *n* : fuel made by heating soft coal

co•la *n* : carbonated soft drink

col•an•der *n* : perforated utensil for draining food

cold *adj* **1** : having a low or below normal temperature **2** : lacking warmth of feeling **3** : suffering from lack of warmth ~ *n* **1** : low temperature **2** : minor respiratory illness — **cold•ly** *adv* — **cold•ness** *n* — **in cold blood** : with premeditation

cold–blood•ed *adj* **1** : cruel or merciless **2** : having a body temperature that varies with the temperature of the environment

cole•slaw *n* : cabbage salad

col•ic *n* : sharp abdominal pain — **col•icky** *adj*

col•i•se•um *n* : arena

col•lab•o•rate *vb* **-rat•ed; -rat•ing 1** : work jointly with others **2** : help the enemy — **col•lab•o•ra•tion** *n* — **col•lab•o•ra•tor** *n*

col•lapse *vb* **-lapsed; -laps•ing 1** : fall in **2** : break down physically or mentally **3** : fold down ~ *n* : breakdown — **col•laps•ible** *adj*

col•lar *n* : part of a garment around the neck ~ *vb* **1** : seize by the collar **2** : grab — **col•lar•less** *adj*

col•lar•bone *n* : bone joining the breastbone and the shoulder blade

col•lards *n pl* : kale

col•late *vb* **-lat•ed; -lat•ing 1** : compare carefully **2** : assemble in order

col•lat•er•al *adj* **1** : secondary **2** : descended from the same ancestors but not in the same line **3** : similar ~ *n* : property used as security for a loan

col•league *n* : associate

col•lect *vb* **1** : bring, come, or gather together **2** : receive payment of ~ *adv or adj* : to be paid for by the receiver — **col•lect•ible, col•lect•able** *adj* — **col•lec•tion** *n* — **col•lec•tor** *n*

col•lec•tive *adj* : denoting or shared by a group ~ *n* : a cooperative unit — **col•lec•tive•ly** *adv*

col•lege *n* : institution of higher learning granting a bachelor's degree — **col•le•gian** *n* — **col•le•giate** *adj*

col•lide *vb* **-lid•ed; -lid•ing** : strike together — **col•li•sion** *n*

col•lie *n* : large long-haired dog

col•loid *n* : tiny particles in suspension in a fluid — **col•loi•dal** *adj*

col•lo•qui•al *adj* : used in informal conversation — **col•lo•qui•al•ism** *n*

col•lo•quy *n, pl* **-quies** : formal conversation or conference

col•lu•sion *n* : secret cooperation for deceit — **col•lu•sive** *adj*

co•logne *n* : perfumed liquid

¹**co•lon** *n, pl* **colons** *or* **co•la** : lower part of the large intestine — **co•lon•ic** *adj*

²**colon** *n, pl* **colons** : punctuation mark : used esp. to direct attention to following matter

col•o•nel *n* : commissioned officer (as in the army) ranking next below a brigadier general

col•o•nize *vb* **-nized; -niz•ing 1** : establish a colony in **2** : settle — **col•o•ni•za•tion** *n* — **col•o•niz•er** *n*

col•on•nade *n* : row of supporting columns

col•o•ny *n, pl* **-nies 1** : people who inhabit a new territory or the territory itself **2** : animals of one kind (as bees) living together — **co•lo•nial** *adj or n* — **col•o•nist** *n*

col•or *n* **1** : quality of visible things distinct from shape that results from light reflection **2** *pl* : flag **3** : liveliness ~ *vb* **1** : give color to **2** : blush — **col•or•fast** *adj* — **col•or•ful** *adj* — **col•or•less** *adj*

col•or–blind *adj* : unable to distinguish colors — **color blindness** *n*

col•ored *adj* **1** : having color **2** : of a race other than the white ~ *n, pl* **colored** *or* **coloreds** : colored person

co•los•sal *adj* : very large or great

co•los•sus *n, pl* **-si** : something of great size or scope

colt *n* : young male horse — **colt•ish** *adj*

col•umn *n* **1** : vertical section of a printed page **2** : regular feature article (as in a newspaper) **3** : pillar **4** : row (as of soldiers) — **co•lum•nar** *adj* — **col•um•nist** *n*

co•ma *n* : deep prolonged unconsciousness — **co•ma•tose** *adj*

comb *n* **1** : toothed instrument for arranging the hair **2** : crest on a fowl's head — **comb** *vb* — **combed** *adj*

com•bat *vb* **-bat•ed** *or* **-bat•ted; -bat•ing** *or* **-bat•ting** : fight — **com•bat** *n* — **com•bat•ant** *n* — **com•bat•ive** *adj*

com•bi•na•tion *n* **1** : process or result of combining **2** : code for opening a lock

com•bine *vb* **-bined; -bin•ing** : join together ~ *n* **1** : association for business or political advantage **2** : harvesting machine

com•bus•ti•ble *adj* : apt to catch fire — **com•bus•ti•bil•i•ty** *n* — **combustible** *n*

com•bus•tion *n* : process of burning

come *vb* **came ; come; com•ing 1** : move toward or arrive at something **2** : reach a state **3** : originate or exist **4** : amount — **come clean** *vb* : confess — **come into** *vb* : acquire, achieve — **come off** *vb* : succeed — **come to** *vb* : regain consciousness — **come to pass** : happen — **come to terms** : reach an agreement

come•back *n* **1** : retort **2** : return to a former position — **come back** *vb*

co•me•di•an *n* **1** : comic actor **2** : funny person **3** : entertainer specializing in comedy

co•me•di•enne *n* : a woman who is a comedian

com•e•dy *n, pl* **-dies 1** : an amusing play **2** : humorous entertainment

come•ly *adj* **-li•er; -est** : attractive — **come•li•ness** *n*

com•et *n* : small bright celestial body having a tail

com•fort *n* **1** : consolation **2** : well-being or something that gives it ~ *vb* **1** : give hope to **2** : console — **com•fort•able** *adj* — **com•fort•ably** *adv* — **com•fort•less** *adj*

com•fort•er *n* **1** : one that comforts **2** : quilt

com•ic *adj* **1** : relating to comedy **2** : funny ~ *n* **1** : comedian **2** : sequence of cartoons — **com•i•cal** *adj*

com•ing *adj* : next

com•ma *n* : punctuation mark , used esp. to separate sentence parts

com•mand *vb* **1** : order **2** : control ~ *n* **1** : act of commanding **2** : an order given **3** : mastery **4** : troops under a commander — **com•man•dant** *n*

com•man•deer *vb* : seize by force

com•mand•er *n* **1** : officer commanding an army or subdivision of an army **2** : commissioned officer in the navy ranking next below a captain

com•mand•ment *n* : order

command sergeant major *n* : noncommissioned officer in the army ranking above a first sergeant

com•mem•o•rate *vb* **-rat•ed; -rat•ing** : celebrate or honor — **com•mem•o•ra•tion** *n* — **com•mem•o•ra•tive** *adj*

com•mence *vb* **-menced; -menc•ing** : start

com•mence•ment *n* **1** : beginning **2** : graduation ceremony

com•mend *vb* **1** : entrust **2** : recommend **3** : praise — **commend•able** *adj* — **com•men•da•tion** *n*

com•men•su•rate *adj* : equal in measure or extent

com•ment *n* : statement of opinion or remark — **comment** *vb*

com•men•tary *n, pl* **-tar•ies** : series of comments

com•men•ta•tor *n* : one who discusses news

com•merce *n* : business

com•mer•cial *adj* : designed for profit or for mass appeal ~ *n* : broadcast advertisement — **com•mer•cial•ize** *vb* — **com•mer•cial•ly** *adv*

com•min•gle *vb* : mix

com•mis•er•ate *vb* **-at•ed; at•ing** : sympathize — **com•mis•er•a•tion** *n*

com•mis•sary *n, pl* **-sar•ies** : store esp. for military personnel

com•mis•sion *n* **1** : order granting power or rank **2** : panel to judge, approve, or act **3** : the doing of an act **4** : agent's fee ~ *vb* **1** : confer rank or authority to or for **2** : request something be done

com•mis•sion•er *n* **1** : member of a commission **2** : head of a government department

com•mit *vb* **-tt- 1** : turn over to someone for safekeeping or confinement **2** : perform or do **3** : pledge — **com•mit•ment** *n*

com•mit•tee *n* : panel that examines or acts on something

com•mo•di•ous *adj* : spacious

com•mod•i•ty *n, pl* **-ties** : article for sale

com·mo·dore *n* **1** : former commissioned officer in the navy ranking next below a rear admiral **2** : officer commanding a group of merchant ships

com·mon *adj* **1** : public **2** : shared by several **3** : widely known, found, or observed **4** : ordinary ~ *n* : community land — **com·mon·ly** *adv* — **in common** : shared together

com·mon·place *n* : cliché ~ *adj* : ordinary

common sense *n* : good judgment

com·mon·weal *n* : general welfare

com·mon·wealth *n* : state

com·mo·tion *n* : disturbance

¹com·mune *vb* **-muned; -mun·ing** : communicate intimately

²com·mune *n* : community that shares all ownership and duties — **com·mu·nal** *adj*

com·mu·ni·cate *vb* **-cat·ed; -cat·ing 1** : make known **2** : transmit **3** : exchange information or opinions — **com·mu·ni·ca·ble** *adj* — **com·mu·ni·ca·tion** *n* — **com·mu·ni·ca·tive** *adj*

Com·mu·nion *n* : Christian sacrament of partaking of bread and wine

com·mu·ni·qué *n* : official bulletin

com·mu·nism *n* **1** : social organization in which goods are held in common **2** *cap* : political doctrine based on revolutionary Marxist socialism — **com·mu·nist** *n or adj, often cap* — **com·mu·nis·tic** *adj, often cap*

com·mu·ni·ty *n, pl* **-ties** : body of people living in the same place under the same laws

com·mute *vb* **-mut·ed; -mut·ing 1** : reduce (a punishment) **2** : travel back and forth regularly ~ *n* : trip made in commuting — **com·mu·ta·tion** *n* — **com·mut·er** *n*

¹com·pact *adj* **1** : hard **2** : small or brief ~ *vb* : pack together ~ *n* **1** : cosmetics case **2** : small car — **com·pact·ly** *adv* — **com·pact·ness** *n*

²com·pact *n* : agreement

compact disc *n* : plastic-coated disc with laser-readable recorded music

com·pan·ion *n* **1** : close friend **2** : one of a pair — **com·pan·ion·able** *adj* — **com·pan·ion·ship** *n*

com·pa·ny *n, pl* **-nies 1** : business organization **2** : group of performers **3** : guests **4** : infantry unit

com·par·a·tive *adj* **1** : relating to or being an adjective or adverb form that denotes increase **2** : relative — **comparative** *n* — **com·par·a·tive·ly** *adv*

com·pare *vb* **-pared; -par·ing 1** : represent as similar **2** : check for likenesses or differences ~ *n* : comparison — **com·pa·ra·ble** *adj*

com·par·i·son *n* **1** : act of comparing **2** : change in the form and meaning of an adjective or adverb to show different levels of quality, quantity, or relation

com·part·ment *n* : section or room

com·pass *n* **1** : scope **2** : device for drawing circles **3** : device for determining direction

com·pas·sion *n* : pity — **com·pas·sion·ate** *adj*

com·pat·i·ble *adj* : harmonious — **com·pat·i·bil·i·ty** *n*

com·pa·tri·ot *n* : fellow countryman

com·pel *vb* **-ll-** : cause through necessity

com·pen·di·ous *adj* **1** : concise and comprehensive **2** : comprehensive

com·pen·di·um *n, pl* **-di·ums** *or* **-dia** : summary

com·pen·sate *vb* **-sat·ed; -sat·ing 1** : offset or balance **2** : repay — **com·pen·sa·tion** *n* — **com·pen·sa·to·ry** *adj*

com·pete *vb* **-pet·ed; -pet·ing** : strive to win — **com·pe·ti·tion** *n* — **com·pet·i·tive** *adj* — **com·pet·i·tive·ness** *n* — **com·pet·i·tor** *n*

com·pe·tent *adj* : capable — **com·pe·tence** *n* — **com·pe·ten·cy** *n*

com·pile *vb* **-piled; -pil·ing** : collect or compose from several sources — **com·pi·la·tion** *n* — **com·pil·er** *n*

com·pla·cen·cy *n* : self-satisfaction — **com·pla·cent** *adj*

com·plain *vb* **1** : express grief, pain, or discontent **2** : make an accusation — **com·plain·ant** *n* — **com·plain·er** *n*

com·plaint *n* **1** : expression of grief or discontent **2** : ailment **3** : formal accusation

com·ple·ment *n* **1** : something that completes **2** : full number or amount ~ *vb* : complete — **com·ple·men·ta·ry** *adj*

com·plete *adj* **-plet·er; -est 1** : having all parts **2** : finished **3** : total ~ *vb* **-plet·ed; -plet·ing 1** : make whole **2** : finish — **com·plete·ly** *adv* — **com·plete·ness** *n* — **com·ple·tion** *n*

com·plex *adj* **1** : having many parts **2** : intricate ~ *n* : psychological problem — **com·plex·i·ty** *n*

com·plex·ion *n* : hue or appearance of the skin esp. of the face — **com·plex·ioned** *adj*

com·pli·cate *vb* **-cat·ed; -cat·ing** : make complex or hard to understand — **com·pli·cat·ed** *adj* — **com·pli·ca·tion** *n*

com·plic·i·ty *n, pl* **-ties** : participation in guilt

com·pli·ment *n* **1** : flattering remark **2** *pl* : greeting ~ *vb* : pay a compliment to

com·pli·men·ta·ry *adj* **1** : praising **2** : free

com·ply *vb* **-plied; -ply·ing** : conform or yield — **com·pli·ance** *n* — **com·pli·ant** *n*

com·po·nent *n* : part of something larger ~ *adj* : serving as a component

com·port *vb* **1** : agree **2** : behave — **com·port·ment** *n*

com·pose *vb* **-posed; -pos·ing 1** : create (as by writing) or put together **2** : calm **3** : set type — **com·pos·er** *n* — **com·po·si·tion** *n*

com·pos·ite *adj* : made up of diverse parts — **composite** *n*

com·post *n* : decayed organic fertilizing material

com·po·sure *n* : calmness

com·pote *n* : fruits cooked in syrup

¹com·pound *vb* **1** : combine or add **2** : pay (interest) on principal and accrued interest ~ *adj* : made up of 2 or more parts ~ *n* : something that is compound

²com·pound *n* : enclosure

com·pre·hend *vb* **1** : understand **2** : include — **com·pre·hen·si·ble** *adj* — **com·pre·hen·sion** *n* — **com·pre·hen·sive** *adj*

com·press *vb* : squeeze together ~ *n* : pad for pressing on a wound — **com·pres·sion** *n* — **com·pres·sor** *n*

compressed air *n* : air under pressure greater than that of the atmosphere

com·prise *vb* **-prised; -pris·ing 1** : contain or cover **2** : be made up of

com·pro·mise *vb* **-mised; -mis·ing** : settle differences by mutual concessions — **compromise** *n*

comp·trol·ler *n* : financial officer

com·pul·sion *n* **1** : coercion **2** : irresistible impulse — **com·pul·sive** *adj* — **com·pul·so·ry** *adj*

com·punc·tion *n* : remorse

com·pute *vb* **-put·ed; -put·ing** · : calculate — **com·pu·ta·tion** *n*

com·put·er *n* : electronic data processing machine — **com·put·er·i·za·tion** *n* — **com·put·er·ize** *vb*

com·rade *n* : companion — **com·rade·ship** *n*

¹con *adv* : against ~ *n* : opposing side or person

²con *vb* **-nn-** : swindle

con·cave *adj* : curved like the inside of a sphere — **con·cav·i·ty** *n*

con·ceal *vb* : hide — **con·ceal·ment** *n*

con·cede *vb* **-ced·ed; -ced·ing** : grant

con·ceit *n* : excessively high opinion of oneself — **con·ceit·ed** *adj*

con·ceive *vb* **-ceived; -ceiv·ing 1** : become preg-

nant **2** : think of — **con·ceiv·able** *adj* — **con·ceiv·ably** *adv*

con·cen·trate *vb* **-trat·ed; -trat·ing 1** : gather together **2** : make stronger **3** : fix one's attention ~ *n* : something concentrated — **con·cen·tra·tion** *n*

con·cen·tric *adj* : having a common center

con·cept *n* : thought or idea

con·cep·tion *n* **1** : act of conceiving **2** : idea

con·cern *vb* **1** : relate to **2** : involve ~ *n* **1** : affair **2** : worry **3** : business — **con·cerned** *adj* — **con·cern·ing** *prep*

con·cert *n* **1** : agreement or joint action **2** : public performance of music — **con·cert·ed** *adj*

con·cer·ti·na *n* : accordionlike instrument

con·cer·to *n, pl* **-ti** *or* **-tos** : orchestral work with solo instruments

con·ces·sion *n* **1** : act of conceding **2** : something conceded **3** : right to do business on a property

conch *n, pl* **conchs** *or* **conch·es** : large spiral-shelled marine mollusk

con·cil·ia·to·ry *adj* : mollifying

con·cise *adj* : said in few words — **con·cise·ly** *adv* — **con·cise·ness** *n* — **con·ci·sion** *n*

con·clave *n* : private meeting

con·clude *vb* **-clud·ed; -clud·ing 1** : end **2** : decide — **con·clu·sion** *n* — **con·clu·sive** *adj* — **con·clu·sive·ly** *adv*

con·coct *vb* : prepare or devise — **con·coc·tion** *n*

con·com·i·tant *adj* : accompanying — **concomitant** *n*

con·cord *n* : agreement

con·cor·dance *n* **1** : agreement **2** : index of words — **con·cor·dant** *adj*

con·course *n* : open space where crowds gather

con·crete *adj* **1** : naming something real **2** : actual or substantial **3** : made of concrete ~ *n* : hard building material made of cement, sand, gravel, and water

con·cre·tion *n* : hard mass

con·cu·bine *n* : mistress

con·cur *vb* **-rr-** : agree — **con·cur·rence** *n*

con·cur·rent *adj* : happening at the same time

con·cus·sion *n* **1** : shock **2** : brain injury from a blow

con·demn *vb* **1** : declare to be wrong, guilty, or unfit for use **2** : sentence — **con·dem·na·tion** *n*

con·dense *vb* **-densed; -dens·ing 1** : make or become more compact **2** : change from vapor to liquid — **con·den·sa·tion** *n* — **con·dens·er** *n*

con·de·scend *vb* **1** : lower oneself **2** : act haughtily — **con·de·scen·sion** *n*

con·di·ment *n* : pungent seasoning

con·di·tion *n* **1** : necessary situation or stipulation **2** *pl* : state of affairs **3** : state of being ~ *vb* : put into proper condition — **con·di·tion·al** *adj* — **con·di·tion·al·ly** *adv*

con·do·lence *n* : expression of sympathy — usu. pl.

con·do·min·i·um *n, pl* **-ums** : individually owned apartment

con·done *vb* **-doned; -don·ing** : overlook or forgive

con·dor *n* : large western American vulture

con·du·cive *adj* : tending to help or promote

con·duct *n* **1** : management **2** : behavior ~ *vb* **1** : guide **2** : manage or direct **3** : be a channel for **4** : behave — **con·duc·tion** *n* — **con·duc·tive** *adj* — **con·duc·tiv·i·ty** *n* — **con·duc·tor** *n*

con·duit *n* : channel (as for conveying fluid)

cone *n* **1** : scaly fruit of pine and related trees **2** : solid figure having a circular base and tapering sides

con·fec·tion *n* : sweet dish or candy — **con·fec·tion·er** *n*

con·fed·er·a·cy *n, pl* **-cies 1** : league **2** *cap* : 11 southern states that seceded from the U.S. in 1860 and 1861

con·fed·er·ate adj 1 : united in a league 2 cap : relating to the Confederacy ~ n 1 : ally 2 cap : adherent of the Confederacy ~ vb -at·ed; -at·ing : unite — **con·fed·er·a·tion** n

con·fer vb -rr- 1 : give 2 : meet to exchange views — **con·fer·ee** n — **con·fer·ence** n

con·fess vb 1 : acknowledge or disclose one's misdeed, fault, or sin 2 : declare faith in — **con·fes·sion** n — **con·fes·sion·al** n or adj

con·fes·sor n 1 : one who confesses 2 : priest who hears confessions

con·fet·ti n : bits of paper or ribbon thrown in celebration

con·fi·dant n : one to whom secrets are confided

con·fide vb -fid·ed; -fid·ing 1 : share private thoughts 2 : reveal in confidence

con·fi·dence n 1 : trust 2 : self-assurance 3 : something confided — **con·fi·dent** adj — **con·fi·den·tial** adj — **con·fi·den·tial·ly** adv — **con·fi·dent·ly** adv

con·fig·u·ra·tion n : arrangement

con·fine vb -fined; -fin·ing 1 : restrain or restrict to a limited area 2 : imprison — **con·fine·ment** n — **con·fin·er** n

confines n pl : bounds

con·firm vb 1 : ratify 2 : verify 3 : admit as a full member of a church or synagogue — **con·fir·ma·tion** n

con·fis·cate vb -cat·ed; -cat·ing : take by authority — **con·fis·ca·tion** n — **con·fis·ca·to·ry** adj

con·fla·gra·tion n : great fire

con·flict n 1 : war 2 : clash of ideas ~ vb : clash

con·form vb 1 : make or be like 2 : obey — **con·for·mi·ty** n

con·found vb : confuse

con·front vb : oppose or face — **con·fron·ta·tion** n

con·fuse vb -fused; -fus·ing 1 : make mentally uncertain 2 : jumble — **con·fu·sion** n

con·fute vb -fut·ed; -fut·ing : overwhelm by argument

con·geal vb 1 : freeze 2 : become thick and solid

con·ge·nial adj : kindred or agreeable — **con·ge·ni·al·i·ty** n

con·gen·i·tal adj : existing from birth

con·gest vb : overcrowd or overfill — **con·ges·tion** n — **con·ges·tive** adj

con·glom·er·ate adj : made up of diverse parts ~ vb -at·ed; -at·ing : form into a mass ~ n : diversified corporation — **con·glom·er·a·tion** n

con·grat·u·late vb -lat·ed; -lat·ing : express pleasure to for good fortune — **con·grat·u·la·tion** n — **con·grat·u·la·to·ry** adj

con·gre·gate vb -gat·ed; -gat·ing : assemble

con·gre·ga·tion n 1 : assembly of people at worship 2 : religious group — **con·gre·ga·tion·al** adj

con·gress n : assembly of delegates or of senators and representatives — **con·gres·sio·nal** adj — **con·gress·man** n — **con·gress·wom·an** n

con·gru·ence n : likeness — **con·gru·ent** adj

con·gru·ity n : correspondence between things — **con·gru·ous** adj

con·ic adj : relating to or like a cone — **con·i·cal** adj

co·ni·fer n : cone-bearing tree — **co·nif·er·ous** adj

con·jec·ture n or vb : guess — **con·jec·tur·al** adj

con·join vb : join together — **con·joint** adj

con·ju·gal adj : relating to marriage

con·ju·gate vb -gat·ed; -gat·ing : give the inflected forms of (a verb) — **con·ju·ga·tion** n

con·junc·tion n 1 : combination 2 : occurrence at the same time 3 : a word that joins other words together — **con·junc·tive** adj

con·jure vb -jured; -jur·ing 1 : summon by sor-cery 2 : practice sleight of hand 3 : entreat — **con·jur·er, con·ju·ror** n

con·nect vb : join or associate — **con·nect·able** adj — **con·nec·tion** n — **con·nec·tive** n or adj — **con·nec·tor** n

con·nive vb -nived; -niv·ing 1 : pretend ignorance of wrongdoing 2 : cooperate secretly — **con·niv·ance** n

con·nois·seur n : expert judge esp. of art

con·note vb -not·ed; -not·ing : suggest additional meaning — **con·no·ta·tion** n

con·nu·bi·al adj : relating to marriage

con·quer vb : defeat or overcome — **con·quer·or** n

con·quest n 1 : act of conquering 2 : something conquered

con·science n : awareness of right and wrong

con·sci·en·tious adj : honest and hard-working — **con·sci·en·tious·ly** adv

con·scious adj 1 : aware 2 : mentally awake or alert 3 : intentional — **con·scious·ly** adv — **con·scious·ness** n

con·script vb : draft for military service — **con·script** n — **con·scrip·tion** n

con·se·crate vb -crat·ed; -crat·ing 1 : declare sacred 2 : devote to a solemn purpose — **con·se·cra·tion** n

con·sec·u·tive adj : following in order — **con·sec·u·tive·ly** adv

con·sen·sus n 1 : agreement in opinion 2 : collective opinion

con·sent vb : give permission or approval — **con·sent** n

con·se·quence n 1 : result or effect 2 : importance — **con·se·quent** adj — **con·se·quent·ly** adv

con·se·quen·tial adj : important

con·ser·va·tion n : planned management of natural resources — **con·ser·va·tion·ist** n

con·ser·va·tive adj 1 : disposed to maintain the status quo 2 : cautious — **con·ser·va·tism** n — **conservative** n — **con·ser·va·tive·ly** adv

con·ser·va·to·ry n, pl -ries : school for art or music

con·serve vb -served; -serv·ing : keep from wasting ~ n : candied fruit or fruit preserves

con·sid·er vb 1 : think about 2 : give thoughtful attention to 3 : think that — **con·sid·er·ate** adj — **con·sid·er·a·tion** n

con·sid·er·able adj 1 : significant 2 : noticeably large — **con·sid·er·a·bly** adv

con·sid·er·ing prep : taking notice of

con·sign vb 1 : transfer 2 : send to an agent for sale — **con·sign·ee** n — **con·sign·ment** n — **con·sign·or** n

con·sist vb 1 : be inherent — used with in 2 : be made up — used with of

con·sis·ten·cy n, pl -cies 1 : degree of thickness or firmness 2 : quality of being consistent

con·sis·tent adj : being steady and regular — **con·sis·tent·ly** adv

¹**con·sole** vb -soled; -sol·ing : soothe the grief of — **con·so·la·tion** n

²**con·sole** n : cabinet or part with controls

con·sol·i·date vb -dat·ed; -dat·ing : unite or compact — **con·sol·i·da·tion** n

con·som·mé n : clear soup

con·so·nance n : agreement or harmony — **con·so·nant** adj — **con·so·nant·ly** adv

con·so·nant n 1 : speech sound marked by constriction or closure in the breath channel 2 : letter other than a, e, i, o, and u — **con·so·nan·tal** adj

con·sort n : spouse ~ vb : keep company

con·spic·u·ous adj : very noticeable — **con·spic·u·ous·ly** adv

con·spire vb -spired; -spir·ing : secretly plan an unlawful act — **con·spir·a·cy** n — **con·spir·a·tor** n — **con·spir·a·to·ri·al** adj

con·sta·ble n : police officer

con·stab·u·lary n, pl -lar·ies : police force

con·stant adj 1 : steadfast or faithful 2 : not varying 3 : continually recurring ~ n : something unchanging — **con·stan·cy** n — **con·stant·ly** adv

con·stel·la·tion n : group of stars

con·ster·na·tion n : amazed dismay

con·sti·pa·tion n : difficulty of defecation — **con·sti·pate** vb

con·stit·u·ent adj 1 : component 2 : having power to elect ~ n 1 : component part 2 : one who may vote for a representative — **con·stit·u·en·cy** n

con·sti·tute vb -tut·ed; -tut·ing 1 : establish 2 : be all or a basic part of

con·sti·tu·tion n 1 : physical composition or structure 2 : the basic law of an organized body or the document containing it — **con·sti·tu·tion·al** adj — **con·sti·tu·tion·al·i·ty** n

con·strain vb 1 : compel 2 : confine 3 : restrain — **con·straint** n

con·strict vb : draw or squeeze together — **con·stric·tion** n — **con·stric·tive** adj

con·struct vb : build or make — **con·struc·tion** n — **con·struc·tive** adj

con·strue vb -strued; -stru·ing : explain or interpret

con·sul n 1 : Roman magistrate 2 : government commercial official in a foreign country — **con·sul·ar** adj — **con·sul·ate** n

con·sult vb 1 : ask the advice or opinion of 2 : confer — **con·sul·tant** n — **con·sul·ta·tion** n

con·sume vb -sumed; -sum·ing : eat or use up — **con·sum·able** adj — **con·sum·er** n

con·sum·mate adj : complete or perfect ~ vb -mat·ed; -mat·ing : make complete — **con·sum·ma·tion** n

con·sump·tion n 1 : act of consuming 2 : use of goods 3 : tuberculosis — **con·sump·tive** adj or n

con·tact n 1 : a touching 2 : association or relationship 3 : connection or communication ~ vb 1 : come or bring into contact 2 : communicate with

con·ta·gion n 1 : spread of disease by contact 2 : disease spread by contact — **con·ta·gious** adj

con·tain vb 1 : enclose or include 2 : have or hold within 3 : restrain — **con·tain·er** n — **con·tain·ment** n

con·tam·i·nate vb -nat·ed; -nat·ing : soil or infect by contact or association — **con·tam·i·na·tion** n

con·tem·plate vb -plat·ed; -plat·ing : view or consider thoughtfully — **con·tem·pla·tion** n — **con·tem·pla·tive** adj

con·tem·po·ra·ne·ous adj : contemporary

con·tem·po·rary adj 1 : occurring or existing at the same time 2 : of the same age — **contemporary** n

con·tempt n 1 : feeling of scorn 2 : state of being despised 3 : disobedience to a court or legislature — **con·tempt·ible** adj

con·temp·tu·ous adj : feeling or expressing contempt — **con·temp·tu·ous·ly** adv

con·tend vb 1 : strive against rivals or difficulties 2 : argue 3 : maintain or claim — **con·tend·er** n

¹**con·tent** adj : satisfied ~ vb : satisfy ~ n : ease of mind — **con·tent·ed** adj — **con·tent·ed·ly** adv — **con·tent·ed·ness** n — **con·tent·ment** n

²**con·tent** n 1 pl : something contained 2 pl : subject matter (as of a book) 3 : essential meaning 4 : proportion contained

con·ten·tion n : state of contending — **con·ten·tious** adj — **con·ten·tious·ly** adv

con·test vb : dispute or challenge ~ n 1 : struggle 2 : game — **con·test·able** adj — **con·tes·tant** n

con·text n : words surrounding a word or phrase

con·tig·u·ous adj : connected to or adjoining — **con·ti·gu·i·ty** n

con·ti·nence n : self-restraint — **con·ti·nent** adj

con·ti·nent n : great division of land on the globe — **con·ti·nen·tal** adj

con·tin·gen·cy n, pl **-cies** : possible event

con·tin·gent adj : dependent on something else ~ n : a quota from an area or group

con·tin·u·al adj 1 : continuous 2 : steadily recurring — **con·tin·u·al·ly** adv

con·tin·ue vb **-tin·ued; -tinu·ing** 1 : remain in a place or condition 2 : endure 3 : resume after an intermission 4 : extend — **con·tin·u·ance** n — **con·tin·u·a·tion** n

con·tin·u·ous adj : continuing without interruption — **con·ti·nu·ity** n — **con·tin·u·ous·ly** adv

con·tort vb : twist out of shape — **con·tor·tion** n

con·tour n 1 : outline 2 pl : shape

con·tra·band n : illegal goods

con·tra·cep·tion n : prevention of conception — **con·tra·cep·tive** adj or n

con·tract n : binding agreement ~ vb 1 : establish or undertake by contract 2 : become ill with 3 : make shorter — **con·trac·tion** n — **con·trac·tor** n — **con·trac·tu·al** adj — **con·trac·tu·al·ly** adv

con·tra·dict vb : state the contrary of — **con·tra·dic·tion** n — **con·tra·dic·to·ry** adj

con·tral·to n, pl **-tos** : lowest female singing voice

con·trap·tion n : device or contrivance

con·trary adj 1 : opposite in character, nature, or position 2 : mutually opposed 3 : unfavorable 4 : uncooperative or stubborn — **con·trari·ly** adv — **con·trari·wise** adv — **contrary** n

con·trast n 1 : unlikeness shown by comparing 2 : unlike color or tone of adjacent parts ~ vb 1 : show differences 2 : compare so as to show differences

con·tra·vene vb **-vened; -ven·ing** : go or act contrary to

con·trib·ute vb **-ut·ed; -ut·ing** : give or help along with others — **con·tri·bu·tion** n — **con·trib·u·tor** n — **con·trib·u·to·ry** adj

con·trite adj : repentant — **con·tri·tion** n

con·trive vb **-trived; -triv·ing** 1 : devise or make with ingenuity 2 : bring about — **con·triv·ance** n — **con·triv·er** n

con·trol vb **-ll-** 1 : exercise power over 2 : dominate or rule ~ n 1 : power to direct or regulate 2 : restraint 3 : regulating device — **con·trol·la·ble** adj — **con·trol·ler** n

con·tro·ver·sy n, pl **-sies** : clash of opposing views — **con·tro·ver·sial** adj

con·tro·vert vb : contradict — **con·tro·vert·ible** adj

con·tu·ma·cious adj : rebellious

con·tu·me·ly n : rudeness

con·tu·sion n : bruise — **con·tuse** vb

co·nun·drum n : riddle

con·va·lesce vb **-lesced; -lesc·ing** : gradually recover health — **con·va·les·cence** n — **con·va·les·cent** adj or n

con·vec·tion n : circulation in fluids due to warmer portions rising and colder ones sinking — **con·vec·tion·al** adj — **con·vec·tive** adj

con·vene vb **-vened; -ven·ing** : assemble or meet

con·ve·nience n 1 : personal comfort or ease 2 : device that saves work

con·ve·nient adj 1 : suited to one's convenience 2 : near at hand — **con·ve·nient·ly** adv

con·vent n : community of nuns

con·ven·tion n 1 : agreement esp. between nations 2 : large meeting 3 : body of delegates 4 : accepted usage or way of behaving — **con·ven·tion·al** adj — **con·ven·tion·al·ly** adv

con·verge vb **-verged; -verg·ing** : approach a single point — **con·ver·gence** — **con·ver·gent** adj

con·ver·sant adj : having knowledge and experience

con·ver·sa·tion n : an informal talking together — **con·ver·sa·tion·al** adj

¹**con·verse** vb **-versed; -vers·ing** : engage in conversation — **con·verse** n

²**con·verse** adj : opposite — **con·verse** n — **con·verse·ly** adv

con·ver·sion n 1 : change 2 : adoption of religion

con·vert vb 1 : turn from one belief or party to another 2 : change — n : one who has undergone religious conversion — **con·vert·er, con·ver·tor** n — **con·vert·ible** adj

con·vert·ible n : automobile with a removable top

con·vex adj : curved or rounded like the outside of a sphere — **con·vex·i·ty** n

con·vey vb **-veyed; -vey·ing** : transport or transmit — **con·vey·ance** n — **con·vey·or** n

con·vict vb : find guilty ~ n : person in prison

con·vic·tion n 1 : act of convicting 2 : strong belief

con·vince vb **-vinced; -vinc·ing** : cause to believe — **con·vinc·ing·ly** adv

con·viv·ial adj : cheerful or festive — **con·viv·i·al·i·ty** n

con·voke vb **-voked; -vok·ing** : call together to a meeting — **con·vo·ca·tion** n

con·vo·lut·ed adj 1 : intricately folded 2 : intricate

con·vo·lu·tion n : convoluted structure

con·voy vb : accompany for protection ~ n : group of vehicles or ships moving together

con·vul·sion n : violent involuntary muscle contraction — **con·vulse** vb — **con·vul·sive** adj

coo n : sound of a pigeon — **coo** vb

cook n : one who prepares food ~ vb : prepare food — **cook·book** n — **cook·er** n — **cook·ery** n — **cook·ware** n

cook·ie, cooky n, pl **-ies** : small sweet flat cake

cool adj 1 : moderately cold 2 : not excited 3 : unfriendly ~ vb : make or become cool ~ n 1 : cool time or place 2 : composure — **cool·ant** n — **cool·er** n — **cool·ly** adv — **cool·ness** n

coo·lie n : unskilled Oriental laborer

coop n : enclosure usu. for poultry ~ vb : confine in or as if in a coop

co-op n : cooperative

coo·per n : barrel maker — **cooper** vb

co·op·er·ate vb : act jointly — **co·op·er·a·tion** n

co·op·er·a·tive adj : willing to work with others ~ n : enterprise owned and run by those using its services

co-opt vb 1 : elect as a colleague 2 : take over

co·or·di·nate adj : equal esp. in rank ~ n : any of a set of numbers used in specifying the location of a point on a surface or in space ~ vb **-nat·ed; -nat·ing** 1 : make or become coordinate 2 : work or act together harmoniously — **co·or·di·nate·ly** adv — **co·or·di·na·tion** n — **co·or·di·na·tor** n

coot n 1 : dark-colored ducklike bird 2 : harmless simple person

cop n : police officer

¹**cope** n : cloaklike ecclesiastical vestment

²**cope** vb **coped; cop·ing** : deal with difficulties

co·pi·lot n : assistant airplane pilot

cop·ing n : top layer of a wall

co·pi·ous adj : very abundant — **co·pi·ous·ly** adv — **co·pi·ous·ness** n

cop·per n 1 : malleable reddish metallic chemical element 2 : penny — **cop·pery** adj

cop·per·head n : largely coppery brown venomous snake

co·pra n : dried coconut meat

copse n : thicket

cop·u·la n : verb linking subject and predicate — **cop·u·la·tive** adj

cop·u·late vb **-lat·ed; -lat·ing** : engage in sexual intercourse — **cop·u·la·tion** n

copy n, pl **cop·ies** 1 : imitation or reproduction of an original 2 : writing to be set for printing ~ vb **cop·ied; copy·ing** 1 : make a copy of 2 : imitate — **copi·er** n — **copyist** n

copy·right n : sole right to a literary or artistic work ~ vb : get a copyright on

co·quette n : flirt

cor·al n 1 : skeletal material of colonies of tiny sea polyps 2 : deep pink — **coral** adj

cord n 1 : usu. heavy string 2 : long slender anatomical structure 3 : measure of firewood equal to 128 cu. ft. 4 : small electrical cable ~ vb 1 : tie or furnish with a cord 2 : pile (wood) in cords

cor·dial adj : warmly welcoming ~ n : liqueur — **cor·di·al·i·ty** n — **cor·dial·ly** adv

cor·don n : encircling line of troops or police — **cordon** vb

cor·do·van n : soft fine-grained leather

cor·du·roy n 1 : heavy ribbed fabric 2 pl : trousers of corduroy

core n 1 : central part of some fruits 2 : inmost part ~ vb **cored; cor·ing** : take out the core of — **cor·er** n

cork n 1 : tough elastic bark of a European oak (**cork oak**) 2 : stopper of cork ~ vb : stop up with a cork — **corky** adj

cork·screw n : device for drawing corks from bottles

cor·mo·rant n : dark seabird

¹**corn** n : cereal grass or its seeds ~ vb : cure or preserve in brine — **corn·meal** n — **corn·stalk** n — **corn·starch** n

²**corn** n : local hardening and thickening of skin

corn·cob n : axis on which the kernels of Indian corn are arranged

cor·nea n : transparent part of the coat of the eyeball — **cor·ne·al** adj

cor·ner n 1 : point or angle formed by the meeting of lines or sides 2 : place where two streets meet 3 : inescapable position 4 : control of the supply of something ~ vb 1 : drive into a corner 2 : get a corner on 3 : turn a corner

cor·ner·stone n 1 : stone at a corner of a wall 2 : something basic

cor·net n : trumpetlike instrument

cor·nice n : horizontal wall projection

cor·nu·co·pia n : goat's horn filled with fruits and grain emblematic of abundance

co·rol·la n : petals of a flower

cor·ol·lary n, pl **-lar·ies** 1 : logical deduction 2 : consequence or result

co·ro·na n : shining ring around the sun seen during eclipses

cor·o·nary adj : relating to the heart or its blood vessels ~ n 1 : thrombosis of an artery supplying the heart 2 : heart attack

cor·o·na·tion n : crowning of a monarch

cor·o·ner n : public official who investigates causes of suspicious deaths

¹**cor·po·ral** adj : bodily

²**corporal** n : noncommissioned officer ranking next below a sergeant

cor·po·ra·tion n : legal creation with the rights and liabilities of a person — **cor·po·rate** adj

cor·po·re·al adj : physical or material — **cor·po·re·al·ly** adv

corps n, pl **corps** 1 : subdivision of a military force 2 : working group

corpse n : dead body

cor·pu·lence n : obesity — **cor·pu·lent** adj

cor·pus n, pl **-po·ra** 1 : corpse 2 : body of writings

cor·pus·cle n : blood cell

cor·ral n : enclosure for animals — **corral** vb

cor·rect vb 1 : make right 2 : chastise ~ adj 1 : true or factual 2 : conforming to a standard — **cor·rec·tion** n — **cor·rec·tive** adj — **cor·rect·ly** adv — **cor·rect·ness** n

cor·re·late vb -lat·ed; -lat·ing : show a connection between — **cor·re·late** n — **cor·re·la·tion** n

cor·rel·a·tive adj : regularly used together — **correlative** n

cor·re·spond vb 1 : match 2 : communicate by letter — **cor·re·spon·dence** n — **cor·re·spond·ing·ly** adv

cor·re·spon·dent n 1 : person one writes to 2 : reporter

cor·ri·dor n : passageway connecting rooms

cor·rob·o·rate vb -rat·ed; -rat·ing : support with evidence — **cor·rob·o·ra·tion** n

cor·rode vb -rod·ed; -rod·ing : wear away by chemical action — **cor·ro·sion** n — **cor·ro·sive** adj or n

cor·ru·gate vb -gat·ed; -gat·ing : form into ridges and grooves — **cor·ru·gat·ed** adj — **cor·ru·ga·tion** n

cor·rupt vb 1 : change from good to bad 2 : bribe ~ adj : morally debased — **cor·rupt·ible** adj — **cor·rup·tion** n

cor·sage n : bouquet worn by a woman

cor·set n : woman's stiffened undergarment

cor·tege n : funeral procession

cor·tex n, pl -ti·ces or -tex·es : outer or covering layer of an organism or part (as the brain) — **cor·ti·cal** adj

cor·ti·sone n : adrenal hormone

cos·met·ic n : beautifying preparation ~ adj : relating to beautifying

cos·mic adj 1 : relating to the universe 2 : vast or grand

cos·mo·naut n : Soviet or Russian astronaut

cos·mo·pol·i·tan adj : belonging to all the world — **cos·mopolitan** n

cos·mos n : universe

cos·sack n : Russian czarist cavalryman

cost n 1 : amount paid for something 2 : loss or penalty ~ vb **cost; cost·ing** 1 : require so much in payment 2 : cause to pay, suffer, or lose — **cost·li·ness** n — **cost·ly** adj

cos·tume n : clothing

co·sy var of COZY

cot n : small bed

cote n : small shed or coop

co·te·rie n : exclusive group of persons

co·til·lion n : formal ball

cot·tage n : small house

cot·ton n : soft fibrous plant substance or thread or cloth made of it — **cot·ton·seed** n — **cot·tony** adj

cot·ton·mouth n : poisonous snake

couch vb 1 : lie or place on a couch 2 : phrase ~ n : bed or sofa

cou·gar n : large tawny wild American cat

cough vb : force air from the lungs with short sharp noises — **cough** n

could past of CAN

coun·cil n 1 : assembly or meeting 2 : body of lawmakers — **coun·cil·lor, coun·cil·or** n — **coun·cil·man** n — **coun·cil·wom·an** n

coun·sel n 1 : advice 2 : deliberation together 3 pl -sel : lawyer ~ vb -seled or -selled; -sel·ing or -sel·ling 1 : advise 2 : consult together — **coun·sel·or, coun·sel·lor** n

¹count vb 1 : name or indicate one by one to find the total number 2 : recite numbers in order 3 : rely 4 : be of value or account ~ n 1 : act of counting or the total obtained by counting 2 : charge in an indictment — **count·able** adj

²count n : European nobleman

coun·te·nance n : face or facial expression ~ vb -nanced; -nanc·ing : allow or encourage

¹count·er n 1 : piece for reckoning or games 2 : surface over which business is transacted

²count·er n : one that counts

³coun·ter vb : oppose ~ adv : in an opposite direction ~ n : offsetting force or move ~ adj : contrary

counter- prefix 1 : contrary or opposite 2 : opposing 3 : retaliatory

counteraccusation	counterploy
counteraggression	counterpower
counterargue	counterpressure
counterassault	counterpropaganda
counterattack	counterproposal
counterbid	counterprotest
counterblockade	counterquestion
counterblow	counterraid
countercampaign	counterrally
countercharge	counterreform
counterclaim	counterresponse
countercomplaint	counterretaliation
countercoup	counterrevolution
countercriticism	counterrevolutionary
counterdemand	counterstrategy
counterdemonstration	counterstyle
counterdemonstrator	countersue
countereffort	countersuggestion
counterevidence	countersuit
counterguerrilla	countertendency
counterinflationary	counterterror
counterinfluence	counterterrorism
countermeasure	counterterrorist
countermove	counterthreat
countermovement	counterthrust
counteroffer	countertrend
counterpetition	

coun·ter·act vb : lessen the force of — **coun·ter·ac·tive** adj

coun·ter·bal·ance n : balancing influence or weight ~ vb : oppose or balance

coun·ter·clock·wise adv or adj : opposite to the way a clock's hands move

coun·ter·feit vb 1 : copy in order to deceive 2 : pretend ~ adj : spurious ~ n : fraudulent copy — **coun·ter·feit·er** n

coun·ter·mand vb : supersede with a contrary order

coun·ter·pane n : bedspread

coun·ter·part n : one that is similar or corresponds

coun·ter·point n : music with interwoven melodies

coun·ter·sign n : secret signal ~ vb : add a confirming signature to

count·ess n : wife or widow of a count or an earl or a woman holding that rank in her own right

count·less adj : too many to be numbered

coun·try n, pl -tries 1 : nation 2 : rural area ~ adj : rural — **coun·try·man** n

coun·try·side n : rural area or its people

coun·ty n, pl -ties : local government division esp. of a state

coup n, pl **coups** 1 : brilliant sudden action or plan 2 : sudden overthrow of a government

coupe n : 2-door automobile with an enclosed body

cou·ple vb -pled; -pling : link together ~ n 1 : pair 2 : two persons closely associated or married

cou·pling n : connecting device

cou·pon n : certificate redeemable for goods or a cash discount

cour·age n : ability to conquer fear or despair — **cou·ra·geous** adj

cou·ri·er n : messenger

course n 1 : progress 2 : ground over which something moves 3 : part of a meal served at one time 4 : method of procedure 5 : subject taught in a series of classes ~ vb **coursed; cours·ing** 1 : hunt with dogs 2 : run speedily — **of course** : as might be expected

court n 1 : residence of a sovereign 2 : sovereign and his or her officials and advisers 3 : area enclosed by a building 4 : space marked for playing a game 5 : place where justice is administered ~ vb : woo — **court·house** n — **court·room** n — **court·ship** n

cour·te·ous adj : showing politeness and respect for others — **cour·te·ous·ly** adv

cour·te·san n : prostitute

cour·te·sy n, pl -sies : courteous behavior

cour·ti·er n : person in attendance at a royal court

court·ly adj -li·er; -est : polite or elegant — **court·li·ness** n

court–mar·tial n, pl **courts–martial** : military trial court — **court–martial** vb

court·yard n : enclosure open to the sky that is attached to a house

cous·in n : child of one's uncle or aunt

cove n : sheltered inlet or bay

co·ven n : group of witches

cov·e·nant n : binding agreement — **cov·e·nant** vb

cov·er vb 1 : place something over or upon 2 : protect or hide 3 : include or deal with ~ n : something that covers — **cov·er·age** n

cov·er·let n : bedspread

co·vert adj : secret ~ n : thicket that shelters animals

cov·et vb : desire enviously — **cov·et·ous** adj

cov·ey n, pl -eys 1 : bird with her young 2 : small flock (as of quail)

¹cow n : large adult female animal (as of cattle) — **cow·hide** n

²cow vb : intimidate

cow·ard n : one who lacks courage — **cow·ard·ice** n — **cow·ard·ly** adv or adj

cow·boy n : a mounted ranch hand who tends cattle

cow·er vb : shrink from fear or cold

cow·girl n : woman ranch hand who tends cattle

cowl n : monk's hood

cow·lick n : turned-up tuft of hair that resists control

cow·slip n : yellow flower

cox·swain n : person who steers a boat

coy adj : shy or pretending shyness

coy·ote n, pl **coy·otes** or **coyote** : small No. American wolf

coz·en vb : cheat

co·zy adj -zi·er; -est : snug

crab n : short broad shellfish with pincers

crab·by adj -bi·er; -est : cross

¹crack vb 1 : break with a sharp sound 2 : fail in tone 3 : break without completely separating ~ n 1 : sudden sharp noise 2 : witty remark 3 : narrow break 4 : sharp blow 5 : try

²crack adj : extremely proficient

crack·down n : disciplinary action — **crack down** vb

crack·er n : thin crisp bakery product

crack·le vb -led; -ling 1 : make snapping noises 2 : develop fine cracks in a surface — **crackle** n

crack·pot n : eccentric

crack–up n : crash

cra·dle n : baby's bed ~ vb -dled; -dling 1 : place in a cradle 2 : hold securely

craft n 1 : occupation requiring special skill 2 : craftiness 3 pl usu **craft** : structure designed to provide transportation 4 pl usu **craft** : small boat — **crafts·man** n — **crafts·man·ship** n

crafty adj **craft·i·er; -est** : sly — **craft·i·ness** n

crag n : steep cliff — **crag·gy** adj

cram vb -mm- 1 : eat greedily 2 : pack in tight 3 : study intensely for a test

cramp n 1 : sudden painful contraction of muscle

2 *pl* : sharp abdominal pains ~ *vb* **1** : affect with cramp **2** : restrain

cran•ber•ry *n* : red acid berry of a trailing plant

crane *n* **1** : tall wading bird **2** : machine for lifting heavy objects ~ *vb* **craned; cran•ing** : stretch one's neck to see

cra•ni•um *n, pl* **-ni•ums** *or* **-nia** : skull — **cra•ni•al** *adj*

crank *n* **1** : bent lever turned to operate a machine **2** : eccentric ~ *vb* : start or operate by turning a crank

cranky *adj* **crank•i•er; -est** : irritable

cran•ny *n, pl* **-nies** : crevice

craps *n* : dice game

crash *vb* **1** : break noisily **2** : fall and hit something with noise and damage ~ *n* **1** : loud sound **2** : action of crashing **3** : failure

crass *adj* : crude or unfeeling

crate *n* : wooden shipping container — **crate** *vb*

cra•ter *n* : volcanic depression

cra•vat *n* : necktie

crave *vb* **craved; crav•ing** : long for — **crav•ing** *n*

cra•ven *adj* : cowardly — **cra•ven** *n*

craw•fish *n* : crayfish

crawl *vb* **1** : move slowly (as by drawing the body along the ground) **2** : swarm with creeping things ~ *n* : very slow pace

cray•fish *n* : lobsterlike freshwater crustacean

cray•on *n* : stick of chalk or wax used for drawing or coloring — **crayon** *vb*

craze *vb* **crazed; craz•ing** : make or become insane ~ *n* : fad

cra•zy *adj* **cra•zi•er; -est** **1** : mentally disordered **2** : wildly impractical — **cra•zi•ly** *adv* — **cra•zi•ness** *n*

creak *vb or n* : squeak — **creaky** *adj*

cream *n* **1** : yellowish fat-rich part of milk **2** : thick smooth sauce, confection, or cosmetic **3** : choicest part ~ *vb* : beat into creamy consistency — **creamy** *adj*

cream•ery *n, pl* **-er•ies** : place where butter and cheese are made

crease *n* : line made by folding — **crease** *vb*

cre•ate *vb* **-at•ed; -at•ing** : bring into being — **cre•ation** *n* — **cre•ative** *adj* — **cre•ativ•i•ty** *n* — **cre•ator** *n*

crea•ture *n* : lower animal or human being

cre•dence *n* : belief

cre•den•tials *n* : evidence of qualifications or authority

cred•i•ble *adj* : believable — **cred•i•bil•i•ty** *n*

cred•it *n* **1** : balance in a person's favor **2** : time given to pay for goods **3** : belief **4** : esteem **5** : source of honor ~ *vb* **1** : believe **2** : give credit to

cred•it•able *adj* : worthy of esteem or praise — **cred•it•ably** *adv*

cred•i•tor *n* : person to whom money is owed

cred•u•lous *adj* : easily convinced — **cre•du•li•ty** *n*

creed *n* : statement of essential beliefs

creek *n* : small stream

creel *n* : basket for carrying fish

creep *vb* **crept; creep•ing** **1** : crawl **2** : grow over a surface like ivy — **creep** *n* — **creep•er** *n*

cre•mate *vb* **-mat•ed; -mat•ing** : burn up (a corpse) — **cre•ma•tion** *n* — **cre•ma•to•ry** *n*

cre•o•sote *n* : oily wood preservative

crepe, crêpe *n* : light crinkled fabric

cres•cen•do *adv or adj* : growing louder — **crescendo** *n*

cres•cent *n* : shape of the moon between new moon and first quarter

crest *n* **1** : tuft on a bird's head **2** : top of a hill or wave **3** : part of a coat of arms ~ *vb* : rise to a crest — **crest•ed** *adj*

crest•fall•en *adj* : sad

cre•tin *n* : stupid person

cre•vasse *n* : deep fissure esp. in a glacier

crev•ice *n* : narrow fissure

crew *n* : body of workers (as on a ship) — **crew•man** *n*

crib *n* **1** : manger **2** : grain storage bin **3** : baby's bed ~ *vb* **-bb-** : put in a crib

crib•bage *n* : card game scored by moving pegs on a board (**cribbage board**)

crick *n* : muscle spasm

¹crick•et *n* : insect noted for the chirping of the male

²cricket *n* : bat and ball game played on a field with wickets

cri•er *n* : one who calls out announcements

crime *n* : serious violation of law

crim•i•nal *adj* : relating to or being a crime or its punishment ~ *n* : one who commits a crime

crimp *vb* : cause to become crinkled, wavy, or bent — **crimp** *n*

crim•son *n* : deep red — **crimson** *adj*

cringe *vb* **cringed; cring•ing** : shrink in fear

crin•kle *vb* **-kled; -kling** : wrinkle — **crinkle** *n* — **crin•kly** *adj*

crin•o•line *n* **1** : stiff cloth **2** : full stiff skirt or petticoat

crip•ple *n* : disabled person ~ *vb* **-pled; -pling** : disable

cri•sis *n, pl* **cri•ses** : decisive or critical moment

crisp *adj* **1** : easily crumbled **2** : firm and fresh **3** : lively **4** : invigorating — **crisp** *vb* — **crisp•ly** *adv* — **crisp•ness** *n* — **crispy** *adj*

criss•cross *n* : pattern of crossed lines ~ *vb* : mark with or follow a crisscross

cri•te•ri•on *n, pl* **-ria** : standard

crit•ic *n* : judge of literary or artistic works

crit•i•cal *adj* **1** : inclined to criticize **2** : being a crisis **3** : relating to criticism or critics — **crit•i•cal•ly** *adv*

crit•i•cize *vb* **-cized; -cizing** **1** : judge as a critic **2** : find fault — **crit•i•cism** *n*

cri•tique *n* : critical estimate

croak *n* : hoarse harsh cry (as of a frog) — **croak** *vb*

cro•chet *n* : needlework done with a hooked needle — **crochet** *vb*

crock *n* : thick earthenware pot or jar — **crock•ery** *n*

croc•o•dile *n* : large reptile of tropical waters

cro•cus *n, pl* **-cus•es** : herb with spring flowers

crone *n* : ugly old woman

cro•ny *n, pl* **-nies** : chum

crook *n* **1** : bent or curved tool or part **2** : thief ~ *vb* : curve sharply

crook•ed *adj* **1** : bent **2** : dishonest — **crook•ed•ness** *n*

croon *vb* : sing softly — **croon•er** *n*

crop *n* **1** : pouch in the throat of a bird or insect **2** : short riding whip **3** : something that can be harvested ~ *vb* **-pp-** **1** : trim **2** : appear unexpectedly : — used with *up*

cro•quet *n* : lawn game of driving balls through wickets

cro•quette *n* : mass of minced food deep-fried

cro•sier *n* : bishop's staff

cross *n* **1** : figure or structure consisting of an upright and a cross piece **2** : interbreeding of unlike strains ~ *vb* **1** : intersect **2** : cancel **3** : go or extend across **4** : interbreed ~ *adj* **1** : going across **2** : contrary **3** : marked by bad temper — **cross•ing** *n* — **cross•ly** *adv*

cross•bow *n* : short bow mounted on a rifle stock

cross•breed *vb* **-bred; -breed•ing** : hybridize

cross–ex•am•ine *vb* : question about earlier testimony — **cross–ex•am•i•na•tion** *n*

cross–eyed *adj* : having the eye turned toward the nose

cross–re•fer *vb* : refer to another place (as in a book) — **cross–ref•er•ence** *n*

cross•roads *n* : place where 2 roads cross

cross section *n* : representative portion

cross•walk *n* : path for pedestrians crossing a street

cross•ways *adv* : crosswise

cross•wise *adv* : so as to cross something — **cross•wise** *adj*

crotch *n* : angle formed by the parting of 2 legs or branches

crotch•ety *adj* : cranky, illnatured

crouch *vb* : stoop over — **crouch** *n*

croup *n* : laryngitis of infants

crou•ton *n* : bit of toast

¹crow *n* : large glossy black bird

²crow *vb* **1** : make the loud sound of the cock **2** : gloat ~ *n* : cry of the cock

crow•bar *n* : metal bar used as a pry or lever

crowd *vb* : collect or cram together ~ *n* : large number of people

crown *n* **1** : wreath of honor or victory **2** : royal headdress **3** : top or highest part ~ *vb* **1** : place a crown on **2** : honor — **crowned** *adj*

cru•cial *adj* : vitally important

cru•ci•ble *n* : heat-resisting container

cru•ci•fix *n* : representation of Christ on the cross

cru•ci•fix•ion *n* : act of crucifying

cru•ci•fy *vb* **-fied; -fy•ing** **1** : put to death on a cross **2** : persecute

crude *adj* **crud•er; -est** **1** : not refined **2** : lacking grace or elegance ~ *n* : unrefined petroleum — **crude•ly** *adv* — **cru•di•ty** *n*

cru•el *adj* **-el•er** *or* **-el•ler; -el•est** *or* **-el•lest** : causing suffering to others — **cru•el•ly** *adv* — **cru•el•ty** *n*

cru•et *n* : bottle for salad dressings

cruise *vb* **cruised; cruis•ing** **1** : sail to several ports **2** : travel at the most efficient speed — **cruise** *n*

cruis•er *n* **1** : warship **2** : police car

crumb *n* : small fragment

crum•ble *vb* **-bled; -bling** : break into small pieces — **crum•bly** *adj*

crum•ple *vb* **-pled; -pling** **1** : crush together **2** : collapse

crunch *vb* : chew or press with a crushing noise ~ *n* : crunching sound — **crunchy** *adj*

cru•sade *n* **1** *cap* : medieval Christian expedition to the Holy Land **2** : reform movement — **crusade** *vb* — **cru•sad•er** *n*

crush *vb* **1** : squeeze out of shape **2** : grind or pound to bits **3** : suppress ~ *n* **1** : severe crowding **2** : infatuation

crust *n* **1** : hard outer part of bread or a pie **2** : hard surface layer — **crust•al** *adj* — **crusty** *adj*

crus•ta•cean *n* : aquatic arthropod having a firm shell

crutch *n* : support for use by the disabled in walking

crux *n, pl* **crux•es** **1** : hard problem **2** : crucial point

cry *vb* **cried; cry•ing** **1** : call out **2** : weep ~ *n, pl* **cries** **1** : shout **2** : fit of weeping **3** : characteristic sound of an animal

crypt *n* : underground chamber

cryp•tic *adj* : enigmatic

cryp•tog•ra•phy *n* : coding and decoding of messages — **cryp•tog•ra•pher** *n*

crys•tal *n* **1** : transparent quartz **2** : something (as glass) like crystal **3** : body formed by solidification that has a regular repeating atomic arrangement — **crys•tal•line** *adj*

crys•tal•lize *vb* **-lized; -liz•ing** : form crystals or a definite shape — **crys•tal•li•za•tion** *n*

cub *n* : young animal

cub•by•hole *n* : small confined space

cube *n* **1** : solid having 6 equal square sides **2** : product obtained by taking a number 3 times as a factor ~ *vb* **cubed; cub•ing** **1** : raise to the 3d power **2** : form into a cube **3** : cut into cubes — **cu·bic** *adj*

cu·bi·cle *n* : small room

cu·bit *n* : ancient unit of length equal to about 18 inches

cuck·old *n* : man whose wife is unfaithful — **cuckold** *vb*

cuck·oo *n*, *pl* **-oos** : brown European bird ~ *adj* : silly

cu·cum·ber *n* : fleshy fruit related to the gourds

cud *n* : food chewed again by ruminating animals

cud·dle *vb* **-dled; -dling** : lie close

cud·gel *n or vb* : club

¹**cue** *n* : signal — **cue** *vb*

²**cue** *n* : stick used in pool

¹**cuff** *n* **1** : part of a sleeve encircling the wrist **2** : folded trouser hem

²**cuff** *vb or n* : slap

cui·sine *n* : manner of cooking

cu·li·nary *adj* : of or relating to cookery

cull *vb* : select

cul·mi·nate *vb* **-nat·ed; -nat·ing** : rise to the highest point — **cul·mi·na·tion** *n*

cul·pa·ble *adj* : deserving blame

cul·prit *n* : guilty person

cult *n* **1** : religious system **2** : faddish devotion — **cult·ist** *n*

cul·ti·vate *vb* **-vat·ed; -vat·ing 1** : prepare for crops **2** : foster the growth of **3** : refine — **cul·ti·va·tion** *n*

cul·ture *n* **1** : cultivation **2** : refinement of intellectual and artistic taste **3** : particular form or stage of civilization — **cul·tur·al** *adj* — **cul·tured** *adj*

cul·vert *n* : drain crossing under a road or railroad

cum·ber·some *adj* : awkward to handle due to bulk

cu·mu·la·tive *adj* : increasing by additions

cu·mu·lus *n*, *pl* **-li** : massive rounded cloud

cun·ning *adj* **1** : crafty **2** : clever **3** : appealing ~ *n* **1** : skill **2** : craftiness

cup *n* **1** : small drinking vessel **2** : contents of a cup **3** : a half pint ~ *vb* **-pp-** : shape like a cup — **cup·ful** *n*

cup·board *n* : small storage closet

cup·cake *n* : small cake

cu·pid·i·ty *n*, *pl* **-ties** : excessive desire for money

cu·po·la *n* : small rooftop structure

cur *n* : mongrel dog

cu·rate *n* : member of the clergy — **cu·ra·cy** *n*

cu·ra·tor *n* : one in charge of a museum or zoo

curb *n* **1** : restraint **2** : raised edging along a street ~ *vb* : hold back

curd *n* : coagulated milk

cur·dle *vb* **-dled; -dling 1** : form curds **2** : sour

cure *n* **1** : recovery from disease **2** : remedy ~ *vb* **cured; cur·ing 1** : restore to health **2** : process for storage or use — **cur·able** *adj*

cur·few *n* : requirement to be off the streets at a set hour

cu·rio *n*, *pl* **-ri·os** : rare or unusual article

cu·ri·ous *adj* **1** : eager to learn **2** : strange — **cu·ri·os·i·ty** *n* — **cu·ri·ous·ness** *n*

curl *vb* **1** : form into ringlets **2** : curve ~ *n* **1** : ringlet of hair **2** : something with a spiral form — **curl·er** *n* — **curly** *adj*

cur·lew *n*, *pl* **-lews** *or* **-lew** : long-legged brownish bird

curli·cue *n* : fanciful curve

cur·rant *n* **1** : small seedless raisin **2** : berry of a shrub

cur·ren·cy *n*, *pl* **-cies 1** : general use or acceptance **2** : money

cur·rent *adj* : occurring in or belonging to the present ~ *n* **1** : swiftest part of a stream **2** : flow of electricity

cur·ric·u·lum *n*, *pl* **-la** : course of study

¹**cur·ry** *vb* **-ried; -ry·ing** : brush (a horse) with a wire brush (**cur·ry·comb**) — **curry fa·vor** : seek favor by flattery

²**curry** *n*, *pl* **-ries** : blend of pungent spices or a food seasoned with this

curse *n* **1** : a calling down of evil or harm upon one **2** : affliction ~ *vb* **cursed; curs·ing 1** : call down injury upon **2** : swear at **3** : afflict

cur·sor *n* : indicator on a computer screen

cur·so·ry *adj* : hastily done

curt *adj* : rudely abrupt — **curt·ly** *adv* — **curt·ness** *n*

cur·tail *vb* : shorten — **cur·tail·ment** *n*

cur·tain *n* : hanging screen that can be drawn back or raised — **curtain** *vb*

curt·sy, curt·sey *n*, *pl* **-sies** *or* **-seys** : courteous bow made by bending the knees — **curtsy, curt·sey** *vb*

cur·va·ture *n* : amount or state of curving

curve *vb* **curved; curv·ing** : bend from a straight line or course ~ *n* **1** : a bending without angles **2** : something curved

cush·ion *n* **1** : soft pillow **2** : something that eases or protects ~ *vb* **1** : provide with a cushion **2** : soften the force of

cusp *n* : pointed end

cus·pid *n* : a canine tooth

cus·pi·dor *n* : spittoon

cus·tard *n* : sweetened cooked mixture of milk and eggs

cus·to·dy *n*, *pl* **-dies** : immediate care or charge — **cus·to·di·al** *adj* — **cus·to·di·an** *n*

cus·tom *n* **1** : habitual course of action **2** *pl* : import taxes ~ *adj* : made to personal order — **cus·tomar·i·ly** *adv* — **custom·ary** *adj* — **cus·tom–built** *adj* — **cus·tom–made** *adj*

cus·tom·er *n* : buyer

cut *vb* **cut; cut·ting 1** : penetrate or divide with a sharp edge **2** : experience the growth of (a tooth) through the gum **3** : shorten **4** : remove by severing **5** : intersect ~ *n* **1** : something separated by cutting **2** : reduction — **cut in** *vb* : thrust oneself between others

cu·ta·ne·ous *adj* : relating to the skin

cute *adj* **cut·er; -est** : pretty

cu·ti·cle *n* : outer layer (as of skin)

cut·lass *n* : short heavy curved sword

cut·lery *n* : cutting utensils

cut·let *n* : slice of meat

cut·ter *n* **1** : tool or machine for cutting **2** : small armed motorboat **3** : light sleigh

cut·throat *n* : murderer ~ *adj* : ruthless

-cy *n suffix* **1** : action or practice **2** : rank or office **3** : body **4** : state or quality

cy·a·nide *n* : poisonous chemical salt

cy·cle *n* **1** : period of time for a series of repeated events **2** : recurring round of events **3** : long period of time **4** : bicycle or motorcycle ~ *vb* **-cled; -cling** : ride a cycle — **cy·clic** , **cy·cli·cal** *adj* — **cy·clist** *n*

cy·clone *n* : tornado — **cy·clon·ic** *adj*

cy·clo·pe·dia, cy·clo·pae·dia *n* : encyclopedia

cyl·in·der *n* **1** : long round body or figure **2** : rotating chamber in a revolver **3** : piston chamber in an engine — **cy·lin·dri·cal** *adj*

cym·bal *n* : one of 2 concave brass plates clashed together

cyn·ic *n* : one who attributes all actions to selfish motives — **cyn·i·cal** *adj* — **cyn·i·cism** *n*

cy·no·sure *n* : center of attraction

cy·press *n* : evergreen tree related to the pines

cyst *n* : abnormal bodily sac — **cys·tic** *adj*

czar *n* : ruler of Russia until 1917 — **czar·ist** *n or adj*

D

d *n*, *pl* **d's** *or* **ds** : 4th letter of the alphabet

¹**dab** *n* : gentle touch or stroke ~ *vb* **-bb-** : touch or apply lightly

²**dab** *n* : small amount

dab·ble *vb* **-bled; -bling 1** : splash **2** : work without serious effort — **dab·bler** *n*

dachs·hund *n* : small dog with a long body and short legs

dad *n* : father

dad·dy *n*, *pl* **-dies** : father

daf·fo·dil *n* : narcissus with trumpetlike flowers

daft *adj* : foolish — **daft·ness** *n*

dag·ger *n* : knife for stabbing

dahl·ia *n* : tuberous herb with showy flowers

dai·ly *adj* **1** : occurring, done, or used every day or every weekday **2** : computed in terms of one day ~ *n*, *pl* **-lies** : daily newspaper — **daily** *adv*

dain·ty *n*, *pl* **-ties** : something delicious ~ *adj* **-ti·er; -est** : delicately pretty — **dain·ti·ly** *adv* — **dain·ti·ness** *n*

dairy *n*, *pl* **-ies** : farm that produces or company

that processes milk — **dairy·maid** *n* — **dairy·man** *n*

da·is *n* : raised platform (as for a speaker)

dai·sy *n*, *pl* **-sies** : tall leafy-stemmed plant bearing showy flowers

dale *n* : valley

dal·ly *vb* **-lied; -ly·ing 1** : flirt **2** : dawdle — **dal·li·ance** *n*

dal·ma·tian *n* : large dog having a spotted white coat

¹**dam** *n* : female parent of a domestic animal

²**dam** *n* : barrier to hold back water — **dam** *vb*

dam·age *n* **1** : loss or harm due to injury **2** *pl* : compensation for loss or injury ~ *vb* **-aged; -ag·ing** : do damage to

dam·ask *n* : firm lustrous figured fabric

dame *n* : woman of rank or authority

damn *vb* **1** : condemn to hell **2** : curse — **dam·na·ble** *adj* — **dam·na·tion** *n* — **damned** *adj*

damp *n* : moisture ~ *vb* **1** : reduce the draft in **2**

: restrain **3** : moisten ~ *adj* : moist — **damp·ness** *n*

damp·en *vb* **1** : diminish in activity or vigor **2** : make or become damp

damp·er *n* : movable plate to regulate a flue draft

dam·sel *n* : young woman

dance *vb* **danced; danc·ing** : move rhythmically to music ~ *n* : act of dancing or a gathering for dancing — **danc·er** *n*

dan·de·li·on *n* : common yellow-flowered herb

dan·der *n* : temper

dan·druff *n* : whitish thin dry scales of skin on the scalp

dan·dy *n*, *pl* **-dies 1** : man too concerned with clothes **2** : something excellent ~ *adj* **-di·er; -est** : very good

dan·ger *n* **1** : exposure to injury or evil **2** : something that may cause injury — **dan·ger·ous** *adj*

dan·gle *vb* **-gled; -gling 1** : hang and swing freely **2** : be left without support or connection **3** : allow or cause to hang **4** : offer as an inducement

dank *adj* : unpleasantly damp

dap•per *adj* : neat and stylishly dressed

dap•ple *vb* **-pled; -pling** : mark with colored spots

dare *vb* **dared; dar•ing 1** : have sufficient courage **2** : urge or provoke to contend — **dare** *n* — **dar•ing** *n or adj*

dare•dev•il *n* : recklessly bold person

dark *adj* **1** : having little or no light **2** : not light in color **3** : gloomy ∼ *n* : absence of light — **dark•en** *vb* — **dark•ly** *adv* — **dark•ness** *n*

dar•ling *n* **1** : beloved **2** : favorite ∼ *adj* **1** : dearly loved **2** : very pleasing

darn *vb* : mend with interlacing stitches — **darn•er** *n*

dart *n* **1** : small pointed missile **2** *pl* : game of throwing darts at a target **3** : tapering fold in a garment **4** : quick movement ∼ *vb* : move suddenly or rapidly

dash *vb* **1** : smash **2** : knock or hurl violently **3** : ruin **4** : perform or finish hastily **5** : move quickly ∼ *n* **1** : sudden burst, splash, or stroke **2** : punctuation mark — **3** : tiny amount **4** : showiness or liveliness **5** : sudden rush **6** : short race **7** : dashboard

dash•board *n* : instrument panel

dash•ing *adj* : dapper and charming

das•tard *n* : one who sneakingly commits malicious acts

das•tard•ly *adj* : base or malicious

da•ta *n sing or pl* : factual information

da•ta•base *n* : data organized for computer search

¹date *n* : edible fruit of a palm

²date *n* **1** : day, month, or year when something is done or made **2** : historical time period **3** : social engagement or the person one goes out with ∼ *vb* **dat•ed; dat•ing 1** : determine or record the date of **2** : have a date with **3** : originate — **to date** : up to now

dat•ed *adj* : old-fashioned

da•tum *n, pl* **-ta** *or* **-tums** : piece of data

daub *vb* : smear ∼ *n* : something daubed on — **daub•er** *n*

daugh•ter *n* : human female offspring

daugh•ter–in–law *n, pl* **daughters–in–law** : wife of one's son

daunt *vb* : lessen the courage of

daunt•less *adj* : fearless

dav•en•port *n* : sofa

daw•dle *vb* **-dled; -dling 1** : waste time **2** : loiter

dawn *vb* **1** : grow light as the sun rises **2** : begin to appear, develop, or be understood ∼ *n* : first appearance (as of daylight)

day *n* **1** : period of light between one night and the next **2** : 24 hours **3** : specified date **4** : particular time or age **5** : period of work for a day — **day•light** *n* — **day•time** *n*

day•break *n* : dawn

day•dream *n* : fantasy of wish fulfillment — **day•dream** *vb*

daylight saving time *n* : time one hour ahead of standard time

daze *vb* **dazed; daz•ing 1** : stun by a blow **2** : dazzle — **daze** *n*

daz•zle *vb* **-zled; -zling 1** : overpower with light **2** : impress greatly — **dazzle** *n*

DDT *n* : long-lasting insecticide

dea•con *n* : subordinate church officer

dea•con•ess *n* : woman who assists in church ministry

dead *adj* **1** : lifeless **2** : unresponsive or inactive **3** : exhausted **4** : obsolete **5** : precise ∼ *n, pl* **dead 1** : one that is dead — usu. with *the***2** : most lifeless time ∼ *adv* **1** : completely **2** : directly — **dead•en** *vb*

dead•beat *n* : one who will not pay debts

dead end *n* : end of a street with no exit — **dead–end** *adj*

dead heat *n* : tie in a contest

dead•line *n* : time by which something must be finished

dead•lock *n* : struggle that neither side can win — **deadlock** *vb*

dead•ly *adj* **-li•er; -est 1** : capable of causing death **2** : very accurate **3** : fatal to spiritual progress **4** : suggestive of death **5** : very great ∼ *adv* : extremely — **dead•li•ness** *n*

dead•pan *adj* : expressionless — **dead•pan** *n or vb or adv*

dead•wood *n* : something useless

deaf *adj* : unable or unwilling to hear — **deaf•en** *vb* — **deaf•ness** *n*

deaf–mute *n* : deaf person unable to speak

deal *n* **1** : indefinite quantity **2** : distribution of playing cards **3** : negotiation or agreement **4** : treatment received **5** : bargain ∼ *vb* **dealt ; deal•ing 1** : distribute playing cards **2** : be concerned with **3** : administer or deliver **4** : take action **5** : sell **6** : reach a state of acceptance — **deal•er** *n* — **deal•ing** *n*

dean *n* **1** : head of a group of clergy members **2** : university or school administrator **3** : senior member

dear *adj* **1** : highly valued or loved **2** : expensive ∼ *n* : loved one — **dear•ly** *adv* — **dear•ness** *n*

dearth *n* : scarcity

death *n* **1** : end of life **2** : cause of loss of life **3** : state of being dead **4** : destruction or extinction — **death•less** *adj* — **death•ly** *adj or adv*

de•ba•cle *n* : disaster or fiasco

de•bar *vb* : bar from something

de•bark *vb* : disembark — **de•bar•ka•tion** *n*

de•base *vb* : disparage — **de•base•ment** *n*

de•bate *vb* **-bat•ed; -bat•ing** : discuss a question by argument — **de•bat•able** *adj* — **debate** *n* — **de•bat•er** *n*

de•bauch *vb* : seduce or corrupt — **de•bauch•ery** *n*

de•bil•i•tate *vb* **-tat•ed; -tat•ing** : make ill or weak

de•bil•i•ty *n, pl* **-ties** : physical weakness

deb•it *n* : account entry of a payment or debt ∼ *vb* : record as a debit

deb•o•nair *adj* : suave

de•bris *n, pl* **-bris** : remains of something destroyed

debt *n* **1** : sin **2** : something owed **3** : state of owing — **debt•or** *n*

de•bunk *vb* : expose as false

de•but *n* **1** : first public appearance **2** : formal entrance into society — **debut** *vb* — **deb•u•tante** *n*

de•cade *n* : 10 years

dec•a•dence *n* : deterioration — **dec•a•dent** *adj or n*

de•cal *n* : picture or design for transfer from prepared paper

de•camp *vb* : depart suddenly

de•cant *vb* : pour gently

de•cant•er *n* : ornamental bottle

de•cap•i•tate *vb* **-tat•ed; -tat•ing** : behead — **de•cap•i•ta•tion** *n*

de•cay *vb* **1** : decline in condition **2** : decompose — **decay** *n*

de•cease *n* : death — **decease** *vb*

de•ceit *n* **1** : deception **2** : dishonesty — **de•ceit•ful** *adj* — **de•ceit•ful•ly** *adv* — **de•ceit•ful•ness** *n*

de•ceive *vb* **-ceived; -ceiv•ing** : trick or mislead — **de•ceiv•er** *n*

de•cel•er•ate *vb* **-at•ed; -at•ing** : slow down

De•cem•ber *n* : 12th month of the year having 31 days

de•cent *adj* **1** : good, right, or just **2** : clothed **3** : not obscene **4** : fairly good — **de•cen•cy** *n* — **de•cent•ly** *adv*

de•cep•tion *n* **1** : act or fact of deceiving **2** : fraud — **de•cep•tive** *adj* — **de•cep•tive•ly** *adv* — **de•cep•tive•ness** *n*

de•cide *vb* **-cid•ed; -cid•ing 1** : make a choice or judgment **2** : bring to a conclusion **3** : cause to decide

de•cid•ed *adj* **1** : unquestionable **2** : resolute — **de•cid•ed•ly** *adv*

de•cid•u•ous *adj* : having leaves that fall annually

dec•i•mal *n* : fraction in which the denominator is a power of 10 expressed by a point (**decimal point**) placed at the left of the numerator — **decimal** *adj*

de•ci•pher *vb* : make out the meaning of — **de•ci•pher•able** *adj*

de•ci•sion *n* **1** : act or result of deciding **2** : determination

de•ci•sive *adj* **1** : having the power to decide **2** : conclusive **3** : showing determination — **de•ci•sive•ly** *adv* — **de•ci•sive•ness** *n*

deck *n* **1** : floor of a ship **2** : pack of playing cards ∼ *vb* **1** : array or dress up **2** : knock down

de•claim *vb* : speak loudly or impressively — **dec•la•ma•tion** *n*

de•clare *vb* **-clared; -clar•ing 1** : make known formally **2** : state emphatically — **dec•la•ra•tion** *n* — **de•clar•a•tive** *adj* — **de•clar•a•to•ry** *adj* — **de•clar•er** *n*

de•clen•sion *n* : inflectional forms of a noun, pronoun, or adjective

de•cline *vb* **-clined; -clin•ing 1** : turn or slope downward **2** : wane **3** : refuse to accept **4** : inflect ∼ *n* **1** : gradual wasting away **2** : change to a lower state or level **3** : a descending slope — **dec•li•na•tion** *n*

de•code *vb* : decipher (a coded message) — **de•cod•er** *n*

de•com•mis•sion *vb* : remove from service

de•com•pose *vb* **1** : separate into parts **2** : decay — **de•com•po•si•tion** *n*

de•con•ges•tant *n* : agent that relieves congestion

de•cor, dé•cor *n* : room design or decoration

dec•o•rate *vb* **-rat•ed; -rat•ing 1** : add something attractive to **2** : honor with a medal — **dec•o•ra•tion** *n* — **dec•o•ra•tive** *adj* — **dec•o•ra•tor** *n*

de•co•rum *n* : proper behavior — **dec•o•rous** *adj*

de•coy *n* : something that tempts or draws attention from another ∼ *vb* : tempt

de•crease *vb* **-creased; -creas•ing** : grow or cause to grow less — **decrease** *n*

de•cree *n* : official order — **de•cree** *vb*

de•crep•it *adj* : impaired by age

de•cre•scen•do *adv or adj* : with a decrease in volume

de•cry *vb* : express strong disapproval of

ded•i•cate *vb* **-cat•ed; -cat•ing 1** : set apart for a purpose (as honor or worship) **2** : address to someone as a compliment — **ded•i•ca•tion** *n* — **ded•i•ca•to•ry** *adj*

de•duce *vb* **-duced; -duc•ing** : derive by reasoning — **de•duc•ible** *adj*

de•duct *vb* : subtract — **deduct•ible** *adj*

de•duc•tion *n* **1** : subtraction **2** : reasoned conclusion — **de•duc•tive** *adj*

deed *n* **1** : exploit **2** : document showing ownership ∼ *vb* : convey by deed

deem *vb* : think

deep *adj* **1** : extending far or a specified distance down, back, within, or outward **2** : occupied **3** : dark and rich in color **4** : low in tone ∼ *adv* **1** : deeply **2** : far along in time ∼ *n* : deep place — **deep•en** *vb* — **deep•ly** *adv*

deep–seat•ed *adj* : firmly established

deer *n, pl* **deer** : ruminant mammal with antlers in the male — **deer•skin** *n*

de•face vb : mar the surface of — **de•face•ment** n — **de•fac•er** n

de•fame vb **-famed; -fam•ing** : injure the reputation of — **def•a•ma•tion** n — **de•fam•a•to•ry** adj

de•fault n : failure in a duty — **default** vb — **de•fault•er** n

de•feat vb 1 : frustrate 2 : win victory over ~ n : loss of a battle or contest

def•e•cate vb **-cat•ed; -cat•ing** : discharge feces from the bowels — **def•e•ca•tion** n

de•fect n : imperfection ~ vb : desert — **de•fec•tion** n — **de•fec•tor** n

de•fec•tive adj : faulty or deficient — **defective** n

de•fend vb 1 : protect from danger or harm 2 : take the side of — **de•fend•er** n

de•fen•dant n : person charged or sued in a court

de•fense n 1 : act of defending 2 : something that defends 3 : party, group, or team that opposes another — **de•fense•less** adj — **de•fen•si•ble** adj — **de•fen•sive** adj or n

¹de•fer vb **-rr-** : postpone — **de•fer•ment** n — **de•fer•ra•ble** adj

²defer vb **-rr-** : yield to the opinion or wishes of another — **def•er•ence** n — **def•er•en•tial** adj

de•fi•ance n : disposition to resist — **de•fi•ant** adj

de•fi•cient adj 1 : lacking something necessary 2 : not up to standard — **de•fi•cien•cy** n

def•i•cit n : shortage esp. in money

de•file vb **-filed; -fil•ing** 1 : make filthy or corrupt 2 : profane or dishonor — **de•file•ment** n

de•fine vb **-fined; -fin•ing** 1 : fix or mark the limits of 2 : clarify in outline 3 : set forth the meaning of — **de•fin•able** adj — **de•fin•ably** adv — **de•fin•er** n — **def•i•ni•tion** n

def•i•nite adj 1 : having distinct limits 2 : clear in meaning, intent, or identity 3 : typically designating an identified or immediately identifiable person or thing — **def•i•nite•ly** adv

de•fin•i•tive adj 1 : conclusive 2 : authoritative

de•flate vb **-flat•ed; -flat•ing** 1 : release air or gas from 2 : reduce — **de•fla•tion** n

de•flect vb : turn aside — **de•flec•tion** n

de•fog vb : remove condensed moisture from — **de•fog•ger** n

de•fo•li•ate vb **-at•ed; -at•ing** : deprive of leaves esp. prematurely — **de•fo•li•ant** n — **de•fo•li•a•tion** n

de•form vb 1 : distort 2 : disfigure — **de•for•ma•tion** n — **de•for•mi•ty** n

de•fraud vb : cheat

de•fray vb : pay

de•frost vb 1 : thaw out 2 : free from ice — **de•frost•er** n

deft adj : quick and skillful — **deft•ly** adv — **deft•ness** n

de•funct adj : dead

de•fy vb **-fied; -fy•ing** 1 : challenge 2 : boldly refuse to obey

de•gen•er•ate adj : degraded or corrupt ~ n : degenerate person ~ vb : become degenerate — **de•gen•er•a•cy** n — **de•gen•er•a•tion** n — **de•gen•er•a•tive** adj

de•grade vb 1 : reduce from a higher to a lower rank or degree 2 : debase 3 : decompose =**m•de•grad•able** adj — **deg•ra•da•tion** n

de•gree n 1 : step in a series 2 : extent, intensity, or scope 3 : title given to a college graduate 4 : a 360th part of the circumference of a circle 5 : unit for measuring temperature

de•hy•drate vb 1 : remove water from 2 : lose liquid — **de•hy•dra•tion** n

de•i•fy vb **-fied; -fy•ing** : make a god of — **de•i•fi•ca•tion** n

deign vb : condescend

de•i•ty n, pl **-ties** 1 cap : God 2 : a god or goddess

de•ject•ed adj : sad — **de•jec•tion** n

de•lay n : a putting off of something ~ vb 1 : postpone 2 : stop or hinder for a time

de•lec•ta•ble adj : delicious

del•e•gate n : representative ~ vb **-gat•ed; -gat•ing** 1 : entrust to another 2 : appoint as one's delegate — **del•e•ga•tion** n

de•lete vb **-let•ed; -let•ing** : eliminate something written — **de•le•tion** n

del•e•te•ri•ous adj : harmful

de•lib•er•ate adj 1 : determined after careful thought 2 : intentional 3 : not hurried ~ vb **-at•ed; -at•ing** : consider carefully — **de•lib•er•ate•ly** adv — **de•lib•er•ateness** n — **de•lib•er•a•tion** n — **de•lib•er•a•tive** adj

del•i•ca•cy n, pl **-cies** 1 : something special and pleasing to eat 2 : fineness 3 : frailty

del•i•cate adj 1 : subtly pleasing to the senses 2 : dainty and charming 3 : sensitive or fragile 4 : requiring fine skill or tact — **del•i•cate•ly** adv

del•i•ca•tes•sen n : store that sells ready-to-eat food

de•li•cious adj : very pleasing esp. in taste or aroma — **de•li•cious•ly** adv — **de•li•cious•ness** n

de•light n 1 : great pleasure 2 : source of great pleasure ~ vb 1 : take great pleasure 2 : satisfy greatly — **de•light•ful** adj — **de•light•ful•ly** adv

de•lin•eate vb **-eat•ed; -eat•ing** : sketch or portray — **de•lin•ea•tion** n

de•lin•quent n : delinquent person ~ adj 1 : violating duty or law 2 : overdue in payment — **de•lin•quen•cy** n

de•lir•i•um n : mental disturbance — **de•lir•i•ous** adj

de•liv•er vb 1 : set free 2 : hand over 3 : assist in birth 4 : say or speak 5 : send to an intended destination — **de•liv•er•ance** n — **de•liv•er•er** n — **de•liv•ery** n

dell n : small secluded valley

del•ta n : triangle of land at the mouth of a river

de•lude vb **-lud•ed; -lud•ing** : mislead or deceive

del•uge n 1 : flood 2 : drenching rain ~ vb **-uged; -ug•ing** 1 : flood 2 : overwhelm

de•lu•sion n : false belief

de•luxe adj : very luxurious or elegant

delve vb **delved; delv•ing** 1 : dig 2 : seek information in records

dem•a•gogue, dem•a•gog n : politician who appeals to emotion and prejudice — **dem•a•gogu•ery** n — **dem•a•gogy** n

de•mand n 1 : act of demanding 2 : something claimed as due 3 : ability and desire to buy 4 : urgent need ~ vb 1 : ask for with authority 2 : require

de•mar•cate vb **-cat•ed; -cat•ing** : mark the limits of — **de•mar•ca•tion** n

de•mean vb : degrade

de•mean•or n : behavior

de•ment•ed adj : crazy

de•mer•it n : mark given an offender

demi•god n : mythological being less powerful than a god

de•mise n 1 : death 2 : loss of status

demi•tasse n : small cup of coffee

de•mo•bi•lize vb : disband from military service — **de•mo•bi•li•za•tion** n

de•moc•ra•cy n, pl **-cies** 1 : government in which the supreme power is held by the people 2 : political unit with democratic government

dem•o•crat n : adherent of democracy

dem•o•crat•ic adj : relating to or favoring democracy — **dem•o•crat•i•cal•ly** adv — **de•moc•ra•tize** vb

de•mol•ish vb 1 : tear down or smash 2 : put an end to — **de•mo•li•tion** n

de•mon n : evil spirit — **de•mon•ic** adj

dem•on•strate vb **-strat•ed; -strat•ing** 1 : show clearly or publicly 2 : prove 3 : explain — **de•mon•stra•ble** adj — **de•mon•stra•bly** adv — **dem•on•stra•tion** n — **de•mon•stra•tive** adj or n — **dem•on•stra•tor** n

de•mor•al•ize vb : destroy the enthusiasm of

de•mote vb **-mot•ed; -mot•ing** : reduce to a lower rank — **de•mo•tion** n

de•mur vb **-rr-** : object — **de•mur** n

de•mure adj : modest — **de•mure•ly** adv

den n 1 : animal's shelter 2 : hiding place 3 : cozy private little room

de•na•ture vb **-tured; -tur•ing** : make (alcohol) unfit for drinking

de•ni•al n : rejection of a request or of the validity of a statement

den•i•grate vb **-grat•ed; -grat•ing** : speak ill of

den•im n 1 : durable twilled cotton fabric 2 pl : pants of denim

den•i•zen n : inhabitant

de•nom•i•na•tion n 1 : religious body 2 : value or size in a series — **de•nom•i•na•tion•al** adj

de•nom•i•na•tor n : part of a fraction below the line

de•note vb 1 : mark out plainly 2 : mean — **de•no•ta•tion** n — **de•no•ta•tive** adj

de•noue•ment n : final outcome (as of a drama)

de•nounce vb **-nounced; -nounc•ing** 1 : pronounce blameworthy or evil 2 : inform against

dense adj **dens•er; -est** 1 : thick, compact, or crowded 2 : stupid — **dense•ly** adv — **dense•ness** n — **den•si•ty** n

dent n : small depression — **dent** vb

den•tal adj : relating to teeth or dentistry

den•ti•frice n : preparation for cleaning teeth

den•tin , den•tine n : bonelike component of teeth

den•tist n : one who cares for and replaces teeth — **den•tist•ry** n

den•ture n : artificial teeth

de•nude vb **-nud•ed; -nud•ing** : strip of covering

de•nun•ci•a•tion n : act of denouncing

de•ny vb **-nied; -ny•ing** 1 : declare untrue 2 : disavow 3 : refuse to grant

de•odor•ant n : preparation to prevent unpleasant odors — **de•odor•ize** vb

de•part vb 1 : go away or away from 2 : die — **de•par•ture** n

de•part•ment n 1 : area of responsibility or interest 2 : functional division — **de•part•men•tal** adj

de•pend vb 1 : rely for support 2 : be determined by or based on something else — **de•pend•abil•i•ty** n — **de•pend•able** adj — **de•pen•dence** n — **de•pen•den•cy** n — **de•pen•dent** adj or n

de•pict vb : show by or as if by a picture — **de•pic•tion** n

de•plete vb **-plet•ed; -plet•ing** : use up resources of — **de•ple•tion** n

de•plore vb **-plored; -plor•ing** : regret strongly — **de•plor•able** adj

de•ploy vb : spread out for battle — **de•ploy•ment** n

de•port vb 1 : behave 2 : send out of the country — **de•por•ta•tion** n — **de•port•ment** n

de•pose vb **-posed; -pos•ing** 1 : remove (a ruler) from office 2 : testify — **de•po•si•tion** n

de•pos•it vb **-it•ed; -it•ing •:** place esp. for safekeeping ~ n 1 : state of being deposited 2 : something deposited 3 : act of depositing 4 : natural accumulation — **de•pos•i•tor** n

de•pos•i•to•ry n, pl **-ries** : place for deposit

de•pot n 1 : place for storage 2 : bus or railroad station

de•prave vb **-praved; -prav- ing** : corrupt morally — **de•praved** adj — **de•prav•i•ty** n

dep•re•cate vb **-cat•ed; -cat•ing** 1 : express disapproval of **2** : belittle — **dep•re•ca•tion** *n* — **dep•re•ca•tory** *adj*

de•pre•ci•ate *vb* **-at•ed; -at•ing 1** : lessen in value **2** : belittle — **de•pre•ci•a•tion** *n*

dep•re•da•tion *n* : a laying waste or plundering — **dep•re•date** *vb*

de•press *vb* **1** : press down **2** : lessen the activity or force of **3** : discourage **4** : decrease the market value of — **de•pres•sant** *n or adj* — **de•pressed** *adj* — **de•pres•sive** *adj or n* — **de•pres•sor** *n*

de•pres•sion *n* **1** : act of depressing or state of being depressed **2** : depressed place **3** : period of low economic activity

de•prive *vb* **-prived; -priv•ing** : take or keep something away from — **de•pri•va•tion** *n*

depth *n, pl* **depths 1** : something that is deep **2** : distance down from a surface **3** : distance from front to back **4** : quality of being deep

dep•u•ta•tion *n* : delegation

dep•u•ty *n, pl* **-ties** : person appointed to act for another — **dep•u•tize** *vb*

de•rail *vb* : leave the rails — **de•rail•ment** *n*

de•range *vb* **-ranged; -rang•ing 1** : disarrange or upset **2** : make insane — **de•range•ment** *n*

der•by *n, pl* **-bies 1** : horse race **2** : stiff felt hat with dome-shaped crown

de•reg•u•late *vb* : remove restrictions on — **de•reg•u•la•tion** *n*

der•e•lict *adj* **1** : abandoned **2** : negligent ~ *n* **1** : something abandoned **2** : bum — **der•e•lic•tion** *n*

de•ride *vb* **-rid•ed; -rid•ing** : make fun of — **de•ri•sion** *n* — **de•ri•sive** *adj* — **de•ri•sive•ly** *adv* — **de•ri•sive•ness** *n*

de•rive *vb* **-rived; -riv•ing 1** : obtain from a source or parent **2** : come from a certain source **3** : infer or deduce — **der•i•va•tion** *n* — **de•riv•a•tive** *adj or n*

der•ma•tol•o•gy *n* : study of the skin and its disorders — **der•ma•tol•o•gist** *n*

de•rog•a•tive *adj* : derogatory

de•rog•a•to•ry *adj* : intended to lower the reputation

der•rick *n* **1** : hoisting apparatus **2** : framework over an oil well

de•scend *vb* **1** : move or climb down **2** : derive **3** : extend downward **4** : appear suddenly (as in an attack) — **de•scen•dant, de•scen•dent** *adj or n* — **de•scent** *n*

de•scribe *vb* **-scribed; -scrib•ing** : represent in words — **de•scrib•able** *adj* — **de•scrip•tion** *n* — **de•scrip•tive** *adj*

de•scry *vb* **-scried; -scry•ing** : catch sight of

des•e•crate *vb* **-crat•ed; -crat•ing** : treat (something sacred) with disrespect — **des•e•cra•tion** *n*

de•seg•re•gate *vb* : eliminate esp. racial segregation in — **de•seg•re•ga•tion** *n*

¹des•ert *n* : dry barren region — **desert** *adj*

²de•sert *n* : what one deserves

³de•sert *vb* : abandon — **de•sert•er** *n* — **de•ser•tion** *n*

de•serve *vb* **-served; -serv•ing** : be worthy of

des•ic•cate *vb* **-cat•ed; -cat•ing** : dehydrate — **des•ic•ca•tion** *n*

de•sign *vb* **1** : create and work out the details of **2** : make a pattern or sketch of ~ *n* **1** : mental project or plan **2** : purpose **3** : preliminary sketch **4** : underlying arrangement of elements **5** : decorative pattern — **de•sign•er** *n*

des•ig•nate *vb* **-nat•ed; -nat•ing 1** : indicate, specify, or name **2** : appoint — **des•ig•na•tion** *n*

de•sire *vb* **-sired; -sir•ing 1** : feel desire for **2** : request ~ *n* **1** : strong conscious impulse to have, be, or do something **2** : something desired — **de•sir•abil•i•ty** *n* — **de•sir•able** *adj* — **de•sir•able•ness** *n* — **de•sir•ous** *adj*

de•sist *vb* : stop

desk *n* : table esp. for writing and reading

des•o•late *adj* **1** : lifeless **2** : disconsolate ~ *vb* **-lat•ed; -lat•ing** : lay waste — **des•o•la•tion** *n*

de•spair *vb* : lose all hope ~ *n* : loss of hope

des•per•a•do *n, pl* **-does** *or* **-dos** : desperate criminal

des•per•ate *adj* **1** : hopeless **2** : rash **3** : extremely intense — **des•per•ate•ly** *adv* — **des•per•a•tion** *n*

des•pi•ca•ble *adj* : deserving scorn

de•spise *vb* **-spised; -spis•ing** : feel contempt for

de•spite *prep* : in spite of

de•spoil *vb* : strip of possessions or value

de•spon•den•cy *n* : dejection — **de•spon•dent** *adj*

des•pot *n* : tyrant — **des•pot•ic** *adj* — **des•po•tism** *n*

des•sert *n* : sweet food, fruit, or cheese ending a meal

des•ti•na•tion *n* : place where something or someone is going

des•tine *vb* **-tined; -tin•ing 1** : designate, assign, or determine in advance **2** : direct

des•ti•ny *n, pl* **-nies** : that which is to happen in the future

des•ti•tute *adj* **1** : lacking something **2** : very poor — **des•ti•tu•tion** *n*

de•stroy *vb* : kill or put an end to

de•stroy•er *n* **1** : one that destroys **2** : small speedy warship

de•struc•tion *n* **1** : action of destroying **2** : ruin — **de•struc•ti•bil•i•ty** *n* — **de•struc•ti•ble** *adj* — **de•struc•tive** *adj*

des•ul•to•ry *adj* : aimless

de•tach *vb* : separate

de•tached *adj* **1** : separate **2** : aloof or impartial

de•tach•ment *n* **1** : separation **2** : troops or ships on special service **3** : aloofness **4** : impartiality

de•tail *n* : small item or part ~ *vb* : give details of

de•tain *vb* **1** : hold in custody **2** : delay

de•tect *vb* : discover — **detect•able** *adj* — **de•tec•tion** *n* — **de•tec•tor** *n*

de•tec•tive *n* : one who investigates crime

dé•tente *n* : relaxation of tensions between nations

de•ten•tion *n* : confinement

de•ter *vb* **-rr-** : discourage or prevent — **de•ter•rence** *n* — **de•ter•rent** *adj or n*

de•ter•gent *n* : cleansing agent

de•te•ri•o•rate *vb* **-rat•ed; -rat•ing** : make or become worse — **de•te•ri•o•ra•tion** *n*

de•ter•mi•na•tion *n* **1** : act of deciding or fixing **2** : firm purpose

de•ter•mine *vb* **-mined; -min•ing 1** : decide on, establish, or settle **2** : find out **3** : bring about as a result

de•test *vb* : hate — **de•test•able** *adj* — **de•tes•ta•tion** *n*

det•o•nate *vb* **-nat•ed; -nat•ing** : explode — **det•o•na•tion** *n* — **det•o•na•tor** *n*

de•tour *n* : temporary indirect route — **detour** *vb*

de•tract *vb* : take away — **de•trac•tion** *n* — **de•trac•tor** *n*

det•ri•ment *n* : damage — **det•ri•men•tal** *adj* — **det•ri•men•tal•ly** *adv*

deuce *n* **1** : 2 in cards or dice **2** : tie in tennis **3** : devil — used as an oath

deut•sche mark *n* : monetary unit of Germany

de•val•ue *vb* : reduce the value of — **de•val•u•a•tion** *n*

dev•as•tate *vb* **-tat•ed; -tat•ing** : ruin — **dev•as•ta•tion** *n*

de•vel•op *vb* **1** : grow, increase, or evolve gradually **2** : cause to grow, increase, or reach full potential — **de•vel•op•er** *n* — **de•vel•op•ment** *n* — **de•vel•op•men•tal** *adj*

de•vi•ate *vb* **-at•ed; -at•ing** : change esp. from a course or standard — **de•vi•ant** *adj or n* — **de•vi•ate** *n* — **de•vi•a•tion** *n*

de•vice *n* **1** : specialized piece of equipment or tool **2** : design

dev•il *n* **1** : personified supreme spirit of evil **2** : demon **3** : wicked person ~ *vb* **-iled** *or* **-illed; -il•ing** *or* **-il•ling 1** : season highly **2** : pester — **dev•il•ish** *adj* — **dev•il•ry** , **dev•il•try** *n*

de•vi•ous *adj* : tricky

de•vise *vb* **-vised; -vis•ing 1** : invent **2** : plot **3** : give by will

de•void *adj* : entirely lacking

de•vote *vb* **-vot•ed; -vot•ing** : set apart for a special purpose

de•vot•ed *adj* : faithful

dev•o•tee *n* : ardent follower

de•vo•tion *n* **1** : prayer — usu. pl. **2** : loyalty and dedication — **de•vo•tion•al** *adj*

de•vour *vb* : consume ravenously — **de•vour•er** *n*

de•vout *adj* **1** : devoted to religion **2** : serious — **de•vout•ly** *adv* — **de•vout•ness** *n*

dew *n* : moisture condensed at night — **dew•drop** *n* — **dewy** *adj*

dex•ter•ous *adj* : skillful with the hands — **dex•ter•i•ty** *n* — **dex•ter•ous•ly** *adv*

dex•trose *n* : plant or blood sugar

di•a•be•tes *n* : disorder in which the body has too little insulin and too much sugar — **di•a•bet•ic** *adj or n*

di•a•bol•ic , **di•a•bol•i•cal** *adj* : fiendish

di•a•crit•ic *n* : mark accompanying a letter and indicating a specific sound value — **di•a•crit•i•cal** *adj*

di•a•dem *n* : crown

di•ag•no•sis *n, pl* **-no•ses** : identifying of a disease from its symptoms — **di•ag•nose** *vb* — **di•ag•nos•tic** *adj*

di•ag•o•nal *adj* : extending from one corner to the opposite corner ~ *n* : diagonal line, direction, or arrangement — **di•ag•o•nal•ly** *adv*

di•a•gram *n* : explanatory drawing or plan ~ *vb* **-gramed** *or* **-grammed; -gram•ing** *or* **gram•ming** : represent by a diagram — **di•a•gram•mat•ic** *adj*

di•al *n* **1** : face of a clock, meter, or gauge **2** : control knob or wheel ~ *vb* **-aled** *or* **-alled; -al•ing** *or* **-al•ling** : turn a dial to call, operate, or select

di•a•lect *n* : variety of language confined to a region or group

di•a•logue *n* : conversation

di•am•e•ter *n* **1** : straight line through the center of a circle **2** : thickness

di•a•met•ric , **di•a•met•ri•cal** *adj* : completely opposite — **di•a•met•ri•cal•ly** *adv*

di•a•mond *n* **1** : hard brilliant mineral that consists of crystalline carbon **2** : flat figure having 4 equal sides, 2 acute angles, and 2 obtuse angles **3** : playing card of a suit marked with a red diamond **4** : baseball field

di•a•per *n* : baby's garment for receiving bodily wastes ~ *vb* : put a diaper on

di•a•phragm *n* **1** : sheet of muscle between the chest and abdominal cavity **2** : contraceptive device

di•ar•rhea *n* : abnormally watery discharge from bowels

di•a•ry *n, pl* **-ries** : daily record of personal experiences — **di•a•rist** *n*

di•a•tribe *n* : biting or abusive denunciation

dice *n, pl* **dice** : die or a game played with dice ~ *vb* **diced; dic•ing** : cut into small cubes

dick•er *vb* : bargain

dic•tate *vb* **-tat•ed; -tat•ing 1** : speak for a person or a machine to record **2** : command ~ *n* : order — **dic•ta•tion** *n*

dic•ta•tor *n* : person ruling absolutely and often

brutally — **dic•ta•to•ri•al** *adj* — **dic•ta•tor•ship** *n*

dic•tion *n* **1** : choice of the best word **2** : precise pronunciation

dic•tio•nary *n, pl* **-nar•ies** : reference book of words with information about their meanings

dic•tum *n, pl* **-ta** : authoritative or formal statement

did *past of* DO

di•dac•tic *adj* : intended to teach a moral lesson

¹die *vb* **died; dy•ing 1** : stop living **2** : pass out of existence **3** : stop or subside **4** : long

²die *n* **1** *pl* **dice** : small marked cube used in gambling **2** *pl* **dies** : form for stamping or cutting

die•sel *n* : engine in which high compression causes ignition of the fuel

di•et *n* : food and drink regularly consumed (as by a person) ~ *vb* : eat less or according to certain rules — **di•etary** *adj or n* — **di•et•er** *n*

di•etet•ics *n sing or pl* : science of nutrition — **di•etet•ic** *adj* — **di•eti•tian, di•eti•cian** *n*

dif•fer *vb* **1** : be unlike **2** : vary **3** : disagree — **dif•fer•ence** *n*

dif•fer•ent *adj* : not the same — **dif•fer•ent•ly** *adv*

dif•fer•en•ti•ate *vb* **-at•ed; -at•ing 1** : make or become different **2** : distinguish — **dif•fer•en•ti•a•tion** *n*

dif•fi•cult *adj* : hard to do, understand, or deal with

dif•fi•cul•ty *n, pl* **-ties 1** : difficult nature **2** : great effort **3** : something hard to do, understand, or deal with

dif•fi•dent *adj* : reserved — **dif•fi•dence** *n*

dif•fuse *adj* **1** : wordy **2** : not concentrated ~ *vb* **-fused; -fus•ing** : pour out or spread widely — **dif•fu•sion** *n*

dig *vb* **dug; dig•ging 1** : turn up soil **2** : hollow out or form by removing earth **3** : uncover by turning up earth ~ *n* **1** : thrust **2** : cutting remark — **dig in** *vb* **1** : establish a defensive position **2** : begin working or eating — **dig up** *vb* : discover

¹di•gest *n* : body of information in shortened form

²di•gest *vb* **1** : think over **2** : convert (food) into a form that can be absorbed **3** : summarize — **di•gest•ible** *adj* — **di•ges•tion** *n* — **di•ges•tive** *adj*

dig•it *n* **1** : any of the figures 1 to 9 inclusive and usu. the symbol 0 **2** : finger or toe

dig•i•tal *adj* : providing information in numerical digits — **dig•i•tal•ly** *adv*

dig•ni•fy *vb* **-fied; -fy•ing** : give dignity or attention to

dig•ni•tary *n, pl* **-taries** : person of high position

dig•ni•ty *n, pl* **-ties 1** : quality or state of being worthy or honored **2** : formal reserve (as of manner)

di•gress *vb* : wander from the main subject — **di•gres•sion** *n*

dike *n* : earth bank or dam

di•lap•i•dat•ed *adj* : fallen into partial ruin — **di•lap•i•da•tion** *n*

di•late *vb* **-lat•ed; -lat•ing** : swell or expand — **dil•a•ta•tion** *n* — **di•la•tion** *n*

dil•a•to•ry *adj* **1** : delaying **2** : tardy or slow

di•lem•ma *n* **1** : undesirable choice **2** : predicament

dil•et•tante *n, pl* **-tantes** *or* **-tan•ti** : one who dabbles in a field of interest

dil•i•gent *adj* : attentive and busy — **dil•i•gence** *n* — **dil•i•gent•ly** *adv*

dill *n* : herb with aromatic leaves and seeds

dil•ly•dal•ly *vb* : waste time by delay

di•lute *vb* **-lut•ed; -lut•ing** : lessen the consistency or strength of= by mixing with something else ~ = *adj* : weak — **di•lu•tion** *n*

dim *adj* **-mm- 1** : not bright or distinct **2** : having no luster **3** : not seeing or understanding clearly

— **dim** *vb* — **dim•ly** *adv* — **dim•mer** *n* — **dim•ness** *n*

dime *n* : U.S. coin worth 1/10 dollar

di•men•sion *n* **1** : measurement of extension (as in length, height, or breadth) **2** : extent — **di•men•sion•al** *adj*

di•min•ish *vb* **1** : make less or cause to appear less **2** : dwindle

di•min•u•tive *adj* : extremely small

dim•ple *n* : small depression esp. in the cheek or chin

din *n* : loud noise

dine *vb* **dined; din•ing** : eat dinner

din•er *n* **1** : person eating dinner **2** : railroad dining car or restaurant resembling one

din•ghy *n, pl* **-ghies** : small boat

din•gy *adj* **-gi•er; -est 1** : dirty **2** : shabby — **din•gi•ness** *n*

din•ner *n* : main daily meal

di•no•saur *n* : extinct often huge reptile

dint *n* : force — in the phrase **by dint of**

di•o•cese *n, pl* **-ces•es** : territorial jurisdiction of a bishop — **di•oc•e•san** *adj or n*

dip *vb* **-pp- 1** : plunge into a liquid **2** : take out with a ladle **3** : lower and quickly raise again **4** : sink or slope downward suddenly ~ *n* **1** : plunge into water for sport **2** : sudden downward movement or incline — **dip•per** *n*

diph•the•ria *n* : acute contagious disease

diph•thong *n* : two vowel sounds joined to form one speech sound (as **ou** in **out**)

di•plo•ma *n, pl* **-mas** : record of graduation from a school

di•plo•ma•cy *n* **1** : business of conducting negotiations between nations **2** : tact — **dip•lo•mat** *n* — **dip•lo•mat•ic** *adj*

dire *adj* **dir•er; -est 1** : very horrible **2** : extreme

di•rect *vb* **1** : address **2** : cause to move or to follow a certain course **3** : show (someone) the way **4** : regulate the activities or course of **5** : request with authority ~ *adj* **1** : leading to or coming from a point without deviation or interruption **2** : frank — **direct** *adv* — **di•rect•ly** *adv* — **di•rect•ness** *n* — **di•rec•tor** *n*

direct current *n* : electric current flowing in one direction only

di•rec•tion *n* **1** : supervision **2** : order **3** : course along which something moves — **di•rec•tion•al** *adj*

di•rec•tive *n* : order

di•rec•to•ry *n, pl* **-ries** : alphabetical list of names and addresses

dirge *n* : funeral hymn

di•ri•gi•ble *n* : airship

dirt *n* **1** : mud, dust, or grime that makes something unclean **2** : soil

dirty *adj* **dirt•i•er; -est 1** : not clean **2** : unfair **3** : indecent ~ *vb* **dirt•ied; dirty•ing** : make or become dirty — **dirt•i•ness** *n*

dis•able *vb* **-abled; -abling** : make unable to function — **dis•abil•i•ty** *n*

dis•abuse *vb* : free from error or misconception

dis•ad•van•tage *n* : something that hinders success — **dis•ad•van•ta•geous** *adj*

dis•af•fect *vb* : cause discontent in — **dis•af•fec•tion** *n*

dis•agree *vb* **1** : fail to agree **2** : differ in opinion — **dis•agree•ment** *n*

dis•agree•able *adj* : unpleasant

dis•al•low *vb* : refuse to admit or recognize

dis•ap•pear *vb* **1** : pass out of sight **2** : cease to be — **dis•ap•pear•ance** *n*

dis•ap•point *vb* : fail to fulfill the expectation or hope of — **dis•ap•point•ment** *n*

dis•ap•prove *vb* **1** : condemn or reject **2** : feel or express dislike or rejection — **dis•ap•prov•al** *n* — **dis•ap•prov•ing•ly** *adv*

dis•arm *vb* **1** : take weapons from **2** : reduce

armed forces **3** : make harmless or friendly — **dis•ar•ma•ment** *n*

dis•ar•range *vb* : throw into disorder — **dis•ar•range•ment** *n*

dis•ar•ray *n* : disorder

di•sas•ter *n* : sudden great misfortune — **di•sas•trous** *adj*

dis•avow *vb* : deny responsibility for — **dis•avow•al** *n*

dis•band *vb* : break up the organization of

dis•bar *vb* : expel from the legal profession — **dis•bar•ment** *n*

dis•be•lieve *vb* : hold not worthy of belief — **dis•be•lief** *n*

dis•burse *vb* **-bursed; -burs•ing** : pay out — **dis•burse•ment** *n*

disc *var of* DISK

dis•card *vb* : get rid of as unwanted — **dis•card** *n*

dis•cern *vb* : discover with the eyes or the mind — **dis•cern•ible** *adj* — **dis•cern•ment** *n*

dis•charge *vb* **1** : unload **2** : shoot **3** : set free **4** : dismiss from service **5** : let go or let off **6** : give forth fluid ~ *n* **1** : act of discharging **2** : a flowing out (as of blood) **3** : dismissal

dis•ci•ple *n* : one who helps spread another's teachings

dis•ci•pli•nar•i•an *n* : one who enforces order

dis•ci•pline *n* **1** : field of study **2** : training that corrects, molds, or perfects **3** : punishment **4** : control gained by obedience or training ~ *vb* **-plined; -plin•ing 1** : punish **2** : train in self-control — **dis•ci•plin•ary** *adj*

dis•claim *vb* : disavow

dis•close *vb* : reveal — **dis•clo•sure** *n*

dis•col•or *vb* : change the color of esp. for the worse — **dis•col•or•ation** *n*

dis•com•fit *vb* : upset — **dis•com•fi•ture** *n*

dis•com•fort *n* : uneasiness

dis•con•cert *vb* : upset

dis•con•nect *vb* : undo the connection of

dis•con•so•late *adj* : hopelessly sad

dis•con•tent *n* : uneasiness of mind — **dis•con•tent•ed** *adj*

dis•con•tin•ue *vb* : end — **dis•con•tin•u•ance** *n* — **dis•con•ti•nu•i•ty** *n* — **dis•con•tin•u•ous** *adj*

dis•cord *n* : lack of harmony — **dis•cor•dant** *adj* — **dis•cor•dant•ly** *adv*

dis•count *n* : reduction from a regular price ~ *vb* **1** : reduce the amount of **2** : disregard — **discount** *adj* — **dis•count•er** *n*

dis•cour•age *vb* **-aged; -ag•ing 1** : deprive of courage, confidence, or enthusiasm **2** : dissuade — **dis•cour•age•ment** *n*

dis•course *n* **1** : conversation **2** : formal treatment of a subject ~ *vb* **-coursed; -cours•ing** : talk at length

dis•cour•te•ous *adj* : lacking courtesy — **dis•cour•te•ous•ly** *adv* — **dis•cour•te•sy** *n*

dis•cov•er *vb* **1** : make known **2** : obtain the first sight or knowledge of **3** : find out — **dis•cov•er•er** *n* — **dis•cov•ery** *n*

dis•cred•it *vb* **1** : disbelieve **2** : destroy confidence in ~ *n* **1** : loss of reputation **2** : disbelief — **dis•cred•it•able** *adj*

dis•creet *adj* : capable of keeping a secret — **dis•creet•ly** *adv*

dis•crep•an•cy *n, pl* **-cies** : difference or disagreement

dis•crete *adj* : individually distinct

dis•cre•tion *n* **1** : discreet quality **2** : power of decision or choice — **dis•cre•tion•ary** *adj*

dis•crim•i•nate *vb* **-nat•ed; -nat•ing 1** : distinguish **2** : show favor or disfavor unjustly — **dis•crim•i•na•tion** *n* — **dis•crim•i•na•to•ry** *adj*

dis•cur•sive *adj* : passing from one topic to another — **dis•cur•sive•ly** *adv* — **dis•cur•sive•ness** *n*

dis·cus *n, pl* **-cus·es** : disk hurled for distance in a contest

dis·cuss *vb* : talk about or present — **dis·cus·sion** *n*

dis·dain *n* : feeling of contempt ~ *vb* : look upon or reject with disdain — **dis·dain·ful** *adj* — **dis·dain·ful·ly** *adv*

dis·ease *n* : condition of a body that impairs its functioning — **dis·eased** *adj*

dis·em·bark *vb* : get off a ship — **dis·em·bar·ka·tion** *n*

dis·em·bod·ied *adj* : having no substance or reality

dis·en·chant *vb* : to free from illusion — **dis·en·chant·ment** *n*

dis·en·chant·ed *adj* : disappointed

dis·en·gage *vb* : release — **dis·en·gage·ment** *n*

dis·en·tan·gle *vb* : free from entanglement

dis·fa·vor *n* : disapproval

dis·fig·ure *vb* : spoil the appearance of — **dis·fig·ure·ment** *n*

dis·fran·chise *vb* : deprive of the right to vote — **dis·fran·chise·ment** *n*

dis·gorge *vb* : spew forth

dis·grace *vb* : bring disgrace to ~ *n* **1** : shame **2** : cause of shame — **dis·grace·ful** *adj* — **dis·grace·ful·ly** *adv*

dis·grun·tle *vb* **-tled; -tling** : put in bad humor

dis·guise *vb* **-guised; -guis·ing** : hide the true identity or nature of ~ *n* : something that conceals

dis·gust *n* : strong aversion ~ *vb* : provoke disgust in — **dis·gust·ed·ly** *adv* — **dis·gust·ing·ly** *adv*

dish *n* **1** : vessel for serving food or the food it holds **2** : food prepared in a particular way ~ *vb* : put in a dish — **dish·cloth** *n* — **dish·rag** *n* — **dish·wash·er** *n* — **dish·wa·ter** *n*

dis·har·mo·ny *n* : lack of= harmony — **dis·har·mo·ni·ous** *adj*

dis·heart·en *vb* : discourage

di·shev·el *vb* **-eled** *or* **-elled; -el·ing** *or* **-el·ling** : throw into disorder — **di·shev·eled, di·shev·elled** *adj*

dis·hon·est *adj* : not honest — **dis·hon·est·ly** *adv* — **dis·hon·es·ty** *n*

dis·hon·or *n or vb* : disgrace — **dis·hon·or·able** *adj* — **dis·hon·or·ably** *adv*

dis·il·lu·sion *vb* : to free from illusion — **dis·il·lu·sion·ment** *n*

dis·in·cli·na·tion *n* : slight aversion — **dis·in·cline** *vb*

dis·in·fect *vb* : destroy disease germs in or on — **dis·in·fec·tant** *adj or n* — **dis·in·fec·tion** *n*

dis·in·gen·u·ous *adj* : lacking in candor

dis·in·her·it *vb* : prevent from inheriting property

dis·in·te·grate *vb* : break into parts or small bits — **dis·in·te·gra·tion** *n*

dis·in·ter·est·ed *adj* **1** : not interested **2** : not prejudiced — **dis·in·ter·est·ed·ness** *n*

dis·joint·ed *adj* **1** : separated at the joint **2** : incoherent

disk *n* : something round and flat

dis·like *vb* : regard with dislike ~ *n* : feeling that something is unpleasant and to be avoided

dis·lo·cate *vb* : move out of the usual or proper place — **dis·lo·ca·tion** *n*

dis·lodge *vb* : force out of a place

dis·loy·al *adj* : not loyal — **dis·loy·al·ty** *n*

dis·mal *adj* : showing or causing gloom — **dis·mal·ly** *adv*

dis·man·tle *vb* **-tled; -tling** : take apart

dis·may *vb* **-mayed; -may·ing** : discourage — **dismay** *n*

dis·mem·ber *vb* : cut into pieces — **dis·mem·ber·ment** *n*

dis·miss *vb* **1** : send away **2** : remove from service **3** : put aside or out of mind — **dis·miss·al** *n*

dis·mount *vb* **1** : get down from something **2** : take apart

dis·obey *vb* : refuse to obey — **dis·obe·di·ence** *n* — **dis·obe·di·ent** *adj*

dis·or·der *n* **1** : lack of order **2** : breach of public order **3** : abnormal state of body or mind — **disorder** *vb* — **dis·or·der·li·ness** *n* — **dis·or·der·ly** *adj*

dis·or·ga·nize *vb* : throw into disorder — **dis·or·ga·ni·za·tion** *n*

dis·own *vb* : repudiate

dis·par·age *vb* **-aged; -ag·ing** : say bad things about — **dis·par·age·ment** *n*

dis·pa·rate *adj* : different in quality or character — **dis·par·i·ty** *n*

dis·pas·sion·ate *adj* : not influenced by strong feeling — **dis·pas·sion·ate·ly** *adv*

dis·patch *vb* **1** : send **2** : kill **3** : attend to rapidly **4** : defeat ~ *n* **1** : message **2** : news item from a correspondent **3** : promptness and efficiency — **dis·patch·er** *n*

dis·pel *vb* **-ll-** : clear away

dis·pen·sa·ry *n, pl* **-ries** : place where medical or dental aid is provided

dis·pen·sa·tion *n* **1** : system of principles or rules **2** : exemption from a rule **3** : act of dispensing

dis·pense *vb* **-pensed; -pens·ing** **1** : portion out **2** : make up and give out (remedies) — **dis·pens·er** *n* — **dispense with** : do without

dis·perse *vb* **-persed; -pers·ing** : scatter — **dis·per·sal** *n* — **dis·per·sion** *n*

dis·place *vb* **1** : expel or force to flee from home or native land **2** : take the place of — **dis·place·ment** *n*

dis·play *vb* : present to view — **display** *n*

dis·please *vb* : arouse the dislike of — **dis·plea·sure** *n*

dis·port *vb* **1** : amuse **2** : frolic

dis·pose *vb* **-posed; -pos·ing** **1** : give a tendency to **2** : settle — **dis·pos·able** *adj* — **dis·pos·al** *n* — **dis·pos·er** *n* — **dispose of** **1** : determine the fate, condition, or use of **2** : get rid of

dis·po·si·tion *n* **1** : act or power of disposing of **2** : arrangement **3** : natural attitude

dis·pos·sess *vb* : deprive of possession or occupancy — **dis·pos·ses·sion** *n*

dis·pro·por·tion *n* : lack of proportion — **dis·pro·por·tion·ate** *adj*

dis·prove *vb* : prove false — **dis·proof** *n*

dis·pute *vb* **-put·ed; -put·ing** **1** : argue **2** : deny the truth or rightness of **3** : struggle against or over ~ *n* : debate or quarrel — **dis·put·able** *adj* — **dis·pu·ta·tion** *n*

dis·qual·i·fy *vb* : make ineligible — **dis·qual·i·fi·ca·tion** *n*

dis·qui·et *vb* : make uneasy or restless ~ *n* : anxiety

dis·re·gard *vb* : pay no attention to ~ *n* : neglect

dis·re·pair *n* : need of repair

dis·rep·u·ta·ble *adj* : having a bad reputation

dis·re·pute *n* : low regard

dis·re·spect *n* : lack of respect — **dis·re·spect·ful** *adj*

dis·robe *vb* : undress

dis·rupt *vb* : throw into disorder — **dis·rup·tion** *n* — **dis·rup·tive** *adj*

dis·sat·is·fac·tion *n* : lack of satisfaction

dis·sat·is·fy *vb* : fail to satisfy

dis·sect *vb* : cut into parts esp. to examine — **dis·sec·tion** *n*

dis·sem·ble *vb* **-bled; -bling** : disguise feelings or intention — **dis·sem·bler** *n*

dis·sem·i·nate *vb* **-nat·ed; -nat·ing** : spread around — **dis·sem·i·na·tion** *n*

dis·sen·sion *n* : discord

dis·sent *vb* : object or disagree ~ *n* : difference of opinion — **dis·sent·er** *n* — **dis·sen·tient** *adj or n*

dis·ser·ta·tion *n* : long written study of a subject

dis·ser·vice *n* : injury

dis·si·dent *n* : one who differs openly with an establishment — **dis·si·dence** *n* — **dissident** *adj*

dis·sim·i·lar *adj* : different — **dis·sim·i·lar·i·ty** *n*

dis·si·pate *vb* **-pat·ed; -pat·ing** **1** : break up and drive off **2** : squander — **dis·si·pa·tion** *n*

dis·so·ci·ate *vb* **-at·ed; -at·ing** : separate from association — **dis·so·ci·a·tion** *n*

dis·so·lute *adj* : loose in morals or conduct

dis·so·lu·tion *n* : act or process of dissolving

dis·solve *vb* **1** : break up or bring to an end **2** : pass or cause to pass into solution

dis·so·nance *n* : discord — **dis·so·nant** *adj*

dis·suade *vb* **-suad·ed; -suad·ing** : persuade not to do something — **dis·sua·sion** *n*

dis·tance *n* **1** : measure of separation in space or time **2** : reserve

dis·tant *adj* **1** : separate in space **2** : remote in time, space, or relationship **3** : reserved — **dis·tant·ly** *adv*

dis·taste *n* : dislike — **dis·taste·ful** *adj*

dis·tem·per *n* : serious virus disease of dogs

dis·tend *vb* : swell out — **dis·ten·sion, dis·ten·tion** *n*

dis·till *vb* : obtain by distillation — **dis·til·late** *n* — **dis·till·er** *n* — **dis·till·ery** *n*

dis·til·la·tion *n* : purification of liquid by evaporating then condensing

dis·tinct *adj* **1** : distinguishable from others **2** : readily discerned — **dis·tinc·tive** *adj* — **dis·tinc·tive·ly** *adv* — **dis·tinc·tive·ness** *n* — **dis·tinct·ly** *adv* — **dis·tinct·ness** *n*

dis·tinc·tion *n* **1** : act of distinguishing **2** : difference **3** : special recognition

dis·tin·guish *vb* **1** : perceive as different **2** : set apart **3** : discern **4** : make outstanding — **dis·tin·guish·able** *adj* — **dis·tin·guished** *adj*

dis·tort *vb* : twist out of shape, condition, or true meaning — **dis·tor·tion** *n*

dis·tract *vb* : divert the mind or attention of — **dis·trac·tion** *n*

dis·traught *adj* : agitated with mental conflict

dis·tress *n* **1** : suffering **2** : misfortune **3** : state of danger or great need ~ *vb* : subject to strain or distress — **dis·tress·ful** *adj*

dis·trib·ute *vb* **-ut·ed; -ut·ing** **1** : divide among many **2** : spread or hand out — **dis·tri·bu·tion** *n* — **dis·trib·u·tive** *adj* — **dis·trib·u·tor** *n*

dis·trict *n* : territorial division

dis·trust *vb or n* : mistrust — **dis·trust·ful** *adj*

dis·turb *vb* **1** : interfere with **2** : destroy the peace, composure, or order of — **dis·tur·bance** *n* — **dis·turb·er** *n*

dis·use *n* : lack of use

ditch *n* : trench ~ *vb* **1** : dig a ditch in **2** : get rid of

dith·er *n* : highly nervous or excited state

dit·to *n, pl* **-tos** : more of the same

dit·ty *n, pl* **-ties** : short simple song

di·uret·ic *adj* : tending to increase urine flow — **diuretic** *n*

di·ur·nal *adj* **1** : daily **2** : of or occurring in the daytime

di·van *n* : couch

dive *vb* **dived** *or* **dove; dived; div·ing** **1** : plunge into water headfirst **2** : submerge **3** : descend quickly ~ *n* **1** : act of diving **2** : sharp decline — **div·er** *n*

di·verge *vb* **-verged; -verg·ing** **1** : move in different directions **2** : differ — **di·ver·gence** *n* — **di·ver·gent** *adj*

di·vers *adj* : various

di·verse *adj* : involving different forms — **di·ver·si·fi·ca·tion** *n* — **di·ver·si·fy** *vb* — **di·ver·si·ty** *n*

di·vert *vb* **1** : turn from a course or purpose **2** : distract **3** : amuse — **di·ver·sion** *n*

di·vest *vb* : strip of clothing, possessions, or rights

di·vide *vb* **-vid·ed; -vid·ing 1** : separate **2** : distribute **3** : share **4** : subject to mathematical division ~ *n* : watershed — **di·vid·er** *n*

div·i·dend *n* **1** : individual share **2** : bonus **3** : number to be divided

div·i·na·tion *n* : practice of trying to foretell future events

di·vine *adj* **-vin·er; -est 1** : relating to or being God or a god **2** : supremely good ~ *n* : clergy member — *vb* **-vined; -vin·ing 1** : infer **2** : prophesy — **di·vine·ly** *adv* — **divin·er** *n* — **di·vin·i·ty** *n*

di·vis·i·ble *adj* : capable of being divided — **di·vis·i·bil·i·ty** *n*

di·vi·sion *n* **1** : distribution **2** : part of a whole **3** : disagreement **4** : process of finding out how many times one number is contained in another

di·vi·sive *adj* : creating dissension

di·vi·sor *n* : number by which a dividend is divided

di·vorce *n* : legal breaking up of a marriage — **divorce** *vb*

di·vor·cée *n* : divorced woman

di·vulge *vb* **-vulged; -vulg·ing** : reveal

diz·zy *adj* **-zi·er; -est 1** : having a sensation of whirling **2** : causing or caused by giddiness — **diz·zi·ly** *adv* — **diz·zi·ness** *n*

DNA *n* : compound in cell nuclei that is the basis of heredity

do *vb* **did ; done ; do·ing ; does 1** : work to accomplish (an action or task) **2** : behave **3** : prepare or fix up **4** : fare **5** : finish **6** : serve the needs or purpose of **7** — used as an auxiliary verb — **do away with 1** : get rid of **2** : destroy — **do by** : deal with — **do·er** *n* — **do in** *vb* **1** : ruin **2** : kill

doc·ile *adj* : easily managed — **do·cil·i·ty** *n*

¹**dock** *vb* **1** : shorten **2** : reduce

²**dock** *n* **1** : berth between 2 piers to receive ships **2** : loading wharf or platform ~ *vb* : bring or come into dock — **dock·work·er** *n*

³**dock** *n* : place in a court for a prisoner

dock·et *n* **1** : record of the proceedings in a legal action **2** : list of legal causes to be tried — **docket** *vb*

doc·tor *n* **1** : person holding one of the highest academic degrees **2** : one (as a surgeon) skilled in healing arts ~ *vb* **1** : give medical treatment to **2** : repair or alter — **doc·tor·al** *adj*

doc·trine *n* : something taught — **doc·tri·nal** *adj*

doc·u·ment *n* : paper that furnishes information or legal proof — **doc·u·ment** *vb* — **doc·u·men·ta·tion** *n* — **doc·u·ment·er** *n*

doc·u·men·ta·ry *adj* **1** : of or relating to documents **2** : giving a factual presentation — **documentary** *n*

dod·der *vb* : become feeble usu. from age

dodge *vb* **dodged; dodg·ing 1** : move quickly aside or out of the way of **2** : evade — **dodge** *n*

do·do *n, pl* **-does** *or* **-dos 1** : heavy flightless extinct bird **2** : stupid person

doe *n, pl* **does** *or* **doe** : adult female deer — **doe·skin** *n*

does *pres 3d sing of* DO

doff *vb* : remove

dog *n* : flesh-eating domestic mammal ~ *vb* **1** : hunt down or track like a hound **2** : harass — **dog·catch·er** *n* — **dog·gy** *n or adj* — **dog·house** *n*

dog–ear *n* : turned-down corner of a page — **dog-near** *vb* — **dog–eared** *adj*

dog·ged *adj* : stubbornly determined

dog·ma *n* : tenet or code of tenets

dog·ma·tism *n* : unwarranted stubbornness of opinion — **dog·ma·tic** *adj*

dog·wood *n* : flowering tree

doi·ly *n, pl* **-lies** : small decorative mat

do·ings *n pl* : events

dol·drums *n pl* : spell of listlessness, despondency, or stagnation

dole *n* : distribution esp. of money to the needy or unemployed — **dole out** *vb* : give out esp. in small portions

dole·ful *adj* : sad — **dole·ful·ly** *adv*

doll *n* : small figure of a person used esp. as a child's toy

dol·lar *n* : any of various basic monetary units (as in the U.S. and Canada)

dol·ly *n, pl* **-lies** : small cart or wheeled platform

dol·phin *n* **1** : sea mammal related to the whales **2** : saltwater food fish

dolt *n* : stupid person — **dolt·ish** *adj*

-dom *n suffix* **1** : office or realm **2** : state or fact of being **3** : those belonging to a group

do·main *n* **1** : territory over which someone reigns **2** : sphere of activity or knowledge

dome *n* **1** : large hemispherical roof **2** : roofed stadium

do·mes·tic *adj* **1** : relating to the household or family **2** : relating and limited to one's own country **3** : tame ~ *n* : household servant — **do·mes·ti·cal·ly** *adv*

do·mes·ti·cate *vb* **-cat·ed; -cat·ing** : tame — **do·mes·ti·ca·tion** *n*

dom·i·cile *n* : home — **domicile** *vb*

dom·i·nance *n* : control — **dom·i·nant** *adj*

dom·i·nate *vb* **-nat·ed; -nat·ing 1** : have control over **2** : rise high above — **dom·i·na·tion** *n*

dom·i·neer *vb* : exercise arbitrary control

do·min·ion *n* **1** : supreme authority **2** : governed territory

dom·i·no *n, pl* **-noes** *or* **-nos** : flat rectangular block used as a piece in a game (**dominoes**)

don *vb* **-nn-** : put on (clothes)

do·nate *vb* **-nat·ed; -nat·ing** : make a gift of — **do·na·tion** *n*

¹**done** *past part of* DO

²**done** *adj* **1** : finished or ended **2** : cooked sufficiently

don·key *n, pl* **-keys** : sturdy domestic ass

do·nor *n* : one that gives

doo·dle *vb* **-dled; -dling** : draw or scribble aimlessly — **doodle** *n*

doom *n* **1** : judgment **2** : fate **3** : ruin — **doom** *vb*

door *n* : passage for entrance or a movable barrier that can open or close such a passage — **door·jamb** *n* — **door·knob** *n* — **door·mat** *n* — **door·step** *n* — **door·way** *n*

dope **1** : narcotic preparation **2** : stupid person **3** : information ~ *vb* **doped; dop·ing** : drug

dor·mant *adj* : not actively growing or functioning — **dor·man·cy** *n*

dor·mer *n* : window built upright in a sloping roof

dor·mi·to·ry *n, pl* **-ries** : residence hall (as at a college)

dor·mouse *n* : squirrellike rodent

dor·sal *adj* : relating to or on the back — **dor·sal·ly** *adv*

do·ry *n, pl* **-ries** : flat-bottomed boat

dose *n* : quantity (as of medicine) taken at one time ~ *vb* **dosed; dos·ing** : give medicine to — **dos·age** *n*

dot *n* **1** : small spot **2** : small round mark made with or as if with a pen ~ *vb* **-tt-** : mark with dots

dot·age *n* : senility

dote *vb* **dot·ed; dot·ing 1** : act feebleminded **2** : be foolishly fond

dou·ble *adj* **1** : consisting of 2 members or parts **2** : being twice as great or as many **3** : folded in two ~ *n* **1** : something twice another **2** : one that resembles another ~ *adv* : doubly ~ *vb* **-bled; -bling 1** : make or become twice as great **2** : fold or bend **3** : clench

dou·ble–cross *vb* : deceive by trickery — **double–cross·er** *n*

dou·bly *adv* : to twice the degree

doubt *vb* **1** : be uncertain about **2** : mistrust **3** : consider unlikely ~ *n* **1** : uncertainty **2** : mistrust **3** : inclination not to believe — **doubt·ful** *adj* — **doubt·ful·ly** *adv* — **doubt·less** *adv*

douche *n* : jet of fluid for cleaning a body part

dough *n* : stiff mixture of flour and liquid — **doughy** *adj*

dough·nut *n* : small fried ring-shaped cake

dough·ty *adj* **-ti·er; -est** : able, strong, or valiant

dour *adj* **1** : severe **2** : gloomy or sullen — **dour·ly** *adv*

douse *vb* **doused; dous·ing 1** : plunge into or drench with water **2** : extinguish

¹**dove** *n* : small wild pigeon

²**dove** *past of* DIVE

dove·tail *vb* : fit together neatly

dow·a·ger *n* **1** : widow with wealth or a title **2** : dignified elderly woman

dowdy *adj* **dowd·i·er; -est** : lacking neatness and charm

dow·el *n* **1** : peg used for fastening two pieces **2** : wooden rod

dow·er *n* : property given a widow for life ~ *vb* : supply with a dower

¹**down** *adv* **1** : toward or in a lower position or state **2** : to a lying or sitting position **3** : as a cash deposit **4** : on paper ~ *adj* **1** : lying on the ground **2** : directed or going downward **3** : being at a low level ~ *prep* : toward the bottom of ~ *vb* **1** : cause to go down **2** : defeat

²**down** *n* : fluffy feathers

down·cast *adj* **1** : sad **2** : directed down

down·fall *n* : ruin or cause of ruin

down·grade *n* : downward slope ~ *vb* : lower in grade or position

down·heart·ed *adj* : sad

down·pour *n* : heavy rain

down·right *adv* : thoroughly ~ *adj* : absolute or thorough

downs *n pl* : rolling treeless uplands

down·size *vb* : reduce in size

down·stairs *adv* : on or to a lower floor and esp. the main floor — **downstairs** *adj or n*

down–to–earth *adj* : practical

down·town *adv* : to, toward, or in the business center of a town — **down·town** *n or adj*

down·trod·den *adj* : suffering oppression

down·ward, down·wards *adv* : to a lower place or condition — **downward** *adj*

down·wind *adv or adj* : in the direction the wind is blowing

downy *adj* **-i·er; -est** : resem·bling or covered with down

dow·ry *n, pl* **-ries** : property a woman gives her husband in marriage

dox·ol·o·gy *n, pl* **-gies** : hymn of praise to God

doze *vb* **dozed; doz·ing** : sleep lightly — **doze** *n*

doz·en *n, pl* **-ens** *or* **-en** : group of 12 — **doz·enth** *adj*

drab *adj* **-bb-** : dull — **drab·ly** *adv* — **drab·ness** *n*

dra·co·ni·an *adj, often cap* : harsh, cruel

draft *n* **1** : act of drawing or hauling **2** : act of drinking **3** : amount drunk at once **4** : preliminary outline or rough sketch **5** : selection from a pool or the selection process **6** : order for the payment of money **7** : air current ~ *vb* **1** : select usu. on a compulsory basis **2** : make a preliminary sketch, version, or plan of ~ *adj* : drawn from a container — **draft·ee** *n* — **drafty** *adj*

drafts·man *n* : person who draws plans

drag *n* **1** : something dragged over a surface or through water **2** : something that hinders progress or is boring **3** : act or an instance of dragging ~ *vb* **-gg- 1** : haul **2** : move or work with difficulty **3** : pass slowly **4** : search or fish with a drag — **drag·ger** *n*

drag·net n 1 : trawl 2 : planned actions for finding a criminal

dra·gon n : fabled winged serpent

drag·on·fly n : large 4-winged insect

drain vb 1 : draw off or flow off gradually or completely 2 : exhaust ~ n : means or act of draining — **drain·age** n — **drain·er** n — **drain·pipe** n

drake n : male duck

dra·ma n 1 : composition for theatrical presentation esp. on a serious subject 2 : series of events involving conflicting forces — **dra·mat·ic** adj — **dra·mat·i·cal·ly** adv — **dram·a·tist** n — **dram·a·ti·za·tion** n — **dra·ma·tize** vb

drank past of DRINK

drape vb **draped; drap·ing** 1 : cover or adorn with folds of cloth 2 : cause to hang in flowing lines or folds ~ n : curtain

drap·ery n, pl **-er·ies** : decorative fabric hung esp. as a heavy curtain

dras·tic adj : extreme or harsh — **dras·ti·cal·ly** adj

draught , draughty chiefly Brit var of DRAFT, DRAFTY

draw vb **drew ; drawn ; draw·ing** 1 : move or cause to move (as by pulling) 2 : attract or provoke 3 : extract 4 : take or receive (as money) 5 : bend a bow in preparation for shooting 6 : leave a contest undecided 7 : sketch 8 : write out 9 : deduce ~ n 1 : act, process, or result of drawing 2 : tie — **draw out** : cause to speak candidly — **draw up** 1 : write out 2 : pull oneself erect 3 : bring or come to a stop

draw·back n : disadvantage

draw·bridge n : bridge that can be raised

draw·er n 1 : one that draws 2 : sliding boxlike compartment 3 pl : underpants

draw·ing n 1 : occasion of choosing by lot 2 : act or art of making a figure, plan, or sketch with lines 3 : something drawn

drawl vb : speak slowly — **drawl** n

dread vb : feel extreme fear or reluctance ~ n : great fear ~ adj : causing dread — **dread·ful** adj — **dread·ful·ly** adv

dream n 1 : series of thoughts or visions during sleep 2 : dreamlike vision 3 : something notable 4 : ideal ~ vb **dreamed** or **dreamt dream·ing** 1 : have a dream 2 : imagine — **dream·er** n — **dream·like** adj — **dreamy** adj

drea·ry adj **-ri·er; -est** : dismal — **drea·ri·ly** adv

¹dredge n : machine for removing earth esp. from under water ~ vb **dredged; dredg·ing** : dig up or search with a dredge — **dredg·er** n

²dredge vb **dredged; dredg·ing** : coat (food) with flour

dregs n pl 1 : sediment 2 : most worthless part

drench vb : wet thoroughly

dress vb 1 : put clothes on 2 : decorate 3 : prepare (as a carcass) for use 4 : apply dressings, remedies, or fertilizer to ~ n 1 : apparel 2 : single garment of bodice and skirt ~ adj : suitable for a formal event — **dress·mak·er** n — **dress·mak·ing** n

dress·er n : bureau with a mirror

dress·ing n 1 : act or process of dressing 2 : sauce or a seasoned mixture 3 : material to cover an injury

dressy adj **dress·i·er; -est** 1 : showy in dress 2 : stylish

drew past of DRAW

drib·ble vb **-bled; -bling** 1 : fall or flow in drops 2 : drool — **dribble** n

drier comparative of DRY

driest superlative of DRY

drift n 1 : motion or course of something drifting 2 : mass piled up by wind 3 : general intention or meaning ~ vb 1 : float or be driven along (as by a current) 2 : wander without purpose 3 : pile up under force — **drift·er** n — **drift·wood** n

¹drill vb 1 : bore with a drill 2 : instruct by repetition ~ n 1 : tool for boring holes 2 : regularly practiced exercise — **drill·er** n

²drill n : seed-planting implement

³drill n : twill-weave cotton fabric

drily var of DRYLY

drink vb **drank ; drunk** or **drank; drink·ing** 1 : swallow liquid 2 : absorb 3 : drink alcoholic beverages esp. to excess ~ n 1 : beverage 2 : alcoholic liquor — **drink·able** adj — **drink·er** n

drip vb **-pp-** : fall or let fall in drops ~ n 1 : a dripping 2 : sound of falling drops

drive vb **drove ; driv·en ; driv·ing** 1 : urge or force onward 2 : direct the movement or course of 3 : compel 4 : cause to become 5 : propel forcefully ~ n 1 : trip in a vehicle 2 : intensive campaign 3 : aggressive or dynamic quality 4 : basic need — **driv·er** n

drive–in adj : accommodating patrons in cars — **drive–in** n

driv·el vb **-eled** or **-elled; -el·ing** or **el·ling** 1 : drool 2 : talk stupidly ~ n : nonsense

drive·way n : usu. short private road from the street to a house

driz·zle n : fine misty rain — **drizzle** vb

droll adj : humorous or whimsical — **droll·ery** n — **drol·ly** adv

drom·e·dary n, pl **-dar·ies** : speedy one-humped camel

drone n 1 : male honeybee 2 : deep hum or buzz ~ vb **droned; dron·ing** : make a dull monotonous sound

drool vb : let liquid run from the mouth

droop vb 1 : hang or incline downward 2 : lose strength or spirit — **droop** n — **droopy** adj

drop n 1 : quantity of fluid in one spherical mass 2 pl : medicine used by drops 3 : decline or fall 4 : distance something drops ~ vb **-pp-** 1 : fall in drops 2 : let fall 3 : convey 4 : go lower or become less strong or less active — **drop·let** n — **drop back** vb : move toward the rear — **drop behind** : fail to keep up — **drop in** vb : pay an unexpected visit

drop·per n : device that dispenses liquid by drops

drop·sy n : edema

dross n : waste matter

drought n : long dry spell

¹drove n : crowd of moving people or animals

²drove past of DRIVE

drown vb 1 : suffocate in water 2 : overpower or become overpowered

drowse vb **drowsed; drows·ing** : doze — **drowse** n

drowsy adj **drows·i·er; -est** : sleepy — **drows·i·ly** adv — **drows·i·ness** n

drub vb **-bb-** : beat severely

drudge vb **drudged; drudg·ing** : do hard or boring work — **drudge** n — **drudg·ery** n

drug n 1 : substance used as or in medicine 2 : narcotic ~ vb **-gg-** : affect with drugs — **drug·gist** n — **drug·store** n

dru·id n : ancient Celtic priest

drum n 1 : musical instrument that is a skin-covered cylinder beaten usu. with sticks 2 : drum-shaped object (as a container) ~ vb **-mm-** 1 : beat a drum 2 : drive, force, or bring about by steady effort — **drum·beat** n — **drum·mer** n

drum·stick n 1 : stick for beating a drum 2 : lower part of a fowl's leg

drunk adj : having the faculties impaired by alcohol ~ n : one who is drunk — **drunk·ard** n — **drunk·en** adj — **drunk·en·ly** adv — **drunk·en·ness** n

dry adj **dri·er ; dri·est** 1 : lacking water or moisture 2 : thirsty 3 : marked by the absence of alcoholic beverages 4 : uninteresting 5 : not sweet ~ vb **dried; dry·ing** : make or become dry — **dry·ly** adv — **dry·ness** n

dry–clean vb : clean (fabrics) chiefly with solvents other than water — **dry cleaning** n

dry·er n : device for drying

dry goods n pl : textiles, clothing, and notions

dry ice n : solid carbon dioxide

du·al adj : twofold — **du·al·ism** n — **du·al·i·ty** n

dub vb **-bb-** : name

du·bi·ous adj 1 : uncertain 2 : questionable — **du·bi·ous·ly** adv — **du·bi·ous·ness** n

du·cal adj : relating to a duke or dukedom

duch·ess n 1 : wife of a duke 2 : woman holding a ducal title

duchy n, pl **-ies** : territory of a duke or duchess

¹duck n, pl : swimming bird related to the goose and swan ~ vb 1 : thrust or plunge under water 2 : lower the head or body suddenly 3 : evade — **duck·ling** n

²duck n : cotton fabric

duct n : canal for conveying a fluid — **duct·less** adj

duc·tile adj : able to be drawn out or shaped — **duc·til·i·ty** n

dude n 1 : dandy 2 : guy

dud·geon n : ill humor

due adj 1 : owed 2 : appropriate 3 : attributable 4 : scheduled ~ n 1 : something due 2 pl : fee ~ adv : directly

du·el n : combat between 2 persons — **duel** vb — **du·el·ist** n

du·et n : musical composition for 2 performers

due to prep : because of

dug past of DIG

dug·out n 1 : boat made by hollowing out a log 2 : shelter made by digging

duke n : nobleman of the highest rank — **duke·dom** n

dull adj 1 : mentally slow 2 : blunt 3 : not brilliant or interesting — **dull** vb — **dul·lard** n — **dull·ness** n — **dul·ly** adv

du·ly adv : in a due manner or time

dumb adj 1 : mute 2 : stupid — **dumb·ly** adv

dumb·bell n 1 : short bar with weights on the ends used for exercise 2 : stupid person

dumb·found, dum·found vb : amaze

dum·my n, pl **-mies** 1 : stupid person 2 : imitative substitute

dump vb : let fall in a pile ~ n : place for dumping something (as refuse) — **in the dumps** : sad

dump·ling n : small mass of boiled or steamed dough

dumpy adj **dump·i·er; -est** : short and thick in build

¹dun adj : brownish gray

²dun vb **-nn-** : hound for payment of a debt

dunce n : stupid person

dune n : hill of sand

dung n : manure

dun·ga·ree n 1 : blue denim 2 pl : work clothes made of dungaree

dun·geon n : underground prison

dunk vb : dip or submerge temporarily in liquid

duo n, pl **du·os** : pair

du·o·de·num n, pl **-na** or **-nums** : part of the small intestine nearest the stomach — **du·o·de·nal** adj

dupe n : one easily deceived or cheated — **dupe** vb

du·plex adj : double ~ n : 2-family house

du·pli·cate adj 1 : consisting of 2 identical items 2 : being just like another ~ n : exact copy ~ vb **-cat·ed; -cat·ing** 1 : make an exact copy of 2 : repeat or equal — **du·pli·ca·tion** n — **du·pli·ca·tor** n

du·plic·i·ty n, pl **-ties** : deception

du·ra·ble adj : lasting a long time — **du·ra·bil·i·ty** n

du·ra·tion n : length of time something lasts

du·ress n : coercion

dur•ing *prep* 1 : throughout 2 : at some point in

dusk *n* : twilight — **dusky** *adj*

dust *n* : powdered matter ~ *vb* 1 : remove dust from 2 : sprinkle with fine particles — **dust•er** *n* — **dust•pan** *n* — **dusty** *adj*

du•ty *n, pl* **-ties** 1 : action required by one's occupation or position 2 : moral or legal obligation 3 : tax — **du•te•ous** *adj* — **du•ti•able** *adj* — **du•ti•ful** *adj*

dwarf *n, pl* **dwarfs** *or* **dwarves** : one that is much below normal size ~ *vb* 1 : stunt 2 : cause to seem smaller — **dwarf•ish** *adj*

dwell *vb* **dwelt** *or* **dwelled ; dwell•ing** 1 : reside 2 : keep the attention directed — **dwell•er** *n* — **dwell•ing** *n*

dwin•dle *vb* **-dled; -dling** : become steadily less

dye *n* : coloring material ~ *vb* **dyed; dye•ing** : give a new color to

dying *pres part of* DIE

dyke *var of* DIKE

dy•nam•ic *adj* 1 : relating to physical force producing motion 2 : energetic or forceful

dy•na•mite *n* : explosive made of nitroglycerin — **dynamite** *vb*

dy•na•mo *n, pl* **-mos** : electrical generator

dy•nas•ty *n, pl* **-ties** : succession of rulers of the same family — **dy•nas•tic** *adj*

dys•en•tery *n, pl* **-ter•ies** : disease marked by diarrhea

dys•lex•ia *n* : disturbance of the ability to read — **dys•lex•ic** *adj*

dys•pep•sia *n* : indigestion — **dys•pep•tic** *adj or* *n*

dys•tro•phy *n, pl* **-phies** : disorder involving nervous and muscular tissue

E

e *n, pl* **e's** *or* **es** : 5th letter of the alphabet

each *adj* : being one of the class named ~ *pron* : every individual one ~ *adv* : apiece

ea•ger *adj* : enthusiastic or anxious — **ea•ger•ly** *adv* — **ea•ger•ness** *n*

ea•gle *n* : large bird of prey

-ean —see -AN

¹**ear** *n* : organ of hearing or the outer part of this — **ear•ache** *n* — **eared** *adj* — **ear•lobe** *n*

²**ear** *n* : fruiting head of a cereal

ear•drum *n* : thin membrane that receives and transmits sound waves in the ear

earl *n* : British nobleman — **earl•dom** *n*

ear•ly *adj* **-li•er; -est** 1 : relating to or occurring near the beginning or before the usual time 2 : ancient — **early** *adv*

ear•mark *vb* : designate for a specific purpose

earn *vb* 1 : receive as a return for service 2 : deserve

ear•nest *n* : serious state of mind — **earnest** *adj* — **ear•nest•ly** *adv* — **ear•nest•ness** *n*

earn•ings *n pl* : something earned

ear•phone *n* : device that reproduces sound and is worn over or in the ear

ear•ring *n* : earlobe ornament

ear•shot *n* : range of hearing

earth *n* 1 : soil or land 2 : planet inhabited by man — **earth•li•ness** *n* — **earth•ly** *adj* — **earth•ward** *adv*

earth•en *adj* : made of earth or baked clay — **earth•en•ware** *n*

earth•quake *n* : shaking or trembling of the earth

earth•worm *n* : long segmented worm

earthy *adj* **earth•i•er; -est** 1 : relating to or consisting of earth 2 : practical 3 : coarse — **earth•i•ness** *n*

ease *n* 1 : comfort 2 : naturalness of manner 3 : freedom from difficulty ~ *vb* **eased; eas•ing** 1 : relieve from distress 2 : lessen the tension of 3 : make easier

ea•sel *n* : frame to hold a painter's canvas

east *adv* : to or toward the east ~ *adj* : situated toward or at or coming from the east ~ *n* 1 : direction of sunrise 2 *cap* : regions to the east — **east•er•ly** *adv or adj* — **east•ward** *adv or adj* — **east•wards** *adv*

Eas•ter *n* : church feast celebrating Christ's resurrection

east•ern *adj* 1 *cap* : relating to a region designated East 2 : lying toward or coming from the east — **East•ern•er** *n*

easy *adj* **eas•i•er; -est** 1 : marked by ease 2 : lenient — **eas•i•ly** *adv* — **eas•i•ness** *n*

easy•go•ing *adj* : relaxed and casual

eat *vb* **ate ; eat•en ; eat•ing** 1 : take in as food 2 : use up or corrode — **eat•able** *adj or* *n* — **eat•er** *n*

eaves *n pl* : overhanging edge of a roof

eaves•drop *vb* : listen secretly — **eaves•drop•per** *n*

ebb *n* 1 : outward flow of the tide 2 : decline ~ *vb* 1 : recede from the flood state 2 : wane

eb•o•ny *n, pl* **-nies** : hard heavy wood of tropical trees ~ *adj* 1 : made of ebony 2 : black

ebul•lient *adj* : exuberant — **ebul•lience** *n*

ec•cen•tric *adj* 1 : odd in behavior 2 : being off center — **eccen•tric** *n* — **ec•cen•tri•cal•ly** *adv* — **ec•cen•tric•i•ty** *n*

ec•cle•si•as•tic *n* : clergyman

ec•cle•si•as•ti•cal , ecclesiastic *adj* : relating to a church — **ec•cle•si•as•ti•cal•ly** *adv*

ech•e•lon *n* 1 : steplike arrangement 2 : level of authority

echo *n, pl* **ech•oes** : repetition of a sound caused by a reflection of the sound waves — **echo** *vb*

éclair *n* : custard-filled pastry

eclec•tic *adj* : drawing or drawn from varied sources

eclipse *n* : total or partial obscuring of one celestial body by another — **eclipse** *vb*

ecol•o•gy *n, pl* **-gies** : science concerned with the interaction of organisms and their environment — **eco•log•i•cal** *adj* — **eco•log•i•cal•ly** *adv* — **ecol•o•gist** *n*

eco•nom•ic *adj* : relating to the producing and the buying and selling of goods and services

eco•nom•ics *n* : branch of knowledge dealing with goods and services — **econ•o•mist** *n*

econ•o•mize *vb* **-mized; -miz•ing** : be thrifty — **econ•o•miz•er** *n*

econ•o•my *n, pl* **-mies** 1 : thrifty use of resources 2 : economic sys- tem — **eco•nom•i•cal** *adj* — **ec•o•nom•i•cal•ly** *adv* — **economy** *adj*

ecru *n* : beige

ec•sta•sy *n, pl* **-sies** : extreme emotional excitement — **ec•stat•ic** *adj* — **ec•stat•i•cal•ly** *adv*

ec•u•men•i•cal *adj* : promoting worldwide Christian unity

ec•ze•ma *n* : itching skin inflammation

¹**-ed** *vb suffix or adj suffix* 1 — used to form the past participle of regular verbs 2 : having or having the characteristics of

²**-ed** *vb suffix* — used to form the past tense of regular verbs

ed•dy *n, pl* **-dies** : whirlpool — **eddy** *vb*

ede•ma *n* : abnormal accumulation of fluid in the body tissues — **edem•a•tous** *adj*

Eden *n* : paradise

edge *n* 1 : cutting side of a blade 2 : line where something begins or ends ~ *vb* **edged; edg•ing** 1 : give or form an edge 2 : move gradually 3 : narrowly defeat — **edg•er** *n*

edge•wise *adv* : sideways

edgy *adj* **edg•i•er; -est** : nervous — **edg•i•ness** *n*

ed•i•ble *adj* : fit or safe to be eaten — **ed•i•bil•i•ty** *n* — **edible** *n*

edict *n* : order or decree

ed•i•fi•ca•tion *n* : instruction or information — **ed•i•fy** *vb*

ed•i•fice *n* : large building

ed•it *vb* 1 : revise and prepare for publication 2 : delete — **ed•i•tor** *n* — **ed•i•tor•ship** *n*

edi•tion *n* 1 : form in which a text is published 2 : total number published at one time

ed•i•to•ri•al *adj* 1 : relating to an editor or editing 2 : expressing opinion ~ *n* : article (as in a newspaper) expressing the views of an editor — **ed•i•to•ri•al•ize** *vb* — **ed•i•to•ri•al•ly** *adv*

ed•u•cate *vb* **-cat•ed; -cat•ing** 1 : give instruction to 2 : develop mentally and morally 3 : provide with information — **ed•u•ca•ble** *adj* — **ed•u•ca•tion** *n* — **ed•u•ca•tion•al** *adj* — **ed•u•ca•tor** *n*

eel *n* : snakelike fish

ee•rie *adj* **-ri•er; -est** : weird — **ee•ri•ly** *adv*

ef•face *vb* **-faced; -fac•ing** •: obliterate by rubbing out — **ef•face•ment** *n*

ef•fect *n* 1 : result 2 : meaning 3 : influence 4 *pl* : goods or possessions ~ *vb* : cause to happen — **in effect** : in substance

ef•fec•tive *adj* 1 : producing a strong or desired effect 2 : being in operation — **ef•fec•tive•ly** *adv* — **ef•fec•tive•ness** *n*

ef•fec•tu•al *adj* : producing an intended effect — **ef•fec•tu•al•ly** *adv* — **ef•fec•tu•al•ness** *n*

ef•fem•i•nate *adj* : unsuitably womanish — **ef•fem•i•na•cy** *n*

ef•fer•vesce *vb* **-vesced; -vesc•ing** 1 : bubble and hiss as gas escapes 2 : show exhilaration — **ef•fer•ves•cence** *n* — **ef•fer•ves•cent** *adj* — **ef•fer•ves•cent•ly** *adv*

ef•fete *adj* 1 : worn out 2 : weak or decadent 3 : effeminate

ef•fi•ca•cious *adj* : effective — **ef•fi•ca•cy** *n*

ef•fi•cient *adj* : working well with little waste — **ef•fi•cien•cy** *n* — **ef•fi•cient•ly** *adv*

ef•fi•gy *n, pl* **-gies** : usu. crude image of a person

ef•flu•ent *n* : something that flows out — **efflu•ent** *adj*

ef•fort *n* 1 : a putting forth of strength 2 : use of resources toward a goal 3 : product of effort — **ef•fort•less** *adj* — **ef•fort•less•ly** *adv*

ef•fron•tery *n, pl* **-ter•ies** : insolence

ef•fu•sion *n* : a gushing forth — **ef•fu•sive** *adj* — **ef•fu•sive•ly** *adv*

¹**egg** *vb* : urge to action

²**egg** *n* 1 : rounded usu. hard-shelled reproductive body esp. of birds and reptiles from which the young hatches 2 : ovum — **egg•shell** *n*

egg•nog *n* : rich drink of eggs and cream

egg•plant *n* : edible purplish fruit of a plant related to the potato

ego *n, pl* **egos** : self-esteem

ego•cen•tric *adj* : self-centered

ego•tism *n* : exaggerated sense of self-importance — **ego•tist** *n* — **ego•tis•tic, ego•tis•ti•cal** *adj* — **ego•tis•ti•cal•ly** *adv*

egre•gious *adj* : notably bad — **egre•gious•ly** *adv*

egress *n* : a way out

egret *n* : long-plumed heron

ei•der•down *n* : soft down obtained from a northern sea duck (**eider**)

eight *n* **1** : one more than 7 **2** : 8th in a set or series **3** : something having 8 units — **eight** *adj or pron* — **eighth** *adj or adv or n*

eigh•teen *n* : one more than 17 — **eigh•teen** *adj or pron* — **eigh•teenth** *adj or n*

eighty *n, pl* **eight•ies** : 8 times 10 — **eight•i•eth** *adj or n* — **eighty** *adj or pron*

ei•ther *adj* **1** : both **2** : being the one or the other of two ~ *pron* : one of two or more ~ *conj* : one or the other

ejac•u•late *vb* -**lat•ed; -lat•ing 1** : say suddenly **2** : eject a fluid (as semen) — **ejac•u•la•tion** *n*

eject *vb* : drive or throw out — **ejec•tion** *n*

eke *vb* **eked; ek•ing** : barely gain with effort — usu. with *out*

elab•o•rate *adj* **1** : planned in detail **2** : complex and ornate ~ *vb* -**rat•ed; -rat•ing** : work out in detail — **elab•o•rate•ly** *adv* — **elab•o•rate•ness** *n* — **elab•o•ra•tion** *n*

elapse *vb* **elapsed; elaps•ing** : slip by

elas•tic *adj* **1** : springy **2** : flexible ~ *n* **1** : elastic material **2** : rubber band — **elas•tic•i•ty** *n*

elate *vb* **elat•ed; elat•ing** : fill with joy — **ela•tion** *n*

el•bow *n* **1** : joint of the arm **2** : elbow-shaped bend or joint ~ *vb* : push aside with the elbow

el•der *adj* : older — *n* **1** : one who is older **2** : church officer

el•der•ber•ry *n* : edible black or red fruit or a tree or shrub bearing these

el•der•ly *adj* : past middle age

el•dest *adj* : oldest

elect *adj* : elected but not yet in office ~ *n* **elect** *pl* : exclusive group ~ *vb* : choose esp. by vote — **elec•tion** *n* — **elec•tive** *n or adj* — **elec•tor** *n* — **elec•tor•al** *adj*

elec•tor•ate *n* : body of persons entitled to vote

elec•tric *adj* **1** *or* **elec•tri•cal** : relating to or run by electricity **2** : thrilling — **elec•tri•cal•ly** *adv*

elec•tri•cian *n* : person who installs or repairs electrical equipment

elec•tric•i•ty *n, pl* -**ties 1** : fundamental form of energy occurring naturally (as in lightning) or produced artificially **2** : electric current

elec•tri•fy *vb* -**fied; -fy•ing 1** : charge with electricity **2** : equip for use of electric power **3** : thrill — **elec•tri•fi•ca•tion** *n*

elec•tro•car•dio•gram *n* : tracing made by an electrocardiograph

elec•tro•car•dio•graph *n* : instrument for monitoring heart function

elec•tro•cute *vb* -**cut•ed; -cut•ing** : kill by an electric shock — **elec•tro•cu•tion** *n*

elec•trode *n* : conductor at a nonmetallic part of a circuit

elec•trol•y•sis *n* **1** : production of chemical changes by passage of an electric current through a substance **2** : destruction of hair roots with an electric current — **elec•tro•lyt•ic** *adj*

elec•tro•lyte *n* : nonmetallic electric conductor

elec•tro•mag•net *n* : magnet made using electric current

elec•tro•mag•ne•tism *n* : natural force responsible for interactions between charged particles — **elec•tro•mag•net•ic** *adj* — **elec•tro•mag•net•i•cal•ly** *adv*

elec•tron *n* : negatively charged particle within the atom

elec•tron•ic *adj* : relating to electrons or electronics — **elec•tron•i•cal•ly** *adv*

elec•tron•ics *n* : physics of electrons and their use esp. in devices

elec•tro•plate *vb* : coat (as with metal) by electrolysis

el•e•gance *n* : refined gracefulness — **el•e•gant** *adj* — **el•e•gant•ly** *adv*

el•e•gy *n, pl* -**gies** : poem expressing grief for one who is dead — **ele•gi•ac** *adj*

el•e•ment *n* **1** *pl* : weather conditions **2** : natural environment **3** : constituent part **4** *pl* : simplest principles **5** : substance that has atoms of only one kind — **el•e•men•tal** *adj*

el•e•men•ta•ry *adj* **1** : simple **2** : relating to the basic subjects of education

el•e•phant *n* : huge mammal with a trunk and 2 ivory tusks

el•e•vate *vb* -**vat•ed; -vat•ing 1** : lift up **2** : exalt

el•e•va•tion *n* : height or a high place

el•e•va•tor *n* **1** : cage or platform for raising or lowering something **2** : grain storehouse

elev•en *n* **1** : one more than 10 **2** : 11th in a set or series **3** : something having 11 units — **eleven** *adj or pron* — **elev•enth** *adj or n*

elf *n, pl* **elves** : mischievous fairy — **elf•in** *adj* — **elf•ish** *adj*

elic•it *vb* : draw forth

el•i•gi•ble *adj* : qualified to participate or to be chosen — **el•i•gi•bil•i•ty** *n* — **eligible** *n*

elim•i•nate *vb* -**nat•ed; -nat•ing** : get rid of — **elim•i•na•tion** *n*

elite *n* : choice or select group

elix•ir *n* : medicinal solution

elk *n* : large deer

el•lipse *n* : oval

el•lip•sis *n, pl* -**lip•ses 1** : omission of a word **2** : marks (as . . .) to show omission

el•lip•ti•cal , **el•lip•tic** *adj* **1** : relating to or shaped like an ellipse **2** : relating to or marked by ellipsis

elm *n* : tall shade tree

el•o•cu•tion *n* : art of public speaking

elon•gate *vb* -**gat•ed; -gat•ing** : make or grow longer — **elon•ga•tion** *n*

elope *vb* **eloped; elop•ing** : run away esp. to be married — **elope•ment** *n* — **elop•er** *n*

el•o•quent *adj* : forceful and persuasive in speech — **el•o•quence** *n* — **el•o•quent•ly** *adv*

else *adv* **1** : in a different way, time, or place **2** : otherwise ~ *adj* **1** : other **2** : more

else•where *adv* : in or to another place

elu•ci•date *vb* -**dat•ed; -dat•ing** : explain — **elu•ci•da•tion** *n*

elude *vb* **elud•ed; elud•ing** : evade — **elu•sive** *adj* — **elu•sive•ly** *adv* — **elu•sive•ness** *n*

elves *pl of* ELF

ema•ci•ate *vb* -**at•ed; -at•ing** : become or make very thin — **ema•ci•a•tion** *n*

em•a•nate *vb* -**nat•ed; -nat•ing** : come forth — **em•a•na•tion** *n*

eman•ci•pate *vb* -**pat•ed; -pat•ing** : set free — **eman•ci•pa•tion** *n* — **eman•ci•pa•tor** *n*

emas•cu•late *vb* -**lat•ed; -lat•ing 1** : castrate **2** : weaken — **emas•cu•la•tion** *n*

em•balm *vb* : preserve (a corpse) — **em•balm•er** *n*

em•bank•ment *n* : protective barrier of earth

em•bar•go *n, pl* -**goes** : ban on trade — **embargo** *vb*

em•bark *vb* **1** : go on board a ship or airplane **2** : make a start — **em•bar•ka•tion** *n*

em•bar•rass *vb* : cause distress and self-consciousness — **em•bar•rass•ment** *n*

em•bas•sy *n, pl* -**sies** : residence and offices of an ambassador

em•bed *vb* -**dd-** : fix firmly

em•bel•lish *vb* : decorate — **em•bel•lish•ment** *n*

em•ber *n* : smoldering fragment from a fire

em•bez•zle *vb* -**zled; -zling** : steal (money) by falsifying records — **em•bez•zle•ment** *n* — **em•bez•zler** *n*

em•bit•ter *vb* : make bitter

em•bla•zon *vb* : display conspicuously

em•blem *n* : symbol — **em•blem•at•ic** *adj*

em•body *vb* -**bod•ied; -body•ing** : give definite form or expression to — **em•bodi•ment** *n*

em•boss *vb* : ornament with raised work

em•brace *vb* -**braced; -brac•ing 1** : clasp in the arms **2** : welcome **3** : include — **embrace** *n*

em•broi•der *vb* : ornament with or do needlework — **em•broi•dery** *n*

em•broil *vb* : involve in conflict or difficulties

em•bryo *n* : living being in its earliest stages of development — **em•bry•on•ic** *adj*

emend *vb* : correct — **emen•da•tion** *n*

em•er•ald *n* : green gem ~ *adj* : bright green

emerge *vb* **emerged; emerg•ing** : rise, come forth, or ap- pear — **emer•gence** *n* — **emer•gent** *adj*

emer•gen•cy *n, pl* -**cies** : condition requiring prompt action

em•ery *n, pl* -**er•ies** : dark granular mineral used for grinding

emet•ic *n* : agent that induces vomiting — **emetic** *adj*

em•i•grate *vb* -**grat•ed; -grat•ing** : leave a country to settle elsewhere — **em•i•grant** *n* — **em•i•gra•tion** *n*

em•i•nence *n* **1** : prominence or superiority **2** : person of high rank

em•i•nent *adj* : prominent — **em•i•nent•ly** *adv*

em•is•sary *n, pl* -**sar•ies** : agent

emis•sion *n* : substance discharged into the air

emit *vb* -**tt-** : give off or out

emol•u•ment *n* : salary or fee

emote *vb* **emot•ed; emot•ing** : express emotion

emo•tion *n* : intense feeling — **emo•tion•al** *adj* — **emo•tion•al•ly** *adv*

em•per•or *n* : ruler of an empire

em•pha•sis *n, pl* -**pha•ses** : stress

em•pha•size *vb* -**sized; -siz•ing** : stress

em•phat•ic *adj* : uttered with emphasis — **em•phat•i•cal•ly** *adv*

em•pire *n* : large state or a group of states

em•pir•i•cal *adj* : based on observation — **em•pir•i•cal•ly** *adv*

em•ploy *vb* **1** : use **2** : occupy ~ *n* : paid occupation — **em•ploy•ee, em•ploye** *n* — **em•ploy•er** *n* — **em•ploy•ment** *n*

em•pow•er *vb* : give power to — **em•pow•er•ment** *n*

em•press *n* **1** : wife of an emperor **2** : woman emperor

emp•ty *adj* **1** : containing nothing **2** : not occupied **3** : lacking value, sense, or purpose ~ *vb* -**tied; -ty•ing** : make or become empty — **emp•ti•ness** *n*

emu *n* : Australian bird related to the ostrich

em•u•late *vb* -**lat•ed; -lat•ing** : try to equal or excel — **em•u•la•tion** *n*

emul•si•fy *vb* -**fied; -fy•ing** : convert into an emulsion — **emul•si•fi•ca•tion** *n* — **emul•si•fi•er** *n*

emul•sion *n* **1** : mixture of mutually insoluble liquids **2** : light-sensitive coating on photographic film

-en *vb suffix* **1** : become or cause to be **2** : cause or come to have

en•able *vb* -**abled; -abling** : give power, capacity, or ability to

en•act *vb* **1** : make into law **2** : act out — **en•act•ment** *n*

enam•el *n* **1** : glasslike substance used to coat metal or pottery **2** : hard outer layer of a tooth **3** : glossy paint — **enamel** *vb*

en•am•or *vb* : excite with love

en•camp *vb* : make camp — **en•camp•ment** *n*

en•case *vb* : enclose in or as if in a case

-ence *n suffix* **1** : action or process **2** : quality or state

en·ceph·a·li·tis *n, pl* **-lit·i·des** : inflammation of the brain

en·chant *vb* **1** : bewitch **2** : fascinate — **en·chant·er** *n* — **en·chant·ment** *n* — **en·chant·ress** *n*

en·cir·cle *vb* : surround

en·close *vb* **1** : shut up or surround **2** : include — **en·clo·sure** *n*

en·co·mi·um *n, pl* **-mi·ums** *or* **-mia** : high praise

en·com·pass *vb* : surround or include

en·core *n* : further performance

en·coun·ter *vb* **1** : fight **2** : meet unexpectedly — **encounter** *n*

en·cour·age *vb* **-aged; -ag·ing 1** : inspire with courage and hope **2** : foster — **en·cour·age·ment** *n*

en·croach *vb* : enter upon another's property or rights — **en·croach·ment** *n*

en·crust *vb* : form a crust on

en·cum·ber *vb* : burden — **en·cum·brance** *n*

-en·cy *n suffix* : -ence

en·cyc·li·cal *adj* : papal letter to bishops

en·cy·clo·pe·dia *n* : reference work on many subjects — **en·cy·clo·pe·dic** *adj*

end *n* **1** : point at which something stops or no longer exists **2** : cessation **3** : purpose ~ *vb* **1** : stop or finish **2** : be at the end of — **end·ed** *adj* — **end·less** *adj* — **end·less·ly** *adv*

en·dan·ger *vb* : bring into danger

en·dear *vb* : make dear — **en·dear·ment** *n*

en·deav·or *vb or n* : attempt

end·ing *n* : end

en·dive *n* : salad plant

en·do·crine *adj* : producing secretions distributed by the bloodstream

en·dorse *vb* **-dorsed; -dors·ing 1** : sign one's name to **2** : approve — **en·dorse·ment** *n*

en·dow *vb* **1** : furnish with funds **2** : furnish naturally — **en·dow·ment** *n*

en·dure *vb* **-dured; -dur·ing 1** : last **2** : suffer patiently **3** : tolerate — **en·dur·able** *adj* — **en·dur·ance** *n*

en·e·ma *n* : injection of liquid into the rectum

en·e·my *n, pl* **-mies** : one that attacks or tries to harm another

en·er·get·ic *adj* : full of energy or activity — **en·er·get·i·cal·ly** *adv*

en·er·gize *vb* **-gized; -giz·ing** : give energy to

en·er·gy *n, pl* **-gies 1** : capacity for action **2** : vigorous action **3** : capacity for doing work

en·er·vate *vb* **-vat·ed; -vat·ing** : make weak or listless — **en·er·va·tion** *n*

en·fold *vb* : surround or embrace

en·force *vb* **1** : compel **2** : carry out — **en·force·able** *adj* — **en·force·ment** *n*

en·fran·chise *vb* **-chised; -chis·ing** : grant voting rights to — **en·fran·chise·ment** *n*

en·gage *vb* **-gaged; -gag·ing 1** : participate or cause to participate **2** : bring or come into working contact **3** : bring into conflict **4** : hire **5** : bring or enter into conflict — **en·gage·ment** *n*

en·gag·ing *adj* : attractive

en·gen·der *vb* **-dered; -der·ing** : create

en·gine *n* **1** : machine that converts energy into mechanical motion **2** : locomotive

en·gi·neer *n* **1** : one trained in engineering **2** : engine operator ~ *vb* : lay out or manage as an engineer

en·gi·neer·ing *n* : practical application of science and mathematics

en·grave *vb* **-graved; -grav·ing** : cut into a surface — **en·grav·er** *n* — **en·grav·ing** *n*

en·gross *vb* : occupy fully

en·gulf *vb* : swallow up

en·hance *vb* **-hanced; -hanc·ing** : improve in value — **en·hance·ment** *n*

enig·ma *n* : puzzle or mystery — **enig·mat·ic** *adj* — **enig·mat·i·cal·ly** *adv*

en·join *vb* **1** : command **2** : forbid

en·joy *vb* : take pleasure in — **en·joy·able** *adj* — **en·joy·ment** *n*

en·large *vb* **-larged; -larg·ing** : make or grow larger — **en·large·ment** *n* — **en·larg·er** *n*

en·light·en *vb* : give knowledge or spiritual insight to — **en·light·en·ment** *n*

en·list *vb* **1** : join the armed forces **2** : get the aid of — **en·list·ee** *n* — **en·list·ment** *n*

en·liv·en *vb* : give life or spirit to

en·mi·ty *n, pl* **-ties** : mutual hatred

en·no·ble *vb* **-bled; -bling** : make noble

en·nui *n* : boredom

enor·mi·ty *n, pl* **-ties 1** : great wickedness **2** : huge size

enor·mous *adj* : great in size, number, or degree — **enor·mous·ly** *adv* — **enor·mous·ness** *n*

enough *adj* : adequate ~ *adv* **1** : in an adequate manner **2** : in a tolerable degree ~ *pron* : adequate number, quantity, or amount

en·quire , **en·qui·ry** *var of* INQUIRE, INQUIRY

en·rage *vb* : fill with rage

en·rich *vb* : make rich — **en·rich·ment** *n*

en·roll, en·rol *vb* **-rolled; -roll·ing 1** : enter on a list **2** : become enrolled — **en·roll·ment** *n*

en route *adv or adj* : on or along the way

en·sconce *vb* **-sconced; -sconc·ing** : settle snugly

en·sem·ble *n* **1** : small group **2** : complete costume

en·shrine *vb* **1** : put in a shrine **2** : cherish

en·sign *n* **1** : flag **2** : lowest ranking commissioned officer in the navy

en·slave *vb* : make a slave of — **en·slave·ment** *n*

en·snare *vb* : trap

en·sue *vb* **-sued; -su·ing** : follow as a consequence

en·sure *vb* **-sured; -sur·ing** : guarantee

en·tail *vb* : involve as a necessary result

en·tan·gle *vb* : tangle — **en·tan·gle·ment** *n*

en·ter *vb* **1** : go or come in or into **2** : start **3** : set down (as in a list)

en·ter·prise *n* **1** : an undertaking **2** : business organization **3** : initiative

en·ter·pris·ing *adj* : showing initiative

en·ter·tain *vb* **1** : treat or receive as a guest **2** : hold in mind **3** : amuse — **en·ter·tain·er** *n* — **en·ter·tain·ment** *n*

en·thrall, en·thral *vb* **-thralled; -thrall·ing** : hold spellbound

en·thu·si·asm *n* : strong excitement of feeling or its cause — **en·thu·si·ast** *n* — **en·thu·si·as·tic** *adj* — **en·thu·si·as·ti·cal·ly** *adv*

en·tice *vb* **-ticed; -tic·ing** : tempt — **en·tice·ment** *n*

en·tire *adj* : complete or whole — **en·tire·ly** *adv* — **en·tire·ty** *n*

en·ti·tle *vb* **-tled; -tling 1** : name **2** : give a right to

en·ti·ty *n, pl* **-ties** : something with separate existence

en·to·mol·o·gy *n* : study of insects — **en·to·mo·log·i·cal** *adj* — **en·to·mol·o·gist** *n*

en·tou·rage *n* : retinue

en·trails *n pl* : intestines

¹en·trance *n* **1** : act of entering **2** : means or place of entering — **en·trant** *n*

²en·trance *vb* **-tranced; -tranc·ing** : fascinate or delight

en·trap *vb* : trap — **en·trap·ment** *n*

en·treat *vb* : ask urgently — **en·treaty** *n*

en·trée, en·tree *n* : principal dish of the meal

en·trench *vb* : establish in a strong position — **en·trench·ment** *n*

en·tre·pre·neur *n* : organizer or promoter of an enterprise

en·trust *vb* : commit to another with confidence

en·try *n, pl* **-tries 1** : entrance **2** : an entering in a record or an item so entered

en·twine *vb* : twine together or around

enu·mer·ate *vb* **-at·ed; -at·ing 1** : count **2** : list — **enu·mer·a·tion** *n*

enun·ci·ate *vb* **-at·ed; -at·ing 1** : announce **2** : pronounce — **enun·ci·a·tion** *n*

en·vel·op *vb* : surround — **en·vel·op·ment** *n*

en·ve·lope *n* : paper container for a letter

en·vi·ron·ment *n* : surroundings — **en·vi·ron·men·tal** *adj*

en·vi·ron·men·tal·ist *n* : person concerned about the environment

en·vi·rons *n pl* : vicinity

en·vis·age *vb* **-aged; -ag·ing** : have a mental picture of

en·vi·sion *vb* : picture to oneself

en·voy *n* : diplomat

en·vy *n* **1** : resentful awareness of another's advantage **2** : object of envy ~ *vb* **-vied; -vy·ing** : feel envy toward or on account of — **en·vi·able** *adj* — **en·vi·ous** *adj* — **en·vi·ous·ly** *adv*

en·zyme *n* : biological catalyst

eon *var of* AEON

ep·au·let *n* : shoulder ornament on a uniform

ephem·er·al *adj* : short-lived

ep·ic *n* : long poem about a hero — **epic** *adj*

ep·i·cure *n* : person with fastidious taste esp. in food and wine — **ep·i·cu·re·an** *n or adj*

ep·i·dem·ic *adj* : affecting many persons at one time — **epidemic** *n*

epi·der·mis *n* : outer layer of skin

ep·i·gram *n* : short witty poem or saying — **ep·i·gram·mat·ic** *adj*

ep·i·lep·sy *n, pl* **-sies** : nervous disorder marked by convulsive attacks — **ep·i·lep·tic** *adj or n*

epis·co·pal *adj* : governed by bishops

ep·i·sode *n* : occurrence — **ep·i·sod·ic** *adj*

epis·tle *n* : letter

ep·i·taph *n* : inscription in memory of a dead person

ep·i·thet *n* : characterizing often abusive word or phrase

epit·o·me *n* **1** : summary **2** : ideal example — **epit·o·mize** *vb*

ep·och *n* : extended period — **ep·och·al** *adj*

ep·oxy *n* : synthetic resin used esp. in adhesives ~ *vb* **-ox·ied** *or* **-oxyed; -oxy·ing** : glue with epoxy

equa·ble *adj* : free from unpleasant extremes — **eq·ua·bil·i·ty** *n* — **eq·ua·bly** *adv*

equal *adj* : of the same quantity, value, quality, number, or status as another ~ *n* : one that is equal ~ *vb* **equaled** *or* **equalled; equal·ing** *or* **equal·ling** : be or become equal to — **equal·i·ty** *n* — **equal·ize** *vb* — **equal·ly** *adv*

equa·nim·i·ty *n, pl* **-ties** : calmness

equate *vb* **equat·ed; equat·ing** : treat or regard as equal

equa·tion *n* : mathematical statement that two things are equal

equa·tor *n* : imaginary circle that separates the northern and southern hemispheres — **equa·to·ri·al** *adj*

eques·tri·an *adj* : relating to horseback riding ~ *n* : horseback rider

equi·lat·er·al *adj* : having equal sides

equi·lib·ri·um *n, pl* **-ri·ums** *or* **-ria** : state of balance

equine *adj* : relating to the horse — **equine** *n*

equi·nox *n* : time when day and night are everywhere of equal length

equip *vb* **-pp-** : furnish with needed resources — **equip·ment** *n*

eq·ui·ta·ble *adj* : fair

eq·ui·ty *n, pl* **-ties 1** : justice **2** : value of a property less debt

equiv·a·lent *adj* : equal — **equiv·a·lence** *n* — **equivalent** *n*

equiv·o·cal *adj* : ambiguous or uncertain

equiv•o•cate *vb* **-cat•ed; -cat•ing 1** : use misleading language **2** : avoid answering definitely — **equiv•o•ca•tion** *n*

[1]-er *adj suffix or adv suffix* — used to form the comparative degree of adjectives and adverbs and esp. those of one or two syllables

[2]-er -ier , -yer *n suffix* **1** : one that is associated with **2** : one that performs or is the object of an action **3** : one that is

era *n* : period of time associated with something

erad•i•cate *vb* **-cat•ed; -cat•ing** : do away with

erase *vb* **erased; eras•ing** : rub or scratch out — **eras•er** *n* — **era•sure** *n*

ere *prep or conj* : before

erect *adj* : not leaning or lying down ~ *vb* **1** : build **2** : bring to an upright position — **erection** *n*

er•mine *n* : weasel with white winter fur or its fur

erode *vb* **erod•ed; erod•ing** : wear away gradually

ero•sion *n* : process of eroding

erot•ic *adj* : sexually arousing — **erot•i•cal•ly** *adv* — **erot•i•cism** *n*

err *vb* : be or do wrong

er•rand *n* : short trip taken to do something often for another

er•rant *adj* **1** : traveling about **2** : going astray

er•rat•ic *adj* **1** : eccentric **2** : inconsistent — **er•rat•i•cal•ly** *adv*

er•ro•ne•ous *adj* : wrong — **er•ro•ne•ous•ly** *adv*

er•ror *n* **1** : something that is not accurate **2** : state of being wrong

er•satz *adj* : phony

erst•while *adv* : in the past ~ *adj* : former

er•u•di•tion *n* : great learning — **er•u•dite** *adj*

erupt *vb* : burst forth esp. suddenly and violently — **erup•tion** *n* — **erup•tive** *adj*

-ery *n suffix* **1** : character or condition **2** : practice **3** : place of doing

[1]-es *n pl suffix* — used to form the plural of some nouns

[2]-es *vb suffix* — used to form the 3d person singular present of some verbs

es•ca•late *vb* **-lat•ed; -lat•ing** : become quickly larger or greater — **es•ca•la•tion** *n*

es•ca•la•tor *n* : moving stairs

es•ca•pade *n* : mischievous adventure

es•cape *vb* **-caped; -cap•ing** : get away or get away from ~ *n* **1** : flight from or avoidance of something unpleasant **2** : leakage **3** : means of escape ~ *adj* : providing means of escape — **es•cap•ee** *n*

es•ca•role *n* : salad green

es•carp•ment *n* : cliff

es•chew *vb* : shun

es•cort *n* : one accompanying another — **es•cort** *vb*

es•crow *n* : deposit to be delivered upon fulfillment of a condition

esoph•a•gus *n, pl* **-gi** : muscular tube connecting the mouth and stomach

es•o•ter•ic *adj* : mysterious or secret

es•pe•cial•ly *adv* : particularly or notably

es•pi•o•nage *n* : practice of spying

es•pous•al *n* **1** : betrothal **2** : wedding **3** : a taking up as a supporter — **es•pouse** *vb*

espres•so *n, pl* **-sos** : strong steam-brewed coffee

es•py *vb* **-pied; -py•ing** : catch sight of

es•quire *n* — used as a title of courtesy

-ess *n suffix* : female

es•say *n* : literary composition ~ *vb* : attempt — **es•say•ist** *n*

es•sence *n* **1** : fundamental nature or quality **2** : extract **3** : perfume

es•sen•tial *adj* : basic or necessary — **essential** *n* — **es•sen•tial•ly** *adv*

-est *adj suffix or adv suffix* — used to form the

superlative degree of adjectives and adverbs and esp. those of 1 or 2 syllables

es•tab•lish *vb* **1** : bring into existence **2** : put on a firm basis **3** : cause to be recognized

es•tab•lish•ment *n* **1** : business or a place of business **2** : an establishing or being established **3** : controlling group

es•tate *n* **1** : one's possessions **2** : large piece of land with a house

es•teem *n or vb* : regard

es•ter *n* : organic chemical compound

esthetic *var of* AESTHETIC

es•ti•ma•ble *adj* : worthy of esteem

es•ti•mate *vb* **-mat•ed; -mat•ing** : judge the approximate value, size, or cost ~ *n* **1** : rough or approximate calculation **2** : statement of the cost of a job — **es•ti•ma•tion** *n* — **es•ti•ma•tor** *n*

es•trange *vb* **-tranged; -trang•ing** : make hostile — **es•trange•ment** *n*

es•tro•gen *n* : hormone that produces female characteristics

es•tu•ary *n, pl* **-ar•ies** : arm of the sea at a river's mouth

et cet•era : and others esp. of the same kind

etch *vb* : produce by corroding parts of a surface with acid — **etch•er** *n* — **etch•ing** *n*

eter•nal *adj* : lasting forever — **eter•nal•ly** *adv*

eter•ni•ty *n, pl* **-ties** : infinite duration

eth•ane *n* : gaseous hydrocarbon

eth•a•nol *n* : alcohol

ether *n* : light flammable liquid used as an anesthetic

ethe•re•al *adj* **1** : celestial **2** : exceptionally delicate

eth•i•cal *adj* **1** : relating to ethics **2** : honorable — **eth•i•cal•ly** *adv*

eth•ics *n sing or pl* **1** : study of good and evil and moral duty **2** : moral principles or practice

eth•nic *adj* : relating to races or groups of people with common customs ~ *n* : member of a minority ethnic group

eth•nol•o•gy *n* : study of the races of human beings — **eth•no•log•i•cal** *adj* — **eth•nol•o•gist** *n*

et•i•quette *n* : good manners

et•y•mol•o•gy *n, pl* **-gies 1** : history of a word **2** : study of etymologies — **et•y•mo•log•i•cal** *adj* — **et•y•mol•o•gist** *n*

eu•ca•lyp•tus *n, pl* **-ti** *or* **-tus•es** : Australian evergreen tree

Eu•cha•rist *n* : Communion — **eu•cha•ris•tic** *adj*

eu•lo•gy *n, pl* **-gies** : speech in praise — **eu•lo•gis•tic** *adj* — **eu•lo•gize** *vb*

eu•nuch *n* : castrated man

eu•phe•mism *n* : substitution of a pleasant expression for an unpleasant or offensive one — **eu•phe•mis•tic** *adj*

eu•pho•ni•ous *adj* : pleasing to the ear — **eu•pho•ny** *n*

eu•pho•ria *n* : elation — **eu•phor•ic** *adj*

eu•tha•na•sia *n* : mercy killing

evac•u•ate *vb* **-at•ed; -at•ing 1** : discharge wastes from the body **2** : remove or withdraw from — **evac•u•a•tion** *n*

evade *vb* **evad•ed; evad•ing** : manage to avoid

eval•u•ate *vb* **-at•ed; -at•ing** : appraise — **eval•u•a•tion** *n*

evan•gel•i•cal *adj* : relating to the Christian gospel

evan•ge•lism *n* : the winning or revival of personal commitments to Christ — **evan•ge•list** *n* — **evan•ge•lis•tic** *adj*

evap•o•rate *vb* **-rat•ed; -rat•ing 1** : pass off in or convert into vapor **2** : disappear quickly — **evap•o•ra•tion** *n* — **evap•o•ra•tor** *n*

eva•sion *n* : act or instance of evading — **eva•sive** *adj* — **eva•sive•ness** *n*

eve *n* : evening

even *adj* **1** : smooth **2** : equal or fair **3** : fully revenged **4** : divisible by 2 ~ *adv* **1** : already **2** — used for emphasis ~ *vb* : make or become even — **even•ly** *adv* — **even•ness** *n*

eve•ning *n* : early part of the night

event *n* **1** : occurrence **2** : noteworthy happening **3** : eventuality — **event•ful** *adj*

even•tu•al *adj* : later — **even•tu•al•ly** *adv*

even•tu•al•i•ty *n, pl* **-ties** : possible occurrence or outcome

ev•er *adv* **1** : always **2** : at any time **3** : in any case

ev•er•green *adj* : having foliage that remains green — **evergreen** *n*

ev•er•last•ing *adj* : lasting forever

ev•ery *adj* **1** : being each one of a group **2** : all possible

ev•ery•body *pron* : every person

ev•ery•day *adj* : ordinary

ev•ery•one *pron* : every person

ev•ery•thing *pron* : all that exists

ev•ery•where *adv* : in every place or part

evict *vb* : force (a person) to move from a property — **evic•tion** *n*

ev•i•dence *n* **1** : outward sign **2** : proof or testimony

ev•i•dent *adj* : clear or obvious — **ev•i•dent•ly** *adv*

evil *adj* **evil•er** *or* **evil•ler; evil•est** *or* **evil•lest** : wicked ~ *n* **1** : sin **2** : source of sorrow or distress — **evil•do•er** *n* — **evil•ly** *adv*

evince *vb* **evinced; evinc•ing** : show

evis•cer•ate *vb* **-at•ed; -at•ing** : remove the viscera of — **evis•cer•a•tion** *n*

evoke *vb* **evoked; evok•ing** : call forth or up — **evo•ca•tion** *n* — **evoc•a•tive** *adj*

evo•lu•tion *n* : process of change by degrees — **evo•lu•tion•ary** *adj*

evolve *vb* **evolved; evolv•ing** : develop or change by degrees

ewe *n* : female sheep

ew•er *n* : water pitcher

ex•act *vb* : compel to furnish ~ *adj* : precisely correct — **ex•act•ing** *adj* — **ex•ac•tion** *n* — **ex•ac•ti•tude** *n* — **ex•act•ly** *adv* — **ex•act•ness** *n*

ex•ag•ger•ate *vb* **-at•ed; -at•ing** : say more than is true — **ex•ag•ger•at•ed•ly** *adv* — **ex•ag•ger•a•tion** *n* — **ex•ag•ger•a•tor** *n*

ex•alt *vb* : glorify — **ex•al•ta•tion** *n*

ex•am *n* : examination

ex•am•ine *vb* **-ined; -in•ing 1** : inspect closely **2** : test by questioning — **ex•am•i•na•tion** *n*

ex•am•ple *n* **1** : representative sample **2** : model **3** : problem to be solved for teaching purposes

ex•as•per•ate *vb* **-at•ed; -at•ing** : thoroughly annoy — **ex•as•per•a•tion** *n*

ex•ca•vate *vb* **-vat•ed; -vat•ing** : dig or hollow out — **ex•ca•va•tion** *n* — **ex•ca•va•tor** *n*

ex•ceed *vb* **1** : go or be beyond the limit of **2** : do better than

ex•ceed•ing•ly *adv* : extremely

ex•cel *vb* **-ll-** : do extremely well or far better than

ex•cel•lence *n* : quality of being excellent

ex•cel•len•cy *n, pl* **-cies** — used as a title of honor

ex•cel•lent *adj* : very good — **ex•cel•lent•ly** *adv*

ex•cept *vb* : omit ~ *prep* : excluding ~ *conj* : but — **ex•cep•tion** *n*

ex•cep•tion•al *adj* : superior — **ex•cep•tion•al•ly** *adv*

ex•cerpt *n* : brief passage ~ *vb* : select an excerpt

ex•cess *n* : amount left over — **excess** *adj* — **ex•ces•sive** *adj* — **ex•ces•sive•ly** *adv*

ex•change *n* **1** : the giving or taking of one thing in return for another **2** : marketplace esp. for securities ~ *vb* **-changed; -chang•ing** : transfer in return for some equivalent — **ex•change•able** *adj*

[1]ex•cise *n* : tax

[2]ex•cise *vb* **-cised; -cis•ing** : cut out — **ex•ci•sion** *n*

ex·cite *vb* **-cit·ed; -cit·ing 1** : stir up **2** : kindle the emotions of — **ex·cit·abil·i·ty** *n* — **ex·cit·able** *adj* — **ex·ci·ta·tion** *n* — **ex·cit·ed·ly** *adv* — **ex·cite·ment** *n*

ex·claim *vb* : cry out esp. in delight — **ex·cla·ma·tion** *n* — **ex·clam·a·to·ry** *adj*

exclamation point *n* : punctuation mark ! used esp. after an interjection or exclamation

ex·clude *vb* **-clud·ed; -clud·ing** : leave out — **ex·clu·sion** *n*

ex·clu·sive *adj* **1** : reserved for particular persons **2** : stylish **3** : sole — **exclusive** *n* — **ex·clu·sive·ly** *adv* — **ex·clu·sive·ness** *n*

ex·com·mu·ni·cate *vb* : expel from a church — **ex·com·mu·ni·ca·tion** *n*

ex·cre·ment *n* : bodily waste — **ex·cre·men·tal** *adj*

ex·crete *vb* **-cret·ed; -cret·ing** : eliminate wastes from the body — **ex·cre·tion** *n* — **ex·cre·to·ry** *adj*

ex·cru·ci·at·ing *adj* : intensely painful — **ex·cru·ci·at·ing·ly** *adv*

ex·cul·pate *vb* **-pat·ed; -pat·ing** : clear from alleged fault

ex·cur·sion *n* : pleasure trip

ex·cuse *vb* **-cused; -cus·ing 1** : pardon **2** : release from an obligation **3** : justify ~ *n* **1** : justification **2** : apology

ex·e·cute *vb* **-cut·ed; -cut·ing 1** : carry out fully **2** : enforce **3** : put to death — **ex·e·cu·tion** *n* — **ex·e·cu·tion·er** *n*

ex·ec·u·tive *adj* : relating to the carrying out of decisions, plans, or laws ~ *n* **1** : branch of government with executive duties **2** : administrator

ex·ec·u·tor *n* : person named in a will to execute it

ex·ec·u·trix *n, pl* **ex·ec·u·tri·ces** *or* **ex·ec·u·trix·es** : woman executor

ex·em·pla·ry *adj* : so commendable as to serve as a model

ex·em·pli·fy *vb* **-fied; -fy·ing** : serve as an example of — **ex·em·pli·fi·ca·tion** *n*

ex·empt *adj* : being free from some liability ~ *vb* : make exempt — **ex·emp·tion** *n*

ex·er·cise *n* **1** : a putting into action **2** : exertion to develop endurance or a skill **3** *pl* : public ceremony ~ *vb* **-cised; -cis·ing 1** : exert **2** : engage in exercise — **ex·er·cis·er** *n*

ex·ert *vb* : put into action — **ex·er·tion** *n*

ex·hale *vb* **-haled; -hal·ing** : breathe out — **ex·ha·la·tion** *n*

ex·haust *vb* **1** : draw out or develop completely **2** : use up **3** : tire or wear out — *n* : waste steam or gas from an engine or a system for removing it — **ex·haus·tion** *n* — **ex·haus·tive** *adj*

ex·hib·it *vb* : display esp. publicly ~ *n* **1** : act of exhibiting **2** : something exhibited — **ex·hi·bi·tion** *n* — **ex·hib·i·tor** *n*

ex·hil·a·rate *vb* **-rat·ed; -rat·ing** : thrill — **ex·hil·a·ra·tion** *n*

ex·hort *vb* : urge earnestly — **ex·hor·ta·tion** *n*

ex·hume *vb* **-humed; -hum·ing** : dig up (a buried corpse) — **ex·hu·ma·tion** *n*

ex·i·gen·cies *n pl* : requirements (as of a situation)

ex·ile *n* **1** : banishment **2** : person banished from his or her country — **exile** *vb*

ex·ist *vb* **1** : have real or actual being **2** : live — **ex·is·tence** *n* — **ex·is·tent** *adj*

ex·it *n* **1** : departure **2** : way out of an enclosed space **3** : way off an expressway — **exit** *vb*

ex·o·dus *n* : mass departure

ex·on·er·ate *vb* **-at·ed; -at·ing** : free from blame — **ex·on·er·a·tion** *n*

ex·or·bi·tant *adj* : exceeding what is usual or proper

ex·or·cise *vb* **-cised; -cis·ing** : drive out (as an evil spirit) — **ex·or·cism** *n* — **ex·or·cist** *n*

ex·ot·ic *adj* : foreign or strange — **exotic** *n* — **ex·ot·i·cal·ly** *adv*

ex·pand *vb* : enlarge

ex·panse *n* : very large area

ex·pan·sion *n* **1** : act or process of expanding **2** : expanded part

ex·pan·sive *adj* **1** : tending to expand **2** : warmly benevolent **3** : of large extent — **ex·pan·sive·ly** *adv* — **ex·pan·sive·ness** *n*

ex·pa·tri·ate *n* : exile — **expatriate** *adj or vb*

ex·pect *vb* **1** : look forward to **2** : consider probable or one's due — **ex·pec·tan·cy** *n* — **ex·pec·tant** *adj* — **ex·pec·tant·ly** *adv* — **ex·pec·ta·tion** *n*

ex·pe·di·ent *adj* : convenient or advantageous rather than right or just ~ *n* : convenient often makeshift means to an end

ex·pe·dite *vb* **-dit·ed; -dit·ing** : carry out or handle promptly — **ex·pe·dit·er** *n*

ex·pe·di·tion *n* : long journey for work or research or the people making this

ex·pe·di·tious *adj* : prompt and efficient

ex·pel *vb* **-ll-** : force out

ex·pend *vb* **1** : pay out **2** : use up — **ex·pend·able** *adj*

ex·pen·di·ture *n* : act of using or spending

ex·pense *n* : cost — **ex·pen·sive** *adj* — **ex·pen·sive·ly** *adv*

ex·pe·ri·ence *n* **1** : a participating in or living through an event **2** : an event that affects one **3** : knowledge from doing ~ *vb* **-enced; -enc·ing** : undergo

ex·per·i·ment *n* : test to discover something ~ *vb* : make experiments — **ex·per·i·men·tal** *adj* — **ex·per·i·menta·tion** *n* — **ex·per·i·men·ter** *n*

ex·pert *adj* : thoroughly skilled ~ *n* : person with special skill — **ex·pert·ly** *adv* — **ex·pert·ness** *n*

ex·per·tise *n* : skill

ex·pi·ate *vb* : make amends for — **ex·pi·a·tion** *n*

ex·pire *vb* **-pired; -pir·ing 1** : breathe out **2** : die **3** : end — **ex·pi·ra·tion** *n*

ex·plain *vb* **1** : make clear **2** : give the reason for — **ex·plain·able** *adj* — **ex·pla·na·tion** *n* — **ex·plan·a·to·ry** *adj*

ex·ple·tive *n* : usu. profane exclamation

ex·pli·ca·ble *adj* : capable of being explained

ex·plic·it *adj* : absolutely clear or precise — **ex·plic·it·ly** *adv* — **ex·plic·it·ness** *n*

ex·plode *vb* **-plod·ed; -plod·ing 1** : discredit **2** : burst or cause to burst violently **3** : increase rapidly

ex·ploit *n* : heroic act ~ *vb* **1** : utilize **2** : use unfairly — **ex·ploi·ta·tion** *n*

ex·plore *vb* **-plored; -plor·ing** : examine or range over thoroughly — **ex·plo·ra·tion** *n* — **ex·plor·a·to·ry** *adj* — **ex·plor·er** *n*

ex·plo·sion *n* : process or instance of exploding

ex·plo·sive *adj* : able to cause explosion **2** : likely to explode — **explosive** *n* — **ex·plo·sive·ly** *adv*

ex·po·nent *n* **1** : mathematical symbol showing how many times a number is to be repeated as a factor **2** : advocate — **ex·po·nen·tial** *adj* — **ex·po·nen·tial·ly** *adv*

ex·port *vb* : send to foreign countries — **export** *n* — **ex·por·ta·tion** *n* — **ex·port·er** *n*

ex·pose *vb* **-posed; -pos·ing 1** : deprive of shelter or protection **2** : subject (film) to light **3** : make known — **ex·po·sure** *n*

ex·po·sé, ex·po·se *n* : exposure of something discreditable

ex·po·si·tion *n* : public exhibition

ex·pound *vb* : set forth or explain in detail

1ex·press *adj* **1** : clear **2** : specific **3** : traveling at high speed with few stops — **express** *adv or n* — **ex·press·ly** *adv*

2express *vb* **1** : make known in words or appearance **2** : press out (as juice)

ex·pres·sion *n* **1** : utterance **2** : mathematical symbol **3** : significant word or phrase **4** : look on one's face — **ex·pres·sion·less** *adj* — **ex·pres·sive** *adj* — **ex·pres·sive·ness** *n*

ex·press·way *n* : high-speed divided highway with limited access

ex·pul·sion *n* : an expelling or being expelled

ex·pur·gate *vb* **-gat·ed; -gat·ing** : censor — **ex·pur·ga·tion** *n*

ex·qui·site *adj* **1** : flawlessly beautiful and delicate **2** : keenly discriminating

ex·tant *adj* : existing

ex·tem·po·ra·ne·ous *adj* : impromptu — **ex·tem·po·ra·ne·ous·ly** *adv*

ex·tend *vb* **1** : stretch forth or out **2** : prolong **3** : enlarge — **ex·tend·able** *adj*

ex·ten·sion *n* **1** : an extending or being extended **2** : additional part **3** : extra telephone line

ex·ten·sive *adj* : of considerable extent — **ex·ten·sive·ly** *adv*

ex·tent *n* : range, space, or degree to which something extends

ex·ten·u·ate *vb* **-at·ed; -at·ing** : lessen the seriousness of — **ex·ten·u·a·tion** *n*

ex·te·ri·or *adj* : external ~ *n* : external part or surface

ex·ter·mi·nate *vb* **-nat·ed; -nat·ing** : destroy utterly — **ex·ter·mi·na·tion** *n* — **ex·ter·mi·na·tor** *n*

ex·ter·nal *adj* : relating to or on the outside — **ex·ter·nal·ly** *adv*

ex·tinct *adj* : no longer existing — **ex·tinc·tion** *n*

ex·tin·guish *vb* : cause to stop burning — **ex·tin·guish·able** *adj* — **ex·tin·guish·er** *n*

ex·tir·pate *vb* **-pat·ed; -pat·ing** : destroy

ex·tol *vb* **-ll-** : praise highly

ex·tort *vb* : obtain by force or improper pressure — **ex·tor·tion** *n* — **ex·tor·tion·er** *n* — **ex·tor·tion·ist** *n*

ex·tra *adj* **1** : additional **2** : superior — **extra** *n or adv*

extra- *prefix* : outside or beyond

ex·tract *vb* **1** : pull out forcibly **2** : withdraw (as a juice) ~ *n* **1** : excerpt **2** : product (as a juice) obtained by extracting — **ex·tract·able** *adj* — **ex·trac·tion** *n* — **ex·trac·tor** *n*

ex·tra·cur·ric·u·lar *adj* : lying outside the regular curriculum

ex·tra·dite *vb* **-dit·ed; -dit·ing** : bring or deliver a suspect to a different jurisdiction for trial — **ex·tra·di·tion** *n*

ex·tra·mar·i·tal *adj* : relating to sexual relations of a married person outside of the marriage

ex·tra·ne·ous *adj* : not essential or relevant — **ex·tra·ne·ous·ly** *adv*

ex·traor·di·nary *adj* : notably unusual or exceptional — **ex·traor·di·nari·ly** *adv*

ex·tra·sen·so·ry *adj* : outside the ordinary senses

ex·tra·ter·res·tri·al *n* : one existing or coming from outside the earth ~ *adj* : relating to an extraterrestrial

ex·trav·a·gant *adj* : wildly excessive, lavish, or costly — **ex·trav·a·gance** *n* — **ex·trav·a·gant·ly** *adv*

ex·trav·a·gan·za *n* : spectacular event

ex·tra·ve·hic·u·lar *adj* : occurring outside a spacecraft

ex·treme *adj* **1** : very great or intense **2** : very severe **3** : not moderate **4** : most remote ~ *n* **1** : extreme state **2** : something located at one end or the other of a range — **ex·treme·ly** *adv*

ex·trem·i·ty *n, pl* **-ties 1** : most remote part **2** : human hand or foot **3** : extreme degree or state (as of need)

ex·tri·cate *vb* **-cat·ed; -cat·ing** : set or get free from an entanglement or difficulty — **ex•tri•ca•ble** *adj* **ex•tri•ca•tion** *n*

ex•tro•vert *n* : gregarious person — **ex•tro•ver•sion** *n* — **ex•tro•vert•ed** *adj*

ex•trude *vb* **-trud•ed; -trud•ing** : to force or push out

ex•u•ber•ant *adj* : joyously unrestrained — **ex•u•ber•ance** *n* — **ex•u•ber•ant•ly** *adv*

ex•ude *vb* **-ud•ed; -ud•ing** 1 : discharge slowly through pores 2 : display conspicuously

ex•ult *vb* : rejoice — **ex•ul•tant** *adj* — **ex•ul•tant•ly** *adv* — **ex•ul•ta•tion** *n*

-ey —see -Y

eye *n* 1 : organ of sight consisting of a globular structure (**eye•ball**) in a socket of the skull with thin movable covers (**eye•lids**) bordered with hairs (**eye•lash•es**) 2 : vision 3 : judgment 4 : something suggesting an eye ~ *vb* **eyed; eye•ing** *or* **ey•ing** : look at — **eye•brow** *n* — **eyed** *adj* — **eye•strain** *n*

eye•drop•per *n* : dropper

eye•glass•es *n pl* : glasses

eye•let *n* : hole (as in cloth) for a lacing or rope

eye–open•er *n* : something startling — **eye–open•ing** *adj*

eye•piece *n* : lens at the eye end of an optical instrument

eye•sight *n* : sight

eye•sore *n* : unpleasant sight

eye•tooth *n* : upper canine tooth

eye•wit•ness *n* : person who actually sees something happen

ey•rie *var of* AERIE

F

f *n, pl* **f's** *or* **fs** : 6th letter of the alphabet

fa•ble *n* 1 : legendary story 2 : story that teaches a lesson — **fa•bled** *adj*

fab•ric *n* 1 : structure 2 : material made usu. by weaving or knitting fibers

fab•ri•cate *vb* **-cat•ed; -cat•ing** 1 : construct 2 : invent — **fab•ri•ca•tion** *n*

fab•u•lous *adj* 1 : like, told in, or based on fable 2 : incredible or marvelous — **fab•u•lous•ly** *adv*

fa•cade *n* 1 : principal face of a building 2 : false or superficial appearance

face *n* 1 : front or principal surface (as of the head) 2 : presence 3 : facial expression 4 : grimace 5 : outward appearance ~ *vb* **faced; fac•ing** 1 : challenge or resist firmly or brazenly 2 : cover with different material 3 : sit or stand with the face toward 4 : have the front oriented toward — **faced** *adj* — **face•less** *adj* — **fa•cial** *adj or n*

face•down *adv* : with the face downward

face–lift *n* 1 : cosmetic surgery on the face 2 : modernization

fac•et *n* 1 : surface of a cut gem 2 : phase — **fac•et•ed** *adj*

fa•ce•tious *adj* : jocular — **fa•ce•tious•ly** *adv* — **fa•ce•tious•ness** *n*

fac•ile *adj* 1 : easy 2 : fluent

fa•cil•i•tate *vb* **-tat•ed; -tat•ing** : make easier

fa•cil•i•ty *n, pl* **-ties** 1 : ease in doing or using 2 : something built or installed to serve a purpose or facilitate an activity

fac•ing *n* : lining or covering or material for this

fac•sim•i•le *n* : exact copy

fact *n* 1 : act or action 2 : something that exists or is real 3 : piece of information — **fac•tu•al** *adj* — **fac•tu•al•ly** *adv*

fac•tion *n* : part of a larger group — **fac•tion•al•ism** *n*

fac•tious *adj* : causing discord

fac•ti•tious *adj* : artificial

fac•tor *n* 1 : something that has an effect 2 : gene 3 : number used in multiplying

fac•to•ry *n, pl* **-ries** : place for manufacturing

fac•to•tum *n* : person (as a servant) with varied duties

fac•ul•ty *n, pl* **-ties** 1 : ability to act 2 : power of the mind or body 3 : body of teachers or department of instruction

fad *n* : briefly popular practice or interest — **fad•dish** *adj* — **fad•dist** *n*

fade *vb* **fad•ed; fad•ing** 1 : wither 2 : lose or cause to lose freshness or brilliance 3 : grow dim 4 : vanish

fag *vb* **-gg-** 1 : drudge 2 : tire or exhaust

fag•ot, fag•got *n* : bundle of twigs

Fahr•en•heit *adj* : relating to a thermometer scale with the boiling point at 212 degrees and the freezing point at 32 degrees

fail *vb* 1 : decline in health 2 : die away 3 : stop functioning 4 : be unsuccessful 5 : become bank-

rupt 6 : disappoint 7 : neglect ~ *n* : act of failing

fail•ing *n* : slight defect in character or conduct ~ *prep* : in the absence or lack of

faille *n* : closely woven ribbed fabric

fail•ure *n* 1 : absence of expected action or performance 2 : bankruptcy 3 : deficiency 4 : one that has failed

faint *adj* 1 : cowardly or spiritless 2 : weak and dizzy 3 : lacking vigor 4 : indistinct ~ *vb* : lose consciousness ~ *n* : act or condition of fainting — **faint•heart•ed** *adj* — **faint•ly** *adv* — **faint•ness** *n*

¹fair *adj* 1 : pleasing in appearance 2 : not stormy or cloudy 3 : just or honest 4 : conforming with the rules 5 : open to legitimate pursuit or attack 6 : light in color 7 : adequate — **fair•ness** *n*

²fair *adv, chiefly Brit* : FAIRLY

³fair *n* : exhibition for judging or selling — **fair•ground** *n*

fair•ly *adv* 1 : in a manner of speaking 2 : without bias 3 : somewhat

fairy *n, pl* **fair•ies** : usu. small imaginary being — **fairy tale** *n*

fairy•land *n* 1 : land of fairies 2 : beautiful or charming place

faith *n, pl* **faiths** 1 : allegiance 2 : belief and trust in God 3 : confidence 4 : system of religious beliefs — **faith•ful** *adj* — **faith•ful•ly** *adv* — **faith•ful•ness** *n* — **faith•less** *adj* — **faith•less•ly** *adv* — **faith•less•ness** *n*

fake *vb* **faked; fak•ing** 1 : falsify 2 : counterfeit ~ *n* : copy, fraud, or impostor ~ *adj* : not genuine — **fak•er** *n*

fa•kir *n* : wandering beggar of India

fal•con *n* : small long-winged hawk used esp. for hunting — **fal•con•ry** *n*

fall *vb* **fell; fall•en; fall•ing** 1 : go down by gravity 2 : hang freely 3 : go lower 4 : be defeated or ruined 5 : commit a sin 6 : happen at a certain time 7 : become gradually ~ *n* 1 : act of falling 2 : autumn 3 : downfall 4 *pl* : waterfall 5 : distance something falls

fal•la•cy *n, pl* **-cies** 1 : false idea 2 : false reasoning — **fal•la•cious** *adj*

fal•li•ble *adj* : capable of making a mistake — **fal•li•bly** *adv*

fall•out *n* 1 : radioactive particles from a nuclear explosion 2 : secondary effects

fal•low *adj* 1 : plowed but not planted 2 : dormant — **fallow** *n or vb*

false *adj* **fals•er; fals•est** 1 : not genuine, true, faithful, or permanent 2 : misleading — **false•ly** *adv* — **false•ness** *n* — **fal•si•fi•ca•tion** *n* — **fal•si•fy** *vb* — **fal•si•ty** *n*

false•hood *n* : lie

fal•set•to *n, pl* **-tos** : artificially high singing voice

fal•ter *vb* **-tered; -ter•ing** 1 : move unsteadily 2 : hesitate — **fal•ter•ing•ly** *adv*

fame *n* : public reputation — **famed** *adj*

fa•mil•ial *adj* : relating to a family

¹fa•mil•iar *n* 1 : companion 2 : guardian spirit

²familiar *adj* 1 : closely acquainted 2 : forward 3 : frequently seen or experienced — **fa•mil•iar•i•ty** *n* — **fa•mil•iar•ize** *vb* — **fa•mil•iar•ly** *adv*

fam•i•ly *n, pl* **-lies** 1 : persons of common ancestry 2 : group living together 3 : parents and children 4 : group of related individuals

fam•ine *n* : extreme scarcity of food

fam•ish *vb* : starve

fa•mous *adj* : widely known or celebrated

fa•mous•ly *adv* : very well

¹fan *n* : device for producing a current of air ~ *vb* **-nn-** 1 : move air with a fan 2 : direct a current of air upon 3 : stir to activity

²fan *n* : enthusiastic follower or admirer

fa•nat•ic , fa•nat•i•cal *adj* : excessively enthusiastic or devoted — **fanatic** *n* — **fa•nat•i•cism** *n*

fan•ci•er *n* : one devoted to raising a particular plant or animal

fan•cy *n, pl* **-cies** 1 : liking 2 : whim 3 : imagination ~ *vb* **-cied; -cy•ing** 1 : like 2 : imagine ~ *adj* **-cier; -est** 1 : not plain 2 : of superior quality — **fan•ci•ful** *adj* — **fan•ci•ful•ly** *adv* — **fan•ci•ly** *adv*

fan•dan•go *n, pl* **-gos** : lively Spanish dance

fan•fare *n* 1 : a sounding of trumpets 2 : showy display

fang *n* : long sharp tooth

fan•light *n* : semicircular window

fan•ta•sia *n* : music written to fancy rather than to form

fan•tas•tic *adj* 1 : imaginary or unrealistic 2 : exceedingly or unbelievably great — **fan•tas•ti•cal•ly** *adv*

fan•ta•sy *n* 1 : imagination 2 : product (as a daydream) of the imagination 3 : fantasia — **fan•ta•size** *vb*

far *adv* **far•ther** *or* **fur•ther ; far•thest** *or* **furthest** 1 : at or to a distance 2 : much 3 : to a degree 4 : to an advanced point or extent ~ *adj* **farther** *or* **further; far•thest** *or* **furthest** 1 : remote 2 : long 3 : being more distant

far•away *adj* : distant

farce *n* 1 : satirical comedy with an improbable plot 2 : ridiculous display — **far•ci•cal** *adj*

¹fare *vb* **fared; far•ing** : get along

²fare *n* 1 : price of transportation 2 : range of food

fare•well *n* 1 : wish of welfare at parting 2 : departure — **farewell** *adj*

far–fetched *adj* : improbable

fa•ri•na *n* : fine meal made from cereal grains

farm *n* : place where something is raised for food ~ *vb* 1 : use (land) as a farm 2 : raise plants or animals for food — **farm•er** *n* — **farm•hand** *n* — **farm•house** *n* — **farm•ing** *n* — **farm•land** *n* — **farm•yard** *n*

far–off *adj* : remote in time or space

far•ri•er *n* : blacksmith who shoes horses

far•row *vb* : give birth to a litter of pigs — **farrow** *n*

far•sight•ed *adj* **1** : better able to see distant things than near **2** : judicious or shrewd — **far•sight•ed•ness** *n*

far•ther *adv* **1** : at or to a greater distance or more advanced point **2** : to a greater degree or extent ~ *adj* : more distant

far•ther•most *adj* : most distant

far•thest *adj* : most distant ~ *adv* **1** : to or at the greatest distance **2** : to the most advanced point **3** : by the greatest extent

fas•ci•cle *n* **1** : small bundle **2** : division of a book published in parts — **fas•ci•cled** *adj*

fas•ci•nate *vb* **-nat•ed; -nat•ing** : transfix and hold spellbound — **fas•ci•na•tion** *n*

fas•cism *n* : dictatorship that exalts nation and race — **fas•cist** *n or adj* — **fas•cis•tic** *adj*

fash•ion *n* **1** : manner **2** : prevailing custom or style ~ *vb* : form or construct — **fash•ion•able** *adj* — **fash•ion•ably** *adv*

¹fast *adj* **1** : firmly fixed, bound, or shut **2** : faithful **3** : moving or acting quickly **4** : indicating ahead of the correct time **5** : deep and undisturbed **6** : permanently dyed **7** : wild or promiscuous ~ *adv* **1** : so as to be secure or bound **2** : soundly or deeply **3** : swiftly

²fast *vb* : abstain from food or eat sparingly ~ *n* : act or time of fasting

fas•ten *vb* : attach esp. by pinning or tying — **fas•ten•er** *n* — **fas•ten•ing** *n*

fas•tid•i•ous *adj* : hard to please — **fas•tid•i•ous•ly** *adv* — **fas•tid•i•ous•ness** *n*

fat *adj* **-tt-** **1** : having much fat **2** : thick ~ *n* : animal tissue rich in greasy or oily matter — **fat•ness** *n* — **fat•ten** *vb* — **fat•ty** *adj or n*

fa•tal *adj* : causing death or ruin — **fa•tal•i•ty** *n* — **fa•tal•ly** *adv*

fa•tal•ism *n* : belief that fate determines events — **fa•tal•ist** *n* — **fa•tal•is•tic** *adj* — **fa•tal•is•ti•cal•ly** *adv*

fate *n* **1** : principle, cause, or will held to determine events **2** : end or outcome — **fat•ed** *adj* — **fate•ful** *adj* — **fate•ful•ly** *adv*

fa•ther *n* **1** : male parent **2** *cap* : God **3** : originator — **father** *vb* — **fa•ther•hood** *n* — **fa•ther•land** *n* — **fa•ther•less** *adj* — **fa•ther•ly** *adj*

father–in–law *n, pl* **fa•thers–in–law** : father of one's spouse

fath•om *n* : nautical unit of length equal to 6 feet ~ *vb* : understand — **fath•om•able** *adj* — **fath•om•less** *adj*

fa•tigue *n* **1** : weariness from labor or use **2** : tendency to break under repeated stress ~ *vb* **-tigued; -tigu•ing** : tire out

fat•u•ous *adj* : foolish or stupid — **fat•u•ous•ly** *adv* — **fat•u•ous•ness** *n*

fau•cet *n* : fixture for drawing off a liquid

fault *n* **1** : weakness in character **2** : something wrong or imperfect **3** : responsibility for something wrong **4** : fracture in the earth's crust ~ *vb* : find fault in or with — **fault•find•er** *n* — **fault•find•ing** *n* — **fault•i•ly** *adv* — **fault•less** *adj* — **fault•less•ly** *adv* — **faulty** *adj*

fau•na *n* : animals or animal life esp. of a region — **fau•nal** *adj*

faux pas *n, pl* **faux pas** : social blunder

fa•vor *n* **1** : approval **2** : partiality **3** : act of kindness ~ *vb* : regard or treat with favor — **fa•vor•able** *adj* — **fa•vor•ably** *adv*

fa•vor•ite *n* : one favored — **favorite** *adj* — **fa•vor•it•ism** *n*

¹fawn *vb* : seek favor by groveling

²fawn *n* : young deer

faze *vb* **fazed; faz•ing** : disturb the composure of

fear *n* : unpleasant emotion caused by expectation or awareness of danger ~ *vb* : be afraid of — **fear•ful** *adj* — **fear•ful•ly** *adv* — **fear•less** *adj* — **fear•less•ly** *adv* — **fear•less•ness** *n* — **fear•some** *adj*

fea•si•ble *adj* : capable of being done — **fea•si•bil•i•ty** *n* — **fea•si•bly** *adv*

feast *n* **1** : large or fancy meal **2** : religious festival ~ *vb* : eat plentifully

feat *n* : notable deed

feath•er *n* : one of the light horny outgrowths that form the external covering of a bird's body — **feather** *vb* — **feath•ered** *adj* — **feath•er•less** *adj* — **feath•ery** *adj*

fea•ture *n* **1** : shape or appearance of the face **2** : part of the face **3** : prominent characteristic **4** : special attraction ~ *vb* : give prominence to — **fea•ture•less** *adj*

Feb•ru•ary *n* : 2d month of the year having 28 and in leap years 29 days

fe•ces *n pl* : intestinal body waste — **fe•cal** *adj*

feck•less *adj* : irresponsible

fe•cund *adj* : prolific — **fe•cun•di•ty** *n*

fed•er•al *adj* : of or constituting a government with power distributed between a central authority and constituent units — **fed•er•al•ism** *n* — **fed•er•al•ist** *n or adj* — **fed•er•al•ly** *adv*

fed•er•ate *vb* **-at•ed; -at•ing** : join in a federation

fed•er•a•tion *n* : union of organizations

fe•do•ra *n* : soft felt hat

fed up *adj* : out of patience

fee *n* : fixed charge

fee•ble *adj* **-bler; -blest** : weak or ineffective — **fee•ble•mind•ed** *adj* — **fee•ble•mind•ed•ness** *n* — **fee•ble•ness** *n* — **fee•bly** *adv*

feed *vb* **fed; feed•ing** **1** : give food to **2** : eat **3** : furnish ~ *n* : food for livestock — **feed•er** *n*

feel *vb* **felt; feel•ing** **1** : perceive or examine through physical contact **2** : think or believe **3** : be conscious of **4** : seem **5** : have sympathy ~ *n* **1** : sense of touch **2** : quality of a thing imparted through touch — **feel•er** *n*

feel•ing *n* **1** : sense of touch **2** : state of mind **3** *pl* : sensibilities **4** : opinion

feet *pl of* FOOT

feign *vb* : pretend

feint *n* : mock attack intended to distract attention — **feint** *vb*

fe•lic•i•tate *vb* **-tat•ed; -tat•ing** : congratulate — **fe•lic•i•ta•tion** *n*

fe•lic•i•tous *adj* : aptly expressed — **fe•lic•i•tous•ly** *adv*

fe•lic•i•ty *n, pl* **-ties** **1** : great happiness **2** : pleasing faculty esp. in art or language

fe•line *adj* : relating to cats — **feline** *n*

¹fell *vb* : cut or knock down

²fell *past of* FALL

fel•low *n* **1** : companion or associate **2** : man or boy — **fel•low•ship** *n*

fel•low•man *n* : kindred human being

fel•on *n* : one who has committed a felony

fel•o•ny *n, pl* **-nies** : serious crime — **fe•lo•ni•ous** *adj*

¹felt *n* : cloth made of pressed wool and fur

²felt *past of* FEEL

fe•male *adj* : relating to or being the sex that bears young — **female** *n*

fem•i•nine *adj* : relating to the female sex — **fem•i•nin•i•ty** *n*

fem•i•nism *n* : organized activity on behalf of women's rights — **fem•i•nist** *n or adj*

fe•mur *n, pl* **fe•murs** *or* **fem•o•ra** : long bone of the thigh — **fem•o•ral** *adj*

fence *n* : enclosing barrier esp. of wood or wire ~ *vb* **fenced; fenc•ing** **1** : enclose with a fence **2** : practice fencing — **fenc•er** *n*

fenc•ing *n* **1** : combat with swords for sport **2** : material for building fences

fend *vb* : ward off

fend•er *n* : guard over an automobile wheel

fen•nel *n* : herb related to the carrot

fer•ment *vb* : cause or undergo fermentation ~ *n* : agitation

fer•men•ta•tion *n* : chemical decomposition of an organic substance in the absence of oxygen

fern *n* : flowerless seedless green plant

fe•ro•cious *adj* : fierce or savage — **fe•ro•cious•ly** *adv* — **fe•ro•cious•ness** *n* — **fe•roc•i•ty** *n*

fer•ret *n* : white European polecat ~ *vb* : find out by searching

fer•ric, fer•rous *adj* : relating to or containing iron

fer•rule *n* : metal band or ring

fer•ry *vb* **-ried; -ry•ing** : carry by boat over water ~ *n, pl* **-ries** : boat used in ferrying — **fer•ry•boat** *n*

fer•tile *adj* **1** : producing plentifully **2** : capable of developing or reproducing — **fer•til•i•ty** *n*

fer•til•ize *vb* **-ized; -iz•ing** : make fertile — **fer•til•iza•tion** *n* — **fer•til•iz•er** *n*

fer•vid *adj* : ardent or zealous — **fer•vid•ly** *adv*

fer•vor *n* : passion — **fer•ven•cy** *n* — **fer•vent** *adj* — **fer•vent•ly** *adv*

fes•ter *vb* **1** : form pus **2** : become more bitter or malignant

fes•ti•val *n* : time of celebration

fes•tive *adj* : joyous or happy — **fes•tive•ly** *adv* — **fes•tiv•i•ty** *n*

fes•toon *n* : decorative chain or strip hanging in a curve — **festoon** *vb*

fe•tal *adj* : of, relating to, or being a fetus

fetch *vb* **1** : go or come after and bring or take back **2** : sell for

fetch•ing *adj* : attractive — **fetch•ing•ly** *adv*

fête *n* : lavish party ~ *vb* **fêt•ed; fêt•ing** : honor or commemorate with a fête

fet•id *adj* : having an offensive smell

fe•tish *n* **1** : object believed to have magical powers **2** : object of unreasoning devotion or concern

fet•lock *n* : projection on the back of a horse's leg above the hoof

fet•ter *n* : chain or shackle for the feet — **fet•ter** *vb*

fet•tle *n* : state of fitness

fe•tus *n* : vertebrate not yet born or hatched

feud *n* : prolonged quarrel — **feud** *vb*

feu•dal *adj* : of or relating to feudalism

feu•dal•ism *n* : medieval political order in which land is granted in return for service — **feu•dal•is•tic** *adj*

fe•ver *n* **1** : abnormal rise in body temperature **2** : state of heightened emotion — **fe•ver•ish** *adj* — **fe•ver•ish•ly** *adv*

few *pron* : not many ~ *adj* : some but not many — often with *a* ~ *n* : small number — often with *a*

few•er *pron* : smaller number of things

fez *n, pl* **fez•zes** : round flat-crowned hat

fi•an•cé *n* : man one is engaged to

fi•an•cée *n* : woman one is engaged to

fi•as•co *n, pl* **-coes** : ridiculous failure

fi•at *n* : decree

fib *n* : trivial lie — **fib** *vb* — **fib•ber** *n*

fi•ber, fi•bre *n* **1** : threadlike substance or structure (as a muscle cell or fine root) **2** : indigestible material in food **3** : element that gives texture or substance — **fi•brous** *adj*

fi•ber•board *n* : construction material made of compressed fibers

fi•ber•glass *n* : glass in fibrous form in various products (as insulation)

fi•bril•la•tion *n* : rapid irregular contractions of heart muscle — **fib•ril•late** *vb*

fib•u•la *n, pl* **-lae** *or* **-las** : outer of the two leg bones below the knee — **fib•u•lar** *adj*

fick•le *adj* : unpredictably changeable — **fick•le•ness** *n*

fic·tion *n* : a made-up story or literature consisting of these — **fic·tion·al** *adj*

fic·ti·tious *adj* : made up or pretended

fid·dle *n* : violin ~ *vb* **-dled; -dling 1** : play on the fiddle **2** : move the hands restlessly — **fid·dler** *n*

fid·dle·sticks *n* : nonsense — used as an interjection

fi·del·i·ty *n, pl* **-ties 1** : quality or state of being faithful **2** : quality of reproduction

fid·get *n* **1** *pl* : restlessness **2** : one that fidgets ~ *vb* : move restlessly — **fid·gety** *adj*

fi·du·cia·ry *adj* : held or holding in trust — **fidu·ciary** *n*

field *n* **1** : open country **2** : cleared land **3** : land yielding some special product **4** : sphere of activity **5** : area for sports **6** : region or space in which a given effect (as magnetism) exists ~ *vb* : put into the field — **field** *adj* — **field·er** *n*

fiend *n* **1** : devil **2** : extremely wicked person — **fiend·ish** *adj* — **fiend·ish·ly** *adv*

fierce *adj* **fierc·er; -est 1** : violently hostile or aggressive **2** : intense **3** : menacing looking — **fierce·ly** *adv* — **fierce·ness** *n*

fi·ery *adj* **fi·er·i·er; -est 1** : burning **2** : hot or passionate — **fi·eri·ness** *n*

fi·es·ta *n* : festival

fife *n* : small flute

fif·teen *n* : one more than 14 — **fifteen** *adj or pron* — **fif·teenth** *adj or n*

fifth *n* **1** : one that is number 5 in a countable series **2** : one of 5 equal parts of something — **fifth** *adj or adv*

fif·ty *n, pl* **-ties** : 5 times 10 — **fif·ti·eth** *adj or n* — **fifty** *adj or pron*

fif·ty–fif·ty *adv or adj* : shared equally

fig *n* : pear-shaped edible fruit

fight *vb* **fought ; fight·ing 1** : contend against another in battle **2** : box **3** : struggle ~ *n* **1** : hostile encounter **2** : boxing match **3** : verbal disagreement — **fight·er** *n*

fig·ment *n* : something imagined or made up

fig·u·ra·tive *adj* : metaphorical — **fig·u·ra·tive·ly** *adv*

fig·ure *n* **1** : symbol representing a number **2** *pl* : arithmetical calculations **3** : price **4** : shape or outline **5** : illustration **6** : pattern or design **7** : prominent person ~ *vb* **-ured; -ur·ing 1** : be important **2** : calculate — **fig·ured** *adj*

fig·u·rine *n* : small statue

fil·a·ment *n* : fine thread or threadlike part — **fil·a·men·tous** *adj*

fil·bert *n* : edible nut of a European hazel

filch *vb* : steal furtively

¹file *n* : tool for smoothing or sharpening ~ *vb* **filed; fil·ing** : rub or smooth with a file

²file *vb* **filed; fil·ing 1** : arrange in order **2** : enter or record officially ~ *n* : device for keeping papers in order

³file *n* : row of persons or things one behind the other — *vb* **filed; fil·ing** : march in file

fil·ial *adj* : relating to a son or daughter

fil·i·bus·ter *n* : long speeches to delay a legislative vote — **filibuster** *vb* — **fil·i·bus·ter·er** *n*

fil·i·gree *n* : ornamental designs of fine wire — **fil·i·greed** *adj*

fill *vb* **1** : make or become full **2** : stop up **3** : feed **4** : satisfy **5** : occupy fully **6** : spread through ~ *n* **1** : full supply **2** : material for filling — **fill·er** *n* — **fill in** *vb* **1** : provide information to or for **2** : substitute

fil·let *n* : piece of boneless meat or fish ~ *vb* : cut into fillets

fill·ing *n* : material used to fill something

fil·ly *n, pl* **-lies** : young female horse

film *n* **1** : thin skin or membrane **2** : thin coating or layer **3** : strip of material used in taking pictures **4** : movie ~ *vb* : make a movie of — **filmy** *adj*

film·strip *n* : strip of film with photographs for still projection

fil·ter *n* **1** : device for separating matter from a fluid **2** : device (as on a camera lens) that absorbs light ~ *vb* **1** : pass through a filter **2** : remove by means of a filter — **fil·ter·able** *adj* — **fil·tra·tion** *n*

filth *n* : repulsive dirt or refuse — **filth·i·ness** *n* — **filthy** *adj*

fin *n* **1** : thin external process controlling movement in an aquatic animal **2** : fin-shaped part (as on an airplane) **3** : flipper — **finned** *adj*

fi·na·gle *vb* **-gled; -gling** : get by clever or tricky means — **fi·na·gler** *n*

fi·nal *adj* **1** : not to be changed **2** : ultimate **3** : coming at the end — **final** *n* — **fi·nal·ist** *n* — **fi·nal·i·ty** *n* — **fi·nal·ize** *vb* — **fi·nal·ly** *adv*

fi·na·le *n* : last or climactic part

fi·nance *n* **1** *pl* : money resources **2** : management of money affairs ~ *vb* **-nanced; -nanc·ing 1** : raise funds for **2** : give necessary funds to **3** : sell on credit

fi·nan·cial *adj* : relating to finance — **fi·nan·cial·ly** *adv*

fi·nan·cier *n* : person who invests large sums of money

finch *n* : songbird (as a sparrow or linnet) with a strong bill

find *vb* **found ; find·ing 1** : discover or encounter **2** : obtain by effort **3** : experience or feel **4** : gain or regain the use of **5** : decide on (a verdict) ~ *n* **1** : act or instance of finding **2** : something found — **find·er** *n* — **find·ing** *n* — **find out** *vb* : learn, discover, or verify something

fine *n* : money paid as a penalty ~ *vb* **fined; fin·ing** : impose a fine on ~ *adj* **fin·er; -est 1** : free from impurity **2** : small or thin **3** : not coarse **4** : superior in quality or appearance ~ *adv* : finely — **fine·ly** *adv* — **fine·ness** *n*

fin·ery *n, pl* **-er·ies** : showy clothing and jewels

fi·nesse *n* **1** : delicate skill **2** : craftiness — **fi·nesse** *vb*

fin·ger *n* **1** : one of the 5 divisions at the end of the hand and esp. one other than the thumb **2** : something like a finger **3** : part of a glove for a finger ~ *vb* **1** : touch with the fingers **2** : identify as if by pointing — **fin·gered** *adj* — **fin·ger·nail** *n* — **fin·ger·tip** *n*

fin·ger·ling *n* : small fish

fin·ger·print *n* : impression of the pattern of marks on the tip of a finger — **fingerprint** *vb*

fin·icky *adj* : excessively particular in taste or standards

fin·ish *vb* **1** : come or bring to an end **2** : use or dispose of entirely **3** : put a final coat or surface on ~ *n* **1** : end **2** : final treatment given a surface — **fin·ish·er** *n*

fi·nite *adj* : having definite limits

fink *n* : contemptible person

fiord *var of* FJORD

fir *n* : erect evergreen tree or its wood

fire *n* **1** : light or heat and esp. the flame of something burning **2** : destructive burning (as of a house) **3** : enthusiasm **4** : the shooting of weapons ~ *vb* **fired; fir·ing 1** : kindle **2** : stir up or enliven **3** : dismiss from employment **4** : shoot **5** : bake — **fire·bomb** *n or vb* — **fire·fight·er** *n* — **fire·less** *adj* — **fire·proof** *adj or vb* — **fire·wood** *n*

fire·arm *n* : weapon (as a rifle) that works by an explosion of gunpowder

fire·ball *n* **1** : ball of fire **2** : brilliant meteor

fire·boat *n* : boat equipped for fighting fire

fire·box *n* **1** : chamber (as of a furnace) that contains a fire **2** : fire-alarm box

fire·break *n* : cleared land for checking a forest fire

fire·bug *n* : person who deliberately sets destructive fires

fire·crack·er *n* : small firework that makes noise

fire·fly *n* : night-flying beetle that produces a soft light

fire·man *n* **1** : person trained to put out fires **2** : stoker

fire·place *n* : opening made in a chimney to hold an open fire

fire·plug *n* : hydrant

fire·side *n* **1** : place near the fire or hearth **2** : home ~ *adj* : having an informal quality

fire·trap *n* : place apt to catch on fire

fire·work *n* : device that explodes to produce noise or a display of light

¹firm *adj* **1** : securely fixed in place **2** : strong or vigorous **3** : not subject to change **4** : resolute ~ *vb* : make or become firm — **firm·ly** *adv* — **firm·ness** *n*

²firm *n* : business enterprise

fir·ma·ment *n* : sky

first *adj* **1** : being number one **2** : foremost ~ *adv* **1** : before any other **2** : for the first time ~ *n* **1** : number one **2** : one that is first — **first class** *n* — **first–class** *adj or adv* — **first·ly** *adv* — **first–rate** *adj or adv*

first aid *n* : emergency care

first lieutenant *n* : commissioned officer ranking next below a captain

first sergeant *n* **1** : noncommissioned officer serving as the chief assistant to the commander of a military unit **2** : rank in the army below a command sergeant major and in the marine corps below a sergeant major

firth *n* : estuary

fis·cal *adj* : relating to money — **fis·cal·ly** *adv*

fish *n, pl* **fish** *or* **fish·es** : water animal with fins, gills, and usu. scales ~ *vb* **1** : try to catch fish **2** : grope — **fish·er** *n* — **fish·hook** *n* — **fish·ing** *n*

fish·er·man *n* : one who fishes

fish·ery *n, pl* **-er·ies** : fishing business or a place for this

fishy *adj* **fish·i·er; -est 1** : relating to or like fish **2** : questionable

fis·sion *n* : splitting of an atomic nucleus — **fis·sion·able** *adj*

fis·sure *n* : crack

fist *n* : hand doubled up — **fist·ed** *adj* — **fist·ful** *n*

fist·i·cuffs *n pl* : fist fight

¹fit *n* : sudden attack of illness or emotion

²fit *adj* **-tt- 1** : suitable **2** : qualified **3** : sound in body ~ *vb* **-tt- 1** : be suitable to **2** : insert or adjust correctly **3** : make room for **4** : supply or equip **5** : belong ~ *n* : state of fitting or being fitted — **fit·ly** *adv* — **fit·ness** *n* — **fit·ter** *n*

fit·ful *adj* : restless — **fit·ful·ly** *adv*

fit·ting *adj* : suitable ~ *n* : a small part

five *n* **1** : one more than 4 **2** : 5th in a set or series **3** : something having 5 units — **five** *adj or pron*

fix *vb* **1** : attach **2** : establish **3** : make right **4** : prepare **5** : improperly influence ~ *n* **1** : predicament **2** : determination of location — **fix·er** *n*

fix·a·tion *n* : obsessive attachment — **fix·ate** *vb*

fixed *adj* **1** : stationary **2** : settled — **fixed·ly** *adv* — **fixed·ness** *n*

fix·ture *n* : permanent part of something

fizz *vb* : make a hissing sound ~ *n* : effervescence

fiz·zle *vb* **-zled; -zling 1** : fizz **2** : fail ~ *n* : failure

fjord *n* : inlet of the sea between cliffs

flab *n* : flabby flesh

flab·ber·gast *vb* : astound

flab·by *adj* **-bi·er; -est** : not firm — **flab·bi·ness** *n*

flac·cid *adj* : not firm

¹flag *n* : flat stone

²flag *n* **1** : fabric that is a symbol (as of a country) **2**

: something used to signal ~ *vb* **-gg-** : signal with a flag — **flag·pole** *n* — **flag·staff** *n*

³**flag** *vb* **-gg-** : lose strength or spirit

flag·el·late *vb* **-lat·ed; -lat·ing** : whip — **flag·el·la·tion** *n*

flag·on *n* : container for liquids

fla·grant *adj* : conspicuously bad — **fla·grant·ly** *adv*

flag·ship *n* : ship carrying a commander

flag·stone *n* : flag

flail *n* : tool for threshing grain ~ *vb* : beat with or as if with a flail

flair *n* : natural aptitude

flak *n, pl* **flak** **1** : antiaircraft fire **2** : criticism

flake *n* : small flat piece ~ *vb* **flaked; flak·ing** : separate or form into flakes

flam·boy·ant *adj* : showy — **flam·boy·ance** *n* — **flam·boy·ant·ly** *adv*

flame *n* **1** : glowing part of a fire **2** : state of combustion **3** : burning passion — **flame** *vb* — **flam·ing** *adj*

fla·min·go *n, pl* **-gos** : long-legged long-necked tropical water bird

flam·ma·ble *adj* : easily ignited

flange *n* : rim

flank *n* : side of something ~ *vb* **1** : attack or go around the side of **2** : be at the side of

flan·nel *n* : soft napped fabric

flap *n* **1** : slap **2** : something flat that hangs loose ~ *vb* **-pp- 1** : move (wings) up and down **2** : swing back and forth noisily

flap·jack *n* : pancake

flare *vb* **flared; flar·ing** : become suddenly bright or excited ~ *n* : blaze of light

flash *vb* **1** : give off a sudden flame or burst of light **2** : appear or pass suddenly ~ *n* **1** : sudden burst of light or inspiration **2** : instant ~ *adj* : coming suddenly

flash·light *n* : small battery-operated light

flashy *adj* **flash·i·er; -est** : showy — **flash·i·ly** *adv* — **flash·i·ness** *n*

flask *n* : flattened bottle

flat *adj* **-tt- 1** : smooth **2** : broad and thin **3** : definite **4** : uninteresting **5** : deflated **6** : below the true pitch ~ *n* **1** : level surface of land **2** : flat note in music **3** : apartment **4** : deflated tire ~ *adv* **-tt- 1** : exactly **2** : below the true pitch ~ *vb* **-tt-** : make flat — **flat·ly** *adv* — **flat·ness** *n* — **flat·ten** *vb*

flat·car *n* : railroad car without sides

flat·fish *n* : flattened fish with both eyes on the upper side

flat·foot *n, pl* **flat·feet** : foot condition in which the arch is flattened — **flat–foot·ed** *adj*

flat–out *adj* **1** : being maximum effort or speed **2** : downright

flat·ter *vb* **1** : praise insincerely **2** : judge or represent too favorably — **flat·ter·er** *n* — **flat·tery** *n*

flat·u·lent *adj* : full of gas — **flat·u·lence** *n*

flat·ware *n* : eating utensils

flaunt *vb* : display ostentatiously — **flaunt** *n*

fla·vor *n* **1** : quality that affects the sense of taste **2** : something that adds flavor ~ *vb* : give flavor to — **fla·vor·ful** *adj* — **fla·vor·ing** *n* — **fla·vor·less** *adj*

flaw *n* : fault — **flaw·less** *adj* — **flaw·less·ly** *adv* — **flaw·less·ness** *n*

flax *n* : plant from which linen is made

flax·en *adj* : made of or like flax

flay *vb* **1** : strip off the skin of **2** : criticize harshly

flea *n* : leaping bloodsucking insect

fleck *vb or n* : streak or spot

fledg·ling *n* : young bird

flee *vb* **fled ; flee·ing** : run away

fleece *n* : sheep's wool ~ *vb* **fleeced; fleec·ing 1** : shear **2** : get money from dishonestly — **fleecy** *adj*

¹**fleet** *vb* : pass rapidly ~ *adj* : swift — **fleet·ing** *adj* — **fleet·ness** *n*

²**fleet** *n* : group of ships

fleet admiral *n* : commissioned officer of the highest rank in the navy

flesh *n* **1** : soft parts of an animal's body **2** : soft plant tissue (as fruit pulp) — **fleshed** *adj* — **flesh out** *vb* : make fuller — **fleshy** *adj*

flesh·ly *adj* : sensual

flew *past of* FLY

flex *vb* : bend

flex·i·ble *adj* **1** : capable of being flexed **2** : adaptable — **flex·i·bil·i·ty** *n* — **flex·i·bly** *adv*

flick *n* : light jerky stroke ~ *vb* **1** : strike lightly **2** : flutter

flick·er *vb* **1** : waver **2** : burn unsteadily ~ *n* **1** : sudden movement **2** : wavering light

fli·er *n* **1** : aviator **2** : advertising circular

¹**flight** *n* **1** : act or instance of flying **2** : ability to fly **3** : a passing through air or space **4** : series of stairs — **flight·less** *adj*

²**flight** *n* : act or instance of running away

flighty *adj* **flight·i·er; -est** : capricious or silly — **flight·i·ness** *n*

flim·flam *n* : trickery

flim·sy *adj* **-si·er; -est 1** : not strong or well made **2** : not believable — **flim·si·ly** *adv* — **flim·si·ness** *n*

flinch *vb* : shrink from pain

fling *vb* **flung ; fling·ing 1** : move brusquely **2** : throw ~ *n* **1** : act or instance of flinging **2** : attempt **3** : period of self-indulgence

flint *n* : hard quartz that gives off sparks when struck with steel — **flinty** *adj*

flip *vb* **-pp- 1** : cause to turn over quickly or many times **2** : move with a quick push ~ *adj* : insolent — **flip** *n*

flip·pant *adj* : not serious enough — **flip·pan·cy** *n*

flip·per *n* : paddlelike limb (as of a seal) for swimming

flirt *vb* **1** : be playfully romantic **2** : show casual interest ~ *n* : one who flirts — **flir·ta·tion** *n* — **flir·ta·tious** *adj*

flit *vb* **-tt-** : dart

float *n* **1** : something that floats **2** : vehicle carrying an exhibit ~ *vb* **1** : rest on or in a fluid without sinking **2** : wander **3** : finance by issuing stock or bonds — **float·er** *n*

flock *n* : group of animals (as birds) or people ~ *vb* : gather or move as a group

floe *n* : mass of floating ice

flog *vb* **-gg-** : beat with a rod or whip — **flog·ger** *n*

flood *n* **1** : great flow of water over the land **2** : overwhelming volume ~ *vb* : cover or fill esp. with water — **flood·wa·ter** *n*

floor *n* **1** : bottom of a room on which one stands **2** : story of a building **3** : lower limit ~ *vb* **1** : furnish with a floor **2** : knock down **3** : amaze — **floor·board** *n* — **floor·ing** *n*

floo·zy, floo·zie *n, pl* **-zies** : promiscuous young woman

flop *vb* **-pp- 1** : flap **2** : slump heavily **3** : fail — **flop** *n*

flop·py *adj* **-pi·er; -est** : soft and flexible

flo·ra *n* : plants or plant life of a region

flo·ral *adj* : relating to flowers

flor·id *adj* **1** : very flowery in style **2** : reddish

flo·rist *n* : flower dealer

floss *n* **1** : soft thread for embroidery **2** : thread used to clean between teeth — **floss** *vb*

flo·ta·tion *n* : process or instance of floating

flo·til·la *n* : small fleet

flot·sam *n* : floating wreckage

¹**flounce** *vb* **flounced; flounc·ing** : move with exaggerated jerky motions — **flounce** *n*

²**flounce** *n* : fabric border or wide ruffle

¹**floun·der** *n, pl* **flounder** *or* **flounders** : flatfish

²**flounder** *vb* **1** : struggle for footing **2** : proceed clumsily

flour *n* : finely ground meal ~ *vb* : coat with flour — **floury** *adj*

flour·ish *vb* **1** : thrive **2** : wave threateningly ~ *n* **1** : embellishment **2** : fanfare **3** : wave **4** : showiness of action

flout *vb* : treat with disdain

flow *vb* **1** : move in a stream **2** : proceed smoothly and readily ~ *n* : uninterrupted stream

flow·er *n* **1** : showy plant shoot that bears seeds **2** : state of flourishing ~ *vb* **1** : produce flowers **2** : flourish — **flow·ered** *adj* — **flow·er·i·ness** *n* — **flow·er·less** *adj* — **flow·er·pot** *n* — **flow·ery** *adj*

flown *past part of* FLY

flu *n* **1** : influenza **2** : minor virus ailment

flub *vb* **-bb-** : bungle — **flub** *n*

fluc·tu·ate *vb* **-at·ed; -at·ing** : change rapidly esp. up and down — **fluc·tu·a·tion** *n*

flue *n* : smoke duct

flu·ent *adj* : speaking with ease — **flu·en·cy** *n* — **flu·ent·ly** *adv*

fluff *n* **1** : something soft and light **2** : blunder ~ *vb* **1** : make fluffy **2** : make a mistake — **fluffy** *adj*

flu·id *adj* : flowing ~ *n* : substance that can flow — **flu·id·i·ty** *n* — **flu·id·ly** *adv*

fluid ounce *n* : unit of liquid measure equal to $\frac{1}{16}$ pint

fluke *n* : stroke of luck

flume *n* : channel for water

flung *past of* FLING

flunk *vb* : fail in school work

flun·ky, flun·key *n, pl* **-kies** *or* **keys** : lackey

flu·o·res·cence *n* : emission of light after initial absorption — **flu·o·resce** *vb* — **flu·o·res·cent** *adj*

flu·o·ri·date *vb* **-dat·ed; -dat·ing** : add fluoride to — **flu·o·ri·da·tion** *n*

flu·o·ride *n* : compound of fluorine

flu·o·rine *n* : toxic gaseous chemical element

flu·o·ro·car·bon *n* : compound containing fluorine and carbon

flu·o·ro·scope *n* : instrument for internal examination — **flu·o·ro·scop·ic** *adj* — **flu·o·ros·co·py** *n*

flur·ry *n, pl* **-ries 1** : light snowfall **2** : bustle **3** : brief burst of activity — **flurry** *vb*

¹**flush** *vb* : cause (a bird) to fly from cover

²**flush** *n* **1** : sudden flow (as of water) **2** : surge of emotion **3** : blush ~ *vb* **1** : blush **2** : wash out with a rush of liquid ~ *adj* **1** : filled to overflowing **2** : of a reddish healthy color **3** : smooth or level **4** : abutting — **flush** *adv*

³**flush** *n* : cards of the same suit

flus·ter *vb* : upset — **fluster** *n*

flute *n* **1** : pipelike musical instrument **2** : groove — **flut·ed** *adj* — **flut·ing** *n* — **flut·ist** *n*

flut·ter *vb* **1** : flap the wings rapidly **2** : move with quick wavering or flapping motions **3** : behave in an agitated manner ~ *n* **1** : a fluttering **2** : state of confusion — **flut·tery** *adj*

flux *n* : state of continuous change

¹**fly** *vb* **flew ; flown ; fly·ing 1** : move through the air with wings **2** : float or soar **3** : flee **4** : move or pass swiftly **5** : operate an airplane

²**fly** *n, pl* **flies** : garment closure

³**fly** *n, pl* **flies** : winged insect

fly·er *var of* FLIER

fly·pa·per *n* : sticky paper for catching flies

fly·speck *n* **1** : speck of fly dung **2** : something tiny

fly·wheel *n* : rotating wheel that regulates the speed of machinery

foal *n* : young horse — **foal** *vb*

foam *n* **1** : mass of bubbles on top of a liquid **2** : material of cellular form ~ *vb* : form foam — **foamy** *adj*

fob *n* : short chain for a pocket watch

fo'•c'sle *var of* FORECASTLE

fo•cus *n, pl* **-ci 1** : point at which reflected or refracted rays meet **2** : adjustment (as of eyeglasses) for clear vision **3** : central point ~ *vb* : bring to a focus — **fo•cal** *adj* — **fo•cal•ly** *adv*

fod•der *n* : food for livestock

foe *n* : enemy

fog *n* **1** : fine particles of water suspended near the ground **2** : mental confusion ~ *vb* **-gg-** : obscure or be obscured with fog — **fog•gy** *adj*

fog•horn *n* : warning horn sounded in a fog

fo•gy *n, pl* **-gies** : person with old-fashioned ideas

foi•ble *n* : minor character fault

¹foil *vb* : defeat ~ *n* : light fencing sword

²foil *n* **1** : thin sheet of metal **2** : one that sets off another by contrast

foist *vb* : force another to accept

¹fold *n* **1** : enclosure for sheep **2** : group with a common interest

²fold *vb* **1** : lay one part over another **2** : embrace ~ *n* : part folded

fold•er *n* **1** : one that folds **2** : circular **3** : folded cover or envelope for papers

fol•de•rol *n* : nonsense

fo•liage *n* : plant leaves

fo•lio *n, pl* **-li•os** : sheet of paper folded once

folk *n, pl* **folk** *or* **folks 1** : people in general **2** *folks pl* : one's family ~ *adj* : relating to the common people

folk•lore *n* : customs and traditions of a people — **folk•lor•ist** *n*

folksy *adj* **folks•i•er; -est** : friendly and informal

fol•li•cle *n* : small anatomical cavity or gland

fol•low *vb* **1** : go or come after **2** : pursue **3** : obey **4** : proceed along **5** : keep one's attention fixed on **6** : result from — **fol•low•er** *n*

fol•low•ing *adj* : next ~ *n* : group of followers ~ *prep* : after

fol•ly *n, pl* **-lies** : foolishness

fo•ment *vb* : incite

fond *adj* **1** : strongly attracted **2** : affectionate **3** : dear — **fond•ly** *adv* — **fond•ness** *n*

fon•dle *vb* **-dled; -dling** : touch lovingly

fon•due *n* : preparation of melted cheese

font *n* **1** : baptismal basin **2** : fountain

food *n* : material eaten to sustain life

fool *n* **1** : stupid person **2** : jester ~ *vb* **1** : waste time **2** : meddle **3** : deceive — **fool•ery** *n* — **fool•ish** *adj* — **fool•ish•ly** *adv* — **fool•ish•ness** *n* — **fool•proof** *adj*

fool•har•dy *adj* : rash — **fool•har•di•ness** *n*

foot *n, pl* **feet 1** : end part of a leg **2** : unit of length equal to ⅓ yard **3** : unit of verse meter **4** : bottom — **foot•age** *n* — **foot•ed** *adj* — **foot•path** *n* — **foot•print** *n* — **foot•race** *n* — **foot•rest** *n* — **foot•wear** *n*

foot•ball *n* : ball game played by 2 teams on a rectangular field

foot•bridge *n* : bridge for pedestrians

foot•hill *n* : hill at the foot of higher hills

foot•hold *n* : support for the feet

foot•ing *n* **1** : foothold **2** : basis

foot•lights *n pl* : stage lights along the floor

foot•lock•er *n* : small trunk

foot•loose *adj* : having no ties

foot•man *n* : male servant

foot•note *n* : note at the bottom of a page

foot•step *n* **1** : step **2** : distance covered by a step **3** : footprint

foot•stool *n* : stool to support the feet

foot•work *n* : skillful movement of the feet (as in boxing)

fop *n* : dandy — **fop•pery** *n* — **fop•pish** *adj*

for *prep* **1** — used to show preparation or purpose **2** : because of **3** — used to show a recipient **4** : in support of **5** : so as to support or help cure **6** : so as to be equal to **7** : concerning **8** : through the period of ~ *conj* : because

for•age *n* : food for animals ~ *vb* **-aged; -ag•ing 1** : hunt food **2** : search for provisions

for•ay *n or vb* : raid

¹for•bear *vb* **-bore ; -borne ; -bear•ing 1** : refrain from **2** : be patient — **for•bear•ance** *n*

²forbear *var of* FOREBEAR

for•bid *vb* **-bade** *or* **-bad ; -bid•den ; -bid•ding 1** : prohibit **2** : order not to do something

for•bid•ding *adj* : tending to discourage

force *n* **1** : exceptional strength or energy **2** : military strength **3** : body (as of persons) available for a purpose **4** : violence **5** : influence (as a push or pull) that causes motion ~ *vb* **forced; forc•ing 1** : compel **2** : gain against resistance **3** : break open — **force•ful** *adj* — **force•ful•ly** *adv* — **in force 1** : in great numbers **2** : valid

for•ceps *n, pl* **forceps** : surgical instrument for grasping objects

forc•ible *adj* **1** : done by force **2** : showing force — **forc•i•bly** *adv*

ford *n* : place to wade across a stream ~ *vb* : wade across

fore *adv* : in or toward the front ~ *adj* : being or coming before in time, place, or order ~ *n* : front

fore–and–aft *adj* : lengthwise

fore•arm *n* : part of the arm between the elbow and the wrist

fore•bear *n* : ancestor

fore•bod•ing *n* : premonition of disaster — **fore•bod•ing** *adj*

fore•cast *vb* **-cast; -cast•ing** : predict — **forecast** *n* — **fore•cast•er** *n*

fore•cas•tle *n* : forward part of a ship

fore•close *vb* : take legal measures to terminate a mortgage — **fore•clo•sure** *n*

fore•fa•ther *n* : ancestor

fore•fin•ger *n* : finger next to the thumb

fore•foot *n* : front foot of a quadruped

fore•front *n* : foremost position or place

¹fore•go *vb* **-went; -gone; -go•ing** : precede

²forego *var of* FORGO

fore•go•ing *adj* : preceding

fore•gone *adj* : determined in advance

fore•ground *n* : part of a scene nearest the viewer

fore•hand *n* : stroke (as in tennis) made with the palm of the hand turned forward — **fore•hand** *adj*

fore•head *n* : part of the face above the eyes

for•eign *adj* **1** : situated outside a place or country and esp. one's own country **2** : belonging to a different place or country **3** : not pertinent **4** : related to or dealing with other nations — **for•eign•er** *n*

fore•know *vb* **-knew; -known; -know•ing** : know beforehand — **fore•knowl•edge** *n*

fore•leg *n* : front leg

fore•lock *n* : front lock of hair

fore•man *n* **1** : spokesman of a jury **2** : workman in charge

fore•most *adj* : first in time, place, or order — **foremost** *adv*

fore•noon *n* : morning

fo•ren•sic *adj* : relating to courts or public speaking or debate

fo•ren•sics *n pl* : art or study of speaking or debating

fore•or•dain *vb* : decree beforehand

fore•quar•ter *n* : front half on one side of the body of a quadruped

fore•run•ner *n* : one that goes before

fore•see *vb* **-saw; -seen; -see•ing** : see or realize beforehand — **fore•see•able** *adj*

fore•shad•ow *vb* : hint or suggest beforehand

fore•sight *n* : care or provision for the future — **fore•sight•ed** *adj* — **fore•sight•ed•ness** *n*

for•est *n* : large thick growth of trees and underbrush — **for•est•ed** *adj* — **for•est•er** *n* — **for•est•land** *n* — **for•est•ry** *n*

fore•stall *vb* : prevent by acting in advance

foreswear *var of* FORSWEAR

fore•taste *n* : advance indication or notion ~ *vb* : anticipate

fore•tell *vb* **-told; -tell•ing** : predict

fore•thought *n* : foresight

for•ev•er *adv* **1** : for a limitless time **2** : always

for•ev•er•more *adv* : forever

fore•warn *vb* : warn beforehand

fore•word *n* : preface

for•feit *n* : something forfeited ~ *vb* : lose or lose the right to by an error or crime — **for•fei•ture** *n*

¹forge *n* : smithy ~ *vb* **forged; forg•ing 1** : form (metal) by heating and hammering **2** : imitate falsely esp. to defraud — **forg•er** *n* — **forg•ery** *n*

²forge *vb* **forged; forg•ing** : move ahead steadily

for•get *vb* **-got ; -got•ten** *or* **-got; -get•ting 1** : be unable to think of or recall **2** : fail to think of at the proper time — **for•get•ta•ble** *adj* — **for•get•ful** *adj* — **for•get•ful•ly** *adv*

forget–me–not *n* : small herb with blue or white flowers

for•give *vb* **-gave ; -giv•en ; -giv•ing** : pardon — **for•giv•able** *adj* — **for•give•ness** *n*

for•giv•ing *adj* **1** : able to forgive **2** : allowing room for error or weakness

for•go, fore•go *vb* **-went; -gone; -go•ing** : do without

fork *n* **1** : implement with prongs for lifting, holding, or digging **2** : forked part **3** : a dividing into branches or a place where something branches ~ *vb* **1** : divide into branches **2** : move with a fork — **forked** *adj*

fork•lift *n* : machine for lifting with steel fingers

for•lorn *adj* **1** : deserted **2** : wretched — **for•lorn•ly** *adv*

form *n* **1** : shape **2** : set way of doing or saying something **3** : document with blanks to be filled in **4** : manner of performing with respect to what is expected **5** : mold **6** : kind or variety **7** : one of the ways in which a word is changed to show difference in use ~ *vb* **1** : give form or shape to **2** : train **3** : develop **4** : constitute — **for•ma•tive** *adj* — **form•less** *adj*

for•mal *adj* : following established custom ~ *n* : formal social event — **for•mal•i•ty** *n* — **for•mal•ize** *vb* — **for•mal•ly** *adv*

form•al•de•hyde *n* : colorless pungent gas used as a preservative and disinfectant

for•mat *n* : general style or arrangement of something — **format** *vb*

for•ma•tion *n* **1** : a giving form to something **2** : something formed **3** : arrangement

for•mer *adj* : coming before in time — **for•mer•ly** *adv*

for•mi•da•ble *adj* **1** : causing fear or dread **2** : very difficult — **for•mi•da•bly** *adv*

for•mu•la *n, pl* **-las** *or* **-lae 1** : set form of words for ceremonial use **2** : recipe **3** : milk mixture for a baby **4** : group of symbols or figures briefly expressing information **5** : set form or method

for•mu•late *vb* **-lat•ed; -lat•ing** : design, devise — **for•mu•la•tion** *n*

for•ni•ca•tion *n* : illicit sexual intercourse — **for•ni•cate** *vb* — **for•ni•ca•tor** *n*

for•sake *vb* **-sook ; -sak•en ; -sak•ing** : renounce completely

for•swear *vb* **-swore; -sworn; -swear•ing 1** : renounce under oath **2** : perjure

for•syth•ia *n* : shrub grown for its yellow flowers

fort *n* **1** : fortified place **2** : permanent army post

forte *n* : something at which a person excels

forth *adv* : forward

forth•com•ing *adj* **1** : coming or available soon **2** : open and direct

forth•right *adj* : direct — **forth•right•ly** *adv* — **forth•right•ness** *n*

forth•with *adv* : immediately

for·ti·fy *vb* **-fied; -fy·ing** : make strong — **for·ti·fi·ca·tion** *n*

for·ti·tude *n* : ability to endure

fort·night *n* : 2 weeks — **fort·night·ly** *adj or adv*

for·tress *n* : strong fort

for·tu·itous *adj* : accidental

for·tu·nate *adj* **1** : coming by good luck **2** : lucky — **for·tu·nate·ly** *adv*

for·tune *n* **1** : prosperity attained partly through luck **2** : good or bad luck **3** : destiny **4** : wealth

for·tune–tell·er *n* : one who foretells a person's future — **for·tune–tell·ing** *n or adj*

for·ty *n, pl* **forties** : 4 times 10 — **for·ti·eth** *adj or n* — **forty** *adj or pron*

fo·rum *n, pl* **-rums 1** : Roman marketplace **2** : medium for open discussion

for·ward *adj* **1** : being near or at or belonging to the front **2** : brash ~ *adv* : toward what is in front ~ *n* : player near the front of his team ~ *vb* **1** : help onward **2** : send on — **for·ward·er** *n* — **for·ward·ness** *n*

for·wards *adv* : forward

fos·sil *n* : preserved trace of an ancient plant or animal ~ *adj* : being or originating from a fossil — **fos·sil·ize** *vb*

fos·ter *adj* : being, having, or relating to substitute parents ~ *vb* : help to grow or develop

fought *past of* FIGHT

foul *adj* **1** : offensive **2** : clogged with dirt **3** : abusive **4** : wet and stormy **5** : unfair ~ *n* : a breaking of the rules in a game ~ *adv* : foully ~ *vb* **1** : make or become foul or filthy **2** : tangle — **foul·ly** *adv* — **foul·mouthed** *adj* — **foul·ness** *n*

fou·lard *n* : lightweight silk

foul–up *n* : error or state of confusion — **foul up** *vb* : bungle

¹found *past of* FIND

²found *vb* : establish — **found·er** *n*

foun·da·tion *n* **1** : act of founding **2** : basis for something **3** : endowed institution **4** : supporting structure — **foun·da·tion·al** *adj*

foun·der *vb* : sink

found·ling *n* : abandoned infant that is found

found·ry *n, pl* **-dries** : place where metal is cast

fount *n* : fountain

foun·tain *n* **1** : spring of water **2** : source **3** : artificial jet of water

four *n* **1** : one more than 3 **2** : 4th in a set or series **3** : something having 4 units — **four** *adj or pron*

four·fold *adj* : quadruple — **four·fold** *adv*

four·score *adj* : 80

four·some *n* : group of 4

four·teen *n* : one more than 13 — **fourteen** *adj or pron* — **four·teenth** *adj or n*

fourth *n* **1** : one that is 4th **2** : one of 4 equal parts of something — **fourth** *adj or adv*

fowl *n, pl* **fowl** *or* **fowls 1** : bird **2** : chicken

fox *n, pl* **fox·es 1** : small mammal related to wolves **2** : clever person ~ *vb* : trick — **foxy** *adj*

fox·glove *n* : flowering plant that provides digitalis

fox·hole *n* : pit for protection against enemy fire

foy·er *n* : entrance hallway

fra·cas *n, pl* **-cas·es** : brawl

frac·tion *n* **1** : number indicating one or more equal parts of a whole **2** : portion — **frac·tion·al** *adj* — **frac·tion·al·ly** *adv*

frac·tious *adj* : hard to control

frac·ture *n* : a breaking of something — **fracture** *vb*

frag·ile *adj* : easily broken — **fra·gil·i·ty** *n*

frag·ment *n* : part broken off ~ *vb* : break into parts — **frag·men·tary** *adj* — **frag·men·ta·tion** *n*

fra·grant *adj* : sweet-smelling — **fra·grance** *n* — **fra·grant·ly** *adv*

frail *adj* : weak or delicate — **frail·ty** *n*

frame *vb* **framed; fram·ing 1** : plan **2** : formulate **3** : construct or arrange **4** : enclose in a frame **5** : make appear guilty ~ *n* **1** : makeup of the body **2** : supporting or enclosing structure **3** : state or disposition (as of mind) — **frame·work** *n*

franc *n* : monetary unit (as of France)

fran·chise *n* **1** : special privilege **2** : the right to vote — **fran·chi·see** *n*

fran·gi·ble *adj* : breakable — **fran·gi·bil·i·ty** *n*

¹frank *adj* : direct and sincere — **frank·ly** *adv* — **frank·ness** *n*

²frank *vb* : mark (mail) with a sign showing it can be mailed free ~ *n* : sign on franked mail

frank·furt·er , frank·furt *n* : cooked sausage

frank·in·cense *n* : incense resin

fran·tic *adj* : wildly excited — **fran·ti·cal·ly** *adv*

fra·ter·nal *adj* **1** : brotherly **2** : of a fraternity — **fra·ter·nal·ly** *adv*

fra·ter·ni·ty *n, pl* **-ties** : men's student social group

frat·er·nize *vb* **-nized; -niz·ing 1** : mingle as friends **2** : associate with members of a hostile group — **frat·er·ni·za·tion** *n*

frat·ri·cide *n* : killing of a sibling — **frat·ri·cid·al** *adj*

fraud *n* : trickery — **fraud·u·lent** *adj* — **fraud·u·lent·ly** *adv*

fraught *adj* : full of or accompanied by something specified

¹fray *n* : fight

²fray *vb* **1** : wear by rubbing **2** : separate the threads of **3** : irritate

fraz·zle *vb* **-zled; -zling** : wear out ~ *n* : exhaustion

freak *n* **1** : something abnormal or unusual **2** : enthusiast — **freak·ish** *adj* — **freak out** *vb* **1** : experience nightmarish hallucinations from drugs **2** : distress or become distressed

freck·le *n* : brown spot on the skin — **freckle** *vb*

free *adj* **fre·er; fre·est 1** : having liberty or independence **2** : not taxed **3** : given without charge **4** : voluntary **5** : not in use **6** : not fastened ~ *adv* : without charge ~ *vb* **freed; free·ing** : set free — **free** *adv* — **free·born** *adj* — **free·dom** *n* — **free·ly** *adv*

free·boo·ter *n* : pirate

free–for–all *n* : fight with no rules

free·load *vb* : live off another's generosity — **free·load·er** *n*

free·stand·ing *adj* : standing without support

free·way *n* : expressway

free will *n* : independent power to choose — **free·will** *adj*

freeze *vb* **froze ; fro·zen ; freez·ing 1** : harden into ice **2** : become chilled **3** : damage by frost **4** : stick fast **5** : become motionless **6** : fix at one stage or level ~ *n* **1** : very cold weather **2** : state of being frozen — **freez·er** *n*

freeze–dry *vb* : preserve by freezing then drying — **freeze–dried** *adj*

freight *n* **1** : carrying of goods or payment for this **2** : shipped goods ~ *vb* : load or ship goods — **freigh·ter** *n*

french fry *vb* : fry in deep fat — **french fry** *n*

fre·net·ic *adj* : frantic — **fre·net·i·cal·ly** *adv*

fren·zy *n, pl* **-zies** : violent agitation — **fren·zied** *adj*

fre·quen·cy *n, pl* **-cies 1** : frequent or regular occurrence **2** : number of cycles or sound waves per second

fre·quent *adj* : happening often ~ *vb* : go to habitually — **fre·quent·er** *n* — **fre·quent·ly** *adv*

fres·co *n, pl* **-coes** : painting on fresh plaster

fresh *adj* **1** : not salt **2** : pure **3** : not preserved **4** : not stale **5** : like new **6** : insolent — **fres·hen** *vb* — **fresh·ly** *adv* — **fresh·ness** *n*

fresh·et *n* : overflowing stream

fresh·man *n* : first-year student

fresh·wa·ter *n* : water that is not salty

fret *vb* **-tt- 1** : worry or become irritated **2** : fray **3** : agitate ~ *n* **1** : worn spot **2** : irritation — **fret·ful** *adj* — **fret·ful·ly** *adv* — **fret·ful·ness** *n*

fri·a·ble *adj* : easily pulverized

fri·ar *n* : member of a religious order

fri·ary *n, pl* **-ar·ies** : monastery of friars

fric·as·see *n* : meat stewed in a gravy ~ *vb* **-seed; -see·ing** : stew in gravy

fric·tion *n* **1** : a rubbing between 2 surfaces **2** : clash of opinions — **fric·tion·al** *adj*

Fri·day *n* : 6th day of the week

friend *n* : person one likes — **friend·less** *adj* — **friend·li·ness** *n* — **friend·ly** *adj* — **friend·ship** *n*

frieze *n* : ornamental band around a room

frig·ate *n* : warship smaller than a destroyer

fright *n* : sudden fear — **frigh·ten** *vb* — **fright·ful** *adj* — **fright·ful·ly** *adv* — **fright·ful·ness** *n*

frig·id *adj* : intensely cold — **fri·gid·i·ty** *n*

frill *n* **1** : ruffle **2** : pleasing but nonessential addition — **frilly** *adj*

fringe *n* **1** : ornamental border of short hanging threads or strips **2** : edge — **fringe** *vb*

frisk *vb* **1** : leap about **2** : search (a person) esp. for weapons

frisky *adj* **frisk·i·er; -est** : playful — **frisk·i·ly** *adv* — **frisk·i·ness** *n*

¹frit·ter *n* : fried batter containing fruit or meat

²fritter *vb* : waste little by little

friv·o·lous *adj* : not important or serious — **fri·vol·i·ty** *n* — **friv·o·lous·ly** *adv*

frizz *vb* : curl tightly — **frizz** *n* — **frizzy** *adj*

fro *adv* : away

frock *n* **1** : loose outer garment **2** : dress

frog *n* **1** : leaping amphibian **2** : hoarseness **3** : ornamental braid fastener **4** : small holder for flowers

frog·man *n* : underwater swimmer

frol·ic *vb* **-icked; -ick·ing** : romp ~ *n* : fun — **frol·ic·some** *adj*

from *prep* — used to show a starting point

frond *n* : fern or palm leaf

front *n* **1** : face **2** : behavior **3** : main side of a building **4** : forward part **5** : boundary between air masses ~ *vb* **1** : have the main side adjacent to something **2** : serve as a front — **fron·tal** *adj*

front·age *n* : length of boundary line on a street

fron·tier *n* : outer edge of settled territory — **fron·tiers·man** *n*

fron·tis·piece *n* : illustration facing a title page

frost *n* **1** : freezing temperature **2** : ice crystals on a surface ~ *vb* **1** : cover with frost **2** : put icing on (a cake) — **frosty** *adj*

frost·bite *n* : partial freezing of part of the body — **frost·bit·ten** *adj*

frost·ing *n* : icing

froth *n, pl* **froths** : bubbles on a liquid — **frothy** *adj*

fro·ward *adj* : willful

frown *vb or n* : scowl

frow·sy, frow·zy *adj* **-si·er** *or* **-zi·er; -est** : untidy

froze *past of* FREEZE

frozen *past part of* FREEZE

fru·gal *adj* : thrifty — **fru·gal·i·ty** *n* — **fru·gal·ly** *adv*

fruit *n* **1** : usu. edible and sweet part of a seed plant **2** : result ~ *vb* : bear fruit — **fruit·cake** *n* — **fruit·ed** *adj* — **fruit·ful** *adj* — **fruit·ful·ness** *n* — **fruit·less** *adj* — **fruit·less·ly** *adv* — **fruity** *adj*

fru·ition *n* : completion

frumpy *adj* **frump·i·er; -est** : dowdy

frus·trate *vb* **-trat·ed; -trat·ing 1** : block **2** : cause to fail — **frus·trat·ing·ly** *adv* — **frus·tra·tion** *n*

¹fry *vb* **fried; fry·ing 1** : cook esp. with fat or oil **2** : be cooked by frying ~ *n, pl* **fries 1** : something fried **2** : social gathering with fried food

²**fry** *n, pl* **fry** : recently hatched fish

fud·dle *vb* **-dled; -dling** : muddle

fud·dy-dud·dy *n, pl* **-dies** : one who is old-fashioned or unimaginative

fudge *vb* **fudged; fudg·ing** : cheat or exaggerate ~ *n* : creamy candy

fu·el *n* : material burned to produce heat or power ~ *vb* **-eled** *or* **-elled; -el·ing** *or* **-el·ling** : provide with or take in fuel

fu·gi·tive *adj* **1** : running away or trying to escape **2** : not lasting — **fugitive** *n*

-ful *adj suffix* **1** : full of **2** : having the qualities of **3** : -able ~ *n suffix* : quantity that fills

ful·crum *n, pl* **-crums** *or* **-cra** : support on which a lever turns

ful·fill, ful·fil *vb* **-filled; -fill·ing 1** : perform **2** : satisfy — **ful·fill·ment** *n*

¹**full** *adj* **1** : filled **2** : complete **3** : rounded **4** : having an abundance of something ~ *adv* : entirely ~ *n* : utmost degree — **full·ness** *n* — **ful·ly** *adv*

²**full** *vb* : shrink and thicken woolen cloth — **full·er** *n*

full-fledged *adj* : fully developed

ful·some *adj* : copious verging on excessive

fum·ble *vb* **-bled; -bling** : fail to hold something properly — **fumble** *n*

fume *n* : irritating gas ~ *vb* **fumed; fum·ing 1** : give off fumes **2** : show annoyance

fu·mi·gate *vb* **-gat·ed; -gat·ing** : treat with pest-killing fumes — **fu·mi·gant** *n* — **fu·mi·ga·tion** *n*

fun *n* **1** : something providing amusement or enjoyment **2** : enjoyment ~ *adj* : full of fun

func·tion *n* **1** : special purpose **2** : formal ceremony or social affair ~ *vb* : have or carry on a function — **func·tion·al** *adj* — **func·tion·al·ly** *adv*

func·tion·ary *n, pl* **-ar·ies** : official

fund *n* **1** : store **2** : sum of money intended for a special purpose **3** *pl* : available money ~ *vb* : provide funds for

fun·da·men·tal *adj* **1** : basic **2** : of central importance or necessity — **fundamental** *n* — **fun·da·men·tal·ly** *adv*

fu·ner·al *n* : ceremony for a dead person — **funeral** *adj* — **fu·ne·re·al** *adj*

fun·gi·cide *n* : agent that kills fungi — **fun·gi·cid·al** *adj*

fun·gus *n, pl* **fun·gi** : lower plant that lacks chlorophyll — **fun·gal** *adj* — **fun·gous** *adj*

funk *n* : state of depression

funky *adj* **funk·i·er; -est** : unconventional and unsophisticated

fun·nel *n* **1** : cone-shaped utensil with a tube for directing the flow of a liquid **2** : ship's smokestack ~ *vb* **-neled; -nel·ing** : move to a central point or into a central channel

fun·nies *n pl* : section of comic strips

fun·ny *adj* **-ni·er; -est 1** : amusing **2** : strange

fur *n* **1** : hairy coat of a mammal **2** : article of clothing made with fur — **fur** *adj* — **furred** *adj* — **fur·ry** *adj*

fur·bish *vb* : make lustrous or new looking

fu·ri·ous *adj* : fierce or angry — **fu·ri·ous·ly** *adv*

fur·long *n* : a unit of distance equal to 220 yards

fur·lough *n* : authorized absence from duty — **furlough** *vb*

fur·nace *n* : enclosed structure in which heat is produced

fur·nish *vb* **1** : provide with what is needed **2** : make available for use

fur·nish·ings *n pl* **1** : articles or accessories of dress **2** : furniture

fur·ni·ture *n* : movable articles for a room

fu·ror *n* **1** : anger **2** : sensational craze

fur·ri·er *n* : dealer in furs

fur·row *n* **1** : trench made by a plow **2** : wrinkle or groove — **furrow** *vb*

fur·ther *adv* **1** : at or to a more advanced point **2** : more ~ *adj* : additional ~ *vb* : promote — **fur·ther·ance** *n*

fur·ther·more *adv* : in addition

fur·ther·most *adj* : most distant

fur·thest *adv or adj* : farthest

fur·tive *adj* : slyly or secretly done — **fur·tive·ly** *adv* — **fur·tive·ness** *n*

fu·ry *n, pl* **-ries 1** : intense rage **2** : violence

¹**fuse** *n* **1** : cord lighted to transmit fire to an explosive **2** *usu* **fuze** : device for exploding a charge ~, **fuze** *vb* **fused** *or* **fuzed; fus·ing** *or* **fuz·ing** : equip with a fuse

²**fuse** *vb* **fused; fus·ing 1** : melt and run together **2** : unite ~ *n* : electrical safety device — **fus·ible** *adj*

fu·se·lage *n* : main body of an aircraft

fu·sil·lade *n* : volley of fire

fu·sion *n* **1** : process of merging by melting **2** : union of atomic nuclei

fuss *n* **1** : needless bustle or excitement **2** : show of attention **3** : objection or protest ~ *vb* : make a fuss

fuss·bud·get *n* : one who fusses or is fussy about trifles

fussy *adj* **fuss·i·er; -est 1** : irritable **2** : paying very close attention to details — **fuss·i·ly** *adv* — **fuss·i·ness** *n*

fu·tile *adj* : useless or vain — **fu·til·i·ty** *n*

fu·ture *adj* : coming after the present ~ *n* **1** : time yet to come **2** : what will happen — **fu·tur·is·tic** *adj*

fuze *var of* FUSE

fuzz *n* : fine particles or fluff

fuzzy *adj* **fuzz·i·er; -est 1** : covered with or like fuzz **2** : indistinct — **fuzz·i·ness** *n*

-fy *vb suffix* : make — **-fi·er** *n suffix*

G

g *n, pl* **g's** *or* **gs 1** : 7th letter of the alphabet **2** : unit of gravitational force

gab *vb* **-bb-** : chatter — **gab** *n* — **gab·by** *adj*

gab·ar·dine *n* : durable twilled fabric

ga·ble *n* : triangular part of the end of a building — **ga·bled** *adj*

gad *vb* **-dd-** : roam about — **gad·der** *n*

gad·fly *n* : persistently critical person

gad·get *n* : device — **gad·get·ry** *n*

gaff *n* : metal hook for lifting fish — **gaff** *vb*

gaffe *n* : social blunder

gag *vb* **-gg- 1** : prevent from speaking or crying out by stopping up the mouth **2** : retch or cause to retch ~ *n* **1** : something that stops up the mouth **2** : laugh-provoking remark or act

gage *var of* GAUGE

gag·gle *n* : flock of geese

gai·ety *n, pl* **-eties** : high spirits

gai·ly *adv* : in a gay manner

gain *n* **1** : profit **2** : obtaining of profit or possessions **3** : increase ~ *vb* **1** : get possession of **2** : win **3** : arrive at **4** : increase or increase in **5** : profit — **gain·er** *n* — **gain·ful** *adj* — **gain·ful·ly** *adv*

gain·say *vb* **-said; -say·ing; -says** : deny or dispute — **gain·say·er** *n*

gait *n* : manner of walking or running — **gait·ed** *adj*

gal *n* : girl

ga·la *n* : festive celebration — **gala** *adj*

gal·axy *n, pl* **-ax·ies** : very large group of stars — **ga·lac·tic** *adj*

gale *n* **1** : strong wind **2** : outburst

¹**gall** *n* **1** : bile **2** : insolence

²**gall** *n* **1** : skin sore caused by chafing **2** : swelling of plant tissue caused by parasites ~ *vb* **1** : chafe **2** : irritate or vex

gal·lant *n* : man very attentive to women ~ *adj* **1** : splendid **2** : brave **3** : polite and attentive to women — **gal·lant·ly** *adv* — **gal·lant·ry** *n*

gall·blad·der *n* : pouch attached to the liver in which bile is stored

gal·le·on *n* : large sailing ship formerly used esp. by the Spanish

gal·lery *n, pl* **-ler·ies 1** : outdoor balcony **2** : long narrow passage or hall **3** : room or building for exhibiting art **4** : spectators — **gal·ler·ied** *adj*

gal·ley *n, pl* **-leys 1** : old ship propelled esp. by oars **2** : kitchen of a ship or airplane

gal·li·um *n* : bluish white metallic chemical element

gal·li·vant *vb* : travel or roam about for pleasure

gal·lon *n* : unit of liquid measure equal to 4 quarts

gal·lop *n* : fast 3-beat gait of a horse — **gallop** *vb* — **gal·lop·er** *n*

gal·lows *n, pl* **-lows** *or* **-lows·es** : upright frame for hanging criminals

gall·stone *n* : abnormal concretion in the gallbladder or bile passages

ga·lore *adj* : in abundance

ga·losh *n* : overshoe — usu. pl.

gal·va·nize *vb* **-nized; -niz·ing 1** : shock into action **2** : coat (iron or steel) with zinc — **gal·va·ni·za·tion** *n* — **gal·va·niz·er** *n*

gam·bit *n* **1** : opening tactic in chess **2** : stratagem

gam·ble *vb* **-bled; -bling 1** : play a game for stakes **2** : bet **3** : take a chance ~ *n* : risky undertaking — **gam·bler** *n*

gam·bol *vb* **-boled** *or* **-bolled; -bol·ing** *or* **-bol·ling** : skip about in play — **gambol** *n*

game *n* **1** : playing activity **2** : competition according to rules **3** : animals hunted for sport or food ~ *vb* **gamed; gam·ing** : gamble ~ *adj* **1** : plucky **2** : lame — **game·ly** *adv* — **game·ness** *n*

game·cock *n* : fighting cock

game·keep·er *n* : person in charge of game animals or birds

gam·ete *n* : mature germ cell — **ga·met·ic** *adj*

ga·mine *n* : charming tomboy

gam·ut *n* : entire range or series

gamy *or* **gam·ey** *adj* **gam·i·er; -est** : having the flavor of game esp. when slightly tainted — **gam·i·ness** *n*

¹**gan·der** *n* : male goose

²**gander** *n* : glance

gang *n* **1** : group of persons working together **2** : group of criminals ~ *vb* : attack in a gang — with *up*

gan·gling *adj* : lanky

gan·gli·on *n, pl* **-glia** : mass of nerve cells

gang·plank *n* : platform used in boarding or leaving a ship

gan·grene *n* : local death of body tissue — **gan·grene** *vb* — **gan·gre·nous** *adj*

gang·ster *n* : member of criminal gang

gang·way *n* : passage in or out

gan·net *n* : large fish-eating marine bird

gan•try *n, pl* **-tries** : frame structure supported over or around something

gap *n* **1** : break in a barrier **2** : mountain pass **3** : empty space

gape *vb* **gaped; gap•ing 1** : open widely **2** : stare with mouth open — **gape** *n*

ga•rage *n* : shelter or repair shop for automobiles ~ *vb* **-raged; -rag•ing** : put or keep in a garage

garb *n* : clothing ~ *vb* : dress

gar•bage *n* **1** : food waste **2** : trash — **gar•bage•man** *n*

gar•ble *vb* **-bled; -bling** : distort the meaning of

gar•den *n* **1** : plot for growing fruits, flowers, or vegetables **2** : public recreation area ~ *vb* : work in a garden — **gar•den•er** *n*

gar•de•nia *n* : tree or shrub with fragrant white or yellow flowers or the flower

gar•gan•tuan *adj* : having tremendous size or volume

gar•gle *vb* **-gled; -gling** : rinse the throat with liquid — **gargle** *n*

gar•goyle *n* : waterspout in the form of a grotesque human or animal

gar•ish *adj* : offensively bright or gaudy

gar•land *n* : wreath ~ *vb* : form into or deck with a garland

gar•lic *n* : herb with pungent bulbs used in cooking — **gar•licky** *adj*

gar•ment *n* : article of clothing

gar•ner *vb* : acquire by effort

gar•net *n* : deep red mineral

gar•nish *vb* : add decoration to (as food) — **garnish** *n*

gar•nish•ee *vb* **-eed; -ee•ing** : take (as a debtor's wages) by legal authority

gar•nish•ment *n* : attachment of property to satisfy a creditor

gar•ret *n* : attic

gar•ri•son *n* : military post or the troops stationed there — **garrison** *vb*

gar•ru•lous *adj* : talkative — **•gar•ru•li•ty** *n* — **gar•ru•lous•ly** *adv* — **gar•ru•lous•ness** *n*

gar•ter *n* : band to hold up a stocking or sock

gas *n, pl* **gas•es 1** : fluid (as hydrogen or air) that tends to expand indefinitely **2** : gasoline ~ *vb* **gassed; gas•sing 1** : treat with gas **2** : fill with gasoline — **gas•eous** *adj*

gash *n* : deep long cut — **gash** *vb*

gas•ket *n* : material or a part used to seal a joint

gas•light *n* : light of burning illuminating gas

gas•o•line *n* : flammable liquid from petroleum

gasp *vb* **1** : catch the breath audibly **2** : breathe laboriously — **gasp** *n*

gas•tric *adj* : relating to or located near the stomach

gas•tron•o•my *n* : art of good eating — **gas•tro•nom•ic** *adj*

gate *n* : an opening for passage in a wall or fence — **gate•keep•er** *n* — **gate•post** *n*

gate•way *n* : way in or out

gath•er *vb* **1** : bring or come together **2** : harvest **3** : pick up little by little **4** : deduce — **gath•er•er** *n* — **gath•er•ing** *n*

gauche *adj* : crude or tactless

gaudy *adj* **gaud•i•er; -est** : tastelessly showy — **gaud•i•ly** *adv* — **gaud•i•ness** *n*

gauge *n* : instrument for measuring ~ *vb* **gauged; gaug•ing** : measure

gaunt *adj* : thin or emaciated — **gaunt•ness** *n*

¹gaunt•let *n* **1** : protective glove **2** : challenge to combat

²gauntlet *n* : ordeal

gauze *n* : thin often transparent fabric — **gauzy** *adj*

gave *past of* GIVE

gav•el *n* : mallet of a presiding officer, auctioneer, or judge

gawk *vb* : stare stupidly

gawky *adj* **gawk•i•er; -est** : clumsy

gay *adj* **1** : merry **2** : bright and lively **3** : homosexual — **gay** *n*

gaze *vb* **gazed; gaz•ing** : fix the eyes in a steady intent look — **gaze** *n* — **gaz•er** *n*

ga•zelle *n* : small swift antelope

ga•zette *n* : newspaper

gaz•et•teer *n* : geographical dictionary

gear *n* **1** : clothing **2** : equipment **3** : toothed wheel — **gear** *vb*

gear•shift *n* : mechanism by which automobile gears are shifted

geek *n* : socially inept person

geese *pl of* GOOSE

gei•sha *n, pl* **-sha** *or* **-shas** : Japanese girl or woman trained to entertain men

gel•a•tin *n* : sticky substance obtained from animal tissues by boiling — **ge•lat•i•nous** *adj*

geld *vb* : castrate

geld•ing *n* : castrated horse

gem *n* : cut and polished valuable stone — **gem•stone** *n*

gen•der *n* **1** : sex **2** : division of a class of words (as nouns) that determines agreement of other words

gene *n* : segment of DNA that controls inheritance of a trait

ge•ne•al•o•gy *n, pl* **-gies** : study of family pedigrees — **ge•ne•a•log•i•cal** *adj* — **ge•ne•a•log•i•cal•ly** *adv* — **ge•ne•al•o•gist** *n*

genera *pl of* GENUS

gen•er•al *adj* **1** : relating to the whole **2** : applicable to all of a group **3** : common or widespread ~ *n* **1** : something that involves or is applicable to the whole **2** : commissioned officer in the army, air force, or marine corps ranking above a lieutenant general — **gen•er•al•ly** *adv* — **in general** : for the most part

gen•er•al•i•ty *n, pl* **-ties** : general statement

gen•er•al•ize *vb* **-ized; -iz•ing** : reach a general conclusion esp. on the basis of particular instances — **gen•er•al•iza•tion** *n*

general of the air force : commissioned officer of the highest rank in the air force

general of the army : commissioned officer of the highest rank in the army

gen•er•ate *vb* **-at•ed; -at•ing** : create or produce

gen•er•a•tion *n* **1** : living beings constituting a single step in a line of descent **2** : production — **gen•er•a•tive** *adj*

gen•er•a•tor *n* **1** : one that generates **2** : machine that turns mechanical into electrical energy

ge•ner•ic *adj* **1** : general **2** : not protected by a trademark **3** : relating to a genus — **generic** *n*

gen•er•ous *adj* : freely giving or sharing — **gen•er•os•i•ty** *n* — **gen•er•ous•ly** *adv* — **gen•er•ous•ness** *n*

ge•net•ics *n* : biology dealing with heredity and variation — **ge•net•ic** *adj* — **ge•net•i•cal•ly** *adv* — **ge•net•i•cist** *n*

ge•nial *adj* : cheerful — **ge•nial•i•ty** *n* — **ge•nial•ly** *adv*

ge•nie *n* : supernatural spirit that often takes human form

gen•i•tal *adj* : concerned with reproduction — **gen•i•tal•ly** *adv*

gen•i•ta•lia *n pl* : external genital organs

gen•i•tals *n pl* : genitalia

ge•nius *n* **1** : single strongly marked capacity **2** : extraordinary intellectual power or a person having such power

geno•cide *n* : systematic destruction of a racial or cultural group

genre *n* : category esp. of literary composition

gen•teel *adj* : polite or refined

gen•tile *n* : person who is not Jewish — **gentile** *adj*

gen•til•i•ty *n, pl* **-ties 1** : good birth and family **2** : good manners

gen•tle *adj* **-tler; -tlest 1** : of a family of high social station **2** : not harsh, stern, or violent **3** : soft or delicate ~ *vb* **-tled; -tling** : make gentle — **gen•tle•ness** *n* — **gen•tly** *adv*

gen•tle•man *n* : man of good family or manners — **gen•tle•man•ly** *adv*

gen•tle•wom•an *n* : woman of good family or breeding

gen•try *n, pl* **-tries** : people of good birth or breeding

gen•u•flect *vb* : bend the knee in worship — **gen•u•flec•tion** *n*

gen•u•ine *adj* : being the same in fact as in appearance — **gen•u•ine•ly** *adv* — **gen•u•ine•ness** *n*

ge•nus *n, pl* **gen•era** : category of biological classification

ge•ode *n* : stone having a mineral-lined cavity

geo•de•sic *adj* : made of a framework of linked polygons

ge•og•ra•phy *n* **1** : study of the earth and its climate, products, and inhabitants **2** : natural features of a region — **ge•og•ra•pher** *n* — **geo•graph•ic, geo•graph•i•cal** *adj* — **geo•graph•i•cal•ly** *adv*

ge•ol•o•gy *n* : study of the history of the earth and its life esp. as recorded in rocks — **geo•log•ic, geo•log•i•cal** *adj* — **geo•log•i•cal•ly** *adv* — **ge•ol•o•gist** *n*

ge•om•e•try *n, pl* **-tries** : mathematics of the relations, properties, and measurements of solids, surfaces, lines, and angles — **geo•met•ric, geo•met•ri•cal** *adj*

geo•ther•mal *adj* : relating to or derived from the heat of the earth's interior

ge•ra•ni•um *n* : garden plant with clusters of white, pink, or scarlet flowers

ger•bil *n* : burrowing desert rodent

ge•ri•at•ric *adj* **1** : relating to aging or the aged **2** : old

ge•ri•at•rics *n* : medicine dealing with the aged and aging

germ *n* **1** : microorganism **2** : source or rudiment

ger•mane *adj* : relevant

ger•ma•ni•um *n* : grayish white hard chemical element

ger•mi•cide *n* : agent that destroys germs — **ger•mi•cid•al** *adj*

ger•mi•nate *vb* **-nat•ed; -nat•ing** : begin to develop — **ger•mi•na•tion** *n*

ger•ry•man•der *vb* : divide into election districts so as to give one political party an advantage — **gerrymander** *n*

ger•und *n* : word having the characteristics of both verb and noun

ge•sta•po *n, pl* **-pos** : secret police

ges•ta•tion *n* : pregnancy or incubation — **gestate** *vb*

ges•ture *n* **1** : movement of the body or limbs that expresses something **2** : something said or done for its effect on the attitudes of others — **ges•tur•al** *adj* — **gesture** *vb*

ge•sund•heit *interj* — used to wish good health to one who has just sneezed

get *vb* **got; got** *or* **got•ten; get•ting 1** : gain or be in possession of **2** : succeed in coming or going **3** : cause to come or go or to be in a certain condition or position **4** : become **5** : be subjected to **6** : understand **7** : be obliged — **get along** *vb* **1** : get by **2** : be on friendly terms — **get by** *vb* : meet one's needs

get•away *n* **1** : escape **2** : a starting or getting under way

gey•ser *n* : spring that intermittently shoots up hot water and steam

ghast•ly *adj* **-li•er; -est** : horrible or shocking

gher·kin *n* : small pickle

ghet·to *n, pl* **-tos** *or* **-toes** : part of a city in which members of a minority group live

ghost *n* : disembodied soul — **ghost·ly** *adv*

ghost·write *vb* **-wrote; -writ·ten** : write for and in the name of another — **ghost·writ·er** *n*

ghoul *n* : legendary evil being that feeds on corpses — **ghoul·ish** *adj*

GI *n, pl* **GI's** *or* **GIs** : member of the U.S. armed forces

gi·ant *n* **1** : huge legendary being **2** : something very large or very powerful — **giant** *adj*

gib·ber *vb* **-bered; -ber·ing** : speak rapidly and foolishly

gib·ber·ish *n* : unintelligible speech or language

gib·bon *n* : manlike ape

gibe *vb* **gibed; gib·ing** : jeer at — **gibe** *n*

gib·lets *n pl* : edible fowl viscera

gid·dy *adj* **-di·er; -est** **1** : silly **2** : dizzy — **gid·di·ness** *n*

gift *n* **1** : something given **2** : talent — **gift·ed** *adj*

gi·gan·tic *adj* : very big

gig·gle *vb* **-gled; -gling** : laugh in a silly manner — **giggle** *n* — **gig·gly** *adj*

gig·o·lo *n, pl* **-los** : man living on the earnings of a woman

Gi·la monster *n* : large venomous lizard

gild *vb* **gild·ed** *or* **gilt; gild·ing** : cover with or as if with gold

gill *n* : organ of a fish for obtaining oxygen from water

gilt *adj* : gold-colored ~ *n* : gold or goldlike substance on the surface of an object

gim·bal *n* : device that allows something to incline freely

gim·let *n* : small tool for boring holes

gim·mick *n* : new and ingenious scheme, feature, or device — **gim·mick·ry** *n* — **gim·micky** *adj*

gimpy *adj* : lame

¹gin *n* : machine to separate seeds from cotton — **gin** *vb*

²gin *n* : clear liquor flavored with juniper berries

gin·ger *n* : pungent aromatic spice from a tropical plant — **gin·ger·bread** *n*

gin·ger·ly *adj* : very cautious or careful — **gingerly** *adv*

ging·ham *n* : cotton clothing fabric

gin·gi·vi·tis *n* : inflammation of the gums

gink·go *n, pl* **-goes** *or* **-gos** : tree of eastern China

gin·seng *n* : aromatic root of a Chinese herb

gi·raffe *n* : African mammal with a very long neck

gird *vb* **gird·ed** *or* **girt; gird·ing** **1** : encircle or fasten with or as if with a belt **2** : prepare

gird·er *n* : horizontal supporting beam

gir·dle *n* : woman's supporting undergarment ~ *vb* : surround

girl *n* **1** : female child **2** : young woman **3** : sweetheart — **girl·hood** *n* — **girl·ish** *adj*

girlfriend *n* : frequent or regular female companion of a boy or man

girth *n* : measure around something

gist *n* : main point or part

give *vb* **gave; giv·en; giv·ing** **1** : put into the possession or keeping of another **2** : pay **3** : perform **4** : contribute or donate **5** : produce **6** : utter **7** : yield to force, strain, or pressure — ~ *n* : capacity or tendency to yield to force or strain — **give in** *vb* : surrender — **give out** *vb* : become used up or exhausted — **give up** *vb* **1** : let out of one's control **2** : cease from trying, doing, or hoping

give·away *n* **1** : unintentional betrayal **2** : something given free

giv·en *adj* **1** : prone or disposed **2** : having been specified

giz·zard *n* : muscular usu. horny-lined enlargement following the crop of a bird

gla·cial *adj* **1** : relating to glaciers **2** : very slow — **gla·cial·ly** *adv*

gla·cier *n* : large body of ice moving slowly

glad *adj* **-dd- 1** : experiencing or causing pleasure, joy, or delight **2** : very willing — **glad·den** *vb* — **glad·ly** *adv* — **glad·ness** *n*

glade *n* : grassy open space in a forest

glad·i·a·tor *n* : one who fought to the death for the entertainment of ancient Romans — **glad·i·a·to·ri·al** *adj*

glad·i·o·lus *n, pl* **-li** : plant related to the irises

glam·our, glam·or *n* : romantic or exciting attractiveness — **glam·or·ize** *vb* — **glam·or·ous** *adj*

glance *vb* **glanced; glanc·ing** **1** : strike and fly off to one side **2** : give a quick look ~ *n* : quick look

gland *n* : group of cells that secretes a substance — **glan·du·lar** *adj*

glans *n, pl* **glan·des** : conical vascular body forming the end of the penis or clitoris

glare *vb* **glared; glar·ing** **1** : shine with a harsh dazzling light **2** : stare angrily ~ *n* **1** : harsh dazzling light **2** : angry stare

glar·ing *adj* : painfully obvious — **glar·ing·ly** *adv*

glass *n* **1** : hard usu. transparent material made by melting sand and other materials **2** : something made of glass **3** *pl* : lenses used to correct defects of vision — **glass** *adj* — **glass·ful** *n* — **glass·ware** *n* — **glassy** *adj*

glass·blow·ing *n* : art of shaping a mass of molten glass by blowing air into it — **glass·blow·er** *n*

glau·co·ma *n* : state of increased pressure within the eyeball

glaze *vb* **glazed; glaz·ing** **1** : furnish with glass **2** : apply glaze to ~ *n* : glassy surface or coating

gla·zier *n* : one who sets glass in window frames

gleam *n* **1** : transient or partly obscured light **2** : faint trace ~ *vb* : send out gleams

glean *vb* : collect little by little — **glean·able** *adj* — **glean·er** *n*

glee *n* : joy — **glee·ful** *adj*

glen *n* : narrow hidden valley

glib *adj* **-bb-** : speaking or spoken with ease — **glib·ly** *adv*

glide *vb* **glid·ed; glid·ing** : move or descend smoothly and effortlessly — **glide** *n*

glid·er *n* **1** : winged aircraft having no engine **2** : swinging porch seat

glim·mer *vb* : shine faintly or unsteadily ~ *n* **1** : faint light **2** : small amount

glimpse *vb* **glimpsed; glimps·ing** : take a brief look at — **glimpse** *n*

glint *vb* : gleam or sparkle — **glint** *n*

glis·ten *vb* : shine or sparkle by reflection — **glisten** *n*

glit·ter *vb* : shine with brilliant or metallic luster ~ *n* : small glittering ornaments — **glit·tery** *adj*

gloat *vb* : think of something with triumphant delight

glob *n* : large rounded lump

glob·al *adj* : worldwide — **glob·al·ly** *adv*

globe *n* **1** : sphere **2** : the earth or a model of it

glob·u·lar *adj* **1** : round **2** : made up of globules

glob·ule *n* : tiny ball

glock·en·spiel *n* : portable musical instrument consisting of tuned metal bars

gloom *n* **1** : darkness **2** : sadness — **gloom·i·ly** *adv* — **gloom·i·ness** *n* — **gloomy** *adj*

glop *n* : messy mass or mixture

glo·ri·fy *vb* **-fied; -fy·ing** **1** : make to seem glorious **2** : worship — **glo·ri·fi·ca·tion** *n*

glo·ry *n, pl* **-ries** **1** : praise or honor offered in worship **2** : cause for praise or renown **3** : magnificence **4** : heavenly bliss ~ *vb* **-ried, -ry·ing** : rejoice proudly — **glo·ri·ous** *adj* — **glo·ri·ous·ly** *adv*

¹gloss *n* : luster — **gloss·i·ly** *adv* — **gloss·i·ness**

n — **gloss over** *vb* **1** : mask the true nature of **2** : deal with only superficially — **glossy** *adj*

²gloss *n* : brief explanation or translation ~ *vb* : translate or explain

glos·sa·ry *n, pl* **-ries** : dictionary — **glos·sar·i·al** *adj*

glove *n* : hand covering with sections for each finger

glow *vb* **1** : shine with or as if with intense heat **2** : show exuberance ~ *n* : brightness or warmth of color or feeling

glow·er *vb* : stare angrily — **glower** *n*

glow·worm *n* : insect or insect larva that emits light

glu·cose *n* : sugar found esp. in blood, plant sap, and fruits

glue *n* : substance used for sticking things together — **glue** *vb* — **glu·ey** *adj*

glum *adj* **-mm- 1** : sullen **2** : dismal

glut *vb* **-tt-** : fill to excess — **glut** *n*

glu·ten *n* : gluey protein substance in flour

glu·ti·nous *adj* : sticky

glut·ton *n* : one who eats to excess — **glut·ton·ous** *adj* — **glut·tony** *n*

gnarled *adj* **1** : knotty **2** : gloomy or sullen

gnash *vb* : grind (as teeth) together

gnat *n* : small biting fly

gnaw *vb* : bite or chew on — **gnaw·er** *n*

gnome *n* : dwarf of folklore — **gnom·ish** *adj*

gnu *n, pl* **gnu** *or* **gnus** : large African antelope

go *vb* **went; gone; go·ing; goes 1** : move, proceed, run, or pass **2** : leave **3** : extend or lead **4** : sell or amount — with *for* **5** : happen **6** — used in present participle to show intent or imminent action **7** : become **8** : fit or harmonize **9** : belong ~ *n, pl* **goes 1** : act or manner of going **2** : vigor **3** : attempt — **go back on** : betray — **go by the board** : be discarded — **go for** : favor — **go off** : explode — **go one better** : outdo — **go over 1** : examine **2** : study — **go to town** : be very successful — **on the go** : constantly active

goad *n* : something that urges — **goad** *vb*

goal *n* **1** : mark to reach in a race **2** : purpose **3** : object in a game through which a ball is propelled

goal·ie *n* : player who defends the goal

goal·keep·er *n* : goalie

goat *n* : horned ruminant mammal related to the sheep — **goat·skin** *n*

goa·tee *n* : small pointed beard

gob *n* : lump

¹gob·ble *vb* **-bled; -bling** : eat greedily

²gobble *vb* **-bled; -bling** : make the noise of a turkey (**gobbler**)

gob·ble·dy·gook *n* : nonsense

gob·let *n* : large stemmed drinking glass

gob·lin *n* : ugly mischievous sprite

god *n* **1** *cap* : supreme being **2** : being with supernatural powers — **god·like** *adj* — **god·ly** *adj*

god·child *n* : person one sponsors at baptism — **god·daugh·ter** *n* — **god·son** *n*

god·dess *n* : female god

god·less *adj* : not believing in God — **god·less·ness** *n*

god·par·ent *n* : sponsor at baptism — **god·fa·ther** *n* — **god·moth·er** *n*

god·send *n* : something needed that comes unexpectedly

goes *pres 3d sing of* GO

go-get·ter *n* : enterprising person — **go-get·ting** *adj or n*

gog·gle *vb* **-gled; -gling** : stare wide-eyed

gog·gles *n pl* : protective glasses

go·ings-on *n pl* : events

goi·ter *n* : abnormally enlarged thyroid gland

gold *n* : malleable yellow metallic chemical element — **gold·smith** *n*

gold·brick *n* : person who shirks duty — **gold·brick** *vb*

gold·en *adj* **1** : made of, containing, or relating to gold **2** : having the color of gold **3** : precious or favorable

gold·en·rod *n* : herb having tall stalks with tiny yellow flowers

gold·finch *n* : yellow American finch

gold·fish *n* : small usu. orange or golden carp

golf *n* : game played by hitting a small ball (**golf ball**) with clubs (**golf clubs**) into holes placed in a field (**golf course**) — **golf** *vb* — **golf·er** *n*

go·nad *n* : sex gland

gon·do·la *n* **1** : long narrow boat used on the canals of Venice **2** : car suspended from a cable

gon·do·lier *n* : person who propels a gondola

gone *adj* **1** : past **2** : involved

gon·er *n* : hopeless case

gong *n* : metallic disk that makes a deep sound when struck

gon·or·rhea *n* : bacterial inflammatory venereal disease of the genital tract — **gon·or·rhe·al** *adj*

goo *n* : thick or sticky substance — **goo·ey** *adj*

good *adj* **bet·ter; best 1** : satisfactory **2** : salutary **3** : considerable **4** : desirable **5** : well-behaved, kind, or virtuous ~ *n* **1** : something good **2** : benefit **3** *pl* : personal property **4** *pl* : wares ~ *adv* : well — **good–heart·ed** *adj* — **good–look·ing** *adj* — **good–na·tured** *adj* — **good·ness** *n* — **good–tem·pered** *adj* — **for good** : forever

good–bye, good–by *n* : parting remark

good–for–noth·ing *n* : idle worthless person

Good Friday *n* : Friday before Easter observed as the anniversary of the crucifixion of Christ

good·ly *adj* **-li·er; -est** : considerable

good·will *n* **1** : good intention **2** : kindly feeling

goody *n, pl* **good·ies** : something that is good esp. to eat

goody–goody *adj* : affectedly or annoyingly sweet or self-righteous — **goody–goody** *n*

goof *vb* **1** : blunder **2** : waste time — usu. with *off* or *around* — **goof** *n* — **goof–off** *n*

goofy *adj* **goof·i·er; -est** : crazy — **goof·i·ness** *n*

goose *n, pl* **geese** : large bird with webbed feet

goose·ber·ry *n* : berry of a shrub related to the currant

goose bumps *n pl* : roughening of the skin caused by fear, excitement, or cold

goose·flesh *n* : goose bumps

goose pimples *n pl* : goose bumps

go·pher *n* : burrowing rodent

¹**gore** *n* : blood

²**gore** *vb* **gored; gor·ing** : pierce or wound with a horn or tusk

¹**gorge** *n* : narrow ravine

²**gorge** *vb* **gorged; gorg·ing** : eat greedily

gor·geous *adj* : supremely beautiful

go·ril·la *n* : African manlike ape

gory *adj* **gor·i·er; -est** : bloody

gos·hawk *n* : long-tailed hawk with short rounded wings

gos·ling *n* : young goose

gos·pel *n* **1** : teachings of Christ and the apostles **2** : something accepted as infallible truth — **gospel** *adj*

gos·sa·mer *n* **1** : film of cobweb **2** : light filmy substance

gos·sip *n* **1** : person who reveals personal information **2** : rumor or report of an intimate nature ~ *vb* : spread gossip — **gos·sipy** *adj*

got *past of* GET

Goth·ic *adj* : relating to a medieval style of architecture

gotten *past part of* GET

gouge *n* **1** : rounded chisel **2** : cavity or groove scooped out ~ *vb* **gouged; goug·ing 1** : cut or scratch a groove in **2** : overcharge

gou·lash *n* : beef stew with vegetables and paprika

gourd *n* **1** : any of a group of vines including the cucumber, squash, and melon **2** : inedible hard-shelled fruit of a gourd

gour·mand *n* : person who loves good food and drink

gour·met *n* : connoisseur of food and drink

gout *n* : disease marked by painful inflammation and swelling of the joints — **gouty** *adj*

gov·ern *vb* **1** : control and direct policy in **2** : guide or influence strongly **3** : restrain — **gov·ern·ment** *n* — **gov·ern·men·tal** *adj*

gov·ern·ess *n* : female teacher in a private home

gov·er·nor *n* **1** : head of a political unit **2** : automatic speed-control device — **gov·er·nor·ship** *n*

gown *n* **1** : loose flowing outer garment **2** : woman's formal evening dress — **gown** *vb*

grab *vb* **-bb-** : take by sudden grasp — **grab** *n*

grace *n* **1** : unmerited divine assistance **2** : short prayer before or after a meal **3** : respite **4** : ease of movement or bearing ~ *vb* **graced; grac·ing 1** : honor **2** : adorn — **grace·ful** *adj* — **grace·ful·ly** *adv* — **grace·ful·ness** *n* — **grace·less** *adj*

gra·cious *adj* : marked by kindness and courtesy or charm and taste — **gra·cious·ly** *adv* — **gra·cious·ness** *n*

grack·le *n* : American blackbird

gra·da·tion *n* : step, degree, or stage in a series

grade *n* **1** : stage in a series, order, or ranking **2** : division of school representing one year's work **3** : mark of accomplishment in school **4** : degree of slope ~ *vb* **grad·ed; grad·ing 1** : arrange in grades **2** : make level or evenly sloping **3** : give a grade to — **grad·er** *n*

grade school *n* : school including the first 4 or 8 grades

gra·di·ent *n* : slope

grad·u·al *adj* : going by steps or degrees — **grad·u·al·ly** *adv*

grad·u·ate *n* : holder of a diploma ~ *adj* : of or relating to studies beyond the bachelor's degree ~ *vb* **-at·ed; -at·ing 1** : grant or receive a diploma **2** : mark with degrees of measurement — **grad·u·a·tion** *n*

graf·fi·to *n, pl* **-ti** : inscription on a wall

graft *vb* : join one thing to another so that they grow together ~ *n* **1** : grafted plant **2** : the getting of money dishonestly or the money so gained — **graft·er** *n*

grain *n* **1** : seeds or fruits of cereal grasses **2** : small hard particle **3** : arrangement of fibers in wood — **grained** *adj* — **grainy** *adj*

gram *n* : metric unit of weight equal to 1/1000 kilogram

gram·mar *n* : study of words and their functions and relations in the sentence — **gram·mar·i·an** *n* — **gram·mat·i·cal** *adj* — **gram·mat·i·cal·ly** *adv*

grammar school *n* : grade school

gra·na·ry *n, pl* **-ries** : storehouse for grain

grand *adj* **1** : large or striking in size or scope **2** : fine and imposing **3** : very good — **grand·ly** *adv* — **grand·ness** *n*

grand·child *n* : child of one's son or daughter — **grand·daugh·ter** *n* — **grand·son** *n*

gran·deur *n* : quality or state of being grand

gran·dil·o·quence *n* : pompous speaking — **gran·dil·o·quent** *adj*

gran·di·ose *adj* **1** : impressive **2** : affectedly splendid — **gran·di·ose·ly** *adv*

grand·par·ent *n* : parent of one's father or mother — **grand·fa·ther** *n* — **grand·moth·er** *n*

grand·stand *n* : usu. roofed stand for spectators

grange *n* : farmers association

gran·ite *n* : hard igneous rock

grant *vb* **1** : consent to **2** : give **3** : admit as true ~ *n* **1** : act of granting **2** : something granted — **grant·ee** *n* — **grant·er** *n* — **grant·or** *n*

gran·u·late *vb* **-lat·ed; -lat·ing** : form into grains or crystals — **gran·u·la·tion** *n*

gran·ule *n* : small particle — **gran·u·lar** *adj* — **gran·u·lar·i·ty** *n*

grape *n* : smooth juicy edible berry of a woody vine (**grape·vine**)

grape·fruit *n* : large edible yellow-skinned citrus fruit

graph *n* : diagram that shows relationships between things — **graph** *vb*

graph·ic *adj* **1** : vividly described **2** : relating to the arts (**graphic arts**) of representation and printing on flat surfaces ~ *n* **1** : picture used for illustration **2** *pl* : computer screen display — **graph·i·cal·ly** *adv*

graph·ite *n* : soft carbon used for lead pencils and lubricants

grap·nel *n* : small anchor with several claws

grap·ple *vb* **-pled; -pling 1** : seize or hold with or as if with a hooked implement **2** : wrestle

grasp *vb* **1** : take or seize firmly **2** : understand ~ *n* **1** : one's hold or control **2** : one's reach **3** : comprehension

grass *n* : plant with jointed stem and narrow leaves — **grassy** *adj*

grass·hop·per *n* : leaping plant-eating insect

grass·land *n* : land covered with grasses

¹**grate** *n* **1** : grating **2** : frame of iron bars to hold burning fuel

²**grate** *vb* **grat·ed; -ing 1** : pulverize by rubbing against something rough **2** : irritate — **grat·er** *n* — **grat·ing·ly** *adv*

grate·ful *adj* : thankful or appreciative — **grate·ful·ly** *adv* — **grate·ful·ness** *n*

grat·i·fy *vb* **-fied; -fy·ing** : give pleasure to — **grat·i·fi·ca·tion** *n*

grat·ing *n* : framework with bars across it

gra·tis *adv or adj* : free

grat·i·tude *n* : state of being grateful

gra·tu·itous *adj* **1** : free **2** : uncalled-for

gra·tu·ity *n, pl* **-ities** : tip

¹**grave** *n* : place of burial — **grave·stone** *n* — **grave·yard** *n*

²**grave** *adj* **grav·er; grav·est 1** : threatening great harm or danger **2** : solemn — **grave·ly** *adv* — **grave·ness** *n*

grav·el *n* : loose rounded fragments of rock — **grav·el·ly** *adj*

grav·i·tate *vb* **-tat·ed; -tat·ing** : move toward something

grav·i·ta·tion *n* : natural force of attraction that tends to draw bodies together — **grav·i·ta·tion·al** *adj* — **grav·i·ta·tion·al·ly** *adv*

grav·i·ty *n, pl* **-ties 1** : serious importance **2** : gravitation

gra·vy *n, pl* **-vies** : sauce made from thickened juices of cooked meat

gray *adj* **1** : of the color gray **2** : having gray hair ~ *n* : neutral color between black and white ~ *vb* : make or become gray — **gray·ish** *adj* — **gray·ness** *n*

¹**graze** *vb* **grazed; graz·ing** : feed on herbage or pasture — **graz·er** *n*

²**graze** *vb* **grazed; graz·ing** : touch lightly in passing

grease *n* : thick oily material or fat ~ *vb* **greased; greas·ing** : smear or lubricate with grease — **greasy** *adj*

great *adj* **1** : large in size or number **2** : larger than usual — **great·ly** *adv* — **great·ness** *n*

grebe *n* : diving bird related to the loon

greed *n* : selfish desire beyond reason — **greed·i·ly** *adv* — **greed·i·ness** *n* — **greedy** *adj*

green *adj* **1** : of the color green **2** : unripe **3** : inexperienced ~ *vb* : become green ~ *n* **1** : color between blue and yellow **2** *pl* : leafy parts of plants — **green•ish** adj — **green•ness** n

green•ery n, pl **-er•ies** : green foliage or plants

green•horn n : inexperienced person

green•house n : glass structure for the growing of plants

greet vb 1 : address with expressions of kind wishes 2 : react to — **greet•er** n

greet•ing n 1 : friendly address on meeting 2 pl : best wishes

gre•gar•i•ous adj : social or companionable — **gre•gar•i•ous•ly** adv — **gre•gar•i•ous•ness** n

grem•lin n : small mischievous gnome

gre•nade n : small missile filled with explosive or chemicals

grew past of GROW

grey var of GRAY

grey•hound n : tall slender dog noted for speed

grid n 1 : grating 2 : evenly spaced horizontal and vertical lines (as on a map)

grid•dle n : flat metal surface for cooking

grid•iron n 1 : grate for broiling 2 : football field

grief n 1 : emotional suffering caused by or as if by bereavement 2 : disaster

griev•ance n : complaint

grieve vb **grieved; griev•ing** : feel or cause to feel grief or sorrow

griev•ous adj 1 : oppressive 2 : causing grief or sorrow — **griev•ous•ly** adv

grill vb 1 : cook on a grill 2 : question intensely ~ n 1 : griddle 2 : informal restaurant

grille, grill n : grating forming a barrier or screen — **grill•work** n

grim adj **-mm-** 1 : harsh and forbidding in appearance 2 : relentless — **grim•ly** adv — **grim•ness** n

gri•mace n : facial expression of disgust — **gri•mace** vb

grime n : embedded or accumulated dirt — **grimy** adj

grin vb **-nn-** : smile so as to show the teeth — **grin** n

grind vb **ground; grind•ing** 1 : reduce to powder 2 : wear down or sharpen by friction 3 : operate or produce by turning a crank ~ n : monotonous labor or routine — **grind•er** n — **grind•stone** n

grip vb **-pp-** : seize or hold firmly ~ n 1 : grasp 2 : control 3 : device for holding

gripe vb **griped; grip•ing** 1 : cause pains in the bowels 2 : complain — **gripe** n

grippe n : influenza

gris•ly adj **-li•er; -est** : horrible or gruesome

grist n : grain to be ground or already ground — **grist•mill** n

gris•tle n : cartilage — **gris•tly** adj

grit n 1 : hard sharp granule 2 : material composed of granules 3 : unyielding courage ~ vb **-tt-** : press with a grating noise — **grit•ty** adj

grits n pl : coarsely ground hulled grain

griz•zled adj : streaked with gray

groan vb 1 : moan 2 : creak under a strain — **groan** n

gro•cer n : food dealer — **gro•cery** n

grog n : rum diluted with water

grog•gy adj **-gi•er; -est** : dazed and unsteady on the feet — **grog•gi•ly** adv — **grog•gi•ness** n

groin n : juncture of the lower abdomen and inner thigh

grom•met n : eyelet

groom n 1 : one who cares for horses 2 : bridegroom ~ vb 1 : clean and care for (as a horse) 2 : make neat or attractive 3 : prepare

groove n 1 : long narrow channel 2 : fixed routine — **groove** vb

grope vb **groped; grop•ing** : search for by feeling

gros•beak n : finch with large conical bill

¹**gross** adj 1 : glaringly noticeable 2 : bulky 3 : consisting of an overall total exclusive of deductions 4 : vulgar ~ n : the whole before any deductions ~ vb : earn as a total — **gross•ly** adv — **gross•ness** n

²**gross** n, pl **gross** : 12 dozen

gro•tesque adj 1 : absurdly distorted or repulsive 2 : ridiculous — **gro•tesque•ly** adv

grot•to n, pl **-toes** : cave

grouch n : complaining person — **grouch** vb — **grouchy** adj

¹**ground** n 1 : bottom of a body of water 2 pl : sediment 3 : basis for something 4 : surface of the earth 5 : conductor that makes electrical connection with the earth or a framework ~ vb 1 : force or bring down to the ground 2 : give basic knowledge to 3 : connect with an electrical ground — **ground•less** adj

²**ground** past of GRIND

ground•hog n : woodchuck

ground•wa•ter n : underground water

ground•work n : foundation

group n : number of associated individuals ~ vb : gather or collect into groups

grou•per n : large fish of warm seas

grouse n, pl **grouse** or **grouses** : ground-dwelling game bird

grout n : mortar for filling cracks — **grout** vb

grove n : small group of trees

grov•el vb **-eled** or **-elled; -el•ing** or **-el•ling** : abase oneself

grow vb **grew; grown; grow•ing** 1 : come into existence and develop to maturity 2 : be able to grow 3 : advance or increase 4 : become 5 : cultivate — **grow•er** n

growl vb : utter a deep threatening sound — **growl** n

grown–up n : adult — **grown–up** adj

growth n 1 : stage in growing 2 : process of growing 3 : result of something growing

grub vb **-bb-** 1 : root out by digging 2 : search about ~ n 1 : thick wormlike larva 2 : food

grub•by adj **-bi•er; -est** : dirty — **grub•bi•ness** n

grub•stake n : supplies for a prospector

grudge vb **grudged; grudg•ing** : be reluctant to give ~ n : feeling of ill will

gru•el n : thin porridge

gru•el•ing, gru•el•ling adj : requiring extreme effort

grue•some adj : horribly repulsive

gruff adj : rough in speech or manner — **gruff•ly** adv

grum•ble vb **-bled; -bling** : mutter in discontent — **grum•bler** n

grumpy adj **grump•i•er; -est** : cross — **grump•i•ly** adv — **grump•i•ness** n

grun•ion n : fish of the California coast

grunt n : deep guttural sound — **grunt** vb

gua•no n : excrement of seabirds used as fertilizer

guar•an•tee n 1 : assurance of the fulfillment of a condition 2 : something given or held as a security ~ vb **-teed; -tee•ing** 1 : promise to be responsible for 2 : state with certainty — **guar•an•tor** n

guar•an•ty n, pl **-ties** 1 : promise to answer for another's failure to pay a debt 2 : guarantee 3 : pledge ~ vb **-tied; -ty•ing** : guarantee

guard n 1 : defensive position 2 : act of protecting 3 : an individual or group that guards against danger 4 : protective or safety device ~ vb 1 : protect or watch over 2 : take precautions — **guard•house** n — **guard•room** n

guard•ian n : one who has responsibility for the care of the person or property of another — **guard•ian•ship** n

gua•va n : shrubby tropical tree or its mildly acid fruit

gu•ber•na•to•ri•al adj : relating to a governor

guer•ril•la, gue•ril•la n : soldier engaged in small-scale harassing tactics

guess vb 1 : form an opinion from little evidence 2 : state correctly solely by chance 3 : think or believe — **guess** n

guest n 1 : person to whom hospitality (as of a house) is extended 2 : patron of a commercial establishment (as a hotel) 3 : person not a regular cast member who appears on a program

guf•faw n : loud burst of laughter — **guf•faw** vb

guide n 1 : one that leads or gives direction to another 2 : device on a machine to direct motion ~ vb **guid•ed; guid•ing** 1 : show the way to 2 : direct — **guid•able** adj — **guid•ance** n — **guide•book** n

guide•line n : summary of procedures regarding policy or conduct

guild n : association

guile n : craftiness — **guile•ful** adj — **guile•less** adj — **guile•less•ness** n

guil•lo•tine n : machine for beheading persons — **guillotine** vb

guilt n 1 : fact of having committed an offense 2 : feeling of responsibility for offenses — **guilt•i•ly** adv — **guilt•i•ness** n — **guilty** adj

guin•ea n 1 : old gold coin of United Kingdom 2 : 21 shillings

guinea pig n : small So. American rodent

guise n : external appearance

gui•tar n : 6-stringed musical instrument played by plucking

gulch n : ravine

gulf n 1 : extension of an ocean or a sea into the land 2 : wide gap

¹**gull** n : seabird with webbed feet

²**gull** vb : make a dupe of ~ n : dupe — **gull•ible** adj

gul•let n : throat

gul•ly n, pl **-lies** : trench worn by running water

gulp vb : swallow hurriedly or greedily — **gulp** n

¹**gum** n : tissue along the jaw at the base of the teeth

²**gum** n 1 : sticky plant substance 2 : gum usu. of sweetened chicle prepared for chewing — **gum•my** adj

gum•bo n : thick soup

gum•drop n : gumlike candy

gump•tion n : initiative

gun n 1 : cannon 2 : portable firearm 3 : discharge of a gun 4 : something like a gun ~ vb **-nn-** : hunt with a gun — **gun•fight** n — **gun•fight•er** n — **gun•fire** n — **gun•man** n — **gun•pow•der** n — **gun•shot** n — **gun•smith** n

gun•boat n : small armed ship

gun•ner n : person who uses a gun

gun•nery sergeant n : noncommissioned officer in the marine corps ranking next below a first sergeant

gun•ny•sack n : burlap sack

gun•sling•er n : skilled gunman in the old West

gun•wale n : upper edge of a boat's side

gup•py n, pl **-pies** : tiny tropical fish

gur•gle vb **-gled; -gling** : make a sound like that of a flowing and gently splashing liquid — **gurgle** n

gu•ru n, pl **-rus** 1 : personal religious teacher in Hinduism 2 : expert

gush vb : pour forth violently or enthusiastically — **gush•er** n

gushy adj **gush•i•er; -est** : effusively sentimental

gust n 1 : sudden brief rush of wind 2 : sudden outburst — **gust** vb — **gusty** adj

gus•ta•to•ry adj : relating to the sense of taste

gus•to *n* : zest
gut *n* **1** *pl* : intestines **2** : digestive canal **3** *pl* : courage ~ *vb* **-tt-** : eviscerate
gut•ter *n* : channel for carrying off rainwater
gut•tur•al *adj* : sounded in the throat — **gut•tural** *n*
¹**guy** *n* : rope, chain, or rod attached to something to steady it — **guy** *vb*
²**guy** *n* : person

guz•zle *vb* **-zled; -zling** : drink greedily
gym *n* : gymnasium
gym•na•si•um *n, pl* **-si•ums** *or* **-sia** : place for indoor sports
gym•nas•tics *n* : physical exercises performed in a gymnasium — **gym•nast** *n* — **gym•nas•tic** *adj*
gy•ne•col•o•gy *n* : branch of medicine dealing with the diseases of women — **gy•ne•co•logic,**

gy•ne•co•log•i•cal *adj* — **gy•ne•col•o•gist** *n*
gyp *n* **1** : cheat **2** : trickery — **gyp** *vb*
gyp•sum *n* : calcium-containing mineral
gy•rate *vb* **-rat•ed; -rat•ing** : revolve around a center — **gy•ra•tion** *n*
gy•ro•scope *n* : wheel mounted to spin rapidly about an axis that is free to turn in various directions

H

h *n, pl* **h's** *or* **hs** : 8th letter of the alphabet
hab•er•dash•er *n* : men's clothier — **hab•er•dash•ery** *n*
hab•it *n* **1** : monk's or nun's clothing **2** : usual behavior **3** : addiction — **hab•it-form•ing** *adj*
hab•it•able *adj* : capable of being lived in
hab•i•tat *n* : place where a plant or animal naturally occurs
hab•i•ta•tion *n* **1** : occupancy **2** : dwelling place
ha•bit•u•al *adj* **1** : commonly practiced or observed **2** : doing, practicing, or acting by habit — **ha•bit•u•al•ly** *adv* — **ha•bit•u•al•ness** *n*
ha•bit•u•ate *vb* **-at•ed; -at•ing** : accustom
ha•ci•en•da *n* : ranch house
¹**hack** *vb* **1** : cut with repeated irregular blows **2** : cough in a short dry manner **3** : manage successfully — **hack** *n* — **hack•er** *n*
²**hack** *n* **1** : horse or vehicle for hire **2** : saddle horse **3** : writer for hire — **hack** *adj* — **hack•man** *n*
hack•le *n* **1** : long feather on the neck or back of a bird **2** *pl* : hairs that can be erected **3** *pl* : temper
hack•ney *n, pl* **-neys** **1** : horse for riding or driving **2** : carriage for hire
hack•neyed *adj* : trite
hack•saw *n* : saw for metal
had *past of* HAVE
had•dock *n, pl* **haddock** : Atlantic food fish
Ha•des *n* **1** : mythological abode of the dead **2** : *often not cap* : hell
haft *n* : handle of a weapon or tool
hag *n* **1** : witch **2** : ugly old woman
hag•gard *adj* : worn or emaciated — **hag•gard•ly** *adv*
hag•gle *vb* **-gled; -gling** : argue in bargaining — **hag•gler** *n*
¹**hail** *n* **1** : precipitation in small lumps of ice **2** : something like a rain of hail ~ *vb* : rain hail — **hail•stone** *n* — **hail•storm** *n*
²**hail** *vb* **1** : greet or salute **2** : summon ~ *n* : expression of greeting or praise — often used as an interjection
hair *n* : threadlike growth from the skin — **hair•brush** *n* — **hair•cut** *n* — **hair•dress•er** *n* — **haired** *adj* — **hair•i•ness** *n* — **hair•less** *adj* — **hair•pin** *n* — **hair•style** *n* — **hair•styl•ing** *n* — **hair•styl•ist** *n* — **hairy** *adj*
hair•breadth, hairs•breadth *n* : tiny distance or margin
hair•do *n, pl* **-dos** : style of wearing hair
hair•line *n* **1** : thin line **2** : outline of the hair on the head
hair•piece *n* : toupee
hair–rais•ing *adj* : causing terror or astonishment
hake *n* : marine food fish
hal•cy•on *adj* : prosperous or most pleasant
¹**hale** *adj* : healthy or robust
²**hale** *vb* **haled; hal•ing** **1** : - haul **2** : - compel to go
half *n, pl* **halves** : either of 2 equal parts ~ *adj* **1** : being a half or nearly a half **2** : partial — **half** *adv*

half brother *n* : brother related through one parent only
half–heart•ed *adj* : without enthusiasm — **half–heart•ed•ly** *adv* — **half–heart•ed•ness** *n*
half–life *n* : time for half of something to undergo a process
half sister *n* : sister related through one parent only
half•way *adj* : midway between 2 points — **half•way** *adv*
half–wit *n* : foolish person — **half–wit•ted** *adj*
hal•i•but *n, pl* **halibut** : large edible marine flatfish
hal•i•to•sis *n* : bad breath
hall *n* **1** : large public or college or university building **2** : lobby **3** : auditorium
hal•le•lu•jah *interj* — used to express praise, joy, or thanks
hall•mark *n* : distinguishing characteristic
hal•low *vb* : consecrate — **hal•lowed** *adj*
Hal•low•een *n* : evening of October 31 observed esp. by children in merrymaking and masquerading
hal•lu•ci•na•tion *n* : perception of objects that are not real — **hal•lu•ci•nate** *vb* — **hal•lu•ci•na•to•ry** *adj*
hal•lu•ci•no•gen *n* : substance that induces hallucinations — **hal•lu•ci•no•gen•ic** *adj*
hall•way *n* : entrance hall
ha•lo *n, pl* **-los** *or* **-loes** : circle of light appearing to surround a shining body
¹**halt** *adj* : lame
²**halt** *vb* : stop or cause to stop — **halt** *n*
hal•ter *n* **1** : rope or strap for leading or tying an animal **2** : brief blouse held up by straps ~ *vb* : catch (an animal) with a halter
halt•ing *adj* : uncertain — **halt•ing•ly** *adv*
halve *vb* **halved; halv•ing** **1** : divide into halves **2** : reduce to half
halves *pl of* HALF
ham *n* **1** : thigh — usu. pl. **2** : cut esp. of pork from the thigh **3** : showy actor **4** : amateur radio operator ~ *vb* **-mm-** : overplay a part — **ham** *adj*
ham•burg•er, ham•burg *n* : ground beef or a sandwich made with this
ham•let *n* : small village
ham•mer *n* **1** : hand tool for pounding **2** : gun part whose striking explodes the charge ~ *vb* : beat, drive, or shape with a hammer — **hammer out** *vb* : produce with effort
ham•mer•head *n* **1** : striking part of a hammer **2** : shark with a hammerlike head
ham•mock *n* : swinging bed hung by cords at each end
¹**ham•per** *vb* : impede
²**hamper** *n* : large covered basket
ham•ster *n* : stocky shorttailed rodent
ham•string *vb* **-strung; -string•ing** **1** : cripple by cutting the leg tendons **2** : make ineffective or powerless
hand *n* **1** : end of a front limb adapted for grasping **2** : - side **3** : - promise of marriage **4** : handwrit-

ing **5** : assistance or participation **6** : applause **7** : cards held by a player **8** : worker ~ *vb* : lead, assist, give, or pass with the hand — **hand•clasp** *n* — **hand•craft** *vb* — **hand•ful** *n* — **hand•gun** *n* — **hand•less** *adj* — **hand•made** *adj* — **hand•rail** *n* — **hand•saw** *n* — **hand•wo•ven** *adj* — **hand•writ•ing** *n* — **hand•writ•ten** *adj*
hand•bag *n* : woman's purse
hand•ball *n* : game played by striking a ball with the hand
hand•bill *n* : printed advertisement or notice distributed by hand
hand•book *n* : concise reference book
hand•cuffs *n pl* : locking bracelets that bind the wrists together — **handcuff** *vb*
hand•i•cap *n* **1** : advantage given or disadvantage imposed to equalize a competition **2** : disadvantage — **handicap** *vb* — **hand•i•capped** *adj* — **hand•i•cap•per** *n*
hand•i•craft *n* **1** : manual skill **2** : article made by hand — **•hand•i•craft•er** *n* — **hand•i•crafts•man** *n*
hand•i•work *n* : work done personally or by the hands
hand•ker•chief *n, pl* **-chiefs** : small piece of cloth carried for personal use
han•dle *n* : part to be grasped ~ *vb* **-dled; -dling** **1** : touch, hold, or manage with the hands **2** : deal with **3** : deal or trade in — **han•dle•bar** *n* — **han•dled** *adj* — **han•dler** *n*
hand•maid•en *n* : female attendant
hand•out *n* : something given out
hand•pick *vb* : select personally
hand•shake *n* : clasping of hands (as in greeting)
hand•some *adj* **-som•er; -est** **1** : sizable **2** : generous **3** : nice-looking — **hand•some•ly** *adv* — **hand•some•ness** *n*
hand•spring *n* : somersault on the hands
hand•stand *n* : a balancing upside down on the hands
handy *adj* **hand•i•er; -est** **1** : conveniently near **2** : easily used **3** : dexterous — **hand•i•ly** *adv* — **hand•i•ness** *n*
handy•man *n* : one who does odd jobs
hang *vb* **hung hang•ing** **1** : fasten or remain fastened to an elevated point without support from below **2** : suspend by the neck until dead — past tense often *hanged* **3** : droop ~ *n* **1** : way a thing hangs **2** : an understanding of something — **hang•er** *n* — **hang•ing** *n*
han•gar *n* : airplane shelter
hang•dog *adj* : ashamed or guilty
hang•man *n* : public executioner
hang•nail *n* : loose skin near a fingernail
hang•out *n* : place where one likes to spend time
hang•over *n* : sick feeling following heavy drinking
hank *n* : coil or loop
han•ker *vb* : desire strongly — **han•ker•ing** *n*
han•ky–pan•ky *n* : questionable or underhanded activity
han•som *n* : 2-wheeled covered carriage

Ha·nuk·kah *n* : 8-day Jewish holiday commemorating the rededication of the Temple of Jerusalem after its defilement by Antiochus of Syria

hap·haz·ard *adj* : having no plan or order — **hap·haz·ard·ly** *adv*

hap·less *adj* : unfortunate — **hap·less·ly** *adv* — **hap·less·ness** *n*

hap·pen *vb* 1 : take place 2 : be fortunate to encounter something unexpectedly — often used with infinitive

hap·pen·ing *n* : occurrence

hap·py *adj* **-pi·er; -est** 1 : fortunate 2 : content, pleased, or joyous — **hap·pi·ly** *adv* — **hap·pi·ness** *n*

ha·rangue *n* : ranting or scolding speech — **harangue** *vb* — **ha·rangu·er** *n*

ha·rass *vb* 1 : disturb and impede by repeated raids 2 : annoy continually — **ha·rass·ment** *n*

har·bin·ger *n* : one that announces or foreshadows what is coming

har·bor *n* : protected body of water suitable for anchorage ~ *vb* 1 : give refuge to 2 : hold as a thought or feeling

hard *adj* 1 : not easily penetrated 2 : firm or definite 3 : close or searching 4 : severe or unfeeling 5 : strenuous or difficult 6 : physically strong or intense — **hard** *adv* — **hard·ness** *n*

hard·en *vb* : make or become hard or harder — **hard·en·er** *n*

hard·head·ed *adj* 1 : stubborn 2 : realistic — **hard·head·ed·ly** *adv* — **hard·head·ed·ness** *n*

hard·heart·ed *adj* : lacking sympathy — **hard·heart·ed·ly** *adv* — **hard·heart·ed·ness** *n*

hard·ly *adv* 1 : only just 2 : certainly not

hard·nosed *adj* : tough or uncompromising

hard·ship *n* : suffering or privation

hard·tack *n* : hard biscuit

hard·ware *n* 1 : cutlery or tools made of metal 2 : physical components of a vehicle or apparatus

hard·wood *n* : wood of a broad-leaved usu. deciduous tree — **hardwood** *adj*

har·dy *adj* **-di·er; -est** : able to withstand adverse conditions — **har·di·ly** *adv* — **har·di·ness** *n*

hare *n, pl* **hare** *or* **hares** : long-eared mammal related to the rabbit

hare·brained *adj* : foolish

hare·lip *n* : deformity in which the upper lip is vertically split — **hare·lipped** *adj*

ha·rem *n* : house or part of a house allotted to women in a Muslim household or the women and servants occupying it

hark *vb* : listen

har·le·quin *n* : clown

har·lot *n* : prostitute

harm *n* 1 : physical or mental damage 2 : mischief ~ *vb* : cause harm — **harm·ful** *adj* — **harm·ful·ly** *adv* — **harm·ful·ness** *n* — **harm·less** *adj* — **harm·less·ly** *adv* — **harm·less·ness** *n*

har·mon·ic *adj* 1 : of or relating to musical harmony 2 : pleasing to hear — **har·mon·i·cal·ly** *adv*

har·mon·i·ca *n* : small wind instrument with metallic reeds

har·mo·ny *n, pl* **-nies** 1 : musical combination of sounds 2 : pleasing arrangement of parts 3 : lack of conflict 4 : internal calm — **har·mo·ni·ous** *adj* — **har·mo·ni·ous·ly** *adv* — **har·mo·ni·ous·ness** *n* — **har·mo·ni·za·tion** *n* — **har·mo·nize** *vb*

har·ness *n* : gear of a draft animal ~ *vb* 1 : put a harness on 2 : put to use

harp *n* : musical instrument with many strings plucked by the fingers ~ *vb* 1 : play on a harp 2 : dwell on a subject tiresomely — **harp·er** *n* — **harp·ist** *n*

har·poon *n* : barbed spear used in hunting whales — **harpoon** *vb* — **har·poon·er** *n*

harp·si·chord *n* : keyboard instrument with strings that are plucked

har·py *n, pl* **-pies** : shrewish woman

har·row *n* : implement used to break up soil ~ *vb* 1 : cultivate with a harrow 2 : distress

har·ry *vb* **-ried; -ry·ing** : torment by or as if by constant attack

harsh *adj* 1 : disagreeably rough 2 : severe — **harsh·ly** *adv* — **harsh·ness** *n*

har·um–scar·um *adv* : recklessly

har·vest *n* 1 : act or time of gathering in a crop 2 : mature crop — **harvest** *vb* — **har·vest·er** *n*

has *pres 3d sing of* HAVE

hash *vb* : chop into small pieces ~ *n* : chopped meat mixed with potatoes and browned

hasp *n* : hinged strap fastener esp. for a door

has·sle *n* 1 : quarrel 2 : struggle 3 : cause of annoyance — **hassle** *vb*

has·sock *n* : cushion used as a seat or leg rest

haste *n* 1 : rapidity of motion 2 : rash action 3 : excessive eagerness — **hast·i·ly** *adv* — **hast·i·ness** *n* — **hasty** *adj*

has·ten *vb* : hurry

hat *n* : covering for the head

¹hatch *n* : small door or opening — **hatch·way** *n*

²hatch *vb* : emerge from an egg — **hatch·ery** *n*

hatch·et *n* : short-handled ax

hate *n* : intense hostility and aversion ~ *vb* **hat·ed; hat·ing** 1 : express or feel hate 2 : dislike — **hate·ful** *adj* — **hate·ful·ly** *adv* — **hate·ful·ness** *n* — **hat·er** *n*

ha·tred *n* : hate

hat·ter *n* : one that makes or sells hats

haugh·ty *adj* **-ti·er; -est** : disdainfully proud — **haugh·ti·ly** *adv* — **haugh·ti·ness** *n*

haul *vb* 1 : draw or pull 2 : transport or carry ~ *n* 1 : amount collected 2 : load or the distance it is transported — **haul·er** *n*

haunch *n* : hip or hindquarter — usu. pl.

haunt *vb* 1 : visit often 2 : visit or inhabit as a ghost ~ *n* : place frequented — **haunt·er** *n* — **haunt·ing·ly** *adv*

have *vb* **had; hav·ing; has** 1 : hold in possession, service, or affection 2 : be compelled or forced to 3 — used as an auxiliary with the past participle to form the present perfect, past perfect, or future perfect 4 : obtain or receive 5 : undergo 6 : cause to 7 : bear — **have to do with** : have in the way of connection or relation with or effect on

ha·ven *n* : place of safety

hav·oc *n* 1 : wide destruction 2 : great confusion

¹hawk *n* : bird of prey with a strong hooked bill and sharp talons

²hawk *vb* : offer for sale by calling out in the street — **hawk·er** *n*

haw·ser *n* : large rope

haw·thorn *n* : spiny shrub or tree with pink or white fragrant flowers

hay *n* : herbs (as grass) cut and dried for use as fodder — **hay** *vb* — **hay·loft** *n* — **hay·mow** *n* — **hay·stack** *n*

hay·cock *n* : small pile of hay

hay·rick *n* : large outdoor stack of hay

hay·seed *n* : bumpkin

hay·wire *adj* : being out of order

haz·ard *n* 1 : source of danger 2 : chance ~ *vb* : venture or risk — **haz·ard·ous** *adj*

¹haze *n* : fine dust, smoke, or light vapor in the air that reduces visibility

²haze *vb* **hazed; haz·ing** : harass by abusive and humiliating tricks

ha·zel *n* 1 : shrub or small tree bearing edible nuts (**ha·zel·nuts**) 2 : light brown color

hazy *adj* **haz·i·er; -est** 1 : obscured by haze 2 : vague or indefinite — **haz·i·ly** *adv* — **haz·i·ness** *n*

he *pron* 1 : that male one 2 : a or the person

head *n* 1 : front or upper part of the body 2 : mind 3 : upper or higher end 4 : director or leader 5 : place of leadership or honor ~ *adj* : principal or chief ~ *vb* 1 : provide with or form a head 2 : put, stand, or be at the head 3 : point or proceed in a certain direction — **head·ache** *n* — **head·band** *n* — **head·dress** *n* — **head·ed** *adj* — **head·first** *adv or adj* — **head·gear** *n* — **head·less** *adj* — **head·rest** *n* — **head·ship** *n* — **head·wait·er** *n*

head·ing *n* 1 : direction in which a plane or ship heads 2 : something (as a title) standing at the top or beginning

head·land *n* : promontory

head·light *n* : light on the front of a vehicle

head·line *n* : introductory line of a newspaper story printed in large type

head·long *adv* 1 : head foremost 2 : in a rash or reckless manner — **head·long** *adj*

head·mas·ter *n* : man who is head of a private school

head·mis·tress *n* : woman who is head of a private school

head–on *adj* : having the front facing in the direction of initial contact — **head–on** *adv*

head·phone *n* : an earphone held on by a band over the head — usu. pl.

head·quar·ters *n sing or pl* : command or administrative center

head·stone *n* : stone at the head of a grave

head·strong *adj* : stubborn or willful

head·wa·ters *n pl* : source of a stream

head·way *n* : forward motion

heady *adj* **head·i·er; -est** 1 : - intoxicating 2 : shrewd

heal *vb* : make or become sound or whole — **heal·er** *n*

health *n* : sound physical or mental condition

health·ful *adj* : beneficial to health — **health·ful·ly** *adv* — **health·ful·ness** *n*

healthy *adj* **health·i·er; -est** : enjoying or typical of good health — **health·i·ly** *adv* — **health·i·ness** *n*

heap *n* : pile ~ *vb* : throw or lay in a heap

hear *vb* **heard; hear·ing** 1 : perceive by the ear 2 : heed 3 : learn

hear·ing *n* 1 : process or power of perceiving sound 2 : earshot 3 : session in which witnesses are heard

hear·ken *vb* : give attention

hear·say *n* : rumor

hearse *n* : vehicle for carrying the dead to the grave

heart *n* 1 : hollow muscular organ that keeps up the circulation of the blood 2 : playing card of a suit marked with a red heart 3 : whole personality or the emotional or moral part of it 4 : courage 5 : essential part — **heart·beat** *n* — **heart·ed** *adj*

heart·ache *n* : anguish of mind

heart·break *n* : crushing grief — **heart·break·er** *n* — **heart·break·ing** *adj* — **heart·bro·ken** *adj*

heart·burn *n* : burning distress in the heart area after eating

heart·en *vb* : encourage

hearth *n* 1 : area in front of a fireplace 2 : home — **hearth·stone** *n*

heart·less *adj* : cruel

heart·rend·ing *adj* : causing intense grief or anguish

heart·sick *adj* : very despondent — **heart·sick·ness** *n*

heart·strings *n pl* : deepest emotions

heart·throb *n* : sweetheart

heart·warm·ing *adj* : inspiring sympathetic feeling

heart·wood *n* : central portion of wood

hearty *adj* **heart·i·er; -est** 1 : vigorously healthy 2 : nourishing — **heart·i·ly** *adv* — **heart·i·ness** *n*

heat *vb* : make or become warm or hot — *n* **1** : condition of being hot **2** : form of energy that causes a body to rise in temperature **3** : intensity of feeling — **heat•ed•ly** *adv* — **heat•er** *n*

heath *n* **1** : often evergreen shrubby plant of wet acid soils **2** : tract of wasteland — **heathy** *adj*

hea•then *n, pl* **-thens** *or* **-then** : uncivilized or godless person — **heathen** *adj*

heath•er *n* : evergreen heath with lavender flowers — **heath•ery** *adj*

heat•stroke *n* : disorder that follows prolonged exposure to excessive heat

heave *vb* **heaved** *or* **hove; heav•ing 1** : rise or lift upward **2** : throw **3** : rise and fall ~ *n* **1** : an effort to lift or raise **2** : throw

heav•en *n* **1** *pl* : sky **2** : abode of the Deity and of the blessed dead **3** : place of supreme happiness — **heav•en•ly** *adj* — **heav•en•ward** *adv or adj*

heavy *adj* **heavi•er; -est 1** : - having great weight **2** : hard to bear **3** : greater than the average — **heav•i•ly** *adv* — **heavi•ness** *n* — **heavy•weight** *n*

heavy–du•ty *adj* : able to withstand unusual strain

heavy•set *adj* : stocky and compact in build

heck•le *vb* **-led; -ling** : harass with gibes — **heck•ler** *n*

hec•tic *adj* : filled with excitement, activity, or confusion — **hec•ti•cal•ly** *adv*

hedge *n* **1** : fence or boundary of shrubs or small trees **2** : means of protection ~ *vb* **hedged; hedg•ing 1** : protect oneself against loss **2** : evade the risk of commitment — **hedg•er** *n*

hedge•hog *n* : spiny mammal (as a porcupine)

he•do•nism *n* : way of life devoted to pleasure — **he•do•nist** *n* — **he•do•nis•tic** *adj*

heed *vb* : pay attention ~ *n* : attention — **heed•ful** *adj* — **heed•ful•ly** *adv* — **heed•ful•ness** *n* — **heed•less** *adj* — **heed•less•ly** *adv* — **heed•less•ness** *n*

¹heel *n* **1** : back of the foot **2** : crusty end of a loaf of bread **3** : solid piece forming the back of the sole of a shoe — **heel•less** *adj*

²heel *vb* : tilt to one side

heft *n* : weight ~ *vb* : judge the weight of by lifting

hefty *adj* **heft•i•er; -est** : big and bulky

he•ge•mo•ny *n* : - preponderant influence over others

heif•er *n* : young cow

height *n* **1** : highest part or point **2** : distance from bottom to top **3** : altitude

height•en *vb* : increase in amount or degree

hei•nous *adj* : shockingly evil — **hei•nous•ly** *adv* — **hei•nous•ness** *n*

heir *n* : one who inherits or is entitled to inherit property

heir•ess *n* : female heir esp. to great wealth

heir•loom *n* : something handed on from one generation to another

held *past of* HOLD

he•li•cal *adj* : spiral

he•li•cop•ter *n* : aircraft supported in the air by rotors

he•lio•trope *n* : garden herb with small fragrant white or purple flowers

he•li•um *n* : very light nonflammable gaseous chemical element

he•lix *n, pl* **-li•ces** : something spiral

hell *n* **1** : nether world in which the dead continue to exist **2** : realm of the devil **3** : place or state of torment or destruction — **hell•ish** *adj*

hell•gram•mite *n* : aquatic insect larva

hel•lion *n* : troublesome person

hel•lo *n, pl* **-los** : expression of greeting

helm *n* : lever or wheel for steering a ship — **helms•man** *n*

hel•met *n* : protective covering for the head

help *vb* **1** : supply what is needed **2** : be of

use **3** : refrain from or prevent ~ *n* **1** : something that helps or a source of help **2** : one who helps another — **help•er** *n* — **help•ful** *adj* — **help•ful•ly** *adv* — **help•ful•ness** *n* — **help•less** *adj* — **help•less•ly** *adv* — **help•less•ness** *n*

help•ing *n* : portion of food

help•mate *n* **1** : helper **2** : wife

help•meet *n* : helpmate

hel•ter–skel•ter *adv* : in total disorder

hem *n* : border of an article of cloth doubled back and stitched down ~ *vb* **-mm- 1** : sew a hem **2** : surround restrictively — **hem•line** *n*

he•ma•tol•o•gy *n* : study of the blood and blood-forming organs — **hema•to•log•ic** *adj* — **he•ma•tol•o•gist** *n*

hemi•sphere *n* : one of the halves of the earth divided by the equator into northern and southern parts (**northern hemisphere, southern hemisphere**) or by a meridian into eastern and western parts (**eastern hemisphere, western hemisphere**) — **hemi•spher•ic, hemi•spher•i•cal** *adj*

hem•lock *n* **1** : poisonous herb related to the carrot **2** : evergreen tree related to the pines

he•mo•glo•bin *n* : iron-containing compound found in red blood cells

he•mo•phil•ia *n* : hereditary tendency to severe prolonged bleeding — **he•mo•phil•i•ac** *adj or n*

hem•or•rhage *n* : large discharge of blood — **hemorrhage** *vb* — **hem•or•rhag•ic** *adj*

hem•or•rhoids *n pl* : swollen mass of dilated veins at or just within the anus

hemp *n* : tall Asian herb grown for its tough fiber — **hemp•en** *adj*

hen *n* : female domestic fowl

hence *adv* **1** : away **2** : therefore **3** : from this source or origin

hence•forth *adv* : from this point on

hence•for•ward *adv* : henceforth

hench•man *n* : trusted follower

hen•na *n* : reddish brown dye from a tropical shrub used esp. on hair

hen•peck *vb* : subject (one's husband) to persistent nagging

he•pat•ic *adj* : relating to or resembling the liver

hep•a•ti•tis *n, pl* **-tit•i•des** : disease in which the liver becomes inflamed

her *adj* : of or relating to her or herself ~ *pron, objective case of* SHE

her•ald *n* **1** : official crier or messenger **2** : harbinger ~ *vb* : give notice

her•ald•ry *n, pl* **-ries** : practice of devising and granting stylized emblems (as for a family) — **he•ral•dic** *adj*

herb *n* **1** : seed plant that lacks woody tissue **2** : plant or plant part valued for medicinal or savory qualities — **her•ba•ceous** *adj* — **herb•age** *n* — **herb•al** *n or adj* — **herb•al•ist** *n*

her•bi•cide *n* : agent that destroys plants — **her•bi•cid•al** *adj*

her•biv•o•rous *adj* : feeding on plants — **her•bi•vore** *n*

her•cu•le•an *adj* : of extraordinary power, size, or difficulty

herd *n* : group of animals of one kind ~ *vb* : assemble or move in a herd — **herd•er** *n* — **herds•man** *n*

here *adv* **1** : in, at, or to this place **2** : now **3** : at or in this point or particular **4** : in the present life or state ~ *n* : this place — **here•abouts, here•about** *adv*

here•af•ter *adv* : in some future time or state ~ *n* : existence beyond earthly life

here•by *adv* : by means of this

he•red•i•tary *adj* **1** : genetically passed or passable from parent to offspring **2** : passing by inheritance

he•red•i•ty *n* : the passing of characteristics from parent to offspring

here•in *adv* : in this

here•of *adv* : of this

here•on *adv* : on this

her•e•sy *n, pl* **-sies** : opinion or doctrine contrary to church dogma — **her•e•tic** *n* — **he•re•ti•cal** *adj*

here•to *adv* : to this document

here•to•fore *adv* : up to this time

here•un•der *adv* : under this

here•un•to *adv* : to this

here•upon *adv* : on this

here•with *adv* **1** : with this **2** : hereby

her•i•tage *n* **1** : inheritance **2** : birthright

her•maph•ro•dite *n* : - animal or plant having both male and female reproductive organs — **her•maphrodite** *adj* — **her•maph•ro•dit•ic** *adj*

her•met•ic *adj* : sealed airtight — **her•met•i•cal•ly** *adv*

her•mit *n* : one who lives in solitude

her•nia *n, pl* **-ni•as** *or* **-ni•ae** : protrusion of a bodily part through the weakened wall of its enclosure — **her•ni•ate** *vb*

he•ro *n, pl* **-roes** : one that is much admired or shows great courage — **he•ro•ic** *adj* — **he•ro•i•cal•ly** *adv* — **he•ro•ics** *n pl* — **her•o•ism** *n*

her•o•in *n* : strongly addictive narcotic

her•o•ine *n* : woman of heroic achievements or qualities

her•on *n* : long-legged long-billed wading bird

her•pes *n* : virus disease characterized by the formation of blisters

her•pe•tol•o•gy *n* : study of reptiles and amphibians — **her•pe•tol•o•gist** *n*

her•ring *n, pl* **-ring** *or* **-rings** : narrow-bodied Atlantic food fish

hers *pron* : one or the ones belonging to her

her•self *pron* : she, her — used reflexively or for emphasis

hertz *n, pl* **hertz** : unit of frequency equal to one cycle per second

hes•i•tant *adj* : tending to hesitate — **hes•i•tance** *n* — **hes•i•tan•cy** *n* — **hes•i•tant•ly** *adv*

hes•i•tate *vb* **-tat•ed; -tat•ing 1** : hold back esp. in doubt **2** : pause — **hes•i•ta•tion** *n*

het•er•o•ge•neous *adj* : consisting of dissimilar ingredients or constituents — **het•er•o•ge•ne•ity** *n* — **het•ero•ge•neous•ly** *adv*

het•ero•sex•u•al *adj* : oriented toward the opposite sex — **heterosexual** *n* — **het•ero•sex•u•al•i•ty** *n*

hew *vb* **hewed; hewed** *or* **hewn; hew•ing 1** : cut or shape with or as if with an ax **2** : conform strictly — **hew•er** *n*

hex *vb* : put an evil spell on — **hex** *n*

hexa•gon *n* : 6-sided polygon — **hex•ag•o•nal** *adj*

hey•day *n* : time of flourishing

hi•a•tus *n* : lapse in continuity

hi•ba•chi *n* : brazier

hi•ber•nate *vb* **-nat•ed; -nat•ing** : pass the winter in a torpid or resting state — **hi•ber•na•tion** *n* — **hi•ber•na•tor** *n*

hic•cup *vb* **-cuped; -cup•ing** : to inhale spasmodically and make a peculiar sound ~ *n pl* : attack of hiccuping

hick *n* : awkward provincial person — **hick** *adj*

hick•o•ry *n, pl* **-ries** : No. American hardwood tree — **hickory** *adj*

¹hide *vb* **hid; hid•den** *or* **hid; hid•ing** : put or remain out of sight — **hid•er** *n*

²hide *n* : animal skin

hide•bound *adj* : inflexible or conservative

hid•eous *adj* : very ugly — **hid•eous•ly** *adv* — **hid•eous•ness** *n*

hie *vb* **hied; hy•ing** *or* **hie•ing** : hurry

hi•er•ar•chy n, pl **-chies** : persons or things arranged in a graded series — **hi•er•ar•chi•cal** adj

hi•er•o•glyph•ic n : character in the picture writing of the ancient Egyptians

high adj 1 : having large extension upward 2 : elevated in pitch 3 : exalted in character 4 : of greater degree or amount than average 5 : expensive 6 : excited or stupefied by alcohol or a drug ~ adv : at or to a high place or degree ~ n 1 : elevated point or level 2 : automobile gear giving the highest speed — **highly** adv

high•boy n : high chest of drawers on legs

high•brow n : person of superior learning or culture — **highbrow** adj

high–flown adj : pretentious

high–hand•ed adj : willful and arrogant — **high–hand•ed•ly** adv — **high–hand•ed•ness** n

high•land n : hilly country — **high•land•er** n

high•light n : event or detail of major importance ~ vb 1 : emphasize 2 : be a highlight of

high•ness n 1 : quality or degree of being high 2 — used as a title (as for kings)

high–rise adj : having several stories

high school n : school usu. including grades 9 to 12 or 10 to 12

high–spir•it•ed adj : lively

high–strung adj : very nervous or sensitive

high•way n : public road

high•way•man n : one who robs travelers on a road

hi•jack vb : steal esp. by commandeering a vehicle — **hijack** n — **hi•jack•er** n

hike vb **hiked; hik•ing** 1 : raise quickly 2 : take a long walk ~ n 1 : long walk 2 : increase — **hik•er** n

hi•lar•i•ous adj : extremely funny — **hi•lar•i•ous•ly** adv — **hi•lar•i•ty** n

hill n : place where the land rises — **hill•side** n — **hill•top** n — **hilly** adj

hill•bil•ly n, pl **-lies** : person from a backwoods area

hill•ock n : small hill

hilt n : handle of a sword

him pron, objective case of HE

him•self pron : he, him — used reflexively or for emphasis

¹hind n : female deer

²hind adj : back

hin•der vb : obstruct or hold back

hind•most adj : farthest to the rear

hind•quar•ter n : back half of a complete side of a carcass

hin•drance n : something that hinders

hind•sight n : understanding of an event after it has happened

Hin•du•ism n : body of religious beliefs and practices native to India — **Hin•du** n or adj

hinge n : jointed piece on which a swinging part (as a door) turns ~ vb **hinged; hing•ing** 1 : attach by or furnish with hinges 2 : depend

hint n 1 : indirect suggestion 2 : clue 3 : very small amount — **hint** vb

hin•ter•land n : remote region

hip n : part of the body on either side just below the waist — **hip•bone** n

hip•po•pot•a•mus n, pl **-mus•es** or **-mi** : large thick-skinned African river animal

hire n 1 : payment for labor 2 : employment 3 : one who is hired ~ vb **hired; hir•ing** : employ for pay

hire•ling n : one who serves another only for gain

hir•sute adj : hairy

his adj : of or belonging to him ~ pron : ones belonging to him

hiss vb 1 : make a sibilant sound 2 : show dislike by hissing — **hiss** n

his•to•ri•an n : writer of history

his•to•ry n, pl **-ries** 1 : chronological record of significant events 2 : study of past events 3 : an established record — **his•tor•ic, his•tor•i•cal** adj — **his•tor•i•cal•ly** adv

his•tri•on•ics n pl : exaggerated display of emotion

hit vb **hit; hit•ting** 1 : reach with a blow 2 : come or cause to come in contact 3 : affect detrimentally ~ n 1 : blow 2 : great success — **hit•ter** n

hitch vb 1 : move by jerks 2 : catch by a hook 3 : hitchhike ~ n 1 : jerk 2 : sudden halt

hitch•hike vb : travel by securing free rides from passing vehicles — **hitch•hik•er** n

hith•er adv : to this place

hith•er•to adv : up to this time

hive n 1 : container housing honeybees 2 : colony of bees — **hive** vb

hives n sing or pl : allergic disorder with itchy skin patches

HMO n : comprehensive health-care organization financed by clients

hoard n : hidden accumulation — **hoard** vb — **hoard•er** n

hoar•frost n : frost

hoarse adj **hoars•er; -est** 1 : harsh in sound 2 : speaking in a harsh strained voice — **hoarse•ly** adv — **hoarse•ness** n

hoary adj **hoar•i•er; -est** : gray or white with age — **hoar•i•ness** n

hoax n : act intended to trick or dupe — **hoax** vb — **hoax•er** n

hob•ble vb **-bled; -bling** : limp along ~ n : hobbling movement

hob•by n, pl **-bies** : interest engaged in for relaxation — **hob•by•ist** n

hob•gob•lin n 1 : mischievous goblin 2 : bogey

hob•nail n : short nail for studding shoe soles — **hob-nailed** adj

hob•nob vb **-bb-** : associate socially

ho•bo n, pl **-boes** : tramp

¹hock n : joint or region in the hind limb of a quadruped corresponding to the human ankle

²hock n or vb : pawn

hock•ey n : game played on ice or a field by 2 teams

hod n : carrier for bricks or mortar

hodge•podge n : heterogeneous mixture

hoe n : long-handled tool for cultivating or weeding — **hoe** vb

hog n 1 : domestic adult swine 2 : glutton ~ vb : take selfishly — **hog•gish** adj

hogs•head n : large cask or barrel

hog•wash n : nonsense

hoist vb : lift ~ n 1 : lift 2 : apparatus for hoisting

hok•ey adj **hok•i•er; -est** 1 : tiresomely simple or sentimental 2 : phony

¹hold vb **held; hold•ing** 1 : possess 2 : restrain 3 : have a grasp on 4 : remain or keep in a particular situation or position 5 : contain 6 : regard 7 : cause to occur 8 : occupy esp. by appointment or election ~ n 1 : act or manner of holding 2 : restraining or controlling influence — **hold•er** n — **hold forth** : speak at length — **hold to** : adhere to — **hold with** : agree with

²hold n : cargo area of a ship

hold•ing n : property owned — usu. pl.

hold•up n 1 : robbery at the point of a gun 2 : delay

hole n 1 : opening into or through something 2 : hollow place (as a pit) 3 : den — **hole** vb

hol•i•day n 1 : day of freedom from work 2 : vacation — **holiday** vb

ho•li•ness n : quality or state of being holy — used as a title for a high religious official

ho•lis•tic adj : relating to a whole (as the body)

hol•ler vb : cry out — **holler** n

hol•low adj **-low•er; -est** 1 : sunken 2 : having a cavity within 3 : sounding like a noise made in an empty place 4 : empty of value or meaning ~ vb : make or become hollow ~ n 1 : surface depression 2 : cavity — **hol•low•ness** n

hol•ly n, pl **-lies** : evergreen tree or shrub with glossy leaves

hol•ly•hock n : tall perennial herb with showy flowers

ho•lo•caust n : thorough destruction esp. by fire

hol•stein n : large black-and-white dairy cow

hol•ster n : case for a pistol

ho•ly adj **-li•er; -est** 1 : sacred 2 : spiritually pure

hom•age n : reverent regard

home n 1 : residence 2 : congenial environment 3 : place of origin or refuge ~ vb **homed; hom•ing** : go or return home — **home•bred** adj — **home•com•ing** n — **home•grown** adj — **home•land** n — **home•less** adj — **home•made** adj

home•ly adj **-li•er; -est** : plain or unattractive — **home•li•ness** n

home•mak•er n : one who manages a household — **home•mak•ing** n

home•sick adj : longing for home — **home•sick•ness** n

home•spun adj : simple

home•stead n : home and land occupied and worked by a family — **home•stead•er** n

home•stretch n 1 : last part of a racetrack 2 : final stage

home•ward, home•wards adv : toward home — **home•ward** adj

home•work n : school lessons to be done outside the classroom

hom•ey adj **hom•i•er; -est** : characteristic of home

ho•mi•cide n : the killing of one human being by another — **hom•i•cid•al** adj

hom•i•ly n, pl **-lies** : sermon

hom•i•ny n : type of processed hulled corn

ho•mo•ge•neous adj : of the same or a similar kind — **ho•mo•ge•ne•i•ty** n — **ho•mo•ge•neous•ly** adv

ho•mog•e•nize vb **-nized; -niz•ing** : make the particles in (as milk) of uniform size and even distribution — **ho•mog•e•ni•za•tion** n — **ho•mog•e•niz•er** n

ho•mo•graph n : one of 2 or more words (as the noun conduct and the verb conduct) spelled alike but different in origin or meaning or pronunciation

hom•onym n 1 : homophone 2 : homograph 3 : one of 2 or more words (as pool of water and pool the game) spelled and pronounced alike but different in meaning

ho•mo•phone n : one of 2 or more words (as to, too, and two) pronounced alike but different in origin or meaning or spelling

Ho•mo sa•pi•ens n : humankind

ho•mo•sex•u•al adj : oriented toward one's own sex — **homosexual** n — **ho•mo•sex•u•al•i•ty** n

hone vb : sharpen with or as if with an abrasive stone

hon•est adj 1 : free from deception 2 : trustworthy 3 : frank — **hon•est•ly** adv — **hon•esty** n

hon•ey n, pl **-eys** : sweet sticky substance made by bees (**hon•ey•bees**) from the nectar of flowers

hon•ey•comb n : mass of 6-sided wax cells built by honeybees or something like it ~ vb : make or become full of holes like a honeycomb

hon•ey•moon n : holiday taken by a newly married couple — **honeymoon** vb

hon•ey•suck•le n : shrub or vine with flowers rich in nectar

honk n : cry of a goose or a similar sound — **honk** vb — **honk•er** n

hon•or n 1 : good name 2 : outward respect or symbol of this 3 : privilege 4 : person of superior rank or position — used esp. as a title **5** : something or someone worthy of respect **6** : integrity ~ *vb* **1** : regard with honor **2** : confer honor on **3** : fulfill the terms of — **hon•or•able** *adj* — **hon•or•ably** *adv* — **hon•or•ari•ly** *adv* — **hon•or•ary** *adj* — **hon•or•ee** *n*

hood *n* **1** : part of a garment that covers the head **2** : covering over an automobile engine compartment — **hood•ed** *adj*

-hood *n suffix* **1** : state, condition, or quality **2** : individuals sharing a state or character

hood•lum *n* : thug

hood•wink *vb* : deceive

hoof *n, pl* **hooves** or **hoofs** : horny covering of the toes of some mammals (as horses or cattle) — **hoofed** *adj*

hook *n* : curved or bent device for catching, holding, or pulling ~ *vb* : seize or make fast with a hook — **hook•er** *n*

hook•worm *n* : parasitic intestinal worm

hoo•li•gan *n* : thug

hoop *n* : circular strip, figure, or object

hoot *vb* **1** : shout in contempt **2** : make the cry of an owl — **hoot** *n* — **hoot•er** *n*

¹hop *vb* **-pp-** : move by quick springy leaps — **hop** *n*

²hop *n* : vine whose ripe dried flowers are used to flavor malt liquors

hope *vb* **hoped; hop•ing** : desire with expectation of fulfillment ~ *n* **1** : act of hoping **2** : something hoped for — **hope•ful** *adj* — **hope•fully** *adv* — **hope•ful•ness** *n* — **hope•less** *adj* — **hope•less•ly** *adv* — **hope•less•ness** *n*

hop•per *n* : container that releases its contents through the bottom

horde *n* : throng or swarm

ho•ri•zon *n* : apparent junction of earth and sky

hor•i•zon•tal *adj* : parallel to the horizon — **hor•i•zon•tal•ly** *adv*

hor•mone *n* : cell product in body fluids that has a specific effect on other cells — **hor•mon•al** *adj*

horn *n* **1** : hard bony projection on the head of a hoofed animal **2** : brass wind instrument — **horned** *adj* — **horn•less** *adj*

hor•net *n* : large social wasp

horny *adj* **horn•i•er; -est** **1** : made of horn **2** : hard or callous **3** : sexually aroused

horo•scope *n* : astrological forecast

hor•ren•dous *adj* : horrible

hor•ri•ble *adj* **1** : having or causing horror **2** : highly disagreeable — **hor•ri•ble•ness** *n* — **hor•ri•bly** *adv*

hor•rid *adj* : horrible — **hor•rid•ly** *adv*

hor•ri•fy *vb* **-fied; -fy•ing** : cause to feel horror

hor•ror *n* **1** : intense fear, dread, or dismay **2** : intense repugnance **3** : something horrible

hors d'oeuvre *n, pl* **hors d'oeuvres** : appetizer

horse *n* : large solid-hoofed domesticated mammal — **horse•back** *n or adv* — **horse•hair** *n* — **horse•hide** *n* — **horse•less** *adj* — **horse•man** *n* — **horse•man•ship** *n* — **horse•wom•an** *n* — **hors•ey, horsy** *adj*

horse•fly *n* : large fly with bloodsucking female

horse•play *n* : rough boisterous play

horse•pow•er *n* : unit of mechanical power

horse•rad•ish *n* : herb with a pungent root used as a condiment

horse•shoe *n* : U-shaped protective metal plate fitted to the rim of a horse's hoof

hor•ti•cul•ture *n* : science of growing fruits, vegetables, and flowers — **hor•ti•cul•tur•al** *adj* — **hor•ti•cul•tur•ist** *n*

ho•san•na *interj* — used as a cry of acclamation and adoration — **hosanna** *n*

hose *n* **1** *pl* **hose** : stocking or sock **2** *pl* **hos•es** : flexible tube for conveying fluids ~ *vb* **hosed; hos•ing** : spray, water, or wash with a hose

ho•siery *n* : stockings or socks

hos•pice *n* **1** : lodging (as for travelers) maintained by a religious order **2** : facility or program for caring for dying persons

hos•pi•ta•ble *adj* : given to generous and cordial reception of guests — **hos•pi•ta•bly** *adv*

hos•pi•tal *n* : institution where the sick or injured receive medical care — **hos•pi•tal•i•za•tion** *n* — **hos•pi•tal•ize** *vb*

hos•pi•tal•i•ty *n, pl* **-ties** : hospitable treatment, reception, or disposition

¹host *n* **1** : army **2** : multitude

²host *n* : one who receives or entertains guests — **host** *vb*

³host *n* : eucharistic bread

hos•tage *n* : person held to guarantee that promises be kept or demands met

hos•tel *n* : lodging for youth — **hos•tel•er** *n*

hos•tel•ry *n, pl* **-ries** : hotel

host•ess *n* : woman who is host

hos•tile *adj* : openly or actively unfriendly or opposed to someone or something — **hostile** *n* — **hos•tile•ly** *adv* — **hos•til•i•ty** *n*

hot *adj* **-tt-** **1** : having a high temperature **2** : giving a sensation of heat or burning **3** : ardent **4** : pungent — **hot** *adv* — **hot•ly** *adv* — **hot•ness** *n*

hot•bed *n* : environment that favors rapid growth

hot dog *n* : frankfurter

ho•tel *n* : building where lodging and personal services are provided

hot•head•ed *adj* : impetuous — **hot•head** *n* — **hot•head•ed•ly** *adv* — **hot•head•ed•ness** *n*

hot•house *n* : greenhouse

hound *n* : long-eared hunting dog ~ *vb* : pursue relentlessly

hour *n* **1** : 24th part of a day **2** : time of day — **hour•ly** *adv or adj*

hour•glass *n* : glass vessel for measuring time

house *n, pl* **hous•es** **1** : building to live in **2** : household **3** : legislative body **4** : business firm ~ *vb* **housed; hous•ing** : provide with or take shelter — **house•boat** *n* — **house•clean** *vb* — **house•clean•ing** *n* — **house•ful** *n* — **house•maid** *n* — **house•wares** *n pl* — **house•work** *n*

house•bro•ken *adj* : trained in excretory habits acceptable in indoor living

house•fly *n* : two-winged fly common about human habitations

house•hold *n* : those who dwell as a family under the same roof ~ *adj* **1** : domestic **2** : common or familiar — **house•hold•er** *n*

house•keep•ing *n* : care and management of a house or institution — **house•keep•er** *n*

house•warm•ing *n* : party to celebrate moving into a house

house•wife *n* : married woman in charge of a household — **house•wife•ly** *adj* — **house•wif•ery** *n*

hous•ing *n* **1** : dwellings for people **2** : protective covering

hove *past of* HEAVE

hov•el *n* : small wretched house

hov•er *vb* **1** : remain suspended in the air **2** : move about in the vicinity

how *adv* **1** : in what way or condition **2** : for what reason **3** : to what extent ~ *conj* : the way or manner in which

how•ev•er *conj* : in whatever manner ~ *adv* **1** : to whatever degree or in whatever manner **2** : in spite of that

how•it•zer *n* : short cannon

howl *vb* : emit a loud long doleful sound like a dog — **howl** *n* — **howl•er** *n*

hoy•den *n* : girl or woman of saucy or carefree behavior

hub *n* : central part of a circular object (as of a wheel) — **hub•cap** *n*

hub•bub *n* : uproar

hu•bris *n* : excessive pride

huck•le•ber•ry *n* **1** : shrub related to the blueberry or its berry **2** : blueberry

huck•ster *n* : peddler

hud•dle *vb* **-dled; -dling** **1** : crowd together **2** : confer — **huddle** *n*

hue *n* : color or gradation of color — **hued** *adj*

huff *n* : fit of pique — **huffy** *adj*

hug *vb* **-gg-** **1** : press tightly in the arms **2** : stay close to — **hug** *n*

huge *adj* **hug•er; hug•est** : very large or extensive — **huge•ly** *adv* — **huge•ness** *n*

hu•la *n* : Polynesian dance

hulk *n* **1** : bulky or unwieldy person or thing **2** : old ship unfit for service — **hulk•ing** *adj*

hull *n* **1** : outer covering of a fruit or seed **2** : frame or body of a ship or boat ~ *vb* : remove the hulls of — **hull•er** *n*

hul•la•ba•loo *n, pl* **-loos** : uproar

hum *vb* **-mm-** **1** : make a prolonged sound like that of the speech sound **2** : be busily active **3** : run smoothly **4** : sing with closed lips — **hum** *n* — **hum•mer** *n*

hu•man *adj* **1** : of or relating to the species people belong to **2** : by, for, or like people — **human** *n* — **hu•man•kind** *n* — **hu•man•ly** *adv* — **hu•man•ness** *n*

hu•mane *adj* : showing compassion or consideration for others — **hu•mane•ly** *adv* — **hu•mane•ness** *n*

hu•man•ism *n* : doctrine or way of life centered on human interests or values — **hu•man•ist** *n or adj* — **hu•man•is•tic** *adj*

hu•man•i•tar•i•an *n* : person promoting human welfare — **humanitarian** *adj* — **hu•man•i•tari•an•ism** *n*

hu•man•i•ty *n, pl* **-ties** **1** : human or humane quality or state **2** : the human race

hu•man•ize *vb* **-ized; -iz•ing** : make human or humane — **hu•man•iza•tion** *n* — **hu•man•iz•er** *n*

hu•man•oid *adj* : having human form — **humanoid** *n*

hum•ble *adj* **-bler; -blest** **1** : not proud or haughty **2** : not pretentious ~ *vb* **-bled; -bling** : make humble — **hum•ble•ness** *n* — **hum•bler** *n* — **hum•bly** *adv*

hum•bug *n* : nonsense

hum•drum *adj* : monotonous

hu•mid *adj* : containing or characterized by moisture — **hu•mid•i•fi•ca•tion** *n* — **hu•mid•i•fi•er** *n* — **hu•mid•i•fy** *vb* — **hu•mid•ly** *adv*

hu•mid•i•ty *n, pl* **-ties** : atmospheric moisture

hu•mi•dor *n* : - humidified storage case (as for cigars)

hu•mil•i•ate *vb* **-at•ed; -at•ing** : injure the self-respect of — **hu•mil•i•at•ing•ly** *adv* — **hu•mil•i•ation** *n*

hu•mil•i•ty *n* : humble quality or state

hum•ming•bird *n* : tiny American bird that can hover

hum•mock *n* : mound or knoll — **hum•mocky** *adj*

hu•mor *n* **1** : mood **2** : quality of being laughably ludicrous or incongruous **3** : appreciation of what is ludicrous or incongruous **4** : something intended to be funny ~ *vb* : comply with the wishes or mood of — **hu•mor•ist** *n* — **hu•mor•less** *adj* — **hu•mor•less•ly** *adv* — **hu•mor•less•ness** *n* — **hu•mor•ous** *adj* — **hu•mor•ous•ly** *adv* — **hu•mor•ous•ness** *n*

hump *n* : rounded protuberance — **humped** *adj*

hump•back *n* : hunchback — **hump•backed** *adj*

hu•mus *n* : dark organic part of soil

hunch *vb* : assume or cause to assume a bent or crooked posture ~ *n* : strong intuitive feeling

hunch•back *n* **1** : back with a hump **2** : person with a crooked back — **hunch•backed** *adj*

hun·dred *n, pl* **-dreds** *or* **-dred** : 10 times 10 — **hundred** *adj* — **hun·dredth** *adj or n*

¹**hung** *past of* HANG

²**hung** *adj* : unable to reach a verdict

hun·ger *n* **1** : craving or urgent need for food **2** : strong desire — **hunger** *vb* — **hun·gri·ly** *adv* — **hun·gry** *adj*

hunk *n* : large piece

hun·ker *vb* : settle in for a sustained period — used with *down*

hunt *vb* **1** : pursue for food or sport **2** : try to find ~ *n* : act or instance of hunting — **hunt·er** *n*

hur·dle *n* **1** : barrier to leap over in a race **2** : obstacle — **hurdle** *vb* — **hur·dler** *n*

hurl *vb* : throw with violence — **hurl** *n* — **hurl·er** *n*

hur·rah *interj* — used to express joy or approval

hur·ri·cane *n* : tropical storm with winds of 74 miles per hour or greater

hur·ry *vb* **-ried; -ry·ing** : go or cause to go with haste — ~ *n* : extreme haste — **hur·ried·ly** *adv* — **hur·ried·ness** *n*

hurt *vb* **hurt; hurt·ing** **1** : feel or cause pain **2** : do harm to — ~ *n* **1** : bodily injury **2** : harm — **hurt·ful** *adj* — **hurt·ful·ness** *n*

hur·tle *vb* **-tled; -tling** : move rapidly or forcefully

hus·band *n* : married man ~ *vb* : manage prudently

hus·band·ry *n* **1** : careful use **2** : agriculture

hush *vb* : make or become quiet ~ *n* : silence

husk *n* : outer covering of a seed or fruit ~ *vb* : strip the husk from — **husk·er** *n*

¹**hus·ky** *adj* **-ki·er; -est** : hoarse — **hus·ki·ly** *adv* — **hus·ki·ness** *n*

²**husky** *adj* **-ki·er; -est** : burly — **husk·i·ness** *n*

³**husky** *n, pl* **-kies** : working dog of the arctic

hus·sy *n, pl* **-sies** **1** : brazen woman **2** : mischievous girl

hus·tle *vb* **-tled; -tling** **1** : hurry **2** : work energetically — **hustle** *n* — **hus·tler** *n*

hut *n* : small often temporary dwelling

hutch *n* **1** : cupboard with open shelves **2** : pen for an animal

hy·a·cinth *n* : bulbous herb grown for bell-shaped flowers

hy·brid *n* : offspring of genetically differing parents — **hybrid** *adj* — **hy·brid·iza·tion** *n* — **hy·brid·ize** *vb* — **hy·brid·iz·er** *n*

hy·drant *n* : pipe from which water may be drawn to fight fires

hy·drau·lic *adj* : operated by liquid forced through a small hole — **hy·drau·lics** *n*

hy·dro·car·bon *n* : organic compound of carbon and hydrogen

hy·dro·elec·tric *adj* : producing electricity by waterpower — **hy·dro·elec·tric·i·ty** *n*

hy·dro·gen *n* : very light gaseous colorless odorless flammable chemical element

hydrogen bomb *n* : powerful bomb that derives its energy from the union of atomic nuclei

hy·dro·pho·bia *n* : rabies

hy·dro·plane *n* : speedboat that skims the water

hy·drous *adj* : containing water

hy·e·na *n* : nocturnal carnivorous mammal of Asia and Africa

hy·giene *n* : conditions or practices conducive to health — **hy·gien·ic** *adj* — **hy·gien·i·cal·ly** *adv* — **hy·gien·ist** *n*

hy·grom·e·ter *n* : instrument for measuring atmospheric humidity

hying *pres part of* HIE

hymn *n* : song of praise esp. to God — **hymn** *vb*

hym·nal *n* : book of hymns

hype *vb* **hyped; hyp·ing** : publicize extravagantly — **hype** *n*

hyper- *prefix* **1** : above or beyond **2** : excessively or excessive

hyperacid	hypercorrect
hyperacidity	hypercritical
hyperactive	hyperemotional
hyperacute	hyperenergetic
hyperaggressive	hyperexcitable
hypercautious	hyperfastidious

hyperintense	hypersensitiveness
hypermasculine	hypersensitivity
hypernationalistic	hypersexual
hyperreactive	hypersusceptible
hyperrealistic	hypertense
hyperromantic	hypervigilant
hypersensitive	

hy·per·bo·le *n* : extravagant exaggeration

hy·per·ten·sion *n* : high blood pressure — **hy·per·ten·sive** *adj or n*

hy·phen *n* : punctuation mark - used to divide or compound words — **hyphen** *vb*

hy·phen·ate *vb* **-at·ed; -at·ing** : connect or divide with a hyphen — **hy·phen·ation** *n*

hyp·no·sis *n, pl* **-no·ses** : induced state like sleep in which the subject is responsive to suggestions of the inducer (**hyp·no·tist**) — **hyp·no·tism** *n* — **hyp·no·tiz·able** *adj* — **hyp·no·tize** *vb*

hyp·not·ic *adj* : relating to hypnosis — **hypnotic** *n* — **hyp·not·i·cal·ly** *adv*

hy·po·chon·dria *n* : morbid concern for one's health — **hy·po·chon·dri·ac** *adj or n*

hy·poc·ri·sy *n, pl* **-sies** : a feigning to be what one is not — **hyp·o·crite** *n* — **hyp·o·crit·i·cal** *adj* — **hyp·o·crit·i·cal·ly** *adv*

hy·po·der·mic *adj* : administered or used in making an injection beneath the skin ~ *n* : hypodermic syringe

hy·pot·e·nuse *n* : side of a right-angled triangle opposite the right angle

hy·poth·e·sis *n, pl* **-e·ses** : assumption made in order to test its consequences — **hy·poth·e·size** *vb* — **hy·po·thet·i·cal** *adj* — **hy·po·thet·i·cal·ly** *adv*

hys·ter·ec·to·my *n, pl* **-mies** : surgical removal of the uterus

hys·te·ria *n* : uncontrollable fear or outburst of emotion — **hys·ter·i·cal** *adj* — **hys·ter·i·cal·ly** *adv*

hys·ter·ics *n pl* : uncontrollable laughter or crying

I

i *n, pl* **i's** *or* **is** : 9th letter of the alphabet

I *pron* : the speaker

-ial *adj suffix* : of, relating to, or characterized by

-ian — see -AN

ibis *n, pl* **ibis** *or* **ibis·es** : wading bird with a down-curved bill

-ible — see -ABLE

ibu·pro·fen *n* : drug used to relieve inflammation, pain, and fever

-ic *adj suffix* **1** : of, relating to, or being **2** : containing **3** : characteristic of **4** : marked by **5** : caused by

-i·cal *adj suffix* : -ic — **-i·cal·ly** *adv suffix*

ice *n* **1** : frozen water **2** : flavored frozen dessert ~ *vb* **iced; ic·ing** **1** : freeze **2** : chill **3** : cover with icing

ice·berg *n* : large floating mass of ice

ice·box *n* : refrigerator

ice·break·er *n* : ship equipped to cut through ice

ice cream *n* : sweet frozen food

ice–skate *vb* : skate on ice — **ice skater** *n*

ich·thy·ol·o·gy *n* : study of fishes — **ich·thy·ol·o·gist** *n*

ici·cle *n* : hanging mass of ice

ic·ing *n* : sweet usu. creamy coating for baked goods

icon *n* **1** : religious image **2** : small picture on a computer screen identified with an available function

icon·o·clast *n* : attacker of cherished beliefs or institutions — **icon·o·clasm** *n*

icy *adj* **ic·i·er; -est** **1** : covered with or consisting of ice **2** : very cold — **ic·i·ly** *adv* — **ic·i·ness** *n*

id *n* : unconscious instinctual part of the mind

idea *n* **1** : something imagined in the mind **2** : purpose or plan

ide·al *adj* **1** : imaginary **2** : perfect ~ *n* **1** : standard of excellence **2** : model **3** : aim — **ide·al·ly** *adv*

ide·al·ism *n* : adherence to ideals — **ide·al·ist** *n* — **ide·al·is·tic** *adj* — **ide·al·is·ti·cal·ly** *adv*

ide·al·ize *vb* **-ized; -iz·ing** : think of or represent as ideal — **ide·al·i·za·tion** *n*

iden·ti·cal *adj* **1** : being the same **2** : exactly or essentially alike

iden·ti·fi·ca·tion *n* **1** : act of identifying **2** : evidence of identity

iden·ti·fy *vb* **-fied; -fy·ing** **1** : associate **2** : establish the identity of — **iden·ti·fi·able** *adj* — **iden·ti·fi·er** *n*

iden·ti·ty *n, pl* **-ties** **1** : sameness of essential character **2** : individuality **3** : fact of being what is supposed

ide·ol·o·gy *n, pl* **-gies** : body of beliefs — **ide·o·log·i·cal** *adj*

id·i·om *n* **1** : language peculiar to a person or group **2** : expression with a special meaning — **id·i·om·at·ic** *adj* — **id·i·om·at·i·cal·ly** *adv*

id·io·syn·cra·sy *n, pl* **-sies** : personal peculiarity — **id·io·syn·crat·ic** *adj* — **id·io·syn·crat·i·cal·ly** *adv*

id·i·ot *n* : mentally retarded or foolish person — **id·i·o·cy** *n* — **id·i·ot·ic** *adj* — **id·i·ot·i·cal·ly** *adv*

idle *adj* **idler; idlest** **1** : worthless **2** : inactive **3** : lazy — *vb* **idled; idling** : spend time doing nothing — **idle·ness** *n* — **idler** *n* — **idly** *adv*

idol *n* **1** : image of a god **2** : object of devotion — **idol·iza·tion** *n* — **idol·ize** *vb*

idol·a·ter, idol·a·tor *n* : worshiper of idols — **idol·a·trous** *adj* — **idol·a·try** *n*

idyll *n* : period of peace and contentment — **idyl·lic** *adj*

-ier — see -ER

if *conj* **1** : in the event that **2** : whether **3** : even though

-i·fy *vb suffix* : -fy

ig·loo *n, pl* **-loos** : hut made of snow blocks

ig·nite *vb* **-nit·ed; -nit·ing** : set afire or catch fire — **ig·nit·able** *adj*

ig·ni·tion *n* **1** : a setting on fire **2** : process or means of igniting fuel

ig·no·ble *adj* : not honorable — **ig·no·bly** *adv*

ig·no·min·i·ous *adj* **1** : dishonorable **2** : humiliating — **ig·no·min·i·ous·ly** *adv* — **ig·no·mi·ny** *n*

ig·no·ra·mus *n* : ignorant person

ig·no·rant *adj* **1** : lacking knowledge **2** : showing a lack of knowledge or intelligence **3** : unaware — **ig·no·rance** *n* — **ig·no·rant·ly** *adv*

ig·nore *vb* **-nored; -nor·ing** : refuse to notice

igua·na *n* : large tropical American lizard

ilk *n* : kind

ill *adj* **worse; worst 1** : sick **2** : bad **3** : rude or unacceptable **4** : hostile ~ *adv* **worse; worst 1** : with displeasure **2** : harshly **3** : scarcely **4** : badly ~ *n* **1** : evil **2** : misfortune **3** : sickness

il·le·gal *adj* : not lawful — **il·le·gal·i·ty** *n* — **il·le·gal·ly** *adv*

il·leg·i·ble *adj* : not legible — **il·leg·i·bil·i·ty** *n* — **il·leg·i·bly** *adv*

il·le·git·i·mate *adj* **1** : born of unmarried parents **2** : illegal — **il·le·git·i·ma·cy** *n* — **il·le·git·i·mate·ly** *adv*

il·lic·it *adj* : not lawful — **illic·it·ly** *adv*

il·lim·it·able *adj* : boundless — **il·lim·it·ably** *adv*

il·lit·er·ate *adj* : unable to read or write — **il·lit·er·a·cy** *n* — **illiterate** *n*

ill–na·tured *adj* : cross — **ill–na·tured·ly** *adv*

ill·ness *n* : sickness

il·log·i·cal *adj* : contrary to sound reasoning — **il·log·i·cal·ly** *adv*

ill–starred *adj* : unlucky

il·lu·mi·nate *vb* **-nat·ed; -nat·ing 1** : light up **2** : make clear — **il·lu·mi·nat·ing·ly** *adv* — **il·lu·mi·na·tion** *n*

ill–use *vb* : abuse — **ill–use** *n*

il·lu·sion *n* **1** : mistaken idea **2** : misleading visual image

il·lu·so·ry *adj* : based on or producing illusion

il·lus·trate *vb* **-trat·ed; -trating 1** : explain by example **2** : provide with pictures or figures — **il·lus·tra·tor** *n*

il·lus·tra·tion *n* **1** : example that explains **2** : pictorial explanation

il·lus·tra·tive *adj* : designed to illustrate — **il·lus·tra·tive·ly** *adv*

il·lus·tri·ous *adj* : notably or brilliantly outstanding — **il·lus·tri·ous·ness** *n*

ill will *n* : unfriendly feeling

im·age *n* **1** : likeness **2** : visual counterpart of an object formed by a lens or mirror **3** : mental picture ~ *vb* **-aged; -ag·ing** : create a representation of

im·ag·ery *n* **1** : images **2** : figurative language

imag·i·nary *adj* : existing only in the imagination

imag·i·na·tion *n* **1** : act or power of forming a mental image **2** : creative ability — **imag·i·na·tive** *adj* — **imag·i·na·tive·ly** *adv*

imag·ine *vb* **-ined; -in·ing** : form a mental picture of something not present — **imag·in·able** *adj* — **imag·in·ably** *adv*

im·bal·ance *n* : lack of balance

im·be·cile *n* : idiot — **imbecile, im·be·cil·ic** *adj* — **im·be·cil·i·ty** *n*

im·bibe *vb* **-bibed; -bib·ing** : drink — **im·bib·er** *n*

im·bro·glio *n, pl* **-glios** : complicated situation

im·bue *vb* **-bued; -bu·ing** : fill (as with color or a feeling)

im·i·tate *vb* **-tat·ed; -tat·ing 1** : follow as a model **2** : mimic — **im·i·ta·tive** *adj* — **im·i·ta·tor** *n*

im·i·ta·tion *n* **1** : act of imitating **2** : copy — **imitation** *adj*

im·mac·u·late *adj* : without stain or blemish — **im·mac·u·late·ly** *adv*

im·ma·te·ri·al *adj* **1** : spiritual **2** : not relevant — **im·ma·te·ri·al·i·ty** *n*

im·ma·ture *adj* : not yet mature — **im·ma·tu·ri·ty** *n*

im·mea·sur·able *adj* : indefinitely extensive — **immea·sur·ably** *adv*

im·me·di·a·cy *n, pl* **-cies** : quality or state of being urgent

im·me·di·ate *adj* **1** : direct **2** : being next in line **3** : made or done at once **4** : not distant — **im·me·di·ate·ly** *adv*

im·me·mo·ri·al *adj* : old beyond memory

im·mense *adj* : vast — **immense·ly** *adv* — **im·men·si·ty** *n*

im·merse *vb* **-mersed; -mersing 1** : plunge or dip esp. into liquid **2** : engross — **im·mer·sion** *n*

im·mi·grant *n* : one that immigrates

im·mi·grate *vb* **-grat·ed; -grat·ing** : come into a place and take up residence — **im·mi·gra·tion** *n*

im·mi·nent *adj* : ready to take place — **im·mi·nence** *n* — **im·mi·nent·ly** *adv*

im·mo·bile *adj* : incapable of being moved — **im·mo·bil·i·ty** *n* — **im·mo·bi·lize** *vb*

im·mod·er·ate *adj* : not moderate — **im·mod·er·a·cy** *n* — **im·mod·er·ate·ly** *adv*

im·mod·est *adj* : not modest — **im·mod·est·ly** *adv* — **im·mod·es·ty** *n*

im·mo·late *vb* **-lat·ed; -lat·ing** : offer in sacrifice — **im·mo·la·tion** *n*

im·mor·al *adj* : not moral — **im·mo·ral·i·ty** *n* — **im·mor·al·ly** *adv*

im·mor·tal *adj* **1** : not mortal **2** : having lasting fame ~ *n* : one exempt from death or oblivion — **im·mor·tal·i·ty** *n* — **im·mor·tal·ize** *vb*

im·mov·able *adj* **1** : stationary **2** : unyielding — **im·mov·abil·i·ty** *n* — **im·mov·ably** *adv*

im·mune *adj* : not liable esp. to disease — **im·mu·ni·ty** *n* — **im·mu·ni·za·tion** *n* — **im·mu·nize** *vb*

im·mu·nol·o·gy *n* : science of immunity to disease — **im·mu·no·log·ic, im·mu·no·log·i·cal** *adj* — **im·mu·nol·o·gist** *n*

im·mu·ta·ble *adj* : unchangeable — **im·mu·ta·bil·i·ty** *n* — **im·mu·ta·bly** *adv*

imp *n* **1** : demon **2** : mischievous child

im·pact *vb* **1** : press upon **2** : have an effect on ~ *n* **1** : forceful contact **2** : influence

im·pact·ed *adj* : wedged between the jawbone and another tooth

im·pair *vb* : diminish in quantity, value, or ability — **im·pair·ment** *n*

im·pa·la *n, pl* **impalas** *or* **impala** : large African antelope

im·pale *vb* **-paled; -pal·ing** : pierce with something pointed

im·pal·pa·ble *adj* : incapable of being felt — **im·pal·pa·bly** *adv*

im·pan·el *vb* : enter in or on a panel

im·part *vb* : give from or as if from a store

im·par·tial *adj* : not partial — **im·par·tial·i·ty** *n* — **im·par·tial·ly** *adv*

im·pass·able *adj* : not passable — **im·pass·ably** *adv*

im·passe *n* : inescapable predicament

im·pas·sioned *adj* : filled with passion

im·pas·sive *adj* : showing no feeling or interest — **im·pas·sive·ly** *adv* — **im·pas·siv·i·ty** *n*

im·pa·tiens *n* : annual herb with showy flowers

im·pa·tient *adj* : not patient — **im·pa·tience** *n* — **im·pa·tient·ly** *adv*

im·peach *vb* **1** : charge (an official) with misconduct **2** : cast doubt on **3** : remove from office for misconduct — **im·peach·ment** *n*

im·pec·ca·ble *adj* : faultless — **im·pec·ca·bly** *adv*

im·pe·cu·nious *adj* : broke — **im·pe·cu·nious·ness** *n*

im·pede *vb* **-ped·ed; -ped·ing** : interfere with

im·ped·i·ment *n* **1** : hindrance **2** : speech defect

im·pel *vb* **-pelled; -pel·ling** : urge forward

im·pend *vb* : be about to occur

im·pen·e·tra·ble *adj* : incapable of being penetrated or understood — **im·pen·e·tra·bil·i·ty** *n* — **im·pen·e·tra·bly** *adv*

im·pen·i·tent *adj* : not penitent — **im·pen·i·tence** *n*

im·per·a·tive *adj* **1** : expressing a command **2** : urgent ~ *n* **1** : imperative mood or verb form **2** : unavoidable fact, need, or obligation — **im·per·a·tive·ly** *adv*

im·per·cep·ti·ble *adj* : not perceptible — **im·per·cep·ti·bly** *adv*

im·per·fect *adj* : not perfect — **im·per·fec·tion** *n* — **im·per·fect·ly** *adv*

im·pe·ri·al *adj* **1** : relating to an empire or an emperor **2** : royal

im·pe·ri·al·ism *n* : policy of controlling other nations — **im·pe·ri·al·ist** *n or adj* — **im·pe·ri·al·is·tic** *adj* — **im·pe·ri·al·is·ti·cal·ly** *adv*

im·per·il *vb* **-iled** *or* **-illed; -il·ing** *or* **-il·ling** : endanger

im·pe·ri·ous *adj* : arrogant or domineering — **im·pe·ri·ous·ly** *adv*

im·per·ish·able *adj* : not perishable

im·per·ma·nent *adj* : not permanent — **im·per·ma·nent·ly** *adv*

im·per·me·able *adj* : not permeable

im·per·mis·si·ble *adj* : not permissible

im·per·son·al *adj* : not involving human personality or emotion — **im·per·son·al·i·ty** *n* — **im·per·son·al·ly** *adv*

im·per·son·ate *vb* **-at·ed; -at·ing** : assume the character of — **im·per·son·ation** *n* — **im·per·son·ator** *n*

im·per·ti·nent *adj* **1** : irrelevant **2** : insolent — **im·per·ti·nence** *n* — **im·per·ti·nent·ly** *adv*

im·per·turb·able *adj* : calm and steady

im·per·vi·ous *adj* : incapable of being penetrated or affected

im·pet·u·ous *adj* : impulsive — **im·pet·u·os·i·ty** *n* — **im·pet·u·ous·ly** *adv*

im·pe·tus *n* : driving force

im·pi·ety *n* : quality or state of being impious

im·pinge *vb* **-pinged; -ping·ing** : encroach — **im·pinge·ment** *n*

im·pi·ous *adj* : not pious

imp·ish *adj* : mischievous — **imp·ish·ly** *adv* — **imp·ish·ness** *n*

im·pla·ca·ble *adj* : not capable of being appeased or changed — **im·pla·ca·bil·i·ty** *n* — **im·pla·ca·bly** *adv*

im·plant *vb* **1** : set firmly or deeply **2** : fix in the mind or spirit ~ *n* : something implanted in tissue — **im·plan·ta·tion** *n*

im·plau·si·ble *adj* : not plausible — **im·plau·si·bil·i·ty** *n*

im·ple·ment *n* : tool, utensil ~ *vb* : put into practice — **im·ple·men·ta·tion** *n*

im·pli·cate *vb* **-cat·ed; -cat·ing** : involve

im·pli·ca·tion *n* **1** : an implying **2** : something implied

im·plic·it *adj* **1** : understood though only implied **2** : complete and unquestioning — **im·plic·it·ly** *adv*

im·plode *vb* **-plod·ed; -ploding** : burst inward — **im·plo·sion** *n* — **im·plo·sive** *adj*

im·plore *vb* **-plored; -plor·ing** : entreat

im·ply *vb* **-plied; -ply·ing** : express indirectly

im·po·lite *adj* : not polite

im·pol·i·tic *adj* : not politic

im·pon·der·a·ble *adj* : incapable of being precisely evaluated — **imponderable** *n*

im·port *vb* **1** : mean **2** : bring in from an external source ~ *n* **1** : meaning **2** : importance **3** : something imported — **im·por·ta·tion** *n* — **im·port·er** *n*

im·por·tant *adj* : having great worth, significance, or influence — **im·por·tance** *n* — **impor·tant·ly** *adv*

im·por·tu·nate *adj* : troublesomely persistent or urgent

im·por·tune *vb* **-tuned; -tun·ing** : urge or beg persistently — **im·por·tu·ni·ty** *n*

im·pose *vb* **-posed; -pos·ing 1** : establish as compulsory **2** : take unwarranted advantage of — **im·po·si·tion** *n*

im·pos·ing *adj* : impressive — **im·pos·ing·ly** *adv*

im·pos·si·ble *adj* **1** : incapable of occurring **2** : enormously difficult — **im·pos·si·bil·i·ty** *n* — **im·pos·si·bly** *adv*

im·post *n* : tax

im·pos·tor, im·pos·ter *n* : one who assumes an identity or title to deceive — **im·pos·ture** *n*

im·po·tent *adj* **1** : lacking power **2** : sterile — **im·po·tence** *n* — **im·po·ten·cy** *n* — **im·po·tent·ly** *adv*

im·pound *vb* : seize and hold in legal custody — **im·pound·ment** *n*

im·pov·er·ish *vb* : make poor — **im·pov·er·ish·ment** *n*

im·prac·ti·ca·ble *adj* : not practicable

im·prac·ti·cal *adj* : not practical

im·pre·cise *adj* : not precise — **im·pre·cise·ly** *adv* — **im·pre·cise·ness** *n* — **im·pre·ci·sion** *n*

im·preg·na·ble *adj* : able to resist attack — **im·preg·na·bil·i·ty** *n*

im·preg·nate *vb* **-nat·ed; -nat·ing 1** : make pregnant **2** : cause to be filled, permeated, or saturated — **im·preg·na·tion** *n*

im·pre·sa·rio *n, pl* **-ri·os** : one who sponsors an entertainment

¹im·press *vb* **1** : apply with or produce by pressure **2** : press, stamp, or print in or upon **3** : produce a vivid impression of **4** : affect (as the mind) forcibly

²im·press *vb* : force into naval service — **im·press·ment** *n*

im·pres·sion *n* **1** : mark made by impressing **2** : marked influence or effect **3** : printed copy **4** : vague notion or recollection — **impres·sion·able** *adj*

im·pres·sive *adj* : making a marked impression — **im·pres·sive·ly** *adv* — **im·pres·sive·ness** *n*

im·pri·ma·tur *n* : official approval (as of a publication by a censor)

im·print *vb* : stamp or mark by or as if by pressure ~ *n* : something imprinted or printed

im·pris·on *vb* : put in prison — **im·pris·on·ment** *n*

im·prob·a·ble *adj* : unlikely to be true or to occur — **im·prob·a·bil·i·ty** *n* — **im·prob·a·bly** *adv*

im·promp·tu *adj* : not planned beforehand — **impromptu** *adv or n*

im·prop·er *adj* : not proper — **im·prop·er·ly** *adv*

im·pro·pri·ety *n, pl* **-eties** : state or instance of being improper

im·prove *vb* **-proved; -proving** : grow or make better — **im·prov·able** *adj* — **im·prove·ment** *n*

im·prov·i·dent *adj* : not providing for the future — **improv·i·dence** *n*

im·pro·vise *vb* **-vised; -vis·ing** : make, invent, or arrange offhand — **im·pro·vi·sa·tion** *n* — **im·pro·vis·er, im·pro·vi·sor** *n*

im·pru·dent *adj* : not prudent — **im·pru·dence** *n*

im·pu·dent *adj* : insolent — **im·pu·dence** *n* — **im·pu·dent·ly** *adv*

im·pugn *vb* : attack as false

im·pulse *n* **1** : moving force **2** : sudden inclination

im·pul·sive *adj* : acting on impulse — **im·pul·sive·ly** *adv* — **impul·sive·ness** *n*

im·pu·ni·ty *n* : exemption from punishment or harm

im·pure *adj* : not pure — **im·pu·ri·ty** *n*

im·pute *vb* **-put·ed; -put·ing** : credit to or blame on a person or cause — **im·pu·ta·tion** *n*

in *prep* **1** — used to indicate location, inclusion, situation, or manner **2** : into **3** : during ~ *adv* : to or toward the inside ~ *adj* : located inside

in- *prefix* **1** : not **2** : lack of

inability	incorrect
inaccessibility	incorrectly
inaccessible	incorrectness
inaccuracy	incorruptible
inaccurate	inculpable
inaction	incurable
inactive	incurious
inactivity	indecency
inadequacy	indecent
inadequate	indecently
inadequately	indecipherable
inadmissibility	indecisive
inadmissible	indecisively
inadvisability	indecisiveness
inadvisable	indecorous
inapparent	indecorously
inapplicable	indecorousness
inapposite	indefensible
inappositely	indefinable
inappositeness	indefinably
inappreciative	indescribable
inapproachable	indescribably
inappropriate	indestructibility
inappropriately	indestructible
inappropriateness	indigestible
inapt	indiscernible
inarguable	indiscreet
inartistic	indiscreetly
inartistically	indiscretion
inattentive	indisputable
inattentively	indisputably
inattentiveness	indistinct
inaudible	indistinctly
inaudibly	indistinctness
inauspicious	indivisibility
inauthentic	indivisible
incapability	ineducable
incapable	ineffective
incautious	ineffectively
incoherence	ineffectiveness
incoherent	ineffectual
incoherently	ineffectually
incombustible	ineffectualness
incommensurate	inefficiency
incommodious	inefficient
incommunicable	inefficiently
incompatibility	inelastic
incompatible	inelasticity
incomplete	inelegance
incompletely	inelegant
incompleteness	ineligibility
incomprehensible	ineligible
inconclusive	ineradicable
incongruent	inessential
inconsecutive	inexact
inconsiderate	inexactly
inconsiderately	inexpedient
inconsiderateness	inexpensive
inconsistency	inexperience
inconsistent	inexperienced
inconsistently	inexpert
inconspicuous	inexpertly
inconspicuously	inexpertness
inconstancy	inexplicable
inconstant	inexplicably
inconstantly	inexplicit
inconsumable	inexpressible
incontestable	inexpressibly
incontestably	inextinguishable
incorporeal	inextricable
incorporeally	infeasibility

infeasible	insincerity
infelicitous	insolubility
infelicity	insoluble
infertile	instability
infertility	insubstantial
inflexibility	insufficiency
inflexible	insufficient
inflexibly	insufficiently
infrequent	insupportable
infrequently	intangibility
inglorious	intangible
ingloriously	intangibly
ingratitude	intolerable
inhumane	intolerably
inhumanely	intolerance
injudicious	intolerant
injudiciously	intractable
injudiciousness	invariable
inoffensive	invariably
inoperable	inviable
inoperative	invisibility
insalubrious	invisible
insensitive	invisibly
insensitivity	involuntarily
inseparable	involuntary
insignificant	invulnerability
insincere	invulnerable
insincerely	invulnerably

in·ad·ver·tent *adj* : unintentional — **in·ad·ver·tence** *n* — **in·ad·ver·ten·cy** *n* — **in·ad·ver·tent·ly** *adv*

in·alien·able *adj* : incapable of being transferred or given up — **in·alien·abil·i·ty** *n* — **in·alien·ably** *adv*

inane *adj* **inan·er; -est** : silly or stupid — **inan·i·ty** *n*

in·an·i·mate *adj* : not animate or animated — **in·an·i·mate·ly** *adv* — **in·an·i·mate·ness** *n*

in·ap·pre·cia·ble *adj* : too small to be perceived — **in·ap·pre·cia·bly** *adv*

in·ar·tic·u·late *adj* : without the power of speech or effective expression — **in·ar·tic·u·late·ly** *adv*

in·as·much as *conj* : because

in·at·ten·tion *n* : failure to pay attention

in·au·gu·ral *adj* : relating to an inauguration ~ *n* **1** : inaugural speech **2** : inauguration

in·au·gu·rate *vb* **-rat·ed; -rat·ing 1** : install in office **2** : start — **in·au·gu·ra·tion** *n*

in·board *adv* : inside a vehicle or craft — **in·board** *adj*

in·born *adj* : present from birth

in·bred *adj* : deeply ingrained in one's nature

in·breed·ing *n* : interbreeding of closely related individuals — **in·breed** *vb*

in·cal·cu·la·ble *adj* : too large to be calculated — **in·cal·cu·la·bly** *adv*

in·can·des·cent *adj* **1** : glowing with heat **2** : brilliant — **in·can·des·cence** *n*

in·can·ta·tion *n* : use of spoken or sung charms or spells as a magic ritual

in·ca·pac·i·tate *vb* **-tat·ed; -tat·ing** : disable

in·ca·pac·i·ty *n, pl* **-ties** : quality or state of being incapable

in·car·cer·ate *vb* **-at·ed; -at·ing** : imprison — **in·car·cer·a·tion** *n*

in·car·nate *adj* : having bodily form and substance — **in·car·nate** *vb* — **in·car·na·tion** *n*

in·cen·di·ary *adj* **1** : pertaining to or used to ignite fire **2** : tending to excite — **incendiary** *n*

in·cense *n* : material burned to produce a fragrant odor or its smoke ~ *vb* **-censed; -cens·ing** : make very angry

in·cen·tive *n* : inducement to do something

in·cep·tion *n* : beginning

in·ces·sant *adj* : continuing without interruption — **in·ces·sant·ly** *adv*

in·cest *n* : sexual intercourse between close relatives — **in·ces·tu·ous** *adj*

inch *n* : unit of length equal to {frac112} foot ~ *vb* : move by small degrees

in·cho·ate *adj* : new and not fully formed or ordered

in·ci·dent *n* : occurrence — **in·ci·dence** *n* — **incident** *adj*

in·ci·den·tal *adj* 1 : subordinate, nonessential, or attendant 2 : met by chance ~ *n* 1 : something incidental 2 *pl* : minor expenses that are not itemized — **in·ci·den·tal·ly** *adv*

in·cin·er·ate *vb* -at·ed; -at·ing : burn to ashes — **in·cin·er·a·tor** *n*

in·cip·i·ent *adj* : beginning to be or appear

in·cise *vb* -cised; -cis·ing : carve into

in·ci·sion *n* : surgical cut

in·ci·sive *adj* : keen and discerning — **in·ci·sive·ly** *adv*

in·ci·sor *n* : tooth for cutting

in·cite *vb* -cit·ed; -cit·ing : arouse to action — **in·cite·ment** *n*

in·ci·vil·i·ty *n* : rudeness

in·clem·ent *adj* : stormy — **in·clem·en·cy** *n*

in·cline *vb* -clined; -clin·ing 1 : bow 2 : tend toward an opinion 3 : slope ~ *n* : slope — **in·cli·na·tion** *n* — **in·clin·er** *n*

inclose, inclosure *var of* ENCLOSE, ENCLOSURE

in·clude *vb* -clud·ed; -clud·ing : take in or comprise — **in·clu·sion** *n* — **in·clu·sive** *adj*

in·cog·ni·to *adv or adj* : with one's identity concealed

in·come *n* : money gained (as from work or investment)

in·com·ing *adj* : coming in

in·com·mu·ni·ca·do *adv or adj* : without means of communication

in·com·pa·ra·ble *adj* : eminent beyond comparison

in·com·pe·tent *adj* : lacking sufficient knowledge or skill — **in·com·pe·tence** *n* — **in·com·pe·ten·cy** *n* — **incompetent** *n*

in·con·ceiv·able *adj* 1 : impossible to comprehend 2 : unbelievable — **in·con·ceiv·ably** *adv*

in·con·gru·ous *adj* : inappropriate or out of place — **incon·gru·i·ty** *n* — **in·con·gru·ous·ly** *adv*

in·con·se·quen·tial *adj* : unimportant — **incon·se·quence** *n* — **in·con·se·quen·tial·ly** *adv*

in·con·sid·er·able *adj* : trivial

in·con·sol·able *adj* : incapable of being consoled — **in·con·sol·ably** *adv*

in·con·ve·nience *n* 1 : discomfort 2 : something that causes trouble or annoyance ~ *vb* : cause inconvenience to — **in·con·ve·nient** *adj* — **incon·ve·nient·ly** *adv*

in·cor·po·rate *vb* -rat·ed; -rat·ing 1 : blend 2 : form into a legal body — **in·cor·po·rat·ed** *adj* — **in·cor·po·ra·tion** *n*

in·cor·ri·gi·ble *adj* : incapable of being corrected or reformed — **in·cor·ri·gi·bil·i·ty** *n*

in·crease *vb* -creased; -creas·ing : make or become greater ~ *n* 1 : enlargement in size 2 : something added — **in·creas·ing·ly** *adv*

in·cred·i·ble *adj* : too extraordinary to be believed — **incred·i·bil·i·ty** *n* — **in·cred·i·bly** *adv*

in·cred·u·lous *adj* : skeptical — **in·cre·du·li·ty** *n* — **in·cred·u·lous·ly** *adv*

in·cre·ment *n* : increase or amount of increase — **incre·men·tal** *adj*

in·crim·i·nate *vb* -nat·ed; -nat·ing : show to be guilty of a crime — **in·crim·i·na·tion** *n* — **in·crim·i·na·to·ry** *adj*

in·cu·bate *vb* -bat·ed; -bat·ing : keep (as eggs) under conditions favorable for development — **in·cu·ba·tion** *n* — **in·cu·ba·tor** *n*

in·cul·cate *vb* -cat·ed; -cat·ing : instill by repeated teaching — **in·cul·ca·tion** *n*

in·cum·bent *n* : holder of an office ~ *adj* : obligatory — **incum·ben·cy** *n*

in·cur *vb* -rr- : become liable or subject to

in·cur·sion *n* : invasion

in·debt·ed *adj* : owing something — **in·debt·ed·ness** *n*

in·de·ci·sion *n* : inability to decide

in·deed *adv* : without question

in·de·fat·i·ga·ble *adj* : not tiring — **in·de·fat·i·ga·bly** *adv*

in·def·i·nite *adj* 1 : not defining or identifying 2 : not precise 3 : having no fixed limit — **in·def·i·nite·ly** *adv*

in·del·i·ble *adj* : not capable of being removed or erased — **in·del·i·bly** *adv*

in·del·i·cate *adj* : improper — **in·del·i·ca·cy** *n*

in·dem·ni·fy *vb* -fied; -fy·ing : repay for a loss — **in·dem·ni·fi·ca·tion** *n*

in·dem·ni·ty *n, pl* -ties : security against loss or damage

¹**in·dent** *vb* : leave a space at the beginning of a paragraph

²**indent** *vb* : force inward so as to form a depression or dent

in·den·ta·tion *n* 1 : notch, recess, or dent 2 : action of indenting 3 : space at the beginning of a paragraph

in·den·ture *n* : contract binding one person to work for another for a given period — usu. in pl. ~ *vb* -tured; -tur·ing : bind by indentures

Independence Day *n* : July 4 observed as a legal holiday in commemoration of the adoption of the Declaration of Independence in 1776

in·de·pen·dent *adj* 1 : not governed by another 2 : not requiring or relying on something or somebody else 3 : not easily influenced — **in·de·pen·dence** *n* — **independent** *n* — **in·de·pen·dent·ly** *adv*

in·de·ter·mi·nate *adj* : not definitely determined — **in·de·ter·mi·na·cy** *n* — **in·de·ter·mi·nate·ly** *adv*

in·dex *n, pl* -dex·es *or* -di·ces 1 : alphabetical list of items (as topics in a book) 2 : a number that serves as a measure or indicator of something ~ *vb* 1 : provide with an index 2 : serve as an index of

index finger *n* : forefinger

in·di·cate *vb* -cat·ed; -cat·ing 1 : point out or to 2 : show indirectly 3 : state briefly — **in·di·ca·tion** *n* — **in·di·ca·tor** *n*

in·dic·a·tive *adj* : serving to indicate

in·dict *vb* : charge with a crime — **in·dict·able** *adj* — **in·dict·ment** *n*

in·dif·fer·ent *adj* 1 : having no preference 2 : showing neither interest nor dislike 3 : mediocre — **in·dif·fer·ence** *n* — **in·dif·fer·ent·ly** *adv*

in·dig·e·nous *adj* : native to a particular region

in·di·gent *adj* : needy — **in·di·gence** *n*

in·di·ges·tion *n* : discomfort from inability to digest food

in·dig·na·tion *n* : anger aroused by something unjust or unworthy — **in·dig·nant** *adj* — **in·dig·nant·ly** *adv*

in·dig·ni·ty *n, pl* -ties 1 : offense against self-respect 2 : humiliating treatment

in·di·go *n, pl* -gos *or* -goes 1 : blue dye 2 : deep reddish blue color

in·di·rect *adj* : not straight or straightforward — **in·di·rec·tion** *n* — **in·di·rect·ly** *adv* — **in·di·rect·ness** *n*

in·dis·crim·i·nate *adj* 1 : not careful or discriminating 2 : haphazard — **in·dis·crim·i·nate·ly** *adv*

in·dis·pens·able *adj* : absolutely essential — **in·dis·pens·abil·i·ty** *n* — **indis·pensable** *n* — **in·dis·pens·ably** *adv*

in·dis·posed *adj* : slightly ill — **in·dis·po·si·tion** *n*

in·dis·sol·u·ble *adj* : not capable of being dissolved or broken

in·di·vid·u·al *n* 1 : single member of a category 2 : person — **individual** *adj* — **in·di·vid·u·al·ly** *adv*

in·di·vid·u·al·ist *n* : person who is markedly independent in thought or action

in·di·vid·u·al·i·ty *n* : special quality that distinguishes an individual

in·di·vid·u·al·ize *vb* -ized; -iz·ing 1 : make individual 2 : treat individually

in·doc·tri·nate *vb* -nat·ed; -nat·ing : instruct in fundamentals (as of a doctrine) — **in·doc·tri·na·tion** *n*

in·do·lent *adj* : lazy — **in·do·lence** *n*

in·dom·i·ta·ble *adj* : invincible — **in·dom·i·ta·bly** *adv*

in·door *adj* : relating to the inside of a building

in·doors *adv* : in or into a building

in·du·bi·ta·ble *adj* : being beyond question — **in·du·bi·ta·bly** *adv*

in·duce *vb* -duced; -duc·ing 1 : persuade 2 : bring about — **in·duce·ment** *n* — **in·duc·er** *n*

in·duct *vb* 1 : put in office 2 : admit as a member 3 : enroll (as for military service) — **in·duct·ee** *n*

in·duc·tion *n* 1 : act or instance of inducting 2 : reasoning from particular instances to a general conclusion

in·duc·tive *adj* : reasoning by induction

in·dulge *vb* -dulged; -dulg·ing : yield to the desire of or for — **indul·gence** *n* — **in·dul·gent** *adj* — **in·dul·gent·ly** *adv*

in·dus·tri·al *adj* 1 : relating to industry 2 : heavy-duty — **in·dus·tri·al·ist** *n* — **in·dus·tri·al·iza·tion** *n* — **in·dus·tri·al·ize** *vb* — **in·dus·tri·al·ly** *adv*

in·dus·tri·ous *adj* : diligent or busy — **in·dus·tri·ous·ly** *adv* — **in·dus·tri·ous·ness** *n*

in·dus·try *n, pl* -tries 1 : diligence 2 : manufacturing enterprises or activity

in·ebri·at·ed *adj* : drunk — **ine·bri·a·tion** *n*

in·ef·fa·ble *adj* : incapable of being expressed in words — **in·ef·fa·bly** *adv*

in·ept *adj* 1 : inappropriate or foolish 2 : generally incompetent — **in·ep·ti·tude** *n* — **in·ept·ly** *adv* — **in·ept·ness** *n*

in·equal·i·ty *n* : quality of being unequal or uneven

in·ert *adj* 1 : powerless to move or act 2 : sluggish — **in·ert·ly** *adv* — **in·ert·ness** *n*

in·er·tia *n* : tendency of matter to remain at rest or in motion — **in·er·tial** *adj*

in·es·cap·able *adj* : inevitable — **in·es·cap·ably** *adv*

in·es·ti·ma·ble *adj* : incapable of being estimated — **in·es·ti·ma·bly** *adv*

in·ev·i·ta·ble *adj* : incapable of being avoided or escaped — **in·ev·i·ta·bil·i·ty** *n* — **in·ev·i·ta·bly** *adv*

in·ex·cus·able *adj* : being without excuse or justification — **in·ex·cus·ably** *adv*

in·ex·haust·ible *adj* : incapable of being used up or tired out — **in·ex·haust·ibly** *adv*

in·ex·o·ra·ble *adj* : unyielding or relentless — **in·ex·o·ra·bly** *adv*

in·fal·li·ble *adj* : incapable of error — **in·fal·li·bil·i·ty** *n* — **in·fal·li·bly** *adv*

in·fa·mous *adj* : having the worst kind of reputation — **in·fa·mous·ly** *adv*

in·fa·my *n, pl* -mies : evil reputation

in·fan·cy *n, pl* -cies 1 : early childhood 2 : early period of existence

in·fant *n* : baby

in·fan·tile *adj* 1 : relating to infants 2 : childish

in·fan·try *n, pl* -tries : soldiers that fight on foot

in·fat·u·ate *vb* **-at·ed; -at·ing** : inspire with foolish love or admiration — **in·fat·u·a·tion** *n*

in·fect *vb* : contaminate with disease-producing matter — **in·fec·tion** *n* — **in·fec·tious** *adj* — **in·fec·tive** *adj*

in·fer *vb* **-rr-** : deduce — **in·fer·ence** *n* — **in·fer·en·tial** *adj*

in·fe·ri·or *adj* **1** : being lower in position, degree, rank, or merit **2** : of lesser quality — **inferior** *n* — **in·fe·ri·or·i·ty** *n*

in·fer·nal *adj* : of or like hell — often used as a general expression of disapproval — **in·fer·nal·ly** *adv*

in·fer·no *n, pl* **-nos** : place or condition suggesting hell

in·fest *vb* : swarm or grow in or over — **in·fes·ta·tion** *n*

in·fi·del *n* : one who does not believe in a particular religion

in·fi·del·i·ty *n, pl* **-ties** : lack of faithfulness

in·field *n* : baseball field inside the base lines — **in·field·er** *n*

in·fil·trate *vb* **-trat·ed; -trat·ing** : enter or become established in without being noticed — **in·fil·tra·tion** *n*

in·fi·nite *adj* **1** : having no limit or extending indefinitely **2** : vast — **infinite** *n* — **in·fi·nite·ly** *adv* — **in·fin·i·tude** *n*

in·fin·i·tes·i·mal *adj* : immeasurably small — **in·fin·i·tes·i·mal·ly** *adv*

in·fin·i·tive *n* : verb form in English usu. used with *to*

in·fin·i·ty *n, pl* **-ties** **1** : quality or state of being infinite **2** : indefinitely great number or amount

in·firm *adj* : feeble from age — **in·fir·mi·ty** *n*

in·fir·ma·ry *n, pl* **-ries** : place for the care of the sick

in·flame *vb* **-flamed; -flam·ing** **1** : excite to intense action or feeling **2** : affect or become affected with inflammation — **in·flam·ma·to·ry** *adj*

in·flam·ma·ble *adj* : flammable

in·flam·ma·tion *n* : response to injury in which an affected area becomes red and painful and congested with blood

in·flate *vb* **-flat·ed; -flat·ing** **1** : swell or puff up (as with gas) **2** : expand or increase abnormally — **in·flat·able** *adj*

in·fla·tion *n* **1** : act of inflating **2** : continual rise in prices — **in·fla·tion·ary** *adj*

in·flec·tion *n* **1** : change in pitch or loudness of the voice **2** : change in form of a word — **in·flect** *vb* — **in·flec·tion·al** *adj*

in·flict *vb* : give by or as if by hitting — **in·flic·tion** *n*

in·flu·ence *n* **1** : power or capacity of causing an effect in indirect or intangible ways **2** : one that exerts influence ~ *vb* **-enced; -enc·ing** : affect or alter by influence — **in·flu·en·tial** *adj*

in·flu·en·za *n* : acute very contagious virus disease

in·flux *n* : a flowing in

in·form *vb* : give information or knowledge to — **in·for·mant** *n* — **in·form·er** *n*

in·for·mal *adj* **1** : without formality or ceremony **2** : for ordinary or familiar use — **in·for·mal·i·ty** *n* — **in·for·mal·ly** *adv*

in·for·ma·tion *n* : knowledge obtained from investigation, study, or instruction — **infor·ma·tion·al** *adj*

in·for·ma·tive *adj* : giving knowledge

in·frac·tion *n* : violation

in·fra·red *adj* : being, relating to, or using radiation of wavelengths longer than those of red light — **infrared** *n*

in·fra·struc·ture *n* : foundation of a system or organization

in·fringe *vb* **-fringed; -fring·ing** : violate another's right or privilege — **in·fringe·ment** *n*

in·fu·ri·ate *vb* **-at·ed; -at·ing** : make furious — **in·fu·ri·at·ing·ly** *adv*

in·fuse *vb* **-fused; -fus·ing** **1** : instill a principle or quality in **2** : steep in liquid without boiling — **in·fu·sion** *n*

¹-ing *vb suffix or adj suffix* — used to form the present participle and sometimes an adjective resembling a present participle

²-ing *n suffix* **1** : action or process **2** : something connected with or resulting from an action or process

in·ge·nious *adj* : very clever — **in·ge·nious·ly** *adv* — **in·ge·nious·ness** *n*

in·ge·nue, in·gé·nue *n* : naive young woman

in·ge·nu·i·ty *n, pl* **-ities** : skill or cleverness in planning or inventing

in·gen·u·ous *adj* : innocent and candid — **in·gen·u·ous·ly** *adv* — **in·gen·u·ous·ness** *n*

in·gest *vb* : eat — **in·ges·tion** *n*

in·gle·nook *n* : corner by the fireplace

in·got *n* : block of metal

in·grained *adj* : deep-seated

in·grate *n* : ungrateful person

in·gra·ti·ate *vb* **-at·ed; -at·ing** : gain favor for (oneself) — **in·gra·ti·at·ing** *adj*

in·gre·di·ent *n* : one of the substances that make up a mixture

in·grown *adj* : grown in and esp. into the flesh

in·hab·it *vb* : live or dwell in — **in·hab·it·able** *adj* — **in·hab·it·ant** *n*

in·hale *vb* **-haled; -hal·ing** : breathe in — **in·hal·ant** *n* — **in·ha·la·tion** *n* — **in·hal·er** *n*

in·here *vb* **-hered; -her·ing** : be inherent

in·her·ent *adj* : being an essential part of something — **in·her·ent·ly** *adv*

in·her·it *vb* : receive from one's ancestors — **in·her·it·able** *adj* — **in·her·i·tance** *n* — **in·her·i·tor** *n*

in·hib·it *vb* : hold in check — **in·hi·bi·tion** *n*

in·hu·man *adj* : cruel or impersonal — **in·hu·man·i·ty** *n* — **in·hu·man·ly** *adv* — **in·hu·man·ness** *n*

in·im·i·cal *adj* : hostile or harmful — **in·im·i·cal·ly** *adv*

in·im·i·ta·ble *adj* : not capable of being imitated

in·iq·ui·ty *n, pl* **-ties** : wickedness — **in·iq·ui·tous** *adj*

ini·tial *adj* **1** : of or relating to the beginning **2** : first ~ *n* : 1st letter of a word or name ~ *vb* **-tialed** *or* **-tialled; -tial·ing** *or* **-tial·ling** : put initials on — **ini·tial·ly** *adv*

ini·ti·ate *vb* **-at·ed; -at·ing** **1** : start **2** : induct into membership **3** : instruct in the rudiments of something — **initiate** *n* — **ini·ti·a·tion** *n* — **ini·tia·to·ry** *adj*

ini·tia·tive *n* **1** : first step **2** : readiness to undertake something on one's own

in·ject *vb* : force or introduce into something — **in·jec·tion** *n*

in·junc·tion *n* : court writ requiring one to do or to refrain from doing a specified act

in·jure *vb* **-jured; -jur·ing** : do damage, hurt, or a wrong to

in·ju·ry *n, pl* **-ries** **1** : act that injures **2** : hurt, damage, or loss sustained — **in·ju·ri·ous** *adj*

in·jus·tice *n* : unjust act

ink *n* : usu. liquid and colored material for writing and printing ~ *vb* : put ink on — **ink·well** *n* — **inky** *adj*

in·kling *n* : hint or idea

in·land *n* : interior of a country — **inland** *adj or adv*

in–law *n* : relative by marriage

in·lay *vb* **-laid; -lay·ing** : set into a surface for decoration ~ *n* **1** : inlaid work **2** : shaped filling cemented into a tooth

in·let *n* : small bay

in·mate *n* : person confined to an asylum or prison

in me·mo·ri·am *prep* : in memory of

in·most *adj* : deepest within

inn *n* : hotel

in·nards *n pl* : internal parts

in·nate *adj* **1** : inborn **2** : inherent — **in·nate·ly** *adv*

in·ner *adj* : being on the inside

in·ner·most *adj* : farthest inward

in·ner·sole *n* : insole

in·ning *n* : baseball team's turn at bat

inn·keep·er *n* : owner of an inn

in·no·cent *adj* **1** : free from guilt **2** : harmless **3** : not sophisticated — **in·no·cence** *n* — **innocent** *n* — **in·no·cent·ly** *adv*

in·noc·u·ous *adj* **1** : harmless **2** : inoffensive

in·no·va·tion *n* : new idea or method — **in·no·vate** *vb* — **in·no·va·tive** *adj* — **in·no·va·tor** *n*

in·nu·en·do *n, pl* **-dos** *or* **-does** : insinuation

in·nu·mer·a·ble *adj* : countless

in·oc·u·late *vb* **-lat·ed; -lat·ing** : treat with something esp. to establish immunity — **in·oc·u·la·tion** *n*

in·op·por·tune *adj* : inconvenient — **in·op·por·tune·ly** *adv*

in·or·di·nate *adj* : unusual or excessive — **in·or·di·nate·ly** *adv*

in·or·gan·ic *adj* : made of mineral matter

in·pa·tient *n* : patient who stays in a hospital

in·put *n* : something put in — **input** *vb*

in·quest *n* : inquiry esp. before a jury

in·quire *vb* **-quired; -quir·ing** **1** : ask **2** : investigate — **in·quir·er** *n* — **in·quir·ing·ly** *adv* — **in·qui·ry** *n*

in·qui·si·tion *n* **1** : official inquiry **2** : severe questioning — **in·quis·i·tor** *n* — **in·quis·i·to·ri·al** *adj*

in·quis·i·tive *adj* : curious — **in·quis·i·tive·ly** *adv* — **in·quis·i·tive·ness** *n*

in·road *n* : encroachment

in·rush *n* : influx

in·sane *adj* **1** : not sane **2** : absurd — **in·sane·ly** *adv* — **in·san·i·ty** *n*

in·sa·tia·ble *adj* : incapable of being satisfied — **in·sa·tia·bil·i·ty** *n* — **in·sa·tia·bly** *adv*

in·scribe *vb* **1** : write **2** : engrave **3** : dedicate (a book) to someone — **in·scrip·tion** *n*

in·scru·ta·ble *adj* : mysterious — **in·scru·ta·bly** *adv*

in·seam *n* : inner seam (of a garment)

in·sect *n* : small usu. winged animal with 6 legs

in·sec·ti·cide *n* : insect poison — **in·sec·ti·cid·al** *adj*

in·se·cure *adj* **1** : uncertain **2** : unsafe **3** : fearful — **in·se·cure·ly** *adv* — **in·se·cu·ri·ty** *n*

in·sem·i·nate *vb* **-nat·ed; -nat·ing** : introduce semen into — **in·sem·i·na·tion** *n*

in·sen·si·ble *adj* **1** : unconscious **2** : unable to feel **3** : unaware — **in·sen·si·bil·i·ty** *n* — **in·sen·si·bly** *adv*

in·sen·tient *adj* : lacking feeling — **in·sen·tience** *n*

in·sert *vb* : put in — **insert** *n* — **in·ser·tion** *n*

in·set *vb* **inset** *or* **in·set·ted; in·set·ting** : set in — **inset** *n*

in·shore *adj* **1** : situated near shore **2** : moving toward shore ~ *adv* : toward shore

in·side *n* **1** : inner side **2** *pl* : innards ~ *prep* **1** : in or into the inside of **2** : within ~ *adv* **1** : on the inner side **2** : into the interior — **in·side** *adj* — **in·sid·er** *n*

inside of *prep* : inside

in·sid·i·ous *adj* **1** : treacherous **2** : seductive — **in·sid·i·ous·ly** *adv* — **in·sid·i·ous·ness** *n*

in·sight *n* : understanding — **in·sight·ful** *adj*

in•sig•nia, in•sig•ne *n, pl* **-nia** *or* **-ni•as** : badge of authority or office

in•sin•u•ate *vb* **-at•ed; -at•ing 1** : imply **2** : bring in artfully — **in•sin•u•a•tion** *n*

in•sip•id *adj* **1** : tasteless **2** : not stimulating — **in•si•pid•i•ty** *n*

in•sist *vb* : be firmly demanding — **in•sis•tence** *n* — **insis•tent** *adj* — **in•sis•tent•ly** *adv*

insofar as *conj* : to the extent that

in•sole *n* : inside sole of a shoe

in•so•lent *adj* : contemptuously rude — **in•so•lence** *n*

in•sol•vent *adj* : unable or insufficient to pay debts — **in•sol•ven•cy** *n*

in•som•nia *n* : inability to sleep

in•so•much as *conj* : inasmuch as

insomuch that *conj* : to such a degree that

in•sou•ci•ance *n* : lighthearted indifference — **insou•ci•ant** *adj*

in•spect *vb* : view closely and critically — **inspec•tion** *n* — **in•spec•tor** *n*

in•spire *vb* **-spired; -spir•ing 1** : inhale **2** : influence by example **3** : bring about **4** : stir to action — **in•spi•ra•tion** *n* — **in•spi•ra•tion•al** *adj* — **in•spir•er** *n*

in•stall, in•stal *vb* **-stalled; -stall•ing 1** : induct into office **2** : set up for use — **in•stal•la•tion** *n*

in•stall•ment *n* : partial payment

in•stance *n* **1** : request or instigation **2** : example

in•stant *n* : moment ~ *adj* **1** : immediate **2** : ready to mix — **in•stan•ta•neous** *adj* — **in•stan•ta•neous•ly** *adv* — **in•stant•ly** *adv*

in•stead *adv* : as a substitute or alternative

instead of *prep* : as a substitute for or alternative to

in•step *n* : part of the foot in front of the ankle

in•sti•gate *vb* **-gat•ed; -gat•ing** : incite — **in•sti•ga•tion** *n* — **in•sti•ga•tor** *n*

in•still *vb* **-stilled; -still•ing** : impart gradually

in•stinct *n* **1** : natural talent **2** : natural inherited or subconsciously motivated behavior — **in•stinc•tive** *adj* — **in•stinc•tive•ly** *adv* — **in•stinc•tu•al** *adj*

in•sti•tute *vb* **-tut•ed; -tut•ing** : establish, start, or organize ~ *n* **1** : organization promoting a cause **2** : school

in•sti•tu•tion *n* **1** : act of instituting **2** : custom **3** : corporation or society of a public character — **in•sti•tu•tion•al** *adj* — **in•sti•tu•tion•al•ize** *vb* — **in•sti•tu•tion•al•ly** *adv*

in•struct *vb* **1** : teach **2** : give an order to — **in•struc•tion** *n* — **in•struc•tion•al** *adj* — **in•struc•tive** *adj* — **in•struc•tor** *n* — **in•struc•tor•ship** *n*

in•stru•ment *n* **1** : something that produces music **2** : means **3** : device for doing work and esp. precision work **4** : legal document — **in•stru•men•tal** *adj* — **in•stru•men•tal•ist** *n* — **in•stru•men•tal•i•ty** *n* — **in•stru•men•ta•tion** *n*

in•sub•or•di•nate *adj* : not obeying — **in•sub•or•di•na•tion** *n*

in•suf•fer•able *adj* : unbearable — **in•suf•fer•ably** *adv*

in•su•lar *adj* **1** : relating to or residing on an island **2** : narrow-minded — **in•su•lar•i•ty** *n*

in•su•late *vb* **-lat•ed; -lat•ing** : protect from heat loss or electricity — **in•su•la•tion** *n* — **in•su•la•tor** *n*

in•su•lin *n* : hormone used by diabetics

in•sult *vb* : treat with contempt ~ *n* : insulting act or remark — **in•sult•ing•ly** *adv*

in•su•per•a•ble *adj* : too difficult — **in•su•per•a•bly** *adv*

in•sure *vb* **-sured; -sur•ing 1** : guarantee against loss **2** : make certain — **in•sur•able** *adj* — **in•sur•ance** *n* — **in•sured** *n* — **in•sur•er** *n*

in•sur•gent *n* : rebel — **in•sur•gence** *n* — **in•sur•gen•cy** *n* — **in•sur•gent** *adj*

in•sur•mount•able *adj* : too great to be overcome — **in•sur•mount•ably** *adv*

in•sur•rec•tion *n* : revolution — **in•sur•rec•tion•ist** *n*

in•tact *adj* : undamaged

in•take *n* **1** : opening through which something enters **2** : act of taking in **3** : amount taken in

in•te•ger *n* : number that is not a fraction and does not include a fraction

in•te•gral *adj* : essential

in•te•grate *vb* **-grat•ed; -grat•ing 1** : unite **2** : end segregation of or at — **in•te•gra•tion** *n*

in•teg•ri•ty *n* **1** : soundness **2** : adherence to a code of values **3** : completeness

in•tel•lect *n* : power of knowing or thinking — **in•tel•lec•tu•al** *adj or n* — **in•tel•lec•tu•al•ism** *n* — **in•tel•lec•tu•al•ly** *adv*

in•tel•li•gence *n* **1** : ability to learn and understand **2** : mental acuteness **3** : information

in•tel•li•gent *adj* : having or showing intelligence — **in•tel•li•gent•ly** *adv*

in•tel•li•gi•ble *adj* : understandable — **in•tel•li•gi•bil•i•ty** *n* — **in•tel•li•gi•bly** *adv*

in•tem•per•ance *n* : lack of moderation — **in•tem•per•ate** *adj* — **in•tem•per•ate•ness** *n*

in•tend *vb* : have as a purpose

in•tend•ed *n* : engaged person — **intended** *adj*

in•tense *adj* **1** : extreme **2** : deeply felt — **in•tense•ly** *adv* — **in•ten•si•fi•ca•tion** *n* — **in•ten•si•fy** *vb* — **in•ten•si•ty** *n* — **in•ten•sive** *adj* — **in•ten•sive•ly** *adv*

¹in•tent *n* : purpose — **in•ten•tion** *n* — **in•ten•tion•al** *adj* — **in•ten•tion•al•ly** *adv*

²intent *adj* : concentrated — **in•tent•ly** *adv* — **in•tent•ness** *n*

in•ter *vb* **-rr-** : bury

inter- *prefix* : between or among

interagency	interisland
interatomic	interlibrary
interbank	intermolecular
interborough	intermountain
intercampus	interoceanic
interchurch	interoffice
intercity	interparticle
interclass	interparty
intercoastal	interpersonal
intercollegiate	interplanetary
intercolonial	interpopulation
intercommunal	interprovincial
intercommunity	interracial
intercompany	interregional
intercontinental	interreligious
intercounty	interscholastic
intercultural	intersectional
interdenominational	interstate
interdepartmental	interstellar
interdivisional	intersystem
interelectronic	interterm
interethnic	interterminal
interfaculty	intertribal
interfamily	intertroop
interfiber	intertropical
interfraternity	interuniversity
intergalactic	interurban
intergang	intervalley
intergovernmental	intervillage
intergroup	interwar
interhemispheric	interzonal
interindustry	interzone
interinstitutional	

in•ter•ac•tion *n* : mutual influence — **in•ter•act** *vb* — **in•ter•ac•tive** *adj*

in•ter•breed *vb* **-bred; -breed•ing** : breed together

in•ter•ca•late *vb* **-lat•ed; -lat•ing** : insert — **in•ter•ca•la•tion** *n*

in•ter•cede *vb* **-ced•ed; -ced•ing** : act to reconcile — **in•ter•ces•sion** *n* — **in•ter•ces•sor** *n*

in•ter•cept *vb* : interrupt the progress of — **in•tercept** *n* — **in•ter•cep•tion** *n* — **in•ter•cep•tor** *n*

in•ter•change *vb* **1** : exchange **2** : change places ~ *n* **1** : exchange **2** : junction of highways — **in•ter•change•able** *adj*

in•ter•course *n* **1** : relations between persons or nations **2** : copulation

in•ter•de•pen•dent *adj* : mutually dependent — **in•ter•de•pen•dence** *n*

in•ter•dict *vb* **1** : prohibit **2** : destroy or cut (an enemy supply line) — **in•ter•dic•tion** *n*

in•ter•est *n* **1** : right **2** : benefit **3** : charge for borrowed money **4** : readiness to pay special attention **5** : quality that causes interest ~ *vb* **1** : concern **2** : get the attention of — **in•ter•est•ing** *adj* — **in•ter•est•ing•ly** *adv*

in•ter•face *n* : common boundary — **in•ter•fa•cial** *adj*

in•ter•fere *vb* **-fered; -fer•ing 1** : collide or be in opposition **2** : try to run the affairs of others — **in•ter•fer•ence** *n*

in•ter•im *n* : time between — **interim** *adj*

in•te•ri•or *adj* : being on the inside ~ *n* **1** : inside **2** : inland area

in•ter•ject *vb* : stick in between

in•ter•jec•tion *n* : an exclamatory word — **in•ter•jec•tion•al•ly** *adv*

in•ter•lace *vb* : cross or cause to cross one over another

in•ter•lin•ear *adj* : between written or printed lines

in•ter•lock *vb* **1** : interlace **2** : connect for mutual effect — **inter•lock** *n*

in•ter•lop•er *n* : intruder or meddler

in•ter•lude *n* : intervening period

in•ter•mar•ry *vb* **1** : marry each other **2** : marry within a group — **in•ter•mar•riage** *n*

in•ter•me•di•ary *n, pl* **-ar•ies** : agent between individuals or groups — **intermediary** *adj*

in•ter•me•di•ate *adj* : between extremes — **intermediate** *n*

in•ter•ment *n* : burial

in•ter•mi•na•ble *adj* : endless — **in•ter•mi•na•bly** *adv*

in•ter•min•gle *vb* : mingle

in•ter•mis•sion *n* : break in a performance

in•ter•mit•tent *adj* : coming at intervals — **in•ter•mit•tent•ly** *adv*

in•ter•mix *vb* : mix together — **in•ter•mix•ture** *n*

¹in•tern *vb* : confine esp. during a war — **in•tern•ee** *n* — **in•tern•ment** *n*

²intern *n* : advanced student (as in medicine) gaining supervised experience ~ *vb* : act as an intern — **in•tern•ship** *n*

in•ter•nal *adj* **1** : inward **2** : inside of the body **3** : relating to or existing in the mind — **in•ter•nal•ly** *adv*

in•ter•na•tion•al *adj* : affecting 2 or more nations ~ *n* : something having international scope — **in•ter•na•tion•al•ism** *n* — **in•ter•na•tion•al•ize** *vb* — **in•ter•na•tion•ally** *adv*

in•ter•nist *n* : specialist in nonsurgical medicine

in•ter•play *n* : interaction

in•ter•po•late *vb* **-lat•ed; -lat•ing** : insert — **in•ter•po•la•tion** *n*

in•ter•pose *vb* **-posed; -pos•ing 1** : place between **2** : intrude — **in•ter•po•si•tion** *n*

in•ter•pret *vb* : explain the meaning of — **in•ter•pre•ta•tion** *n* — **in•ter•pre•ta•tive** *adj* — **in•ter•pret•er** *n* — **in•ter•pre•tive** *adj*

in•ter•re•late *vb* : have a mutual relationship —

in·ter·re·lat·ed·ness n — **in·ter·re·la·tion** n — **in·ter·re·la·tion·ship** n

in·ter·ro·gate vb **-gat·ed; -gat·ing** : question — **in·ter·ro·ga·tion** n — **in·ter·rog·a·tive** adj or n — **in·ter·rog·a·tor** n — **in·ter·rog·a·to·ry** adj

in·ter·rupt vb : intrude so as to hinder or end continuity — **in·ter·rupt·er** n — **in·ter·rup·tion** n — **in·ter·rup·tive** adv

in·ter·sect vb 1 : cut across or divide 2 : cross — **in·ter·sec·tion** n

in·ter·sperse vb **-spersed; -spers·ing** : insert at intervals — **in·ter·sper·sion** n

in·ter·stice n, pl **-stic·es** : space between — **in·ter·sti·tial** adj

in·ter·twine vb : twist together — **in·ter·twine·ment** n

in·ter·val n 1 : time between 2 : space between

in·ter·vene vb **-vened; -ven·ing** 1 : happen between events 2 : intercede — **in·ter·ven·tion** n

in·ter·view n : a meeting to get information — interview vb — **in·ter·view·er** n

in·ter·weave vb **-wove; -wo·ven; -weav·ing** : weave together — **in·ter·wo·ven** adj

in·tes·tate adj : not leaving a will

in·tes·tine n : tubular part of the digestive system after the stomach including a long narrow upper part (**small intestine**) followed by a broader shorter lower part (**large intestine**) — **in·tes·ti·nal** adj

in·ti·mate vb **-mat·ed; -mat·ing** : hint ~ adj 1 : very friendly 2 : suggesting privacy 3 : very personal ~ n : close friend — **in·ti·ma·cy** n — **in·ti·mate·ly** adv — **in·ti·ma·tion** n

in·tim·i·date vb **-dat·ed; -dat·ing** : make fearful — **in·tim·i·da·tion** n

in·to prep 1 : to the inside of 2 : to the condition of 3 : against

in·to·na·tion n : way of singing or speaking

in·tone vb **-toned; -ton·ing** : chant

in·tox·i·cate vb **-cat·ed; -cat·ing** : make drunk — **in·tox·i·cant** n or adj — **in·tox·i·ca·tion** n

in·tra·mu·ral adj : within a school

in·tran·si·gent adj : uncompromising — **in·tran·si·gence** n — **intransigent** n

in·tra·ve·nous adj : by way of the veins — **in·tra·ve·nous·ly** adv

in·trep·id adj : fearless — **in·tre·pid·i·ty** n

in·tri·cate adj : very complex and delicate — **in·tri·ca·cy** n — **in·tri·cate·ly** adv

in·trigue vb **-trigued; -trigu·ing** 1 : scheme 2 : arouse curiosity of ~ n : secret scheme — **in·trigu·ing·ly** adv

in·trin·sic adj : essential — **in·trin·si·cal·ly** adv

in·tro·duce vb **-duced; -duc·ing** 1 : bring in esp. for the 1st time 2 : cause to be acquainted 3 : bring to notice 4 : put in — **in·tro·duc·tion** n — **in·tro·duc·to·ry** adj

in·tro·spec·tion n : examination of one's own thoughts or feelings — **in·tro·spec·tive** adj — **in·tro·spec·tive·ly** adv

in·tro·vert n : shy or reserved person — **in·tro·ver·sion** n — **introvert** adj — **in·tro·vert·ed** adj

in·trude vb **-trud·ed; -trud·ing** 1 : thrust in 2 : encroach — **in·trud·er** n — **in·tru·sion** n — **in·tru·sive** adj — **in·tru·sive·ness** n

in·tu·ition n : quick and ready insight — **in·tu·it** vb — **in·tu·i·tive** adj — **in·tu·i·tive·ly** adv

in·un·date vb **-dat·ed; -dat·ing** : flood — **in·un·da·tion** n

in·ure vb **-ured; -ur·ing** : accustom to accept something undesirable

in·vade vb **-vad·ed; -vad·ing** : enter for conquest — **in·vad·er** n — **in·va·sion** n

¹**in·val·id** adj : not true or legal — **in·val·id·i·ty** n — **in·val·id·ly** adv

²**in·va·lid** adj : sickly ~ n : one chronically ill

in·val·i·date vb : make invalid — **in·val·i·da·tion** n

in·valu·able adj : extremely valuable

in·va·sive adj : involving entry into the body

in·vec·tive n : abusive language — **invective** adj

in·veigh vb : protest or complain forcefully

in·vei·gle vb **-gled; -gling** : win over or get by flattery

in·vent vb 1 : think up 2 : create for the 1st time — **in·ven·tion** n — **in·ven·tive** adj — **in·ven·tive·ness** n — **in·ven·tor** n

in·ven·to·ry n, pl **-ries** 1 : list of goods 2 : stock — **inventory** vb

in·verse adj or n : opposite — **in·verse·ly** adv

in·vert vb 1 : turn upside down or inside out 2 : reverse — **in·ver·sion** n

in·ver·te·brate adj : lacking a backbone ~ n : invertebrate animal

in·vest vb 1 : give power or authority to 2 : endow with a quality 3 : commit money to someone else's use in hope of profit — **in·vest·ment** n — **in·ves·tor** n

in·ves·ti·gate vb **-gat·ed; -gat·ing** : study closely and systematically — **in·ves·ti·ga·tion** n — **in·ves·ti·ga·tive** adj — **in·ves·ti·ga·tor** n

in·ves·ti·ture n : act of establishing in office

in·vet·er·ate adj : acting out of habit

in·vid·i·ous adj : harmful or obnoxious — **in·vid·i·ous·ly** adv

in·vig·o·rate vb **-rat·ed; -rat·ing** : give life and energy to — **in·vig·o·ra·tion** n

in·vin·ci·ble adj : incapable of being conquered — **in·vin·ci·bil·i·ty** n — **in·vin·ci·bly** adv

in·vi·o·la·ble adj : safe from violation or desecration — **in·vi·o·la·bil·i·ty** n

in·vi·o·late adj : not violated or profaned

in·vite vb **-vit·ed; -vit·ing** 1 : entice 2 : increase the likelihood of 3 : request the presence or participation of 4 : encourage — **in·vi·ta·tion** n — **in·vit·ing** n

in·vo·ca·tion n 1 : prayer 2 : incantation

in·voice n : itemized bill for goods shipped ~ vb **-voiced; -voic·ing** : bill

in·voke vb **-voked; -vok·ing** 1 : call on for help 2 : cite as authority 3 : conjure 4 : carry out

in·volve vb **-volved; -volv·ing** 1 : draw in as a participant 2 : relate closely 3 : require as a necessary part 4 : occupy fully — **in·volve·ment** n

in·volved adj : intricate

¹**in·ward** adj : inside

²**inward, in·wards** adv : toward the inside, center, or inner being

in·ward·ly adv 1 : mentally or spiritually 2 : internally 3 : to oneself

io·dide n : compound of iodine

io·dine n 1 : nonmetallic chemical element 2 : solution of iodine used as an antiseptic

io·dize vb **-dized; -diz·ing** : treat with iodine or an iodide

ion n : electrically charged particle — **ion·ic** adj — **ion·iz·able** adj — **ion·iza·tion** n — **ion·ize** vb — **ion·iz·er** n

-ion n suffix 1 : act or process 2 : state or condition

iono·sphere n : layer of the upper atmosphere containing ionized gases — **ion·o·spher·ic** adj

io·ta n : small quantity

IOU n : acknowledgment of a debt

iras·ci·ble adj : marked by hot temper — **iras·ci·bil·i·ty** n

irate adj : roused to intense anger — **irate·ly** adv

ire n : anger

ir·i·des·cence n : rainbowlike play of colors — **ir·i·des·cent** adj

iris n, pl **iris·es** or **iri·des** 1 : colored part around the pupil of the eye 2 : plant with long leaves and large showy flowers

irk vb : annoy — **irk·some** adj — **irk·some·ly** adv

iron n 1 : heavy metallic chemical element 2 : something made of iron 3 : heated device for pressing clothes 4 : hardness, determination ~ vb : press or smooth out with an iron — **iron·ware** n — **iron·work** n — **iron·work·er** n — **iron·works** n pl

iron·clad adj 1 : sheathed in iron armor 2 : strict or exacting

iron·ing n : clothes to be ironed

iron·wood n : tree or shrub with very hard wood or this wood

iro·ny n, pl **-nies** 1 : use of words to express the opposite of the literal meaning 2 : incongruity between the actual and expected result of events — **iron·ic, iron·i·cal** adj — **iron·i·cal·ly** adv

ir·ra·di·ate vb **-at·ed; -at·ing** : treat with radiation — **ir·ra·di·a·tion** n

ir·ra·tio·nal adj 1 : incapable of reasoning 2 : not based on reason — **ir·ra·tio·nal·i·ty** n — **ir·ra·tio·nal·ly** adv

ir·rec·on·cil·able adj : impossible to reconcile — **irrec·on·cil·abil·i·ty** n

ir·re·cov·er·able adj : not capable of being recovered — **ir·re·cov·er·ably** adv

ir·re·deem·able adj : not redeemable

ir·re·duc·ible adj : not reducible — **ir·re·duc·ibly** adv

ir·re·fut·able adj : impossible to refute

ir·reg·u·lar adj : not regular or normal — **ir·regular** n — **irreg·u·lar·i·ty** n — **ir·reg·u·lar·ly** adv

ir·rel·e·vant adj : not relevant — **ir·rel·e·vance** n

ir·re·li·gious adj : not following religious practices

ir·rep·a·ra·ble adj : impossible to make good, undo, or remedy

ir·re·place·able adj : not replaceable

ir·re·press·ible adj : impossible to repress or control

ir·re·proach·able adj : blameless

ir·re·sist·ible adj : impossible to successfully resist — **ir·re·sist·ibly** adv

ir·res·o·lute adj : uncertain — **ir·res·o·lute·ly** adv — **ir·res·o·lu·tion** n

ir·re·spec·tive of prep : without regard to

ir·re·spon·si·ble adj : not responsible — **ir·re·spon·si·bil·i·ty** n — **ir·re·spon·si·bly** adv

ir·re·triev·able adj : not retrievable

ir·rev·er·ence n 1 : lack of reverence 2 : irreverent act or utterance — **ir·rev·er·ent** adj

ir·re·vers·ible adj : incapable of being reversed

ir·rev·o·ca·ble adj : incapable of being revoked — **ir·rev·o·ca·bly** adv

ir·ri·gate vb **-gat·ed; -gat·ing** : supply with water by artificial means — **ir·ri·ga·tion** n

ir·ri·tate vb **-tat·ed; -tat·ing** 1 : excite to anger 2 : make sore or inflamed — **ir·ri·ta·bil·i·ty** n — **ir·ri·ta·ble** adj — **ir·ri·ta·bly** adv — **ir·ri·tant** adj or n — **ir·ri·tat·ing·ly** adv — **ir·ri·ta·tion** n

is pres 3d sing of BE

-ish adj suffix 1 : characteristic of 2 : somewhat

Is·lam n : religious faith of Muslims — **Is·lam·ic** adj

is·land n : body of land surrounded by water — **is·land·er** n

isle n : small island

is·let n : small island

-ism n suffix 1 : act or practice 2 : characteristic manner 3 : condition 4 : doctrine

iso·late vb **-lat·ed; -lat·ing** : place or keep by itself — **iso·la·tion** n

iso·met·rics n sing or pl : exercise against unmoving resistance — **isometric** adj

isos·ce·les adj : having 2 equal sides

iso·tope n : species of atom of a chemical element — **iso·to·pic** adj

is·sue vb **-sued; -su·ing** 1 : go, come, or flow out

2 : descend from a specified ancestor 3 : emanate or result 4 : put forth or distribute officially ~ n 1 : action of issuing 2 : offspring 3 : result 4 : point of controversy 5 : act of giving out or printing 6 : quantity given out or printed — **is•su•ance** n — **is•su•er** n

-ist n suffix 1 : one that does 2 : one that plays 3 : one that specializes in 4 : follower of a doctrine

isth•mus n : narrow strip of land connecting 2 larger portions

it pron 1 : that one — used of a lifeless thing or an abstract entity 2 — used as an anticipatory subject or object ~ n : player who tries to catch others (as in a game of tag)

ital•ic n : style of type with slanting letters — **italic** adj — **ital•i•ci•za•tion** n — **ital•i•cize** vb

itch n 1 : uneasy irritating skin sensation 2 : skin disorder 3 : persistent desire — **itch** vb — **itchy** adj

item n 1 : particular in a list, account, or series 2 : piece of news — **item•iza•tion** n — **item•ize** vb

itin•er•ant adj : traveling from place to place

itin•er•ary n, pl **-ar•ies** : route or outline of a journey

its adj : relating to it

it•self pron : it — used reflexively or for emphasis

-ity n suffix : quality, state, or degree

-ive adj suffix : that performs or tends toward an action

ivo•ry n, pl **-ries** 1 : hard creamy-white material of elephants' tusks 2 : pale yellow color

ivy n, pl **ivies** : trailing woody vine with evergreen leaves

-ize vb suffix 1 : cause to be, become, or resemble 2 : subject to an action 3 : treat or combine with 4 : engage in an activity

J

j n, pl **j's** or **js** : 10th letter of the alphabet

jab vb **-bb-** : thrust quickly or abruptly ~ n : short straight punch

jab•ber vb : talk rapidly or unintelligibly — **jab•ber** n

jack n 1 : mechanical device to raise a heavy body 2 : small flag 3 : small 6-pointed metal object used in a game (**jacks**) 4 : electrical socket ~ vb 1 : raise with a jack 2 : increase

jack•al n : wild dog

jack•ass n 1 : male ass 2 : stupid person

jack•et n : garment for the upper body

jack•ham•mer n : pneumatic tool for drilling

jack•knife n : pocketknife ~ vb : fold like a jackknife

jack–o'–lan•tern n : lantern made of a carved pumpkin

jack•pot n : sum of money won

jack•rab•bit n : large hare of western No. America

jade n : usu. green gemstone

jad•ed adj : dulled or bored by having too much

jag•ged adj : sharply notched

jag•uar n : black-spotted tropical American cat

jai alai n : game with a ball propelled by a basket on the hand

jail n : prison — **jail** vb — **jail•break** n — **jail•er**, **jail•or** n

ja•la•pe•ño n : Mexican hot pepper

ja•lopy n, pl **-lopies** : dilapidated vehicle

jal•ou•sie n : door or window with louvers

jam vb **-mm-** 1 : press into a tight position 2 : cause to become wedged and unworkable ~ n 1 : crowded mass that blocks or impedes 2 : difficult situation 3 : thick sweet food made of cooked fruit

jamb n : upright framing piece of a door

jam•bo•ree n : large festive gathering

jan•gle vb **-gled; -gling** : make a harsh ringing sound — **jangle** n

jan•i•tor n : person who has the care of a building — **jan•i•to•ri•al** adj

Jan•u•ary n : 1st month of the year having 31 days

¹jar vb **-rr-** 1 : have a harsh or disagreeable effect 2 : vibrate or shake ~ n 1 : jolt 2 : painful effect

²jar n : wide-mouthed container

jar•gon n : special vocabulary of a group

jas•mine n : climbing shrub with fragrant flowers

jas•per n : red, yellow, or brown opaque quartz

jaun•dice n : yellowish discoloration of skin, tissues, and body fluids

jaun•diced adj : exhibiting envy or hostility

jaunt n : short pleasure trip

jaun•ty adj **-ti•er; -est** : lively in manner or appearance — **jaun•ti•ly** adv — **jaun•ti•ness** n

jav•e•lin n : light spear

jaw n 1 : either of the bony or cartilaginous structures that support the mouth 2 : one of 2 movable parts for holding or crushing ~ vb : talk indignantly or at length — **jaw•bone** n — **jawed** adj

jay n : noisy brightly colored bird

jay•bird n : jay

jay•walk vb : cross a street carelessly — **jay•walk•er** n

jazz vb : enliven ~ n 1 : kind of American music involving improvisation 2 : empty talk — **jazzy** adj

jeal•ous adj : suspicious of a rival or of one believed to enjoy an advantage — **jeal•ous•ly** adv — **jeal•ou•sy** n

jeans n pl : pants made of durable twilled cotton cloth

jeep n : 4-wheel army vehicle

jeer vb 1 : speak or cry out in derision 2 : ridicule ~ n : taunt

Je•ho•vah n : God

je•june adj : dull or childish

jell vb 1 : come to the consistency of jelly 2 : take shape

jel•ly n, pl **-lies** : a substance (as food) with a soft somewhat elastic consistency — **jelly** vb

jel•ly•fish n : sea animal with a saucer-shaped jellylike body

jen•ny n, pl **-nies** : female bird or donkey

jeop•ar•dy n : exposure to death, loss, or injury — **jeop•ar•dize** vb

jerk vb 1 : give a sharp quick push, pull, or twist 2 : move in short abrupt motions ~ n 1 : short quick pull or twist 2 : stupid or foolish person — **jerk•i•ly** adv — **jerky** adj

jer•kin n : close-fitting sleeveless jacket

jer•ry–built adj : built cheaply and flimsily

jer•sey n, pl **-seys** 1 : plain knit fabric 2 : knitted shirt

jest n : witty remark — **jest** vb

jest•er n : one employed to entertain a court

¹jet n : velvet-black coal used for jewelry

²jet vb **-tt-** 1 : spout or emit in a stream 2 : travel by jet ~ n 1 : forceful rush of fluid through a narrow opening 2 : jet-propelled airplane

jet–propelled adj : driven by an engine (**jet engine**) that produces propulsion (**jet propulsion**) by the rearward discharge of a jet of fluid

jet•sam n : jettisoned goods

jet•ti•son vb 1 : throw (goods) overboard 2 : discard — **jettison** n

jet•ty n, pl **-ties** : pier or wharf

Jew n : one whose religion is Judaism — **Jew•ish** adj

jew•el n 1 : ornament of precious metal 2 : gem ~ vb **-eled** or **-elled; -el•ing** or **-el•ling** : adorn with jewels — **jew•el•er**, **jew•el•ler** n — **jew•el•ry** n

jib n : triangular sail

jibe vb **jibed; jib•ing** : be in agreement

jif•fy n, pl **-fies** : short time

jig n : lively dance ~ vb **-gg-** : dance a jig

jig•ger n : measure used in mixing drinks

jig•gle vb **-gled; -gling** : move with quick little jerks — **jiggle** n

jig•saw n : machine saw with a narrow blade that moves up and down

jilt vb : drop (a lover) unfeelingly

jim•my n, pl **-mies** : small crowbar ~ vb **-mied; -my•ing** : pry open

jim•son•weed n : coarse poisonous weed

jin•gle vb **-gled; -gling** : make a light tinkling sound ~ n 1 : light tinkling sound 2 : short verse or song

jin•go•ism n : extreme chauvinism or nationalism — **jin•go•ist** n — **jin•go•is•tic** adj

jinx n : one that brings bad luck — **jinx** vb

jit•ney n, pl **-neys** : small bus

jit•ters n pl : extreme nervousness — **jit•tery** adj

job n 1 : something that has to be done 2 : regular employment — **job•hold•er** n — **job•less** adj

job•ber n : middleman

jock•ey n, pl **-eys** : one who rides a horse in a race ~ vb **-eyed; -ey•ing** : manipulate or maneuver adroitly

jo•cose adj : jocular

joc•u•lar adj : marked by jesting — **joc•u•lar•i•ty** n — **joc•u•lar•ly** adv

jo•cund adj : full of mirth or gaiety

jodh•purs n pl : riding breeches

¹jog vb **-gg-** 1 : give a slight shake or push to 2 : run or ride at a slow pace ~ n 1 : slight shake 2 : slow pace — **jog•ger** n

²jog n : brief abrupt change in direction or line

join vb 1 : come or bring together 2 : become a member of — **join•er** n

joint n 1 : point of contact between bones 2 : place where 2 parts connect 3 : often disreputable place ~ adj : common to 2 or more — **joint•ed** adj — **joint•ly** adv

joist n : beam supporting a floor or ceiling

joke n : something said or done to provoke laughter — vb **joked; jok•ing** : make jokes — **jok•er** n — **jok•ing•ly** adv

jol•li•ty n, pl **-ties** : gaiety or merriment

jol•ly adj **-li•er; -est** : full of high spirits

jolt vb 1 : move with a sudden jerky motion 2 : give a jolt to ~ n 1 : abrupt jerky blow or movement 2 : sudden shock — **jolt•er** n

jon•quil n : narcissus with white or yellow flowers

josh vb : tease or joke

jos•tle vb **-tled; -tling** : push or shove

jot n : least bit ~ vb **-tt-** : write briefly and hurriedly

jounce vb **jounced; jounc•ing** : jolt — **jounce** n

jour•nal n 1 : brief account of daily events 2 : periodical (as a newspaper)

jour•nal•ism n : business of reporting or printing news — **jour•nal•ist** n — **jour•nal•is•tic** adj

jour•ney n, pl **-neys** : a going from one place to another ~ vb **-neyed; -ney•ing** : make a journey

jour•ney•man *n* : worker who has learned a trade and works for another person

joust *n* : combat on horseback between 2 knights with lances — **joust** *vb*

jo•vial *adj* : marked by good humor — **jo•vi•al•i•ty** *n* — **jo•vi•al•ly** *adv*

¹jowl *n* : loose flesh about the lower jaw or throat

²jowl *n* 1 : lower jaw 2 : cheek

joy *n* 1 : feeling of happiness 2 : source of happiness — **joy** *vb* — **joy•ful** *adj* — **joy•ful•ly** *adv* — **joy•less** *adj* — **joy•ous** *adj* — **joy•ous•ly** *adv* — **joy•ous•ness** *n*

joy•ride *n* : reckless ride for pleasure — **joy•rid•er** *n* — **joy•rid•ing** *n*

ju•bi•lant *adj* : expressing great joy — **ju•bi•lant•ly** *adv* — **ju•bi•la•tion** *n*

ju•bi•lee *n* 1 : 50th anniversary 2 : season or occasion of celebration

Ju•da•ism *n* : religion developed among the ancient Hebrews — **Ju•da•ic** *adj*

judge *vb* **judged; judg•ing** 1 : form an opinion 2 : decide as a judge ~ *n* 1 : public official authorized to decide questions brought before a court 2 : one who gives an authoritative opinion — **judge•ship** *n*

judg•ment, judge•ment *n* 1 : decision or opinion given after judging 2 : capacity for judging — **judg•men•tal** *adj* — **judg•men•tal•ly** *adv*

ju•di•ca•ture *n* : administration of justice

ju•di•cial *adj* : relating to judicature or the judiciary — **ju•di•cial•ly** *adv*

ju•di•cia•ry *n* : system of courts of law or the judges of them — **judiciary** *adj*

ju•di•cious *adj* : having or characterized by sound judgment — **ju•di•cious•ly** *adv*

ju•do *n* : form of wrestling — **judo•ist** *n*

jug *n* : large deep container with a narrow mouth and a handle

jug•ger•naut *n* : massive inexorable force or object

jug•gle *vb* **-gled; -gling** 1 : keep several objects in motion in the air at the same time 2 : manipulate for an often tricky purpose — **jug•gler** *n*

jug•u•lar *adj* : in or on the throat or neck

juice *n* 1 : extractable fluid contents of cells or tissues 2 : electricity — **juic•er** *n* — **juic•i•ly** *adv* — **juic•i•ness** *n* — **juicy** *adj*

ju•jube *n* : gummy candy

juke•box *n* : coin-operated machine for playing music recordings

ju•lep *n* : mint-flavored bourbon drink

Ju•ly *n* : 7th month of the year having 31 days

jum•ble *vb* **-bled; -bling** : mix in a confused mass — **jumble** *n*

jum•bo *n, pl* **-bos** : very large version — **jumbo** *adj*

jump *vb* 1 : rise into or through the air esp. by muscular effort 2 : pass over 3 : give a start 4 : rise or increase sharply ~ *n* 1 : a jumping 2 : sharp sudden increase 3 : initial advantage

¹jump•er *n* : one that jumps

²jumper *n* : sleeveless one-piece dress

jumpy *adj* **jump•i•er; -est** : nervous or jittery

junc•tion *n* 1 : a joining 2 : place or point of meeting

junc•ture *n* 1 : joint or connection 2 : critical time or state of affairs

June *n* : 6th month of the year having 30 days

jun•gle *n* : thick tangled mass of tropical vegetation

ju•nior *n* 1 : person who is younger or of lower rank than another 2 : student in the next-to-last year ~ *adj* : younger or lower in rank

ju•ni•per *n* : evergreen shrub or tree

¹junk *n* 1 : discarded articles 2 : shoddy product ~ *vb* : discard or scrap — **junky** *adj*

²junk *n* : flat-bottomed ship of Chinese waters

jun•ket *n* : trip made by an official at public expense

jun•ta *n* : group of persons controlling a government

ju•ris•dic•tion *n* 1 : right or authority to interpret and apply the law 2 : limits within which authority may be exercised — **ju•ris•dic•tion•al** *adj*

ju•ris•pru•dence *n* 1 : system of laws 2 : science or philosophy of law

ju•rist *n* : judge

ju•ror *n* : member of a jury

ju•ry *n, pl* **-ries** : body of persons sworn to give a verdict on a matter

just *adj* 1 : reasonable 2 : correct or proper 3 : morally or legally right 4 : deserved ~ *adv* 1 : exactly 2 : very recently 3 : barely 4 : only 5 : quite 6 : possibly — **just•ly** *adv* — **just•ness** *n*

jus•tice *n* 1 : administration of what is just 2 : judge 3 : administration of law 4 : fairness

jus•ti•fy *vb* **-fied; -fy•ing** : prove to be just, right, or reasonable — **jus•ti•fi•able** *adj* — **jus•ti•fi•ca•tion** *n*

jut *vb* **-tt-** : stick out

jute *n* : strong glossy fiber from a tropical plant

ju•ve•nile *adj* : relating to children or young people ~ *n* : young person

jux•ta•pose *vb* **-posed; -pos•ing** : place side by side — **jux•ta•po•si•tion** *n*

K

k *n, pl* **k's** *or* **ks** : 11th letter of the alphabet

kai•ser *n* : German ruler

kale *n* : curly cabbage

ka•lei•do•scope *n* : device containing loose bits of colored material reflecting in many patterns — **ka•lei•do•scop•ic** *adj* — **ka•lei•do•scop•i•cal•ly** *adv*

kan•ga•roo *n, pl* **-roos** : large leaping Australian mammal

ka•o•lin *n* : fine white clay

kar•at *n* : unit of gold content

ka•ra•te *n* : art of self-defense by crippling kicks and punches

ka•ty•did *n* : large American grasshopper

kay•ak *n* : Eskimo canoe

ka•zoo *n, pl* **-zoos** : toy musical instrument

keel *n* : central lengthwise strip on the bottom of a ship — **keeled** *adj*

keen *adj* 1 : sharp 2 : severe 3 : enthusiastic 4 : mentally alert — **keen•ly** *adv* — **keen•ness** *n*

keep *vb* **kept; keep•ing** 1 : perform 2 : guard 3 : maintain 4 : retain in one's possession 5 : detain 6 : continue in good condition 7 : refrain ~ *n* 1 : fortress 2 : means by which one is kept — **keep•er** *n*

keep•ing *n* : conformity

keep•sake *n* : souvenir

keg *n* : small cask or barrel

kelp *n* : coarse brown seaweed

ken *n* : range of sight or understanding

ken•nel *n* : dog shelter — **ken•nel** *vb*

ker•chief *n* : square of cloth worn as a head covering

ker•nel *n* 1 : inner softer part of a seed or nut 2 : whole seed of a cereal 3 : central part

ker•o•sene, ker•o•sine *n* : thin flammable oil from petroleum

ketch•up *n* : spicy tomato sauce

ket•tle *n* : vessel for boiling liquids

ket•tle•drum *n* : brass or copper kettle-shaped drum

¹key *n* 1 : usu. metal piece to open a lock 2 : explanation 3 : lever pressed by a finger in playing an instrument or operating a machine 4 : leading individual or principle 5 : system of musical tones or pitch ~ *vb* : attune ~ *adj* : basic — **key•hole** *n* — **key up** *vb* : make nervous

²key *n* : low island or reef

key•board *n* : arrangement of keys

key•note *n* 1 : 1st note of a scale 2 : central fact, idea, or mood ~ *vb* 1 : set the keynote of 2 : deliver the major speech

key•stone *n* : wedge-shaped piece at the crown of an arch

kha•ki *n* : light yellowish brown color

khan *n* : Mongol leader

kib•butz *n, pl* **-but•zim** : Israeli communal farm or settlement

ki•bitz•er *n* : one who offers unwanted advice — **kib•itz** *vb*

kick *vb* 1 : strike out or hit with the foot 2 : object strongly 3 : recoil ~ *n* 1 : thrust with the foot 2 : recoil of a gun 3 : stimulating effect — **kick•er** *n*

kid *n* 1 : young goat 2 : child ~ *vb* **-dd-** 1 : deceive as a joke 2 : tease — **kid•der** *n* — **kid•ding•ly** *adv*

kid•nap *vb* **-napped** *or* **-naped; -nap•ping** *or* **-nap•ing** : carry a person away by illegal force — **kid•nap•per, kid•nap•er** *n*

kid•ney *n, pl* **-neys** : either of a pair of organs that excrete urine

kill *vb* 1 : deprive of life 2 : finish 3 : use up (time) ~ *n* : act of killing — **kill•er** *n*

kiln *n* : heated enclosure for burning, firing, or drying — **kiln** *vb*

ki•lo *n, pl* **-los** : kilogram

kilo•cy•cle *n* : kilohertz

ki•lo•gram *n* : basic metric mass unit nearly equal to the mass of 1000 cubic centimeters of water at its maximum density

ki•lo•hertz *n* : 1000 hertz

ki•lo•me•ter *n* : 1000 meters

ki•lo•volt *n* : 1000 volts

kilo•watt *n* : 1000 watts

kilt *n* : knee-length pleated skirt

kil•ter *n* : proper condition

ki•mo•no *n, pl* **-nos** : loose robe

kin *n* 1 : one's relatives 2 : kinsman

kind *n* 1 : essential quality 2 : group with common traits 3 : variety ~ *adj* 1 : of a sympathetic nature 2 : arising from sympathy — **kind•heart•ed** *adj* — **kind•ness** *n*

kin•der•gar•ten *n* : class for young children — **kin•der•gart•ner** *n*

kin•dle *vb* **-dled; -dling** 1 : set on fire or start burning 2 : stir up

kin•dling *n* : material for starting a fire

kind•ly *adj* **-li•er; -est** : of a sympathetic nature ~ *adv* 1 : sympathetically 2 : courteously — **kind•li•ness** *n*

kin•dred *n* 1 : related individuals 2 : kin ~ *adj* : of a like nature

kin•folk, kinfolks *n pl* : kin

king *n* : male sovereign — **king•dom** *n* — **king•less** *adj* — **king•ly** *adj* — **king•ship** *n*

king•fish•er *n* : bright-colored crested bird

kink *n* 1 : short tight twist or curl 2 : cramp —

kinky *adj*

kin•ship *n* : relationship

kins•man *n* : male relative

kins•wom•an *n* : female relative

kip•per *n* : dried or smoked fish — **kipper** *vb*

kiss *vb* : touch with the lips as a mark of affection — **kiss** *n*

kit *n* : set of articles (as tools or parts)

kitch•en *n* : room with cooking facilities

kite *n* 1 : small hawk 2 : covered framework flown at the end of a string

kith *n* : familiar friends

kit•ten *n* : young cat — **kit•ten•ish** *adj*

¹kit•ty *n*, *pl* **-ties** : kitten

²kitty *n*, *pl* **-ties** : fund or pool (as in a card game)

kit•ty–cor•ner, kit•ty–cor•nered *var of* CATER-CORNER

ki•wi *n* : small flightless New Zealand bird

klep•to•ma•nia *n* : neurotic impulse to steal — **klep•to•ma•ni•ac** *n*

knack *n* 1 : clever way of doing something 2 : natural aptitude

knap•sack *n* : bag for carrying supplies on one's back

knave *n* : rogue — **knav•ery** *n* — **knav•ish** *adj*

knead *vb* 1 : work and press with the hands 2 : massage — **knead•er** *n*

knee *n* : joint in the middle part of the leg — **kneed** *adj*

knee•cap *n* : bone forming the front of the knee

kneel *vb* **knelt** *or* **kneeled; kneel•ing** : rest on one's knees

knell *n* : stroke of a bell

knew *past of* KNOW

knick•ers *n pl* : pants gathered at the knee

knick•knack *n* : small decorative object

knife *n*, *pl* **knives** : sharp blade with a handle — *vb*.**knifed; knif•ing** : stab or cut with a knife

knight *n* 1 : mounted warrior of feudal times 2 : man honored by a sovereign ~ *vb* : make a knight of — **knight•hood** *n* — **knight•ly** *adv*

knit *vb* **knit** *or* **knit•ted; knit•ting** 1 : link firmly or closely 2 : form a fabric by interlacing yarn or thread ~ *n* : knitted garment — **knit•ter** *n*

knob *n* : rounded protuberance or handle — **knobbed** *adj* — **knob•by** *adj*

knock *vb* 1 : strike with a sharp blow 2 : collide 3 : find fault with ~ *n* : sharp blow — **knock out** *vb* : make unconscious

knock•er *n* : device hinged to a door to knock with

knoll *n* : small round hill

knot *n* 1 : interlacing (as of string) that forms a lump 2 : base of a woody branch in the stem 3 : group 4 : one nautical mile per hour ~ *vb* -**tt-** : tie in or with a knot — **knot•ty** *adj*

know *vb* **knew; known; know•ing** 1 : perceive directly or understand 2 : be familiar with — **know•able** *adj* — **know•er** *n*

know•ing *adj* : shrewdly and keenly alert — **know•ing•ly** *adv*

knowl•edge *n* 1 : understanding gained by experience 2 : range of information — **knowl•edge•able** *adj*

knuck•le *n* : rounded knob at a finger joint

ko•ala *n* : gray furry Australian animal

kohl•ra•bi *n*, *pl* **-bies** : cabbage that forms no head

Ko•ran *n* : book of Islam containing revelations made to Muhammad by Allah

ko•sher *adj* : ritually fit for use according to Jewish law

kow•tow *vb* : show excessive deference

kryp•ton *n* : gaseous chemical element used in lamps

ku•dos *n* : fame and renown

kum•quat *n* : small citrus fruit

L

l *n*, *pl* **l's** *or* **ls** : 12th letter of the alphabet

lab *n* : laboratory

la•bel *n* 1 : identification slip 2 : identifying word or phrase ~ *vb* **-beled** *or* **-belled; -bel•ing** *or* **-bel•ling** : put a label on

la•bi•al *adj* : of or relating to the lips

la•bor *n* 1 : physical or mental effort 2 : physical efforts of childbirth 3 : task 4 : people who work manually ~ *vb* : work esp. with great effort — **la•bor•er** *n*

lab•o•ra•to•ry *n*, *pl* **-ries** : place for experimental testing

Labor Day *n* : 1st Monday in September observed as a legal holiday in recognition of working people

la•bo•ri•ous *adj* : requiring great effort — **la•bo•ri•ous•ly** *adv*

lab•y•rinth *n* : maze — **lab•y•rin•thine** *adj*

lace *n* 1 : cord or string for tying 2 : fine net usu. figured fabric ~ *vb* **laced; lac•ing** 1 : tie 2 : adorn with lace — **lacy** *adj*

lac•er•ate *vb* **-at•ed; -at•ing** : tear roughly — **lac•er•a•tion** *n*

lach•ry•mose *adj* : tearful

lack *vb* : be missing or deficient in ~ *n* : deficiency

lack•a•dai•si•cal *adj* : lacking spirit — **lack•a•dai•si•cal•ly** *adv*

lack•ey *n*, *pl* **-eys** 1 : footman or servant 2 : toady

lack•lus•ter *adj* : dull

la•con•ic *adj* : sparing of words — **la•con•i•cal•ly** *adv*

lac•quer *n* : glossy surface coating — **lacquer** *vb*

la•crosse *n* : ball game played with long-handled rackets

lac•tate *vb* **-tat•ed; -tat•ing** : secrete milk — **lac•ta•tion** *n*

lac•tic *adj* : relating to milk

la•cu•na *n*, *pl* **-nae** *or* **-nas** : blank space or missing part

lad *n* : boy

lad•der *n* : device with steps or rungs for climbing

lad•en *adj* : loaded

la•dle *n* : spoon with a deep bowl — **ladle** *vb*

la•dy *n*, *pl* **-dies** 1 : woman of rank or authority 2 : woman

la•dy•bird *n* : ladybug

la•dy•bug *n* : brightly colored beetle

lag *vb* **-gg-** : fail to keep up ~ *n* 1 : a falling behind 2 : interval

la•ger *n* : beer

lag•gard *adj* : slow ~ *n* : one that lags — **lag•gard•ly** *adv or adj* — **lag•gard•ness** *n*

la•gniappe *n* : bonus

la•goon *n* : shallow sound, channel, or pond near or connecting with a larger body of water

laid *past of* LAY

lain *past part of* LIE

lair *n* : den

lais•sez–faire *n* : doctrine opposing government interference in business

la•ity *n* : people of a religious faith who are not clergy members

lake *n* : inland body of water

la•ma *n* : Buddhist monk

lamb *n* : young sheep or its flesh used as food

lam•baste, lam•bast *vb* 1 : beat 2 : censure

lam•bent *adj* : light or bright — **lam•ben•cy** *n* — **lam•bent•ly** *adv*

lame *adj* **lam•er; lam•est** 1 : having a limb disabled 2 : weak ~ *vb* **lamed; lam•ing** : make lame — **lame•ly** *adv* — **lame•ness** *n*

la•mé *n* : cloth with tinsel threads

lame•brain *n* : fool

la•ment *vb* 1 : mourn 2 : express sorrow for ~ *n* 1 : mourning 2 : complaint — **lam•en•ta•ble** *adj* — **lam•en•ta•bly** *adv* — **lam•en•ta•tion** *n*

lam•i•nat•ed *adj* : made of thin layers of material — **lam•i•nate** *vb* — **lam•i•nate** *n or adj* — **lam•i•na•tion** *n*

lamp *n* : device for producing light or heat

lam•poon *n* : satire — **lam•poon** *vb*

lam•prey *n*, *pl* **-preys** : sucking eellike fish

lance *n* : spear ~ *vb* **lanced; lanc•ing** : pierce or open with a lancet

lance corporal *n* : enlisted man in the marine corps ranking above a private first class and below a corporal

lan•cet *n* : pointed surgical instrument

land *n* 1 : solid part of the surface of the earth 2 : country ~ *vb* 1 : go ashore 2 : catch or gain 3 : touch the ground or a surface — **land•less** *adj* — **land•own•er** *n*

land•fill *n* : dump

land•ing *n* 1 : action of one that lands 2 : place for loading passengers and cargo 3 : level part of a staircase

land•la•dy *n* : woman landlord

land•locked *adj* : enclosed by land

land•lord *n* : owner of property

land•lub•ber *n* : one with little sea experience

land•mark *n* 1 : object that marks a boundary or serves as a guide 2 : event that marks a turning point

land•scape *n* : view of natural scenery ~ *vb* **-scaped; -scap•ing** : beautify a piece of land (as by decorative planting)

land•slide *n* 1 : slipping down of a mass of earth 2 : overwhelming victory

land•ward *adj* : toward the land — **landward** *adv*

lane *n* : narrow way

lan•guage *n* : words and the methods of combining them for communication

lan•guid *adj* 1 : weak 2 : sluggish — **lan•guid•ly** *adv* — **lan•guid•ness** *n*

lan•guish *vb* : become languid or discouraged

lan•guor *n* : listless indolence — **lan•guor•ous** *adj* — **lan•guor•ous•ly** *adv*

lank *adj* 1 : thin 2 : limp

lanky *adj* **lank•i•er; -est** : tall and thin

lan•o•lin *n* : fatty wax from sheep's wool used in ointments

lan•tern *n* : enclosed portable light

¹lap *n* 1 : front part of the lower trunk and thighs of a seated person 2 : overlapping part 3 : one complete circuit completing a course (as around a track or pool) ~ *vb* **-pp-** : fold over

²lap *vb* **-pp-** 1 : scoop up with the tongue 2 : splash gently

lap•dog *n* : small dog

la•pel *n* : fold of the front of a coat

lap•i•dary *n* : one who cuts and polishes gems ~ *adj* : relating to gems

lapse *n* 1 : slight error 2 : termination of a right or privilege 3 : interval ~ *vb* **lapsed; laps•ing** 1 : slip 2 : subside 3 : cease

lap•top *adj* : of a size that may be used on one's lap

lar•board n : port side

lar•ce•ny n, pl **-nies** : theft — **lar•ce•nous** adj

larch n : tree like a pine that loses its needles

lard n : pork fat

lar•der n : pantry

large adj **larg•er; larg•est** : greater than average — **large•ly** adv — **large•ness** n

lar•gesse, lar•gess n : liberal giving

lar•i•at n : lasso

¹lark n : small songbird

²lark vb or n : romp

lar•va n, pl **-vae** : wormlike form of an insect — **lar•val** adj

lar•yn•gi•tis n : inflammation of the larynx

lar•ynx n, pl **-ryn•ges** or **-ynx•es** : upper part of the trachea — **la•ryn•ge•al** adj

la•sa•gna n : flat noodles baked usu. with tomato sauce, meat, and cheese

las•civ•i•ous adj : lewd — **las•civ•i•ous•ness** n

la•ser n : device that produces an intense light beam

¹lash vb : whip ∼ n **1** : stroke esp. of a whip **2** : eyelash

²lash vb : bind with a rope or cord

lass n : girl

lass•ie n : girl

las•si•tude n **1** : fatigue **2** : listlessness

las•so n, pl **-sos** or **-soes** : rope with a noose for catching livestock — **lasso** vb

¹last vb : continue in existence or operation

²last adj **1** : final **2** : previous **3** : least likely ∼ adv **1** : at the end **2** : most recently **3** : in conclusion ∼ n : something that is last — **last•ly** adv — **at last** : finally

³last n : form on which a shoe is shaped

latch vb : catch or get hold ∼ n : catch that holds a door closed

late adj **lat•er; lat•est 1** : coming or staying after the proper time **2** : advanced toward the end **3** : recently deceased **4** : recent — **late** adv — **late•com•er** n — **late•ly** adv — **late•ness** n

la•tent adj : present but not visible or expressed — **la•ten•cy** n

lat•er•al adj : on or toward the side — **lat•er•al•ly** adv

la•tex n, pl **-ti•ces** or **-tex•es** : emulsion of synthetic rubber or plastic

lath n, pl **laths** or **lath** : building material (as a thin strip of wood) used as a base for plaster — **lath** vb — **lath•ing** n

lathe n : machine that rotates material for shaping

lath•er n **1** : foam ∼ vb : form or spread lather

lat•i•tude n **1** : distance north or south from the earth's equator **2** : freedom of action

la•trine n : toilet

lat•ter adj **1** : more recent **2** : being the second of 2 — **lat•ter•ly** adv

lat•tice n : framework of crossed strips

laud vb or n : praise — **laud•able** adj — **laud•ably** adv

laugh vb : show mirth, joy, or scorn with a smile and explosive sound — **laugh** n — **laugh•able** adj — **laugh•ing•ly** adv

laugh•ing•stock n : object of ridicule

laugh•ter n : action or sound of laughing

¹launch vb **1** : hurl or send off **2** : set afloat **3** : start — **launch** n — **launch•er** n

²launch n : small open boat

laun•der vb : wash or iron fabrics — **laun•der•er** n — **laun•dress** n — **laun•dry** n

lau•re•ate n : recipient of honors — **laureate** adj

lau•rel n **1** : small evergreen tree **2** : honor

la•va n : volcanic molten rock

lav•a•to•ry n, pl **-ries** : bathroom

lav•en•der n **1** : aromatic plant used for perfume **2** : pale purple color

lav•ish adj : expended profusely ∼ vb : expend or give freely — **lav•ish•ly** adv — **lav•ish•ness** n

law n **1** : established rule of conduct **2** : body of such laws **3** : principle of construction or procedure **4** : rule stating uniform behavior under uniform conditions **5** : lawyer's profession — **law•break•er** n — **law•giv•er** n — **law•less** adj — **law•less•ly** adv — **law•less•ness** n — **law•mak•er** n — **law•man** n — **law•suit** n

law•ful adj : permitted by law — **law•ful•ly** adv

lawn n : grass-covered yard

law•yer n : legal practitioner

lax adj : not strict or tense — **lax•i•ty** n — **lax•ly** adv

lax•a•tive n : drug relieving constipation

¹lay vb **laid; lay•ing 1** : put or set down **2** : produce eggs **3** : bet **4** : impose as a duty or burden **5** : put forward ∼ n : way something lies or is laid

²lay past of LIE

³lay n : song

⁴lay adj : of the laity — **lay•man** n — **lay•wom•an** n

lay•er n **1** : one that lays **2** : one thickness over or under another

lay•off n : temporary dismissal of a worker

lay•out n : arrangement

la•zy adj **-zi•er; -est** : disliking activity or exertion — **la•zi•ly** adv — **la•zi•ness** n

lea n : meadow

leach vb : remove (a soluble part) with a solvent

¹lead vb **led; lead•ing 1** : guide on a way **2** : direct the activity of **3** : go at the head of **4** : tend to a definite result ∼ n : position in front — **lead•er** n — **lead•er•less** adj — **lead•er•ship** n

²lead n **1** : heavy bluish white chemical element **2** : marking substance in a pencil — **lead•en** adj

leaf n, pl **leaves 1** : green outgrowth of a plant stem **2** : leaflike thing ∼ vb **1** : produce leaves **2** : turn book pages — **leaf•age** n — **leafed** adj — **leaf•less** adj — **leafy** adj — **leaved** adj

leaf•let n : pamphlet

¹league n : unit of distance equal to about 3 miles

²league n : association for a common purpose — **league** vb — **leagu•er** n

leak vb **1** : enter or escape through a leak **2** : become or make known ∼ n : opening that accidentally admits or lets out a substance — **leak•age** n — **leaky** adj

¹lean vb **1** : bend from a vertical position **2** : rely on for support **3** : incline in opinion — **lean** n

²lean adj **1** : lacking in flesh **2** : lacking richness — **lean•ness** n

leap vb **leapt** or **leaped; leap•ing** : jump — **leap** n

leap year n : 366-day year

learn vb **1** : gain understanding or skill by study or experience **2** : memorize **3** : find out — **learn•er** n

learn•ed adj : having great learning — **learn•ed•ness** n

learn•ing n : knowledge

lease n : contract transferring real estate for a term and usu. for rent ∼ vb **leased; leas•ing** : grant by or hold under a lease

leash n : line to hold an animal — **leash** vb

least adj **1** : lowest in importance or position **2** : smallest **3** : scantiest ∼ n : one that is least ∼ adv : in the smallest or lowest degree

leath•er n : dressed animal skin — **leath•ern** adj — **leathery** adj

¹leave vb **left; leav•ing 1** : bequeath **2** : allow or cause to remain **3** : have as a remainder **4** : go away ∼ n **1** : permission **2** : authorized absence **3** : departure

²leave vb **leaved; leav•ing** : leaf

leav•en n : substance for producing fermentation ∼ vb : raise dough with a leaven

leaves pl of LEAF

lech•ery n : inordinate indulgence in sex — **lech-**

er n — **lech•er•ous** adj — **lech•er•ous•ly** adv — **lech•er•ous•ness** n

lec•ture n **1** : instructive talk **2** : reprimand — **lecture** vb — **lec•tur•er** n — **lec•ture•ship** n

led past of LEAD

ledge n : shelflike projection

led•ger n : account book

lee n : side sheltered from the wind — **lee** adj

leech n : segmented freshwater worm that feeds on blood

leek n : onionlike herb

leer n : suggestive or malicious look — **leer** vb

leery adj : suspicious or wary

lees n pl : dregs

lee•ward adj : situated away from the wind ∼ n : the lee side

lee•way n : allowable margin

¹left adj : on the same side of the body as the heart ∼ n : left hand — **left** adv

²left past of LEAVE

leg n **1** : limb of an animal that supports the body **2** : something like a leg **3** : clothing to cover the leg ∼ vb **-gg-** : walk or run — **legged** adj — **leg•less** adj

leg•a•cy n, pl **-cies** : inheritance

le•gal adj **1** : relating to law or lawyers **2** : lawful — **le•gal•is•tic** adj — **le•gal•i•ty** n — **le•gal•ize** vb — **le•gal•ly** adv

leg•ate n : official representative

le•ga•tion n **1** : diplomatic mission **2** : official residence and office of a diplomat

leg•end n **1** : story handed down from the past **2** : inscription **3** : explanation of map symbols — **leg•end•ary** adj

leg•er•de•main n : sleight of hand

leg•ging, leg•gin n : leg covering

leg•i•ble adj : capable of being read — **leg•i•bil•i•ty** n — **leg•i•bly** adv

le•gion n **1** : large army unit **2** : multitude **3** : association of former servicemen — **le•gion•ary** n — **le•gion•naire** n

leg•is•late vb **-lat•ed; -lat•ing** : enact or bring about with laws — **leg•is•la•tion** n — **leg•is•la•tive** adj — **leg•is•la•tor** n

leg•is•la•ture n : organization with authority to make laws

le•git•i•mate adj **1** : lawfully begotten **2** : genuine **3** : conforming with law or accepted standards — **le•git•i•ma•cy** n — **le•git•i•mate•ly** adv — **le•git•i•mize** vb

le•gume n : plant bearing pods — **le•gu•mi•nous** adj

lei n : necklace of flowers

lei•sure n **1** : free time **2** : ease **3** : convenience — **lei•sure•ly** adj or adv

lem•ming n : short-tailed rodent

lem•on n : yellow citrus fruit — **lem•ony** adj

lem•on•ade n : sweetened lemon beverage

lend vb **lent; lend•ing 1** : give for temporary use **2** : furnish — **lend•er** n

length n **1** : longest dimension **2** : duration in time **3** : piece to be joined to others — **length•en** vb — **length•wise** adv or adj — **lengthy** adj

le•nient adj : of mild and tolerant disposition or effect — **le•ni•en•cy** n — **le•ni•ent•ly** adv

len•i•ty n : leniency

lens n **1** : curved piece for forming an image in an optical instrument **2** : transparent body in the eye that focuses light rays

Lent n : 40-day period of penitence and fasting from Ash Wednesday to Easter — **Lent•en** adj

len•til n : legume with flat edible seeds

le•o•nine adj : like a lion

leop•ard n : large tawny black-spotted cat

le•o•tard n : close-fitting garment

lep•er n : person with leprosy

lep•re•chaun n : mischievous Irish elf

lep·ro·sy *n* : chronic bacterial disease — **lep-rous** *adj*

les·bi·an *n* : female homosexual — **lesbian** *adj* — **les·bi·an·ism** *n*

le·sion *n* : abnormal area in the body due to injury or disease

less *adj* 1 : fewer 2 : of lower rank, degree, or importance 3 : smaller ~ *adv* : to a lesser degree ~ *n, pl* **less** : smaller portion ~ *prep* : minus — **less·en** *vb*

-less *adj suffix* 1 : not having 2 : unable to act or be acted on

les·see *n* : tenant under a lease

less·er *adj* : of less size, quality, or significance

les·son *n* 1 : reading or exercise to be studied by a pupil 2 : something learned

les·sor *n* : one who transfers property by a lease

lest *conj* : for fear that

¹let *n* : hindrance or obstacle

²let *vb* **let; let·ting** 1 : cause to 2 : rent 3 : permit

-let *n suffix* : small one

le·thal *adj* : deadly — **le·thal·ly** *adv*

leth·ar·gy *n* 1 : drowsiness 2 : state of being lazy or indifferent — **le·thar·gic** *adj*

let·ter *n* 1 : unit of an alphabet 2 : written or printed communication 3 *pl* : literature or learning 4 : literal meaning ~ *vb* : mark with letters — **let·ter·er** *n*

let·tuce *n* : garden plant with crisp leaves

leu·ke·mia *n* : cancerous blood disease — **leu-ke·mic** *adj* or *n*

lev·ee *n* : embankment to prevent flooding

lev·el *n* 1 : device for establishing a flat surface 2 : horizontal surface 3 : position in a scale ~ *vb* **-eled** *or* **-elled; -el·ing** *or* **-el·ling** 1 : make flat or level 2 : aim 3 : raze ~ *adj* 1 : having an even surface 2 : of the same height or rank — **lev·el·er** *n* — **lev·el·ly** *adv* — **lev·el·ness** *n*

le·ver *n* : bar for prying or dislodging something — **le·ver·age** *n*

le·vi·a·than *n* 1 : large sea animal 2 : enormous thing

lev·i·ty *n* : unseemly frivolity

levy *n, pl* **lev·ies** : imposition or collection of a tax ~ *vb* **lev·ied; levy·ing** 1 : impose or collect legally 2 : enlist for military service 3 : wage

lewd *adj* 1 : sexually unchaste 2 : vulgar — **lewd·ly** *adv* — **lewd·ness** *n*

lex·i·cog·ra·phy *n* : dictionary making — **lex·i·cog·rapher** *n* — **lex·i·co·graph·i·cal** *or* **lex·i·co·graph·ic** *adj*

lex·i·con *n, pl* **-i·ca** *or* **-icons** : dictionary

li·a·ble *adj* 1 : legally obligated 2 : probable 3 : susceptible — **li·a·bil·i·ty** *n*

li·ai·son *n* 1 : close bond 2 : communication between groups

li·ar *n* : one who lies

li·bel *n* : action, crime, or an instance of injuring a person's reputation esp. by something written ~ *vb* **-beled** *or* **-belled; -bel·ing** *or* **-bel·ling** : make or publish a libel — **li·bel·er** *n* — **li·bel·ist** *n* — **li·bel·ous, li·bel·lous** *adj*

lib·er·al *adj* : not stingy, narrow, or conservative — **liberal** *n* — **lib·er·al·ism** *n* — **lib·er·al·i·ty** *n* — **lib·er·al·ize** *vb* — **lib·er·al·ly** *adv*

lib·er·ate *vb* **-at·ed; -at·ing** : set free — **lib·er·a·tion** *n* — **lib·er·a·tor** *n*

lib·er·tine *n* : one who leads a dissolute life

lib·er·ty *n, pl* **-ties** 1 : quality or state of being free 2 : action going beyond normal limits

li·bi·do *n, pl* **-dos** : sexual drive — **li·bid·i·nal** *adj* — **li·bid·i·nous** *adj*

li·brary *n, pl* **-brar·ies** 1 : place where books are kept for use 2 : collection of books — **li·brar·i·an** *n*

li·bret·to *n, pl* **-tos** *or* **-ti** : text of an opera — **li·bret·tist** *n*

lice *pl of* LOUSE

li·cense, li·cence *n* 1 : legal permission to engage in some activity 2 : document or tag providing proof of a license 3 : irresponsible use of freedom — **license** *vb* — **li·cens·ee** *n*

li·cen·tious *adj* : disregarding sexual restraints — **li·cen·tious·ly** *adv* — **li·cen·tious·ness** *n*

li·chen *n* : complex lower plant made up of an alga and a fungus

lic·it *adj* : lawful

lick *vb* 1 : draw the tongue over 2 : beat ~ *n* 1 : stroke of the tongue 2 : small amount

lic·o·rice *n* : dried root of a European legume or candy flavored by it

lid *n* 1 : movable cover 2 : eyelid

¹lie *vb* **lay; lain; ly·ing** 1 : be in, rest in, or assume a horizontal position 2 : occupy a certain relative position ~ *n* : position in which something lies

²lie *vb* **lied; ly·ing** : tell a lie ~ *n* : untrue statement

liege *n* : feudal superior or vassal

lien *n* : legal claim on the property of another

lieu·ten·ant *n* 1 : representative 2 : first lieutenant or second lieutenant 3 : commissioned officer in the navy ranking next below a lieutenant commander — **lieu·ten·an·cy** *n*

lieutenant colonel *n* : commissioned officer (as in the army) ranking next below a colonel

lieutenant commander *n* : commissioned officer in the navy ranking next below a commander

lieutenant general *n* : commissioned officer (as in the army) ranking next below a general

lieutenant junior grade *n, pl* **lieutenants junior grade** : commissioned officer in the navy ranking next below a lieutenant

life *n, pl* **lives** 1 : quality that distinguishes a vital and functional being from a dead body or inanimate matter 2 : physical and mental experiences of an individual 3 : biography 4 : period of existence 5 : way of living 6 : liveliness — **life·less** *adj* — **life·like** *adj*

life·blood *n* : basic source of strength and vitality

life·boat *n* : boat for saving lives at sea

life·guard *n* : one employed to safeguard bathers

life·long *adj* : continuing through life

life·sav·ing *n* : art or practice of saving lives — **life·sav·er** *n*

life·style *n* : a way of life

life·time *n* : duration of an individual's existence

lift *vb* 1 : move upward or cause to move upward 2 : put an end to — **lift** *n* — **lift·er** *n*

lift·off *n* : vertical takeoff by a rocket

lig·a·ment *n* : band of tough tissue that holds bones together

lig·a·ture *n* : something that binds or ties

¹light *n* 1 : radiation that makes vision possible 2 : daylight 3 : source of light 4 : public knowledge 5 : aspect 6 : celebrity 7 : flame for lighting ~ *adj* 1 : bright 2 : weak in color ~ *vb* **lit** *or* **light·ed; light·ing** 1 : make or become light 2 : cause to burn — **light·er** *n* — **light·ness** *n* — **light·proof** *adj*

²light *adj* : not heavy, serious, or abundant — **light** *adv* — **light·ly** *adv* — **light·ness** *n* — **light·weight** *adj*

³light *vb* **light·ed** *or* **lit; light·ing** : settle or dismount

¹light·en *vb* 1 : make light or bright 2 : give out flashes of lightning

²lighten *vb* 1 : relieve of a burden 2 : become lighter

light·heart·ed *adj* : free from worry — **light-heart·ed·ly** *adv* — **light·heart·ed·ness** *n*

light·house *n* : structure with a powerful light for guiding sailors

light·ning *n* : flashing discharge of atmospheric electricity

light–year *n* : distance traveled by light in one year equal to about 5.88 trillion miles

lig·nite *n* : brownish black soft coal

¹like *vb* **liked; lik·ing** 1 : enjoy 2 : desire ~ *n* : preference — **lik·able, like·able** *adj*

²like *adj* : similar ~ *prep* 1 : similar or similarly to 2 : typical of 3 : such as ~ *n* : counterpart ~ *conj* : as or as if — **like·ness** *n* — **like·wise** *adv*

-like *adj comb form* : resembling or characteristic of

like·li·hood *n* : probability

like·ly *adj* **-li·er; -est** 1 : probable 2 : believable ~ *adv* : in all probability

lik·en *vb* : compare

lik·ing *n* : favorable regard

li·lac *n* : shrub with clusters of fragrant pink, purple, or white flowers

lilt *n* : rhythmical swing or flow

lily *n, pl* **lil·ies** : tall bulbous herb with funnel-shaped flowers

lima bean *n* : flat edible seed of a plant or the plant itself

limb *n* 1 : projecting appendage used in moving or grasping 2 : tree branch — **limb·less** *adj*

lim·ber *adj* : supple or agile ~ *vb* : make or become limber

lim·bo *n, pl* **-bos** : place or state of confinement or oblivion

¹lime *n* : caustic white oxide of calcium

²lime *n* : small green lemonlike citrus fruit — **lime·ade** *n*

lime·light *n* : center of public attention

lim·er·ick *n* : light poem of 5 lines

lime·stone *n* : rock that yields lime when burned

lim·it *n* 1 : boundary 2 : something that restrains or confines ~ *vb* : set limits on — **lim·i·ta·tion** *n* — **lim·it·less** *adj*

lim·ou·sine *n* : large luxurious sedan

limp *vb* : walk lamely ~ *n* : limping movement or gait ~ *adj* : lacking firmness and body — **limp·ly** *adv* — **limp·ness** *n*

lim·pid *adj* : clear or transparent

lin·den *n* : tree with large heart-shaped leaves

¹line *vb* **lined; lin·ing** : cover the inner surface of — **lin·ing** *n*

²line *n* 1 : cord, rope, or wire 2 : row or something like a row 3 : note 4 : course of action or thought 5 : state of agreement 6 : occupation 7 : limit 8 : transportation system 9 : long narrow mark ~ *vb* **lined; lin·ing** 1 : mark with a line 2 : place in a line 3 : form a line

lin·eage *n* : descent from a common ancestor

lin·eal *adj* 1 : linear 2 : in a direct line of ancestry

lin·ea·ments *n pl* : features or contours esp. of a face

lin·ear *adj* 1 : straight 2 : long and narrow

lin·en *n* 1 : cloth or thread made of flax 2 : household articles made of linen cloth

lin·er *n* 1 : one that lines 2 : ship or airplane belonging to a line

line·up *n* 1 : line of persons for inspection or identification 2 : list of players in a game

-ling *n suffix* 1 : one linked with 2 : young, small, or minor one

lin·ger *vb* : be slow to leave or act — **lin·ger·er** *n*

lin·ge·rie *n* : women's underwear

lin·go *n, pl* **-goes** : usu. strange language

lin·guist *n* 1 : person skilled in speech or languages 2 : student of language — **lin·guis·tic** *adj* — **lin·guis·tics** *n pl*

lin·i·ment *n* : liquid medication rubbed on the skin

link *n* 1 : connecting structure (as a ring of a chain) 2 : bond — **link** *vb* — **link·age** *n* — **link·er** *n*

li·no·leum *n* : floor covering with hard surface

lin·seed *n* : seeds of flax yielding an oil (**lin-seed oil**)

lint *n* : fine fluff or loose short fibers from fabric

lin•tel *n* : horizontal piece over a door or window

li•on *n* : large cat of Africa and Asia — **li•on•ess** *n*

li•on•ize *vb* **-ized; -iz•ing** : treat as very important — **li•on•iza•tion** *n*

lip *n* **1** : either of the 2 fleshy folds surrounding the mouth **2** : edge of something hollow — **lipped** *adj* — **lip•read•ing** *n*

li•po•suc•tion *n* : surgical removal of fat deposits (as from the thighs)

lip•stick *n* : stick of cosmetic to color lips

liq•ue•fy *vb* **-fied; -fy•ing** : make or become liquid — **liq•ue•fi•er** *n*

li•queur *n* : sweet or aromatic alcoholic liquor

liq•uid *adj* **1** : flowing freely like water **2** : neither solid nor gaseous **3** : of or convertible to cash — **liquid** *n* — **li•quid•i•ty** *n*

liq•ui•date *vb* **-dat•ed; -dat•ing 1** : pay off **2** : dispose of — **liq•ui•da•tion** *n*

li•quor *n* : liquid substance and esp. a distilled alcoholic beverage

lisp *vb* : pronounce *s* and *z* imperfectly — **lisp** *n*

lis•some *adj* : supple or agile

¹list *n* **1** : series of names or items *~ vb* **1** : make a list of **2** : put on a list

²list *vb* : tilt or lean over *~ n* : slant

lis•ten *vb* **1** : pay attention in order to hear **2** : heed — **lis•ten•er** *n*

list•less *adj* : having no desire to act — **list•less•ly** *adv* — **list•less•ness** *n*

lit *past of* LIGHT

lit•a•ny *n, pl* **-nies 1** : prayer said as a series of responses to a leader **2** : long recitation

li•ter *n* : unit of liquid measure equal to about 1.06 quarts

lit•er•al *adj* : being exactly as stated — **lit•er•al•ly** *adv*

lit•er•ary *adj* : relating to literature

lit•er•ate *adj* : able to read and write — **lit•er•a•cy** *n*

lit•er•a•ture *n* : writings of enduring interest

lithe *adj* **1** : supple **2** : graceful — **lithe•some** *adj*

lith•o•graph *n* : print from a drawing on metal or stone — **li•thog•ra•pher** *n* — **lith•o•graph•ic** *adj* — **li•thog•ra•phy** *n*

lit•i•gate *vb* **-gat•ed; -gat•ing** : carry on a lawsuit — **lit•i•gant** *n* — **lit•i•ga•tion** *n* — **li•ti•gious** *adj* — **li•ti•gious•ness** *n*

lit•mus *n* : coloring matter that turns red in acid solutions and blue in alkaline

lit•ter *n* **1** : animal offspring of one birth **2** : stretcher **3** : rubbish **4** : material to absorb animal waste *~ vb* **1** : give birth to young **2** : strew with litter

lit•tle *adj* **lit•tler** *or* **less** *or* **less•er; lit•tlest** *or* **least 1** : not big **2** : not much **3** : not important *~ adv* **less; least 1** : slightly **2** : not often *~ n* : small amount — **lit•tle•ness** *n*

lit•ur•gy *n, pl* **-gies** : rite of worship — **li•tur•gi•cal** *adj* — **li•tur•gi•cal•ly** *adv* — **lit•ur•gist** *n*

liv•able *adj* : suitable for living in or with — **liv•a•bil•i•ty** *n*

¹live *vb* **lived; liv•ing 1** : be alive **2** : conduct one's life **3** : subsist **4** : reside

²live *adj* **1** : having life **2** : burning **3** : connected to electric power **4** : not exploded **5** : of continuing interest **6** : involving the actual presence of real people

live•li•hood *n* : means of subsistence

live•long *adj* : whole

live•ly *adj* **-li•er; -est** : full of life and vigor — **live•li•ness** *n*

liv•en *vb* : enliven

liv•er *n* : organ that secretes bile

liv•ery *n, pl* **-er•ies 1** : servant's uniform **2** : care of horses for pay — **liv•er•ied** *adj* — **liv•ery•man** *n*

lives *pl of* LIFE

live•stock *n* : farm animals

liv•id *adj* **1** : discolored by bruising **2** : pale **3** : enraged

liv•ing *adj* : having life *~ n* : livelihood

liz•ard *n* : reptile with 4 legs and a long tapering tail

lla•ma *n* : So. American mammal related to the camel

load *n* **1** : cargo **2** : supported weight **3** : burden **4** : a large quantity — usu. pl. *~ vb* **1** : put a load on **2** : burden **3** : put ammunition in

¹loaf *n, pl* **loaves** : mass of bread

²loaf *vb* : waste time — **loaf•er** *n*

loam *n* : soil — **loamy** *adj*

loan *n* **1** : money borrowed at interest **2** : something lent temporarily **3** : grant of use *~ vb* : lend

loath *adj* : very reluctant

loathe *vb* **loathed; loath•ing** : hate

loath•ing *n* : extreme disgust

loath•some *adj* : repulsive

lob *vb* **-bb-** : throw or hit in a high arc — **lob** *n*

lob•by *n, pl* **-bies 1** : public waiting room at the entrance of a building **2** : persons lobbying *~ vb* **-bied; -by•ing** : try to influence legislators — **lob•by•ist** *n*

lobe *n* : rounded part — **lo•bar** *adj* — **lobed** *adj*

lo•bot•o•my *n, pl* **-mies** : surgical severance of nerve fibers in the brain

lob•ster *n* : marine crustacean with 2 large pincerlike claws

lo•cal *adj* : confined to or serving a limited area — **local** *n* — **lo•cal•ly** *adv*

lo•cale *n* : setting for an event

lo•cal•i•ty *n, pl* **-ties** : particular place

lo•cal•ize *vb* **-ized; -iz•ing** : confine to a definite place — **lo•cal•i•za•tion** *n*

lo•cate *vb* **-cat•ed; -cat•ing 1** : settle **2** : find a site for **3** : discover the place of — **lo•ca•tion** *n*

¹lock *n* : tuft or strand of hair

²lock *n* **1** : fastener using a bolt **2** : enclosure in a canal to raise or lower boats *~ vb* **1** : make fast with a lock **2** : confine **3** : interlock

lock•er *n* : storage compartment

lock•et *n* : small case worn on a necklace

lock•jaw *n* : tetanus

lock•out *n* : closing of a plant by an employer during a labor dispute

lock•smith *n* : one who makes or repairs locks

lo•co•mo•tion *n* : power of moving — **lo•co•mo•tive** *adj*

lo•co•mo•tive *n* : vehicle that moves railroad cars

lo•co•weed *n* : western plant poisonous to livestock

lo•cust *n* **1** : migratory grasshopper **2** : cicada **3** : tree with hard wood or this wood

lo•cu•tion *n* : way of saying something

lode *n* : ore deposit

lode•stone *n* : magnetic rock

lodge *vb* **lodged; lodg•ing 1** : provide quarters for **2** : come to rest **3** : file *~ n* **1** : special house (as for hunters) **2** : animal's den **3** : branch of a fraternal organization — **lodg•er** *n* — **lodg•ing** *n* — **lodg•ment, lodge•ment** *n*

loft *n* **1** : attic **2** : upper floor (as of a warehouse)

lofty *adj* **loft•i•er; -est 1** : noble **2** : proud **3** : tall or high — **loft•i•ly** *adv* — **loft•i•ness** *n*

log *n* **1** : unshaped timber **2** : daily record of a ship's or plane's progress *~ vb* **-gg- 1** : cut (trees) for lumber **2** : enter in a log — **log•ger** *n*

log•a•rithm *n* : exponent to which a base number is raised to produce a given number

loge *n* : box in a theater

log•ger•head *n* : large Atlantic sea turtle — **at loggerheads** : in disagreement

log•ic *n* **1** : science of reasoning **2** : sound reasoning — **log•i•cal** *adj* — **log•i•cal•ly** *adv* — **lo•gi•cian** *n*

lo•gis•tics *n sing or pl* : procurement and movement of people and supplies — **lo•gis•tic** *adj*

logo *n, pl* **log•os** : advertising symbol

loin *n* **1** : part of the body on each side of the spine between the hip and lower ribs **2** *pl* : pubic regions

loi•ter *vb* : remain around a place idly — **loi•ter•er** *n*

loll *vb* : lounge

lol•li•pop, lol•ly•pop *n* : hard candy on a stick

lone *adj* **1** : alone or isolated **2** : only — **lone•li•ness** *n* — **lone•ly** *adj* — **lon•er** *n*

lone•some *adj* : sad from lack of company — **lone•some•ly** *adv* — **lone•some•ness** *n*

long *adj* **lon•ger; longest 1** : extending far or for a considerable time **2** : having a specified length **3** : tedious **4** : well supplied — used with *on ~ adv* : for a long time *~ n* : long period *~ vb* : feel a strong desire — **long•ing** *n* — **long•ing•ly** *adv*

lon•gev•i•ty *n* : long life

long•hand *n* : handwriting

long•horn *n* : cattle with long horns

lon•gi•tude *n* : angular distance east or west from a meridian

lon•gi•tu•di•nal *adj* : lengthwise — **lon•gi•tu•di•nal•ly** *adv*

long•shore•man *n* : one who loads and unloads ships

look *vb* **1** : see **2** : seem **3** : direct one's attention **4** : face *~ n* **1** : action of looking **2** : appearance of the face **3** : aspect — **look after** : take care of — **look for 1** : expect **2** : search for

look•out *n* **1** : one who watches **2** : careful watch

¹loom *n* : frame or machine for weaving

²loom *vb* : appear large and indistinct or impressive

loon *n* : black-and-white diving bird

loo•ny, loo•ney *adj* **-ni•er; -est** : crazy

loop *n* **1** : doubling of a line that leaves an opening **2** : something like a loop — **loop** *vb*

loop•hole *n* : means of evading

loose *adj* **loos•er; -est 1** : not fixed tight **2** : not restrained **3** : not dense **4** : slack **5** : not exact *~ vb* **loosed; loos•ing 1** : release **2** : untie or relax — **loose** *adv* — **loose•ly** *adv* — **loos•en** *vb* — **loose•ness** *n*

loot *n or vb* : plunder — **loot•er** *n*

lop *vb* **-pp-** : cut off

lope *n* : bounding gait — **lope** *vb*

lop•sid•ed *adj* **1** : leaning to one side **2** : not symmetrical — **lop•sid•ed•ly** *adv* — **lop•sid•ed•ness** *n*

lo•qua•cious *adj* : very talkative — **lo•quac•i•ty** *n*

lord *n* **1** : one with authority over others **2** : British nobleman

lord•ly *adj* **-li•er; -est** : haughty

lord•ship *n* : rank of a lord

Lord's Supper *n* : Communion

lore *n* : traditional knowledge

lose *vb* **lost; los•ing 1** : have pass from one's possession **2** : be deprived of **3** : waste **4** : be defeated in **5** : fail to keep to or hold **6** : get rid of — **los•er** *n*

loss *n* **1** : something lost **2** *pl* : killed, wounded, or captured soldiers **3** : failure to win

lost *adj* **1** : not used, won, or claimed **2** : unable to find the way

lot *n* **1** : object used in deciding something by chance **2** : share **3** : fate **4** : plot of land **5** : much

loth *var of* LOATH

lo•tion *n* : liquid to rub on the skin

lot•tery *n, pl* **-ter•ies** : drawing of lots with prizes going to winners

lo•tus *n* **1** : legendary fruit that causes forgetfulness **2** : water lily

loud adj **1** : high in volume of sound **2** : noisy **3** : obtrusive in color or pattern — **loud** adv — **loud•ly** adv — **loud•ness** n

loud•speak•er n : device that amplifies sound

lounge vb **lounged; loung•ing** : act or move lazily ~ n : room with comfortable furniture

lour var of LOWER

louse n, pl **lice** : parasitic wingless usu. flat insect

lousy adj **lous•i•er; -est 1** : infested with lice **2** : not good — **lous•i•ly** adv — **lous•i•ness** n

lout n : stupid awkward person — **lout•ish** adj — **lout•ish•ly** adv

lou•ver, lou•vre n : opening having parallel slanted slats for ventilation or such a slat

love n **1** : strong affection **2** : warm attachment **3** : beloved person ~ vb **loved; lov•ing 1** : feel affection for **2** : enjoy greatly — **lov•able** adj — **love•less** adj — **lov•er** n — **lov•ing•ly** adv

love•lorn adj : deprived of love or of a lover

love•ly adj **-li•er; -est** : beautiful — **love•li•ness** n — **lovely** adv

¹**low** vb or n : moo

²**low** adj **low•er; low•est 1** : not high or tall **2** : below normal level **3** : not loud **4** : humble **5** : sad **6** : less than usual **7** : falling short of a standard **8** : unfavorable ~ n **1** : something low **2** : automobile gear giving the slowest speed — **low** adv — **low•ness** n

low•brow n : person with little taste or intellectual interest

¹**low•er** vb **1** : scowl **2** : become dark and threatening

²**low•er** adj : relatively low (as in rank)

³**low•er** vb **1** : drop **2** : let descend **3** : reduce in amount

low•land n : low flat country

low•ly adj **-li•er; -est 1** : humble **2** : low in rank — **low•li•ness** n

loy•al adj : faithful to a country, cause, or friend — **loy•al•ist** n — **loy•al•ly** adv — **loy•al•ty** n

loz•enge n : small medicated candy

lu•bri•cant n : material (as grease) to reduce friction

lu•bri•cate vb **-cat•ed; -cat•ing** : apply a lubricant to — **lu•bri•ca•tion** n — **lu•bri•ca•tor** n

lu•cid adj **1** : mentally sound **2** : easily understood — **lu•cid•i•ty** n — **lu•cid•ly** adv — **lu•cid•ness** n

luck n **1** : chance **2** : good fortune — **luck•i•ly** adv — **luck•i•ness** n — **luck•less** adj — **lucky** adj

lu•cra•tive adj : profitable — **lu•cra•tive•ly** adv — **lu•cra•tive•ness** n

lu•di•crous adj : comically ridiculous — **lu•di•crous•ly** adv — **lu•di•crous•ness** n

lug vb **-gg-** : drag or carry laboriously

lug•gage n : baggage

lu•gu•bri•ous adj : mournful often to an exaggerated degree — **lu•gu•bri•ous•ly** adv — **lu•gu•bri•ous•ness** n

luke•warm adj **1** : moderately warm **2** : not enthusiastic

lull vb : make or become quiet or relaxed ~ n : temporary calm

lul•la•by n, pl **-bies** : song to lull children to sleep

lum•ba•go n : rheumatic back pain

lum•ber n : timber dressed for use ~ vb : cut logs — **lum•ber•man** n — **lum•ber•yard** n

lum•ber•jack n : logger

lu•mi•nary n, pl **-nar•ies** : very famous person

lu•mi•nes•cence n : low-temperature emission of light — **lu•mi•nes•cent** adj

lu•mi•nous adj : emitting light — **lu•mi•nance** n — **lu•mi•nos•i•ty** n — **lu•mi•nous•ly** adv

lump n **1** : mass of irregular shape **2** : abnormal swelling ~ vb : heap together — **lump•ish** adj — **lumpy** adj

lu•na•cy n, pl **-cies** : state of insanity

lu•nar adj : of the moon

lu•na•tic adj : insane — **lunatic** n

lunch n : noon meal — vb : eat lunch

lun•cheon n : usu. formal lunch

lung n : breathing organ in the chest — **lunged** adj

lunge n **1** : sudden thrust **2** : sudden move forward — **lunge** vb

lurch n : sudden swaying — **lurch** vb

lure n **1** : something that attracts **2** : artificial fish bait ~ vb **lured; lur•ing** : attract

lu•rid adj **1** : gruesome **2** : sensational — **lu•rid•ly** adv

lurk vb : lie in wait

lus•cious adj **1** : pleasingly sweet in taste or smell **2** : sensually appealing — **lus•cious•ly** adv — **lus•cious•ness** n

lush adj : covered with abundant growth

lust n **1** : intense sexual desire **2** : intense longing — **lust** vb — **lust•ful** adj

lus•ter, lus•tre n **1** : brightness from reflected light **2** : magnificence — **lus•ter•less** adj — **lus•trous** adj

lusty adj **lust•i•er; -est** : full of vitality — **lust•i•ly** adv — **lust•i•ness** n

lute n : pear-shaped stringed instrument — **lute•nist, lu•ta•nist** n

lux•u•ri•ant adj **1** : growing plentifully **2** : rich and varied — **lux•u•ri•ance** n — **lux•u•ri•ant•ly** adv

lux•u•ri•ate vb **-at•ed; -at•ing** : revel

lux•u•ry n, pl **-ries 1** : great comfort **2** : something adding to pleasure or comfort — **lux•u•ri•ous** adj — **lux•u•ri•ous•ly** adv

-ly adv suffix **1** : in a specified way **2** : from a specified point of view

ly•ce•um n : hall for public lectures

lye n : caustic alkaline substance

lying pres part of LIE

lymph n : bodily liquid consisting chiefly of blood plasma and white blood cells — **lym•phat•ic** adj

lynch vb : put to death by mob action — **lynch•er** n

lynx n, pl **lynx** or **lynx•es** : wildcat

lyre n : ancient Greek stringed instrument

lyr•ic adj **1** : suitable for singing **2** : expressing direct personal emotion ~ n **1** : lyric poem **2** pl : words of a song — **lyr•i•cal** adj

M

m n, pl **m's** or **ms** : 13th letter of the alphabet

ma'am n : madam

ma•ca•bre adj : gruesome

mac•ad•am n : pavement of cemented broken stone — **mac•ad•am•ize** vb

mac•a•ro•ni n : tube-shaped pasta

mac•a•roon n : cookie of ground almonds or coconut

ma•caw n : large long-tailed parrot

¹**mace** n **1** : heavy spiked club **2** : ornamental staff as a symbol of authority

²**mace** n : spice from the fibrous coating of the nutmeg

ma•chete n : large heavy knife

mach•i•na•tion n : plot or scheme — **mach•i•nate** vb

ma•chine n : combination of mechanical or electrical parts ~ vb **-chined; -chin•ing** : modify by machine-operated tools — **ma•chin•able** adj — **ma•chin•ery** n — **ma•chin•ist** n

mack•er•el n, pl **-el** or **-els** : No. Atlantic food fish

mack•i•naw n : short heavy plaid coat

mac•ra•mé n : coarse lace or fringe made by knotting

mac•ro adj : very large

mac•ro•cosm n : universe

mad adj **-dd- 1** : insane or rabid **2** : rash and foolish **3** : angry **4** : carried away by enthusiasm — **mad•**

den vb — **mad•den•ing•ly** adv — **mad•ly** adv — **mad•ness** n

mad•am n, pl **mes•dames** — used in polite address to a woman

ma•dame n, pl **mes•dames** — used as a title for a woman not of English-speaking nationality

mad•cap adj : wild or zany — **madcap** n

made past of MAKE

Ma•dei•ra n : amber-colored dessert wine

ma•de•moi•selle n, pl **ma•de•moi•selles** or **mes•de•moi•selles** : an unmarried girl or woman — used as a title for a woman esp. of French nationality

mad•house n **1** : insane asylum **2** : place of great uproar or confusion

mad•man n : lunatic

mad•ri•gal n : elaborate song for several voice parts

mad•wom•an n : woman who is insane

mael•strom n **1** : whirlpool **2** : tumult

mae•stro n, pl **-stros** or **-stri** : eminent composer or conductor

Ma•fia n : secret criminal organization

ma•fi•o•so n, pl **-si** : member of the Mafia

mag•a•zine n **1** : storehouse **2** : publication issued at regular intervals **3** : cartridge container in a gun

ma•gen•ta n : deep purplish red color

mag•got n : wormlike fly larva — **mag•goty** adj

mag•ic n **1** : art of using supernatural powers **2** : extraordinary power or influence **3** : sleight of hand — **magic, mag•i•cal** adj — **mag•i•cal•ly** adv — **ma•gi•cian** n

mag•is•te•ri•al adj **1** : authoritative **2** : relating to a magistrate

mag•is•trate n : judge — **mag•is•tra•cy** n

mag•ma n : molten rock

mag•nan•i•mous adj : noble or generous — **mag•na•nim•i•ty** n — **mag•nan•i•mous•ly** adv — **mag•nan•i•mous•ness** n

mag•ne•sia n : oxide of magnesium used as a laxative

mag•ne•sium n : silver-white metallic chemical element

mag•net n **1** : body that attracts iron **2** : something that attracts — **mag•net•ic** adj — **mag•net•i•cal•ly** adv — **mag•ne•tism** n

mag•ne•tite n : black iron ore

mag•ne•tize vb **-tized; -tiz•ing 1** : attract like a magnet **2** : give magnetic properties to — **mag•ne•tiz•able** adj — **mag•ne•ti•za•tion** n — **mag•ne•tiz•er** n

mag•nif•i•cent adj : splendid — **mag•nif•i•cence** n — **mag•nif•i•cent•ly** adv

mag•ni•fy vb **-fied; -fy•ing 1** : intensify **2** : enlarge — **mag•ni•fi•ca•tion** n — **mag•ni•fi•er** n

mag·ni·tude *n* 1 : greatness of size or extent 2 : quantity

mag·no·lia *n* : shrub with large fragrant flowers

mag·pie *n* : long-tailed black-and-white bird

ma·hog·a·ny *n, pl* **-nies** : tropical evergreen tree or its reddish brown wood

maid *n* 1 : unmarried young woman 2 : female servant

maid·en *n* : unmarried young woman ~ *adj* 1 : unmarried 2 : first — **maid·en·hood** *n* — **maid·en·ly** *adj*

maid·en·hair *n* : fern with delicate feathery fronds

¹mail *n* 1 : something sent or carried in the postal system 2 : postal system ~ *vb* : send by mail — **mail·box** *n* — **mail·man** *n*

²mail *n* : armor of metal links or plates

maim *vb* : seriously wound or disfigure

main *n* 1 : force 2 : ocean 3 : principal pipe, duct, or circuit of a utility system ~ *adj* : chief — **main·ly** *adv*

main·frame *n* : large fast computer

main·land *n* : part of a country on a continent

main·stay *n* : chief support

main·stream *n* : prevailing current or direction of activity or influence — **mainstream** *adj*

main·tain *vb* 1 : keep in an existing state (as of repair) 2 : sustain 3 : declare — **main·tain·abil·i·ty** *n* — **main·tain·able** *adj* — **main·te·nance** *n*

mai·tre d'hô·tel *n* : head of a dining room staff

maize *n* : corn

maj·es·ty *n, pl* **-ties** 1 : sovereign power or dignity — used as a title 2 : grandeur or splendor — **ma·jes·tic** *adj* — **ma·jes·ti·cal·ly** *adv*

ma·jor *adj* 1 : larger or greater 2 : noteworthy or conspicuous ~ *n* 1 : commissioned officer (as in the army) ranking next below a lieutenant colonel 2 : main field of study ~ *vb* **-jored; -jor·ing** : pursue an academic major

ma·jor·do·mo *n, pl* **-mos** : head steward

major general *n* : commissioned officer (as in the army) ranking next below a lieutenant general

ma·jor·i·ty *n, pl* **-ties** 1 : age of full civil rights 2 : quantity more than half

make *vb* **made; mak·ing** 1 : cause to exist, occur, or appear 2 : fashion or manufacture 3 : formulate in the mind 4 : constitute 5 : prepare 6 : cause to be or become 7 : carry out or perform 8 : compel 9 : gain 10 : have an effect — used with *for* ~ *n* : brand — **mak·er** *n* — **make do** *vb* : get along with what is available — **make good** *vb* 1 : repay 2 : succeed — **make out** *vb* 1 : draw up or write 2 : discern or understand 3 : fare — **make up** *vb* 1 : invent 2 : become reconciled 3 : compensate for

make–be·lieve *n* : a pretending to believe ~ *adj* : imagined or pretended

make·shift *n* : temporary substitute — **make·shift** *adj*

make·up *n* 1 : way in which something is constituted 2 : cosmetics

mal·ad·just·ed *adj* : poorly adjusted (as to one's environment) — **mal·ad·just·ment** *n*

mal·adroit *adj* : clumsy or inept

mal·a·dy *n, pl* **-dies** : disease or disorder

mal·aise *n* : sense of being unwell

mal·a·mute *n* : powerful heavy-coated dog

mal·a·prop·ism *n* : humorous misuse of a word

ma·lar·ia *n* : disease transmitted by a mosquito — **ma·lar·i·al** *adj*

ma·lar·key *n* : foolishness

mal·con·tent *n* : discontented person — **malcontent** *adj*

male *adj* 1 : relating to the sex that performs a fertilizing function 2 : masculine ~ *n* : male individual — **male·ness** *n*

male·dic·tion *n* : curse

male·fac·tor *n* : one who commits an offense esp. against the law

ma·lef·i·cent *adj* : harmful

ma·lev·o·lent *adj* : malicious or spiteful — **ma·lev·o·lence** *n*

mal·fea·sance *n* : misconduct by a public official

mal·for·ma·tion *n* : distortion or faulty formation — **mal·formed** *adj*

mal·func·tion *vb* : fail to operate properly — **malfunction** *n*

mal·ice *n* : desire to cause pain or injury to another — **ma·li·cious** *adj* — **ma·li·cious·ly** *adv*

ma·lign *adj* 1 : wicked 2 : malignant ~ *vb* : speak evil of

ma·lig·nant *adj* 1 : harmful 2 : likely to cause death — **ma·lig·nan·cy** *n* — **ma·lig·nant·ly** *adv* — **ma·lig·ni·ty** *n*

ma·lin·ger *vb* : pretend illness to avoid duty — **ma·lin·ger·er** *n*

mall *n* 1 : shaded promenade 2 : concourse providing access to rows of shops

mal·lard *n, pl* **-lard** *or* **-lards** : common wild duck

mal·lea·ble *adj* 1 : easily shaped 2 : adaptable — **mal·le·a·bil·i·ty** *n*

mal·let *n* : hammerlike tool

mal·nour·ished *adj* : poorly nourished

mal·nu·tri·tion *n* : inadequate nutrition

mal·odor·ous *adj* : foul-smelling — **mal·odor·ous·ly** *adv* — **mal·odor·ous·ness** *n*

mal·prac·tice *n* : failure of professional duty

malt *n* : sprouted grain used in brewing

mal·treat *vb* : treat badly — **mal·treat·ment** *n*

ma·ma, mam·ma *n* : mother

mam·mal *n* : warm-blooded vertebrate animal that nourishes its young with milk — **mam·ma·li·an** *adj* or *n*

mam·ma·ry *adj* : relating to the milk-secreting glands (**mammary glands**) of mammals

mam·mo·gram *n* : X-ray photograph of the breasts

mam·moth *n* : large hairy extinct elephant ~ *adj* : enormous

man *n, pl* **men** 1 : human being 2 : adult male 3 : mankind ~ *vb* **-nn-** : supply with people for working — **man·hood** *n* — **man·hunt** *n* — **man·like** *adj* — **man·li·ness** *n* — **man·ly** *adj or adv* — **man·made** *adj* — **man·nish** *adj* — **man·nish·ly** *adv* — **man·nish·ness** *n* — **man·size, man·sized** *adj*

man·a·cle *n* : shackle for the hands or wrists — **manacle** *vb*

man·age *vb* **-aged; -ag·ing** 1 : control 2 : direct or carry on business or affairs 3 : cope — **man·age·abil·i·ty** *n* — **man·age·able** *adj* — **man·age·able·ness** *n* — **man·age·ably** *adv* — **man·age·ment** *n* — **man·ag·er** *n* — **man·a·ge·ri·al** *adj*

man·da·rin *n* : Chinese imperial official

man·date *n* : authoritative command

man·da·to·ry *adj* : obligatory

man·di·ble *n* : lower jaw — **man·dib·u·lar** *adj*

man·do·lin *n* : stringed musical instrument

man·drake *n* : herb with a large forked root

mane *n* : animal's neck hair — **maned** *adj*

ma·neu·ver *n* 1 : planned movement of troops or ships 2 : military training exercise 3 : clever or skillful move or action — **maneuver** *vb* — **ma·neu·ver·abil·i·ty** *n*

man·ful *adj* : courageous — **man·ful·ly** *adv*

man·ga·nese *n* : gray metallic chemical element

mange *n* : skin disease of domestic animals — **mangy** *adj*

man·ger *n* : feeding trough for livestock

man·gle *vb* **-gled; -gling** 1 : mutilate 2 : bungle — **man·gler** *n*

man·go *n, pl* **-goes** : juicy yellowish red tropical fruit

man·grove *n* : tropical tree growing in salt water

man·han·dle *vb* : handle roughly

man·hole *n* : entry to a sewer

ma·nia *n* 1 : insanity marked by uncontrollable emotion or excitement 2 : excessive enthusiasm — **ma·ni·ac** *n* — **ma·ni·a·cal** *adj* — **man·ic** *adj or n*

man·i·cure *n* : treatment for the fingernails ~ *vb* **-cured; -cur·ing** 1 : do manicure work on 2 : trim precisely — **man·i·cur·ist** *n*

¹man·i·fest *adj* : clear to the senses or to the mind ~ *vb* : make evident — **man·i·fes·ta·tion** *n* — **man·i·fest·ly** *adv*

²manifest *n* : invoice of cargo or list of passengers

man·i·fes·to *n, pl* **-tos** *or* **-toes** : public declaration of policy or views

man·i·fold *adj* : marked by diversity or variety ~ *n* : pipe fitting with several outlets for connections

ma·nila paper *n* : durable brownish paper

ma·nip·u·late *vb* **-lat·ed; -lat·ing** 1 : treat or operate manually or mechanically 2 : influence esp. by cunning — **ma·nip·u·la·tion** *n* — **ma·nip·u·la·tive** *adj* — **ma·nip·u·la·tor** *n*

man·kind *n* : human race

man·na *n* : something valuable that comes unexpectedly

manned *adj* : carrying or performed by a man

man·ne·quin *n* : dummy used to display clothes

man·ner *n* 1 : kind 2 : usual way of acting 3 : artistic method 4 *pl* : social conduct

man·nered *adj* 1 : having manners of a specified kind 2 : artificial

man·ner·ism *n* : individual peculiarity of action

man·ner·ly *adj* : polite — **man·ner·li·ness** *n* — **mannerly** *adv*

man–of–war *n, pl* **men–of–war** : warship

man·or *n* : country estate — **ma·no·ri·al** *adj*

man·pow·er *n* : supply of people available for service

man·sard *n* : roof with two slopes on all sides and the lower slope the steeper

manse *n* : parsonage

man·ser·vant *n, pl* **men·ser·vants** : a male servant

man·sion *n* : very big house

man·slaugh·ter *n* : unintentional killing of a person

man·tel *n* : shelf above a fireplace

man·tis *n, pl* **-tis·es** *or* **-tes** : large green insect-eating insect with stout forelegs

man·tle *n* 1 : sleeveless cloak 2 : something that covers, enfolds, or envelops — **mantle** *vb*

man·tra *n* : mystical chant

man·u·al *adj* : involving the hands or physical force ~ *n* : handbook — **man·u·al·ly** *adv*

man·u·fac·ture *n* : process of making wares by hand or by machinery ~ *vb* **-tured; -tur·ing** : make from raw materials — **man·u·fac·tur·er** *n*

ma·nure *n* : animal excrement used as fertilizer

manu·script *n* 1 : something written or typed 2 : document submitted for publication

many *adj* **more; most** : consisting of a large number — **many** *n or pron*

map *n* : representation of a geographical area ~ *vb* **-pp-** 1 : make a map of 2 : plan in detail — **map·pa·ble** *adj* — **map·per** *n*

ma·ple *n* : tree with hard light-colored wood

mar *vb* **-rr-** : damage

mar·a·schi·no *n, pl* **-nos** : preserved cherry

mar·a·thon *n* 1 : long-distance race 2 : test of endurance — **mar·a·thon·er** *n*

ma·raud *vb* : roam about in search of plunder — **ma·raud·er** *n*

mar·ble *n* 1 : crystallized limestone 2 : small glass ball used in a children's game (**marbles**)

mar·bling *n* : intermixture of fat and lean in meat

march *vb* : move with regular steps or in a purposeful manner ~ *n* **1** : distance covered in a march **2** : measured stride **3** : forward movement **4** : music for marching — **march·er** *n*

March *n* : 3d month of the year having 31 days

mar·chio·ness *n* : woman holding the rank of a marquess

Mar·di Gras *n* : Tuesday before the beginning of Lent often observed with parades and merry-making

mare *n* : female horse

mar·ga·rine *n* : butter substitute made usu. from vegetable oils

mar·gin *n* **1** : edge **2** : spare amount, measure, or degree

mar·gin·al *adj* **1** : relating to or situated at a border or margin **2** : close to the lower limit of acceptability — **mar·gin·al·ly** *adv*

mari·gold *n* : garden plant with showy flower heads

mar·i·jua·na *n* : intoxicating drug obtained from the hemp plant

ma·ri·na *n* : place for mooring pleasure boats

mar·i·nate *vb* **-nat·ed; -nat·ing** : soak in a savory sauce

ma·rine *adj* **1** : relating to the sea **2** : relating to marines ~ *n* : infantry soldier associated with a navy

mar·i·ner *n* : sailor

mar·i·o·nctte *n* : puppet

mar·i·tal *adj* : relating to marriage

mar·i·time *adj* : relating to the sea or commerce on the sea

mar·jo·ram *n* : aromatic mint used as a seasoning

mark *n* **1** : something aimed at **2** : something (as a line) designed to record position **3** : visible sign **4** : written symbol **5** : grade **6** : lasting impression **7** : blemish ~ *vb* **1** : designate or set apart by a mark or make a mark on **2** : characterize **3** : remark — **mark·er** *n*

marked *adj* : noticeable — **mark·ed·ly** *adv*

mar·ket *n* **1** : buying and selling of goods or the place this happens **2** : demand for commodities **3** : store ~ *vb* : sell — **mar·ket·able** *adj*

mar·ket·place *n* **1** : market **2** : world of trade or economic activity

marks·man *n* : good shooter — **marks·man·ship** *n*

mar·lin *n* : large oceanic fish

mar·ma·lade *n* : jam with pieces of fruit and rind

mar·mo·set *n* : small bushy-tailed monkey

mar·mot *n* : burrowing rodent

¹ma·roon *vb* : isolate without hope of escape

²maroon *n* : dark red color

mar·quee *n* : canopy over an entrance

mar·quess, mar·quis, *pl* **-quess·es** *or* **-quis·es** *or* **-quis** : British noble ranking next below a duke

mar·quise *n, pl* **mar·quises** : marchioness

mar·riage *n* **1** : state of being married **2** : wedding ceremony — **mar·riage·able** *adj*

mar·row *n* : soft tissue in the cavity of bone

mar·ry *vb* **-ried; -ry·ing 1** : join as husband and wife **2** : take or give in marriage — **mar·ried** *adj or n*

marsh *n* : soft wet land — **marshy** *adj*

mar·shal *n* **1** : leader of ceremony **2** : usu. high military or administrative officer ~ *vb* **-shaled** *or* **-shalled; -shal·ing** *or* **-shal·ling 1** : arrange in order, rank, or position **2** : lead with ceremony

marsh·mal·low *n* : spongy candy

mar·su·pi·al *n* : mammal that nourishes young in an abdominal pouch — **marsupial** *adj*

mart *n* : market

mar·ten *n, pl* **-ten** *or* **-tens** : weasellike mammal with soft fur

mar·tial *adj* **1** : relating to war or an army **2** : warlike

mar·tin *n* : small swallow

mar·ti·net *n* : strict disciplinarian

mar·tyr *n* : one who dies or makes a great sacrifice for a cause ~ *vb* : make a martyr of — **mar·tyr·dom** *n*

mar·vel *vb* **-veled** *or* **-velled; -vel·ing** *or* **-vel·ling** : feel surprise or wonder ~ *n* : something amazing — **mar·vel·ous, mar·vel·lous** *adj* — **mar·vel·ous·ly** *adv* — **mar·vel·ous·ness** *n*

Marx·ism *n* : political and social principles of Karl Marx — **Marx·ist** *n or adj*

mas·cara *n* : eye cosmetic

mas·cot *n* : one believed to bring good luck

mas·cu·line *adj* : relating to the male sex — **mas·cu·lin·i·ty** *n*

mash *n* **1** : crushed steeped grain for fermenting **2** : soft pulpy mass ~ *vb* **1** : reduce to a pulpy mass **2** : smash — **mash·er** *n*

mask *n* : disguise for the face ~ *vb* **1** : disguise **2** : cover to protect — **mask·er** *n*

mas·och·ism *n* : pleasure in being abused — **mas·och·ist** *n* — **mas·och·is·tic** *adj*

ma·son *n* : workman who builds with stone or brick — **ma·son·ry** *n*

mas·quer·ade *n* **1** : costume party **2** : disguise ~ *vb* **-ad·ed; -ad·ing 1** : disguise oneself **2** : take part in a costume party — **mas·quer·ad·er** *n*

mass *n* **1** : large amount of matter or number of things **2** : expanse or magnitude **3** : great body of people — usu. pl. ~ *vb* : form into a mass — **mass·less** *adj* — **massy** *adj*

Mass *n* : worship service of the Roman Catholic Church

mas·sa·cre *n* : wholesale slaughter — **massa·cre** *vb*

mas·sage *n* : a rubbing of the body — **massage** *vb*

mas·seur *n* : man who massages

mas·seuse *n* : woman who massages

mas·sive *adj* **1** : being a large mass **2** : large in scope — **mas·sive·ly** *adv* — **mas·sive·ness** *n*

mast *n* : tall pole esp. for supporting sails — **mast·ed** *adj*

mas·ter *n* **1** : male teacher **2** : holder of an academic degree between a bachelor's and a doctor's **3** : one highly skilled **4** : one in authority ~ *vb* **1** : subdue **2** : become proficient in — **mas·ter·ful** *adj* — **mas·ter·ful·ly** *adv* — **mas·ter·ly** *adj* — **mas·tery** *n*

master chief petty officer *n* : petty officer of the highest rank in the navy

master gunnery sergeant *n* : noncommissioned officer in the marine corps ranking above a master sergeant

mas·ter·piece *n* : great piece of work

master sergeant *n* **1** : noncommissioned officer in the army ranking next below a sergeant major **2** : noncommissioned officer in the air force ranking next below a senior master sergeant **3** : noncommissioned officer in the marine corps ranking next below a master gunnery sergeant

mas·ter·work *n* : masterpiece

mas·tic *n* : pasty glue

mas·ti·cate *vb* **-cat·ed; -cat·ing** : chew — **mas·ti·ca·tion** *n*

mas·tiff *n* : large dog

mast·odon *n* : extinct elephantlike animal

mas·toid *n* : bone behind the ear — **mastoid** *adj*

mas·tur·ba·tion *n* : stimulation of sex organs by hand — **mas·tur·bate** *vb*

¹mat *n* **1** : coarse woven or plaited fabric **2** : mass of tangled strands **3** : thick pad ~ *vb* **-tt-** : form into a mat

²mat *vb* **-tt- 1** : make matte **2** : provide (a picture) with a mat ~ *or* **matt** *or* **matte** *n* : border around a picture

³mat *var of* MATTE

mat·a·dor *n* : bullfighter

¹match *n* **1** : one equal to another **2** : one able to

cope with another **3** : suitable pairing **4** : game **5** : marriage ~ *vb* **1** : set in competition **2** : marry **3** : be or provide the equal of **4** : fit or go together — **match·less** *adj* — **match·mak·er** *n*

²match *n* : piece of wood or paper material with a combustible tip

mate *n* **1** : companion **2** : subordinate officer on a ship **3** : one of a pair ~ *vb* **mat·ed; mat·ing 1** : fit together **2** : come together as a pair **3** : copulate

ma·te·ri·al *adj* **1** : natural **2** : relating to matter **3** : important **4** : of a physical or worldly nature ~ *n* : stuff something is made of — **ma·te·ri·al·ly** *adv*

ma·te·ri·al·ism *n* **1** : theory that matter is the only reality **2** : preoccupation with material and not spiritual things — **ma·te·ri·al·ist** *n or adj* — **ma·te·ri·al·is·tic** *adj*

ma·te·ri·al·ize *vb* **-ized; -iz·ing** : take or cause to take bodily form — **ma·te·ri·al·i·za·tion** *n*

ma·té·ri·el, ma·te·ri·el *n* : military supplies

ma·ter·nal *adj* : motherly — **ma·ter·nal·ly** *adv*

ma·ter·ni·ty *n, pl* **-ties 1** : state of being a mother **2** : hospital's childbirth facility ~ *adj* **1** : worn during pregnancy **2** : relating to the period close to childbirth

math *n* : mathematics

math·e·mat·ics *n pl* : science of numbers and of shapes in space — **math·e·mat·i·cal** *adj* — **math·e·mat·i·cal·ly** *adv* — **math·e·ma·ti·cian** *n*

mat·i·nee, mat·i·née *n* : afternoon performance

mat·ins *n* : morning prayers

ma·tri·arch *n* : woman who rules a family — **ma·tri·ar·chal** *adj* — **ma·tri·ar·chy** *n*

ma·tri·cide *n* : murder of one's mother — **ma·tri·cid·al** *adj*

ma·tric·u·late *vb* **-lat·ed; -lat·ing** : enroll in school — **ma·tric·u·la·tion** *n*

mat·ri·mo·ny *n* : marriage — **mat·ri·mo·ni·al** *adj* — **mat·ri·mo·ni·al·ly** *adv*

ma·trix *n, pl* **-tri·ces** *or* **-trix·es** : something (as a mold) that gives form, foundation, or origin to something else enclosed in it

ma·tron *n* **1** : dignified mature woman **2** : woman supervisor — **ma·tron·ly** *adj*

matte *adj* : not shiny

mat·ter *n* **1** : subject of interest **2** *pl* : circumstances **3** : trouble **4** : physical substance ~ *vb* : be important

mat·tock *n* : a digging tool

mat·tress *n* : pad to sleep on

ma·ture *adj* **-tur·er; -est 1** : carefully considered **2** : fully grown or developed **3** : due for payment ~ *vb* **-tured; -tur·ing** : become mature — **mat·u·ra·tion** *n* — **ma·ture·ly** *adv* — **ma·tu·ri·ty** *n*

maud·lin *adj* : excessively sentimental

maul *n* : heavy hammer ~ *vb* **1** : beat **2** : handle roughly

mau·so·le·um *n, pl* **-leums** *or* **-lea** : large above-ground tomb

mauve *n* : lilac color

ma·ven, ma·vin *n* : expert

mav·er·ick *n* **1** : unbranded range animal **2** : nonconformist

maw *n* **1** : stomach **2** : throat, esophagus, or jaws

mawk·ish *adj* : sickly sentimental — **mawk·ish·ly** *adv* — **mawk·ish·ness** *n*

max·im *n* : proverb

max·i·mum *n, pl* **-ma** *or* **-mums 1** : greatest quantity **2** : upper limit **3** : largest number — **maximum** *adj* — **max·i·mize** *vb*

may *verbal auxiliary, past might; pres sing & pl* **may 1** : have permission **2** : be likely to **3** — used to express desire, purpose, or contingency

May *n* : 5th month of the year having 31 days

may·ap·ple *n* : woodland herb having edible fruit

may·be *adv* : perhaps

may·flow·er *n* : spring-blooming herb

may·fly *n* : fly with an aquatic larva

may·hem *n* **1** : crippling or mutilation of a person **2** : needless damage

may·on·naise *n* : creamy white sandwich spread

may·or *n* : chief city official — **may·or·al** *adj* — **may·or·al·ty** *n*

maze *n* : confusing network of passages — **mazy** *adj*

ma·zur·ka *n* : Polish dance

me *pron, objective case of* I

mead *n* : alcoholic beverage brewed from honey

mead·ow *n* : low-lying usu. level grassland — **mead·ow·land** *n*

mead·ow·lark *n* : songbird with a yellow breast

mea·ger, mea·gre *adj* **1** : thin **2** : lacking richness or strength — **mea·ger·ly** *adv* — **mea·ger·ness** *n*

¹meal *n* **1** : food to be eaten at one time **2** : act of eating — **meal·time** *n*

²meal *n* : ground grain — **mealy** *adj*

¹mean *adj* **1** : humble **2** : worthy of or showing little regard **3** : stingy **4** : malicious — **mean·ly** *adv* — **mean·ness** *n*

²mean *vb* **meant; mean·ing 1** : intend **2** : serve to convey, show, or indicate **3** : be important

³mean *n* **1** : middle point **2** *pl* : something that helps gain an end **3** *pl* : material resources **4** : sum of several quantities divided by the number of quantities ~ *adj* : being a mean

me·an·der *vb* **-dered; -der·ing 1** : follow a winding course **2** : wander aimlessly — **meander** *n*

mean·ing *n* **1** : idea conveyed or intended to be conveyed **2** : aim — **mean·ing·ful** *adj* — **mean·ing·ful·ly** *adv* — **mean·ing·less** *adj*

mean·time *n* : intervening time — **meantime** *adv*

mean·while *n* : meantime ~ *adv* **1** : meantime **2** : at the same time

mea·sles *n pl* : disease that is marked by red spots on the skin

mea·sly *adj* **-sli·er; -est** : contemptibly small in amount

mea·sure *n* **1** : moderate amount **2** : dimensions or amount **3** : something to show amount **4** : unit or system of measurement **5** : act of measuring **6** : means to an end ~ *vb* **-sured; -sur·ing 1** : find out or mark off size or amount of **2** : have a specified measurement — **mea·sur·able** *adj* — **mea·sur·ably** *adv* — **mea·sure·less** *adj* — **mea·sure·ment** *n* — **mea·sur·er** *n*

meat *n* **1** : food **2** : animal flesh used as food — **meat·ball** *n* — **meaty** *adj*

me·chan·ic *n* : worker who repairs cars

me·chan·i·cal *adj* **1** : relating to machines or mechanics **2** : involuntary — **me·chan·i·cal·ly** *adv*

me·chan·ics *n sing or pl* **1** : branch of physics dealing with energy and forces in relation to bodies **2** : mechanical details

mech·a·nism *n* **1** : piece of machinery **2** : technique for gaining a result **3** : basic processes producing a phenomenon — **mech·a·nis·tic** *adj* — **mech·a·ni·za·tion** *n* — **mech·a·nize** *vb* — **mech·a·niz·er** *n*

med·al *n* **1** : religious pin or pendant **2** : coinlike commemorative metal piece

med·al·ist, med·al·list *n* : person awarded a medal

me·dal·lion *n* : large medal

med·dle *vb* **-dled; -dling** : interfere — **med·dler** *n* — **med·dle·some** *adj*

me·dia *n pl* : communications organizations

me·di·an *n* : middle value in a range — **median** *adj*

me·di·ate *vb* **-at·ed; -at·ing** : help settle a dispute — **me·di·a·tion** *n* — **me·di·a·tor** *n*

med·ic *n* : medical worker esp. in the military

med·i·ca·ble *adj* : curable

med·ic·aid *n* : government program of medical aid for the poor

med·i·cal *adj* : relating to medicine — **med·i·cal·ly** *adv*

medi·care *n* : government program of medical care for the aged

med·i·cate *vb* **-cat·ed; -cat·ing** : treat with medicine

med·i·ca·tion *n* **1** : act of medicating **2** : medicine

med·i·cine *n* **1** : preparation used to treat disease **2** : science dealing with the cure of disease — **me·dic·i·nal** *adj* — **me·dic·i·nal·ly** *adv*

me·di·eval, me·di·ae·val *adj* : of or relating to the Middle Ages — **me·di·eval·ist** *n*

me·di·o·cre *adj* : not very good — **me·di·oc·ri·ty** *n*

med·i·tate *vb* **-tat·ed; -tat·ing** : contemplate — **med·i·ta·tion** *n* — **med·i·ta·tive** *adj* — **med·i·ta·tive·ly** *adv*

me·di·um *n, pl* **-diums** *or* **-dia 1** : middle position or degree **2** : means of effecting or conveying something **3** : surrounding substance **4** : means of communication **5** : mode of artistic expression — **medium** *adj*

med·ley *n, pl* **-leys** : series of songs performed as one

meek *adj* **1** : mild-mannered **2** : lacking spirit — **meek·ly** *adv* — **meek·ness** *n*

meer·schaum *n* : claylike tobacco pipe

¹meet *vb* **met; meet·ing 1** : run into **2** : join **3** : oppose **4** : assemble **5** : satisfy **6** : be introduced to ~ *n* : sports team competition

²meet *adj* : proper

meet·ing *n* : a getting together — **meet·ing·house** *n*

mega·byte *n* : unit of computer storage capacity

mega·hertz *n* : one million hertz

mega·phone *n* : cone-shaped device to intensify or direct the voice

mel·an·choly *n* : depression — **mel·an·chol·ic** *adj* — **melancholy** *adj*

mel·a·no·ma *n, pl* **-mas** : usu. malignant skin tumor

me·lee *n* : brawl

me·lio·rate *vb* **-rat·ed; -rat·ing** : improve — **me·lio·ra·tion** *n* — **me·lio·ra·tive** *adj*

mel·lif·lu·ous *adj* : sweetly flowing — **mel·lif·lu·ous·ly** *adv* — **mel·lif·lu·ous·ness** *n*

mel·low *adj* **1** : grown gentle or mild **2** : rich and full — **mellow** *vb* — **mel·low·ness** *n*

melo·dra·ma *n* : overly theatrical play — **melo·dra·mat·ic** *adj* — **melo·dra·mat·i·cal·ly** *adv*

mel·o·dy *n, pl* **-dies 1** : agreeable sound **2** : succession of musical notes — **me·lod·ic** *adj* — **me·lod·i·cal·ly** *adv* — **me·lo·di·ous** *adj* — **me·lo·di·ous·ly** *adv* — **me·lo·di·ous·ness** *n*

mel·on *n* : gourdlike fruit

melt *vb* **1** : change from solid to liquid usu. by heat **2** : dissolve or disappear gradually **3** : move or be moved emotionally

mem·ber *n* **1** : part of a person, animal, or plant **2** : one of a group **3** : part of a whole — **mem·ber·ship** *n*

mem·brane *n* : thin layer esp. in an organism — **mem·bra·nous** *adj*

me·men·to *n, pl* **-tos** *or* **-toes** : souvenir

memo *n, pl* **mem·os** : memorandum

mem·oirs *n pl* : autobiography

mem·o·ra·bil·ia *n pl* **1** : memorable things **2** : mementos

mem·o·ra·ble *adj* : worth remembering — **mem·o·ra·bil·i·ty** *n* — **mem·o·ra·ble·ness** *n* — **mem·o·ra·bly** *adv*

mem·o·ran·dum *n, pl* **-dums** *or* **-da** : informal note

me·mo·ri·al *n* : something (as a monument) meant to keep remembrance alive — **memorial** *adj* — **me·mo·ri·al·ize** *vb*

Memorial Day *n* : last Monday in May or formerly May 30 observed as a legal holiday in commemoration of dead servicemen

mem·o·ry *n, pl* **-ries 1** : power of remembering **2** : something remembered **3** : commemoration **4** : time within which past events are remembered — **mem·o·ri·za·tion** *n* — **mem·o·rize** *vb* — **mem·o·riz·er** *n*

men *pl of* MAN

men·ace *n* : threat of danger ~ *vb* **-aced; -ac·ing 1** : threaten **2** : endanger — **men·ac·ing·ly** *adv*

me·nag·er·ie *n* : collection of wild animals

mend *vb* **1** : improve **2** : repair **3** : heal — **mend** *n* — **mend·er** *n*

men·da·cious *adj* : dishonest — **men·da·cious·ly** *adv* — **men·dac·i·ty** *n*

men·di·cant *n* : beggar — **men·di·can·cy** *n* — **mendicant** *adj*

men·ha·den *n, pl* **-den** : fish related to the herring

me·nial *adj* **1** : relating to servants **2** : humble ~ *n* : domestic servant — **me·ni·al·ly** *adv*

men·in·gi·tis *n, pl* **-git·i·des** : disease of the brain and spinal cord

meno·pause *n* : time when menstruation ends — **meno·paus·al** *adj*

me·no·rah *n* : candelabrum used in Jewish worship

men·stru·a·tion *n* : monthly discharge of blood from the uterus — **men·stru·al** *adj* — **men·stru·ate** *vb*

-ment *n suffix* **1** : result or means of an action **2** : action or process **3** : place of an action **4** : state or condition

men·tal *adj* : relating to the mind or its disorders — **men·tal·i·ty** *n* — **men·tal·ly** *adv*

men·thol *n* : soothing substance from oil of peppermint — **men·tho·lat·ed** *adj*

men·tion *vb* : refer to — **mention** *n*

men·tor *n* : instructor

menu *n* **1** : restaurant's list of food **2** : list of offerings

me·ow *n* : characteristic cry of a cat — **meow** *vb*

mer·can·tile *adj* : relating to merchants or trade

mer·ce·nary *n, pl* **-nar·ies** : hired soldier ~ *adj* : serving only for money

mer·chan·dise *n* : goods bought and sold ~ *vb* **-dised; -dis·ing** : buy and sell — **mer·chan·dis·er** *n*

mer·chant *n* : one who buys and sells

merchant marine *n* : commercial ships

mer·cu·ri·al *adj* : unpredictable — **mer·cu·ri·al·ly** *adv* — **mer·cu·ri·al·ness** *n*

mer·cu·ry *n* : heavy liquid metallic chemical element

mer·cy *n, pl* **-cies 1** : show of pity or leniency **2** : divine blessing — **mer·ci·ful** *adj* — **mer·ci·ful·ly** *adv* — **mer·ci·less** *adj* — **mer·ci·less·ly** *adv* — **mercy** *adj*

mere *adj, superlative* **mer·est** : nothing more than — **mere·ly** *adv*

merge *vb* **merged; merg·ing 1** : unite **2** : blend — **merg·er** *n*

me·rid·i·an *n* : imaginary circle on the earth's surface passing through the poles — **meridian** *adj*

me·ringue *n* : baked dessert topping of beaten egg whites

me·ri·no *n, pl* **-nos 1** : kind of sheep **2** : fine soft woolen yarn

mer·it *n* **1** : praiseworthy quality **2** *pl* : rights and wrongs of a legal case ~ *vb* : deserve — **mer·i·to·ri·ous** *adj* — **mer·i·to·ri·ous·ly** *adv* — **mer·i·to·ri·ous·ness** *n*

mer·maid *n* : legendary female sea creature

mer·ry *adj* **-ri·er; -est** : full of high spirits — **mer·ri·ly** *adv* — **mer·ri·ment** *n* — **mer·ry·mak·er** *n* — **mer·ry·mak·ing** *n*

merry–go–round *n* : revolving amusement ride

me·sa n : steep flat-topped hill

mesdames pl of MADAM or of MADAME or of MRS.

mesdemoiselles pl of MADEMOISELLE

mesh n 1 : one of the openings in a net 2 : net fabric 3 : working contact ~ vb : fit together properly — **meshed** adj

mes·mer·ize vb **-ized; -iz·ing** : hypnotize

mess n 1 : meal eaten by a group 2 : confused, dirty, or offensive state ~ vb 1 : make dirty or untidy 2 : putter 3 : interfere — **messy** adj

mes·sage n : news, information, or a command sent by one person to another

mes·sen·ger n : one who carries a message or does an errand

Mes·si·ah n 1 : expected deliverer of the Jews 2 : Jesus Christ 3 not cap : great leader

messieurs pl of MONSIEUR

Messrs. pl of MR.

mes·ti·zo n, pl **-zos** : person of mixed blood

met past of MEET

me·tab·o·lism n : biochemical processes necessary to life — **met·a·bol·ic** adj — **me·tab·o·lize** vb

met·al n : shiny substance that can be melted and shaped and conducts heat and electricity — **me·tal·lic** adj — **met·al·ware** n — **met·al·work** n — **met·al·work·er** n — **met·al·work·ing** n

met·al·lur·gy n : science of metals — **met·al·lur·gi·cal** adj — **met·al·lur·gist** n

meta·mor·pho·sis n, pl **-pho·ses** : sudden and drastic change (as of form) — **metamor·phose** vb

met·a·phor n : use of a word denoting one kind of object or idea in place of another to suggest a likeness between them — **met·a·phor·i·cal** adj

meta·phys·ics n : study of the causes and nature of things — **meta·phys·i·cal** adj

mete vb **met·ed; met·ing** : allot

me·te·or n : small body that produces a streak of light as it burns up in the atmosphere

me·te·or·ic adj 1 : relating to a meteor 2 : sudden and spectacular — **me·te·or·i·cal·ly** adv

me·te·or·ite n : meteor that reaches the earth

me·te·o·rol·o·gy n : science of weather — **me·te·o·ro·log·ic, me·te·o·ro·log·i·cal** adj — **me·te·o·rol·o·gist** n

¹me·ter n : rhythm in verse or music

²meter n : unit of length equal to 39.37 inches

³meter n : measuring instrument

meth·a·done n : synthetic addictive narcotic

meth·ane n : colorless odorless flammable gas

meth·a·nol n : volatile flammable poisonous liquid

meth·od n 1 : procedure for achieving an end 2 : orderly arrangement or plan — **me·thod·i·cal** adj — **me·thod·i·cal·ly** adv — **me·thod·i·cal·ness** n

me·tic·u·lous adj : extremely careful in attending to details — **me·tic·u·lous·ly** adv — **me·tic·u·lous·ness** n

met·ric, met·ri·cal adj : relating to meter or the metric system — **met·ri·cal·ly** adv

metric system n : system of weights and measures using the meter and kilogram

met·ro·nome n : instrument that ticks regularly to mark a beat in music

me·trop·o·lis n : major city — **met·ro·pol·i·tan** adj

met·tle n : spirit or courage — **met·tle·some** adj

mez·za·nine n 1 : intermediate level between 2 main floors 2 : lowest balcony

mez·zo-so·pra·no n : voice between soprano and contralto

mi·as·ma n 1 : noxious vapor 2 : harmful influence — **mi·as·mic** adj

mi·ca n : mineral separable into thin transparent sheets

mice pl of MOUSE

mi·cro adj : very small

mi·crobe n : disease-causing microorganism — **mi·cro·bi·al** adj

mi·cro·bi·ol·o·gy n : biology dealing with microscopic life — **mi·cro·bi·o·log·i·cal** adj — **mi·cro·bi·ol·o·gist** n

mi·cro·com·put·er n : small computer that uses a microprocessor

mi·cro·cosm n : one thought of as a miniature universe

mi·cro·film n : small film recording printed matter — microfilm vb

mi·crom·e·ter n : instrument for measuring minute distances

mi·cro·min·ia·tur·ized adj : reduced to a very small size — **mi·cro·min·ia·tur·iza·tion** n

mi·cron n : one millionth of a meter

mi·cro·or·gan·ism n : very tiny living thing

mi·cro·phone n : instrument for changing sound waves into variations of an electric current

mi·cro·pro·ces·sor n : miniaturized computer processing unit on a single chip

mi·cro·scope n : optical device for magnifying tiny objects — **mi·cro·scop·ic** adj — **mi·cro·scop·i·cal·ly** adv — **mi·cros·copy** n

mi·cro·wave n 1 : short radio wave 2 : oven that cooks food using microwaves ~ vb : heat or cook in a microwave oven — **mi·cro·wav·able, mi·cro·wave·able** adj

mid adj : middle — **mid·point** n — **mid·stream** n — **mid·sum·mer** n — **mid·town** n or adj — **mid·week** n — **mid·win·ter** n — **mid·year** n

mid·air n : a point in the air well above the ground

mid·day n : noon

mid·dle adj 1 : equally distant from the extremes 2 : being at neither extreme ~ n : middle part or point

Middle Ages n pl : period from about A.D. 500 to about 1500

mid·dle·man n : dealer or agent between the producer and consumer

mid·dling adj 1 : of middle or medium size, degree, or quality 2 : mediocre

midge n : very tiny fly

midg·et n : very small person or thing

mid·land n : interior of a country

mid·most adj : being nearest the middle — **mid·most** adv

mid·night n : 12 o'clock at night

mid·riff n : mid-region of the torso

mid·ship·man n : student naval officer

midst n : position close to or surrounded by others — **midst** prep

mid·way n : concessions and amusements at a carnival ~ adv : in the middle

mid·wife n : person who aids at childbirth — **mid·wife·ry** n

mien n : appearance

miff vb : upset or peeve

¹might past of MAY — used to express permission or possibility or as a polite alternative to may

²might n : power or resources

mighty adj **might·i·er; -est** 1 : very strong 2 : great — **might·i·ly** adv — **might·i·ness** n — **mighty** adv

mi·graine n : severe headache often with nausea

mi·grant n : one who moves frequently to find work

mi·grate vb **-grat·ed; -grat·ing** 1 : move from one place to another 2 : pass periodically from one region or climate to another — **mi·gra·tion** n — **mi·gra·to·ry** adj

mild adj 1 : gentle in nature or behavior 2 : moderate in action or effect — **mild·ly** adv — **mild·ness** n

mil·dew n : whitish fungal growth — **mildew** vb

mile n : unit of length equal to 5280 feet

mile·age n 1 : allowance per mile for traveling expenses 2 : amount or rate of use expressed in miles

mile·stone n : significant point in development

mi·lieu n, pl **-lieus** or **-lieux** : surroundings or setting

mil·i·tant adj : aggressively active or hostile — **mil·i·tan·cy** n — **militant** n — **mil·i·tant·ly** adv

mil·i·ta·rism n : dominance of military ideals or of a policy of aggressive readiness for war — **mil·i·ta·rist** n — **mil·i·ta·ris·tic** adj

mil·i·tary adj 1 : relating to soldiers, arms, or war 2 : relating to or performed by armed forces ~ n : armed forces or the people in them — **mil·i·tar·i·ly** adv

mil·i·tate vb **-tat·ed; -tat·ing** : have an effect

mi·li·tia n : civilian soldiers — **mi·li·tia·man** n

milk n : white nutritive fluid secreted by female mammals for feeding their young ~ vb 1 : draw off the milk of 2 : draw something from as if by milking — **milk·er** n — **milk·i·ness** n — **milky** adj

milk·man n : man who sells or delivers milk

milk·weed n : herb with milky juice

¹mill n 1 : building in which grain is ground into flour 2 : manufacturing plant 3 : machine used esp. for forming or processing ~ vb 1 : subject to a process in a mill 2 : move in a circle — **mill·er** n

²mill n : 1/10 cent

mil·len·ni·um n, pl **-nia** or **-niums** : a period of 1000 years

mil·let n : cereal and forage grass with small seeds

mil·li·gram n : 1/1000 gram

mil·li·li·ter n : 1/1000 liter

mil·li·me·ter n : 1/1000 meter

mil·li·ner n : person who makes or sells women's hats — **mil·li·nery** n

mil·lion n, pl **millions** or **mil·lion** : 1000 thousands — **million** adj — **mil·lionth** adj or n

mil·lion·aire n : person worth a million or more (as of dollars)

mil·li·pede n : longbodied arthropod with 2 pairs of legs on most segments

mill·stone n : either of 2 round flat stones used for grinding grain

mime n 1 : mimic 2 : pantomime — **mime** vb

mim·eo·graph n : machine for making many stencil copies — **mimeograph** vb

mim·ic n : one that mimics ~ vb **-icked; -ick·ing** 1 : imitate closely 2 : ridicule by imitation — **mim·ic·ry** n

min·a·ret n : tower attached to a mosque

mince vb **minced; minc·ing** 1 : cut into small pieces 2 : choose (one's words) carefully 3 : walk in a prim affected manner

mind n 1 : memory 2 : the part of an individual that feels, perceives, and esp. reasons 3 : intention 4 : normal mental condition 5 : opinion 6 : intellectual ability ~ vb 1 : attend to 2 : obey 3 : be concerned about 4 : be careful — **mind·ed** adj — **mind·less** adj — **mind·less·ly** adv — **mind·less·ness** n

mind·ful adj : aware or attentive — **mind·ful·ly** adv — **mind·ful·ness** n

¹mine pron : that which belongs to me

²mine n 1 : excavation from which minerals are taken 2 : explosive device placed in the ground or water for destroying enemy vehicles or vessels that later pass ~ vb **mined; min·ing** 1 : get ore from 2 : place military mines in — **mine·field** n — **min·er** n

min·er·al n 1 : crystalline substance not of organic origin 2 : useful natural substance (as coal) obtained from the ground — **mineral** adj

min·er·al·o·gy n : science dealing with minerals

— **min•er•al•og•i•cal** *adj* — **min•er•al•o•gist** *n*

min•gle *vb* **-gled; -gling** : bring together or mix

mini- *comb form* : miniature or of small dimensions

min•ia•ture *n* : tiny copy or very small version — **miniature** *adj* — **min•ia•tur•ist** *n* — **min•ia•tur•ize** *vb*

mini•bike *n* : small motorcycle

mini•bus *n* : small bus

mini•com•put•er *n* : computer intermediate between a mainframe and a microcomputer in size and speed

mini•course *n* : short course of study

min•i•mal *adj* : relating to or being a minimum — **min•i•mal•ly** *adv*

min•i•mize *vb* **-mized; -miz•ing** 1 : reduce to a minimum 2 : underestimate intentionally

min•i•mum *n, pl* **-ma** *or* **-mums** : lowest quantity or amount — **minimum** *adj*

min•ion *n* 1 : servile dependent 2 : subordinate official

mini•se•ries *n* : television story in several parts

mini•skirt *n* : very short skirt

min•is•ter *n* 1 : Protestant member of the clergy 2 : high officer of state 3 : diplomatic representative ~ *vb* : give aid or service — **min•is•te•ri•al** *adj* — **min•is•tra•tion** *n*

min•is•try *n, pl* **-tries** 1 : office or duties of a minister 2 : body of ministers 3 : government department headed by a minister

mini•van *n* : small van

mink *n, pl* **mink** *or* **minks** : weasellike mammal or its soft brown fur

min•now *n, pl* **-nows** : small freshwater fish

mi•nor *adj* 1 : less in size, importance, or value 2 : not serious ~ *n* 1 : person not yet of legal age 2 : secondary field of academic specialization

mi•nor•i•ty *n, pl* **-ties** 1 : time or state of being a minor 2 : smaller number (as of votes) 3 : part of a population differing from others (as in race or religion)

min•strel *n* 1 : medieval singer of verses 2 : performer in a program usu. of black American songs and jokes — **min•strel•sy** *n*

¹**mint** *n* 1 : fragrant herb that yields a flavoring oil 2 : mint-flavored piece of candy — **minty** *adj*

²**mint** *n* 1 : place where coins are made 2 : vast sum ~ *adj* : unused — **mint** *vb* — **mint•er** *n*

min•u•et *n* : slow graceful dance

mi•nus *prep* 1 : diminished by 2 : lacking ~ *n* : negative quantity or quality

mi•nus•cule, min•is•cule *adj* : very small

¹**min•ute** *n* 1 : 60th part of an hour or of a degree 2 : short time 3 *pl* : official record of a meeting

²**mi•nute** *adj* **-nut•er; -est** 1 : very small 2 : marked by close attention to details — **mi•nute•ly** *adv* — **mi•nute•ness** *n*

mir•a•cle *n* 1 : extraordinary event taken as a sign of divine intervention in human affairs 2 : marvel — **mi•rac•u•lous** *adj* — **mi•rac•u•lous•ly** *adv*

mi•rage *n* : distant illusion caused by atmospheric conditions (as in the desert)

mire *n* : heavy deep mud ~ *vb* **mired; mir•ing** : stick or sink in mire — **miry** *adj*

mir•ror *n* : smooth surface (as of glass) that reflects images ~ *vb* : reflect in or as if in a mirror

mirth *n* : gladness and laughter — **mirth•ful** *adj* — **mirth•ful•ly** *adv* — **mirth•ful•ness** *n* — **mirth•less** *adj*

mis•an•thrope *n* : one who hates mankind — **mis•an•throp•ic** *adj* — **mis•an•thro•py** *n*

mis•ap•pre•hend *vb* : misunderstand — **mis•ap•pre•hen•sion** *n*

mis•ap•pro•pri•ate *vb* : take dishonestly for one's own use — **mis•ap•pro•pri•a•tion** *n*

mis•be•got•ten *adj* 1 : illegitimate 2 : ill-conceived

mis•be•have *vb* : behave improperly — **mis•be•hav•er** *n* — **mis•be•hav•ior** *n*

mis•cal•cu•late *vb* : calculate wrongly — **mis•cal•cu•la•tion**

mis•car•ry *vb* 1 : give birth prematurely before the fetus can survive 2 : go wrong or be unsuccessful — **mis•car•riage** *n*

mis•ce•ge•na•tion *n* : marriage between persons of different races

mis•cel•la•neous *adj* : consisting of many things of different kinds — **mis•cel•la•neous•ly** *adv* — **mis•cel•la•neous•ness** *n*

mis•cel•la•ny *n, pl* **-nies** : collection of various things

mis•chance *n* : bad luck

mis•chief *n* : conduct esp. of a child that annoys or causes minor damage

mis•chie•vous *adj* 1 : causing annoyance or minor injury 2 : irresponsibly playful — **mis•chie•vous•ly** *adv* — **mis•chie•vous•ness** *n*

mis•con•ceive *vb* : interpret incorrectly — **mis•con•cep•tion** *n*

mis•con•duct *n* 1 : mismanagement 2 : bad behavior

mis•con•strue *vb* : misinterpret — **mis•con•struc•tion** *n*

mis•cre•ant *n* : one who behaves criminally or viciously — **mis•creant** *adj*

mis•deed *n* : wrong deed

mis•de•mean•or *n* : crime less serious than a felony

mi•ser *n* : person who hoards and is stingy with money — **mi•ser•li•ness** *n* — **mi•ser•ly** *adj*

mis•er•a•ble *adj* 1 : wretchedly deficient 2 : causing extreme discomfort 3 : shameful — **mis•er•a•ble•ness** *n* — **mis•er•a•bly** *adv*

mis•ery *n, pl* **-er•ies** : suffering and want caused by distress or poverty

mis•fire *vb* 1 : fail to fire 2 : miss an intended effect — **mis•fire** *n*

mis•fit *n* : person poorly adjusted to his environment

mis•for•tune *n* 1 : bad luck 2 : unfortunate condition or event

mis•giv•ing *n* : doubt or concern

mis•guid•ed *adj* : mistaken, uninformed, or deceived

mis•hap *n* : accident

mis•in•form *vb* : give wrong information to — **mis•in•for•ma•tion** *n*

mis•in•ter•pret *vb* : understand or explain wrongly — **mis•in•ter•pre•ta•tion** *n*

mis•judge *vb* : judge incorrectly or unjustly — **mis•judg•ment** *n*

mis•lay *vb* **-laid; -lay•ing** : misplace

mis•lead *vb* **-led; -lead•ing** : lead in a wrong direction or into error — **mis•lead•ing•ly** *adv*

mis•man•age *vb* : manage badly — **mis•man•age•ment** *n*

mis•no•mer *n* : wrong name

mi•sog•y•nist *n* : one who hates or distrusts women — **mi•sog•y•nis•tic** *adj* — **mi•sog•y•ny** *n*

mis•place *vb* : put in a wrong or unremembered place

mis•print *n* : error in printed matter

mis•pro•nounce *vb* : pronounce incorrectly — **mis•pro•nun•ci•a•tion** *n*

mis•quote *vb* : quote incorrectly — **mis•quo•ta•tion** *n*

mis•read *vb* **-read; -read•ing** : read or interpret incorrectly

mis•rep•re•sent *vb* : represent falsely or unfairly — **mis•rep•re•sen•ta•tion** *n*

mis•rule *vb* : govern badly ~ *n* 1 : bad or corrupt government 2 : disorder

¹**miss** *vb* 1 : fail to hit, reach, or contact 2 : notice the absence of 3 : fail to obtain 4 : avoid 5 : omit — **miss** *n*

²**miss** *n* : young unmarried woman or girl — often used as a title

mis•sal *n* : book containing what is said at mass during the year

mis•shap•en *adj* : distorted

mis•sile *n* : object (as a stone or rocket) thrown or shot

miss•ing *adj* : absent or lost

mis•sion *n* 1 : ministry sent by a church to spread its teaching 2 : group of diplomats sent to a foreign country 3 : task

mis•sion•ary *adj* : relating to religious missions ~ *n, pl* **-ar•ies** : person sent to spread religious faith

mis•sive *n* : letter

mis•spell *vb* : spell incorrectly — **mis•spell•ing** *n*

mis•state *vb* : state incorrectly — **mis•state•ment** *n*

mis•step *n* 1 : wrong step 2 : mistake

mist *n* : particles of water falling as fine rain

mis•take *n* 1 : misunderstanding or wrong belief 2 : wrong action or statement — **mistake** *vb*

mis•tak•en *adj* : having a wrong opinion or incorrect information — **mis•tak•en•ly** *adv*

mis•ter *n* : sir — used without a name in addressing a man

mis•tle•toe *n* : parasitic green shrub with waxy white berries

mis•treat *vb* : treat badly — **mis•treat•ment** *n*

mis•tress *n* 1 : woman in control 2 : a woman not his wife with whom a married man has recurrent sexual relations

mis•tri•al *n* : trial that has no legal effect

mis•trust *n* : lack of confidence ~ *vb* : have no confidence in — **mis•trust•ful** *adj* — **mis•trust•ful•ly** *adv* — **mis•trust•ful•ness** *n*

misty *adj* **mist•i•er; -est** 1 : obscured by mist 2 : tearful — **mist•i•ly** *adv* — **mist•i•ness** *n*

mis•un•der•stand *vb* 1 : fail to understand 2 : interpret incorrectly

mis•un•der•stand•ing *n* 1 : wrong interpretation 2 : disagreement

mis•use *vb* 1 : use incorrectly 2 : mistreat — **mis•use** *n*

mite *n* 1 : tiny spiderlike animal 2 : small amount

mi•ter, mi•tre *n* 1 : bishop's headdress 2 : angular joint in wood ~ *vb* **-tered** *or* **-tred; -ter•ing** *or* **-tring** : bevel the ends of for a miter joint

mit•i•gate *vb* **-gat•ed; -gat•ing** : make less severe — **mit•i•ga•tion** *n* — **mit•i•ga•tive** *adj*

mi•to•sis *n, pl* **-to•ses** : process of forming 2 cell nuclei from one — **mi•tot•ic** *adj*

mitt *n* : mittenlike baseball glove

mit•ten *n* : hand covering without finger sections

mix *vb* : combine or join into one mass or group ~ *n* : commercially prepared food mixture — **mix•able** *adj* — **mix•er** *n* — **mix up** *vb* : confuse

mix•ture *n* : act or product of mixing

mix–up *n* : instance of confusion

mne•mon•ic *adj* : relating to or assisting memory

moan *n* : low prolonged sound of pain or grief — **moan** *vb*

moat *n* : deep wide trench around a castle

mob *n* 1 : large disorderly crowd 2 : criminal gang ~ *vb* **-bb-** : crowd around and attack or annoy

mo•bile *adj* : capable of moving or being moved ~ *n* : suspended art construction with freely moving parts — **mo•bil•i•ty** *n*

mo•bi•lize *vb* **-lized; -liz•ing** : assemble and make ready for war duty — **mo•bi•li•za•tion** *n*

moc•ca•sin *n* 1 : heelless shoe 2 : venomous U.S. snake

mo•cha *n* 1 : mixture of coffee and chocolate 2 : dark brown color

mock *vb* 1 : ridicule 2 : mimic in derision ~ *adj* 1

: simulated **2** : phony — **mock•er** n — **mock•ery** n — **mock•ing•ly** adv

mock•ing•bird n : songbird that mimics other birds

mode n **1** : particular form or variety **2** : style — **mod•al** adj — **mod•ish** adj

mod•el n **1** : structural design **2** : miniature representation **3** : something worthy of copying **4** : one who poses for an artist or displays clothes **5** : type or design ~ vb **-eled** or **-elled; -el•ing** or **-el•ling 1** : shape **2** : work as a model ~ adj **1** : serving as a pattern **2** : being a miniature representation of

mo•dem n : device by which a computer communicates with another computer over telephone lines

mod•er•ate adj : avoiding extremes ~ vb **-at•ed; -at•ing 1** : lessen the intensity of **2** : act as a moderator — **moderate** n — **mod•er•ate•ly** adv — **mod•er•ate•ness** n — **mod•er•a•tion** n

mod•er•a•tor n : one who presides

mod•ern adj : relating to or characteristic of the present — **mod•ern** n — **mo•der•ni•ty** n — **mod•ern•iza•tion** n — **mod•ern•ize** vb — **mod•ern•iz•er** n — **mod•ern•ly** adv — **modern•ness** n

mod•est adj **1** : having a moderate estimate of oneself **2** : reserved or decent in thoughts or actions **3** : limited in size, amount, or aim — **mod•est•ly** adv — **mod•es•ty** n

mod•i•cum n : small amount

mod•i•fy vb **-fied; -fy•ing 1** : limit the meaning of **2** : change — **mod•i•fi•ca•tion** n — **mod•i•fi•er** n

mod•u•lar adj : built with standardized units — **mod•u•lar•ized** adj

mod•u•late vb **-lat•ed; -lat•ing 1** : keep in proper measure or proportion **2** : vary a radio wave — **mod•u•la•tion** n — **mod•u•la•tor** n — **mod•u•la•to•ry** adj

mod•ule n : standardized unit

mo•gul n : important person

mo•hair n : fabric made from the hair of the Angora goat

moist adj : slightly or moderately wet — **moist•en** vb — **moist•en•er** n — **moist•ly** adv — **moist•ness** n

mois•ture n : small amount of liquid that causes dampness — **mois•tur•ize** vb — **mois•tur•iz•er** n

mo•lar n : grinding tooth — **molar** adj

mo•las•ses n : thick brown syrup from raw sugar

¹mold n : crumbly organic soil

²mold n : frame or cavity for forming ~ vb : shape in or as if in a mold — **mold•er** n

³mold n : surface growth of fungus ~ vb : become moldy — **mold•i•ness** n — **moldy** adj

mold•er vb : crumble

mold•ing n : decorative surface, plane, or strip

¹mole n : spot on the skin

²mole n : small burrowing mammal — **mole•hill** n

mol•e•cule n : small particle of matter — **mo•lec•u•lar** adj

mole•skin n : heavy cotton fabric

mo•lest vb **1** : annoy or disturb **2** : force physical and usu. sexual contact on — **mo•les•ta•tion** n — **mo•lest•er** n

mol•li•fy vb **-fied; -fy•ing** : soothe in temper — **mol•li•fi•ca•tion** n

mol•lusk, mol•lusc n : shelled aquatic invertebrate — **mol•lus•can** adj

mol•ly•cod•dle vb **-dled; -dling** : pamper

molt vb : shed hair, feathers, outer skin, or horns periodically — **molt** n — **molt•er** n

mol•ten adj : fused or liquefied by heat

mom n : mother

mo•ment n **1** : tiny portion of time **2** : time of excellence **3** : importance

mo•men•tari•ly adv **1** : for a moment **2** : at any moment

mo•men•tary adj : continuing only a moment — **mo•men•tar•i•ness** n

mo•men•tous adj : very important — **mo•men•tous•ly** adv — **mo•men•tous•ness** n

mo•men•tum n, pl **-ta** or **-tums** : force of a moving body

mon•arch n : ruler of a kingdom or empire — **mo•nar•chi•cal** adj

mon•ar•chist n : believer in monarchical government — **mon•ar•chism** n

mon•ar•chy n, pl **-chies** : realm of a monarch

mon•as•tery n, pl **-ter•ies** : house for monks

mo•nas•tic adj : relating to monasteries, monks, or nuns — **mo•nastic** n — **mo•nas•ti•cal•ly** adv — **mo•nas•ti•cism** n

Mon•day n : 2d day of the week

mon•e•tary adj : relating to money

mon•ey n, pl **-eys** or **-ies 1** : something (as coins or paper currency) used in buying **2** : wealth — **mon•eyed** adj — **mon•ey•lend•er** n

mon•ger n : dealer

mon•gol•ism n : congenital mental retardation — **Mon•gol•oid** adj or n

mon•goose n, pl **-goos•es** : small agile mammal esp. of India

mon•grel n : offspring of mixed breed

mon•i•tor n **1** : student assistant **2** : television screen ~ vb : watch or observe esp. for quality

monk n : member of a religious order living in a monastery — **monk•ish** adj

mon•key n, pl **-keys** : small long-tailed arboreal primate ~ vb **1** : fool **2** : tamper

mon•key•shines n pl : pranks

monks•hood n : poisonous herb with showy flowers

mon•o•cle n : eyeglass for one eye

mo•nog•a•my n **1** : marriage with one person at a time **2** : practice of having a single mate for a period of time — **mo•nog•a•mist** n — **mo•nog•a•mous** adj

mono•gram n : sign of identity made of initials — **mono•gram** vb

mono•graph n : learned treatise

mono•lin•gual adj : using only one language

mono•lith n **1** : single great stone **2** : single uniform massive whole — **mono•lith•ic** adj

mono•logue n : long speech — **mono•logu•ist, mo•no•lo•gist** n

mono•nu•cle•o•sis n : acute infectious disease

mo•nop•o•ly n, pl **-lies 1** : exclusive ownership or control of a commodity **2** : one controlling a monopoly — **mo•nop•o•list** n — **mo•nop•o•lis•tic** adj — **mo•nop•o•li•za•tion** n — **mo•nop•o•lize** vb

mono•rail n : single rail for a vehicle or a vehicle or system using it

mono•syl•lab•ic adj : consisting of or using words of only one syllable — **mono•syl•la•ble** n

mono•the•ism n : doctrine or belief that there is only one deity — **mono•the•ist** n — **mono•the•is•tic** adj

mono•tone n : succession of words in one unvarying tone

mo•not•o•nous adj **1** : sounded in one unvarying tone **2** : tediously uniform — **mo•not•o•nous•ly** adv — **mo•not•o•nous•ness** n — **mo•not•o•ny** n

mon•ox•ide n : oxide containing one atom of oxygen in a molecule

mon•sieur n, pl **mes•sieurs** : man of high rank or station — used as a title for a man esp. of French nationality

mon•si•gnor n, pl **mon•si•gnors** or **mon•si•gno•ri** : Roman Catholic prelate — used as a title

mon•soon n : periodic rainy season

mon•ster n **1** : abnormal or terrifying animal **2** : ugly, wicked, or cruel person — **mon•stros•i•ty** n — **mon•strous** adj — **mon•strous•ly** adv

mon•tage n : artistic composition of several different elements

month n : 12th part of a year — **month•ly** adv or adj or n

mon•u•ment n : structure erected in remembrance

mon•u•men•tal adj **1** : serving as a monument **2** : outstanding **3** : very great — **mon•u•men•tal•ly** adv

moo vb : make the noise of a cow — **moo** n

mood n : state of mind or emotion

moody adj **mood•i•er; -est 1** : sad **2** : subject to changing moods and esp. to bad moods — **mood•i•ly** adv — **mood•i•ness** n

moon n : natural satellite (as of earth) — **moon•beam** n — **moon•light** n — **moon•lit** adj

moon•light vb **-ed; -ing** : hold a 2d job — **moon•light•er** n

moon•shine n **1** : moonlight **2** : meaningless talk **3** : illegally distilled liquor

¹moor n : open usu. swampy wasteland — **moor•land** n

²moor vb : fasten with line or anchor

moor•ing n : place where boat can be moored

moose n, pl **moose** : large heavy-antlered deer

moot adj : open to question

mop n : floor-cleaning implement ~ vb **-pp-** : use a mop on

mope vb **moped; mop•ing** : be sad or listless

mo•ped n : low-powered motorbike

mo•raine n : glacial deposit of earth and stones

mor•al adj **1** : relating to principles of right and wrong **2** : conforming to a standard of right behavior **3** : relating to or acting on the mind, character, or will ~ n **1** : point of a story **2** pl : moral practices or teachings — **mor•al•ist** n — **mor•al•is•tic** adj — **mor•al•i•ty** n — **mor•al•ize** vb — **mor•al•ly** adv

mo•rale n : emotional attitude

mo•rass n : swamp

mor•a•to•ri•um n, pl **-ri•ums** or **-ria** : suspension of activity

mo•ray n : savage eel

mor•bid adj **1** : relating to disease **2** : gruesome — **mor•bid•i•ty** n — **mor•bid•ly** adv — **mor•bid•ness** n

mor•dant adj : sarcastic — **mor•dant•ly** adv

more adj **1** : greater **2** : additional ~ adv **1** : in addition **2** : to a greater degree ~ n **1** : greater quantity **2** : additional amount ~ pron : additional ones

mo•rel n : pitted edible mushroom

more•over adv : in addition

mo•res n, pl : customs

morgue n : temporary holding place for dead bodies

mor•i•bund adj : dying

morn n : morning

morn•ing n : time from sunrise to noon

mo•ron n **1** : mentally retarded person **2** : very stupid person — **mo•ron•ic** adj — **mo•ron•i•cal•ly** adv

mo•rose adj : sullen — **mo•rose•ly** adv — **mo•rose•ness** n

mor•phine n : addictive painkilling drug

mor•row n : next day

Morse code n : code of dots and dashes or long and short sounds used for transmitting messages

mor•sel n : small piece or quantity

mor•tal adj **1** : causing or subject to death **2** : extreme — **mortal** n — **mor•tal•i•ty** n — **mor•tal•ly** adv

mor•tar n **1** : strong bowl **2** : short-barreled cannon **3** : masonry material used to cement bricks or stones in place — **mortar** vb

mort•gage n : transfer of property rights as security for a loan — **mortgage** vb — **mort•gag•ee** n — **mort•ga•gor** n

mor•ti•fy vb **-fied; -fy•ing 1** : subdue by abstinence or self-inflicted pain **2** : humiliate — **mor•ti•fi•ca•tion** n

mor•tu•ary n, pl **-ar•ies** : place where dead bodies are kept until burial

mo•sa•ic n : inlaid stone decoration — **mosaic** adj

Mos•lem var of MUSLIM

mosque n : building where Muslims worship

mos•qui•to n, pl **-toes** : biting bloodsucking insect

moss n : green seedless plant — **mossy** adj

most adj **1** : majority of **2** : greatest ~ adv : to the greatest or a very great degree ~ n : greatest amount ~ pron : greatest number or part

-most adj suffix : most : most toward

most•ly adv : mainly

mote n : small particle

mo•tel n : hotel with rooms accessible from the parking lot

moth n : small pale insect related to the butterflies

moth•er n **1** : female parent **2** : source ~ vb **1** : give birth to **2** : cherish or protect — **moth•er•hood** n — **moth•er•land** n — **moth•er•less** adj — **moth•er•ly** adj

moth•er–in–law n, pl **mothers–in–law** : spouse's mother

mo•tif n : dominant theme

mo•tion n **1** : act or instance of moving **2** : proposal for action ~ vb : direct by a movement — **mo•tion•less** adj — **mo•tion•less•ly** adv — **mo•tion•less•ness** n

motion picture n : movie

mo•ti•vate vb **-vat•ed; -vat•ing** : provide with a motive — **mo•ti•va•tion** n — **mo•ti•va•tor** n

mo•tive n : cause of a person's action ~ adj **1** : moving to action **2** : relating to motion — **mo•tive•less** adj

mot•ley adj : of diverse colors or elements

mo•tor n : unit that supplies power or motion ~ vb : travel by automobile — **mo•tor•ist** n — **mo•tor•ize** vb

mo•tor•bike n : lightweight motorcycle

mo•tor•boat n : engine-driven boat

mo•tor•car n : automobile

mo•tor•cy•cle n : 2-wheeled automotive vehicle — **mo•tor•cy•clist** n

mo•tor•truck n : automotive truck

mot•tle vb **-tled; -tling** : mark with spots of different color

mot•to n, pl **-toes** : brief guiding rule

mould var of MOLD

mound n : pile (as of earth)

¹mount n : mountain

²mount vb **1** : increase in amount **2** : get up on **3** : put in position ~ n **1** : frame or support **2** : horse to ride — **mount•able** adj — **mount•er** n

moun•tain n : elevated land higher than a hill — **moun•tain•ous** adj — **moun•tain•top** n

moun•tain•eer n : mountain resident or climber

moun•te•bank n : impostor

mourn vb : feel or express grief — **mourn•er** n — **mourn•ful** adj — **mourn•ful•ly** adv — **mourn•ful•ness** n — **mourn•ing** n

mouse n, pl **mice 1** : small rodent **2** : device for controlling cursor movement on a computer display — **mouse•trap** n or vb — **mousy, mous•ey** adj

mousse n **1** : light chilled dessert **2** : foamy hairstyling preparation

mous•tache var of MUSTACHE

mouth n : opening through which an animal takes in food ~ vb **1** : speak **2** : repeat without comprehension or sincerity **3** : form soundlessly with the lips — **mouthed** adj — **mouth•ful** n

mouth•piece n **1** : part (as of a musical instrument) held in or to the mouth **2** : spokesman

mou•ton n : processed sheepskin

move vb **moved; mov•ing 1** : go or cause to go to another point **2** : change residence **3** : change or cause to change position **4** : take or cause to take action **5** : make a formal request **6** : stir the emotions ~ n **1** : act or instance of moving **2** : step taken to achieve a goal — **mov•able, move•able** adj — **move•ment** n — **mov•er** n

mov•ie n : projected picture in which persons and objects seem to move

¹mow n : part of a barn where hay or straw is stored

²mow vb **mowed; mowed** or **mown; mow•ing** : cut with a machine — **mow•er** n

Mr. n, pl **Messrs.** — conventional title for a man

Mrs. n, pl **Mes•dames** — conventional title for a married woman

Ms. n — conventional title for a woman

much adj **more; most** : great in quantity, extent, or degree ~ adv **more; most** : to a great degree or extent ~ n : great quantity, extent, or degree

mu•ci•lage n : weak glue

muck n : manure, dirt, or mud — **mucky** adj

mu•cus n : slippery protective secretion of membranes (**mucous membranes**) lining body cavities — **mu•cous** adj

mud n : soft wet earth — **mud•di•ly** adv — **mud•di•ness** n — **mud•dy** adj or vb

mud•dle vb **-dled; -dling 1** : make, be, or act confused **2** : make a mess of — **muddle** n — **mud•dle•head•ed** adj

mu•ez•zin n : Muslim who calls the hour of daily prayer

¹muff n : tubular hand covering

²muff vb : bungle — **muff** n

muf•fin n : soft cake baked in a cup-shaped container

muf•fle vb **-fled; -fling 1** : wrap up **2** : dull the sound of — **muf•fler** n

muf•ti n : civilian clothes

¹mug n : drinking cup ~ vb **-gg-** : make faces

²mug vb **-gg-** : assault with intent to rob — **mug•ger** n

mug•gy adj **-gi•er; -est** : hot and humid — **mug•gi•ness** n

Mu•ham•mad•an n : Muslim — **Mu•ham•mad•an•ism** n

mu•lat•to n, pl **-toes** or **-tos** : person of mixed black and white ancestry

mul•ber•ry n : tree with small edible fruit

mulch n : protective ground covering — **mulch** vb

mulct n or vb : fine

¹mule n **1** : offspring of a male ass and a female horse **2** : stubborn person — **mul•ish** adj — **mul•ish•ly** adv — **mu•lish•ness** n

²mule n : backless shoe

mull vb : ponder

mul•let n, pl **-let** or **-lets** : marine food fish

multi- comb form **1** : many or multiple **2** : many times over

multiarmed	multidimensional
multibarreled	multidirectional
multibillion	multidisciplinary
multibranched	multidiscipline
multibuilding	multidivisional
multicenter	multifaceted
multichambered	multifamily
multichannel	multifilament
multicolored	multifunction
multicounty	multifunctional
multicultural	multigrade
multiheaded	multiroom
multihospital	multisense
multihued	multiservice
multilane	multisided
multilevel	multispeed
multimedia	multistage
multimember	multistep
multimillion	multistory
multimillionaire	multisyllabic
multipart	multitalented
multipartite	multitrack
multiparty	multiunion
multiplant	multiunit
multipolar	multiuse
multiproblem	multivitamin
multiproduct	multiwarhead
multipurpose	multiyear
multiracial	

mul•ti•far•i•ous adj : diverse

mul•ti•lat•er•al adj : having many sides or participants

mul•ti•lin•gual adj : knowing or using several languages — **mul•ti•lin•gual•ism** n

mul•ti•na•tion•al adj **1** : relating to several nations or nationalities **2** : having divisions in several countries — **multinational** n

mul•ti•ple adj **1** : several or many **2** : various ~ n : product of one number by another

multiple sclerosis n : brain or spinal disease affecting muscle control

mul•ti•pli•ca•tion n **1** : increase **2** : short method of repeated addition

mul•ti•plic•i•ty n, pl **-ties** : great number or variety

mul•ti•ply vb **-plied; -ply•ing 1** : increase in number **2** : perform multiplication — **mul•ti•pli•er** n

mul•ti•tude n : great number — **mul•ti•tu•di•nous** adj

¹mum adj : silent

²mum n : chrysanthemum

mum•ble vb **-bled; -bling** : speak indistinctly — **mumble** n — **mum•bler** n

mum•mer n **1** : actor esp. in a pantomime **2** : disguised merrymaker — **mum•mery** n

mum•my n, pl **-mies** : embalmed body — **mum•mi•fi•ca•tion** n — **mum•mi•fy** vb

mumps n sing or pl : virus disease with swelling esp. of the salivary glands

munch vb : chew

mun•dane adj **1** : relating to the world **2** : lacking concern for the ideal or spiritual — **mun•dane•ly** adv

mu•nic•i•pal adj : of or relating to a town or city — **mu•nic•i•pal•i•ty** n

mu•nif•i•cent adj : generous — **mu•nif•i•cence** n

mu•ni•tion n : armaments

mu•ral adj : relating to a wall ~ n : wall painting — **mu•ra•list** n

mur•der n : unlawful killing of a person ~ vb : commit a murder — **mur•der•er** n — **mur•der•ess** n — **mur•der•ous** adj — **mur•der•ous•ly** adv

murk n : darkness — **murk•i•ly** adv — **murk•i•ness** n — **murky** adj

mur•mur n **1** : muttered complaint **2** : low indistinct sound — **murmur** vb — **mur•mur•er** n — **mur•mur•ous** adj

mus•ca•tel n : sweet wine

mus•cle n **1** : body tissue capable of contracting to produce motion **2** : strength ~ vb **-cled; -cling** : force one's way — **mus•cled** adj — **mus•cu•lar** adj — **mus•cu•lar•i•ty** n

muscular dystrophy n : disease marked by progressive wasting of muscles

mus•cu•la•ture n : bodily muscles

¹muse *vb* **mused; mus·ing** : ponder — **mus·ing·ly** *adv*

²muse *n* : source of inspiration

mu·se·um *n* : institution displaying objects of interest

mush *n* **1** : corn meal boiled in water or something of similar consistency **2** : sentimental nonsense — **mushy** *adj*

mush·room *n* : caplike organ of a fungus ~ *vb* : grow rapidly

mu·sic *n* : vocal or instrumental sounds — **mu·si·cal** *adj or n* — **mu·si·cal·ly** *adv*

mu·si·cian *n* : composer or performer of music — **mu·si·cian·ly** *adj* — **mu·si·cian·ship** *n*

musk *n* : strong-smelling substance from an Asiatic deer used in perfume — **musk·i·ness** *n* — **musky** *adj*

mus·kel·lunge *n, pl* **-lunge** : large No. American pike

mus·ket *n* : former shoulder firearm — **mus·ke·teer** *n*

musk·mel·on *n* : small edible melon

musk–ox *n* : shaggy-coated wild ox of the arctic

musk·rat *n, pl* **-rat** *or* **-rats** : No. American aquatic rodent

Mus·lim *n* : adherent of Islam — **Muslim** *adj*

mus·lin *n* : cotton fabric

muss *n* : untidy state ~ *vb* : disarrange — **muss·i·ly** *adv* — **muss·i·ness** *n* — **mussy** *adj*

mus·sel *n* : edible mollusk

must *vb* — used as an auxiliary esp. to express a command, obligation, or necessity ~ *n* : something necessary

mus·tache *n* : hair of the human upper lip

mus·tang *n* : wild horse of Western America

mus·tard *n* : pungent yellow seasoning

mus·ter *vb* **1** : assemble **2** : rouse ~ *n* : assembled group

musty *adj* **mus·ti·er; -est** : stale — **must·i·ly** *adv* — **must·i·ness** *n*

mu·ta·ble *adj* : changeable — **mu·ta·bil·i·ty** *n*

mu·tant *adj* : relating to or produced by mutation — **mutant** *n*

mu·tate *vb* **-tat·ed; -tat·ing** : undergo mutation — **mu·ta·tive** *adj*

mu·ta·tion *n* : change in a hereditary character — **mu·ta·tion·al** *adj*

mute *adj* **mut·er; -est 1** : unable to speak **2** : silent ~ *n* **1** : one who is mute **2** : muffling device ~ *vb* **mut·ed; mut·ing** : muffle — **mute·ly** *adv* — **mute·ness** *n*

mu·ti·late *vb* **-lat·ed; -lat·ing** : damage seriously (as by cutting off or altering an essential part) — **mu·ti·la·tion** *n* — **mu·ti·la·tor** *n*

mu·ti·ny *n, pl* **-nies** : rebellion — **mu·ti·neer** *n* — **mu·ti·nous** *adj* — **mu·ti·nous·ly** *adv* — **mutiny** *vb*

mutt *n* : mongrel

mut·ter *vb* **1** : speak indistinctly or softly **2** : grumble — **mutter** *n*

mut·ton *n* : flesh of a mature sheep — **mut·tony** *adj*

mu·tu·al *adj* **1** : given or felt by one another in equal amount **2** : common — **mu·tu·al·ly** *adv*

muz·zle *n* **1** : nose and jaws of an animal **2** : muzzle covering to immobilize an animal's jaws **3** : discharge end of a gun ~ *vb* **-zled; -zling** : restrain with or as if with a muzzle

my *adj* **1** : relating to me or myself **2** — used interjectionally esp. to express surprise

my·nah, my·na *n* : dark crested Asian bird

my·o·pia *n* : nearsightedness — **my·o·pic** *adj* — **my·o·pi·cal·ly** *adv*

myr·i·ad *n* : indefinitely large number — **myriad** *adj*

myrrh *n* : aromatic plant gum

myr·tle *n* : shiny evergreen

my·self *pron* : I, me — used reflexively or for emphasis

mys·tery *n, pl* **-ter·ies 1** : religious truth **2** : something not understood **3** : puzzling or secret quality or state — **mys·te·ri·ous** *adj* — **mys·te·ri·ous·ly** *adv* — **mys·te·ri·ous·ness** *n*

mys·tic *adj* : mystical or mysterious ~ *n* : one who has mystical experiences — **mys·ti·cism** *n*

mys·ti·cal *adj* **1** : spiritual **2** : relating to direct communion with God — **mys·ti·cal·ly** *adj*

mys·ti·fy *vb* **-fied; -fy·ing** : perplex — **mys·ti·fi·ca·tion** *n*

mys·tique *n* : aura of mystery surrounding something

myth *n* **1** : legendary narrative explaining a belief or phenomenon **2** : imaginary person or thing — **myth·i·cal** *adj*

my·thol·o·gy *n, pl* **-gies** : body of myths — **myth·o·log·i·cal** *adj* — **my·thol·o·gist** *n*

N

n *n, pl* **n's** *or* **ns** : 14th letter of the alphabet

nab *vb* **-bb- 1** : seize or arrest

na·dir *n* : lowest point

¹nag *n* : old or decrepit horse

²nag *vb* **-gg- 1** : complain **2** : scold or urge continually **3** : be persistently annoying ~ *n* : one who nags habitually

na·iad *n, pl* **-iads** *or* **-ia·des** : mythological water nymph

nail *n* **1** : horny sheath at the end of each finger and toe **2** : pointed metal fastener ~ *vb* : fasten with a nail — **nail·er** *n*

na·ive, na·ïve *adj* **-iv·er; -est 1** : innocent and unsophisticated **2** : easily deceived — **na·ive·ly** *adv* — **na·ive·ness** *n*

na·ïve·té *n* : quality or state of being naive

na·ked *adj* **1** : having no clothes on **2** : uncovered **3** : plain or obvious **4** : unaided — **na·ked·ly** *adv* — **na·ked·ness** *n*

nam·by–pam·by *adj* : weak or indecisive

name *n* **1** : word by which a person or thing is known **2** : disparaging word for someone **3** : distinguished reputation ~ *vb* **named; nam·ing 1** : give a name to **2** : mention or identify by name **3** : nominate or appoint ~ *adj* **1** : relating to a name **2** : prominent — **name·able** *adj* — **name·less** *adj* — **name·less·ly** *adv*

name·ly *adv* : that is to say

name·sake *n* : one named after another

¹nap *vb* **-pp- 1** : sleep briefly **2** : be off guard ~ *n* : short sleep

²nap *n* : soft downy surface — **nap·less** *adj* — **napped** *adj*

na·palm *n* : gasoline in the form of a jelly

nape *n* : back of the neck

naph·tha *n* : flammable solvent

nap·kin *n* : small cloth for use at the table

nar·cis·sism *n* : self-love — **nar·cis·sist** *n or adj* — **nar·cis·sis·tic** *adj*

nar·cis·sus *n, pl* **-cis·sus** *or* **-cis·sus·es** *or* **-cis·si** : plant with flowers usu. borne separately

nar·cot·ic *n* : painkilling addictive drug — **narcotic** *adj*

nar·rate *vb* **nar·rat·ed; nar·rat·ing** : tell (a story) — **nar·ra·tion** *n* — **nar·ra·tive** *n or adj* — **nar·ra·tor** *n*

nar·row *adj* **1** : of less than standard width **2** : limited **3** : not liberal **4** : barely successful ~ *vb* : make narrow — **nar·row·ly** *adv* — **nar·row·ness** *n*

nar·row–mind·ed *adj* : shallow, provincial, or bigoted

nar·rows *n pl* : narrow passage

nar·whal *n* : sea mammal with a tusk

nasal *adj* : relating to or uttered through the nose — **na·sal·ly** *adv*

nas·tur·tium *n* : herb with showy flowers

nas·ty *adj* **nas·ti·er; -est 1** : filthy **2** : indecent **3** : malicious or spiteful **4** : difficult or disagreeable **5** : unfair — **nas·ti·ly** *adv* — **nas·ti·ness** *n*

na·tal *adj* : relating to birth

na·tion *n* **1** : people of similar characteristics **2** : community with its own territory and government — **na·tion·al** *adj or n* — **na·tion·al·ly** *adv* — **na·tion·wide** *adj*

na·tion·al·ism *n* : devotion to national interests, unity, and independence — **na·tion·al·ist** *n or adj* — **na·tion·al·is·tic** *adj*

na·tion·al·i·ty *n, pl* **-ties 1** : national character **2** : membership in a nation **3** : political independence **4** : ethnic group

na·tion·al·ize *vb* **-ized; -iz·ing 1** : make national **2** : place under government control — **na·tion·al·i·za·tion** *n*

na·tive *adj* **1** : belonging to a person at or by way of birth **2** : born or produced in a particular place ~ *n* : one who belongs to a country by birth

Na·tiv·i·ty *n, pl* **-ties 1** : birth of Christ **2** *not cap* : birth

nat·ty *adj* **-ti·er; -est** : smartly dressed — **nat·ti·ly** *adv* — **nat·ti·ness** *n*

nat·u·ral *adj* **1** : relating to or determined by nature **2** : not artificial **3** : simple and sincere **4** : lifelike ~ *n* : one having an innate talent — **nat·u·ral·ness** *n*

nat·u·ral·ism *n* : realism in art and literature — **nat·u·ral·is·tic** *adj*

nat·u·ral·ist *n* **1** : one who practices naturalism **2** : student of animals or plants

nat·u·ral·ize *vb* **-ized; -iz·ing 1** : become or cause to become established **2** : confer citizenship on — **nat·u·ral·i·za·tion** *n*

nat·u·ral·ly *adv* **1** : in a natural way **2** : as might be expected

na·ture *n* **1** : basic quality of something **2** : kind **3** : disposition **4** : physical universe **5** : natural environment

naught *n* **1** : nothing **2** : zero

naugh·ty *adj* **-ti·er; -est 1** : disobedient or misbehaving **2** : improper — **naught·i·ly** *adv* — **naught·i·ness** *n*

nau·sea *n* **1** : sickness of the stomach with a desire to vomit **2** : extreme disgust — **nau·seous** *adj*

nau·se·ate *vb* **-ated; -at·ing** : affect or become affected with nausea — **nau·se·at·ing·ly** *adv*

nau·ti·cal *adj* : relating to ships and sailing — **nau·ti·cal·ly** *adv*

nau·ti·lus *n, pl* **-lus·es** *or* **-li** : sea mollusk with a spiral shell

na·val *adj* : relating to a navy

nave *n* : central part of a church

na·vel *n* : depression in the abdomen

nav·i·ga·ble *adj* : capable of being navigated — **nav·i·ga·bil·i·ty** *n*

nav·i·gate *vb* **-gat·ed; -gat·ing 1** : sail on or

through 2 : direct the course of — **nav•i•ga•tion** n — **nav•i•ga•tor** n

na•vy n, pl **-vies** 1 : fleet 2 : nation's organization for sea warfare

nay adv : no — used in oral voting ~ n : negative vote

Na•zi n : member of a German fascist party from 1933 to 1945 — **Nazi** adj — **Na•zism, Na•zi•ism** n

near adv : at or close to ~ prep : close to ~ adj 1 : not far away 2 : very much like ~ vb : approach — **near•ly** adv — **near•ness** n

near•by adv or adj : near

near•sight•ed adj : seeing well at short distances only — **near•sight•ed•ly** adv — **near•sight•ed•ness** n

neat adj 1 : not diluted 2 : tastefully simple 3 : orderly and clean — **neat** adv — **neat•ly** adv — **neat•ness** n

neb•u•la n, pl **-lae** : large cloud of interstellar gas — **neb•u•lar** adj

neb•u•lous adj : indistinct

nec•es•sary n, pl **-saries** : indispensable item ~ adj 1 : inevitable 2 : compulsory 3 : positively needed — **nec•es•sar•i•ly** adv

ne•ces•si•tate vb **-tat•ed; -tat•ing** : make necessary

ne•ces•si•ty n, pl **-ties** 1 : very great need 2 : something that is necessary 3 : poverty 4 : circumstances that cannot be changed

neck n 1 : body part connecting the head and trunk 2 : part of a garment at the neck 3 : narrow part ~ vb : kiss and caress — **necked** adj

neck•er•chief n, pl **-chiefs** : cloth worn tied about the neck

neck•lace n : ornament worn around the neck

neck•tie n : ornamental cloth tied under a collar

nec•ro•man•cy n : art of conjuring up the spirits of the dead — **nec•ro•man•cer** n

ne•cro•sis n, pl **-cro•ses** : death of body tissue

nec•tar n : sweet plant secretion

nec•tar•ine n : smooth-skinned peach

née, nee adj — used to identify a married woman by maiden name

need n 1 : obligation 2 : lack of something or what is lacking 3 : poverty ~ vb 1 : be in want 2 : have cause for 3 : be under obligation — **need•ful** adj — **need•less** adj — **need•less•ly** adv — **needy** adj

nee•dle n 1 : pointed sewing implement or something like it 2 : movable bar in a compass 3 : hollow instrument for injecting or withdrawing material ~ vb **-dled; -dling** : incite to action by repeated gibes — **nee•dle•work** n

nee•dle•point n 1 : lace fabric 2 : embroidery on canvas — **needlepoint** adj

ne•far•i•ous adj : very wicked — **ne•far•i•ous•ly** adv

ne•gate vb **-gat•ed; -gat•ing** 1 : deny 2 : nullify — **ne•ga•tion** n

neg•a•tive adj 1 : marked by denial or refusal 2 : showing a lack of something suspected or desirable 3 : less than zero 4 : having more electrons than protons 5 : having light and shadow images reversed ~ n 1 : negative word or vote 2 : a negative number 3 : negative photographic image — **neg•a•tive•ly** adv — **neg•a•tive•ness** n — **neg•a•tiv•i•ty** n

ne•glect vb 1 : disregard 2 : leave unattended to ~ n 1 : act of neglecting 2 : condition of being neglected — **ne•glect•ful** adj

neg•li•gee n : woman's loose robe

neg•li•gent adj : marked by neglect — **neg•li•gence** n — **neg•li•gent•ly** adv

neg•li•gi•ble adj : insignificant

ne•go•ti•ate vb **-at•ed; -at•ing** 1 : confer with another to settle a matter 2 : obtain cash for 3

: get through successfully — **ne•go•tia•ble** adj — **ne•go•ti•a•tion** n — **ne•go•ti•a•tor** n

Ne•gro n, pl **-groes** : member of the black race — **Negro** adj — **Ne•groid** n or adj, often not cap

neigh n : cry of a horse — **neigh** vb

neigh•bor n 1 : one living nearby 2 : fellowman ~ vb : be near or next to — **neigh•bor•hood** n — **neigh•bor•li•ness** n — **neigh•bor•ly** adv

nei•ther pron or adj : not the one or the other ~ conj 1 : not either 2 : nor

nem•e•sis n, pl **-e•ses** 1 : old and usu. frustrating rival 2 : retaliation

ne•ol•o•gism n : new word

ne•on n : gaseous colorless chemical element that emits a reddish glow in electric lamps — **neon** adj

neo•phyte n : beginner

neph•ew n : a son of one's brother, sister, brother-in-law, or sister-in-law

nep•o•tism n : favoritism shown in hiring a relative

nerd n : one who is not stylish or socially at ease — **nerdy** adj

nerve n 1 : strand of body tissue that connects the brain with other parts of the body 2 : self-control 3 : daring 4 pl : nervousness — **nerved** adj — **nerve•less** adj

ner•vous adj 1 : relating to or made up of nerves 2 : easily excited 3 : timid or fearful — **ner•vous•ly** adv — **ner•vous•ness** n

nervy adj **nerv•i•er; -est** : insolent or presumptuous

-ness n suffix : condition or quality

nest n 1 : shelter prepared by a bird for its eggs 2 : place where eggs (as of insects or fish) are laid and hatched 3 : snug retreat 4 : set of objects fitting one inside or under another ~ vb : build or occupy a nest

nes•tle vb **-tled; -tling** : settle snugly (as in a nest)

¹net n : fabric with spaces between strands or something made of this ~ vb **-tt-** : cover with or catch in a net

²net adj : remaining after deductions ~ vb **-tt-** : have as profit

neth•er adj : situated below

net•tle n : coarse herb with stinging hairs ~ vb **-tled; -tling** : provoke or vex — **net•tle•some** adj

net•work n : system of crossing or connected elements

neu•ral adj : relating to a nerve

neu•ral•gia n : pain along a nerve — **neu•ral•gic** adj

neu•ri•tis n, pl **-rit•i•des** or **-ri•tis•es** : inflammation of a nerve

neu•rol•o•gy n : study of the nervous system — **neu•ro•log•i•cal, neu•ro•log•ic** adj — **neu•rol•o•gist** n

neu•ro•sis n, pl **-ro•ses** : nervous disorder

neu•rot•ic adj : relating to neurosis ~ n : unstable person — **neu•rot•i•cal•ly** adv

neu•ter adj : neither masculine nor feminine ~ vb : castrate or spay

neu•tral adj 1 : not favoring either side 2 : being neither one thing nor the other 3 : not decided in color 4 : not electrically charged ~ n 1 : one that is neutral 2 : position of gears that are not engaged — **neu•tral•i•za•tion** n — **neu•tral•ize** vb

neu•tral•i•ty n : state of being neutral

neu•tron n : uncharged atomic particle

nev•er adv 1 : not ever 2 : not in any degree, way, or condition

nev•er•more adv : never again

nev•er•the•less adv : in spite of that

new adj 1 : not old or familiar 2 : different from the former 3 : recently discovered or learned 4

: not accustomed 5 : refreshed or regenerated 6 : being such for the first time — adv : newly — **new•ish** adj — **new•ness** n

new•born adj 1 : recently born 2 : born anew — n, pl **-born** or **-borns** : newborn individual

new•ly adv : recently

news n : report of recent events — **news•let•ter** n — **news•mag•a•zine** n — **news•man** n — **news•pa•per** n — **news•pa•per•man** n — **news•stand** n — **news•wom•an** n — **news•wor•thy** adj

news•cast n : broadcast of news — **news•cast•er** n

news•print n : paper made from wood pulp

newsy adj **news•i•er; -est** : filled with news

newt n : small salamander

New Year n : New Year's Day

New Year's Day n : January 1 observed as a legal holiday

next adj : immediately preceding or following ~ adv 1 : in the time or place nearest 2 : at the first time yet to come ~ prep : nearest to

nex•us n, pl **-us•es** or **-us** : connection

nib n : pen point

nib•ble vb **-bled; -bling** : bite gently or bit by bit ~ n : small bite

nice adj **nic•er; nic•est** 1 : fastidious 2 : very precise or delicate 3 : pleasing 4 : respectable — **nice•ly** adv — **nice•ness** n

nice•ty n, pl **-ties** 1 : dainty or elegant thing 2 : fine detail 3 : exactness

niche n 1 : recess in a wall 2 : fitting place, work, or use

nick n 1 : small broken area or chip 2 : critical moment ~ vb : make a nick in

nick•el n 1 : hard silver-white metallic chemical element used in alloys 2 : U.S. 5-cent piece

nick•name n : informal substitute name — **nick•name** vb

nic•o•tine n : poisonous and addictive substance in tobacco

niece n : a daughter of one's brother, sister, brother-in-law, or sister-in-law

nig•gard•ly adj : stingy — **nig•gard** n — **nig•gard•li•ness** n

nig•gling adj : petty and annoying

nigh adv or adj or prep : near

night n 1 : period between dusk and dawn 2 : the coming of night — **night** adj — **night•ly** adj or adv — **night•time** n

night•clothes n pl : garments worn in bed

night•club n : place for drinking and entertainment open at night

night crawler n : earthworm

night•fall n : the coming of night

night•gown n : gown worn for sleeping

night•in•gale n : Old World thrush that sings at night

night•mare n : frightening dream — **nightmare** adj — **night•mar•ish** adj

night•shade n : group of plants that include poisonous forms and food plants (as the potato and eggplant)

nil n : nothing

nim•ble adj **-bler; -blest** 1 : agile 2 : clever — **nim•ble•ness** n — **nim•bly** adv

nine n 1 : one more than 8 2 : 9th in a set or series — **nine** adj or pron — **ninth** adj or adv or n

nine•pins n : bowling game using 9 pins

nine•teen n : one more than 18 — **nineteen** adj or pron — **nine•teenth** adj or n

nine•ty n, pl **-ties** : 9 times 10 — **nine•ti•eth** adj or n — **ninety** adj or pron

nin•ny n, pl **nin•nies** : fool

¹nip vb **-pp-** 1 : catch hold of and squeeze tightly 2 : pinch or bite off 3 : destroy the growth or fulfillment of ~ n 1 : biting cold 2 : tang 3 : pinch or bite

²**nip** *n* : small quantity of liquor ~ *vb* **-pp-** : take liquor in nips

nip•per *n* **1** : one that nips **2** *pl* : pincers **3** : small boy

nip•ple *n* : tip of the breast or something resembling it

nip•py *adj* **-pi•er; -est 1** : pungent **2** : chilly

nir•va•na *n* : state of blissful oblivion

nit *n* : egg of a parasitic insect

ni•ter *n* : potassium nitrate used in gunpowder or fertilizer or in curing meat

ni•trate *n* : chemical salt used esp. in curing meat

ni•tric acid *n* : liquid acid used in making dyes, explosives, and fertilizers

ni•trite *n* : chemical salt used in curing meat

ni•tro•gen *n* : tasteless odorless gaseous chemical element

ni•tro•glyc•er•in, ni•tro•glyc•er•ine *n* : heavy oily liquid used as an explosive and as a blood-vessel relaxer

nit•wit *n* : stupid person

no *adv* **1** — used to express the negative **2** : in no respect or degree **3** : not so **4** — used as an interjection of surprise or doubt ~ *adj* **1** : not any **2** : not a ~ *n, pl* **noes** *or* **nos 1** : refusal **2** : negative vote

no•bil•i•ty *n* **1** : quality or state of being noble **2** : class of people of noble rank

no•ble *adj* **-bler; -blest 1** : illustrious **2** : aristocratic **3** : stately **4** : of outstanding character ~ *n* : nobleman — **no•ble•ness** *n* — **no•bly** *adv*

no•ble•man *n* : member of the nobility

no•ble•wom•an *n* : a woman of noble rank

no•body *pron* : no person ~ *n, pl* **-bod•ies** : person of no influence or importance

noc•tur•nal *adj* : relating to, occurring at, or active at night

noc•turne *n* : dreamy musical composition

nod *vb* **-dd- 1** : bend the head downward or forward (as in bowing or going to sleep or as a sign of assent) **2** : move up and down **3** : show by a nod of the head — **nod** *n*

node *n* : stem part from which a leaf arises — **nod•al** *adj*

nod•ule *n* : small lump or swelling — **nod•u•lar** *adj*

no•el *n* **1** : Christmas carol **2** *cap* : Christmas season

noes *pl of* NO

nog•gin *n* **1** : small mug **2** : person's head

no•how *adv* : in no manner

noise *n* : loud or unpleasant sound ~ *vb* **noised; nois•ing** : spread by rumor — **noise•less** *adj* — **noise•less•ly** *adv* — **noise•mak•er** *n* — **nois•i•ly** *adv* — **nois•i•ness** *n* — **noisy** *adj*

noi•some *adj* : harmful or offensive

no•mad *n* : one who has no permanent home — **nomad** *adj* — **no•mad•ic** *adj*

no•men•cla•ture *n* : system of names

nom•i•nal *adj* **1** : being something in name only **2** : small or negligible — **nom•i•nal•ly** *adv*

nom•i•nate *vb* **-nat•ed; -nat•ing** : propose or choose as a candidate — **nom•i•na•tion** *n*

nom•i•na•tive *adj* : relating to or being a grammatical case marking typically the subject of a verb — **nominative** *n*

nom•i•nee *n* : person nominated

non- *prefix* **1** : not, reverse of, or absence of **2** : not important

nonabrasive	nonadjustable
nonabsorbent	nonaffiliated
nonacademic	nonaggression
nonaccredited	nonalcoholic
nonacid	nonaligned
nonaddictive	nonappearance
nonadhesive	nonautomatic
nonadjacent	nonbeliever

nonbinding	nonmember
nonbreakable	nonmetal
noncancerous	nonmetallic
noncandidate	nonmilitary
non-Catholic	nonmusical
non-Christian	nonnative
nonchurchgoer	nonnegotiable
noncitizen	nonobjective
nonclassical	nonobservance
nonclassified	nonorthodox
noncombat	nonparallel
noncombatant	nonparticipant
noncombustible	nonparticipating
noncommercial	nonpaying
noncommunist	nonpayment
noncompliance	nonperformance
nonconflicting	nonperishable
nonconforming	nonphysical
nonconsecutive	nonpoisonous
nonconstructive	nonpolitical
noncontagious	nonpolluting
noncontrollable	nonporous
noncontroversial	nonpregnant
noncorrosive	nonproductive
noncriminal	nonprofessional
noncritical	nonprofit
noncumulative	nonracial
noncurrent	nonradioactive
nondeductible	nonrated
nondeferrable	nonrealistic
nondegradable	nonrecurring
nondelivery	nonrefillable
nondemocratic	nonrefundable
nondenominational	nonreligious
nondestructive	nonrenewable
nondiscrimination	nonrepresentative
nondiscriminatory	nonresident
noneducational	nonresponsive
nonelastic	nonrestricted
nonelected	nonreversible
nonelective	nonsalable
nonelectric	nonscientific
nonelectronic	nonscientist
nonemotional	nonsegregated
nonenforcement	non-self-governing
nonessential	nonsexist
nonexclusive	nonsexual
nonexistence	nonsignificant
nonexistent	nonskier
nonexplosive	nonsmoker
nonfat	nonsmoking
nonfatal	nonspeaking
nonfattening	nonspecialist
nonfictional	nonspecific
nonflammable	nonstandard
nonflowering	nonstick
nonfunctional	nonstop
nongovernmental	nonstrategic
nongraded	nonstudent
nonhazardous	nonsugar
nonhereditary	nonsurgical
nonindustrial	nonswimmer
nonindustrialized	nontaxable
noninfectious	nonteaching
noninflationary	nontechnical
nonintegrated	nontoxic
nonintellectual	nontraditional
noninterference	nontransferable
nonintoxicating	nontropical
noninvasive	nontypical
non-Jewish	nonunion
nonlegal	nonuser
nonlethal	nonvenomous
nonliterary	nonverbal
nonliving	nonvoter
nonmagnetic	nonwhite
nonmalignant	nonworker
nonmedical	

non•age *n* : period of youth and esp. legal minority

nonce *n* : present occasion ~ *adj* : occurring, used, or made only once

non•cha•lant *adj* : showing indifference — **non•cha•lance** *n* — **non•cha•lant•ly** *adv*

non•com•mis•sioned officer *n* : subordinate officer in the armed forces appointed from enlisted personnel

non•com•mit•tal *adj* : indicating neither consent nor dissent

non•con•duc•tor *n* : substance that is a very poor conductor

non•con•form•ist *n* : one who does not conform to an established belief or mode of behavior — **non•con•for•mi•ty** *n*

non•de•script *adj* : lacking distinctive qualities

none *pron* : not any ~ *adv* : not at all

non•en•ti•ty *n* : one of no consequence

none•the•less *adv* : nevertheless

non•pa•reil *adj* : having no equal ~ *n* **1** : one who has no equal **2** : chocolate candy disk

non•par•ti•san *adj* : not influenced by political party bias

non•per•son *n* : person without social or legal status

non•plus *vb* **-ss-** : perplex

non•pre•scrip•tion *adj* : available without a doctor's prescription

non•pro•lif•er•a•tion *n* : aimed at ending increased use of nuclear arms

non•sched•uled *adj* : licensed to carry by air without a regular schedule

non•sense *n* : foolish or meaningless words or actions — **non•sen•si•cal** *adj* — **non•sen•si•cal•ly** *adv*

non•sup•port *n* : failure in a legal obligation to provide for someone's needs

non•vi•o•lence *n* : avoidance of violence esp. in political demonstrations — **non•vi•o•lent** *adj*

noo•dle *n* : ribbon-shaped food paste

nook *n* **1** : inside corner **2** : private place

noon *n* : middle of the day — **noon** *adj*

noon•day *n* : noon

no one *pron* : no person

noon•time *n* : noon

noose *n* : rope loop that slips down tight

nor *conj* : and not — used esp. after *neither* to introduce and negate the 2d member of a series

norm *n* **1** : standard usu. derived from an average **2** : typical widespread practice or custom

nor•mal *adj* : average, regular, or standard — **nor•mal•cy** *n* — **nor•mal•i•ty** *n* — **nor•mal•i•za•tion** *n* — **nor•mal•ize** *vb* — **nor•mal•ly** *adv*

north *adv* : to or toward the north ~ *adj* : situated toward, at, or coming from the north ~ *n* **1** : direction to the left of one facing east **2** *cap* : regions to the north — **north•er•ly** *adv or adj* — **north•ern** *adj* — **North•ern•er** *n* — **north•ern•most** *adj* — **north•ward** *adv or adj* — **north•wards** *adv*

north•east *n* **1** : direction between north and east **2** *cap* : regions to the northeast — **northeast** *adj or adv* — **north•east•er•ly** *adv or adj* — **north•east•ern** *adj*

northern lights *n pl* : aurora borealis

north pole *n* : northernmost point of the earth

north•west *n* **1** : direction between north and west **2** *cap* : regions to the northwest — **north•west** *adj or adv* — **north•west•er•ly** *adv or adj* — **north•west•ern** *adj*

nose *n* **1** : part of the face containing the nostrils **2** : sense of smell **3** : front part ~ *vb* **nosed; nos•ing 1** : detect by smell **2** : push aside with the nose **3** : pry **4** : inch ahead — **nose•bleed** *n* — **nosed** *adj* — **nose out** *vb* : narrowly defeat

nose•gay *n* : small bunch of flowers

nos•tal•gia *n* : wistful yearning for something past — **nos•tal•gic** *adj*

nos•tril *n* : opening of the nose

nos•trum *n* : questionable remedy

nosy, nos•ey *adj* **nos•i•er; -est** : tending to pry

not *adv* — used to make a statement negative

no•ta•ble *adj* 1 : noteworthy 2 : distinguished ~ *n* : notable person — **no•ta•bil•i•ty** *n* — **no•ta•bly** *adv*

no•ta•rize *vb* **-rized; -riz•ing** : attest as a notary public

no•ta•ry public *n, pl* **-ries public** *or* **-ry publics** : public official who attests writings to make them legally authentic

no•ta•tion *n* 1 : note 2 : act, process, or method of making things down

notch *n* : V-shaped hollow — **notch** *vb*

note *vb* **not•ed; not•ing** 1 : notice 2 : write down ~ *n* 1 : musical tone 2 : written comment or record 3 : short informal letter 4 : notice or heed — **note•book** *n*

not•ed *adj* : famous

note•wor•thy *adj* : worthy of special mention

noth•ing *pron* 1 : no thing 2 : no part 3 : one of no value or importance ~ *adv* : not at all — *n* 1 : something that does not exist 2 : zero 3 : one of little or no importance — **noth•ing•ness** *n*

no•tice *n* 1 : warning or announcement 2 : attention ~ *vb* **-ticed; -tic•ing** : take notice of — **no•tice•able** *adj* — **no•tice•ably** *adv*

no•ti•fy *vb* **-fied; -fy•ing** : give notice of or to — **no•ti•fi•ca•tion** *n*

no•tion *n* 1 : idea or opinion 2 : whim

no•to•ri•ous *adj* : widely and unfavorably known — **no•to•ri•ety** *n* — **no•to•ri•ous•ly** *adv*

not•with•stand•ing *prep* : in spite of ~ *adv* : nevertheless ~ *conj* : although

nou•gat *n* : nuts or fruit pieces in a sugar paste

nought *var of* NAUGHT

noun *n* : word that is the name of a person, place, or thing

nour•ish *vb* : promote the growth of — **nour•ish•ing** *adj* — **nour•ish•ment** *n*

no•va *n, pl* **-vas** *or* **-vae** : star that suddenly brightens and then fades gradually

nov•el *adj* : new or strange ~ *n* : long invented prose story — **nov•el•ist** *n*

nov•el•ty *n, pl* **-ties** 1 : something new or unusual 2 : newness 3 : small manufactured article — usu. pl.

No•vem•ber *n* : 11th month of the year having 30 days

nov•ice *n* 1 : one preparing to take vows in a religious order 2 : one who is inexperienced or untrained

no•vi•tiate *n* : period or state of being a novice

now *adv* 1 : at the present time or moment 2 : forthwith 3 : under these circumstances ~ *conj* : in view of the fact ~ *n* : present time

now•a•days *adv* : now

no•where *adv* : not anywhere — **no•where** *n*

nox•ious *adj* : harmful

noz•zle *n* : device to direct or control a flow of fluid

nu•ance *n* : subtle distinction or variation

nub *n* 1 : knob or lump 2 : gist

nu•bile *adj* 1 : of marriageable condition or age 2 : sexually attractive

nu•cle•ar *adj* 1 : relating to the atomic nucleus or atomic energy 2 : relating to a weapon whose power is from a nuclear reaction

nu•cle•us *n, pl* **-clei** : central mass or part (as of a cell or an atom)

nude *adj* **nud•er; nud•est** : naked ~ *n* : nude human figure — **nu•di•ty** *n*

nudge *vb* **nudged; nudg•ing** : touch or push gently — **nudge** *n*

nud•ism *n* : practice of going nude — **nud•ist** *n*

nug•get *n* : lump of gold

nui•sance *n* : something annoying

null *adj* : having no legal or binding force — **nul•li•ty** *n*

nul•li•fy *vb* **-fied; -fy•ing** : make null or valueless — **nul•li•fi•ca•tion** *n*

numb *adj* : lacking feeling — **numb** *vb* — **numb•ly** *adv* — **numbness** *n*

num•ber *n* 1 : total of individuals taken together 2 : indefinite total 3 : unit of a mathematical system 4 : numeral 5 : one in a sequence ~ *vb* 1 : count 2 : assign a number to 3 : comprise in number — **num•ber•less** *adj*

nu•mer•al *n* : conventional symbol representing a number

nu•mer•a•tor *n* : part of a fraction above the line

nu•mer•i•cal, nu•meric *adj* 1 : relating to numbers 2 : expressed in or involving numbers — **nu•mer•i•cal•ly** *adv*

nu•mer•ol•o•gy *n* : occult study of numbers — **nu•mer•ol•o•gist** *n*

nu•mer•ous *adj* : consisting of a great number

nu•mis•mat•ics *n* : study or collection of monetary objects — **nu•mis•mat•ic** *adj* — **nu•mis•ma•tist** *n*

num•skull *n* : stupid person

nun *n* : woman belonging to a religious order — **nun•nery** *n*

nup•tial *adj* : relating to marriage or a wedding ~ *n* : marriage or wedding — usu. pl.

nurse *n* 1 : one hired to care for children 2 : person trained to care for sick people ~ *vb* **nursed; nurs•ing** 1 : suckle 2 : care for

nurs•ery *n, pl* **-er•ies** 1 : place where children are cared for 2 : place where young plants are grown

nursing home *n* : private establishment providing care for persons who are unable to care for themselves

nur•ture *n* 1 : training or upbringing 2 : food or nourishment ~ *vb* **-tured; -tur•ing** 1 : care for or feed 2 : educate

nut *n* 1 : dry hard-shelled fruit or seed with a firm inner kernel 2 : metal block with a screw hole through it 3 : foolish, eccentric, or crazy person 4 : enthusiast — **nut•crack•er** *n* — **nut•shell** *n* — **nut•ty** *adj*

nut•hatch *n* : small bird

nut•meg *n* : nutlike aromatic seed of a tropical tree

nu•tri•ent *n* : something giving nourishment — **nutrient** *adj*

nu•tri•ment *n* : nutrient

nu•tri•tion *n* : act or process of nourishing esp. with food — **nu•tri•tion•al** *adj* — **nu•tri•tious** *adj* — **nu•tri•tive** *adj*

nuts *adj* 1 : enthusiastic 2 : crazy

nuz•zle *vb* **-zled; -zling** 1 : touch with or as if with the nose 2 : snuggle

ny•lon *n* 1 : tough synthetic material used esp. in textiles 2 *pl* : stockings made of nylon

nymph *n* 1 : lesser goddess in ancient mythology 2 : girl 3 : immature insect

O

o *n, pl* **o's** *or* **os** 1 : 15th letter of the alphabet 2 : zero

O *var of* OH

oaf *n* : stupid or awkward person — **oaf•ish** *adj*

oak *n, pl* **oaks** *or* **oak** : tree bearing a thin-shelled nut or its wood — **oak•en** *adj*

oar *n* : pole with a blade at the end used to propel a boat

oar•lock *n* : u-shaped device for holding an oar

oa•sis *n, pl* **oa•ses** : fertile area in a desert

oat *n* : cereal grass or its edible seed — **oat•cake** *n* — **oat•en** *adj* — **oat•meal** *n*

oath *n, pl* **oaths** 1 : solemn appeal to God as a pledge of sincerity 2 : profane utterance

ob•du•rate *adj* : stubbornly resistant — **ob•du•ra•cy** *n*

obe•di•ent *adj* : willing to obey — **obe•di•ence** *n* — **obe•di•ent•ly** *adv*

obei•sance *n* : bow of respect or submission

obe•lisk *n* : 4-sided tapering pillar

obese *adj* : extremely fat — **obe•si•ty** *n*

obey *vb* **obeyed; obey•ing** 1 : follow the commands or guidance of 2 : behave in accordance with

ob•fus•cate *vb* **-cat•ed; -cat•ing** : confuse — **ob•fus•ca•tion** *n*

obit•u•ary *n, pl* **-ar•ies** : death notice

¹ob•ject *n* 1 : something that may be seen or felt 2 : purpose 3 : noun or equivalent toward which the action of a verb is directed or which follows a preposition

²ob•ject *vb* : offer opposition or disapproval — **ob•jec•tion** *n* — **ob•jec•tion•able** *adj* — **ob•jec•tion•ably** *adv* — **ob•jec•tor** *n*

ob•jec•tive *adj* 1 : relating to an object or end 2 : existing outside an individual's thoughts or feelings 3 : treating facts without distortion 4 : relating to or being a grammatical case marking objects ~ *n* : aim or end of action — **ob•jec•tive•ly** *adv* — **ob•jec•tive•ness** *n* — **ob•jec•tiv•i•ty** *n*

ob•li•gate *vb* **-gat•ed; -gat•ing** : bind legally or morally — **ob•li•ga•tion** *n* — **oblig•a•to•ry** *adj*

oblige *vb* **obliged; oblig•ing** 1 : compel 2 : do a favor for — **oblig•ing** *adj* — **oblig•ing•ly** *adv*

oblique *adj* 1 : lying at a slanting angle 2 : indirect — **oblique•ly** *adv* — **oblique•ness** *n* — **obliq•ui•ty** *n*

oblit•er•ate *vb* **-at•ed; -at•ing** : completely remove or destroy — **oblit•er•a•tion** *n*

obliv•i•on *n* 1 : state of having lost conscious awareness 2 : state of being forgotten

obliv•i•ous *adj* : not aware or mindful—with *to* or *of* — **obliv•i•ous•ly** *adv* — **obliv•i•ous•ness** *n*

ob•long *adj* : longer in one direction than in the other with opposite sides parallel — **ob•long** *n*

ob•lo•quy *n, pl* **-quies** 1 : strongly condemning utterance 2 : bad repute

ob•nox•ious *adj* : repugnant — **ob•nox•ious•ly** *adv* — **ob•nox•ious•ness** *n*

oboe *n* : slender woodwind instrument with a reed mouthpiece — **obo•ist** *n*

ob•scene *adj* : repugnantly indecent — **ob•scene•ly** *adv* — **ob•scen•i•ty** *n*

ob•scure *adj* 1 : dim or hazy 2 : not well known 3 : vague ~ *vb* : make indistinct or unclear — **ob•scure•ly** *adv* — **ob•scu•ri•ty** *n*

ob•se•quies *n pl* : funeral or burial rite

ob·se·qui·ous *adj* : excessively attentive or flattering — **ob·se·qui·ous·ly** *adv* — **ob·se·qui·ous·ness** *n*

ob·ser·va·to·ry *n, pl* **-ries** : place for observing astronomical phenomena

ob·serve *vb* **-served; -serv·ing** 1 : conform to 2 : celebrate 3 : see, watch, or notice 4 : remark — **ob·serv·able** *adj* — **ob·ser·vance** *n* — **ob·ser·vant** *adj* — **ob·ser·va·tion** *n*

ob·sess *vb* : preoccupy intensely or abnormally — **ob·ses·sion** *n* — **ob·ses·sive** *adj* — **ob·ses·sive·ly** *adv*

ob·so·les·cent *adj* : going out of use — **ob·so·les·cence** *n*

ob·so·lete *adj* : no longer in use

ob·sta·cle *n* : something that stands in the way or opposes

ob·stet·rics *n sing or pl* : branch of medicine that deals with childbirth — **ob·stet·ric, ob·stet·ri·cal** *adj* — **ob·ste·tri·cian** *n*

ob·sti·nate *adj* : stubborn — **ob·sti·na·cy** *n* — **ob·sti·nate·ly** *adv*

ob·strep·er·ous *adj* : uncontrollably noisy or defiant — **ob·strep·er·ous·ness** *n*

ob·struct *vb* : block or impede — **ob·struc·tion** *n* — **ob·struc·tive** *adj* — **ob·struc·tor** *n*

ob·tain *vb* 1 : gain by effort 2 : be generally recognized — **ob·tain·able** *adj*

ob·trude *vb* **-trud·ed; -trud·ing** 1 : thrust out 2 : intrude — **ob·tru·sion** *n* — **ob·tru·sive** *adj* — **ob·tru·sive·ly** *adv* — **ob·tru·sive·ness** *n*

ob·tuse *adj* 1 : slow-witted 2 : exceeding 90 but less than 180 degrees — **ob·tuse·ly** *adv* — **obtuse·ness** *n*

ob·verse *n* : principal side (as of a coin)

ob·vi·ate *vb* **-at·ed; -at·ing** : make unnecessary — **ob·vi·a·tion** *n*

ob·vi·ous *adj* : plain or unmistakable — **ob·vi·ous·ly** *adv* — **obvi·ous·ness** *n*

oc·ca·sion *n* 1 : favorable opportunity 2 : cause 3 : time of an event 4 : special event ~ *vb* : cause — **oc·ca·sion·al** *adj* — **oc·ca·sion·al·ly** *adv*

oc·ci·den·tal *adj* : western — **Occidental** *n*

oc·cult *adj* 1 : secret or mysterious 2 : relating to supernatural agencies — **oc·cult·ism** *n* — **oc·cult·ist** *n*

oc·cu·pan·cy *n, pl* **-cies** : an occupying

oc·cu·pant *n* : one who occupies

oc·cu·pa·tion *n* 1 : vocation 2 : action or state of occupying — **oc·cu·pa·tion·al** *adj* — **oc·cu·pa·tion·al·ly** *adv*

oc·cu·py *vb* **-pied; -py·ing** 1 : engage the attention of 2 : fill up 3 : take or hold possession of 4 : reside in — **oc·cu·pi·er** *n*

oc·cur *vb* **-rr-** 1 : be found or met with 2 : take place 3 : come to mind

oc·cur·rence *n* : something that takes place

ocean *n* 1 : whole body of salt water 2 : very large body of water — **ocean·front** *n* — **ocean·go·ing** *adj* — **oce·an·ic** *adj*

ocean·og·ra·phy *n* : science dealing with the ocean — **ocean·og·ra·pher** *n* — **ocean·o·graph·ic** *adj*

oce·lot *n* : medium-sized American wildcat

ocher, ochre *n* : red or yellow pigment

o'·clock *adv* : according to the clock

oc·ta·gon *n* : 8-sided polygon — **oc·tag·o·nal** *adj*

oc·tave *n* : musical interval of 8 steps or the notes within this interval

Oc·to·ber *n* : 10th month of the year having 31 days

oc·to·pus *n, pl* **-pus·es** *or* **-pi** : sea mollusk with 8 arms

oc·u·lar *adj* : relating to the eye

oc·u·list *n* 1 : ophthalmologist 2 : optometrist

odd *adj* 1 : being only one of a pair or set 2 : not divisible by two without a remainder 3 : additional to what is usual or to the number mentioned 4 : queer — **odd·ly** *adv* — **odd·ness** *n*

odd·i·ty *n, pl* **-ties** : something odd

odds *n pl* 1 : difference by which one thing is favored 2 : disagreement 3 : ratio between winnings and the amount of the bet

ode *n* : solemn lyric poem

odi·ous *adj* : hated — **odi·ous·ly** *adv* — **odi·ous·ness** *n*

odi·um *n* 1 : merited loathing 2 : disgrace

odor *n* : quality that affects the sense of smell — **odor·less** *adj* — **odor·ous** *adj*

od·ys·sey *n, pl* **-seys** : long wandering

o'er *adv or prep* : OVER

of *prep* 1 : from 2 : distinguished by 3 : because of 4 : made or written by 5 : made with, being, or containing 6 : belonging to or connected with 7 : about 8 : that is 9 : concerning 10 : before

off *adv* 1 : from a place 2 : unattached or removed 3 : to a state of being no longer in use 4 : away from work 5 : at a distance in time or space ~ *prep* 1 : away from 2 : at the expense of 3 : not engaged in or abstaining from 4 : below the usual level of ~ *adj* 1 : not operating, up to standard, or correct 2 : remote 3 : provided for

of·fal *n* 1 : waste 2 : viscera and trimmings of a butchered animal

of·fend *vb* 1 : sin or act in violation 2 : hurt, annoy, or insult — **of·fend·er** *n*

of·fense, of·fence *n* : attack, misdeed, or insult

of·fen·sive *adj* : causing offense ~ *n* : attack — **of·fen·sive·ly** *adv* — **of·fen·sive·ness** *n*

of·fer *vb* 1 : present for acceptance 2 : propose 3 : put up (an effort) ~ *n* 1 : proposal 2 : bid — **of·fer·ing** *n*

of·fer·to·ry *n, pl* **-ries** : presentation of offerings or its musical accompaniment

off·hand *adv or adj* : without previous thought or preparation

of·fice *n* 1 : position of authority (as in government) 2 : rite 3 : place where a business is transacted — **of·fice·hold·er** *n*

of·fi·cer *n* 1 : one charged with law enforcement 2 : one who holds an office of trust or authority 3 : one who holds a commission in the armed forces

of·fi·cial *n* : one in office ~ *adj* : authorized or authoritative — **of·fi·cial·dom** *n* — **of·fi·cial·ly** *adv*

of·fi·ci·ant *n* : clergy member who officiates at a religious rite

of·fi·ci·ate *vb* **-at·ed; -at·ing** : perform a ceremony or function

of·fi·cious *adj* : volunteering one's services unnecessarily — **of·fi·cious·ly** *adv* — **of·fi·cious·ness** *n*

off·ing *n* : future

off·set *vb* **-set; -set·ting** : provide an opposite or equaling effect to

off·shoot *n* : outgrowth

off·shore *adv* : at a distance from the shore ~ *adj* : moving away from or situated off the shore

off·spring *n, pl* **offspring** : one coming into being through animal or plant reproduction

of·ten *adv* : many times — **of·ten·times, oft·times** *adv*

ogle *vb* **ogled; ogling** : stare at lustily — **ogle** *n* — **ogler** *n*

ogre *n* 1 : monster 2 : dreaded person

oh *interj* 1 — used to express an emotion 2 — used in direct address

ohm *n* : unit of electrical resistance — **ohm·ic** *adj* — **ohm·me·ter** *n*

oil *n* 1 : greasy liquid substance 2 : petroleum ~ *vb* : put oil in or on — **oil·er** *n* — **oil·i·ness** *n* — **oily** *adj*

oil·cloth *n* : cloth treated with oil or paint and used for coverings

oil·skin *n* : oiled waterproof cloth

oink *n* : natural noise of a hog — **oink** *vb*

oint·ment *n* : oily medicinal preparation

OK *or* **okay** *adv or adj* : all right ~ *vb* **OK'd** *or* **okayed; OK'·ing** *or* **okay·ing** : approve ~ *n* : approval

okra *n* : leafy vegetable with edible green pods

old *adj* 1 : of long standing 2 : of a specified age 3 : relating to a past era 4 : having existed a long time — **old·ish** *adj*

old·en *adj* : of or relating to a bygone era

old–fash·ioned *adj* 1 : out-of-date 2 : conservative

old maid *n* : spinster

old–tim·er *n* 1 : veteran 2 : one who is old

ole·an·der *n* : poisonous evergreen shrub

oleo·mar·ga·rine *n* : margarine

ol·fac·to·ry *adj* : relating to the sense of smell

oli·gar·chy *n, pl* **-chies** 1 : government by a few people 2 : those holding power in an oligarchy — **oli·garch** *n* — **oli·gar·chic, oli·gar·chi·cal** *adj*

ol·ive *n* 1 : evergreen tree bearing small edible fruit or the fruit 2 : dull yellowish green color

om·buds·man *n, pl* **-men** : complaint investigator

om·e·let, om·e·lette *n* : beaten eggs lightly fried and folded

omen *n* : sign or warning of the future

om·i·nous *adj* : presaging evil — **om·i·nous·ly** *adv* — **om·i·nous·ness** *n*

omit *vb* **-tt-** 1 : leave out 2 : fail to perform — **omis·si·ble** *adj* — **omis·sion** *n*

om·nip·o·tent *adj* : almighty — **om·nip·o·tence** *n* — **om·nip·o·tent·ly** *adv*

om·ni·pres·ent *adj* : ever-present — **om·ni·pres·ence** *n*

om·ni·scient *adj* : all-knowing — **om·ni·science** *n* — **om·ni·scient·ly** *adv*

om·niv·o·rous *adj* 1 : eating both meat and vegetables 2 : avid — **om·niv·o·rous·ly** *adv*

on *prep* 1 : in or to a position over and in contact with 2 : at or to 3 : about 4 : from 5 : with regard to 6 : in a state or process 7 : during the time of ~ *adv* 1 : in or into contact with 2 : forward 3 : into operation

once *adv* 1 : one time only 2 : at any one time 3 : formerly ~ *n* : one time ~ *conj* : as soon as ~ *adj* : former — **at once** 1 : simultaneously 2 : immediately

once–over *n* : swift examination

on·com·ing *adj* : approaching

one *adj* 1 : being a single thing 2 : being one in particular 3 : being the same in kind ~ *pron* 1 : certain indefinitely indicated person or thing 2 : a person in general ~ *n* 1 : 1st in a series 2 : single person or thing — **one·ness** *n*

oner·ous *adj* : imposing a burden

one·self *pron* : one's own self — usu. used reflexively or for emphasis

one–sid·ed *adj* 1 : occurring on one side only 2 : partial

one·time *adj* : former

one–way *adj* : made or for use in only one direction

on·go·ing *adj* : continuing

on·ion *n* : plant grown for its pungent edible bulb or this bulb

on·ly *adj* : alone in its class ~ *adv* 1 : merely or exactly 2 : solely 3 : at the very least 4 : as a result ~ *conj* : but

on·set *n* : start

on·shore *adj* 1 : moving toward shore 2 : lying on or near the shore — **on·shore** *adv*

on·slaught *n* : attack

on·to *prep* : to a position or point on

onus *n* : burden (as of obligation or blame)

on·ward *adv or adj* : forward

on·yx *n* : quartz used as a gem

¹ooze *n* : soft mud ~ *vb* **oozed; ooz·ing** : flow or leak out slowly — **oozy** *adj*

opac·i·ty *n* : quality or state of being opaque or an opaque spot

opal *n* : gem with delicate colors

opaque *adj* **1** : blocking light **2** : not easily understood **3** : dull-witted — **opaque·ly** *adv*

open *adj* **1** : not shut or shut up **2** : not secret or hidden **3** : frank or generous **4** : extended **5** : free from controls **6** : not decided ~ *vb* **1** : make or become open **2** : make or become functional **3** : start ~ *n* : outdoors — **open·er** *n* — **open·ly** *adv* — **open·ness** *n*

open-hand·ed *adj* : generous — **open-hand·ed·ly** *adv*

open·ing *n* **1** : act or instance of making open **2** : something that is open **3** : opportunity

op·era *n* : drama set to music — **op·er·at·ic** *adj*

op·er·a·ble *adj* **1** : usable or in working condition **2** : suitable for surgical treatment

op·er·ate *vb* **-at·ed; -at·ing 1** : perform work **2** : perform an operation **3** : manage — **op·er·a·tor** *n*

op·er·a·tion *n* **1** : act or process of operating **2** : surgical work on a living body **3** : military action or mission — **op·er·a·tion·al** *adj*

op·er·a·tive *adj* : working or having an effect

op·er·et·ta *n* : light opera

oph·thal·mol·o·gy *n* : branch of medicine dealing with the eye — **oph·thal·mol·o·gist** *n*

opi·ate *n* : preparation or derivative of opium

opine *vb* **opined; opin·ing** : express an opinion

opin·ion *n* **1** : belief **2** : judgment **3** : formal statement by an expert

opin·ion·at·ed *adj* : stubborn in one's opinions

opi·um *n* : addictive narcotic drug that is the dried juice of a poppy

opos·sum *n* : common tree-dwelling nocturnal mammal

op·po·nent *n* : one that opposes

op·por·tune *adj* : suitable or timely — **op·por·tune·ly** *adv*

op·por·tun·ism *n* : a taking advantage of opportunities — **op·por·tun·ist** *n* — **op·por·tu·nis·tic** *adj*

op·por·tu·ni·ty *n, pl* **-ties** : favorable time

op·pose *vb* **-posed; -pos·ing 1** : place opposite or against something **2** : resist — **op·po·si·tion** *n*

op·po·site *n* : one that is opposed ~ *adj* **1** : set facing something that is at the other side or end **2** : opposed or contrary ~ *adv* : on opposite sides ~ *prep* : across from — **op·po·site·ly** *adv*

op·press *vb* **1** : persecute **2** : weigh down — **op·pres·sion** *n* — **op·pres·sive** *adj* — **op·pres·sive·ly** *adv* — **op·pres·sor** *n*

op·pro·bri·ous *adj* : expressing or deserving opprobrium — **op·pro·bri·ous·ly** *adv*

op·pro·bri·um *n* **1** : something that brings disgrace **2** : infamy

opt *vb* : choose

op·tic *adj* : relating to vision or the eye

op·ti·cal *adj* : relating to optics, vision, or the eye

op·ti·cian *n* : maker of or dealer in eyeglasses

op·tics *n pl* : science of light and vision

op·ti·mal *adj* : most favorable — **op·ti·mal·ly** *adv*

op·ti·mism *n* : tendency to hope for the best — **op·ti·mist** *n* — **op·ti·mis·tic** *adj* — **op·ti·mis·ti·cal·ly** *adv*

op·ti·mum *n, pl* **-ma** : amount or degree of something most favorable to an end — **optimum** *adj*

op·tion *n* **1** : ability to choose **2** : right to buy or sell a stock **3** : alternative — **op·tion·al** *adj*

op·tom·e·try *n* : profession of examining the eyes — **op·tom·e·trist** *n*

op·u·lent *adj* : lavish — **op·u·lence** *n* — **op·u·lent·ly** *adv*

opus *n, pl* **opera** : work esp. of music

or *conj* — used to indicate an alternative

-or *n suffix* : one that performs an action

or·a·cle **1** : one held to give divinely inspired answers or revelations **2** : wise person or an utterance of such a person — **orac·u·lar** *adj*

oral *adj* **1** : spoken **2** : relating to the mouth — **oral·ly** *adv*

or·ange *n* **1** : reddish yellow citrus fruit **2** : color between red and yellow — **or·ange·ade** *n*

orang·u·tan *n* : large reddish brown ape

ora·tion *n* : elaborate formal speech

or·a·tor *n* : one noted as a public speaker

or·a·to·rio *n, pl* **-ri·os** : major choral work

or·a·to·ry *n* : art of public speaking — **or·a·tor·i·cal** *adj*

orb *n* : spherical body

or·bit *n* : path made by one body revolving around another ~ *vb* : revolve around — **or·bit·al** *adj* — **or·bit·er** *n*

or·chard *n* : place where fruit or nut trees are grown — **or·chard·ist** *n*

or·ches·tra *n* **1** : group of musicians **2** : front seats of a theater's main floor — **or·ches·tral** *adj* — **or·ches·tral·ly** *adv*

or·ches·trate *vb* **-trat·ed; -trat·ing 1** : compose or arrange for an orchestra **2** : arrange or combine for best effect — **or·ches·tra·tion** *n*

or·chid *n* : plant with showy 3-petal flowers or its flower

or·dain *vb* **1** : admit to the clergy **2** : decree

or·deal *n* : severely trying experience

or·der *n* **1** : rank, class, or special group **2** : arrangement **3** : rule of law **4** : authoritative regulation or instruction **5** : working condition **6** : special request for a purchase or what is purchased ~ *vb* **1** : arrange **2** : give an order to **3** : place an order for

or·der·ly *adj* **1** : being in order or tidy **2** : well behaved ~ *n, pl* **-lies 1** : officer's attendant **2** : hospital attendant — **or·der·li·ness** *n*

or·di·nal *n* : number indicating order in a series

or·di·nance *n* : municipal law

or·di·nary *adj* : of common occurrence, quality, or ability — **or·di·nar·i·ly** *adv*

or·di·na·tion *n* : act of ordaining

ord·nance *n* : military supplies

ore *n* : mineral containing a valuable constituent

oreg·a·no *n* : mint used as a seasoning and source of oil

or·gan *n* **1** : air-powered or electronic keyboard instrument **2** : animal or plant structure with special function **3** : periodical

or·gan·ic *adj* **1** : relating to a bodily organ **2** : relating to living things **3** : relating to or containing carbon or its compounds **4** : relating to foods produced without the use of laboratory-made products — **or·gan·i·cal·ly** *adv*

or·gan·ism *n* : a living thing

or·gan·ist *n* : organ player

or·ga·nize *vb* **-nized; -niz·ing** : form parts into a functioning whole — **or·ga·ni·za·tion** *n* — **or·ga·ni·za·tion·al** *adj* — **or·ga·niz·er** *n*

or·gasm *n* : climax of sexual excitement — **or·gas·mic** *adj*

or·gy *n, pl* **-gies** : unrestrained indulgence (as in sexual activity)

ori·ent *vb* **1** : set in a definite position **2** : acquaint with a situation — **ori·en·ta·tion** *n*

ori·en·tal *adj* : Eastern — **Oriental** *n*

or·i·fice *n* : opening

or·i·gin *n* **1** : ancestry **2** : rise, beginning, or derivation from a source — **orig·i·nate** *vb* — **orig·i·na·tor** *n*

orig·i·nal *n* : something from which a copy is made ~ *adj* **1** : first **2** : not copied from something else **3** : inventive — **orig·i·nal·i·ty** *n* — **orig·i·nal·ly** *adv*

ori·ole *n* : American songbird

or·na·ment *n* : something that adorns ~ *vb* : provide with ornament — **or·na·men·tal** *adj* — **or·na·men·ta·tion** *n*

or·nate *adj* : elaborately decorated — **or·nate·ly** *adv* — **or·nate·ness** *n*

or·nery *adj* : irritable

or·ni·thol·o·gy *n, pl* **-gies** : study of birds — **or·ni·tho·log·i·cal** *adj* — **or·ni·thol·o·gist** *n*

or·phan *n* : child whose parents are dead — **orphan** *vb* — **or·phan·age** *n*

or·tho·don·tics *n* : dentistry dealing with straightening teeth — **or·tho·don·tist** *n*

or·tho·dox *adj* **1** : conforming to established doctrine **2** *cap* : of or relating to a Christian church originating in the Eastern Roman Empire — **or·tho·doxy** *n*

or·thog·ra·phy *n* : spelling — **or·tho·graph·ic** *adj*

or·tho·pe·dics *n sing or pl* : correction or prevention of skeletal deformities — **or·tho·pe·dic** *adj* — **or·tho·pe·dist** *n*

-o·ry *adj suffix* **1** : of, relating to, or characterized by **2** : serving for, producing, or maintaining

os·cil·late *vb* **-lat·ed; -lat·ing** : swing back and forth — **os·cil·la·tion** *n*

os·mo·sis *n* : diffusion esp. of water through a membrane — **os·mot·ic** *adj*

os·prey *n, pl* **-preys** : large fish-eating hawk

os·si·fy *vb* **-fied; -fy·ing** : make or become hardened or set in one's ways

os·ten·si·ble *adj* : seeming — **os·ten·si·bly** *adv*

os·ten·ta·tion *n* : pretentious display — **os·ten·ta·tious** *adj* — **os·ten·ta·tious·ly** *adv*

os·te·op·a·thy *n* : system of healing that emphasizes manipulation (as of joints) — **os·te·o·path** *n* — **os·te·o·path·ic** *adj*

os·te·o·po·ro·sis *n, pl* **-ro·ses** : condition characterized by fragile and porous bones

os·tra·cize *vb* **-cized; -ciz·ing** : exclude by common consent — **ostra·cism** *n*

os·trich *n* : very large flightless bird

oth·er *adj* **1** : being the one left **2** : alternate **3** : additional ~ *pron* **1** : remaining one **2** : different one

oth·er·wise *adv* **1** : in a different way **2** : in different circumstances **3** : in other respects — **otherwise** *adj*

ot·ter *n* : fish-eating mammal with webbed feet

ot·to·man *n* : upholstered footstool

ought *verbal auxiliary* — used to express obligation, advisability, or expectation

ounce *n* **1** : unit of weight equal to about 28.3 grams **2** : unit of capacity equal to about 29.6 milliliters

our *adj* : of or relating to us

ours *pron* : that which belongs to us

our·selves *pron* : we, us — used reflexively or for emphasis

-ous *adj suffix* : having or having the qualities of

oust *vb* : expel or eject

oust·er *n* : expulsion

out *adv* **1** : away from the inside or center **2** : beyond control **3** : to extinction, exhaustion, or completion **4** : in or into the open ~ *vb* : become known ~ *adj* **1** : situated outside **2** : absent ~ *prep* **1** : out through **2** : outward on or along — **out·bound** *adj* — **out·build·ing** *n*

out·age *n* : period of no electricity

out·board *adv* : outside a boat or ship — **outboard** *adj*

out·break *n* : sudden occurrence

out·burst *n* : violent expression of feeling

out·cast *n* : person cast out by society

out•come n : result

out•crop n : part of a rock stratum that appears above the ground — **outcrop** vb

out•cry n : loud cry

out•dat•ed adj : out-of-date

out•dis•tance vb : go far ahead of

out•do vb -**did**; -**done**; -**do•ing**; -**does** : do better than

out•doors adv : in or into the open air ~ n : open air — **out•door** adj

out•er adj 1 : external 2 : farther out — **out•er•most** adj

out•field n : baseball field beyond the infield — **out•field•er** n

out•fit n 1 : equipment for a special purpose 2 : group ~ vb -**tt**- : equip — **out•fit•ter** n

out•go n, pl outgoes : expenditure

out•go•ing adj 1 : retiring from a position 2 : friendly

out•grow vb -**grew**; -**grown**; -**grow•ing** 1 : grow faster than 2 : grow too large for

out•growth n 1 : product of growing out 2 : consequence

out•ing n : excursion

out•land•ish adj : very strange — **out•land•ish•ly** adv

out•last vb : last longer than

out•law n : lawless person ~ vb : make illegal

out•lay n : expenditure

out•let n 1 : exit 2 : means of release 3 : market for goods 4 : electrical device that gives access to wiring

out•line n 1 : line marking the outer limits 2 : summary ~ vb 1 : draw the outline of 2 : indicate the chief parts of

out•live vb : live longer than

out•look n 1 : viewpoint 2 : prospect for the future

out•ly•ing adj : far from a central point

out•ma•neu•ver vb : defeat by more skillful maneuvering

out•mod•ed adj : out-of-date

out•num•ber vb : exceed in number

out of prep 1 : out from within 2 : beyond the limits of 3 : among 4 — used to indicate absence or loss 5 : because of 6 : from or with

out–of–date adj : no longer in fashion or in use

out•pa•tient n : person treated at a hospital who does not stay overnight

out•post n : remote military post

out•put n : amount produced ~ vb -**put•ted** or -**put**; -**put•ting** : produce

out•rage n 1 : violent or shameful act 2 : injury or insult 3 : extreme anger ~ vb -**raged**; -**rag•ing** 1 : subject to violent injury 2 : make very angry

out•ra•geous adj : extremely offensive or shameful — **out•ra•geous•ly** adv — **out•ra•geous•ness** n

out•right adv 1 : completely 2 : instantly ~ adj 1 : complete 2 : given without reservation

out•set n : beginning

out•side n 1 : place beyond a boundary 2 : exterior 3 : utmost limit — adj 1 : outer 2 : coming from without 3 : remote — adv : on or to the outside ~ prep 1 : on or to the outside of 2 : beyond the limits of

outside of prep 1 : outside 2 : besides

out•sid•er n : one who does not belong to a group

out•skirts n pl : outlying parts (as of a city)

out•smart vb : outwit

out•spo•ken adj : direct and open in speech — **out•spo•ken•ness** n

out•stand•ing adj 1 : unpaid 2 : very good — **out•stand•ing•ly** adv

out•strip vb 1 : go faster than 2 : surpass

¹out•ward adj 1 : being toward the outside 2 : showing outwardly

²outward, out•wards adv : toward the outside — **out•ward•ly** adv

out•wit vb : get the better of by superior cleverness

ova pl of OVUM

oval adj : egg-shaped — **oval** n

ova•ry n, pl -**ries** 1 : egg-producing organ 2 : seed-producing part of a flower — **ovar•i•an** adj

ova•tion n : enthusiastic applause

ov•en n : chamber (as in a stove) for baking

over adv 1 : across 2 : upside down 3 : in excess or addition 4 : above 5 : at an end 6 : again ~ prep 1 : above in position or authority 2 : more than 3 : along, through, or across 4 : because of ~ adj 1 : upper 2 : remaining 3 : ended

over- prefix 1 : so as to exceed or surpass 2 : excessive or excessively

overabundance	overenergetic
overabundant	overenthusiastic
overachiever	overestimate
overactive	overexaggerate
overaggressive	overexaggeration
overambitious	overexcite
overanalyze	overexcited
overanxiety	overexercise
overanxious	overexert
overarousal	overexertion
overassertive	overexpand
overbake	overexpansion
overbid	overexplain
overbill	overexploit
overbold	overexpose
overborrow	overextend
overbright	overextension
overbroad	overexuberant
overbuild	overfamiliar
overburden	overfatigued
overbusy	overfeed
overbuy	overfertilize
overcapacity	overfill
overcapitalize	overfond
overcareful	overgeneralization
overcautious	overgeneralize
overcharge	overgenerous
overcivilized	overglamorize
overclean	overgraze
overcommit	overharvest
overcompensate	overhasty
overcomplicate	overheat
overconcern	overidealize
overconfidence	overimaginative
overconfident	overimpress
overconscientious	overindebtedness
overconsume	overindulge
overconsumption	overindulgence
overcontrol	overindulgent
overcook	overinflate
overcorrect	overinsistent
overcritical	overintense
overcrowd	overintensity
overdecorate	overinvestment
overdependence	overladen
overdependent	overlarge
overdevelop	overlend
overdose	overload
overdramatic	overlong
overdramatize	overloud
overdress	overmedicate
overdrink	overmodest
overdue	overmuch
overeager	overobvious
overeat	overoptimistic
overeducated	overorganize
overelaborate	overparticular
overemotional	overpay
overemphasis	overpayment
overemphasize	overplay

overpopulated	oversimple
overpraise	oversimplify
overprescribe	oversolicitous
overpressure	overspecialize
overprice	overspend
overprivileged	overstaff
overproduce	overstimulation
overproduction	overstock
overpromise	overstrain
overprotect	overstress
overprotective	overstretch
overqualified	oversubtle
overrate	oversupply
overreact	oversuspicious
overreaction	oversweeten
overrefined	overtax
overregulate	overtighten
overregulation	overtip
overreliance	overtired
overrepresented	overtrain
overrespond	overtreat
overripe	overuse
oversaturate	overutilize
oversell	overvalue
oversensitive	overweight
overserious	overwork
oversexed	overzealous

¹over•age adj : too old

²over•age n : surplus

over•all adj : including everything

over•alls n pl : pants with an extra piece covering the chest

over•awe vb : subdue by awe

over•bear•ing adj : arrogant

over•blown adj : pretentious

over•board adv : over the side into the water

over•cast adj : clouded over ~ n : cloud covering

over•coat n : outer coat

over•come vb -**came**; -**come**; -**com•ing** 1 : defeat 2 : make helpless or exhausted

over•do vb -**did**; -**done**; -**do•ing**; -**does** : do too much

over•draft n : overdrawn sum

over•draw vb -**drew**; -**drawn**; -**draw•ing** : write checks for more than one's bank balance

over•flow vb 1 : flood 2 : flow over — **over•flow** n

over•grow vb -**grew**; -**grown**; -**grow•ing** : grow over

over•hand adj : made with the hand brought down from above — **over•hand** adv — **over•hand•ed** adv or adj

over•hang vb -**hung**; -**hang•ing** : jut out over ~ n : something that overhangs

over•haul vb 1 : repair 2 : overtake

over•head adv : aloft ~ adj : situated above ~ n : general business expenses

over•hear vb -**heard**; -**hear•ing** : hear without the speaker's knowledge

over•joyed adj : filled with joy

over•kill n : large excess

over•land adv or adj : by, on, or across land

over•lap vb : lap over — **over•lap** n

over•lay vb -**laid**; -**lay•ing** : lay over or across — **over•lay** n

over•look vb 1 : look down on 2 : fail to see 3 : ignore 4 : pardon 5 : supervise ~ n : observation point

over•ly adv : excessively

over•night adv 1 : through the night 2 : suddenly — **overnight** adj

over•pass n : bridge over a road

over•pow•er vb : conquer

over•reach vb : try or seek too much

over•ride vb -**rode**; -**rid•den**; -**rid•ing** : neutralize action of

over•rule vb : rule against or set aside

over·run *vb* **-ran; -run·ning 1** : swarm or flow over **2** : go beyond ~ *n* : an exceeding of estimated costs

over·seas *adv or adj* : beyond or across the sea

over·see *vb* **-saw; -seen; -seeing** : supervise — **over·seer** *n*

over·shad·ow *vb* : exceed in importance

over·shoe *n* : protective outer shoe

over·shoot *vb* **-shot; -shoot·ing** : shoot or pass beyond

over·sight *n* : inadvertent omission or error

over·sleep *vb* **-slept; -sleep·ing** : sleep longer than intended

over·spread *vb* **-spread; -spread·ing** : spread over or above

over·state *vb* : exaggerate — **over·statement** *n*

over·stay *vb* : stay too long

over·step *vb* : exceed

overt *adj* : not secret — **overt·ly** *adv*

over·take *vb* **-took; -tak·en; -tak·ing** : catch up with

over·throw *vb* **-threw; -thrown; -throw·ing 1** : upset **2** : defeat — **over·throw** *n*

over·time *n* : extra working time — **overtime** *adv*

over·tone *n* **1** : higher tone in a complex musical tone **2** : suggestion

over·ture *n* **1** : opening offer **2** : musical introduction

over·turn *vb* **1** : turn over **2** : nullify

over·view *n* : brief survey

over·ween·ing *adj* **1** : arrogant **2** : excessive

over·whelm *vb* : overcome completely — **over·whelm·ing·ly** *adv*

over·wrought *adj* : extremely excited

ovoid, ovoi·dal *adj* : egg-shaped

ovu·late *vb* **-lat·ed; -lat·ing** : produce eggs from an ovary — **ovu·la·tion** *n*

ovum *n*, *pl* **ova** : female germ cell

owe *vb* **owed; ow·ing 1** : have an obligation to pay **2** : be indebted to or for

owing to *prep* : because of

owl *n* : nocturnal bird of prey — **owl·ish** *adj* — **owl·ish·ly** *adv*

own *adj* : belonging to oneself ~ *vb* **1** : have as property **2** : acknowledge ~ *pron* : one or ones belonging to oneself — **own·er** *n* — **own·er·ship** *n*

ox *n*, *pl* **ox·en** : bovine mammal and esp. a castrated bull

ox·ide *n* : compound of oxygen

ox·i·dize *vb* **-dized; -diz·ing** : combine with oxygen — **ox·i·da·tion** — **ox·i·diz·er** *n*

ox·y·gen *n* : gaseous chemical element essential for life

oys·ter *n* : bivalve mollusk — **oys·ter·ing** *n*

ozone *n* : very reactive bluish form of oxygen

P

p *n*, *pl* **p's** *or* **ps** : 16th letter of the alphabet

pace *n* **1** : walking step **2** : rate of progress ~ *vb* **paced; pac·ing 1** : go at a pace **2** : cover with slow steps **3** : set the pace of

pace·mak·er *n* : electrical device to regulate heartbeat

pachy·derm *n* : elephant

pa·cif·ic *adj* : calm or peaceful

pac·i·fism *n* : opposition to war or violence — **pac·i·fist** *n or adj* — **pac·i·fis·tic** *adj*

pac·i·fy *vb* **-fied; -fy·ing** : make calm — **pac·i·fi·ca·tion** — **pac·i·fi·er** *n*

pack *n* **1** : compact bundle **2** : group of animals ~ *vb* **1** : put into a container **2** : fill tightly or completely **3** : send without ceremony — **pack·er** *n*

pack·age *n* : items bundled together ~ *vb* **-aged; -ag·ing** : enclose in a package

pack·et *n* : small package

pact *n* : agreement

pad *n* **1** : cushioning part or thing **2** : floating leaf of a water plant **3** : tablet of paper ~ *vb* **-dd- 1** : furnish with a pad **2** : expand with needless matter — **pad·ding** *n*

pad·dle *n* : implement with a flat blade ~ *vb* **-dled; -dling** : move, beat, or stir with a paddle

pad·dock *n* : enclosed area for racehorses

pad·dy *n*, *pl* **-dies** : wet land where rice is grown

pad·lock *n* : lock with a U-shaped catch — **pad·lock** *vb*

pae·an *n* : song of praise

pa·gan *n or adj* : heathen — **pa·gan·ism** *n*

¹page *n* : messenger ~ *vb* **paged; pag·ing** : summon by repeated calls — **pag·er** *n*

²page *n* : single leaf (as of a book) or one side of the leaf

pag·eant *n* : elaborate spectacle or procession — **pag·eant·ry** *n*

pa·go·da *n* : tower with roofs curving upward

paid *past of* PAY

pail *n* : cylindrical container with a handle — **pail·ful** *n*

pain *n* **1** : punishment or penalty **2** : suffering of body or mind **3** *pl* : great care ~ *vb* : cause or experience pain — **pain·ful** *adj* — **pain·ful·ly** *adv* — **pain·kill·er** *n* — **pain·kill·ing** *adj* — **pain·less** *adj* — **pain·less·ly** *adv*

pains·tak·ing *adj* : taking pains — **painstaking** *n* — **pains·tak·ing·ly** *adv*

paint *vb* **1** : apply color or paint to **2** : portray esp. in color — *n* : mixture of pigment and liquid — **paint·brush** *n* — **paint·er** *n* — **paint·ing** *n*

pair *n* : a set of two ~ *vb* : put or go together as a pair

pa·ja·mas *n pl* : loose suit for sleeping

pal *n* : close friend

pal·ace *n* **1** : residence of a chief of state **2** : mansion — **pa·la·tial** *adj*

pal·at·able *adj* : agreeable to the taste

pal·ate *n* **1** : roof of the mouth **2** : taste — **pal·a·tal** *adj*

pa·la·ver *n* : talk — **palaver** *vb*

¹pale *adj* **pal·er; pal·est 1** : lacking in color or brightness **2** : light in color or shade ~ *vb* **paled; pal·ing** : make or become pale — **pale·ness** *n*

²pale *n* **1** : fence stake **2** : enclosed place

pa·le·on·tol·o·gy *n* : branch of biology dealing with ancient forms of life known from fossils — **pa·le·on·tol·o·gist** *n*

pal·ette *n* : board on which paints are laid and mixed

pal·i·sade *n* **1** : high fence **2** : line of cliffs

¹pall *n* **1** : cloth draped over a coffin **2** : something that produces gloom

²pall *vb* : lose in interest or attraction

pall·bear·er *n* : one who attends the coffin at a funeral

¹pal·let *n* : makeshift bed

²pallet *n* : portable storage platform

pal·li·ate *vb* **-at·ed; -at·ing 1** : ease without curing **2** : cover or conceal by excusing — **pal·li·a·tion** *n* — **pal·li·a·tive** *adj or n*

pal·lid *adj* : pale

pal·lor *n* : paleness

¹palm *n* **1** : tall tropical tree crowned with large leaves **2** : symbol of victory

²palm *n* : underside of the hand ~ *vb* **1** : conceal in the hand **2** : impose by fraud

palm·ist·ry *n* : reading a person's character or future in his palms — **palm·ist** *n*

palmy *adj* **palm·i·er; -est** : flourishing

pal·o·mi·no *n*, *pl* **-nos** : light-colored horse

pal·pa·ble *adj* **1** : capable of being touched **2** : obvious — **pal·pa·bly** *adv*

pal·pi·tate *vb* **-tat·ed; -tat·ing** : beat rapidly — **pal·pi·ta·tion** *n*

pal·sy *n*, *pl* **-sies 1** : paralysis **2** : condition marked by tremor — **pal·sied** *adj*

pal·try *adj* **-tri·er; -est** : trivial

pam·per *vb* : spoil or indulge

pam·phlet *n* : unbound publication — **pam·phle·teer** *n*

pan *n* : broad, shallow, and open container ~ *vb* **1** : wash gravel in a pan to search for gold **2** : criticize severely

pan·a·cea *n* : remedy for all ills or difficulties

pan·cake *n* : fried flat cake

pan·cre·as *n* : gland that produces insulin — **pan·cre·at·ic** *adj*

pan·da *n* : black-and-white bearlike animal

pan·de·mo·ni·um *n* : wild uproar

pan·der *n* **1** : pimp **2** : one who caters to others' desires or weaknesses ~ *vb* : act as a pander

pane *n* : sheet of glass

pan·e·gyr·ic *n* : eulogistic oration — **pan·e·gyr·ist** *n*

pan·el *n* **1** : list of persons (as jurors) **2** : discussion group **3** : flat piece of construction material **4** : board with instruments or controls ~ *vb* -**eled** *or* -**elled; -el·ing** *or* -**el·ling** : decorate with panels — **pan·el·ing** *n* — **pan·el·ist** *n*

pang *n* : sudden sharp pain

pan·han·dle *vb* **-dled; -dling** : ask for money on the street — **pan·han·dler** *n*

pan·ic *n* : sudden overpowering fright ~ *vb* **-icked; -ick·ing** : affect or be affected with panic — **pan·icky** *adj*

pan·o·ply *n*, *pl* **-plies 1** : full suit of armor **2** : impressive array

pan·o·ra·ma *n* : view in every direction — **pan·o·ram·ic** *adj*

pan·sy *n*, *pl* **-sies** : low-growing garden herb with showy flowers

pant *vb* **1** : breathe with great effort **2** : yearn ~ *n* : panting sound

pan·ta·loons *n pl* : pants

pan·the·on *n* **1** : the gods of a people **2** : group of famous people

pan·ther *n* : large wild cat

pant·ies *n pl* : woman's or child's short underpants

pan·to·mime *n* **1** : play without words **2** : expression by bodily or facial movements ~ *vb* : represent by pantomime

pan·try *n*, *pl* **-tries** : storage room for food and dishes

pants *n pl* **1** : 2-legged outer garment **2** : panties

pap *n* : soft food

pa·pa·cy *n*, *pl* **-cies 1** : office of pope **2** : reign of a pope

pa·pal *adj* : relating to the pope

pa·pa·ya *n* : tropical tree with large yellow edible fruit

pa·per *n* **1** : pliable substance used to write or print on, to wrap things in, or to cover walls **2** : printed or written document **3** : newspaper — **paper** *adj or vb* — **pa·per·hang·er** *n* — **pa·per·weight** *n* — **pa·pery** *adj*

pa·per·board *n* : cardboard

pa·pier–mâ·ché *n* : molding material of waste paper

pa•poose n : young child of American Indian parents

pa•pri•ka n : mild red spice from sweet peppers

pa•py•rus n, pl **-rus•es** or **-ri** 1 : tall grasslike plant 2 : paper from papyrus

par n 1 : stated value 2 : common level 3 : accepted standard or normal condition — **par** adj

par•a•ble n : simple story illustrating a moral truth

para•chute n : large umbrella-shaped device for making a descent through air — **parachute** vb — **para•chut•ist** n

pa•rade n 1 : pompous display 2 : ceremonial formation and march ~ vb **-rad•ed; -rad•ing** 1 : march in a parade 2 : show off

par•a•digm n : model

par•a•dise n : place of bliss

par•a•dox n : statement that seems contrary to common sense yet is perhaps true — **par•a•dox•i•cal** adj — **par•a•dox•i•cal•ly** adv

par•af•fin n : white waxy substance used esp. for making candles and sealing foods

par•a•gon n : model of perfection

para•graph n : unified division of a piece of writing ~ vb : divide into paragraphs

par•a•keet n : small slender parrot

par•al•lel adj 1 : lying or moving in the same direction but always the same distance apart 2 : similar ~ n 1 : parallel line, curve, or surface 2 : line of latitude 3 : similarity ~ vb 1 : compare 2 : correspond to — **par•al•lel•ism** n

par•al•lel•o•gram n : 4-sided polygon with opposite sides equal and parallel

pa•ral•y•sis n, pl **-y•ses** : loss of function and esp. of voluntary motion — **par•a•lyt•ic** adj or n

par•a•lyze vb **-lyzed; -lyz•ing** : affect with paralysis — **par•a•lyz•ing•ly** adv

para•med•ic n : person trained to provide initial emergency medical treatment

pa•ram•e•ter n : characteristic element — **para•met•ric** adj

par•a•mount adj : superior to all others

par•amour n : illicit lover

para•noia n : mental disorder marked by irrational suspicion — **para•noid** adj or n

par•a•pet n : protecting rampart in a fort

par•a•pher•na•lia n sing or pl : equipment

para•phrase n : restatement of a text giving the meaning in different words — **paraphrase** vb

para•ple•gia n : paralysis of the lower trunk and legs — **para•ple•gic** adj or n

par•a•site n : organism living on another — **par•a•sit•ic** adj — **par•a•sit•ism** n

para•sol n : umbrella used to keep off the sun

para•troops n pl : troops trained to parachute from an airplane — **para•troop•er** n

par•boil vb : boil briefly

par•cel n 1 : lot 2 : package ~ vb **-celed** or **-celled; -cel•ing** or **-cel•ling** : divide into portions

parch vb : toast or shrivel with dry heat

parch•ment n : animal skin prepared to write on

par•don n : excusing of an offense ~ vb : free from penalty — **par•don•able** adj — **par•don•er** n

pare vb **pared; par•ing** 1 : trim off an outside part 2 : reduce as if by paring — **par•er** n

par•e•gor•ic n : tincture of opium and camphor

par•ent n : one that begets or brings up offspring — **par•ent•age** n — **pa•ren•tal** adj — **par•ent•hood** n

pa•ren•the•sis n, pl **-the•ses** 1 : word or phrase inserted in a passage 2 : one of a pair of punctuation marks ( ) — **par•en•thet•ic** or **par•en•thet•i•cal** adj — **par•en•thet•i•cal•ly** adv

par•fait n : layered cold dessert

pa•ri•ah n : outcast

par•ish n : local church community

pa•rish•io•ner n : member of a parish

par•i•ty n, pl **-ties** : equality

park n : land set aside for recreation or for its beauty ~ vb : leave a vehicle standing

par•ka n : usu. hooded heavy jacket

park•way n : broad landscaped thoroughfare

par•lance n : manner of speaking

par•lay n : the risking of a stake plus its winnings — **parlay** vb

par•ley n, pl **-leys** : conference about a dispute — **parley** vb

par•lia•ment n : legislative assembly — **par•lia•men•tar•i•an** n — **par•lia•men•ta•ry** adj

par•lor n 1 : reception room 2 : place of business

pa•ro•chi•al adj 1 : relating to a church parish 2 : provincial — **pa•ro•chi•al•ism** n

par•o•dy n, pl **-dies** : humorous or satirical imitation — **parody** vb

pa•role n : conditional release of a prisoner — **parole** vb — **pa•rol•ee** n

par•ox•ysm n : convulsion

par•quet n : flooring of patterned wood inlay

par•ra•keet var of PARAKEET

par•rot n : bright-colored tropical bird

par•ry vb **-ried; -ry•ing** 1 : ward off a blow 2 : evade adroitly — **parry** n

parse vb **parsed; pars•ing** : analyze grammatically

par•si•mo•ny n : extreme frugality — **par•si•mo•ni•ous** adj — **par•si•mo•ni•ous•ly** adv

pars•ley n : garden plant used as a seasoning or garnish

pars•nip n : carrotlike vegetable with a white edible root

par•son n : minister

par•son•age n : parson's house

part n 1 : one of the units into which a larger whole is divided 2 : function or role ~ vb 1 : take leave 2 : separate 3 : go away 4 : give up

par•take vb **-took; -tak•en; -tak•ing** : have or take a share — **par•tak•er** n

par•tial adj 1 : favoring one over another 2 : affecting a part only — **par•tial•i•ty** n — **par•tial•ly** adv

par•tic•i•pate vb **-pat•ed; -pat•ing** : take part in something — **par•tic•i•pant** adj or n — **par•tic•i•pa•tion** n — **par•tic•i•pa•to•ry** adj

par•ti•ci•ple n : verb form with functions of both verb and adjective — **par•ti•cip•i•al** adj

par•ti•cle n : small bit

par•tic•u•lar adj 1 : relating to a specific person or thing 2 : individual 3 : hard to please ~ n : detail — **par•tic•u•lar•ly** adv

par•ti•san n 1 : adherent 2 : guerrilla — **partisan** adj — **par•ti•san•ship** n

par•tite adj : divided into parts

par•ti•tion n 1 : distribution 2 : something that divides — **partition** vb

part•ly adv : in some degree

part•ner n 1 : associate 2 : companion 3 : business associate — **part•ner•ship** n

part of speech : class of words distinguished esp. according to function

par•tridge n, pl **-tridge** or **-tridg•es** : stout-bodied game bird

par•ty n, pl **-ties** 1 : political organization 2 : participant 3 : company of persons esp. with a purpose 4 : social gathering

par•ve•nu n : social upstart

pass vb 1 : move past, over, or through 2 : go away or die 3 : allow to elapse 4 : go unchallenged 5 : transfer or undergo transfer 6 : render a judgment 7 : occur 8 : enact 9 : undergo testing successfully 10 : be regarded 11 : decline ~ n 1 : low place in a mountain range 2 : act of passing 3 : accomplishment 4 : permission to leave, enter, or move about — **pass•able** adj — **pass•ably** adv — **pass•er** n — **pass•er•by** n

pas•sage n 1 : process of passing 2 : means of passing 3 : voyage 4 : right to pass 5 : literary selection — **pas•sage•way** n

pass•book n : bankbook

pas•sé adj : out-of-date

pas•sen•ger n : traveler in a conveyance

pass•ing n : death

pas•sion n 1 : strong feeling esp. of anger, love, or desire 2 : object of affection or enthusiasm — **pas•sion•ate** adj — **pas•sion•ate•ly** adv — **pas•sion•less** adj

pas•sive adj 1 : not active but acted upon 2 : submissive — **passive** n — **pas•sive•ly** adv — **pas•siv•i•ty** n

Pass•over n : Jewish holiday celebrated in March or April in commemoration of the Hebrews' liberation from slavery in Egypt

pass•port n : government document needed for travel abroad

pass•word n 1 : word or phrase spoken to pass a guard 2 : sequence of characters needed to get into a computer system

past adj 1 : ago 2 : just gone by 3 : having existed before the present 4 : expressing past time ~ prep or adv : beyond ~ n 1 : time gone by 2 : verb tense expressing time gone by 3 : past life

pas•ta n : fresh or dried shaped dough

paste n 1 : smooth ground food 2 : moist adhesive ~ vb **past•ed; past•ing** : attach with paste — **pasty** adj

paste•board n : cardboard

pas•tel n : light color — **pastel** adj

pas•teur•ize vb **-ized; -iz•ing** : heat (as milk) so as to kill germs — **pas•teur•i•za•tion** n

pas•time n : amusement

pas•tor n : priest or minister serving a church or parish — **pas•tor•ate** n

pas•to•ral adj 1 : relating to rural life 2 : of or relating to spiritual guidance or a pastor ~ n : literary work dealing with rural life

past•ry n, pl **-ries** : sweet baked goods

pas•ture n : land used for grazing ~ vb **-tured; -tur•ing** : graze

pat n 1 : light tap 2 : small mass ~ vb **-tt-** : tap gently ~ adj or adv 1 : apt or glib 2 : unyielding

patch n 1 : piece used for mending 2 : small area distinct from surrounding area ~ vb 1 : mend with a patch 2 : make of fragments 3 : repair hastily — **patchy** adj

patch•work n : something made of pieces of different materials, shapes, or colors

pate n : crown of the head

pa•tel•la n, pl **-lae** or **-las** : kneecap

pa•tent adj 1 : obvious 2 : protected by a patent ~ n : document conferring or securing a right ~ vb : secure by patent — **pat•ent•ly** adv

pa•ter•nal adj 1 : fatherly 2 : related through or inherited from a father — **pa•ter•nal•ly** adv

pa•ter•ni•ty n : fatherhood

path n 1 : trodden way 2 : route or course — **path•find•er** n — **path•way** n — **path•less** adj

pa•thet•ic adj : pitiful — **pa•thet•i•cal•ly** adv

pa•thol•o•gy n, pl **-gies** 1 : study of disease 2 : physical abnormality — **path•o•log•i•cal** adj — **pa•thol•o•gist** n

pa•thos n : element evoking pity

pa•tience n : habit or fact of being patient

pa•tient adj : bearing pain or trials without complaint ~ n : one under medical care — **pa•tient•ly** adv

pa•ti•na n, pl **-nas** or **-nae** : green film formed on copper and bronze

pa•tio n, pl **-ti•os** 1 : courtyard 2 : paved recreation area near a house

pa•tri•arch n 1 : man revered as father or founder 2 : venerable old man — **pa•tri•ar•chal** adj — **pa•tri•ar•chy** n

pa·tri·cian *n* : person of high birth — **patrician** *adj*

pat·ri·mo·ny *n* : something inherited — **pat·ri·mo·ni·al** *adj*

pa·tri·ot *n* : one who loves his or her country — **pa·tri·ot·ic** *adj* — **pa·tri·ot·i·cal·ly** *adv* — **pa·tri·o·tism** *n*

pa·trol *n* **1** : a going around for observation or security **2** : group on patrol ~ *vb* **-ll-** : carry out a patrol

pa·trol·man *n* : police officer

pa·tron *n* **1** : special protector **2** : wealthy supporter **3** : customer

pa·tron·age *n* **1** : support or influence of a patron **2** : trade of customers **3** : control of government appointments

pa·tron·ess *n* : woman who is a patron

pa·tron·ize *vb* **-ized; -iz·ing 1** : be a customer of **2** : treat with condescension

¹pat·ter *vb* : talk glibly or mechanically ~ *n* : rapid talk

²patter *vb* : pat or tap rapidly ~ *n* : quick succession of pats or taps

pat·tern *n* **1** : model for imitation or for making things **2** : artistic design **3** : noticeable formation or set of characteristics ~ *vb* : form according to a pattern

pat·ty *n, pl* **-ties** : small flat cake

pau·ci·ty *n* : shortage

paunch *n* : large belly — **paunchy** *adj*

pau·per *n* : poor person — **pau·per·ism** *n* — **pau·per·ize** *vb*

pause *n* : temporary stop ~ *vb* **paused; paus·ing** : stop briefly

pave *vb* **paved; pav·ing** : cover to smooth or firm the surface — **pave·ment** *n* — **pav·ing** *n*

pa·vil·ion *n* **1** : large tent **2** : light structure used for entertainment or shelter

paw *n* : foot of a 4-legged clawed animal ~ *vb* **1** : handle clumsily or rudely **2** : touch or strike with a paw

pawn *n* **1** : goods deposited as security for a loan **2** : state of being pledged ~ *vb* : deposit as a pledge — **pawn·bro·ker** *n* — **pawn·shop** *n*

pay *vb* **paid; pay·ing 1** : make due return for goods or services **2** : discharge indebtedness for **3** : requite **4** : give freely or as fitting **5** : be profitable ~ *n* **1** : status of being paid **2** : something paid — **pay·able** *adj* — **pay·check** *n* — **pay·ee** *n* — **pay·er** *n* — **pay·ment** *n*

PC *n, pl* **PCs** *or* **PC's** : microcomputer

pea *n* : round edible seed of a leguminous vine

peace *n* **1** : state of calm and quiet **2** : absence of war or strife — **peace·able** *adj* — **peace·ably** *adv* — **peace·ful** *adj* — **peace·ful·ly** *adv* — **peace·keep·er** *n* — **peace·keep·ing** *n* — **peace·mak·er** *n* — **peace·time** *n*

peach *n* : sweet juicy fruit of a flowering tree or this tree

pea·cock *n* : brilliantly colored male pheasant

peak *n* **1** : pointed or projecting part **2** : top of a hill **3** : highest level ~ *vb* : reach a maximum — **peak** *adj*

peak·ed *adj* : sickly

peal *n* : loud sound (as of ringing bells) ~ *vb* : give out peals

pea·nut *n* : annual herb that bears underground pods or the pod or the edible seed inside

pear *n* : fleshy fruit of a tree related to the apple

pearl *n* : gem formed within an oyster — **pearly** *adj*

peas·ant *n* : tiller of the soil — **peas·ant·ry** *n*

peat *n* : decayed organic deposit often dried for fuel — **peaty** *adj*

peb·ble *n* : small stone — **peb·bly** *adj*

pe·can *n* : hickory tree bearing a smooth-shelled nut or the nut

pec·ca·dil·lo *n, pl* **-loes** *or* **-los** : slight offense

¹peck *n* : unit of dry measure equal to 8 quarts

²peck *vb* : strike or pick up with the bill ~ *n* : quick sharp stroke

pec·tin *n* : water-soluble plant substance that causes fruit jellies to set — **pec·tic** *adj*

pec·to·ral *adj* : relating to the breast or chest

pe·cu·liar *adj* **1** : characteristic of only one **2** : strange — **pe·cu·liar·i·ty** *n* — **pe·cu·liar·ly** *adv*

pe·cu·ni·ary *adj* : relating to money

ped·a·go·gy *n* : art or profession of teaching — **ped·a·gog·ic** **ped·a·gog·i·cal** *adj* — **ped·a·gogue** *n*

ped·al *n* : lever worked by the foot ~ *adj* : relating to the foot ~ *vb* : use a pedal

ped·ant *n* : learned bore — **pe·dan·tic** *adj* — **ped·ant·ry** *n*

ped·dle *vb* **-dled; -dling** : offer for sale — **ped·dler** *n*

ped·es·tal *n* : support or foot of something upright

pe·des·tri·an *adj* **1** : ordinary **2** : walking ~ *n* : person who walks

pe·di·at·rics *n* : branch of medicine dealing with children — **pe·di·at·ric** *adj* — **pe·di·a·tri·cian** *n*

ped·i·gree *n* : line of ancestors or a record of it

ped·i·ment *n* : triangular gablelike decoration on a building

peek *vb* **1** : look furtively **2** : glance — **peek** *n*

peel *vb* **1** : strip the skin or rind from **2** : lose the outer layer ~ *n* : skin or rind — **peel·ing** *n*

¹peep *vb or n* : cheep

²peep *vb* **1** : look slyly **2** : begin to emerge ~ *n* : brief look — **peep·er** *n* — **peep·hole** *n*

¹peer *n* **1** : one's equal **2** : nobleman — **peer·age** *n*

²peer *vb* : look intently or curiously

peer·less *adj* : having no equal

peeve *vb* **peeved; peev·ing** : make resentful ~ *n* : complaint — **peev·ish** *adj* — **peev·ish·ly** *adv* — **peev·ish·ness** *n*

peg *n* : small pinlike piece ~ *vb* **-gg- 1** : put a peg into **2** : fix or mark with or as if with pegs

pei·gnoir *n* : negligee

pe·jo·ra·tive *adj* : having a negative or degrading effect ~ *n* : a degrading word or phrase — **pe·jo·ra·tive·ly** *adv*

pel·i·can *n* : large-billed seabird

pel·la·gra *n* : protein-deficiency disease

pel·let *n* : little ball — **pel·let·al** *adj* — **pel·let·ize** *vb*

pell–mell *adv* : in confusion or haste

pel·lu·cid *adj* : very clear

¹pelt *n* : skin of a fur-bearing animal

²pelt *vb* : strike with blows or missiles

pel·vis *n, pl* **-vis·es** *or* **-ves** : cavity formed by the hip bones — **pel·vic** *adj*

¹pen *n* : enclosure for animals ~ *vb* **-nn-** : shut in a pen

²pen *n* : tool for writing with ink ~ *vb* **-nn-** : write

pe·nal *adj* : relating to punishment

pe·nal·ize *vb* **-ized; -iz·ing** : put a penalty on

pen·al·ty *n, pl* **-ties 1** : punishment for crime **2** : disadvantage, loss, or hardship due to an action

pen·ance *n* : act performed to show repentance

pence *pl of* PENNY

pen·chant *n* : strong inclination

pen·cil *n* : writing or drawing tool with a solid marking substance (as graphite) as its core ~ *vb* **-ciled** *or* **-cilled; -cil·ing** *or* **-cil·ling** : draw or write with a pencil

pen·dant *n* : hanging ornament

pen·dent, pen·dant *adj* : hanging

pend·ing *prep* : while awaiting ~ *adj* : not yet decided

pen·du·lous *adj* : hanging loosely

pen·du·lum *n* : a hanging weight that is free to swing

pen·e·trate *vb* **-trat·ed; -trat·ing 1** : enter into **2** : permeate **3** : see into — **pen·e·tra·ble** *adj* — **pen·e·tra·tion** *n* — **pen·e·tra·tive** *adj*

pen·guin *n* : short-legged flightless seabird

pen·i·cil·lin *n* : antibiotic usu. produced by a mold

pen·in·su·la *n* : land extending out into the water — **pen·in·su·lar** *adj*

pe·nis *n, pl* **-nes** *or* **-nis·es** : male organ of copulation

pen·i·tent *adj* : feeling sorrow for sins or offenses ~ *n* : penitent person — **pen·i·tence** *n* — **pen·i·ten·tial** *adj*

pen·i·ten·tia·ry *n, pl* **-ries** : state or federal prison

pen·man·ship *n* : art or practice of writing

pen·nant *n* : nautical or championship flag

pen·ny *n, pl* **-nies** *or* **pence 1** : monetary unit equal to 1/100 pound **2** *pl* **-nies** : cent — **pen·ni·less** *adj*

pen·sion *n* : retirement income ~ *vb* : pay a pension to — **pen·sion·er** *n*

pen·sive *adj* : thoughtful — **pen·sive·ly** *adv*

pent *adj* : confined

pent·a·gon *n* : 5-sided polygon — **pen·tag·o·nal** *adj*

pen·tam·e·ter *n* : line of verse containing 5 metrical feet

pent·house *n* : rooftop apartment

pen·u·ry *n* **1** : poverty **2** : thrifty or stingy manner — **pe·nu·ri·ous** *adj*

pe·on *n, pl* **-ons** *or* **-o·nes** : landless laborer in Spanish America — **pe·on·age** *n*

pe·o·ny *n, pl* **-nies** : garden plant having large flowers

peo·ple *n, pl* **people 1** *pl* : human beings in general **2** *pl* : human beings in a certain group (as a family) or community **3** *pl* **peoples** : tribe, nation, or race ~ *vb* **-pled; -pling** : constitute the population of

pep *n* : brisk energy ~ *vb* **pepped; pep·ping** : put pep into — **pep·py** *adj*

pep·per *n* **1** : pungent seasoning from the berry (**peppercorn**) of a shrub **2** : vegetable grown for its hot or sweet fruit ~ *vb* : season with pepper — **pep·pery** *adj*

pep·per·mint *n* : pungent aromatic mint

pep·per·o·ni *n* : spicy beef and pork sausage

pep·tic *adj* : relating to digestion or the effect of digestive juices

per *prep* **1** : by means of **2** : for each **3** : according to

per·am·bu·late *vb* **-lat·ed; -lat·ing** : walk — **per·am·bu·la·tion** *n*

per·cale *n* : fine woven cotton cloth

per·ceive *vb* **-ceived; -ceiv·ing 1** : realize **2** : become aware of through the senses — **per·ceiv·able** *adj*

per·cent *adv* : in each hundred ~ *n, pl* **-cent** *or* **-cents 1** : one part in a hundred **2** : percentage

per·cent·age *n* : part expressed in hundredths

per·cen·tile *n* : standing on a scale of 0–100

per·cep·ti·ble *adj* : capable of being perceived — **per·cep·ti·bly** *adv*

per·cep·tion *n* **1** : act or result of perceiving **2** : ability to understand

per·cep·tive *adj* : showing keen perception — **per·cep·tive·ly** *adv*

¹perch *n* : roost for birds ~ *vb* : roost

²perch *n, pl* **perch** *or* **perch·es** : freshwater spiny-finned food fish

per·co·late *vb* **-lat·ed; -lat·ing** : trickle or filter down through a substance — **per·co·la·tor** *n*

per·cus·sion *n* **1** : sharp blow **2** : musical instrument sounded by striking

pe•remp•to•ry adj 1 : imperative 2 : domineering — **pe•remp•to•ri•ly** adv

pe•ren•ni•al adj 1 : present at all seasons 2 : continuing from year to year 3 : recurring regularly ~ n : perennial plant — **pe•ren•ni•al•ly** adv

per•fect adj 1 : being without fault or defect 2 : exact 3 : complete ~ vb : make perfect — **per•fect•ibil•i•ty** n — **per•fect•ible** adj — **per•fect•ly** adv — **per•fect•ness** n

per•fec•tion n 1 : quality or state of being perfect 2 : highest degree of excellence — **per•fec•tion•ist** n

per•fid•i•ous adj : treacherous — **per•fid•i•ous•ly** adv

per•fo•rate vb -rat•ed; -rat•ing : make a hole in — **per•fo•ra•tion** n

per•force adv : of necessity

per•form vb 1 : carry out 2 : do in a set manner 3 : give a performance — **per•form•er** n

per•for•mance n 1 : act or process of performing 2 : public presentation

per•fume n 1 : pleasant odor 2 : something that gives a scent ~ vb -fumed; -fum•ing : add scent to

per•func•to•ry adj : done merely as a duty — **per•func•to•ri•ly** adv

per•haps adv : possibly but not certainly

per•il n : danger — **per•il•ous** adj — **per•il•ous•ly** adv

pe•rim•e•ter n : outer boundary of a body or figure

pe•ri•od n 1 : punctuation mark . used esp. to mark the end of a declarative sentence or an abbreviation 2 : division of time 3 : stage in a process or development

pe•ri•od•ic adj : occurring at regular intervals — **pe•ri•od•i•cal•ly** adv

pe•ri•od•i•cal n : newspaper or magazine

pe•riph•ery n, pl -er•ies : outer boundary — **pe•riph•er•al** adj

peri•scope n : optical instrument for viewing from a submarine

per•ish vb : die or spoil — **per•ish•able** adj or n

per•ju•ry n : lying under oath — **per•jure** vb — **per•jur•er** n

¹**perk** vb 1 : thrust (as the head) up jauntily 2 : freshen 3 : gain vigor or spirit — **perky** adj

²**perk** vb : percolate

³**perk** n : privilege or benefit in addition to regular pay

per•ma•nent adj : lasting ~ n : hair wave — **per•ma•nence** n — **per•ma•nent•ly** adv

per•me•able adj : permitting fluids to seep through — **per•me•a•bil•i•ty** n

per•me•ate vb -at•ed; -at•ing 1 : seep through 2 : pervade — **per•me•ation** n

per•mis•si•ble adj : that may be permitted

per•mis•sion n : formal consent

per•mis•sive adj : granting freedom esp. to excess — **per•miss•ive•ly** adv — **per•mis•sive•ness** n

per•mit vb -tt- 1 : approve 2 : make possible ~ n : license

per•ni•cious adj : very harmful — **per•ni•cious•ly** adv

per•ox•ide n : compound (as hydrogen peroxide) in which oxygen is joined to oxygen

per•pen•dic•u•lar adj 1 : vertical 2 : meeting at a right angle — **perpendicular** n — **per•pen•dic•u•lar•i•ty** n — **per•pen•dic•u•lar•ly** adv

per•pe•trate vb -trat•ed; -trat•ing : be guilty of doing — **per•pe•tra•tion** n — **per•pe•tra•tor** n

per•pet•u•al adj 1 : continuing forever 2 : occurring continually — **per•pet•u•al•ly** adv — **per•pe•tu•ity** n

per•pet•u•ate vb -at•ed; -at•ing : make perpetual — **per•pet•u•a•tion** n

per•plex vb : confuse — **per•plex•i•ty** n

per•se•cute vb -cut•ed; -cut•ing : harass, afflict — **per•se•cu•tion** n — **per•se•cu•tor** n

per•se•vere vb -vered; -ver•ing : persist — **per•se•ver•ance** n

per•sist vb 1 : go on resolutely in spite of difficulties 2 : continue to exist — **per•sis•tence** n — **per•sis•ten•cy** n — **per•sis•tent** adj — **per•sis•tent•ly** adv

per•son n 1 : human being 2 : human being's body or individuality 3 : reference to the speaker, one spoken to, or one spoken of

per•son•able adj : having a pleasing personality

per•son•age n : person of rank or distinction

per•son•al adj 1 : relating to a particular person 2 : done in person 3 : affecting one's body 4 : offensive to a certain individual — **per•son•al•ly** adv

per•son•al•i•ty n, pl -ties 1 : manner and disposition of an individual 2 : distinctive or well-known person

per•son•al•ize vb -ized; -iz•ing : mark as belonging to a particular person

per•son•i•fy vb -fied; -fy•ing 1 : represent as a human being 2 : be the embodiment of — **per•son•i•fi•ca•tion** n

per•son•nel n : body of persons employed

per•spec•tive n 1 : apparent depth and distance in painting 2 : view of things in their true relationship or importance

per•spi•ca•cious adj : showing keen understanding or discernment — **per•spi•cac•i•ty** n

per•spire vb -spired; -spir•ing : sweat — **per•spi•ra•tion** n

per•suade vb -suad•ed; -suad•ing : win over to a belief or course of action by argument or entreaty — **per•sua•sion** n — **per•sua•sive** adj — **per•sua•sive•ly** adv — **per•sua•sive•ness** n

pert adj : flippant or irreverent

per•tain vb 1 : belong 2 : relate

per•ti•nent adj : relevant — **per•ti•nence** n

per•turb vb : make uneasy — **per•tur•ba•tion** n

pe•ruse vb -rused; -rus•ing : read attentively — **pe•rus•al** n

per•vade vb -vad•ed; -vad•ing : spread through every part of — **per•va•sive** adj

per•verse adj 1 : corrupt 2 : unreasonably contrary — **per•verse•ly** adv — **per•verse•ness** n — **per•ver•sion** n — **per•ver•si•ty** n

per•vert vb : corrupt or distort ~ n : one that is perverted

pe•so n, pl -sos : monetary unit (as of Mexico)

pes•si•mism n : inclination to expect the worst — **pes•si•mist** n — **pes•si•mis•tic** adj

pest n 1 : nuisance 2 : plant or animal detrimental to humans or their crops — **pes•ti•cide** n

pes•ter vb -tered; -ter•ing : harass with petty matters

pes•ti•lence n : plague — **pes•ti•lent** adj

pes•tle n : implement for grinding substances in a mortar

pet n 1 : domesticated animal kept for pleasure 2 : favorite ~ vb -tt- : stroke gently or lovingly

pet•al n : modified leaf of a flower head

pe•tite adj : having a small trim figure

pe•ti•tion n : formal written request ~ vb : make a request — **pe•ti•tion•er** n

pet•ri•fy vb -fied; -fy•ing 1 : change into stony material 2 : make rigid or inactive (as from fear) — **pet•ri•fac•tion** n

pe•tro•leum n : raw oil obtained from the ground

pet•ti•coat n : skirt worn under a dress

pet•ty adj -ti•er; -est 1 : minor 2 : of no importance 3 : narrow-minded or mean — **pet•ti•ly** adv — **pet•ti•ness** n

petty officer n : subordinate officer in the navy or coast guard

pet•u•lant adj : irritable — **pet•u•lance** n — **pet•u•lant•ly** adv

pe•tu•nia n : tropical herb with bright flowers

pew n : bench with a back used in a church

pew•ter n : alloy of tin used for household utensils

pH n : number expressing relative acidity and alkalinity

pha•lanx n, pl -lanx•es or -lan•ges 1 : body (as of troops) in compact formation 2 pl phalanges : digital bone of the hand or foot

phal•lus n, pl -li or -lus•es : penis — **phal•lic** adj

phantasy var of FANTASY

phan•tom n : something that only appears to be real — **phantom** adj

pha•raoh n : ruler of ancient Egypt

phar•ma•ceu•ti•cal adj : relating to pharmacy or the making and selling of medicinal drugs — **pharmaceutical** n

phar•ma•col•o•gy n : science of drugs esp. as related to medicinal uses — **phar•ma•co•log•i•cal** adj — **phar•ma•col•o•gist** n

phar•ma•cy n, pl -cies 1 : art or practice of preparing and dispensing medical drugs 2 : drugstore — **phar•ma•cist** n

phar•ynx n, pl -ynx•es or pha•ryn•ges : space behind the mouth into which the nostrils, esophagus, and windpipe open — **pha•ryn•ge•al** adj

phase n 1 : particular appearance or stage in a recurring series of changes 2 : stage in a process — **phase in** vb : introduce in stages — **phase out** vb : discontinue gradually

pheas•ant n, pl -ant or -ants : long-tailed brilliantly colored game bird

phe•nom•e•non n, pl -na or -nons 1 : observable fact or event 2 pl -nons : prodigy — **phe•nom•e•nal** adj

phi•lan•der•er n : one who makes love without serious intent

phi•lan•thro•py n, pl -pies : charitable act or gift or an organization that distributes such gifts — **phil•an•throp•ic** adj — **phi•lan•thro•pist** n

phi•lat•e•ly n : collection and study of postage stamps — **phi•lat•e•list** n

phi•lis•tine n : one who is smugly indifferent to intellectual or artistic values — **philistine** adj

philo•den•dron n, pl -drons or -dra : plant grown for its showy leaves

phi•los•o•pher n 1 : reflective thinker 2 : student of philosophy

phi•los•o•phy n, pl -phies 1 : critical study of fundamental beliefs 2 : sciences and liberal arts exclusive of medicine, law, and theology 3 : system of ideas 4 : sum of personal convictions — **phil•o•soph•ic** **phil•o•soph•i•cal** adj — **phil•o•soph•i•cal•ly** adv — **phi•los•o•phize** vb

phle•bi•tis n : inflammation of a vein

phlegm n : thick mucus in the nose and throat

phlox n, pl phlox or phlox•es : herb grown for its flower clusters

pho•bia n : irrational persistent fear

phoe•nix n : legendary bird held to burn itself to death and rise fresh and young from its ashes

phone n : telephone ~ vb **phoned; phon•ing** : call on a telephone

pho•neme n : basic distinguishable unit of speech — **pho•ne•mic** adj

pho•net•ics n : study of speech sounds — **pho•net•ic** adj — **pho•ne•ti•cian** n

pho•nics n : method of teaching reading by stressing sound values of syllables and words

pho•no•graph n : instrument that reproduces sounds from a grooved disc

pho•ny, pho•ney adj -ni•er; -est : not sincere or genuine — **phony** n

phos•phate n : chemical salt used in fertilizers — **phos•phat•ic** adj

phos•phor n : phosphorescent substance

phos•pho•res•cence n : luminescence from absorbed radiation — **phos•pho•res•cent** adj — **phos•pho•res•cent•ly** adv

phos·pho·rus *n* : poisonous waxy chemical element — **phos·phor·ic** *adj* — **phos·pho·rous** *adj*

pho·to *n, pl* **-tos** : photograph — **photo** *vb or adj*

pho·to·copy *n* : photographic copy (as of a printed page) — **photocopy** *vb*

pho·to·elec·tric *adj* : relating to an electrical effect due to the interaction of light with matter

pho·to·gen·ic *adj* : suitable for being photographed

pho·to·graph *n* : picture taken by photography — **photograph** *vb* — **pho·tog·ra·pher** *n*

pho·tog·ra·phy *n* : process of using light to produce images on a sensitized surface — **pho·to·graph·ic** *adj* — **pho·to·graph·i·cal·ly** *adv*

pho·to·syn·the·sis *n* : formation of carbohydrates by chlorophyll-containing plants exposed to sunlight — **pho·to·syn·the·size** *vb* — **pho·to·syn·thet·ic** *adj*

phrase *n* **1** : brief expression **2** : group of related words that express a thought ~ *vb* **phrased**; **phras·ing** : express in a particular manner

phrase·ol·o·gy *n, pl* **-gies** : manner of phrasing

phy·lum *n, pl* **-la** : major division of the plant or animal kingdom

phys·i·cal *adj* **1** : relating to nature **2** : material as opposed to mental or spiritual **3** : relating to the body ~ *n* : medical examination — **phys·i·cal·ly** *adv*

phy·si·cian *n* : doctor of medicine

physician's assistant *n* : person certified to provide basic medical care under a physician's supervision

phys·i·cist *n* : specialist in physics

phys·ics *n* : science that deals with matter and motion

phys·i·og·no·my *n, pl* **-mies** : facial appearance esp. as a reflection of inner character

phys·i·ol·o·gy *n* : functional processes in an organism — **phys·i·o·log·i·cal phys·i·o·log·ic** *adj* — **phys·i·ol·o·gist** *n*

phy·sique *n* : build of a person's body

pi *n, pl* **pis** : symbol π denoting the ratio of the circumference of a circle to its diameter or the ratio itself

pi·a·nist *n* : one who plays the piano

pi·ano *n, pl* **-anos** : musical instrument with strings sounded by hammers operated from a keyboard

pi·az·za *n, pl* **-zas** *or* **-ze** : public square in a town

pic·a·yune *adj* : trivial or petty

pic·co·lo *n, pl* **-los** : small shrill flute

¹pick *vb* **1** : break up with a pointed instrument **2** : remove bit by bit **3** : gather by plucking **4** : select **5** : rob **6** : provoke **7** : unlock with a wire **8** : eat sparingly ~ *n* **1** : act of choosing **2** : choicest one — **pick·er** *n* — **pick up** *vb* **1** : improve **2** : put in order

²pick *n* : pointed digging tool

pick·ax *n* : pick

pick·er·el *n, pl* **-el** *or* **-els** : small pike

pick·et *n* **1** : pointed stake (as for a fence) **2** : worker demonstrating on strike ~ *vb* : demonstrate as a picket

pick·le *n* **1** : brine or vinegar solution for preserving foods or a food preserved in a pickle **2** : bad state — **pickle** *vb*

pick·pock·et *n* : one who steals from pockets

pick·up *n* **1** : revival or acceleration **2** : light truck with an open body

pic·nic *n* : outing with food usu. eaten in the open ~ *vb* **-nicked**; **-nick·ing** : go on a picnic

pic·to·ri·al *adj* : relating to pictures

pic·ture *n* **1** : representation by painting, drawing, or photography **2** : vivid description **3** : copy **4** : movie ~ *vb* **-tured**; **-tur·ing** : form a mental image of

pic·tur·esque *adj* : attractive or charming enough for a picture — **pic·tur·esque·ness** *n*

pie *n* : pastry crust and a filling

pie·bald *adj* : blotched with white and black

piece *n* **1** : part of a whole **2** : one of a group or set **3** : single item **4** : product of creative work ~ *vb* **pieced**; **piec·ing** : join into a whole

piece·meal *adv or adj* : gradually

pied *adj* : colored in blotches

pier *n* **1** : support for a bridge span **2** : deck or wharf built out over water **3** : pillar

pierce *vb* **pierced**; **pierc·ing 1** : enter or thrust into or through **2** : penetrate **3** : see through

pi·ety *n, pl* **-eties** : devotion to religion

pig *n* **1** : young swine **2** : dirty or greedy individual **3** : iron casting — **pig·gish** *adj* — **pig·let** *n* — **pig·pen** *n* — **pig·sty** *n*

pi·geon *n* : stout-bodied short-legged bird

pi·geon·hole *n* : small open compartment for letters or documents ~ *vb* **1** : place in a pigeonhole **2** : classify

pig·gy·back *adv or adj* : up on the back and shoulders

pig·head·ed *adj* : stubborn

pig·ment *n* : coloring matter — **pig·men·ta·tion** *n*

pigmy *var of* PYGMY

pig·tail *n* : tight braid of hair

¹pike *n, pl* **pike** *or* **pikes** : large freshwater fish

²pike *n* : former weapon consisting of a long wooden staff with a steel point

³pike *n* : turnpike

pi·laf, pi·laff, pi·lau *n* : dish of seasoned rice

¹pile *n* : supporting pillar driven into the ground

²pile *n* : quantity of things thrown on one another ~ *vb* **piled**; **pil·ing** : heap up, accumulate

³pile *n* : surface of fine hairs or threads — **piled** *adj*

piles *n pl* : hemorrhoids

pil·fer *vb* : steal in small quantities

pil·grim *n* **1** : one who travels to a shrine or holy place in devotion **2** *cap* : one of the English settlers in America in 1620

pil·grim·age *n* : pilgrim's journey

pill *n* : small rounded mass of medicine — **pill·box** *n*

pil·lage *vb* **-laged**; **-lag·ing** : loot and plunder — **pillage** *n*

pil·lar *n* : upright usu. supporting column — **pil·lared** *adj*

pil·lo·ry *n, pl* **-ries** : wooden frame for public punishment with holes for the head and hands ~ *vb* **-ried**; **-ry·ing 1** : set in a pillory **2** : expose to public scorn

pil·low *n* : soft cushion for the head — **pil·low·case** *n*

pi·lot *n* **1** : helmsman **2** : person licensed to take ships into and out of a port **3** : guide **4** : one that flies an aircraft or spacecraft ~ *vb* : act as pilot of — **pi·lot·less** *adj*

pi·men·to *n, pl* **-tos** *or* **-to 1** : allspice **2** : pimiento

pi·mien·to *n, pl* **-tos** : mild red sweet pepper

pimp *n* : man who solicits clients for a prostitute — **pimp** *vb*

pim·ple *n* : small inflamed swelling on the skin — **pim·ply** *adj*

pin *n* **1** : fastener made of a small pointed piece of wire **2** : ornament or emblem fastened to clothing with a pin **3** : wooden object used as a target in bowling ~ *vb* **-nn- 1** : fasten with a pin **2** : hold fast or immobile — **pin·hole** *n*

pin·a·fore *n* : sleeveless dress or apron fastened at the back

pin·cer *n* **1** *pl* : gripping tool with 2 jaws **2** : pincerlike claw

pinch *vb* **1** : squeeze between the finger and thumb or between the jaws of a tool **2** : compress painfully **3** : restrict **4** : steal ~ *n* **1** : emergency

2 : painful effect **3** : act of pinching **4** : very small quantity

pin·cush·ion *n* : cushion for storing pins

¹pine *n* : evergreen cone-bearing tree or its wood

²pine *vb* **pined**; **pin·ing 1** : lose health through distress **2** : yearn for intensely

pine·ap·ple *n* : tropical plant bearing an edible juicy fruit

pin·feath·er *n* : new feather just coming through the skin

¹pinion *vb* : restrain by binding the arms

²pinion *n* : small gear

¹pink *n* **1** : plant with narrow leaves and showy flowers **2** : highest degree

²pink *n* : light red color — **pink** *adj* — **pink·ish** *adj*

pink·eye *n* : contagious eye inflammation

pin·na·cle *n* : highest point

pi·noch·le *n* : card game played with a 48-card deck

pin·point *vb* : locate, hit, or aim with great precision

pint *n* : 1/2 quart

pin·to *n, pl* **pintos** : spotted horse or pony

pin·worm *n* : small parasitic intestinal worm

pi·o·neer *n* **1** : one that originates or helps open up a new line of thought or activity **2** : early settler ~ *vb* : act as a pioneer

pi·ous *adj* **1** : conscientious in religious practices **2** : affectedly religious — **pi·ous·ly** *adv*

pipe *n* **1** : tube that produces music when air is forced through **2** : bagpipe **3** : long tube for conducting a fluid **4** : smoking tool ~ *vb* **piped**; **pip·ing 1** : play on a pipe **2** : speak in a high voice **3** : convey by pipes — **pip·er** *n*

pipe·line *n* **1** : line of pipe **2** : channel for information

pip·ing *n* **1** : music of pipes **2** : narrow fold of material used to decorate edges or seams

pi·quant *adj* **1** : tangy **2** : provocative or charming — **pi·quan·cy** *n*

pique *n* : resentment ~ *vb* **piqued**; **piqu·ing 1** : offend **2** : arouse by provocation

pi·qué, pi·que *n* : durable ribbed clothing fabric

pi·ra·cy *n, pl* **-cies 1** : robbery on the seas **2** : unauthorized use of another's production or invention

pi·ra·nha *n* : small So. American fish with sharp teeth

pi·rate *n* : one who commits piracy — **pirate** *vb* — **pi·rat·i·cal** *adj*

pir·ou·ette *n* : ballet turn on the toe or ball of one foot — **pirouette** *vb*

pis *pl of* PI

pis·ta·chio *n, pl* **-chios** : small tree bearing a greenish edible seed or its seed

pis·til *n* : female reproductive organ in a flower — **pis·til·late** *adj*

pis·tol *n* : firearm held with one hand

pis·ton *n* : sliding piece that receives and transmits motion usu. inside a cylinder

¹pit *n* **1** : hole or shaft in the ground **2** : sunken or enclosed place for a special purpose **3** : hell **4** : hollow or indentation ~ *vb* **-tt- 1** : form pits in **2** : become marred with pits

²pit *n* : stony seed of some fruits ~ *vb* **-tt-** : remove the pit from

pit bull *n* : powerful compact dog bred for fighting

¹pitch *n* : resin from conifers — **pitchy** *adj*

²pitch *vb* **1** : erect and fix firmly in place **2** : throw **3** : set at a particular tone level **4** : fall headlong ~ *n* **1** : action or manner of pitching **2** : degree of slope **3** : relative highness of a tone **4** : sales talk — **pitched** *adj*

¹pitch·er *n* : container for liquids

²pitch·er *n* : one that pitches (as in baseball)

pitch·fork *n* : long-handled fork for pitching hay

pit·e·ous *adj* : arousing pity — **pit·e·ous·ly** *adv*

pit·fall *n* : hidden danger

pith *n* **1** : spongy plant tissue **2** : essential or meaningful part — **pithy** *adj*

piti·able *adj* : pitiful

piti·ful *adj* **1** : arousing or deserving pity **2** : contemptible — **piti·ful·ly** *adv*

pit·tance *n* : small portion or amount

pi·tu·itary *adj* : relating to or being a small gland attached to the brain

pity *n, pl* **pi·ties 1** : sympathetic sorrow **2** : something to be regretted ~ *vb* **pit·ied; pity·ing** : feel pity for — **piti·less** *adj* — **piti·less·ly** *adv*

piv·ot *n* : fixed pin on which something turns ~ *vb* : turn on or as if on a pivot — **piv·ot·al** *adj*

pix·ie, pixy *n, pl* **pix·ies** : mischievous sprite

piz·za *n* : thin pie of bread dough spread with a spiced mixture (as of tomatoes, cheese, and meat)

piz·zazz, pi·zazz *n* : glamour

piz·ze·ria *n* : pizza restaurant

plac·ard *n* : poster ~ *vb* : display placards in or on

pla·cate *vb* **-cat·ed; -cat·ing** : appease — **pla·ca·ble** *adj*

place *n* **1** : space or room **2** : indefinite area **3** : a particular building, locality, area, or part **4** : relative position in a scale or se- quence **5** : seat **6** : job ~ *vb* **placed; plac·ing 1** : put in a place **2** : iden- tify — **place·ment** *n*

place·bo *n, pl* **-bos** : something inactive prescribed as a remedy for its psychological effect

pla·cen·ta *n, pl* **-tas** *or* **-tae** : structure in a uterus by which a fetus is nourished — **pla·cen·tal** *adj*

plac·id *adj* : undisturbed or peaceful — **pla·cid·i·ty** *n* — **plac·id·ly** *adv*

pla·gia·rize *vb* **-rized; -riz·ing** : use (words or ideas) of another as if your own — **pla·gia·rism** *n* — **pla·gia·rist** *n*

plague *n* **1** : disastrous evil **2** : destructive contagious bacterial disease ~ *vb* **plagued; plagu·ing 1** : afflict with disease or disaster **2** : harass

plaid *n* : woolen fabric with a pattern of crossing stripes or the pattern itself — **plaid** *adj*

plain *n* : expanse of relatively level treeless country ~ *adj* **1** : lacking ornament **2** : not concealed or disguised **3** : easily understood **4** : frank **5** : not fancy or pretty — **plain·ly** *adv* — **plain·ness** *n*

plain·tiff *n* : complaining party in a lawsuit

plain·tive *adj* : expressive of suffering or woe — **plain·tive·ly** *adv*

plait *n* **1** : pleat **2** : braid of hair or straw — **plait** *vb*

plan *n* **1** : drawing or diagram **2** : method for accomplishing something ~ *vb* **-nn- 1** : form a plan of **2** : intend — **plan·less** *adj* — **plan·ner** *n*

¹**plane** *vb* **planed; plan·ing** : smooth or level off with a plane ~ *n* : smoothing or shaping tool — **plan·er** *n*

²**plane** *n* **1** : level surface **2** : level of existence, consciousness, or development **3** : airplane ~ *adj* **1** : flat **2** : dealing with flat surfaces or figures

plan·et *n* : celestial body that revolves around the sun — **plan·e·tary** *adj*

plan·e·tar·i·um *n, pl* **-iums** *or* **-ia** : building or room housing a device to project images of celestial bodies

plank *n* **1** : heavy thick board **2** : article in the platform of a political party — **plank·ing** *n*

plank·ton *n* : tiny aquatic animal and plant life — **plank·ton·ic** *adj*

plant *vb* **1** : set in the ground to grow **2** : place firmly or forcibly ~ *n* **1** : living thing without sense organs that cannot move about **2** : land, buildings, and machinery used esp. in manufacture

¹**plan·tain** *n* : short-stemmed herb with tiny greenish flowers

²**plantain** *n* : banana plant with starchy greenish fruit

plan·ta·tion *n* : agricultural estate usu. worked by resident laborers

plant·er *n* **1** : plantation owner **2** : plant container

plaque *n* **1** : commemorative tablet **2** : film layer on a tooth

plas·ma *n* : watery part of blood — **plas·mat·ic** *adj*

plas·ter *n* **1** : medicated dressing **2** : hardening paste for coating walls and ceilings ~ *vb* : cover with plaster — **plas·ter·er** *n*

plas·tic *adj* : capable of being molded ~ *n* : material that can be formed into rigid objects, films, or filaments — **plas·tic·i·ty** *n*

plate *n* **1** : flat thin piece **2** : plated metalware **3** : shallow usu. circular dish **4** : denture or the part of it that fits to the mouth **5** : something printed from an engraving ~ *vb* **plat·ed; plat·ing** : overlay with metal — **plat·ing** *n*

pla·teau *n, pl* **-teaus** *or* **-teaux** : large level area of high land

plat·form *n* **1** : raised flooring or stage **2** : declaration of principles for a political party

plat·i·num *n* : heavy grayish-white metallic chemical element

plat·i·tude *n* : trite remark — **plat·i·tu·di·nous** *adj*

pla·toon *n* : small military unit

platoon sergeant *n* : noncommissioned officer in the army ranking below a first sergeant

plat·ter *n* : large serving plate

platy·pus *n* : small aquatic egg-laying mammal

plau·dit *n* : act of applause

plau·si·ble *adj* : reasonable or believable — **plau·si·bil·i·ty** *n* — **plau·si·bly** *adv*

play *n* **1** : action in a game **2** : recreational activity **3** : light or fitful movement **4** : free movement **5** : stage representation of a drama ~ *vb* **1** : engage in recreation **2** : move or toy with aimlessly **3** : perform music **4** : act in a drama — **play·act·ing** *n* — **play·er** *n* — **play·ful** *adj* — **play·ful·ly** *adv* — **play·ful·ness** *n* — **play·pen** *n* — **play·suit** *n* — **play·thing** *n*

play·ground *n* : place for children to play

play·house *n* **1** : theater **2** : small house for children to play in

playing card *n* : one of a set of 24 to 78 cards marked to show its rank and suit and used to play a game of cards

play·mate *n* : companion in play

play·off *n* : contest or series of contests to determine a champion

play·wright *n* : writer of plays

pla·za *n* **1** : public square **2** : shopping mall

plea *n* **1** : defendant's answer to charges **2** : urgent request

plead *vb* **plead·ed** *or* **pled; plead·ing 1** : argue for or against in court **2** : answer to a charge or indictment **3** : appeal earnestly — **plead·er** *n*

pleas·ant *adj* **1** : giving pleasure **2** : marked by pleasing behavior or appearance — **pleas·ant·ly** *adv* — **pleas·ant·ness** *n*

pleas·ant·ries *n pl* : pleasant and casual conversation

please *vb* **pleased; pleas·ing 1** : give pleasure or satisfaction to **2** : desire or intend

pleas·ing *adj* : giving pleasure — **pleas·ing·ly** *adv*

plea·sur·able *adj* : pleasant — **plea·sur·ably** *adv*

plea·sure *n* **1** : desire or inclination **2** : enjoyment **3** : source of delight

pleat *vb* : arrange in pleats ~ *n* : fold in cloth

ple·be·ian *n* : one of the common people ~ *adj* : ordinary

pledge *n* **1** : something given as security **2** : promise or vow ~ *vb* **pledged; pledg·ing 1** : offer as or bind by a pledge **2** : promise

ple·na·ry *adj* : full

pleni·po·ten·tia·ry *n* : diplomatic agent having full authority — **plenipotenti·ary** *adj*

plen·i·tude *n* **1** : completeness **2** : abundance

plen·te·ous *adj* : existing in plenty

plen·ty *n* : more than adequate number or amount — **plen·ti·ful** *adj* — **plen·ti·ful·ly** *adv*

pleth·o·ra *n* : excess

pleu·ri·sy *n* : inflammation of the chest membrane

pli·able *adj* : flexible

pli·ant *adj* : flexible — **pli·an·cy** *n*

pli·ers *n pl* : pinching or gripping tool

¹**plight** *vb* : pledge

²**plight** *n* : bad state

plod *vb* **-dd- 1** : walk heavily or slowly **2** : work laboriously and monotonously — **plod·der** *n* — **plod·ding·ly** *adv*

plot *n* **1** : small area of ground **2** : ground plan **3** : main story development (as of a book or movie) **4** : secret plan for doing something ~ *vb* **-tt- 1** : make a plot or plan of **2** : plan or contrive — **plot·ter** *n*

plo·ver *n, pl* **-ver** *or* **-vers** : shorebird related to the sandpiper

plow, plough *n* **1** : tool used to turn soil **2** : device for pushing material aside ~ *vb* **1** : break up with a plow **2** : cleave or move through like a plow — **plow·man** *n*

plow·share *n* : plow part that cuts the earth

ploy *n* : clever maneuver

pluck *vb* **1** : pull off or out **2** : tug or twitch ~ *n* **1** : act or instance of plucking **2** : spirit or courage

plucky *adj* **pluck·i·er; -est** : courageous or spirited

plug *n* **1** : something for sealing an opening **2** : electrical connector at the end of a cord **3** : piece of favorable publicity ~ *vb* **-gg- 1** : stop or make tight or secure by inserting a plug **2** : publicize

plum *n* **1** : smooth-skinned juicy fruit **2** : fine reward

plum·age *n* : feathers of a bird **plum·aged** *adj*

plumb *n* : weight on the end of a line (**plumb line**) to show vertical direction ~ *adv* **1** : vertically **2** : completely ~ *vb* : sound or test with a plumb ~ *adj* : vertical

plumb·er *n* : one who repairs usu. water pipes and fixtures

plumb·ing *n* : system of water pipes in a building

plume *n* : large, conspicuous, or showy feather ~ *vb* **plumed; plum·ing 1** : provide or deck with feathers **2** : indulge in pride — **plumed** *adj*

plum·met *vb* : drop straight down

¹**plump** *vb* : drop suddenly or heavily ~ *adv* **1** : straight down **2** : in a direct manner

²**plump** *adj* : having a full rounded form — **plump·ness** *n*

plun·der *vb* : rob or take goods by force (as in war) ~ *n* : something taken in plundering — **plun·der·er** *n*

plunge *vb* **plunged; plung·ing 1** : thrust or drive with force **2** : leap or dive into water **3** : begin an action suddenly **4** : dip or move suddenly forward or down ~ *n* : act or instance of plunging — **plung·er** *n*

plu·ral *adj* : relating to a word form denoting more than one — **plu·ral** *n*

plu·ral·i·ty *n, pl* **-ties** : greatest number of votes cast when not a majority

plu·ral·ize *vb* **-ized; -iz·ing** : make plural — **plu·ral·i·za·tion** *n*

plus *prep* : with the addition of ~ *n* **1** : sign + (**plus sign**) in mathematics to indicate addition **2** : added or positive quantity **3** : advantage ~ *adj* : being more or in addition — *conj* : and

plush *n* : fabric with a long pile ~ *adj* : luxurious — **plush·ly** *adv* — **plushy** *adj* — **plush·ness** *n*

plu·toc·ra·cy *n, pl* **-cies 1** : government by the wealthy **2** : a controlling class of the wealthy — **plu·to·crat** *n* — **plu·to·crat·ic** *adj*

plu·to·ni·um *n* : radioactive chemical element

¹**ply** *n, pl* **plies** : fold, thickness, or strand of which something is made

²**ply** *vb* **plied; ply·ing 1** : use or work at **2** : keep supplying something to **3** : travel regularly usu. by sea

ply·wood *n* : sheets of wood glued and pressed together

pneu·mat·ic *adj* **1** : moved by air pressure **2** : filled with compressed air — **pneu·mat·i·cal·ly** *adv*

pneu·mo·nia *n* : inflammatory lung disease

¹**poach** *vb* : cook in simmering liquid

²**poach** *vb* : hunt or fish illegally — **poach·er** *n*

pock *n* : small swelling on the skin or its scar — **pock·mark** *n* — **pock·marked** *adj*

pock·et *n* **1** : small open bag sewn into a garment **2** : container or receptacle **3** : isolated area or group ~ *vb* : put in a pocket — **pock·et·ful** *n*

pock·et·book *n* **1** : purse **2** : financial resources

pock·et·knife *n* : knife with a folding blade carried in the pocket

pod *n* **1** : dry fruit that splits open when ripe **2** : compartment on a ship or craft

po·di·a·try *n* : branch of medicine dealing with the foot — **po·di·a·trist** *n*

po·di·um *n, pl* **-di·ums** *or* **-dia** : dais

po·em *n* : composition in verse

po·et *n* : writer of poetry

po·et·ry *n* **1** : metrical writing **2** : poems — **po·et·ic, po·et·i·cal** *adj*

po·grom *n* : organized massacre

poi·gnant *adj* **1** : emotionally painful **2** : deeply moving — **poi·gnan·cy** *n*

poin·set·tia *n* : showy tropical American plant

point *n* **1** : individual often essential detail **2** : purpose **3** : particular place, time, or stage **4** : sharp end **5** : projecting piece of land **6** : dot or period **7** : division of the compass **8** : unit of counting ~ *vb* **1** : sharpen **2** : indicate direction by extending a finger **3** : direct attention to **4** : aim — **point·ed·ly** *adv* — **point·less** *adj*

point-blank *adj* **1** : so close to a target that a missile fired goes straight to it **2** : direct — **point-blank** *adv*

point·er *n* **1** : one that points out **2** : large short-haired hunting dog **3** : hint or tip

poise *vb* **poised; pois·ing** : balance ~ *n* : self-possessed calmness

poi·son *n* : chemical that can injure or kill ~ *vb* **1** : injure or kill with poison **2** : apply poison to **3** : affect destructively — **poi·son·er** *n* — **poi·son·ous** *adj*

poke *vb* **poked; pok·ing 1** : prod **2** : dawdle ~ *n* : quick thrust

¹**pok·er** *n* : rod for stirring a fire

²**po·ker** *n* : card game for gambling

po·lar *adj* : relating to a geographical or magnetic pole

po·lar·ize *vb* **-ized; -iz·ing 1** : cause to have magnetic poles **2** : break up into opposing groups — **po·lar·i·za·tion** *n*

¹**pole** *n* : long slender piece of wood or metal

²**pole** *n* **1** : either end of the earth's axis **2** : battery terminal **3** : either end of a magnet

pole·cat *n, pl* **polecats** *or* **polecat 1** : European carnivorous mammal **2** : skunk

po·lem·ics *n sing or pl* : practice of disputation — **po·lem·i·cal** *adj* — **po·lem·i·cist** *n*

po·lice *n, pl* **police 1** : department of government that keeps public order and enforces the laws **2** : members of the police ~ *vb* **-liced; -lic·ing** : regulate and keep in order — **po·lice·man** *n* — **po·lice·wom·an** *n*

police officer *n* : member of the police

¹**pol·i·cy** *n, pl* **-cies** : course of action selected to guide decisions

²**policy** *n, pl* **-cies** : insurance contract — **pol·i·cy·hold·er** *n*

po·lio *n* : poliomyelitis — **polio** *adj*

po·lio·my·eli·tis *n* : acute virus disease of the spinal cord

pol·ish *vb* **1** : make smooth and glossy **2** : develop or refine ~ *n* **1** : shiny surface **2** : refinement

po·lite *adj* **-lit·er; -est** : marked by courteous social conduct — **po·lite·ly** *adv* — **po·lite·ness** *n*

pol·i·tic *adj* : shrewdly tactful

politically correct *adj* : seeking to avoid offending members of a different group

pol·i·tics *n sing or pl* : practice of government and managing of public affairs — **po·lit·i·cal** *adj* — **po·lit·i·cal·ly** *adv* — **pol·i·ti·cian** *n*

pol·ka *n* : lively couple dance — **polka** *vb*

pol·ka dot *n* : one of a series of regular dots in a pattern

poll *n* **1** : head **2** : place where votes are cast — usu. pl. **3** : a sampling of opinion ~ *vb* **1** : cut off **2** : receive or record votes **3** : question in a poll — **poll·ster** *n*

pol·len *n* : spores of a seed plant

pol·li·na·tion *n* : the carrying of pollen to fertilize the seed — **pol·li·nate** *vb* — **pol·li·na·tor** *n*

pol·lute *vb* **-lut·ed; -lut·ing** : contaminating with waste products — **pol·lut·ant** *n* — **pol·lut·er** *n* — **pol·lu·tion** *n*

pol·ly·wog, pol·li·wog *n* : tadpole

po·lo *n* : game played by 2 teams on horseback using long-handled mallets to drive a wooden ball

pol·ter·geist *n* : mischievous ghost

pol·troon *n* : coward

poly·es·ter *n* : synthetic fiber

po·lyg·a·my *n* : marriage to several spouses at the same time — **po·lyg·a·mist** *n* — **po·lyg·a·mous** *adj*

poly·gon *n* : closed plane figure with straight sides

poly·mer *n* : chemical compound of molecules joined in long strings — **po·lym·er·i·za·tion** *n* — **po·lym·er·ize** *vb*

poly·tech·nic *adj* : relating to many technical arts or applied sciences

poly·the·ism *n* : worship of many gods — **poly·the·ist** *adj or n*

poly·un·sat·u·rat·ed *adj* : having many double or triple bonds in a molecule

pome·gran·ate *n* : tropical reddish fruit with many seeds

pom·mel *n* **1** : knob on the hilt of a sword **2** : knob at the front of a saddle ~ *vb* **-meled** *or* **-melled; -mel·ing** *or* **-mel·ling** : pummel

pomp *n* **1** : brilliant display **2** : ostentation

pomp·ous *adj* : pretentiously dignified — **pom·pos·i·ty** *n* — **pomp·ous·ly** *adv*

pon·cho *n, pl* **-chos** : blanketlike cloak

pond *n* : small body of water

pon·der *vb* : consider

pon·der·ous *adj* **1** : very heavy **2** : clumsy **3** : oppressively dull

pon·tiff *n* : pope — **pon·tif·i·cal** *adj*

pon·tif·i·cate *vb* **-cat·ed; -cat·ing** : talk pompously

pon·toon *n* : flat-bottomed boat or float

po·ny *n, pl* **-nies** : small horse

po·ny·tail *n* : hair arrangement like the tail of a pony

poo·dle *n* : dog with a curly coat

¹**pool** *n* **1** : small body of water **2** : puddle

²**pool** *n* **1** : amount contributed by participants in a joint venture **2** : game of pocket billiards ~ *vb* : combine in a common fund

poor *adj* **1** : lacking material possessions **2** : less than adequate **3** : arousing pity **4** : unfavorable — **poor·ly** *adv*

¹**pop** *vb* **-pp- 1** : move suddenly **2** : burst with or make a sharp sound **3** : protrude ~ *n* **1** : sharp explosive sound **2** : flavored soft drink

²**pop** *adj* : popular

pop·corn *n* : corn whose kernels burst open into a light mass when heated

pope *n, often cap* : head of the Roman Catholic Church

pop·lar *n* : slender quick-growing tree

pop·lin *n* : strong plain-woven fabric with cross-wise ribs

pop·over *n* : hollow muffin made from egg-rich batter

pop·py *n, pl* **-pies** : herb with showy flowers

pop·u·lace *n* **1** : common people **2** : population

pop·u·lar *adj* **1** : relating to the general public **2** : widely accepted **3** : commonly liked — **pop·u·lar·i·ty** *n* — **pop·u·lar·ize** *vb* — **pop·u·lar·ly** *adv*

pop·u·late *vb* **-lat·ed; -lat·ing** : inhabit or occupy

pop·u·la·tion *n* : people or number of people in an area

pop·u·list *n* : advocate of the rights of the common people — **pop·u·lism** *n*

pop·u·lous *adj* : densely populated — **pop·u·lous·ness** *n*

por·ce·lain *n* : fine-grained ceramic ware

porch *n* : covered entrance

por·cu·pine *n* : mammal with sharp quills

¹**pore** *vb* **pored; por·ing** : read attentively

²**pore** *n* : tiny hole (as in the skin) — **pored** *adj*

pork *n* : pig meat

pork barrel *n* : government projects benefiting political patrons

por·nog·ra·phy *n* : depiction of erotic behavior intended to cause sexual excitement — **por·no·graph·ic** *adj*

po·rous *adj* : permeable to fluids — **po·ros·i·ty** *n*

por·poise *n* **1** : small whale with a blunt snout **2** : dolphin

por·ridge *n* : soft boiled cereal

por·rin·ger *n* : low one-handled metal bowl or cup

¹**port** *n* **1** : harbor **2** : city with a harbor

²**port** *n* **1** : inlet or outlet (as in an engine) for a fluid **2** : porthole

³**port** *n* : left side of a ship or airplane looking forward — **port** *adj*

⁴**port** *n* : sweet wine

por·ta·ble *adj* : capable of being carried — **port·able** *n*

por·tage *n* : carrying of boats overland between navigable bodies of water or the route where this is done — **portage** *vb*

por·tal *n* : entrance

por·tend *vb* : give a warning of beforehand

por·tent *n* : something that foreshadows a coming event — **por·ten·tous** *adj*

por·ter *n* : baggage carrier

por·ter·house *n* : choice cut of steak

port·fo·lio *n, pl* **-lios 1** : portable case for papers **2** : office or function of a diplomat **3** : investor's securities

port·hole *n* : window in the side of a ship or aircraft

por·ti·co *n, pl* **-coes** *or* **-cos** : colonnade forming a porch

por·tion *n* : part or share of a whole ~ *vb* : divide into or allot portions

port·ly *adj* **-li·er; -est** : somewhat stout

por·trait *n* : picture of a person — **por·trait·ist** *n* — **por·trai·ture** *n*

por·tray *vb* **1** : make a picture of **2** : describe in words **3** : play the role of — **por·tray·al** *n*

por·tu·la·ca *n* : tropical herb with showy flowers

pose *vb* **posed; pos·ing 1** : assume a posture or attitude **2** : propose **3** : pretend to be what one is not ~ *n* **1** : sustained posture **2** : pretense — **pos·er** *n*

posh *adj* : elegant

po·si·tion n 1 : stand taken on a question 2 : place or location 3 : status 4 : job — **position** vb

pos·i·tive adj 1 : definite 2 : confident 3 : relating to or being an adjective or adverb form that denotes no increase 4 : greater than zero 5 : having a deficiency of electrons 6 : affirmative — **pos·i·tive·ly** adv — **pos·i·tive·ness** n

pos·se n : emergency assistants of a sheriff

pos·sess vb 1 : have as property or as a quality 2 : control — **pos·ses·sion** n — **pos·ses·sor** n

pos·ses·sive adj 1 : relating to a grammatical case denoting ownership 2 : jealous — **possessive** n — **pos·ses·sive·ness** n

pos·si·ble adj 1 : that can be done 2 : potential — **pos·si·bil·i·ty** n — **pos·si·bly** adv

pos·sum n : opossum

¹**post** n : upright stake serving to support or mark ~ vb : put up or announce by a notice

²**post** vb 1 : mail 2 : inform

³**post** n 1 : sentry's station 2 : assigned task 3 : army camp ~ vb : station

post- prefix : after or subsequent to postadolescent

postattack	postmarital
postbaccalaureate	postmenopausal
postbiblical	postnatal
postcollege	postnuptial
postcolonial	postproduction
postelection	postpuberty
postexercise	postrecession
postflight	postretirement
postgame	postrevolutionary
postgraduate	postseason
postgraduation	postsecondary
postharvest	postsurgical
posthospital	posttreatment
postimperial	posttrial
postinaugural	postvaccination
postindustrial	postwar
postinoculation	

post·age n : fee for mail

post·al adj : relating to the mail

post·card n : card for mailing a message

post·date vb : assign a date to that is later than the actual date of execution

post·er n : large usu. printed notice

pos·te·ri·or adj 1 : later 2 : situated behind ~ n : buttocks

pos·ter·i·ty n : all future generations

post·haste adv : speedily

post·hu·mous adj : occurring after one's death — **post·hu·mous·ly** adv

post·man n : mail carrier

post·mark n : official mark on mail — **post·mark** vb

post·mas·ter n : chief of a post office

post me·ri·di·em adj : being after noon

post·mor·tem adj : occurring or done after death ~ n 1 : medical examination of a corpse 2 : analysis after an event

post office n : agency or building for mail service

post·op·er·a·tive adj : following surgery

post·paid adv : with postage paid by the sender

post·par·tum adj : following childbirth — **postpartum** adv

post·pone vb -**poned; -pon·ing** : put off to a later time — **post·pone·ment** n

post·script n : added note

pos·tu·lant n : candidate for a religious order

pos·tu·late vb -**lat·ed; -lat·ing** : assume as true ~ n : assumption

pos·ture n : bearing of the body ~ vb -**tured; -tur·ing** : strike a pose

po·sy n, pl -**sies** : flower or bunch of flowers

pot n : rounded container ~ vb -**tt-** : place in a pot — **pot·ful** n

po·ta·ble adj : drinkable

pot·ash n : white chemical salt of potassium used esp. in agriculture

po·tas·si·um n : silver-white metallic chemical element

po·ta·to n, pl -**toes** : edible plant tuber

pot·bel·ly n : paunch — **pot·bel·lied** adj

po·tent adj : powerful or effective — **po·ten·cy** n

po·ten·tate n : powerful ruler

po·ten·tial adj : capable of becoming actual ~ n 1 : something that can become actual 2 : degree of electrification with reference to a standard — **po·ten·ti·al·i·ty** n — **po·ten·tial·ly** adv

poth·er n : fuss

pot·hole n : large hole in a road surface

po·tion n : liquid medicine or poison

pot·luck n : whatever food is available

pot·pour·ri n 1 : mix of flowers, herbs, and spices used for scent 2 : miscellaneous collection

pot·shot n 1 : casual or easy shot 2 : random critical remark

pot·ter n : pottery maker

pot·tery n, pl -**ter·ies** : objects (as dishes) made from clay

pouch n 1 : small bag 2 : bodily sac

poul·tice n : warm medicated dressing — **poultice** vb

poul·try n : domesticated fowl

pounce vb **pounced; pounc·ing** : spring or swoop upon and seize

¹**pound** n 1 : unit of weight equal to 16 ounces 2 : monetary unit (as of the United Kingdom) — **pound·age** n

²**pound** n : shelter for stray animals

³**pound** vb 1 : crush by beating 2 : strike heavily 3 : drill 4 : move along heavily

pour vb 1 : flow or supply esp. copiously 2 : rain hard

pout vb : look sullen — **pout** n

pov·er·ty n 1 : lack of money or possessions 2 : poor quality

pow·der n : dry material of fine particles ~ vb : sprinkle or cover with powder — **pow·dery** adj

pow·er n 1 : position of authority 2 : ability to act 3 : one that has power 4 : physical might 5 : force or energy used to do work ~ vb : supply with power — **pow·er·ful** adj — **pow·er·ful·ly** adv — **pow·er·less** adj

pow·er·house n : dynamic or energetic person

pow·wow n : conference

pox n, pl **pox** or **pox·es** : disease marked by skin rash

prac·ti·ca·ble adj : feasible — **prac·ti·ca·bil·i·ty** n

prac·ti·cal adj 1 : relating to practice 2 : virtual 3 : capable of being put to use 4 : inclined to action as opposed to speculation — **prac·ti·cal·i·ty** n — **prac·ti·cal·ly** adv

prac·tice, prac·tise vb -**ticed** or -**tised; -tic·ing** or -**tis·ing** 1 : perform repeatedly to become proficient 2 : do or perform customarily 3 : be professionally engaged in ~ n 1 : actual performance 2 : habit 3 : exercise for proficiency 4 : exercise of a profession

prac·ti·tio·ner n : one who practices a profession

prag·ma·tism n : practical approach to problems — **prag·mat·ic** adj — **prag·mat·i·cal·ly** adv

prai·rie n : broad grassy rolling tract of land

praise vb **praised; prais·ing** 1 : express approval of 2 : glorify — **praise** n — **praise·wor·thy** adj

prance vb **pranced; pranc·ing** 1 : spring from the hind legs 2 : swagger — **prance** n — **prancer** n

prank n : playful or mischievous act — **prankster** n

prate vb **prat·ed; prat·ing** : talk long and foolishly

prat·fall n : fall on the buttocks

prat·tle vb -**tled; -tling** : babble — **prattle** n

prawn n : shrimplike crustacean

pray vb 1 : entreat 2 : ask earnestly for something 3 : address God or a god

prayer n 1 : earnest request 2 : an addressing of God or a god 3 : words used in praying — **prayer·ful** adj — **prayer·ful·ly** adv

praying mantis n : mantis

pre- prefix : before, prior to, or in advance

preadmission	premenstrual
preadolescence	premix
preadolescent	premodern
preadult	premodify
preanesthetic	premoisten
prearrange	premold
prearrangement	prenatal
preassembled	prenotification
preassign	prenotify
prebattle	prenuptial
prebiblical	preopening
prebreakfast	preoperational
precalculus	preoperative
precancel	preordain
precancellation	prepackage
preclear	prepay
preclearance	preplan
precollege	preprocess
precolonial	preproduction
precombustion	preprofessional
precompute	preprogram
preconceive	prepubertal
preconception	prepublication
preconcert	prepunch
precondition	prepurchase
preconstructed	prerecorded
preconvention	preregister
precook	preregistration
precool	prerehearsal
precut	prerelease
predawn	preretirement
predefine	prerevolutionary
predeparture	prerinse
predesignate	presale
predetermine	preschool
predischarge	preseason
predrill	preselect
preelection	preset
preelectric	preshrink
preemployment	preshrunk
preestablish	presoak
preexist	presort
preexistence	prestamp
preexistent	presterilize
prefight	prestrike
preform	presurgery
pregame	presweeten
preheat	pretape
preinaugural	pretelevision
preindustrial	pretournament
preinterview	pretreat
prejudge	pretreatment
prekindergarten	pretrial
prelaunch	prewar
prelife	prewash
premarital	prewrap
premenopausal	

preach vb 1 : deliver a sermon 2 : advocate earnestly — **preach·er** n — **preach·ment** n

pre·am·ble n : introduction

pre·can·cer·ous adj : likely to become cancerous

pre·car·i·ous adj : dangerously insecure — **pre·car·i·ous·ly** adv — **pre·car·i·ous·ness** n

pre·cau·tion n : care taken beforehand — **pre·cau·tion·ary** adj

pre·cede vb -**ced·ed; -ced·ing** : be, go, or come ahead of — **pre·ce·dence** n

prec•e•dent *n* : something said or done earlier that serves as an example

pre•cept *n* : rule of action or conduct

pre•cinct *n* **1** : district of a city **2** *pl* : vicinity

pre•cious *adj* **1** : of great value **2** : greatly cherished **3** : affected

prec•i•pice *n* : steep cliff

pre•cip•i•tate *vb* **-tat•ed; -tat•ing 1** : cause to happen quickly or abruptly **2** : cause to separate out of a liquid **3** : fall as rain, snow, or hail ~ *n* : solid matter precipitated from a liquid ~ *adj* : unduly hasty — **pre•cip•i•tate•ly** *adv* — **pre•cip•i•tate•ness** *n* — **pre•cip•i•tous** *adj* — **pre•cip•i•tous•ly** *adv*

pre•cip•i•ta•tion *n* **1** : rash haste **2** : rain, snow, or hail

pré•cis *n, pl* **pré•cis** : concise summary of essentials

pre•cise *adj* **1** : definite **2** : highly accurate — **pre•cise•ly** *adv* — **pre•cise•ness** *n*

pre•ci•sion *n* : quality or state of being precise

pre•clude *vb* **-clud•ed; -clud•ing** : make impossible

pre•co•cious *adj* : exceptionally advanced — **pre•co•cious•ly** *adv* — **pre•coc•i•ty** *n*

pre•cur•sor *n* : harbinger

pred•a•to•ry *adj* : preying upon others — **pred•a•tor** *n*

pre•de•ces•sor *n* : a previous holder of a position

pre•des•tine *vb* : settle beforehand — **pre•des•ti•na•tion** *n*

pre•dic•a•ment *n* : difficult situation

pred•i•cate *n* : part of a sentence that states something about the subject ~ *vb* **-cat•ed; -cat•ing 1** : affirm **2** : establish — **pred•i•ca•tion** *n*

pre•dict *vb* : declare in advance — **pre•dict•abil•i•ty** *n* — **pre•dict•able** *adj* — **pre•dict•ably** *adv* — **pre•dic•tion** *n*

pre•di•lec•tion *n* : established preference

pre•dis•pose *vb* : cause to be favorable or susceptible to something beforehand — **pre•dis•po•si•tion** *n*

pre•dom•i•nate *vb* : be superior — **pre•dom•i•nance** *n* — **pre•dom•i•nant** *adj* — **pre•dom•i•nant•ly** *adv*

pre•em•i•nent *adj* : having highest rank — **pre•em•i•nence** *n* — **pre•em•i•nent•ly** *adv*

pre•empt *vb* **1** : seize for oneself **2** : take the place of — **pre•emp•tion** *n* — **pre•emp•tive** *adj*

preen *vb* : dress or smooth up (as feathers)

pre•fab•ri•cat•ed *adj* : manufactured for rapid assembly elsewhere — **pre•fab•ri•ca•tion** *n*

pref•ace *n* : introductory comments ~ *vb* **-aced; -ac•ing** : introduce with a preface — **pref•a•to•ry** *adj*

pre•fect *n* : chief officer or judge — **pre•fec•ture** *n*

pre•fer *vb* **-rr- 1** : like better **2** : bring (as a charge) against a person — **pref•er•a•ble** *adj* — **pref•er•a•bly** *adv* — **pref•er•ence** *n* — **pref•er•en•tial** *adj*

pre•fer•ment *n* : promotion

pre•fig•ure *vb* : foreshadow

¹pre•fix *vb* : place before

²prefix *n* : affix at the beginning of a word

preg•nant *adj* **1** : containing unborn young **2** : meaningful — **preg•nan•cy** *n*

pre•hen•sile *adj* : adapted for grasping

pre•his•tor•ic, pre•his•tor•i•cal *adj* : relating to the period before written history

prej•u•dice *n* **1** : damage esp. to one's rights **2** : unreasonable attitude for or against something ~ *vb* **-diced; -dic•ing 1** : damage **2** : cause to have prejudice — **prej•u•di•cial** *adj*

prel•ate *n* : clergy member of high rank — **prel•a•cy** *n*

pre•lim•i•nary *n, pl* **-nar•ies** : something that precedes or introduces — **preliminary** *adj*

pre•lude *n* : introductory performance, event, or musical piece

pre•ma•ture *adj* : coming before the usual or proper time — **pre•ma•ture•ly** *adv*

pre•med•i•tate *vb* : plan beforehand — **pre•med•i•ta•tion** *n*

pre•mier *adj* : first in rank or importance ~ *n* : prime minister — **pre•mier•ship** *n*

pre•miere *n* : 1st performance ~ *vb* **-miered; -mier•ing** : give a 1st performance of

prem•ise *n* **1** : statement made or implied as a basis of argument **2** *pl* : piece of land with the structures on it

pre•mi•um *n* **1** : bonus **2** : sum over the stated value **3** : sum paid for insurance **4** : high value

pre•mo•ni•tion *n* : feeling that something is about to happen — **pre•mon•i•to•ry** *adj*

pre•oc•cu•pied *adj* : lost in thought

pre•oc•cu•py *vb* : occupy the attention of — **pre•oc•cu•pa•tion** *n*

pre•pare *vb* **-pared; -par•ing 1** : make or get ready often beforehand **2** : put together or compound — **prep•a•ra•tion** *n* — **pre•pa•ra•to•ry** *adj* — **pre•pared•ness** *n*

pre•pon•der•ant *adj* : having great weight, power, importance, or numbers — **pre•pon•der•ance** *n* — **pre•pon•der•ant•ly** *adv*

prep•o•si•tion *n* : word that combines with a noun or pronoun to form a phrase — **prep•o•si•tion•al** *adj*

pre•pos•sess•ing *adj* : tending to create a favorable impression

pre•pos•ter•ous *adj* : absurd

pre•req•ui•site *n* : something required beforehand — **prerequisite** *adj*

pre•rog•a•tive *n* : special right or power

pre•sage *vb* **-saged; -sag•ing 1** : give a warning of **2** : predict — **pres•age** *n*

pres•by•ter *n* : priest or minister

pre•science *n* : foreknowledge of events — **pre•scient** *adj*

pre•scribe *vb* **-scribed; -scrib•ing 1** : lay down as a guide **2** : direct the use of as a remedy

pre•scrip•tion *n* : written direction for the preparation and use of a medicine or the medicine prescribed

pres•ence *n* **1** : fact or condition of being present **2** : appearance or bearing

¹pres•ent *n* : gift

²pres•ent *vb* **1** : introduce **2** : bring before the public **3** : make a gift to or of **4** : bring before a court for inquiry — **pre•sent•able** *adj* — **pre•sen•ta•tion** *n* — **pre•sent•ment** *n*

³pres•ent *adj* : now existing, in progress, or attending ~ *n* : present time

pre•sen•ti•ment *n* : premonition

pres•ent•ly *adv* **1** : soon **2** : now

present participle *n* : participle that typically expresses present action

pre•serve *vb* **-served; -serv•ing 1** : keep safe from danger or spoilage **2** : maintain ~ *n* **1** : preserved fruit — often in pl. **2** : area for protection of natural resources — **pres•er•va•tion** *n* — **pre•ser•va•tive** *adj or n* — **pre•serv•er** *n*

pre•side *vb* **-sid•ed; -sid•ing 1** : act as chairman **2** : exercise control

pres•i•dent *n* **1** : one chosen to preside **2** : chief official (as of a company or nation) — **pres•i•den•cy** *n* — **pres•i•den•tial** *adj*

press *n* **1** : crowded condition **2** : machine or device for exerting pressure and esp. for printing **3** : pressure **4** : printing or publishing establishment **5** : news media and esp. newspapers ~ *vb* **1** : lie against and exert pressure on **2** : smooth with an iron or squeeze with something heavy **3** : urge **4** : crowd **5** : force one's way — **press•er** *n*

press•ing *adj* : urgent

pres•sure *n* **1** : burden of distress or urgent business **2** : direct application of force — **pressure** *vb* — **pres•sur•i•za•tion** *n* — **pres•sur•ize** *vb*

pres•ti•dig•i•ta•tion *n* : sleight of hand

pres•tige *n* : estimation in the eyes of people — **pres•ti•gious** *adj*

pres•to *adv or adj* : quickly

pre•sume *vb* **-sumed; -sum•ing 1** : assume authority without right to do so **2** : take for granted — **pre•sum•able** *adj* — **pre•sum•ably** *adv*

pre•sump•tion *n* **1** : presumptuous attitude or conduct **2** : belief supported by probability — **pre•sump•tive** *adj*

pre•sump•tu•ous *adj* : too bold or forward — **pre•sump•tu•ous•ly** *adv*

pre•sup•pose *vb* : take for granted — **pre•sup•po•si•tion** *n*

pre•tend *vb* **1** : act as if something is real or true when it is not **2** : act in a way that is false **3** : lay claim — **pre•tend•er** *n*

pre•tense, pre•tence *n* **1** : insincere effort **2** : deception — **pre•ten•sion** *n*

pre•ten•tious *adj* : overly showy or self-important — **pre•ten•tious•ly** *adv* — **pre•ten•tious•ness** *n*

pre•ter•nat•u•ral *adj* **1** : exceeding what is natural **2** : inexplicable by ordinary means — **pre•ter•nat•u•ral•ly** *adv*

pre•text *n* : falsely stated purpose

pret•ty *adj* **-ti•er; -est** : pleasing by delicacy or attractiveness ~ *adv* : in some degree ~ *vb* **-tied; -ty•ing** : make pretty — **pret•ti•ly** *adv* — **pret•ti•ness** *n*

pret•zel *n* : twisted thin bread that is glazed and salted

pre•vail *vb* **1** : triumph **2** : urge successfully **3** : be frequent, widespread, or dominant

prev•a•lent *adj* : widespread — **prev•a•lence** *n*

pre•var•i•cate *vb* **-cat•ed; -cat•ing** : deviate from the truth — **pre•var•i•ca•tion** *n* — **pre•var•i•ca•tor** *n*

pre•vent *vb* : keep from happening or acting — **pre•vent•able** *adj* — **pre•ven•tion** *n* — **pre•ven•tive** *adj or n* — **pre•ven•ta•tive** *adj or n*

pre•view *vb* : view or show beforehand — **pre•view** *n*

pre•vi•ous *adj* : having gone, happened, or existed before — **pre•vi•ous•ly** *adv*

prey *n, pl* **preys 1** : animal taken for food by another **2** : victim ~ *vb* **1** : seize and devour animals as prey **2** : have a harmful effect on

price *n* : cost ~ *vb* **priced; pric•ing** : set a price on

price•less *adj* : too precious to have a price

pric•ey *adj* **pric•i•er; -est** : expensive

prick *n* **1** : tear or small wound made by a point **2** : something sharp or pointed ~ *vb* : pierce slightly with a sharp point — **prick•er** *n*

prick•le *n* **1** : small sharp spine or thorn **2** : slight stinging pain ~ *vb* **-led; -ling** : tingle — **prick•ly** *adj*

pride *n* : quality or state of being proud ~ *vb* **prid•ed; prid•ing** : indulge in pride — **pride•ful** *adj*

priest *n* : person having authority to perform the sacred rites of a religion — **priest•hood** *n* — **priest•li•ness** *n* — **priest•ly** *adj*

priest•ess *n* : woman who is a priest

prig *n* : one who irritates by rigid or pointed observance of proprieties — **prig•gish** *adj* — **prig•gish•ly** *adv*

prim *adj* **-mm-** : stiffly formal and proper — **prim•ly** *adv* — **prim•ness** *n*

pri•mal *adj* **1** : original or primitive **2** : most important

pri•ma•ry *adj* : first in order of time, rank, or importance ~ *n, pl* **-ries** : preliminary election — **pri•mar•i•ly** *adv*

primary school *n* : elementary school

pri•mate n 1 : highest-ranking bishop 2 : mammal of the group that includes humans and monkeys

prime n : earliest or best part or period ~ adj : standing first (as in significance or quality) ~ vb **primed; prim•ing** 1 : fill or load 2 : lay a preparatory coating on

prime minister n : chief executive of a parliamentary government

¹**prim•er** n : small introductory book

²**prim•er** n 1 : device for igniting an explosive 2 : material for priming a surface

pri•me•val adj : relating to the earliest ages

prim•i•tive adj 1 : relating to or characteristic of an early stage of development 2 : of or relating to a tribal people or culture ~ n : one that is primitive — **prim•i•tive•ly** adv — **prim•i•tive•ness** n

pri•mor•di•al adj : primeval

primp vb : dress or groom in a finicky manner

prim•rose n : low herb with clusters of showy flowers

prince n 1 : ruler 2 : son of a king or queen — **prince•ly** adj

prin•cess n 1 : daughter of a king or queen 2 : wife of a prince

prin•ci•pal adj : most important ~ n 1 : leading person 2 : head of a school 3 : sum lent at interest — **prin•ci•pal•ly** adv

prin•ci•pal•i•ty n, pl -**ties** : territory of a prince

prin•ci•ple n 1 : general or fundamental law 2 : rule or code of conduct or devotion to such a code

print n 1 : mark or impression made by pressure 2 : printed state or form 3 : printed matter 4 : copy made by printing 5 : cloth with a figure stamped on it ~ vb 1 : produce impressions of (as from type) 2 : write in letters like those of printer's type — **print•able** adj — **print•er** n

print•ing n : art or business of a printer

print•out n : printed output produced by a computer — **print out** vb

¹**pri•or** n : head of a religious house — **pri•o•ry** n

²**prior** adj : coming before in time, order, or importance — **pri•or•i•ty** n

pri•or•ess n : nun who is head of a religious house

prism n : transparent 3-sided object that separates light into colors — **pris•mat•ic** adj

pris•on n : place where criminals are confined

pris•on•er n : person on trial or in prison

pris•sy adj -**si•er, -est** : overly prim — **pris•si•ness** n

pris•tine adj : pure

pri•va•cy n, pl -**cies** : quality or state of being apart from others

pri•vate adj 1 : belonging to a particular individual or group 2 : carried on independently 3 : withdrawn from company or observation ~ n : enlisted person of the lowest rank in the marine corps or of one of the two lowest ranks in the army — **pri•vate•ly** adv

pri•va•teer n : private ship armed to attack enemy ships and commerce

private first class n : enlisted person ranking next below a corporal in the army and next below a lance corporal in the marine corps

pri•va•tion n : lack of what is needed for existence

priv•i•lege n : right granted as an advantage or favor — **priv•i•leged** adj

privy adj 1 : private or secret 2 : having access to private or secret information ~ n, pl **priv•ies** : outdoor toilet — **priv•i•ly** adv

¹**prize** n 1 : something offered or striven for in competition or in contests of chance 2 : something very desirable — **prize** adj — **prize•win•ner** n — **prize•win•ning** adj

²**prize** vb **prized; priz•ing** : value highly

³**prize** vb **prized; priz•ing** : pry

prize•fight n : professional boxing match — **prize•fight•er** n — **prize•fight•ing** n

¹**pro** n : favorable argument or person ~ adv : in favor

²**pro** n or adj : professional

prob•a•ble adj : seeming true or real or to have a good chance of happening — **prob•a•bil•i•ty** n — **prob•a•bly** adv

pro•bate n : judicial determination of the validity of a will ~ vb -**bat•ed; -bat•ing** : establish by probate

pro•ba•tion n 1 : period of testing and trial 2 : freedom for a convict during good behavior under supervision — **pro•ba•tion•ary** adj — **pro•ba•tion•er** n

probe n 1 : slender instrument for examining a cavity 2 : investigation ~ vb **probed; prob•ing** 1 : examine with a probe 2 : investigate

pro•bi•ty n : honest behavior

prob•lem n 1 : question to be solved 2 : source of perplexity or vexation — **problem** adj — **prob•lem•at•ic** adj — **prob•lem•at•i•cal** adj

pro•bos•cis n, pl -**cis•es** also -**ci•des** : long flexible snout

pro•ce•dure n 1 : way of doing something 2 : series of steps in= regular order — **pro•ce•dur•al** adj

pro•ceed vb 1 : come forth 2 : go on in an orderly way 3 : begin and carry on an action 4 : advance

pro•ceed•ing n 1 : procedure 2 pl : something said or done or its official record

pro•ceeds n pl : total money taken in

pro•cess n, pl -**cess•es** 1 : something going on 2 : natural phenomenon marked by gradual changes 3 : series of actions or operations directed toward a result 4 : summons 5 : projecting part ~ vb : subject to a process — **pro•ces•sor** n

pro•ces•sion n : group moving along in an orderly way

pro•ces•sion•al n : music for a procession

pro•claim vb : announce publicly or with conviction — **proc•la•ma•tion** n

pro•cliv•i•ty n, pl -**ties** : inclination

pro•cras•ti•nate vb -**nat•ed; -nat•ing** : put something off until later — **pro•cras•ti•na•tion** n — **pro•cras•ti•na•tor** n

pro•cre•ate vb -**at•ed; -at•ing** : produce offspring — **pro•cre•ation** n — **pro•cre•ative** adj — **pro•cre•ator** n

proc•tor n : supervisor of students (as at an examination) — **proc•tor** vb

pro•cure vb -**cured; -cur•ing** : get possession of — **pro•cur•able** adj — **pro•cure•ment** n — **pro•cur•er** n

prod vb -**dd-** : push with or as if with a pointed instrument — **prod** n

prod•i•gal adj : recklessly extravagant or wasteful — **prodigal** n — **prod•i•gal•i•ty** n

pro•di•gious adj : extraordinary in size or degree — **pro•di•gious•ly** adv

prod•i•gy n, pl -**gies** : extraordinary person or thing

pro•duce vb -**duced; -duc•ing** 1 : present to view 2 : give birth to 3 : bring into existence ~ n 1 : product 2 : agricultural products — **pro•duc•er** n

prod•uct n 1 : number resulting from multiplication 2 : something produced

pro•duc•tion n : act, process, or result of producing — **pro•duc•tive** adj — **pro•duc•tive•ness** n — **pro•duc•tiv•i•ty** n

pro•fane vb -**faned; -fan•ing** : treat with irreverence ~ adj 1 : not concerned with religion 2 : serving to debase what is holy — **pro•fane•ly** adv — **pro•fane•ness** n — **pro•fan•i•ty** n

pro•fess vb 1 : declare openly 2 : confess one's faith in — **pro•fessed•ly** adv

pro•fes•sion n 1 : open declaration of belief 2 : oc-cupation requiring specialized knowledge and academic training

pro•fes•sion•al adj 1 : of, relating to, or engaged in a profession 2 : playing sport for pay — **profes•sional** n — **pro•fes•sion•al•ism** n — **pro•fes•sion•al•ize** vb — **pro•fes•sion•al•ly** adv

pro•fes•sor n : university or college teacher — **pro•fes•so•ri•al** adj — **pro•fes•sor•ship** n

prof•fer vb -**fered; -fer•ing** : offer — **proffer** n

pro•fi•cient adj : very good at something — **pro•fi•cien•cy** n — **proficient** n — **pro•fi•cient•ly** adv

pro•file n : picture in outline — **profile** vb

prof•it n 1 : valuable return 2 : excess of the selling price of goods over cost ~ vb : gain a profit — **prof•it•able** adj — **prof•it•ably** adv — **prof•it•less** adj

prof•i•teer n : one who makes an unreasonable profit — **profiteer** vb

prof•li•gate adj 1 : shamelessly immoral 2 : wildly extravagant — **prof•li•ga•cy** n — **profligate** n — **prof•li•gate•ly** adv

pro•found adj 1 : marked by intellectual depth or insight 2 : deeply felt — **pro•found•ly** adv — **pro•fun•di•ty** n

pro•fuse adj : pouring forth liberally — **pro•fuse•ly** adv — **pro•fu•sion** n

pro•gen•i•tor n : direct ancestor

prog•e•ny n, pl -**nies** : offspring

pro•ges•ter•one n : female hormone

prog•no•sis n, pl -**no•ses** : prospect of recovery from disease

prog•nos•ti•cate vb -**cat•ed; -cat•ing** : predict from signs or symptoms — **prog•nos•ti•ca•tion** n — **prog•nos•ti•ca•tor** n

pro•gram n 1 : outline of the order to be pursued or the subjects included (as in a performance) 2 : plan of procedure 3 : coded instructions for a computer ~ vb -**grammed** or -**gramed; -gram•ming** or -**gram•ing** 1 : enter in a program 2 : provide a computer with a program — **pro•gram•ma•bil•i•ty** n — **pro•gram•ma•ble** adj — **pro•gram•mer** n

prog•ress n : movement forward or to a better condition — vb 1 : move forward 2 : improve — **pro•gres•sive** adj — **pro•gres•sive•ly** adv

pro•gres•sion n 1 : act of progressing 2 : continuous connected series

pro•hib•it vb : prevent by authority

pro•hi•bi•tion n 1 : act of prohibiting 2 : legal restriction on sale or manufacture of alcoholic beverages — **pro•hi•bi•tion•ist** n — **pro•hib•i•tive** adj — **pro•hib•i•tive•ly** adv — **pro•hib•i•to•ry** adj

proj•ect n : planned undertaking ~ vb 1 : design or plan 2 : protrude 3 : throw forward — **pro•jec•tion** n

pro•jec•tile n : missile hurled by external force

pro•jec•tor n : device for projecting pictures on a screen

pro•le•tar•i•an n : member of the proletariat — **prole•tarian** adj

pro•le•tar•i•at n : laboring class

pro•lif•er•ate vb -**at•ed; -at•ing** : grow or increase in number rapidly — **pro•lif•er•a•tion** n

pro•lif•ic adj : producing abundantly — **pro•lif•i•cal•ly** adv

pro•logue n : preface

pro•long vb : lengthen in time or extent — **pro•lon•ga•tion** n

prom n : formal school dance

prom•e•nade n 1 : leisurely walk 2 : place for strolling — **promenade** vb

prom•i•nence n 1 : quality, state, or fact of being readily noticeable or distinguished 2 : something that stands out — **prom•i•nent** adj — **prom•i•nent•ly** adv

pro·mis·cu·ous adj : having a number of sexual partners — **prom·is·cu·ity** n — **pro·mis·cu·ous·ly** adv — **pro·mis·cu·ous·ness** n

prom·ise n 1 : statement that one will do or not do something 2 : basis for expectation — **promise** vb — **prom·is·so·ry** adj

prom·is·ing adj : likely to succeed — **prom·is·ing·ly** adv

prom·on·to·ry n, pl -ries : point of land jutting into the sea

pro·mote vb -mot·ed; -mot·ing 1 : advance in rank 2 : contribute to the growth, development, or prosperity of — **pro·mot·er** n — **pro·mo·tion** n — **pro·mo·tion·al** adj

¹prompt vb 1 : incite 2 : give a cue to (an actor or singer) — **prompt·er** n

²prompt adj : ready and quick — **prompt·ly** adv — **prompt·ness** n

prone adj 1 : having a tendency 2 : lying face downward — **prone·ness** n

prong n : sharp point of a fork — **pronged** adj

pro·noun n : word used as a substitute for a noun

pro·nounce vb -nounced; -nounc·ing 1 : utter officially or as an opinion 2 : say or speak esp. correctly — **pro·nounce·able** adj — **pro·nounce·ment** n — **pro·nun·ci·a·tion** n

pro·nounced adj : decided

¹proof n 1 : evidence of a truth or fact 2 : trial impression or print

²proof adj : designed for or successful in resisting or repelling

proof·read vb : read and mark corrections in — **proof·read·er** n

prop vb -pp- 1 : support 2 : sustain — **prop** n

pro·pa·gan·da n : the spreading of ideas or information to further or damage a cause — **pro·pa·gan·dist** n — **pro·pa·gan·dize** vb

prop·a·gate vb -gat·ed; -gat·ing 1 : reproduce biologically 2 : cause to spread — **prop·a·ga·tion** n

pro·pane n : heavy flammable gaseous fuel

pro·pel vb -ll- : drive forward — **pro·pel·lant, pro·pel·lent** n or adj

pro·pel·ler n : hub with revolving blades that propels a craft

pro·pen·si·ty n, pl -ties : particular interest or inclination

prop·er adj 1 : suitable or right 2 : limited to a specified thing 3 : correct 4 : strictly adhering to standards of social manners, dignity, or good taste — **prop·er·ly** adv

prop·er·ty n, pl -ties 1 : quality peculiar to an individual 2 : something owned 3 : piece of real estate 4 : ownership

proph·e·cy n, pl -cies : prediction

proph·e·sy vb -sied; -sy·ing : predict — **proph·e·si·er** n

proph·et n : one who utters revelations or predicts events — **proph·et·ess** n — **pro·phet·ic, pro·phet·i·cal** adj — **pro·phet·i·cal·ly** adv

pro·pin·qui·ty n : nearness

pro·pi·ti·ate vb -at·ed; -at·ing : gain or regain the favor of — **pro·pi·ti·a·tion** n — **pro·pi·ti·a·to·ry** adj

pro·pi·tious adj : favorable

pro·po·nent n : one who argues in favor of something

pro·por·tion n 1 : relation of one part to another or to the whole with respect to magnitude, quantity, or degree 2 : symmetry 3 : share ~ vb : adjust in size in relation to others — **pro·por·tion·al** adj — **pro·por·tion·al·ly** adv — **pro·por·tion·ate** adj — **pro·por·tion·ate·ly** adv

pro·pose vb -posed; -pos·ing 1 : plan or intend 2 : make an offer of marriage 3 : present for consideration — **pro·pos·al** n

prop·o·si·tion n : something proposed ~ vb : suggest sexual intercourse to

pro·pound vb : set forth for consideration

pro·pri·etor n : owner — **pro·pri·e·tary** adj — **pro·pri·etor·ship** n — **pro·pri·etress** n

pro·pri·ety n, pl -eties : standard of acceptability in social conduct

pro·pul·sion n 1 : action of propelling 2 : driving power — **pro·pul·sive** adj

pro·sa·ic adj : dull

pro·scribe vb -scribed; -scrib·ing : prohibit — **pro·scrip·tion** n

prose n : ordinary language

pros·e·cute vb -cut·ed; -cut·ing 1 : follow to the end 2 : seek legal punishment of — **pros·e·cu·tion** n — **pros·e·cu·tor** n

pros·e·lyte n : new convert — **pros·e·ly·tize** vb

pros·pect n 1 : extensive view 2 : something awaited 3 : potential buyer ~ vb : look for mineral deposits — **pro·spec·tive** adj — **pro·spec·tive·ly** adv — **pros·pec·tor** n

pro·spec·tus n : introductory description of an enterprise

pros·per vb : thrive or succeed — **pros·per·ous** adj

pros·per·i·ty n : economic well-being

pros·tate n : glandular body about the base of the male urethra — **prostate** adj

pros·the·sis n, pl -the·ses : artificial replacement for a body part — **pros·thet·ic** adj

pros·ti·tute vb -tut·ed; -tut·ing 1 : offer sexual activity for money 2 : put to corrupt or unworthy purposes ~ n : one who engages in sexual activities for money — **pros·ti·tu·tion** n

pros·trate adj : stretched out with face on the ground ~ vb -trat·ed; -trat·ing 1 : fall or throw (oneself) into a prostrate position 2 : reduce to helplessness — **pros·tra·tion** n

pro·tag·o·nist n : main character in a drama or story

pro·tect vb : shield from injury — **pro·tec·tor** n

pro·tec·tion n 1 : act of protecting 2 : one that protects — **pro·tec·tive** adj

pro·tec·tor·ate n : state dependent upon the authority of another state

pro·té·gé n : one under the care and protection of an influential person

pro·tein n : complex combination of amino acids present in living matter

pro·test n 1 : organized public demonstration of disapproval 2 : strong objection ~ vb 1 : assert positively 2 : object strongly — **pro·tes·ta·tion** n — **pro·test·er, pro·tes·tor** n

Prot·es·tant n : Christian not of a Catholic or Orthodox church — **Prot·es·tant·ism** n

pro·to·col n : diplomatic etiquette

pro·ton n : positively charged atomic particle

pro·to·plasm n : complex colloidal living substance of plant and animal cells — **pro·to·plas·mic** adj

pro·to·type n : original model

pro·to·zo·an n : single-celled lower invertebrate animal

pro·tract vb : prolong

pro·trac·tor n : instrument for drawing and measuring angles

pro·trude vb -trud·ed; -trud·ing : stick out or cause to stick out — **pro·tru·sion** n

pro·tu·ber·ance n : something that protrudes — **pro·tu·ber·ant** adj

proud adj 1 : having or showing excessive self-esteem 2 : highly pleased 3 : having proper self-respect 4 : glorious — **proud·ly** adv

prove vb proved; proved or prov·en; prov·ing 1 : test by experiment or by a standard 2 : establish the truth of by argument or evidence 3 : turn out esp. after trial or test — **prov·able** adj

prov·en·der n : dry food for domestic animals

prov·erb n : short meaningful popular saying — **pro·ver·bi·al** adj

pro·vide vb -vid·ed; -vid·ing 1 : take measures beforehand 2 : make a stipulation 3 : supply what is needed — **pro·vid·er** n

pro·vid·ed conj : if

prov·i·dence n 1 often cap : divine guidance 2 cap : God 3 : quality of being provident

prov·i·dent adj 1 : making provision for the future 2 : thrifty — **prov·i·dent·ly** adv

prov·i·den·tial adj 1 : relating to Providence 2 : opportune

pro·vid·ing conj : provided

prov·ince n 1 : administrative district 2 pl : all of a country outside the metropolis 3 : sphere

pro·vin·cial adj 1 : relating to a province 2 : limited in outlook — **pro·vin·cial·ism** n

pro·vi·sion n 1 : act of providing 2 : stock of food — usu. in pl. 3 : stipulation ~ vb : supply with provisions

pro·vi·sion·al adj : provided for a temporary need — **pro·vi·sion·al·ly** adv

pro·vi·so n, pl -sos or -soes : stipulation

pro·voke vb -voked; -vok·ing 1 : incite to anger 2 : stir up on purpose — **prov·o·ca·tion** n — **pro·voc·a·tive** adj

prow n : bow of a ship

prow·ess n 1 : valor 2 : extraordinary ability

prowl vb : roam about stealthily — **prowl** n — **prowl·er** n

prox·i·mate adj : very near

prox·im·i·ty n : nearness

proxy n, pl prox·ies : authority to act for another — **proxy** adj

prude n : one who shows extreme modesty — **prud·ery** n — **prud·ish** adj

pru·dent adj 1 : shrewd 2 : cautious 3 : thrifty — **pru·dence** n — **pru·den·tial** adj — **pru·dent·ly** adv

¹prune n : dried plum

²prune vb pruned; prun·ing : cut off unwanted parts

pru·ri·ent adj : lewd — **pru·ri·ence** n

¹pry vb pried; pry·ing : look closely or inquisitively

²pry vb pried; pry·ing : raise, move, or pull apart with a lever

psalm n : sacred song or poem — **psalm·ist** n

pseu·do·nym n : fictitious name — **pseu·don·y·mous** adj

pso·ri·a·sis n : chronic skin disease

psy·che n : soul or mind

psy·chi·a·try n : branch of medicine dealing with mental, emotional, and behavioral disorders — **psy·chi·at·ric** adj — **psy·chi·a·trist** n

psy·chic adj 1 : relating to the psyche 2 : sensitive to supernatural forces ~ n : person sensitive to supernatural forces — **psy·chi·cal·ly** adv

psy·cho·anal·y·sis n : study of the normally hidden content of the mind esp. to resolve conflicts — **psy·cho·an·a·lyst** n — **psy·cho·an·al·yt·ic** adj — **psy·cho·an·a·lyze** vb

psy·chol·o·gy n, pl -gies 1 : science of mind and behavior 2 : mental and behavioral aspect (as of an individual) — **psy·cho·log·i·cal** adj — **psy·cho·log·i·cal·ly** adv — **psy·chol·o·gist** n

psy·cho·path n : mentally ill or unstable person — **psy·cho·path·ic** adj

psy·cho·sis n, pl -cho·ses : mental derangement (as paranoia) — **psy·chot·ic** adj or n

psy·cho·so·mat·ic adj : relating to bodily symptoms caused by mental or emotional disturbance

psy·cho·ther·a·py n : treatment of mental disorder by psychological means — **psy·cho·ther·a·pist** n

pto·maine n : bacterial decay product

pu·ber·ty n : time of sexual maturity

pu·bic adj : relating to the lower abdominal region

pub·lic adj 1 : relating to the people as a whole 2 : civic 3 : not private 4 : open to all 5 : well-known

~ *n* : people as a whole — **pub·lic·ly** *adv*

pub·li·ca·tion *n* **1** : process of publishing **2** : published work

pub·lic·i·ty *n* **1** : news information given out to gain public attention **2** : public attention

pub·li·cize *vb* **-cized; -ciz·ing** : bring to public attention — **pub·li·cist** *n*

pub·lish *vb* **1** : announce publicly **2** : reproduce for sale esp. by printing — **pub·lish·er** *n*

puck·er *vb* : pull together into folds or wrinkles **~** *n* : wrinkle

pud·ding *n* : creamy dessert

pud·dle *n* : very small pool of water

pudgy *adj* **pudg·i·er; -est** : short and plump

pu·er·ile *adj* : childish

puff *vb* **1** : blow in short gusts **2** : pant **3** : enlarge **~** *n* **1** : short discharge (as of air) **2** : slight swelling **3** : something light and fluffy — **puffy** *adj*

pug *n* : small stocky dog

pu·gi·lism *n* : boxing — **pu·gi·list** *n* — **pu·gi·lis·tic** *adj*

pug·na·cious *adj* : prone to fighting — **pug·nac·i·ty** *n*

puke *vb* **puked; puk·ing** : vomit — **puke** *n*

pul·chri·tude *n* : beauty — **pul·chri·tu·di·nous** *adj*

pull *vb* **1** : exert force so as to draw (something) toward or out **2** : move **3** : stretch or tear **~** *n* **1** : act of pulling **2** : influence **3** : device for pulling something — **pull·er** *n*

pul·let *n* : young hen

pul·ley *n, pl* **-leys** : wheel with a grooved rim

Pull·man *n* : railroad car with berths

pull·over *adj* : put on by being pulled over the head — **pullover** *n*

pul·mo·nary *adj* : relating to the lungs

pulp *n* **1** : soft part of a fruit or vegetable **2** : soft moist mass (as of mashed wood) — **pulpy** *adj*

pul·pit *n* : raised desk used in preaching

pul·sate *vb* **-sat·ed; -sat·ing** : expand and contract rhythmically — **pul·sa·tion** *n*

pulse *n* : arterial throbbing caused by heart contractions — **pulse** *vb*

pul·ver·ize *vb* **-ized; -iz·ing** : beat or grind into a powder

pu·ma *n* : cougar

pum·ice *n* : light porous volcanic glass used in polishing

pum·mel *vb* **-meled; -mel·ing** : beat

¹pump *n* : device for moving or compressing fluids **~** *vb* **1** : raise (as water) with a pump **2** : fill by means of a pump — with *up* **3** : move like a pump — **pump·er** *n*

²pump *n* : woman's low shoe

pum·per·nick·el *n* : dark rye bread

pump·kin *n* : large usu. orange fruit of a vine related to the gourd

pun *n* : humorous use of a word in a way that suggests two or more interpretations — **pun** *vb*

¹punch *vb* **1** : strike with the fist **2** : perforate with a punch **~** *n* : quick blow with the fist — **punch·er** *n*

²punch *n* : tool for piercing or stamping

³punch *n* : mixed beverage often including fruit juice

punc·til·i·ous *adj* : marked by precise accordance with conventions

punc·tu·al *adj* : prompt — **punc·tu·al·i·ty** *n* — **punc·tu·al·ly** *adv*

punc·tu·ate *vb* **-at·ed; -at·ing** : mark with punctuation

punc·tu·a·tion *n* : standardized marks in written matter to clarify the meaning and separate parts

punc·ture *n* : act or result of puncturing **~** *vb* **-tured; -tur·ing** : make a hole in

pun·dit *n* **1** : learned person **2** : expert or critic

pun·gent *adj* : having a sharp or stinging odor or taste — **pun·gen·cy** *n* — **pun·gent·ly** *adv*

pun·ish *vb* : impose a penalty on or for — **pun·ish·able** *adj* — **pun·ish·ment** *n*

pu·ni·tive *adj* : inflicting punishment

pun·kin *var of* PUMPKIN

¹punt *n* : long narrow flat-bottomed boat **~** *vb* : propel (a boat) by pushing with a pole

²punt *vb* : kick a ball dropped from the hands **~** *n* : act of punting a ball

pu·ny *adj* **-ni·er; -est** : slight in power or size

pup *n* : young dog

pu·pa *n, pl* **-pae** *or* **-pas** : insect (as a moth) when it is in a cocoon — **pu·pal** *adj*

¹pu·pil *n* : young person in school

²pupil *n* : dark central opening of the iris of the eye

pup·pet *n* : small doll moved by hand or by strings — **pup·pe·teer** *n*

pup·py *n, pl* **-pies** : young dog

pur·chase *vb* **-chased; -chas·ing** : obtain in exchange for money **~** *n* **1** : act of purchasing **2** : something purchased **3** : secure grasp — **pur·chas·er** *n*

pure *adj* **pur·er; pur·est** : free of foreign matter, contamination, or corruption — **pure·ly** *adv*

pu·ree *n* : thick liquid mass of food — **puree** *vb*

pur·ga·to·ry *n, pl* **-ries** : intermediate state after death for purification by expiating sins — **pur·ga·tor·i·al** *adj*

purge *vb* **purged; purg·ing** **1** : purify esp. from sin **2** : have or cause emptying of the bowels **3** : to get rid of **~** *n* **1** : act or result of purging **2** : something that purges — **pur·ga·tive** *adj or n*

pu·ri·fy *vb* **-fied; -fy·ing** : make or become pure — **pu·ri·fi·ca·tion** *n* — **pu·ri·fi·er** *n*

Pu·rim *n* : Jewish holiday celebrated in February or March in commemoration of the deliverance of the Jews from the massacre plotted by Haman

pu·ri·tan *n* : one who practices or preaches a very strict moral code — **pu·ri·tan·i·cal** *adj* — **pu·ri·tan·i·cal·ly** *adv*

pu·ri·ty *n* : quality or state of being pure

purl *n* : stitch in knitting **~** *vb* : knit in purl stitch

pur·loin *vb* : steal

pur·ple *n* : bluish red color — **pur·plish** *adj*

pur·port *vb* : convey outwardly as the meaning **~** *n* : meaning — **pur·port·ed·ly** *adv*

pur·pose *n* **1** : something (as a result) aimed at **2** : resolution **~** *vb* **-posed; -pos·ing** : intend — **pur·pose·ful** *adj* — **pur·pose·ful·ly** *adv* — **pur·pose·less** *adj* — **pur·pose·ly** *adv*

purr *n* : low murmur typical of a contented cat — **purr** *vb*

¹purse *n* **1** : bag or pouch for money and small objects **2** : financial resource **3** : prize money

²purse *vb* **pursed; purs·ing** : pucker

pur·su·ance *n* : act of carrying out or into effect

pursuant to *prep* : according to

pur·sue *vb* **-sued; -su·ing** **1** : follow in order to overtake **2** : seek to accomplish **3** : proceed along **4** : engage in — **pur·su·er** *n*

pur·suit *n* **1** : act of pursuing **2** : occupation

pur·vey *vb* **-veyed; -vey·ing** : supply (as provisions) usu. as a business — **pur·vey·or** *n*

pus *n* : thick yellowish fluid (as in a boil)

push *vb* **1** : press against to move forward **2** : urge on or provoke **~** *n* **1** : vigorous effort **2** : act of pushing — **push·cart** *n* — **push·er** *n*

pushy *adj* **push·i·er; -est** : objectionably aggressive

pu·sil·lan·i·mous *adj* : cowardly

pussy *n, pl* **puss·ies** : cat

pus·tule *n* : pus-filled pimple

put *vb* **put; put·ting** **1** : bring to a specified position or condition **2** : subject to pain, suffering, or death **3** : impose or cause to exist **4** : express **5** : cause to be used or employed — **put off** *vb* : postpone or delay — **put out** *vb* : bother or inconvenience — **put up** *vb* **1** : prepare for storage **2** : lodge **3** : contribute or pay — **put up with** : endure

pu·tre·fy *vb* **-fied; -fy·ing** : make or become putrid — **pu·tre·fac·tion** *n*

pu·trid *adj* : rotten — **pu·trid·i·ty** *n*

put·ty *n, pl* **-ties** : doughlike cement — **putty** *vb*

puz·zle *vb* **-zled; -zling** **1** : confuse **2** : attempt to solve — with *out* or *over* **~** *n* : something that confuses or tests ingenuity — **puz·zle·ment** *n* — **puz·zler** *n*

pyg·my *n, pl* **-mies** : dwarf — **pygmy** *adj*

py·lon *n* : tower or tall post

pyr·a·mid *n* : structure with a square base and 4 triangular sides meeting at a point

pyre *n* : material heaped for a funeral fire

py·ro·ma·nia *n* : irresistible impulse to start fires — **py·ro·ma·ni·ac** *n*

py·ro·tech·nics *n pl* : spectacular display (as of fireworks) — **py·ro·tech·nic** *adj*

Pyr·rhic *adj* : achieved at excessive cost

py·thon *n* : very large constricting snake

Q

q *n, pl* **q's** *or* **qs** : 17th letter of the alphabet

¹quack *vb* : make a cry like that of a duck — **quack** *n*

²quack *n* : one who pretends to have medical or healing skill — **quack** *adj* — **quack·ery** *n* — **quack·ish** *adj*

quad·ran·gle *n* : rectangular courtyard

quad·rant *n* : ¼ of a circle

quad·ri·lat·er·al *n* : 4-sided polygon

qua·drille *n* : square dance for 4 couples

quad·ru·ped *n* : animal having 4 feet

qua·dru·ple *vb* **-pled; -pling** : multiply by 4 **~** *adj* : being 4 times as great or as many

qua·dru·plet *n* : one of 4 offspring born at one birth

quaff *vb* : drink deeply or repeatedly — **quaff** *n*

quag·mire *n* : soft land or bog

qua·hog *n* : thick-shelled clam

¹quail *n, pl* **quail** *or* **quails** : short-winged plump game bird

²quail *vb* : cower in fear

quaint *adj* : pleasingly old-fashioned or odd — **quaint·ly** *adv* — **quaint·ness** *n*

quake *vb* **quaked; quak·ing** : shake or tremble **~** *n* : earthquake

qual·i·fi·ca·tion *n* **1** : limitation or stipulation **2** : special skill or experience for a job

qual·i·fy *vb* **-fied; -fy·ing** **1** : modify or limit **2** : fit by skill or training for some purpose **3** : become eligible — **qual·i·fied** *adj* — **qual·i·fi·er** *n*

qual·i·ty *n, pl* **-ties** **1** : peculiar and essential character, nature, or feature **2** : excellence or distinction

qualm *n* : sudden feeling of doubt or uneasiness

quan·da·ry *n, pl* **-ries** : state of perplexity or doubt

quan·ti·ty n, pl **-ties 1** : something that can be measured or numbered **2** : considerable amount
quan·tum theory n : theory in physics that radiant energy (as light) is composed of separate packets of energy
quar·an·tine n **1** : restraint on the movements of persons or goods to prevent the spread of pests or disease **2** : place or period of quarantine — **quarantine** vb
quar·rel n : basis of conflict — **quarrel** vb — **quar·rel·some** adj
¹quar·ry n, pl **quarries** : prey
²quarry n, pl **-ries** : excavation for obtaining stone — **quarry** vb
quart n : unit of liquid measure equal to .95 liter or of dry measure equal to 1.10 liters
quar·ter n **1** : 1/4 part **2** : 1/4 of a dollar **3** : city district **4** pl : place to live esp. for a time **5** : mercy ~ vb : divide into 4 equal parts
quar·ter·ly adv or adj : at 3-month intervals ~ n, pl **-lies** : periodical published 4 times a year
quar·ter·mas·ter n **1** : ship's helmsman **2** : army supply officer
quar·tet n **1** : music for 4 performers **2** : group of 4
quar·to n, pl **-tos** : book printed on pages cut 4 from a sheet
quartz n : transparent crystalline mineral
quash vb **1** : set aside by judicial action **2** : suppress summarily and completely
qua·si adj : similar or nearly identical
qua·train n : unit of 4 lines of verse
qua·ver vb : tremble or trill — **quaver** n
quay n : wharf
quea·sy adj **-si·er; -est** : nauseated — **quea·si·ly** adv — **quea·si·ness** n
queen n **1** : wife or widow of a king **2** : female monarch **3** : woman of rank, power, or attractiveness **4** : fertile female of a social insect — **queen·ly** adj

queer adj : differing from the usual or normal — **queer·ly** adv — **queer·ness** n
quell vb : put down by force
quench vb **1** : put out **2** : satisfy (a thirst) — **quench·able** adj — **quench·er** n
quer·u·lous adj : fretful or whining — **quer·u·lous·ly** adv — **quer·u·lous·ness** n
que·ry n, pl **-ries** : question — **query** vb
quest n or vb : search
ques·tion n **1** : something asked **2** : subject for debate **3** : dispute ~ vb **1** : ask questions **2** : doubt or dispute **3** : subject to analysis — **ques·tion·er** n
ques·tion·able adj **1** : not certain **2** : of doubtful truth or morality — **ques·tion·ably** adv
question mark n : a punctuation mark ? used esp. at the end of a sentence to indicate a direct question
ques·tion·naire n : set of questions
queue n **1** : braid of hair **2** : a waiting line ~ vb **queued; queu·ing** or **queue·ing** : line up
quib·ble n : minor objection — **quibble** vb — **quib·bler** n
quick adj **1** : rapid **2** : alert or perceptive ~ n : sensitive area of living flesh — **quick** adv — **quick·ly** adv — **quick·ness** n
quick·en vb **1** : come to life **2** : increase in speed
quick·sand n : deep mass of sand and water
quick·sil·ver n : mercury
qui·es·cent adj : being at rest — **qui·es·cence** n
qui·et adj **1** : marked by little motion or activity **2** : gentle **3** : free from noise **4** : not showy **5** : secluded ~ vb : pacify — **quiet** adv or n — **qui·et·ly** adv — **qui·et·ness** n
qui·etude n : quietness or repose
quill n **1** : a large stiff feather **2** : porcupine's spine
quilt n : padded bedspread ~ vb : stitch or sew in layers with padding in between
quince n : hard yellow applelike fruit

qui·nine n : bitter drug used against malaria
quin·tes·sence n **1** : purest essence of something **2** : most typical example — **quint·es·sen·tial** adj — **quin·tes·sen·tial·ly** adv
quin·tet n **1** : music for 5 performers **2** : group of 5
quin·tu·ple adj **1** : having 5 units or members **2** : being 5 times as great or as many — **quintuple** n or vb
quin·tu·plet n : one of 5 offspring at one birth
quip vb **-pp-** : make a clever remark — **quip** n
quire n : 24 or 25 sheets of paper of the same size and quality
quirk n : peculiarity of action or behavior — **quirky** adj
quit vb **quit; quit·ting 1** : stop **2** : leave — **quit·ter** n
quite adv **1** : completely **2** : to a considerable extent
quits adj : even or equal with another (as by repaying a debt)
¹quiv·er n : case for arrows
²quiver vb : shake or tremble — **quiver** n
quix·ot·ic adj : idealistic to an impractical degree — **quix·ot·i·cal·ly** adv
quiz n, pl **quiz·zes** : short test ~ vb **-zz-** : question closely
quiz·zi·cal adj **1** : teasing **2** : curious
quoit n : ring thrown at a peg in a game (**quoits**)
quon·dam adj : former
quo·rum n : required number of members present
quo·ta n : proportional part or share
quotation mark n : one of a pair of punctuation marks " " or ' ' used esp. to indicate the beginning and the end of a quotation
quote vb **quot·ed; quot·ing 1** : repeat (another's words) exactly **2** : state (a price) — **quot·able** adj — **quo·ta·tion** n — **quote** n
quo·tient n : number obtained from division

R

r n, pl **r's** or **rs** : 18th letter of the alphabet
rab·bet n : groove in a board
rab·bi n : Jewish religious leader — **rab·bin·ic** **rab·bin·i·cal** adj
rab·bin·ate n : office of a rabbi
rab·bit n, pl **-bit** or **-bits** : long-eared burrowing mammal
rab·ble n : mob
ra·bid adj **1** : violent **2** : fanatical **3** : affected with rabies — **ra·bid·ly** adv
ra·bies n, pl **rabies** : acute deadly virus disease
rac·coon n, pl **-coon** or **-coons** : tree-dwelling mammal with a black mask and a bushy ringed tail
¹race n **1** : strong current of water **2** : contest of speed **3** : election campaign ~ vb **raced; rac·ing 1** : run in a race **2** : rush — **race·course** n — **rac·er** n — **race·track** n
²race n **1** : family, tribe, people, or nation of the same stock **2** : division of mankind based on hereditary traits — **ra·cial** adj — **ra·cial·ly** adv
race·horse n : horse used for racing
rac·ism n : discrimination based on the belief that some races are by nature superior — **rac·ist** n
rack n **1** : framework for display or storage **2** : instrument that stretches the body for torture ~ vb : torture with or as if with a rack
¹rack·et n : bat with a tight netting across an open frame
²racket n **1** : confused noise **2** : fraudulent scheme — **rack·e·teer** n — **rack·e·teer·ing** n
ra·con·teur n : storyteller
racy adj **rac·i·er; -est** : risqué — **rac·i·ly** adv — **rac·i·ness** n

ra·dar n : radio device for determining distance and direction of distant objects
ra·di·al adj : having parts arranged like rays coming from a common center — **ra·di·al·ly** adv
ra·di·ant adj **1** : glowing **2** : beaming with happiness **3** : transmitted by radiation — **ra·di·ance** n — **ra·di·ant·ly** adv
ra·di·ate vb **-at·ed; -at·ing 1** : issue rays or in rays **2** : spread from a center — **ra·di·a·tion** n
ra·di·a·tor n : cooling or heating device
rad·i·cal adj **1** : fundamental **2** : extreme ~ n : person favoring extreme changes — **rad·i·cal·ism** n — **rad·i·cal·ly** adv
radii pl of RADIUS
ra·dio n, pl **-di·os 1** : wireless transmission or reception of sound by means of electric waves **2** : radio receiving set ~ vb : send a message to by radio — **radio** adj
ra·dio·ac·tiv·i·ty n : property of an element that emits energy through nuclear disintegration — **ra·dio·ac·tive** adj
ra·di·ol·o·gy n : medical use of radiation — **ra·di·ol·o·gist** n
rad·ish n : pungent fleshy root usu. eaten raw
ra·di·um n : metallic radioactive chemical element
ra·di·us n, pl **-dii 1** : line from the center of a circle or sphere to the circumference or surface **2** : area defined by a radius
ra·don n : gaseous radioactive chemical element
raff·ish adj : flashily vulgar — **raff·ish·ly** adv — **raff·ish·ness** n

raf·fle n : lottery among people who have bought tickets ~ vb **-fled; -fling** : offer in a raffle
¹raft n : flat floating platform ~ vb : travel or transport by raft
²raft n : large amount or number
raf·ter n : beam supporting a roof
¹rag n : waste piece of cloth
²rag n : composition in ragtime
rag·a·muf·fin n : ragged dirty person
rage n **1** : violent anger **2** : vogue ~ vb **raged; rag·ing 1** : be extremely angry or violent **2** : be out of control
rag·ged adj : torn — **rag·ged·ly** adv — **rag·ged·ness** n
ra·gout n : meat stew
rag·time n : syncopated music
rag·weed n : coarse weedy herb with allergenic pollen
raid n : sudden usu. surprise attack — **raid** vb — **raid·er** n
¹rail n **1** : bar serving as a guard or barrier **2** : bar forming a track for wheeled vehicles **3** : railroad
²rail vb : scold someone vehemently — **rail·er** n
rail·ing n : rail or a barrier of rails
rail·lery n, pl **-ler·ies** : good-natured ridicule
rail·road n : road for a train laid with iron rails and wooden ties ~ vb : force something hastily — **rail·road·er** n — **rail·road·ing** n
rail·way n : railroad
rai·ment n : clothing
rain **1** : water falling in drops from the clouds **2** : shower of objects ~ vb : fall as or like rain

— **rain•coat** *n* — **rain•drop** *n* — **rain•fall** *n* — **rain•mak•er** *n* — **rain•mak•ing** *n* — **rain•storm** *n* — **rain•water** *n* — **rainy** *adj*

rain•bow *n* : arc of colors formed by the sun shining through moisture

raise *vb* **raised; rais•ing 1** : lift **2** : arouse **3** : erect **4** : collect **5** : breed, grow, or bring up **6** : increase **7** : make light ~ *n* : increase esp. in pay — **rais•er** *n*

rai•sin *n* : dried grape

ra•ja, ra•jah *n* : Indian prince

¹rake *n* : garden tool for smoothing or sweeping ~ *vb* **raked; rak•ing 1** : gather, loosen, or smooth with or as if with a rake **2** : sweep with gunfire

²rake *n* : dissolute man

rak•ish *adj* : smart or jaunty — **rak•ish•ly** *adv* — **rak•ish•ness** *n*

ral•ly **-lied; -ly•ing 1** : bring or come together **2** : revive or recover **3** : make a comeback ~ *n*, *pl* **-lies 1** : act of rallying **2** : mass meeting

ram *n* **1** : male sheep **2** : beam used in battering down walls or doors ~ *vb* **-mm- 1** : force or drive in or through **2** : strike against violently

RAM *n* : main internal storage area in a computer

ram•ble *vb* **-bled; -bling** : wander — **ramble** *n* — **ram•bler** *n*

ram•bunc•tious *adj* : unruly

ram•i•fi•ca•tion *n* : consequence

ram•i•fy *vb* **-fied; -fy•ing** : branch out

ramp *n* : sloping passage or connecting roadway

ram•page *vb* **-paged; -pag•ing** : rush about wildly ~ *n* : violent or riotous action or behavior

ram•pant *adj* : widespread — **ram•pant•ly** *adv*

ram•part *n* : embankment of a fortification

ram•rod *n* : rod used to load or clean a gun ~ *adj* : strict or inflexible

ram•shack•le *adj* : shaky

ran *past of* RUN

ranch *n* **1** : establishment for the raising of cattle, sheep, or horses **2** : specialized farm ~ *vb* : operate a ranch — **ranch•er** *n*

ran•cid *adj* : smelling or tasting as if spoiled — **ran•cid•i•ty** *n*

ran•cor *n* : bitter deep-seated ill will — **ran•cor•ous** *adj*

ran•dom *adj* : occurring by chance — **ran•dom•ly** *adv* — **random•ness** *n* — **at random** : without definite aim or method

ran•dom•ize *vb* **-ized; -izing** : select, assign, or arrange in a random way

rang *past of* RING

range *n* **1** : series of things in a row **2** : open land for grazing **3** : cooking stove **4** : variation within limits **5** : place for target practice **6** : extent ~ *vb* **ranged; rang•ing 1** : arrange **2** : roam at large, freely, or over **3** : vary within limits

rang•er *n* : officer who manages and protects public lands

rangy *adj* **rang•i•er; -est** : being slender with long limbs — **rang•i•ness** *n*

¹rank *adj* **1** : vigorous in growth **2** : unpleasantly strong-smelling — **rank•ly** *adv* — **rank•ness** *n*

²rank *n* **1** : line of soldiers **2** : orderly arrangement **3** : grade of official standing **4** : position within a group ~ *vb* **1** : arrange in formation or according to class **2** : take or have a relative position

rank and file *n* : general membership

ran•kle *vb* **-kled; -kling** : cause anger, irritation, or bitterness

ran•sack *vb* : search through and rob

ran•som *n* : something demanded for the freedom of a captive ~ *vb* : gain the freedom of by paying a price — **ran•som•er** *n*

rant *vb* : talk or scold violently — **rant•er** *n* — **rant•ing•ly** *adv*

¹rap *n* : sharp blow or rebuke ~ *vb* **-pp-** : strike or criticize sharply

²rap *vb* **-pp-** : talk freely

ra•pa•cious *adj* **1** : excessively greedy **2** : ravenous — **ra•pacious•ly** *adv* — **ra•pa•cious•ness** *n* — **ra•pac•i•ty** *n*

¹rape *n* : herb grown as a forage crop and for its seeds (**rape•seed**)

²rape *vb* **raped; rap•ing** : force to have sexual intercourse — **rape** *n* — **rap•er** *n* — **rap•ist** *n*

rap•id *adj* : very fast — **ra•pid•i•ty** *n* — **rap•id•ly** *adv*

rap•ids *n pl* : place in a stream where the current is swift

ra•pi•er *n* : narrow 2-edged sword

rap•ine *n* : plunder

rap•port *n* : harmonious relationship

rapt *adj* : engrossed — **rapt•ly** *adv* — **rapt•ness** *n*

rap•ture *n* : spiritual or emotional ecstasy — **rap•tur•ous** *adj* — **rap•tur•ous•ly** *adv*

¹rare *adj* **rar•er; rar•est** : having a portion relatively uncooked

²rare *adj* **rar•er; rar•est 1** : not dense **2** : unusually fine **3** : seldom met with — **rare•ly** *adv* — **rare•ness** *n* — **rar•i•ty** *n*

rar•e•fy *vb* **-fied; -fy•ing** : make or become rare, thin, or less dense — **rar•e•fac•tion** *n*

rar•ing *adj* : full of enthusiasm

ras•cal *n* : mean, dishonest, or mischievous person — **ras•cal•i•ty** *n* — **ras•cal•ly** *adj*

¹rash *adj* : too hasty in decision or action — **rash•ly** *adv* — **rash•ness** *n*

²rash *n* : a breaking out of the skin with red spots

rasp *vb* **1** : rub with or as if with a rough file **2** : to speak in a grating tone ~ *n* : coarse file

rasp•ber•ry *n* : edible red or black berry

rat *n* : destructive rodent larger than the mouse ~ *vb* : betray or inform on

ratch•et *n* : notched device for allowing motion in one direction

rate *n* **1** : quantity, amount, or degree measured in relation to some other quantity **2** : rank ~ *vb* **rat•ed; rat•ing 1** : estimate or determine the rank or quality of **2** : deserve

rath•er *adv* **1** : preferably **2** : on the other hand **3** : more properly **4** : somewhat

rat•i•fy *vb* **-fied; -fy•ing** : approve and accept formally — **rat•i•fi•ca•tion** *n*

rat•ing *n* : classification according to grade

ra•tio *n*, *pl* **-tios** : relation in number, quantity, or degree between things

ra•tion *n* : share or allotment (as of food) ~ *vb* : use or allot sparingly

ra•tio•nal *adj* **1** : having reason or sanity **2** : relating to reason — **ra•tio•nal•ly** *adv*

ra•tio•nale *n* **1** : explanation of principles of belief or practice **2** : underlying reason

ra•tio•nal•ize *vb* **-ized; -iz•ing** : justify (as one's behavior or weaknesses) esp. to oneself — **ra•tio•nal•i•za•tion** *n*

rat•tan *n* : palm with long stems used esp. for canes and wickerwork

rat•tle *vb* **-tled; -tling 1** : make a series of clattering sounds **2** : say briskly **3** : confuse or upset ~ *n* **1** : series of clattering sounds **2** : something (as a toy) that rattles

rat•tler *n* : rattlesnake

rat•tle•snake *n* : American venomous snake with a rattle at the end of the tail

rat•ty *adj* **rat•ti•er; -est** : shabby

rau•cous *adj* : harsh or boisterous — **rau•cous•ly** *adv* — **rau•cousness** *n*

rav•age *n* : destructive effect ~ *vb* **-aged; -ag•ing** : lay waste — **rav•ag•er** *n*

rave *vb* **raved; rav•ing 1** : talk wildly in or as if in

delirium **2** : talk with extreme enthusiasm ~ *n* **1** : act of raving **2** : enthusiastic praise

rav•el *vb* **-eled** *or* **-elled; -el•ing** *or* **-el•ling 1** : unravel **2** : tangle ~ *n* **1** : something tangled **2** : loose thread

ra•ven *n* : large black bird ~ *adj* : black and shiny

rav•en•ous *adj* : very hungry — **rav•en•ous•ly** *adv* — **rav•en•ousness** *n*

ra•vine *n* : narrow steep-sided valley

rav•ish *vb* **1** : seize and take away by violence **2** : overcome with joy or delight **3** : rape — **rav•ish•er** *n* — **rav•ish•ment** *n*

raw *adj* **raw•er; raw•est 1** : not cooked **2** : not processed **3** : not trained **4** : having the surface rubbed off **5** : cold and damp **6** : vulgar — **raw•ness** *n*

raw•hide *n* : untanned skin of cattle

ray *n* **1** : thin beam of radiant energy (as light) **2** : tiny bit

ray•on *n* : fabric made from cellulose fiber

raze *vb* **razed; raz•ing** : destroy or tear down

ra•zor *n* : sharp cutting instrument used to shave off hair

re- *prefix* **1** : again or anew **2** : back or backward

reaccelerate	recharge
reaccept	rechargeable
reacclimatize	recheck
reaccredit	rechristen
reacquaint	recirculate
reacquire	recirculation
reactivate	reclassification
reactivation	reclassify
readdress	recolonize
readjust	recombine
readjustment	recompute
readmit	reconceive
readopt	reconnect
reaffirm	reconquer
realign	reconquest
realignment	reconsider
reallocate	reconsideration
reanalysis	reconsolidate
reanalyze	reconstruct
reappear	recontaminate
reappearance	reconvene
reapply	reconvict
reappoint	recopy
reapportion	re-create
reappraisal	recross
reappraise	redecorate
reapprove	rededicate
reargue	rededication
rearrange	redefine
rearrest	redeposit
reassemble	redesign
reassert	redevelop
reassess	rediscover
reassessment	rediscovery
reassign	redissolve
reassignment	redistribute
reattach	redraft
reattain	redraw
reawaken	reemerge
rebalance	reemergence
rebaptize	reemphasize
rebid	reenergize
rebind	reengage
reborn	reenlist
rebroadcast	reenlistment
rebuild	reenroll
rebury	reenter
recalculate	reequip
recapture	reestablish
recast	reestablishment
recertification	reestimate
recertify	reevaluate
rechannel	reevaluation

reexamination
reexamine
refinance
refire
refloat
refocus
refold
reformulate
refreeze
refuel
regain
regrow
regrowth
rehear
reheat
rehire
rehospitalization
rehospitalize
reidentify
reignite
reimplant
reimpose
reincorporate
reindict
reinfection
reinflate
reinject
reinjection
reinoculate
reinsert
reinsertion
reinspect
reinstall
reinstitute
reintegrate
reintegration
reinter
reintroduce
reinvent
reinvestigate
reinvestigation
reinvigorate
rejudge
rekindle
reknit
relabel
relandscape
relaunch
relearn
relight
reline
reload
remarriage
remarry
rematch
remelt
remobilize
remoisten
remold
remotivate
rename
renegotiate
reoccupy
reoccur
reoccurrence
reoperate
reorchestrate
reorganization
reorganize
reorient
repack
repave

rephotograph
replan
replaster
replay
replot
repolish
repopulate
repressurize
reprice
reprint
reprocess
reprogram
reread
rereading
rerecord
reregister
reroof
reroute
resalable
resale
reschedule
reseal
resegregate
resell
resentence
reset
resettle
resew
reshoot
reshow
resocialization
resod
resolidify
restage
restart
restate
restatement
restimulate
restock
restructure
restudy
restyle
resubmit
resupply
resurface
resurvey
resynthesis
resynthesize
retarget
reteach
retell
retest
rethink
retighten
retrain
retranslate
retransmit
retry
retune
retype
reupholster
reusable
reuse
reutilize
revaccinate
revaccination
revisit
rewash
reweave
rewind
rewire
rewrap

reach vb 1 : stretch out 2 : touch or try to touch or grasp 3 : extend to or arrive at 4 : communicate with ~ n 1 : act of reaching 2 : distance one can reach 3 : ability to reach — **reach•able** adj — **reach•er** n

re•act vb 1 : act in response to some influence or stimulus 2 : undergo chemical change — **re•active** adj

re•ac•tion n 1 : action or emotion caused by and directly related or counter to another action 2 : chemical change

re•ac•tion•ary adj : relating to or favoring return to an earlier political order or policy — **reactionary** n

re•ac•tor n 1 : one that reacts 2 : device for the controlled release of nuclear energy

read vb read; read•ing 1 : understand written language 2 : utter aloud printed words 3 : interpret 4 : study 5 : indicate ~ adj : informed by reading — **read•a•bil•i•ty** n — **read•able** adj — **read•ably** adv — **read•er** n — **read•er•ship** n

read•ing n 1 : something read or for reading 2 : particular version, interpretation, or performance 3 : data indicated by an instrument

ready adj readi•er; -est 1 : prepared or available for use or action 2 : willing to do something ~ vb read•ied; ready•ing : make ready ~ n : state of being ready — **read•i•ly** adv — **read•i•ness** n

re•al adj 1 : relating to fixed or immovable things (as land) 2 : genuine 3 : not imaginary ~ adv : very — **re•al•ness** n — **for real** 1 : in earnest 2 : genuine

real estate n : property in houses and land

re•al•ism n 1 : disposition to deal with facts practically 2 : faithful portrayal of reality — **re•al•ist** adj or n — **re•al•is•tic** adj — **re•al•is•ti•cal•ly** adv

re•al•i•ty n, pl -ties 1 : quality or state of being real 2 : something real

re•al•ize vb -ized; -iz•ing 1 : make actual 2 : obtain 3 : be aware of — **re•al•iz•able** adj — **re•al•i•za•tion** n

re•al•ly adv : in truth

realm n 1 : kingdom 2 : sphere

¹ream n : quantity of paper that is 480, 500, or 516 sheets

² ream vb : enlarge, shape, or clean with a specially shaped tool (**reamer**)

reap vb : cut or clear (as a crop) with a scythe or machine — **reap•er** n

¹ rear vb 1 : raise upright 2 : breed or bring up 3 : rise on the hind legs

² rear n 1 : back 2 : position at the back of something ~ adj : being at the back — **rear•ward** adj or adv

rear admiral n : commissioned officer in the navy or coast guard ranking next below a vice admiral

rea•son n 1 : explanation or justification 2 : motive for action or belief 3 : power or process of thinking ~ vb 1 : use the faculty of reason 2 : try to persuade another — **rea•son•er** n — **rea•son•ing** n

rea•son•able adj 1 : being within the bounds of reason 2 : inexpensive — **rea•son•able•ness** n — **rea•son•ably** adv

re•as•sure vb : restore one's confidence — **re•as•sur•ance** n — **re•as•sur•ing•ly** adv

re•bate n : return of part of a payment — **rebate** vb

reb•el n : one that resists authority ~ vb -belled; -bel•ling 1 : resist authority 2 : feel or exhibit anger — **rebel** adj

re•bel•lion n : resistance to authority and esp. to one's government

re•bel•lious adj 1 : engaged in rebellion 2 : inclined to resist authority — **re•bel•lious•ly** adv — **re•bel•lious•ness** n

re•birth n 1 : new or second birth 2 : revival

re•bound vb 1 : spring back on striking something 2 : recover from a reverse ~ n 1 : action of rebounding 2 : reaction to a reverse

re•buff vb : refuse or repulse rudely — **rebuff** n

re•buke vb -buked; -buk•ing : reprimand sharply — **rebuke** n

re•bus n : riddle representing syllables or words with pictures

re•but vb -but•ted; -but•ting : refute — **re•but•ter** n

re•but•tal n : opposing argument

re•cal•ci•trant adj 1 : stubbornly resisting authority 2 : resistant to handling or treatment — **re•cal•ci•trance** n

re•call vb 1 : call back 2 : remember 3 : revoke ~ n 1 : a summons to return 2 : remembrance 3 : act of revoking

re•cant vb : take back (something said) publicly

re•ca•pit•u•late vb : summarize — **re•ca•pit•u•la•tion** n

re•cede vb -ced•ed; -ced•ing 1 : move back or away 2 : slant backward

re•ceipt n 1 : act of receiving 2 : something (as payment) received — usu. in pl. 3 : writing acknowledging something received

re•ceive vb -ceived; -ceiv•ing 1 : take in or accept 2 : greet or entertain (visitors) 3 : pick up radio waves and convert into sounds or pictures — **re•ceiv•able** adj

re•ceiv•er n 1 : one that receives 2 : one having charge of property or money involved in a lawsuit 3 : apparatus for receiving radio waves — **re•ceiv•er•ship** n

re•cent adj 1 : having lately come into existence 2 : of the present time or time just past — **re•cent•ly** adv — **re•cent•ness** n

re•cep•ta•cle n : container

re•cep•tion n 1 : act of receiving 2 : social gathering at which guests are formally welcomed

re•cep•tion•ist n : person employed to greet callers

re•cep•tive adj : open and responsive to ideas, impressions, or suggestions — **re•cep•tive•ly** adv — **re•cep•tive•ness** n — **re•cep•tiv•i•ty** n

re•cess n 1 : indentation in a line or surface 2 : suspension of a session for rest ~ vb 1 : make a recess in or put into a recess 2 : interrupt a session for a recess

re•ces•sion n 1 : departing procession 2 : period of reduced economic activity

rec•i•pe n : instructions for making something

re•cip•i•ent n : one that receives

re•cip•ro•cal adj 1 : affecting each in the same way 2 : so related that one is equivalent to the other — **re•cip•ro•cal•ly** adv — **re•ci•proc•i•ty** n

re•cip•ro•cate vb : make a return for something done or given — **re•cip•ro•ca•tion** n

re•cit•al n 1 : public reading or recitation 2 : music or dance concert or exhibition by pupils — **re•cit•al•ist** n

rec•i•ta•tion n : a reciting or recital

re•cite vb -cit•ed; -cit•ing 1 : repeat verbatim 2 : recount — **re•cit•er** n

reck•less adj : lacking caution — **reck•less•ly** adv — **reck•less•ness** n

reck•on vb 1 : count or calculate 2 : consider

reck•on•ing n 1 : act or instance of reckoning 2 : settling of accounts

re•claim vb 1 : change to a desirable condition 2 : obtain from a waste product or by-product 3 : demand or obtain the return of — **re•claim•able** adj — **rec•la•ma•tion** n

re•cline vb -clined; -clin•ing : lean backward or lie down

rec•luse n : one who leads a secluded or solitary life

rec•og•ni•tion n : act of recognizing or state of being recognized

re•cog•ni•zance n : promise recorded before a court

rec•og•nize vb 1 : identify as previously known 2 : take notice of 3 : acknowledge esp. with appreciation — **rec•og•niz•able** adj — **rec•og•niz•ably** adv

re•coil vb : draw or spring back= ~ n : action of recoiling

rec•ol•lect vb : remember

rec•ol•lec•tion n 1 : act or power of recollecting 2 : something recollected

rec•om•mend vb 1 : present as deserving of acceptance or trial 2 : advise — **rec•om•mend•able** adj

rec•om•men•da•tion n 1 : act of recommending 2 : something recommended or that recommends

rec•om•pense n : compensation — **recompense** vb

rec•on•cile vb -ciled; -cil•ing 1 : cause to be friendly again 2 : adjust or settle 3 : bring to acceptance — **rec•on•cil•able** adj — **rec•on•cile•ment** n — **rec•on•cil•er** n — **rec•on•cil•i•a•tion** n

re•con•dite adj 1 : hard to understand 2 : little known

re•con•di•tion vb : restore to good condition

re•con•nais•sance n : exploratory survey of enemy territory

re•con•noi•ter, re•con•noi•tre vb -tered or -tred; -ter•ing or -tring : make a reconnaissance of

re•cord vb 1 : set down in writing 2 : register permanently 3 : indicate 4 : preserve (as sound or images) for later reproduction ~ n 1 : something recorded 2 : best performance

re•cord•er n 1 : person or device that records 2 : wind instrument with finger holes

¹**re•count** vb : relate in detail

²**re•count** vb : count again — **recount** n

re•coup vb : make up for (an expense or loss)

re•course n : source of aid or a turning to such a source

re•cov•er vb 1 : regain position, poise, or health 2 : recoup — **re•cov•er•able** adj — **re•cov•ery** n

rec•re•a•tion n : a refreshing of strength or spirits as a change from work or study — **rec•re•a•tion•al** adj

re•crim•i•na•tion n : retaliatory accusation — **re•crim•i•nate** vb

re•cruit n : newly enlisted member ~ vb : enlist the membership or services of — **re•cruit•er** n — **re•cruit•ment** n

rect•an•gle n : 4-sided figure with 4 right angles — **rect•an•gu•lar** adj

rec•ti•fy vb -fied; -fy•ing : make or set right — **rec•ti•fi•ca•tion** n

rec•ti•tude n : moral integrity

rec•tor n : pastor

rec•to•ry n, pl -ries : rector's residence

rec•tum n, pl -tums or -ta : last part of the intestine joining the colon and anus — **rec•tal** adj

re•cum•bent adj : lying down

re•cu•per•ate vb -at•ed; -at•ing : recover (as from illness) — **re•cu•per•a•tion** n — **re•cu•per•a•tive** adj

re•cur vb -rr- 1 : return in thought or talk 2 : occur again — **re•cur•rence** n — **re•cur•rent** adj

re•cy•cle vb : process (as glass or cans) in order to regain a material for human use — **re•cy•cla•ble** adj

red n 1 : color of blood or of the ruby 2 cap : communist — **red** adj — **red•dish** adj — **red•ness** n

red•den vb : make or become red or reddish

re•deem vb 1 : regain, free, or rescue by paying a price 2 : atone for 3 : free from sin 4 : convert into something of value — **re•deem•able** adj — **re•deem•er** n

re•demp•tion n : act of redeeming — **re•demp•tive** adj — **re•demp•to•ry** adj

red•head n : one having red hair — **red•head•ed** adj

red•o•lent adj 1 : having a fragrance 2 : suggestive — **red•o•lence** n — **red•o•lent•ly** adv

re•dou•ble vb 1 : make twice as great in size or amount 2 : intensify

re•doubt n : small fortification

re•doubt•able adj : arousing dread

re•dound vb : have an effect

re•dress vb : set right ~ n 1 : relief or remedy 2 : compensation

red tape n : complex obstructive official routine

re•duce vb 1 : lessen 2 : put in a lower rank 3 : lose weight — **re•duc•er** n — **re•duc•ible** adj

re•duc•tion n 1 : act of reducing 2 : amount lost in reducing 3 : something made by reducing

re•dun•dant adj : using more words than necessary — **re•dun•dan•cy** n — **re•dun•dant•ly** adv

red•wood n : tall coniferous timber tree

reed n 1 : tall slender grass of wet areas 2 : elastic strip that vibrates to produce tones in certain wind instruments — **reedy** adj

reef n : ridge of rocks or sand at or near the surface of the water

reek n : strong or disagreeable fume or odor ~ vb : give off a reek

¹**reel** n : revolvable device on which something flexible is wound or a quantity of something wound on it ~ vb 1 : wind on a reel 2 : pull in by reeling — **reel•able** adj — **reel•er** n

²**reel** vb 1 : whirl or waver as from a blow 2 : walk or move unsteadily ~ n : reeling motion

³**reel** n : lively dance

re•fer vb -rr- 1 : direct or send to some person or place 2 : submit for consideration or action 3 : have connection 4 : mention or allude to something — **re•fer•able** adj — **re•fer•ral** n

ref•er•ee n 1 : one to whom an issue is referred for settlement 2 : sports official ~ vb -eed; -ee•ing : act as referee

ref•er•ence n 1 : act of referring 2 : a bearing on a matter 3 : consultation for information 4 : person who can speak for one's character or ability or a recommendation given by such a person

ref•er•en•dum n, pl -da or -dums : a submitting of legislative measures for voters' approval or rejection

re•fill vb : fill again — **re•fill** n — **re•fill•able** adj

re•fine vb -fined; -fin•ing 1 : free from impurities or waste matter 2 : improve or perfect 3 : free or become free of what is coarse or uncouth — **re•fine•ment** n — **re•fin•er** n

re•fin•ery n, pl -er•ies : place for refining (as oil or sugar)

re•flect vb 1 : bend or cast back (as light or heat) 2 : bring as a result 3 : cast reproach or blame 4 : ponder — **re•flec•tion** n — **re•flec•tive** adj — **re•flec•tor** n

re•flex n : automatic response to a stimulus ~ adj 1 : bent back 2 : relating to a reflex — **re•flex•ly** adv

re•flex•ive adj : of or relating to an action directed back upon the doer or the grammatical subject — **reflexive** n — **re•flex•ive•ly** adv — **re•flex•ive•ness** n

re•form vb : make or become better esp. by correcting bad habits — **reform** n — **re•form•able** adj — **refor•ma•tive** adj — **reform•er** n

re•for•ma•to•ry n, pl -ries : penal institution for reforming young offenders

re•fract vb : subject to refraction

re•frac•tion n : the bending of a ray (as of light) when it passes from one medium into another — **re•frac•tive** adj

re•frac•to•ry adj : obstinate or unmanageable

re•frain vb : hold oneself back ~ n : verse recurring regularly in a song — **re•frain•ment** n

re•fresh vb 1 : make or become fresh or fresher 2 : supply or take refreshment — **re•fresh•er** n — **re•fresh•ing•ly** adv

re•fresh•ment n 1 : act of refreshing 2 pl : light meal

re•frig•er•ate vb -at•ed; -at•ing : chill or freeze (food) for preservation — **re•frig•er•ant** adj or n — **re•frig•er•a•tion** n — **re•frig•er•a•tor** n

ref•uge n 1 : protection from danger 2 : place that provides protection

ref•u•gee n : person who flees for safety

re•fund vb : give or put back (money) ~ n 1 : act of refunding 2 : sum refunded — **refund•able** adj

re•fur•bish vb : renovate

¹**re•fuse** vb -fused; -fus•ing : decline to accept, do, or give — **re•fus•al** n

²**ref•use** n : worthless matter

re•fute vb -fut•ed; -fut•ing : prove to be false — **ref•u•ta•tion** n — **re•fut•er** n

re•gal adj 1 : befitting a king 2 : stately — **re•gal•ly** adv

re•gale vb -galed; -gal•ing 1 : entertain richly or agreeably 2 : delight

re•ga•lia n pl 1 : symbols of royalty 2 : insignia of an office or order 3 : finery

re•gard n 1 : consideration 2 : feeling of approval and liking 3 pl : friendly greetings 4 : relation ~ vb 1 : pay attention to 2 : show respect for 3 : have an opinion of 4 : look at 5 : relate to — **re•gard•ful** adj — **regard•less** adj

re•gard•ing prep : concerning

regardless of prep : in spite of

re•gen•er•ate adj 1 : formed or created again 2 : spiritually reborn ~ vb 1 : reform completely 2 : replace (a lost body part) by new tissue growth 3 : give new life to — **re•gen•er•a•tion** n — **re•gen•er•a•tive** adj — **re•gen•er•a•tor** n

re•gent n 1 : person who rules during the childhood, absence, or incapacity of the sovereign 2 : member of a governing board — **re•gen•cy** n

re•gime n : government in power

reg•i•men n : systematic course of treatment or training

reg•i•ment n : military unit ~ vb 1 : organize rigidly for control 2 : make orderly — **reg•i•men•tal** adj — **reg•i•men•ta•tion** n

re•gion n : indefinitely defined area — **re•gion•al** adj — **re•gion•al•ly** adv

reg•is•ter n 1 : record of items or details or a book for keeping such a record 2 : device to regulate ventilation 3 : counting or recording device 4 : range of a voice or instrument ~ vb 1 : enter in a register 2 : record automatically 3 : get special care for mail by paying more postage

reg•is•trar n : official keeper of records

reg•is•tra•tion n 1 : act of registering 2 : entry in a register

reg•is•try n, pl -tries 1 : enrollment 2 : place of registration 3 : official record book

re•gress vb : go or cause to go back or to a lower level — **re•gres•sion** n — **re•gres•sive** adj

re•gret vb -tt- 1 : mourn the loss or death of 2 : be very sorry for ~ n 1 : sorrow or the expression of sorrow 2 pl : message declining an invitation — **re•gret•ful** adj — **re•gret•ful•ly** adv — **re•gret•ta•ble** adj — **re•gret•ta•bly** adv — **re•gret•ter** n

reg•u•lar adj 1 : conforming to what is usual, normal, or average 2 : steady, uniform, or unvarying — **regular** n — **reg•u•lar•i•ty** n — **reg•u•lar•ize** vb — **reg•u•lar•ly** adv

reg•u•late vb -lat•ed; -lat•ing 1 : govern according to rule 2 : adjust to a standard — **reg•u•la•tive** adj — **reg•u•la•tor** n — **reg•u•la•to•ry** adj

reg•u•la•tion *n* 1 : act of regulating 2 : rule dealing with details of procedure

re•gur•gi•tate *vb* **-tat•ed; -tat•ing** : vomit — **re•gur•gi•ta•tion** *n*

re•ha•bil•i•tate *vb* **-tat•ed; -tat•ing** 1 : reinstate 2 : make good or usable again — **re•ha•bil•i•tation** *n*

re•hears•al *n* : practice session or performance

re•hearse *vb* **-hearsed; -hearsing** 1 : repeat or recount 2 : engage in a rehearsal of — **re•hears•er** *n*

reign *n* : sovereign's authority or rule ~ *vb* : rule as a sovereign

re•im•burse *vb* **-bursed; -burs•ing** : repay — **re•im•burs•able** *adj* — **re•im•burse•ment** *n*

rein *n* 1 : strap fastened to a bit to control an animal 2 : restraining influence ~ *vb* : direct by reins

re•in•car•na•tion *n* : rebirth of the soul — **re•in•car•nate** *vb*

rein•deer *n* : caribou

re•in•force *vb* : strengthen or support — **re•in•force•ment** *n* — **re•in•forc•er** *n*

re•in•state *vb* : restore to a former position — **re•in•state•ment** *n*

re•it•er•ate *vb* : say again — **re•it•er•a•tion** *n*

re•ject *vb* 1 : refuse to grant or consider 2 : refuse to admit, believe, or receive 3 : throw out as useless or unsatisfactory ~ *n* : rejected person or thing — **re•jec•tion** *n*

re•joice *vb* **-joiced; -joic•ing** : feel joy — **re•joic•er** *n*

re•join *vb* 1 : join again 2 : say in answer

re•join•der *n* : answer

re•ju•ve•nate *vb* **-nat•ed; -nat•ing** : make young again — **re•ju•ve•na•tion** *n*

re•lapse *n* : recurrence of illness after a period of improvement ~ *vb* : suffer a relapse

re•late *vb* **-lat•ed; -lat•ing** 1 : give a report of 2 : show a connection between 3 : have a relationship — **re•lat•able** *adj* — **re•lat•er, re•la•tor** *n*

re•la•tion *n* 1 : account 2 : connection 3 : relationship 4 : reference 5 *pl* : dealings

re•la•tion•ship *n* : the state of being related or interrelated

rel•a•tive *n* : person connected with another by blood or marriage ~ *adj* : considered in comparison with something else — **rel•a•tive•ly** *adv* — **rel•a•tive•ness** *n*

re•lax *vb* 1 : make or become less tense or rigid 2 : make less severe 3 : seek rest or recreation — **re•lax•er** *n*

re•lax•a•tion *n* 1 : lessening of tension 2 : recreation

re•lay *n* : fresh supply (as of horses or people) arranged to relieve others ~ *vb* **-layed; -lay•ing** : pass along in stages

re•lease *vb* **-leased; -leas•ing** 1 : free from confinement or oppression 2 : relinquish 3 : permit publication, performance, exhibition, or sale ~ *n* 1 : relief from trouble 2 : discharge from an obligation 3 : act of releasing or what is released

rel•e•gate *vb* **-gat•ed; -gat•ing** 1 : remove to some less prominent position 2 : assign to a particular class or sphere — **rel•e•ga•tion** *n*

re•lent *vb* : become less severe

re•lent•less *adj* : mercilessly severe or persistent — **re•lent•less•ly** *adv* — **re•lent•less•ness** *n*

rel•e•vance *n* : relation to the matter at hand — **rel•e•vant** *adj* — **rel•e•vant•ly** *adv*

re•li•able *adj* : fit to be trusted — **re•li•abil•i•ty** *n* — **re•li•able•ness** *n* — **re•li•ably** *adv*

re•li•ance *n* : act or result of relying

re•li•ant *adj* : dependent

rel•ic *n* 1 : object venerated because of its association with a saint or martyr 2 : remaining trace

re•lief *n* 1 : lightening of something oppressive 2 : welfare

re•lieve *vb* **-lieved; -liev•ing** 1 : free from a burden or distress 2 : release from a post or duty 3 : break the monotony of — **re•liev•er** *n*

re•li•gion *n* 1 : service and worship of God 2 : set or system of religious beliefs — **re•li•gion•ist** *n*

re•li•gious *adj* 1 : relating or devoted to an ultimate reality or deity 2 : relating to religious beliefs or observances 3 : faithful, fervent, or zealous — **re•li•gious•ly** *adv*

re•lin•quish *vb* 1 : renounce 2 : let go of — **re•lin•quish•ment** *n*

rel•ish *n* 1 : keen enjoyment 2 : highly seasoned sauce (as of pickles) ~ *vb* : enjoy — **rel•ish•able** *adj*

re•live *vb* : live over again (as in the imagination)

re•lo•cate *vb* : move to a new location — **re•lo•ca•tion** *n*

re•luc•tant *adj* : feeling or showing doubt or unwillingness — **re•luc•tance** *n* — **re•luc•tant•ly** *adv*

re•ly *vb* **-lied; -ly•ing** : place faith or confidence — often with *on*

re•main *vb* 1 : be left after others have been removed 2 : be something yet to be done 3 : stay behind 4 : continue unchanged

re•main•der *n* : that which is left over

re•mains *n pl* 1 : remaining part or trace 2 : dead body

re•mark *vb* : express as an observation ~ *n* : passing comment

re•mark•able *adj* : extraordinary — **re•mark•able•ness** *n* — **re•mark•ably** *adv*

re•me•di•al *adj* : intended to remedy or improve

rem•e•dy *n, pl* **-dies** 1 : medicine that cures 2 : something that corrects an evil or compensates for a loss ~ *vb* **-died; -dy•ing** : provide or serve as a remedy for

re•mem•ber *vb* 1 : think of again 2 : keep from forgetting 3 : convey greetings from

re•mem•brance *n* 1 : act of remembering 2 : something that serves to bring to mind

re•mind *vb* : cause to remember — **re•mind•er** *n*

rem•i•nisce *vb* **-nisced; -nisc•ing** : indulge in reminiscence

rem•i•nis•cence *n* 1 : recalling of a past experience 2 : account of a memorable experience

rem•i•nis•cent *adj* 1 : relating to reminiscence 2 : serving to remind — **rem•i•nis•cent•ly** *adv*

re•miss *adj* : negligent or careless in performance of duty — **re•miss•ly** *adv* — **re•miss•ness** *n*

re•mis•sion *n* 1 : act of forgiving 2 : a period of relief from or easing of symptoms of a disease

re•mit *vb* **-tt-** 1 : pardon 2 : send money in payment

re•mit•tance *n* : sum of money remitted

rem•nant *n* : small part or trace remaining

re•mod•el *vb* : alter the structure of

re•mon•strance *n* : act or instance of remonstrating

re•mon•strate *vb* **-strat•ed; -strat•ing** : speak in protest, reproof, or opposition — **re•mon•stra•tion** *n*

re•morse *n* : distress arising from a sense of guilt — **re•morse•ful** *adj* — **re•morse•less** *adj*

re•mote *adj* **-mot•er; -est** 1 : far off in place or time 2 : hard to reach or find 3 : acting, acted on, or controlled indirectly or from afar 4 : slight 5 : distant in manner — **re•mote•ly** *adv* — **re•mote•ness** *n*

re•move *vb* **-moved; -mov•ing** 1 : move by lifting or taking off or away 2 : get rid of — **re•mov•able** *adj* — **re•mov•al** *n* — **re•mov•er** *n*

re•mu•ner•ate *vb* **-at•ed; -at•ing** : pay — **re•mu•ner•a•tion** *n* — **re•mu•ner•a•tor** *n*

re•mu•ner•a•tive *adj* : gainful

re•nais•sance *n* : rebirth or revival

re•nal *adj* : relating to the kidneys

rend *vb* **rent; rend•ing** : tear apart forcibly

ren•der *vb* 1 : extract by heating 2 : hand over or give up 3 : do (a service) for another 4 : cause to be or become

ren•dez•vous *n, pl* **ren•dez•vous** 1 : place appointed for a meeting 2 : meeting at an appointed place ~ *vb* **-voused; -vous•ing** : meet at a rendezvous

ren•di•tion *n* : version

ren•e•gade *n* : deserter of one faith or cause for another

re•nege *vb* **-neged; -neg•ing** : go back on a promise — **re•neg•er** *n*

re•new *vb* 1 : make or become new, fresh, or strong again 2 : begin again 3 : grant or obtain an extension of — **re•new•able** *adj* — **renew•al** *n* — **re•new•er** *n*

re•nounce *vb* **-nounced; -nounc•ing** : give up, refuse, or resign — **re•nounce•ment** *n*

ren•o•vate *vb* **-vat•ed; -vating** : make like new again — **ren•o•va•tion** *n* — **ren•o•va•tor** *n*

re•nown *n* : state of being widely known and honored — **renowned** *adj*

¹rent *n* : money paid or due periodically for the use of another's property ~ *vb* : hold or give possession and use of for rent — **rent•al** *n or adj* — **rent•er** *n*

²rent *n* : a tear in cloth

re•nun•ci•a•tion *n* : act of renouncing

¹re•pair *vb* : go

²repair *vb* : restore to good condition ~ *n* 1 : act or instance of repairing 2 : condition — **re•pair•er** *n* — **re•pairman** *n*

rep•a•ra•tion *n* : money paid for redress — usu. pl.

rep•ar•tee *n* : clever replies

re•past *n* : meal

re•pa•tri•ate *vb* **-at•ed; -ating** : send back to one's own country — **re•pa•tri•ate** *n* — **re•pa•tri•a•tion** *n*

re•pay *vb* **-paid; -pay•ing** : pay back — **re•pay•able** *adj* — **re•payment** *n*

re•peal *vb* : annul by legislative action — **repeal** *n* — **re•peal•er** *n*

re•peat *vb* : say or do again ~ *n* 1 : act of repeating 2 : something repeated — **re•peat•able** *adj* — **re•peat•ed•ly** *adv* — **re•peat•er** *n*

re•pel *vb* **-pelled; -pel•ling** 1 : drive away 2 : disgust — **re•pel•lent** *adj or n*

re•pent *vb* 1 : turn from sin 2 : regret — **re•pen•tance** *n* — **re•pen•tant** *adj*

re•per•cus•sion *n* : effect of something done or said

rep•er•toire *n* : pieces a company or performer can present

rep•er•to•ry *n, pl* **-ries** 1 : repertoire 2 : theater with a resident company doing several plays

rep•e•ti•tion *n* : act or instance of repeating

rep•e•ti•tious *adj* : tediously repeating — **rep•e•ti•tious•ly** *adv* — **rep•e•ti•tious•ness** *n*

re•pet•i•tive *adj* : repetitious — **re•pet•i•tive•ly** *adv* — **re•pet•i•tive•ness** *n*

re•pine *vb* **re•pined; re•pin•ing** : feel or express discontent

re•place *vb* 1 : restore to a former position 2 : take the place of 3 : put something new in the place of — **re•place•able** *adj* — **re•place•ment** *n* — **re•plac•er** *n*

re•plen•ish *vb* : stock or supply anew — **re•plen•ish•ment** *n*

re•plete *adj* : full — **re•pleteness** *n* — **re•ple•tion** *n*

rep•li•ca *n* : exact copy

rep•li•cate *vb* **-cat•ed; -cating** : duplicate or repeat — **rep•li•cate** *n* — **rep•li•ca•tion** *n*

re•ply *vb* **-plied; -ply•ing** : say or do in answer ~ *n, pl* **-plies** : answer

re·port *n* 1 : rumor 2 : statement of information (as events or causes) 3 : explosive noise ~ *vb* 1 : give an account of 2 : present an account of (an event) as news 3 : present oneself 4 : make known to authorities — **re·port·age** *n* — **re·port·ed·ly** *adv* — **re·port·er** *n* — **re·por·to·ri·al** *adj*

re·pose *vb* **-posed; -pos·ing** : lay or lie at rest ~ *n* 1 : state of resting 2 : calm or peace — **re·pose·ful** *adj*

re·pos·i·to·ry *n, pl* **-ries** : place where something is stored

re·pos·sess *vb* : regain possession and legal ownership of — **repos·ses·sion** *n*

rep·re·hend *vb* : censure — **rep·re·hen·sion** *n*

rep·re·hen·si·ble *adj* : deserving condemnation — **rep·re·hen·si·bly** *adv*

rep·re·sent *vb* 1 : serve as a sign or symbol of 2 : act or speak for 3 : describe as having a specified quality or character — **rep·re·sen·ta·tion** *n*

rep·re·sen·ta·tive *adj* 1 : standing or acting for another 2 : carried on by elected representatives ~ *n* 1 : typical example 2 : one that represents another 3 : member of usu. the lower house of a legislature — **rep·re·sen·ta·tive·ly** *adv* — **rep·re·sen·ta·tive·ness** *n*

re·press *vb* : restrain or suppress — **re·pres·sion** *n* — **re·pres·sive** *adj*

re·prieve *n* 1 : a delay in punishment 2 : temporary respite — **reprieve** *vb*

rep·ri·mand *n* : formal or severe criticism — **reprimand** *vb*

re·pri·sal *n* : act in retaliation

re·prise *n* : musical repetition

re·proach *n* 1 : disgrace 2 : rebuke ~ *vb* : express disapproval to — **re·proach·ful** *adj* — **re·proachful·ly** *adv* — **re·proach·ful·ness** *n*

rep·ro·bate *n* : scoundrel — **reprobate** *adj*

rep·ro·ba·tion *n* : strong disapproval

re·pro·duce *vb* 1 : produce again or anew 2 : produce offspring — **re·pro·duc·ible** *adj* — **re·pro·duc·tion** *n* — **re·pro·duc·tive** *adj*

re·proof *n* : blame or censure for a fault

re·prove *vb* **-proved; -prov·ing** : express disapproval to or of

rep·tile *n* : air-breathing scaly vertebrate — **rep·til·ian** *adj or n*

re·pub·lic *n* : country with representative government

re·pub·li·can *adj* 1 : relating to or resembling a republic 2 : supporting a republic — **republican** *n* — **re·pub·li·can·ism** *n*

re·pu·di·ate *vb* **-at·ed; -at·ing** : refuse to have anything to do with — **re·pu·di·a·tion** *n*

re·pug·nant *adj* : contrary to one's tastes or principles — **re·pug·nance** *n* — **re·pug·nant·ly** *adv*

re·pulse *vb* **-pulsed; -puls·ing** 1 : drive or beat back 2 : rebuff 3 : be repugnant to — **repulse** *n* — **re·pul·sion** *n*

re·pul·sive *adj* : arousing aversion or disgust — **re·pul·sive·ly** *adv* — **re·pul·sive·ness** *n*

rep·u·ta·ble *adj* : having a good reputation — **rep·u·ta·bly** *adv*

rep·u·ta·tion *n* : one's character or public esteem

re·pute *vb* **-put·ed; -put·ing** : think of as being ~ *n* : reputation — **re·put·ed** *adj* — **re·put·ed·ly** *adv*

re·quest *n* : act or instance of asking for something or a thing asked for ~ *vb* 1 : make a request of 2 : ask for — **re·quest·er** *n*

re·qui·em *n* : Mass for a dead person or a musical setting for this

re·quire *vb* **-quired; -quir·ing** 1 : insist on 2 : call for as essential — **re·quire·ment** *n*

req·ui·site *adj* : necessary — **requisite** *n*

req·ui·si·tion *n* : formal application or demand — **requisition** *vb*

re·quite *vb* **-quit·ed; -quit·ing** : make return for or to — **re·quit·al** *n*

re·scind *vb* : repeal or cancel — **re·scis·sion** *n*

res·cue *vb* **-cued; -cu·ing** : set free from danger or confinement — **rescue** *n* — **res·cu·er** *n*

re·search *n* : careful or diligent search esp. for new knowledge — **research** *vb* — **re·search·er** *n*

re·sem·ble *vb* **-sem·bled; -sem·bling** : be like or similar to — **re·sem·blance** *n*

re·sent *vb* : feel or show annoyance at — **re·sent·ful** *adj* — **re·sent·ful·ly** *adv* — **re·sent·ment** *n*

res·er·va·tion *n* 1 : act of reserving or something reserved 2 : limiting condition

re·serve *vb* **-served; -serv·ing** 1 : store for future use 2 : set aside for special use ~ *n* 1 : something reserved 2 : restraint in words or bearing 3 : military forces withheld from action or not part of the regular services — **re·served** *adj*

res·er·voir *n* : place where something (as water) is kept in store

re·side *vb* **-sid·ed; -sid·ing** 1 : make one's home 2 : be present

res·i·dence *n* 1 : act or fact of residing in a place 2 : place where one lives — **res·i·dent** *adj or n* — **res·i·den·tial** *adj*

res·i·due *n* : part remaining — **re·sid·u·al** *adj*

re·sign *vb* 1 : give up deliberately 2 : give (oneself) over without resistance — **res·ig·na·tion** *n* — **re·sign·ed·ly** *adv*

re·sil·ience *n* : ability to recover or adjust easily

re·sil·ien·cy *n* : resilience

re·sil·ient *adj* : elastic

res·in *n* : substance from the gum or sap of trees — **res·in·ous** *adj*

re·sist *vb* 1 : withstand the force or effect of 2 : fight against — **re·sist·ible** *adj* — **re·sist·less** *adj*

re·sis·tance *n* 1 : act of resisting 2 : ability of an organism to resist disease 3 : opposition to electric current

re·sis·tant *adj* : giving resistance

res·o·lute *adj* : having a fixed purpose — **res·o·lute·ly** *adv* — **res·o·lute·ness** *n*

res·o·lu·tion *n* 1 : process of resolving 2 : firmness of purpose 3 : statement of the opinion, will, or intent of a body

re·solve *vb* **-solved; -solv·ing** 1 : find an answer to 2 : make a formal resolution ~ *n* 1 : something resolved 2 : steadfast purpose — **re·solv·able** *adj*

res·o·nant *adj* 1 : continuing to sound 2 : relating to intensification or prolongation of sound (as by a vibrating body) — **res·o·nance** *n* — **res·o·nant·ly** *adv*

re·sort *n* 1 : source of help 2 : place to go for vacation ~ *vb* 1 : go often or habitually 2 : have recourse

re·sound *vb* : become filled with sound

re·sound·ing *adj* : impressive — **re·sound·ing·ly** *adv*

re·source *n* 1 : new or reserve source 2 *pl* : available funds 3 : ability to handle situations — **re·source·ful** *adj* — **re·source·ful·ness** *n*

re·spect *n* 1 : relation to something 2 : high or special regard 3 : detail ~ *vb* : consider deserving of high regard — **re·spect·er** *n* — **respect·ful** *adj* — **re·spect·ful·ly** *adv* — **re·spect·ful·ness** *n*

re·spect·able *adj* 1 : worthy of respect 2 : fair in size, quantity, or quality — **re·spect·abil·i·ty** *n* — **re·spect·ably** *adv*

re·spec·tive *adj* : individual and specific

re·spec·tive·ly *adv* 1 : as relating to each 2 : each in the order given

res·pi·ra·tion *n* : act or process of breathing — **re·spi·ra·to·ry** *adj* — **re·spire** *vb*

res·pi·ra·tor *n* : device for artificial respiration

re·spite *n* : temporary delay or rest

re·splen·dent *adj* : shining brilliantly — **re·splen·dence** *n* — **re·splen·dent·ly** *adv*

re·spond *vb* 1 : answer 2 : react — **re·spon·dent** *n or adj* — **re·spond·er** *n*

re·sponse *n* 1 : act of responding 2 : answer

re·spon·si·ble *adj* 1 : answerable for acts or decisions 2 : able to fulfill obligations 3 : having important duties — **re·spon·si·bil·i·ty** *n* — **re·spon·si·ble·ness** *n* — **re·spon·si·bly** *adv*

re·spon·sive *adj* : quick to respond — **re·spon·sive·ly** *adv* — **re·spon·sive·ness** *n*

¹rest *n* 1 : sleep 2 : freedom from work or activity 3 : state of inactivity 4 : something used as a support ~ *vb* 1 : get rest 2 : cease action or motion 3 : give rest to 4 : sit or lie fixed or supported 5 : depend — **rest·ful** *adj* — **rest·ful·ly** *adv*

²rest *n* : remainder

res·tau·rant *n* : public eating place

res·ti·tu·tion *n* : act or fact of restoring something or repaying someone

res·tive *adj* : uneasy or fidgety — **res·tive·ly** *adv* — **res·tive·ness** *n*

rest·less *adj* 1 : lacking or giving no rest 2 : always moving 3 : uneasy — **rest·less·ly** *adv* — **rest·less·ness** *n*

re·store *vb* **-stored; -stor·ing** 1 : give back 2 : put back into use or into a former state — **re·stor·able** *adj* — **res·to·ra·tion** *n* — **re·stor·ative** *n or adj* — **re·stor·er** *n*

re·strain *vb* : limit or keep under control — **re·strain·able** *adj* — **re·strained** *adj* — **re·strain·ed·ly** *adv* — **re·strain·er** *n*

restraining order *n* : legal order directing one person to stay away from another

re·straint *n* 1 : act of restraining 2 : restraining force 3 : control over feelings

re·strict *vb* 1 : confine within bounds 2 : limit use of — **re·stric·tion** *n* — **re·stric·tive** *adj* — **re·stric·tive·ly** *adv*

re·sult *vb* : come about because of something else ~ *n* 1 : thing that results 2 : something obtained by calculation or investigation — **re·sul·tant** *adj or n*

re·sume *vb* **-sumed; -sum·ing** : return to or take up again after interruption — **re·sump·tion** *n*

ré·su·mé, re·su·me, re·su·mé *n* : summary of one's career and qualifications

re·sur·gence *n* : a rising again — **re·sur·gent** *adj*

res·ur·rect *vb* 1 : raise from the dead 2 : bring to attention or use again — **res·ur·rec·tion** *n*

re·sus·ci·tate *vb* **-tat·ed; -tat·ing** : bring back from apparent death — **re·sus·ci·ta·tion** *n* — **re·sus·ci·ta·tor** *n*

re·tail *vb* : sell in small quantities directly to the consumer ~ *n* : business of selling to consumers — **retail** *adj or adv* — **re·tail·er** *n*

re·tain *vb* 1 : keep or hold onto 2 : engage the services of

re·tain·er *n* 1 : household servant 2 : retaining fee

re·tal·i·ate *vb* **-at·ed; -at·ing** : return (as an injury) in kind — **re·tal·i·a·tion** *n* — **re·tal·ia·to·ry** *adj*

re·tard *vb* : hold back — **re·tar·da·tion** *n*

re·tard·ed *adj* : slow or limited in intellectual development

retch *vb* : try to vomit

re·ten·tion *n* 1 : state of being retained 2 : ability to retain — **re·ten·tive** *adj*

ret·i·cent *adj* : tending not to talk — **ret·i·cence** *n* — **ret·i·cent·ly** *adv*

ret·i·na *n, pl* **-nas** *or* **-nae** : sensory membrane lining the eye — **ret·i·nal** *adj*

ret·i·nue *n* : attendants or followers of a distinguished person

re·tire *vb* **-tired; -tir·ing** 1 : withdraw for privacy

2 : end a career **3** : go to bed — **re•tir•ee** n — **re•tire•ment** n

re•tir•ing adj : shy

re•tort vb : say in reply ~ n : quick, witty, or cutting answer

re•trace vb : go over again or in reverse

re•tract vb **1** : draw back or in **2** : withdraw a charge or promise — **re•tract•able** adj — **re•trac•tion** n

re•treat n **1** : act of withdrawing **2** : place of privacy or safety or meditation and study ~ vb : make a retreat

re•trench vb : cut down (as expenses) — **re•trench•ment** n

ret•ri•bu•tion n : retaliation — **re•trib•u•tive** adj — **re•trib•u•to•ry** adj

re•trieve vb **-trieved; -triev•ing 1** : search for and bring in game **2** : recover — **re•triev•able** adj — **retriev•al** n

re•triev•er n : dog for retrieving game

ret•ro•ac•tive adj : made effective as of a prior date — **ret•ro•ac•tive•ly** adv

ret•ro•grade adj **1** : moving backward **2** : becoming worse

ret•ro•gress vb : move backward — **ret•ro•gres•sion** n

ret•ro•spect n : review of past events — **ret•ro•spec•tion** n — **ret•ro•spec•tive** adj — **ret•ro•spec•tive•ly** adv

re•turn vb **1** : go or come back **2** : pass, give, or send back to an earlier possessor **3** : answer **4** : bring in as a profit **5** : give or do in return ~ n **1** : act of returning or something returned **2** pl : report of balloting results **3** : statement of taxable income **4** : profit — **return** adj — **re•turn•able** adj or n — **re•turn•er** n

re•union n **1** : act of reuniting **2** : a meeting of persons after a separation

re•vamp vb : renovate or revise

re•veal vb **1** : make known **2** : show plainly

rev•eil•le n : military signal sounded about sunrise

rev•el vb **-eled** or **-elled; -el•ing** or **-el•ling 1** : take part in a revel **2** : take great pleasure ~ n : wild party or celebration — **rev•el•er, rev•el•ler** n — **rev•el•ry** n

rev•e•la•tion n **1** : act of revealing **2** : something enlightening or astonishing

re•venge vb : avenge ~ n **1** : desire for retaliation **2** : act of retaliation — **re•venge•ful** adj — **re•veng•er** n

rev•e•nue n : money collected by a government

re•ver•ber•ate vb **-at•ed; -at•ing** : resound in a series of echoes — **re•ver•ber•a•tion** n

re•vere vb **-vered; -ver•ing** : show honor and devotion to — **rev•er•ence** n — **rev•er•ent** adj — **rev•er•ent•ly** adv

rev•er•end adj : worthy of reverence ~ n : clergy member

rev•er•ie n, pl **-er•ies** : daydream

re•verse adj **1** : opposite to a previous or normal condition **2** : acting in an opposite way ~ vb **-versed; -vers•ing 1** : turn upside down or completely around **2** : change to the contrary or in the opposite direction ~ n **1** : something contrary **2** : change for the worse **3** : back of something — **re•ver•sal** n — **re•verse•ly** adv — **re•vers•ible** adj

re•vert vb : return to an original type or condition — **re•ver•sion** n

re•view n **1** : formal inspection **2** : general survey **3** : critical evaluation **4** : second or repeated study or examination ~ vb **1** : examine or study again **2** : reexamine judicially **3** : look back over **4** : examine critically **5** : inspect — **re•view•er** n

re•vile vb **-viled; -vil•ing** : abuse verbally — **re•vile•ment** n — **re•vil•er** n

re•vise vb **-vised; -vis•ing 1** : look over something written to correct or improve **2** : make a new version of — **re•vis•able** adj — **revise** n — **re•vis•er, re•vi•sor** n — **re•vi•sion** n

re•viv•al n **1** : act of reviving or state of being revived **2** : evangelistic meeting

re•vive vb **-vived; -viv•ing** : bring back to life or consciousness or into use — **re•viv•er** n

re•vo•ca•tion n : act or instance of revoking

re•voke vb **-voked; -vok•ing** : annul by recalling — **re•vok•er** n

re•volt vb **1** : throw off allegiance **2** : cause or experience disgust or shock ~ n : rebellion or revolution — **re•volt•er** n

re•volt•ing adj : extremely offensive — **re•volt•ing•ly** adv

rev•o•lu•tion n **1** : rotation **2** : progress in an orbit **3** : sudden, radical, or complete change (as overthrow of a government) — **rev•o•lu•tion•ary** adj or n

rev•o•lu•tion•ize vb **-ized; -izing** : change radically — **rev•o•lu•tion•iz•er** n

re•volve vb **-volved; -volv•ing 1** : ponder **2** : move in an orbit **3** : rotate — **re•volv•able** adj

re•volv•er n : pistol with a revolving cylinder

re•vue n : theatrical production of brief numbers

re•vul•sion n : complete dislike or repugnance

re•ward vb : give a reward to or for ~ n : something offered for service or achievement

re•write vb **-wrote; -writ•ten; -writ•ing** : revise — **rewrite** n

rhap•so•dy n, pl **-dies 1** : expression of extravagant praise **2** : flowing free-form musical composition — **rhap•sod•ic** adj — **rhap•sod•i•cal•ly** adv — **rhap•so•dize** vb

rhet•o•ric n : art of speaking or writing effectively — **rhe•tor•i•cal** adj — **rhet•o•ri•cian** n

rheu•ma•tism n : disorder marked by inflammation or pain in muscles or joints — **rheu•mat•ic** adj

rhine•stone n : a colorless imitation gem

rhi•no n, pl **-no** or **-nos** : rhinoceros

rhi•noc•er•os n, pl **-noc•er•os** or **-noc•eri** : large thick-skinned mammal with 1 or 2 horns on the snout

rho•do•den•dron n : flowering evergreen shrub

rhom•bus n, pl **-bus•es** or **-bi** : parallelogram with equal sides

rhu•barb n : garden plant with edible stalks

rhyme n **1** : correspondence in terminal sounds **2** : verse that rhymes ~ vb **rhymed; rhym•ing** : make or have rhymes

rhythm n : regular succession of sounds or motions — **rhyth•mic, rhyth•mi•cal** adj — **rhyth•mi•cal•ly** adv

rhythm and blues n : popular music based on blues and black folk music

rib n **1** : curved bone joined to the spine **2** : riblike thing ~ vb **-bb- 1** : furnish or mark with ribs **2** : tease — **rib•ber** n

rib•ald adj : coarse or vulgar — **rib•ald•ry** n

rib•bon n **1** : narrow strip of fabric used esp. for decoration **2** : strip of inked cloth (as in a typewriter)

ri•bo•fla•vin n : growth-promoting vitamin

rice n, pl **rice** : starchy edible seeds of an annual cereal grass

rich adj **1** : having a lot of money or possessions **2** : valuable **3** : containing much sugar, fat, or seasoning **4** : abundant **5** : deep and pleasing in color or tone **6** : fertile — **rich•ly** adv — **rich•ness** n

rich•es n pl : wealth

rick•ets n : childhood bone disease

rick•ety adj : shaky

rick•sha, rick•shaw n : small covered 2-wheeled carriage pulled by one person

ric•o•chet vb **-cheted** or **-chet•ted; -chet•ing** or **-chet•ting** : bounce off at an angle — **rico•chet** n

rid vb **rid; rid•ding** : make free of something unwanted — **rid•dance** n

rid•den adj : overburdened with — used in combination

¹rid•dle n : puzzling question ~ vb **-dled; -dling** : speak in riddles

²riddle vb **-dled; -dling** : fill full of holes

ride vb **rode; rid•den; rid•ing 1** : be carried along **2** : sit on and cause to move **3** : travel over a surface **4** : tease or nag ~ n **1** : trip on an animal or in a vehicle **2** : mechanical device ridden for amusement

rid•er n **1** : one that rides **2** : attached clause or document — **rid•er•less** adj

ridge n **1** : range of hills **2** : raised line or strip **3** : line of intersection of 2 sloping surfaces — **ridgy** adj

rid•i•cule vb : laugh at or make fun of — **ridi•cule** n

ri•dic•u•lous adj : arousing ridicule — **ri•dic•u•lous•ly** adv — **ri•dic•u•lous•ness** n

rife adj : abounding — **rife** adv

riff•raff n : mob

¹ri•fle vb **-fled; -fling** : ransack esp. with intent to steal — **ri•fler** n

²rifle n : long shoulder weapon with spiral grooves in the bore — **ri•fleman** n — **ri•fling** n

rift n : separation — **rift** vb

¹rig vb **-gg- 1** : fit out with rigging **2** : set up esp. as a makeshift ~ n **1** : distinctive shape, number, and arrangement of sails and masts of a sailing ship **2** : equipment **3** : carriage with its horse

²rig vb **-gg-** : manipulate esp. by deceptive or dishonest means

rig•ging n : lines that hold and move the masts, sails, and spars of a sailing ship

right adj **1** : meeting a standard of conduct **2** : correct **3** : genuine **4** : normal **5** : opposite of left ~ n **1** : something that is correct, just, proper, or honorable **2** : something to which one has a just claim **3** : something that is on the right side ~ adv **1** : according to what is right **2** : immediately **3** : completely **4** : on or to the right ~ vb **1** : restore to a proper state **2** : bring or become upright again — **right•er** n — **right•ness** n — **right•ward** adj

right angle n : angle whose sides are perpendicular to each other — **right-an•gled** or **right-an•gle** adj

righ•teous adj : acting or being in accordance with what is just or moral — **righ•teous•ly** adv — **righteous•ness** n

right•ful adj : lawful — **right•ful•ly** adv — **right•ful•ness** n

right•ly adv **1** : justly **2** : properly **3** : correctly

rig•id adj : lacking flexibility — **ri•gid•i•ty** n — **rig•id•ly** adv

rig•ma•role n **1** : meaningless talk **2** : complicated often unnecessary procedure

rig•or n : severity — **rig•or•ous** adj — **rig•or•ous•ly** adv

rig•or mor•tis n : temporary stiffness of muscles occurring after death

rile vb **riled; ril•ing** : anger

rill n : small brook

rim n : edge esp. of something curved ~ vb **-mm-** : border

¹rime n : frost — **rimy** adj

²rime var of RHYME

rind n : usu. hard or tough outer layer

¹ring n **1** : circular band used as an ornament or for holding or fastening **2** : something circular **3** : place for contest or display **4** : group with a selfish or dishonest aim ~ vb : surround — **ringed** adj — **ring•like** adj

²ring vb **rang; rung; ringing 1** : sound resonantly when struck **2** : cause to make a metallic sound by striking **3** : resound **4** : call esp. by a bell ~ **n 1** : resonant sound or tone **2** : act or instance of ringing

ring•er *n* **1** : one that sounds by ringing **2** : illegal substitute **3** : one that closely resembles another

ring•lead•er *n* : leader esp. of troublemakers

ring•let *n* : long curl

ring•worm *n* : contagious skin disease caused by fungi

rink *n* : enclosed place for skating

rinse *vb* **rinsed; rins•ing 1** : cleanse usu. with water only **2** : treat (hair) with a rinse ~ *n* : liquid used for rinsing — **rins•er** *n*

ri•ot *n* **1** : violent public disorder **2** : random or disorderly profusion — **riot** *vb* — **ri•ot•er** *n* — **ri•ot•ous** *adj*

rip *vb* **-pp-** : cut or tear open ~ *n* : rent made by ripping — **rip•per** *n*

ripe *adj* **rip•er; rip•est** : fully grown, developed, or prepared — **ripe•ly** *adv* — **rip•en** *vb* — **ripe•ness** *n*

rip–off *n* : theft — **rip off** *vb*

rip•ple *vb* **-pled; -pling 1** : become lightly ruffled on the surface **2** : sound like rippling water — **ripple** *n*

rise *vb* **rose; ris•en; ris•ing 1** : get up from sitting, kneeling, or lying **2** : take arms **3** : appear above the horizon **4** : ascend **5** : gain a higher position or rank **6** : increase ~ *n* **1** : act of rising **2** : origin **3** : elevation **4** : increase **5** : upward slope **6** : area of high ground — **ris•er** *n*

risk *n* : exposure to loss or injury — **risk** *vb* — **risk•i•ness** *n* — **risky** *adj*

ris•qué *adj* : nearly indecent

rite *n* **1** : set form for conducting a ceremony **2** : liturgy of a church **3** : ceremonial action

rit•u•al *n* : rite — **ritual** *adj* — **rit•u•al•ism** *n* — **rit•u•al•is•tic** *adj* — **rit•u•al•is•ti•cal•ly** *adv* — **rit•u•al•ly** *adv*

ri•val *n* **1** : competitor **2** : peer ~ *vb* **-valed** *or* **-valled; -val•ing** *or* **-val•ling 1** : be in competition with **2** : equal — **rival** *adj* — **ri•val•ry** *n*

riv•er *n* : large natural stream of water — **riv•er•bank** *n* — **riv•er•bed** *n* — **riv•er•boat** *n* — **riv•er•side** *n*

riv•et *n* : headed metal bolt ~ *vb* : fasten with a rivet — **riv•et•er** *n*

riv•u•let *n* : small stream

roach *n* : cockroach

road *n* : open way for vehicles, persons, and animals — **road•bed** *n* — **road•side** *n* or *adj* — **road•way** *n*

road•block *n* : obstruction on a road

road•run•ner *n* : large fast-running bird

roam *vb* : wander

roan *adj* : of a dark color sprinkled with white ~ *n* : animal with a roan coat

roar *vb* : utter a full loud prolonged sound — **roar** *n* — **roar•er** *n*

roast *vb* **1** : cook by dry heat **2** : criticize severely ~ *n* : piece of meat suitable for roasting — **roast** *adj* — **roast•er** *n*

rob *vb* **-bb- 1** : steal from **2** : commit robbery — **rob•ber** *n*

rob•bery *n, pl* **-ber•ies** : theft of something from a person by use of violence or threat

robe *n* **1** : long flowing outer garment **2** : covering for the lower body ~ *vb* **robed; rob•ing** : clothe with or as if with a robe

rob•in *n* : No. American thrush with a reddish breast

ro•bot *n* **1** : machine that looks and acts like a human being **2** : efficient but insensitive person — **ro•bot•ic** *adj*

ro•bust *adj* : strong and vigorously healthy — **ro•bust•ly** *adv* — **ro•bust•ness** *n*

¹rock *vb* : sway or cause to sway back and forth ~

n **1** : rocking movement **2** : popular music marked by repetition and a strong beat

²rock *n* : mass of hard mineral material — **rock** *adj* — **rocky** *adj*

rock•er *n* **1** : curved piece on which a chair rocks **2** : chair that rocks

rock•et *n* **1** : self-propelled firework or missile **2** : jet engine that carries its own oxygen ~ *vb* : rise abruptly and rapidly — **rock•et•ry** *n*

rod *n* **1** : straight slender stick **2** : unit of length equal to 5 yards

rode *past of* RIDE

ro•dent *n* : usu. small gnawing mammal

ro•deo *n, pl* **-de•os** : contest of cowboy skills

roe *n* : fish eggs

rogue *n* : dishonest or mischievous person — **rogu•ery** *n* — **rogu•ish** *adj* — **rogu•ish•ly** *adv* — **rogu•ish•ness** *n*

roil *vb* **1** : make cloudy or muddy by stirring up **2** : make angry

role *n* **1** : part to play **2** : function

roll *n* **1** : official record or list of names **2** : something rolled up or rounded **3** : bread baked in a small rounded mass **4** : sound of rapid drum strokes **5** : heavy reverberating sound **6** : rolling movement ~ *vb* **1** : move by turning over **2** : move on wheels **3** : flow in a continuous stream **4** : swing from side to side **5** : shape or be shaped in rounded form **6** : press with a roller

roll•er *n* **1** : revolving cylinder **2** : rod on which something is rolled up **3** : long heavy ocean wave

roller skate *n* : a skate with wheels instead of a runner — **roller-skate** *vb*

rol•lick•ing *adj* : full of good spirits

Ro•man Catholic *n* : member of a Christian church led by a pope — **Roman Catholic** *adj* — **Roman Catholicism** *n*

ro•mance *n* **1** : medieval tale of knightly adventure **2** : love story **3** : love affair ~ *vb* **-manced; -manc•ing 1** : have romantic fancies **2** : have a love affair with — **ro•manc•er** *n*

ro•man•tic *adj* **1** : visionary or imaginative **2** : appealing to one's emotions — **ro•man•ti•cal•ly** *adv*

romp *vb* : play actively and noisily — **romp** *n*

roof *n, pl* **roofs** : upper covering part of a building ~ *vb* : cover with a roof — **roofed** *adj* — **roof•ing** *n* — **roof•less** *adj* — **roof•top** *n*

¹rook *n* : crowlike bird

²rook *vb* : cheat

rook•ie *n* : novice

room *n* **1** : sufficient space **2** : partitioned part of a building ~ *vb* : occupy lodgings — **room•er** *n* — **room•ful** *n* — **roomy** *adj*

room•mate *n* : one sharing the same lodgings

roost *n* : support on which birds perch ~ *vb* : settle on a roost

roost•er *n* : adult male domestic chicken

¹root *n* **1** : leafless underground part of a seed plant **2** : rootlike thing or part **3** : source **4** : essential core ~ *vb* : form, fix, or become fixed by roots — **root•less** *adj* — **root•let** *n* — **root•like** *adj*

²root *vb* : turn up with the snout

³root *vb* : applaud or encourage noisily — **root•er** *n*

rope *n* : large strong cord of strands of fiber ~ *vb* **roped; rop•ing 1** : tie with a rope **2** : lasso

ro•sa•ry *n, pl* **-ries 1** : string of beads used in praying **2** : Roman Catholic devotion

¹rose *past of* RISE

²rose *n* **1** : prickly shrub with bright flowers **2** : purplish red — **rose** *adj* — **rose•bud** *n* — **rose•bush** *n*

rose•mary *n, pl* **-mar•ies** : fragrant shrubby mint

ro•sette *n* : rose-shaped ornament

Rosh Ha•sha•nah *n* : Jewish New Year observed as a religious holiday in September or October

ros•in *n* : brittle resin

ros•ter *n* : list of names

ros•trum *n, pl* **-trums** *or* **-tra** : speaker's platform

rosy *adj* **ros•i•er; -est 1** : of the color rose **2** : hopeful — **ros•i•ly** *adv* — **ros•i•ness** *n*

rot *vb* **-tt-** : undergo decomposition ~ *n* **1** : decay **2** : disease in which tissue breaks down

ro•ta•ry *adj* **1** : turning on an axis **2** : having a rotating part

ro•tate *vb* **-tat•ed; -tat•ing 1** : turn about an axis or a center **2** : alternate in a series — **ro•ta•tion** *n* — **ro•ta•tor** *n*

rote *n* : repetition from memory

ro•tor *n* **1** : part that rotates **2** : system of rotating horizontal blades for supporting a helicopter

rot•ten *adj* **1** : having rotted **2** : corrupt **3** : extremely unpleasant or inferior — **rot•ten•ness** *n*

ro•tund *adj* : rounded — **rotun•di•ty** *n*

ro•tun•da *n* : building or room with a dome

roué *n* : man given to debauched living

rouge *n* : cosmetic for the cheeks — **rouge** *vb*

rough *adj* **1** : not smooth **2** : not calm **3** : harsh, violent, or rugged **4** : crudely or hastily done ~ *n* : rough state or something in that state ~ *vb* **1** : roughen **2** : manhandle **3** : make roughly — **rough•ly** *adv* — **rough•ness** *n*

rough•age *n* : coarse bulky food

rough•en *vb* : make or become rough

rough•neck *n* : rowdy

rou•lette *n* : gambling game using a whirling numbered wheel

¹round *adj* **1** : having every part the same distance from the center **2** : cylindrical **3** : complete **4** : approximate **5** : blunt **6** : moving in or forming a circle ~ *n* **1** : round or curved thing **2** : series of recurring actions or events **3** : period of time or a unit of action **4** : fired shot **5** : cut of beef ~ *vb* **1** : make or become round **2** : go around **3** : finish **4** : express as an approximation — **round•ish** *adj* — **round•ly** *adv* — **round•ness** *n*

²round *prep or adv* : around

round•about *adj* : indirect

round•up *n* **1** : gathering together of range cattle **2** : summary — **round up** *vb*

rouse *vb* **roused; rous•ing 1** : wake from sleep **2** : stir up

rout *n* **1** : state of wild confusion **2** : disastrous defeat ~ *vb* : defeat decisively

route *n* : line of travel ~ *vb* **rout•ed; rout•ing** : send by a selected route

rou•tine *n* **1** : regular course of procedure **2** : an often repeated speech, formula, or part — **routine** *adj* — **rou•tine•ly** *adv*

rove *vb* **roved; rov•ing** : wander or roam — **rov•er** *n*

¹row *vb* **1** : propel a boat with oars **2** : carry in a rowboat ~ *n* : act of rowing — **row•boat** *n* — **row•er** *n*

²row *n* : number of objects in a line

³row *n* : noisy quarrel — **row** *vb*

row•dy *adj* **-di•er; -est** : coarse or boisterous in behavior — **row•di•ness** *n* — **rowdy** *n*

roy•al *adj* : relating to or befitting a king ~ *n* : person of royal blood — **roy•al•ly** *adv*

roy•al•ty *n, pl* **-ties 1** : state of being royal **2** : royal persons **3** : payment for use of property

rub *vb* **-bb- 1** : use pressure and friction on a body **2** : scour, polish, erase, or smear by pressure and friction **3** : chafe with friction ~ *n* : difficulty

rub•ber *n* **1** : one that rubs **2** : waterproof elastic substance or something made of it — **rubber** *adj* — **rub•ber•ize** *vb* — **rub•bery** *adj*

rub•bish *n* : waste or trash

rub•ble *n* : broken fragments esp. of a destroyed building

ru•ble *n* : monetary unit of Russia

ru•by *n, pl* **-bies** : precious red stone or its color — **ruby** *adj*

rud•der n : steering device at the rear of a ship or aircraft

rud•dy adj **-di•er; -est** : reddish — **rud•di•ness** n

rude adj **rud•er; rud•est 1** : roughly made **2** : impolite — **rude•ly** adv — **rude•ness** n

ru•di•ment n **1** : something not fully developed **2** : elementary principle — **ru•di•men•ta•ry** adj

rue vb **rued; ru•ing** : feel regret for ~ n : regret — **rue•ful** adj — **rue•ful•ly** adv — **rue•ful•ness** n

ruf•fi•an n : brutal person

ruf•fle vb **-fled; -fling 1** : draw into or provide with pleats **2** : roughen the surface of **3** : irritate ~ n : strip of fabric pleated on one edge — **ruf•fly** adj

rug n : piece of heavy fabric used as a floor covering

rug•ged adj **1** : having a rough uneven surface **2** : severe **3** : strong — **rug•ged•ly** adv — **rug•ged•ness** n

ru•in n **1** : complete collapse or destruction **2** : remains of something destroyed — usu. in pl. **3** : cause of destruction ~ vb **1** : destroy **2** : damage beyond repair **3** : bankrupt

ru•in•ous adj : causing ruin — **ruin•ous•ly** adv

rule n **1** : guide or principle for governing action **2** : usual way of doing something **3** : government **4** : straight strip (as of wood or metal) marked off in units for measuring ~ vb **ruled; rul•ing 1** : govern **2** : give as a decision — **rul•er** n

rum n : liquor made from molasses or sugarcane

rum•ble vb **-bled; -bling** : make a low heavy rolling sound — **rumble** n

ru•mi•nant n : hoofed mammal (as a cow or deer) that chews the cud — **ruminant** adj

ru•mi•nate vb **-nat•ed; -nat•ing** : contemplate — **ru•mi•na•tion** n

rum•mage vb **-maged; -maging** : search thoroughly

rum•my n : card game

ru•mor n **1** : common talk **2** : widespread statement not authenticated — **rumor** vb

rump n : rear part of an animal

rum•ple vb **-pled; -pling** : tousle or wrinkle — **rumple** n

rum•pus n : disturbance

run vb **ran; run; run•ning 1** : go rapidly or hurriedly **2** : enter a race or election **3** : operate **4** : continue in force **5** : flow rapidly **6** : take a certain direction **7** : manage **8** : incur ~ n **1** : act of running **2** : brook **3** : continuous series **4** : usual kind **5** : freedom of movement **6** : lengthwise ravel

run•around n : evasive or delaying action esp. in response to a request

run•away n : fugitive ~ adj **1** : fugitive **2** : out of control

run-down adj : being in poor condition

¹rung past part of RING

²rung n : horizontal piece of a chair or ladder

run•ner n **1** : one that runs **2** : thin piece or part on which something slides **3** : slender creeping branch of a plant

run•ner–up n, pl **run•ners–up** : competitor who finishes second

run•ning adj **1** : flowing **2** : continuous

runt n : small person or animal — **runty** adj

run•way n : strip on which aircraft land and take off

ru•pee n : monetary unit (as of India)

rup•ture n **1** : breaking or tearing apart **2** : hernia ~ vb **-tured; -tur•ing** : cause or undergo rupture

ru•ral adj : relating to the country or agriculture

ruse n : trick

¹rush n : grasslike marsh plant

²rush vb **1** : move forward or act with too great haste **2** : perform in a short time ~ n **1** : violent forward motion ~ adj : requiring speed — **rush•er** n

rus•set n **1** : reddish brown color **2** : a baking potato — **russet** adj

rust n **1** : reddish coating on exposed iron **2** : reddish brown color — **rust** vb — **rusty** adj

rus•tic adj : relating to or suitable for the country or country dwellers ~ n : rustic person — **rus•ti•cal•ly** adv

rus•tle vb **-tled; -tling 1** : make or cause a rustle **2** : forage food **3** : steal cattle from the range ~ n : series of small sounds — **rus•tler** n

rut n **1** : track worn by wheels or feet **2** : set routine — **rut•ted** adj

ruth•less adj : having no pity — **ruth•less•ly** adv — **ruth•less•ness** n

-ry n suffix : -ery

rye n **1** : cereal grass grown for grain **2** : whiskey from rye

S

s n, pl **s's** or **ss** : 19th letter of the alphabet

¹-s — used to form the plural of most nouns

²-s vb suffix — used to form the 3d person singular present of most verbs

Sab•bath n **1** : Saturday observed as a day of worship by Jews and some Christians **2** : Sunday observed as a day of worship by Christians

sa•ber, sa•bre n : curved cavalry sword

sa•ble n **1** : black **2** : dark brown mammal or its fur

sab•o•tage n : deliberate destruction or hampering ~ vb **-taged; -tag•ing** : wreck through sabotage

sab•o•teur n : person who sabotages

sac n : anatomical pouch

sac•cha•rin n : low-calorie artificial sweetener

sac•cha•rine adj : nauseatingly sweet

sa•chet n : small bag with perfumed powder (**sachet powder**)

¹sack n : bag — vb : fire

²sack vb : plunder a captured place

sack•cloth n : rough garment worn as a sign of penitence

sac•ra•ment n : formal religious act or rite — **sac•ra•men•tal** adj

sa•cred adj **1** : set apart for or worthy of worship **2** : worthy of reverence **3** : relating to religion — **sa•cred•ly** adv — **sa•cred•ness** n

sac•ri•fice n **1** : the offering of something precious to a deity or the thing offered **2** : loss or deprivation — vb **-ficed; -fic•ing** : offer or give up as a sacrifice — **sac•ri•fi•cial** adj

sac•ri•lege n : violation of something sacred — **sac•ri•le•gious** adj

sac•ro•sanct adj : sacred

sad adj **-dd- 1** : affected with grief or sorrow **2** : causing sorrow — **sad•den** vb — **sad•ly** adv — **sad•ness** n

sad•dle n : seat for riding on horseback ~ vb **-dled; -dling** : put a saddle on

sa•dism n : delight in cruelty — **sa•dist** n — **sa•dis•tic** adj — **sa•dis•ti•cal•ly** adv

sa•fa•ri n : hunting expedition in Africa

safe adj **saf•er; saf•est 1** : free from harm **2** : providing safety ~ n : container to keep valuables safe — **safe•keep•ing** n — **safe•ly** adv

safe•guard n : measure or device for preventing accidents — **safeguard** vb

safe•ty n, pl **-ties 1** : freedom from danger **2** : protective device

saf•flow•er n : herb with seeds rich in edible oil

saf•fron n : orange powder from a crocus flower used in cooking

sag vb **-gg-** : droop, sink, or settle — **sag** n

sa•ga n : story of heroic deeds

sa•ga•cious adj : shrewd — **sa•gac•i•ty** n

¹sage adj : wise or prudent ~ n : wise man — **sage•ly** adv

²sage n : mint used in flavoring

sage•brush n : low shrub of the western U.S.

said past of SAY

sail n **1** : fabric used to catch the wind and move a boat or ship **2** : trip on a sailboat ~ vb **1** : travel on a ship or sailboat **2** : move with ease or grace — **sail•boat** n — **sail•or** n

sail•fish n : large fish with a very large dorsal fin

saint n : holy or godly person — **saint•ed** adj — **saint•hood** n — **saint•li•ness** n — **saint•ly** adj

¹sake n **1** : purpose or reason **2** : one's good or benefit

²sa•ke, sa•ki n : Japanese rice wine

sa•la•cious adj : sexually suggestive — **sa•la•cious•ly** adv

sal•ad n : dish usu. of raw lettuce, vegetables, or fruit

sal•a•man•der n : lizardlike amphibian

sa•la•mi n : highly seasoned dried sausage

sal•a•ry n, pl **-ries** : regular payment for services

sale n **1** : transfer of ownership of property for money **2** : selling at bargain prices **3** **sales** pl : activities involved in selling — **sal•able, saleable** adj — **sales•man** n — **sales•per•son** n — **sales•wom•an** n

sa•lient adj : standing out conspicuously

sa•line adj : containing salt — **sa•lin•i•ty** n

sa•li•va n : liquid secreted into the mouth — **sal•i•vary** adj — **sal•i•vate** vb — **sal•i•va•tion** n

sal•low adj : of a yellowish sickly color

sal•ly n, pl **-lies 1** : quick attack on besiegers **2** : witty remark — **sally** vb

salm•on n, pl **salmon 1** : food fish with pink or red flesh **2** : deep yellowish pink color

sa•lon n : elegant room or shop

sa•loon n **1** : public cabin on a passenger ship **2** : barroom

sal•sa n : spicy sauce of tomatoes, onions, and hot peppers

salt n **1** : white crystalline substance that consists of sodium and chlorine **2** : compound formed usu. from acid and metal — **salt** vb or adj — **salt•i•ness** n — **salty** adj

salt•wa•ter adj : relating to or living in salt water

sa•lu•bri•ous adj : good for health

sal•u•tary adj : health-giving or beneficial

sal•u•ta•tion n : greeting

sa•lute vb **-lut•ed; -lut•ing** : honor by ceremony or formal movement — **salute** n

sal·vage n : something saved from destruction ~ vb **-vaged; -vag·ing** : rescue or save

sal·va·tion n : saving of a person from sin or danger

salve n : medicinal ointment ~ vb **salved; salv·ing** : soothe

sal·ver n : small tray

sal·vo n, pl **-vos** or **-voes** : simultaneous discharge of guns

same adj : being the one referred to ~ pron : the same one or ones ~ adv : in the same manner — **same·ness** n

sam·ple n : piece or part that shows the quality of a whole ~ vb **-pled; -pling** : judge by a sample

sam·pler n : piece of needlework testing skill in embroidering

san·a·to·ri·um n, pl **-riums** or **-ria** : hospital for the chronically ill

sanc·ti·fy vb **-fied; -fy·ing** : make holy — **sanc·ti·fi·ca·tion** n

sanc·ti·mo·nious adj : hypocritically pious — **sanc·ti·mo·nious·ly** adv

sanc·tion n 1 : authoritative approval 2 : coercive measure — usu. pl ~ vb : approve

sanc·ti·ty n, pl **-ties** : quality or state of being holy or sacred

sanc·tu·ary n, pl **-ar·ies** 1 : consecrated place 2 : place of refuge

sand n : loose granular particles of rock ~ vb : smooth with an abrasive — **sand·bank** n — **sand·er** n — **sand·storm** n — **sandy** adj

san·dal n : shoe consisting of a sole strapped to the foot

sand·pa·per n : abrasive paper — **sandpaper** vb

sand·pip·er n : long-billed shorebird

sand·stone n : rock made of naturally cemented sand

sand·wich n : 2 or more slices of bread with a filling between them ~ vb : squeeze or crowd in

sane adj **san·er; san·est** 1 : mentally healthy 2 : sensible — **sane·ly** adv

sang past of SING

san·gui·nary adj : bloody

san·guine adj 1 : reddish 2 : cheerful

san·i·tar·i·um n, pl **-i·ums** or **-ia** : sanatorium

san·i·tary adj 1 : relating to health 2 : free from filth or infective matter

san·i·ta·tion n : protection of health by maintenance of sanitary conditions

san·i·ty n : soundness of mind

sank past of SINK

¹**sap** n 1 : fluid that circulates through a plant 2 : gullible person

²**sap** vb **-pp-** 1 : undermine 2 : weaken or exhaust gradually

sa·pi·ent adj : wise — **sa·pi·ence** n

sap·ling n : young tree

sap·phire n : hard transparent blue gem

sap·py adj **-pi·er; -est** 1 : full of sap 2 : overly sentimental

sap·suck·er n : small No. American woodpecker

sar·casm n 1 : cutting remark 2 : ironical criticism or reproach — **sar·cas·tic** adj — **sar·cas·ti·cal·ly** adv

sar·coph·a·gus n, pl **-gi** : large stone coffin

sar·dine n : small fish preserved for use as food

sar·don·ic adj : disdainfully humorous — **sar·don·i·cal·ly** adv

sa·rong n : loose garment worn esp. by Pacific islanders

sar·sa·pa·ril·la n : dried roots of a tropical American plant used esp. for flavoring or a carbonated drink flavored with this

sar·to·ri·al adj : relating to a tailor or men's clothes

¹**sash** n : broad band worn around the waist or over the shoulder

²**sash** n, pl **sash** 1 : frame for a pane of glass in a door or window 2 : movable part of a window

sas·sa·fras n : No. American tree or its dried root bark

sassy adj **sass·i·er; -est** : saucy

sat past of SIT

Sa·tan n : devil — **sa·tan·ic** adj — **sa·tan·i·cal·ly** adv

satch·el n : small bag

sate vb **sat·ed; sat·ing** : satisfy fully

sat·el·lite n 1 : toady 2 : body or object that revolves around a larger celestial body

sa·ti·ate vb **-at·ed; -at·ing** : sate — **sa·ti·ety** n

sat·in n : glossy fabric — **sat·iny** adj

sat·ire n : literary ridicule done with humor — **sa·tir·ic** **sa·tir·i·cal** adj — **sa·tir·i·cal·ly** adv — **sat·i·rist** n — **sat·i·rize** vb

sat·is·fac·tion n : state of being satisfied — **sat·is·fac·to·ri·ly** adv — **sat·is·fac·to·ry** adj

sat·is·fy vb **-fied; -fy·ing** 1 : make happy 2 : pay what is due to or on — **sat·is·fy·ing·ly** adv

sat·u·rate vb **-rat·ed; -rat·ing** : soak or charge thoroughly — **sat·u·ra·tion** n

Sat·ur·day n : 7th day of the week

sat·ur·nine adj : sullen

sa·tyr n : pleasure-loving forest god of ancient Greece

sauce n : fluid dressing or topping for food — **sauce·pan** n

sau·cer n : small shallow dish under a cup

saucy adj **sauc·i·er; -est** : insolent — **sauc·i·ly** adv — **sauc·i·ness** n

sau·er·kraut n : finely cut and fermented cabbage

sau·na n : steam or dry heat bath or a room or cabinet used for such a bath

saun·ter vb : stroll

sau·sage n : minced and highly seasoned meat

sau·té vb **-téed** or **-téd; -té·ing** : fry in a little fat — **sauté** n

sav·age adj 1 : wild 2 : cruel ~ n : person belonging to a primitive society — **sav·age·ly** adv — **sav·age·ness** n — **sav·age·ry** n

¹**save** vb **saved; sav·ing** 1 : rescue from danger 2 : guard from destruction 3 : redeem from sin 4 : put aside as a reserve — **sav·er** n

²**save** prep : except

sav·ior, sav·iour n 1 : one who saves 2 cap : Jesus Christ

sa·vor n : special flavor ~ vb : taste with pleasure — **sa·vory** adj

¹**saw** past of SEE

²**saw** n : cutting tool with teeth ~ vb **sawed; sawed** or **sawn; saw·ing** : cut with a saw — **saw·dust** n — **saw·mill** n — **saw·yer** n

saw·horse n : support for wood being sawed

sax·o·phone n : wind instrument with a reed mouthpiece and usu. a bent metal body

say vb **said say·ing says** 1 : express in words 2 : state positively ~ n, pl **says** 1 : expression of opinion 2 : power of decision

say·ing n : commonly repeated statement

scab n 1 : protective crust over a sore or wound 2 : worker taking a striker's job ~ vb **-bb-** 1 : become covered with a scab 2 : work as a scab — **scab·by** adj

scab·bard n : sheath for the blade of a weapon

scaf·fold n 1 : raised platform for workmen 2 : platform on which a criminal is executed

scald vb 1 : burn with hot liquid or steam 2 : heat to the boiling point

¹**scale** n : weighing device ~ vb **scaled; scal·ing** : weigh

²**scale** n 1 : thin plate esp. on the body of a fish or reptile 2 : thin coating or layer ~ vb **scaled; scal·ing** : strip of scales — **scaled** adj — **scale·less** adj — **scaly** adj

³**scale** n 1 : graduated series 2 : size of a sample

(as a model) in proportion to the size of the actual thing 3 : standard of estimation or judgment 4 : series of musical tones ~ vb **scaled; scal·ing** 1 : climb by a ladder 2 : arrange in a graded series

scal·lion n : bulbless onion

scal·lop n 1 : marine mollusk 2 : rounded projection on a border

scalp n : skin and flesh of the head ~ vb 1 : remove the scalp from 2 : resell at a greatly increased price — **scalp·er** n

scal·pel n : surgical knife

scamp n : rascal

scam·per vb : run nimbly — **scamper** n

scan vb **-nn-** 1 : read (verses) so as to show meter 2 : examine closely or hastily 3 : examine with a sensing device — **scan** n — **scan·ner** n

scan·dal n 1 : disgraceful situation 2 : malicious gossip — **scandal·ize** vb — **scan·dal·ous** adj

scant adj : barely sufficient ~ vb : stint — **scant·i·ly** adv — **scanty** adj

scape·goat n : one that bears the blame for others

scap·u·la n, pl **-lae** or **-las** : shoulder blade

scar n : mark where a wound has healed — **scar** vb

scar·ab n : large dark beetle or an ornament representing one

scarce adj **scarc·er; scarc·est** : lacking in quantity or number — **scar·ci·ty** n

scarce·ly adv 1 : barely 2 : almost not

scare vb **scared; scar·ing** : frighten ~ n : fright — **scary** adj

scare·crow n : figure for scaring birds from crops

scarf n, pl **scarves** or **scarfs** : cloth worn about the shoulders or the neck

scar·let n : bright red color — **scarlet** adj

scarlet fever n : acute contagious disease marked by fever, sore throat, and red rash

scath·ing adj : bitterly severe

scat·ter vb 1 : spread about irregularly 2 : disperse

scav·en·ger n 1 : person that collects refuse or waste 2 : animal that feeds on decayed matter — **scav·enge** vb

sce·nar·io n, pl **-i·os** 1 : plot of a play or movie 2 : possible sequence of events

scene n 1 : single situation in a play or movie 2 : stage setting 3 : view 4 : display of emotion — **sce·nic** adj

scen·ery n, pl **-er·ies** 1 : painted setting for a stage 2 : picturesque view

scent vb 1 : smell 2 : fill with odor ~ n 1 : odor 2 : sense of smell 3 : perfume — **scent·ed** adj

scep·ter n : staff signifying authority

scep·tic var of SKEPTIC

sched·ule n : list showing sequence of events ~ vb **-uled; -ul·ing** : make a schedule of

scheme n 1 : crafty plot 2 : systematic design ~ vb **schemed; schem·ing** : form a plot — **sche·mat·ic** adj — **schem·er** n

schism n : split — **schismat·ic** n or adj

schizo·phre·nia n : severe mental illness — **schiz·oid** adj or n — **schizo·phren·ic** adj or n

schol·ar n : student or learned person — **schol·ar·ly** adj

schol·ar·ship n 1 : qualities or learning of a scholar 2 : money given to a student to pay for education

scho·las·tic adj : relating to schools, scholars, or scholarship

¹**school** n 1 : institution for learning 2 : pupils in a school 3 : group with shared beliefs ~ vb : teach — **school·boy** n — **school·girl** n — **school·house** n — **school·mate** n — **school·room** n — **school·teach·er** n

²**school** n : large number of fish swimming together

schoo·ner n : sailing ship

sci·ence n : branch of systematic study esp. of the physical world — **sci·en·tif·ic** adj — **sci·en·tif·i·cal·ly** adv — **sci·en·tist** n

scin·til·late vb **-lat·ed; -lat·ing** : flash — **scin·til·la·tion** n

scin·til·lat·ing adj : brilliantly lively or witty

sci·on n : descendant

scis·sors n pl : small shears

scoff vb : mock — **scoff·er** n

scold n : person who scolds ~ vb : criticize severely

scoop n : shovellike utensil ~ vb **1** : take out with a scoop **2** : dig out

scoot vb : move swiftly

scoot·er n : child's foot-propelled vehicle

¹scope n **1** : extent **2** : room for development

²scope n : viewing device (as a microscope)

scorch vb : burn the surface of

score n, pl **scores 1** or pl **score** : twenty **2** : cut **3** : record of points made (as in a game) **4** : debt **5** : music of a composition ~ vb **scored; scor·ing 1** : record **2** : mark with lines **3** : gain in a game **4** : assign a grade to **5** : compose a score for — **score·less** adj — **scor·er** n

scorn n : emotion involving both anger and disgust ~ vb : hold in contempt — **scorn·er** n — **scorn·ful** adj — **scorn·ful·ly** adv

scor·pi·on n : poisonous long-tailed animal

scoun·drel n : villain

¹scour vb : examine thoroughly

²scour vb : rub in order to clean

scourge n **1** : whip **2** : punishment ~ vb **scourged; scourg·ing 1** : lash **2** : punish severely

scout vb : inspect or observe to get information ~ n : person sent out to get information

scow n : large flat-bottomed boat with square ends

scowl vb : make a frowning expression of displeasure — **scowl** n

scrag·gly adj : irregular or unkempt

scram vb **-mm-** : go away at once

scram·ble vb **-bled; -bling 1** : clamber clumsily around **2** : struggle for possession of something **3** : mix together **4** : cook (eggs) by stirring during frying — **scramble** n

¹scrap n **1** : fragment **2** : discarded material ~ vb **-pp-** : get rid of as useless

²scrap vb **-pp-** : fight — **scrap** n — **scrap·per** n

scrap·book n : blank book in which mementos are kept

scrape vb **scraped; scrap·ing 1** : remove by drawing a knife over **2** : clean or smooth by rubbing **3** : draw across a surface with a grating sound **4** : damage by contact with a rough surface **5** : gather or proceed with difficulty ~ n **1** : act of scraping **2** : predicament — **scrap·er** n

scratch vb **1** : scrape or dig with or as if with claws or nails **2** : cause to move gratingly **3** : delete by or as if by drawing a line through ~ n : mark or sound made in scratching — **scratchy** adj

scrawl vb : write hastily and carelessly — **scrawl** n

scraw·ny adj **-ni·er; -est** : very thin

scream vb : cry out loudly and shrilly ~ n : loud shrill cry

screech vb or n : shriek

screen n **1** : device or partition used to protect or decorate **2** : surface on which pictures appear (as in movies) ~ vb : shield or separate with or as if with a screen

screw n **1** : grooved fastening device **2** : propeller ~ vb **1** : fasten by means of a screw **2** : move spirally

screw·driv·er n : tool for turning screws

scrib·ble vb **-bled; -bling** : write hastily or carelessly — **scribble** n — **scrib·bler** n

scribe n : one who writes or copies writing

scrimp vb : economize greatly

scrip n **1** : paper money for less than a dollar **2** : certificate entitling one to something (as stock)

script n : text (as of a play)

scrip·ture n : sacred writings of a religion — **scrip·tur·al** adj

scroll n **1** : roll of paper for writing a document **2** : spiral or coiled design

scro·tum n, pl **-ta** or **-tums** : pouch containing the testes

scrounge vb **scrounged; scroung·ing** : collect by or as if by foraging

¹scrub n : stunted tree or shrub or a growth of these — **scrub** adj — **scrub·by** adj

²scrub vb **-bb-** : clean or wash by rubbing — **scrub** n

scruff n : loose skin of the back of the neck

scrump·tious adj : delicious

scru·ple n : reluctance due to ethical considerations — **scruple** vb — **scru·pu·lous** adj — **scru·pu·lous·ly** adv

scru·ti·ny n, pl **-nies** : careful inspection — **scru·ti·nize** vb

scud vb **-dd-** : move speedily

scuff vb : scratch, scrape, or wear away — **scuff** n

scuf·fle vb **-fled; -fling 1** : struggle at close quarters **2** : shuffle one's feet — **scuffle** n

scull n **1** : oar **2** : racing shell propelled with sculls ~ vb : propel a boat by an oar over the stern

scul·lery n, pl **-ler·ies** : room for cleaning dishes and cookware

sculpt vb : sculpture

sculp·ture n : work of art carved or molded ~ vb **-tured; -tur·ing** : form as sculpture — **sculp·tor** n — **sculp·tur·al** adj

scum n : slimy film on a liquid

scur·ri·lous adj : vulgar or abusive

scur·ry vb **-ried; -ry·ing** : scamper

scur·vy n : vitamin-deficiency disease

¹scut·tle n : pail for coal

²scuttle vb **-tled; -tling** : sink (a ship) by cutting holes in its bottom

³scuttle vb **-tled; -tling** : scamper

scythe n : tool for mowing by hand — **scythe** vb

sea n **1** : large body of salt water **2** : ocean **3** : rough water — **sea** adj — **sea·coast** n — **sea·food** n — **sea·port** n — **sea·shore** n — **sea·wa·ter** n

sea·bird n : bird frequenting the open ocean

sea·board n : country's seacoast

sea·far·er n : seaman — **sea·far·ing** adj or n

sea horse n : small fish with a horselike head

¹seal n : large sea mammal of cold regions — **seal·skin** n

²seal n **1** : device for stamping a design **2** : something that closes ~ vb **1** : affix a seal to **2** : close up securely **3** : determine finally — **seal·ant** n — **seal·er** n

sea lion n : large Pacific seal with external ears

seam n **1** : line of junction of 2 edges **2** : layer of a mineral ~ vb : join by sewing — **seam·less** adj

sea·man n **1** : one who helps to handle a ship **2** : naval enlisted man ranking next below a petty officer third class — **sea·man·ship** n

seaman apprentice n : naval enlisted man ranking next below a seaman

seaman recruit n : naval enlisted man of the lowest rank

seam·stress n : woman who sews

seamy adj **seam·i·er; -est** : unpleasant or sordid

sé·ance n : meeting for communicating with spirits

sea·plane n : airplane that can take off from and land on the water

sear vb : scorch — **sear** n

search vb **1** : look through **2** : seek — **search** n — **search·er** n — **search·light** n

sea·sick adj : nauseated by the motion of a ship — **sea·sick·ness** n

¹sea·son n **1** : division of the year **2** : customary time for something — **sea·son·al** adj — **sea·son·al·ly** adv

²season vb **1** : add spice to (food) **2** : make strong or fit for use — **sea·son·ing** n

sea·son·able adj : occurring at a suitable time — **sea·son·ably** adv

seat n **1** : place to sit **2** : chair, bench, or stool for sitting on **3** : place that serves as a capital or center ~ vb **1** : place in or on a seat **2** : provide seats for

sea·weed n : marine alga

sea·wor·thy adj : strong enough to hold up to a sea voyage

se·cede vb **-ced·ed; -ced·ing** : withdraw from a body (as a nation)

se·clude vb **-clud·ed; -clud·ing** : shut off alone — **se·clu·sion** n

¹sec·ond adj : next after the 1st ~ n **1** : one that is second **2** : one who assists (as in a duel) — **second, sec·ond·ly** adv

²second n **1** : 60th part of a minute **2** : moment

sec·ond·ary adj **1** : second in rank or importance **2** : coming after the primary or elementary

sec·ond·hand adj **1** : not original **2** : used before

second lieutenant n : lowest ranking commissioned officer of the army, air force, or marines

se·cret adj **1** : hidden **2** : kept from general knowledge — **se·cre·cy** n — **secret** n — **se·cre·tive** adj — **se·cret·ly** adv

sec·re·tar·i·at n : administrative department

sec·re·tary n, pl **-tar·ies 1** : one hired to handle correspondence and other tasks for a superior **2** : official in charge of correspondence or records **3** : head of a government department — **sec·re·tari·al** adj

¹se·crete vb **-cret·ed; -cret·ing** : produce as a secretion

²se·crete vb **-cret·ed; -cret·ing** : hide

se·cre·tion n **1** : process of secreting **2** : product of glandular activity

sect n : religious group

sec·tar·i·an adj **1** : relating to a sect **2** : limited in character or scope ~ n : member of a sect

sec·tion n : distinct part — **sec·tion·al** adj

sec·tor n **1** : part of a circle between 2 radii **2** : distinctive part

sec·u·lar adj **1** : not sacred **2** : not monastic

se·cure adj **-cur·er; -est** : free from danger or loss ~ vb **1** : fasten safely **2** : get — **se·cure·ly** adv

se·cu·ri·ty n, pl **-ties 1** : safety **2** : something given to guarantee payment **3** pl : bond or stock certificates

se·dan n **1** : chair carried by 2 men **2** : enclosed automobile

¹se·date adj : quiet and dignified — **se·date·ly** adv

²sedate vb **-dat·ed; -dat·ing** : dose with sedatives — **se·da·tion** n

sed·a·tive adj : serving to relieve tension ~ n : sedative drug

sed·en·tary adj : characterized by much sitting

sedge n : grasslike marsh plant

sed·i·ment n : material that settles to the bottom of a liquid or is deposited by water or a glacier — **sed·i·men·ta·ry** adj — **sed·i·men·ta·tion** n

se·di·tion n : revolution against a government — **se·di·tious** adj

se·duce vb **-duced; -duc·ing 1** : lead astray **2** : entice to sexual intercourse — **se·duc·er** n — **se·duc·tion** n — **se·duc·tive** adj

sed·u·lous adj : diligent

¹see vb **saw; seen; see·ing 1** : perceive by the eye **2** : have experience of **3** : understand **4** : make sure **5** : meet with or escort

²see n : jurisdiction of a bishop

seed n, pl **seed** or **seeds 1** : part by which a plant is propagated **2** : source ~ vb **1** : sow **2** : remove seeds from — **seed·less** adj

seed·ling n : young plant grown from seed

seedy *adj* **seed·i·er; -est 1** : full of seeds **2** : shabby

seek *vb* **sought; seek·ing 1** : search for **2** : try to reach or obtain — **seek·er** *n*

seem *vb* : give the impression of being — **seem·ing·ly** *adv*

seem·ly *adj* **seem·li·er; -est** : proper or fit

seep *vb* : leak through fine pores or cracks — **seep·age** *n*

seer *n* : one who foresees or predicts events

seer·suck·er *n* : light puckered fabric

see·saw *n* : board balanced in the middle — **seesaw** *vb*

seethe *vb* **seethed; seeth·ing** : become violently agitated

seg·ment *n* : division of a thing — **seg·ment·ed** *adj*

seg·re·gate *vb* **-gat·ed; -gat·ing 1** : cut off from others **2** : separate by races — **seg·re·ga·tion** *n*

seine *n* : large weighted fishing net ~ *vb* : fish with a seine

seis·mic *adj* : relating to an earthquake

seis·mo·graph *n* : apparatus for detecting earthquakes

seize *vb* **seized; seiz·ing** : take by force — **sei·zure** *n*

sel·dom *adv* : not often

se·lect *adj* **1** : favored **2** : discriminating ~ *vb* : take by preference — **se·lec·tive** *adj*

se·lec·tion *n* : act of selecting or thing selected

se·lect·man *n* : New England town official

self *n, pl* **selves** : essential person distinct from others

self- *comb form* **1** : oneself or itself **2** : of oneself or itself **3** : by oneself or automatic **4** : to, for, or toward oneself

self-addressed	self-governing
self-administered	self-government
self-analysis	self-help
self-appointed	self-image
self-assertive	self-importance
self-assurance	self-important
self-assured	self-imposed
self-awareness	self-improvement
self-cleaning	self-indulgence
self-closing	self-indulgent
self-complacent	self-inflicted
self-conceit	self-interest
self-confessed	self-love
self-confidence	self-operating
self-confident	self-pity
self-contained	self-portrait
self-contempt	self-possessed
self-contradiction	self-possession
self-contradictory	self-preservation
self-control	self-proclaimed
self-created	self-propelled
self-criticism	self-propelling
self-defeating	self-protection
self-defense	self-reliance
self-denial	self-reliant
self-denying	self-respect
self-destruction	self-respecting
self-destructive	self-restraint
self-determination	self-sacrifice
self-determined	self-satisfaction
self-discipline	self-satisfied
self-doubt	self-service
self-educated	self-serving
self-employed	self-starting
self-employment	self-styled
self-esteem	self-sufficiency
self-evident	self-sufficient
self-explanatory	self-supporting
self-expression	self-taught
self-fulfilling	self-winding
self-fulfillment	

self–cen·tered *adj* : concerned only with one's own self

self–con·scious *adj* : uncomfortably aware of oneself as an object of observation — **self–con·scious·ly** *adv* — **self–con·scious·ness** *n*

self·ish *adj* : excessively or exclusively concerned with one's own well-being — **self·ish·ly** *adv* — **self·ish·ness** *n*

self·less *adj* : unselfish — **self·less·ness** *n*

self–made *adj* : having succeeded by one's own efforts

self–righ·teous *adj* : strongly convinced of one's own righteousness

self·same *adj* : precisely the same

sell *vb* **sold; sell·ing 1** : transfer (property) esp. for money **2** : deal in as a business **3** : be sold — **sell·er** *n*

selves *pl of* SELF

se·man·tic *adj* : relating to meaning in language — **se·man·tics** *n sing or pl*

sem·a·phore *n* **1** : visual signaling apparatus **2** : signaling by flags

sem·blance *n* : appearance

se·men *n* : male reproductive fluid

se·mes·ter *n* : half a school year

semi- *prefix* **1** : half **2** : partial

semi·co·lon *n* : punctuation mark;

semi·con·duc·tor *n* : substance between a conductor and a nonconductor in ability to conduct electricity — **semi·con·duct·ing** *adj*

semi·fi·nal *adj* : being next to the final — **semi·final** *n*

semi·for·mal *adj* : being or suitable for an occasion of moderate formality

sem·i·nal *adj* **1** : relating to seed or semen **2** : causing or influencing later development

sem·i·nar *n* : conference or conferencelike study

sem·i·nary *n, pl* **-nar·ies** : school and esp. a theological school — **sem·i·nar·i·an** *n*

sen·ate *n* : upper branch of a legislature — **sen·a·tor** *n* — **sen·a·to·ri·al** *adj*

send *vb* **sent; send·ing 1** : cause to go **2** : propel — **send·er** *n*

se·nile *adj* : mentally deficient through old age — **se·nil·i·ty** *n*

se·nior *adj* : older or higher ranking — **senior** *n* — **se·nior·i·ty** *n*

senior chief petty officer *n* : petty officer in the navy or coast guard ranking next below a master chief petty officer

senior master sergeant *n* : noncommissioned officer in the air force ranking next below a chief master sergeant

sen·sa·tion *n* **1** : bodily feeling **2** : condition of excitement or the cause of it — **sen·sa·tion·al** *adj*

sense *n* **1** : meaning **2** : faculty of perceiving something physical **3** : sound mental capacity ~ *vb* **sensed; sens·ing 1** : perceive by the senses **2** : detect automatically — **sense·less** *adj* — **sense·less·ly** *adv*

sen·si·bil·i·ty *n, pl* **-ties** : delicacy of feeling

sen·si·ble *adj* **1** : capable of sensing or being sensed **2** : aware or conscious **3** : reasonable — **sen·si·bly** *adv*

sen·si·tive *adj* **1** : subject to excitation by or responsive to stimuli **2** : having power of feeling **3** : easily affected — **sen·si·tive·ness** *n* — **sen·si·tiv·i·ty** *n*

sen·si·tize *vb* **-tized; -tiz·ing** : make or become sensitive

sen·sor *n* : device that responds to a physical stimulus

sen·so·ry *adj* : relating to sensation or the senses

sen·su·al *adj* **1** : pleasing the senses **2** : devoted to the pleasures of the senses — **sen·su·al·ist** *n* — **sen·su·al·i·ty** *n* — **sen·su·al·ly** *adv*

sen·su·ous *adj* : having strong appeal to the senses

sent *past of* SEND

sen·tence *n* **1** : judgment of a court **2** : grammatically self-contained speech unit ~ *vb* **-tenced; -tenc·ing** : impose a sentence on

sen·ten·tious *adj* : using pompous language

sen·tient *adj* : capable of feeling

sen·ti·ment *n* **1** : belief **2** : feeling

sen·ti·men·tal *adj* : influenced by tender feelings — **sen·ti·men·tal·ism** *n* — **sen·ti·men·tal·ist** *n* — **sen·ti·men·tal·i·ty** *n* — **sen·ti·men·tal·ize** *vb* — **sen·ti·men·tal·ly** *adv*

sen·ti·nel *n* : sentry

sen·try *n, pl* **-tries** : one who stands guard

se·pal *n* : modified leaf in a flower calyx

sep·a·rate *vb* **-rat·ed; -rat·ing 1** : set or keep apart **2** : become divided or detached ~ *adj* **1** : not connected or shared **2** : distinct from each other — **sep·a·ra·ble** *adj* — **sep·a·rate·ly** *adv* — **sep·a·ra·tion** *n* — **sep·a·ra·tor** *n*

se·pia *n* : brownish gray

Sep·tem·ber *n* : 9th month of the year having 30 days

sep·ul·chre, sep·ul·cher *n* : burial vault — **se·pul·chral** *adj*

se·quel *n* **1** : consequence or result **2** : continuation of a story

se·quence *n* : continuous or connected series — **se·quen·tial** *adj* — **se·quen·tial·ly** *adv*

se·ques·ter *vb* : segregate

se·quin *n* : spangle

se·quoia *n* : huge California coniferous tree

sera *pl of* SERUM

ser·aph *n, pl* **-a·phim** *or* **-aphs** : angel — **se·raph·ic** *adj*

sere *adj* : dried up or withered

ser·e·nade *n* : music sung or played esp. to a woman being courted — **serenade** *vb*

ser·en·dip·i·ty *n* : good luck in finding things not sought for — **ser·en·dip·i·tous** *adj*

se·rene *adj* : tranquil — **se·rene·ly** *adv* — **se·ren·i·ty** *n*

serf *n* : peasant obligated to work the land — **serf·dom** *n*

serge *n* : twilled woolen cloth

ser·geant *n* : noncommissioned officer (as in the army) ranking next below a staff sergeant

sergeant first class *n* : noncommissioned officer in the army ranking next below a master sergeant

sergeant major *n, pl* **sergeants major** *or* **sergeant majors 1** : noncommissioned officer serving as an enlisted adviser in a headquarters **2** : noncommissioned officer in the marine corps ranking above a first sergeant

se·ri·al *adj* : being or relating to a series or sequence ~ *n* : story appearing in parts — **se·ri·al·ly** *adv*

se·ries *n, pl* **series** : number of things in order

se·ri·ous *adj* **1** : subdued in appearance or manner **2** : sincere **3** : of great importance — **se·ri·ous·ly** *adv* — **se·ri·ous·ness** *n*

ser·mon *n* : lecture on religion or behavior

ser·pent *n* : snake — **ser·pen·tine** *adj*

ser·rated *adj* : saw-toothed

se·rum *n, pl* **-rums** *or* **-ra** : watery part of blood

ser·vant *n* : person employed for domestic work

serve *vb* **served; serv·ing 1** : work through or perform a term of service **2** : be of use **3** : prove adequate **4** : hand out (food or drink) **5** : be of service to — **serv·er** *n*

ser·vice *n* **1** : act or means of serving **2** : meeting for worship **3** : branch of public employment or the persons in it **4** : set of dishes or silverware **5** : benefit ~ *vb* **-viced; -vic·ing** : repair — **ser·vice·able** *adj* — **ser·vice·man** *n* — **ser·vice·wom·an** *n*

ser·vile *adj* : behaving like a slave — **ser·vil·i·ty** *n*

serv·ing *n* : helping

ser·vi·tude *n* : slavery

ses·a·me *n* : annual herb or its seeds that are used in flavoring

ses·sion *n* : meeting

set *vb* **set; set·ting 1** : cause to sit **2** : place **3** : settle, arrange, or adjust **4** : cause to be or do **5** : become fixed or solid **6** : sink below the horizon ~ *adj* : settled ~ *n* **1** : group classed together **2** : setting for the scene of a play or film **3** : electronic apparatus **4** : collection of mathematical elements — **set forth** : begin a trip — **set off** *vb* : set forth — **set out** *vb* : begin a trip or undertaking — **set up** *vb* **1** : assemble or erect **2** : cause

set·back *n* : reverse

set·tee *n* : bench or sofa

set·ter *n* : large long-coated hunting dog

set·ting *n* : the time, place, and circumstances in which something occurs

set·tle *vb* **-tled; -tling 1** : come to rest **2** : sink gradually **3** : establish in residence **4** : adjust or arrange **5** : calm **6** : dispose of (as by paying) **7** : decide or agree on — **set·tle·ment** *n* — **set·tler** *n*

sev·en *n* : one more than 6 — **seven** *adj or pron* — **sev·enth** *adj or adv or n*

sev·en·teen *n* : one more than 16 — **seventeen** *adj or pron* — **sev·en·teenth** *adj or n*

sev·en·ty *n, pl* **-ties** : 7 times 10 — **sev·en·ti·eth** *adj or n* — **seventy** *adj or pron*

sev·er *vb* **-ered; -er·ing** : cut off or apart — **sev·er·ance** *n*

sev·er·al *adj* **1** : distinct **2** : consisting of an indefinite but not large number — **sev·er·al·ly** *adv*

se·vere *adj* **-ver·er; -est 1** : strict **2** : restrained or unadorned **3** : painful or distressing **4** : hard to endure — **se·vere·ly** *adv* — **se·ver·i·ty** *n*

sew *vb* **sewed; sewn** *or* **sewed; sew·ing** : join or fasten by stitches — **sew·ing** *n*

sew·age *n* : liquid household waste

¹**sew·er** *n* : one that sews

²**sew·er** *n* : pipe or channel to carry off waste matter

sex *n* **1** : either of 2 divisions into which organisms are grouped according to their reproductive roles or the qualities which differentiate them **2** : copulation — **sexed** *adj* — **sex·less** *adj* — **sex·u·al** *adj* — **sex·u·al·i·ty** *n* — **sex·u·al·ly** *adv* — **sexy** *adj*

sex·ism *n* : discrimination based on sex and esp. against women — **sex·ist** *adj or n*

sex·tant *n* : instrument for navigation

sex·tet *n* **1** : music for 6 performers **2** : group of 6

sex·ton *n* : church caretaker

shab·by *adj* **-bi·er; -est 1** : worn and faded **2** : dressed in worn clothes **3** : not generous or fair — **shab·bi·ly** *adv* — **shab·bi·ness** *n*

shack *n* : hut

shack·le *n* : metal device to bind legs or arms ~ *vb* **-led; -ling** : bind or fasten with shackles

shad *n* : Atlantic food fish

shade *n* **1** : space sheltered from the light esp. of the sun **2** : gradation of color **3** : small difference **4** : something that shades ~ *vb* **shad·ed; shad·ing 1** : shelter from light and heat **2** : add shades of color to **3** : show slight differences esp. in color or meaning

shad·ow *n* **1** : shade cast upon a surface by something blocking light **2** : trace **3** : gloomy influence ~ *vb* **1** : cast a shadow **2** : follow closely — **shad·owy** *adj*

shady *adj* **shad·i·er; -est 1** : giving shade **2** : of dubious honesty

shaft *n* **1** : long slender cylindrical part **2** : deep vertical opening (as of a mine)

shag *n* : shaggy tangled mat

shag·gy *adj* **-gi·er; -est 1** : covered with long hair or wool **2** : not neat and combed

shake *vb* **shook; shak·en; shak·ing 1** : move or cause to move quickly back and forth **2** : distress

3 : clasp (hands) as friendly gesture — **shake** *n* — **shak·er** *n*

shake-up *n* : reorganization

shaky *adj* **shak·i·er; -est** : not sound, stable, or reliable — **shak·i·ly** *adv* — **shak·i·ness** *n*

shale *n* : stratified rock

shall *vb, past* **should** *pres sing & pl* **shall** — used as an auxiliary to express a command, futurity, or determination

shal·low *adj* **1** : not deep **2** : not intellectually profound

shal·lows *n pl* : area of shallow water

sham *adj or n or vb* : fake

sham·ble *vb* **-bled; -bling** : shuffle along — **sham·ble** *n*

sham·bles *n* : state of disorder

shame *n* **1** : distress over guilt or disgrace **2** : cause of shame or regret ~ *vb* **shamed; sham·ing 1** : make ashamed **2** : disgrace — **shame·ful** *adj* — **shame·ful·ly** *adv* — **shame·less** *adj* — **shameless·ly** *adv*

shame·faced *adj* : ashamed

sham·poo *vb* : wash one's hair ~ *n, pl* **-poos** : act of or preparation used in shampooing

sham·rock *n* : plant of legend with 3-lobed leaves

shank *n* : part of the leg between the knee and ankle

shan·ty *n, pl* **-ties** : hut

shape *vb* **shaped; shap·ing** : form esp. in a particular structure or appearance ~ *n* **1** : distinctive appearance or arrangement of parts **2** : condition — **shape·less** *adj* — **shape·li·ness** *n* — **shape·ly** *adj*

shard *n* : broken piece

share *n* **1** : portion belonging to one **2** : interest in a company's stock ~ *vb* **shared; shar·ing** : divide or use with others — **share·hold·er** *n* — **shar·er** *n*

share·crop·per *n* : farmer who works another's land in return for a share of the crop — **share·crop** *vb*

shark *n* : voracious sea fish

sharp *adj* **1** : having a good point or cutting edge **2** : alert, clever, or sarcastic **3** : vigorous or fierce **4** : having prominent angles or a sudden change in direction **5** : distinct **6** : higher than the true pitch ~ *adv* : exactly ~ *n* : sharp note — **sharp·ly** *adv* — **sharp·ness** *n*

shar·pen *vb* : make sharp — **sharp·en·er** *n*

sharp·shoot·er *n* : expert marksman — **sharp·shoot·ing** *n*

shat·ter *vb* : smash or burst into fragments — **shat·ter·proof** *adj*

shave *vb* **shaved; shaved** *or* **shav·en; shav·ing 1** : cut off with a razor **2** : make bare by cutting the hair from **3** : slice very thin ~ *n* : act or instance of shaving — **shav·er** *n*

shawl *n* : loose covering for the head or shoulders

she *pron* : that female one

sheaf *n, pl* **sheaves** : bundle esp. of grain stalks

shear *vb* **sheared; sheared;** *or* **shorn shear·ing 1** : trim wool from **2** : cut off with scissorlike action

shears *n pl* : cutting tool with 2 blades fastened so that the edges slide by each other

sheath *n, pl* **sheaths** : covering (as for a blade)

sheathe *vb* **sheathed; sheath·ing** : put into a sheath

shed *vb* **shed; shed·ding 1** : give off (as tears or hair) **2** : cause to flow or diffuse ~ *n* : small storage building

sheen *n* : subdued luster

sheep *n, pl* **sheep** : domesticated mammal covered with wool — **sheep·skin** *n*

sheep·ish *adj* : embarrassed by awareness of a fault

sheer *adj* **1** : pure **2** : very steep **3** : very thin or transparent — **sheer** *adv*

sheet *n* : broad flat piece (as of cloth or paper)

sheikh, sheik *n* : Arab chief — **sheikh·dom, sheikdom** *n*

shelf *n, pl* **shelves 1** : flat narrow structure used for storage or display **2** : sandbank or rock ledge

shell *n* **1** : hard or tough outer covering **2** : case holding explosive powder and projectile for a weapon **3** : light racing boat with oars ~ *vb* **1** : remove the shell of **2** : bombard — **shelled** *adj* — **shell·er** *n*

shel·lac *n* : varnish ~ *vb* **-lacked; -lack·ing 1** : coat with shellac **2** : defeat — **shel·lack·ing** *n*

shell·fish *n* : water animal with a shell

shel·ter *n* : something that gives protection ~ *vb* : give refuge to

shelve *vb* **shelved; shelv·ing 1** : place or store on shelves **2** : dismiss or put aside

she·nan·i·gans *n pl* : mischievous or deceitful conduct

shep·herd *n* : one that tends sheep ~ *vb* : act as a shepherd or guardian

shep·herd·ess *n* : woman who tends sheep

sher·bet, sher·bert *n* : fruit-flavored frozen dessert

sher·iff *n* : county law officer

sher·ry *n, pl* **-ries** : type of wine

shield *n* **1** : broad piece of armor carried on the arm **2** : something that protects — **shield** *vb*

shier *comparative of* SHY

shiest *superlative of* SHY

shift *vb* **1** : change place, position, or direction **2** : get by ~ *n* **1** : loose-fitting dress **2** : an act or instance of shifting **3** : scheduled work period

shift·less *adj* : lazy

shifty *adj* **shift·i·er; -est** : tricky or untrustworthy

shil·le·lagh *n* : club or stick

shil·ling *n* : former British coin

shilly-shally *vb* **-shall·ied; -shally·ing 1** : hesitate **2** : dawdle

shim·mer *vb or n* : glimmer

shin *n* : front part of the leg below the knee ~ *vb* **-nn-** : climb by sliding the body close along

shine *vb* **shone** *or* **shined; shin·ing 1** : give off or cause to give off light **2** : be outstanding **3** : polish ~ *n* : brilliance

shin·gle *n* **1** : small thin piece used in covering roofs or exterior walls — **shingle** *vb*

shin·gles *n pl* : acute inflammation of spinal nerves

shin·ny *vb* **-nied; -ny·ing** : shin

shiny *adj* **shin·i·er; -est** : bright or polished

ship *n* **1** : large oceangoing vessel **2** : aircraft or spacecraft ~ *vb* **-pp- 1** : put on a ship **2** : transport by carrier — **ship·board** *n* — **ship·build·er** *n* — **ship·per** *n* — **ship·wreck** *n or vb* — **ship·yard** *n*

-ship *n suffix* **1** : state, condition, or quality **2** : rank or profession **3** : skill **4** : something showing a state or quality

ship·ment *n* : an act of shipping or the goods shipped

ship·ping *n* **1** : ships **2** : transportation of goods

ship·shape *adj* : tidy

shire *n* : British county

shirk *vb* : evade — **shirk·er** *n*

shirr *vb* **1** : gather (cloth) by drawing up parallel lines of stitches **2** : bake (eggs) in a dish

shirt *n* : garment for covering the torso — **shirt·less** *adj*

shiv·er *vb* : tremble — **shiver** *n* — **shiv·ery** *adj*

shoal *n* : shallow place (as in a river)

¹**shock** *n* : pile of sheaves set up in a field

²**shock** *n* **1** : forceful impact **2** : violent mental or emotional disturbance **3** : effect of a charge of electricity **4** : depression of the vital bodily processes ~ *vb* **1** : strike with surprise, horror,

or disgust **2** : subject to an electrical shock — **shock•proof** *adj*

³**shock** *n* : bushy mass (as of hair)

shod•dy *adj* **-di•er; -est** : poorly made or done — **shod•di•ly** *adv* — **shod•di•ness** *n*

shoe *n* **1** : covering for the human foot **2** : horseshoe ~ *vb* **shod; shoe•ing** : put horseshoes on — **shoe•lace** *n* — **shoe•ma•ker** *n*

shone *past of* SHINE

shook *past of* SHAKE

shoot *vb* **shot; shoot•ing 1** : propel (as an arrow or bullet) **2** : wound or kill with a missile **3** : discharge (a weapon) **4** : drive (as a ball) at a goal **5** : photograph **6** : move swiftly ~ *n* : new plant growth — **shoot•er** *n*

shop *n* : place where things are made or sold ~ *vb* **-pp-** : visit stores — **shop•keep•er** *n* — **shop•per** *n*

shop•lift *vb* : steal goods from a store — **shop•lift•er** *n*

¹**shore** *n* : land along the edge of water — **shore•line** *n*

²**shore** *vb* **shored; shor•ing** : prop up ~ *n* : something that props

shore•bird *n* : bird of the seashore

shorn *past part of* SHEAR

short *adj* **1** : not long or tall or extending far **2** : brief in time **3** : curt **4** : not having or being enough ~ *adv* : curtly ~ *n* **1** *pl* : short drawers or trousers **2** : short circuit — **short•en** *vb* — **short•ly** *adv* — **short•ness** *n*

short•age *n* : deficiency

short•cake *n* : dessert of biscuit with sweetened fruit

short•change *vb* : cheat esp. by giving too little change

short circuit *n* : abnormal electric connection — **short–circuit** *vb*

short•com•ing *n* : fault or failing

short•cut *n* **1** : more direct route than that usu. taken **2** : quicker way of doing something

short•hand *n* : method of speed writing

short–lived *adj* : of short life or duration

short–sight•ed *adj* : lacking foresight

shot *n* **1** : act of shooting **2** : attempt (as at making a goal) **3** : small pellets forming a charge **4** : range or reach **5** : photograph **6** : injection of medicine **7** : small serving of liquor — **shot•gun** *n*

should *past of* SHALL — used as an auxiliary to express condition, obligation, or probability

shoul•der *n* **1** : part of the body where the arm joins the trunk **2** : part that projects or lies to the side ~ *vb* : push with or bear on the shoulder

shoulder blade *n* : flat triangular bone at the back of the shoulder

shout *vb* : give voice loudly — **shout** *n*

shove *vb* **shoved; shov•ing** : push along or away — **shove** *n*

shov•el *n* : broad tool for digging or lifting ~ *vb* **-eled** *or* **-elled; -el•ing** *or* **-el•ling** : take up or dig with a shovel

show *vb* **showed; shown** *or* **showed; show•ing 1** : present to view **2** : reveal or demonstrate **3** : teach **4** : prove **5** : conduct or escort **6** : appear or be noticeable ~ *n* **1** : demonstrative display **2** : spectacle **3** : theatrical, radio, or television program — **show•case** *n* — **show off** *vb* **1** : display proudly **2** : act so as to attract attention — **show up** *vb* : arrive

show•down *n* : decisive confrontation

show•er *n* **1** : brief fall of rain **2** : bath in which water sprinkles down on the person or a facility for such a bath **3** : party at which someone gets gifts ~ *vb* **1** : rain or fall in a shower **2** : bathe in a shower — **show•ery** *adj*

showy *adj* **show•i•er; -est** : very noticeable or overly elaborate — **show•i•ly** *adv* — **show•i•ness** *n*

shrap•nel *n, pl* **shrapnel** : metal fragments of a bomb

shred *n* : narrow strip cut or torn off ~ *vb* **-dd-** : cut or tear into shreds

shrew 1 : scolding woman **2** : mouselike mammal — **shrew•ish** *adj*

shrewd *adj* : clever — **shrewd•ly** *adv* — **shrewd•ness** *n*

shriek *n* : shrill cry — **shriek** *vb*

shrill *adj* : piercing and high-pitched — **shril•ly** *adv*

shrimp *n* : small sea crustacean

shrine *n* **1** : tomb of a saint **2** : hallowed place

shrink *vb* **shrank; shrunk** *or* **shrunk•en; shrink•ing 1** : draw back or away **2** : become smaller — **shrink•able** *adj*

shrink•age *n* : amount lost by shrinking

shriv•el *vb* **-eled** *or* **-elled; -el•ing** *or* **-el•ling** : shrink or wither into wrinkles

shroud *n* **1** : cloth put over a corpse **2** : cover or screen ~ *vb* : veil or screen from view

shrub *n* : low woody plant — **shrub•by** *adj*

shrub•bery *n, pl* **-ber•ies** : growth of shrubs

shrug *vb* **-gg-** : hunch the shoulders up in doubt, indifference, or uncertainty — **shrug** *n*

shuck *vb* : strip of a shell or husk — **shuck** *n*

shud•der *vb* : tremble — **shudder** *n*

shuf•fle *vb* **-fled; -fling 1** : mix together **2** : walk with a sliding movement — **shuffle** *n*

shuf•fle•board *n* : game of sliding disks into a scoring area

shun *vb* **-nn-** : keep away from

shunt *vb* : turn off to one side

shut *vb* **shut; shut•ting 1** : bar passage into or through (as by moving a lid or door) **2** : suspend activity — **shut out** : exclude — **shut up** *vb* : stop or cause to stop talking

shut–in *n* : invalid

shut•ter *n* **1** : movable cover for a window **2** : camera part that exposes film

shut•tle *n* **1** : part of a weaving machine that carries thread back and forth **2** : vehicle traveling back and forth over a short route ~ *vb* **-tled; -tling** : move back and forth frequently

shut•tle•cock *n* : light conical object used in badminton

shy *adj* **shi•er** *or* **shy•er; shi•est** *or* **shy•est 1** : sensitive and hesitant in dealing with others **2** : wary **3** : lacking ~ *vb* **shied; shy•ing** : draw back (as in fright) — **shy•ly** *adv* — **shy•ness** *n*

sib•i•lant *adj* : having the sound of the *s* or the *sh* in *sash* — **sibilant** *n*

sib•ling *n* : brother or sister

sick *adj* **1** : not in good health **2** : nauseated **3** : relating to or meant for the sick — **sick•bed** *n* — **sick•en** *vb* — **sick•ly** *adj* — **sick•ness** *n*

sick•le *n* : curved short-handled blade

side *n* **1** : part to left or right of an object or the torso **2** : edge or surface away from the center or at an angle to top and bottom or ends **3** : contrasting or opposing position or group — **sid•ed** *adj*

side•board *n* : piece of dining-room furniture for table service

side•burns *n pl* : whiskers in front of the ears

side•long *adv or adj* : to or along the side

side•show *n* : minor show at a circus

side•step *vb* **1** : step aside **2** : avoid

side•swipe *vb* : strike with a glancing blow — **sideswipe** *n*

side•track *vb* : lead aside or astray

side•walk *n* : paved walk at the side of a road

side•ways *adv or adj* **1** : to or from the side **2** : with one side to the front

sid•ing *n* **1** : short railroad track **2** : material for covering the outside of a building

si•dle *vb* **-dled; -dling** : move sideways or unobtrusively

siege *n* : persistent attack (as on a fortified place)

si•es•ta *n* : midday nap

sieve *n* : utensil with holes to separate particles

sift *vb* **1** : pass through a sieve **2** : examine carefully — **sift•er** *n*

sigh *n* : audible release of the breath (as to express weariness) — **sigh** *vb*

sight *n* **1** : something seen or worth seeing **2** : process, power, or range of seeing **3** : device used in aiming **4** : view or glimpse ~ *vb* : get sight of — **sight•ed** *adj* — **sight•less** *adj* — **sight–see•ing** *adj* — **sight•seer** *n*

sign *n* **1** : symbol **2** : gesture expressing a command or thought **3** : public notice to advertise or warn **4** : trace ~ *vb* **1** : mark with or make a sign **2** : write one's name on — **sign•er** *n*

sig•nal *n* **1** : sign of command or warning **2** : electronic transmission ~ *vb* **-naled** *or* **-nalled; -nal•ing** *or* **-nal•ling** : communicate or notify by signals ~ *adj* : distinguished

sig•na•to•ry *n, pl* **-ries** : person or government that signs jointly with others

sig•na•ture *n* : one's name written by oneself

sig•net *n* : small seal

sig•nif•i•cance *n* **1** : meaning **2** : importance — **sig•nif•i•cant** *adj* — **sig•nif•i•cant•ly** *adv*

sig•ni•fy *vb* **-fied; -fy•ing 1** : show by a sign **2** : mean — **sig•ni•fi•ca•tion** *n*

si•lence *n* : state of being without sound ~ *vb* **-lenced; -lenc•ing** : keep from making noise or sound — **si•lenc•er** *n*

si•lent *adj* : having or producing no sound — **si•lent•ly** *adv*

sil•hou•ette *n* : outline filled in usu. with black ~ *vb* **-ett•ed; -ett•ing** : represent by a silhouette

sil•i•ca *n* : mineral found as quartz and opal

sil•i•con *n* : nonmetallic chemical element

silk *n* **1** : fine strong lustrous protein fiber from moth larvae (**silkworms**) **2** : thread or cloth made from silk — **silk•en** *adj* — **silky** *adj*

sill *n* : bottom part of a window frame or a doorway

sil•ly *adj* **sil•li•er; -est** : foolish or stupid — **sil•li•ness** *n*

si•lo *n, pl* **-los** : tall building for storing animal feed

silt *n* : fine earth carried by rivers ~ *vb* : obstruct or cover with silt

sil•ver *n* **1** : white ductile metallic chemical element **2** : silverware ~ *adj* : having the color of silver — **sil•very** *adj*

sil•ver•ware *n* : eating and serving utensils esp. of silver

sim•i•lar *adj* : resembling each other in some ways — **sim•i•lar•i•ty** *n* — **sim•i•lar•ly** *adv*

sim•i•le *n* : comparison of unlike things using *like* or *as*

sim•mer *vb* : stew gently

sim•per *vb* : give a silly smile — **simper** *n*

sim•ple *adj* **-pler; -plest 1** : free from dishonesty, vanity, or pretense **2** : of humble origin or modest position **3** : not complex **4** : lacking education, experience, or intelligence — **sim•ple•ness** *n* — **sim•ply** *adv*

sim•ple•ton *n* : fool

sim•plic•i•ty *n* : state or fact of being simple

sim•pli•fy *vb* **-fied; -fy•ing** : make easier — **sim•pli•fi•ca•tion** *n*

sim•u•late *vb* **-lat•ed; -lat•ing** : create the effect or appearance of — **sim•u•la•tion** *n* — **sim•u•la•tor** *n*

si•mul•ta•ne•ous *adj* : occurring or operating at the same time — **si•mul•ta•ne•ous•ly** *adv* — **simul•ta•ne•ous•ness** *n*

sin *n* : offense against God ~ *vb* **-nn-** : commit a sin — **sin•ful** *adj* — **sin•less** *adj* — **sin•ner** *n*

since *adv* **1** : from a past time until now **2** : backward in time ~ *prep* **1** : in the period after **2** : continuously from ~ *conj* **1** : from the time when **2** : because

sin·cere *adj* **-cer·er; -cer·est** : genuine or honest — **sin·cere·ly** *adv* — **sin·cer·i·ty** *n*

si·ne·cure *n* : well-paid job that requires little work

sin·ew *n* **1** : tendon **2** : physical strength — **sin·ewy** *adj*

sing *vb* **sang** *or* **sung sung; sing·ing** : produce musical tones with the voice — **sing·er** *n*

singe *vb* **singed; singe·ing** : scorch lightly

sin·gle *adj* **1** : one only **2** : unmarried ~ *n* : separate one — **single·ness** *n* — **sin·gly** *adv* — **single out** *vb* : select or set aside

sin·gu·lar *adj* **1** : relating to a word form denoting one **2** : outstanding or superior **3** : queer — **singular** *n* — **sin·gu·lar·i·ty** *n* — **sin·gu·lar·ly** *adv*

sin·is·ter *adj* : threatening evil

sink *vb* **sank** *or* **sunk; sunk; sink·ing 1** : submerge or descend **2** : grow worse **3** : make by digging or boring **4** : invest ~ *n* : basin with a drain

sink·er *n* : weight to sink a fishing line

sin·u·ous *adj* : winding in and out — **sin·u·os·i·ty** *n* — **sin·u·ous·ly** *adv*

si·nus *n* : skull cavity usu. connecting with the nostrils

sip *vb* **-pp-** : drink in small quantities — **sip** *n*

si·phon *n* : tube that draws liquid by suction — **siphon** *vb*

sir *n* **1** — used before the first name of a knight or baronet **2** — used as a respectful form of address

sire *n* : father ~ *vb* **sired; sir·ing** : beget

si·ren *n* **1** : seductive woman **2** : wailing warning whistle

sir·loin *n* : cut of beef

sirup *var of* SYRUP

si·sal *n* : strong rope fiber

sis·sy *n, pl* **-sies** : timid or effeminate boy

sis·ter *n* : female sharing one or both parents with another person — **sis·ter·hood** *n* — **sis·ter·ly** *adj*

sis·ter–in–law *n, pl* **sis·ters–in–law** : sister of one's spouse or wife of one's brother

sit *vb* **sat; sit·ting 1** : rest on the buttocks or haunches **2** : roost **3** : hold a session **4** : pose for a portrait **5** : have a location **6** : rest or fix in place — **sit·ter** *n*

site *n* : place

sit·u·at·ed *adj* : located

sit·u·a·tion *n* **1** : location **2** : condition **3** : job

six *n* : one more than 5 — **six** *adj or pron* — **sixth** *adj or adv or n*

six·teen *n* : one more than 15 — **sixteen** *adj or pron* — **six·teenth** *adj or n*

six·ty *n, pl* **-ties** : 6 times 10 — **six·ti·eth** *adj or n* — **sixty** *adj or pron*

siz·able, size·able *adj* : quite large — **siz·ably** *adv*

size *n* : measurement of the amount of space something takes up ~ *vb* : grade according to size

siz·zle *vb* **-zled; -zling** : fry with a hissing sound — **sizzle** *n*

skate *n* **1** : metal runner on a shoe for gliding over ice **2** : roller skate — **skate** *vb* — **skat·er** *n*

skein *n* : loosely twisted quantity of yarn or thread

skel·e·ton *n* : bony framework — **skel·e·tal** *adj*

skep·tic *n* : one who is critical or doubting — **skep·ti·cal** *adj* — **skep·ti·cism** *n*

sketch *n* **1** : rough drawing **2** : short story or essay — **sketch** *vb* — **sketchy** *adj*

skew·er *n* : long pin for holding roasting meat — **skewer** *vb*

ski *n, pl* **skis** : long strip for gliding over snow or water — **ski** *vb* — **ski·er** *n*

skid *n* **1** : plank for supporting something or on which it slides **2** : act of skidding ~ *vb* **-dd-** : slide sideways

skiff *n* : small boat

skill *n* : developed or learned ability — **skilled** *adj* — **skill·ful** *adj* — **skill·ful·ly** *adv*

skil·let *n* : pan for frying

skim *vb* **-mm- 1** : take off from the top of a liquid **2** : read or move over swiftly ~ *adj* : having the cream removed — **skim·mer** *n*

skimp *vb* : give too little of something — **skimpy** *adj*

skin *n* **1** : outer layer of an animal body **2** : rind ~ *vb* **-nn-** : take the skin from — **skin·less** *adj* — **skinned** *adj* — **skin·tight** *adj*

skin diving *n* : sport of swimming under water with a face mask and flippers

skin·flint *n* : stingy person

skin·ny *adj* **-ni·er; -est** : very thin

skip *vb* **-pp- 1** : move with leaps **2** : read past or ignore — **skip** *n*

skip·per *n* : ship's master — **skipper** *vb*

skir·mish *n* : minor combat — **skirmish** *vb*

skirt *n* : garment or part of a garment that hangs below the waist ~ *vb* : pass around the edge of

skit *n* : brief usu. humorous play

skit·tish *adj* : easily frightened

skulk *vb* : move furtively

skull *n* : bony case that protects the brain

skunk *n* : mammal that can forcibly eject an ill-smelling fluid

sky *n, pl* **skies 1** : upper air **2** : heaven — **sky·line** *n* — **sky·ward** *adv or adj*

sky·lark *n* : European lark noted for its song

sky·light *n* : window in a roof or ceiling

sky·rock·et *n* : shooting firework ~ *vb* : rise suddenly

sky·scrap·er *n* : very tall building

slab *n* : thick slice

slack *adj* **1** : careless **2** : not taut **3** : not busy ~ *n* **1** : part hanging loose **2** *pl* : casual trousers — **slack·en** *vb* — **slack·ly** *adv* — **slack·ness** *n*

slag *n* : waste from melting of ores

slain *past part of* SLAY

slake *vb* **slaked; slak·ing** : quench

slam *n* : heavy jarring impact ~ *vb* **-mm-** : shut, strike, or throw violently and loudly

slan·der *n* : malicious gossip ~ *vb* : hurt (someone) with slander — **slan·der·er** *n* — **slan·der·ous** *adj*

slang *n* : informal nonstandard vocabulary — **slangy** *adj*

slant *vb* **1** : slope **2** : present with a special viewpoint ~ *n* : sloping direction, line, or plane

slap *vb* **-pp-** : strike sharply with the open hand — **slap** *n*

slash *vb* **1** : cut with sweeping strokes **2** : reduce sharply ~ *n* : gash

slat *n* : thin narrow flat strip

slate *n* **1** : dense fine-grained layered rock **2** : roofing tile or writing tablet of slate **3** : list of candidates ~ *vb* **slat·ed; slat·ing** : designate

slat·tern *n* : untidy woman — **slat·tern·ly** *adj*

slaugh·ter *n* **1** : butchering of livestock for market **2** : great and cruel destruction of lives ~ *vb* : commit slaughter upon — **slaughter·house** *n*

slave *n* : one owned and forced into service by another ~ *vb* **slaved; slav·ing** : work as or like a slave — **slave** *adj* — **slav·ery** *n*

sla·ver *vb or n* : slobber

slav·ish *adj* : of or like a slave — **slav·ish·ly** *adv*

slay *vb* **slew slain slay·ing** : kill — **slay·er** *n*

slea·zy *adj* **-zi·er; -est** : shabby or shoddy

sled *n* : vehicle on runners — **sled** *vb*

¹sledge *n* : sledgehammer

²sledge *n* : heavy sled

sledge·ham·mer *n* : heavy long-handled hammer — **sledgehammer** *adj or vb*

sleek *adj* : smooth or glossy — **sleek** *vb*

sleep *n* : natural suspension of consciousness ~ *vb* **slept; sleep·ing** : rest in a state of sleep — **sleep·er** *n* — **sleep·less** *adj* — **sleep·walk·er** *n*

sleepy *adj* **sleep·i·er; -est 1** : ready for sleep **2** : quietly inactive — **sleep·i·ly** *adv* — **sleep·i·ness** *n*

sleet *n* : frozen rain — **sleet** *vb* — **sleety** *adj*

sleeve *n* : part of a garment for the arm — **sleeve·less** *adj*

sleigh *n* : horse-drawn sled with seats ~ *vb* : drive or ride in a sleigh

sleight of hand : skillful manual manipulation or a trick requiring it

slen·der *adj* **1** : thin esp. in physique **2** : scanty

sleuth *n* : detective

slew *past of* SLAY

slice *n* : thin flat piece ~ *vb* **sliced; slic·ing** : cut a slice from

slick *adj* **1** : very smooth **2** : clever — **slick** *vb*

slick·er *n* : raincoat

slide *vb* **slid; slid·ing** : move smoothly along a surface ~ *n* **1** : act of sliding **2** : surface on which something slides **3** : transparent picture for projection

slier *comparative of* SLY

sliest *superlative of* SLY

slight *adj* **1** : slender **2** : frail **3** : small in degree ~ *vb* **1** : ignore or treat as unimportant — **slight** *n* — **slight·ly** *adv*

slim *adj* **-mm- 1** : slender **2** : scanty ~ *vb* **-mm-** : make or become slender

slime *n* : dirty slippery film (as on water) — **slimy** *adj*

sling *vb* **slung; sling·ing** : hurl with or as if with a sling ~ *n* **1** : strap for swinging and hurling stones **2** : looped strap or bandage to lift or support

sling·shot *n* : forked stick with elastic bands for shooting pebbles

slink *vb* **slunk; slink·ing** : move stealthily or sinuously — **slinky** *adj*

¹slip *vb* **-pp- 1** : escape quietly or secretly **2** : slide along smoothly **3** : make a mistake **4** : to pass without being noticed or done **5** : fall off from a standard ~ *n* **1** : ship's berth **2** : sudden mishap **3** : mistake **4** : woman's undergarment

²slip *n* **1** : plant shoot **2** : small strip (as of paper)

slip·per *n* : shoe that slips on easily

slip·pery *adj* **-peri·er; -est 1** : slick enough to slide on **2** : tricky — **slip·peri·ness** *n*

slip·shod *adj* : careless

slit *vb* **slit; slit·ting** : make a slit in ~ *n* : long narrow cut

slith·er *vb* : glide along like a snake — **slith·ery** *adj*

sliv·er *n* : splinter

slob *n* : untidy person

slob·ber *vb* : dribble saliva — **slobber** *n*

slo·gan *n* : word or phrase expressing the aim of a cause

sloop *n* : one-masted sailboat

slop *n* : food waste for animal feed ~ *vb* **-pp-** : spill

slope *vb* **sloped; slop·ing** : deviate from the vertical or horizontal ~ *n* : upward or downward slant

slop·py *adj* **-pi·er; -est 1** : muddy **2** : untidy

slot *n* : narrow opening

sloth *n, pl* **sloths 1** : laziness **2** : slow-moving mammal — **sloth·ful** *adj*

slouch *n* **1** : drooping posture **2** : lazy or incompetent person ~ *vb* : walk or stand with a slouch

¹slough *n* : swamp

²slough; sluff *vb* : cast off (old skin)

slov·en·ly *adj* : untidy

slow *adj* **1** : sluggish or stupid **2** : moving, working, or happening at less than the usual speed ~ *vb* **1** : make slow **2** : go slower — **slow** *adv* — **slow·ly** *adv* — **slow·ness** *n*

sludge *n* : slushy mass (as of treated sewage)

slug *n* **1** : mollusk related to the snails **2** : bullet **3** : metal disk ~ *vb* **-gg-** : strike forcibly — **slug·ger** *n*

slug•gish *adj* : slow in movement or flow — **slug-gish•ly** *adv* — **slug•gish•ness** *n*

sluice *n* : channel for water ~ *vb* **sluiced; sluic-ing** : wash in running water

slum *n* : thickly populated area marked by poverty

slum•ber *vb or n* : sleep

slump *vb* **1** : sink suddenly **2** : slouch — **slump** *n*

slung past of SLING

slunk past of SLINK

¹slur *vb* **-rr-** : run (words or notes) together — **slur** *n*

²slur *n* : malicious or insulting remark

slurp *vb* : eat or drink noisily — **slurp** *n*

slush *n* : partly melted snow — **slushy** *adj*

slut *n* **1** : untidy woman **2** : lewd woman — **slut•tish** *adj*

sly *adj* **sli•er; sli•est** : given to or showing secrecy and deception — **sly•ly** *adv* — **sly•ness** *n*

¹smack *n* : characteristic flavor ~ *vb* : have a taste or hint

²smack *vb* **1** : move (the lips) so as to make a sharp noise **2** : kiss or slap with a loud noise ~ *n* **1** : sharp noise made by the lips **2** : noisy slap

³smack *adv* : squarely and sharply

⁴smack *n* : fishing boat

small *adj* **1** : little in size or amount **2** : few in number **3** : trivial — **small•ish** *adj* — **small•ness** *n*

small•pox *n* : contagious virus disease

smart *vb* **1** : cause or feel stinging pain **2** : endure distress ~ *adj* **1** : intelligent or resourceful **2** : stylish — **smart** *n* — **smart•ly** *adv* — **smart•ness** *n*

smash *vb* : break or be broken into pieces ~ *n* **1** : smashing blow **2** : act or sound of smashing

smat•ter•ing *n* **1** : superficial knowledge **2** : small scattered number or amount

smear *n* : greasy stain ~ *vb* **1** : spread (something sticky) **2** : smudge **3** : slander

smell *vb* **smelled** *or* **smelt; smell•ing 1** : perceive the odor of **2** : have or give off an odor ~ *n* **1** : sense by which one perceives odor **2** : odor — **smelly** *adj*

¹smelt *n, pl* **smelts** *or* **smelt** : small food fish

²smelt *vb* : melt or fuse (ore) in order to separate the metal — **smelt•er** *n*

smile *n* : facial expression with the mouth turned up usu. to show pleasure — **smile** *vb*

smirk *vb* : wear a conceited smile — **smirk** *n*

smite *vb* **smote; smit•ten** *or* **smote; smit•ing 1** : strike heavily or kill **2** : affect strongly

smith *n* : worker in metals and esp. a blacksmith

smithy *n, pl* **smith•ies** : a smith's workshop

smock *n* : loose dress or protective coat

smog *n* : fog and smoke — **smog•gy** *adj*

smoke *n* : sooty gas from burning ~ *vb* **smoked; smok•ing 1** : give off smoke **2** : inhale the fumes of burning tobacco **3** : cure (as meat) with smoke — **smoke•less** *adj* — **smok•er** *n* — **smoky** *adj*

smoke•stack *n* : chimney through which smoke is discharged

smol•der, smoul•der *vb* **1** : burn and smoke without flame **2** : be suppressed but active — **smolder** *n*

smooth *adj* **1** : having a surface without irregularities **2** : not jarring or jolting ~ *vb* : make smooth — **smooth•ly** *adv* — **smooth•ness** *n*

smor•gas•bord *n* : buffet consisting of many foods

smoth•er *vb* **1** : kill by depriving of air **2** : cover thickly

smudge *vb* **smudged; smudg•ing** : soil or blur by rubbing ~ *n* **1** : thick smoke **2** : dirty spot

smug *adj* **-gg-** : content in one's own virtue or accomplishment — **smug•ly** *adv* — **smug•ness** *n*

smug•gle *vb* **-gled; -gling** : import or export secretly or illegally — **smug•gler** *n*

smut *n* **1** : something that soils **2** : indecent lan-guage or matter **3** : disease of plants caused by fungi — **smut•ty** *adj*

snack *n* : light meal

snag *n* : unexpected difficulty ~ *vb* **-gg-** : become caught on something that sticks out

snail *n* : small mollusk with a spiral shell

snake *n* : long-bodied limbless reptile — **snake-bite** *n*

snap *vb* **-pp-** **1** : bite at something **2** : utter angry words **3** : break suddenly with a sharp sound ~ *n* **1** : act or sound of snapping **2** : fastening that closes with a click **3** : something easy to do — **snap•per** *n* — **snap•pish** *adj* — **snap-py** *adj*

snap•drag•on *n* : garden plant with spikes of showy flowers

snap•shot *n* : casual photograph

snare *n* : trap for catching game ~ *vb* : capture or hold with or as if with a snare

¹snarl *n* : tangle ~ *vb* : cause to become knotted

²snarl *vb or n* : growl

snatch *vb* **1** : try to grab something suddenly **2** : seize or take away suddenly ~ *n* **1** : act of snatching **2** : something brief or fragmentary

sneak *vb* : move or take in a furtive manner ~ *n* : one who acts in a furtive manner — **sneak•i•ly** *adv* — **sneak•ing•ly** *adv* — **sneaky** *adj*

sneak•er *n* : sports shoe

sneer *vb* : smile scornfully — **sneer** *n*

sneeze *vb* **sneezed; sneez•ing** : force the breath out with sudden and involuntary violence — **sneeze** *n*

snick•er *n* : partly suppressed laugh — **snicker** *vb*

snide *adj* : subtly ridiculing

sniff *vb* **1** : draw air audibly up the nose **2** : detect by smelling — **sniff** *n*

snip *n* : fragment snipped off ~ *vb* **-pp-** : cut off by bits

¹snipe *n, pl* **snipes** *or* **snipe** : game bird of marshy areas

²snipe *vb* **sniped; snip•ing** : shoot at an enemy from a concealed position — **snip•er** *n*

snips *n pl* : scissorslike tool

sniv•el *vb* **-eled** *or* **-elled; -el•ing** *or* **-el•ling 1** : have a running nose **2** : whine

snob *n* : one who acts superior to others — **snob-bery** *n* — **snob•bish** *adj* — **snob•bish•ly** *adv* — **snob•bish•ness** *n*

snoop *vb* : pry in a furtive way ~ *n* : prying person

snooze *vb* **snoozed; snooz•ing** : take a nap — **snooze** *n*

snore *vb* **snored; snor•ing** : breathe with a hoarse noise while sleeping — **snore** *n*

snort *vb* : force air noisily through the nose — **snort** *n*

snout *n* : long projecting muzzle (as of a swine)

snow *n* : crystals formed from water vapor ~ *vb* : fall as snow — **snow•ball** *n* — **snow•bank** *n* — **snow•drift** *n* — **snow•fall** *n* — **snow•plow** *n* — **snow•storm** *n* — **snowy** *adj*

snow•shoe *n* : frame of wood strung with thongs for walking on snow

snub *vb* **-bb-** : ignore or avoid through disdain — **snub** *n*

¹snuff *vb* : put out (a candle) — **snuff•er** *n*

²snuff *vb* : draw forcibly into the nose ~ *n* : pulverized tobacco

snug *adj* **-gg-** **1** : warm, secure, and comfortable **2** : fitting closely — **snug•ly** *adv* — **snug•ness** *n*

snug•gle *vb* **-gled; -gling** : curl up comfortably

so *adv* **1** : in the manner or to the extent indicated **2** : in the same way **3** : therefore **4** : finally **5** : thus ~ *conj* : for that reason

soak *vb* **1** : lie in a liquid **2** : absorb ~ *n* : act of soaking

soap *n* : cleaning substance — **soap** *vb* — **soapy** *adj*

soar *vb* : fly upward on or as if on wings

sob *vb* **-bb-** : weep with convulsive heavings of the chest — **sob** *n*

so•ber *adj* **1** : not drunk **2** : serious or solemn — **so•ber•ly** *adv*

so•bri•ety *n* : quality or state of being sober

soc•cer *n* : game played by kicking a ball

so•cia•ble *adj* : friendly — **so•cia•bil•i•ty** *n* — **socia•bly** *adv*

so•cial *adj* **1** : relating to pleasant companionship **2** : naturally living or growing in groups **3** : relating to human society ~ *n* : social gathering — **so•cial•ly** *adv*

so•cial•ism *n* : social system based on government control of the production and distribution of goods — **so•cial•ist** *n or adj* — **so•cial•is-tic** *adj*

so•cial•ize *vb* **-ized; -iz•ing 1** : regulate by socialism **2** : adapt to social needs **3** : participate in a social gathering — **so•cial•i•za•tion** *n*

social work *n* : services concerned with aiding the poor and socially maladjusted — **social worker** *n*

so•ci•ety *n, pl* **-et•ies 1** : companionship **2** : community life **3** : rich or fashionable class **4** : voluntary group

so•ci•ol•o•gy *n* : study of social relationships — **so•ci•o•log•i•cal** *adj* — **so•ci•ol•o•gist** *n*

¹sock *n, pl* **socks** *or* **sox** : short stocking

²sock *vb or n* : punch

sock•et *n* : hollow part that holds something

sod *n* : turf ~ *vb* **-dd-** : cover with sod

so•da *n* **1** : carbonated water or a soft drink **2** : ice cream drink made with soda

sod•den *adj* **1** : lacking spirit **2** : soaked or soggy

so•di•um *n* : soft waxy silver white metallic chemical element

so•fa *n* : wide padded chair

soft *adj* **1** : not hard, rough, or harsh **2** : nonalcoholic — **soft•en** *vb* — **soft•en•er** *n* — **soft•ly** *adv* — **soft•ness** *n*

soft•ball *n* : game like baseball

soft•ware *n* : computer programs

sog•gy *adj* **-gi•er; -est** : heavy with moisture — **sog•gi•ness** *n*

¹soil *vb* : make or become dirty ~ *n* : embedded dirt

²soil *n* : loose surface material of the earth

so•journ *n* : temporary stay ~ *vb* : reside temporarily

so•lace *n or vb* : comfort

so•lar *adj* : relating to the sun or the energy in sunlight

sold past of SELL

sol•der *n* : metallic alloy melted to join metallic surfaces ~ *vb* : cement with solder

sol•dier *n* : person in military service ~ *vb* : serve as a soldier — **sol•dier•ly** *adj or adv*

¹sole *n* : bottom of the foot or a shoe — **soled** *adj*

²sole *n* : flatfish caught for food

³sole *adj* : single or only — **sole•ly** *adv*

sol•emn *adj* **1** : dignified and ceremonial **2** : highly serious — **so•lem•ni•ty** *n* — **sol•emn•ly** *adv*

so•lic•it *vb* : ask for — **so•lic•i•ta•tion** *n*

so•lic•i•tor *n* **1** : one that solicits **2** : lawyer

so•lic•i•tous *adj* : showing or expressing concern — **so•lic•i•tous•ly** *adv* — **so•lic•i•tude** *n*

sol•id *adj* **1** : not hollow **2** : having 3 dimensions **3** : hard **4** : of good quality **5** : of one character ~ *n* **1** : 3-dimensional figure **2** : substance in solid form — **solid** *adv* — **so•lid•i•ty** *n* — **sol•id•ly** *adv* — **sol•id•ness** *n*

sol•i•dar•i•ty *n* : unity of purpose

so•lid•i•fy *vb* **-fied; -fy•ing** : make or become solid — **so•lid•i•fi•ca•tion** *n*

so•lil•o•quy *n, pl* **-quies** : dramatic monologue — **so•lil•o•quize** *vb*

sol•i•taire *n* **1** : solitary gem **2** : card game for one person

sol·i·tary *adj* **1** : alone **2** : secluded **3** : single

sol·i·tude *n* : state of being alone

so·lo *n, pl* **-los** : performance by only one person ~ *adv* : alone — **solo** *adj or vb* — **so·lo·ist** *n*

sol·stice *n* : time of the year when the sun is farthest north or south of the equator

sol·u·ble *adj* **1** : capable of being dissolved **2** : capable of being solved — **sol·u·bil·i·ty** *n*

so·lu·tion *n* **1** : answer to a problem **2** : homogeneous liquid mixture

solve *vb* **solved; solv·ing** : find a solution for — **solv·able** *adj*

sol·vent *adj* **1** : able to pay all debts **2** : dissolving or able to dissolve ~ *n* : substance that dissolves or disperses another substance — **sol·ven·cy** *n*

som·ber, som·bre *adj* **1** : dark **2** : grave — **som·ber·ly** *adv*

som·bre·ro *n, pl* **-ros** : broad-brimmed hat

some *adj* **1** : one unspecified **2** : unspecified or indefinite number of **3** : at least a few or a little ~ *pron* : a certain number or amount

-some *adj suffix* : characterized by a thing, quality, state, or action

some·body *pron* : some person

some·day *adv* : at some future time

some·how *adv* : by some means

some·one *pron* : some person

som·er·sault *n* : body flip — **somersault** *vb*

some·thing *pron* : some undetermined or unspecified thing

some·time *adv* : at a future, unknown, or unnamed time

some·times *adv* : occasionally

some·what *adv* : in some degree

some·where *adv* : in, at, or to an unknown or unnamed place

som·no·lent *adj* : sleepy — **som·no·lence** *n*

son *n* : male offspring

so·nar *n* : device that detects and locates underwater objects using sound waves

so·na·ta *n* : instrumental composition

song *n* : music and words to be sung

song·bird *n* : bird with musical tones

son·ic *adj* : relating to sound waves or the speed of sound

son–in–law *n, pl* **sons–in–law** : husband of one's daughter

son·net *n* : poem of 14 lines

so·no·rous *adj* **1** : loud, deep, or rich in sound **2** : impressive — **so·nor·i·ty** *n*

soon *adv* **1** : before long **2** : promptly **3** : early

soot *n* : fine black substance formed by combustion — **sooty** *adj*

soothe *vb* **soothed; sooth·ing** : calm or comfort — **sooth·er** *n*

sooth·say·er *n* : prophet — **sooth·say·ing** *n*

sop *n* : conciliatory bribe, gift, or concession ~ *vb* **-pp-** **1** : dip in a liquid **2** : soak **3** : mop up

so·phis·ti·cat·ed *adj* **1** : complex **2** : wise, cultured, or shrewd in human affairs — **so·phis·ti·ca·tion** *n*

soph·ist·ry *n* : subtly fallacious reasoning or argument — **sophist** *n*

soph·o·more *n* : 2d-year student

so·po·rif·ic *adj* : causing sleep or drowsiness

so·pra·no *n, pl* **-nos** : highest singing voice

sor·cery *n* : witchcraft — **sor·cer·er** *n* — **sor·cer·ess** *n*

sor·did *adj* : filthy or vile — **sor·did·ly** *adv* — **sor·did·ness** *n*

sore *adj* **sor·er; sor·est** **1** : causing pain or distress **2** : severe or intense **3** : angry ~ *n* : sore usu. infected spot on the body — **sore·ly** *adv* — **sore·ness** *n*

sor·ghum *n* : forage grass

so·ror·i·ty *n, pl* **-ties** : women's student social group

¹sor·rel *n* : brownish orange to light brown color or an animal of this color

²sorrel *n* : herb with sour juice

sor·row *n* : deep distress, sadness, or regret or a cause of this — **sor·row·ful** *adj* — **sor·row·ful·ly** *adv*

sor·ry *adj* **-ri·er; -est** **1** : feeling sorrow, regret, or penitence **2** : dismal

sort *n* **1** : kind **2** : nature ~ *vb* : classify — **out of sorts** : grouchy

sor·tie *n* : military attack esp. against besiegers

SOS *n* : call for help

so–so *adj or adv* : barely acceptable

sot *n* : drunkard — **sot·tish** *adj*

souf·flé *n* : baked dish made light with beaten egg whites

sought *past of* SEEK

soul *n* **1** : immaterial essence of an individual life **2** : essential part **3** : person

soul·ful *adj* : full of or expressing deep feeling — **soul·ful·ly** *adv*

¹sound *adj* **1** : free from fault, error, or illness **2** : firm or hard **3** : showing good judgment — **sound·ly** *adv* — **sound·ness** *n*

²sound *n* **1** : sensation of hearing **2** : energy of vibration sensed in hearing **3** : something heard ~ *vb* **1** : make or cause to make a sound **2** : seem — **sound·less** *adj* — **sound·less·ly** *adv* — **sound·proof** *adj or vb*

³sound *n* : wide strait ~ *vb* **1** : measure the depth of (water) **2** : investigate

soup *n* : broth usu. containing pieces of solid food — **soupy** *adj*

sour *adj* **1** : having an acid or tart taste **2** : disagreeable ~ *vb* : become or make sour — **sour·ish** *adj* — **sour·ly** *adv* — **sour·ness** *n*

source *n* **1** : point of origin **2** : one that provides something needed

souse *vb* **soused; sous·ing** **1** : pickle **2** : immerse **3** : intoxicate ~ *n* **1** : something pickled **2** : drunkard

south *adv* **1** : to or toward the south ~ *adj* : situated toward, at, or coming from the south ~ *n* **1** : direction to the right of sunrise **2** *cap* : regions to the south — **south·er·ly** *adv or adj* — **south·ern** *adj* — **South·ern·er** *n* — **south·ern·most** *adj* — **southward** *adv or adj* — **south·wards** *adv*

south·east *n* **1** : direction between south and east **2** *cap* : regions to the southeast — **southeast** *adj or adv* — **south·east·er·ly** *adv or adj* — **south·east·ern** *adj*

south pole *n* : the southernmost point of the earth

south·west *n* **1** : direction between south and west **2** *cap* : regions to the southwest — **south·west** *adj or adv* — **south·west·er·ly** *adv or adj* — **south·west·ern** *adj*

sou·ve·nir *n* : something that is a reminder of a place or event

sov·er·eign *n* **1** : supreme ruler **2** : gold coin of the United Kingdom ~ *adj* **1** : supreme **2** : independent — **sov·er·eign·ty** *n*

¹sow *n* : female swine

²sow *vb* **sowed; sown** *or* **sowed, sow·ing** **1** : plant or strew with seed **2** : scatter abroad — **sow·er** *n*

sox *pl of* SOCK

soy·bean *n* : legume with edible seeds

spa *n* : resort at a mineral spring

space *n* **1** : period of time **2** : area in, around, or between **3** : region beyond earth's atmosphere **4** : accommodations ~ *vb* **spaced; spac·ing** : place at intervals — **space·craft** *n* — **space·flight** *n* — **space·man** *n* — **space·ship** *n*

spa·cious *adj* : large or roomy — **spa·cious·ly** *adv* — **spa·cious·ness** *n*

¹spade *n or vb* : shovel — **spade·ful** *n*

²spade *n* : playing card marked with a black figure like an inverted heart

spa·ghet·ti *n* : pasta strings

span *n* **1** : amount of time **2** : distance between supports ~ *vb* **-nn-** : extend across

span·gle *n* : small disk of shining metal or plastic — **spangle** *vb*

span·iel *n* : small or medium-sized dog with drooping ears and long wavy hair

spank *vb* : hit on the buttocks with an open hand

¹spar *n* : pole or boom

²spar *vb* **-rr-** : practice boxing

spare *adj* **1** : held in reserve **2** : thin or scanty ~ *vb* **spared; spar·ing** **1** : reserve or avoid using **2** : avoid punishing or killing — **spare** *n*

spar·ing *adj* : thrifty — **spar·ing·ly** *adv*

spark *n* **1** : tiny hot and glowing particle **2** : smallest beginning or germ **3** : visible electrical discharge ~ *vb* **1** : emit or produce sparks **2** : stir to activity

spar·kle *vb* **-kled; -kling** **1** : flash **2** : effervesce ~ *n* : gleam — **spar·kler** *n*

spar·row *n* : small singing bird

sparse *adj* **spars·er; spars·est** : thinly scattered — **sparse·ly** *adv*

spasm *n* **1** : involuntary muscular contraction **2** : sudden, violent, and temporary effort or feeling — **spas·mod·ic** *adj* — **spas·mod·i·cal·ly** *adv*

spas·tic *adj* : relating to, marked by, or affected with muscular spasm — **spastic** *n*

¹spat *past of* SPIT

²spat *n* : petty dispute

spa·tial *adj* : relating to space — **spa·tial·ly** *adv*

spat·ter *vb* : splash with drops of liquid — **spatter** *n*

spat·u·la *n* : flexible knifelike utensil

spawn *vb* **1** : produce eggs or offspring **2** : bring forth ~ *n* : egg cluster — **spawn·er** *n*

spay *vb* : remove the ovaries of (a female)

speak *vb* **spoke; spo·ken; speak·ing** **1** : utter words **2** : express orally **3** : address an audience **4** : use (a language) in talking — **speak·er** *n*

spear *n* : long pointed weapon ~ *vb* : strike or pierce with a spear

spear·head *n* : leading force, element, or influence — **spearhead** *vb*

spear·mint *n* : aromatic garden mint

spe·cial *adj* **1** : unusual or unique **2** : particularly favored **3** : set aside for a particular use — **special** *n* — **spe·cial·ly** *adv*

spe·cial·ist *n* **1** : person who specializes in a particular branch of learning or activity **2** : any of four enlisted ranks in the army corresponding to the grades of corporal through sergeant first class

spe·cial·ize *vb* **-ized; -iz·ing** : concentrate one's efforts — **spe·cial·i·za·tion** *n*

spe·cial·ty *n, pl* **-ties** : area or field in which one specializes

spe·cie *n* : money in coin

spe·cies *n, pl* **spe·cies** : biological grouping of closely related organisms

spe·cif·ic *adj* : definite or exact — **spe·cif·i·cal·ly** *adv*

spec·i·fi·ca·tion *n* **1** : act or process of specifying **2** : detailed description of work to be done — usu. pl.

spec·i·fy *vb* **-fied; -fy·ing** : mention precisely or by name

spec·i·men *n* : typical example

spe·cious *adj* : apparently but not really genuine or correct

speck *n* : tiny particle or blemish — **speck** *vb*

speck·led *adj* : marked with spots

spec·ta·cle *n* **1** : impressive public display **2** *pl* : eyeglasses

spec·tac·u·lar *adj* : sensational or showy

spec·ta·tor *n* : person who looks on

spec•ter, spec•tre n 1 : ghost 2 : haunting vision

spec•tral adj : relating to or resembling a specter or spectrum

spec•trum n, pl **-tra** or **-trums** : series of colors formed when white light is dispersed into its components

spec•u•late vb **-lat•ed; -lat•ing** 1 : think about things yet unknown 2 : risk money in a business deal in hope of high profit — **spec•u•la•tion** n — **spec•u•la•tive** adj — **spec•u•la•tor** n

speech n 1 : power, act, or manner of speaking 2 : talk given to an audience — **speech•less** adj

speed n 1 : quality of being fast 2 : rate of motion or performance ~ vb **sped** or **speed•ed; speed•ing** : go at a great or excessive rate of speed — **speed•boat** n — **speed•er** n — **speed•i•ly** adv — **speedup** n — **speedy** adj

speed•om•e•ter n : instrument for indicating speed

¹spell n : influence of or like magic

²spell vb : name, write, or print the letters of 2 : mean — **spell•er** n

³spell vb : substitute for or relieve (someone) ~ n 1 : turn at work 2 : period of time

spell•bound adj : held by a spell

spend vb **spent; spend•ing** 1 : pay out 2 : cause or allow to pass — **spend•er** n

spend•thrift n : wasteful person

sperm n, pl **sperm** or **sperms** : semen or a germ cell in it

spew vb : gush out in a stream

sphere n 1 : figure with every point on its surface at an equal distance from the center 2 : round body 3 : range of action or influence — **spher•i•cal** adj

spher•oid n : spherelike figure

spice n 1 : aromatic plant product for seasoning food 2 : interesting quality — **spice** vb — **spicy** adj

spi•der n : small insectlike animal with 8 legs — **spi•dery** adj

spig•ot n : faucet

spike n : very large nail ~ vb **spiked; spik•ing** : fasten or pierce with a spike — **spiked** adj

spill vb 1 : fall, flow, or run out unintentionally 2 : divulge ~ n 1 : act of spilling 2 : something spilled — **spill•able** adj

spill•way n : passage for surplus water

spin vb **spun; spin•ning** 1 : draw out fiber and twist into thread 2 : form thread from a sticky body fluid 3 : revolve or cause to revolve extremely fast ~ n : rapid rotating motion — **spin•ner** n

spin•ach n : garden herb with edible leaves

spi•nal adj : relating to the backbone — **spi•nal•ly** adv

spinal cord n : thick strand of nervous tissue that extends from the brain along the back within the backbone

spin•dle n 1 : stick used for spinning thread 2 : shaft around which something turns

spin•dly adj : tall and slender

spine n 1 : backbone 2 : stiff sharp projection on a plant or animal — **spine•less** adj — **spiny** adj

spin•et n : small piano

spin•ster n : woman who has never married

spi•ral adj : circling or winding around a single point or line — **spiral** n or vb — **spi•ral•ly** adv

spire n : steeple — **spiry** adj

spir•it n 1 : life-giving force 2 cap : presence of God 3 : ghost 4 : mood 5 : vivacity or enthusiasm 6 pl : alcoholic liquor ~ vb : carry off secretly — **spir•it•ed** adj — **spir•it•less** adj

spir•i•tu•al adj 1 : relating to the spirit or sacred matters 2 : deeply religious ~ n : religious folk song — **spir•i•tu•al•i•ty** n — **spir•i•tu•al•ly** adv

spir•i•tu•al•ism n : belief that spirits commu-

nicate with the living — **spir•i•tu•al•ist** n or adj

¹spit n 1 : rod for holding and turning meat over a fire 2 : point of land that runs into the water

²spit vb **spit** or **spat; spit•ting** : eject saliva from the mouth ~ n 1 : saliva 2 : perfect likeness

spite n : petty ill will ~ vb **spit•ed; spit•ing** : annoy or offend — **spite•ful** adj — **spite•ful•ly** adv — **in spite of** : in defiance or contempt of

spit•tle n : saliva

spit•toon n : receptacle for spit

splash vb : scatter a liquid on — **splash** n

splat•ter vb : spatter — **splatter** n

splay vb : spread out or apart — **splay** n or adj

spleen n 1 : organ for maintenance of the blood 2 : spite or anger

splen•did adj 1 : impressive in beauty or brilliance 2 : outstanding — **splen•did•ly** adv

splen•dor n 1 : brilliance 2 : magnificence

splice vb **spliced; splic•ing** : join (2 things) end to end — **splice** n

splint n 1 : thin strip of wood 2 : something that keeps an injured body part in place

splin•ter n : thin needlelike piece ~ vb : break into splinters

split vb **split; split•ting** : divide lengthwise or along a grain — **split** n

splotch n : blotch

splurge vb **splurged; splurg•ing** : indulge oneself — **splurge** n

splut•ter n : sputter — **splutter** vb

spoil n : plunder ~ vb **spoiled** or **spoilt; spoil•ing** 1 : pillage 2 : ruin 3 : rot — **spoil•age** n — **spoil•er** n

¹spoke past of SPEAK

²spoke n : rod from the hub to the rim of a wheel

spo•ken past part of SPEAK

spokes•man n : person who speaks for others

spokes•wom•an n : woman who speaks for others

sponge n 1 : porous water-absorbing mass that forms the skeleton of some marine animals 2 : spongelike material used for wiping ~ vb **sponged; spong•ing** 1 : wipe with a sponge 2 : live at another's expense — **spongy** adj

spon•sor n : one who assumes responsibility for another or who provides financial support — **sponsor** vb — **spon•sor•ship** n

spon•ta•ne•ous adj : done, produced, or occurring naturally or without planning — **spon•ta•ne•i•ty** n — **spon•ta•ne•ous•ly** adv

spoof vb : make good-natured fun of — **spoof** n

spook n : ghost ~ vb : frighten — **spooky** adj

spool n : cylinder on which something is wound

spoon n : utensil consisting of a small shallow bowl with a handle — **spoon** vb — **spoon•ful** n

spoor n : track or trail esp. of a wild animal

spo•rad•ic adj : occasional — **spo•rad•i•cal•ly** adv

spore n : primitive usu. one-celled reproductive body

sport vb 1 : frolic 2 : show off ~ n 1 : physical activity engaged in for pleasure 2 : jest 3 : person who shows good sportsmanship — **sport•ive** adj — **sporty** adj

sports•cast n : broadcast of a sports event — **sports•cast•er** n

sports•man n : one who enjoys hunting and fishing

sports•man•ship n : ability to be gracious in winning or losing

spot n 1 : blemish 2 : distinctive small part 3 : location ~ vb **-tt-** 1 : mark with spots 2 : see or recognize ~ adj : made at random or in limited numbers — **spot•less** adj — **spot•less•ly** adv

spot•light n 1 : intense beam of light 2 : center of public interest — **spotlight** vb

spot•ty adj **-ti•er; -est** : uneven in quality

spouse n : one's husband or wife

spout vb 1 : shoot forth in a stream 2 : say pompously ~ n 1 : opening through which liquid spouts 2 : jet of liquid

sprain n : twisting injury to a joint ~ vb : injure with a sprain

sprat n : small or young herring

sprawl vb : lie or sit with limbs spread out — **sprawl** n

¹spray n : branch or arrangement of flowers

²spray n 1 : mist 2 : device that discharges liquid as a mist — **spray** vb — **spray•er** n

spread vb **spread; spread•ing** 1 : open up or unfold 2 : scatter or smear over a surface 3 : cause to be known or to exist over a wide area ~ n 1 : extent to which something is spread 2 : cloth cover 3 : something intended to be spread — **spread•er** n

spread•sheet n : accounting program for a computer

spree n : burst of indulging in something

sprig n : small shoot or twig

spright•ly adj **-li•er; -est** : lively — **spright•li•ness** n

spring vb **sprang** or **sprung; sprung; spring•ing** 1 : move or grow quickly or by elastic force 2 : come from by descent 3 : make known suddenly ~ n 1 : source 2 : flow of water from underground 3 : season between winter and summer 4 : elastic body or device (as a coil of wire) 5 : leap 6 : elastic power — **springy** adj

sprin•kle vb **-kled; -kling** : scatter in small drops or particles ~ n : light rainfall — **sprin•kler** n

sprint n : short run at top speed — **sprint** vb — **sprint•er** n

sprite n : elf or elfish person

sprock•et n : toothed wheel whose teeth engage the links of a chain

sprout vb : send out new growth ~ n : plant shoot

¹spruce n : conical evergreen tree

²spruce adj **spruc•er; spruc•est** : neat and stylish in appearance ~ vb **spruced; spruc•ing** : make or become neat

spry adj **spri•er** or **spry•er; spri•est** or **spry•est** : agile and active

spume n : froth

spun past of SPIN

spunk n : courage — **spunky** adj

spur n 1 : pointed device used to urge on a horse 2 : something that urges to action 3 : projecting part ~ vb **-rr-** : urge on — **spurred** adj

spu•ri•ous adj : not genuine

spurn vb : reject

¹spurt n : burst of effort, speed, or activity ~ vb : make a spurt

²spurt vb : gush out ~ n : sudden gush

sput•ter vb 1 : talk hastily and indistinctly in excitement 2 : make popping sounds — **sputter** n

spy vb **spied; spy•ing** : watch or try to gather information secretly — **spy** n

squab n, pl **squabs** or **squab** : young pigeon

squab•ble n or vb : dispute

squad n : small group

squad•ron n : small military unit

squal•id adj : filthy or wretched

squall n : sudden violent brief storm — **squally** adj

squa•lor n : quality or state of being squalid

squan•der vb : waste

square n 1 : instrument for measuring right angles 2 : flat figure that has 4 equal sides and 4 right angles 3 : open area in a city 4 : product of number multiplied by itself ~ adj **squar•er; squar•est** 1 : being a square in form 2 : having sides meet at right angles 3 : multiplied by itself 4 : being a square unit of area 5 : honest ~ vb **squared; squar•ing** 1 : form into a square 2 : multiply (a number) by itself 3 : conform 4 : settle — **square•ly** adv

¹**squash** *vb* **1** : press flat **2** : suppress

²**squash** *n, pl* **squash·es** *or* **squash** : garden vegetable

squat *vb* **-tt-** **1** : stoop or sit on one's heels **2** : settle on land one does not own ~ *n* : act or posture of squatting ~ *adj* **squat·ter; squat·test** : short and thick — **squat·ter** *n*

squaw *n* : American Indian woman

squawk *n* : harsh loud cry — **squawk** *vb*

squeak *vb* : make a thin high-pitched sound — **squeak** *n* — **squeaky** *adj*

squeal *vb* **1** : make a shrill sound or cry **2** : protest — **squeal** *n*

squea·mish *adj* : easily nauseated or disgusted

squeeze *vb* **squeezed; squeez·ing** **1** : apply pressure to **2** : extract by pressure — **squeeze** *n* — **squeez·er** *n*

squelch *vb* : suppress (as with a retort) — **squelch** *n*

squid *n, pl* **squid** *or* **squids** : 10-armed long-bodied sea mollusk

squint *vb* : look with the eyes partly closed — **squint** *n or adj*

squire *n* **1** : knight's aide **2** : country landholder **3** : lady's devoted escort ~ *vb* **squired; squir·ing** : escort

squirm *vb* : wriggle

squir·rel *n* : rodent with a long bushy tail

squirt *vb* : eject liquid in a spurt — **squirt** *n*

stab *n* **1** : wound made by a pointed weapon **2** : quick thrust **3** : attempt ~ *vb* **-bb-** : pierce or wound with or as if with a pointed weapon

¹**sta·ble** *n* : building for domestic animals ~ *vb* **-bled; -bling** : keep in a stable

²**stable** *adj* **sta·bler; sta·blest** **1** : firmly established **2** : mentally and emotionally healthy **3** : steady — **sta·bil·i·ty** *n* — **sta·bil·iza·tion** *n* — **sta·bi·lize** *vb* — **sta·bi·liz·er** *n*

stac·ca·to *adj* : disconnected

stack *n* : large pile ~ *vb* : pile up

sta·di·um *n* : outdoor sports arena

staff *n, pl* **staffs** *or* **staves** **1** : rod or supporting cane **2** : people assisting a leader **3** : 5 horizontal lines on which music is written ~ *vb* : supply with workers — **staff·er** *n*

staff sergeant *n* : noncommissioned officer ranking next above a sergeant in the army, air force, or marine corps

stag *n, pl* **stags** *or* **stag** : male deer ~ *adj* : only for men ~ *adv* : without a date

stage *n* **1** : raised platform for a speaker or performers **2** : theater **3** : step in a process ~ *vb* **staged; stag·ing** : produce (a play)

stage·coach *n* : passenger coach

stag·ger *vb* **1** : reel or cause to reel from side to side **2** : overlap or alternate — **stagger** *n* — **stag·ger·ing·ly** *adv*

stag·nant *adj* : not moving or active — **stag·nate** *vb* — **stag·na·tion** *n*

¹**staid** *adj* : sedate

²**staid** *past of* STAY

stain *vb* **1** : discolor **2** : dye (as wood) **3** : disgrace ~ *n* **1** : discolored area **2** : mark of guilt **3** : coloring preparation — **stain·less** *adj*

stair *n* **1** : step in a series for going from one level to another **2** *pl* : flight of steps — **stair·way** *n*

stair·case *n* : series of steps with their framework

stake *n* **1** : usu. small post driven into the ground **2** : bet **3** : prize in a contest ~ *vb* **staked; stak·ing** **1** : mark or secure with a stake **2** : bet

sta·lac·tite *n* : icicle-shaped deposit hanging in a cavern

sta·lag·mite *n* : icicle-shaped deposit on a cavern floor

stale *adj* **stal·er; stal·est** **1** : having lost good taste and quality from age **2** : no longer new, strong, or effective — **stale·ness** *n*

stale·mate *n* : deadlock — **stalemate** *vb*

¹**stalk** *vb* **1** : walk stiffly or proudly **2** : pursue stealthily

²**stalk** *n* : plant stem — **stalked** *adj*

¹**stall** *n* **1** : compartment in a stable **2** : booth where articles are sold

²**stall** *vb* : bring or come to a standstill unintentionally

³**stall** *vb* : delay, evade, or keep a situation going to gain advantage or time

stal·lion *n* : male horse

stal·wart *adj* : strong or brave

sta·men *n* : flower organ that produces pollen

stam·i·na *n* : endurance

stam·mer *vb* : hesitate in speaking — **stammer** *n*

stamp *vb* **1** : pound with the sole of the foot or a heavy implement **2** : impress or imprint **3** : cut out with a die **4** : attach a postage stamp to ~ *n* **1** : device for stamping **2** : act of stamping **3** : government seal showing a tax or fee has been paid

stam·pede *n* : headlong rush of frightened animals ~ *vb* **-ped·ed; -ped·ing** : flee in panic

stance *n* : way of standing

¹**stanch** *vb* : stop the flow of (as blood)

²**stanch** *var of* STAUNCH

stan·chion *n* : upright support

stand *vb* **stood; stand·ing** **1** : be at rest in or assume an upright position **2** : remain unchanged **3** : be steadfast **4** : maintain a relative position or rank **5** : set upright **6** : undergo or endure ~ *n* **1** : act or place of standing, staying, or resisting **2** : sales booth **3** : structure for holding something upright **4** : group of plants growing together **5** *pl* : tiered seats **6** : opinion or viewpoint

stan·dard *n* **1** : symbolic figure or flag **2** : model, rule, or guide **3** : upright support — **standard** *adj* — **stan·dard·i·za·tion** *n* — **stan·dard·ize** *vb*

standard time *n* : time established over a region or country

stand·ing *n* **1** : relative position or rank **2** : duration

stand·still *n* : state of rest

stank *past of* STINK

stan·za *n* : division of a poem

¹**sta·ple** *n* : U-shaped wire fastener — **staple** *vb* — **sta·pler** *n*

²**staple** *n* : chief commodity or item — **staple** *adj*

star *n* **1** : celestial body visible as a point of light **2** : 5- or 6-pointed figure representing a star **3** : leading performer ~ *vb* **-rr-** **1** : mark with a star **2** : play the leading role — **star·dom** *n* — **star·less** *adj* — **star·light** *n* — **star·ry** *adj*

star·board *n* : right side of a ship or airplane looking forward — **starboard** *adj*

starch *n* : nourishing carbohydrate from plants also used in adhesives and laundering ~ *vb* : stiffen with starch — **starchy** *adj*

stare *vb* **stared; star·ing** : look intently with wide-open eyes — **stare** *n* — **star·er** *n*

stark *adj* **1** : absolute **2** : severe or bleak ~ *adv* : completely — **stark·ly** *adv*

star·ling *n* : bird related to the crows

start *vb* **1** : twitch or jerk (as from surprise) **2** : perform or show performance of the first part of an action or process ~ *n* **1** : sudden involuntary motion **2** : beginning — **start·er** *n*

star·tle *vb* **-tled; -tling** : frighten or surprise suddenly

starve *vb* **starved; starv·ing** **1** : suffer or die from hunger **2** : kill with hunger — **star·va·tion** *n*

stash *vb* : store in a secret place for future use — **stash** *n*

state *n* **1** : condition of being **2** : condition of mind **3** : nation or a political unit within it ~ *vb* **stat·ed; stat·ing** **1** : express in words **2** : establish — **state·hood** *n*

state·ly *adj* **-li·er; -est** : having impressive dignity — **state·li·ness** *n*

state·ment *n* **1** : something stated **2** : financial summary

state·room *n* : private room on a ship

states·man *n* : one skilled in government or diplomacy — **states·man·like** *adj* — **states·man·ship** *n*

stat·ic *adj* **1** : relating to bodies at rest or forces in equilibrium **2** : not moving **3** : relating to stationary charges of electricity ~ *n* : noise on radio or television from electrical disturbances

sta·tion *n* **1** : place of duty **2** : regular stop on a bus or train route **3** : social standing **4** : place where radio or television programs originate ~ *vb* : assign to a station

sta·tion·ary *adj* **1** : not moving or not movable **2** : not changing

sta·tio·nery *n* : letter paper with envelopes

sta·tis·tic *n* : single item of statistics

sta·tis·tics *n pl* : numerical facts collected for study — **sta·tis·ti·cal** *adj* — **sta·tis·ti·cal·ly** *adv* — **stat·is·ti·cian** *n*

stat·u·ary *n, pl* **-ar·ies** : collection of statues

stat·ue *n* : solid 3-dimensional likeness — **stat·u·ette** *n*

stat·u·esque *adj* : tall and shapely

stat·ure *n* **1** : height **2** : status gained by achievement

sta·tus *n* : relative situation or condition

sta·tus quo *n* : existing state of affairs

stat·ute *n* : law — **stat·u·to·ry** *adj*

staunch *adj* : steadfast — **staunch·ly** *adv*

stave *n* : narrow strip of wood ~ *vb* **staved** *or* **stove; stav·ing** **1** : break a hole in **2** : drive away

staves *pl of* STAFF

¹**stay** *n* : support ~ *vb* **stayed; stay·ing** : prop up

²**stay** *vb* **stayed** *or* **staid; stay·ing** **1** : pause **2** : remain **3** : reside **4** : stop or postpone **5** : satisfy for a time ~ *n* : a staying

stead *n* : one's place, job, or function — **in good stead** : to advantage

stead·fast *adj* : faithful or determined — **stead·fast·ly** *adv*

steady *adj* **steadi·er; -est** **1** : firm in position or sure in move- ment **2** : calm or reliable **3** : constant **4** : regular ~ *vb* **stead·ied; steady·ing** : make or become steady — **steadi·ly** *adv* — **steadi·ness** *n* — **steady** *adv*

steak *n* : thick slice of meat

steal *vb* **stole; sto·len; steal·ing** **1** : take and carry away wrongfully and with intent to keep **2** : move secretly or slowly

stealth *n* : secret or unobtrusive procedure — **stealth·i·ly** *adv* — **stealthy** *adj*

steam *n* : vapor of boiling water ~ *vb* : give off steam — **steam·boat** *n* — **steam·ship** *n* — **steamy** *adj*

steed *n* : horse

steel *n* : tough carbon-containing iron ~ *vb* : fill with courage — **steel** *adj* — **steely** *adj*

¹**steep** *adj* : having a very sharp slope or great elevation — **steep·ly** *adv* — **steep·ness** *n*

²**steep** *vb* : soak in a liquid

stee·ple *n* : usu. tapering church tower

stee·ple·chase *n* : race over hurdles

¹**steer** *n* : castrated ox

²**steer** *vb* **1** : direct the course of (as a ship or car) **2** : guide

steer·age *n* : section in a ship for people paying the lowest fares

stein *n* : mug

stel·lar *adj* : relating to stars or resembling a star

¹**stem** *n* : main upright part of a plant ~ *vb* **-mm-** **1** : derive **2** : make progress against — **stem·less** *adj* — **stemmed** *adj*

²**stem** *vb* **-mm-** : stop the flow of

stench *n* : stink

sten·cil *n* : printing sheet cut with letters to let ink pass through — **stencil** *vb*

ste·nog·ra·phy *n* : art or process of writing in shorthand — **ste·nog·ra·pher** *n* — **steno·graph·ic** *adj*

sten·to·ri·an *adj* : extremely loud and powerful

step *n* **1** : single action of a leg in walking or running **2** : rest for the foot in going up or down **3** : degree, rank, or stage **4** : way of walking ~ *vb* **-pp- 1** : move by steps **2** : press with the foot

step- *comb form* : related by a remarriage and not by blood

step·lad·der *n* : light portable set of steps in a hinged frame

steppe *n* : dry grassy treeless land esp. of Asia

-ster *n suffix* **1** : one that does, makes, or uses **2** : one that is associated with or takes part in **3** : one that is

ste·reo *n, pl* **-reos** : stereophonic sound system — **stereo** *adj*

ste·reo·phon·ic *adj* : relating to a 3-dimensional effect of reproduced sound

ste·reo·type *n* : gross often mistaken generalization — **stereotype** *vb* — **ste·reo·typ·i·cal** *adj* — **ste·reo·typi·cal·ly** *adv*

ste·reo·typed *adj* : lacking originality or individuality

ster·ile *adj* **1** : unable to bear fruit, crops, or offspring **2** : free from disease germs — **ste·ril·i·ty** *n* — **ster·il·i·za·tion** *n* — **ster·il·ize** *vb* — **ster·il·iz·er** *n*

ster·ling *adj* **1** : being or made of an alloy of 925 parts of silver with 75 parts of copper **2** : excellent

¹stern *adj* : severe — **stern·ly** *adv* — **stern·ness** *n*

²stern *n* : back end of a boat

ster·num *n, pl* **-nums** *or* **-na** : long flat chest bone joining the 2 sets of ribs

stetho·scope *n* : instrument used for listening to sounds in the chest

ste·ve·dore *n* : worker who loads and unloads ships

stew *n* **1** : dish of boiled meat and vegetables **2** : state of worry or agitation — **stew** *vb*

stew·ard *n* **1** : manager of an estate or an organization **2** : person on a ship or airliner who looks after passenger comfort — **stew·ard·ship** *n*

stew·ard·ess *n* : woman who is a steward (as on an airplane)

¹stick *n* **1** : cut or broken branch **2** : long thin piece of wood or something resembling it

²stick *vb* **stuck; stick·ing 1** : stab **2** : thrust or project **3** : hold fast to something **4** : attach **5** : become jammed or fixed

stick·er *n* : adhesive label

stick·ler *n* : one who insists on exactness or completeness

sticky *adj* **stick·i·er; -est 1** : adhesive or gluey **2** : muggy **3** : difficult

stiff *adj* **1** : not bending easily **2** : tense **3** : formal **4** : strong **5** : severe — **stiff·en** *vb* — **stiff·en·er** *n* — **stiff·ly** *adv* — **stiff·ness** *n*

sti·fle *vb* **-fled; -fling 1** : smother or suffocate **2** : suppress

stig·ma *n, pl* **-ma·ta** *or* **-mas** : mark of disgrace — **stig·ma·tize** *vb*

stile *n* : steps for crossing a fence

sti·let·to *n, pl* **-tos** *or* **-toes** : slender dagger

¹still *adj* **1** : motionless **2** : silent ~ *vb* : make or become still ~ *adv* **1** : without motion **2** : up to and during this time **3** : in spite of that ~ *n* : silence — **still·ness** *n*

²still *n* : apparatus used in distillation

still·born *adj* : born dead — **still·birth** *n*

stilt *n* : one of a pair of poles for walking

stilt·ed *adj* : not easy and natural

stim·u·lant *n* : substance that temporarily increases the activity of an organism — **stimu·lant** *adj*

stim·u·late *vb* **-lat·ed; -lat·ing** : make active — **stim·u·la·tion** *n*

stim·u·lus *n, pl* **-li** : something that stimulates

sting *vb* **stung; sting·ing 1** : prick painfully **2** : cause to suffer acutely ~ *n* : act of stinging or a resulting wound — **sting·er** *n*

stin·gy *adj* **stin·gi·er; -est** : not generous — **stin·gi·ness** *n*

stink *vb* **stank** *or* **stunk; stunk; stink·ing** : have a strong offensive odor — **stink** *n* — **stink·er** *n*

stint *vb* : be sparing or stingy ~ *n* **1** : restraint **2** : quantity or period of work

sti·pend *n* : money paid periodically

stip·ple *vb* **-pled; -pling** : engrave, paint, or draw with dots instead of lines — **stipple** *n*

stip·u·late *vb* **-lat·ed; -lat·ing** : demand as a condition — **stip·u·la·tion** *n*

stir *vb* **-rr- 1** : move slightly **2** : prod or push into activity **3** : mix by continued circular movement ~ *n* : act or result of stirring

stir·rup *n* : saddle loop for the foot

stitch *n* **1** : loop formed by a needle in sewing **2** : sudden sharp pain ~ *vb* **1** : fasten or decorate with stitches **2** : sew

stock *n* **1** : block or part of wood **2** : original from which others derive **3** : farm animals **4** : supply of goods **5** : money invested in a large business **6** *pl* : instrument of punishment like a pillory with holes for the feet or feet and hands ~ *vb* : provide with stock

stock·ade *n* : defensive or confining enclosure

stock·ing *n* : close-fitting covering for the foot and leg

stock·pile *n* : reserve supply — **stockpile** *vb*

stocky *adj* **stock·i·er; -est** : short and relatively thick

stock·yard *n* : yard for livestock to be slaughtered or shipped

stodgy *adj* **stodg·i·er; -est 1** : dull **2** : old-fashioned

sto·ic, sto·i·cal *adj* : showing indifference to pain — **stoic** *n* — **sto·ical·ly** *adv* — **sto·i·cism** *n*

stoke *vb* **stoked; stok·ing** : stir up a fire or supply fuel to a furnace — **stok·er** *n*

¹stole *past of* STEAL

²stole *n* : long wide scarf

stolen *past part of* STEAL

stol·id *adj* : having or showing little or no emotion — **stol·id·ly** *adv*

stom·ach *n* **1** : saclike digestive organ **2** : abdomen **3** : appetite or desire ~ *vb* : put up with — **stom·ach·ache** *n*

stomp *vb* : stamp

stone *n* **1** : hardened earth or mineral matter **2** : small piece of rock **3** : seed that is hard or has a hard covering ~ *vb* **stoned; ston·ing** : pelt or kill with stones — **stony** *adj*

stood *past of* STAND

stool *n* **1** : seat usu. without back or arms **2** : footstool **3** : discharge of feces

¹stoop *vb* **1** : bend over **2** : lower oneself ~ *n* **1** : act of bending over **2** : bent position of shoulders

²stoop *n* : small porch at a house door

stop *vb* **-pp- 1** : block an opening **2** : end or cause to end **3** : pause for rest or a visit in a journey ~ *n* **1** : plug **2** : act or place of stopping **3** : delay in a journey — **stop·light** *n* — **stop·page** *n* — **stop·per** *n*

stop·gap *n* : temporary measure or thing

stor·age *n* : safekeeping of goods (as in a warehouse)

store *vb* **stored; stor·ing** : put aside for future use ~ *n* **1** : something stored **2** : retail business establishment — **store·house** *n* — **store·keep·er** *n* — **store·room** *n*

stork *n* : large wading bird

storm *n* **1** : heavy fall of rain or snow **2** : violent outbreak ~ *vb* **1** : rain or snow heavily **2** : rage **3** : make an attack against — **stormy** *adj*

¹sto·ry *n, pl* **-ries 1** : narrative **2** : report — **sto·ry·tell·er** *n*

²story *n, pl* **-ries** : floor of a building

stout *adj* **1** : firm or strong **2** : thick or bulky — **stout·ly** *adv* — **stout·ness** *n*

¹stove *n* : apparatus for providing heat (as for cooking or heating)

²stove *past of* STAVE

stow *vb* **1** : pack in a compact mass **2** : put or hide away

strad·dle *vb* **-dled; -dling** : stand over or sit on with legs on opposite sides — **straddle** *n*

strafe *vb* **strafed; straf·ing** : fire upon with machine guns from a low-flying airplane

strag·gle *vb* **-gled; -gling** : wander or become separated from others — **strag·gler** *n*

straight *adj* **1** : having no bends, turns, or twists **2** : just, proper, or honest **3** : neat and orderly ~ *adv* : in a straight manner — **straight·en** *vb*

straight·for·ward *adj* : frank or honest

straight·way *adv* : immediately

¹strain *n* **1** : lineage **2** : trace

²strain *n* **1** : exert to the utmost **2** : filter or remove by filtering **3** : injure by improper use ~ *n* **1** : excessive tension or exertion **2** : bodily injury from excessive effort — **strain·er** *n*

strait *n* **1** : narrow channel connecting 2 bodies of water **2** *pl* : distress

strait·en *vb* **1** : hem in **2** : make distressing or difficult

¹strand *vb* **1** : drive or cast upon the shore **2** : leave helpless

²strand *n* **1** : twisted fiber of a rope **2** : length of something ropelike

strange *adj* **strang·er; strang·est 1** : unusual or queer **2** : new — **strange·ly** *adv* — **strange·ness** *n*

strang·er *n* : person with whom one is not acquainted

stran·gle *vb* **-gled; -gling** : choke to death — **stran·gler** *n*

stran·gu·la·tion *n* : act or process of strangling

strap *n* : narrow strip of flexible material used esp. for fastening — *vb* **1** : secure with a strap **2** : beat with a strap — **strap·less** *n*

strap·ping *adj* : robust

strat·a·gem *n* : deceptive scheme or maneuver

strat·e·gy *n, pl* **-gies** : carefully worked out plan of action — **stra·te·gic** *adj* — **strat·e·gist** *n*

strat·i·fy *vb* **-fied; -fy·ing** : form or arrange in layers — **strat·i·fi·ca·tion** *n*

strato·sphere *n* : earth's atmosphere from about 7 to 31 miles above the surface

stra·tum *n, pl* **-ta** : layer

straw *n* **1** : grass stems after grain is removed **2** : tube for drinking ~ *adj* : made of straw

straw·ber·ry *n* : juicy red pulpy fruit

stray *vb* : wander or deviate ~ *n* : person or animal that strays ~ *adj* : separated from or not related to anything close by

streak *n* **1** : mark of a different color **2** : narrow band of light **3** : trace **4** : run (as of luck) or series ~ *vb* **1** : form streaks in or on **2** : move fast

stream *n* **1** : flow of water on land **2** : steady flow (as of water or air) ~ *vb* **1** : flow in a stream **2** : pour out streams

stream·er *n* : long ribbon or ribbonlike flag

stream·lined *adj* **1** : made with contours to reduce air or water resistance **2** : simplified **3** : modernized — **streamline** *vb*

street *n* : thoroughfare esp. in a city or town

street·car *n* : passenger vehicle running on rails in the streets

strength *n* **1** : quality of being strong **2** : toughness **3** : intensity

strength•en *vb* : make, grow, or become stronger — **strength•en•er** *n*

stren•u•ous *adj* 1 : vigorous 2 : requiring or showing energy — **stren•u•ous•ly** *adv*

stress *n* 1 : pressure or strain that tends to distort a body 2 : relative prominence given to one thing among others 3 : state of physical or mental tension or something inducing it ~ *vb* : put stress on — **stress•ful** *adj*

stretch *vb* 1 : spread or reach out 2 : draw out in length or breadth 3 : make taut 4 : exaggerate 5 : become extended without breaking ~ *n* : act of extending beyond normal limits

stretch•er *n* : device for carrying a sick or injured person

strew *vb* **strewed; strewed** *or* **strewn; strewing** 1 : scatter 2 : cover by scattering something over

strick•en *adj* : afflicted with disease

strict *adj* 1 : allowing no escape or evasion 2 : precise — **strict•ly** *adv* — **strict•ness** *n*

stric•ture *n* : hostile criticism

stride *vb* **strode; strid•den; strid•ing** : walk or run with long steps ~ *n* 1 : long step 2 : manner of striding

stri•dent *adj* : loud and harsh

strife *n* : conflict

strike *vb* **struck; struck; strik•ing** 1 : hit sharply 2 : delete 3 : produce by impressing 4 : cause to sound 5 : afflict 6 : occur to or impress 7 : cause (a match) to ignite by rubbing 8 : refrain from working 9 : find 10 : take on (as a pose) ~ *n* 1 : act or instance of striking 2 : work stoppage 3 : military attack — **strik•er** *n* — **strike out** *vb* : start out vigorously — **strike up** *vb* : start

strik•ing *adj* : very noticeable — **strik•ing•ly** *adv*

string *n* 1 : line usu. of twisted threads 2 : series 3 *pl* : stringed instruments ~ *vb* **strung; string•ing** 1 : thread on or with a string 2 : hang or fasten by a string

stringed *adj* : having strings

strin•gent *adj* : severe

stringy *adj* **string•i•er; -est** : tough or fibrous

¹**strip** *vb* **-pp-** 1 : take the covering or clothing from 2 : undress — **strip•per** *n*

²**strip** *n* : long narrow flat piece

stripe *n* : distinctive line or long narrow section ~ *vb* **striped; strip•ing** : make stripes on — **striped** *adj*

strive *vb* **strove; striv•en** *or* **strived; striv•ing** 1 : struggle 2 : try hard

strode *past of* STRIDE

stroke *vb* **stroked; strok•ing** : rub gently ~ *n* 1 : act of swinging or striking 2 : sudden action

stroll *vb* : walk leisurely — **stroll** *n* — **stroll•er** *n*

strong *adj* 1 : capable of exerting great force or of withstanding stress or violence 2 : healthy 3 : zealous — **strong•ly** *adv*

strong•hold *n* : fortified place

struck *past of* STRIKE

struc•ture *n* 1 : building 2 : arrangement of elements ~ *vb* **-tured; -tur•ing** : make into a structure — **struc•tur•al** *adj*

strug•gle *vb* **-gled; -gling** 1 : make strenuous efforts to over- come an adversary 2 : proceed with great effort ~ *n* 1 : strenuous effort 2 : intense competition for superiority

strum *vb* **-mm-** : play (a musical instrument) by brushing the strings with the fingers

strum•pet *n* : prostitute

strung *past of* STRING

strut *vb* **-tt-** : walk in a proud or showy manner ~ *n* 1 : proud walk 2 : supporting bar or rod

strych•nine *n* : bitter poisonous substance

stub *n* : short end or section ~ *vb* **-bb-** : strike against something

stub•ble *n* : short growth left after cutting — **stub•bly** *adj*

stub•born *adj* 1 : determined not to yield 2 : hard to control — **stub•born•ly** *adv* — **stub•born•ness** *n*

stub•by *adj* : short, blunt, and thick

stuc•co, *pl* **-cos** *or* **-coes** : plaster for coating outside walls — **stuc•coed** *adj*

stuck *past of* STICK

stuck–up *adj* : conceited

¹**stud** *n* : male horse kept for breeding

²**stud** *n* 1 : upright beam for holding wall material 2 : projecting nail, pin, or rod ~ *vb* **-dd-** : supply or dot with studs

stu•dent *n* : one who studies

stud•ied *adj* : premeditated

stu•dio *n*, *pl* **-dios** 1 : artist's workroom 2 : place where movies are made or television or radio shows are broadcast

stu•di•ous *adj* : devoted to study — **stu•di•ous•ly** *adv*

study *n*, *pl* **stud•ies** 1 : act or process of learning about something 2 : branch of learning 3 : careful examination 4 : room for reading or studying ~ *vb* **stud•ied; study•ing** : apply the attention and mind to a subject

stuff *n* 1 : personal property 2 : raw or fundamental material 3 : unspecified material or things ~ *vb* : fill by packing things in — **stuff•ing** *n*

stuffy *adj* **stuff•i•er; -est** 1 : lacking fresh air 2 : unimaginative or pompous

stul•ti•fy *vb* **-fied; -fy•ing** 1 : cause to appear foolish 2 : impair or make ineffective 3 : have a dulling effect on

stum•ble *vb* **-bled; -bling** 1 : lose one's balance or fall in walking or running 2 : speak or act clumsily 3 : happen by chance — **stumble** *n*

stump *n* : part left when something is cut off ~ *vb* : confuse — **stumpy** *adj*

stun *vb* **-nn-** 1 : make senseless or dizzy by or as if by a blow 2 : bewilder

stung *past of* STING

stunk *past of* STINK

stun•ning *adj* 1 : astonishing or incredible 2 : strikingly beautiful — **stun•ning•ly** *adv*

¹**stunt** *vb* : hinder the normal growth or progress of

²**stunt** *n* : spectacular feat

stu•pe•fy *vb* **-fied; -fy•ing** 1 : make insensible by or as if by drugs 2 : amaze

stu•pen•dous *adj* : very big or impressive — **stu•pen•dous•ly** *adv*

stu•pid *adj* : not sensible or intelligent — **stu•pid•i•ty** *n* — **stu•pid•ly** *adv*

stu•por *n* : state of being conscious but not aware or sensible

stur•dy *adj* **-di•er; -est** : strong — **stur•di•ly** *adv* — **stur•di•ness** *n*

stur•geon *n* : fish whose roe is caviar

stut•ter *vb* *or* *n* : stammer

¹**sty** *n*, *pl* **sties** : pig pen

²**sty, stye** *n*, *pl* **sties** *or* **styes** : inflamed swelling on the edge of an eyelid

style *n* 1 : distinctive way of speaking, writing, or acting 2 : elegant or fashionable way of living ~ *vb* **styled; styl•ing** 1 : name 2 : give a particular design or style to — **stylish** *adj* — **styl•ish•ly** *adv* — **styl•ish•ness** *n* — **styl•ist** *n* — **styl•ize** *vb*

sty•lus *n*, *pl* **-li** 1 : pointed writing tool 2 : phonograph needle

sty•mie *vb* **-mied; -mie•ing** : block or frustrate

suave *adj* : well-mannered and gracious — **suave•ly** *adv*

¹**sub** *n* *or* *vb* : substitute

²**sub** *n* : submarine

sub- *prefix* 1 : under or beneath 2 : subordinate or secondary 3 : subordinate portion of 4 : with repetition of a process so as to form, stress, or deal with subordinate parts or relations 5 : somewhat 6 : nearly

subacute	subindustry
subagency	sublease
subagent	sublethal
subarctic	sublevel
subarea	subliterate
subatmospheric	subnetwork
subaverage	suboceanic
subbase	suborder
subbasement	subpar
subbranch	subpart
subcabinet	subplot
subcategory	subpolar
subclass	subprincipal
subclassification	subprocess
subclassify	subprogram
subcommission	subproject
subcommittee	subregion
subcommunity	subsea
subcomponent	subsection
subcontract	subsense
subcontractor	subspecialty
subculture	subspecies
subdean	substage
subdepartment	subsurface
subdistrict	subsystem
subentry	subtemperate
subfamily	subtheme
subfreezing	subtopic
subgroup	subtotal
subhead	subtreasury
subheading	subtype
subhuman	subunit
subindex	subvariety

sub•con•scious *adj* : existing without conscious awareness ~ *n* : part of the mind concerned with subconscious activities — **sub•con•scious•ly** *adv*

sub•di•vide *vb* 1 : divide into several parts 2 : divide (land) into building lots — **sub•di•vi•sion** *n*

sub•due *vb* **-dued; -du•ing** 1 : bring under control 2 : reduce the intensity of

sub•ject *n* 1 : person under the authority of another 2 : something being discussed or studied 3 : word or word group about which something is said in a sentence ~ *adj* 1 : being under one's authority 2 : prone 3 : dependent on some condition or act ~ *vb* 1 : bring under control 2 : cause to undergo — **sub•jec•tion** *n*

sub•jec•tive *adj* : deriving from an individual viewpoint or bias — **sub•jec•tive•ly** *adv* — **sub•jec•tiv•i•ty** *n*

sub•ju•gate *vb* **-gat•ed; -gat•ing** : bring under one's control — **sub•ju•ga•tion** *n*

sub•junc•tive *adj* : relating to a verb form which expresses possibility or contingency — **subjunctive** *n*

sub•let *vb* **-let; -let•ting** : rent (a property) from a lessee

sub•lime *adj* : splendid — **sub•lime•ly** *adv*

sub•ma•rine *adj* : existing, acting, or growing under the sea ~ *n* : underwater boat

sub•merge *vb* **-merged; -merg•ing** : put or plunge under the surface of water — **sub•mergence** *n* — **sub•mers•ible** *adj* *or* *n* — **sub•mer•sion** *n*

sub•mit *vb* **-tt-** 1 : yield 2 : give or offer — **sub•mis•sion** *n* — **sub•mis•sive** *adj*

sub•nor•mal *adj* : falling below what is normal

sub•or•di•nate *adj* : lower in rank ~ *n* : one that is subordinate ~ *vb* **-nat•ed; -nat•ing** : place in a lower rank or class — **sub•or•di•na•tion** *n*

sub•poe•na *n* : summons to appear in court ~ *vb* **-naed; -na•ing** : summon with a subpoena

sub·scribe *vb* **-scribed; -scrib·ing 1** : give consent or approval **2** : agree to support or to receive and pay for — **sub·scrib·er** *n*

sub·scrip·tion *n* : order for regular receipt of a publication

sub·se·quent *adj* : following after — **sub·se·quent·ly** *adv*

sub·ser·vi·ence *n* : obsequious submission — **sub·ser·vi·en·cy** *n* — **sub·ser·vi·ent** *adj*

sub·side *vb* **-sid·ed; -sid·ing** : die down in intensity

sub·sid·iary *adj* **1** : furnishing support **2** : of secondary importance ~ *n* : company controlled by another company

sub·si·dize *vb* **-dized; -diz·ing** : aid with a subsidy

sub·si·dy *n, pl* **-dies** : gift of supporting funds

sub·sist *vb* : acquire the necessities of life — **sub·sis·tence** *n*

sub·stance *n* **1** : essence or essential part **2** : physical material **3** : wealth

sub·stan·dard *adj* : falling short of a standard or norm

sub·stan·tial *adj* **1** : plentiful **2** : considerable — **substan·tial·ly** *adv*

sub·stan·ti·ate *vb* **-at·ed; -at·ing** : verify — **sub·stan·ti·a·tion** *n*

sub·sti·tute *n* : replacement ~ *vb* **-tut·ed; -tut·ing** : put or serve in place of another — **substi·tute** *adj* — **sub·sti·tu·tion** *n*

sub·ter·fuge *n* : deceptive trick

sub·ter·ra·nean *adj* : lying or being underground

sub·ti·tle *n* : movie caption

sub·tle *adj* **-tler -tlest 1** : hardly noticeable **2** : clever — **sub·tle·ty** *n* — **sub·tly** *adv*

sub·tract *vb* : take away (as one number from another) — **sub·trac·tion** *n*

sub·urb *n* : residential area adjacent to a city — **sub·ur·ban** *adj or n* — **sub·ur·ban·ite** *n*

sub·vert *vb* : overthrow or ruin — **sub·ver·sion** *n* — **sub·ver·sive** *adj*

sub·way *n* : underground electric railway

suc·ceed *vb* **1** : follow (someone) in a job, role, or title **2** : attain a desired object or end

suc·cess *n* **1** : favorable outcome **2** : gaining of wealth and fame **3** : one that succeeds — **suc·cess·ful** *adj* — **suc·cess·ful·ly** *adv*

suc·ces·sion *n* **1** : order, act, or right of succeeding **2** : series

suc·ces·sive *adj* : following in order — **suc·ces·sive·ly** *adv*

suc·ces·sor *n* : one that succeeds another

suc·cinct *adj* : brief — **suc·cinct·ly** *adv* — **suc·cinct·ness** *n*

suc·cor *n or vb* : help

suc·co·tash *n* : beans and corn cooked together

suc·cu·lent *adj* : juicy — **suc·cu·lence** *n* — **succulent** *n*

suc·cumb *vb* **1** : yield **2** : die

such *adj* **1** : of this or that kind **2** : having a specified quality — **such** *pron or adv*

suck *vb* **1** : draw in liquid with the mouth **2** : draw liquid from by or as if by mouth — **suck** *n*

suck·er *n* **1** : one that sucks or clings **2** : easily deceived person

suck·le *vb* **-led; -ling** : give or draw milk from the breast or udder

suck·ling *n* : young unweaned mammal

su·crose *n* : cane or beet sugar

suc·tion *n* **1** : act of sucking **2** : act or process of drawing in by partially exhausting the air

sud·den *adj* **1** : happening unexpectedly **2** : steep **3** : hasty — **sud·den·ly** *adv* — **sud·den·ness** *n*

suds *n pl* : soapy water esp. when frothy — **sudsy** *adj*

sue *vb* **sued; su·ing 1** : petition **2** : bring legal action against

suede, suède *n* : leather with a napped surface

su·et *n* : hard beef fat

suf·fer *vb* **1** : experience pain, loss, or hardship **2** : permit — **suf·fer·er** *n*

suf·fer·ing *n* : pain or hardship

suf·fice *vb* **-ficed; -fic·ing** : be sufficient

suf·fi·cient *adj* : adequate — **suf·fi·cien·cy** *n* — **suf·fi·cient·ly** *adv*

suf·fix *n* : letters added at the end of a word — **suffix** *vb* — **suf·fix·a·tion** *n*

suf·fo·cate *vb* **-cat·ed; -cat·ing** : suffer or die or cause to die from lack of air — **suf·fo·cat·ing·ly** *adv* — **suf·fo·ca·tion** *n*

suf·frage *n* : right to vote

suf·fuse *vb* **-fused; -fus·ing** : spread over or through

sug·ar *n* : sweet substance ~ *vb* : mix, cover, or sprinkle with sugar — **sug·ar·cane** *n* — **sug·ary** *adj*

sug·gest *vb* **1** : put into someone's mind **2** : remind one by association of ideas — **sug·gest·ible** *adj* — **sug·ges·tion** *n*

sug·ges·tive *adj* : suggesting something improper — **sug·ges·tive·ly** *adv* — **sug·ges·tive·ness** *n*

su·i·cide *n* **1** : act of killing oneself purposely **2** : one who commits suicide — **su·i·cid·al** *adj*

suit *n* **1** : action in court to recover a right or claim **2** : number of things used or worn together **3** : one of the 4 sets of playing cards ~ *vb* **1** : be appropriate or becoming to **2** : meet the needs of — **suit·abil·i·ty** *n* — **suit·able** *adj* — **suit·ably** *adv*

suit·case *n* : case for a traveler's clothing

suite *n* **1** : group of rooms **2** : set of matched furniture

suit·or *n* : one who seeks to marry a woman

sul·fur *n* : nonmetallic yellow chemical element — **sul·fu·ric** *adj* — **sul·fu·rous** *adj*

sulk *vb* : be moodily silent or irritable — **sulk** *n*

sulky *adj* : inclined to sulk ~ *n* : light 2-wheeled horse-drawn cart — **sulk·i·ly** *adv* — **sulk·i·ness** *n*

sul·len *adj* **1** : gloomily silent **2** : dismal — **sul·len·ly** *adv* — **sul·lenness** *n*

sul·ly *vb* **-lied; -ly·ing** : cast doubt or disgrace on

sul·tan *n* : sovereign of a Muslim state — **sul·tan·ate** *n*

sul·try *adj* **-tri·er; -est 1** : very hot and moist **2** : sexually arousing

sum *n* **1** : amount **2** : gist **3** : result of addition ~ *vb* **-mm-** : find the sum of

su·mac *n* : shrub with spikes of berries

sum·ma·ry *adj* **1** : concise **2** : done without delay or formality ~ *n, pl* **-ries** : concise statement — **sum·mar·i·ly** *adv* — **sum·ma·rize** *vb*

sum·ma·tion *n* : a summing up esp. in court

sum·mer *n* : season in which the sun shines most directly — **sum·mery** *adj*

sum·mit *n* **1** : highest point **2** : high-level conference

sum·mon *vb* **1** : send for or call together **2** : order to appear in court — **sum·mon·er** *n*

sum·mons *n, pl* **sum·mons·es** : an order to answer charges in court

sump·tu·ous *adj* : lavish

sun *n* **1** : shining celestial body around which the planets revolve **2** : light of the sun ~ *vb* **-nn-** : expose to the sun — **sun·beam** *n* — **sun·block** *n* — **sun·burn** *n or vb* — **sun·glass·es** *n pl* — **sun·light** *n* — **sun·ny** *adj* — **sun·rise** *n* — **sun·set** *n* — **sun·shine** *n* — **sun·tan** *n*

sun·dae *n* : ice cream with topping

Sun·day *n* : 1st day of the week

sun·di·al *n* : device for showing time by the sun's shadow

sun·dries *n, pl* : various small articles

sun·dry *adj* : several

sun·fish *n* : perchlike freshwater fish

sun·flow·er *n* : tall plant grown for its oil-rich seeds

sung *past of* SING

sunk *past of* SINK

sunk·en *adj* **1** : submerged **2** : fallen in

sun·spot *n* : dark spot on the sun

sun·stroke *n* : heatstroke from the sun

sup *vb* **-pp-** : eat the evening meal

super *adj* : very fine

super- *prefix* **1** : higher in quantity, quality, or degree than **2** : in addition **3** : exceeding a norm **4** : in excessive degree or intensity **5** : surpassing others of its kind **6** : situated above, on, or at the top of **7** : more inclusive than **8** : superior in status or position

superabundance	superpolite
superabundant	superport
superambitious	superpowerful
superathlete	superrich
superbomb	supersalesman
superclean	superscout
supercolossal	supersecrecy
superconvenient	supersecret
supercop	supersensitive
superdense	supersize
supereffective	supersized
superefficiency	superslick
superefficient	supersmooth
superfast	supersoft
supergood	superspecial
supergovernment	superspecialist
supergroup	superspy
superhero	superstar
superheroine	superstate
superhuman	superstrength
superintellectual	superstrong
superintelligence	supersystem
superintelligent	supertanker
superman	superthick
supermodern	superthin
superpatriot	supertight
superpatriotic	superweapon
superpatriotism	superwoman
superplane	

su·perb *adj* : outstanding — **su·perb·ly** *adv*

su·per·cil·ious *adj* : haughtily contemptuous

su·per·fi·cial *adj* : relating to what is only apparent — **su·per·fi·ci·al·i·ty** *n* — **su·per·fi·cial·ly** *adv*

su·per·flu·ous *adj* : more than necessary — **su·per·flu·i·ty** *n*

su·per·im·pose *vb* : lay over or above something

su·per·in·tend *vb* : have charge and oversight of — **su·per·in·ten·dence** *n* — **su·per·in·ten·den·cy** *n* — **su·per·in·ten·dent** *n*

su·pe·ri·or *adj* **1** : higher, better, or more important **2** : haughty — **superior** *n* — **su·pe·ri·or·i·ty** *n*

su·per·la·tive *adj* **1** : relating to or being an adjective or adverb form that denotes an extreme level **2** : surpassing others — **superlative** *n* — **su·per·la·tive·ly** *adv*

su·per·mar·ket *n* : self-service grocery store

su·per·nat·u·ral *adj* : beyond the observable physical world — **su·per·nat·u·ral·ly** *adv*

su·per·pow·er *n* : politically and militarily dominant nation

su·per·sede *vb* **-sed·ed; -sed·ing** : take the place of

su·per·son·ic *adj* : faster than the speed of sound

su·per·sti·tion *n* : beliefs based on ignorance, fear of the unknown, or trust in magic — **su·per·sti·tious** *adj*

su·per·struc·ture *n* : something built on a base or as a vertical extension

su·per·vise *vb* **-vised; -vis·ing** : have charge of

— **su·per·vi·sion** n — **su·per·vi·sor** n — **su·per·vi·so·ry** adj

su·pine adj 1 : lying on the back 2 : indifferent or abject

sup·per n : evening meal

sup·plant vb : take the place of

sup·ple adj **-pler; -plest** : able to bend easily

sup·ple·ment n : something that adds to or makes up for a lack — **supplement** vb — **sup·ple·men·tal** adj — **sup·ple·men·ta·ry** adj

sup·pli·ant n : one who supplicates

sup·pli·cate vb **-cat·ed; -cat·ing** 1 : pray to God 2 : ask earnestly and humbly — **sup·pli·cant** n — **sup·pli·ca·tion** n

sup·ply vb **-plied; -ply·ing** : furnish ~ n, pl **-plies** 1 : amount needed or available 2 pl : provisions — **sup·pli·er** n

sup·port vb 1 : take sides with 2 : provide with food, clothing, and shelter 3 : hold up or serve as a foundation for — **support** n — **sup·port·able** adj — **sup·port·er** n

sup·pose vb **-posed; -pos·ing** 1 : assume to be true 2 : expect 3 : think probable — **sup·po·si·tion** n

sup·pos·i·to·ry n, pl **-ries** : medicated material for insertion (as into the rectum)

sup·press vb 1 : put an end to by authority 2 : keep from being known 3 : hold back — **sup·pres·sant** n — **sup·pres·sion** n

su·prem·a·cy n, pl **-cies** : supreme power or authority

su·preme adj 1 : highest in rank or authority 2 : greatest possible — **su·preme·ly** adv

Supreme Being n : God

sur·charge n 1 : excessive load or burden 2 : extra fee or cost

sure adj **sur·er; sur·est** 1 : confident 2 : reliable 3 : not to be disputed 4 : bound to happen ~ adv : surely — **sure·ness** n

sure·ly adv 1 : in a sure manner 2 : without doubt 3 : indeed

sure·ty n, pl **-ties** 1 : guarantee 2 : one who gives a guarantee for another person

surf n : waves that break on the shore ~ vb : ride the surf — **surfboard** n — **surf·er** n — **surf·ing** n

sur·face n 1 : the outside of an object 2 : outward aspect ~ vb **-faced; -fac·ing** : rise to the surface

sur·feit n 1 : excess 2 : excessive indulgence (as in food or drink) 3 : disgust caused by excess ~ vb : feed, supply, or indulge to the point of surfeit

surge vb **surged; surg·ing** : rise and fall in or as if in waves ~ n : sudden increase

sur·geon n : physician who specializes in surgery

sur·gery n, pl **-ger·ies** : medical treatment involving cutting open the body

sur·gi·cal adj : relating to surgeons or surgery — **sur·gi·cal·ly** adv

sur·ly adj **-li·er; -est** : having a rude nature — **sur·li·ness** n

sur·mise vb **-mised; -mis·ing** : guess — **surmise** n

sur·mount vb 1 : prevail over 2 : get to or be the top of

sur·name n : family name

sur·pass vb : go beyond or exceed — **sur·pass·ing·ly** adv

sur·plice n : loose white outer ecclesiastical vestment

sur·plus n : quantity left over

sur·prise vb **-prised; -pris·ing** 1 : come upon or affect unexpectedly 2 : amaze — **surprise** n — **sur·pris·ing** adj — **sur·pris·ing·ly** adv

sur·ren·der vb : give up oneself or a possession to another ~ n : act of surrendering

sur·rep·ti·tious adj : done, made, or acquired by stealth — **sur·rep·ti·tious·ly** adv

sur·rey n, pl **-reys** : horse-drawn carriage

sur·ro·gate n : substitute

sur·round vb : enclose on all sides

sur·round·ings n pl : objects, conditions, or area around something

sur·veil·lance n : careful watch

sur·vey vb **-veyed; -vey·ing** 1 : look over and examine closely 2 : make a survey of (as a tract of land) ~ n, pl **-veys** 1 : inspection 2 : process of measuring (as land) — **sur·vey·or** n

sur·vive vb **-vived; -viv·ing** 1 : remain alive or in existence 2 : outlive or outlast — **sur·viv·al** n — **sur·vi·vor** n

sus·cep·ti·ble adj : likely to allow or be affected by something — **sus·cep·ti·bil·i·ty** n

sus·pect adj 1 : regarded with suspicion 2 : questionable ~ n : one who is suspected (as of a crime) ~ vb 1 : have doubts of 2 : believe guilty without proof 3 : guess

sus·pend vb 1 : temporarily stop or keep from a function or job 2 : withhold (judgment) temporarily 3 : hang

sus·pend·er n : one of 2 supporting straps holding up trousers and passing over the shoulders

sus·pense n : excitement and uncertainty as to outcome — **sus·pense·ful** adj

sus·pen·sion n : act of suspending or the state or period of being suspended

sus·pi·cion n 1 : act of suspecting something 2 : trace

sus·pi·cious adj 1 : arousing suspicion 2 : inclined to suspect — **sus·pi·cious·ly** adv

sus·tain vb 1 : provide with nourishment 2 : keep going 3 : hold up 4 : suffer 5 : support or prove

sus·te·nance n 1 : nourishment 2 : something that sustains or supports

svelte adj : slender and graceful

swab n 1 : mop 2 : wad of absorbent material for applying medicine ~ vb **-bb-** : use a swab on

swad·dle vb **-dled; -dling** : bind (an infant) in bands of cloth

swag·ger vb **-gered; -ger·ing** 1 : walk with a conceited swing 2 : boast — **swagger** n

¹**swal·low** n : small migratory bird

²**swallow** vb 1 : take into the stomach through the throat 2 : envelop or take in 3 : accept too easily — **swallow** n

swam past of SWIM

swamp n : wet spongy land ~ vb : deluge (as with water) — **swampy** adj

swan n : white long-necked swimming bird

swap vb **-pp-** : trade — **swap** n

swarm n 1 : mass of honeybees leaving a hive to start a new colony 2 : large crowd ~ vb : gather in a swarm

swar·thy adj **-thi·er; -est** : dark in complexion

swash·buck·ler n : swaggering or daring soldier or adventurer — **swash·buck·ling** adj

swat vb **-tt-** : hit sharply — **swat** n — **swat·ter** n

swatch n : sample piece (as of fabric)

swath, swathe n : row or path cut (as through grass)

swathe vb **swathed; swath·ing** : wrap with or as if with a bandage

sway vb 1 : swing gently from side to side 2 : influence ~ n 1 : gentle swinging from side to side 2 : controlling power or influence

swear vb **swore; sworn; swear·ing** 1 : make or cause to make a solemn statement under oath 2 : use profane language — **swear·er** n — **swear·ing** n

sweat vb **sweat** or **sweat·ed; sweat·ing** 1 : excrete salty moisture from skin glands 2 : form drops of moisture on the surface 3 : work or cause to work hard — **sweat** n — **sweaty** adj

sweat·er n : knitted jacket or pullover

sweat·shirt n : loose collarless heavy cotton jersey pullover

sweep vb **swept; sweep·ing** 1 : remove or clean by a brush or a single forceful wipe (as of the hand) 2 : move over with speed and force (as of the hand) 3 : move or extend in a wide curve ~ n 1 : a clearing off or away 2 : single forceful wipe or swinging movement 3 : scope — **sweep·er** n — **sweep·ing** adj

sweep·stakes n, pl **sweep·stakes** : contest in which the entire prize may go to the winner

sweet adj 1 : being or causing the pleasing taste typical of sugar 2 : not stale or spoiled 3 : not salted 4 : pleasant 5 : much loved ~ n : something sweet — **sweet·en** vb — **sweet·ly** adv — **sweet·ness** n — **sweet·en·er** n

sweet·heart n : person one loves

sweet potato n : sweet yellow edible root of a tropical vine

swell vb **swelled; swelled** or **swol·len; swell·ing** 1 : enlarge 2 : bulge 3 : fill or be filled with emotion ~ n 1 : long rolling ocean wave 2 : condition of bulging — **swell·ing** n

swel·ter vb : be uncomfortable from excessive heat

swept past of SWEEP

swerve vb **swerved; swerv·ing** : move abruptly aside from a course — **swerve** n

¹**swift** adj 1 : moving with great speed 2 : occurring suddenly — **swift·ly** adv — **swift·ness** n

²**swift** n : small insect-eating bird

swig vb **-gg-** : drink in gulps — **swig** n

swill vb : swallow greedily ~ n 1 : animal food of refuse and liquid 2 : garbage

swim vb **swam; swum; swim·ming** 1 : propel oneself in water 2 : float in or be surrounded with a liquid 3 : be dizzy ~ n : act or period of swimming — **swim·mer** n

swin·dle vb **-dled; -dling** : cheat (someone) of money or property — **swindle** n — **swin·dler** n

swine n, pl **swine** : short-legged hoofed mammal with a snout — **swin·ish** adj

swing vb **swung; swing·ing** 1 : move or cause to move rapidly in an arc 2 : sway or cause to sway back and forth 3 : hang so as to sway or sag 4 : turn on a hinge or pivot 5 : manage or handle successfully ~ n 1 : act or instance of swinging 2 : swinging movement (as in trying to hit something) 3 : suspended seat for swinging — **swing** adj — **swing·er** n

swipe n : strong sweeping blow ~ vb **swiped; swip·ing** 1 : strike or wipe with a sweeping motion 2 : steal esp. with a quick movement

swirl vb : move or cause to move in a circle — **swirl** n

swish n : hissing, sweeping, or brushing sound — **swish** vb

switch n 1 : slender flexible whip or twig 2 : blow with a switch 3 : shift, change, or reversal 4 : device that opens or closes an electrical circuit ~ vb 1 : punish or urge on with a switch 2 : change or reverse roles, positions, or subjects 3 : operate a switch of

switch·board n : panel of switches to make and break telephone connections

swiv·el vb **-eled** or **-elled; -el·ing** or **-el·ling** : swing or turn on a pivot — **swivel** n

swollen past part of SWELL

swoon n : faint — **swoon** vb

swoop vb : make a swift diving attack — **swoop** n

sword n : thrusting or cutting weapon with a long blade

sword·fish n : large ocean fish with a long sword-like projection

swore past of SWEAR

sworn past part of SWEAR

swum past part of SWIM

swung past of SWING

syc·a·more n : shade tree

sy·co·phant n : servile flatterer — **syc·o·phan·tic** adj

syl•la•ble *n* : unit of a spoken word — **syl•lab•ic** *adj*

syl•la•bus *n, pl* **-bi** *or* **-bus•es** : summary of main topics (as of a course of study)

syl•van *adj* **1** : living or located in a wooded area **2** : abounding in woods

sym•bol *n* : something that represents or suggests another thing — **sym•bol•ic** *adj* — **symbol•i•cal•ly** *adv*

sym•bol•ism *n* : representation of meanings with symbols

sym•bol•ize *vb* **-ized; -izing** : serve as a symbol of — **sym•bol•i•za•tion** *n*

sym•me•try *n, pl* **-tries** : regularity and balance in the arrangement of parts — **sym•met•ri•cal** *adj* — **sym•met•ri•cal•ly** *adv*

sym•pa•thize *vb* **-thized; -thiz•ing** : feel or show sympathy — **sym•pa•thiz•er** *n*

sym•pa•thy *n, pl* **-thies** **1** : ability to understand or share the feelings of another **2** : expression of sorrow for another's misfortune — **sym•pa•thet•ic** *adj* — **sym•pa•thet•i•cal•ly** *adv*

sym•pho•ny *n, pl* **-nies** : composition for an orchestra or the orchestra itself — **sym•phon•ic** *adj*

sym•po•sium *n, pl* **-sia** *or* **-siums** : conference at which a topic is discussed

symp•tom *n* : unusual feeling or reaction that is a sign of disease — **symp•tom•at•ic** *adj*

syn•a•gogue, syn•a•gog *n* : Jewish house of worship

syn•chro•nize *vb* **-nized; -niz•ing** **1** : occur or cause to occur at the same instant **2** : cause to agree in time — **syn•chro•ni•za•tion** *n*

syn•co•pa•tion *n* : shifting of the regular musical accent to the weak beat — **syn•co•pate** *vb*

syn•di•cate *n* : business association ~ *vb* **-cat•ed; -cat•ing** **1** : form a syndicate **2** : publish through a syndicate — **syn•di•ca•tion** *n*

syn•drome *n* : particular group of symptoms

syn•onym *n* : word with the same meaning as another — **syn•on•y•mous** *adj* — **syn•on•y•my** *n*

syn•op•sis *n, pl* **-op•ses** : condensed statement or outline

syn•tax *n* : way in which words are put together — **syn•tac•tic** *or* **syn•tac•ti•cal** *adj*

syn•the•sis *n, pl* **-the•ses** : combination of parts or elements into a whole — **syn•the•size** *vb*

syn•thet•ic *adj* : artificially made — **synthetic** *n* — **syn•thet•i•cal•ly** *adv*

syph•i•lis *n* : venereal disease

sy•ringe *n* : plunger device for injecting or withdrawing liquids

syr•up *n* : thick sticky sweet liquid — **syr•upy** *adj*

sys•tem *n* **1** : arrangement of units that function together **2** : regular order — **sys•tem•at•ic** *adj* — **sys•tem•at•i•cal•ly** *adv* — **sys•tem•a•tize** *vb*

sys•tem•ic *adj* : relating to the whole body

T

t *n, pl* **t's** *or* **ts** : 20th letter of the alphabet

tab *n* **1** : short projecting flap **2** *pl* : careful watch

tab•by *n, pl* **-bies** : domestic cat

tab•er•na•cle *n* : house of worship

ta•ble *n* **1** : piece of furniture having a smooth slab fixed on legs **2** : supply of food **3** : arrangement of data in columns **4** : short list — **ta•ble•cloth** *n* — **ta•ble•top** *n* — **ta•ble•ware** *n* — **tab•u•lar** *adj*

tab•leau *n, pl* **-leaux** **1** : graphic description **2** : depiction of a scene by people in costume

ta•ble•spoon *n* **1** : large serving spoon **2** : measuring spoon holding ½ fluid ounce — **ta•ble•spoon•ful** *n*

tab•let *n* **1** : flat slab suited for an inscription **2** : collection of sheets of paper glued together at one edge **3** : disk-shaped pill

tab•loid *n* : newspaper of small page size

ta•boo *adj* : banned esp. as immoral or dangerous — **taboo** *n or vb*

tab•u•late *vb* **-lat•ed; -lat•ing** : put in the form of a table — **tab•u•la•tion** *n* — **tab•u•la•tor** *n*

tac•it *adj* : implied but not expressed — **tac•it•ly** *adv* — **tac•it•ness** *n*

tac•i•turn *adj* : not inclined to talk

tack *n* **1** : small sharp nail **2** : course of action ~ *vb* **1** : fasten with tacks **2** : add on

tack•le *n* **1** : equipment **2** : arrangement of ropes and pulleys **3** : act of tackling ~ *vb* **-led; -ling 1** : seize or throw down **2** : start dealing with

¹**tacky** *adj* **tack•i•er; -est** : sticky to the touch

²**tacky** *adj* **tack•i•er; -est** : cheap or gaudy

tact *n* : sense of the proper thing to say or do — **tact•ful** *adj* — **tact•ful•ly** *adv* — **tact•less** *adj* — **tact•less•ly** *adv*

tac•tic *n* : action as part of a plan

tac•tics *n sing or pl* **1** : science of maneuvering forces in combat **2** : skill of using available means to reach an end — **tac•ti•cal** *adj* — **tac•ti•cian** *n*

tac•tile *adj* : relating to or perceptible through the sense of touch

tad•pole *n* : larval frog or toad with tail and gills

taf•fe•ta *n* : crisp lustrous fabric (as of silk)

taf•fy *n, pl* **-fies** : candy stretched until porous

¹**tag** *n* : piece of hanging or attached material ~ *vb* **-gg- 1** : provide or mark with a tag **2** : follow closely

²**tag** *n* : children's game of trying to catch one another ~ *vb* : touch a person in tag

tail *n* **1** : rear end or a growth extending from the rear end of an animal **2** : back or last part **3** : the reverse of a coin ~ *vb* : follow — **tailed** *adj* — **tail•less** *adj*

tail•gate *n* : hinged gate on the back of a vehicle that can be lowered for loading ~ *vb* **-gat•ed; -gat•ing** : drive too close behind another vehicle

tail•light *n* : red warning light at the back of a vehicle

tai•lor *n* : one who makes or alters garments ~ *vb* **1** : fashion or alter (clothes) **2** : make or adapt for a special purpose

tail•spin *n* : spiral dive by an airplane

taint *vb* : affect or become affected with something bad and esp. decay ~ *n* : trace of decay or corruption

take *vb* **took; tak•en; tak•ing 1** : get into one's possession **2** : become affected by **3** : receive into one's body (as by eating) **4** : pick out or remove **5** : use for transportation **6** : need or make use of **7** : lead, carry, or cause to go to another place **8** : undertake and do, make, or perform ~ *n* : amount taken — **take•over** *n* — **tak•er** *n* — **take advantage of** : profit by — **take exception** : object — **take off** *vb* **1** : remove **2** : go away **3** : mimic **4** : begin flight — **take over** *vb* : assume control or possession of or responsibility for — **take place** : happen

take•off *n* : act or instance of taking off

talc *n* : soft mineral used in making toilet powder (**tal•cum powder**)

tale *n* **1** : story or anecdote **2** : falsehood

tal•ent *n* : natural mental or creative ability — **tal•ent•ed** *adj*

tal•is•man *n, pl* **-mans** : object thought to act as a charm

talk *vb* **1** : express one's thoughts in speech **2** : discuss **3** : influence to a position or course of action by talking ~ *n* **1** : act of talking **2** : formal discussion **3** : rumor **4** : informal lecture — **talk•a•tive** *adj* — **talk•er** *n*

tall *adj* : extending to a great or specified height — **tall•ness** *n*

tal•low *n* : hard white animal fat used esp. in candles

tal•ly *n, pl* **-lies** : recorded amount ~ *vb* **-lied; -ly•ing 1** : add or count up **2** : match

tal•on *n* : bird's claw

tam *n* : tam-o'-shanter

tam•bou•rine *n* : small drum with loose disks at the sides

tame *adj* **tam•er; tam•est 1** : changed from being wild to being controllable by man **2** : docile **3** : dull ~ *vb* **tamed; tam•ing** : make or become tame — **tam•able, tame•able** *adj* — **tame•ly** *adv* — **tam•er** *n*

tam-o'-shan•ter *n* : Scottish woolen cap with a wide flat circular crown

tamp *vb* : drive down or in by a series of light blows

tam•per *vb* : interfere so as to change for the worse

tan *vb* **-nn- 1** : change (hide) into leather esp. by soaking in a liquid containing tannin **2** : make or become brown (as by exposure to the sun) ~ *n* **1** : brown skin color induced by the sun **2** : light yellowish brown — **tan•ner** *n* — **tan•nery** *n*

tan•dem *adv* : one behind another

tang *n* : sharp distinctive flavor — **tangy** *adj*

tan•gent *adj* : touching a curve or surface at only one point ~ *n* **1** : tangent line, curve, or surface **2** : abrupt change of course — **tan•gen•tial** *adj*

tan•ger•ine *n* : deep orange citrus fruit

tan•gi•ble *adj* **1** : able to be touched **2** : substantially real — **tan•gi•bly** *adv*

tan•gle *vb* **-gled; -gling** : unite in intricate confusion ~ *n* : tangled twisted mass

tan•go *n, pl* **-gos** : dance of Latin-American origin — **tango** *vb*

tank *n* **1** : large artificial receptacle for liquids **2** : armored military vehicle — **tank•ful** *n*

tan•kard *n* : tall one-handled drinking vessel

tank•er *n* : vehicle or vessel with tanks for transporting a liquid

tan•nin *n* : substance of plant origin used in tanning and dyeing

tan•ta•lize *vb* **-lized; -liz•ing** : tease or torment by keeping something desirable just out of reach — **tan•ta•liz•er** *n* — **tan•ta•liz•ing•ly** *adv*

tan•ta•mount *adj* : equivalent in value or meaning

tan•trum *n* : fit of bad temper

¹**tap** *n* **1** : faucet **2** : act of tapping ~ *vb* **-pp- 1** : pierce so as to draw off fluid **2** : connect into — **tap•per** *n*

²**tap** *vb* **-pp-** : rap lightly ~ *n* : light stroke or its sound

tape *n* 1 : narrow flexible strip (as of cloth, plastic, or metal) 2 : tape measure ~ *vb* **taped; tap•ing** 1 : fasten with tape 2 : record on tape

tape measure *n* : strip of tape marked in units for use in measuring

ta•per *n* 1 : slender wax candle 2 : gradual lessening of width in a long object ~ *vb* 1 : make or become smaller toward one end 2 : diminish gradually

tap•es•try *n, pl* **-tries** : heavy handwoven ruglike wall hanging

tape•worm *n* : long flat intestinal worm

tap•i•o•ca *n* : a granular starch used esp. in puddings

tar *n* : thick dark sticky liquid distilled (as from coal) ~ *vb* **-rr-** : treat or smear with tar

ta•ran•tu•la *n* : large hairy usu. harmless spider

tar•dy *adj* **-di•er; -est** : late — **tar•di•ly** *adv* — **tar•di•ness** *n*

tar•get *n* 1 : mark to shoot at 2 : goal to be achieved ~ *vb* 1 : make a target of 2 : establish as a goal

tar•iff *n* 1 : duty or rate of duty imposed on imported goods 2 : schedule of tariffs, rates, or charges

tar•nish *vb* : make or become dull or discolored — **tarnish** *n*

tar•pau•lin *n* : waterproof protective covering

¹tar•ry *vb* **-ried; -ry•ing** : be slow in leaving

²tar•ry *adj* : resembling or covered with tar

¹tart *adj* 1 : pleasantly sharp to the taste 2 : caustic — **tart•ly** *adv* — **tart•ness** *n*

²tart *n* : small pie

tar•tan *n* : woolen fabric with a plaid design

tar•tar *n* : hard crust on the teeth

task *n* : assigned work

task•mas•ter *n* : one that burdens another with labor

tas•sel *n* : hanging ornament made of a bunch of cords fastened at one end

taste *vb* **tast•ed; tast•ing** 1 : test or determine the flavor of 2 : eat or drink in small quantities 3 : have a specific flavor ~ *n* 1 : small amount tasted 2 : bit 3 : special sense that identifies sweet, sour, bitter, or salty qualities 4 : individual preference 5 : critical appreciation of quality — **taste•ful** *adj* — **taste•ful•ly** *adv* — **taste•less** *adj* — **taste•less•ly** *adv* — **tast•er** *n*

tasty *adj* **tast•i•er; -est** : pleasing to the sense of taste — **tast•i•ness** *n*

tat•ter *n* 1 : part torn and left hanging 2 *pl* : tattered clothing ~ *vb* : make or become ragged

tat•tle *vb* **-tled; -tling** : inform on someone — **tat•tler** *n*

tat•tle•tale *n* : one that tattles

tat•too *vb* : mark the skin with indelible designs or figures — **tattoo** *n*

taught *past of* TEACH

taunt *n* : sarcastic challenge or insult — **taunt** *vb* — **taunt•er** *n*

taut *adj* : tightly drawn — **taut•ly** *adv* — **taut•ness** *n*

tav•ern *n* : establishment where liquors are sold to be drunk on the premises

taw•dry *adj* **-dri•er; -est** : cheap and gaudy — **taw•dri•ly** *adv*

taw•ny *adj* **-ni•er; -est** : brownish orange

tax *vb* 1 : impose a tax on 2 : charge 3 : put under stress ~ *n* 1 : charge by authority for public purposes 2 : strain — **tax•able** *adj* — **tax•a•tion** *n* — **tax•pay•er** *n* — **tax•pay•ing** *adj*

taxi *n, pl* **tax•is** : automobile transporting passengers for a fare ~ *vb* **tax•ied; taxi•ing** *or* **taxy•ing; tax•is** *or* **tax•ies** 1 : transport or go by taxi 2 : move along the ground before takeoff or after landing

taxi•cab *n* : taxi

taxi•der•my *n* : skill or job of stuffing and mounting animal skins — **taxi•der•mist** *n*

tea *n* : cured leaves of an oriental shrub or a drink made from these — **tea•cup** *n* — **tea•pot** *n*

teach *vb* **taught; teaching** 1 : tell or show the fundamentals or skills of something 2 : cause to know the consequences 3 : impart knowledge of — **teach•able** *adj* — **teach•er** *n* — **teach•ing** *n*

teak *n* : East Indian timber tree or its wood

tea•ket•tle *n* : covered kettle with a handle and spout for boiling water

teal *n, pl* **teal** *or* **teals** : small short-necked wild duck

team *n* 1 : draft animals harnessed together 2 : number of people organized for a game or work ~ *vb* : form or work together as a team — **team** *adj* — **team•mate** *n* — **team•work** *n*

team•ster *n* 1 : one that drives a team of animals 2 : one that drives a truck

¹tear *n* : drop of salty liquid that moistens the eye — **tear•ful** *adj* — **tear•ful•ly** *adv*

²tear *vb* **tore; torn; tear•ing** 1 : separate or pull apart by force 2 : move or act with violence or haste ~ *n* : act or result of tearing

tease *vb* **teased; teas•ing** : annoy by goading, coaxing, or tantalizing ~ *n* 1 : act of teasing or state of being teased 2 : one that teases

tea•spoon *n* 1 : small spoon for stirring or sipping 2 : measuring spoon holding ⅙ fluid ounce — **tea•spoon•ful** *n*

teat *n* : protuberance through which milk is drawn from an udder or breast

tech•ni•cal *adj* 1 : having or relating to special mechanical or scientific knowledge 2 : by strict interpretation of rules — **tech•ni•cal•ly** *adv*

tech•ni•cal•i•ty *n, pl* **-ties** : detail meaningful only to a specialist

technical sergeant *n* : noncommissioned officer in the air force ranking next below a master sergeant

tech•ni•cian *n* : person with the technique of a specialized skill

tech•nique *n* : manner of accomplishing something

tech•nol•o•gy *n, pl* **-gies** : applied science — **tech•no•log•i•cal** *adj*

te•dious *adj* : wearisome from length or dullness — **te•dious•ly** *adv* — **te•dious•ness** *n*

te•di•um *n* : tedious state or quality

tee *n* : mound or peg on which a golf ball is placed before beginning play — **tee** *vb*

teem *vb* : become filled to overflowing

teen•age, teen•aged *adj* : relating to people in their teens — **teen•ag•er** *n*

teens *n pl* : years 13 to 19 in a person's life

tee•pee *var of* TEPEE

tee•ter *vb* 1 : move unsteadily 2 : seesaw — **teeter** *n*

teeth *pl of* TOOTH

teethe *vb* **teethed; teeth•ing** : grow teeth

tele•cast *vb* **-cast; -cast•ing** : broadcast by television — **telecast** *n* — **tele•cast•er** *n*

tele•com•mu•ni•ca•tion *n* : communication at a distance (as by radio or telephone)

tele•gram *n* : message sent by telegraph

tele•graph *n* : system for communication by electrical transmission of coded signals ~ *vb* : send by telegraph — **te•leg•ra•pher** *n* — **tele•graph•ic** *adj*

te•lep•a•thy *n* : apparent communication without known sensory means — **tele•path•ic** *adj* — **tele•path•i•cal•ly** *adv*

tele•phone *n* : instrument or system for electrical transmission of spoken words ~ *vb* **-phoned; -phon•ing** : communicate with by telephone — **tele•phon•er** *n*

tele•scope *n* : tube-shaped optical instrument for viewing distant objects ~ *vb* **-scoped; -scop-**

ing : slide or cause to slide inside another similar section — **tele•scop•ic** *adj*

tele•vise *vb* **-vised; -vis•ing** : broadcast by television

tele•vi•sion *n* : transmission and reproduction of images by radio waves

tell *vb* **told; tell•ing** 1 : count 2 : relate in detail 3 : reveal 4 : give information or an order to 5 : find out by observing

tell•er *n* 1 : one that relates or counts 2 : bank employee handling money

te•mer•i•ty *n, pl* **-ties** : boldness

temp *n* 1 : temperature 2 : temporary worker

tem•per *vb* 1 : dilute or soften 2 : toughen ~ *n* 1 : characteristic attitude or feeling 2 : toughness 3 : disposition or control over one's emotions

tem•per•a•ment *n* : characteristic frame of mind — **tem•per•a•men•tal** *adj*

tem•per•ance *n* : moderation in or abstinence from indulgence and esp. the use of intoxicating drink

tem•per•ate *adj* : moderate

tem•per•a•ture *n* 1 : degree of hotness or coldness 2 : fever

tem•pest *n* : violent storm — **tem•pes•tu•ous** *adj*

¹tem•ple *n* : place of worship

²temple *n* : flattened space on each side of the forehead

tem•po *n, pl* **-pi** *or* **-pos** : rate of speed

tem•po•ral *adj* : relating to time or to secular concerns

tem•po•rary *adj* : lasting for a short time only — **tem•po•rar•i•ly** *adv*

tempt *vb* 1 : coax or persuade to do wrong 2 : attract or provoke — **tempt•er** *n* — **tempt•ing•ly** *adv* — **tempt•ress** *n*

temp•ta•tion *n* 1 : act of tempting 2 : something that tempts

ten *n* 1 : one more than 9 2 : 10th in a set or series 3 : thing having 10 units — **ten** *adj or pron* — **tenth** *adj or adv or n*

ten•a•ble *adj* : capable of being held or defended — **ten•a•bil•i•ty** *n*

te•na•cious *adj* 1 : holding fast 2 : retentive — **te•na•cious•ly** *adv* — **te•nac•i•ty** *n*

ten•ant *n* : one who occupies a rented dwelling — **ten•an•cy** *n*

¹tend *vb* : take care of or supervise something

²tend *vb* 1 : move in a particular direction 2 : show a tendency

ten•den•cy *n, pl* **-cies** : likelihood to move, think, or act in a particular way

¹ten•der *adj* 1 : soft or delicate 2 : expressing or responsive to love or sympathy 3 : sensitive (as to touch) — **ten•der•ly** *adv* — **ten•der•ness** *n*

²tend•er *n* 1 : one that tends 2 : boat providing transport to a larger ship 3 : vehicle attached to a steam locomotive for carrying fuel and water

³ten•der *n* 1 : offer of a bid for a contract 2 : something that may be offered in payment — **tender** *vb*

ten•der•ize *vb* **-ized; -iz•ing** : make (meat) tender — **ten•der•iz•er** *n*

ten•der•loin *n* : tender beef or pork strip from near the backbone

ten•don *n* : cord of tissue attaching muscle to bone — **ten•di•nous** *adj*

ten•dril *n* : slender coiling growth of some climbing plants

ten•e•ment *n* 1 : house divided into apartments 2 : shabby dwelling

te•net *n* : principle of belief

ten•nis *n* : racket-and-ball game played across a net

ten•or *n* 1 : general drift or meaning 2 : highest natural adult male voice

ten•pin *n* : bottle-shaped pin bowled at in a game (**tenpins**)

¹**tense** *n* : distinct verb form that indicates time

²**tense** *adj* **tens•er; tens•est 1** : stretched tight **2** : marked by nervous tension — **tense** *vb* — **tense•ly** *adv* — **tense•ness** *n* — **ten•si•ty** *n*

ten•sile *adj* : relating to tension

ten•sion *n* **1** : tense condition **2** : state of mental unrest or of potential hostility or opposition

tent *n* : collapsible shelter

ten•ta•cle *n* : long flexible projection of an insect or mollusk — **ten•ta•cled** *adj* — **ten•tac•u•lar** *adj*

ten•ta•tive *adj* : subject to change or discussion — **ten•ta•tive•ly** *adv*

ten•u•ous *adj* **1** : not dense or thick **2** : flimsy or weak — **ten•u•ous•ly** *adv* — **ten•u•ous•ness** *n*

ten•ure *n* : act, right, manner, or period of holding something — **ten•ured** *adj*

te•pee *n* : conical tent

tep•id *adj* : moderately warm

term *n* **1** : period of time **2** : mathematical expression **3** : special word or phrase **4** *pl* : conditions **5** *pl* : relations ~ *vb* : name

ter•min•al *n* **1** : end **2** : device for making an electrical connection **3** : station at end of a transportation line — **terminal** *adj*

ter•mi•nate *vb* **-nat•ed; -nat•ing** : bring or come to an end — **ter•mi•na•ble** *adj* — **ter•mi•na•tion** *n*

ter•mi•nol•o•gy *n* : terms used in a particular subject

ter•mi•nus *n, pl* **-ni** *or* **-nus•es 1** : end **2** : end of a transportation line

ter•mite *n* : wood-eating insect

tern *n* : small sea bird

ter•race *n* **1** : balcony or patio **2** : bank with a flat top ~ *vb* **-raced; -rac•ing** : landscape in a series of banks

ter•ra-cot•ta *n* : reddish brown earthenware

ter•rain *n* : features of the land

ter•ra•pin *n* : No. American turtle

ter•rar•i•um *n, pl* **-ia** *or* **-i•ums** : container for keeping plants or animals

ter•res•tri•al *adj* **1** : relating to the earth or its inhabitants **2** : living or growing on land

ter•ri•ble *adj* **1** : exciting terror **2** : distressing **3** : intense **4** : of very poor quality — **ter•ri•bly** *adv*

ter•ri•er *n* : small dog

ter•rif•ic *adj* **1** : exciting terror **2** : extraordinary

ter•ri•fy *vb* **-fied; -fy•ing** : fill with terror — **ter•ri•fy•ing•ly** *adv*

ter•ri•to•ry *n, pl* **-ries** : particular geographical region — **ter•ri•to•ri•al** *adj*

ter•ror *n* : intense fear and panic or a cause of it

ter•ror•ism *n* : systematic covert warfare to produce terror for political coercion — **ter•ror•ist** *adj or n*

ter•ror•ize *vb* **-ized; -iz•ing 1** : fill with terror **2** : coerce by threat or violence

ter•ry *n, pl* **-ries** : absorbent fabric with a loose pile

terse *adj* **ters•er; ters•est** : concise — **terse•ly** *adv* — **terse•ness** *n*

ter•tia•ry *adj* : of 3d rank, importance, or value

test *n* : examination or evaluation ~ *vb* : examine by a test — **test•er** *n*

tes•ta•ment *n* **1** *cap* : division of the Bible **2** : will — **tes•ta•men•ta•ry** *adj*

tes•ti•cle *n* : testis

tes•ti•fy *vb* **-fied; -fy•ing 1** : give testimony **2** : serve as evi- dence

tes•ti•mo•ni•al *n* **1** : favorable recommendation **2** : tribute — **testimonial** *adj*

tes•ti•mo•ny *n, pl* **-nies** : statement given as evidence in court

tes•tis *n, pl* **-tes** : male reproductive gland

tes•ty *adj* **-ti•er; -est** : easily annoyed

tet•a•nus *n* : bacterial disease producing violent spasms

tête-à-tête *adv* : privately ~ *n* : private conversation ~ *adj* : private

teth•er *n* : leash ~ *vb* : restrain with a leash

text *n* **1** : author's words **2** : main body of printed or written matter on a page **3** : textbook **4** : scriptural passage used as the theme of a sermon **5** : topic — **tex•tu•al** *adj*

text•book *n* : book on a school subject

tex•tile *n* : fabric

tex•ture *n* **1** : feel and appearance of something **2** : structure

than *conj or prep* — used in comparisons

thank *vb* : express gratitude to

thank•ful *adj* : giving thanks — **thank•ful•ly** *adv* — **thank•ful•ness** *n*

thank•less *adj* : not appreciated

thanks *n pl* : expression of gratitude

Thanks•giv•ing *n* : 4th Thursday in November observed as a legal holiday for giving thanks for divine goodness

that *pron, pl* **those 1** : something indicated or understood **2** : the one farther away ~ *adj, pl* **those** : being the one mentioned or understood or farther away ~ *conj or pron* — used to introduce a clause ~ *adv* : to such an extent

thatch *vb* : cover with thatch ~ *n* : covering of matted straw

thaw *vb* : melt or cause to melt — **thaw** *n*

the *definite article* : that particular one ~ *adv* — used before a comparative or superlative

the•ater, the•atre *n* **1** : building or room for viewing a play or movie **2** : dramatic arts

the•at•ri•cal *adj* **1** : relating to the theater **2** : involving exaggerated emotion

thee *pron, archaic objective case of* THOU

theft *n* : act of stealing

their *adj* : relating to them

theirs *pron* : their one or ones

the•ism *n* : belief in the existence of a god or gods — **the•ist** *n or adj* — **the•is•tic** *adj*

them *pron, objective case of* THEY

theme *n* **1** : subject matter **2** : essay **3** : melody developed in a piece of music — **the•mat•ic** *adj*

them•selves *pron pl* : they, them — used reflexively or for emphasis

then *adv* **1** : at that time **2** : soon after that **3** : in addition **4** : in that case **5** : consequently ~ *n* : that time ~ *adj* : existing at that time

thence *adv* : from that place or fact

the•oc•ra•cy *n, pl* **-cies** : government by officials regarded as divinely inspired — **the•o•crat•ic** *adj*

the•ol•o•gy *n, pl* **-gies** : study of religion — **the•o•lo•gian** *n* — **the•o•log•i•cal** *adj*

the•o•rem *n* : provable statement of truth

the•o•ret•i•cal *adj* : relating to or being theory — **the•o•ret•i•cal•ly** *adv*

the•o•rize *vb* **-rized; -riz•ing** : put forth theories — **the•o•rist** *n*

the•o•ry *n, pl* **-ries 1** : general principles of a subject **2** : plausible or scientifically acceptable explanation **3** : judgment, guess, or opinion

ther•a•peu•tic *adj* : offering or relating to remedy — **ther•a•peu•ti•cal•ly** *adv*

ther•a•py *n, pl* **-pies** : treatment for mental or physical disorder — **ther•a•pist** *n*

there *adv* **1** : in, at, or to that place **2** : in that respect ~ *pron* — used to introduce a sentence or clause ~ *n* : that place or point

there•abouts, there•about *adv* : near that place, time, number, or quantity

there•af•ter *adv* : after that

there•by *adv* **1** : by that **2** : connected with or with reference to that

there•fore *adv* : for that reason

there•in *adv* **1** : in or into that place, time, or thing **2** : in that respect

there•of *adv* **1** : of that or it **2** : from that

there•upon *adv* **1** : on that matter **2** : therefore **3** : immediately after that

there•with *adv* : with that

ther•mal *adj* : relating to, caused by, or conserving heat — **ther•mal•ly** *adv*

ther•mo•dy•nam•ics *n* : physics of heat

ther•mom•e•ter *n* : instrument for measuring temperature — **ther•mo•met•ric** *adj* — **ther•mo•met•ri•cal•ly** *adv*

ther•mos *n* : double-walled bottle used to keep liquids hot or cold

ther•mo•stat *n* : automatic temperature control — **ther•mo•stat•ic** *adj* — **ther•mo•stat•i•cal•ly** *adv*

the•sau•rus *n, pl* **-sau•ri** *or* **-sau•rus•es** : book of words and esp. synonyms

these *pl of* THIS

the•sis *n, pl* **the•ses 1** : proposition to be argued for **2** : essay embodying results of original research

thes•pi•an *adj* : dramatic ~ *n* : actor

they *pron* **1** : those ones **2** : people in general

thi•a•mine *n* : essential vitamin

thick *adj* **1** : having relatively great mass from front to back or top to bottom **2** : viscous ~ *n* : most crowded or thickest part — **thick•ly** *adv* — **thick•ness** *n*

thick•en *vb* : make or become thick — **thick•en•er** *n*

thick•et *n* : dense growth of bushes or small trees

thick–skinned *adj* : insensitive to criticism

thief *n, pl* **thieves** : one that steals

thieve *vb* **thieved; thiev•ing** : steal — **thiev•ery** *n*

thigh *n* : upper part of the leg

thigh•bone *n* : femur

thim•ble *n* : protective cap for the finger in sewing — **thim•ble•ful** *n*

thin *adj* **-nn- 1** : having relatively little mass from front to back or top to bottom **2** : not closely set or placed **3** : relatively free flowing **4** : lacking substance, fullness, or strength ~ *vb* **-nn-** : make or become thin — **thin•ly** *adv* — **thin•ness** *n*

thing *n* **1** : matter of concern **2** : event or act **3** : object **4** *pl* : possessions

think *vb* **thought; think•ing 1** : form or have in the mind **2** : have as an opinion **3** : ponder **4** : devise by thinking **5** : imagine — **think•er** *n*

thin–skinned *adj* : extremely sensitive to criticism

third *adj* : being number 3 in a countable series ~ *n* **1** : one that is third **2** : one of 3 equal parts — **third, third•ly** *adv*

third dimension *n* : thickness or depth — **third–dimensional** *adj*

third world *n* : less developed nations of the world

thirst *n* **1** : dryness in mouth and throat **2** : intense desire ~ *vb* : feel thirst — **thirsty** *adj*

thir•teen *n* : one more than 12 — **thirteen** *adj or pron* — **thir•teenth** *adj or n*

thir•ty *n, pl* **thirties** : 3 times 10 — **thir•ti•eth** *adj or n* — **thirty** *adj or pron*

this *pron, pl* **these** : something close or under immediate discussion ~ *adj, pl* **these** : being the one near, present, just mentioned, or more immediately under observation ~ *adv* : to such an extent or degree

this•tle *n* : tall prickly herb

thith•er *adv* : to that place

thong *n* : strip of leather or hide

tho•rax *n, pl* **-rax•es** *or* **-races 1** : part of the body between neck and abdomen **2** : middle of 3 divisions of an insect body — **tho•rac•ic** *adj*

thorn n : sharp spike on a plant or a plant bearing these — **thorny** adj

thor•ough adj : omitting or overlooking nothing — **thor•ough•ly** adv — **thor•ough•ness** n

thor•ough•bred n **1** cap : light speedy racing horse **2** : one of excellent quality — **thorough-bred** adj

thor•ough•fare n : public road

those pl of THAT

thou pron, archaic : you

though adv : however ~ conj **1** : despite the fact that **2** : granting that

thought past of THINK ~ n **1** : process of thinking **2** : serious consideration **3** : idea

thought•ful adj **1** : absorbed in or showing thought **2** : considerate of others — **thought-ful•ly** adv — **thought•ful•ness** n

thought•less adj **1** : careless or reckless **2** : lacking concern for others — **thought•less•ly** adv

thou•sand n, pl **-sands** or **-sand** : 10 times 100 — **thousand** adj — **thou•sandth** adj or n

thrash vb **1** : thresh **2** : beat **3** : move about violently — **thrash•er** n

thread n **1** : fine line of fibers **2** : train of thought **3** : ridge around a screw ~ vb **1** : pass thread through **2** : put together on a thread **3** : make one's way through or between

thread•bare adj **1** : worn so that the thread shows **2** : trite

threat n **1** : expression of intention to harm **2** : thing that threatens

threat•en vb **1** : utter threats **2** : show signs of being near or impending — **threat•en•ing•ly** adv

three n **1** : one more than 2 **2** : 3d in a set or series — **three** adj or pron

three•fold adj : triple — **three•fold** adv

three•score adj : being 3 times 20

thresh vb : beat to separate grain — **thresh•er** n

thresh•old n **1** : sill of a door **2** : beginning stage

threw past of THROW

thrice adv : 3 times

thrift n : careful management or saving of money — **thrift•i•ly** adv — **thrift•less** adj — **thrifty** adj

thrill vb **1** : have or cause to have a sudden sharp feeling of excitement **2** : tremble — **thrill** n — **thrill•er** n — **thrill•ing•ly** adv

thrive vb **throve** or **thrived**; **thriv•en** : grow vigorously **2** : prosper

throat n **1** : front part of the neck **2** : passage to the stomach — **throat•ed** adj — **throaty** adj

throb vb **-bb-** : pulsate — **throb** n

throe n **1** : pang or spasm **2** pl : hard or painful struggle

throne n : chair representing power or sovereignty

throng n or vb : crowd

throt•tle vb **-tled**; **-tling** : choke ~ n : valve regulating volume of fuel and air delivered to engine cylinders

through prep **1** : into at one side and out at the other side of **2** : by way of **3** : among, between, or all around **4** : because of **5** : throughout the time of ~ adv **1** : from one end or side to the other **2** : from beginning to end **3** : to the core **4** : into the open ~ adj **1** : going directly from origin to destination **2** : finished

through•out adv **1** : everywhere **2** : from beginning to end ~ prep **1** : in or to every part of **2** : during the whole of

throve past of THRIVE

throw vb **threw**; **thrown**; **throw•ing 1** : propel through the air **2** : cause to fall or fall off **3** : put suddenly in a certain position or condition **4** : move quickly as if throwing **5** : put on or off hastily — **throw** n — **throw•er** n — **throw up** vb : vomit

thrush n : songbird

thrust vb **thrust**; **thrust•ing 1** : shove forward **2** : stab or pierce — **thrust** n

thud n : dull sound of something falling — **thud** vb

thug n : ruffian or gangster

thumb n **1** : short thick division of the hand opposing the fingers **2** : glove part for the thumb ~ vb : leaf through with the thumb — **thumb•nail** n

thump vb : strike with something thick or heavy causing a dull sound — **thump** n

thun•der n : sound following lightning — **thun-der** vb — **thun•der•clap** n — **thun•der•ous** adj — **thun•der•ous•ly** adv

thun•der•bolt n : discharge of lightning with thunder

thun•der•show•er n : shower with thunder and lightning

thun•der•storm n : storm with thunder and lightning

Thurs•day n : 5th day of the week

thus adv **1** : in this or that way **2** : to this degree or extent **3** : because of this or that

thwart vb : block or defeat

thy adj, archaic : your

thyme n : cooking herb

thy•roid adj : relating to a large endocrine gland (**thyroid gland**)

thy•self pron, archaic : yourself

ti•ara n : decorative formal headband

tib•ia n, pl **-i•ae** : bone between the knee and ankle

tic n : twitching of facial muscles

¹tick n : small 8-legged blood-sucking animal

²tick n **1** : light rhythmic tap or beat **2** : check mark ~ vb **1** : make ticks **2** : mark with a tick **3** : operate

tick•er n **1** : something (as a watch) that ticks **2** : telegraph instrument that prints on paper tape

tick•et n **1** : tag showing price, payment of a fee or fare, or a traffic offense **2** : list of candidates ~ vb : put a ticket on

tick•ing n : fabric covering of a mattress

tick•le vb **-led**; **-ling 1** : please or amuse **2** : touch lightly causing uneasiness, laughter, or spasmodic movements — **tickle** n

tick•lish adj **1** : sensitive to tickling **2** : requiring delicate handling — **tick•lish•ly** adv — **tick-lish•ness** n

tid•al wave n : high sea wave following an earthquake

tid•bit n : choice morsel

tide n : alternate rising and falling of the sea ~ vb **tid•ed**; **tid•ing** : be enough to allow (one) to get by for a time — **tid•al** adj — **tide•wa•ter** n

tid•ings n pl : news or message

ti•dy adj **-di•er**; **-est 1** : well ordered and cared for **2** : large or substantial — **ti•di•ness** n — **tidy** vb

tie n **1** : line or ribbon for fastening, uniting, or closing **2** : cross support to which railroad rails are fastened **3** : uniting force **4** : equality in score or tally or a deadlocked contest **5** : necktie ~ vb **tied**; **ty•ing** or **tie•ing 1** : fasten or close by wrapping and knotting a tie **2** : form a knot in **3** : gain the same score or tally as an opponent

tier n : one of a steplike series of rows

tiff n : petty quarrel — **tiff** vb

ti•ger n : very large black-striped cat — **ti•ger•ish** adj — **ti•gress** n

tight adj **1** : fitting close together esp. so as not to allow air or water in **2** : held very firmly **3** : taut **4** : fitting too snugly **5** : difficult **6** : stingy **7** : evenly contested **8** : low in supply — **tight** adv — **tight•en** vb — **tight•ly** adv — **tight•ness** n

tights n pl : skintight garments

tight•wad n : stingy person

tile n : thin piece of stone or fired clay used on roofs, floors, or walls ~ vb : cover with tiles

¹till prep or conj : until

²till vb : cultivate (soil) — **till•able** adj

³till n : money drawer

¹till•er n : one that cultivates soil

²til•ler n : lever for turning a boat's rudder

tilt vb : cause to incline ~ n : slant

tim•ber n **1** : cut wood for building **2** : large squared piece of wood **3** : wooded land or trees for timber ~ vb : cover, frame, or support with timbers — **tim•bered** adj — **tim•ber•land** n

tim•bre n : sound quality

time n **1** : period during which something exists or continues or can be accomplished **2** : point at which something happens **3** : customary hour **4** : age **5** : tempo **6** : moment, hour, day, or year as indicated by a clock or calendar **7** : one's experience during a particular period ~ vb **timed**; **tim•ing 1** : arrange or set the time of **2** : determine or record the time, duration, or rate of — **time•keep•er** n — **time•less** adj — **time-less•ness** n — **time•li•ness** n — **time•ly** adv — **tim•er** n

time•piece n : device to show time

times prep : multiplied by

time•ta•ble n : table of departure and arrival times

tim•id adj : lacking in courage or self-confidence — **ti•mid•i•ty** n — **tim•id•ly** adv

tim•o•rous adj : fearful — **tim•o•rous•ly** adv — **tim•o•rous•ness** n

tim•pa•ni n pl : set of kettledrums — **tim•pa•nist** n

tin n **1** : soft white metallic chemical element **2** : metal food can

tinc•ture n : alcoholic solution of a medicine

tin•der n : substance used to kindle a fire

tine n : one of the points of a fork

tin•foil n : thin metal sheeting

tinge vb **tinged**; **tinge•ing** or **ting•ing 1** : color slightly **2** : affect with a slight odor ~ n : slight coloring or flavor

tin•gle vb **-gled**; **-gling** : feel a ringing, stinging, or thrilling sensation — **tingle** n

tin•ker vb : experiment in repairing something — **tin•ker•er** n

tin•kle vb **-kled**; **-kling** : make or cause to make a high ringing sound — **tinkle** n

tin•sel n : decorative thread or strip of glittering metal or paper

tint n **1** : slight or pale coloration **2** : color shade ~ vb : give a tint to

ti•ny adj **-ni•er**; **-est** : very small

¹tip vb **-pp- 1** : overturn **2** : lean ~ n : act or state of tipping

²tip n : pointed end of something ~ vb **-pp- 1** : furnish with a tip **2** : cover the tip of

³tip n : small sum given for a service performed ~ vb : give a tip to

⁴tip n : piece of confidential information ~ vb **-pp-** : give confidential information to

tip–off n : indication

tip•ple vb **-pled**; **-pling** : drink intoxicating liquor esp. habitually or excessively — **tip•pler** n

tip•sy adj **-si•er**; **-est** : unsteady or foolish from alcohol

tip•toe n : the toes of the feet ~ adv or adj : supported on tiptoe ~ vb **-toed**; **-toe•ing** : walk quietly or on tiptoe

tip–top n : highest point ~ adj : excellent

ti•rade n : prolonged speech of abuse

¹tire vb **tired**; **tir•ing 1** : make or become weary **2** : wear out the patience of — **tire•less** adj — **tire•less•ly** adv — **tire•less•ness** n — **tire-some** adj — **tire•some•ly** adv — **tire•some-ness** n

²tire n : rubber cushion encircling a car wheel

tired adj : weary

tis•sue n **1** : soft absorbent paper **2** : layer of cells forming a basic structural element of an animal or plant body

ti•tan•ic *adj* : gigantic

ti•ta•ni•um *n* : gray light strong metallic chemical element

tithe *n* : tenth part paid or given esp. for the support of a church — **tithe** *vb* — **tith•er** *n*

tit•il•late *vb* **-lat•ed; -lat•ing** : excite pleasurably — **tit•il•la•tion** *n*

ti•tle *n* 1 : legal ownership 2 : distinguishing name 3 : designation of honor, rank, or office 4 : championship — **ti•tled** *adj*

tit•ter *n* : nervous or affected laugh — **titter** *vb*

tit•u•lar *adj* 1 : existing in title only 2 : relating to or bearing a title

tiz•zy *n, pl* **tizzies** : state of agitation or worry

TNT *n* : high explosive

to *prep* 1 : in the direction of 2 : at, on, or near 3 : resulting in 4 : before or until 5 — used to show a relationship or object of a verb 6 — used with an infinitive ~ *adv* 1 : forward 2 : to a state of consciousness

toad *n* : tailless leaping amphibian

toad•stool *n* : mushroom esp. when inedible or poisonous

toady *n, pl* **toad•ies** : one who flatters to gain favors — **toady** *vb*

toast *vb* 1 : make (as a slice of bread) crisp and brown 2 : drink in honor of someone or something 3 : warm ~ *n* 1 : toasted sliced bread 2 : act of drinking in honor of someone — **toast•er** *n*

to•bac•co *n, pl* **-cos** : broad-leaved herb or its leaves prepared for smoking or chewing

to•bog•gan *n* : long flat-bottomed light sled ~ *vb* : coast on a toboggan

to•day *adv* 1 : on or for this day 2 : at the present time ~ *n* : present day or time

tod•dle *vb* **-dled; -dling** : walk with tottering steps like a young child — **toddle** *n* — **tod•dler** *n*

to–do *n, pl* **to–dos** : disturbance or fuss

toe *n* : one of the 5 end divisions of the foot — **toe•nail** *n*

tof•fee, tof•fy *n, pl* **toffees** *or* **toffies** : candy made of boiled sugar and butter

to•ga *n* : loose outer garment of ancient Rome

to•geth•er *adv* 1 : in or into one place or group 2 : in or into contact or association 3 : at one time 4 : as a group — **to•geth•er•ness** *n*

togs *n pl* : clothing

toil *vb* : work hard and long — **toil** *n* — **toil•er** *n* — **toil•some** *adj*

toi•let *n* 1 : dressing and grooming oneself 2 : bathroom 3 : water basin to urinate and defecate in

to•ken *n* 1 : outward sign or expression of something 2 : small part representing the whole 3 : piece resembling a coin

told *past of* TELL

tol•er•a•ble *adj* 1 : capable of being endured 2 : moderately good — **tol•er•a•bly** *adv*

tol•er•ance *n* 1 : lack of opposition for beliefs or practices differing from one's own 2 : capacity for enduring 3 : allowable deviation — **tol•er•ant** *adj* — **tol•er•ant•ly** *adv*

tol•er•ate *vb* **-at•ed; -at•ing** 1 : allow to be or to be done without opposition 2 : endure or resist the action of — **tol•er•a•tion** *n*

¹toll *n* 1 : fee paid for a privilege or service 2 : cost of achievement in loss or suffering — **toll•booth** *n* — **toll•gate** *n*

²toll *vb* 1 : cause the sounding of (a bell) 2 : sound with slow measured strokes ~ *n* : sound of a tolling bell

tom•a•hawk *n* : light ax used as a weapon by American Indians

to•ma•to *n, pl* **-toes** : tropical American herb or its fruit

tomb *n* : house, vault, or grave for burial

tom•boy *n* : girl who behaves in a manner usu. considered boyish

tomb•stone *n* : stone marking a grave

tom•cat *n* : male cat

tome *n* : large or weighty book

to•mor•row *adv* : on or for the day after today — **tomorrow** *n*

tom–tom *n* : small-headed drum beaten with the hands

ton *n* : unit of weight equal to 2000 pounds

tone *n* 1 : vocal or musical sound 2 : sound of definite pitch 3 : manner of speaking that expresses an emotion or attitude 4 : color quality 5 : healthy condition 6 : general character or quality ~ *vb* : soften or muffle — often used with *down* — **ton•al** *adj* — **to•nal•i•ty** *n*

tongs *n pl* : grasping device of 2 joined or hinged pieces

tongue *n* 1 : fleshy movable organ of the mouth 2 : language 3 : something long and flat and fastened at one end — **tongued** *adj* — **tongue•less** *adj*

ton•ic *n* : something (as a drug) that invigorates or restores health — **tonic** *adj*

to•night *adv* : on this night ~ *n* : present or coming night

ton•sil *n* : either of a pair of oval masses in the throat — **ton•sil•lec•to•my** *n* — **ton•sil•li•tis** *n*

too *adv* 1 : in addition 2 : excessively

took *past of* TAKE

tool *n* : device worked by hand ~ *vb* : shape or finish with a tool

toot *vb* : sound or cause to sound esp. in short blasts — **toot** *n*

tooth *n, pl* **teeth** 1 : one of the hard structures in the jaws for chewing 2 : one of the projections on the edge of a gear wheel — **tooth•ache** *n* — **tooth•brush** *n* — **toothed** *adj* — **tooth•less** *adj* — **tooth•paste** *n* — **tooth•pick** *n*

tooth•some *adj* 1 : delicious 2 : attractive

¹top *n* 1 : highest part or level of something 2 : lid or covering ~ *vb* **-pp-** 1 : cover with a top 2 : surpass 3 : go over the top of ~ *adj* : being at the top — **topped** *adj*

²top *n* : spinning toy

to•paz *n* : hard gem

top•coat *n* : lightweight overcoat

top•ic *n* : subject for discussion or study

top•i•cal *adj* 1 : relating to or arranged by topics 2 : relating to current or local events — **top•i•cal•ly** *adv*

top•most *adj* : highest of all

top–notch *adj* : of the highest quality

to•pog•ra•phy *n* 1 : art of mapping the physical features of a place 2 : outline of the form of a place — **to•pog•ra•pher** *n* — **top•o•graph•ic** *adj* — **top•o•graph•i•cal** *adj*

top•ple *vb* **-pled; -pling** : fall or cause to fall

top•sy–tur•vy *adv or adj* 1 : upside down 2 : in utter confusion

torch *n* : flaming light — **torch•bear•er** *n* — **torch•light** *n*

tore *past of* TEAR

tor•ment *n* : extreme pain or anguish or a source of this ~ *vb* 1 : cause severe anguish to 2 : harass — **tor•men•tor** *n*

torn *past part of* TEAR

tor•na•do *n, pl* **-does** *or* **-dos** : violent destructive whirling wind

tor•pe•do *n, pl* **-does** : self-propelled explosive submarine missile ~ *vb* : hit with a torpedo

tor•pid *adj* 1 : having lost motion or the power of exertion 2 : lacking vigor — **tor•pid•i•ty** *n*

tor•por *n* : extreme sluggishness or lethargy

torque *n* : turning force

tor•rent *n* 1 : rushing stream 2 : tumultuous outburst — **tor•ren•tial** *adj*

tor•rid *adj* 1 : parched with heat 2 : impassioned

tor•sion *n* : a twisting or being twisted — **tor•sion•al** *adj* — **tor•sion•al•ly** *adv*

tor•so *n, pl* **-sos** *or* **-si** : trunk of the human body

tor•ti•lla *n* : round flat cornmeal or wheat flour bread

tor•toise *n* : land turtle

tor•tu•ous *adj* 1 : winding 2 : tricky

tor•ture *n* 1 : use of pain to punish or force 2 : agony ~ *vb* **-tured; -tur•ing** : inflict torture on — **tor•tur•er** *n*

toss *vb* 1 : move to and fro or up and down violently 2 : throw with a quick light motion 3 : move restlessly — **toss** *n*

toss–up *n* 1 : a deciding by flipping a coin 2 : even chance

tot *n* : small child

to•tal *n* : entire amount ~ *vb* **-taled** *or* **-talled; -tal•ing** *or* **-tal•ling** 1 : add up 2 : amount to — **total** *adj* — **to•tal•ly** *adv*

to•tal•i•tar•i•an *adj* : relating to a political system in which the government has complete control over the people — **totalitarian** *n* — **to•tal•i•tar•i•an•ism** *n*

to•tal•i•ty *n, pl* **-ties** : whole amount or entirety

tote *vb* **tot•ed; tot•ing** : carry

to•tem *n* : often carved figure used as a family or tribe emblem

tot•ter *vb* 1 : sway as if about to fall 2 : stagger

touch *vb* 1 : make contact with so as to feel 2 : be or cause to be in contact 3 : take into the hands or mouth 4 : treat or mention a subject 5 : relate or concern 6 : move to sympathetic feeling ~ *n* 1 : light stroke 2 : act or fact of touching or being touched 3 : sense of feeling 4 : trace 5 : state of being in contact — **touch up** *vb* : improve with minor changes

touch•down *n* : scoring of 6 points in football

touch•stone *n* : test or criterion of genuineness or quality

touchy *adj* **touch•i•er; -est** 1 : easily offended 2 : requiring tact

tough *adj* 1 : strong but elastic 2 : not easily chewed 3 : severe or disciplined 4 : stubborn ~ *n* : rowdy — **tough•ly** *adv* — **tough•ness** *n*

tough•en *vb* : make or become tough

tou•pee *n* : small wig for a bald spot

tour *n* 1 : period of time spent at work or on an assignment 2 : journey with a return to the starting point ~ *vb* : travel over to see the sights — **tour•ist** *n*

tour•na•ment *n* 1 : medieval jousting competition 2 : championship series of games

tour•ney *n, pl* **-neys** : tournament

tour•ni•quet *n* : tight bandage for stopping blood flow

tou•sle *vb* **-sled; -sling** : dishevel (as someone's hair)

tout *vb* : praise or publicize loudly

tow *vb* : pull along behind — **tow** *n*

to•ward, to•wards *prep* 1 : in the direction of 2 : with respect to 3 : in part payment on

tow•el *n* : absorbent cloth or paper for wiping or drying

tow•er *n* : tall structure ~ *vb* : rise to a great height — **tow•ered** *adj* — **tow•er•ing** *adj*

tow•head *n* : person having whitish blond hair — **tow•head•ed** *adj*

town *n* 1 : small residential area 2 : city — **towns•peo•ple** *n pl*

town•ship *n* 1 : unit of local government 2 : 36 square miles of U.S. public land

tox•ic *adj* : poisonous — **tox•ic•i•ty** *n*

tox•in *n* : poison produced by an organism

toy *n* : something for a child to play with ~ *vb* : amuse oneself or play with something ~ *adj* 1 : designed as a toy 2 : very small

¹trace *vb* **traced; trac•ing** 1 : mark over the lines of (a drawing) **2** : follow the trail or the development of ~ *n* **1** : track **2** : tiny amount or residue — **trace•able** *adj* — **trac•er** *n*

²**trace** *n* : line of a harness

tra•chea *n, pl* **-che•ae** : windpipe — **tra•che•al** *adj*

track *n* **1** : trail left by wheels or footprints **2** : racing course **3** : train rails **4** : awareness of a progression **5** : looped belts propelling a vehicle ~ *vb* **1** : follow the trail of **2** : make tracks on — **track•er** *n*

track–and–field *adj* : relating to athletic contests of running, jumping, and throwing events

¹**tract** *n* **1** : stretch of land **2** : system of body organs

²**tract** *n* : pamphlet of propaganda

trac•ta•ble *adj* : easily controlled

trac•tion *n* : gripping power to permit movement — **trac•tion•al** *adj* — **trac•tive** *adj*

trac•tor *n* **1** : farm vehicle used esp. for pulling **2** : truck for hauling a trailer

trade *n* **1** : one's regular business **2** : occupation requiring skill **3** : the buying and selling of goods **4** : act of trading ~ *vb* **trad•ed; trad•ing 1** : give in exchange for something **2** : buy and sell goods **3** : be a regular customer — **trades•peo•ple** *n pl*

trade-in *n* : an item traded to a merchant at the time of a purchase

trade•mark *n* : word or mark identifying a manufacturer — **trademark** *vb*

trades•man *n* : shopkeeper

tra•di•tion *n* : belief or custom passed from generation to generation — **tra•di•tion•al** *adj* — **tra•di•tion•al•ly** *adv*

tra•duce *vb* **-duced; -duc•ing** : lower the reputation of — **tra•duc•er** *n*

traf•fic *n* **1** : business dealings **2** : movement along a route ~ *vb* : do business — **traf•fick•er** *n* — **traffic light** *n*

trag•e•dy *n, pl* **-dies 1** : serious drama describing a conflict and having a sad end **2** : disastrous event

trag•ic *adj* : being a tragedy — **trag•i•cal•ly** *adv*

trail *vb* **1** : hang down and drag along the ground **2** : draw along behind **3** : follow the track of **4** : dwindle ~ *n* **1** : something that trails **2** : path or evidence left by something

trail•er *n* **1** : vehicle intended to be hauled **2** : dwelling designed to be towed to a site

train *n* **1** : trailing part of a gown **2** : retinue or procession **3** : connected series **4** : group of linked railroad cars ~ *vb* **1** : cause to grow as desired **2** : make or become prepared or skilled **3** : point — **train•ee** *n* — **train•er** *n* — **train•load** *n*

traipse *vb* **traipsed; traips•ing** : walk

trait *n* : distinguishing quality

trai•tor *n* : one who betrays a trust or commits treason — **trai•tor•ous** *adj*

tra•jec•to•ry *n, pl* **-ries** : path of something moving through air or space

tram•mel *vb* **-meled** *or* **-melled; -mel•ing** *or* **-mel•ling** : impede — **trammel** *n*

tramp *vb* **1** : walk or hike **2** : tread on ~ *n* : beggar or vagrant

tram•ple *vb* **-pled; -pling** : walk or step on so as to bruise or crush — **trample** *n* — **tram•pler** *n*

tram•po•line *n* : resilient sheet or web supported by springs and used for bouncing — **tram•po•lin•ist** *n*

trance *n* **1** : sleeplike condition **2** : state of mystical absorption

tran•quil *adj* : quiet and undisturbed — **tran•quil•ize** *vb* — **tran•quil•iz•er** *n* — **tran•quil•li•ty** *or* **tran•quil•i•ty** *n* — **tran•quil•ly** *adv*

trans•act *vb* : conduct (business)

trans•ac•tion *n* **1** : business deal **2** *pl* : records of proceedings

tran•scend *vb* : rise above or surpass — **tran•scen•dent** *adj* — **tran•scen•den•tal** *adj*

tran•scribe *vb* **-scribed; -scrib•ing** : make a copy, arrangement, or recording of — **tran•scrip•tion** *n*

tran•script *n* : official copy

tran•sept *n* : part of a church that crosses the nave at right angles

trans•fer *vb* **-rr- 1** : move from one person, place, or situation to another **2** : convey ownership of **3** : print or copy by contact **4** : change to another vehicle or transportation line ~ *n* **1** : act or process of transferring **2** : one that transfers or is transferred **3** : ticket permitting one to transfer — **trans•fer•able** *adj* — **trans•fer•al** *n* — **trans•fer•ence** *n*

trans•fig•ure *vb* **-ured; -ur•ing 1** : change the form or appearance of **2** : glorify — **trans•fig•u•ra•tion** *n*

trans•fix *vb* **1** : pierce through **2** : hold motionless

trans•form *vb* **1** : change in structure, appearance, or character **2** : change (an electric current) in potential or type — **trans•for•ma•tion** *n* — **trans•form•er** *n*

trans•fuse *vb* **-fused; -fus•ing 1** : diffuse into or through **2** : transfer (as blood) into a vein — **trans•fu•sion** *n*

trans•gress *vb* : sin — **trans•gres•sion** *n* — **trans•gres•sor** *n*

tran•sient *adj* : not lasting or staying long — **transient** *n* — **tran•sient•ly** *adv*

tran•sis•tor *n* : small electronic device used in electronic equipment — **tran•sis•tor•ize** *vb*

tran•sit *n* **1** : movement over, across, or through **2** : local and esp. public transportation **3** : surveyor's instrument

tran•si•tion *n* : passage from one state, stage, or subject to another — **tran•si•tion•al** *adj*

tran•si•to•ry *adj* : of brief duration

trans•late *vb* **-lat•ed; -lat•ing** : change into another language — **trans•lat•able** *adj* — **trans•la•tion** *n* — **trans•la•tor** *n*

trans•lu•cent *adj* : not transparent but clear enough to allow light to pass through — **trans•lu•cence** *n* — **trans•lu•cen•cy** *n* — **trans•lu•cent•ly** *adv*

trans•mis•sion *n* **1** : act or process of transmitting **2** : system of gears between a car engine and drive wheels

trans•mit *vb* **-tt- 1** : transfer from one person or place to another **2** : pass on by inheritance **3** : broadcast — **trans•mis•si•ble** *adj* — **trans•mit•ta•ble** *adj* — **trans•mit•tal** *n* — **trans•mit•ter** *n*

tran•som *n* : often hinged window above a door

trans•par•ent *adj* **1** : clear enough to see through **2** : obvious — **trans•par•en•cy** *n* — **trans•par•ent•ly** *adv*

tran•spire *vb* **-spired; -spir•ing** : take place — **tran•spi•ra•tion** *n*

trans•plant *vb* **1** : dig up and move to another place **2** : transfer from one body part or person to another — **transplant** *n* — **trans•plan•ta•tion** *n*

trans•port *vb* **1** : carry or deliver to another place **2** : carry away by emotion ~ *n* **1** : act of transporting **2** : rapture **3** : ship or plane for carrying troops or supplies — **trans•por•ta•tion** *n* — **trans•port•er** *n*

trans•pose *vb* **-posed; -pos•ing** : change the position, sequence, or key — **trans•po•si•tion** *n*

trans•ship *vb* : transfer from one mode of transportation to another — **trans•ship•ment** *n*

trans•verse *adj* : lying across — **trans•verse** *n* — **trans•verse•ly** *adv*

trap *n* **1** : device for catching animals **2** : something by which one is caught unawares **3** : device

to allow one thing to pass through while keeping other things out ~ *vb* **-pp-** : catch in a trap — **trap•per** *n*

trap•door *n* : door in a floor or roof

tra•peze *n* : suspended bar used by acrobats

trap•e•zoid *n* : plane 4-sided figure with 2 parallel sides — **trap•e•zoi•dal** *adj*

trap•pings *n pl* **1** : ornamental covering **2** : outward decoration or dress

trash *n* : something that is no good — **trashy** *adj*

trau•ma *n* : bodily or mental injury — **trau•mat•ic** *adj*

tra•vail *n* : painful work or exertion ~ *vb* : labor hard

trav•el *vb* **-eled** *or* **-elled; -el•ing** *or* **-el•ling 1** : take a trip or tour **2** : move or be carried from point to point ~ *n* : journey — often pl. — **trav•el•er, trav•el•ler** *n*

tra•verse *vb* **-versed; -vers•ing** : go or extend across — **traverse** *n*

trav•es•ty *n, pl* **-ties** : imitation that makes crude fun of something — **travesty** *vb*

trawl *vb* : fish or catch with a trawl ~ *n* : large cone-shaped net — **trawl•er** *n*

tray *n* : shallow flat-bottomed receptacle for holding or carrying something

treach•er•ous *adj* : disloyal or dangerous — **treach•er•ous•ly** *adv*

treach•ery *n, pl* **-er•ies** : betrayal of a trust

tread *vb* **trod; trod•den** *or* **trod; tread•ing 1** : step on or over **2** : walk **3** : press or crush with the feet ~ *n* **1** : way of walking **2** : sound made in walking **3** : part on which a thing runs

trea•dle *n* : foot pedal operating a machine — **treadle** *vb*

tread•mill *n* **1** : mill worked by walking persons or animals **2** : wearisome routine

trea•son *n* : attempt to overthrow the government — **trea•son•able** *adj* — **trea•son•ous** *adj*

trea•sure *n* **1** : wealth stored up **2** : something of great value ~ *vb* **-sured; -sur•ing** : keep as precious

trea•sur•er *n* : officer who handles funds

trea•sury *n, pl* **-sur•ies** : place or office for keeping and distributing funds

treat *vb* **1** : have as a topic **2** : pay for the food or entertainment of **3** : act toward or regard in a certain way **4** : give medical care to ~ *n* **1** : food or entertainment paid for by another **2** : something special and enjoyable — **treat•ment** *n*

trea•tise *n* : systematic written exposition or argument

trea•ty *n, pl* **-ties** : agreement between governments

tre•ble *n* **1** : highest part in music **2** : upper half of the musical range ~ *adj* : triple in number or amount ~ *vb* **-bled; -bling** : make triple — **tre•bly** *adv*

tree *n* : tall woody plant ~ *vb* **treed; tree•ing** : force up a tree — **tree•less** *adj*

trek *n* : difficult trip ~ *vb* **-kk-** : make a trek

trel•lis *n* : structure of crossed strips

trem•ble *vb* **-bled; -bling 1** : shake from fear or cold **2** : move or sound as if shaken

tre•men•dous *adj* : amazingly large, powerful, or excellent — **tre•men•dous•ly** *adv*

trem•or *n* : a trembling

trem•u•lous *adj* : trembling or quaking

trench *n* : long narrow cut in land

tren•chant *adj* : sharply perceptive

trend *n* : prevailing tendency, direction, or style ~ *vb* : move in a particular direction — **trendy** *adj*

trep•i•da•tion *n* : nervous apprehension

tres•pass *n* **1** : sin **2** : unauthorized entry onto someone's property ~ *vb* **1** : sin **2** : enter illegally — **tres•pass•er** *n*

tress *n* : long lock of hair

tres•tle *n* **1** : support with a horizontal piece and spreading legs **2** : framework bridge

tri•ad *n* : union of 3

tri•age *n* : system of dealing with cases (as patients) according to priority guidelines intended to maximize success

tri•al *n* **1** : hearing and judgment of a matter in court **2** : source of great annoyance **3** : test use or experimental effort — **trial** *adj*

tri•an•gle *n* : plane figure with 3 sides and 3 angles — **tri•an•gu•lar** *adj*

tribe *n* : social group of numerous families — **trib•al** *adj* — **tribes•man** *n*

trib•u•la•tion *n* : suffering from oppression

tri•bu•nal *n* **1** : court **2** : something that decides

trib•u•tary *n, pl* **-tar•ies** : stream that flows into a river or lake

trib•ute *n* **1** : payment to acknowledge submission **2** : tax **3** : gift or act showing respect

trick *n* **1** : scheme to deceive **2** : prank **3** : deceptive or ingenious feat **4** : mannerism **5** : knack **6** : tour of duty ~ *vb* : deceive by cunning — **trick•ery** *n* — **trick•ster** *n*

trick•le *vb* **-led; -ling** : run in drops or a thin stream — **trickle** *n*

tricky *adj* **trick•i•er; -est 1** : inclined to trickery **2** : requiring skill or caution

tri•cy•cle *n* : 3-wheeled bicycle

tri•dent *n* : 3-pronged spear

tri•en•ni•al *adj* : lasting, occurring, or done every 3 years — **triennial** *n*

tri•fle *n* : something of little value or importance ~ *vb* **-fled; -fling 1** : speak or act in a playful or flirting way **2** : toy — **tri•fler** *n*

tri•fling *adj* : trivial

trig•ger *n* : finger-piece of a firearm lock that fires the gun — *vb* : set into motion — **trigger** *adj* — **trig•gered** *adj*

trig•o•nom•e•try *n* : mathematics dealing with triangular measurement — **trig•o•no•met•ric** *adj*

trill *n* **1** : rapid alternation between 2 adjacent tones **2** : rapid vibration in speaking ~ *vb* : utter in or with a trill

tril•lion *n* : 1000 billions — **trillion** *adj* — **tril•lionth** *adj or n*

tril•o•gy *n, pl* **-gies** : 3-part literary or musical composition

trim *vb* **-mm- 1** : decorate **2** : make neat or reduce by cutting ~ *adj* **-mm-** : neat and compact ~ *n* **1** : state or condition **2** : ornaments — **trim•ly** *adv* — **trim•mer** *n*

trim•ming *n* : something that ornaments or completes

Trin•i•ty *n* : divine unity of Father, Son, and Holy Spirit

trin•ket *n* : small ornament

trio *n, pl* **tri•os 1** : music for 3 performers **2** : group of 3

trip *vb* **-pp- 1** : step lightly **2** : stumble or cause to stumble **3** : make or cause to make a mistake **4** : release (as a spring or switch) ~ *n* **1** : journey **2** : stumble **3** : drug-induced experience

tri•par•tite *adj* : having 3 parts or parties

tripe *n* **1** : animal's stomach used as food **2** : trash

tri•ple *vb* **-pled; -pling** : make 3 times as great ~ *n* : group of 3 ~ *adj* **1** : having 3 units **2** : being 3 times as great or as many

trip•let *n* **1** : group of 3 **2** : one of 3 offspring born together

trip•li•cate *adj* : made in 3 identical copies ~ *n* : one of 3 copies

tri•pod *n* : a stand with 3 legs — **tripod, tri•po•dal** *adj*

tri•sect *vb* : divide into 3 usu. equal parts — **tri•sec•tion** *n*

trite *adj* **trit•er; trit•est** : commonplace

tri•umph *n, pl* **-umphs** : victory or great suc-

cess ~ *vb* : obtain or celebrate victory — **tri•um•phal** *adj* — **tri•um•phant** *adj* — **tri•um•phant•ly** *adv*

tri•um•vi•rate *n* : ruling body of 3 persons

triv•et *n* **1** : 3 legged stand **2** : stand to hold a hot dish

triv•ia *n sing or pl* : unimportant details

triv•i•al *adj* : of little importance — **triv•i•al•i•ty** *n*

trod *past of* TREAD

trod•den *past part of* TREAD

troll *n* : dwarf or giant of folklore inhabiting caves or hills

trol•ley *n, pl* **-leys** : streetcar run by overhead electric wires

trol•lop *n* : untidy or immoral woman

trom•bone *n* : musical instrument with a long sliding tube — **trom•bon•ist** *n*

troop *n* **1** : cavalry unit **2** *pl* : soldiers **3** : collection of people or things ~ *vb* : move or gather in crowds

troop•er *n* **1** : cavalry soldier **2** : police officer on horseback or state police officer

tro•phy *n, pl* **-phies** : prize gained by a victory

trop•ic *n* **1** : either of the 2 parallels of latitude one 23½ degrees north of the equator (**tropic of Cancer**) and one 23½ degrees south of the equator (**tropic of Cap•ri•corn**) **2** *pl* : region lying between the tropics — **tropic, trop•i•cal** *adj*

trot *n* : moderately fast gait esp. of a horse with diagonally paired legs moving together ~ *vb* **-tt-** : go at a trot — **trot•ter** *n*

troth *n* **1** : pledged faithfulness **2** : betrothal

trou•ba•dour *n* : medieval lyric poet

trou•ble *vb* **-bled; -bling 1** : disturb **2** : afflict **3** : make an effort ~ *n* **1** : cause of mental or physical distress **2** : effort — **trou•ble•mak•er** *n* — **trou•ble•some** *adj* — **trou•ble•some•ly** *adv*

trough *n, pl* **troughs 1** : narrow container for animal feed or water **2** : long channel or depression (as between waves)

trounce *vb* **trounced; trounc•ing** : thrash, punish, or defeat severely

troupe *n* : group of stage performers — **troup•er** *n*

trou•sers *n pl* : long pants — **trouser** *adj*

trous•seau *n, pl* **-seaux** *or* **-seaus** : bride's collection of clothing and personal items

trout *n, pl* **trout** : freshwater food and game fish

trow•el *n* **1** : tool for spreading or smoothing **2** : garden scoop — **trowel** *vb*

troy *n* : system of weights based on a pound of 12 ounces

tru•ant *n* : student absent from school without permission — **tru•an•cy** *n* — **truant** *adj*

truce *n* : agreement to halt fighting

truck *n* **1** : wheeled frame for moving heavy objects **2** : automotive vehicle for transporting heavy loads ~ *vb* : transport on a truck — **truck•er** *n* — **truck•load** *n*

truck•le *vb* **-led; -ling** : yield slavishly to another

tru•cu•lent *adj* : aggressively self-assertive — **truc•u•lence** *n* — **truc•u•len•cy** *n* — **tru•cu•lent•ly** *adv*

trudge *vb* **trudged; trudg•ing** : walk or march steadily and with difficulty

true *adj* **tru•er; tru•est 1** : loyal **2** : in agreement with fact or reality **3** : genuine ~ *adv* **1** : truthfully **2** : accurately ~ *vb* **trued; tru•ing** : make balanced or even — **tru•ly** *adv*

true–blue *adj* : loyal

truf•fle *n* **1** : edible fruit of an underground fungus **2** : ball-shaped chocolate candy

tru•ism *n* : obvious truth

trump *n* : card of a designated suit any of whose cards will win over other cards ~ *vb* : take with a trump

trumped–up *adj* : made-up

trum•pet *n* : tubular brass wind instrument with a flaring end ~ *vb* **1** : blow a trumpet **2** : proclaim loudly — **trum•pet•er** *n*

trun•cate *vb* **-cat•ed; -cat•ing** : cut short — **trun•ca•tion** *n*

trun•dle *vb* **-dled; -dling** : roll along

trunk *n* **1** : main part (as of a body or tree) **2** : long muscular nose of an elephant **3** : storage chest **4** : storage space in a car **5** *pl* : shorts

truss *vb* : bind tightly ~ *n* **1** : set of structural parts forming a framework **2** : appliance worn to hold a hernia in place

trust *n* **1** : reliance on another **2** : assured hope **3** : credit **4** : property held or managed in behalf of another **5** : combination of firms that reduces competition **6** : something entrusted to another's care **7** : custody ~ *vb* **1** : depend **2** : hope **3** : entrust **4** : have faith in — **trust•ful** *adj* — **trust•ful•ly** *adv* — **trust•ful•ness** *n* — **trust•worth•i•ness** *n* — **trust•wor•thy** *adj*

trust•ee *n* : person holding property in trust — **trust•ee•ship** *n*

trusty *adj* **trust•i•er; -est** : dependable

truth *n, pl* **truths 1** : real state of things **2** : true or accepted statement **3** : agreement with fact or reality — **truth•ful** *adj* — **truth•ful•ly** *adv* — **truth•ful•ness** *n*

try *vb* **tried; try•ing 1** : conduct the trial of **2** : put to a test **3** : strain **4** : make an effort at ~ *n, pl* **tries** : act of trying

try•out *n* : competitive test of performance esp. for athletes or actors — **try out** *vb*

tryst *n* : secret rendezvous of lovers

tsar *var of* CZAR

T–shirt *n* : collarless pullover shirt with short sleeves

tub *n* **1** : wide bucketlike vessel **2** : bathtub

tu•ba *n* : large low-pitched brass wind instument

tube *n* **1** : hollow cylinder **2** : round container from which a substance can be squeezed **3** : airtight circular tube of rubber inside a tire **4** : electronic device consisting of a sealed usu. glass container with electrodes inside — **tubed** *adj* — **tube•less** *adj*

tu•ber *n* : fleshy underground growth (as of a potato) — **tu•ber•ous** *adj*

tu•ber•cu•lo•sis *n, pl* **-lo•ses** : bacterial disease esp. of the lungs — **tu•ber•cu•lar** *adj* — **tu•ber•cu•lous** *adj*

tub•ing *n* : series or arrangement of tubes

tu•bu•lar *adj* : of or like a tube

tuck *vb* **1** : pull up into a fold **2** : put into a snug often concealing place **3** : make snug in bed — with *in* ~ *n* : fold in a cloth

tuck•er *vb* : fatigue

Tues•day *n* : 3d day of the week

tuft *n* : clump (as of hair or feathers) — **tuft•ed** *adj*

tug *vb* **-gg- 1** : pull hard **2** : move by pulling ~ *n* **1** : act of tugging **2** : tugboat

tug•boat *n* : boat for towing or pushing ships through a harbor

tug–of–war *n, pl* **tugs–of–war** : pulling contest between 2 teams

tu•ition *n* : cost of instruction

tu•lip *n* : herb with cup-shaped flowers

tum•ble *vb* **-bled; -bling 1** : perform gymnastic feats of rolling and turning **2** : fall or cause to fall suddenly **3** : toss ~ *n* : act of tumbling

tum•bler *n* **1** : acrobat **2** : drinking glass **3** : obstruction in a lock that can be moved (as by a key)

tu•mid *adj* : turgid

tum•my *n, pl* **-mies** : belly

tu•mor *n* : abnormal and useless growth of tissue — **tu•mor•ous** *adj*

tu•mult *n* **1** : uproar **2** : violent agitation of mind or feelings — **tu•mul•tu•ous** *adj*

tun *n* : large cask

tu•na *n, pl* **-na** *or* **-nas** : large sea food fish

tun•dra *n* : treeless arctic plain

tune *n* 1 : melody 2 : correct musical pitch 3 : harmonious relationship ~ *vb* **tuned; tun•ing** 1 : bring or come into harmony 2 : adjust in musical pitch 3 : adjust a receiver so as to receive a broadcast 4 : put in first-class working order — **tun•able** *adj* — **tune•ful** *adj* — **tun•er** *n*

tung•sten *n* : metallic element used for electrical purposes and in hardening alloys (as steel)

tu•nic *n* 1 : ancient knee-length garment 2 : hip-length blouse or jacket

tun•nel *n* : underground passageway ~ *vb* **-neled** *or* **-nelled; -nel•ing** *or* **-nel•ling** : make a tunnel through or under something

tur•ban *n* : wound headdress worn esp. by Muslims

tur•bid *adj* 1 : dark with stirred-up sediment 2 : confused — **tur•bid•i•ty** *n*

tur•bine *n* : engine turned by the force of gas or water on fan blades

tur•bo•jet *n* : airplane powered by a jet engine having a turbine-driven air compressor or the engine itself

tur•bo•prop *n* : airplane powered by a propeller turned by a jet engine-driven turbine

tur•bu•lent *adj* 1 : causing violence or disturbance 2 : marked by agitation or tumult — **tur•bu•lence** *n* — **tur•bu•lent•ly** *adv*

tu•reen *n* : deep bowl for serving soup

turf *n* : upper layer of soil bound by grass and roots

tur•gid *adj* 1 : swollen 2 : too highly embellished in style — **tur•gid•i•ty** *n*

tur•key *n, pl* **-keys** : large American bird raised for food

tur•moil *n* : extremely agitated condition

turn *vb* 1 : move or cause to move around an axis 2 : twist (a mechanical part) to operate 3 : wrench 4 : cause to face or move in a different direction 5 : reverse the sides or surfaces of 6 : upset 7 : go around 8 : become or cause to become 9 : seek aid from a source ~ *n* 1 : act or instance of turning 2 : change 3 : place at which something turns 4 : place, time, or opportunity to do something in order — **turn•er** *n* — **turn down** *vb* : decline to accept — **turn in** *vb* 1 : deliver or report to authorities 2 : go to bed — **turn off** *vb* : stop the functioning of — **turn out** *vb* 1 : expel 2 : produce 3 : come together 4 : prove to be in the end — **turn over** *vb* : transfer — **turn up** *vb* 1 : discover or appear 2 : happen unexpectedly

turn•coat *n* : traitor

tur•nip *n* : edible root of an herb

turn•out *n* 1 : gathering of people for a special purpose 2 : size of a gathering

turn•over *n* 1 : upset or reversal 2 : filled pastry 3 : volume of business 4 : movement (as of goods or people) into, through, and out of a place

turn•pike *n* : expressway on which tolls are charged

turn•stile *n* : post with arms pivoted on the top that allows people to pass one by one

turn•ta•ble *n* : platform that turns a phonograph record

tur•pen•tine *n* : oil distilled from pine-tree resin and used as a solvent

tur•pi•tude *n* : inherent baseness

tur•quoise *n* : blue or greenish gray gemstone

tur•ret *n* 1 : little tower on a building 2 : revolving tool holder or gun housing

tur•tle *n* : reptile with the trunk enclosed in a bony shell

tur•tle•dove *n* : wild pigeon

tur•tle•neck *n* : high close-fitting collar that can be turned over or a sweater or shirt with this collar

tusk *n* : long protruding tooth (as of an elephant) — **tusked** *adj*

tus•sle *n or vb* : struggle

tu•te•lage *n* 1 : act of protecting 2 : instruction esp. of an individual

tu•tor *n* : private teacher ~ *vb* : teach usu. individually

tux•e•do *n, pl* **-dos** *or* **-does** : semiformal evening clothes for a man

TV *n* : television

twain *n* : two

twang *n* 1 : harsh sound like that of a plucked bow-string 2 : nasal speech or resonance ~ *vb* : sound or speak with a twang

tweak *vb* : pinch and pull playfully — **tweak** *n*

tweed *n* 1 : rough woolen fabric 2 *pl* : tweed clothing — **tweedy** *adj*

tweet *n* : chirping note — **tweet** *vb*

twee•zers *n pl* : small pincerlike tool

twelve *n* 1 : one more than 11 2 : 12th in a set or series 3 : something having 12 units — **twelfth** *adj or n* — **twelve** *adj or pron*

twen•ty *n, pl* **-ties** : 2 times 10 — **twen•ti•eth** *adj or n* — **twenty** *adj or pron*

twen•ty–twen•ty, 20–20 *adj* : being vision of normal sharpness

twice *adv* 1 : on 2 occasions 2 : 2 times

twig *n* : small branch — **twig•gy** *adj*

twi•light *n* : light from the sky at dusk or dawn — **twilight** *adj*

twill *n* : fabric with a weave that gives an appearance of diagonal lines in the fabric

twilled *adj* : made with a twill weave

twin *n* : either of 2 offspring born together ~ *adj* 1 : born with one another or as a pair at one birth 2 : made up of 2 similar parts

twine *n* : strong twisted thread ~ *vb* **twined; twin•ing** 1 : twist together 2 : coil about a support — **twin•er** *n* — **twiny** *adj*

twinge *vb* **twinged; twing•ing** *or* **twinge•ing** : affect with or feel a sudden sharp pain ~ *n* : sudden sharp stab (as of pain)

twin•kle *vb* **-kled; -kling** : shine with a flickering light ~ *n* 1 : wink 2 : intermittent shining — **twin•kler** *n*

twirl *vb* : whirl round ~ *n* 1 : act of twirling 2 : coil — **twirl•er** *n*

twist *vb* 1 : unite by winding (threads) together 2 : wrench 3 : move in or have a spiral shape 4 : follow a winding course ~ *n* 1 : act or result of twisting 2 : unexpected development

twist•er *n* : tornado

¹twit *n* : fool

²twit *vb* **-tt-** : taunt

twitch *vb* : move or pull with a sudden motion ~ *n* : act of twitching

twit•ter *vb* : make chirping noises ~ *n* : small intermittent noise

two *n, pl* **twos** 1 : one more than one 2 : the 2d in a set or series 3 : something having 2 units — **two** *adj or pron*

two•fold *adj* : double — **two•fold** *adv*

two•some *n* : couple

-ty *n suffix* : quality, condition, or degree

ty•coon *n* : powerful and successful businessman

tying *pres part of* TIE

tyke *n* : small child

tym•pa•num *n, pl* **-na** : eardrum or the cavity which it closes externally — **tym•pan•ic** *adj*

type *n* 1 : class, kind, or group set apart by common characteristics 2 : special design of printed letters ~ *vb* **typed; typ•ing** 1 : write with a typewriter 2 : identify or classify as a particular type

type•writ•er *n* : keyboard machine that produces printed material by striking a ribbon with raised letters — **type•write** *vb*

ty•phoid *adj* : relating to or being a communicable bacterial disease (**typhoid fever**)

ty•phoon *n* : hurricane of the western Pacific ocean

ty•phus *n* : severe disease with fever, delirium, and rash

typ•i•cal *adj* : having the essential characteristics of a group — **typ•i•cal•i•ty** *n* — **typ•i•cal•ly** *adv* — **typ•i•cal•ness** *n*

typ•i•fy *vb* **-fied; -fy•ing** : be typical of

typ•ist *n* : one who operates a typewriter

ty•pog•ra•phy *n* 1 : art of printing with type 2 : style, arrangement, or appearance of printed matter — **ty•po•graph•ic** **ty•po•graph•i•cal** *adj* — **ty•po•graph•i•cal•ly** *adv*

ty•ran•ni•cal *adj* : relating to a tyrant — **ty•ran•ni•cal•ly** *adv*

tyr•an•nize *vb* **-nized; -niz•ing** : rule or deal with in the manner of a tyrant — **tyr•an•niz•er** *n*

tyr•an•ny *n, pl* **-nies** : unjust use of absolute governmental power

ty•rant *n* : harsh ruler having absolute power

ty•ro *n, pl* **-ros** : beginner

tzar *var of* CZAR

U

u *n, pl* **u's** *or* **us** : 21st letter of the alphabet

ubiq•ui•tous *adj* : omnipresent — **ubiq•ui•tous•ly** *adv* — **ubiq•ui•ty** *n*

ud•der *n* : animal sac containing milk glands and nipples

ug•ly *adj* **ug•li•er; -est** 1 : offensive to look at 2 : mean or quarrelsome — **ug•li•ness** *n*

uku•le•le *n* : small 4-string guitar

ul•cer *n* : eroded sore — **ul•cer•ous** *adj*

ul•cer•ate *vb* **-at•ed; -at•ing** : become affected with an ulcer — **ul•cer•a•tion** *n* — **ul•cer•a•tive** *adj*

ul•na *n* : bone of the forearm opposite the thumb

ul•te•ri•or *adj* : not revealed

ul•ti•mate *adj* : final, maximum, or extreme — **ultimate** *n* — **ul•ti•mate•ly** *adv*

ul•ti•ma•tum *n, pl* **-tums** *or* **-ta** : final proposition or demand carrying or implying a threat

ul•tra•vi•o•let *adj* : having a wavelength shorter than visible light

um•bi•li•cus *n, pl* **-li•ci** *or* **-li•cus•es** : small depression on the abdominal wall marking the site of the cord (**umbilical cord**) that joins the unborn fetus to its mother — **um•bil•i•cal** *adj*

um•brage *n* : resentment

um•brel•la *n* : collapsible fabric device to protect from sun or rain

um•pire *n* 1 : arbitrator 2 : sport official — **umpire** *vb*

ump·teen *adj* : very numerous — **ump·teenth** *adj*

un- *prefix* **1** : not **2** : opposite of

unable
unabridged
unacceptable
unaccompanied
unaccounted
unacquainted
unaddressed
unadorned
unadulterated
unafraid
unaided
unalike
unambiguous
unambitious
unannounced
unanswered
unanticipated
unappetizing
unappreciated
unapproved
unarguable
unarguably
unassisted
unattended
unattractive
unauthorized
unavailable
unavoidable
unbearable
unbiased
unbranded
unbreakable
uncensored
unchallenged
unchangeable
unchanged
unchanging
uncharacteristic
uncharged
unchaste
uncivilized
unclaimed
unclear
uncleared
unclothed
uncluttered
uncombed
uncomfortable
uncomfortably
uncomplimentary
unconfirmed
unconsummated
uncontested
uncontrolled
uncontroversial
unconventional
unconventionally
unconverted
uncooked
uncooperative
uncoordinated
uncovered
uncultivated
undamaged
undated
undecided
undeclared
undefeated
undemocratic
undependable
undeserving
undesirable
undetected
undetermined

undeveloped
undeviating
undignified
undisturbed
undivided
undomesticated
undrinkable
unearned
uneducated
unemotional
unending
unendurable
unenforceable
unenlightened
unethical
unexcitable
unexciting
unexplainable
unexplored
unfair
unfairly
unfairness
unfavorable
unfavorably
unfeigned
unfilled
unfinished
unflattering
unforeseeable
unforeseen
unforgivable
unforgiving
unfulfilled
unfurnished
ungenerous
ungentlemanly
ungraceful
ungrammatical
unharmed
unhealthful
unheated
unhurt
unidentified
unimaginable
unimaginative
unimportant
unimpressed
uninformed
uninhabited
uninjured
uninsured
unintelligent
unintelligible
unintelligibly
unintended
unintentional
unintentionally
uninterested
uninteresting
uninterrupted
uninvited
unjust
unjustifiable
unjustified
unjustly
unknowing
unknowingly
unknown
unleavened
unlicensed
unlikable
unlimited
unlovable
unmanageable

unmarked
unmarried
unmerciful
unmercifully
unmerited
unmolested
unmotivated
unmoving
unnamed
unnecessarily
unnecessary
unneeded
unnoticeable
unnoticed
unobjectionable
unobservable
unobservant
unobtainable
unobtrusive
unobtrusively
unofficial
unopened
unopposed
unorganized
unoriginal
unorthodox
unorthodoxy
unpaid
unpardonable
unpatriotic
unpaved
unpleasant
unpleasantly
unpleasantness
unpopular
unpopularity
unposed
unpredictability
unpredictable
unpredictably
unprejudiced
unprepared
unpretentious
unproductive
unprofitable
unprotected
unproved
unproven
unprovoked
unpunished
unqualified
unquenchable
unquestioning
unreachable
unreadable
unready
unrealistic
unreasonable
unreasonably
unrefined
unrelated
unreliable
unremembered
unrepentant
unrepresented
unrequited
unresolved
unresponsive
unrestrained
unrestricted
unrewarding
unripe

unsafe
unsalted
unsanitary
unsatisfactory
unsatisfied
unscented
unscheduled
unseasoned
unseen
unselfish
unselfishly
unselfishness
unshaped
unshaven
unskillful
unskillfully
unsolicited
unsolved
unsophisticated
unsound
unsoundly
unsoundness
unspecified
unspoiled
unsteadily
unsteadiness
unsteady
unstructured
unsubstantiated
unsuccessful
unsuitable
unsuitably
unsuited
unsupervised
unsupported
unsure
unsurprising
unsuspecting
unsweetened
unsympathetic
untamed
untanned
untidy
untouched
untrained
untreated
untrue
untrustworthy
untruthful
unusable
unusual
unvarying
unverified
unwanted
unwarranted
unwary
unwavering
unweaned
unwed
unwelcome
unwholesome
unwilling
unwillingly
unwillingness
unwise
unwisely
unworkable
unworthily
unworthiness
unworthy
unyielding

un·ac·cus·tomed *adj* **1** : not customary **2** : not accustomed

un·af·fect·ed *adj* **1** : not influenced or changed by something **2** : natural and sincere — **un·af·fect·ed·ly** *adv*

unan·i·mous *adj* **1** : showing no disagreement **2** : formed with the agreement of all — **una·nim·i·ty** *n* — **unan·i·mous·ly** *adv*

un·armed *adj* : not armed or armored

un·as·sum·ing *adj* : not bold or arrogant

un·at·tached *adj* **1** : not attached **2** : not married or engaged

un·aware *adv* : unawares ~ *adj* : not aware

un·awares *adv* **1** : without warning **2** : unintentionally

un·bal·anced *adj* **1** : not balanced **2** : mentally unstable

un·beat·en *adj* : not beaten

un·be·com·ing *adj* : not proper or suitable — **un·be·com·ing·ly** *adv*

un·be·liev·able *adj* **1** : improbable **2** : superlative — **un·be·liev·ably** *adv*

un·bend *vb* **-bent; -bend·ing** : make or become more relaxed and friendly

un·bend·ing *adj* : formal and inflexible

un·bind *vb* **-bound; -bind·ing 1** : remove bindings from **2** : release

un·bolt *vb* : open or unfasten by withdrawing a bolt

un·born *adj* : not yet born

un·bo·som *vb* : disclose thoughts or feelings

un·bowed *adj* : not defeated or subdued

un·bri·dled *adj* : unrestrained

un·bro·ken *adj* **1** : not damaged **2** : not interrupted

un·buck·le *vb* : unfasten the buckle of

un·bur·den *vb* : relieve (oneself) of anxieties

un·but·ton *vb* : unfasten the buttons of

un·called–for *adj* : too harsh or rude for the occasion

un·can·ny *adj* **1** : weird **2** : suggesting superhuman powers — **un·can·ni·ly** *adv*

un·ceas·ing *adj* : never ceasing — **un·ceas·ing·ly** *adv*

un·cer·e·mo·ni·ous *adj* : acting without ordinary courtesy — **un·cer·e·mo·ni·ous·ly** *adv*

un·cer·tain *adj* **1** : not determined, sure, or definitely known **2** : subject to chance or change — **un·cer·tain·ly** *adv* — **un·cer·tain·ty** *n*

un·chris·tian *adj* : not consistent with Christian teachings

un·cle *n* **1** : brother of one's father or mother **2** : husband of one's aunt

un·clean *adj* : not clean or pure — **un·clean·ness** *n*

un·clog *vb* : remove an obstruction from

un·coil *vb* : release or become released from a coiled state

un·com·mit·ted *adj* : not pledged to a particular allegiance or course of action

un·com·mon *adj* **1** : rare **2** : superior — **un·com·mon·ly** *adv*

un·com·pro·mis·ing *adj* : not making or accepting a compromise

un·con·cerned *adj* **1** : disinterested **2** : not anxious or upset — **un·con·cerned·ly** *adv*

un·con·di·tion·al *adj* : not limited in any way — **un·con·di·tion·al·ly** *adv*

un·con·scio·na·ble *adj* : shockingly unjust or unscrupulous — **un·con·scio·na·bly** *adv*

un·con·scious *adj* **1** : not awake or aware of one's surroundings **2** : not consciously done ~ *n* : part of one's mental life that one is not aware of — **un·con·scious·ly** *adv* — **un·con·scious·ness** *n*

un·con·sti·tu·tion·al *adj* : not according to or consistent with a constitution

un·con·trol·la·ble *adj* : incapable of being controlled — **un·con·trol·la·bly** *adv*

un·count·ed *adj* : countless

un·couth *adj* : rude and vulgar

un·cov·er *vb* **1** : reveal **2** : expose by removing a covering

unc·tion *n* **1** : rite of anointing **2** : exaggerated or insincere earnestness

unc·tu·ous *adj* **1** : oily **2** : insincerely smooth in speech or manner — **unc·tu·ous·ly** *adv*

un·cut *adj* **1** : not cut down, into, off, or apart **2** : not shaped by cutting **3** : not abridged

un·daunt·ed *adj* : not discouraged — **un·daunt·ed·ly** *adv*

un·de·ni·able *adj* : plainly true — **un·de·ni·ably** *adv*

un·der *adv* : below or beneath something ~ *prep* **1** : lower than and sheltered by **2** : below the surface of **3** : covered or concealed by **4** : subject to the authority of **5** : less than ~ *adj* **1** : lying below or beneath **2** : subordinate **3** : less than usual, proper, or desired

un·der·age *adj* : of less than legal age

un·der·brush *n* : shrubs and small trees growing beneath large trees

un·der·clothes *n pl* : underwear

un·der·cloth·ing *n* : underwear

un·der·cov·er *adj* : employed or engaged in secret investigation

un·der·cur·rent *n* : hidden tendency or opinion

un·der·cut *vb* **-cut; -cut·ting** : offer to sell or to work at a lower rate than

un·der·de·vel·oped *adj* : not normally or adequately developed esp. economically

un·der·dog *n* : contestant given least chance of winning

un·der·done *adj* : not thoroughly done or cooked

un·der·es·ti·mate *vb* : estimate too low

un·der·ex·pose *vb* : give less than normal exposure to — **un·der·ex·po·sure** *n*

un·der·feed *vb* **-fed; -feed·ing** : feed inadequately

un·der·foot *adv* **1** : under the feet **2** : in the way of another

un·der·gar·ment *n* : garment to be worn under another

un·der·go *vb* **-went; -gone; -go·ing 1** : endure **2** : go through (as an experience)

un·der·grad·u·ate *n* : university or college student

un·der·ground *adv* **1** : beneath the surface of the earth **2** : in secret ~ *adj* **1** : being or growing under the surface of the ground **2** : secret ~ *n* : secret political movement or group

un·der·growth *n* : low growth on the floor of a forest

un·der·hand *adv or adj* **1** : with secrecy and deception **2** : with the hand kept below the waist

un·der·hand·ed *adj or adv* : underhand — **un·der·hand·ed·ly** *adv* — **un·der·hand·ed·ness** *n*

un·der·line *vb* **1** : draw a line under **2** : stress — **underline** *n*

un·der·ling *n* : inferior

un·der·ly·ing *adj* : basic

un·der·mine *vb* **1** : excavate beneath **2** : weaken or wear away secretly or gradually

un·der·neath *prep* : directly under ~ *adv* **1** : below a surface or object **2** : on the lower side

un·der·nour·ished *adj* : insufficiently nourished — **un·der·nour·ish·ment** *n*

un·der·pants *n pl* : short undergarment for the lower trunk

un·der·pass *n* : passageway crossing underneath another

un·der·pin·ning *n* : support

un·der·priv·i·leged *adj* : poor

un·der·rate *vb* : rate or value too low

un·der·score *vb* **1** : underline **2** : emphasize — **underscore** *n*

un·der·sea *adj* : being, carried on, or used beneath the surface of the sea ~ **un·der·seas** *adv* : beneath the surface of the sea

un·der sec·re·tary *n* : deputy secretary

un·der·sell *vb* **-sold; -sell·ing** : sell articles cheaper than

un·der·shirt *n* : shirt worn as underwear

un·der·shorts *n pl* : short underpants

un·der·side *n* : side or surface lying underneath

un·der·sized *adj* : unusually small

un·der·stand *vb* **-stood; -stand·ing 1** : be aware of the meaning of **2** : deduce **3** : have a sympathetic attitude — **un·der·stand·able** *adj* — **un·der·stand·ably** *adv*

un·der·stand·ing *n* **1** : intelligence **2** : ability to comprehend and judge **3** : mutual agreement ~ *adj* : sympathetic

un·der·state *vb* **1** : represent as less than is the case **2** : state with restraint — **un·der·state·ment** *n*

un·der·stood *adj* **1** : agreed upon **2** : implicit

un·der·study *vb* : study another actor's part in order to substitute — **understudy** *n*

un·der·take *vb* **-took; -tak·en; -tak·ing 1** : attempt (a task) or assume (a responsibility) **2** : guarantee

un·der·tak·er *n* : one in the funeral business

un·der·tak·ing *n* **1** : something (as work) that is undertaken **2** : promise

under–the–counter *adj* : illicit

un·der·tone *n* : low or subdued tone or utterance

un·der·tow *n* : current beneath the waves that flows seaward

un·der·val·ue *vb* : value too low

un·der·wa·ter *adj* : being or used below the surface of the water — **underwater** *adv*

under way *adv* : in motion or in progress

un·der·wear *n* : clothing worn next to the skin and under ordinary clothes

un·der·world *n* **1** : place of departed souls **2** : world of organized crime

un·der·write *vb* **-wrote; -writ·ten; -writ·ing 1** : provide insurance for **2** : guarantee financial support of — **un·der·writ·er** *n*

un·dies *n pl* : underwear

un·do *vb* **-did; -done; -do·ing 1** : unfasten **2** : reverse **3** : ruin — **un·do·ing** *n*

un·doubt·ed *adj* : certain — **un·doubt·ed·ly** *adv*

un·dress *vb* : remove one's clothes ~ *n* : state of being naked

un·due *adj* : excessive — **un·du·ly** *adv*

un·du·late *vb* **-lat·ed; -lat·ing** : rise and fall regularly — **un·du·la·tion** *n*

un·dy·ing *adj* : immortal or perpetual

un·earth *vb* : dig up or discover

un·earth·ly *adj* : supernatural

un·easy *adj* **1** : awkward or embarrassed **2** : disturbed or worried — **un·eas·i·ly** *adv* — **un·eas·i·ness** *n*

un·em·ployed *adj* : not having a job — **un·em·ploy·ment** *n*

un·equal *adj* : not equal or uniform — **un·equal·ly** *adv*

un·equaled, un·equalled *adj* : having no equal

un·equiv·o·cal *adj* : leaving no doubt — **un·equiv·o·cal·ly** *adv*

un·err·ing *adj* : infallible — **un·err·ing·ly** *adv*

un·even *adj* **1** : not smooth **2** : not regular or consistent — **un·even·ly** *adv* — **un·even·ness** *n*

un·event·ful *adj* : lacking interesting or noteworthy incidents — **un·event·ful·ly** *adv*

un·ex·pect·ed *adj* : not expected — **un·ex·pect·ed·ly** *adv*

un·fail·ing *adj* : steadfast — **un·fail·ing·ly** *adv*

un·faith·ful *adj* : not loyal — **un·faith·ful·ly** *adv* — **un·faith·ful·ness** *n*

un·fa·mil·iar *adj* **1** : not well known **2** : not acquainted — **un·fa·mil·iar·i·ty** *n*

un·fas·ten *vb* : release a catch or lock

un·feel·ing *adj* : lacking feeling or compassion — **un·feel·ing·ly** *adv*

un·fit *adj* : not suitable — **un·fit·ness** *n*

un·flap·pa·ble *adj* : not easily upset or panicked — **un·flap·pa·bly** *adv*

un·fold *vb* **1** : open the folds of **2** : reveal **3** : develop

un·for·get·ta·ble *adj* : memorable — **un·for·get·ta·bly** *adv*

un·for·tu·nate *adj* **1** : not lucky or successful **2** : deplorable — **unfortunate** *n* — **un·for·tu·nate·ly** *adv*

un·found·ed *adj* : lacking a sound basis

un·freeze *vb* **-froze; -fro·zen; -freez·ing** : thaw

un·friend·ly *adj* : not friendly or kind — **un·friend·li·ness** *n*

un·furl *vb* : unfold or unroll

un·gain·ly *adj* : clumsy — **un·gain·li·ness** *n*

un·god·ly *adj* : wicked — **un·god·li·ness** *n*

un·grate·ful *adj* : not thankful for favors — **un·grate·ful·ly** *adv* — **un·grate·ful·ness** *n*

un·guent *n* : ointment

un·hand *vb* : let go

un·hap·py *adj* **1** : unfortunate **2** : sad — **un·hap·pi·ly** *adv* — **un·hap·pi·ness** *n*

un·healthy *adj* **1** : not wholesome **2** : not well

un·heard–of *adj* : unprecedented

un·hinge *vb* **1** : take from the hinges **2** : make unstable esp. mentally

un·hitch *vb* : unfasten

un·ho·ly *adj* : sinister or shocking — **un·ho·li·ness** *n*

un·hook *vb* : release from a hook

uni·cel·lu·lar *adj* : having or consisting of a single cell

uni·corn *n* : legendary animal with one horn in the middle of the forehead

uni·cy·cle *n* : pedal-powered vehicle with only a single wheel

uni·di·rec·tion·al *adj* : working in only a single direction

uni·form *adj* : not changing or showing any variation ~ *n* : distinctive dress worn by members of a particular group — **uni·for·mi·ty** *n* — **u·ni·form·ly** *adv*

uni·fy *vb* **-fied; -fy·ing** : make into a coherent whole — **uni·fi·ca·tion** *n*

uni·lat·er·al *adj* : having, affecting, or done by one side only — **uni·lat·er·al·ly** *adv*

un·im·peach·able *adj* : blameless

un·in·hib·it·ed *adj* : free of restraint — **un·in·hib·it·ed·ly** *adv*

union *n* **1** : act or instance of joining 2 or more things into one or the state of being so joined **2** : confederation of nations or states **3** : organization of workers (**labor union, trade union**)

union·ize *vb* **-ized; -iz·ing** : form into a labor union — **union·i·za·tion** *n*

unique *adj* **1** : being the only one of its kind **2** : very unusual — **unique·ly** *adv* — **unique·ness** *n*

uni·son *n* **1** : sameness in pitch **2** : exact agreement

unit *n* **1** : smallest whole number **2** : definite amount or quantity used as a standard of measurement **3** : single part of a whole — **unit** *adj*

unite *vb* **unit·ed; unit·ing** : put or join together

uni·ty *n, pl* **-ties 1** : quality or state of being united or a unit **2** : harmony

uni·ver·sal *adj* **1** : relating to or affecting everyone or everything **2** : present or occurring everywhere — **uni·ver·sal·ly** *adv*

uni·verse *n* : the complete system of all things that exist

uni·ver·si·ty *n, pl* **-ties** : institution of higher learning

un·kempt *adj* : not neat or combed

un·kind *adj* : not kind or sympathetic — **un·kind·li·ness** *n* — **un·kind·ly** *adv* — **un·kind·ness** *n*

un·law·ful *adj* : illegal — **un·law·ful·ly** *adv*

un•leash *vb* : free from control or restraint

un•less *conj* : except on condition that

un•like *adj* **1** : not similar **2** : not equal ~ *prep* : different from — **un•like•ly** *adv* — **un•like•ness** *n* — **un•like•li•hood** *n*

un•load *vb* **1** : take (cargo) from a vehicle, vessel, or plane **2** : take a load from **3** : discard

un•lock *vb* **1** : unfasten through release of a lock **2** : release or reveal

un•lucky *adj* **1** : experiencing bad luck **2** : likely to bring misfortune — **un•luck•i•ly** *adv*

un•mis•tak•able *adj* : not capable of being mistaken or misunderstood — **un•mis•tak•ably** *adv*

un•moved *adj* **1** : not emotionally affected **2** : remaining in the same place or position

un•nat•u•ral *adj* **1** : not natural or spontaneous **2** : abnormal — **un•nat•u•ral•ly** *adv* — **un•nat•u•ral•ness** *n*

un•nerve *vb* : deprive of courage, strength, or steadiness

un•oc•cu•pied *adj* **1** : not busy **2** : not occupied

un•pack *vb* **1** : remove (things packed) from a container **2** : remove the contents of (a package)

un•par•al•leled *adj* : having no equal

un•plug *vb* **1** : unclog **2** : disconnect from an electric circuit by removing a plug

un•prec•e•dent•ed *adj* : unlike or superior to anything known before

un•prin•ci•pled *adj* : unscrupulous

un•ques•tion•able *adj* : acknowledged as beyond doubt — **un•ques•tion•ably** *adv*

un•rav•el *vb* **1** : separate the threads of **2** : solve

un•re•al *adj* : not real or genuine — **un•re•al•i•ty** *n*

un•rea•son•ing *adj* : not using or being guided by reason

un•re•lent•ing *adj* : not yielding or easing — **un•re•lent•ing•ly** *adv*

un•rest *n* : turmoil

un•ri•valed, un•ri•valled *adj* : having no rival

un•roll *vb* **1** : unwind a roll of **2** : become unrolled

un•ruf•fled *adj* : not agitated or upset

un•ruly *adj* : not readily controlled or disciplined — **un•rul•i•ness** *n*

un•scathed *adj* : unharmed

un•sci•en•tif•ic *adj* : not in accord with the principles and methods of science

un•screw *vb* : loosen or remove by withdrawing screws or by turning

un•scru•pu•lous *adj* : being or acting in total disregard of conscience, ethical principles, or rights of others — **un•scru•pu•lous•ly** *adv* — **un•scru•pu•lous•ness** *n*

un•seal *vb* : break or remove the seal of

un•sea•son•able *adj* : not appropriate or usual for the season — **un•sea•son•ably** *adv*

un•seem•ly *adj* : not polite or in good taste — **un•seem•li•ness** *n*

un•set•tle *vb* : disturb — **un•set•tled** *adj*

un•sight•ly *adj* : not attractive

un•skilled *adj* : not having or requiring a particular skill

un•snap *vb* : loosen by undoing a snap

un•speak•able *adj* : extremely bad — **un•speak•ably** *adv*

un•sta•ble *adj* **1** : not mentally or physically balanced **2** : tending to change

un•stop *vb* **1** : unclog **2** : remove a stopper from

un•stop•pa•ble *adj* : not capable of being stopped

un•strung *adj* : nervously tired or anxious

un•sung *adj* : not celebrated in song or verse

un•tan•gle *vb* **1** : free from a state of being tangled **2** : find a solution to

un•think•able *adj* : not to be thought of or considered possible

un•think•ing *adj* : careless — **un•think•ing•ly** *adv*

un•tie *vb* **-tied; -ty•ing** *or* **-tie•ing** : open by releasing ties

un•til *prep* : up to the time of ~ *conj* : to the time that

un•time•ly *adj* **1** : premature **2** : coming at an unfortunate time

un•to *prep* : to

un•told *adj* **1** : not told **2** : too numerous to count

un•tow•ard *adj* **1** : difficult to manage **2** : inconvenient

un•truth *n* **1** : lack of truthfulness **2** : lie

un•used *adj* **1** : not accustomed **2** : not used

un•well *adj* : sick

un•wieldy *adj* : too big or awkward to manage easily

un•wind *vb* **-wound; -wind•ing** **1** : undo something that is wound **2** : become unwound **3** : relax

un•wit•ting *adj* **1** : not knowing **2** : not intended — **un•wit•ting•ly** *adv*

un•wont•ed *adj* **1** : unusual **2** : not accustomed by experience

un•wrap *vb* : remove the wrappings from

un•writ•ten *adj* : made or passed on only in speech or through tradition

un•zip *vb* : zip open

up *adv* **1** : in or to a higher position or level **2** : from beneath a surface or level **3** : in or into an upright position **4** : out of bed **5** : to or with greater intensity **6** : into existence, evidence, or knowledge **7** : away **8** — used to indicate a degree of success, completion, or finality **9** : in or into parts ~ *adj* **1** : in the state of having risen **2** : raised to or at a higher level **3** : moving, inclining, or directed upward **4** : in a state of greater intensity **5** : at an end ~ *vb* **upped** *or in 1* **up; upped; up•ping; ups** *or in 1* **up 1** : act abruptly **2** : move or cause to move upward ~ *prep* **1** : to, toward, or at a higher point of **2** : along or toward the beginning of

up•braid *vb* : criticize or scold

up•bring•ing *n* : process of bringing up and training

up•com•ing *adj* : approaching

up•date *vb* : bring up to date — **update** *n*

up•end *vb* **1** : stand or rise on end **2** : overturn

up•grade *n* **1** : upward slope **2** : increase ~ *vb* : raise to a higher position

up•heav•al *n* **1** : a heaving up (as of part of the earth's crust) **2** : violent change

up•hill *adv* : upward on a hill or incline ~ *adj* **1** : going up **2** : difficult

up•hold *vb* **-held; -hold•ing** : support or defend — **up•hold•er** *n*

up•hol•ster *vb* : cover (furniture) with padding and fabric (**uphol•stery**) — **up•hol•ster•er** *n*

up•keep *n* : act or cost of keeping up or maintaining

up•land *n* : high land — **upland** *adj*

up•lift *vb* **1** : lift up **2** : improve the condition or spirits of — **up•lift** *n*

up•on *prep* : on

up•per *adj* : higher in position, rank, or order ~ *n* : top part of a shoe

upper•hand *n* : advantage

up•per•most *adv* : in or into the highest or most prominent position — **uppermost** *adj*

up•pi•ty *adj* : acting with a manner of undue importance

up•right *adj* **1** : vertical **2** : erect in posture **3** : morally correct ~ *n* : something that stands upright — **up•right** *adv* — **up•right•ly** *adv* — **up•right•ness** *n*

up•ris•ing *n* : revolt

up•roar *n* : state of commotion or violent disturbance

up•roar•i•ous *adj* **1** : marked by uproar **2** : extremely funny — **up•roar•i•ous•ly** *adv*

up•root *vb* : remove by or as if by pulling up by the roots

up•set *vb* **-set; -set•ting 1** : force or be forced out of the usual position **2** : disturb emotionally or physically ~ *n* **1** : act of throwing into disorder **2** : minor physical disorder ~ *adj* : emotionally disturbed or agitated

up•shot *n* : final result

up•side down *adv* **1** : turned so that the upper and lower parts are reversed **2** : in or into confusion or disorder — **upside-down** *adj*

up•stairs *adv* : up the stairs or to the next floor ~ *adj* : situated on the floor above ~ *n sing or pl* : part of a building above the ground floor

up•stand•ing *adj* : honest

up•start *n* : one who claims more personal importance than is warranted — **up•start** *adj*

up•swing *n* : marked increase (as in activity)

up•tight *adj* **1** : tense **2** : angry **3** : rigidly conventional

up-to-date *adj* : current — **up-to-date•ness** *n*

up•town *n* : upper part of a town or city — **uptown** *adj or adv*

up•turn *n* : improvement or increase

up•ward, up•wards *adv* **1** : in a direction from lower to higher **2** : toward a higher or greater state or number ~ *adj* : directed toward or situated in a higher place — **up•ward•ly** *adv*

up•wind *adv or adj* : in the direction from which the wind is blowing

ura•ni•um *n* : metallic radioactive chemical element

ur•ban *adj* : characteristic of a city

ur•bane *adj* : polished in manner — **ur•ban•i•ty** *n*

ur•ban•ite *n* : city dweller

ur•chin *n* : mischievous youngster

-ure *n suffix* : act or process

ure•thra *n, pl* **-thras** *or* **-thrae** : canal that carries off urine from the bladder — **ure•thral** *adj*

urge *vb* **urged; urging 1** : earnestly plead for or insist on (an action) **2** : try to persuade **3** : impel to a course of activity ~ *n* : force or impulse that moves one to action

ur•gent *adj* **1** : calling for immediate attention **2** : urging insistently — **ur•gen•cy** *n* — **ur•gent•ly** *adv*

uri•nal *n* : receptacle to urinate in

uri•nate *vb* **-nat•ed; -nat•ing** : discharge urine — **uri•na•tion** *n*

urine *n* : liquid waste material from the kidneys — **uri•nary** *adj*

urn *n* **1** : vaselike or cuplike vessel on a pedestal **2** : large coffee pot

us *pron, objective case of* WE

us•able *adj* : suitable or fit for use — **us•abil•i•ty** *n*

us•age *n* **1** : customary practice **2** : way of doing or of using something

use *n* **1** : act or practice of putting something into action **2** : state of being used **3** : way of using **4** : privilege, ability, or power to use something **5** : utility or function **6** : occasion or need to use — *vb* **used; us•ing 1** : put into action or service **2** : consume **3** : behave toward **4** : to make use of **5** — used in the past tense with *to* to indicate a former practice — **use•ful** *adj* — **use•ful•ly** *adv* — **use•ful•ness** *n* — **use•less** *adj* — **use•less•ly** *adv* — **use•less•ness** *n* — **us•er** *n*

used *adj* : not new

ush•er *n* : one who escorts people to their seats ~ *vb* : conduct to a place

ush•er•ette *n* : woman or girl who is an usher

usu•al *adj* : being what is expected according to custom or habit — **usu•al•ly** *adv*

usurp *vb* : seize and hold by force or without right — **usur•pa•tion** *n* — **usurp•er** *n*

usu•ry *n, pl* **-ries 1** : lending of money at excessive interest or the rate or amount of such interest — **usu•rer** *n* — **usu•ri•ous** *adj*

uten•sil *n* **1** : eating or cooking tool **2** : useful tool

uter•us *n, pl* **uteri** : organ for containing and nourishing an unborn offspring — **uter•ine** *adj*

util•i•tar•i•an *adj* : being or meant to be useful rather than beautiful

util•i•ty *n, pl* **-ties 1** : usefulness **2** : regulated business providing a public service (as electricity)

uti•lize *vb* **-lized; -liz•ing** : make use of — **uti•li•za•tion** *n*

ut•most *adj* **1** : most distant **2** : of the greatest or highest degree or amount — **utmost** *n*

uto•pia *n* : place of ideal perfection — **uto•pi•an** *adj or n*

ut•ter *adj* : absolute ~ *vb* : express with the voice — **ut•ter•er** *n* — **ut•ter•ly** *adv*

ut•ter•ance *n* : what one says

V

v *n, pl* **v's** *or* **vs** : 22d letter of the alphabet

va•can•cy *n, pl* **-cies 1** : state of being vacant **2** : unused or unoccupied place or office

va•cant *adj* **1** : not occupied, filled, or in use **2** : devoid of thought or expression — **va•cant•ly** *adv*

va•cate *vb* **-cat•ed; -cat•ing 1** : annul **2** : leave unfilled or unoccupied

va•ca•tion *n* : period of rest from routine — **vacation** *vb* — **va•ca•tion•er** *n*

vac•ci•nate *vb* **-nat•ed; -nat•ing** : administer a vaccine usu. by injection

vac•ci•na•tion *n* : act of or the scar left by vaccinating

vac•cine *n* : substance to induce immunity to a disease

vac•il•late *vb* **-lat•ed; -lat•ing** : waver between courses or opinions — **vac•il•la•tion** *n*

vac•u•ous *adj* **1** : empty **2** : dull or inane — **va•cu•ity** *n* — **vac•u•ous•ly** *adv* — **vac•u•ous•ness** *n*

vac•u•um *n, pl* **vac•u•ums** *or* **vac•ua** : empty space with no air ~ *vb* : clean with a vacuum cleaner

vacuum cleaner *n* : appliance that cleans by suction

vag•a•bond *n* : wanderer with no home — **vagabond** *adj*

va•ga•ry *n, pl* **-ries** : whim

va•gi•na *n, pl* **-nae** *or* **-nas** : canal that leads out from the uterus — **vag•i•nal** *adj*

va•grant *n* : person with no home and no job — **va•gran•cy** *n* — **vagrant** *adj*

vague *adj* **vagu•er; vagu•est** : not clear, definite, or distinct — **vague•ly** *adv* — **vague•ness** *n*

vain *adj* **1** : of no value **2** : unsuccessful **3** : conceited — **vain•ly** *adv*

va•lance *n* : border drapery

vale *n* : valley

vale•dic•to•ri•an *n* : student giving the farewell address at commencement

vale•dic•to•ry *adj* : bidding farewell — **valedictory** *n*

va•lence *n* : degree of combining power of a chemical element

val•en•tine *n* : sweetheart or a card sent to a sweetheart or friend on St. Valentine's Day

va•let *n* : male personal servant

val•iant *adj* : brave or heroic — **val•iant•ly** *adv*

val•id *adj* **1** : proper and legally binding **2** : founded on truth or fact — **va•lid•i•ty** *n* — **val•id•ly** *adv*

val•i•date *vb* **-dat•ed; -dat•ing** : establish as valid — **val•i•da•tion** *n*

va•lise *n* : suitcase

val•ley *n, pl* **-leys** : long depression between ranges of hills

val•or *n* : bravery or heroism — **val•or•ous** *adj*

valu•able *adj* **1** : worth a lot of money **2** : being of great importance or use — **valuable** *n*

val•u•a•tion *n* **1** : act or process of valuing **2** : market value of a thing

val•ue *n* **1** : fair return or equivalent for something exchanged **2** : how much something is worth **3** : distinctive quality (as of a color or sound) **4** : guiding principle or ideal — usu. pl. ~ *vb* **val•ued; valu•ing 1** : estimate the worth of **2** : appreciate the importance of — **val•ue•less** *adj* — **val•u•er** *n*

valve *n* : structure or device to control flow of a liquid or gas — **valved** *adj* — **valve•less** *adj*

vam•pire *n* **1** : legendary night-wandering dead body that sucks human blood **2** : bat that feeds on the blood of animals

¹**van** *n* : vanguard

²**van** *n* : enclosed truck

va•na•di•um *n* : soft ductile metallic chemical element

van•dal *n* : person who willfully defaces or destroys property — **van•dal•ism** *n* — **van•dal•ize** *vb*

vane *n* : bladelike device designed to be moved by force of the air or water

van•guard *n* **1** : troops moving at the front of an army **2** : forefront of an action or movement

va•nil•la *n* : a flavoring made from the pods of a tropical orchid or this orchid

van•ish *vb* : disappear suddenly

van•i•ty *n, pl* **-ties 1** : futility or something that is futile **2** : undue pride in oneself **3** : makeup case or table

van•quish *vb* **1** : overcome in battle or in a contest **2** : gain mastery over

van•tage *n* : position of advantage or perspective

va•pid *adj* : lacking spirit, liveliness, or zest — **va•pid•i•ty** *n* — **vap•id•ly** *adv* — **vap•id•ness** *n*

va•por *n* **1** : fine separated particles floating in and clouding the air **2** : gaseous form of an ordinarily liquid substance — **va•por•ous** *adj*

va•por•ize *vb* **-ized; -iz•ing** : convert into vapor — **va•por•i•za•tion** *n* — **va•por•iz•er** *n*

var•i•able *adj* : apt to vary — **var•i•abil•i•ty** *n* — **var•i•able** *n* — **var•i•ably** *adv*

var•i•ance *n* **1** : instance or degree of variation **2** : disagreement or dispute **3** : legal permission to build contrary to a zoning law

var•i•ant *n* : something that differs from others of its kind — **variant** *adj*

vari•a•tion *n* : instance or extent of varying

var•i•cose *adj* : abnormally swollen and dilated

var•ied *adj* : showing variety — **var•ied•ly** *adv*

var•ie•gat•ed *adj* : having patches, stripes, or marks of different colors — **var•ie•gate** *vb* — **var•ie•ga•tion** *n*

va•ri•ety *n, pl* **-et•ies 1** : state of being different **2** : collection of different things **3** : something that differs from others of its kind

var•i•ous *adj* : being many and unlike — **var•i•ous•ly** *adv*

var•nish *n* : liquid that dries to a hard glossy protective coating ~ *vb* : cover with varnish

var•si•ty *n, pl* **-ties** : principal team representing a school

vary *vb* **var•ied; vary•ing 1** : alter **2** : make or be of different kinds

vas•cu•lar *adj* : relating to a channel for the conveyance of a body fluid (as blood or sap)

vase *n* : tall usu. ornamental container to hold flowers

vas•sal *n* **1** : one acknowledging another as feudal lord **2** : one in a dependent position — **vas•sal•age** *n*

vast *adj* : very great in size, extent, or amount — **vast•ly** *adv* — **vast•ness** *n*

vat *n* : large tub- or barrel-shaped container

vaude•ville *n* : stage entertainment of unrelated acts

¹**vault** *n* **1** : masonry arch **2** : usu. underground storage or burial room — *vb* : form or cover with a vault — **vault•ed** *adj* — **vaulty** *adj*

²**vault** *vb* : spring over esp. with the help of the hands or a pole ~ *n* : act of vaulting — **vault•er** *n*

vaunt *vb* : boast — **vaunt** *n*

veal *n* : flesh of a young calf

veer *vb* : change course esp. gradually — **veer** *n*

veg•e•ta•ble *adj* **1** : relating to or obtained from plants **2** : like that of a plant ~ *n* **1** : plant **2** : plant grown for food

veg•e•tar•i•an *n* : person who eats no meat — **vegetarian** *adj* — **veg•e•tar•i•an•ism** *n*

veg•e•tate *vb* **-tat•ed; -tat•ing** : lead a dull inert life

veg•e•ta•tion *n* : plant life — **veg•e•ta•tion•al** *adj* — **veg•e•ta•tive** *adj*

ve•he•ment *adj* : showing strong esp. violent feeling — **ve•he•mence** *n* — **ve•he•ment•ly** *adv*

ve•hi•cle *n* **1** : medium through which something is expressed, applied, or administered **2** : structure for transporting something esp. on wheels — **ve•hic•u•lar** *adj*

veil *n* **1** : sheer material to hide something or to cover the face and head **2** : something that hides ~ *vb* : cover with a veil

vein *n* **1** : rock fissure filled with deposited mineral matter **2** : vessel that carries blood toward the heart **3** : sap-carrying tube in a leaf **4** : distinctive element or style of expression — **veined** *adj*

ve•loc•i•ty *n, pl* **-ties** : speed

ve•lour, ve•lours *n, pl* **velours** : fabric with a velvetlike pile

vel•vet *n* : fabric with a short soft pile — **velvet** *adj* — **vel•vety** *adj*

ve•nal *adj* : capable of being corrupted esp. by money — **ve•nal•i•ty** *n* — **ve•nal•ly** *adv*

vend *vb* : sell — **vend•ible** *adj* — **ven•dor** *n*

ven•det•ta *n* : feud marked by acts of revenge

ve•neer *n* **1** : thin layer of fine wood glued over a cheaper wood **2** : superficial display ~ *vb* : overlay with a veneer

ven•er•a•ble *adj* : deserving of respect

ven•er•ate *vb* **-at•ed; -at•ing** : respect esp. with reverence — **ven•er•a•tion** *n*

venereal disease *n* : contagious disease spread through copulation

ven•geance *n* : punishment in retaliation for an injury or offense

venge•ful *adj* : filled with a desire for revenge — **venge•ful•ly** *adv*

ve·nial *adj* : capable of being forgiven

ven·i·son *n* : deer meat

ven·om *n* **1** : poison secreted by certain animals **2** : ill will — **ven·om·ous** *adj*

vent *vb* **1** : provide with or let out at a vent **2** : give expression to ~ *n* : opening for passage or for relieving pressure

ven·ti·late *vb* **-lat·ed; -lat·ing** : allow fresh air to circulate through — **ven·ti·la·tion** *n* — **ven·ti·la·tor** *n*

ven·tri·cle *n* : heart chamber that pumps blood into the arteries

ven·tril·o·quist *n* : one who can make the voice appear to come from another source — **ven·tril·o·quism** *n* — **ven·tril·o·quy** *n*

ven·ture *vb* **-tured; -tur·ing 1** : risk or take a chance on **2** : put forward (an opinion) ~ *n* : speculative business enterprise

ven·ture·some *adj* : brave or daring — **ven·ture·some·ly** *adv* — **ven·ture·some·ness** *n*

ven·ue *n* : scene of an action or event

ve·rac·i·ty *n, pl* **-ties** : truthfulness or accuracy — **ve·ra·cious** *adj*

ve·ran·da, ve·ran·dah *n* : large open porch

verb *n* : word that expresses action or existence

ver·bal *adj* **1** : having to do with or expressed in words **2** : oral **3** : relating to or formed from a verb — **ver·bal·i·za·tion** *n* — **ver·bal·ize** *vb* — **ver·bal·ly** *adv*

verbal auxiliary *n* : auxiliary verb

ver·ba·tim *adv or adj* : using the same words

ver·biage *n* : excess of words

ver·bose *adj* : using more words than are needed — **ver·bos·i·ty** *n*

ver·dant *adj* : green with growing plants — **ver·dant·ly** *adv*

ver·dict *n* : decision of a jury

ver·dure *n* : green growing vegetation or its color

verge *vb* **verged; verg·ing** : be almost on the point of happening or doing something ~ *n* **1** : edge **2** : threshold

ver·i·fy *vb* **-fied; -fy·ing** : establish the truth, accuracy, or reality of — **ver·i·fi·able** *adj* — **ver·i·fi·ca·tion** *n*

ver·i·ly *adv* : truly or confidently

veri·si·mil·i·tude *n* : appearance of being true

ver·i·ta·ble *adj* : actual or true — **ver·i·ta·bly** *adv*

ver·i·ty *n, pl* **-ties** : truth

ver·mi·cel·li *n* : thin spaghetti

ver·min *n, pl* **vermin** : small animal pest

ver·mouth *n* : dry or sweet wine flavored with herbs

ver·nac·u·lar *adj* : relating to a native language or dialect and esp. its normal spoken form ~ *n* : vernacular language

ver·nal *adj* : relating to spring

ver·sa·tile *adj* : having many abilities or uses — **ver·sa·til·i·ty** *n*

¹verse *n* **1** : line or stanza of poetry **2** : poetry **3** : short division of a chapter in the Bible

²verse *vb* **versed; vers·ing** : make familiar by experience, study, or practice

ver·sion *n* **1** : translation of the Bible **2** : account or description from a particular point of view

ver·sus *prep* : opposed to or against

ver·te·bra *n, pl* **-brae** *or* **-bras** : segment of the backbone — **ver·te·bral** *adj*

ver·te·brate *n* : animal with a backbone — **verte·brate** *adj*

ver·tex *n, pl* **ver·ti·ces 1** : point of intersection of lines or surfaces **2** : highest point

ver·ti·cal *adj* : rising straight up from a level surface — **vertical** *n* — **ver·ti·cal·i·ty** *n* — **ver·ti·cal·ly** *adv*

ver·ti·go *n, pl* **-goes** *or* **-gos** : dizziness

verve *n* : liveliness or vividness

very *adj* **veri·er; -est 1** : exact **2** : exactly suitable

3 : mere or bare **4** : precisely the same ~ *adv* **1** : to a high degree **2** : in actual fact

ves·i·cle *n* : membranous cavity — **ve·sic·u·lar** *adj*

ves·pers *n pl* : late afternoon or evening worship service

ves·sel *n* **1** : a container (as a barrel, bottle, bowl, or cup) for a liquid **2** : craft for navigation esp. on water **3** : tube in which a body fluid is circulated

¹vest *vb* **1** : give a particular authority, right, or property to **2** : clothe with or as if with a garment

²vest *n* : sleeveless garment usu. worn under a suit coat

ves·ti·bule *n* : enclosed entrance — **ves·tib·u·lar** *adj*

ves·tige *n* : visible trace or remains — **ves·ti·gial** *adj* — **ves·ti·gial·ly** *adv*

vest·ment *n* : clergy member's garment

ves·try *n, pl* **-tries** : church storage room for garments and articles

vet·er·an *n* **1** : former member of the armed forces **2** : person with long experience — **vet·eran** *adj*

Veterans Day *n* : 4th Monday in October or formerly November 11 observed as a legal holiday in commemoration of the end of war in 1918 and 1945

vet·er·i·nar·i·an *n* : doctor of animals — **vet·er·i·nary** *adj*

ve·to *n, pl* **-toes 1** : power to forbid and esp. the power of a chief executive to prevent a bill from becoming law **2** : exercise of the veto ~ *vb* **1** : forbid **2** : reject a legislative bill

vex *vb* **vexed; vex·ing** : trouble, distress, or annoy — **vex·a·tion** *n* — **vex·a·tious** *adj*

via *prep* : by way of

vi·a·ble *adj* **1** : capable of surviving or growing **2** : practical or workable — **vi·a·bil·i·ty** *n* — **vi·a·bly** *adv*

via·duct *n* : elevated roadway or railway bridge

vi·al *n* : small bottle

vi·brant *adj* **1** : vibrating **2** : pulsing with vigor or activity **3** : sounding from vibration — **vi·bran·cy** *n*

vi·brate *vb* **-brat·ed; -brat·ing 1** : move or cause to move quickly back and forth or side to side **2** : respond sympathetically — **vi·bra·tion** *n* — **vi·bra·tor** *n* — **vi·bra·to·ry** *adj*

vic·ar *n* : parish clergy member — **vi·car·i·ate** *n*

vi·car·i·ous *adj* : sharing in someone else's experience through imagination or sympathetic feelings — **vi·car·i·ous·ly** *adv* — **vi·car·i·ous·ness** *n*

vice *n* **1** : immoral habit **2** : depravity

vice- *prefix* : one that takes the place of

vice-chancellor	vice president
vice-consul	vice presidential
vice presidency	vice-regent

vice admiral *n* : commissioned officer in the navy or coast guard ranking above a rear admiral

vice·roy *n* : provincial governor who represents the sovereign

vice ver·sa *adv* : with the order reversed

vi·cin·i·ty *n, pl* **-ties** : surrounding area

vi·cious *adj* **1** : wicked **2** : savage **3** : malicious — **vi·cious·ly** *adv* — **vi·cious·ness** *n*

vi·cis·si·tude *n* : irregular, unexpected, or surprising change — usu. used in pl.

vic·tim *n* : person killed, hurt, or abused

vic·tim·ize *vb* **-ized; -iz·ing** : make a victim of — **vic·tim·i·za·tion** *n* — **vic·tim·iz·er** *n*

vic·tor *n* : winner

Vic·to·ri·an *adj* : relating to the reign of Queen Victoria of England or the art, taste, or standards of her time ~ *n* : one of the Victorian period

vic·to·ri·ous *adj* : having won a victory — **vic·to·ri·ous·ly** *adv*

vic·to·ry *n, pl* **-ries** : success in defeating an enemy or opponent or in overcoming difficulties

vict·uals *n pl* : food

vid·eo *adj* : relating to the television image

vid·eo·cas·sette *n* : cassette containing videotape

vid·eo·tape *vb* : make a recording of (a television production) on special tape — **videotape** *n*

vie *vb* **vied; vy·ing** : contend — **vi·er** *n*

view *n* **1** : process of seeing or examining **2** : opinion **3** : area of landscape that can be seen **4** : range of vision **5** : purpose or object ~ *vb* **1** : look at **2** : think about or consider — **view·er** *n*

view·point *n* : position from which something is considered

vigil *n* **1** : day of devotion before a religious feast **2** : act or time of keeping awake **3** : long period of keeping watch (as over a sick or dying person)

vig·i·lant *adj* : alert esp. to avoid danger — **vig·i·lance** *n* — **vig·i·lant·ly** *adv*

vig·i·lan·te *n* : one of a group independent of the law working to suppress crime

vi·gnette *n* : short descriptive literary piece

vig·or *n* **1** : energy or strength **2** : intensity or force — **vig·or·ous** *adj* — **vig·or·ous·ly** *adv* — **vig·or·ous·ness** *n*

vile *adj* **vil·er; vil·est** : thoroughly bad or contemptible — **vile·ly** *adv* — **vile·ness** *n*

vil·i·fy *vb* **-fied; -fy·ing** : speak evil of — **vil·i·fi·ca·tion** *n* — **vil·i·fi·er** *n*

vil·la *n* : country estate

vil·lage *n* : small country town — **vil·lag·er** *n*

vil·lain *n* : bad person — **vil·lain·ess** *n* — **vil·lainy** *n*

vil·lain·ous *adj* : evil or corrupt — **vil·lain·ous·ly** *adv* — **vil·lain·ous·ness** *n*

vim *n* : energy

vin·di·cate *vb* **-cat·ed; -cat·ing 1** : avenge **2** : exonerate **3** : justify — **vin·di·ca·tion** *n* — **vin·di·ca·tor** *n*

vin·dic·tive *adj* : seeking or meant for revenge — **vin·dic·tive·ly** *adv* — **vin·dic·tive·ness** *n*

vine *n* : climbing or trailing plant

vin·e·gar *n* : acidic liquid obtained by fermentation — **vin·e·gary** *adj*

vine·yard *n* : plantation of grapevines

vin·tage *n* **1** : season's yield of grapes or wine **2** : period of origin ~ *adj* : of enduring interest

vi·nyl *n* : strong plastic

vi·o·la *n* : instrument of the violin family tuned lower than the violin — **vi·o·list** *n*

vi·o·late *vb* **-lat·ed; -lat·ing 1** : act with disrespect or disregard of **2** : rape **3** : desecrate — **vi·o·la·tion** *n* — **vi·o·la·tor** *n*

vi·o·lence *n* : intense physical force that causes or is intended to cause injury or destruction — **vi·o·lent** *adj* — **vi·o·lent·ly** *adv*

vi·o·let *n* **1** : small flowering plant **2** : reddish blue

vi·o·lin *n* : bowed stringed instrument — **vi·o·lin·ist** *n*

VIP *n, pl* **VIPs** : very important person

vi·per *n* **1** : venomous snake **2** : treacherous or malignant person

vi·ra·go *n, pl* **-goes** *or* **-gos** : shrew

vi·ral *adj* : relating to or caused by a virus

vir·gin *n* **1** : unmarried woman **2** : a person who has never had sexual intercourse ~ *adj* **1** : chaste **2** : natural and unspoiled — **vir·gin·al** *adj* — **vir·gin·al·ly** *adv* — **vir·gin·i·ty** *n*

vir·gule *n* : mark / used esp. to denote "or" or "per"

vir·ile *adj* : masculine — **vi·ril·i·ty** *n*

vir·tu·al *adj* : being in effect but not in fact or name — **vir·tu·al·ly** *adv*

vir·tue n 1 : moral excellence 2 : effective or commendable quality 3 : chastity

vir·tu·os·i·ty n, pl **-ties** : great skill (as in music)

vir·tu·o·so n, pl **-sos** or **-si** : highly skilled performer esp. of music — **virtuoso** adj

vir·tu·ous adj 1 : morally good 2 : chaste — **vir·tu·ous·ly** adv

vir·u·lent adj 1 : extremely severe or infectious 2 : full of malice — **vir·u·lence** n — **vir·u·lent·ly** adv

vi·rus n 1 : tiny disease-causing agent 2 : a computer program that performs a malicious action (as destroying data)

vi·sa n : authorization to enter a foreign country

vis·age n : face

vis·cera n pl : internal bodily organs esp. of the trunk

vis·cer·al adj 1 : bodily 2 : instinctive 3 : deeply or crudely emotional — **vis·cer·al·ly** adv

vis·cid adj : viscous — **vis·cid·i·ty** n

vis·count n : British nobleman ranking below an earl and above a baron

vis·count·ess n 1 : wife of a viscount 2 : woman with rank of a viscount

vis·cous adj : having a thick or sticky consistency — **vis·cos·i·ty** n

vise n : device for clamping something being worked on

vis·i·bil·i·ty n, pl **-ties** : degree or range to which something can be seen

vis·i·ble adj 1 : capable of being seen 2 : manifest or apparent — **vis·i·bly** adv

vi·sion n 1 : vivid picture seen in a dream or trance or in the imagination 2 : foresight 3 : power of seeing ~ vb : imagine

vi·sion·ary adj 1 : given to dreaming or imagining 2 : illusory 3 : not practical ~ n : one with great dreams or projects

vis·it vb 1 : go or come to see 2 : stay with for a time as a guest 3 : cause or be a reward, affliction, or punishment ~ n : short stay as a guest — **vis·it·able** adj — **vis·i·tor** n

vis·i·ta·tion n 1 : official visit 2 : divine punishment or favor 3 : severe trial

vi·sor n 1 : front piece of a helmet 2 : part (as on a cap or car windshield) that shades the eyes

vis·ta n : distant view

vi·su·al adj 1 : relating to sight 2 : visible — **vi·su·al·ly** adv

vi·su·al·ize vb **-ized; -iz·ing** : form a mental image of — **vi·su·al·i·za·tion** n — **vi·su·al·iz·er** n

vi·tal adj 1 : relating to, necessary for, or characteristic of life 2 : full of life and vigor 3 : fatal 4 : very important — **vi·tal·ly** adv

vi·tal·i·ty n, pl **-ties** 1 : life force 2 : energy

vital signs n pl : body's pulse rate, respiration, temperature, and usu. blood pressure

vi·ta·min n : natural organic substance essential to health

vi·ti·ate vb **-at·ed; -at·ing** 1 : spoil or impair 2 : invalidate — **vi·ti·a·tion** n — **vi·ti·a·tor** n

vit·re·ous adj : relating to or resembling glass

vit·ri·ol n : something caustic, corrosive, or biting — **vit·ri·ol·ic** adj

vi·tu·per·ate vb **-at·ed; -at·ing** : abuse in words — **vi·tu·per·a·tion** n — **vi·tu·per·a·tive** adj — **vi·tu·per·a·tive·ly** adv

vi·va·cious adj : lively — **vi·va·cious·ly** adv — **vi·va·cious·ness** n — **vi·vac·i·ty** n

viv·id adj 1 : lively 2 : brilliant 3 : intense or sharp — **viv·id·ly** adv — **viv·id·ness** n

viv·i·fy vb **-fied; -fy·ing** : give life or vividness to

vivi·sec·tion n : experimental operation on a living animal

vix·en n 1 : scolding woman 2 : female fox

vo·cab·u·lary n, pl **-lar·ies** 1 : list or collection of words 2 : stock of words used by a person or about a subject

vo·cal adj 1 : relating to or produced by or for the voice 2 : speaking out freely and usu. emphatically

vocal cords n pl : membranous folds in the larynx that are important in making vocal sounds

vo·cal·ist n : singer

vo·cal·ize vb **-ized; -iz·ing** : give vocal expression to

vo·ca·tion n : regular employment — **vo·ca·tion·al** adj

vo·cif·er·ous adj : noisy and insistent — **vo·cif·er·ous·ly** adv

vod·ka n : colorless distilled grain liquor

vogue n : brief but intense popularity — **vogu·ish** adj

voice n 1 : sound produced through the mouth by humans and many animals 2 : power of speaking 3 : right of choice or opinion ~ vb **voiced; voic·ing** : express in words — **voiced** adj

void adj 1 : containing nothing 2 : lacking — with of 3 : not legally binding ~ n 1 : empty space 2 : feeling of hollowness ~ vb 1 : discharge (as body waste) 2 : make (as a contract) void — **void·able** adj — **void·er** n

vol·a·tile adj 1 : readily vaporizing at a relatively low temperature 2 : likely to change suddenly — **vol·a·til·i·ty** n — **vol·a·til·ize** vb

vol·ca·no n, pl **-noes** or **-nos** : opening in the earth's crust from which molten rock and steam come out — **vol·ca·nic** adj

vo·li·tion n : free will — **vo·li·tion·al** adj

vol·ley n, pl **-leys** 1 : flight of missiles (as arrows) 2 : simultaneous shooting of many weapons

vol·ley·ball n : game of batting a large ball over a net

volt n : unit for measuring the force that moves an electric current

volt·age n : quantity of volts

vol·u·ble adj : fluent and smooth in speech — **vol·u·bil·i·ty** n — **vol·u·bly** adv

vol·ume n 1 : book 2 : space occupied as measured by cubic units 3 : amount 4 : loudness of a sound

vo·lu·mi·nous adj : large or bulky

vol·un·tary adj 1 : done, made, or given freely and without expecting compensation 2 : relating to or controlled by the will — **vol·un·tar·i·ly** adv

vol·un·teer n : person who offers to help or work without expecting payment or reward ~ vb 1 : offer or give voluntarily 2 : offer oneself as a volunteer

vo·lup·tuous adj 1 : luxurious 2 : having a full and sexually attractive figure — **vo·lup·tuous·ly** adv — **vo·lup·tuous·ness** n

vom·it vb : throw up the contents of the stomach — **vomit** n

voo·doo n, pl **voodoos** 1 : religion derived from African polytheism and involving sorcery 2 : one who practices voodoo 3 : charm or fetish used in voodoo — **voodoo** adj — **voo·doo·ism** n

vo·ra·cious adj : greedy or exceedingly hungry — **vo·ra·cious·ly** adv — **vo·ra·cious·ness** n — **vo·rac·i·ty** n

vor·tex n, pl **vor·ti·ces** : whirling liquid

vo·ta·ry n, pl **-ries** 1 : devoted participant, adherent, admirer, or worshiper

vote n 1 : individual expression of preference in choosing or reaching a decision 2 : right to indicate one's preference or the preference expressed ~ vb **vot·ed; vot·ing** 1 : cast a vote 2 : choose or defeat by vote — **vote·less** adj — **vot·er** n

vo·tive adj : consisting of or expressing a vow, wish, or desire

vouch vb : give a guarantee or personal assurance

vouch·er n : written record or receipt that serves as proof of a transaction

vouch·safe vb **-safed; -saf·ing** : grant as a special favor

vow n : solemn promise to do something or to live or act a certain way — **vow** vb

vow·el n 1 : speech sound produced without obstruction or friction in the mouth 2 : letter representing such a sound

voy·age n : long journey esp. by water or through space ~ vb **-aged; -ag·ing** : make a voyage — **voy·ag·er** n

vul·ca·nize vb **-nized; -niz·ing** : treat (as rubber) to make more elastic or stronger

vul·gar adj 1 : relating to the common people 2 : lacking refinement 3 : offensive in manner or language — **vul·gar·ism** n — **vul·gar·ize** vb — **vul·gar·ly** adv

vul·gar·i·ty n, pl **-ties** 1 : state of being vulgar 2 : vulgar language or act

vul·ner·a·ble adj : susceptible to attack or damage — **vul·ner·a·bil·i·ty** n — **vul·ner·a·bly** adv

vul·ture n : large flesh-eating bird

vul·va n, pl **-vae** : external genital parts of the female

vying pres part of VIE

W

w n, pl **w's** or **ws** : 23d letter of the alphabet

wad n 1 : little mass 2 : soft mass of fibrous material 3 : pliable plug to retain a powder charge 4 : considerable amount ~ vb 1 : form into a wad 2 : stuff with a wad

wad·dle vb **-dled; -dling** : walk with short steps swaying from side to side — **waddle** n

wade vb **wad·ed; wad·ing** 1 : step in or through (as water) 2 : move with difficulty — **wade** n — **wad·er** n

wa·fer n 1 : thin crisp cake or cracker 2 : waferlike thing

waf·fle n : crisped cake of batter cooked in a hinged utensil (**waffle iron**) ~ vb : vacillate

waft vb : cause to move lightly by wind or waves — **waft** n

¹**wag** vb **-gg-** : sway or swing from side to side or to and fro — **wag** n

²**wag** n : wit — **wag·gish** adj

wage vb **waged; wag·ing** : engage in ~ n 1 : payment for labor or services 2 : compensation

wa•ger *n or vb* : bet

wag•gle *vb* **-gled; -gling** : wag — **waggle** *n*

wag•on *n* **1** : 4-wheeled vehicle drawn by animals **2** : child's 4-wheeled cart

waif *n* : homeless child

wail *vb* **1** : mourn **2** : make a sound like a mournful cry — **wail** *n*

wain•scot *n* : usu. paneled wooden lining of an interior wall — **wainscot** *vb*

waist *n* **1** : narrowed part of the body between chest and hips **2** : waistlike part — **waist•line** *n*

wait *vb* **1** : remain in readiness or expectation **2** : delay **3** : attend as a waiter ~ *n* **1** : concealment **2** : act or period of waiting

wait•er *n* : person who serves others at tables

wait•per•son *n* : a waiter or waitress

wait•ress *n* : woman who serves others at tables

waive *vb* **waived; waiv•ing** : give up claim to

waiv•er *n* : act of waiving right, claim, or privilege

¹wake *vb* **woke; wo•ken; wak•ing 1** : keep watch **2** : bring or come back to consciousness after sleep ~ *n* **1** : state of being awake **2** : watch held over a dead body

²wake *n* : track left by a ship

wake•ful *adj* : not sleeping or able to sleep — **wake•ful•ness** *n*

wak•en *vb* : wake

wale *n* : ridge on cloth

walk *vb* **1** : move or cause to move on foot **2** : pass over, through, or along by walking ~ *n* **1** : a going on foot **2** : place or path for walking **3** : distance to be walked **4** : way of living **5** : way of walking **6** : slow 4 beat gait of a horse — **walk•er** *n*

wall *n* **1** : structure for defense or for enclosing something **2** : upright enclosing part of a building or room **3** : something like a wall ~ *vb* : provide, separate, surround, or close with a wall — **walled** *adj*

wal•la•by *n, pl* **-bies** : small or medium-sized kangaroo

wal•let *n* : pocketbook with compartments

wall•flow•er *n* **1** : mustardlike plant with showy fragrant flowers **2** : one who remains on the sidelines of social activity

wal•lop *n* **1** : powerful blow **2** : ability to hit hard ~ *vb* **1** : beat soundly **2** : hit hard

wal•low *vb* **1** : roll about in deep mud **2** : indulge oneself excessively ~ *n* : place for wallowing

wall•pa•per *n* **1** : decorative paper for walls — **wallpaper** *vb*

wal•nut *n* **1** : nut with a furrowed shell and adherent husk **2** : tree on which this nut grows or its brown wood

wal•rus *n, pl* **-rus** *or* **-rus•es** : large seallike mammal of northern seas having ivory tusks

waltz *n* : gliding dance to music having 3 beats to the measure or the music — **waltz** *vb*

wam•pum *n* : strung shell beads used by No. American Indians as money

wan *adj* **-nn-** : sickly or pale — **wan•ly** *adv* — **wan•ness** *n*

wand *n* : slender staff

wan•der *vb* **1** : move about aimlessly **2** : stray **3** : become delirious — **wan•der•er** *n*

wan•der•lust *n* : strong urge to wander

wane *vb* **waned; wan•ing 1** : grow smaller or less **2** : lose power, prosperity, or influence — **wane** *n*

wan•gle *vb* **-gled; -gling** : obtain by sly or devious means

want *vb* **1** : lack **2** : need **3** : desire earnestly ~ *n* **1** : deficiency **2** : dire need **3** : something wanted

want•ing *adj* **1** : not present or in evidence **2** : falling below standards **3** : lacking in ability ~ *prep* **1** : less or minus **2** : without

wan•ton *adj* **1** : lewd **2** : having no regard for justice or for others' feelings, rights, or safety ~ *n*

: lewd or immoral person ~ *vb* : be wanton — **wan•ton•ly** *adv* — **wan•ton•ness** *n*

wa•pi•ti *n, pl* **-ti** *or* **-tis** : elk

war *n* **1** : armed fighting between nations **2** : state of hostility or conflict **3** : struggle between opposing forces or for a particular end ~ *vb* **-rr-** : engage in warfare — **war•less** *adj* — **war•time** *n*

war•ble *n* **1** : melodious succession of low pleasing sounds **2** : musical trill ~ *vb* **-bled; -bling** : sing or utter in a trilling way

war•bler *n* **1** : small thrushlike singing bird **2** : small bright-col-ored insect-eating bird

ward *n* **1** : a guarding or being under guard or guardianship **2** : division of a prison or hospital **3** : electoral or administrative division of a city **4** : person under protection of a guardian or a law court ~ *vb* : turn aside — **ward•ship** *n*

¹-ward *adj suffix* **1** : that moves, tends, faces, or is directed toward **2** : that occurs or is situated in the direction of

²-ward, -wards *adv suffix* **1** : in a (specified) direction **2** : toward a (specified) point, position, or area

war•den *n* **1** : guardian **2** : official charged with supervisory duties or enforcement of laws **3** : official in charge of a prison

ward•er *n* : watchman or warden

ward•robe *n* **1** : clothes closet **2** : collection of wearing apparel

ware *n* **1** : articles for sale — often pl. **2** : items of fired clay

ware•house *n* : place for storage of merchandise — **warehouse** *vb* — **ware•house•man** *n* — **ware•hous•er** *n*

war•fare *n* **1** : military operations between enemies **2** : struggle

war•head *n* : part of a missile holding the explosive material

war•like *adj* : fond of, relating to, or used in war

warm *adj* **1** : having or giving out moderate or adequate heat **2** : serving to retain heat **3** : showing strong feeling **4** : giving a pleasant impression of warmth, cheerfulness, or friendliness ~ *vb* **1** : make or become warm **2** : give warmth or energy to **3** : experience feelings of affection **4** : become increasingly ardent, interested, or competent — **warm•er** *n* — **warm•ly** *adv* — **warm up** *vb* : make ready by preliminary activity

war•mon•ger *n* : one who attempts to stir up war

warmth *n* **1** : quality or state of being warm **2** : enthusiasm

warn *vb* **1** : put on guard **2** : notify in advance — **warn•ing** *n or adj*

warp *n* **1** : lengthwise threads in a woven fabric **2** : twist ~ *vb* **1** : twist out of shape **2** : lead astray **3** : distort

war•rant *n* **1** : authorization **2** : legal writ authorizing action ~ *vb* **1** : declare or maintain positively **2** : guarantee **3** : approve **4** : justify

warrant officer *n* **1** : officer in the armed forces ranking next below a commissioned officer **2** : commissioned officer in the navy or coast guard ranking below an ensign

war•ran•ty *n, pl* **-ties** : guarantee of the integrity of a product

war•ren *n* : area where rabbits are bred and kept

war•rior *n* : man engaged or experienced in warfare

war•ship *n* : naval vessel

wart *n* **1** : small projection on the skin caused by a virus **2** : wartlike protuberance — **warty** *adj*

wary *adj* **war•i•er; -est** : careful in guarding against danger or deception

was *past 1st & 3d sing of* BE

wash *vb* **1** : cleanse with or as if with a liquid (as water) **2** : wet thoroughly with liquid **3** : flow along the border of **4** : flow in a stream **5** : move or remove by or as if by the action of water **6** : cover

or daub lightly with a liquid **7** : undergo laundering ~ *n* **1** : act of washing or being washed **2** : articles to be washed **3** : surging action of water or disturbed air — **wash•able** *adj*

wash•board *n* : grooved board to scrub clothes on

wash•bowl *n* : large bowl for water for washing hands and face

wash•cloth *n* : cloth used for washing one's face and body

washed–up *adj* : no longer capable or usable

wash•er *n* **1** : machine for washing **2** : ring used around a bolt or screw to ensure tightness or relieve friction

wash•ing *n* : articles to be washed

Washington's Birthday *n* : the 3d Monday in February or formerly February 22 observed as a legal holiday

wash•out *n* **1** : washing out or away of earth **2** : failure

wash•room *n* : bathroom

wasp *n* : slender-bodied winged insect related to the bees and having a formidable sting

wasp•ish *adj* : irritable

was•sail *n* **1** : toast to someone's health **2** : liquor drunk on festive occasions **3** : riotous drinking — **wassail** *vb*

waste *n* **1** : sparsely settled or barren region **2** : act or an instance of wasting **3** : refuse (as garbage or rubbish) **4** : material (as feces) produced but not used by a living body ~ *vb* **wast•ed; wast•ing 1** : ruin **2** : spend or use carelessly **3** : lose substance or energy ~ *adj* **1** : wild and uninhabited **2** : being of no further use — **wast•er** *n* — **waste•ful** *adj* — **waste•ful•ly** *adv* — **waste•ful•ness** *n*

waste•bas•ket *n* : receptacle for refuse

waste•land *n* : barren uncultivated land

wast•rel *n* : one who wastes

watch *vb* **1** : be or stay awake intentionally **2** : be on the lookout for danger **3** : observe **4** : keep oneself informed about ~ *n* **1** : act of keeping awake to guard **2** : close observation **3** : one that watches **4** : period of duty on a ship or those on duty during this period **5** : timepiece carried on the person — **watch•er** *n*

watch•dog *n* **1** : dog kept to guard property **2** : one that protects

watch•ful *adj* : steadily attentive — **watch•ful•ly** *adv* — **watch•ful•ness** *n*

watch•man *n* : person assigned to watch

watch•word *n* **1** : secret word used as a signal **2** : slogan

wa•ter *n* **1** : liquid that descends as rain and forms rivers, lakes, and seas **2** : liquid containing or resembling water ~ *vb* **1** : supply with or get water **2** : dilute with or as if with water **3** : form or secrete watery matter

water buffalo *n* : common oxlike often domesticated Asian buffalo

wa•ter•col•or *n* **1** : paint whose liquid part is water **2** : picture made with watercolors

wa•ter•course *n* : stream of water

wa•ter•cress *n* : perennial salad plant with white flowers

wa•ter•fall *n* : steep descent of the water of a stream

wa•ter•fowl *n* **1** : bird that frequents the water **2** **waterfowl** *pl* : swimming game birds

wa•ter•front *n* : land fronting a body of water

water lily *n* : aquatic plant with floating leaves and showy flowers

wa•ter•logged *adj* : filled or soaked with water

wa•ter•mark *n* **1** : mark showing how high water has risen **2** : a marking in paper visible under light ~ *vb* : mark (paper) with a watermark

wa•ter•mel•on *n* : large fruit with sweet juicy usu. red pulp

water moccasin *n* : venomous snake of the southeastern U.S.

wa·ter·pow·er *n* : power of moving water used to run machinery

wa·ter·proof *adj* : not letting water through ~ *vb* : make waterproof — **wa·ter·proof·ing** *n*

wa·ter·shed *n* : dividing ridge between two drainage areas or one of these areas

water ski *n* : ski used on water when the wearer is towed — **wa·ter–ski** *vb* — **wa·ter–ski·er** *n*

wa·ter·spout *n* **1** : pipe from which water is spouted **2** : tornado over a body of water

wa·ter·tight *adj* **1** : so tight as not to let water in **2** : allowing no possibility for doubt or uncertainty

wa·ter·way *n* : navigable body of water

wa·ter·works *n pl* : system by which water is supplied (as to a city)

wa·tery *adj* **1** : containing, full of, or giving out water **2** : being like water **3** : soft and soggy

watt *n* : unit of electric power — **watt·age** *n*

wat·tle *n* **1** : framework of flexible branches used in building **2** : fleshy process hanging usu. about the head or neck (as of a bird) — **wat·tled** *adj*

wave *vb* **waved; wav·ing 1** : flutter **2** : signal with the hands **3** : wave to and fro with the hand **4** : curve up and down like a wave ~ *n* **1** : moving swell on the surface of water **2** : wave-like shape **3** : waving motion **4** : surge **5** : disturbance that transfers energy from point to point — **wave·let** *n* — **wave·like** *adj* — **wavy** *adj*

wave·length *n* **1** : distance from crest to crest in the line of advance of a wave **2** : line of thought that reveals a common understanding

wa·ver *vb* **1** : fluctuate in opinion, allegiance, or direction **2** : flicker **3** : falter — **waver** *n* — **wa·ver·er** *n* — **wa·ver·ing·ly** *adv*

¹wax *n* **1** : yellowish plastic substance secreted by bees **2** : substance like beeswax ~ *vb* : treat or rub with wax esp. for polishing

²wax *vb* **1** : grow larger **2** : become

wax·en *adj* : made of or resembling wax

waxy *adj* **wax·i·er; -est** : made of, full of, or resembling wax

way *n* **1** : thoroughfare for travel or passage **2** : route **3** : course of action **4** : method **5** : detail **6** : usual or characteristic state of affairs **7** : condition **8** : distance **9** : progress along a course — **by the way** : in a digression — **by way of 1** : for the purpose of **2** : by the route through — **out of the way** : remote

way·bill *n* : paper that accompanies a shipment and gives details of goods, route, and charges

way·far·er *n* : traveler esp. on foot — **way·far·ing** *adj*

way·lay *vb* **-laid; -lay·ing** : lie in wait for

way·side *n* : side of a road

way·ward *adj* **1** : following one's own capricious inclinations **2** : unpredictable

we *pron* — used of a group that includes the speaker or writer

weak *adj* **1** : lacking strength or vigor **2** : deficient in vigor of mind or character **3** : of less than usual strength **4** : not having or exerting authority — **weak·en** *vb* — **weak·ly** *adv*

weak·ling *n* : person who is physically, mentally, or morally weak

weak·ly *adj* : feeble

weak·ness *n* **1** : quality or state of being weak **2** : fault **3** : object of special liking

wealth *n* **1** : abundant possessions or resources **2** : profusion

wealthy *adj* **wealth·i·er; -est** : having wealth

wean *vb* **1** : accustom (a young mammal) to take food by means other than nursing **2** : free from dependence

weap·on *n* **1** : something (as a gun) that may be used to fight with **2** : means by which one contends against another — **weap·on·less** *adj*

wear *vb* **wore; worn; wear·ing 1** : use as an article of clothing or adornment **2** : carry on the person

3 : show an appearance of **4** : decay by use or by scraping **5** : lessen the strength of **6** : endure use ~ *n* **1** : act of wearing **2** : clothing **3** : lasting quality **4** : result of use — **wear·able** *adj* — **wear·er** *n* — **wear out** *vb* **1** : make or become useless by wear **2** : tire

wea·ri·some *adj* : causing weariness — **wea·ri·some·ly** *adv* — **wea·ri·some·ness** *n*

wea·ry *adj* **-ri·er; -est 1** : worn out in strength, freshness, or patience **2** : expressing or characteristic of weariness ~ *vb* **-ried; -ry·ing** : make or become weary — **wea·ri·ly** *adv* — **wea·ri·ness** *n*

wea·sel *n* : small slender flesh-eating mammal

weath·er *n* : state of the atmosphere ~ *vb* **1** : expose to or endure the action of weather **2** : endure

weath·er-beat·en *adj* : worn or damaged by exposure to the weather

weath·er·man *n* : one who forecasts and reports the weather

weath·er·proof *adj* : able to withstand exposure to weather — **weatherproof** *vb*

weather vane *n* : movable device that shows the way the wind blows

weave *vb* **wove** *or* **weaved; wo·ven** *or* **weaved; weav·ing 1** : form by interlacing strands of material **2** : to make as if by weaving together parts **3** : follow a winding course ~ *n* : pattern or method of weaving — **weav·er** *n*

web *n* **1** : cobweb **2** : animal or plant membrane **3** : network ~ *vb* **-bb-** : cover or provide with a web — **webbed** *adj*

web·bing *n* : strong closely woven tape

wed *vb* **-dd- 1** : marry **2** : unite

wed·ding *n* : marriage ceremony and celebration

wedge *n* : V-shaped object used for splitting, raising, forcing open, or tightening ~ *vb* **wedged; wedg·ing 1** : tighten or split with a wedge **2** : force into a narrow space

wed·lock *n* : marriage

Wednes·day *n* : 4th day of the week

wee *adj* : very small

weed *n* : unwanted plant ~ *vb* **1** : remove weeds **2** : get rid of — **weed·er** *n* — **weedy** *adj*

weeds *n pl* : mourning clothes

week *n* **1** : 7 successive days **2** : calendar period of 7 days beginning with Sunday and ending with Saturday **3** : the working or school days of the calendar week

week·day *n* : any day except Sunday and often Saturday

week·end *n* : Saturday and Sunday ~ *vb* : spend the weekend

week·ly *adj* : occurring, appearing, or done every week ~ *n, pl* **-lies** : weekly publication — **weekly** *adv*

weep *vb* **wept; weep·ing** : shed tears — **weep·er** *n* — **weepy** *adj*

wee·vil *n* : small injurious beetle with a long head usu. curved into a snout — **wee·vily, wee·vil·ly** *adj*

weft *n* : crosswise threads or yarn in weaving

weigh *vb* **1** : determine the heaviness of **2** : have a specified weight **3** : consider carefully **4** : raise (an anchor) off the sea floor **5** : press down or burden

weight *n* **1** : amount that something weighs **2** : relative heaviness **3** : heavy object **4** : burden or pressure **5** : importance ~ *vb* **1** : load with a weight **2** : oppress — **weight·less** *adj* — **weight·less·ness** *n* — **weighty** *adj*

weird *adj* **1** : unearthly or mysterious **2** : strange — **weird·ly** *adv* — **weird·ness** *n*

wel·come *vb* **-comed; -com·ing** : accept or greet cordially ~ *adj* : received or permitted gladly ~ *n* : cordial greeting or reception

weld *vb* : unite by heating, hammering, or pressing ~ *n* : union by welding — **weld·er** *n*

wel·fare *n* **1** : prosperity **2** : government aid for those in need

¹well *n* **1** : spring **2** : hole sunk in the earth to obtain a natural deposit (as of oil) **3** : source of supply **4** : open space extending vertically through floors ~ *vb* : flow forth

²well *adv* **bet·ter; best 1** : in a good or proper manner **2** : satisfactorily **3** : fully **4** : intimately **5** : considerably ~ *adj* **1** : satisfactory **2** : prosperous **3** : desirable **4** : healthy

well–adjusted *adj* : well-balanced

well–ad·vised *adj* : prudent

well–balanced *adj* **1** : evenly balanced **2** : emotionally or psychologically sound

well–be·ing *n* : state of being happy, healthy, or prosperous

well–bred *adj* : having good manners

well–done *adj* **1** : properly performed **2** : cooked thoroughly

well–heeled *adj* : financially well-off

well–mean·ing *adj* : having good intentions

well–nigh *adv* : nearly

well–off *adj* : being in good condition esp. financially

well–read *adj* : well informed through reading

well–round·ed *adj* : broadly developed

well·spring *n* : source

well–to–do *adj* : prosperous

welsh *vb* **1** : avoid payment **2** : break one's word

Welsh rabbit *n* : melted often seasoned cheese poured over toast or crackers

Welsh rare·bit *n* : Welsh rabbit

welt *n* **1** : narrow strip of leather between a shoe upper and sole **2** : ridge raised on the skin usu. by a blow ~ *vb* : hit hard

wel·ter *vb* **1** : toss about **2** : wallow ~ *n* : confused jumble

wen *n* : abnormal growth or cyst

wench *n* : young woman

wend *vb* : direct one's course

went *past of* GO

wept *past of* WEEP

were *past 2d sing, past pl, or past subjunctive of* BE

were·wolf *n, pl* **-wolves** : person held to be able to change into a wolf

west *adv* : to or toward the west ~ *adj* : situated toward or at or coming from the west ~ *n* **1** : direction of sunset **2** *cap* : regions to the west — **west·er·ly** *adv or adj* — **west·ward** *adv or adj* — **west·wards** *adv*

west·ern *adj* **1** *cap* : of a region designated West **2** : lying toward or coming from the west — **West·ern·er** *n*

wet *adj* **-tt- 1** : consisting of or covered or soaked with liquid **2** : not dry ~ *n* : moisture ~ *vb* **-tt-** : make or become moist — **wet·ly** *adv* — **wet·ness** *n*

whack *vb* : strike sharply ~ *n* **1** : sharp blow **2** : proper working order **3** : chance **4** : try

¹whale *n, pl* **whales** *or* **whale** : large marine mammal ~ *vb* **whaled; whal·ing** : hunt for whales — **whale·boat** *n* — **whal·er** *n*

²whale *vb* **whaled; whal·ing** : strike or hit vigorously

whale·bone *n* : horny substance attached to the upper jaw of some large whales (**whalebone whales**)

wharf *n, pl* **wharves** : structure alongside which boats lie to load or unload

what *pron* **1** — used to inquire the identity or nature of something **2** : that which **3** : whatever ~ *adv* : in what respect ~ *adj* **1** — used to inquire about the identity or nature of something **2** : how remarkable or surprising **3** : whatever

what·ev·er *pron* **1** : anything or everything that **2** : no matter what ~ *adj* : of any kind at all

what·not *pron* : any of various other things that might be mentioned

what·so·ev·er *pron or adj* : whatever

wheal *n* : a welt on the skin

wheat *n* : cereal grain that yields flour — **wheaten** *adj*

whee·dle *vb* **-dled; -dling** : coax or tempt by flattery

wheel *n* **1** : disk or circular frame capable of turning on a central axis **2** : device of which the main part is a wheel ~ *vb* **1** : convey or move on wheels or a wheeled vehicle **2** : rotate **3** : turn so as to change direction — **wheeled** *adj* — **wheel·er** *n* — **wheelless** *adj*

wheel·bar·row *n* : one-wheeled vehicle for carrying small loads

wheel·base *n* : distance in inches between the front and rear axles of an automotive vehicle

wheel·chair *n* : chair mounted on wheels esp. for the use of disabled persons

wheeze *vb* **wheezed; wheez·ing** : breathe with difficulty and with a whistling sound — **wheeze** *n* — **wheezy** *adj*

whelk *n* : large sea snail

whelp *n* : one of the young of various carnivorous mammals (as a dog) ~ *vb* : bring forth whelps

when *adv* — used to inquire about or designate a particular time ~ *conj* **1** : at or during the time that **2** : every time that **3** : if **4** : although ~ *pron* : what time

whence *adv or conj* : from what place, source, or cause

when·ev·er *conj or adv* : at whatever time

where *adv* **1** : at, in, or to what place **2** : at, in, or to what situation, position, direction, circumstances, or respect ~ *conj* **1** : at, in, or to what place, position, or circumstance **2** : at, in, or to which place ~ *n* : place

where·abouts *adv* : about where ~ *n sing or pl* : place where a person or thing is

where·as *conj* **1** : while on the contrary **2** : since

where·by *conj* : by, through, or in accordance with which

where·fore *adv* **1** : why **2** : therefore ~ *n* : reason

where·in *adv* : in what respect

where·of *conj* : of what, which, or whom

where·up·on *conj* **1** : on which **2** : and then

wher·ev·er *adv* : where ~ *conj* : at, in, or to whatever place or circumstance

where·with·al *n* : resources and esp. money

whet *vb* **-tt- 1** : sharpen by rubbing (as with a stone) **2** : stimulate — **whet·stone** *n*

whether *conj* **1** : if it is or was true that **2** : if it is or was better **3** : whichever is the case

whey *n* : watery part of sour milk

which *adj* **1** : being what one or ones out of a group **2** : whichever ~ *pron* **1** : which one or ones **2** : whichever

which·ev·er *pron or adj* : no matter what one

whiff *n* **1** : slight gust **2** : inhalation of odor, gas, or smoke **3** : slight trace ~ *vb* : inhale an odor

while *n* **1** : period of time **2** : time and effort used ~ *conj* **1** : during the time that **2** : as long as **3** : although ~ *vb* **whiled; whil·ing** : cause to pass esp. pleasantly

whim *n* : sudden wish, desire, or change of mind

whim·per *vb* : cry softly — **whimper** *n*

whim·si·cal *adj* **1** : full of whims **2** : erratic — **whim·si·cal·i·ty** *n* — **whim·si·cal·ly** *adv*

whim·sy, whim·sey *n, pl* **-sies** *or* **-seys 1** : whim **2** : fanciful creation

whine *vb* **whined; whin·ing 1** : utter a usu. high-pitched plaintive cry **2** : complain — **whine** *n* — **whin·er** *n* — **whiny** *adj*

whin·ny *vb* **-nied; -ny·ing** : neigh — **whinny** *n*

whip *vb* **-pp- 1** : move quickly **2** : strike with something slender and flexible **3** : defeat **4** : incite **5** : beat into a froth ~ *n* **1** : flexible device used for whipping **2** : party leader responsible for discipline **3** : thrashing motion — **whip·per** *n*

whip·cord *n* **1** : thin tough cord **2** : cloth made of hard-twisted yarns

whip·lash *n* : injury from a sudden sharp movement of the neck and head

whip·per·snap·per *n* : small, insignificant, or presumptuous person

whip·pet *n* : small swift dog often used for racing

whip·poor·will *n* : American nocturnal bird

whir *vb* **-rr- :** move, fly, or revolve with a whir ~ *n* : continuous fluttering or vibratory sound

whirl *vb* **1** : move or drive in a circle **2** : spin **3** : move or turn quickly **4** : reel ~ *n* **1** : rapid circular movement **2** : state of commotion or confusion **3** : try

whirl·pool *n* : whirling mass of water having a depression in the center

whirl·wind *n* : whirling wind storm

whisk *n* **1** : quick light sweeping or brushing motion **2** : usu. wire kitchen implement for beating ~ *vb* **1** : move or convey briskly **2** : beat **3** : brush lightly

whisk broom *n* : small broom

whis·ker *n* **1** *pl* : beard **2** : long bristle or hair near an animal's mouth — **whis·kered** *adj*

whis·key, whis·ky *n, pl* **-keys** *or* **-kies** : liquor distilled from a fermented mash of grain

whis·per *vb* **1** : speak softly **2** : tell by whispering ~ *n* **1** : soft low sound **2** : rumor

whist *n* : card game

whis·tle *n* **1** : device by which a shrill sound is produced **2** : shrill clear sound made by a whistle or through the lips ~ *vb* **-tled; -tling 1** : make or utter a whistle **2** : signal or call by a whistle **3** : produce by whistling — **whis·tler** *n*

whis·tle-blow·er *n* : informer

whis·tle-stop *n* : brief political appearance

whit *n* : bit

white *adj* **whit·er; -est 1** : free from color **2** : of the color of new snow or milk **3** : having light skin ~ *n* **1** : color of maximum lightness **2** : white part or thing **3** : person who is light-skinned — **white·ness** *n* — **whit·ish** *adj*

white blood cell *n* : blood cell that does not contain hemoglobin

white·cap *n* : wave crest breaking into white foam

white-col·lar *adj* : relating to salaried employees with duties not requiring protective or work clothing

white elephant *n* : something costly but of little use or value

white·fish *n* : freshwater food fish

whit·en *vb* : make or become white — **whit·en·er** *n*

white slave *n* : woman or girl held unwillingly for purposes of prostitution — **white slavery** *n*

white·tail *n* : No. American deer

white·wash *vb* **1** : whiten with a composition (as of lime and water) **2** : gloss over or cover up faults or wrongdoing — **whitewash** *n*

whith·er *adv* **1** : to what place **2** : to what situation, position, degree, or end

¹whit·ing *n* : usu. light or silvery food fish

²whiting *n* : pulverized chalk or limestone

whit·tle *vb* **-tled; -tling 1** : pare **2** : shape by paring **3** : reduce gradually

whiz, whizz *vb* **-zz- :** make a sound like a speeding object — **whiz, whizz** *n*

who *pron* **1** : what or which person or persons **2** : person or persons that **3** : — used to introduce a relative clause

who·dun·it *n* : detective or mystery story

who·ev·er *pron* : no matter who

whole *adj* **1** : being in healthy or sound condition **2** : having all its parts or elements **3** : constituting the total sum of ~ *n* **1** : complete amount or sum **2** : something whole or entire — **on the whole 1** : considering all circumstances **2** : in general — **whole·ness** *n*

whole·heart·ed *adj* : sincere

whole number *n* : integer

whole·sale *n* : sale of goods in quantity usu. for resale by a retail merchant ~ *adj* **1** : of or relating to wholesaling **2** : performed on a large scale ~ *vb* **-saled; -sal·ing** : sell at wholesale — **wholesale** *adv* — **whole·sal·er** *n*

whole·some *adj* **1** : promoting mental, spiritual, or bodily health **2** : healthy — **whole·some·ness** *n*

whole wheat *adj* : made of ground entire wheat kernels

whol·ly *adv* **1** : totally **2** : solely

whom *pron, objective case of* WHO

whom·ev·er *pron, objective case of* WHOEVER

whoop *vb* : shout loudly ~ *n* : shout

whooping cough *n* : infectious disease marked by convulsive coughing fits

whop·per *n* **1** : something unusually large or extreme of its kind **2** : monstrous lie

whop·ping *adj* : extremely large

whore *n* : prostitute

whorl *n* : spiral — **whorled** *adj*

whose *adj* : of or relating to whom or which ~ *pron* : whose one or ones

who·so·ev·er *pron* : whoever

why *adv* : for what reason, cause, or purpose ~ *conj* **1** : reason for which **2** : for which ~ *n, pl* **whys** : reason ~ *interj* — used esp. to express surprise

wick *n* : cord that draws up oil, tallow, or wax to be burned

wick·ed *adj* **1** : morally bad **2** : harmful or troublesome **3** : very unpleasant **4** : very impressive — **wick·ed·ly** *adv* — **wick·ed·ness** *n*

wick·er *n* **1** : small pliant branch **2** : wickerwork — **wicker** *adj*

wick·er·work *n* : work made of wickers

wick·et *n* **1** : small gate, door, or window **2** : frame in cricket or arch in croquet

wide *adj* **wid·er; wid·est 1** : covering a vast area **2** : measured at right angles to the length **3** : having a great measure across **4** : opened fully **5** : far from the thing in question ~ *adv* **wid·er; wid·est 1** : over a great distance **2** : so as to leave considerable space between **3** : fully — **wide·ly** *adv* — **wid·en** *vb*

wide-awake *adj* : alert

wide-eyed *adj* **1** : having the eyes wide open **2** : amazed **3** : naive

wide·spread *adj* : widely extended

wid·ow *n* : woman who has lost her husband by death and has not married again ~ *vb* : cause to become a widow — **wid·ow·hood** *n*

wid·ow·er *n* : man who has lost his wife by death and has not married again

width *n* **1** : distance from side to side **2** : largeness of extent **3** : measured and cut piece of material

wield *vb* **1** : use or handle esp. effectively **2** : exert — **wield·er** *n*

wie·ner *n* : frankfurter

wife *n, pl* **wives** : married woman — **wife·hood** *n* — **wife·less** *adj* — **wife·ly** *adj*

wig *n* : manufactured covering of hair for the head

wig·gle *vb* **-gled; -gling 1** : move with quick jerky or shaking movements **2** : wriggle — **wiggle** *n* — **wig·gler** *n*

wig·gly *adj* **1** : tending to wiggle **2** : wavy

wig·wag *vb* : signal by a flag or light waved according to a code

wig·wam *n* : American Indian hut consisting of a framework of poles overlaid with bark, rush mats, or hides

wild *adj* **1** : living or being in a state of nature and not domesticated or cultivated **2** : unrestrained **3** : turbulent **4** : crazy **5** : uncivilized **6** : erratic ~

n **1** : wilderness **2** : undomesticated state ~ *adv* : without control — **wild•ly** *adv* — **wild•ness** *n*

wild•cat *n* : any of various undomesticated cats (as a lynx) ~ *adj* **1** : not sound or safe **2** : unauthorized

wil•der•ness *n* : uncultivated and uninhabited region

wild•fire *n* : sweeping and destructive fire

wild•fowl *n* : game waterfowl

wild•life *n* : undomesticated animals

wile *n* : trick to snare or deceive ~ *vb* **wiled; wil•ing** : lure

will *vb, past* **would;** *pres sing & pl* **will 1** : wish **2** — used as an auxiliary verb to express (1) desire or willingness (2) customary action (3) simple future time (4) capability (5) determination (6) probability (7) inevitability or (8) a command **3** : dispose of by a will — *n* **1** : often determined wish **2** : act, process, or experience of willing **3** : power of controlling one's actions or emotions **4** : legal document disposing of property after death

will•ful, wil•ful *adj* **1** : governed by will without regard to reason **2** : intentional — **will•ful•ly** *adv*

will•ing *adj* **1** : inclined or favorably disposed in mind **2** : prompt to act **3** : done, borne, or accepted voluntarily or without reluctance — **will•ing•ly** *adv* — **will•ing•ness** *n*

will-o'-the-wisp *n* **1** : light that appears at night over marshy grounds **2** : misleading or elusive goal or hope

wil•low *n* : quick-growing shrub or tree with flexible shoots

wil•lowy *adj* : gracefully tall and slender

will•pow•er *n* : energetic determination

wil•ly-nil•ly *adv or adj* : without regard for one's choice

wilt *vb* **1** : lose or cause to lose freshness and become limp esp. from lack of water **2** : grow weak

wily *adj* **wil•i•er; -est** : full of craftiness — **wil•i•ness** *n*

win *vb* **won; win•ning 1** : get possession of esp. by effort **2** : gain victory in battle or a contest **3** : make friendly or favorable ~ *n* : victory

wince *vb* **winced; winc•ing** : shrink back involuntarily — **wince** *n*

winch *n* : machine for hoisting or pulling with a drum around which rope is wound — **winch** *vb*

¹**wind** *n* **1** : movement of the air **2** : breath **3** : gas in the stomach or intestines **4** : air carrying a scent **5** : intimation ~ *vb* **1** : get a scent of **2** : cause to be out of breath

²**wind** *vb* **wound; wind•ing 1** : have or follow a curving course **2** : move or lie to encircle **3** : encircle or cover with something pliable **4** : tighten the spring of ~ *n* : turn or coil — **wind•er** *n*

wind•break *n* : trees and shrubs to break the force of the wind

wind•break•er *n* : light wind-resistant jacket

wind•fall *n* **1** : thing blown down by wind **2** : unexpected benefit

wind instrument *n* : musical instrument (as a flute or horn) sounded by wind and esp. by the breath

wind•lass *n* : winch esp. for hoisting anchor

wind•mill *n* : machine worked by the wind turning vanes

win•dow *n* **1** : opening in the wall of a building to let in light and air **2** : pane in a window **3** : span of time for something **4** : area of a computer display — **win•dow•less** *adj*

win•dow-shop *vb* : look at the displays in store windows — **win•dow-shop•per** *n*

wind•pipe *n* : passage for the breath from the larynx to the lungs

wind•shield *n* : transparent screen in front of the occupants of a vehicle

wind-up *n* : end — **wind up** *vb*

wind•ward *adj* : being in or facing the direction from which the wind is blowing ~ *n* : direction from which the wind is blowing

windy *adj* **wind•i•er; -est 1** : having wind **2** : indulging in useless talk

wine *n* **1** : fermented grape juice **2** : usu. fermented juice of a plant product (as fruit) used as a beverage ~ *vb* : treat to or drink wine

wing *n* **1** : movable paired appendage for flying **2** : winglike thing **3** *pl* : area at the side of the stage out of sight **4** : faction ~ *vb* **1** : fly **2** : propel through the air — **winged** *adj* — **wing•less** *adj* — **on the wing** : in flight — **under one's wing** : in one's charge or care

wink *vb* **1** : close and open the eyes quickly **2** : avoid seeing or noticing something **3** : twinkle **4** : close and open one eye quickly as a signal or hint ~ *n* **1** : brief sleep **2** : act of winking **3** : instant — **wink•er** *n*

win•ner *n* : one that wins

win•ning *n* **1** : victory **2** : money won at gambling ~ *adj* **1** : victorious **2** : charming

win•now *vb* **1** : remove (as chaff) by a current of air **2** : sort or separate something

win•some *adj* **1** : causing joy **2** : cheerful or gay — **win•some•ly** *adv* — **win•some•ness** *n*

win•ter *n* : season between autumn and spring ~ *adj* : sown in autumn for harvest the next spring or summer — **win•ter•time** *n*

win•ter•green *n* : low heathlike evergreen plant with red berries

win•try *adj* **win•tri•er; -est 1** : characteristic of winter **2** : cold in feeling

wipe *vb* **wiped; wip•ing 1** : clean or dry by rubbing **2** : remove by rubbing **3** : erase completely **4** : destroy **5** : pass over a surface ~ *n* : act or instance of wiping — **wip•er** *n*

wire *n* **1** : thread of metal **2** : work made of wire **3** : telegram or cablegram ~ *vb* **1** : provide with wire **2** : bind or mount with wire **3** : telegraph — **wire•less** *adj*

wire•less *n, chiefly Brit* : radio

wire•tap *vb* : connect into a telephone or telegraph wire to get information — **wiretap** *n* — **wire•tap•per** *n*

wir•ing *n* : system of wires

wiry *adj* **wir•i•er; -est 1** : resembling wire **2** : slender yet strong and sinewy — **wir•i•ness** *n*

wis•dom *n* **1** : accumulated learning **2** : good sense

wisdom tooth *n* : last tooth on each half of each human jaw

¹**wise** *n* : manner

²**wise** *adj* **wis•er; wis•est 1** : having or showing wisdom, good sense, or good judgment **2** : aware of what is going on — **wise•ly** *adv*

wise•crack *n* : clever, smart, or flippant remark ~ *vb* : make a wisecrack

wish *vb* **1** : have a desire **2** : express a wish concerning **3** : request ~ *n* **1** : a wishing or desire **2** : expressed will or desire

wish•bone *n* : forked bone in front of the breastbone in most birds

wish•ful *adj* **1** : expressive of a wish **2** : according with wishes rather than fact

wishy-washy *adj* : weak or insipid

wisp *n* **1** : small bunch of hay or straw **2** : thin strand, strip, fragment, or streak **3** : something frail, slight, or fleeting — **wispy** *adj*

wis•te•ria *n* : pealike woody vine with long clusters of flowers

wist•ful *adj* : full of longing — **wist•ful•ly** *adv* — **wist•ful•ness** *n*

wit *n* **1** : reasoning power **2** : mental soundness — usu. pl. **3** : quickness and cleverness in handling words and ideas **4** : talent for clever remarks or one noted for witty remarks — **wit•less** *adj* — **wit•less•ly** *adv* — **wit•less•ness** *n* — **wit•ted** *adj*

witch *n* **1** : person believed to have magic power **2** : ugly old woman ~ *vb* : bewitch

witch•craft *n* : power or practices of a witch

witch•ery *n, pl* **-er•ies 1** : witchcraft **2** : charm

witch ha•zel *n* **1** : shrub having small yellow flowers in fall **2** : alcoholic lotion made from witch hazel bark

witch-hunt *n* **1** : searching out and persecution of supposed witches **2** : harassment esp. of political opponents

with *prep* **1** : against, to, or toward **2** : in support of **3** : because of **4** : in the company of **5** : having **6** : despite **7** : containing **8** : by means of

with•draw *vb* **-drew; -drawn; -draw•ing 1** : take back or away **2** : call back or retract **3** : go away **4** : terminate one's participation in or use of — **with•draw•al** *n*

with•drawn *adj* : socially detached and unresponsive

with•er *vb* **1** : shrivel **2** : lose or cause to lose energy, force, or freshness

with•ers *n pl* : ridge between the shoulder bones of a horse

with•hold *vb* **-held; -hold•ing 1** : hold back **2** : refrain from giving

with•in *adv* **1** : in or into the interior **2** : inside oneself ~ *prep* **1** : in or to the inner part of **2** : in the limits or compass of

with•out *prep* **1** : outside **2** : lacking **3** : unaccompanied or unmarked by — **without** *adv*

with•stand *vb* **-stood; -stand•ing** : oppose successfully

wit•ness *n* **1** : testimony **2** : one who testifies **3** : one present at a transaction to testify that it has taken place **4** : one who has personal knowledge or experience **5** : something serving as proof ~ *vb* **1** : bear witness **2** : act as legal witness of **3** : furnish proof of **4** : be a witness of **5** : be the scene of

wit•ti•cism *n* : witty saying or phrase

wit•ting *adj* : intentional — **wit•ting•ly** *adv*

wit•ty *adj* **-ti•er; -est** : marked by or full of wit — **wit•ti•ly** *adv* — **wit•ti•ness** *n*

wives *pl of* WIFE

wiz•ard *n* **1** : magician **2** : very clever person — **wiz•ard•ry** *n*

wiz•ened *adj* : dried up

wob•ble *vb* **-bled; -bling 1** : move or cause to move with an irregular rocking motion **2** : tremble **3** : waver — **wobble** *n* — **wob•bly** *adj*

woe *n* **1** : deep suffering **2** : misfortune

woe•be•gone *adj* : exhibiting woe, sorrow, or misery

woe•ful *adj* **1** : full of woe **2** : bringing woe — **woe•ful•ly** *adv*

woke *past of* WAKE

woken *past part of* WAKE

wolf *n, pl* **wolves** : large doglike predatory mammal ~ *vb* : eat greedily — **wolf•ish** *adj*

wol•fram *n* : tungsten

wol•ver•ine *n, pl* **-ines** : flesh-eating mammal related to the weasels

wom•an *n, pl* **wom•en 1** : adult female person **2** : womankind **3** : feminine nature — **wom•an•hood** *n* — **wom•an•ish** *adj*

wom•an•kind *n* : females of the human race

wom•an•ly *adj* : having qualities characteristic of a woman — **wom•an•li•ness** *n*

womb *n* : uterus

won *past of* WIN

won•der *n* **1** : cause of astonishment or surprise **2** : feeling (as of astonishment) aroused by something extraordinary ~ *vb* **1** : feel surprise **2** : feel curiosity or doubt

won•der•ful *adj* **1** : exciting wonder **2** : unusually good — **won•der•ful•ly** *adv* — **won•der•ful•ness** *n*

won•der•land *n* **1** : fairylike imaginary realm **2** : place that excites admiration or wonder

won•der•ment *n* : wonder

won•drous *adj* : wonderful — **won•drous•ly** *adv* — **won•drous•ness** *n*

wont *adj* : accustomed ~ *n* : habit — **wont•ed** *adj*

woo *vb* : try to gain the love or favor of — **woo•er** *n*

wood *n* **1** : dense growth of trees usu. smaller than a forest — often pl. **2** : hard fibrous substance of trees and shrubs beneath the bark **3** : wood prepared for some use (as burning) ~ *adj* : wooden **2** : suitable for working with wood **3** *or* **woods** : living or growing in woods — **wood•chop•per** *n* — **wood•pile** *n* — **wood•shed** *n*

wood•bine *n* : climbing vine

wood•chuck *n* : thick-bodied grizzled animal of No. America

wood•craft *n* **1** : skill and practice in matters relating to the woods **2** : skill in making articles from wood

wood•cut *n* **1** : relief printing surface engraved on wood **2** : print from a woodcut

wood•ed *adj* : covered with woods

wood•en *adj* **1** : made of wood **2** : lacking resilience **3** : lacking ease, liveliness or interest — **wood•en•ly** *adv* — **wood•en•ness** *n*

wood•land *n* : land covered with trees

wood•peck•er *n* : brightly marked bird with a hard bill for drilling into trees

woods•man *n* : person who works in the woods

wood•wind *n* : one of a group of wind instruments (as a flute or oboe)

wood•work *n* : work (as interior house fittings) made of wood

woody *adj* **wood•i•er; -est 1** : abounding with woods **2** : of, containing, or like wood fibers — **wood•i•ness** *n*

woof *n* : weft

wool *n* **1** : soft hair of some mammals and esp. the sheep **2** : something (as a textile) made of wool — **wooled** *adj*

wool•en, wool•len *adj* **1** : made of wool **2** : relating to the manufacture of woolen products ~ *n* **1** : woolen fabric **2** : woolen garments — usu. pl.

wool•gath•er•ing *n* : idle daydreaming

wool•ly *adj* **-li•er; -est 1** : of, relating to, or bearing wool **2** : consisting of or resembling wool **3** : confused or turbulent

woo•zy *adj* **-zi•er; -est 1** : confused **2** : somewhat dizzy, nauseated, or weak — **woo•zi•ness** *n*

word *n* **1** : brief remark **2** : speech sound or series of speech sounds that communicates a meaning **3** : written representation of a word **4** : order **5** : news **6** : promise **7** *pl* : dispute ~ *vb* : express in words — **word•less** *adj*

word•ing *n* : verbal expression

word processing *n* : production of structured and printed documents through a computer program (**word processor**) — **word process** *vb*

wordy *adj* **word•i•er; -est** : using many words — **word•i•ness** *n*

wore *past of* WEAR

work *n* **1** : labor **2** : employment **3** : task **4** : something (as an artistic production) produced by mental effort or physical labor **5** *pl* : place where industrial labor is done **6** *pl* : moving parts of a mechanism **7** : workmanship ~ *adj* **1** : suitable for wear while working **2** : used for work ~ *vb* **worked** *or* **wrought; work•ing 1** : bring to pass **2** : create by expending labor upon **3** : bring or get into a form or condition **4** : set or keep in operation **5** : solve **6** : cause to labor **7** : arrange **8** : excite **9** : labor **10** : perform work regularly for wages **11** : function according to plan or design **12** : produce a desired effect — **work•bench** *n* — **work•man** *n* — **work•room** *n* — **in the works** : in preparation

work•able *adj* **1** : capable of being worked **2** : feasible — **work•able•ness** *n*

work•a•day *adj* **1** : relating to or suited for working days **2** : ordinary

work•a•hol•ic *n* : compulsive worker

work•day *n* **1** : day on which work is done **2** : period of time during which one is working

work•er *n* : person who works esp. for wages

work•horse *n* **1** : horse used for hard work **2** : person who does most of the work of a group task

work•house *n* : place of confinement for persons who have committed minor offenses

work•ing *adj* **1** : adequate to allow work to be done **2** : adopted or assumed to help further work or activity ~ *n* : operation — usu. used in pl.

work•ing•man *n* : worker

work•man•like *adj* : worthy of a good workman

work•man•ship *n* **1** : art or skill of a workman **2** : quality of a piece of work

work•out *n* : exercise to improve one's fitness

work out *vb* **1** : bring about by effort **2** : solve **3** : develop **4** : to be successful **5** : perform exercises

work•shop *n* **1** : small establishment for manufacturing or handicrafts **2** : seminar emphasizing exchange of ideas and practical methods

world *n* **1** : universe **2** : earth with its inhabitants and all things upon it **3** : people in general **4** : great number or quantity **5** : class of persons or their sphere of interest

world•ly *adj* **1** : devoted to this world and its pursuits rather than to religion **2** : sophisticated — **world•li•ness** *n*

world•ly–wise *adj* : possessing understanding of human affairs

world•wide *adj* : extended throughout the entire world — **worldwide** *adv*

worm *n* **1** : earthworm or a similar animal **2** *pl* : disorder caused by parasitic worms ~ *vb* **1** : move or cause to move in a slow and indirect way **2** : to free from worms — **wormy** *adj*

worm•wood *n* **1** : aromatic woody herb (as sagebrush) **2** : something bitter or grievous

worn *past part of* WEAR

worn–out *adj* : exhausted or used up by or as if by wear

wor•ri•some *adj* **1** : causing worry **2** : inclined to worry

wor•ry *vb* **-ried; -ry•ing 1** : shake and mangle with the teeth **2** : disturb **3** : feel or express anxiety ~ *n, pl* **-ries 1** : anxiety **2** : cause of anxiety — **wor•ri•er** *n*

worse *adj, comparative of* BAD *or of* ILL **1** : bad or evil in a greater degree **2** : more unwell ~ *n* **1** : one that is worse **2** : greater degree of badness — *adv, comparative of* BAD *or of* ILL : in a worse manner

wors•en *vb* : make or become worse

wor•ship *n* **1** : reverence toward a divine being or supernatural power **2** : expression of reverence **3** : extravagant respect or devotion ~ *vb* **-shiped** *or* **-shipped; -ship•ing** *or* **-ship•ping 1** : honor or reverence **2** : perform or take part in worship — **wor•ship•er, wor•ship•per** *n*

worst *adj, superlative of* BAD *or of* ILL **1** : most bad, evil, ill, or corrupt **2** : most unfavorable, unpleasant, or painful ~ *n* : one that is worst — *adv, superlative of* ILL *or of* BAD *or* BADLY : to the extreme degree of badness ~ *vb* : defeat

wor•sted *n* : smooth compact wool yarn or fabric made from such yarn

worth *prep* **1** : equal in value to **2** : deserving of ~ *n* **1** : monetary value **2** : value of something measured by its qualities **3** : moral or personal merit

worth•less *adj* **1** : lacking worth **2** : useless — **worth•less•ness** *n*

worth•while *adj* : being worth the time or effort spent

wor•thy *adj* **-thi•er; -est 1** : having worth or value **2** : having sufficient worth ~ *n, pl* **-thies** : worthy person — **wor•thi•ly** *adv* — **wor•thi•ness** *n*

would *past of* WILL — used to express (1) preference (2) intent (3) habitual action (4) contingency (5) probability or (6) a request

would–be *adj* : desiring or pretending to be

¹wound *n* **1** : injury in which the skin is broken **2** : mental hurt ~ *vb* : inflict a wound to or in

²wound *past of* WIND

wove *past of* WEAVE

woven *past part of* WEAVE

wrack *n* : ruin

wraith *n, pl* **wraiths 1** : ghost **2** : insubstantial appearance

wran•gle *vb or n* : quarrel — **wran•gler** *n*

wrap *vb* **-pp- 1** : cover esp. by winding or folding **2** : envelop and secure for transportation or storage **3** : enclose, surround, or conceal wholly **4** : coil, fold, draw, or twine about something ~ *n* **1** : wrapper or wrapping **2** : outer garment (as a shawl)

wrap•per *n* **1** : that in which something is wrapped **2** : one that wraps

wrap•ping *n* : something used to wrap an object

wrath *n* : violent anger — **wrath•ful** *adj*

wreak *vb* **1** : inflict **2** : bring about

wreath *n, pl* **wreaths** : something (as boughs) intertwined into a circular shape

wreathe *vb* **wreathed; wreath•ing 1** : shape into or take on the shape of a wreath **2** : decorate or cover with a wreath

wreck *n* **1** : broken remains (as of a ship or vehicle) after heavy damage **2** : something disabled or in a state of ruin **3** : an individual who has become weak or infirm **4** : action of breaking up or destroying something ~ *vb* : ruin or damage by breaking up

wreck•age *n* **1** : act of wrecking **2** : remains of a wreck

wreck•er *n* **1** : automotive vehicle for removing disabled cars **2** : one that wrecks or tears down and removes buildings

wren *n* : small mostly brown singing bird

wrench *vb* **1** : pull with violent twisting or force **2** : injure or disable by a violent twisting or straining ~ *n* **1** : forcible twisting **2** : tool for exerting a twisting force

wrest *vb* **1** : pull or move by a forcible twisting movement **2** : gain with difficulty ~ *n* : forcible twist

wres•tle *vb* **-tled; -tling 1** : scuffle with and attempt to throw and pin an opponent **2** : compete against in wrestling **3** : struggle (as with a problem) ~ *n* : action or an instance of wrestling — **wres•tler** *n*

wres•tling *n* : sport in which 2 opponents try to throw and pin each other

wretch *n* **1** : miserable unhappy person **2** : vile person

wretch•ed *adj* **1** : deeply afflicted, dejected, or distressed **2** : grievous **3** : inferior — **wretch•ed•ly** *adv* — **wretch•ed•ness** *n*

wrig•gle *vb* **-gled; -gling 1** : twist and turn restlessly **2** : move along by twisting and turning — **wrig•gle** *n* — **wrig•gler** *n*

wring *vb* **wrung; wring•ing 1** : squeeze or twist out moisture **2** : get by or as if by twisting or pressing **3** : twist together in anguish **4** : pain — **wring•er** *n*

wrin•kle *n* : crease or small fold on a surface (as in the skin or in cloth) ~ *vb* **-kled; -kling** : develop or cause to develop wrinkles — **wrin•kly** *adj*

wrist *n* : joint or region between the hand and the arm

writ *n* **1** : something written **2** : legal order in writing

write *vb* **wrote; writ•ten; writ•ing 1** : form letters or words on a surface **2** : form the letters or the words of (as on paper) **3** : make up and set down for others to read **4** : write a letter to — **write off** *vb* : cancel

writ•er *n* : one that writes esp. as a business or occupation

writhe *vb* **writhed; writh•ing** : twist and turn this way and that

writ•ing *n* **1** : act of one that writes **2** : handwriting **3** : something written or printed

wrong *n* **1** : unfair or unjust act **2** : something that is contrary to justice **3** : state of being or doing

wrong ~ *adj* **wrong•er; wrong•est 1** : sinful **2** : not right according to a standard **3** : unsuitable **4** : incorrect ~ *adv* **1** : in a wrong direction or manner **2** : incorrectly ~ *vb* **wronged; wrong•ing 1** : do wrong to **2** : treat unjustly — **wrong•ly** *adv*

wrong•do•er *n* : one who does wrong — **wrong•do•ing** *n*

wrong•ful *adj* **1** : wrong **2** : illegal — **wrong•ful•ly** *adv* — **wrong•ful•ness** *n*

wrong•head•ed *adj* : stubborn in clinging to

wrong opinion or principles — **wrong•head•ed•ly** *adv* — **wrong•head•ed•ness** *n*

wrote *past of* WRITE

wrought *adj* **1** : formed **2** : hammered into shape **3** : deeply stirred

wrung *past of* WRING

wry *adj* **wri•er; wri•est 1** : turned abnormally to one side **2** : twisted **3** : cleverly and often ironically humorous — **wry•ly** *adv* — **wry•ness** *n*

X

x *n, pl* **x's** *or* **xs 1** : 24th letter of the alphabet **2** : unknown quantity ~ *vb* **x-ed; x-ing** *or* **x'ing** : cancel with a series of *x*'s — usu. with *out*

xe•non *n* : heavy gaseous chemical element

xe•no•pho•bia *n* : fear and hatred of foreign people and things — **xe•no•phobe** *n*

Xmas *n* : Christmas

x–ra•di•a•tion *n* **1** : exposure to X rays **2** : radiation consisting of X rays

x–ray *vb* : examine, treat, or photograph with X rays

X ray *n* **1** : radiation of short wavelength that is

able to penetrate solids **2** : photograph taken with X rays — **X-ray** *adj*

xy•lo•phone *n* : musical instrument with wooden bars that are struck — **xy•lo•phon•ist** *n*

Y

y *n, pl* **y's** *or* **ys** : 25th letter of the alphabet

¹-y *adj suffix* **1** : composed or full of **2** : like **3** : performing or apt to perform an action

²-y *n suffix, pl* **-ies 1** : state, condition, or quality **2** : activity, place of business, or goods dealt with **3** : whole group

yacht *n* : luxurious pleasure boat ~ *vb* : race or cruise in a yacht

ya•hoo *n, pl* **-hoos** : uncouth or stupid person

yak *n* : big hairy Asian ox

yam *n* **1** : edible root of a tropical vine **2** : deep orange sweet potato

yam•mer *vb* **1** : whimper **2** : chatter — **yam•mer** *n*

yank *n* : strong sudden pull — **yank** *vb*

Yank *n* : Yankee

Yan•kee *n* : native or inhabitant of New England, the northern U.S., or the U.S.

yap *vb* **-pp- 1** : yelp **2** : chatter — **yap** *n*

¹yard *n* **1** : 3 feet **2** : long spar for supporting and spreading a sail — **yard•age** *n*

²yard *n* **1** : enclosed roofless area **2** : grounds of a building **3** : work area

yard•arm *n* : end of the yard of a square-rigged ship

yard•stick *n* **1** : measuring stick 3 feet long **2** : standard for judging

yar•mul•ke *n* : a small brimless cap worn by Jewish males in a synagogue

yarn *n* **1** : spun fiber for weaving or knitting **2** : tale

yaw *vb* : deviate erratically from a course — **yaw** *n*

yawl *n* : sailboat with 2 masts

yawn *vb* : open the mouth wide ~ *n* : deep breath through a wide-open mouth — **yawn•er** *n*

ye *pron* : you

yea *adv* **1** : yes **2** : truly ~ *n* : affirmative vote

year *n* **1** : period of about 365 days **2** *pl* : age

year•book *n* : annual report of the year's events

year•ling *n* : one that is or is rated as a year old

year•ly *adj* : annual — **yearly** *adv*

yearn *vb* **1** : feel desire esp. for what one cannot have **2** : feel tenderness or compassion

yearn•ing *n* : tender or urgent desire

yeast *n* : froth or sediment in sugary liquids containing a tiny fungus and used in making alcoholic liquors and as a leaven in baking — **yeasty** *adj*

yell *vb* : utter a loud cry — **yell** *n*

yel•low *adj* **1** : of the color yellow **2** : sensational **3** : cowardly ~ *vb* : make or turn yellow ~ *n* **1** : color of lemons **2** : yolk of an egg — **yel•low•ish** *adj*

yellow fever *n* : virus disease marked by prostration, jaundice, fever, and often hemorrhage

yellow jacket *n* : wasp with yellow stripes

yelp *vb* : utter a sharp quick shrill cry — **yelp** *n*

yen *n* : strong desire

yeo•man *n* **1** : attendant or officer in a royal or noble household **2** : small farmer **3** : naval petty officer with clerical duties — **yeo•man•ry** *n*

-yer —*see* -ER

yes *adv* : used to express consent or agreement ~ *n* : affirmative answer

ye•shi•va, ye•shi•vah *n, pl* **yeshivas** *or* **ye•shi•voth** : Jewish school

yes–man *n* : person who agrees with every opinion or suggestion of a boss

yes•ter•day *adv* **1** : on the day preceding today **2** : only a short time ago ~ *n* **1** : day last past **2** : time not long past

yet *adv* **1** : in addition **2** : up to now **3** : so soon as now **4** : nevertheless ~ *conj* : but

yew *n* : evergreen tree or shrubs with dark stiff poisonous needles

yield *vb* **1** : surrender **2** : grant **3** : bear as a crop **4** : produce **5** : cease opposition or resistance ~ *n* : quantity produced or returned

yo•del *vb* **-deled** *or* **-delled; -del•ing** *or* **-del•ling** : sing by abruptly alternating between chest voice and falsetto — **yodel** *n* — **yo•del•er** *n*

yo•ga *n* : system of exercises for attaining bodily or mental control and well-being

yo•gi *n* : person who practices yoga

yo•gurt *n* : fermented slightly acid soft food made from milk

yoke *n* **1** : neck frame for coupling draft animals or for carrying loads **2** : clamp **3** : slavery **4** : tie or link **5** : piece of a garment esp. at the shoulder ~ *vb* **yoked; yok•ing 1** : couple with a yoke **2** : join

yo•kel *n* : naive and gullible country person

yolk *n* : yellow part of an egg — **yolked** *adj*

Yom Kip•pur *n* : Jewish holiday observed in September or October with fasting and prayer as a day of atonement

yon *adj or adv* : yonder

yon•der *adv* : at or to that place ~ *adj* : distant

yore *n* : time long past

you *pron* **1** : person or persons addressed **2** : person in general

young *adj* **youn•ger; youn•gest 1** : being in the first or an early stage of life, growth, or development **2** : recently come into being **3** : youthful ~ *n, pl* **young** : persons or animals that are young — **young•ish** *adj*

young•ster *n* **1** : young person **2** : child

your *adj* : relating to you or yourself

yours *pron* : the ones belonging to you

your•self *pron, pl* **your•selves** : you — used reflexively or for emphasis

youth *n, pl* **youths 1** : period between childhood and maturity **2** : young man **3** : young persons **4** : state or quality of being young, fresh, or vigorous

youth•ful *adj* **1** : relating to or appropriate to youth **2** : young **3** : vigorous and fresh — **youth•ful•ly** *adv* — **youth•ful•ness** *n*

yowl *vb* : utter a loud long mournful cry — **yowl** *n*

yo–yo *n, pl* **-yos** : toy that falls from or rises to the hand as it unwinds and rewinds on a string

yuc•ca *n* : any of several plants related to the lilies that grow in dry regions

yule *n* : Christmas — **yule•tide** *n*

yum•my *adj* **-mi•er; -est** : highly attractive or pleasing

Z

z *n, pl* **z's** *or* **zs** : 26th letter of the alphabet

za•ny *n, pl* **-nies 1** : clown **2** : silly person ~ *adj* **-ni•er; -est** : crazy or foolish — **za•ni•ly** *adv* — **za•ni•ness** *n*

zeal *n* : enthusiasm

zeal•ot *n* : fanatical partisan

zeal•ous *adj* : filled with zeal — **zeal•ous•ly** *adv* — **zeal•ous•ness** *n*

ze•bra *n* : horselike African mammal marked with light and dark stripes

zeit•geist *n* : general spirit of an era

ze•nith *n* : highest point

zeph•yr *n* : gentle breeze

zep•pe•lin *n* : rigid airship like a blimp

ze•ro *n, pl* **-ros 1** : number represented by the symbol 0 or the symbol itself **2** : starting point **3** : lowest point ~ *adj* : having no size or quantity

zest *n* **1** : quality of enhancing enjoyment **2** : keen enjoyment — **zest•ful** *adj* — **zest•ful•ly** *adv* — **zest•ful•ness** *n*

zig•zag *n* : one of a series of short sharp turns or angles ~ *adj* : having zigzags ~ *adv* : in or by a zigzag path ~ *vb* **-gg-** : proceed along a zigzag path

zil•lion *n* : large indeterminate number

zinc *n* : bluish white crystaline metallic chemical element

zing *n* **1** : shrill humming noise **2** : energy — **zing** *vb*

zin•nia *n* : American herb widely grown for its showy flowers

¹zip *vb* **-pp-** : move or act with speed ~ *n* : energy

²zip *vb* **-pp-** : close or open with a zipper

zip code *n* : number that identifies a U.S. postal delivery area

zip•per *n* : fastener consisting of 2 rows of interlocking teeth

zip•py *adj* **-pi•er; -est** : brisk

zir•con *n* : zirconium-containing mineral sometimes used in jewelry

zir•co•ni•um *n* : corrosion-resistant gray metallic element

zith•er *n* : stringed musical instrument played by plucking

zi•ti *n, pl* **ziti** : short tubular pasta

zo•di•ac *n* : imaginary belt in the heavens encompassing the paths of the planets and divided into 12 signs used in astrology — **zo•di•a•cal** *adj*

zom•bie *n* : person thought to have died and been brought back to life without free will

zon•al *adj* : of, relating to, or having the form of a zone — **zon•al•ly** *adv*

zone *n* **1** : division of the earth's surface based on latitude and climate **2** : distinctive area ~ *vb* **zoned; zon•ing 1** : mark off into zones **2** : reserve for special purposes — **zo•na•tion** *n*

zoo *n, pl* **zoos** : collection of living animals usu. for public display — **zoo•keep•er** *n*

zo•ol•o•gy *n* : science of animals — **zo•o•log•i•cal** *adj* — **zo•ol•o•gist** *n*

zoom *vb* **1** : move with a loud hum or buzz **2** : move or increase with great speed — **zoom** *n*

zuc•chi•ni *n, pl* **-ni** *or* **-nis** : summer squash with smooth cylindrical dark green fruits

zwie•back *n* : biscuit of baked, sliced, and toasted bread

zy•gote *n* : cell formed by the union of 2 sexual cells — **zy•got•ic** *adj*

Index

©1995, Encyclopædia Britannica, Inc.